Business and Personal Fi

Teachers

Tools to Help You Teach!

Online Learning Center

- Curriculum correlation
- Chapter Study Organizers
- Chapter feature activities
- WebQuest projects
- Go Figure Math
- Practice Tests
- *BusinessWeek* activities
- Online resources
- Vocabulary puzzles and games

Log on to
finance07.glencoe.com

access code AEB8585BD8 ONLINE TEXT

TEACHER
finance 2
future

Program Resources

- Interactive Student Edition
- *Presentation Plus!*
- *ExamView®* Test Generator
- Student Activity Workbook
- Financial Planner Software
- S&P's Extension Activities
- Your Personal Financial Planner
- Money Matters
- Inclusion in the Business Education Classroom
- Lesson Planner Plus CD-ROM with:
  - – Student Activity Workbook TAE
  - – Blackline Masters
  - – Internet Resources
  - – Lesson Plans
  - – Reproducible Tests

GLENCOE

Business and Personal FINANCE

Teacher Annotated Edition

Jack R. Kapoor
Professor of Business and Economics
Business and Services Division
College of DuPage
Glen Ellyn, Illinois

Les R. Dlabay
Professor of Business
Department of Economics and Business
Lake Forest College
Lake Forest, Illinois

Robert J. Hughes
Professor of Business
Dallas County Community Colleges
Dallas, Texas

William B. Hoyt
Contributing Editor
Wilton High School
Wilton, Connecticut

McGraw Hill Glencoe

Help your students secure their financial future now...

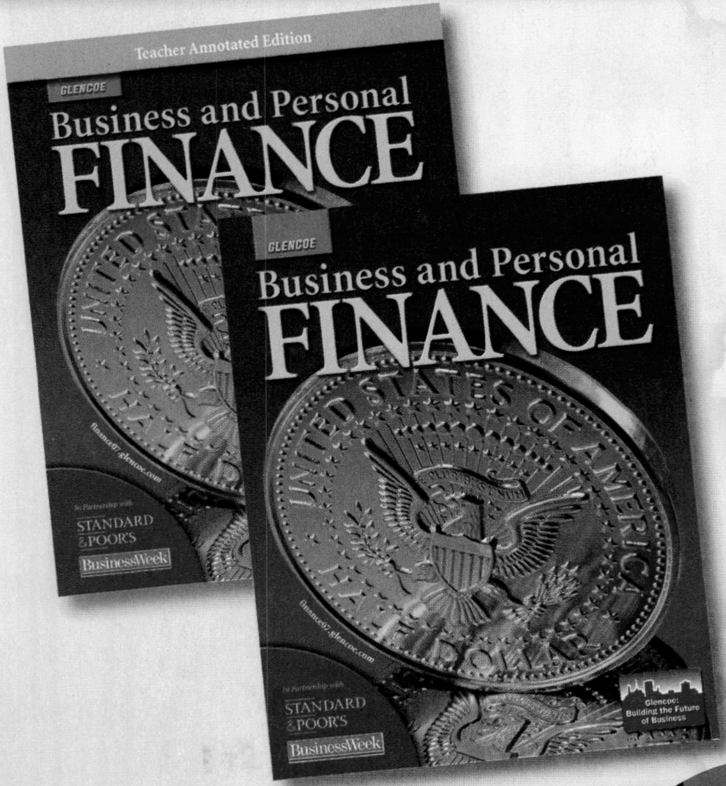

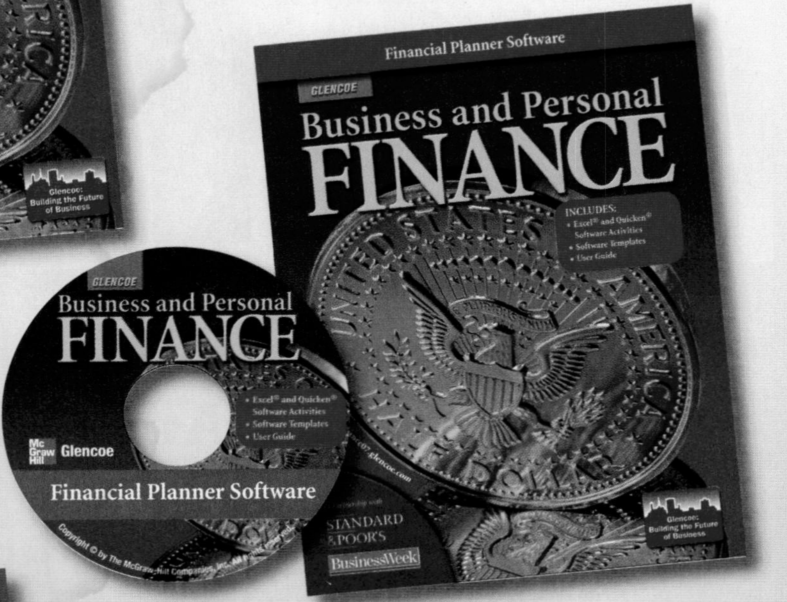

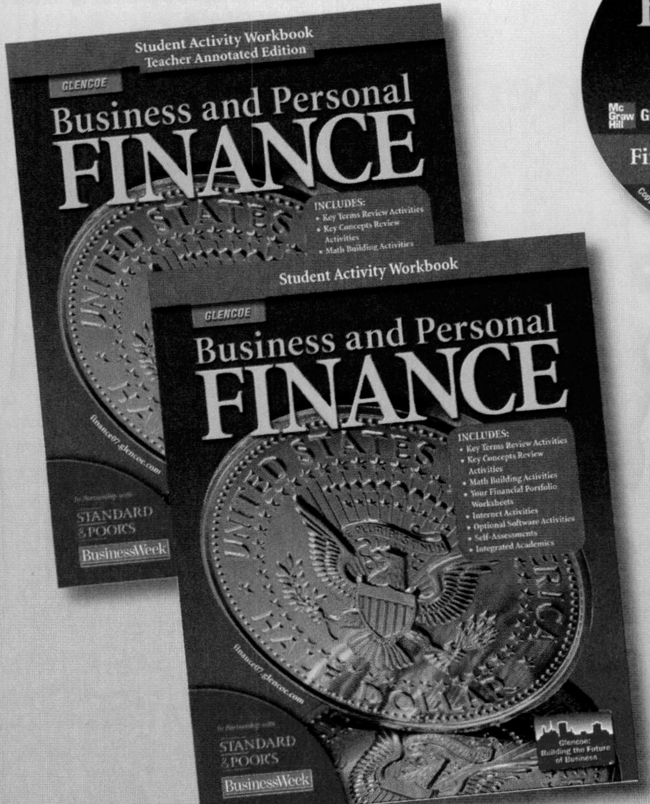

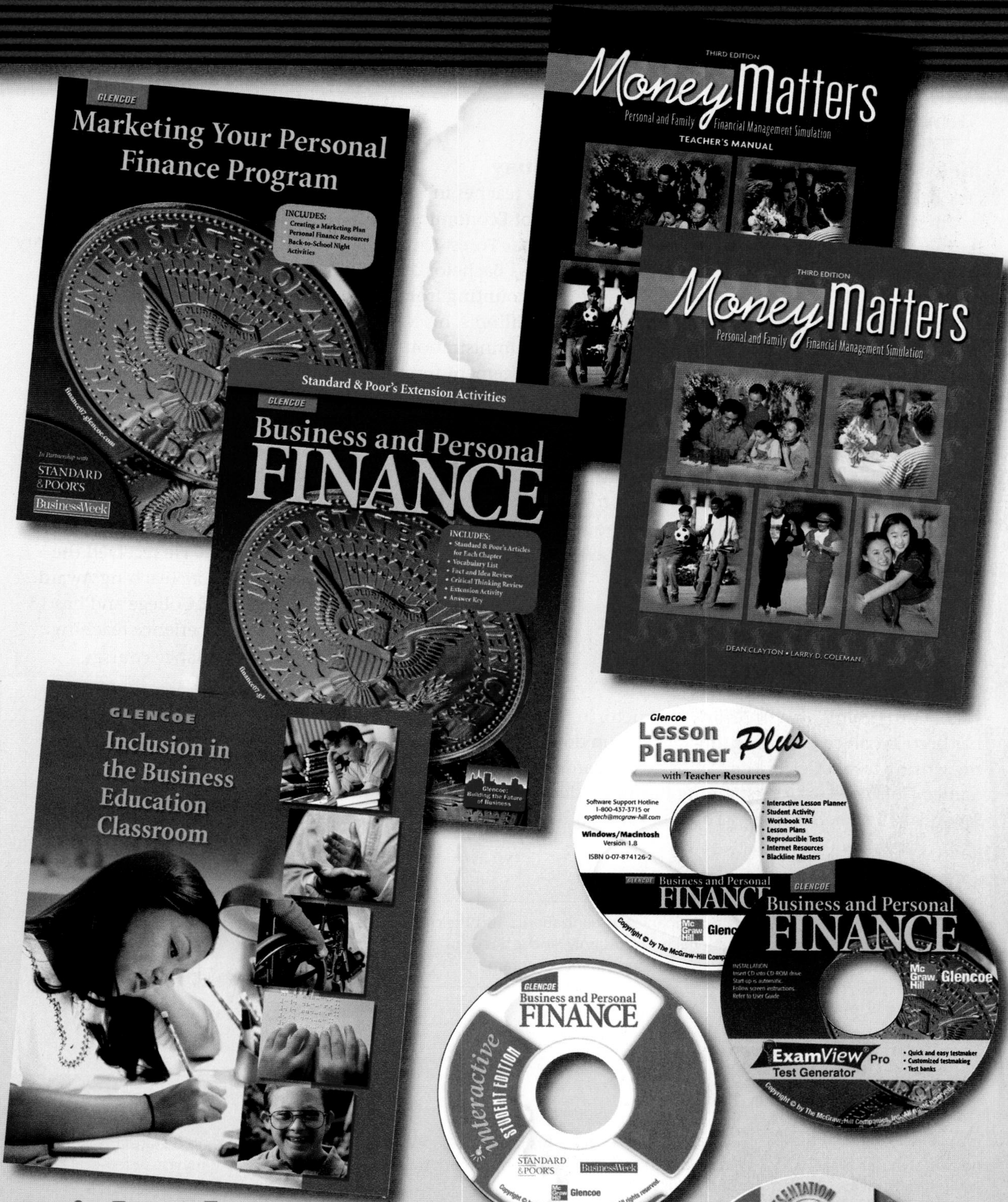

With Glencoe's ***Business and Personal Finance*** Resources

Teacher Manual

About the Authors

Jack R. Kapoor

Jack R. Kapoor is professor of business and economics in the Business and Services Division at College of DuPage, where he has taught since 1969. He received his Bachelor of Arts in Business Administration and Master of Science in International Business from San Francisco State College. He received his Doctor of Education from Northern Illinois University. Dr. Kapoor was awarded the Business and Services Division's Outstanding Professor Award for 1999–2000.

Les R. Dlabay

Les R. Dlabay teaches in the Department of Economics and Business at Lake Forest College. He received his Bachelor of Science in Accounting from University of Illinois, his Master of Business Administration in Business Management from DePaul University, and his Doctor of Education in Business and Economic Education from Northern Illinois University. He is a founding member of the Illinois Consumer Education Association.

Robert J. Hughes

Robert J. Hughes teaches business, management, and finance courses at Dallas County Community Colleges. He received his Bachelor of Arts in Business Administration from Southern Nazarene University and his Master of Business Administration and Doctor of Education from the University of North Texas. Dr. Hughes has taught at the high school, community college, and four-year university levels for 36 years. He received the Excellence in Teaching Award at Richland College and has 15 years of experience teaching personal finance courses.

Contributing Editor

William B. Hoyt

William B. Hoyt is an accounting instructor at Wilton High School in Wilton, Connecticut. He has been involved in accounting curriculum development for many years and was a member of the writing task force for the National Standards for Business Education. In 1996, Mr. Hoyt was named Connecticut's Outstanding Business Educator of the Year and in 1997 was named National Secondary Teacher of the Year by the National Business Education Association.

NOTICE: Information on featured companies, organizations, and their products and services is included for educational purposes only, and it does not present or imply endorsement of the *Business and Personal Finance* program.

McGraw Hill Glencoe

The McGraw·Hill Companies

Printed in the United States of America.

Send all inquiries to:

Glencoe/McGraw-Hill
4400 Easton Commons
Columbus, OH 43219

ISBN-13: 978-0-07-868712-9 (Student Text)
ISBN-10: 0-07-868712-8 (Student Text)

ISBN-13: 978-0-07-869846-0 (Teacher Annotated Edition)
ISBN-10: 0-07-869846-4 (Teacher Annotated Edition)

4 5 6 7 8 9 DOW 12 11 10

Table of Contents

The Importance of Business and Personal Finance

According to a national survey by Teenage Research Unlimited, spending among American teens has risen from $141 billion per year to a staggering $170 billion per year over the past five years. In addition, the teen population in the United States is growing. Researchers predict that by 2010, there will be 35 million teens—and they will be spending a lot of money.

Unfortunately, research also indicates that teens know very little about managing their money. For example, a recent *Consumer Reports* study of 12-year-olds shows that only seven out of ten know that using credit cards is a form of borrowing. Only four out of ten teenagers know that banks charge interest on loans. In fact, many students pay for their college education using credit cards with interest rates as high as 22 percent, when the interest on student loan packages has been as low as 3 to 5 percent.

Consider these additional statistics:

- 48 percent of college students have bounced checks.
- Only two out of five college students balance their checkbooks every month.
- 67 percent of college students have credit cards, and 71 percent of those carry a balance.
- An average high school graduate today may earn more than $1 million during his or her adult life.

In her *Washington Post* column, financial writer Jane Bryant Quinn had this to say about teaching young people to manage their finances: "Young people today are plunged into a world of options from the first day they walk out of school. Credit card or debit cards? Buy a car or lease one? Cash value insurance, term insurance, or none at all? Which mutual fund for your 401(k)? What, by the way, is a mutual fund? Without rudimentary knowledge, how can they possibly make intelligent choices?"

Parents, of course, can educate their children about money, but parents may not have complete knowledge themselves. Financial experts such as Jane Bryant Quinn think classrooms are excellent forums for teaching financial management. Research shows that in states where financial management courses are required in school, adults tend to save more money and have lower bankruptcy rates.

Business and Personal Finance can help students navigate the financial decisions they face today and tomorrow because the text teaches financial management skills. First, it presents and clearly explains financial concepts, such as consumer purchasing strategies, consumer credit, investing, and insurance. Then, with features and activities, such as Document Detective, Common Cents, Savvy Saver, What's Your Financial ID?, and Your Financial Portfolio, students can understand the everyday relevance of newly presented concepts.

Business and Personal Finance will help you teach your students how to use their personal financial resources to enjoy today and be financially secure tomorrow.

Marketing Your Personal Finance Program

Glencoe has provided the following resources in the *Marketing Your Personal Finance Program* supplementary booklet:

- *Your Marketing Plan:* ideas about how to get your message to future students and other decision makers
- *Benefits of Personal Finance:* a table showing the benefits of a personal finance program for students, parents, teachers, department chairs, superintendents, and the community
- *Back-to-School Night Activities:* creative projects
- *Finance Quiz:* suitable for teenagers and adults
- *Personal Finance Resources:* Web sites for young people and educators

Welcome to *Business and Personal Finance*

Do you remember when you first learned that checks had to be backed by money in the bank and that you could not write a check for just any amount? Do you remember the first time you read a table that explained how many years it would take to pay off a credit card balance? Many students today do not fully understand these and other financial concepts.

Business and Personal Finance introduces students to the world of money management and finance. They will learn what to do with their money by learning about their financial options and their responsibilities—and they will learn about the consequences of mismanaged finances.

Business and Personal Finance is a comprehensive text, using the National Standards for Business Education to develop the topics covered in the text. A colorful design, lots of visual interest, clear examples, and an easy-to-read style invite students of all backgrounds and abilities to explore the content.

Teaching the Unit

Business and Personal Finance is divided into six units. The first four units cover personal finance, and the last two units focus on business finance. Each unit covers a specific financial topic and consists of three or four chapters. Each unit-opener spread focuses on the content of the upcoming unit.

Closing the Unit Each unit culminates in a unit lab simulation related to what students have learned throughout the unit.

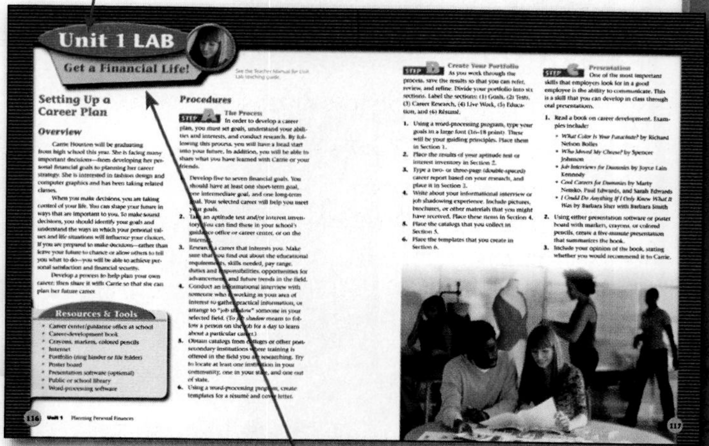

WebQuest This unit activity is continued in each chapter in the unit as it introduces students to a unit topic and directs them to the Online Learning Center to complete a project.

Unit Opener Photo The unit-opener photo illustrates a concept that is related to the unit text so students can get ready for the unit. Ask students: "How does the photo relate to the content of the unit?"

Get a Financial Life! Unit Lab Simulation This unit simulation provides hands-on experience that expands students' understanding of finance as they apply what they have learned to a real-world project.

***BusinessWeek* Finance File** Each unit opens with an excerpt from a *BusinessWeek* article about an aspect of the unit material. The feature directs students to the Online Learning Center to read the complete article and do an activity.

Teacher Manual

Teaching the Chapter

Each chapter of *Business and Personal Finance* is divided into two to four sections in order to facilitate students' ability to manage what they are learning. The chapters are presented in a single-column format to promote readability. Sidebars, features, and colorful illustrations maintain student interest. The chapter-opener resources are designed to preview the chapter topics and help set students' purpose for reading.

Chapter Objectives The learning objectives preview the most important topics covered in the chapter and provide a preview as students familiarize themselves with the new chapter.

Chapter-Opener Photo The chapter-opener photo focuses on the chapter topic as students prepare to read. Ask students: "How does this photo relate to the chapter title?"

In the Real World A brief scenario introduces a chapter concept that relates to the real world as students get ready to begin the chapter.

Reading Strategies The reading strategies listed in the *Reading Strategies* box at the beginning of each chapter can help students to read actively. Also, individual reading strategies are placed throughout the chapter to increase students' understanding.

Ask Standard & Poor's Students get expert financial advice from Standard and Poor's as this feature answers real questions about everyday business and personal finance.

Inside the Student Edition

Teaching the Section

Each chapter of *Business and Personal Finance* is divided into two to four sections. Each section introduces the chapter material in manageable and organized segments.

The Section Open

Focus on Reading Read to Learn lists the concepts that students will learn in the section, providing guidance and structure for the student.

Main Idea explains the main concepts that students learn.

Key Terms list the major terms presented in each section. The key terms are also highlighted and boldface in the text throughout the sections, accompanied by clear, in-context definitions.

Photographs and Figures Throughout each section, relevant photographs, and useful charts and graphs illustrate and expand content. Captions with questions reinforce what students learn.

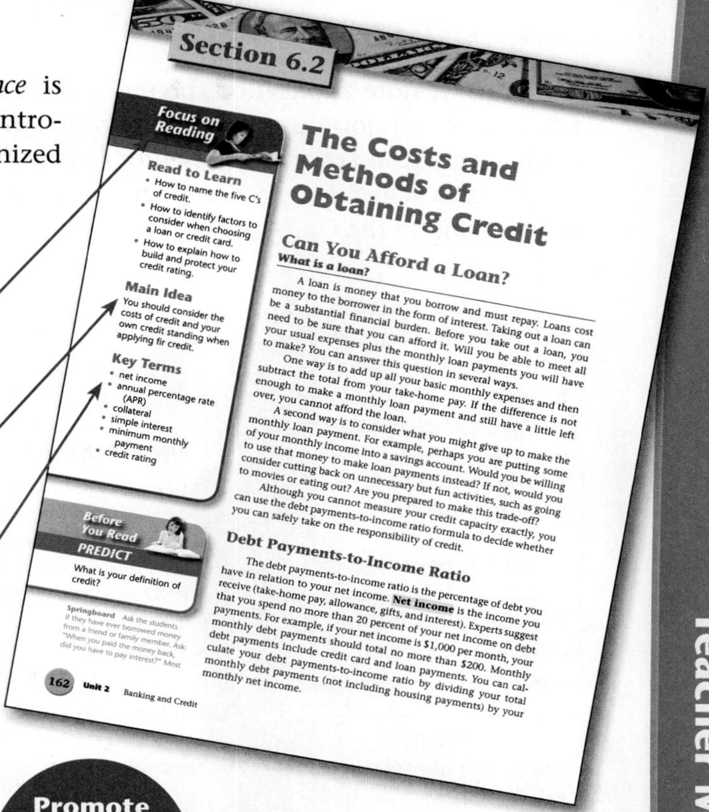

Section 6.2

Focus on Reading

Read to Learn
- How to name the five C's of credit.
- How to identify factors to consider when choosing a loan or credit card.
- How to explain how to build and protect your credit rating.

Main Idea

You should consider the costs of credit and your own credit standing when applying fir credit.

Key Terms
- net income
- annual percentage rate (APR)
- collateral
- simple interest
- minimum monthly payment
- credit rating

Before You Read

PREDICT

What is your definition of credit?

The Costs and Methods of Obtaining Credit

Can You Afford a Loan?

What is a loan?

A loan is money that you borrow and must repay. Loans cost money to the borrower in the form of interest. Taking out a loan can be a substantial financial burden. Before you take out a loan, you need to be sure that you can afford it. Will you be able to meet all your usual expenses plus the monthly loan payments you will have to make? You can answer this question in several ways.

One way is to add up all your basic monthly expenses and then subtract the total from your take-home pay. If the difference is not enough to make a monthly loan payment and still have a little left over, you cannot afford the loan.

A second way is to consider what you might give up to make the monthly loan payment. For example, perhaps you are putting some of your monthly income into a savings account. Would you be willing to use that money to make loan payments instead? If not, would you consider cutting back on unnecessary but fun activities, such as going to movies or eating out? Are you prepared to make this trade-off?

Although you cannot measure your credit capacity exactly, you can use the debt payments-to-income ratio formula to decide whether you can safely take on the responsibility of credit.

Debt Payments-to-Income Ratio

The debt payments-to-income ratio is the percentage of debt you have in relation to your net income. **Net income** is the income you receive (take-home pay, allowance, gifts, and interest). Experts suggest that you spend no more than 20 percent of your net income on debt payments. For example, if your net income is $1,000 per month, your monthly debt payments should total no more than $200. Monthly debt payments include credit card and loan payments. You can calculate your debt payments-to-income ratio by dividing your total monthly debt payments (not including housing payments) by your monthly net income.

Springboard Ask the students if they have ever borrowed money from a friend or family member. Ask: "When you paid the money back, did you have to pay interest?" Most

162 Unit 2 Banking and Credit

Promote Reading and Writing Skills

The Section Close

Quick Check questions relate to the concepts in the section objectives.

Think Critically focuses on the material in the section and cross-curricular skill activities.

Use Communication Skills, Use Math Skills, and **Solve Money Problems** present realistic scenarios requiring students to apply financial concepts and solve financial math problems. Applications include writing, calculating, analyzing, role-playing, and presentation activities.

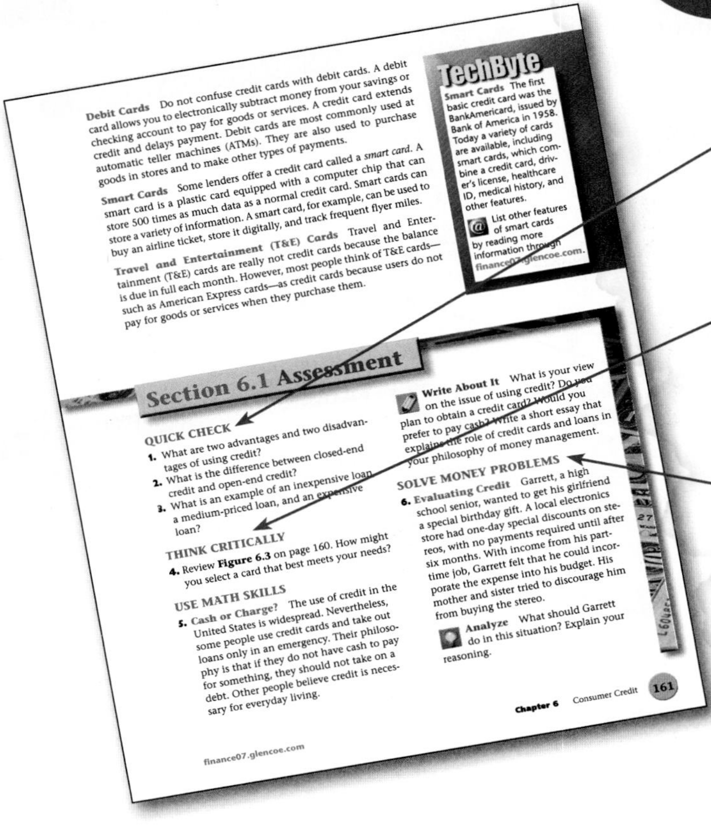

Debit Cards Do not confuse credit cards with debit cards. A debit card allows you to electronically subtract money from your savings or checking account to pay for goods or services. A credit card extends credit and delays payment. Debit cards are most commonly used at automatic teller machines (ATMs). They are also used to purchase goods in stores and to make other types of payments.

Smart Cards Some lenders offer a credit card called a *smart card*. A smart card is a plastic card equipped with a computer chip that can store 500 times as much data as a normal credit card. Smart cards can store a variety of information. A smart card, for example, can be used to buy an airline ticket, store it digitally, and track frequent flyer miles.

Travel and Entertainment (T&E) Cards Travel and Entertainment (T&E) cards are really not credit cards because the balance is due in full each month. However, most people think of T&E cards—such as American Express cards—as credit cards because users do not pay for goods or services when they purchase them.

TechByte

Smart Cards The first basic credit card was the BankAmericard, issued by Bank of America in 1958. Today a variety of cards are available, including smart cards, which combine a credit card, driver's license, healthcare ID, medical history, and other features.

List other features of smart cards by reading more information through finance07.glencoe.com.

Section 6.1 Assessment

QUICK CHECK
1. What are two advantages and two disadvantages of using credit?
2. What is the difference between closed-end credit and open-end credit?
3. What is an example of an inexpensive loan, a medium-priced loan, and an expensive loan?

THINK CRITICALLY
4. Review **Figure 6.3** on page 160. How might you select a card that best meets your needs?

USE MATH SKILLS
5. **Cash or Charge?** The use of credit in the United States is widespread. Nevertheless, some people use credit cards and take out loans only in an emergency. Their philosophy is that if they do not have cash to pay for something, they should not take on a debt. Other people believe credit is necessary for everyday living.

Write About It What is your view on the issue of using credit? Do you plan to obtain a credit card? Would you prefer to pay cash? Write a short essay that explains the role of credit cards and loans in your philosophy of money management.

SOLVE MONEY PROBLEMS
6. **Evaluating Credit** Garrett, a high school senior, wanted to get his girlfriend a special birthday gift. A local electronics store had one-day special discounts on stereos, with no payments required until after six months. With income from his part-time job, Garrett felt that he could incorporate the expense into his budget. His mother and sister tried to discourage him from buying the stereo.

Analyze What should Garrett do in this situation? Explain your reasoning.

finance07.glencoe.com

Chapter 6 Consumer Credit 161

Go Figure—Financial Math

This feature/application presents relevant financial math formulas that clearly illustrate math formulas and concepts presented in the text. The formula is first described in the text and then shown again in the Go Figure box.

Subtitle describes the topic covered.

You Figure gives students on-the-spot application of math formulas.

Synopsis explains the purpose of the math formula.

Example describes a math problem in words.

Formula explains the calculation in words.

Solution demonstrates the numeric calculation.

GO FIGURE — FINANCIAL MATH

UNIT PRICING

Synopsis: Knowing the unit price of an item can help you determine the best buy.

Example: The brand of peppermint mouthwash that Claudia likes is offered in two sizes, 12 ounces for $2.89 and 16 ounces for $3.39. Which is the better buy?

Formula: $\frac{\text{Total Price}}{\text{Unit of Measurement}} = \text{Unit Price}$

Solution: $\frac{\$2.89}{12\text{ oz.}} = \$0.24/\text{oz.}$

$\frac{\$3.39}{16\text{ oz.}} = \$0.21/\text{oz.}$

The 16-ounce size is the better buy at 21 cents per ounce.

YOU FIGURE

You are considering buying soft drinks for your sister's birthday party. The market is offering a six-pack for $2.99 and a liter bottle for $1.29. Which is the better buy?

Math Skills Builder

This appendix feature helps students review real-world math fundamentals, such as multiplying or dividing decimals, reading tables and charts, and problem solving using more than one operation. Each skill-building activity begins with a verbal explanation of the particular math skill:

Example is a numeric example of the problem.

Solution shows step-by-step how to solve the problem.

Problems reinforce the math skill through practice.

Applications show students how to apply the math skill to financial situations.

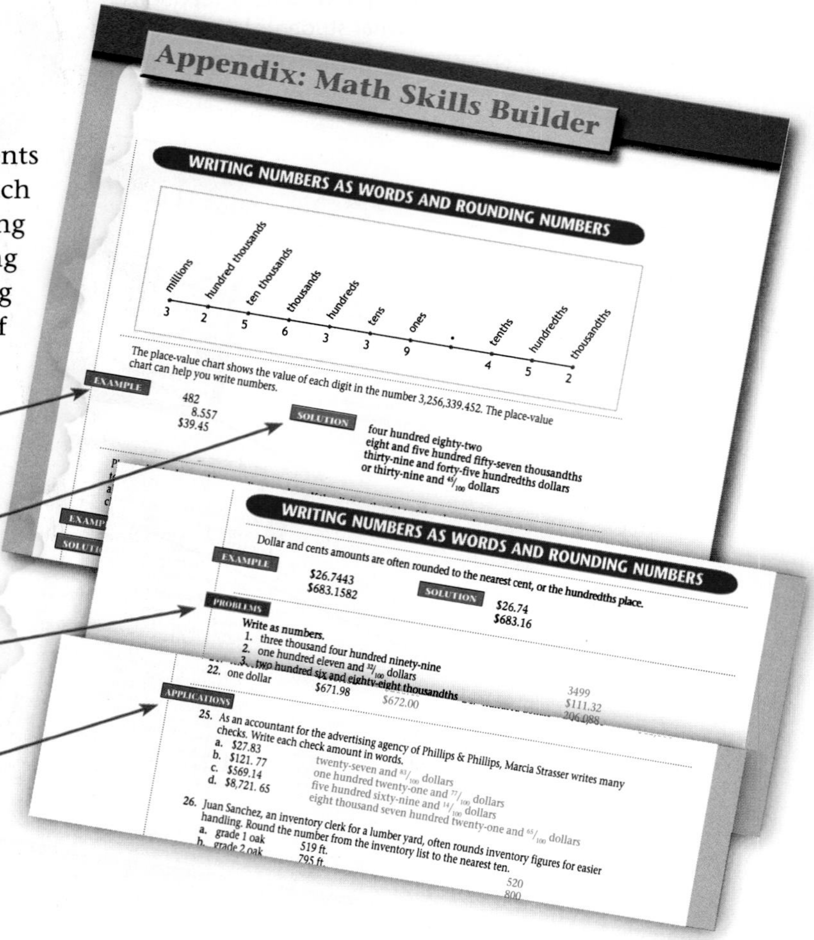

Chapter Review and Activities

Each chapter ends with a four-page review and applications designed to help students recall, use, and expand on the concepts presented in the chapter. *Review and Activities* presents a chapter summary with a key terms activity, recall and review questions, real-world applications, and activities that help you integrate a variety of academics with finance.

What's Your Financial ID? This one-page quick financial assessment quiz helps students evaluate and define their own financial sense or personality.

Your Financial Portfolio This one-page application presents interesting financial situations and gives students information to evaluate and make wise financial decisions. Corresponding worksheets for each chapter are provided in the *Student Activity Workbook*.

Real-World Application Students use their higher-level thinking skills as they consider the basic concepts of the text, connecting real-world finance to other fields of academic study.

Your Financial Figures A real-life financial problem gives students the context for calculating an answer and using software.

Academic Skills Students can reinforce the connection between a variety of academic subjects and finance.

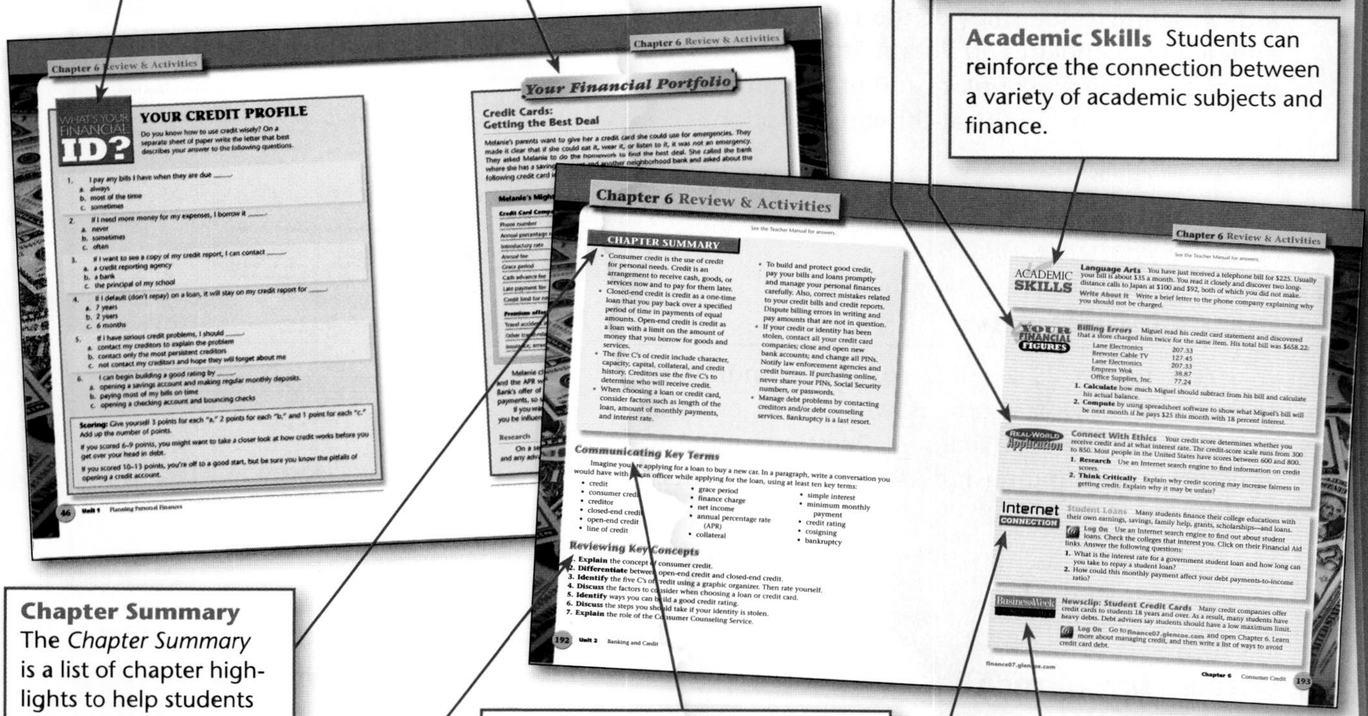

Chapter Summary The *Chapter Summary* is a list of chapter highlights to help students review and remember main points related to a chapter objective.

Communicating Key Terms Students review the financial key terms learned throughout the chapter by applying them in written context.

Reviewing Key Concepts Review questions are correlated to the chapter objectives to help students check their understanding of the text through defining terms and explaining concepts.

Internet Connection This activity challenges students to use the Internet to answer financial questions and solve financial problems through the book's Online Learning Center at **finance07.glencoe.com**.

***BusinessWeek* Online** Students are directed to the Online Learning Center, where they will find complete chapter-related articles to read as they complete an activity.

Inside the Student Edition

Focus on Features

High-interest features in each chapter engage students, enhance their understanding, and increase their involvement with real-world situations. Features incorporate activities, such as critical-thinking questions, that help students integrate what they have learned and apply it.

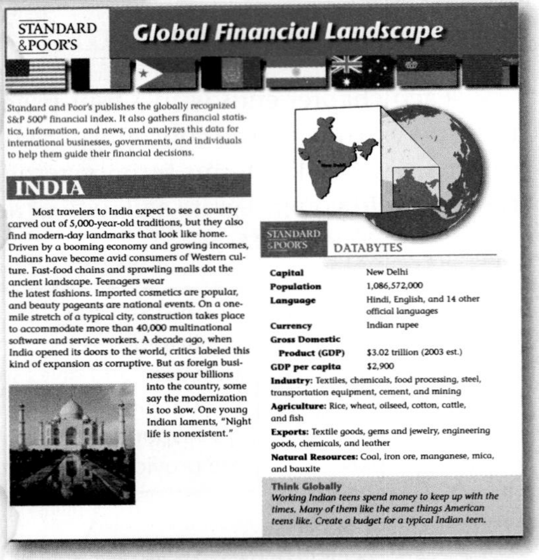

STANDARD &POOR'S

Global Financial Landscape

Standard and Poor's publishes the globally recognized S&P 500® financial index. It also gathers financial statistics, information, and news, and analyzes this data for international businesses, governments, and individuals to help them guide their financial decisions.

INDIA

Most travelers to India expect to see a country carved out of 5,000-year-old traditions, but they also find modern-day landmarks that look like home. Driven by a booming economy and growing incomes, Indians have become avid consumers of Western culture. Fast-food chains and sprawling malls dot the ancient landscape. Teenagers wear the latest fashions. Imported cosmetics are popular, and beauty pageants are national events. On a one-mile stretch of a typical city, construction takes place to accommodate more than 40,000 multinational software and service workers. A decade ago, when India opened its doors to the world, critics labeled this kind of expansion as corruptive. But as foreign businesses pour billions into the country, some say the modernization is too slow. One young Indian laments, "Night life is nonexistent."

STANDARD &POOR'S DATABYTES

Capital	New Delhi
Population	1,086,572,000
Language	Hindi, English, and 14 other official languages
Currency	Indian rupee
Gross Domestic Product (GDP)	$3.02 trillion (2003 est.)
GDP per capita	$2,900

Industry: Textiles, chemicals, food processing, steel, transportation equipment, cement, and mining

Agriculture: Rice, wheat, oilseed, cotton, cattle, and fish

Exports: Textile goods, gems and jewelry, engineering goods, chemicals, and leather

Natural Resources: Coal, iron ore, manganese, mica, and bauxite

Think Globally
Working Indian teens spend money to keep up with the times. Many of them like the same things American teens like. Create a budget for a typical Indian teen.

The S&P's Global Financial Landscape

The *S&P's Global Financial Landscape* feature presents interesting financial profiles of different countries with a DataByte snapshot of the country's statistics gathered by Standard and Poor's. Students will learn about the global marketplace and other cultures, and be challenged with a critical-thinking question.

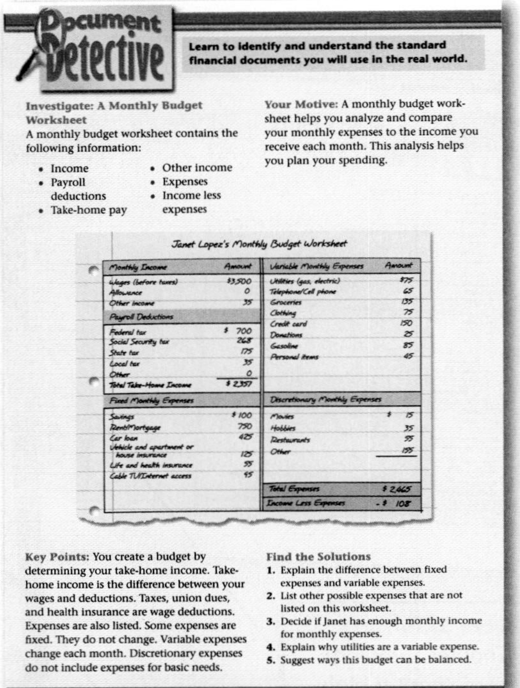

Document Detective

Learn to identify and understand the standard financial documents you will use in the real world.

Investigate: A Monthly Budget Worksheet
A monthly budget worksheet contains the following information:

- Income
- Payroll deductions
- Take-home pay
- Other income
- Expenses
- Income less expenses

Your Motive: A monthly budget worksheet helps you analyze and compare your monthly expenses to the income you receive each month. This analysis helps you plan your spending.

Janet Lopez's Monthly Budget Worksheet

Monthly Income	Amount	Variable Monthly Expenses	Amount
Wages (before taxes)	$3,500	Utilities (gas, electric)	$75
Allowance	0	Telephone/Cell phone	65
Other income	35	Groceries	135
Payroll Deductions		Clothing	75
Federal tax	$ 700	Credit card	150
Social Security tax	268	Donations	25
State tax	175	Gasoline	85
Local tax	35	Personal items	45
Other	0		
Total Take-Home Income	$ 2,357		
Fixed Monthly Expenses		Discretionary Monthly Expenses	
Savings	$ 100	Movies	$ 15
Rent/Mortgage	750	Hobbies	35
Car loan	425	Restaurants	55
Vehicle and apartment or house insurance	125	Other	155
Life and health insurance	55		
Cable TV/Internet access	45		
		Total Expenses	$ 2,465
		Income Less Expenses	- $ 108

Key Points: You create a budget by determining your take-home income. Take-home income is the difference between your wages and deductions. Taxes, union dues, and health insurance are wage deductions. Expenses are also listed. Some expenses are fixed. They do not change. Variable expenses change each month. Discretionary expenses do not include expenses for basic needs.

Find the Solutions
1. Explain the difference between fixed expenses and variable expenses.
2. List other possible expenses that are not listed on this worksheet.
3. Decide if Janet has enough monthly income for monthly expenses.
4. Explain why utilities are a variable expense.
5. Suggest ways this budget can be balanced.

Document Detective

This feature is a guide to understanding the financial documents students will use in everyday business and personal finance. Questions reinforce students' understanding and use of the documents.

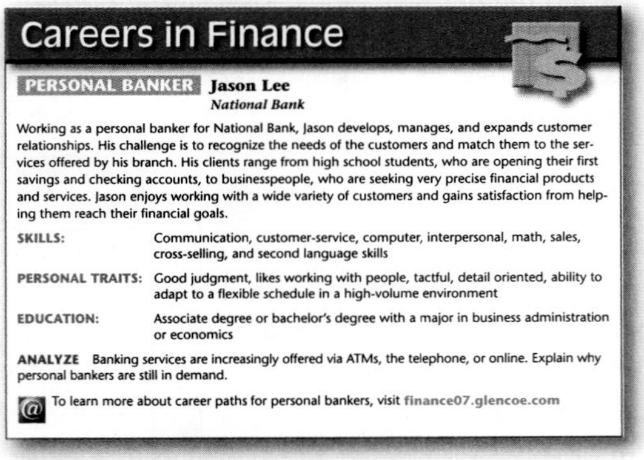

Careers in Finance

PERSONAL BANKER **Jason Lee**
National Bank

Working as a personal banker for National Bank, Jason develops, manages, and expands customer relationships. His challenge is to recognize the needs of the customers and match them to the services offered by his branch. His clients range from high school students, who are opening their first savings and checking accounts, to businesspeople, who are seeking very precise financial products and services. Jason enjoys working with a wide variety of customers and gains satisfaction from helping them reach their financial goals.

SKILLS: Communication, customer-service, computer, interpersonal, math, sales, cross-selling, and second language skills

PERSONAL TRAITS: Good judgment, likes working with people, tactful, detail oriented, ability to adapt to a flexible schedule in a high-volume environment

EDUCATION: Associate degree or bachelor's degree with a major in business administration or economics

ANALYZE Banking services are increasingly offered via ATMs, the telephone, or online. Explain why personal bankers are still in demand.

To learn more about career paths for personal bankers, visit finance07.glencoe.com

Careers in Finance

The *Careers in Finance* feature focuses on and describes a specific career that pertains to a topic presented in the chapter. This feature profiles a field, market, or profession, rather than a particular person, and itemizes characteristics of the career, such as skills, personality, and education. It concludes with a related activity or question.

Inside the Student Edition

TechByte

TechByte Technology is today's number-one trend. This feature highlights the wide range of technological applications that enhance business and personal finance today. An exercise directs students to the book's Online Learning Center at **finance07.glencoe.com**.

Standard & Poor's Put on Your Financial Planner's Cap

Real scenarios provide problems that students can solve as they think like a financial planner.

Academic Connection

This feature connects finance with another field of study, such as art, language arts, history, social science, law, science, health, or other subjects. This interdisciplinary approach helps students integrate academics and perceive interesting links as they observe how finance applies and relates to a variety of pursuits.

$avvy Saver

Lists of interesting tips and facts, such as eating out on a budget or finding the best savings account, help students save money as they learn about business and personal finance.

Common CENTS

Quick finance facts that are related to the chapter topics are reinforced with a critical-thinking application.

WebQuest

Each chapter includes a continuation activity of the WebQuest unit feature that directs students to the Online Learning Center to complete this unit-related project.

Using the Annotations

The annotations provide on-the-spot teaching options and activities. Annotations within the chapter's side columns and in features provide suggestions for teaching the class and ideas for student involvement with the text. Each chapter features the following annotations and answers for figures, photographs, and Go Figure activities.

Springboard serves as a bell-ringer, an activity that helps students "shift gears" from their previous class and focus on the material to be presented.

Motivating Students involves students in chapter content that will be presented in the chapter.

Research suggests independent practice exercises to reinforce learning.

Discussion annotations present topics or open-ended questions that involve students in comprehending and applying the concepts presented.

STEP 2: Develop Your Financial Goals

To develop clear financial goals, think about your attitude toward money and ask yourself some questions: Is it more important to spend your money now or to save for the future? Would you rather get a job right after high school or continue your education? Do your personal values affect your financial decisions? **Values** are the beliefs and principles you consider important, correct, and desirable. Different people value different things.

Needs and Wants Another important aspect of developing financial goals is knowing the difference between your needs and your wants. A *need* is something you must have to survive, such as food, shelter, and clothing. A *want* is something you desire or would like to have or do. For example, if you live in an area where the winter is cold, you need a coat. So you may want a leather jacket, but other less expensive coats would also keep you warm.

Only you can decide what specific goals to pursue. For example, you might want to save money. So, you could save $50 every month or 15 percent of every paycheck.

TechByte

Using Software There are many software products on the market today designed to help you keep track of your personal finances. One of the first and most popular is Quicken®. Features allow you to track and pay bills and see if you have enough money to cover upcoming bills. You can also schedule bill payments and deposits.

@ Describe the information given on the Quicken monthly view screen by reading information through finance07.glencoe.com.

STEP 3: Identify Your Options

It is impossible to make a good decision unless you know all your options. Generally, you have several possible courses of action. Suppose that you are saving $50 a month. You might have these options:

Springboard Ask the students if they feel confident about their ability to make personal financial decisions. Have them explain why or why not.

- **Expand the current situation.** You may decide to increase the amount of money you save every month to $60.
- **Change the current situation.** You could invest in stocks instead of putting your money into a savings account.
- **Start something new.** You could use the $50 to pay off your debts.
- **Continue the same course of action.** You may choose not to change anything.

However, in each case, be aware that the costs of your decision may outweigh the benefits.

▶ MONEY MATTERS Your values affect your spending habits. *Why might people shop at vintage clothing stores or swap meets?*
Answer Answers may include to find bargains, find collectibles, for fun.

finance07.glencoe.com **Chapter 1** Personal Financial Planning 7

Caption Answer provides a possible response to each caption question.

As You Read **QUESTION**

Why should you know the future value of a deposit when making financial plans?

It can help you determine the opportunity costs of spending now or saving for the future.

Future value tables simplify the process of figuring out the effect of compounding. Many online future value calculators are available. The table in Part A of **Figure 1.4** shows the future value of a single deposit of $1. To use the table, find the annual interest rate that your money is earning. Then see what the future value is at Year 5, Year 6, and so on. Multiply the future value figure by the amount of your deposit. For example, if you deposit $1 in a 7 percent account, at the end of Year 7, you would have $1.61:

$$\$1 \times 1.606 = \$1.606$$

Future Value of a Series of Deposits Some savers and investors like to make regular deposits into their savings. A series of equal regular deposits is sometimes called an **annuity**. Use Part B of the chart in Figure 1.4 (future value of a series of equal yearly deposits) to find out the future value of $1,000 a year at 5 percent annual interest for six years. At the end of the six years, you would have $6,802:

$$\$1{,}000 \times 6.802 = \$6{,}802$$

Teaching Activity Divide students into groups of four or five. Tell them that each group has $10,000 to do with as they please. Ask them to discuss options, opportunity costs, interest rates, or any other relevant matters they can come up with. The group is then to determine how they will use the money and prepare a presentation discussing their decisions and how they arrived at them.

Present Value of a Single Deposit You can also calculate the **present value**, which is the amount of money you would need to deposit now in order to have a desired amount in the future. For example, if you want to have $1,000 in five years for a down payment on a car, and your savings account pays 5 percent annual interest, how much money will you need to deposit now to accumulate $1,000? Part C of Figure 1.4 will help you find the answer. Find Year 5 in the left column, and look across to the 5 percent interest-rate column. The value given is 0.784. Multiply this value by the amount of money you want to have in five years:

$$\$1{,}000 \times 0.784 = \$784$$

You need to deposit $784 now to have $1,000 in five years.

Extension Have the students contact local banks to learn what the interest rates are on savings accounts. If the rates differ between banks, ask the students to discuss why they think that occurs.

Present Value of a Series of Deposits You can also use present value calculations to determine how much you would need to deposit so you can take a specific amount of money out of your savings account for a certain number of years. If you want to take $400 out of your account each year for nine years, and your money is earning interest at 8 percent a year, how much money would you need to deposit now? Part D of Figure 1.4 will help you find the answer. Find Year 9 in the left column and look across to the 8 percent interest-rate column. The value given is 6.247. Multiply this value by the amount of money that you want to take out every year:

$$\$400 \times 6.247 = \$2{,}498.80$$

You need to deposit $2,498.80 now to be able to take out $400 each year for nine years. This calculation is used for retirement.

STANDARD & POOR'S **Put on Your Financial Planner's Cap**

If you were planning an investment for yourself, would you choose an annuity? *Why or why not?*

See the Teacher Manual for answer.

22 **Unit 1** Planning Personal Finances

Teaching Activity provides ideas for engaging students of all levels in purposeful activities as they learn.

Critical Thinking encourages higher-level thinking with application.

Extension presents activities that help students explore the content in depth.

Inside the Teacher Annotated Edition

Using the Planning Guides

To help you select activities that will best meet the needs of your students, the *Teacher Annotated Edition* includes a Planning Guide at the beginning of each unit to introduce important concepts. Each chapter also contains a Planning Guide that organizes the chapter's lesson activities into objectives, features, and resources. Additional teaching activities are provided for in-depth coverage of core concepts.

Learning Objectives column lists specific skills and knowledge students can expect to master as they study each chapter. These measurable objectives guide students to read, discuss, and review the chapter.

Features in each section are listed in order of their appearance in the text.

Text and **Technology Resources** columns list pertinent activities from the text and the ancillaries.

National Standards for Business Education chart lists the correlated standards covered by each section.

Teaching Connection provides teaching tips and classroom activities to be applied to the finance classroom.

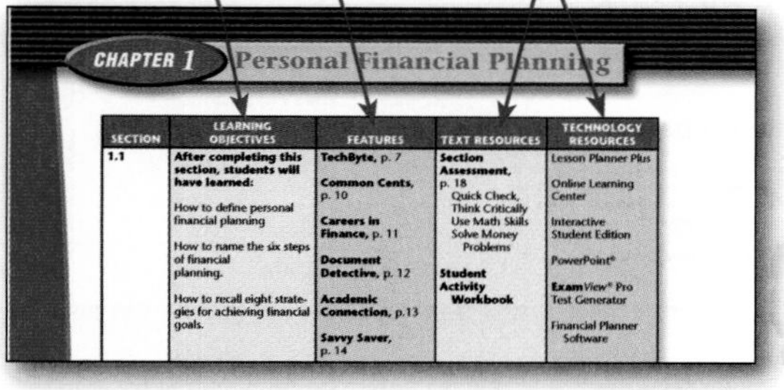

CHAPTER 1 Personal Financial Planning

SECTION	LEARNING OBJECTIVES	FEATURES	TEXT RESOURCES	TECHNOLOGY RESOURCES
1.1	After completing this section, students will have learned: How to define personal financial planning; How to name the six steps of financial planning; How to recall eight strategies for achieving financial goals.	TechByte, p. 7; Common Cents, p. 10; Careers in Finance, p. 11; Document Detective, p. 12; Academic Connection, p. 13; Savvy Saver, p. 14	Section Assessment, p. 18: Quick Check, Think Critically, Use Math Skills, Solve Money Problems; Student Activity Workbook	Lesson Planner Plus; Online Learning Center; Interactive Student Edition; PowerPoint®; ExamView® Pro Test Generator; Financial Planner Software

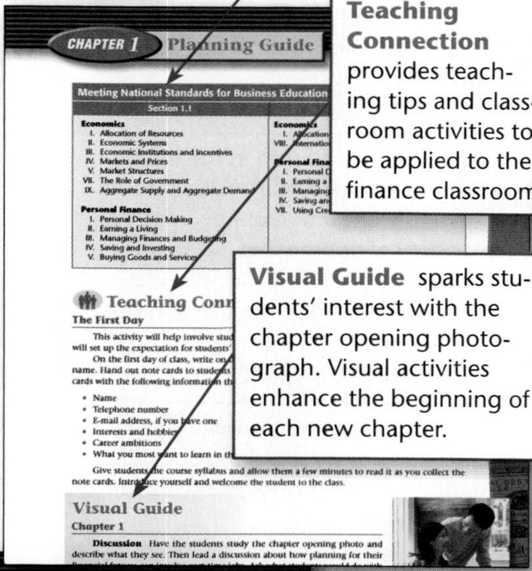

CHAPTER 1 Planning Guide

Meeting National Standards for Business Education

Section 1.1

Economics: I. Allocation of Resources; II. Economic Systems; III. Economic Institutions and Incentives; IV. Markets and Prices; V. Market Structures; VII. The Role of Government; IX. Aggregate Supply and Aggregate Demand

Personal Finance: I. Personal Decision Making; II. Earning a Living; III. Managing Finances and Budgeting; IV. Saving and Investing; V. Buying Goods and Services

Teaching Connection

The First Day

Visual Guide

Chapter 1

Discussion Have the students study the chapter opening photo and describe what they see. Then lead a discussion about how planning for their

Visual Guide sparks students' interest with the chapter opening photograph. Visual activities enhance the beginning of each new chapter.

Workplace Skills and Chapter Correlation chart shows you which foundation skills and workplace competencies are covered in each chapter.

Internet Extension guides your class through an extra Internet activity.

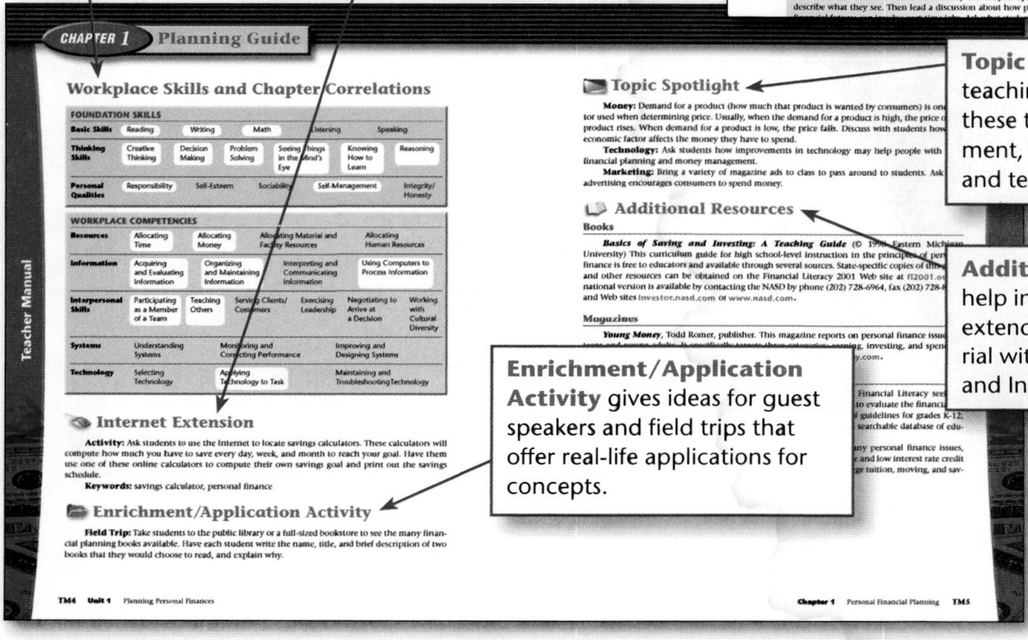

CHAPTER 1 Planning Guide

Workplace Skills and Chapter Correlations

Internet Extension

Activity: Ask students to use the Internet to locate savings calculators. These calculators will compute how much you have to save every day, week, and month to reach your goal. Have them use one of these online calculators to compute their own savings goal and print out the savings schedule.

Keywords: savings calculator, personal finance

Enrichment/Application Activity

Field Trip: Take students to the public library or a full-sized bookstore to see the many financial planning books available. Have each student write the name, title, and brief description of two books that they would choose to read, and explain why.

Topic Spotlight

Additional Resources

Topic Spotlight provides teaching activities related to these topics: ethics, government, marketing, money, and technology.

Additional Resources help instructors or students extend the chapter material with references to books and Internet resources.

Enrichment/Application Activity gives ideas for guest speakers and field trips that offer real-life applications for concepts.

Teacher Manual

Using the Lesson Plans

The Lesson Plans in the *Teacher Annotated Edition* are found in the *Teacher Manual* section and make full and effective use of a mastery approach in four steps: Focus, Teach, Assess, and Close. This widely accepted instructional method develops students' understanding of the subject matter while providing a consistent framework that makes it easy for you to teach the material.

Focus The first step in presenting new material is to capture students' interest. The Lesson Plans suggest a variety of interesting motivational activities to focus students' interest.

Teach The second step in the instructional process encompasses the presentation and exploration of new material. The variety of approaches, strategies, and activities provided allow you to help all students assimilate the content of each chapter.

Assess This third step provides a variety of evaluation and reteaching activities designed to accommodate a wide range of learning abilities.

Close The final step of the instructional method allows students to look back over the new material presented in the lesson. Students summarize what they have learned, evaluate their own learning processes, and relate the new material to their own lives.

CHAPTER 1 Lesson Plans

Teacher Manual

Section 1.1

Focus

Motivation

Ask the student to think about financial goals they might set during the school year. Acknowledge all goals and list them on the board. Then ask the students how they think they will be able to achieve these goals. Use this discussion to introduce this chapter.

Prereading

1. Have the students skim the section, looking at photos and figures, reading captions, and noting headings.
2. Have a student read aloud What You'll Learn on page 4.
3. Dictate each of the key terms to the class. Have students write them on a piece of paper. Then write the key terms on the board. Ask students to guess at the meaning of each term. Leave the list on the board as students study the section.

Teach

Guided Practice

1. Have the student read aloud In the Real World on page 5.
2. Have the students read aloud Ask Standard and Poor's on page 5.
3. Have students silently read the rest of the section, noting and mentally answering the Predict, Relate, Question, and caption questions and reading the features such as Document Detective.

Independent Practice

Have students create a collage of their financial goals for the future. Allow them to use pictures from magazines, Clipart from the computer, or their own artwork. Display the finished collages around the room.

Assess

Reteaching

1. Review the list of key terms that students were unsure about before studying the section.
2. To reteach the concept of supply and demand, choose a popular toy to use as an example. Help the students understand that if demand for a toy is high, then the supply goes down and prices often go up. Then if the popularity of a toy diminishes and the demand goes down, the supply will be high and the prices might be discounted to sell the merchandise.
3. Ask the students to create a list of toys and games (electronic or otherwise) that they think have been affected by this economic concept.

Enrichment

Have the students go to the library or use the Internet to research the Federal Reserve System and the role it plays in our economy. The Web site for the Federal Reserve System is federalreserve.gov.

Assessment

1. Have the students complete the Section 1.1 Assessment.
2. Assign an activity from the *Student Activity Workbook*.

Close

Have students complete this statement: "If I learn and put into action the six steps in the financial planning process, I will...." (Sample response: "...have a solid foundation for making all my financial decisions, now and in the future.")

TM58 Unit 1 Planning Personal Finances

Section 1.2

Focus

Motivation

Ask students to imagine they have just won a million dollars. Generate a discussion about what they would do with that money. Encourage them to think about saving and investing for the future.

Prereading

1. Have the students skim the section, looking at photos and figures, reading captions, and noting headings.
2. Ask a student to read aloud Read to Learn on page 19.
3. Have the students write down each highlighted key term in the section and generate a picture or symbol that identifies it, based on its definition.

Teach

Guided Practice

1. Ask a student to read aloud the paragraph Personal Opportunity Costs.
2. Have students silently read the rest of the section, noting and mentally answering the Predict, Relate, Question, and caption questions and reading the features such as Put on Your Financial Planner's Cap.

Independent Practice

Have students use newspaper or magazine articles to research and report on the current interest rate charged by the Federal Reserve. Then find out what local banks and financial institutions pay you to use your money. Each month throughout the course, research these rates again. Graph the changes in interest rates.

Assess

Reteaching

1. Review the key terms from the section. Make sure the students understand them.
2. To reinforce the concept of the time value of money, ask your students to think about all the times during the last month that they spend, borrowed, saved, or invested money. Then ask them how they might have better used that money.

Enrichment

1. Have the students write an article for the school newspaper on a topic from this chapter. Some ideas might include financial goal setting, the time value of money, or strategies for achieving financial goals.
2. Have the students review the eight strategies for achieving financial goals, found on pages 24–25. Then ask them to create a journal of how they think they will apply the strategies to their own lives now and in the future.

Assessment

1. Have the students complete the Section 1.2 Assessment.
2. Assign the Chapter 1 Review and Activities.
3. Administer the test for Chapter 1 from the Reproducible Tests included in the *Lesson Planner Plus* supplement.

Close

Ask the students to complete this statement: "By learning to use my money wisely now, I will be able to...." (Sample response: "...achieve many of my financial goals.")

ANSWERS

Careers in Finance

Accept all reasonable answers that demonstrate an understanding of the services performed

Chapter 1 Personal Financial Planning TM59

Teacher Manual

Classroom Resources

The *Business and Personal Finance* program offers a complete selection of teacher support materials. Used in conjunction with the **Teacher Annotated Edition**, these materials will enable you to tailor the program to meet the specific needs of your classes.

Student Activity Workbook is designed to reinforce student learning with hands-on activities correlated to chapter content.

Your Personal Financial Planner provides real-world forms and worksheets that help students prepare for real-world personal financial situations.

Standard & Poor's Extension Activities present interesting and relevant articles from Standard & Poor's library of publications that relate to chapter content. The activities enable students to expand their knowledge and sharpen their skills. Each chapter includes a vocabulary list that introduces students to the terms used in the articles. Features also include review questions, critical-thinking activities, and extension activities. Answer keys are provided.

Business Plan Project Workbook is a new textbook workbook that teaches the essential element of a business plan. It provides simple step-by-step directions for students to write their own business plans. A Teacher's Edition is also available that includes teaching suggestions for each chapter section of the business plan, extension activities, review answers, and completed worksheets.

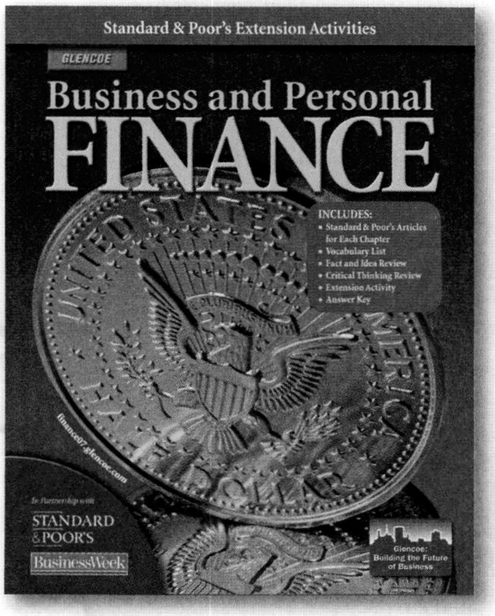

Money Matters: Personal and Family Financial Management Simulation

In the supplement *Money Matters: Personal and Family Financial Management Simulation*, students encounter real-world scenarios and make the same financial decisions made by individuals and families. This simulation combines reality, student creativity, and classroom flexibility, which promotes learning and increases interest.

In this simulation students will learn how financial management is more than just earning an income, paying bills, and saving a few dollars for the future. The five units will help students understand life situations in various stages of the financial life cycle:

- The single person
- The young married couple
- The couple with young children (expanding family)
- The head of household with child
- A couple nearing retirement

Students will see the effects of financial decisions. As they go through the real-life activities, they will have a chance to calculate financial decisions both manually or by using Microsoft® Money, Quicken® Deluxe, or Excel® software.

The **Student Edition** focuses on five personal finance stages in life. Each unit contains a friendly narrative, student activities (with software directions), and business documents.

The **Teacher Manual** provides an overview of the simulation, teaching suggestions, evaluations, master copies of the business forms, and the solutions.

Business and Personal Finance Online Learning Center

The *Business and Personal Finance* Online Learning Center includes information, activities, and exercises that are immensely useful to students, teachers, and families:

- Student resources include links for feature activities, which reinforce financial literacy.
- Teacher resources include a variety of classroom aids, ranging from teaching tips to content correlations.
- Families will find information on how they can best facilitate student learning and study habits, as well as links to other useful Web sites.

Use this Web site to enhance your students' overall learning experience. Various features on the *Business and Personal Finance* Online Learning Center include:

Students
- Chapter Summaries
- Chapter Links
- Note-Taking Guides
- WebQuest activities
- Interactive Games
- Interactive Quizzes
- Student Activities
- Audio Features

Teachers
- Lesson Plans
- Blackline Masters
- NAF Case Studies Tips
- Ethics in Finance
- Selected Teacher Links, including Partners and Associations
- Virtual Business
- Sample Classroom Resources
- Finance Updates

Family
- Letter to Family
- Web Links

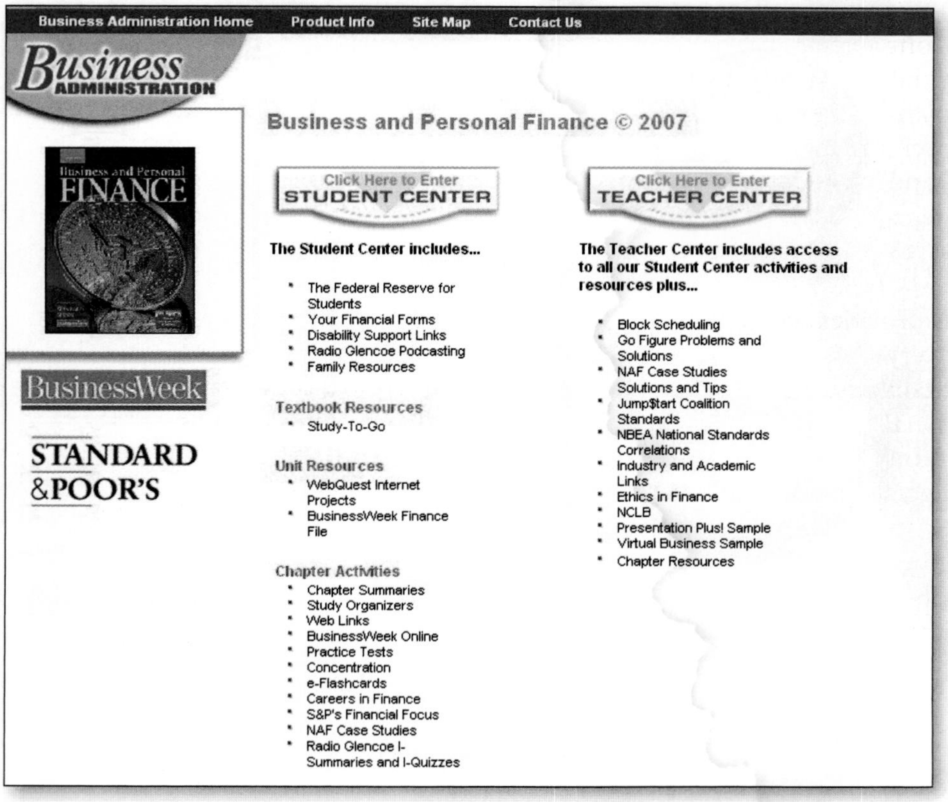

Teacher Classroom Resources

Technology-Based Resources

Lesson Planner Plus CD-ROM gives you instant access to print resources for *Business and Personal Finance:*

- Teacher Annotated Edition of the Student Activity Workbook
- Lesson Plans
- Reproducible Tests
- Internet Resources
- Blackline Masters

ExamView® Pro Test Generator CD-ROM allows you to print out ready-made unit and chapter tests, complete with answer keys. You can also create customized tests. The software can be run by either Macintosh or Windows® platforms.

Financial Planner Software allows students to use popular software programs to carry out authentic financial planning activities. The package includes Quicken® and Excel® spreadsheet templates and solutions, as well as a user guide.

Presentation Plus! provides PowerPoint® lecture aids for every unit, chapter, and section of *Business and Personal Finance*. The presentations can be used as bell-ringers or reviews.

Interactive Student Edition This CD provides the complete digital text of the Student Edition.

Virtual Business® is an exciting visual business simulation to integrate into your business and personal finance classroom. By playing *Virtual Business*, your students will find learning how to run a real-world business energizing, motivating, and most importantly, educational. Included in the package are the *Virtual Business* CD-ROM, an Instructor's Manual, a User's Manual, and five QuickCards. The Instructor's Manual includes 22 student assignments and grading sheets covering topics such as Introduction to Business, Accounting and Finance, Entrepreneurship, and Marketing.

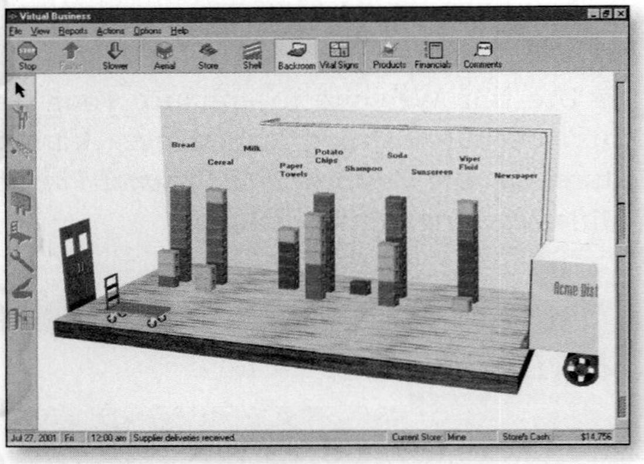

Standard & Poor's and the Student Edition

What comes to mind when you see the name Standard & Poor's? Stock market information? Long-standing reputation? Highly respected investment advice?

Standard & Poor's provides independent financial information, analytical services, advice, and credit ratings to individual investors as well as the world's financial markets. Among the company's many products are the Standard & Poor's 500 Stock Index, the premier U.S. portfolio index; the Standard & Poor's Global 1200 Stock Index, the premier global equity performance benchmark; and credit ratings on more than 290,000 securities and funds worldwide. With more than 5,000 employees located in 19 countries, Standard & Poor's is an integral part of our global infrastructure.

Business and Personal Finance has worked with Standard & Poor's to respond to the kinds of questions and situations faced by today's young people. **Ask Standard & Poor's** question-answer column, Standard & Poor's **Put on Your Financial Planner's Cap**, and **Global Financial Landscape** features are prepared and approved by experts in Standard & Poor's education division. These features add to the real-world emphasis of this text and show students that people their own age have legitimate investment questions and issues.

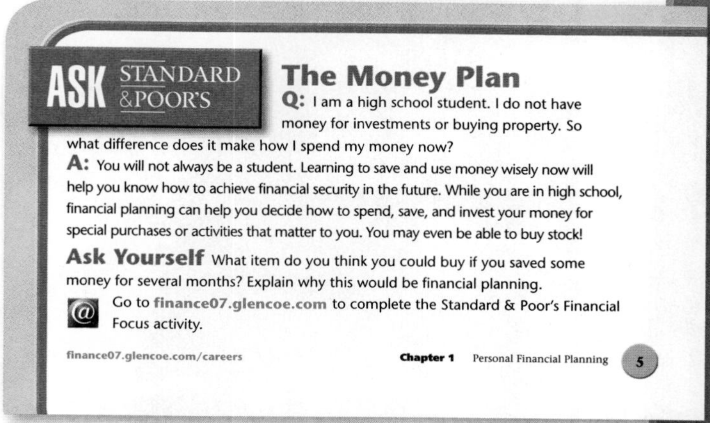

ASK STANDARD & POOR'S

The Money Plan

Q: I am a high school student. I do not have money for investments or buying property. So what difference does it make how I spend my money now?

A: You will not always be a student. Learning to save and use money wisely now will help you know how to achieve financial security in the future. While you are in high school, financial planning can help you decide how to spend, save, and invest your money for special purchases or activities that matter to you. You may even be able to buy stock!

Ask Yourself What item do you think you could buy if you saved some money for several months? Explain why this would be financial planning.

Go to **finance07.glencoe.com** to complete the Standard & Poor's Financial Focus activity.

finance07.glencoe.com/careers **Chapter 1** Personal Financial Planning 5

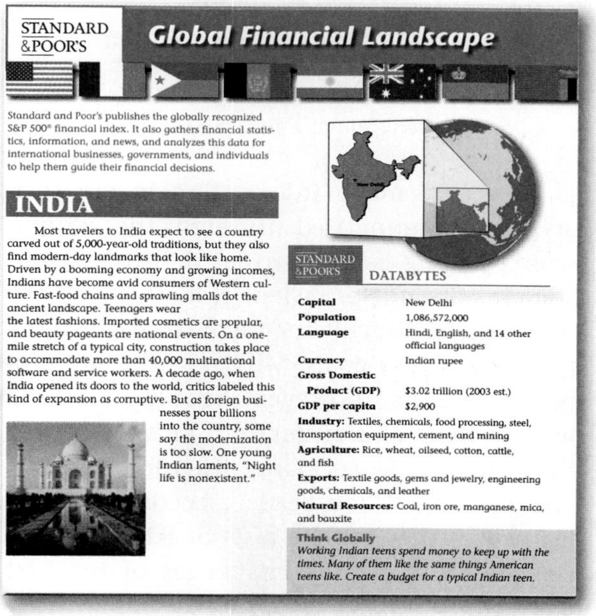

STANDARD & POOR'S **Global Financial Landscape**

Standard and Poor's publishes the globally recognized S&P 500® financial index. It also gathers financial statistics, information, and news, and analyzes this data for international businesses, governments, and individuals to help them guide their financial decisions.

INDIA

Most travelers to India expect to see a country carved out of 5,000-year-old traditions, but they also find modern-day landmarks that look like home. Driven by a booming economy and growing incomes, Indians have become avid consumers of Western culture. Fast-food chains and sprawling malls dot the ancient landscape. Teenagers wear the latest fashions. Imported cosmetics are popular, and beauty pageants are national events. On a one-mile stretch of a typical city, construction takes place to accommodate more than 40,000 multinational software and service workers. A decade ago, when India opened its doors to the world, critics labeled this kind of expansion as corruptive. But as foreign businesses pour billions into the country, some say the modernization is too slow. One young Indian laments, "Night life is nonexistent."

STANDARD & POOR'S DATABYTES

Capital	New Delhi
Population	1,086,572,000
Language	Hindi, English, and 14 other official languages
Currency	Indian rupee
Gross Domestic Product (GDP)	$3.02 trillion (2003 est.)
GDP per capita	$2,900

Industry: Textiles, chemicals, food processing, steel, transportation equipment, cement, and mining

Agriculture: Rice, wheat, oilseed, cotton, cattle, and fish

Exports: Textile goods, gems and jewelry, engineering goods, chemicals, and leather

Natural Resources: Coal, iron ore, manganese, mica, and bauxite

Think Globally

Working Indian teens spend money to keep up with the times. Many of them like the same things American teens like. Create a budget for a typical Indian teen.

STANDARD & POOR'S

Put on Your Financial Planner's Cap

Real scenarios provide problems that students can solve as they think like a financial planner.

Teacher Manual

Reading: The First Skill

"Today a reader, tomorrow a leader."

—Margaret Fuller, American writer and philosopher, 1810–1850

Because much information in our society is communicated through the written word, reading is an essential skill to learn. If students are not proficient readers, it may be much more difficult for them to reach career goals and other goals. Students who are proficient readers, however, usually master a wide variety of transferable skills, including those related to speaking, listening, writing, and viewing. Good readers become lifelong learners as they acquire a set of skills that will prepare them for the challenges of the 21st century.

Research-Based Instruction

The Standards for the English Language Arts state that "all students must have the opportunities and resources to develop the language skills they need to pursue life's goals and to participate fully as informed, productive members of society." The federal government also recognizes the importance of reading for success in life. The No Child Left Behind act (NCLB) emphasizes reading instruction based on scientifically proven methods. NCLB legislation also holds schools and school districts accountable for student progress in this area. Each year, students are given assessments to ensure that they have met the standards of academic proficiency developed by the state.

Accountability

The current emphasis on accountability for student achievement affects you as a teacher of *Business and Personal Finance* because reinforcement of basic literacy skills is a responsibility shared by all educators. As the leading publisher of educational materials, Glencoe is committed to providing teachers and students with a variety of effective reading and related literacy strategies.

Integrating Language Arts

To help you incorporate literacy skills (reading, writing, listening, speaking, and viewing) into your classroom, we have provided a correlation to the language arts standards covered in *Business and Personal Finance*. As you teach this course with and through the *Standards for the English Language Arts**, you will help strengthen your students' literacy performance.

Description	Correlation
Students read a wide variety of print and non-print texts to build an understanding of texts, of themselves, and of the cultures of the United States and the world; to acquire new information; to respond to the needs and demands of society and the workplace; and for personal fulfillment.	*BusinessWeek* Finance File *BusinessWeek* Online
Students adjust their use of spoken, written, and visual language (e.g., conventions, style, and vocabulary) to communicate effectively with a variety of audiences and for different purposes.	Section Assessment Role Plays Chapter Review Role Plays
Students employ a wide range of strategies as they write and use different writing-process elements appropriately to communicate with different audiences for a variety of purposes.	Chapter Review and Activities Write About It *BusinessWeek* Finance File Use Communication Skills Communicating Key Terms
Students apply knowledge of language structure, language conventions (e.g., spelling and punctuation), media techniques, figurative language, and genre to create, critique, and discuss print and non-print texts.	Chapter Review and Activities Write About It Academic Connection Academic Skills
Students conduct research on issues and interests by generating ideas and questions, and by posing problems. They gather, evaluate, and synthesize data from a variety of sources (e.g., print and non-print texts, artifacts, and people) to communicate their discoveries in ways that suit their purpose and audience.	Chapter Review and Activities
Students use a variety of technological and information resources (e.g., libraries, databases, computer networks, and video) to gather and synthesize information and to create and communicate knowledge.	Chapter Review and Activities TechByte *BusinessWeek* Online WebQuest
Students develop an understanding of and respect for diversity in language use, patterns, and dialects across cultures, ethnic groups, geographic regions, and social roles.	Global Financial Landscape

* The information above is published with permission of the *Standards for the English Language Arts*, copublished by the **National Council of Teachers of English** and the **International Reading Association**.

Professional Notes

Reading Strategies

The chart below lists the many reading strategies and activities that you will find throughout Glencoe's *Business and Personal Finance*. Reading specialists have recognized that understanding is increased when students follow pre-reading, during reading, and post-reading strategies. (Some strategies may be effective in all three stages.)

Strategy	Purpose	Activities	Location
Set the purpose	Provide students with purpose for reading	In the Real World Focus on Reading	Section Opener Section Opener
Activate prior knowledge	Prompt students to recall known or related information in a new context	Before You Read Predict As You Read Predict	Margin feature Section Opener
Predict	Ask students to anticipate the content based on visual clues	Before You Read Predict	Section Opener
Identify the main idea	Focus attention on key concepts	The Main Idea Read to Learn What You'll Learn	Section Opener Section Opener Chapter Opener
Pre-teach vocabulary	Explain enriched or above-grade vocabulary	Key Terms	Section Opener
Build comprehension	Reinforce and extend understanding of text material	The Main Idea	Section Opener
Identify key terms	Help students review and reinforce important concepts	Key Terms	Section Opener
Learn with visuals	Support alternative learning styles; help students practice interpreting content using graphics	Chapter Opener Photo In the Real World Photos	Chapter Opener Chapter Opener In Chapter
Organize to learn	Outline main ideas and key sub-points	What You'll Learn Read to Learn	Chapter Opener Section Opener
Summarize	Understand and explain key ideas in original words	Communicating Key Terms	Chapter Review and Activities
Question	Develop critical-thinking and reasoning skills	Think Critically Think Globally As You Read Question	Section Assessment Global Financial Landscape feature In Chapter
Discuss	Grasp details and nuances of concepts; share alternative and interpretive views with other students	After You Read React Quick Check	End of chapter Section Assessment
Make connections	Recognize and build relationships between text and real world	As You Read Relate Academic Connection Real-World Application	In Chapter In Chapter Chapter Review and Activities
Write	Assess comprehension; extend understanding of concepts; offer new interpretations	Write About It Write About It *BusinessWeek* Finance File	Features Section Assessment Chapter Review and Activities Unit Opener

Teacher Manual

Real-World Connections

Making Business and Personal Finance Real

Nothing can bring a classroom topic to life for students like a dose of reality. The Business and Personal Finance teacher can easily take advantage of this. Finance is present in every student's life—at home, in the mall, on the news, and around town. Every day brings another chance to provide real-life examples.

The Internet By visiting the Web sites of financial institutions, financial consultants, and government resources, your students will uncover a wealth of financial information.

Newspapers and Magazines You can bring in clippings or have your students find their own. You can monitor the media's treatment of finance-related issues. Encourage students to challenge the sources of information.

Television Some programs, particularly on Public Broadcasting Service (PBS) stations, bring up-to-the-minute financial news to viewers. Students can take advantage of the easy access to this information.

Guest Speakers Small business owners, bankers, personal financial advisors, and tax accountants are just a few of the experts within easy reach of any community.

Connecting to Careers

Students want to see the connections between course work and the real world. Each chapter's Careers in Finance feature is an excellent starting point for demonstrating how finance knowledge and skills can apply to a wide array of careers. Expand the discussion by referring to this chart, which is based on the 16 "Career Clusters" defined by the U.S. Department of Education.

Career Cluster	Finance-Related Positions
Agriculture, Food & Natural Resources	Loan Officer—Farm Credit Services, Farm Mgr., International Development Specialist
Architecture & Construction	General Contractor, Construction Contract Specialist
Arts, A/V Technology & Communication	Film Production Accountant, Editorial
Business, Management & Administration	Controller, Chief Financial Officer, Commercial Property Mgr.
Education & Training	Accounting Teacher, Public School Budget Administrator
Finance	Account Executive (Stockbroker), Credit Counselor, Personal Banker, Certified Financial Planner, Commercial Loan Officer, Tax Preparer
Government & Public Administration	IRS Auditor, Economic Development Advisor, Policy Analyst
Health Science	Insurance Agent, Director of Finance—Hospital Operations
Hospitality & Tourism	Vice President of Hotel Operations, Executive Chef
Human Services	Income Maintenance Program Advisor, Budget Analyst—U.S. Government, Social Services Grant Administrator
Information Technology	Financial Software Designer, E-Commerce Director
Law, Public Safety & Security	Estate Planning Attorney, FBI Agent, Tax Attorney
Manufacturing	Financial Services—Plant Operations, Production Cost Mgr.
Marketing, Sales & Service	Bank Teller, Real Estate Agent, Personal Property Appraiser
Science, Technology, Engineering & Mathematics	Project Cost Analyst, Industrial Accountant
Transportation, Distribution & Logistics	Purchasing Agent, Transit Authority Contracts Accountant

Assessment Strategies

As a teacher, you will need a variety of ways to assess what your students have learned. One traditional method of measuring student progress is the written test that evaluates recall of subject content. This program contains an **Exam*View*® Pro Testmaker CD-ROM** and **Reproducible Tests** (in the Lesson Planner Plus CD-ROM) as traditional methods of assessment. However, it is also necessary to assess more than students' rote learning skills. Current curriculum objectives focus on the acquisition of knowledge and skills that will help students analyze situations and create plans to address those situations. The acquisition of these skills is not so easily assessed using the traditional paper-and-pencil test.

Performance Assessment

Performance assessment gives you the opportunity to evaluate whether a student has learned to analyze and plan under different sets of circumstances. For example, with limited resources, can the student plan to pay for post-high school training? Does the student understand the discipline necessary to spend less than he or she earns? A paper-and-pencil test will not demonstrate your students' skills in these areas.

Business and Personal Finance provides you with many activities, projects, and situations that create opportunities for alternative assessment. At the end of each section and chapter are skill-building activities, many of which are scenario-based. Students must write or respond to these real-life situations. **Your Financial Figures** requires students to analyze a lifelike, contemporary problem, and **Solve Money Problems** and **Real-World Application** require students to debate and advise others about specific financial situations.

Determining Assessment Strategies

The chart shown on the opposite page can help you determine which assessment strategies will work best for you and your students.

Evaluation of student performance is fundamental to the teaching and learning process.

Professional Notes

Assessment Strategies	Advantages	Disadvantages
• Multiple choice • Matching • Item sets • True/False	• Reliable, easy to validate	• Limited on other measures • Not a good measure of overall performance
Written measures • Essays • Restricted response • Written simulations • Case analysis • Problem-solving exercises	• Face validity (real life) • In-depth assessment • Measures writing skills and higher level skills • Reasonable developmental costs and time	• Subjective scoring • Time consuming and expensive to score • Limited breadth • Difficult to equate • Moderate reliability
Oral measures • Oral examinations • Interviews	• Measures communications and interpersonal skills • In-depth assessment with varied stimulus materials • Learner involvement	• Costly and time consuming • Limited reliability • Narrow sampling of content • Scoring difficult, need multiple raters
Simulated Activities • In-basket • Computer simulations	• Moderate reliability • Performance-based measure	• Costly and time consuming • Difficult to score, administer, and develop
Portfolio and product analysis • Work samples • Projects • Work diaries and logs • Achievement records	• Provides information not normally available • Learner involvement • Face validity (real life) • Easy to collect information	• Costly to administer • Labor and paper intensive • Difficult to validate or equate • Biased toward best samples or outstanding qualities
Performance measures • Demonstrations • Presentations • Performances • Production work • Observation	• Job-related • Relatively easy to administer • In-depth assessment • Face validity	• Rater training required • Hard to equate • Subjective scoring • Time consuming if breadth is needed
Performance records • References • Performance rating forms • Parental rating	• Efficient • Low cost • Easy to administer	• Low reliability • Subjective • Hard to equate • Rate judgment
Self-evaluation	• Learner involvement and empowerment • Learner responsibility • Measures dimensions not available otherwise	• May be biased or unrealistic

Developing Thinking Skills

All educational disciplines strive to teach critical-thinking skills. Your students will need to apply these skills to make important plans and decisions in their own lives now and in the future. When you teach your students critical thinking, you equip them with skills that are essential to achieve success.

Critical thinking is the process of reasonably or logically deciding what to do or believe and involves the abilities to:

- Compare and contrast
- Solve problems
- Make decisions
- Analyze and evaluate
- Synthesize and transfer knowledge
- Conduct metacognitive exercises

Critical-thinking skills are important for the following reasons:

- Critical-thinking skills help students investigate their own ways of solving problems and finding creative resolutions.
- Critical-thinking skills lead students to investigations that compare and contrast what they know with unknowns.
- Critical-thinking skills allow students to make decisions about their own learning and become aware of their own processes.

What Is Thinking?

All learning requires thinking. Benjamin Bloom's taxonomy of the cognitive domain is probably the most widely recognized schema for levels of thinking. Each of Bloom's cognitive categories includes a list of thinking skills that indicates the kinds of behavior students are expected to demonstrate regarding the goals of specific learning tasks:

- *Knowledge:* define, recognize, recall, identify, label, understand, examine, show, collect
- *Comprehension:* translate, interpret, explain, describe, summarize, extrapolate
- *Application:* apply, solve, experiment, show, predict
- *Analysis:* connect, relate, differentiate, classify, arrange, check, group, distinguish, organize, categorize, detect, compare, infer
- *Synthesis:* produce, propose, design, plan, combine, formulate, compose, hypothesize, construct
- *Evaluation:* appraise, judge, criticize, decide

Critical Thinking and Problem Solving in the *Business and Personal Finance* Program

The following are some guidelines for integrating and teaching critical-thinking and problem-solving skills:

- Let students know they are engaging in aspects of critical thinking. For example, at the end of each section within the chapter are **Think Critically** questions. Explain to students that when they answer these questions, they are analyzing and evaluating information. Point out that they regularly analyze and evaluate music, conversations with friends, magazine or newspaper articles, and television programs. This will help demonstrate to students that they have had experience in using these skills.
- Use activities that focus on open-ended problems to foster greater growth for creative problem solving. Examples include **Real-World Application, Put on Your Financial Planner's Cap,** and **Global Financial Landscapes.**
- Use assessments that measure students' growth and performance. Examples include **Reviewing Key Concepts, Communicating Key Terms, Academic Skills,** and **Your Financial Figures.**
- Provide feedback and encourage students to feel comfortable experimenting with new ideas and ways to solve problems.

Cooperative Learning

Studies show that students learn faster and retain more information when they are actively involved in the learning process. Studies also show that in a classroom setting, adolescents often learn more from each other about subject matter than from a traditional teacher-led lecture and discussion. Cooperative learning is one method that gets students actively involved in learning and at the same time allows for peer teaching.

The Basic Elements of Cooperative Learning

Cooperative learning involves assigning students to small groups to work together within a classroom setting. This learning structure is especially effective for more difficult learning tasks, such as problem solving, critical thinking, and conceptual learning. The basic elements of a cooperative learning group are as follows:

- Cooperative learning emphasizes working toward group goals as opposed to the traditional emphasis on individual competition and achievement.
- Students discover that not only must they learn the material themselves, but also they are responsible for helping everyone in the group learn the material.
- The successes or failures of the group are shared by all members of the group.

The Benefits of Cooperative Learning Groups

Cooperative learning offers many benefits:

- The use of higher-level thinking skills draws students into learning situations that require them to be directly involved.
- Students discover how to work with people of all types. Schools with racially or ethnically mixed populations often improve relations among students.
- Communication skills are improved.
- Students learn to work through conflicts.
- Students learn valuable social and problem-solving skills that transfer to real-world occupations and work environments.

Cooperative Learning in this Text

In *Business and Personal Finance*, students and teachers have a variety of materials to assist with cooperative learning activities. Many of the features and section and chapter assessment activities can be completed in a cooperative learning environment:

- **Standard & Poor's Put on Your Financial Planner's Cap** gives students an opportunity to analyze a real financial situation as if they were being approached by a real-life client. The student can make decisions based on the given information.
- **Solve Money Problems** presents a life-like scenario that requires students to apply a newly presented financial concept. Students may also use their communication skills to solve business and personal finance problems. When students solve these problems cooperatively, they see their peers' logic processes.
- **Internet Connection** and **TechByte** can be assigned as a classroom cooperative learning activity, group activity in your media center, or interdisciplinary activity with a related course. Students will need access to the Internet.

Cooperative learning activities that are appropriate for the chapter topic are also included within annotations throughout the **Teacher Annotated Edition**.

Cultural Diversity and Inclusion

Today's diverse classrooms offer unparalleled opportunities for students and teachers alike. A single classroom today may be one in which ten or twelve countries of origin are represented, assorted native languages compete with English, cultures as varied as far eastern or African are represented, and students with physical or emotional disabilities may have the same dreams of success as every other student. Multicultural education incorporates the idea that all students should have an equal opportunity to learn in school. This diversity presents challenges, to be sure, but it also gives great benefits and learning opportunities to the students and the teacher.

Challenges

Some of the challenges you may encounter include:

- Providing a safe classroom for students with physical disabilities,
- Using teaching assists such as tape recorders,
- Having teacher's aides to help students read or take notes,
- Maintaining awareness of language differences and teaching English vocabulary,
- Translating concepts into culture-specific terms.

Benefits and Opportunities

On the other hand, some of the benefits and opportunities you may find include:

- Global perspectives business and personal finance practices,
- Increased cultural understanding for all students,
- A setting which encourages discussion and participation,
- Increased awareness of the needs of the disabled which can enhance accessibility of students' future workplaces,
- Enhanced opportunities to learn about the world–as marketplace and home.

Recognizing these challenges and benefits, Glencoe's *Business and Personal Finance* provides a large variety of activities and exercises, geared to accommodating a diverse school population. Here are some things you can do to foster awareness of diversity:

- Recognize that each student is unique and promote this positively.
- Know, appreciate, and respect your students' diversity.
- Represent this diversity fairly and accurately, ensuring the accuracy of all historical information and the presence of gender equity.
- Use current news or advertising to demonstrate marketplace diversity to students.
- Welcome parent and community involvement.

Including All Students

Today's classroom is composed of students with various backgrounds, skill levels, and characteristics that affect their ability to read and process information at grade level. These students include:

- English Language Learners (ELLs)
- Struggling and striving readers
- Students with physical disabilities
- Students with learning difficulties
- Gifted and talented students

English Language Learners (ELL)

According to the National Assessment of Educational Progress, the number of ELL students is growing two-and-a-half times as fast as the general school population. For students who are English language learners, the focus needs to be on overcoming a language barrier. In the business world and in their personal lives, these individuals will be expected to communicate effectively in oral and written forms.

Individual Needs and Learning Styles

One of your greatest challenges as a teacher is to provide a positive learning environment for all students in your classroom. Because each student has his or her own unique set of abilities, perceptions, and needs, the learning styles and the physical abilities of your students may vary widely.

In order to help you provide all your students with a positive learning experience, this text provides a variety of activities. This diversity will stimulate student interest, motivate learning, and facilitate understanding.

How Do You Prepare?

Students in your classroom may have orthopedic impairments. They may have hearing or vision impairments, learning disabilities, or behavior disorders—all of which may interfere with their ability to learn. The learning styles of your students may also vary. Some students may be visual learners; others may learn more effectively through hands-on activities. Some students may work well independently, while others need the interaction of others. Students may come from a variety of cultural backgrounds, and some may be English language learners.

Teaching Students with Special Needs

Once you determine the special needs of your students, you can identify the areas in the curriculum that may present barriers to them. In order to remove those barriers, you may need to modify your teaching methods.

On the following pages are two charts. The first chart, **Meeting Special Needs**, describes some of the special needs you may encounter with students in your classroom and identifies sources of information. Also provided are tips for modifying your teaching style to accommodate the special needs of your students.

The second chart, **Eight Ways of Learning**, will help you identify your students' learning styles. The chart gives a description of each type of learner; describes the likes of each type, what each type is good at, and how each learns best; and names some famous learners. Once you have identified each student's learning style, you can modify your teaching strategies to best suit his or her needs.

Universal Design for Learning

Every student needs to develop skills in order to succeed in school and in the workplace. To help meet this goal, Glencoe has developed ***Inclusion in the Business Education Classroom.***

This booklet contains reading and learning strategies designed to reach students of all performance levels and abilities. The booklet follows the Universal Design for Learning, a classroom approach that emphasizes how making a classroom inclusive helps every student—challenged or not—to learn and grow.

Meeting Special Needs

Subject	Description	Sources of Information
English Language Learners	Certain students speak English as a second language, or not at all. Customs and behavior of people in the majority culture may be confusing for some of these students. Cultural values may inhibit some of these students from full participation in the classroom.	• *Teaching English as a Second Language* • *Mainstreaming and the Minority Child*
Students with Behavior Disorders	Students with behavior disorders deviate from standards or expectations of behavior and impair the functioning of others and themselves. These students may also be gifted or have learning disabilities.	• *Exceptional Children* • *Journal of Special Education*
Students with Visual Impairments	Students with visual impairments have partial or total loss of sight. Individuals with visual impairments are not significantly different from their sighted peers in ability range or personality. However, a visual impairment may affect cognitive, motor, and social development.	• *Journal of Visual Impairment and Blindness* • *Education of Visually Handicapped* • *American Foundation for the Blind*
Students with Hearing Impairments	Students with hearing impairments have partial or total loss of hearing. Individuals with hearing impairments are not significantly different from their hearing peers in ability, range, or personality. However, a chronic hearing impairment may affect cognitive, motor, social, and speech development.	• *American Annals of the Deaf* • *Journal of Speech and Hearing Research* • *Sign Language Studies*
Students with Physical Impairments	Students with physical impairments fall into two categories—those with orthopedic impairments (use of one or more limbs severely restricted) and those with other health impairments.	• *The Source Book for the Disabled* • *Teaching Exceptional Children*
Gifted Students	Although no formal definition exists, these students can be described as having above average ability, task commitment, and creativity. They rank in the top five percent of their classes. They usually finish work more quickly than other students and are capable of divergent thinking.	• *Gifted Child Quarterly* • *Gifted Creative/Talented* • *Journal for the Education of the Gifted*
Students with Learning Disabilities	Students with learning disabilities have a problem in one or more areas, such as academic learning, language, perception, social-emotional adjustment, memory, or ability to pay attention.	• *Journal of Learning Disabilities* • *Learning Disability Quarterly*

Tips for Instruction
• Remember that students' ability to speak English does not reflect their academic ability. • Try to incorporate students' cultural experiences into your instruction. The help of a bilingual aide may be effective. • Include information about different cultures in your curriculum to help build students' self-image. • Avoid cultural stereotypes. • Encourage students to share their cultures in the classroom
• Work for long-term improvement; do not expect immediate success. • Talk with students about their strengths and weaknesses, and clearly outline objectives. • Structure schedules, rules, room arrangement, and safety for a conducive learning environment. • Model appropriate behavior for students and reinforce proper behavior.
• Modify assignments as needed to help students become independent. • Teach classmates how to serve as guides for students with visual impairments. • Tape lectures and reading assignments for students with visual impairments. • Encourage students to use their sense of touch; provide tactile models whenever possible. • Verbally describe people and events as they occur in the classroom.
• Limit unnecessary noise in the classroom. • Provide a favorable seating arrangement so students with hearing impairments can see speakers and read their lips (or interpreters can assist); avoid visual distractions. • Write out all instructions on paper or on the board; overhead projectors enable you to maintain eye contact while writing. • Avoid standing with your back to the window or light source.
• With the student, determine when you should offer aid. • Help other students and adults understand students with physical impairments. • Learn about special devices or procedures and if any special safety precautions are needed. • Allow students to participate in all activities including field trips, special events, and projects.
• Emphasize concepts, theories, relationships, ideas, and generalizations. • Let students express themselves in a variety of ways including drawing, creative writing, or acting. • Make arrangements for students to work on independent projects. • Make arrangements for students to take selected subjects early.
• Provide assistance and direction; clearly define rules, assignments, and duties. • Allow for pair interaction during class time; utilize peer helpers. • Practice skills frequently. • Allow extra time to complete tests and assignments.

Eight Ways of Learning

Learning Style	Description	Likes to	Is Good at	Learns by
Verbal/ Linguistic Learner	Intelligence is related to words and language, written and spoken.	read, write, tell stories, play word games, and tell jokes and riddles.	memorizing names, dates, places, and trivia; spelling; using descriptive language; and creating imaginary worlds.	saying, hearing, and seeing words.
Logical/ Mathematical Learner	Intelligence deals with inductive and deductive thinking and reasoning, numbers, and abstractions.	perform experiments, solve puzzles, work with numbers, ask questions, and explore patterns and relationships.	math, reasoning, logic, problem solving, computing numbers mentally, moving from concrete to abstract, thinking conceptually, and organizing thoughts.	categorizing, classifying, and working with abstract patterns and relationships.
Visual/ Spatial Learner	Intelligence relies on the sense of sight and being able to visualize an object, including the ability to create mental images.	draw, build, design, and create things, daydream, do jigsaw puzzles and mazes, watch videos, look at photos, and draw maps and charts.	understanding the use of space and how to get around in it, thinking in three-dimensional terms, and imagining things in clear visual images.	visualizing, dreaming, using the mind's eye, and working with colors and pictures.
Musical/ Rhythmic Learner	Intelligence is based on recognition of tonal patterns, including various environmental sounds, and on a sensitivity to rhythm and beats.	sing and hum, listen to music, play an instrument, move body when music is playing, and make up songs.	remembering melodies; keeping time; mimicking beat and rhythm; noticing pitches, rhythms, and background and environmental sounds; and differentiating patterns in sounds.	rhythm, melody, and music.
Bodily/ Kinesthetic Learner	Intelligence is related to physical movement and the brain's motor cortex, which controls bodily motion.	learn by hands-on methods, demonstrate skill in crafts, tinker, perform, display physical endurance, and challenge self physically.	physical activities such as sports, dancing, acting, and crafts.	touching, moving, interacting with space, and processing knowledge through bodily sensations.
Interpersonal Learner	Intelligence operates primarily through person-to-person relationships and communication.	have lots of friends, talk to people, join groups, play cooperative games, solve problems as part of a group, and volunteer help when others need it.	understanding people and their feelings, leading others, organizing, communicating, manipulating, and mediating conflicts.	sharing, comparing, relating, cooperating, and interviewing.
Intrapersonal Learner	Intelligence is related to inner states of being, self-reflection, metacognition, and awareness of spiritual realities.	work alone, pursue own interests, daydream, keep a personal diary or journal, and think about starting own business.	understanding self, focusing inward on feelings/ dreams, following instincts, pursuing interests, setting goals, and being original.	working alone, doing individualized projects, engaging in self-paced instruction, and having own space.
Naturalistic Learner	Intelligence has to do with observing, understanding, and organizing patterns in the natural environment.	spend time outdoors and work with plants, animals, and other parts of the natural environment; good at identifying plants and animals and at hearing and seeing connections to nature.	measuring, charting, mapping, observing plants and animals, keeping journals, collecting, classifying, participating in outdoor activities.	visualizing, hands-on activities, bringing outdoors into the classroom, relating home/classroom to the natural world.

Is Good at...	Learns Best by...	Famous Learners
memorizing names, dates, places, and trivia; spelling; using descriptive language; and creating imaginary worlds.	saying, hearing, and seeing words	Maya Angelou—poet Abraham Lincoln—U.S. President and statesman Jerry Seinfeld—comedian Mary Hatwood Futrell—international teacher, leader, orator
math, reasoning, logic, problem solving, computing numbers, moving from concrete to abstract, thinking conceptually.	categorizing, classifying, and working with abstract patterns and relationships.	Stephen Hawking—physicist Albert Einstein—theoretical physicist Marilyn Burns—math educator Alexa Canady—neurosurgeon
understanding the use of space and how to get around in it, thinking in three-dimensional terms, and imagining things in clear visual images.	visualizing, dreaming, using the mind's eye, and working with colors and pictures.	Pablo Picasso—artist Maria Martinez—Pueblo Indian famous for black pottery Faith Ringgold—painter, quilter, and writer I. M. Pei—architect
remembering melodies; keeping time; mimicking beat and rhythm; noticing pitches, rhythms, and background and environmental sounds.	rhythm, melody, and music.	Henry Mancini—composer Marian Anderson—contralto Daniel Heifetz—violinist Paul McCartney—singer, songwriter, musician
physical activities such as sports, dancing, acting, and crafts.	touching, moving, interacting with space, and processing knowledge through bodily sensations.	Marcel Marceau—mime Jackie Joyner-Kersey—Olympic gold medalist in track and field Katherine Dunham—modern dancer Dr. Christian Bernard—cardiac surgeon
understanding people and their feelings, leading others, organizing, communicating, manipulating, mediating conflicts.	sharing, comparing, relating, cooperating, and interviewing.	Jimmy Carter—U.S. President and statesman Eleanor Roosevelt—former First Lady Lee Iacocca—president of Chrysler Corporation Mother Teresa—winner of Nobel Peace Prize
understanding self, focusing inward on feelings/dreams, following instincts, pursuing interests, and being original.	working alone, doing individualized projects, engaging in self-paced instruction	Marva Collins—educator Maria Montessori—educator and physician Sigmund Freud—psychotherapist Anne Sexton—poet
measuring, charting, mapping, observing plants and animals, keeping journals, collecting, classifying, participating in outdoor activities.	visualizing, hands-on activities, bringing outdoors into the classroom, relating home/classroom to the natural world.	George Washington Carver—agricultural chemist Rachel Carson—scientific writer Charles Darwin—evolutionist John James Audubon—conservationist

No Child Left Behind

The No Child Left Behind Act of 2001, signed into law by President George W. Bush, marks a sweeping reform of the federal government's efforts to improve elementary and secondary education in the United States. Enacted in response to concerns that "too many of our neediest children are being left behind," the Act is built upon four fundamental principles:

- Making districts, schools, and teachers more accountable for results
- Emphasizing doing what works based on scientific research
- Expanding parents' options for their children's education
- Increasing local control and flexibility with regard to using federal funds

Crucial to achieving these objectives is an increased emphasis on standardized testing.

The following chart illustrates how components in the *Business and Personal Finance* textbook correspond to academic disciplines addressed by standardized tests. Two examples of each component are cited for easy reference. (Note that page citations are not exhaustive and are intended to provide only selected instances of each component.)

Academic Area	Component	Benefits	References
English and Language Arts	Reading Strategies	Leads students to become active and effective readers by using a four-step process: Predict, Relate, Question, React.	2, 188
	Communicating Key Terms Solve Money Problems	Reinforces key terms by giving students opportunities to apply the terms in various contexts.	26, 228 18, 53
	Quick Check	Requires students to communicate using various methods including essays, letters, speeches, group discussions, and role-plays.	18, 39
	Think Critically	Helps students to relate each section's content to concepts previewed in "Main Idea."	53, 161
	BusinessWeek Finance File Global Financial Landscape	Leads students to apply concepts to situations outside the scope of the textbook. Questions require oral or written answers.	235, 377 164, 220
	Reviewing Key Concepts	Spotlights a hypothetical scenario relevant to the lives of today's students. Critical thinking questions round out each case study.	192, 228
	Use Communication Skills	Strengthens understanding with questions that require oral or written answers.	276, 318
	Real-World Application	Leads students to relate chapter material to their personal lives.	193, 407
	Academic Connection	Requires students to solve problems using connections to language arts, math, and social studies. Helps students to link finance topics to other disciplines. Each feature includes a related student activity.	13, 174

Professional Notes

Academic Area	Component	Benefits	References
Mathematics	Math Skills Builder Appendix	Reviews math concepts in a 24-page appendix. The exercises can be used as practice problems.	722, 745
	Use Math Skills Solve Money Problems	Reinforces skills by applying mathematical processes to a variety of finance problems.	25, 177 39, 276
	Go Figure	Presents students with relevant math formulas that illustrate a step-by-step approach to solving problems.	21, 163
	Your Financial Portfolio	Presents financial situations in which students must use a rational decision-making process. Calculating costs and analyzing financial activities require students to think critically about real-life financial issues.	195, 231
	Real-World Application	Requires students to solve problems using connections to language arts, math, and social studies.	229, 347
	Academic Connection Academic Skills	Helps students to link finance topics to other disciplines. Each feature includes a related student activity.	217, 385 601, 631
Technology	Internet Connection TechByte *BusinessWeek* Online	Strengthens students' Internet research skills with relevant, practical activities.	27, 193 7, 205 193, 229
	Your Financial Figures	Requires students to use writing, teamwork, role-playing, and other skills to solve real-world financial problems. Activities include an optional Internet or other technology component.	229, 371
	Business and Personal Finance OLC site in chapter opener and throughout chapter	Directs students to Web support, activities, and other online resources.	379, 383
	Global Financial Landscape	Showcases a diversity of countries' economies and contributions to the global marketplace.	15, 220
	Careers in Finance	An Internet-based activity accompanies each feature.	11, 49
	Get a Financial Life!	Each simulation includes a related research activity.	116, 374
	Real-World Application	Provides in-depth financial research and teamwork projects in which students use a variety of resources and procedures to solve problems.	193, 301
	Academic Connection Academic Skills	Requires students to solve problems using connections to language arts, math, and social studies. Helps students to link finance topics to other disciplines. Each feature includes a related student activity.	364, 560 347, 545

Professional Notes

National Standards for Business Education

The National Business Education Association (NBEA) has developed curriculum standards based on a developmental approach. The high-school-level competencies have been integrated into Glencoe's *Business & Personal Finance* program. They are listed in the Planning Guide for each chapter in the Teacher Manual section of the Teacher Annotated Edition, as well as in the chart below.

National Standards for Business Education	Chapters/Sections
ECONOMICS STANDARDS	
I. Allocation of Resources Assess opportunity costs and trade-offs involved in making choices about how to use scarce economic resources.	1.1, 1.2, 2.1, 3.1, 4.1, 5.1, 5.2, 6.2, 6.4, 7.1, 7.2, 7.3, 8.1, 8.2, 9.2, 10.1, 10.4, 11.1, 11.2, 12.1, 12.3, 13.2, 14.1, 15.3, 21.1
II. Economic Systems Explain why societies develop economic systems, identify the basic features of different economic systems, and analyze the major features of the U.S. economic system.	1.1, 2.1, 4.1, 5.2, 9.2, 11.1, 11.2, 12.1, 12.3, 14.1, 18.1, 19.1
III. Economic Institutions and Incentives Analyze the role of core economic institutions and incentives in the U.S. economy.	1.1, 2.1, 2.2, 3.1, 4.1, 4.2, 5.1, 5.2, 6.1, 6.2, 6.3, 6.4, 8.1, 9.2, 10.1, 11.1, 11.2, 12.1, 12.3, 13.3, 14.4, 15.1, 15.2, 15.3, 17.1, 17.2, 19.1, 19.2, 21.1, 22.2
IV. Markets and Prices Analyze the role of markets and prices in the U.S. economy.	1.1, 22.1
V. Market Structures Analyze the different types of market structures and the effect they have on the price and the quality of the goods and services produced.	1.1, 2.1, 8.2, 9.2, 11.1, 11.2, 22.1
VI. Productivity Explain the importance of productivity and analyze how specialization, division of labor, investment in physical and human capital, and technological change affect productivity.	17.2, 18.1, 21.1, 22.2
VII. The Role of Government Analyze the role of government in economic systems, especially the role of government in the U.S. economy.	1.1, 5.1, 6.1, 7.3, 9.3, 10.1, 11.1, 12.1, 12.2, 12.3, 14.2, 14.3, 15.1, 15.2, 15.3, 16.2, 20.1
VIII. International Economic Concepts Examine the role of trade, protectionism, and monetary markets in the global economy.	1.2, 2.1, 3.3, 4.2, 5.2, 6.4, 7.3, 8.1, 9.2, 10.1, 11.2, 12.3, 13.3, 14.4, 15.3, 16.2, 17.2, 19.2, 20.2, 21.2, 22.2
IX. Aggregate Supply and Aggregate Demand Analyze how the U.S. economy functions as a whole and describe selected macroeconomic measures of economic activity.	1.1, 2.1, 3.3, 8.1

Excerpted from *National Standards for Business Education*, copyright © 2001 by National Business Education Association, 1914 Association Dr., Reston VA 21901-1596.

National Standards for Business Education	Chapters/Sections
PERSONAL FINANCE STANDARDS	
I. Personal Decision Making Use a rational decision-making process as it applies to the roles of citizens, workers, and consumers.	1.1, 1.2, 2.1, 2.2, 3.1, 3.2, 3.3, 4.1, 5.1, 5.2, 6.1, 6.2, 6.4, 7.1, 7.2, 7.3, 8.1, 8.2, 8.3, 9.2, 9.3, 10.1, 10.2, 10.3, 10.4, 11.1, 11.2, 12.1, 12.3, 13.1, 13.3, 14.1, 14.2, 14.4, 15.1, 15.2, 15.3, 16.1, 17.1, 17.2, 18.2, 19.1, 22.2
II. Earning a Living Identify various forms of income and analyze factors that affect income as a part of the career decision-making process.	1.1, 1.2, 2.1, 2.2, 3.2, 5.1, 5.2, 7.1, 7.3, 8.1, 8.2, 8.3, 9.1, 9.2, 9.3, 10.1, 10.2, 10.3, 10.4, 11.1, 11.2, 12.1, 12.2, 12.3, 14.1, 15.1, 15.2, 15.3, 16.1, 16.2, 17.1, 17.2, 18.2, 19.1, 19.2, 20.1, 20.2, 21.2, 22.1, 22.2
III. Managing Finances and Budgeting Develop and evaluate a spending/savings plan.	1.1, 1.2, 2.2, 3.2, 3.3, 4.1, 5.1, 5.2, 6.1, 6.2, 6.3, 6.4, 7.1, 7.2, 7.3, 14.4, 15.1, 15.2
IV. Saving and Investing Evaluate savings and investment options to meet short- and long-term goals.	1.1, 1.2, 2.2, 5.1, 5.2, 8.1, 8.2, 8.3, 9.1, 9.2, 9.3, 10.1, 10.2, 10.3, 10.4, 11.1, 11.2, 12.3, 14.4, 15.1, 16.2, 17.2, 19.1
V. Buying Goods and Services Apply a decision-making model to maximize consumer satisfaction when buying goods and services.	1.1, 4.1, 4.2, 5.1, 6.1, 6.2, 6.3, 7.1, 7.2, 7.3, 11.1, 11.2, 12.2, 12.3, 14.2
VI. Banking Evaluate services provided by financial deposit institutions to transfer funds.	5.1, 5.2, 6.3, 11.2, 16.1, 18.1, 21.1
VII. Using Credit Analyze factors that affect the choice of credit, the cost of credit, and the legal aspects of using credit.	1.2, 5.1, 6.1, 6.2, 6.3, 6.4, 7.3, 17.1, 18.2, 19.1, 19.2
VIII. Protecting Against Risk Analyze choices available to consumers for protection against risk and financial loss.	2.2, 3.1, 5.1, 5.2, 7.1, 7.3, 13.1, 13.2, 13.3, 14.1, 14.2, 14.3, 14.4, 18.1, 19.1, 20.2

National Standards for Business Education	*Business and Personal Finance* Ancillaries	
	Student Activity Workbook	**Standard & Poor's Extension Activities**
ECONOMICS STANDARDS		
I. Allocation of Resources Assess opportunity costs and trade-offs involved in making choices about how to use scarce economic resources.	1, 2, 4, 5, 6, 7, 8, 9, 10, 11, 12, 13, 14, 15	2, 3, 4, 5, 6, 9, 14, 16, 17, 19, 21
II. Economic Systems Explain why societies develop economic systems, identify the basic features of different economic systems, and analyze the major features of the U.S. economic system.	11, 22	16, 22
III. Economic Institutions and Incentives Analyze the role of core economic institutions and incentives in the U.S. economy.	1, 2, 4, 5, 7, 8, 9, 10, 11, 12, 14, 15, 17, 19, 20, 21, 22	2, 5, 11, 12, 16, 17, 18, 19, 22
IV. Markets and Prices Analyze the role of markets and prices in the U.S. economy.	9, 22	4, 17, 18
V. Market Structures Analyze the different types of market structures and the effect they have on the price and the quality of the goods and services provided.	7, 22	
VI. Productivity Explain the importance of productivity and analyze how specialization, division of labor, investment in physical and human capital, and technological change affect productivity.	18, 22	
VII. The Role of Government Analyze the role of government in economic systems, especially the role of government in the U.S. economy.	6, 10, 11, 12, 13, 14, 15, 16, 20, 21	2, 5, 8, 11, 12, 13, 15, 17, 18, 21, 22
VIII. International Economic Concepts Examine the role of trade, protectionism, and monetary markets in the global economy.	11, 20	
IX. Aggregate Supply and Aggregate Demand Analyze how the U.S. economy functions as a whole and describe selected macroeconomic measures of economic activity.	2, 3, 11	

Business and Personal Finance Ancillaries			
	Lesson Planner Plus CD-ROM		
Your Personal Financial Planner	Internet Resources	Reproducible Tests	Blackline Masters
1, 2, 3, 4, 5, 6, 7, 8, 9, 10, 11, 12, 13, 14, 15	7, 8, 10, 21	1, 2, 3, 4, 5, 6, 8, 9, 10, 14, 17	1, 4, 5, 6, 7, 21
	12, 14, 15		1, 2
1, 5, 7, 8, 12, 13, 14, 15	1, 2, 4, 7, 8, 9, 10, 11, 12, 13, 14, 15, 16, 17, 18, 19, 21	1, 2, 5, 6, 8, 9, 10, 11, 12, 13, 16, 17, 18, 20, 21	1, 4, 6, 17
		4, 22	
4			1, 11, 22
		3, 18, 22	18, 21
	4, 6, 7, 10, 12, 14, 15, 17, 20, 21	1, 2, 4, 6, 7, 8, 10, 11, 12, 13, 14, 15, 16, 19, 21	1, 7, 12
		2	1, 8

National Standards for Business Education	*Business and Personal Finance* Ancillaries — Student Activity Workbook	*Business and Personal Finance* Ancillaries — Standard & Poor's Extension Activities
PERSONAL FINANCE STANDARDS		
I. Personal Decision Making Use a rational decision-making process as it applies to the roles of citizens, workers, and consumers.	1, 2, 4, 5, 6, 7, 8, 9, 10, 11, 13, 14, 15, 17, 19	2, 7, 9, 11, 14, 15, 16, 17, 19, 20, 21, 22
II. Earning a Living Identify various forms of income and analyze factors that affect income as a part of the career decision-making process.	1, 2, 3, 5, 7, 8, 9, 10, 11, 12, 14, 15, 16, 17, 18, 19, 20, 21, 22	1, 2, 15, 20, 21
III. Managing Finances and Budgeting Develop and evaluate a spending/savings plan.	3, 5, 7, 9, 10, 11, 12, 14, 15, 17	2, 3, 16
IV. Saving and Investing Evaluate savings and investment options to meet short- and long-term goals.	1, 5, 8, 9, 10, 11, 12, 15	1, 5, 8, 9, 10, 11, 15, 20, 21
V. Buying Goods and Services Apply a decision-making model to maximize consumer satisfaction when buying goods and services.	4, 6, 7, 12	5, 9, 12, 14, 15, 17, 19, 22
VI. Banking Evaluate services provided by financial deposit institutions to transfer funds.	5, 6	10
VII. Using Credit Analyze factors that affect the choice of credit, the cost of credit, and the legal aspects of using credit.	1, 4, 5, 6, 7, 11, 17, 19	2, 3, 6, 7, 19
VIII. Protecting Against Risk Analyze choices available to consumers for protection against risk and financial loss.	2, 3, 5, 7, 11, 13, 14, 18, 19, 20, 21	8, 13, 14, 17

Professional Notes

Business and Personal Finance Ancillaries			
	Lesson Planner Plus CD-ROM		
Your Personal Financial Planner	Internet Resources	Reproducible Tests	Blackline Masters
1, 4, 7	7, 8, 10, 21	1, 2, 3, 4, 6, 8, 9, 10, 11, 14, 17	1, 2, 4, 6, 7, 11, 14, 15, 16, 17, 19, 22
2, 12	1, 2, 8, 9, 10, 11, 12, 16, 17, 19, 21	2, 5, 9, 14, 16	1, 2, 3, 7, 12, 15, 16, 17, 18, 19, 20, 21
3, 4, 5, 6, 7, 9, 11, 12, 13, 14, 15	1, 2, 3, 8, 9, 10, 11, 17, 19, 21	1, 2, 3, 5, 8, 9, 10, 11, 16, 17, 20, 21	1, 4, 7, 15
1, 3, 5, 8, 9, 10, 15	1, 8, 9, 10, 11, 14	1, 5, 8, 9, 10, 11, 15	1, 8, 9, 12, 15, 19
4, 5, 6, 7, 11, 12, 13, 14, 15	3, 4, 5, 6, 7, 9, 11	4, 6, 7, 14	4, 6, 7, 14
5	5, 6	5	5, 6
1, 4, 6, 7	6	6, 7, 19, 20	1, 6, 19
1, 2, 13, 14	13, 14	5, 7, 13, 14, 15, 21	3, 7, 13, 14

Building Workplace Skills

Today's business environment is highly competitive and demands skilled employees. Successful employees are able to deal with the varied demands of the fast-paced world of business, which requires insightful decision making, creative problem solving, and skill at interacting with diverse groups —employees, management, investors, customers, or clients.

What skills do your students need in order to prosper in the competitive workplace? In 1991, the U.S. Department of Labor released a report that identified five competencies that, in conjunction with a three-part foundation of skills and personal qualities, lie at the heart of job performance. These Foundation Skills and Workplace Competencies were deemed essential for all workers in the rapidly changing workplace.

Foundation Skills
Basic Skills—reading, writing, math, listening, and speaking
Thinking Skills—creative thinking, decision making, problem solving, seeing things in the mind's eye, knowing how to learn, and reasoning
Personal Qualities—responsibility, self-esteem, sociability, self-management, and integrity and honesty
Workplace Competencies
Resources—allocate time, money, material and facility resources, and human resources
Interpersonal Skills—work in teams, teach others, serve customers, lead, negotiate, and work with people from culturally diverse backgrounds
Information—acquire and evaluate, organize and maintain, interpret and communicate, and use computers to process information
Systems—understand systems, monitor and correct performance, and improve and design systems
Technology—select technology, apply technology to task, and maintain and troubleshoot technology

21st Century Skills

These workplace skills are as essential in the 21st century as they were in the 20th century. However, two major changes have occurred since 1991:

- A dramatic increase in the importance of computer technology
- The passage of the No Child Left Behind Act (NCLB)

These two events prompted educational coalitions to revisit the concept of workplace skills. The most prominent of these, The Partnership for 21st Century Skills, has created a framework integrating technology and the core academic subjects emphasized by the No Child Left Behind Act.

21st Century Skills

Learning Skills	
Information and Communication Skills	**Information and Media Literacy Skills** Analyzing, accessing, managing, integrating, evaluating, and creating information in a variety of forms and media. Understanding the role of media in society.
	Communication Skills Understanding, managing, and creating effective oral, written, and multimedia communication in a variety of forms and contexts.
Thinking and Problem-Solving Skills	**Critical Thinking and Systems Thinking** Exercising sound reasoning in understanding and making complex choices, understanding the interconnections among systems.
	Problem Identification, Formulation, and Solution Ability to frame, analyze, and solve problems.
	Creativity and Intellectual Curiosity Developing, implementing, and communicating new ideas to others, staying open and responsive to new and diverse perspectives.
Interpersonal and Self-Directional Skills	**Interpersonal and Collaborative Skills** Demonstrating teamwork and leadership; adapting to varied roles and responsibilities; working productively with others; exercising empathy; respecting diverse perspectives.
	Self-Direction Monitoring one's own understanding and learning needs, locating appropriate resources, transferring learning from one domain to another.
	Accountability and Adaptability Exercising personal responsibility and flexibility in personal, workplace, and community contexts; setting and meeting high standards and goals for oneself and others; tolerating ambiguity.
	Social Responsibility Acting responsibly with the interests of the larger community in mind; demonstrating ethical behavior in personal, workplace, and community contexts.

Source: Partnership for 21st Century Skills

Workplace Skills Competency Chart

Workplace Skills	Student Edition Correlations
Resources: Identifies, organizes, plans, and allocates resources	
• Allocating time	Chapters 3, 16, 22
• Allocating money	Chapters 2, 3, 4, 5, 6, 7, 8, 9, 16, 18, 19, 20, 21, 22
• Allocating material and facility resources	Chapters 18, 22,
• Allocating human resources	
Information: Acquires and uses information	
• Acquiring information and evaluating information	Chapters 1–22
• Organizing and maintaining information	Chapters 2, 3, 4, 7, 8, 9, 10, 11, 12, 13, 17, 18, 19, 20, 21
• Interpreting and communicating information	Chapters 6, 7, 8, 9, 10, 11, 12, 13, 14, 15, 17
• Using computers to process information	Chapters 1–22
Systems: Understands complex interrelationships	
• Understanding systems	Chapter 21
• Monitoring and correcting performance	Chapter 21
• Correcting systems	Chapter 21
Interpersonal Skills: Works with others	
• Participating as a member of a team	Chapters 1–22
• Teaching others	Chapters 3, 6, 7, 8, 9, 12, 16, 19, 20, 21, 22
• Serving clients/others	Chapters 13, 20
• Exercising leadership	Chapters 5, 16, 18, 19, 22
• Negotiating to arrive at a decision	Chapters 1–22
• Working with cultural diversity	
Technology: Works with a variety of technologies	
• Selecting technology	Chapters 7, 10, 11, 13, 14, 15
• Applying technology to task	Chapters 1–22
• Maintaining and troubleshooting technology	Chapters 1–22
	Chapters 1–22

Foundation Skills	Student Edition Correlations
Personal Qualities:	
• Responsibility, self-management, self-esteem, sociability	Chapters 3, 6, 7, 19, 19
Basic Skills:	
• Reading	Chapters 1–22
• Writing	Chapters 1–22
• Arithmetic/Mathematics	Chapters 1–22
• Speaking and Listening	Chapters 1–22
Thinking Skills:	
• Creative Thinking	Chapters 1–22
• Decision Making	Chapters 1–22
• Problem Solving	Chapters 1–22
• Seeing Things in the Mind's Eye	Chapters 1–22
• Knowing How to Learn	Chapters 1–22
• Reasoning	Chapters 1–22

Resources for New Directions

Academies

Business academies are typically "schools within schools." Students learn school-to-work skills through the collaboration of community businesses, local higher education institutions, and motivated teachers. Students admitted to the academy might engage in field trips, job shadowing, mentoring, and internships as part of their course work. They not only take industry-specific courses like travel and tourism, finance, and information technology, but they must also pass the usual state curriculum for graduation.

Academies attract students by offering preparation for higher education, post-high school career themes, professional development, and community partnerships. Students join a cadre of peers with similar interests and excel at their studies. By adopting what is of interest to them—job placement after high school and business technology—they are entering the world of work armed with skills to understand all aspects of the selected industry.

Each business academy may vary in focus and in core competencies. Generally, assessment occurs in the same methods as in English and language arts, mathematics, science, and social studies. The academy faculty might measure students on portfolios, project-based activities, or scores on tests.

The National Academy Foundation (NAF) operates academies in various career themes, including finance. To learn about the Academy of Finance, visit **www.naf.org**.

Exit Exams

Each state approaches the high school exit examination differently. Some states have implemented it, some have delayed it, and some have ignored it. By 2008, at least 24 states will have an exit exam requirement in place. Public concern about students' low performance and failing schools has prompted state policymakers to endorse the high-stakes testing.

The Center on Education Policy (CEP) reports that multiple-choice items are the predominant type of question on state exit exams, followed by short answers and writing prompts. A writing prompt requires the student to write an essay, letter, or other written product. Recent exit exams have included extended response items.

In order for your students to become successful test takers, they need experience in different assessment methods. Glencoe's *Business and Personal Finance* program offers a variety of assessment options.

For more information on exit exams, visit the High School Exit Examination section of the Center on Education Policy Web site at **www.ctredpol.org**.

Block Scheduling

In most high schools across the United States, the typical school day is made up of six, seven, or eight class periods of 40 to 50 minutes, which meet 180 days a year.

In block scheduling, class sessions are scheduled for longer periods of time over fewer days. For example, a school day of block scheduling might consist of four blocks of 90-minute sessions that run 90 days, or half a school year.

In the following planning guide for *Business and Personal Finance*, to the right of each unit title is the suggested total number of days for that unit, based on a 90-minute class period. The suggested number is the sum of the days estimated to teach each chapter in that unit.

This schedule provides for the presentation of the following components:

- End-of-chapter activities
- Features
- Activities from the Teacher Annotated Edition
- Activities in the Student Activity Workbook
- Unit Tests
- Chapter Tests

Optional activities enhance the chapter but will require more time than given here for each chapter. Typically, optional activities take from one-third to one-half a day each. You may wish to include these optional activities if you find you have some extra time:

- Standard & Poor's Extension Activities
- Your Personal Financial Planner
- Internet Resources
- Financial Planner Software
- Money Matters: Personal and Family Financial Management Simulation
- *Business and Personal Finance* Online Learning Center

Unit/Chapter	DAYS
UNIT 1 Planning Personal Finances	**16**
Chapter 1 Personal Financial Planning	4
Chapter 2 Finances and Career Planning	4
Chapter 3 Money Management Strategy	4
Chapter 4 Consumer Purchasing and Protection	4
Unit 2 Banking and Credit	**13**
Chapter 5 Banking	4
Chapter 6 Consumer Credit	4
Chapter 7 The Finances of Housing	5
Unit 3 Investing Financial Resources	**16**
Chapter 8 Saving and Investing	4
Chapter 9 Stocks	4
Chapter 10 Bonds and Mutual Funds	4
Chapter 11 Real Estate and Other Investments	4

Unit/Chapter	DAYS
Unit 4 Protecting Your Finances	**16**
Chapter 12 Planning Your Tax Strategy	4
Chapter 13 Home and Motor Vehicle Insurance	4
Chapter 14 Health, Disability, and Life Insurance	4
Chapter 15 Retirement and Estate Planning	4
Unit 5 Business Ownership and Planning	**12**
Chapter 16 Types of Business Ownership	4
Chapter 17 Developing a Business Plan	4
Chapter 18 Developing a Financial Plan	4
Unit 6 Business Finance Basics	**17**
Chapter 19 Sources of Funding	4
Chapter 20 Financial Accounting	4
Chapter 21 Managing Payroll and Inventory	4
Chapter 22 Pricing, Costing, and Growth	5

Course Planning Guide

Full-Year Course Schedule—Six-Week Grading System

First	**Unit 1** Chapter 1 Chapter 2 Chapter 3 Chapter 4	**Planning Personal Finances** Personal Financial Planning Finances and Career Planning Money Management Strategy Consumer Purchasing and Protection
Second	**Unit 2** Chapter 5 Chapter 6 Chapter 7	**Banking and Credit** Banking Consumer Credit The Finances of Housing
Third	**Unit 3** Chapter 8 Chapter 9 Chapter 10 Chapter 11	**Investing Financial Resources** Saving and Investing Stocks Bonds and Mutual Funds Real Estate and Other Investments
Fourth	**Unit 4** Chapter 12 Chapter 13 Chapter 14 Chapter 15	**Protecting Your Finances** Planning Your Tax Strategy Home and Motor Vehicle Insurance Health, Disability, and Life Insurance Retirement and Estate Planning
Fifth	**Unit 5** Chapter 16 Chapter 17 Chapter 18	**Business Ownership and Planning** Types of Business Ownership Developing a Business Plan Developing a Financial Plan
Sixth	**Unit 6** Chapter 19 Chapter 20 Chapter 21 Chapter 22	**Business Finance Basics** Sources of Funding Financial Accounting Managing Payroll and Inventory Pricing, Costing, and Growth

Full-Year Course Schedule—Nine-Week Grading System

First	**Unit 1** Chapter 1 Chapter 2 Chapter 3 Chapter 4 **Unit 2** Chapter 5 Chapter 6	**Planning Personal Finances** Personal Financial Planning Finances and Career Planning Money Management Strategy Consumer Purchasing and Protection **Banking and Credit** Banking Consumer Credit
Second	Chapter 7 **Unit 3** Chapter 8 Chapter 9 Chapter 10 Chapter 11	The Finances of Housing **Investing Financial Resources** Saving and Investing Stocks Bonds and Mutual Funds Real Estate and Other Investments
Third	**Unit 4** Chapter 12 Chapter 13 Chapter 14 Chapter 15 **Unit 5** Chapter 16 Chapter 17	**Protecting Your Finances** Planning Your Tax Strategy Home and Motor Vehicle Insurance Health, Disability, and Life Insurance Retirement and Estate Planning **Business Ownership and Planning** Types of Business Ownership Developing a Business Plan
Fourth	Chapter 18 **Unit 6** Chapter 19 Chapter 20 Chapter 21 Chapter 22	Developing a Financial Plan **Business Finance Basics** Sources of Funding Financial Accounting Managing Payroll and Inventory Pricing, Costing, and Growth

Course Planning Guide

Semester Course Schedule—Six-Week Grading System

First	**Unit 1**	**Planning Personal Finances**
	Chapter 1	Personal Financial Planning
	Chapter 2	Finances and Career Planning
	Chapter 3	Money Management Strategy
	Chapter 4	Consumer Purchasing and Protection
	Unit 2	**Banking and Credit**
	Chapter 5	Banking
	Chapter 6	Consumer Credit
	Chapter 7	The Finances of Housing
Second	**Unit 3**	**Investing Financial Resources**
	Chapter 8	Saving and Investing
	Chapter 9	Stocks
	Chapter 10	Bonds and Mutual Funds
	Chapter 11	Real Estate and Other Investments
	Unit 4	**Protecting Your Finances**
	Chapter 12	Planning Your Tax Strategy
	Chapter 13	Home and Motor Vehicle Insurance
	Chapter 14	Health, Disability, and Life Insurance
	Chapter 15	Retirement and Estate Planning
Third	**Unit 5**	**Business Ownership and Planning**
	Chapter 16	Types of Business Ownership
	Chapter 17	Developing a Business Plan
	Chapter 18	Developing a Financial Plan
	Unit 6	**Business Finance Basics**
	Chapter 19	Sources of Funding
	Chapter 20	Financial Accounting
	Chapter 21	Managing Payroll and Inventory
	Chapter 22	Pricing, Costing, and Growth

Semester Course Schedule—Nine-Week Grading System

First	**Unit 1**	**Planning Personal Finances**
	Chapter 1	Personal Financial Planning
	Chapter 2	Finances and Career Planning
	Chapter 3	Money Management Strategy
	Chapter 4	Consumer Purchasing and Protection
	Unit 2	**Banking and Credit**
	Chapter 5	Banking
	Chapter 6	Consumer Credit
	Chapter 7	The Finances of Housing
	Unit 3	**Investing Financial Resources**
	Chapter 8	Saving and Investing
	Chapter 9	Stocks
	Chapter 10	Bonds and Mutual Funds
	Chapter 11	Real Estate and Other Investments
Second	**Unit 4**	**Protecting Your Finances**
	Chapter 12	Planning Your Tax Strategy
	Chapter 13	Home and Motor Vehicle Insurance
	Chapter 14	Health, Disability, and Life Insurance
	Chapter 15	Retirement and Estate Planning
	Unit 5	**Business Ownership and Planning**
	Chapter 16	Types of Business Ownership
	Chapter 17	Developing a Business Plan
	Chapter 18	Developing a Financial Plan
	Unit 6	**Business Finance Basics**
	Chapter 19	Sources of Funding
	Chapter 20	Financial Accounting
	Chapter 21	Managing Payroll and Inventory
	Chapter 22	Pricing, Costing, and Growth

Personal Finances

Plann

1
Financial Planning

ter 2
nces and Career Planning

hapter 3
Money Management Strategy

Chapter 4
Consumer Purchasing and Protection

Unit Overview

This unit introduces students to the concept of financial planning and provides the foundation for using personal financial planning techniques. In Chapter 1, students will learn how to create a financial plan using the six steps of the financial planning process. Chapter 2 discusses the relationship between work, careers, and financial planning. Students will learn how to identify the personal issues to consider when choosing a career and how to apply effective strategies to obtain employment. Chapter 3 explains the relationship between financial documents and money management strategies and how to create a budget, and Chapter 4 describes the importance of wise buying decisions.

Introductory Activity

To introduce the concept of perso financial planning, ask students to spend to 15 minutes writing a description of th they expect for themselves as adults. Ask to describe where they will live, what of work they will do, whether they to have a family, if they would like t and where, and what kind of car the like to own. Then ask them how th to achieve these goals. Finally, ex financial planning helps us achiev goals. Through careful planning, ing, and choosing an appropriate can achieve their goals.

BusinessWeek FINANCE FILE

Which Advisor Knows the Way?

Answer Answers might include that because anyone can claim to be a financial planner, a consumer shoulc watch their own finances t fraud or incompetence.

Teacher Manual

Get a Financial Life!

Setting Up a Career Plan

STEP A The Process

Make sure students have access to all necessary materials. Lead students through the process:

1. Remind them of the future life they wrote about in the unit planning guide introduction. They can use this description to help them develop their goals.
2. Help students arrange to take the aptitude test or interest inventory. Contact the school counselor so he or she is prepared for the students' requests.
3. Give students the list of Web sites from the Additional Resources section of the Chapter 2 Planning Guide. These sites can help students research careers.
4. Help students secure an opportunity to interview or job shadow someone working in their area of interest.
5. If students have questions about how to obtain college catalogs from schools, point out that most colleges will mail information to prospective students. Using the Internet or reference books from the public library, students can obtain the addresses of schools of interest.
6. Explain that by creating templates for a résumé and a cover letter, students will not have to re-enter the text every time they need one of these documents, but they will be able to customize their letters and résumés.

STEP B Create Your Portfolio

Review students' portfolios regularly to make sure they are working on them over time and not waiting until the last minute. Consider creating a schedule for completion of each section in the portfolio.

STEP C Presentation

Evaluate the presentations based on the following criteria:

- Check that students have read their chosen book thoroughly. Allow time for questions to determine how well the students understand what they read.
- Presentations should be clear and easy to understand. They should be interesting and informative.
- Have students explain why they would or would not recommend the book.

Unit Closure

Have each student write a one- or two-page answer to this question: On a scale from one to ten (one being unimportant and ten being very important), how would you rate financial planning and its impact on your life now and in the future?

Evaluation

Administer the Unit 1 test from the **Exam***View*® Pro Testmaker CD-ROM.

Teacher Manual

Personal Financial Planning

pages 4–29

SECTION	LEARNING OBJECTIVES	FEATURES	TEXT RESOURCES	TECHNOLOGY RESOURCES
1.1	**After completing this section, students will have learned:** How to define personal financial planning How to name the six steps of financial planning. How to recall eight strategies for achieving financial goals.	**TechByte,** p. 7 **Common Cents,** p. 10 **Careers in Finance,** p. 11 **Document Detective,** p. 12 **Academic Connection,** p.13 **Savvy Saver,** p. 14 **S&P's Global Financial Landscape,** p. 15	**Section Assessment,** p. 18 Quick Check, Think Critically Use Math Skills Solve Money Problems **Student Activity Workbook**	Lesson Planner Plus Online Learning Center Interactive Student Edition *Presentation Plus!* **Exam***View*® Pro Test Generator Financial Planner Software
1.2	**After completing this section, students will have learned:** How to identify economic factors that affect personal financial decisions. How to explain opportunity costs associated with personal financial decisions. How to identify strategies for achieving financial goals at different stages of life.	**Go Figure—** Calculating Annual Interest, p. 20 **Go Figure—** Calculating the Future Value of a Single Deposit, p. 21 **S&P Put on Your Financial Planner's Cap,** p. 22 **WebQuest,** p. 25	**Section Assessment,** p. 25 Quick Check, Think Critically Use Math Skills Solve Money Problems **Student Activity Workbook**	Lesson Planner Plus Online Learning Center Interactive Student Edition *Presentation Plus!* **Exam***View*® Pro Test Generator Financial Planner Software

Meeting National Standards for Business Education

Section 1.1	Section 2.2
Economics I. Allocation of Resources II. Economic Systems III. Economic Institutions and Incentives IV. Markets and Prices V. Market Structures VII. The Role of Government IX. Aggregate Supply and Aggregate Demand **Personal Finance** I. Personal Decision Making II. Earning a Living III. Managing Finances and Budgeting IV. Saving and Investing V. Buying Goods and Services	**Economics** I. Allocation of Resources VIII. International Economic Concepts **Personal Finance** I. Personal Decision Making II. Earning a Living III. Managing Finances and Budgeting IV. Saving and Investing VII. Using Credit

Teaching Connection

The First Day

This activity will help involve students in the class as soon as they step through the door. It will set up the expectation for students' active participation.

On the first day of class, write on the board the course name, number, and section, and your name. Hand out note cards to students as they walk in the classroom, asking them to fill out the cards with the following information that you write board:

- Name
- Telephone number
- E-mail address, if you have one
- Interests and hobbies
- Career ambitions
- What you most want to learn in this class

Give students the course syllabus and allow them a few minutes to read it as you collect the note cards. Introduce yourself and welcome the students to the class.

Visual Guide

Chapter 1 Opener

Discussion: Have the students study the chapter opening photo and describe what they see. Then lead a discussion about how planning for their financial futures can involve part-time jobs. Ask what students would do with money they might earn while attending high school.

Follow-Up: Ask the students to list three sources of income they might be able to have now.

Teacher Manual

Workplace Skills and Chapter Correlations

FOUNDATION SKILLS

Basic Skills	Reading	Writing	Math	Listening	Speaking	
Thinking Skills	Creative Thinking	Decision Making	Problem Solving	Seeing Things in the Mind's Eye	Knowing How to Learn	Reasoning
Personal Qualities	Responsibility	Self-Esteem	Sociability	Self-Management	Integrity/ Honesty	

WORKPLACE COMPETENCIES

Resources	Allocating Time	Allocating Money	Allocating Material and Facility Resources	Allocating Human Resources		
Information	Acquiring and Evaluating Information	Organizing and Maintaining Information	Interpreting and Communicating Information	Using Computers to Process Information		
Interpersonal Skills	Participating as a Member of a Team	Teaching Others	Serving Clients/ Customers	Exercising Leadership	Negotiating to Arrive at a Decision	Working with Cultural Diversity
Systems	Understanding Systems	Monitoring and Correcting Performance	Improving and Designing Systems			
Technology	Selecting Technology	Applying Technology to Task	Maintaining and TroubleshootingTechnology			

Internet Extension

Activity: Ask students to use the Internet to locate savings calculators. These calculators will compute how much you have to save every day, week, and month to reach your goal. Have the students use one of these online calculators to compute their own savings goal and print out their own savings schedules.

Keywords: savings calculator, personal finance

Enrichment/Application Activity

Field Trip: Take students to the public library or a full-sized bookstore to see the many financial planning books available. Have each student write the name, title, and brief description of two books that they would choose to read, and explain why.

Topic Spotlight

Money: Demand for a product (how much that product is wanted by consumers) is one factor used when determining price. Usually, when the demand for a product is high, the price of the product rises. When demand for a product is low, the price falls. Discuss with students how this economic factor affects the money they have to spend.

Technology: Ask students how improvements in technology may help people with their financial planning and money management.

Marketing: Bring a variety of magazine ads to class to pass around to students. Ask how advertising encourages consumers to spend money.

Additional Resources

Books

Basics of Saving and Investing: A Teaching Guide (©1998 Eastern Michigan University) This curriculum guide for high school-level instruction in the principles of personal finance is free to educators and available through several sources. A national version of this guide is available by contacting the NASD by phone (202) 728-6964, fax (202) 728-8022, and Web sites **investor.nasd.com** or **nasd.com**.

Magazines

Young Money, Todd Romer, publisher. This magazine reports on personal finance issues for teens and young adults. It specifically targets three categories: earning, investing, and spending. Classroom subscription rates are available. Its Web site is **youngmoney.com**.

Internet

www.jumpstartcoalition.org The Jump$tart Coalition for Personal Financial Literacy seeks to improve the personal financial literacy of young adults. Its purpose is to evaluate the financial literacy of young adults; develop, disseminate, and encourage the use of guidelines for grades K–12; and promote the teaching of personal finance. Its Web site provides a searchable database of educational materials for the K–12 age group.

bankrate.com This Web site offers current information on many personal finance issues, such as checking and ATM fees, auto loans, money markets, and no-fee and low interest rate credit cards. It also provides access to financial calculators, such as loan, college tuition, moving, and savings calculators.

Note: Web-site addresses may change.

Section 1.1

Focus

Motivation

Ask the student to think about financial goals they might set during the school year. Acknowledge all goals and list them on the board. Then ask the students how they think they will be able to achieve these goals. Use this discussion to introduce this chapter.

Prereading

1. Have the students skim the section, looking at photos and figures, reading captions, and noting headings.
2. Have a student read aloud What You'll Learn on page 4.
3. Dictate each of the key terms to the class. Have students write them on a piece of paper. Then write the key terms on the board. Ask students to guess at the meaning of each term. Leave the list on the board as students study the section.

Teach

Guided Practice

1. Have the student read aloud In the Real World on page 5.
2. Have the students read aloud Ask Standard and Poor's on page 5.
3. Have students silently read the rest of the section, noting and mentally answering the Predict, Relate, Question, and caption questions and reading the features such as Document Detective.

Independent Practice

Have students create a collage of their financial goals for the future. Allow them to use pictures from magazines, Clipart from the computer, or their own artwork. Display the finished collages around the room.

Assess

Reteaching

1. Review the list of key terms that students were unsure about before studying the section.
2. To reteach the concept of supply and demand, choose a popular toy to use as an example. Help the students understand that if demand for a toy is high, then the supply goes down and prices often go up. Then if the popularity of a toy diminishes and the demand goes down, the supply will be high and the prices might be discounted to sell the merchandise.
3. Ask the students to create a list of toys and games (electronic or otherwise) that they think have been affected by this economic concept.

Enrichment

Have the students go to the library or use the Internet to research the Federal Reserve System and the role it plays in our economy. The Web site for the Federal Reserve System is **federalreserve.gov**.

Assessment

1. Have the students complete the Section 1.1 Assessment.
2. Assign an activity from the *Student Activity Workbook*.

Close

Have students complete this statement: "If I learn and put into action the six steps in the financial planning process, I will...." (Sample response: "...have a solid foundation for making all my financial decisions, now and in the future.")

Section 1.2

Focus

Motivation

Ask students to imagine they have just won a million dollars. Generate a discussion about what they would do with that money. Encourage them to think about saving and investing for the future.

Prereading

1. Have the students skim the section, looking at photos and figures, reading captions, and noting headings.
2. Ask a student to read aloud Read to Learn on page 19.
3. Have the students write down each highlighted key term in the section and generate a picture or symbol that identifies it, based on its definition.

Teach

Guided Practice

1. Ask a student to read aloud the paragraph Personal Opportunity Costs.
2. Have students silently read the rest of the section, noting and mentally answering the Predict, Relate, Question, and caption questions and reading the features such as Put on Your Financial Planner's Cap.

Independent Practice

Have students use newspaper or magazine articles to research and report on the current interest rate charged by the Federal Reserve. Then find out what local banks and financial institutions pay you to use your money. Each month throughout the course, research these rates again. Graph the changes in interest rates.

Assess

Reteaching

1. Review the key terms from the section. Make sure the students understand them.
2. Ask your students to think about all the times during the last month that they spent, borrowed, saved, or invested money. Then ask them how they might have better used that money.

Enrichment

1. Have the students write an article for the school newspaper on a topic from this chapter. Some ideas might include financial goal setting, the time value of money, or strategies for achieving financial goals.
2. Have the students review the eight strategies for achieving financial goals, found on pages 24–25. Then ask them to create a journal of how they think they will apply the strategies to their own lives.

Assessment

1. Have the students complete the Section 1.2 Assessment.
2. Assign the Chapter 1 Review and Activities.
3. Administer the test for Chapter 1 from the Reproducible Tests included in the *Lesson Planner Plus* supplement.

Close

Ask the students to complete this statement: "By learning to use my money wisely now, I will be able to...."

ANSWERS

Careers in Finance

Accept all reasonable answers that demonstrate an understanding of the services performed by personal bankers such as personalized services and answering questions that impersonal ATMs or Web sites cannot answer.

Teacher Manual

Document Detective

1. A fixed expense remains the same amount each month. The amount of a flexible expense changes each month.
2. Answers will vary but could include:
   Fixed: student loan, IRA, etc.
   Flexible: vehicle repairs, dry cleaning, snow removal, etc.
   Other: video rental, CDs, DVDs, sports equipment, etc.
3. No. Janet spends more than she earns.
4. Utilities are flexible because the amount varies each month, depending on usage.
5. Janet could find an extra source of income, such as a second job, or save less each month. Alternatively, Janet could cut back on other expenses, such as discretionary spending.

Academic Connection

Accept all clearly written financial goals that reflect consideration and understanding of the guidelines listed on page 13.

STANDARD &POOR'S Global Financial Landscape

Accept all lists that demonstrate thought and consideration of current trends in teen buying that might be popular among teens in India today. Examples of products might include electronic games and popular music CDs that are priced reasonably.

STANDARD &POOR'S Put on Your Financial Planner's Cap

Accept all reasonable answers.

Section 1.1 Assessment

Quick Check

1. (1) determine your current financial situation, (2) develop your financial goals, (3) identify alternative courses of action (4) evaluate your alternatives, (5) create and use your financial plan of action, and (6) review and revise your plan.
2. Some purchases will be consumable goods, which people buy often and use up quickly. Because they will probably cost less than other goods or services, short-term goals can be set to obtain them. Other purchases will be for durable goods. Set intermediate or long-term goals to obtain these items. Finally, some goals may involve intangibles, which will vary in the time required to achieve them.
3. Students should describe two of the following factors: (1) market forces, (2) financial institutions, (3) global influences, (4) economic conditions.

Think Critically

4. Understanding the difference between what you need and what you want can help develop financial goals.

Use Communication Skills

5. Accept all role plays that demonstrate an understanding of the topics.

Solve Money Problems

6. Answers will vary but should reference the six steps of financial planning: (1) Determine current financial situation; (2) develop financial goals; (3) identify alternative courses of action; (4) evaluate alternatives; (5) create and use a financial plan of action; (6) review and revise the plan.

Section 1.2 Assessment

Quick Check

1. personal opportunity costs and financial opportunity costs
2. It will increase your current income and help your money grow over time.
3. Obtain, plan, spend, save, borrow, invest, manage risk, and retire.

Think Critically

4. Accept all reasonable arguments. For example, the time value of money is the increase in an amount of money as a result of interest earned. If you shop among financial institutions, you might get a higher interest rate. The higher the interest rate, the faster the money will grow.

Use Math Skills

5. Tanya will have $16,578 available in five years. (ANSWER: $3,000 × 5.526 = $16,578) Tanya will need to raise an additional $1,422. (ANSWER: $18,000 – $16,578 = $1,422) Students can use the future value table in Figure 1.4 to answer this question.

Solve Money Problems

6. Group analyses will vary by group.

Chapter 1 Review & Activities

Communicating Key Terms

Accept all reasonable responses that reflect an understanding of the article and chapter topics.

Reviewing Key Concepts

1. Personal financial planning means managing your money (spending, saving, and investing) so that you can achieve financial independence and security.
2. The six steps of financial planning are: (1) Determine your current financial situation; (2) develop your financial goals; (3) identify alternative courses of action; (4) evaluate your alternatives; (5) create and use your financial plan of action; and (6) review and revise your plan.
3. your life situations, your personal values, and outside economic factors
4. For all your financial decisions, you must make choices and give up something. These trade-offs, or opportunity costs, can be personal or financial.
5. The eight strategies are: Obtain, plan, spend wisely, save, borrow wisely, invest, manage risk, and retire.

ACADEMIC SKILLS

Possible answers might be as the market becomes saturated with products over time, popularity diminishes, and thus, inventory is overstocked, causing retail prices to decrease.

YOUR FINANCIAL FIGURES

1. Answers will vary depending on the interest rates used. For example, if the regular savings interest rate is currently 5 percent, the future value rate of the annual deposits is 9.549 percent: .09549 × $1,600 = $152.78; $1,600 + $152.78 = $1,752.78.
2. Answers will vary depending on the interest rates used.

REAL-WORLD Application

Accept all reasonable answers that demonstrate an understanding of the concepts.

Internet CONNECTION

1. Interest rates decrease.
2. Interest rates increase.

BusinessWeek ONLINE

Accept all paragraphs that demonstrate that students have read the online article.

Finances and Career Planning

pages 30–57

SECTION	LEARNING OBJECTIVES	FEATURES	TEXT RESOURCES	TECHNOLOGY RESOURCES
2.1	**After completing this section, students will have learned to:** Identify the personal issues to consider when choosing and planning your career. Explain how education and training affect career advancement. Discuss the factors that influence employment.	**Academic Connection,** p. 34 **Common Cents,** p. 37 **S&P's Global Financial Landscape,** p. 38	**Section Assessment,** p. 39 Quick Check Think Critically Use Communication Skills Solve Money Problems **Student Activity Workbook**	Lesson Planner Plus Online Learning Center Interactive Student Edition *Presentation Plus!* **Exam***View®* Pro Test Generator Financial Planner Software
2.2	**After completing this section, students will have learned to:** Describe effective strategies to obtain employment. Identify sources of career opportunities. Identify the financial and legal issues to consider when looking for employment.	**Document Detective,** p. 42 **TechByte,** p. 43 **S&P's Put on Your Financial Planner's Cap,** p. 48 **Careers in Finance,** p. 49 **Savvy Saver,** p. 41 **WebQuest,** p. 52	**Section Assessment,** p. 53 Quick Check Think Critically Use Math Skills Solve Money Problems **Student Activity Workbook**	Lesson Planner Plus Online Learning Center Interactive Student Edition *Presentation Plus!* **Exam***View®* Pro Test Generator Financial Planner Software

CHAPTER 2 Planning Guide

Meeting National Standards for Business Education	
Section 2.1	**Section 2.2**
Economics I. Allocation of Resources II. Economic Systems III. Economic Institutions and Incentives IV. Markets and Prices VIII. International Economic Concepts IX. Aggregate Supply and Aggregate Demand **Personal Finance** I. Personal Decision Making II. Earning a Living	**Economics** III. Economic Institutions and Incentives **Personal Finance** I. Personal Decision Making II. Earning a Living III. Managing Finances and Budgeting IV. Saving and Investing VIII. Protecting Against Risk

Teaching Connection

Ice Breaker

This exercise will help students relax and clarify expectations. It may also reduce communication breakdown due to different perceptions. Start by pairing students. Tell students they will be timed. One student partner will speak to his or her partner for one minute. Have the speaker describe his or her interests, career ambitions or goals, family or friends, and one experience or trait that makes him or her unique. The second student partner will then do the same for one minute.

Afterward, have the class gather in a large group. Ask partners to introduce their partners. Then lead the class in a discussion about the kinds of things people revealed about themselves and what partners remember most.

Visual Guide

Chapter 2 Opener

Discussion: Have the students study the chapter opening photo and describe what they see. Then lead a discussion about how the choice of a career will affect students' finances in the future. Ask them if money is more important to them than career satisfaction.

Follow-Up: Ask the students to list three careers that they would like to have that might also provide the type of income they would want.

Teacher Manual

Workplace Skills and Chapter Correlations

FOUNDATION SKILLS						
Basic Skills	Reading	Writing	Math	Listening	Speaking	
Thinking Skills	Creative Thinking	Decision Making	Problem Solving	Seeing Things in the Mind's Eye	Knowing How to Learn	Reasoning
Personal Qualities	Responsibility	Self-Esteem	Sociability	Self-Management	Integrity/ Honesty	

WORKPLACE COMPETENCIES						
Resources	Allocating Time	Allocating Money	Allocating Material and Facility Resources	Allocating Human Resources		
Information	Acquiring and Evaluating Information	Organizing and Maintaining Information	Interpreting and Communicating Information	Using Computers to Process Information		
Interpersonal Skills	Participating as a Member of a Team	Teaching Others	Serving Clients/ Customers	Exercising Leadership	Negotiating to Arrive at a Decision	Working with Cultural Diversity
Systems	Understanding Systems	Monitoring and Correcting Performance	Improving and Designing Systems			
Technology	Selecting Technology	Applying Technology to Task	Maintaining and TroubleshootingTechnology			

Internet Extension

Activity: Ask students to use the Internet to find out what kind of career planning information is available online. They should note the different sources of career information that they find and make note of appropriate Web sites.

Keywords: career planning, help with résumé

Enrichment/Application Activity

Guest Speaker: Invite the school counselor to speak to the class about the school-to-work program(s) available through your high school, or invite a career counselor from a university, college, or technical school in your area to talk about the career planning and placement office at his or her institution.

Topic Spotlight

Marketing: Write on the board: "Marketing is the process of developing, promoting, and distributing products in order to satisfy customers' needs and wants." Then discuss with students how finding the right job is like marketing. [EXAMPLE: They are promoting their skills hoping to satisfy the wants and needs of an employer.]

Money: Have each student write a paragraph explaining how important salary is to them and why.

Ethics: Discuss with students this ethical job-hunting situation: You and your best friend are both looking for summer jobs, and you plan to work together. In fact, you have made a pact not to take a job where you both cannot work. You and your friend have applied at a nearby state park that is looking for lifeguards for the summer. You are offered a job, but your friend is not. What would you do and why? How would you feel if the situation were reversed?

Additional Resources

Books

What Color Is Your Parachute? 2005: A Practical Manual for Job-Hunters and Career-Changers by Richard Nelson Bolles, Mark Emery Bolles (Ten Speed Press, ©2005). This popular book is a guide for those who are looking for satisfying and fulfilling employment.

Do What You Are: Discover the Perfect Career for You Through the Secrets of Personality Type—Revised and Updated Edition Featuring E-Careers for the 21st Century by Paul D. Tieger, Barbara Barron-Teiger (Little, Brown, ©2001) Using workbook exercises, this book provides specific job search strategies. It also provides a list of occupations that are popular with students' personality types, including career tracks in growth sectors such as e-commerce, biotechnology, new media, and telecommunications.

Internet

dol.gov/dol/jobs.htm The U.S. Department of Labor offers educational resources at this Web site, such as "Career Exploration and Finding a Job" and "Jobs for Kids Who Like...." Its main Web site is **dol.gov**.

GetThatGig.com This is where young job-seekers (16–21) can find cool summer jobs and internships, and learn about extraordinary career paths in all types of industries. Search for jobs or post your résumé.

monster.com This Web site offers resources for writing and posting résumés, researching companies, getting career advice, and finding jobs.

ja.org This Web site for Junior Achievement (JA) gives information about the programs the organization offers students. JA's purpose is to educate and inspire "young people to value free enterprise, business, and economics to improve the quality of their lives."

Note: Web-site addresses may change.

Section 2.1

Focus

Motivation

Write this statement on the board: "Because of technological changes occurring now, many jobs that will be available in ten years have not been thought of or created." Ask: "How do you plan for a career you know nothing about?"

Prereading

1. Have students skim the section, looking at the pictures, reading the captions, and reading the headings.
2. Ask a student to read aloud Read to Learn on page 32.
3. Have students list the Key Terms in their notebooks, and remind them to enter the definitions.

Teach

Guided Practice

1. Ask students to read aloud In the Real World on page 31 and discuss with them how to make an informed decision.
2. Ask students to read aloud the Standard & Poor's Q&A on page 31; discuss it briefly with them.
3. Have students silently read the rest of the section, noting and mentally answering the Predict, Relate, Question, and caption questions and reading the features such as Global Financial Landscape.

Independent Practice

1. Have students take an aptitude test and/or an interest inventory.
2. Based on the results, have students develop lists of five career possibilities.
3. Ask students to research to discover what kind of education, training, or background is necessary for each potential career.

Assess

Reteaching

1. Go over the list of Key Terms with students, ensuring they have written the correct definitions in their notebooks.
2. Ask students to name the most important elements in the chapter, and write them on the board.
3. Discuss with students the Reading Strategies, the pictures and diagrams and their caption questions, and the features.
4. Write this quote on the board: "It is unwise to devote one's entire education to learning things that everyone else already knows. One must select a vocation for which there is market demand and for which one has talent, and then pursue expertise and excellence within this niche." (John Bishop, Cornell University)

Enrichment

1. Ask students to interview someone who is in one of the career fields selected earlier regarding his/her career path.
2. Have students diagram their interviewee's career path on a poster or some other presentation mode. Select one or two to be presented to the class.
3. As a class, survey the faculty and staff at your school to find out all the different jobs they have had. Ask how they came to choose a career in education.
4. Divide the students into groups. Ask them to prepare a lesson on career planning for middle school/junior high students. Present the lesson to the middle school/junior high students who will be attending your high school.

Assessment

1. Have students complete the Section 2.1 Assessment.
2. Give students a Vocabulary Quiz based on selected words from the Key Terms.
3. Assign an activity from the Chapter 2 *Student Activity Workbook.*

Close

Ask students to prepare an outline of the steps they will take to research and plan their careers; demonstrate outlining on the board.

Section 2.2

Focus

Motivation

Ask students how they would go about searching for a summer job. Ask if they would make a plan, when they would begin their search, what resources they might use.

Prereading

1. Have students skim the section, looking at the pictures, reading the captions, and reading the headings.
2. Ask a student to read aloud Read to Learn on page 40.
3. Have students list the Key Terms in their notebooks, and remind them to enter the definitions.

Teach

Guided Practice

1. Ask a student to read aloud the paragraph answering the question, "What are some of the steps you need to take when searching for a job?"
2. Have students silently read the rest of the section, noting and mentally answering the Predict, Relate, Question, and caption questions and reading the features such as Document Detective.

Independent Practice

1. Although students may not know what careers they will ultimately plan for, ask them to choose a career area (i.e., working with children, computers, animals, medicine, law, etc.) to explore.
2. Ask them to research using library resources, newspapers, and the Internet to locate potential jobs or volunteer work they can do to further their knowledge of the field. Each student is to bring ads for five potential jobs to class.
3. Students are to write letters applying for two of the positions and summarizing why they believe they are qualified.
4. Have the students attend a local job fair. Ask them to be prepared to make a good impression by dressing appropriately and preparing their résumés. When the students return to class, have them share their experiences.

Assess

Reteaching

1. Go over the list of Key Terms with students, ensuring they have written the correct definitions in their notebooks.
2. Ask students to name the most important elements in the chapter, and write them on the board.
3. Discuss with students the Reading Strategies, the pictures and diagrams and their caption questions, and the features.
4. To emphasize the importance of evaluating both the pay and benefits offered by an employer, bring in a list of benefits offered by several employers in your community. Generate a discussion about the types of benefits the students believe are important. Make sure they justify their answers.

Teacher Manual

Enrichment

1. Have students form pairs and ask them to come up with five (5) potential interview questions.
2. Have students exchange questions and, with the questions they have received, conduct practice interviews.
3. Invite some local businesspeople to the class to conduct mock interviews. Ask the guests to evaluate the students' practice questions and each student's interview. Have students dress for such an interview.
4. Invite a lawyer to your class to discuss employee rights with the students. Have the students prepare questions in advance.

Assessment

1. Have students complete the Section 2.2 Assessment and a short vocabulary quiz on this section's key terms.
2. Assign the Chapter Review and Activities.
3. Administer the test for Chapter 2 from the Reproducible Tests in the *Lesson Planner Plus* supplement.

Close

Discuss with students the mock interviews they had with local businesspeople. Ask what they learned.

ANSWERS

STANDARD &POOR'S *Global Financial Landscape*

Answers will vary but may include tourism and food source.

Academic Connection

Accept all reasonable responses.

Document Detective

1. The W-4 form ensures that your employer withholds the correct amount of federal income tax from each pay.
2. A person may choose to withhold more money to cover other income (e.g., rent) that has not had any federal tax withheld. For example, if you receive monthly rent from property you own, you may be required to pay federal taxes on that rent. Additional withholding is a way to pay. A person might also choose additional withholding to receive a tax refund as savings.
3. A person can be exempt if she or he had a right to refund of all federal income taxes because the taxpayer had no tax liability last year, or if the person expects a refund of all federal taxes in the current year.
4. The person must declare that the information he or she provides is correct.
5. A married person can withhold at the higher single rate by checking the appropriate box in item 3.

STANDARD &POOR'S Put on Your Financial Planner's Cap

The friend should gain knowledge about the companies and consider their stability; compare the demands of both jobs; look at the salaries of both but also consider benefits such as health care, retirement, etc.

Careers in Finance

Answers will vary but may include: restaurants and other retail business use cashiers; no experience is required, on-the-job training, learning about financial policies and procedures.

Section 2.1 Assessment

Quick Check

1. Answers will vary but should include three of the characteristics listed on page 33.
   - They work well with others: can function as part of a team
   - They strive to do their best: will probably be rewarded for their excellence.
   - They do not allow conflicts with other employees or changes in their duties to affect their work quality: will stay calm under pressure.
   - They are creative problem-solvers: can make and maintain progress on projects.
   - They read widely and know how to express themselves well: can communicate effectively.
   - They understand themselves and others: will know what is required of them.
2. You can take special tests. Aptitude tests will help you find what you do best; interest inventories help you identify activities you enjoy. Such tests will help match abilities and interests with various other kinds of work.
3. Factors include social influences such as demographic or geographic trends; economic factors such as interest rates, prices, demand for goods and services; and trends in industry and technology, such as increased competition from other countries or further technical innovations.

Think Critically

4. Answers will vary but may include that working parents do not have as much time to provide homemade meals; thus, they rely more on school food services and restaurants.

Use Communication Skills

5. Accept all student surveys that demonstrate sutdent effort.

Solve Money Problems

6. $14,020 (12 × $800 = $9,600; $4 × 5 = $20, and $20 × 52 = $1,040; 52 × $65 = $3,380. $9,600 + $1,040 + $3,380 = $14,020)

Section 2.2 Assessment

Quick Check

1. summer and part-time jobs, temporary work, volunteer work, internships, cooperative education, class projects, and after-school activities
2. Starting salary will depend on education, experience, company size, average salary for that type of job.
3. Answers may include improving communication skills, developing/improving work habits, taking actions when problems arise, keeping up with technological changes, and gaining mentor support.

Think Critically

4. Answers should include the benefits and disadvantages of libraries, mass media, the Internet, school guidance offices, community and professional organizations, and contacts.

Use Math Skills

5. His employment package will be worth approximately $31,923. (Five personal days and five sick days are equal to one week's vacation, or 1/52 of the base pay × 4 = $6,923)

Solve Money Problems

6. Her alternatives might include reimbursement for work-related child-care expenses; a child-care center on site, a flexible work schedule; working from home part-time; and extra health and life insurance for her children. She needs to consider whether she would be allowed to work from home, if she would have to invest in equipment, or make room in her home for an office. She will have to consider if she could work effectively with her children at home. She needs to consider the costs of extra health and life insurance.

Chapter 2 Review & Activities

Communicating Key Terms

Accept all reasonable responses that demonstrate an understanding of the key term definitions.

Reviewing Key Concepts

1. Answers will vary.
2. Factors that affect potential earning power include social influences (demographic trends, geographic trends), economic factors, and industry and technology trends.
3. Who is working (e.g., working parents) and the age of the population affect the growth of various career sectors.
4. Ways to obtain job-related training include: part-time work, volunteer work, internships, cooperative education, class projects, and after-school activities.
5. Sources include libraries, the Internet, newspapers, school guidance offices, community organizations, and your network.
6. Employees are protected against discrimination; in most cases, they must be paid the minimum wage and extra pay for overtime work; and their employers must pay for unemployment insurance, make Social Security contributions, and provide workers' compensation funds.

Academic SKILLS

Accept all essays that reflect an understanding of the concept.

YOUR FINANCIAL FIGURES

From www.homefair.com:

$35,000 in Columbus, Ohio, is equivalent to:
$61,867 in Chicago, Illinois
(76% increase)
$36,466 in Richmond, Virginia
(4.2% increase)
$59,427 in San Diego, California
(70% increase)
Answers to (a) are in parentheses above.
Answers to (b) will vary.

REAL-WORLD Application

Written pieces and role plays will vary but should indicate that students know how to prepare an effective résumé and cover letter.

Internet CONNECTION

Employers are looking for someone who meets their needs, presents him or herself in a positive manner, and emphasizes the skills and capabilities that will help the employer succeed. Your résumé stands out if it is easily read, specific, clear, and brief so the employer can find the needed information easily to make a decision.

BusinessWeek ONLINE

Accept all paragraphs that demonstrate students have read the online article and understand the concept.

Money Management Strategy

pages 58–87

SECTION	LEARNING OBJECTIVES	FEATURES	TEXT RESOURCES	TECHNOLOGY RESOURCES
3.1	**After completing this section, students will have learned to:** Discuss the relationship between opportunity costs and money management. Explain the benefits of keeping financial records and documents. Describe a system to maintain personal financial documents.	**TechByte,** p. 63	**Section Assessment,** p. 64 Quick Check Think Critically Use Communication Skills Solve Money Problems **Student Activity Workbook**	Lesson Planner Plus Online Learning Center Interactive Student Edition *Presentation Plus!* **Exam***View®* Pro Test Generator Financial Planner Software
3.2	**After completing this section, students will have learned to:** Explain the value of a personal balance sheet and cash flow statement. Develop a personal balance sheet and cash flow statement.	**Go Figure**—Net Worth, p. 68 **Careers in Finance,** p. 69 **WebQuest,** p. 71 **Go Figure**—Net Cash Flow, p. 71	**Section Assessment,** p. 73 Quick Check Think Critically, Use Math Skills Solve Money Problems **Student Activity Workbook**	Lesson Planner Plus Online Learning Center Interactive Student Edition *Presentation Plus!* **Exam***View®* Pro Test Generator Financial Planner Software
3.3	**After completing this section, students will have learned to:** Identify the steps of creating a personal budget. Discuss the advantage of increasing your savings.	**Academic Connection,** p. 75 **Savvy Saver,** p. 77 **S&P's Put on Your Financial Planner's Cap,** p. 79 **S&P's Global Financial Landscape,** p. 80 **Document Detective,** p. 81 **Common Cents,** p. 82	**Section Assessment,** p. 83 Quick Check Think Critically Use Communication Skills Solve Money Problems **Student Activity Workbook**	Lesson Planner Plus Online Learning Center Interactive Student Edition *Presentation Plus!* **Exam***View®* Pro Test Generator Financial Planner Software

Meeting National Standards for Business Education		
Section 3.1	**Section 3.2**	**Section 3.3**
Economics I. Allocation of Resources III. Economic Institutions and Incentives **Personal Finance** I. Personal Decision Making VIII. Protecting Against Risk	**Personal Finance** I. Personal Decision Making II. Earning a Living III. Managing Finances and Budgeting	**Economics** VIII. International Economic Concepts IX. Aggregate Supply and Aggregate Demand **Personal Finance** I. Personal Decision Making III. Managing Finances and Budgeting

Teaching Connection

Learning through Role Plays

Think about how you want students to learn concepts. You may want to include various role-playing situations in which students take the role of coach, facilitator, informer, motivator, and/or discussion leader. Throughout the text, there are exercises that allow students to become involved in experiential learning. You can also adapt activities and topics to role-play by following this procedure: 1) Create a situation; 2) analyze the situation; 3) write about the situation; 4) talk about the situation; 5) relate the situation to self; 6) integrate reflections with facts, concepts, and research; 7) experiment and personalize; 8) make it relevant and useful; 9) practice; and 10) analyze the outcomes.

Visual Guide

Chapter 3 Opener

Discussion: Have the students study the chapter opening photo and describe what they see. Then lead a discussion about why it is important for students to manage their money so they have enough to spend it on the necessities of life as well as recreation.

Follow-Up: Ask the students if they think they spend too much money on certain things, tangible and intangible. What are those items? What do they think they should be doing with that money?

Workplace Skills and Chapter Correlations

FOUNDATION SKILLS						
Basic Skills	**Reading**	**Writing**	**Math**	Listening	Speaking	
Thinking Skills	**Creative Thinking**	**Decision Making**	**Problem Solving**	**Seeing Things in the Mind's Eye**	Knowing How to Learn	**Reasoning**
Personal Qualities	**Responsibility**	Self-Esteem	Sociability	**Self-Management**	Integrity/ Honesty	

WORKPLACE COMPETENCIES						
Resources	**Allocating Time**	**Allocating Money**	Allocating Material and Facility Resources	Allocating Human Resources		
Information	**Acquiring and Evaluating Information**	**Organizing and Maintaining Information**	Interpreting and Communicating Information	**Using Computers to Process Information**		
Interpersonal Skills	**Participating as a Member of a Team**	**Teaching Others**	Serving Clients/ Customers	Exercising Leadership	Negotiating to Arrive at a Decision	Working with Cultural Diversity
Systems	Understanding Systems	Monitoring and Correcting Performance	Improving and Designing Systems			
Technology	Selecting Technology	**Applying Technology to Task**	Maintaining and TroubleshootingTechnology			

Internet Extension

Activity: Have students find online budget activities and print them out to share with the class. As a class, compare the different budget activities and determine which one would be most helpful to them now.

Keywords: financial planning

Enrichment/Application Activity

Guest Speaker: If possible, invite to class someone with experience at a kibbutz in Israel or someone with experience as a financial software designer. Ask the speaker to share his or her experiences as they relate to chapter content.

Topic Spotlight

Technology: Have students write one paragraph explaining how technology has affected the ways people record and organize their personal financial records.

Money: Ask students whether net worth is affected by overestimating assets or underestimating liabilities.

Marketing: Discuss with students why a credit card company or bank might sponsor money management Web sites or offer financial planning kits to prospective customers.

Ethics: Discuss with students this ethical job-hunting situation: You and your best friend are both looking for summer jobs, and you plan to work together. In fact, you have made a pact not to take a job where you both cannot work. You and your friend have applied at a nearby state park that is looking for lifeguards for the summer. You are offered a job, but your friend is not. What would you do and why? How would you feel if the situation were reversed?

Additional Resources

Books

Making Allowances: A Dollars and Sense Guide to Teaching Kids About Money by Paul Lermitte (©2002, McGraw-Hill). Financial planner and father of three, Paul Lermitte uses a step-by-step program that provides the principles, structure, and tools to teach kids all about money and how to manage it. This book is packed with tips and ready-to-use worksheets, from an "Allowance Contract" to a "Kid's Loan Contract."

Internet

fleetkids.com/index.html FleetKidsSM: On this site, students can investigate mathematic, financial, and social concepts, including: setting goals, saving and budgeting, and balancing needs and wants. Games and quizzes to engage students in real-world activities.

moneyinstructor.com/interative.asp Money instructor: This interactive learning site features interactive money learning games and exercises, including teaching material for students. This page is for educators to access the interactive lessons and to configure specific lessons for students.

kids.gov/k_money.htm FirstGov for Kids: This is a gateway to other information resources for students seeking answers to financial questions. The site includes a list of organization sites for kids, including Fedville, where kids can actually open a savings account and watch their money grow. They can also shop at local stores, if they earn enough money playing games.

Note: Web site addresses may change.

Section 3.1

Focus

Motivation

Ask students how many of them keep financial records of any sort. If any say "yes," ask what kinds of records, and list them on the board. If no one responds, or after listing responses on the board, ask them why it might be useful to maintain such records; elicit: for budgeting, taxes, making major purchases, etc. Then tell them the upcoming chapter will help them keep records.

Prereading

1. Have students skim the section, looking at the pictures, reading the captions, and reading the headings.
2. Ask a student to read aloud Read to Learn on page 60.
3. Have students list the Key Terms in their notebooks, and remind them to enter the definitions as they learn them.

Teach

Guided Practice

1. Ask students to read aloud In the Real World on page 59 and ask them if they have ever had similar situations; ask them what they did to get out of such situations.
2. Ask students to read aloud the Standard & Poor's Q&A on page 59; discuss it briefly with them.
3. Have students read the rest of the section, noting and mentally answering the Predict, Relate, Question, and caption questions and reading the features such as TechByte.

Independent Practice

1. Have each student design a home filing system on paper to suit his/her needs. They can use various methods: computer databases, file boxes, safe-deposit boxes, etc., and they can integrate two or more methods.
2. Ask several students to present their designs to the class.
3. Have students set up systems, providing file folders or other materials to them.

Assess

Reteaching

1. Go over the list of Key Terms with students, ensuring they have written the correct definitions in their notebooks. Divide students into pairs and have each pair prepare flash cards for the key terms; have them practice, alternating who asks and who answers.
2. Ask students to name the most important elements in the chapter, and write them on the board. To reinforce the concept of opportunity costs, ask students what trade-offs they have made this week.
3. Discuss with students the Reading Strategies, the pictures and diagrams and their caption questions, and the features.

Enrichment

1. Ask students to talk to three people: One must be a local small business owner, and another may be a parent or older sibling. Have them find out what methods they use for organizing their financial records.
2. Have students bring the results of their discussions to class. See how many people use specific methods; for the most used method(s), ask students why they think that method is so popular.

Assessment

1. Have students complete the Section 3.1 Assessment.
2. Give students a Vocabulary Quiz based on selected words from the Key Terms.
3. Assign an activity from Chapter 3 of the *Student Activity Workbook*.

Close

Ask students to reiterate the benefits of maintaining good financial records, and list them on the board. Ask how many students plan to use the home filing systems they created. Tell them you may follow up in a few weeks to see how the system is working out.

Section 3.2

Focus

Motivation

Ask students if they think organizing and filing financial records is sufficient to give them a picture of their financial resources or if they might need other mechanisms to help them reach their financial goals. Then query whether they have any ideas as to what else they might need to do. Tell them this chapter will help them set up ways to follow their financial progress.

Prereading

1. Have students skim the section, looking at the pictures, reading the captions, and reading the headings.
2. Ask a student to read aloud Read to Learn on page 65.
3. Have students list the Key Terms in their notebooks, and remind them to enter the definitions as they learn them. Suggest they make flashcards.

Teach

Guided Practice

1. Ask one or two students to read aloud the section on The Personal Balance Sheet on page 65.
2. Have students silently read the rest of the section, noting and mentally answering the Predict, Relate, Question, and caption questions and reading the features such as Careers in Finance.

Independent Practice

1. Write on the board and have students copy into their notebooks: a date 20 years hence and the headings Income, Fixed Expenses, and Variable Expenses.
2. Ask students to seriously imagine their income/expense situations in 20 years and write down how much they expect to earn and spend in one month.
3. Have students prepare an income statement and balance sheet based on those figures in #1 and #2, following the steps in the text.

Assess

Reteaching

1. Go over the list of Key Terms with students, ensuring they have written the correct definitions in their notebooks. Have students review key terms in pairs using their flashcards.
2. Ask students to name the most important elements in the chapter, and write them on the board.
3. Discuss with students the Reading Strategies, the pictures and diagrams and their caption questions, and the features.

Enrichment

1. Divide students into groups of three. Each group is to devise a survey to determine how people spend discretionary income. The survey should divide each person's discretionary spending into types, i.e., movies, books, clothes, etc.
2. Each student is to survey five (5) people: schoolmates, parents, etc. Each group will then compile the statistics for the group's 15 interviewees. Each group will then prepare a graph showing the averages for each category of discretionary income.

Teacher Manual

Assessment

1. Have students complete the Section 3.2 Assessment.
2. Give students a Vocabulary Quiz based on selected words from the Key Terms.
3. Assign an activity from the *Student Activity Workbook.*

Close

Discuss with students the importance of understanding the financial reports discussed in this section. Explain that most businesses maintain books that have balance sheets, income statements, etc. Also explain that businesses have discretionary income: profits. Ask them how they think businesses might spend this money. Elicit: improvements, growth.

Section 3.3

Focus

Motivation

Ask students if any of them budget their money. (If any say "yes," ask them the benefits of doing so.) Elicit and list on the board reasons to create budgets; then read aloud the paragraph under What is so important about having a budget? on page 74.

Prereading

1. Have students skim the section, looking at the pictures, reading the captions, and reading the headings.
2. Ask a student to read aloud Read to Learn on page 74.
3. Have students list the Key Terms in their notebooks, and remind them to enter the definitions as they learn them. Suggest they make flashcards.

Teach

Guided Practice

1. Ask a student to read aloud the section on Setting Your Financial Goals on page 74.
2. Have students silently read the rest of the section, noting and mentally answering the Predict, Relate, Question, and caption questions and reading the features such as Document Detective.

Independent Practice

1. Tell students they are about to prepare a personal budget. Those students who work or have a regular income should make budgets based on current earnings. Those who do not work can base budgets on imaginary but realistic incomes.
2. Take the students through the steps to create their budgets; estimating income, budgeting for unexpected expenses, budgeting for fixed expenses, and budgeting for variable expenses. Go over how to set up the budget on paper, and tell them to record their expenses for one month.

Assess

Reteaching

1. Go over the list of Key Terms with students, ensuring they have written the correct definitions. Have students review key terms in pairs using their flashcards.
2. Ask students to name the most important elements in the chapter, and write them on the board.
3. Discuss with students the Reading Strategies, the pictures and diagrams and their caption questions, and the features.

Enrichment

Invite a local bank loan officer to speak to your students regarding the significance of savings and credit card debt when considering personal or business loan applications.

Assessment

1. Have students complete the Section 3.3 Assessment and a short vocabulary quiz on this section's Key Terms.
2. Assign the Chapter 3 Assessment.
3. Administer the test for Chapter 3 from the Reproducible Tests in the *Lesson Planner Plus* supplement.

Close

Discuss with students the value of having savings; ask how many of them included deposits to savings accounts in their budgets. Encourage all students to add savings to their budgets and to make savings deposits regularly.

ANSWERS

Careers in Finance

Answer might be a financial advisor helps people reach goals through financial planning, investment services, and risk management.

Academic Connection

Accept all reasonable answers that demonstrate research and an understanding of the concepts.

STANDARD & POOR'S Put on Your Financial Planner's Cap

Answers might include: transportation/vehicle maintenance, clothing, food (lunches), beauty/grooming aids, medical expenses. Other answers are possible.

STANDARD & POOR'S *Global Financial Landscape*

Answers will vary but may include: With the greater focus on education, the Korean children learn skills that will help them compete in the global marketplace and, thus, generate more revenue for the Korean economy.

Document Detective

1. Assets are what a person owns.
2. Liabilities are what a person owes.
3. $44,200
4. A balance sheet tells what assets are available to a person. Banks want to know the net worth of a person when determining whether to loan money to him or her.
5. You determine net worth by subtracting your liabilities from your assets.

Section 3.1 Assessment

Quick Check

1. It will help you plan and measure financial progress, handle routine money matters, determine how much will be available to spend now and in the future, and make savings decisions.
2. Sort through personal financial records, arrange them according to type, and label all files.
3. They are kept in locked, fireproof rooms available only during banking hours, can be opened only with two separate keys, loss from fire and other disasters is rare, and the institution that owns the box is insured for such losses if they occur.

Think Critically

4. Answers and explanations might include decisions to eat in or out, to buy new shoes or wear old ones, to listen to radio or buy a CD, etc.

Use Communication Skills

5. Locations might include home files, home safe, computer (if documents are electronic), or safe-deposit box.

Solve Money Problems

6. Answers might include: pay the bills, record checks and deposits in a register, create and label a folder for each type of document, file documents in the folders.

Section 3.2 Assessment

Quick Check

1. First, determine assets and liabilities. Subtract liabilities from assets; the difference is net worth.
2. Record all income for a month as cash flow; ensuring you record the exact amount available (i.e., record take-home pay, not gross); include any interest income from investments or savings.
3. Borrow money (increasing liabilities) or withdraw savings (decreasing assets).

Think Critically

4. Answers might include automobiles, stereo equipment, jewelry, computers, etc.

Use Math Skills

5. She had a deficit of $125. ($2,375 − ($750 + $1,750) = −$125)

Solve Money Problems

6. Answers might include paying down credit card debt, adding to savings account, or some of each, depending on interest rates for the debt versus for the savings account.

Section 3.3 Assessment

Quick Check

1. Make your best estimates based on your previous months' expenses; when in doubt, guess high. Compare the CPI to your budget to see when you are spending too much.
2. First, determine where your shortfalls occur and decide whether you can make trade-offs in those areas. Then look at your goals: Which purchases fit into your plan for the future? How quickly are you progressing? Do you think you should revise your goals?
3. Answers should include the following: setting aside a fixed amount for savings before you pay your bills, taking a payroll savings deduction, spending less each day and saving money you did not spend.

Think Critically

4. Answers might include car maintenance, entertainment, or telephone bills.

Use Communication Skills

5. Answers will vary, but students may discuss the future problems if Tara does not cut spending. They may suggest ways to cut expenses.

Solve Money Problems

6. Answers will vary, but students should consider car maintenance costs, how long Hiroko must work to pay off the car, whether other expenses can be reduced.

Chapter 3 Review & Activities

Communicating Key Terms

Responses will vary depending on the friend's paycheck and other expenses. Students should indicate an understanding of take-home pay versus gross pay and cash flow.

Reviewing Key Concepts

1. Accept all reasonable answers that indicate that when students decide to purchase something, they close off the option to use that money in other ways.
2. You organize your financial documents to find these materials more easily, to plan financial progress, to handle routine money matters, to determine how much money you have, and to make effective spending decisions.
3. Documents you use often that are not difficult to replace should be kept in home files. Important documents that are not used often and are difficult to replace, such as car titles and mortgage papers, should be kept in a safe-deposit box. Check records and budgets can be kept on a personal computer.

4. You learn from preparing personal financial statements about what you own and what you owe; about progress toward financial goals; how to track your financial activities; and how to organize information for tax filings and credit applications.
5. To prepare a personal balance sheet, determine assets and liabilities and subtract the second from the first to find net worth. To prepare a personal cash flow statement, subtract expenses from income.
6. To prepare a budget: Set your financial goals; estimate your income; budget for savings and unexpected expenses; budget for fixed expenses; budget for variable expenses; record what you spend; and review spending and saving patterns.
7. Your personal financial statements and budget help to identify how you are spending your money, so you can determine where you are vulnerable.

ACADEMIC SKILLS

Reasons include: temptation to buy whatever you want; low incomes and high fixed expenses; and lack of discipline.

YOUR FINANCIAL FIGURES

1. Current earnings: $70 per week x 28 weeks before the trip = $1,960. Fixed expenses: $25 fees per month + $10 per week for bus pass = $75.
2. Fixed expenses for four months are $300. Income – fixed expenses = $1,660. This surplus less the $700 needed for the trip leaves $960 for variable expenses for the time period or additional savings.

REAL-WORLD Application

1. You will work 40 hours/week at rate x plus 10 hours/week at 1.5× for 10 weeks, for a total amount of 400x + 150x = 550x. Estimated expenses are $150 × 10 = $1,500. Add that to the savings needed, and the total you need to earn is $3,500. If 550x = $3,500, then the hourly rate x must be at least $6.36.
2. It is likely that $150 in weekly expenses underestimates the amount needed.

Internet CONNECTION

Answers will vary depending on the city in which the student lives. Answers should show an understanding of fixed and variable expenses.

BusinessWeek ONLINE

Accept all paragraphs that demonstrate students have read the online article and understand the concepts.

CHAPTER 4 Consumer Purchasing and Protection

pages 88–115

SECTION	LEARNING OBJECTIVES	FEATURES	TEXT RESOURCES	TECHNOLOGY RESOURCES
4.1	**After completing this section, students will have learned to:** Determine the factors that influence buying decisions Explain a research-based approach to buying goods and services. Identify strategies for making wise buying decisions.	**Savvy Saver**, p. 95 **WebQuest**, p. 96 **S&P's Put on Your Financial Planner's Cap**, p. 99 **Common Cents**, p. 100 **Go Figure**—Unit Pricing, p. 101 **Document Detective**, p. 102	**Section Assessment**, p. 103 Quick Check Think Critically Use Math Skills Solve Money Problems **Student Activity Workbook**	Lesson Planner Plus Online Learning Center Interactive Student Edition *Presentation Plus!* **Exam***View*® Pro Test Generator Financial Planner Software
4.2	**After completing this section, students will have learned to:** Identify ways to solve consumer problems. Describe the legal alternatives for consumers.	**S&P's Global Financial Landscape**, p. 106 **Academic Connection**, p. 108 **Careers in Finance**, p. 109 **TechByte**, p. 110	**Section Assessment**, p. 111 Quick Check Think Critically Use Communication Skills Solve Money Problems **Student Activity Workbook**	Lesson Planner Plus Online Learning Center Interactive Student Edition *Presentation Plus!* **Exam***View*® Pro Test Generator Financial Planner Software

Meeting National Standards for Business Education	
Section 4.1	**Section 4.2**
Economics I. Allocation of Resources II. Economic Systems III. Economic Institutions and Incentives **Personal Finance** I. Personal Decision Making III. Managing Finances and Budgeting V. Buying Goods and Services	**Economics** III. Economic Institutions and Incentives VIII. International Economic Concepts **Personal Finance** V. Buying Goods and Services

Teaching Connection

Reflection Activity

Reflection provides students with "think time," allowing them the opportunity to process new material or ideas learned in class. It also offers students the chance to ask questions they did not or would not ask during class. Most importantly, it offers students the chance to think about what they want to learn next. Class reflections are a great way for you to keep aware of your students' thinking and of the issues they are having. They help you to plan and to adjust your teaching to meet students' individual needs.

Set aside the last few minutes of your first class period for students to reflect on the first day. Ask students to write their reflections on these questions as a journal activity:

- What did I learn?
- What do I want to know more about?
- What do I want to learn next?

Visual Guide

Chapter 4 Opener

Discussion: Have students study the chapter opening photo and describe what they see. Then lead a discussion about the types of strategies they might use when making a purchase, especially a major purchase such as an automobile. Ask them what might be the most important thing to consider about a major purchase?

Follow-Up: Ask the students to make a list of questions that they might ask a car dealer when considering buying a car.

Workplace Skills and Chapter Correlations

FOUNDATION SKILLS						
Basic Skills	Reading	Writing	Math	Listening	Speaking	
Thinking Skills	Creative Thinking	Decision Making	Problem Solving	Seeing Things in the Mind's Eye	Knowing How to Learn	Reasoning
Personal Qualities	Responsibility	Self-Esteem	Sociability	Self-Management	Integrity/ Honesty	

WORKPLACE COMPETENCIES						
Resources	Allocating Time	Allocating Money	Allocating Material and Facility Resources	Allocating Human Resources		
Information	Acquiring and Evaluating Information	Organizing and Maintaining Information	Interpreting and Communicating Information	Using Computers to Process Information		
Interpersonal Skills	Participating as a Member of a Team	Teaching Others	Serving Clients/ Customers	Exercising Leadership	Negotiating to Arrive at a Decision	Working with Cultural Diversity
Systems	Understanding Systems	Monitoring and Correcting Performance	Improving and Designing Systems			
Technology	Selecting Technology	Applying Technology to Task	Maintaining and TroubleshootingTechnology			

Internet Extension

Activity: Have students access the *Consumer Reports* Web site at **consumerreports.org** and write a brief report on how they might use this Web site before making a major purchase.

Enrichment/Application Activity

Guest Speaker: Take students to the public library or a full-sized bookstore to see the many financial planning books available. Have each student write the name, title, and brief description of two books that they would choose to read, and explain why.

Topic Spotlight

Ethics: Discuss with students what they would do in the following situation. They have recently purchased a CD player with speakers. As they take the boxed CD player out of the car, they accidentally drop the box in the driveway. When they try to turn it on, it does not work. Would they take the CD back and say, "I took it home and it does not work." Would they explain the circumstances and hope to get a new one? Or would they pay to have it fixed?

Marketing: Ask students to describe the kinds of advertisements that they like. Are they on radio or television, billboards, or magazines? Do they think these advertisements really influence them to buy the product? Why or why not?

Money: Tell students that they are shopping for two new pair of jeans. Ask them which sale would be the best buy—jeans that regularly sell for $29.99 on sale for 30 percent off, or jeans priced at $29.99 that are part of a buy one/get one at half price sale? [ANSWER: $29.99 × 30% = 8.99; $29.99 − 8.99 = $21.00; $21.00 × 2 = $42.00; $29.99 × 50% = $14.99; $29.99 + $14.99 = $44.98]

Additional Resources

Books

Living Well on a Shoestring by Christian Millman (paperback: Yankee Publishing, ©2000). This book includes 1,501 ways to spend less money for what kids and adults need and to get more of what they want.

Frugal Living for Dummies by Deborah Taylor-Hough (paperback: For Dummies, ©2003). Spending more money than you make each month is easy to do in a consumer-driven society. This book helps readers make the necessary choices to live within their means.

Consumer Action Handbook (formerly ***Consumer's Resource Handbook***) is published by the Consumer Information Center. Single copies of this handbook are free of charge by writing to CRH, Consumer Information Center, Pueblo, CO 81009, or by accessing the CIC Web site at **pueblo.gsa.gov**. Part One contains information on buying wisely, and Part Two is the Consumer Assistance Directory.

Internet

bbb.org is the Web site of the Better Business Bureau (BBB). It offers a directory of BBB offices, information on marketplace scams, and links to other BBB Web sites.

ftc.gov/bcp/bcp.htm is the Web site of the Bureau of Consumer Protection, an agency of the Federal Trade Commission. This agency is responsible for enforcing consumer protection laws and providing information to consumers in order to protect them from unfair or deceptive business practices. Links to the agency's five divisions are listed on the home page.

Note: Web site addresses may change.

Section 4.1

Focus

Motivation

Ask students for a show of hands: "How many of you think you usually make wise buying decisions?" Then ask them if they can think of things that influence their buying practices; write their answers on the board. Use discussion to introduce the section.

Prereading

1. Have students skim the section, looking at the pictures, reading the captions, and reading the headings.
2. Ask a student to read aloud Read to Learn on page 90.
3. Dictate each of the Key Terms to the class. Have students write them in their notebooks. Then write the Key Terms on the board. Ask students to guess at the meaning of each term. Leave the list on the board, so as students study the section, they can see how close they were to the correct answer.

Teach

Guided Practice

1. Ask students to read aloud In the Real World on page 89 and ask them whether they have had similar situations; ask what they did to get out of such situations.
2. Ask students to read aloud Ask Standard & Poor's on page 89; discuss it briefly.
3. Read the rest of the section with your students, asking them to note and mentally answer the Predict, Relate, Question, and caption questions, and read the features such as Document Detective.

Independent Practice

1. Have students select an expensive product, such as a car or stereo equipment. Ask them to research this product on the Internet, in *Consumer Reports*, and/or through a government agency and any other sources, to determine the product's quality, relative cost, and any other factors related to purchasing.
2. Students are to write a one-page evaluation of the product.

Assess

Reteaching

1. Review the list of Key Terms with students, focusing on the terms students were unsure of initially, and ensuring they have written the correct definitions in their notebooks.
2. To reteach the concept of purchasing as a multi-phase process, divide students into four groups, one for each phase listed on page 91. Have each group (or one student from each group) present to the class what a smart shopper will do during that phase.
3. Discuss with students the Reading Strategies, the pictures and diagrams and their caption questions, and the features.

Enrichment

Describe to students Better Business Bureau and invite a member of the Bureau or another consumer protection agency to speak to the class about consumers' rights.

Assessment

1. Have students complete the Section 4.1 Assessment.
2. Give students a vocabulary quiz based on selected words from the Key Terms.
3. Assign an activity from Chapter 4 of the *Student Activity Workbook*.

Close

Ask students if, after studying this section, they will be wiser shoppers. Ask them in what ways. Then list their answers on the board.

Section 4.2

Focus

Motivation

Ask students if they have ever made purchases which were defective or poorly made or did not live up to the advertising. Have one or two students share their experiences and ask students: "What did you do?" Use this discussion to introduce Section 4.2.

Prereading

1. Have students skim the section, looking at the pictures, reading the captions, and reading the headings.
2. Ask a student to read aloud Read to Learn on page 104.
3. Dictate each of the Key Terms to the class. Have students write them in their notebooks. Then write the key terms on the board. Ask students to generate flashcards for these terms.

Teach

Guided Practice

1. Ask students to read aloud Sources of Common Consumer Complaints on page 104.
2. Read the rest of the section with your students, asking them to note and mentally answer the Predict, Relate, Question, and caption questions, and focus especially on features such as Careers in Finance.

Independent Practice

1. Ask the students to research how the United States sets safety standards for food, drugs, chemicals, and household appliances. Then divide the students into groups of four, and ask each group to research how another country sets the same standards. Have each group prepare a chart or graph that compares the information.
2. Take the class on a field trip to a small claims court to see how cases are presented and disputes resolved. Then have students hold a mock small claims court and role-play a variety of consumer cases.

Assess

Reteaching

1. Have the students work in pairs to practice the Key Terms using their flashcards.
2. To reteach the concept of resolving differences, divide the class into five groups, and assign one of the five methods of dispute resolution to each group. Have each group create a chart explaining the method. Post the charts around the room.
3. Discuss with students the Reading Strategies, the pictures and diagrams and their caption questions, and the features.

Enrichment

Have students each interview a local business owner to find out how that business handles consumer complaints. Have students compile the results and analyze them.

Assessment

1. Have students complete the Section 4.2 Assessment and a short vocabulary quiz on this section's Key Terms.
2. Assign the Chapter 4 Review and Activities.
3. Administer the test for Chapter 4 from the *Reproducible Tests* included in the *Lesson Planner Plus* supplement.

Close

Ask the students if their views on their rights as consumers have changed as a result of studying this section. Ask them what strategies they think they will be most likely to use.

ANSWERS

Standard & Poor's Put on Your Financial Planner's Cap

Trade-offs might include the inability to road test a car and to examine it. If you are buying fresh fruit, you cannot smell and touch the fruit for freshness. If you are buying shoes, you are unable to try them on before purchase.

Document Detective

1. 1 year
2. August 2008
3. repair, replace, or make adjustments
4. The consumer is responsible.
5. No.

Standard & Poor's Global Financial Landscape

Because Ecuador may not have the same consumer protection laws that exist in the United States, consumers there would have a more difficult time resolving complaints.

Academic Connection

Accept all scripts that reflect an understanding of ways to resolve consumer complaints.

Careers in Finance

Because Patagonia is focused on customers and has salespeople who share interest in outdoor sports, the company would benefit from training salespeople to respond cooperatively to customers who have complaints or returns.

Section 4.1 Assessment

Quick Check

1. Answers may include prices, interest rates, product quality, supply and demand, convenience, product safety, brand names, maintenance costs, and warranties.
2. Before you shop: Identify why you need or want the skates, gather information from friends and by reading magazines, and be aware of the marketplace. Then rent skates to understand available choices and compare stores and prices.
3. Answers might include timing purchases to take advantage of sales, selecting the right type of store in which to buy an item, comparing brands, comparing prices and unit prices, reading labels, and evaluating and comparing warranties and service contracts.

Think Critically

4. Accept all reasonable answers that demonstrate students' awareness of economic, social, and personal factors as they apply to scenarios they have created.

Use Math Skills

5. The cat food from the animal hospital is \$2.25/lb. The 25 lb. bag is \$2.38/lb., and the 50 lb. bag is \$1.99/lb. The 50 lb. bag is the best buy in terms of price.

Solve Money Problems

6. Answers might include that Marta can take advantage of sales; she can comparison shop.

Section 4.2 Assessment

Quick Check

1. Complaints involve defective products, poor quality, unexpected cots, deceptive pricing, unsatisfactory repair service, and fraud.
2. 1) Return to the place of purchase; 2) contact the company headquarters; 3) consult a consumer agency; 4) use mediation or arbitration; and 5) take legal action.
3. Advantages include low legal costs; short time; courts often rule in your favor; and no lawyers or juries. Disadvantages include the judge's decision is final; you have to present your own case and evidence; and awards have predetermined limits.

Think Critically

4. Reasons for dissatisfaction might include defective or low quality goods, unexpected costs, deceptive pricing, poor repair service, or fraud.

Use Communication Skills

5. Ways to avoid becoming a victim may include: Do business with reputable companies; do not sign any document you do not understand; be wary of offers that seem too good to be true; and do not rush into what seems to be a good deal.

Solve Money Problems

6. They should first try to resolve the problem by phone to the company; then they should write to the company. Their next step would be to use a consumer agency or a dispute resolution program and then go to small claims court.

Chapter 4 Review & Activities

Communication Key Terms

Accept all responses that demonstrate an understanding of the key term definitions.

Reviewing Key Concepts

1. Economic factors: quality (value for money), price; social factors: style, peer approval; personal factors: amount of disposable income, willingness to spend on a particular item.
2. Before you shop: Identify needs; gather information; and become aware of the marketplace. Weighing alternatives: Decide whether to buy, rent, borrow, or do without; decide what features (performance or design) are important; compare prices; and do comparison shopping. Making the purchase: Negotiate the price; decide on credit or cash; and know the real price. After the purchase: Learn to correctly use the product.
3. Answers will vary but may include that strategies for car buying, for example, may entail more post-purchase effort because of ongoing maintenance and repair needs.
4. Return merchandise to place of purchase; contact the company's headquarters; ask for consumer agency assistance; mediate or arbitrate; or take legal action.
5. Advantages of small claims court: low legal costs; short time span to resolution; ruling often in plaintiff's favor; and no lawyers or juries. Disadvantages of small claims court: The judge's decision is final; you present your own case and evidence; and awards have predetermined limits.

ACADEMIC SKILLS

Answers might include: brand-name product: consistent quality, availability, and reliability; store-brand products: lower price, consistent quality, and reliability related to store.

YOUR FINANCIAL FIGURES

(a) The shoes will cost $75.57 in October. Current total store price is $112.35. Current online price is $105.55. (b) Trade-offs may vary. (c) Answers will vary regarding the comparison of the trade-off.

REAL-WORLD Application

Accept all reasonable answers that demonstrate research and student effort.

Internet CONNECTION

Answers should indicate students' understanding of the advantages and disadvantages on online shopping.

BusinessWeek ONLINE

Accept all lists that demonstrate students have read the online article and understand the concepts.

Banking and Credit

Chapter 5
Banking

Chapter 6
Consumer Credit

Chapter 7
The Finances of Housing

Unit Overview

In Unit 2, students will learn about the wide range of services that can help them plan, manage, and save in order to achieve their financial goals. Chapter 5 discusses the selection and use of financial services, such as the different kinds of savings and checking accounts, longer-term savings (certificates of deposit and U.S. savings bonds), investment services, loans, and other credit services. In Chapter 6, students will learn about the advantages and disadvantages of consumer credit, how to calculate the cost of credit, and how to manage debt. Chapter 7 explains the finances of housing. Students will learn how to calculate the costs of buying a house and describe the process of buying a house.

Introductory Activity

With a show of hands, find out how many students have credit cards, checking accounts, savings accounts, and car loans. Ask students how or where they obtained these financial services. Ask: "Do these financial services cost money or are they free?" If possible, bring brochures from a variety of banks or other financial institutions for students to look through. Then have students write definitions for the terms *financial services* and *financial institutions*. Point out to your students the wide variety of products and services offered by financial institutions and explain that in this unit they will learn how to shop for them.

BusinessWeek
FINANCE FILE

Consumer Debt

Answer Accept all reasonable answers that show student effort. Answers might include not borrowing money, cutting down on credit card use, increasing income, and sticking to a budget.

Get a Financial Life!

Home Ownership

STEP A The Process
Make sure students have access to all necessary materials.

1. $212,500 [ANSWER: $85,000 × 2.5 = $212,500]
2. Features will vary, but students should recognize that the features are typical of a house costing $212,500 or less, and reflect the needs of a young married couple.
3. Remind students that the classified ads of larger newspapers are accessible on the Internet, and the price of the house can be input to locate only the houses in that price range.
4. Give students the names of the Web sites from the Additional Resources section of the Chapter 7 Planning Guide. These sites can help students research amortization tables.
5. If possible, provide students with the names of several insurance agents that would be willing to help.
6. Accept all reasonable costs. Ask the students to explain how they determined the different costs.
7. Students should provide printed examples of their "purchases" to verify costs.
8. Budgets will vary but should include income, emergency and investment savings, mortgage, and variable expenses, such as food, clothing, and utilities.

STEP B Create Your Portfolio
Evaluate students' portfolios based on whether all eight steps of the process are completed, the information seems researched, and the contents are in order. When presenting their summary, have students state the title, date, and author of the publication.

STEP C Presentation
Evaluate students' papers based on completeness and accuracy. Answers will vary, however, look for the following:

1. Students should include researching various lenders and mortgage rates, determining a down payment, qualifying for a mortgage, evaluating points, and considering types of mortgages.
2. Students should include researching various costs such as annual fees, finance charges, and annual percentage rates.
3. Allow students time to review fairly each other's technical papers.

Unit Closure

Have students write one page describing whether they were surprised by the cost of financial services, credit, and housing. If they were surprised, have them explain why. If not, why not?

Evaluation

Administer the Unit 2 test from the **Exam***View*® Pro Testmaker CD-ROM.

CHAPTER 5 Banking

pages 120–151

SECTION	LEARNING OBJECTIVES	FEATURES	TEXT RESOURCES	TECHNOLOGY RESOURCES
5.1	**After completing this section, students will have learned to:** Identify types of financial services. Describe the various types of financial institutions.	**Careers in Finance,** p. 124 **TechByte,** p. 127	**Section Assessment,** p. 131 Quick Check, Think Critically Use Math Skills Solve Money Problems **Student Activity Workbook**	Lesson Planner Plus Online Learning Center Interactive Student Edition *Presentation Plus!* **Exam***View*® Pro Test Generator Financial Planner Software
5.2	**After completing this section, students will have learned to:** Compare the costs and benefits of different savings plans. Explain features of different savings plans. Compare the costs and benefits of different types of checking accounts. Explain how to use a checking account effectively.	**WebQuest,** p. 135 **Go Figure**—Interest Compounded Monthly, p. 136 **Go Figure**—Rate of Return, p. 137 **Document Detective,** p. 138 **S&P's Put on Your Financial Planner's Cap,** p. 139 **S&P's Global Financial Landscape,** p. 140 **Academic Connection,** p. 141 **Savvy Saver,** p. 142 **Common Cents,** p. 144	**Section Assessment,** p. 147 Quick Check, Think Critically Use Communication Skills Solve Money Problems **Student Activity Workbook**	Lesson Planner Plus Online Learning Center Interactive Student Edition *Presentation Plus!* **Exam***View*® Pro Test Generator Financial Planner Software

Meeting National Standards for Business Education	
Section 5.1	**Section 5.2**
Economics I. Allocation of Resources III. Economic Institutions and Incentives VII. The Role of Government **Personal Finance** I. Personal Decision Making II. Earning a Living III. Managing Finances and Budgeting IV. Saving and Investing V. Buying Goods and Services VI. Banking VII. Using Credit VIII. Protecting Against Risk	**Economics** I. Allocation of Resources II. Economic Systems III. Economic Institutions and Incentives VIII. International Economic Concepts **Personal Finance** I. Personal Decision Making II. Earning a Living III. Managing Finances and Budgeting IV. Saving and Investing VI. Banking VIII. Protecting Against Risk

Teaching Connection

Handling Cash

Tape a one-dollar bill on the board. Ask for a volunteer to identify the portraits on $1, $2, $5, $10, $20, $50, and $100 bills. You might use a copy of the $50 or $100 bills. The first student who gets them all correct wins the dollar. Begin a discussion of setting up a savings account with money not spent for non-essential items. Explain that understanding the design and security features of currency can help you detect altered bills or counterfeit currency. Invite a local bank representative to visit the classroom and bring samples of altered bills and counterfeit currency. This basic currency knowledge can be a fun way to learn about handling cash.

Visual Guide

Chapter 5 Opener

Discussion: Have students study the chapter opening photo and describe what they see. Then lead a discussion about the different types of banking services. Ask the students if they have their own bank accounts and what kind. Ask them to explain the advantages of having a savings account and a checking account.

Follow-Up: Have the students make a list of questions they might have regarding bank accounts. Write their questions on the board and have one or two students copy the questions on paper. When the class has finished studying Chapter 5, read those questions aloud and ask if they know the answers.

Workplace Skills and Chapter Correlations

FOUNDATION SKILLS						
Basic Skills	Reading	Writing	Math	Listening	Speaking	
Thinking Skills	Creative Thinking	Decision Making	Problem Solving	Seeing Things in the Mind's Eye	Knowing How to Learn	Reasoning
Personal Qualities	Responsibility	Self-Esteem	Sociability	Self-Management	Integrity/ Honesty	

WORKPLACE COMPETENCIES						
Resources	Allocating Time	Allocating Money	Allocating Material and Facility Resources	Allocating Human Resources		
Information	Acquiring and Evaluating Information	Organizing and Maintaining Information	Interpreting and Communicating Information	Using Computers to Process Information		
Interpersonal Skills	Participating as a Member of a Team	Teaching Others	Serving Clients/ Customers	Exercising Leadership	Negotiating to Arrive at a Decision	Working with Cultural Diversity
Systems	Understanding Systems	Monitoring and Correcting Performance	Improving and Designing Systems			
Technology	Selecting Technology	Applying Technology to Task	Maintaining and TroubleshootingTechnology			

Internet Extension

Activity: Have students use the Internet to locate various bank rates and compare the rates of two banks or two banking plans from one bank. Bank rates can be found at **bankrate.com** or **banx.com**. Students can also enter the name of a particular bank to find out whether it has its own Web site.

Key Words: banking, bank rates

Enrichment/Application Activity

Field Trip: Take students to visit a local bank. Arrange for them to talk with a loan officer, bank manager, and teller. Request information brochures you can copy for the students to study. Have students compare the bank's services with information presented in the chapter.

Topic Spotlight

Ethics: Have students review the personality traits for a bank teller given in the Careers in Finance feature. Ask your students: "What does *personable* mean? Why is it an important trait for a bank teller?"

Technology: Discuss how technology has affected where people do their banking.

Government: Ask students to name two ways the government protects consumers who use banks and other financial institutions.

Additional Resources

Books

Making Allowances: A Dollars and Sense Guide to Teaching Kids About Money by Paul Lermitte (paperback: McGraw-Hill, ©2002). Lermitte, a registered financial planner with 15 years of experience as a family financial adviser, shows kids how use their allowances wisely. He provides guidance on when to start an allowance, how much to give, how to teach kids to value money, when to start saving, and advice on saving for college tuition, including 529 plans.

Banking on Our Future: A Program for Teaching You and Your Kids about Money by John Bryant, Michael Levin (paperback: Beacon Press, ©2002). The book offers advice on how to save money on a weekly basis; when it is the right time for a teenager to open a checking account; how to set financial goals; and budgeting, investing, and car payments.

Internet

app.ny.frb.org/cfpicnic/frame1.cfm The Federal Reserve System has produced many informative, attractive, and free publications. The *Public Information Catalog* is online and lists most publications and audiovisual materials prepared by the 12 Federal Reserve Banks and the Board of Governors of the Federal Reserve System. Publications include *Banking Basics; The Story of American Currency; In Plain English: Making Sense of the Federal Reserve; Electronic Money;* and *The Story of Checks and Electronic Payments.*

aba.com The Web site of the American Bankers Association provides a variety of information about banking services.

newyorkfed.org/education/highschool.html The Federal Reserve Bank of New York Web site features a segment devoted to educating high school students. It includes instructional materials and professional development programs for teachers and active learning opportunities for students. The site also provides three learning activities (with teaching plans) based on existing Web sites to promote understanding about investing, credit, and banking.

Note: Web-site addresses may change.

Section 5.1

Focus

Motivation

Ask your students why they currently use banks. List on the board: savings accounts, ATM cards, etc. Then ask which, if any, of these they consider essential.

Prereading

1. Have students skim the section, looking at the pictures, reading the captions, and reading the headings.
2. Ask a student to read aloud Read to Learn on page 122.
3. Dictate each of the key terms to the class and write them on the board. Have students write them in their notebooks. Ask students to guess at the meaning of each term. Tell them to write the correct definitions in their notebooks as they learn them in the section.
4. Ask the students to discuss the purpose of studying this section.

Teach

Guided Practice

1. Ask students to read aloud In the Real World on page 121 and ask them if, when they needed an account, they went to their parents' bank or if they have ever done any shopping for the right bank.
2. Ask students to read aloud Ask Standard & Poor's on page 121; discuss it briefly with them.
3. Read the rest of the section with your students, asking them to note and mentally answer the Predict, Relate, Question, and caption questions, and read the features such as Careers in Finance.

Independent Practice

Divide the class into four groups. Each group will prepare a presentation and present its results to the class. Assign one of the following projects to each group:

1. Have the first group research and prepare a presentation on how electronic payments are protected against theft. The group should ask and answer: "Will I pay my bills electronically?"
2. Have the second group investigate and prepare a presentation on ATM-related crimes, such as fraud or theft. The group should ask and answer: "Should I moderate my ATM use?"
3. Ask group three to research and prepare a presentation on e-cash—the electronic equivalent of cash used for online purchases. The group should ask and answer: "Is e-cash right for me?"
4. Group four is to compare the services and costs offered by three local commercial banks and three local savings and loan institutions. They are to prepare a presentation on the results. The group should ask and answer: "Which banking institution is right for my needs?"

Assess

Reteaching

1. Review the list of Key Terms with students, ensuring they have written the correct definitions in their notebooks and that they understand all the terms.
2. Ask students to name the most important elements in the section, and write them on the board. To reteach the concept of opportunity costs, ask the students to come up with two additional possible examples of trade-offs to add to the list on page 128. Then divide the class into teams to debate each point.
3. Discuss with students the Reading Strategies, the pictures and diagrams and their caption questions, and the features.

Enrichment

1. Ask your students to compile a list of any local financial institutions that offer special programs for students—savings accounts, checking accounts, ATM cards, credit cards, debit cards, etc.
2. Invite a local bank officer to come to class to discuss and answer questions about banking and potential banking careers.

Assessment

1. Have students complete the Section 5.1 Assessment.
2. Give students a Vocabulary Quiz based on selected words from the Key Terms.
3. Assign an activity from Chapter 5 of the *Student Activity Workbook*.

Close

Ask students: "Which features of financial institutions will best meet your needs today? Will your needs change in five years? Will they change in 15 years? Should people change financial institutions as their needs change?"

Section 5.2

FOCUS

Motivation

Ask for a show of hands of all students planning to go to college or another higher educational institution. Ask how many of these students are saving toward that goal, and then write the percentage on the board. Of the students who are planning on going directly into the workforce, find out how many of them are saving money; write that percentage on the board. Open a discussion on why savings will be useful to them, and use this discussion as an opportunity to introduce the section.

Prereading

1. Have students skim the section, looking at the pictures, reading the captions, and reading the headings.
2. Ask a student to read aloud Read to Learn on page 132.
3. Dictate each of the Key Terms to the class. Have students write them in their notebooks. Then write the Key Terms on the board. Ask students to generate flashcards for these terms.
4. Ask the students to discuss the purpose of studying this section.

Teach

Guided Practice

1. Ask a student to read aloud Types of Savings Plans on page 132. Ask how many students know the differences between the four named types of savings. Then ask two other students to read aloud Regular Savings Accounts also on page 132. Suggest this is the type of savings with which most of them are familiar.
2. Read the rest of the section with your students, asking them to note and mentally answer the Predict, Relate, Question, and caption questions, and focus especially on features such as Document Detective.

Independent Practice

Divide students into five groups. Tell each group to imagine they have $1,000, and this money is to go into savings accounts, money market accounts, CDs, and U.S. Savings Bonds. Each group is to do the following:

- Determine how much of the $1,000 they want to put into each account.
- Find out current interest rates on each type of account.
- Track the interest earned weekly and determine the consequent balance on each type of account, compounding as necessary.

Tell them they should continue doing this for a specific period of time (e.g., one month, six weeks, the entire semester). At the end of that period, tell students they will present their results to the class, revealing how they divided up the initial $1000 and how much they have at that point.

Assess

Reteaching

1. Have the students work in pairs to practice the Key Terms, using their flashcards.
2. To reteach the principle and method of compounding interest, put into a hat some slips of paper noted with various deposit amounts at various interest rates—either simple, compounded daily, monthly, or annually. Ask the students to draw a slip from the hat and determine how much he/she would have after one year.
3. Discuss with students the Reading Strategies, the pictures and diagrams and their caption questions, and the features.

Enrichment

Invite a local banker to class to demonstrate how to do bank reconciliations. If some students are willing to share their statements, ask them to bring them to class as samples.

Assessment

1. Have students complete the Section 5.2 Assessment and a short vocabulary quiz on this section's Key Terms.
2. Assign Chapter 5 Review and Activities.
3. Administer the test for Chapter 5 from the *Reproducible Tests* included in the *Lesson Planner Plus* supplement.

Close

Ask your students what they thought were the most important things they learned in this chapter. List them on the board. Then discuss why these specific items are so important.

ANSWERS

Careers in Finance

Answers will vary but might include that tellers are the main contact with customers; as such, they have the best opportunity to sell additional or new bank services.

Document Detective

1. 1/23/05 to 2/24/05
2. Credits are amounts added to your balance: deposits or interest earned.
3. Debits are amounts subtracted from your balance: checks and charges.
4. Check number 1046 for $2,440.00 cleared.
5. It is the total amount of the checks that cleared the bank during this period.

STANDARD &POOR'S Put on Your Financial Planner's Cap

Answers will vary but should demonstrate that students understand the differences between the different types of accounts, including:

- savings
- money market
- CDs
- U.S. Savings Bonds

STANDARD &POOR'S *Global Financial Landscape*

regular, activity, and interest earning

Academic Connection

Accept all paragraphs that reflect research and an understanding of the Emergency Banking Act.

Section 5.1 Assessment

Quick Check

1. Services include savings, payment services, and borrowing.
2. direct deposit, automatic payments, ATMs, and plastic payments.
3. Deposit institutions include commercial banks, savings and loan associations, mutual savings banks, and credit unions. Non-deposit institutions include life insurance, investment, finance, and mortgage companies.

Think Critically

4. Answers will vary, but currently used services may include savings and checking accounts and ATM cards. In the next five years, students may have more money to manage, so they may need more sophisticated savings and payment and loan services for more expensive purchases such as cars or homes.

Use Math Skills

5. Annual cost = \$234.00
   (3 × 1.50 = \$4.50; 52 × \$4.50 = \$234)

Solve Money Problems

6. Lists will vary, but Dakota would probably best meet his needs by choosing a full-service commercial bank, a savings and loan association, or a credit union. He needs a checking account, a savings account, electronic banking, and borrowing services.

Section 5.2 Assessment

Quick Check

1. Costs: leaving money on deposit for a set period; penalties for early withdrawal, and a minimum investment. Benefits: relatively low risk and higher interest than a savings account.
2. rate of return, inflation, tax considerations, liquidity, and restrictions and fees
3. Regular accounts do not require a minimum balance. If your account does and your account drops below that, you will incur a monthly fee. Some institutions will waive service charges if you maintain a certain balance. Activity accounts require no minimum balance, but institutions charge for each transaction and may also have a monthly fee. Interest-earning accounts offer a low-rate interest, but may require a minimum balance; below that balance, you incur a service charge.

Think Critically

4. Answers might note that standardizing interest calculations and explanations of terms and conditions of savings plans results in consumers who make well-informed decisions when they compare institutions.

Use Communication Skills

5. Accept all posters that demonstrate an understanding of the features of savings or checking accounts.

Solve Money Problems

6. Paragraphs might explain that Matthew will probably want a regular account with overdraft protection; he would not want interest-earning that pays low interest and requires a minimum balance.

Teacher Manual

Chapter 5 Review & Activities

Communicating Key Terms

Accept all promotional copy that reflects an understanding of the Key Terms and the chapter topics.

Reviewing Key Concepts

1. Answers might be advantages of online banking include convenience and faster clearing of deposits.
   Disadvantages include Internet security concerns and identity theft.
2. Commercial banks offer checking, savings, and lending to individuals and businesses. Savings and loan associations specialize in savings accounts and mortgage loans, and also offer checking accounts, business loans, and investment services. Mutual savings banks specialize in savings accounts and mortgage loans; some offer personal and auto loans. Credit unions offer what commercial banks offer.
3. A large, nationally chartered bank may be the safest place to deposit money with protection from the Federal Deposit Insurance Corporation. The size of these banks means they may have more internal controls against employee theft, fraud, etc.
4. You benefit when interest is compounded monthly because the next month's interest is computed on a higher amount—the principal you deposited plus the interest you earned during the prior month.
5. Choose a regular checking account if you write at least a fair number of checks each month and have regular deposits. Choose an activity checking account if you write just a few checks each month and cannot maintain a minimum balance. Choose an interest-bearing checking account if you can maintain a minimum balance but prefer higher liquidity.
6. Keep a record of checks written and deposits made, and reconcile your records with the bank statement you receive every month; also, do not overdraw your checking account.

ACADEMIC SKILLS

Lists might include the following explanations: Use only ATMs affiliated with your bank that do not charge transaction fees. Take out enough cash for an entire week or two-week period. Use other ways of paying for things when you are away from home—because fees for ATM transactions are higher at other banks and in other cities. The trade-off of not using ATMs is less convenience.

YOUR FINANCIAL FIGURES

(a) Bank A is the best deal for someone who can maintain the $300 minimum balance and has a lot of transactions each month. Bank B's offer is the best deal for someone who cannot maintain the larger minimum balance of Bank A, and is unlikely to have more than 35 transactions each month.

(b) Computations should reflect data given.

REAL-WORLD Application

Answers will vary, but students should point out that Check 21 will primarily benefit financial institutions because of reduced costs of clearing and returning checks to customers. Customers who prefer more control over their transactions and want to receive their cancelled paper checks may find Check 21 to be less beneficial.

Internet CONNECTION

Answers will vary but should demonstrate that students visited the Web site and understand the security risks inherent in electronic banking.

(1) Answers might include the presence of SSL encryption.

(2) Electronic banking transactions might include accessing account balance, online statements, ability to transfer funds between accounts and pay bills.

BusinessWeek ONLINE

Accept all answers that demonstrate students have read the online article and understand the concepts.

CHAPTER 6 Consumer Credit

pages 152–195

SECTION	LEARNING OBJECTIVES	FEATURES	TEXT RESOURCES	TECHNOLOGY RESOURCES
6.1	**After completing this section, students will have learned to:** Explain the meaning of consumer credit Differentiate between close-end credit and open-end credit.	**Savvy Saver,** p. 157 **TechByte,** p. 161	**Section Assessment,** p. 161 Quick Check Think Critically Use Communication Skills Solve Money Problems **Student Activity Workbook**	Lesson Planner Plus Online Learning Center Interactive Student Edition *Presentation Plus!* **Exam***View*® Pro Test Generator
6.2	**After completing this section, students will have learned to:** Name the five C's of credit. Identify factors to consider when choosing a loan or credit card. Explain how to build and protect your credit rating.	**Go Figure**—Debt Payments-to-Income Ratio, p. 163 **S&P's Put on Your Financial Planner's Cap,** p. 163 **S&P's Global Financial Landscape,** p. 164 **Go Figure**—Simple Interest on a Loan, p. 166 **Careers in Finance,** p. 167 **Common Cents,** p. 169 **WebQuest,** p. 170 **Document Detective,** p. 171 **Academic Connection,** p. 174	**Section Assessment,** p. 177 Quick Check Think Critically Use Math Skills Solve Money Problems **Student Activity Workbook**	Lesson Planner Plus Online Learning Center Interactive Student Edition *Presentation Plus!* **Exam***View*® Pro Test Generator
6.3	**After completing this section, students will have learned to:** Discuss how to protect yourself from fraud and identify theft		**Section Assessment,** p. 185 Quick Check Think Critically Use Communication Skills Solve Money Problems **Student Activity Workbook**	Lesson Planner Plus Online Learning Center Interactive Student Edition *Presentation Plus!* **Exam***View*® Pro Test Generator
6.4	**After completing this section, students will have learned to:** Identify ways to manage debt problems.		**Section Assessment,** p. 191 Quick Check Think Critically, Use Math Skills, Solve Money Problems **Student Activity Workbook**	Lesson Planner Plus Online Learning Ctr Interactive Student Edition *Presentation Plus!* **Exam***View*® Pro Test Generator

CHAPTER 6 Planning Guide

Meeting National Standards for Business Education	
Section 6.1	**Section 6.2**
Economics III. Economic Institutions and Incentives VII. The Role of Government **Personal Finance** I. Personal Finance I. Personal Decision Making III. Managing Finances and Budgeting V. Buying Goods and Services VII. Using Credit	**Economics** I. Allocation of Resources III. Economic Institutions and Incentives **Personal Finance** I. Personal Decision Making III. Managing Finances and Budgeting V. Buying Goods and Services VII. Using Credit
Section 6.3	**Section 6.4**
Economics III. Economic Institutions and Incentives **Personal Finance** III. Managing Finances and Budgeting V. Buying Goods and Services VI. Banking VII. Using Credit	**Economics** I. Allocation of Resources III. Economic Institutions and Incentives VIII. International Economic Concepts **Personal Finance** I. Personal Decision Making III. Managing Finances and Budgeting VII. Using Credit

Teaching Connection

Journal Writing

Ask students to make a list on a sheet of paper or in a journal of ten words that come to mind when they think of consumer credit. Ask them to share their lists of credit-related words with the rest of the class. Write the words on the board. Have students discuss the meanings of the words. Then compare the list of words to the Key Terms listed in the Chapter 6 Chapter Review and Activities section on page 192. Write on the board any of the key terms that were not identified and ask students what they might mean. Then ask students to write one paragraph on a sheet of paper or in a journal about what they think it means to have good credit. Ask volunteers to read paragraphs.

Visual Guide

Chapter 6 Opener

Discussion: Have students study the chapter opening photo and describe what they see. Then lead a discussion about consumer credit in the United States today and why people use credit cards. Ask students if they think most people have good credit or have too much credit debt. Lead a discussion about using credit and paying for it.

Follow-Up: Have the students make a list of possible types of credit besides credit through credit card companies.

Teacher Manual

Workplace Skills and Chapter Correlations

FOUNDATION SKILLS						
Basic Skills	Reading	Writing	Math	Listening	Speaking	
Thinking Skills	Creative Thinking	Decision Making	Problem Solving	Seeing Things in the Mind's Eye	Knowing How to Learn	Reasoning
Personal Qualities	Responsibility	Self-Esteem	Sociability	Self-Management	Integrity/ Honesty	

WORKPLACE COMPETENCIES						
Resources	Allocating Time	Allocating Money	Allocating Material and Facility Resources	Allocating Human Resources		
Information	Acquiring and Evaluating Information	Organizing and Maintaining Information	Interpreting and Communicating Information	Using Computers to Process Information		
Interpersonal Skills	Participating as a Member of a Team	Teaching Others	Serving Clients/ Customers	Exercising Leadership	Negotiating to Arrive at a Decision	Working with Cultural Diversity
Systems	Understanding Systems	Monitoring and Correcting Performance	Improving and Designing Systems			
Technology	Selecting Technology	Applying Technology to Task	Maintaining and TroubleshootingTechnology			

Internet Extension

Activity: Have students use the Internet to find credit counseling services. Ask students to research one of the companies or organizations and write a brief report on its services. If necessary, explain to students the concept of debt consolidation.

Key Words: credit counseling, debt counseling

Enrichment/Application Activity

Guest Speaker: Invite to class the credit manager of a large department store or other retail outlet. Ask him or her to bring a credit application for the class to see, and discuss the credit problems he or she has witnessed.

Topic Spotlight

Marketing: Discuss with students why retail outlets encourage the use of credit cards when you make a purchase and in advertisements.

Technology: Invite students to share their ideas about smart cards. Ask them: "How will these be helpful? How do you think they will link the physical world with the Internet? How might these be misused?"

Money: Have students solve this word math problem using simple interest. Rebecca wants to buy a new saddle for her horse. The one she wants usually costs $500, but this week it is on sale for $400. She does not have $400, but she could buy it with $50 down and pay the rest in 6 months with 10 percent interest. Does Rebecca save any money buying the saddle this way? If so, how much does she save? [ANSWER: Yes, she saves $82.50. $400 − $50 = $350; $350 × .10 = $35 per year; $35 × .5 = $17.50 per 6 months; $400 + $17.50 = $417.50; $500 − 417.50 = $82.50]

Additional Resources

Books

The Credit Diet: How to Shed Unwanted Debt and Achieve Fiscal Fitness by John Fuhrman (paperback: Wiley, ©2002) Fuhrman uses his personal life experience of overcoming debt to provide practical and easy instructions to help conquer debt problems.

How to Be More Credit Card and Debt Smart (Volume 1): Powerful Financial Management Strategies for Saving Money on Your Credit Cards and Debt! by Scott Bilker (paperback: Press One, ©2002) This book offers advice on how to stop the banks from taking advantage of credit users. It helps the reader get the best lending deals, get financially organized, pick the right mortgage, make more money, and finance a car.

Internet

edgate.com Students can access Practical Money Skills for Life on the main Web page of this site. This is a money management activity that covers making and sticking to a budget, saving and investing; the danger of irresponsible spending; and maintaining a good credit history.

nfcc.org This is the official site of the National Foundation for Credit Counseling. This accredited counseling agency offers quality credit advice and lists its high level standards of service.

bankrate.com and **banx.com** These sites provide current interest rates for credit cards and consumer loans.

equifax.com, **transunion.com**, and **experian.com** Information on credit reports can be found at these main credit reporting companies.

ftc.gov Credit law information is available at this Web site of the Federal Trade Commission.

Note: Web-site addresses may change.

Section 6.1

Focus

Motivation

Point out to the students that credit card companies have tried to make their cards into status symbols (platinum cards, cards with sports teams pictured, etc.) in an effort to get more people to use them. Ask students why people would want these cards and if using them encourages people to spend beyond their means.

Prereading

1. Have students skim the section, looking at the pictures, reading the captions, and reading the headings.
2. Ask a student to read aloud Read to Learn on page 154.
3. Have students list the key terms in their notebooks, and remind them to enter the definitions as they learn them.

Teach

Guided Practice

1. Ask students to read aloud In the Real World on page 153 and ask them if they have ever had or known someone who has had similar situations; ask them what they did to resolve such situations.
2. Ask students to read aloud Ask Standard and Poor's on page 153 and discuss it briefly with them.
3. Have students silently read the rest of the section, noting and mentally answering the Predict, Relate, Question, and caption questions and reading the features such as TechByte.

Independent Practice

1. Divide students into five groups and assign a credit source (see Figure 6.2 on page 158) to each. The students are to research a local institution of that type and determine if that institution gives only the types of loans that are shown in Figure 6.2; and determine the lending policies of the institution.
2. Each group is to prepare a chart or poster to depict the information that they have gathered.
3. Each group will present its research poster to the class.

Assess

Reteaching

1. Go over the list of Key Terms with students, ensuring they have written the correct definitions in their notebooks. Divide students into two teams and have a Key Terms bee in which teams compete to correctly define the terms.
2. Ask students to name the most important points in the chapter, and write them on the board. Reinforce the Factors to Consider Before Using Credit, ask students to choose an item they would like to buy and test its purchase on credit against the six factors listed.
3. Discuss with students the Reading Strategies and the pictures and figures with their caption questions. Assign features questions to students, and then go over their responses.

Enrichment

Divide students into groups to create a skit, poster, or song representing both the advantages and disadvantages of using credit. Each group will present its creation to the class.

Assessment

1. Have students complete the Section 6.1 Assessment.
2. Give students a vocabulary quiz based on selected terms from the Key Terms.
3. Assign an activity from Chapter 6 of the *Student Activity Workbook*.

Close

Have students react to this statement: "Using credit does not increase your purchasing power, or mean you have more money."

Section 6.2

Focus

Motivation

Write on the board: "If credit card companies are willing to give me credit cards, they must think I am a good risk. Otherwise, why would I get credit offers?" Ask students if they have ever thought this. Then ask students why, if they have no credit history, would credit card companies think they are good risks. Ask what factors motivate these companies.

Prereading

1. Have students skim the section, looking at the pictures, reading the captions, and reading the headings.
2. Ask a student to read aloud Read to Learn on page 162.
3. Have students list the Key Terms in their notebooks, and remind them to enter the definitions as they learn them.

Teach

Guided Practice

1. Ask students to read aloud the section Can You Afford a Loan? on page 162 and consider the main message: Repaying a loan requires sacrifice.
2. Ask a student to read aloud Debt Payments-to-Income Ratio on page 162. Then read Go Figure (page 163) to the class and have them do You Figure.
3. Have students silently read the rest of the section, noting and mentally answering the Predict, Relate, Question, and caption questions and reading the features such as Document Detective.

Independent Practice

1. Divide students into six groups. Assign to each group one of the methods discussed under Calculating the Cost of Credit (page 167). Have each group read and discuss its paragraph until all group members thoroughly understand it.
2. Have each group prepare a lesson plan to teach its method to the rest of the class. They are to create and use some form of visual assistance, such as a chart, a graph, or simple illustration.
3. Have all groups present their lessons.

Assess

Reteaching

1. Go over the list of Key Terms with students, ensuring they have written the correct definitions in their notebooks. Have the students prepare flashcards for all the terms and use them, in pairs, to review the terms.
2. Ask students to close their books and ask for volunteers to recall all of the five C's of credit. Give small prizes to students who succeed in recalling three or more.
3. Discuss with students the Reading Strategies and the pictures and figures with their caption questions. Assign features questions and go over the responses.

Enrichment

Invite a banker to the classroom to discuss topics in this section including: The Cost of Credit, Applying for Credit, and What If Your Application Is Denied?

Assessment

1. Have students complete the Section 6.2 Assessment.
2. Give students a vocabulary quiz based on selected terms from the Key Terms.
3. Assign an activity from Chapter 6 of the *Student Activity Workbook.*

Close

Using a computer or an overhead projector, project a typical credit card application. Go over the most important questions with the students.

Section 6.3

Focus

Motivation

Discuss with your students the word *protection.* Ask them to brainstorm a list of ways they have been protected or protected others. Write the list on the board. Ask the class if protecting their credit is important; have them justify their answers.

Prereading

1. Have students skim the section, looking at the pictures, reading the captions, and reading the headings.
2. Ask a student to read aloud Read to Learn and Main Idea on page 178.
3. Read the Predict question to the students and ask them for their responses.

Teach

Guided Practice

1. Ask students to read aloud the section entitled Billing Errors and Disputes on page 178 and ask them if they have ever been charged for something they did not buy. If any say "yes," have them recount the circumstances and tell what they did to resolve the issue.
2. Have students silently read the rest of the section, noting and mentally answering the Relate, Question, and caption questions.

Independent Practice

1. Divide students into groups of four or five. Have each group create a brochure or flyer on ways to protect their credit. As a class, vote for the best one and distribute it to the students in the school.
2. Discuss with students some of the difficulties with credit security on the Internet. Have them research ways security can be breached as well as ways to protect against such breaches. They are to write a report detailing their findings.

Assess

Reteaching

1. Ask students what they believe is the most critical information they learned in this section and why they think so.
2. Ask students to recall, with books closed, the five consumer protection laws listed on pages 183–184.
3. Discuss with students the Reading Strategies and the pictures and figures with their caption questions.

Enrichment

Invite a lawyer to class to discuss what can be done in cases of identity theft.

Assessment

1. Have students complete the Section 6.3 Assessment.
2. Assign an activity from Chapter 6 of the *Student Activity Workbook*.

Close

Have the students explain this statement: "Your credit is like your reputation—it must be protected. Once lost, it is hard to get back."

Section 6.4

Focus

Motivation

Tell the students that in past centuries people could be imprisoned for debt. Today people are not necessarily sent to prison, but the difficulties of clearing debts are extremely trying. Ask students what they think someone can do about debt problems. Write their responses on the board.

Prereading

1. Have students skim the section, looking at the pictures, reading the captions, and reading the headings.
2. Ask a student to read aloud Read to Learn and Main Idea on page 186.

Teach

Guided Practice

1. Ask students to read aloud the section entitled Signs of Debt Problems on page 186. Read The Warning Signs, stopping after each point for discussion.
2. Have students silently read the rest of the section, noting and mentally answering the Relate, Question, and caption questions.

Independent Practice

1. Ask the students if they know that the federal government and many state governments use credit to pay for many services. Ask them to go online to look up the current national debt.
2. Divide the students into groups of four or five, and ask them to discuss whether they think the government should be able to purchase using credit; if so, should they be able to do so in all circumstances? Why or why not?
3. Break up the discussion groups and have each student write an essay on the questions addressed in discussion.

Assess

Reteaching

1. Ask the students what they think is the most important part of this section. Have them explain why.
2. Direct the students' attention to Figure 6.10 on page 189 and ask them the caption question. Ask them also if they think this is a positive or negative economic sign.
3. Discuss with students the Reading Strategies and the pictures and figures with their caption questions.

Enrichment

Invite a bankruptcy lawyer to speak to the class about the personal bankruptcy laws in your state.

Assessment

1. Have students complete the Section 6.4 Assessment.

2. Assign the Chapter 6 Review and Activities.
3. Administer the test for Chapter 6 from the Reproducible Tests in the *Lesson Planner Plus* supplement.

Close

Ask students to consider the entire chapter and choose the most important lesson(s) they learned. Have volunteers explain why specific areas were vitally important.

ANSWERS

STANDARD & POOR'S Put on Your Financial Planner's Cap

Answers may vary but might include that they would ask the client to cut up all of his or her credit cards.

STANDARD & POOR'S *Global Financial Landscape*

Answers may vary but many might say "yes" because Israel's economy is on the upswing.

Careers in Finance

Accept all reasonable answers that demonstrate an understanding of the concept of credit worthiness and the five C's of credit.

Document Detective

1. five charges and one payment transaction
2. $4,959.40 ($5000 – $40.60 = $4,959.40)
3. $40.60
4. $20
5. 2/28/05

Academic Connection

Accept all reasonable answers. Most students may say "yes" because today it is easy to get credit and amass debt.

Section 6.1 Assessment

Quick Check

1. Students should select from the following. Advantages: You can get goods and services now and pay later; combine purchases and make one monthly payment; it is needed for making hotel reservations, renting a car, catalog or online shopping; no need to carry cash; allows a credit history to develop. Disadvantages: Credit costs money; having available credit is a temptation to buy unaffordable things; a bad credit rating might develop; you can lose income and property.
2. Closed-end is credit as a one-time loan that you will pay back over a specified period of time in payments of equal amounts. Open-end credit is credit as a loan with a certain limit on the amount of money you can borrow for a variety of goods and services.
3. Inexpensive loans with low interest rates are given by parents or other family members; medium-priced loans are from commercial banks, savings and loan associations, and credit unions; expensive loans are from finance companies and retail stores at high interest rates and from cash advances through credit card companies at high interest rates.

Think Critically

4. Answers will vary but might include evaluating interest rates.

Use Communication Skills

5. Accept all reasonable essays that reflect an understanding of responsible use of credit.

Solve Money Problems

6. Accept all reasonable answers that reflect insight into the possible difficulties of spending more money than you have.

Section 6.2 Assessment

Quick Check

1. Answers may include any of the following: Add up all monthly expenses, subtract from take-home pay, and see if you have enough left to make a loan payment and still have money left; consider what you can give up to make the monthly payment; use the debt payment-to-income ratio.
2. character, capacity, capital, collateral, and credit history
3. Maintain an income level; keep current debt low; and pay bills on time.

Think Critically

4. Answers may vary but may include maintaining a good credit rating.

Use Math Skills

5. Kim's debt payments-to-income ratio is 31.85 percent; without the college loan, it is 14.07 percent. According to the 20 percent rule, she cannot afford the college loan unless she pays off her credit card debts. [ANSWER: $820 − $145 = $675; $95 + $120 = $215; $215 ÷ $675 = 31.39%; $120 ÷ $675 = 17.8%)

Solve Money Problems

6. Accept all reasonable discussion that note that Eleanor has the right to know what led to the denial.

Section 6.3 Assessment

Quick Check

1. Notify the creditor in writing, including information to support your claim, and pay the undisputed portion of the bill.
2. Be sure cards are returned when making a purchase; keep records of credit card numbers and immediately notify credit card company if your card is lost or stolen.
3. It allows you to sue any creditor or credit bureau that violates the rules regarding access to your credit records or fails to correct errors in your credit file.

Think Critically

4. Accept all letters that demonstrate an understanding of the guidelines.

Use Communication Skills

5. Accept all letters that demonstrate an understanding of the possible consequences of cosigning.

Solve Money Problems

6. Accept all role plays that demonstrate an understanding of methods of fraud protection. For example, Joel should close his bank accounts and/or change his PIN code.

Section 6.4 Assessment

Quick Check

1. Answers will vary but should be based on the bulleted list of nine signs.
2. The Consumer Credit Counseling Service as well as services at universities, credit unions, military bases, and state and federal housing authorities. Also, banks or local consumer protection offices may offer counseling services.

3. Chapter 7 is a straight bankruptcy in which many debts are forgiven, and many of the debtor's assets are sold to pay creditors. In Chapter 13 bankruptcy, a debtor with a regular income proposes a plan to use future earnings or assets to eliminate debts over a period of time; the debtor normally keeps all or most of his property.

Think Critically

4. Accept all reasonable answers that demonstrate an understanding of the warning signs of debt.

Use Math Skills

5. U.S. bankruptcies experienced a 100 percent increase between 1990 and 2003. (1,500 − 750 = 750; 750 ÷ 750 = 100%) It depends on bankruptcy reforms. Further, if the number of credit cards in use increases, bankruptcies are likely to increase.

Solve Money Problems

6. Plans may vary, but might note that Deanne could contact her creditors and try to work out an adjusted repayment schedule, or she can contact a nonprofit credit counseling program. As a last resort, she can declare bankruptcy.

Chapter 6 Review & Activities

Communicating Key Terms

Accept all paragraphs that reflect an understanding of the Key Terms and chapter topics.

Reviewing Key Concepts

1. Consumer credit is the use of credit for personal needs. Credit is an arrangement to receive cash, goods, or services now and to pay for them later. A common form of consumer credit is a credit card issued by a financial institution. Merchants may provide financing for products they sell, and banks also finance purchases through loans and mortgages.
2. Closed-end credit is credit as a one-time loan that you pay back over a specified period of time in payments of equal amounts. Open-end credit is credit as a loan with a specific limit on the amount of money that you borrow for goods and services.
3. The five C's of credit include character, capacity, capital, collateral, and credit history. Creditors use the five C's to determine who will receive credit. Accept all graphic organizers that demonstrate student effort and an understanding of the concept. Students' ratings will vary but may be generally risky due to lack of capacity, capital, and credit history.
4. When choosing a loan or credit card, consider factors such as length of the loan, amount of monthly payments, and interest rate. Consider whether you can afford the loan or use of a credit card. Figure your own debt-to-income ratio, which is the percentage of debt you have in relation to your net income. It is related to capacity to repay a debt. Twenty percent is the most you should pay on debt payments, but 15 percent is better.
5. To build and protect good credit (as shown in Figure 6.7 on page 175), pay bills and loans promptly and manage your personal finances carefully. If possible, pay balances in full or more than the minimum payment. Also, correct mistakes related to your credit bills and credit reports. Dispute billing errors in writing and pay amounts that are not in question. In addition, younger people who have no credit might begin by obtaining a department store credit card and opening a savings or checking account.

6. If your credit or identity has been stolen, contact all your credit card companies; close and open new bank accounts; and change all PINs. Notify law enforcement agencies and credit bureaus. If purchasing online, never share your PINs, Social Security numbers, or passwords.
7. A variety of consumer counseling services are available through universities, credit unions, military bases, and state and federal authorities. In addition, the Consumer Credit Counseling Service is a nonprofit organization, affiliated with the national foundation for Consumer Credit, which provides debt counseling services for families and individuals with serious financial problems. Services are usually free, however a small fee may be charged for administrative costs for debt repayment plans. The goals are to prevent problems as well as solve them. They help people manage money and set up realistic budgets.

ACADEMIC SKILLS

Letters will vary but should include the exact figures.

YOUR FINANCIAL FIGURES

1) Miguel should subtract $207.33 from his bill leaving a balance of $450.89; 2) $766.60

REAL-WORLD Application

Accept all reasonable answers that demonstrate that students have done research on credit scores and have an understanding of the credit scoring system.

Internet CONNECTION

Answers will vary but should demonstrate that students have done online research and have an understanding of the meaning of the debt payments-to-income ratio.

BusinessWeek ONLINE

Accept all answers that demonstrate students have read the online article and understand the concepts.

CHAPTER 7 The Finances of Housing

pages 196–231

SECTION	LEARNING OBJECTIVES	FEATURES	TEXT RESOURCES	TECHNOLOGY RESOURCES
7.1	**After completing this section, students will have learned to:** Evaluate various housing alternatives.		**Section Assessment,** p. 201 Quick Check Think Critically Use Communication Skills Solve Money Problems **Student Activity Workbook**	Lesson Planner Plus Online Learning Center Interactive Student Edition *Presentation Plus!* **Exam***View®* Pro Test Generator Financial Planner Software
7.2	**After completing this section, students will have learned to:** Assess the advantages and disadvantages of renting. Identify the costs of renting.	**TechByte,** p. 205 **Common Cents,** p. 207	**Section Assessment,** p. 208 Quick Check Think Critically Use Math Skills Solve Money Problems **Student Activity Workbook**	Lesson Planner Plus Online Learning Center Interactive Student Edition *Presentation Plus!* **Exam***View®* Pro Test Generator Financial Planner Software
7.3	**After completing this section, students will have learned to:** Identify the advantages and disadvantages of owning a residence. Explain how to evaluate a property. Discuss the financing involved in purchasing a home. Describe a plan for selling a home.	**Savvy Saver,** p. 212 **Careers in Finance,** p. 213 **Document Detective,** p. 214 **Academic Connection,** p. 217 **S&P's Global Financial Landscape,** p. 220 **S&P's Put on Your Financial Planner's Cap,** p. 221 **WebQuest,** p. 223	**Section Assessment,** p. 227 Quick Check Think Critically Use Communication Skills Solve Money Problems **Student Activity Workbook**	Lesson Planner Plus Online Learning Center Interactive Student Edition *Presentation Plus!* **Exam***View®* Pro Test Generator Financial Planner Software

Meeting National Standards for Business Education		
Section 7.1	**Section 7.2**	**Section 7.3**
Economics I. Allocation of Resources **Personal Finance** I. Personal Decision Making II. Earning a Living III. Managing Finances and Budgeting V. Buying Goods and Services VIII. Protecting Against Risk	**Economics** I. Allocation of Resources **Personal Finance** I. Personal Decision Making III. Managing Finances and Budgeting V. Buying Goods and Services	**Economics** I. Allocation of Resources VII. The Role of Government VIII. International Economic Concepts **Personal Finance** I. Personal Decision Making II. Earning a Living III. Managing Finances and Budgeting V. Buying Goods and Services VII. Using Credit VIII. Protecting Against Risk

Teaching Connection

Demonstration

Bring in the Sunday classified ads section from your town's newspaper. Also bring in a print-out of the home page for online classified ads (recycler.com, for example). Show students the newspaper and the print-out. Ask them how they might go about finding an apartment for rent using these two sources. Then show students the home rental section of the classified ads. Also explain to them that the Web site has several sections within it, one of which is dedicated to apartment and house rentals. Then ask a student to describe an ad for an apartment, e.g., one or two bedrooms with washer/dryer. Find a similar apartment in the newspaper and read the ad aloud to the class without the price. Ask students to guess the rental price, and then read the actual price. Discuss the relationship between size and amenities and price.

Visual Guide

Chapter 7 Opener

Discussion: Have students study the chapter opening photo and describe what they see. Then lead a discussion about the different types of residences available, from apartments to houses. Ask them if they think renting or buying is more expensive in the long run.

Follow-Up: Have the students describe the type of home they would eventually like to have one day. Ask them what steps they might take to obtain their ideal home.

Workplace Skills and Chapter Correlations

FOUNDATION SKILLS						
Basic Skills	Reading	Writing	Math	Listening	Speaking	
Thinking Skills	Creative Thinking	Decision Making	Problem Solving	Seeing Things in the Mind's Eye	Knowing How to Learn	Reasoning
Personal Qualities	Responsibility	Self-Esteem	Sociability	Self-Management	Integrity/ Honesty	

WORKPLACE COMPETENCIES						
Resources	Allocating Time	Allocating Money	Allocating Material and Facility Resources	Allocating Human Resources		
Information	Acquiring and Evaluating Information	Organizing and Maintaining Information	Interpreting and Communicating Information	Using Computers to Process Information		
Interpersonal Skills	Participating as a Member of a Team	Teaching Others	Serving Clients/ Customers	Exercising Leadership	Negotiating to Arrive at a Decision	Working with Cultural Diversity
Systems	Understanding Systems	Monitoring and Correcting Performance	Improving and Designing Systems			
Technology	Selecting Technology	Applying Technology to Task	Maintaining and TroubleshootingTechnology			

Internet Extension

Activity: Have students use the Internet to access the online classified ads section of a large local or regional newspaper. Then have them access the real estate section and write a brief report outlining the available information. They may find home buyers' and sellers' guides, information on local schools and neighborhoods, and virtual home tours.

Keywords: the name of the local or regional newspaper of your choice

Enrichment/Application Activity

Guest Speaker: Invite a real estate agent to class to discuss his or her career and talk about the steps involved in buying a home. Ask him or her to discuss finding and choosing a home, negotiating prices, and financing.

Topic Spotlight

Government: Discuss with students why the United States government helps people secure a home loan.

Marketing: Bring to class advertisements for apartments in your area. (Some areas publish brochures strictly for apartments.) Circulate the ads among the students and ask if the ads are effective. Ask: Would students want to live in a particular apartment complex? Why or why not?

Ethics: Discuss with students the laws concerning discrimination in renting in your area. Ask if landlords can choose to rent only to certain people? What would students do if a landlord refused to rent to them?

Additional Resources

Books

Every Tenant's Legal Guide by Janet Portman, Marcia Stewart (paperback: Nolo.com, ©2002) Choosing a place to live is an extremely important decision, yet many people make bad decisions by spending too much money, picking bad landlords, neighbors, or a bad location. This book serves as a guide to any renter who requires legal, financial, and practical advice.

The Word's Easiest Pocket Guide to Renting Your First Apartment (World's Easiest Guides) by Larry Burkett, Ed Strauss, Ken Save (paperback: Moody Publishers, ©2002) This book provides renter-savvy advice as well as practical guidance on the various financial aspects of moving away from home.

Internet

apartments.about.com/cs/first/a/firstapartment.htm Searching for a first apartment, signing the lease, and getting settled can be intimidating experiences for a young person. This site provides useful tips on budgeting, credit reports, space needs, and amenities. It also includes an Apartment Worksheet.

offcampusnetwork.com/movelearn.asp This site provides moving resources and advice, from signing a lease, moving, and sub-letting to apartment hunting. Living away from home when the time comes can be a fun and rewarding experience if students are informed and use common sense.

homepath.com Fannie Mae is the largest non-bank financial services company in the world and the nation's largest source of financing for home mortgages. Its Web site includes information on home buying, mortgages, refinancing, and other home ownership topics.

hud.gov Housing and mortgage information is available from the Department of Housing and Urban Development on this Web site.

Note: Web site addresses may change.

Section 7.1

Focus

Motivation

Ask each student to imagine he or she will be renting a first apartment and needs a roommate to share expenses. One of the student's oldest friends just graduated with the student and will be living in the same area. Ask: "Do you think it is a good idea to share expenses and living quarters with your friend? Will your roommate choice affect your finances?"

Prereading

1. Have students skim the section, looking at the pictures, reading the captions, and reading the headings.
2. Ask a student to read aloud Read to Learn and Main Idea on page 198.
3. Ask the students what might be the purpose of this section. Also ask the students what they might want to learn from this particular section.

Teach

Guided Practice

1. Ask students to read aloud In the Real World on page 197. Ask them if they think there is a way to resolve this particular situation.
2. Ask students to read aloud Ask Standard and Poor's on page 197 and discuss it briefly with them.
3. Have the students silently read the rest of the section, noting and mentally answering the Predict, Relate, Question, and caption questions.

Independent Practice

Have the students research what is involved in repairing a "fixer-upper" property; they are to base their research on a 2-bedroom, 1-bath house. They should talk to building contractors, real estate agents, and homeowners who have had this experience, and check the Internet for additional information. Have them write their findings in a brief essay which cites the cost.

Assess

Reteaching

1. Ask students to name the most important point in the section, and then write it on the board.
2. Write "Rent vs. Buy" on the board and ask students to name pros and cons of each.
3. Discuss with students the Reading Strategies and the pictures and figures with their caption questions.

Enrichment

Invite an apartment manager to class and ask him or her to bring a sample lease to show to students, explaining the terms of the lease to the class. Have a question-and-answer session after the presentation.

Assessment

1. Have students complete the Section 7.1 Assessment.
2. Assign an activity from Chapter 7 of the *Student Activity Workbook.*

Close

Discuss with students what they need to do to make intelligent housing decisions.

Section 7.2

Focus

Motivation

Ask for a show of hands to answer this question: "How many of you just can't wait to have an apartment of your own?" Ask students what expenses they might have, not including rent, if they lived on their own. List the expenses on the board.

Prereading

1. Have students skim the section, looking at the pictures, reading the captions, and reading the headings.
2. Ask a student to read aloud Read to Learn on page 202.
3. Have students list the key terms in their notebooks, and remind them to enter the definitions as they learn them.

Teach

Guided Practice

1. Ask students to read aloud Selecting a Rental Unit on page 202. Ask students to translate the ads shown in Meet the Press at the bottom of the page.
2. Ask students if they know exactly what they would be looking for if they were renting an apartment. List their ideas on the board and discuss with them.
3. Have students silently read the rest of the section, noting and mentally answering the Predict, Relate, Question, and caption questions and reading the features such as Common Cents.

Independent Practice

1. Have the students research the cost to move into an apartment, including rent, deposits, utility deposits and installation, furniture, etc.
2. Ask the students to also determine what their ongoing monthly expenses would be.
3. Have each student prepare a budget for the first three months' expenses.

Assess

Reteaching

1. Have the students write sentences using each term in the Key Terms list.
2. Ask students what they think are the most important aspects of this section and why.
3. Discuss with students the Reading Strategies and the pictures and figures with their caption questions. Assign features questions to students and go over responses.

Enrichment

Invite an attorney to speak to the class about the legal issues regarding renting in your state.

Assessment

1. Have students complete the Section 7.2 Assessment.
2. Give students a vocabulary quiz based on the Key Terms.
3. Assign an activity from Chapter 7 of the *Student Activity Workbook.*

Close

Have students write a brief paper discussing how this section has reinforced or changed their views on renting an apartment.

Section 7.3

Focus

Motivation

Ask your students how many of them want to buy their own homes one day. Then ask them why they want to own homes. List their responses on the board.

Prereading

1. Have students skim the section, looking at the pictures, reading the captions, and reading the headings.
2. Ask a student to read aloud Read to Learn on page 209.
3. Have students list the Key Terms in their notebooks, and remind them to enter the definitions as they learn them.

Teach

Guided Practice

1. Have students read aloud The Home-Buying Process on page 209. Ask them what they think the process entails, and then list their responses on the board. Leave the list on the board and compare the actual process described in the text to their thoughts.
2. Ask students if they know exactly what they would be looking for if they were looking for a house.
3. Have students silently read the rest of the section, noting and mentally answering the Predict, Relate, Question, and caption questions and reading the features such as Document Detective.

Independent Practice

1. Divide the students into groups of four, and tell them they are buying a home for $250,000. Each group is to speak to mortgage lenders from two types of financial institutions from the following list: commercial banks, savings and loan associations, mutual savings banks, credit unions, mortgage companies, and finance companies.
2. Each group is to determine their down payment, and then speak to the lenders to find out the following information: qualifying criteria, points, interest rates and whether the mortgage interest rate must be fixed or variable.
3. Each group is to prepare a visual display illustrating the results of their work, and then present it to the class.

Assess

Reteaching

1. Go over the list of Key Terms with students, ensuring they have written the correct definitions in their notebooks. Divide students into two teams and have a Key Terms bee in which teams compete to correctly define the terms.
2. Ask students what they think are the most important aspects of this section and why.
3. Discuss with students the Reading Strategies and the pictures and figures with their caption questions. Assign features questions to students and go over responses.

Enrichment

Invite a home appraiser to class to speak to students about the process of determining a home's value. Have the students ask questions they have prepared in advance.

Assessment

1. Have students complete the Section 7.3 Assessment.
2. Assign Chapter 7 Review and Activities.
3. Administer the test for Chapter 7 from the Reproducible Tests in the *Lesson Planner Plus* supplement.

Close

Ask the students to consider the various types of housing they can purchase (see list on pages 210–212). Discuss benefits of each type, and ask the class to vote on their preferences.

ANSWERS

Careers in Finance

Answers might include reliability, promptness, knowledge of the market, etc.

Document Detective

1. Answers might include that some additional expenses could be utilities, rent, Internet access, cable TV, etc.
2. Income taxes are considered a monthly expense because they are deducted from each paycheck.
4. Answers might include that LeBron has not set aside very much money to allow for unexpected expenses.
5. Answers will vary but should note that the total amount of expenses should be cut by $380 or more.

Academic Connection

It would take about 11 years and 2 months. [ANSWER: $97,000 − $9,700 = $87,300; $87,300 × 1.08 = $94,284; $94,284 ÷ $700 = 134.69 months or 11 years 2 months]

STANDARD &POOR'S Global Financial Landscape

Accept all reasonable answers.

STANDARD &POOR'S Put on Your Financial Planner's Cap

The client could afford a house at $135,000 ($135,000 × .20 = $27,000), but that would deplete the savings. If there will be other expenses, perhaps the client would be better off buying a house costing $120,000 ($120,000 × .20 = $24,000), which would leave $3,000 for other costs.

Section 7.1 Assessment

Quick Check

1. your lifestyle and finances
2. Buying is better for people who want stability and more room than an apartment offers, privacy and the freedom to do as they wish, and tax benefits.
3. Sources include the public library, a newspaper's real estate section, friends and family, real estate agents, government agencies, and the Internet.

Think Critically

4. Answers might include that some housing needs include a house big enough for five people, someplace near good schools and shopping, a neighborhood with other children. Most students will answer buy for privacy, pet ownership, and tax and financial reasons.

Use Communication Skills

5. Accept all charts that illustrate comparable rental options.

Solve Money Problems

6. Accept all reasonable answers that reflect an understanding of opportunity costs of purchasing the house. Buying may not be a good choice because Lavani is young, knows few people in town, may encounter high maintenance costs, and she is relying on money she does not have yet.

Section 7.2 Assessment

Quick Check

1. mobility, few responsibilities, and low initial cost
2. few financial benefits, more restricted lifestyle, and various legal concerns
3. rent, utilities (if not included in rent), security deposit, and optional renters insurance

Think Critically

4. Answers might include an apartment with two bedrooms or one large bedroom and recreational space, room for some privacy, and space to store their possessions.

Use Math Skills

5. Raj will save about $75.00 a month or $900.00 a year if he rents the house with Jon. ($900 + $300 = $1200; $1200 ÷ 2 = $600; $675 − $600 = $75; $75 × 12 = $900)

Solve Money Problems

6. Accept all reasonable options, but answers might include negotiating a change in the lease with the landlord, perhaps offering the landlord extra money; trying to sublet her apartment and finding one that allows pets; giving the cat to a friend until the lease is up; and breaking the lease and accepting the consequences.

Section 7.3 Assessment

Quick Check

1. Determine your home ownership needs; find and evaluate a property to purchase; price the property; obtain financing; and close the purchase transaction.
2. Costs include the down payment, mortgage application fee, optional home inspection, earnest money, closing costs, mortgage insurance, points, property taxes, homeowners insurance, and mortgage payments.
3. Prepare the home for sale by fixing things where needed; obtain an appraisal if desired; set a price; and decide whether to sell the home on your own or seek professional help.

Think Critically

4. Answers will vary but may note that an evaluation will tell you what repairs the home needs, what future costs you might incur, the value of the home, and the price the seller is asking.

Use Communication Skills

5. Accept all reasonable answers that demonstrate an understanding of the role of condominium or homeowner's associations.

Solve Money Problems

6. Answers might include: Renee should spend more time looking; she should accurately determine how much she can afford; she should consider how she might feel if she lost the house because of bidding too low; she should make a $110,000 offer, and then see if the offer is accepted.

Chapter 7 Review & Activities

Communicating Key Terms

Accept all role plays that reflect an understanding of the Key Terms and chapter topics.

Reviewing Key Concepts

1. Renting and buying are the two main housing alternatives that are available. When deciding whether to buy or rent, you should consider your lifestyle, family size, and finances.
2. Advantages: mobility and fewer responsibilities, low initial costs. Disadvantages: financial and lifestyle restrictions, legal issues.
3. The factors that affect the cost of renting include: location, living space, utilities, security deposits, and renters insurance.
4. Advantages: sense of stability, individual expression, financial benefits. Disadvantages: financial risk, limited mobility, high expenses.
5. The steps for evaluating a property include: walking through the neighborhood, examining the exterior of the home, assessing the interior of the home, having a professional inspect the home, and reviewing the inspection report.

6. Determine how much you can afford for a down payment and then find out if you qualify for a mortgage. Also consider the points that must be paid to get a lower interest rate on your mortgage.
7. Prepare the home for selling by making needed repairs and painting any exterior and interior areas that appear worn. Keep the house clean and keep the lawn in good shape. Then determine the selling price and choose the real estate agent through whom you would like to sell your property.

ACADEMIC SKILLS

The couple might buy a house in a good neighborhood with good schools, large enough to accommodate two children and two adults. Yard work and maintenance needs should be on the low side because of time constraints. For the single person, one possibility is a rental unit with at least one bedroom in neighborhood close to work and/or entertainment venues.

YOUR FINANCIAL FIGURES

#1: $433.95; #2: $397.13; #3: $452.36

REAL-WORLD Application

1. Accept all answers that show research and an understanding of the concept.
2. A 100 percent mortgage is a good deal for people who have investments that provide a better return than the amount of money that would be saved in mortgage interest payments.

Internet CONNECTION

1. Answers will vary but should demonstrate that students visited the Web site and researched the average prices in their area.
2. Accept all reasonable answers. Students might advise not to sell because the condominium would cost more than what the neighbor could get by selling the current home. Also, he or she may need to pay a premium for benefits of condominium living—such as no maintenance and yard work.

BusinessWeek ONLINE

Accept all answers that demonstrate students have read the online article and understand the concepts.

Investing Financial Resources

Chapter 8
Saving and Investing

Chapter 9
Stocks

Chapter 10
Bonds and Mutual Funds

Chapter 11
Real Estate and Other Investments

Unit Overview

Unit 3 describes how to put financial plans into action through investing. The unit discusses how investing can increase resources, which is an important part of achieving financial goals. In Chapter 8, students learn how to prepare for a savings or an investment program, identify investment alternatives, and obtain investment information. Chapter 9 explains the difference between common and preferred stocks, how to evaluate stocks, and how to buy and sell stocks. Chapter 10 describes corporate bonds, government bonds, and mutual funds. Chapter 11 explores the advantages and disadvantages of real estate investments as well as alternative investments, such as precious metals, gems, and collectibles.

Introductory Activity

Ask students to write a brief definition of the word *invest*. Then explain that to invest is to put your money to use by purchasing or buying something that offers profitable returns, especially interest or income. Tell students that the word *invest* is derived from the Latin *investire*, which means to clothe or surround, and that the garment called a *vest* is also derived from *investire*. Ask your students for ideas about how *investire* came to mean *invest* as we use it today. One idea is that many years ago, when clothing was very expensive for the average person, the word came to mean purchasing something expensive that offered the profitable return of staying warm.

BusinessWeek FINANCE FILE

The Best Homes for Rollover IRAs

Answer Accept all reasonable answers that show student effort. Possible answer might be a 401(k) account would provide more money and that the cost of living goes up. In addition, Social Security payments may be reduced in coming years.

UNIT 3 LAB Teaching Guide

Get a Financial Life!

Investment Strategies

STEP A **The Process**
Make sure students have access to all necessary materials.

1. Remind students that the Careers in Finance feature in Chapter 10 describes a certified financial planner. Students can use this description as a model for preparing their résumés.
2. Accept all reasonable options that fall within the categories of stocks, bonds, mutual funds, and real estate.
3. Give students names of some of the Web sites from the Additional Resources section of the chapter planning guides from this unit. They might include the Sound Money Web site at **soundmoney.org**, *BusinessWeek* at **businessweek.com/investor**, The Wall Street Research Net at **wsrn.com**, **bondsonline.com**, the Commercial Real Estate Network at **ccim.com**, and auction Web sites, such as **ebay.com** and **icollector.com**. Publications include *The Wall Street Journal, BusinessWeek, Money*, and *Kiplinger's Personal Finance*.
4. If you invite a financial planner to class as a guest speaker (see the Chapter 8 Planning Guide), allow students time to ask interview questions after the presentation.

STEP B **Create Your Portfolio**
Evaluate students' portfolios based on whether the four steps were completed, the information seems researched, and the contents are neat and in order.

STEP C **Teamwork**
If necessary, organize the teams for the class. Evaluate the teams' seminars based on the following:

1. Participation from all team members.
2. The information presented should be informative, interesting, and reasonably well researched.
3. The written outline should be presented at the time of the seminar.
4. Information in the handouts should reinforce the information in the presentation.
5. Graphs should indicate the audience's understanding of the subject before and after the seminar.
6. Presentations should be well prepared.

Unit Closure

Have students create crossword puzzles using Key Terms from all the chapters of the unit. Allow students to complete each another's puzzles.

Evaluation

Administer the Unit 2 test from the **Exam***View*® Pro Testmaker CD-ROM.

CHAPTER 8 The Fundamentals of Investing

pages 236–259

SECTION	LEARNING OBJECTIVES	FEATURES	TEXT RESOURCES	TECHNOLOGY RESOURCES
8.1	**After completing this section, students will have learned to:** Explain how to establish goals for a savings or investment program. Discuss ways to obtain funds for investing. Identify the factors that affect their investment choices.	**WebQuest,** p. 241 **TechByte,** p. 244 **Go Figure**—Financial Math, p. 245 **Go Figure**—Financial Math, p. 246 **Academic Connection,** p. 246 **Go Figure**—Financial Math, p. 247	**Section Assessment,** p. 249 Quick Check Think Critically Use Communication Skills Solve Money Problems **Student Activity Workbook**	Lesson Planner Plus Online Learning Center Interactive Student Edition *Presentation Plus!* **Exam***View®* Pro Test Generator Financial Planner Software
8.2	**After completing this section, students will have learned to:** Identify the main types of savings and investment alternatives. Explain the steps involved in developing a personal investment plan.	**Careers in Finance,** p. 252 **Document Detective,** p. 253 **S&P's Put on Your Financial Planner's Cap,** p. 256	**Section Assessment,** p. 256 Quick Check Think Critically Use Communication Skills Solve Money Problems **Student Activity Workbook**	Lesson Planner Plus Online Learning Center Interactive Student Edition *Presentation Plus!* **Exam***View®* Pro Test Generator Financial Planner Software
8.3	**After completing this section, students will have learned to:** Describe their role in a personal investment program. Identify sources of financial information.	**Savvy Saver,** p. 258 **S&P's Global Financial Landscape,** p. 259 **Common Cents,** p. 261	**Section Assessment,** p. 265 Quick Check Think Critically Use Communication Skills Solve Money Problems **Student Activity Workbook**	Lesson Planner Plus Online Learning Center Interactive Student Edition *Presentation Plus!* **Exam***View®* Pro Test Generator Financial Planner Software

Meeting National Standards for Business Education		
Section 8.1	**Section 8.2**	**Section 8.3**
Economics I. Allocation of Resources III. Economic Institutions and Incentives VIII. International Economic Concepts IX. Aggregate Supply and Aggregate Demand **Personal Finance** I. Personal Decision Making II. Earning a Living IV. Saving and Investing	**Economics** I. Allocation of Resources IV. Markets and Prices **Personal Finance** I. Personal Decision Making II. Earning a Living IV. Saving and Investing	**Personal Finance** I. Personal Decision Making II. Earning a Living IV. Saving and Investing

Teaching Connection

Introductory Role-Play

To introduce the topics of saving and investing, have students form pairs. Ask one student to think of some financial goals for the future. Have the student play the part of a young adult who has a job and earns a moderate salary and is asking an investment advisor about types of investments to achieve the goals. Have the other student play the advisor who will name different investments and try to explain which one is best. Ask several volunteers to "perform" the role play for the class. Students may not yet know all the terms or information, but this exercise will draw out their prior knowledge to relate to the chapter.

Visual Guide

Chapter 8 Opener

Discussion: Have students study the chapter opening photo and describe what they see. Then lead a discussion about why it is important to save or invest part of your income to meet long-term financial goals and be prepared for emergencies.

Follow Up: Ask students what their long-term financial goals are. Are they saving part of what they earn or are given in order to meet them?

Workplace Skills and Chapter Correlations

FOUNDATION SKILLS

Basic Skills	Reading	Writing	Math	Listening	Speaking	
Thinking Skills	Creative Thinking	Decision Making	Problem Solving	Seeing Things in the Mind's Eye	Knowing How to Learn	Reasoning
Personal Qualities	Responsibility	Self-Esteem	Sociability	Self-Management	Integrity/ Honesty	

WORKPLACE COMPETENCIES

Resources	Allocating Time	Allocating Money	Allocating Material and Facility Resources	Allocating Human Resources		
Information	Acquiring and Evaluating Information	Organizing and Maintaining Information	Interpreting and Communicating Information	Using Computers to Process Information		
Interpersonal Skills	Participating as a Member of a Team	Teaching Others	Serving Clients/ Customers	Exercising Leadership	Negotiating to Arrive at a Decision	Working with Cultural Diversity
Systems	Understanding Systems	Monitoring and Correcting Performance	Improving and Designing Systems			
Technology	Selecting Technology	Applying Technology to Task	Maintaining and TroubleshootingTechnology			

Internet Extension

Activity: Have students access the Motley Fool Web site and write a one-page report explaining its purpose, the information available, and whether they think it could be helpful to new investors and why.

Keywords: Motley Fool

Enrichment/Application Activity

Guest Speaker: Invite a financial planner to visit the class to discuss beginning investment programs. Ask the planner to explain the different types of investments, how people choose among them, and why investing is important to a person's future.

Topic Spotlight

Government: Ask students why they think the interest earned on most state and municipal bonds is tax-exempt, and explain that tax exemption makes the bonds more attractive to investors.

Marketing: Bring to class sample copies of local real estate brochures and have students look through them for commercial property advertisements. Discuss how the real estate agent for a property presents the property to make it more likely to attract buyers.

Ethics: As a class, list on the board the personal qualities a financial planner should have. Ask how ethics might affect the work of a financial planner.

Additional Resources

Periodicals

The Wall Street Journal, ***BusinessWeek***, ***Money***, and ***Kiplinger's Personal Finance*** are good sources of timely economic and financial information.

Internet

theequator.com/fin/balance.htm A financial layman, Steve Saltman, devised this highly comprehensive tutorial on balance sheets, cash flow statements, and downloadable, free, financial model templates. Saltman uses Microsoft Excel, the same software financial planners use. The site is designed for individuals who are not financial professionals.

beginnersinvest.about.com/cs/investinglessons/1/blles3intro.htm This site provides page-by-page lessons for investment novices. It teaches viewers how to read a company's annual report, income statements, and balance sheets. At the end of each mini-lesson is a quiz to test knowledge acquired.

personalwealth.com This is a comprehensive personal investment site featuring investment recommendations. It is one of several sites developed by Standard & Poor's to provide different kinds of financial information.

quicken.com and **moneycentral.msn.com** These are two more sites where investment planning information can be found.

Note: Web site addresses may change.

Section 8.1

Focus

Motivation

Ask students to define the verb *to grow*; look for the response *to get bigger*. Then ask students if they would like to see their money grow, and most will say "yes." Finally, ask them how they think money can be made to grow; elicit, "wise investment."

Prereading

1. Have students skim the section, looking at the pictures, reading the captions, and reading the headings.
2. Ask a student to read aloud Read to Learn on page 238.
3. Have students list the Key Terms in their notebooks, and remind them to enter the definitions as they learn them.

Teach

Guided Practice

1. Ask students to read aloud In the Real World on page 237, and ask them if they think Nellie Magdaleno should just leave her money in a savings account.
2. Ask students to read aloud Ask Standard and Poor's on page 237, and discuss it briefly with them.
3. Have students silently read the rest of the section, noting and mentally answering the Predict, Relate, Question, and caption questions and reading the features such as TechByte.

Independent Practice

1. Divide class into dyads or triads (the goal is 11 groupings). Assign each pair or trio one of the investment categories in Figure 8.3 (page 243).
2. Have each group use library or Internet resources to research that type of investment to understand what it is and why it is or is not risky. Students should also determine to what type(s) of risk that investment category is vulnerable.
3. Have each group prepare and give a presentation that explains the investment category to the rest of the class.

Assess

Reteaching

1. Have the students write sentences using each term in the Key Terms list.
2. To help students understand the inflation rate's impact on investments, have each student write a word problem showing the effect of inflation on an investment and its answer. Put the students in pairs to solve each other's word problems.
3. Discuss with students the Reading Strategies and the pictures and figures with their caption questions. Assign features questions to students and go over responses.

Enrichment

Invite a stockbroker or financial planner to the class to speak about investments. Have the students prepare questions to ask before he or she visits.

Assessment

1. Have students complete the Section 8.1 Assessment.
2. Give students a vocabulary quiz based on the Key Terms.
3. Assign an activity from Chapter 8 of the *Student Activity Workbook*.

Close

Financial writer Sylvia Porter said, "It is important to forego today's luxuries for tomorrow's necessities." Ask students to respond to this statement.

Section 8.2

Focus

Motivation

Ask students to write down one personal long-term financial goal. When they have done so, ask them what types of investments they think might help them reach that goal, and write their responses on the board. Then open a general discussion to find out what the students know about the investments they have mentioned.

Prereading

1. Have students skim the section, looking at the pictures, reading the captions, and reading the headings.
2. Ask a student to read aloud Read to Learn on page 250.
3. Have students list the Key Terms in their notebooks, and remind them to enter the definitions as they learn them.

Teach

Guided Practice

1. Ask a student to read aloud the section Types of Investments on page 250.
2. Have students silently read the rest of the section, noting and mentally answering the Predict, Relate, Question, and caption questions and reading the features such as Document Detective.
3. Assign an activity from Chapter 8 of the *Student Activity Workbook.*

Independent Practice

1. Ask each student in the class to choose one of three topics: stock or equity financing, corporate and government bonds, or real estate.
2. Each student is to research the chosen investment type thoroughly, focusing on the investments history and outlook.
3. Have each student write an essay discussing the material they have researched.

Assess

Reteaching

1. Have the students make flash cards for each term in the Key Terms list, with the term on one side and the definition on the other. With a partner, they are to use the flash cards to learn the terms.
2. Ask the students to write the eight steps in Developing a Personal Investment Plan (page 255) into their notebooks. Suggest that they type them up and hang them on a wall at home near where they study.
3. Discuss with students the Reading Strategies and the pictures and figures with their caption questions. Assign features questions to students and go over responses.

Enrichment

During the next two weeks, have the students collect newspaper and/or magazine articles about investments and bring them to class. Tell them you will post the articles on a bulletin board for the class to share.

Assessment

1. Have students complete the Section 8.2 Assessment.
2. Give students a vocabulary quiz based on the Key Terms.
3. Assign an activity from Chapter 8 of the *Student Activity Workbook.*

Close

Ask the students to set one investment goal and write it down in their notebooks. Have them write how they intend to reach that goal and how long it will take.

Focus

Motivation

Ask students which they think is harder, school or "real life." Then explain that many lessons they learn in school will apply to real life. Draw a parallel between studying for school and doing the necessary work to make sound financial investments.

Prereading

1. Have students skim the section, looking at the pictures, reading the captions, and reading the headings.
2. Ask a student to read aloud Read to Learn on page 257.
3. Have students list the Key Terms in their notebooks, and remind them to enter the definitions as they learn them.

Teach

Guided Practice

1. Ask students to read aloud the first two paragraphs in the section Financial Planners, page 257. Drawing on the metaphor developed in Motivation, have them compare financial planners to tutors.
2. Ask students to read aloud Types of Financial Planners (page 257) and clarify the distinctions among them.
3. Have students silently read the rest of the section, noting and mentally answering the Predict, Relate, Question, React, and caption questions and reading the features such as Global Financial Landscape.

Independent Practice

1. Have students research the current laws regarding short-term and long-term capital gains; then ask the students to find out what the laws were ten years ago.
2. Have the students write a brief essay in which they compare today's laws to the laws ten years ago. Ask them to evaluate the differences.

Assess

Reteaching

1. Have the students make flash cards for each term in the Key Terms list, giving the term on one side and the definition on the other. With a partner, they are to use the flash cards to learn the terms.
2. Have students reread Managing Your Investments (pages 259–262) then close their books. Ask a student to explain the first step, Evaluating Investments, and other students to explain the other three steps.
3. Discuss with students the Reading Strategies and the pictures and figures with their caption questions. Assign features questions to students and go over responses.

Enrichment

Ask the students to find out how the Dow Jones Industrial Average is computed.

Assessment

1. Have the students complete the Section 8.3 Assessment and a short vocabulary quiz on this section's Key Terms.
2. Assign Chapter 8 Review and Activities.
3. Administer the test for Chapter 8 from the Reproducible Tests in the *Lesson Planner Plus* supplement.

Close

Invite two financial planners to class to speak about the advantages and disadvantages of a career in financial planning.

ANSWERS

Careers in Finance

Events that occur worldwide each day have profound effects on world markets. To do the best job, every analyst needs to keep on top of current news.

Document Detective

1. $25,000 + $15,000 + $490,000 = $530,000
2. $20,000
3. Answers may include other investments, her old car, or things she can sell.
4. Answers may include that she is not able to save as much as she plans *or* she saves more, other investments do very well, and her income changes.
5. adjustments for inflation, changing value of investments, and interest earned

STANDARD & POOR'S Put on Your Financial Planner's Cap

Students may suggest CDs, government bonds, or mutual funds, because these are not high-risk investments.

Academic Connection

Accept all reasonable answers that demonstrate research and an understanding of the concepts.

STANDARD & POOR'S Global Financial Landscape

Answers may include: Hydropower is cleaner, cheaper to produce, and it does not rely on outside sources.

Section 8.1 Assessment

Quick Check

1. Establish investment goals, perform a financial checkup, and obtain the money you need to get started.
2. Answers may include: pay yourself first; take advantage of employer-sponsored retirement programs and elective savings programs; make a special savings effort one or two months each year; take advantage of gifts, inheritances, and windfalls.
3. One factor is the amount of risk you are willing to take and examining the five components of risk in relation to your investment: inflation, interest rate, business failure, the financial market, and global investment. You also have to consider each investment's potential for income and growth as well as its liquidity.

Think Critically

4. Students may suggest investing in CDs, bonds, or stable mutual funds.

Use Communication Skills

5. Students may answer that inflation will affect everyone, no matter the type of investment chosen.

Solve Money Problems

6. The emergency fund should have at least $7,800, three months' living expenses (3 × $2,600 = $7,800), but because they are worried and have very little insurance, they may want to have nine months' expenses, $23,400 (9 × $2,600 = $23,400), in a liquid savings account.

Section 8.2 Assessment

Quick Check

1. The main types of investments are stocks, bonds, mutual funds, and real estate.
2. Diversification lowers risk by spreading your assets over different types of investments with different risk levels.

3. The steps for an investment plan are (1) establish investment goals; (2) decide how much money you need to reach those goals by a particular date; (3) determine how much you have to invest; (4) list the investments you want to evaluate; (5) evaluate the risks and potential return for the investments on your list; (6) reduce your list; (7) choose at least two investments; and (8) periodically recheck your investment program.

Think Critically

4. A pyramid has a wide base just as your investment program needs a solid foundation of low-risk investments, while the middle level denotes moderate investments, and the small top reflects the idea of limiting (or avoiding altogether) speculative, high-risk investments.

Use Communication Skills

5. The main argument against is this: Collectibles may lose value or become worthless. The main argument for is this: People such as sports fans or those who like antique jewelry may know a lot about these items; they may already have a solid base of safe investments, and so they are willing to speculate.

Solve Money Problems

6. Answers will vary but may include that Trent needs to be more specific about his investment goal: How much does he want? By when? He should follow the steps in developing his personal investment plan.

Section 8.3 Assessment

Quick Check

1. A financial planner should help you assess your current financial situation; offer a clear plan, including investment recommendations, and discuss it with you; help you track your progress; and direct you to other financial services as needed.
2. Evaluate potential investments, monitor your investments, keep accurate records, remember tax considerations, and be selective about sources of information.
3. Internet and online services, newspapers and news programs, business periodicals, government publications, corporate reports, and investor services and newsletters

Think Critically

4. Answers might include that people feel too busy and do not understand what they read, or they do not have enough money to bother. They should track their investments so they can calculate their net worth, and then adjust to changing circumstances.

Use Math Skills

5. \$30 (\$200 × .15 = \$30). Because he held the stock for less than a year, his gain is short-term and taxed as ordinary income.

Solve Money Problems

6. Possible questions may include: Are you licensed or certified? What is your education and training? How is your fee determined? Are you affiliated with a financial services company or do you work alone? May I have a free initial consultation? Do you have client references? May I see a sample written financial plan?

Chapter 8 Review & Activities

Communicating Key Terms

Accept all answers that demonstrate an understanding of the Key Terms and the concept of retirement savings. Answers should discuss the advantages of long-term retirement planning and savings, pre-tax contributions, and the different types of 401(k) investments.

Reviewing Key Concepts

1. An investment goal determines what you need to do, based on your particular values and lifestyle.
2. Sources of funding for investing include employer-sponsored retirement plans, elective savings programs, gifts, inheritances, windfalls, and ongoing individual savings activities.
3. Risk-averse people are often those who have had bad financial experiences. People who lived through the Great Depression of the 1930s or suffered losses in the stock market during the early 2000s are likely to be risk averse. Young people with few family responsibilities are usually more comfortable with more risk.
4. Equities are riskier than the other investment alternatives, but their return is the greatest plus they are liquid. Government bonds are the least risky investment, but their return is lower, and they are less liquid. Corporate bonds are in between in terms of their risk and return. Mutual funds are less risky than individual stocks, and so, their return is somewhat lower, and there may be restrictions on their liquidity. Real estate can be a good investment in terms of return but is not liquid.
5. Answers will vary but should include the eight steps of developing a personal investment plan.
6. The investor needs to evaluate potential investments, monitor the value of those investments, keep accurate records, and consider tax consequences.
7. Answers may include *The Wall Street Journal*, *Barrons*, *Forbes*, and *Morningstar*.

ACADEMIC SKILLS

Answers might include that insurance and an emergency fund are needed because they are quickly available sources of funds to cover financial losses resulting from accidents, medical emergencies, thefts, and job layoffs.

YOUR FINANCIAL FIGURES

1. (a) The best deal is the corporate bond, which pays $93.50 provided it is kept longer than 12 months. The municipal bond pays $90 in annual interest. The corporate bond pays $110 in annual interest less 20 percent ordinary income tax, or $88, if sold in less than 12 months. If the bond is kept longer than 12 months, it pays $110 less 15 percent long-term capital gains tax, or $93.50. (b) The better choice is the municipal bond.
2. Spreadsheets should show the returns calculated in exercise #1.

REAL-WORLD Application

1. Answers will vary.
2. Reasons may include that the fund has performed well in the past, that the managers of the fund have a good track record, that the fund is well diversified (low risk), and that it has a low entry amount, that is, you do not need a large amount for the initial investment.

Internet CONNECTION

1. Student answers will depend on the company selected.
2. Answers will depend on the individuals interviewed. Reasons may include the benefits of pre-tax contributions, the automatic nature of the savings, and the matching contributions.

BusinessWeek ONLINE

Accept all paragraphs that demonstrate students have read the online article and understand the concepts.

pages 270–303

SECTION	LEARNING OBJECTIVES	FEATURES	TEXT RESOURCES	TECHNOLOGY RESOURCES
9.1	**After completing this section, students will have learned to:** Explain the reasons for investing in common stock. Explain the reasons for investing in preferred stock.	**TechByte,** p. 275	**Section Assessment,** p. 276 Quick Check Think Critically Use Communication Skills Solve Money Problems **Student Activity Workbook**	Lesson Planner Plus Online Learning Center Interactive Student Edition *Presentation Plus!* **Exam***View*® Pro Test Generator Financial Planner Software
9.2	**After completing this section, students will have learned to:** Identify the types of stock investments. Identify sources of information to evaluate stock investments. Discuss the factors that affect stock prices.	**S&P's Global Financial Landscape,** p. 279 **Document Detective,** p. 282 **Go Figure**—Current Yield of a Stock Investment, p. 286 **WebQuest,** p. 286 **Go Figure**—Total Return, p. 287 **Go Figure**—Earnings per Share, p. 288 **Go Figure**—Price-Earnings Ratio, p. 288 **Careers in Finance,** p. 289 **S&P's Put on Your Financial Planner's Cap,** p. 290	**Section Assessment,** p. 290 Quick Check Think Critically Use Math Skills Solve Money Problems **Student Activity Workbook**	Lesson Planner Plus Online Learning Center Interactive Student Edition *Presentation Plus!* **Exam***View*® Pro Test Generator Financial Planner Software
9.3	**After completing this section, students will have learned to:** Describe how stocks are bought and sold. Explain the trading strategies used by long-term investors and short-term investors.	**Academic Connection,** p. 292 **Savvy Saver,** p. 296 **Common Cents,** p. 298	**Section Assessment,** p. 299 Quick Check Think Critically, Use Communication Skills Solve Money Problems **Student Activity Workbook**	Lesson Planner Plus Online Learning Center Interactive Student Edition *Presentation Plus!* **Exam***View*® Pro Test Generator Financial Planner Software

Planning Guide

Meeting National Standards for Business Education		
Section 9.1	**Section 9.2**	**Section 9.3**
Personal Finance II. Earning a Living IV. Saving and Investing	**Economics** I. Allocation of Resources II. Economic Systems III. Economic Institutions and Incentives IV. Markets and Prices VIII. International Economic Concepts **Personal Finance** I. Personal Decision Making II. Earning a Living IV. Saving and Investing	**Economics** VII. The Role of Government **Personal Finance** I. Personal Decision Making II. Earning a Living IV. Saving and Investing

Teaching Connection

Learning through Role Plays

Think about how you want students to learn concepts such as the process of buying and selling stocks. For example, you might ask one student to be a customer at a financial institution or bank who is inquiring about how to purchase a stock. Have another student be the financial representative who will answer the questions. The same type of exercise can be applied to most concepts to reinforce student learning through role play.

Visual Guide

Chapter 9 Opener

Discussion: Have students study the chapter opening photo and describe what they see. Then lead a discussion about the advantages (including the chance to earn a high return) and disadvantages (including higher risk) of investing in stocks.

Follow Up: Ask students how the risk of losing their money might influence their investment decisions. How do they think they might lower this risk?

CHAPTER 9 Planning Guide

Workplace Skills and Chapter Correlations

FOUNDATION SKILLS						
Basic Skills	Reading	Writing	Math	Listening	Speaking	
Thinking Skills	Creative Thinking	Decision Making	Problem Solving	Seeing Things in the Mind's Eye	Knowing How to Learn	Reasoning
Personal Qualities	Responsibility	Self-Esteem	Sociability	Self-Management	Integrity/ Honesty	

WORKPLACE COMPETENCIES						
Resources	Allocating Time	Allocating Money	Allocating Material and Facility Resources	Allocating Human Resources		
Information	Acquiring and Evaluating Information	Organizing and Maintaining Information	Interpreting and Communicating Information	Using Computers to Process Information		
Interpersonal Skills	Participating as a Member of a Team	Teaching Others	Serving Clients/ Customers	Exercising Leadership	Negotiating to Arrive at a Decision	Working with Cultural Diversity
Systems	Understanding Systems	Monitoring and Correcting Performance	Improving and Designing Systems			
Technology	Selecting Technology	Applying Technology to Task	Maintaining and TroubleshootingTechnology			

Internet Extension

Activity: Have students print a copy of a quarterly or annual report found on a company Web site. Allow them to compare the different reports and discuss the information they contain.

Keywords: Type in the name of a business, such as Timberland, Barnes & Noble, or Ford Motor Company, then click on Company, Investor Relations, or Investor Information.

Enrichment/Application Activity

Guest Speaker: Invite the editor of the business/finance section of a local or regional newspaper to speak about businesses in the area that have recently issued stock or whose stock is traded. Ask him or her to explain where the stocks are traded (NYSE, AMEX, or NASDAQ), how much the stocks cost to buy, and how well the stocks have been performing.

Topic Spotlight

Government and Ethics: Explain insider trading (the illegal use of insider information for profit in financial trading) and discuss why it is illegal.

Money: In June 2003, the exchange rate for the new peso was 1 U.S. dollar to 10.50 new pesos. Using this exchange rate, how many new pesos equal 5 U.S. dollars? [ANSWER: $5 \times 10.50 = 52.50$ new pesos]

Technology: Discuss with students how the Internet has changed the trading of stocks. Ask students to imagine how stocks were traded before the Internet.

Additional Resources

Periodicals

Stocks & Commodities This magazine provides specific, technical analysis of stocks and commodities securities.

Barron's A comprehensive source of investor information, this magazine offers in-depth industry and investment advice as well as features dealing with world market issues.

Internet

stockmaster.com This site features a directory of sites listing stock trading tips, stock picks, stock charts, and day trading news. There is a real-time streaming market data ticker on the bottom of the site.

smgww.org The Stock Market Game™, a real-world simulation that teaches about economics, finance, and the American economic system, can be found at this site. Participants invest a hypothetical $100,000 in NASDAQ, AMEX, and NYSE-listed common stocks. They research stocks, study how the financial markets work, choose their portfolios, manage budgets, follow companies in the news, and make decisions on whether to buy, sell, or hold. (The Stock Market Game is a trademarked program of the Foundation for Investor Education.)

money.cnn.com and **multex.com** These sites offer information for research.

finance.yahoo.com and **quote.com** This site provides stock quotes and other financial data.

amex.com (American Stock Exchange), **nyse.com** (New York Stock Exchange), and **nasdaq.com** (National Association of Securities Dealers Automated Quotation system). These sites offer information on the activities and resources of the various stock exchanges.

Note: Web site addresses may change.

Section 9.1

Focus

Motivation

Ask students why they think people invest in the stock market; then ask if there is a trade-off for such investments (elicit "risk"). Ask students how many of them are (a) looking forward to investing in stock, (b) would like to invest in stock but are nervous about it, and (c) definitely do not want to touch investments in stock.

Prereading

1. Have students skim the section, looking at the pictures, reading the captions, and reading the headings.
2. Ask a student to read aloud Read to Learn on page 272.
3. Have students list the Key Terms in their notebooks, and remind them to enter the definitions as they learn them.

Teach

Guided Practice

1. Ask students to read aloud In the Real World on page 271, and ask them how they would respond to As You Read. Do they think believing in the company's products and policies is important?
2. Ask students to read aloud Ask Standard and Poor's on page 271, and discuss it briefly with them.
3. Have students silently read the rest of the section, noting and mentally answering the Predict, Relate, Question, and caption questions and reading the features such as TechByte.

Independent Practice

1. Have each student select a well-known corporation that trades its stock publicly.
2. Have students use library or Internet resources to research the following: (a) whether the corporation trades both common and preferred stock, (b) how many shares of each type were outstanding at the end of the last fiscal year, and (c) what year the company stock was first publicly traded. Students should indicate whether they believe in the products and policies of the company.
3. Have students prepare a presentation as if they were selling shares in their corporation to the rest of the class.

Assess

Reteaching

1. Have the students write sentences using each of the Key Terms.
2. Reinforce the differences between common and preferred stock by writing each on the board as a heading and asking students to list the key points of each.
3. Discuss with students the Reading Strategies and the pictures and figures with their caption questions. Assign features questions to students and go over responses.

Enrichment

Invite a stockbroker to class to speak to the students about how to start their stock investment portfolios: how much money they need, how to establish a relationship with a broker, and anything they need to do to prepare to make their first investment in stock.

Assessment

1. Have students complete the Section 9.1 Assessment.
2. Give students a vocabulary quiz based on the Key Terms.
3. Assign an activity from Chapter 9 of the *Student Activity Workbook*.

Close

Reiterate that corporations do not have to repay the money a stockholder pays for stock. Ask the students to write paragraphs in which they state whether they think this is ethical and explain why or why not.

Section 9.2

Focus

Motivation

Ask students to think of ways in which they evaluate bicycles, shops, music—almost everything, including whether they prefer Coke or Pepsi. Ask them to define the word *evaluate,* considering its component parts. List definitions, synonyms, etc., on the board. Explain that this is the process they must use when deciding how to invest.

Prereading

1. Have students skim the section, looking at the pictures, reading the captions, and reading the headings.
2. Ask a student to read aloud Read to Learn on page 277.
3. Have students list the Key Terms in their notebooks and prepare flash cards as they learn the definitions of the terms.

Teach

Guided Practice

1. Read the first paragraph under Types of Stock Investments (page 277) aloud to students, and ask individual students to read aloud each of the paragraphs categorizing stocks (pages 277–280).
2. Have students silently read the rest of the section, noting and mentally answering the Predict, Relate, Question, and caption questions and reading the features such as Document Detective.

Independent Practice

Bring in a copy of *The Wall Street Journal* and ask students to select two stocks, one from the NYSE listing and the other from the AMEX listing. Have students research the stocks they have selected as if they were evaluating them for investment purposes. Each student is to submit a report detailing his or her evaluations.

Assess

Reteaching

1. Have students work in pairs and practice with their flash cards to learn Key Terms.
2. Review the different calculations investors use to evaluate stocks: current yield, total return, earnings per share, and price-earnings ratio.
3. Discuss with students the Reading Strategies and the pictures and figures with their caption questions. Assign features questions to students and go over responses.

Enrichment

Have the students research cyclical stocks. As a class, create a list of these stocks and ask the students to explain why they think the stocks are cyclical.

Assessment

1. Have students complete the Section 9.2 Assessment.
2. Give students a vocabulary quiz based on the Key Terms.
3. Assign an activity from Chapter 9 of the *Student Activity Workbook.*

Close

Have the students determine whether the current stock market is a bear or bull market. Open a discussion in which selected students explain why they think this is so.

Section 9.3

Focus

Motivation

Ask the students the following questions and list their responses on the board: "What are different ways that things are bought and sold?" "Do you know how stocks are bought and sold?" Tell them they will learn how in this section.

Prereading

1. Have students skim the section, looking at the pictures, reading the captions, and reading the headings.
2. Ask a student to read aloud Read to Learn on page 291.
3. Have students list the Key Terms in their notebooks, and remind them to enter the definitions as they learn them.

Teach

Guided Practice

1. Ask students to read aloud The Primary Markets on page 291 and discuss it with them to ensure they all understand the information.
2. Have a student read aloud the first paragraph under The Secondary Markets on page 291 and compare primary and secondary markets.
3. Have students silently read the rest of the section, noting and mentally answering the Predict, Relate, Question, React, and caption questions and reading the features such as Savvy Saver.

Independent Practice

1. Assign one topic to each student: how to buy and sell stock, primary and secondary markets for stocks, types of orders, investment strategies and techniques.
2. Each student is to begin with the explanations and differences explored in this section's text, then research the topic using library or Internet resources, and compare and contrast the component parts.
3. Each student is to prepare a graphic presentation that makes the distinctions between these component parts clear and present their work to the class.

Assess

Reteaching

1. Have the students write sentences using each of the Key Terms.
2. Ask students what areas they think are still unclear, and respond to their questions and concerns.
3. Discuss with students the Reading Strategies and the pictures and figures with their caption questions. Assign features questions to students and go over responses.

Enrichment

With students working in pairs, if possible, have them interview stockbrokers to find out why they chose that occupation, the best and worst parts of the job, what education and training are required, what personality and character traits are useful, etc.

Assessment

1. Have students complete the Section 9.3 Assessment.
2. Assign Chapter 9 Review and Activities.
3. Administer the test for Chapter 9 from the Reproducible Tests in the *Lesson Planner Plus* supplement.

Close

Have students share, compare, and discuss what they learned on their stockbroker interviews; ask how many might be interested in becoming stockbrokers.

ANSWERS

STANDARD & POOR'S Global Financial Landscape

Answers might include that because the LSE is Europe's largest stock exchange it probably lists large-cap stocks—those from companies that have issued a large number of shares.

Document Detective

1. Taylor Financial Services performed the stock transaction.
2. He sold stock.
3. He sold 160 shares of stock.
4. The commission and fees were subtracted from the gross amount.
5. He will receive his money on 05/04/20--.

Careers in Finance

You will have more research information available to you, and an account executive can help you make investment decisions and handle your entire investment portfolio.

STANDARD & POOR'S Put on Your Financial Planner's Cap

You might suggest that they do both: put a portion of the money into a CD for safety but small earnings, and put the other portion in higher-yield investments such as stocks.

Academic Connection

Students' timelines should show the events leading up to the 1987 stock market crash.

Section 9.1 Assessment

Quick Check

1. To raise money to start up their businesses and to help pay for ongoing activities.
2. Investors purchase common stock as a way to make money from dividends, from an increase in the dollar value of the stock, and from an increase in the value of the stock due to a stock split.
3. It gives the owners the advantage of receiving cash dividends before common stockholders, and the investor knows the dividend amount before buying.

Think Critically

4. The company can bring the stock price down to a price it considers reasonable, making the stock more affordable. Also, a split attracts investors who believe a company splits its stock when it is doing well.

Use Communication Skills

5. Answers will vary but may include the wish to influence change, especially if the company is doing badly.

Solve Money Problems

6. $67.50 ($\$45 \times .06 = \$2.70$; $\$2.70 \times 25 = \$67.50$)

Section 9.2 Assessment

Quick Check

1. The different types of stock investments are blue-chip stocks, income stocks, growth stocks, cyclical stocks, defensive stocks, large-cap stocks, small-cap stocks, and penny stocks.
2. Sources for evaluating stocks include: the financial section of the newspaper, the Internet, financial publications, stock advisory services, and corporate news.
3. Numerical measures of corporations include current yield, total return, earnings per share, and price-earnings ratio.

Think Critically

4. The earnings-per-share calculation is related to a company's profitability. A low price-earnings (PE) ratio may indicate a good investment, whereas a high PE ratio may indicate a poor investment.

Use Math Skills

5. \$1,100 (\$.50 × 100 × 2 = \$100; (\$30 − \$20) × 100 = \$1,000; \$1,000 + \$100 = \$1,100)

Solve Money Problems

6. Answers should indicate two items in the newspaper that provide investor information and indicate why investors should track their investments.

Section 9.3 Assessment

Quick Check

1. In the primary market, the investor purchases a corporation's securities through an investment bank or other representative of the corporation. After stocks are sold on the primary market, they are sold in the secondary market, which is the market for existing, currently traded financial securities.
2. Full-service and discount brokerage firms charge higher commissions than online brokerage firms. Full-service firms charge higher commissions for personalized service and free research. Discount and online firms charge lower rates but will charge extra for research.
3. Investors use the buy-and-hold technique, dollar cost averaging, and direct investment and dividend reinvestment plans, while speculators buy and sell investments in a short time, may buy stock on margin, and sell short.

Think Critically

4. Student handouts should present clear explanations of the buy-and-hold technique, dollar cost averaging, direct investment, and dividend reinvestment.

Use Communication Skills

5. Answers will vary, but should demonstrate an understanding of the risks involved in short-term trading.

Solve Money Problems

6. Answers will vary but should emphasize that Bruce must take responsibility for his investments and make all final decisions. Answers should also mention the danger of poor decisions or even dishonesty by the account executive.

Chapter 9 Review & Activities

Communicating Key Terms

Answers will vary but should demonstrate an understanding of concepts as long-term investments, building a portfolio, and retirement funds.

Reviewing Key Concepts

1. With common stock, dividends are not mandatory. Thus, cash flow is all positive to the corporation, and the outflow can be minimized.
2. If you have cumulative preferred stock, the company cannot omit a dividend owed to you, they must pay you any dividends owed to you before they issue dividends to common stockholders. Convertible preferred stock can be converted to common shares, thus providing possible growth opportunities.
3. A company considered to have small capitalization has fewer shares outstanding. It is likely to be a newer firm engaged in developing and marketing new products. The company will, therefore, probably reinvest all earnings into future growth, i.e., not issue dividends.
4. One of the advantages of a stock advisory service is that it is likely to provide a balanced view of a company's potential. A disadvantage is that many such services charge a fee.
5. The price-earnings ratio is a good measure of a stock investment because it compares the value of the stock to its price: If the PE ratio is small, the price of the stock is low relative to its earnings, and the stock is likely to be a "good deal," i.e., undervalued.

6. A market order is a request to buy stock at the current market value. A limit order is a request to buy or sell stock at a specific price. A stop order is a request to sell stock at the first available opportunity after its market price reaches a specific number.
7. The tax advantage of long-term investment strategies is based on the fact that equities held more than one year and then sold are taxed at the lower capital gains rate. Also, you do not pay taxes on gains until you sell the stock.

ACADEMIC SKILLS

Most states require a number of licenses. To obtain these, the would-be broker must pass several tests; to keep the licenses current, the broker must participate in continuing education. The licenses can be revoked if the individual is convicted of fraud or other felonies.

YOUR FINANCIAL FIGURES

(a) $3,400 (b) $1,700 (c) 200 (d) $8,700

REAL-WORLD Application

1. The government wants investors to hold stocks longer than 12 months because it is advantageous to corporations: It may reduce speculation in company stock and fluctuations in the stock price. The government is essentially encouraging investment in profit-making enterprises.
2. The 15 percent tax rate on capital gains for investments held longer than 12 months is lower than the regular rate for many investors—providing a tax incentive for those investors to hold their investments longer than 12 months.

Internet CONNECTION

Answers will vary but should include the source of the information and the reasoning behind the conclusions.

BusinessWeek ONLINE

Accept all answers that demonstrate students have read the online material and understand the concepts. Accept all reasonable lists.

CHAPTER 10 Bonds and Mutual Funds

pages 304–349

SECTION	LEARNING OBJECTIVES	FEATURES	TEXT RESOURCES	TECHNOLOGY RESOURCES
10.1	**After completing this section, students will have learned to:** Describe the characteristics of corporate bonds. Identify the reasons corporations sell bonds. Explain why investors buy corporate bonds. Discuss the reasons governments issue bonds. Identify the types of government bonds.	**Go Figure**—A Bond's Annual Interest, p. 307 **Common Cents,** p. 310 **Go Figure**—Approximate Market Value of a Bond, p. 312 **Savvy Saver,** p. 314 **Go Figure**—Dollar Amount of Return on a T-Bill, p. 315 **Go Figure**—Rate of Return on a T-Bill, p. 316 **TechByte**—Security in an Uncertain Time, p. 316	**Section Assessment,** p. 318 Quick Check Think Critically Use Communication Skills Solve Money Problems **Student Activity Workbook**	Lesson Planner Plus Online Learning Center Interactive Student Edition *Presentation Plus!* **Exam***View®* Pro Test Generator
10.2	**After completing this section, students will have learned to:** Identify sources of information for selecting bond investments	**Academic Connection,** p. 321 **Go Figure**—Current Yield of a Bond Investment, p. 323 **Document Detective,** p. 324	**Section Assessment,** p. 325 Quick Check Think Critically Use Math Skills Solve Money Problems **Student Activity Workbook**	Lesson Planner Plus Online Learning Center Interactive Student Edition *Presentation Plus!* **Exam***View®* Pro Test Generator
10.3	**After completing this section, students will have learned to:** Identify types of mutual funds.	**Go Figure**—Net Asset Value, p. 328 **Careers in Finance**—Certified Financial Planner, p. 329 **S&P's Put on Your Financial Planner's Cap,** p. 332 **S&P's Global Financial Landscape,** p. 333	**Section Assessment,** p. 334 Quick Check Think Critically Use Math Skills Solve Money Problems **Student Activity Workbook**	Lesson Planner Plus Online Learning Center Interactive Student Edition *Presentation Plus!* **Exam***View®* Pro Test Generator
10.4	**After completing this section, students will have learned to:** Discuss sources of information for selecting mutual funds. Describe the methods of buying and selling mutual funds.	**WebQuest,** p. 337 **Go Figure**—Capital Gain, p. 340 **Go Figure**—Percentage of Asset Growth Withdrawal, p. 344	**Section Assessment,** p. 345 Quick Check Think Critically Use Communication Skills Solve Money Problems **Student Activity Workbook**	Lesson Planner Plus Online Learning Center Interactive Student Edition *Presentation Plus!* **Exam***View®* Pro Test Generator

CHAPTER 10 Planning Guide

Meeting National Standards for Business Education	
Section 10.1	**Section 10.2**
Economics I. Allocation of Resources III. Economic Institutions and Incentives VII. The Role of Government VIII. International Economic Concepts **Personal Finance** I. Personal Decision Making II. Earning a Living IV. Saving and Investing	**Personal Finance** I. Personal Decision Making II. Earning a Living IV. Saving and Investing
Section 10.3	**Section 10.4**
Personal Finance II. Earning a Living IV. Saving and Investing	**Economics** I. Allocation of Resources **Personal Finance** I. Personal Decision Making II. Earning a Living IV. Saving and Investing

Teaching Connection

Simulation Activity

Introduce the concept of mutual funds to the class by creating a class mutual fund. Have students form five to eight groups. Ask each group to choose a product or a type of company in which the group would want to invest $1,000 each. Have them think of a name of the company and describe its business, e.g., type of product, international or national, well established or new. Groups must write the description down on a piece of paper and the price of each share of stock and the amount of shares that must total $1,000. Collect each group's stock description and write the name of each company, the price of the stock and total number of shares owned. Ask for suggestions as to what to name the fund; write names on the board and vote for one. Explain to students that this group of stocks is the class mutual fund.

Visual Guide

Chapter 10 Opener

Discussion: Have the students study the chapter opening photo and describe what they see. Then lead a discussion about the ways governments raise funds to finance the building of new sports stadiums, schools, and tracks, including issuing government bonds.

Follow-Up: Ask students whether they would vote for a bond issue to build a new sports stadium in their area. Why or why not? Do they think that would be a good investment?

Teacher Manual

Workplace Skills and Chapter Correlations

FOUNDATION SKILLS						
Basic Skills	Reading	Writing	Math	Listening	Speaking	
Thinking Skills	Creative Thinking	Decision Making	Problem Solving	Seeing Things in the Mind's Eye	Knowing How to Learn	Reasoning
Personal Qualities	Responsibility	Self-Esteem	Sociability	Self-Management	Integrity/ Honesty	

WORKPLACE COMPETENCIES						
Resources	Allocating Time	Allocating Money	Allocating Material and Facility Resources	Allocating Human Resources		
Information	Acquiring and Evaluating Information	Organizing and Maintaining Information	Interpreting and Communicating Information	Using Computers to Process Information		
Interpersonal Skills	Participating as a Member of a Team	Teaching Others	Serving Clients/ Customers	Exercising Leadership	Negotiating to Arrive at a Decision	Working with Cultural Diversity
Systems	Understanding Systems	Monitoring and Correcting Performance	Improving and Designing Systems			
Technology	Selecting Technology	Applying Technology to Task	Maintaining and TroubleshootingTechnology			

Internet Extension

Activity: Have students research investment clubs on the Internet. Ask them: "How can clubs help people with their investments?"

Keywords: investment clubs, National Association of Investors Corporation (NAIC)

Enrichment/Application Activity

Guest Speaker: Invite a representative from an investment club to speak to the class about the club and why he or she joined. Ask the speaker to talk about researching and choosing mutual funds and corporate and government bonds, as well as stocks. NAIC Online lists its chapters throughout the country at **better-investing.org**.

Topic Spotlight

Marketing: Have students look at both corporate and mutual fund annual reports, then discuss how these publications are a form of marketing.

Money: What is the rate of return on a Treasury bill with a face value of $1,000 and a purchase price of $875? [ANSWER: 14.29%: $1,000 − 875 = 125 ÷ 875 = 14.29%]

Technology: Discuss how the Internet has made investment information available to many more people. Then ask how investors know they are getting accurate information. Discuss with students the importance of using reliable sources.

Additional Resources

Books

Find the Right Mutual Fund: Morningstar Mutual Fund Investing Workbook, Level 1 by Christine Benz (paperback: Wiley, ©2004). This book is a tool for readers taking their first steps in the arena of mutual fund investing. It is filled with informative topics such as how to purchase a fund and how to find a fund's total return, as well as important fund documents.

Mutual Funds for Dummies by Eric Tyson, James C. Collins (paperback: For Dummies, ©2004). As a financial advisor and a columnist, author Tyson has seen avoidable mistakes made repeatedly by investors. He highlights these errors and provides helpful insight into mutual fund investing.

Internet

bonds-online.com This site provides information, education, and direction in making bond investment decisions in areas including tracking bond prices, bond market news, self-directed education, and bond trading.

sec.gov The Web site of the U.S. Securities & Exchange Commission (SEC) provides a great deal of information on the securities market, including how the SEC protects investors and the laws that govern the industry.

sec.gov/oiea1.htm This page on the SEC Web site offers investor education and publications.

Morningstar.com and **Lipper.com** These highly detailed sites provide mutual fund ratings, shareholder class data, mutual fund quotes, investing tools, retirement planning, mutual fund comparisons, and fund newsletters.

Note: Web site addresses may change.

Section 10.1

Focus

Motivation

Ask the students if they have ever borrowed money from or loaned money to a friend, and ask them to explain the details: "Was there interest? An IOU? Collateral?" Then tell the students a bond is an organization's IOU—a promise to repay a sum of money at a set interest rate and within a certain amount of time.

Prereading

1. Have students skim the section, looking at the pictures, reading the captions, and reading the headings.
2. Ask a student to read aloud Read to Learn on page 306.
3. Have students list the Key Terms in their notebooks, and remind them to enter the definitions as they learn them.

Teach

Guided Practice

1. Ask students to read aloud In the Real World on page 305, and ask them if they have ever heard people discuss bond issues. Explain that bond issues are another way that governments (and corporations) raise money to spend on specific things.
2. Ask students to read aloud Ask Standard and Poor's on page 305 and discuss it briefly with them.
3. Have students silently read the rest of the section, noting and mentally answering the Predict, Relate, Question, and caption questions and reading the features such as Common Cents.

Independent Practice

1. Assign students one of the following topics: debentures, mortgage bonds, subordinated debentures, convertible bonds, registered bonds, coupon bonds, bearer bonds, zero-coupon bonds.
2. Have students research in the bond market first to find a corporation selling that type of bond they were assigned, then to find information about the corporation.
3. Students are to offer "their" corporate bonds for sale, trying to convince other students to buy by highlighting the strongest points about the corporation and its bonds.

Assess

Reteaching

1. Have the students write sentences using each term in the Key Terms list.
2. To reinforce the section content, have students explain, with books closed, the methods corporations use to repay bonds.
3. Discuss with students the Reading Strategies and the pictures and figures with their caption questions. Assign features questions to students and go over responses.

Enrichment

Tell the students that bearer bonds were made illegal in the United States in 1982, and have them research why.

Assessment

1. Have students complete the Section 10.1 Assessment.
2. Give students a vocabulary quiz based on the Key Terms.
3. Assign an activity from Chapter 10 of the *Student Activity Workbook*.

Close

Discuss with students the major differences between corporate bonds and government bonds.

Section 10.2

Focus

Motivation

Ask the students if any of them have ever received bonds as gifts. If so, ask if they thought these were good gifts when they received them. Ask those who say "no" if they think differently now.

Prereading

1. Have students skim the section, looking at the pictures, reading the captions, and reading the headings.
2. Ask a student to read aloud Read to Learn and Main Idea on page 319.

Teach

Guided Practice

1. Read aloud to students the paragraph under Determining Investment Value on page 319.
2. Ask students to read aloud Bond Price Quotations on page 319, and discuss it briefly with them.
3. Have students silently read the rest of the section, noting and mentally answering the Predict, Relate, Question, and caption questions and reading the features such as Document Detective.

Independent Practice

Ask the students to research in annual reports, newspapers, and business magazines to determine which source offers the best information or which sources combined will give complete information to bond buyers and sellers.

Assess

Reteaching

1. Have the students close their books, and ask for volunteers to explain bond rating. Ask if corporate bonds and government bonds are rated the same way.
2. Discuss with students the Reading Strategies and the pictures and figures with their caption questions. Assign features questions to students and go over responses.

Enrichment

Take the class on a field trip to a bank, and have a bank officer demonstrate how to purchase Treasury bills, notes, and bonds.

Assessment

1. Have students complete the Section 10.2 Assessment.
2. Assign an activity from Chapter 10 of the *Student Activity Workbook.*

Close

Ask the students to explain the advantages and disadvantages of purchasing government bonds and securities.

Section 10.3

Focus

Motivation

Ask the students if they have developed any methods for reviewing all the investment types and strategies they have learned about so far. Have them create a separate area in their notebooks where they can store single page reference guides to each type of investment they study, and allow them to begin.

Prereading

1. Have students skim the section, looking at the pictures, reading the captions, and reading the headings.
2. Ask a student to read aloud Read to Learn and Main Idea on page 326.
3. Have students make flash cards for the Key Terms in Sections 10.2 and 10.3.

Teach

Guided Practice

1. Read aloud to students Defining Mutual Funds on page 326 and have the students begin a page in their notebooks for a reference section.
2. Ask students to read aloud Why Investors Buy Mutual Funds on pages 326–327 and discuss it briefly with them.
3. Have students silently read the rest of the section, noting and mentally answering the Predict, Relate, Question, and caption questions and reading the features such as Careers in Finance.

Independent Practice

1. Assign each student one of the categories of stock mutual funds.
2. Have students talk to a financial planner or use other research sources to find mutual funds in their categories.
3. Students are to evaluate these funds using all the evaluation techniques they have learned. Have them write up their results.

Assess

Reteaching

1. Have the students work with partners to learn the Key Terms using their flash cards.
2. Ask students to close their books and try to come up with the categories of bond mutual funds. If they can not name them, have students study for a few minutes, then close their books and try again.
3. Discuss with students the Reading Strategies and the pictures and figures with their caption questions. Assign features questions to students and go over responses.

Enrichment

Ask students contact a stockbroker, and then discuss the differences between stock and bond mutual funds.

Assessment

1. Have students complete the Section 10.3 Assessment.
2. Give students a vocabulary quiz based on the Key Terms.
3. Assign an activity from Chapter 10 of the *Student Activity Workbook*.

Close

Prepare in advance two word problems requiring students to compute net asset value. Have two student volunteers come to the board and work the problems, and then explain to the class how they solved them.

Section 10.4

Focus

Motivation

Tell students to name situations in which it is important to make informed decisions, and list them on the board. (Examples include: voting, buying a car, and choosing a college.) Ask them what they think are the components of informed decision making.

Prereading

1. Have students skim the section, looking at the pictures, reading the captions, and reading the headings.
2. Ask a student to read aloud Read to Learn on page 335.
3. Have students add the Key Term to their list of Key Terms in their notebooks.

Teach

Guided Practice

1. Read aloud to the students the introductory paragraph under Making an Informed Decision (page 335).
2. Ask students to read aloud Considering Your Financial Goals on page 335 and discuss it briefly with them.
3. Have students silently read the rest of the section, noting and mentally answering the Predict, Relate, Question, React, and caption questions.

Independent Practice

1. Bring to class a number of various mutual fund prospectuses. Provide each student (or group of students) with a mutual fund prospectus.
2. Ask students to locate in the prospectus each of the ten items listed on page 337; if the information is not in the prospectus, then the students should use other research resources to find it.
3. Students are to research any other information that would help them make an informed decision on whether or not to invest in this mutual fund.
4. Have students evaluate the mutual fund based on its prospectus and the additional information they have researched. Ultimately, the students are to decide whether they would invest in their mutual fund.

Assess

Reteaching

1. Ask students what they think are the most important aspects of this section and why.
2. Discuss with students the Reading Strategies and the pictures and figures with their caption questions. Assign features questions to students and go over responses

Enrichment

Invite a tax attorney to speak to the class to explain tax laws as they relate to mutual funds.

Assessment

1. Have students complete the Section 10.4 Assessment.
2. Assign Chapter 10 Review and Activities.
3. Administer the test for Chapter 10 from the Reproducible Tests in the *Lesson Planner Plus* supplement.

Close

Discuss with students whether they now feel better qualified to make wise decisions concerning investing in mutual funds.

ANSWERS

Academic Connection

Accept all reasonable answers that demonstrate research and an understanding of the history and duties of the bureau.

Document Detective

1. She had 721.273 shares at the beginning of the period.
2. The *Shares This Transaction* amount is calculated by dividing the dollar amount deposited in the account by the share price.
3. The value of the mutual fund changes each day depending on the value of the stocks and bonds the fund holds.
4. The ending value is calculated by multiplying the ending share price by the ending share balance.
5. Tanya's account grew by $430.35.

Teacher Manual

Careers in Finance

Answers may include insurance companies, manufacturing companies—virtually all companies that want to optimize their investment strategies and pension and benefit plans.

STANDARD & POOR'S Put on Your Financial Planner's Cap

Students should note that the type of mutual fund recommended depends on a client's investment objectives: how much money is needed, the time frame, and the level of risk.

STANDARD & POOR'S Global Financial Landscape

Brazilian stocks may be included in growth funds, international funds, and global stock funds. The country's changing political climate and the fact that some of these investments may be overvalued make investing in Brazilian stocks risky.

Section 10.1 Assessment

Quick Check

1. interest rate, maturity date, and face value
2. A company might issue corporate bonds in order to finance regular business activities; raise money at a time when it is difficult or impossible to sell stock; and reduce the taxes it must pay.
3. Investors buy corporate bonds because many are safe investments; bonds may help diversify an investment portfolio; most bonds provide interest income; bonds may increase in value; and face value of a bond is repaid at maturity.

Think Critically

4. Like corporate bonds, municipal bonds pay for ongoing activities and special projects. They pay interest to the bondholder. They are redeemed at the maturity date. They may be callable. You can hold them until the maturity date or sell them to another investor.

Use Communication Skills

5. Answers will vary depending on the types of bond chosen. Students should describe characteristics of the bonds. Reasons to add bonds to investment portfolios include they are safer investments than stocks, provide interest income, and may increase in value.

Solve Money Problems

6. Accept all reasonable answers. Students who answer "yes" may say that government bonds are almost risk-free and buying them will help to improve Marie's quality of life. Those who answer "no" may say that other investments may provide more growth.

Section 10.2 Assessment

Quick Check

1. Newspaper bond sections report the price of a bond as a percentage of its face value, the interest rate, and yield. They also report maturity dates for government bonds.
2. Information related to the financial stability of the company is important to investors. Students may list any of the following: detailed financial information about the company; descriptions of its products, services, and activities; information about the company's goals and plans; news about the company's position in its industry and major trends affecting the company and the industry.
3. You could use the Internet to research bonds and the companies that issue them, to track your bond investments, and to buy or sell bonds.

Think Critically

4. Moody's Investors Services, Inc. (*Moody's Bond Survey*) and Standard & Poor's Corporation (*Standard & Poor's Stock and Bond Guide*) are two sources of bond ratings. A bond rating will give you a good idea of the quality and risk of a bond.

Use Math Skills

5. The actual market price of the bond is \$980. [ANSWER: \$1,000 × 98% = \$980]

Solve Money Problems

6. The current yield on each of the AT&T bonds is approximately 7.7 percent. [ANSWER: \$1,000 × 7% = \$70; \$70 ÷ \$910 = 7.69%] The current yield on the Coca-Cola bond is 8.3 percent. [ANSWER: \$1,000 × 8.5% = \$85; \$85 ÷ \$1,020 = 8.3%]

Section 10.3 Assessment

Quick Check

1. A closed-end fund is a mutual fund with a fixed number of shares issued by an investment company when the fund is first organized. After all the original shares have been sold, an investor can buy shares only from another investor.

2. An open-end mutual fund features an unlimited number of shares that are issued and redeemed by an investment company at the investors' request.

3. Answers might include insured municipal bond funds, long-term corporate bond funds, and short-term U.S. bond funds.

Think Critically

4. Answers will vary but should reflect an understanding of the categories of stock mutual funds and bond mutual funds.

Use Math Skills

5. The load that Noah must pay to invest in this mutual fund is \$85. [ANSWER: \$1,000 × 8.5% = \$85] Students should advise Noah to look for a no-load fund because no-load funds have the same advantages as load funds but do not charge a fee.

Solve Money Problems

6. Ana's advice best addresses Hilda's concerns. Utility funds and money-market funds are considered safe and secure investments. The aggressive growth funds and high-yield (junk) bond funds that Jack recommends are risky investments.

Section 10.4 Assessment

Quick Check

1. A mutual fund quotation provides information about a fund's net asset value, objective, performance, and cost.

2. income dividends, capital gain distributions, and capital gains

3. If you have at least \$5,000 worth of shares in a mutual fund, most funds offer you four ways of withdrawing money: 1) investment period withdrawal, in which you withdraw a certain amount each investment period; 2) investment period liquidation, in which you liquidate a certain number of shares each investment period; 3) asset growth withdrawal, in which you withdraw a prearranged percentage of your investment's asset growth; and 4) dividend and distribution withdrawal, in which you withdraw all income from dividends and capital gains.

Think Critically

4. Answers will vary but should discuss one of three sources: newspaper mutual fund quotations, financial magazines, or the Internet. Students' answers should reflect a clear understanding of the type of information provided by the source selected and how that information would be helpful in finding a mutual fund that fits the students' needs.

Use Communication Skills

5. Flyers will vary but should address investor questions such as: What is the fund's past performance? What are the objectives of the fund? What has been the professional manager's past performance? How is the fund diversified?

Solve Money Problems

6. Students might advise Malia to avoid the contractual savings plan because she will pay penalty fees if she does not make the required purchases.

Chapter 10 Review & Activities

Communicating Key Terms

Student answers should demonstrate an understanding of the Key Terms used and the concepts that retirees usually need a steady flow of income and tend to be more risk-averse than younger people because they have less time to recover from financial setbacks. Bonds will provide a flow of income, plus portfolio diversification reduces risk.

Reviewing Key Concepts

1. The call feature on bonds allows a corporation to buy back bonds from bondholders before the maturity date. Corporations use this feature to pay off high-interest rate bonds early if interest rates fall.
2. Corporations sell bonds to raise money when it is difficult to sell stock. They also may prefer to issue bonds because interest payments are tax deductible, while dividend payments are not.
3. The market value of a bond is based on its interest rate compared with overall interest rates. It also reflects the financial condition of the company that issued it. The following formula is used to determine the market value of a bond: Dollar Amount of Annual Interest ÷ Interest Rate of Comparable New Corporate Bonds = Approximate Market Value.
4. States and municipalities may issue bonds to pay for new schools, roads, airports, bridges, emergency communications systems, and so on.
5. A general obligation municipal bond is backed by the full faith and credit of the government issuing it. A revenue municipal bond is repaid with the income generated by the project it is financing. An insured municipal bond is guaranteed by the government that issues it. Interest on municipal bonds is often not taxable.
6. Bonds are rated by independent companies, such as Moody's Investors Service, Inc. These ratings tell investors how secure their investments are and how likely they are to receive interest and principal repayment. Depending on your risk tolerance and level of return you want, you will choose bonds ranging from "junk" to high-grade investment quality.
7. A closed-end fund has a fixed number of shares; an open-end fund has an unlimited number of shares; a load fund requires that a commission be paid every time shares are purchased, with the supposed advantage of sales advice; no-load mutual funds involve no commissions.
8. A mutual fund prospectus is available from the company managing the fund. The prospectus contains all the information about the fund, its objective, its fees, its investments, management, and historical returns.
9. Closed-end funds can be purchased through a stock exchange or in the over-the-counter market. Open-end funds can be purchased from a brokerage firm or by contacting the investment company that sponsors the fund. Purchasing through a brokerage firm is more convenient because it allows you make all your transactions through a single source, and you receive one statement.

ACADEMIC SKILLS

Student essays should reflect research on the history of mutual funds. Answers may include: Mutual funds are popular today because you do not need a large amount of money to start investing in them; they are professionally managed; and risk is reduced because the funds are invested in many different stocks or bonds.

YOUR FINANCIAL FIGURES

1. (a) Annual Interest Income ÷ Current Yield = Current Market Value
   $(0.075 \times \$1000) \div 0.052 = \$1,442.31$
   (b) Total investment value = $\$1,442.31 \times 12 = \$17,307.69$
   (c) Students may answer that the best course of action may be to hold the bonds or to sell them on the secondary market as they are selling at a high price.
2. Student spreadsheets should show the above calculations.

REAL-WORLD Application

Answers will vary but should indicate students' understanding of the need to have readily accessible funds (emergency funds) and longer-term investments. Because credit card interest rates are very high (18% to 24%), it probably would be wise to use the money to pay that down—and commit to avoid using them in the future.

Internet CONNECTION

Answers will vary but should indicate students' understanding of risk and that there is an inverse relationship between risk and return.

BusinessWeek ONLINE

Accept all paragraphs that demonstrate students have read the online article and understand the concepts. Students should show the reasoning behind their investment advice.

CHAPTER 11 Real Estate and Other Investments

pages 350–373

SECTION	LEARNING OBJECTIVES	FEATURES	TEXT RESOURCES	TECHNOLOGY RESOURCES
11.1	**After completing this section, students will have learned to:** Explain the different types of real estate investments. Discuss the advantages and disadvantages of real estate investments.	**Savvy Saver,** p. 354 **Document Detective,** p. 356 **WebQuest,** p. 358 **Careers in Finance,** p. 359	**Section Assessment,** p. 360 Quick Check Think Critically Use Communication Skills Solve Money Problems **Student Activity Workbook**	Lesson Planner Plus Online Learning Center Interactive Student Edition *Presentation Plus!* **Exam***View*® Pro Test Generator Financial Planner Software
11.2	**After completing this section, students will have learned to:** Identify the different types of precious metal and gem investments. Describe collectibles investments. Analyze the risks of investing in precious metals, gems, and collectibles.	**TechByte,** p. 363 **Academic Connection,** p. 364 **S&P's Global Financial Landscape,** p. 365 **S&P's Put on Your Financial Planner's Cap,** p. 366 **Common Cents,** p. 367	**Section Assessment,** p. 369 Quick Check Think Critically Use Math Skills Solve Money Problems **Student Activity Workbook**	Lesson Planner Plus Online Learning Center Interactive Student Edition *Presentation Plus!* **Exam***View*® Pro Test Generator Financial Planner Software

Meeting National Standards for Business Education	
Section 11.1	**Section 11.2**
Economics I. Allocation of Resources II. Economic Systems III. Economic Institutions and Incentives IV. Markets and Prices VII. The Role of Government **Personal Finance** I. Personal Decision Making II. Earning a Living IV. Saving and Investing V. Buying Goods and Services VIII. Protecting Against Risk	**Economics** I. Allocation of Resources II. Economic Systems III. Economic Institutions and Incentives IV. Markets and Prices VII. The Role of Government **Personal Finance** I. Personal Decision Making II. Earning a Living IV. Saving and Investing V. Buying Goods and Services VI. Banking

Teaching Connection

Show and Tell

To introduce the concept of collectibles, ask students if any of them own collections of special items, such as sports cards, dolls, vinyl records, or any other collectibles. Ask them if they would like to bring an item or two or photos of the collection to class and explain why they enjoy collecting and why some people think the items are valuable. After collections are shown in class, ask students if they think they will become more valuable in 25 years. Also ask students if they can think of any contemporary items that might become collectibles in the future.

Visual Guide

Chapter 11 Opener

Discussion: Have students study the chapter opening photo and describe what they see. Then lead a discussion about investments in collectibles, such as old records, antiques, and dolls.

Follow-Up: Ask students whether they have collections that may be valuable some day. What do they collect? Do they think investing in real estate is a better choice?

Workplace Skills and Chapter Correlations

FOUNDATION SKILLS

Basic Skills	Reading	Writing	Math	Listening	Speaking	
Thinking Skills	Creative Thinking	Decision Making	Problem Solving	Seeing Things in the Mind's Eye	Knowing How to Learn	Reasoning
Personal Qualities	Responsibility	Self-Esteem	Sociability	Self-Management	Integrity/ Honesty	

WORKPLACE COMPETENCIES

Resources	Allocating Time	Allocating Money	Allocating Material and Facility Resources	Allocating Human Resources		
Information	Acquiring and Evaluating Information	Organizing and Maintaining Information	Interpreting and Communicating Information	Using Computers to Process Information		
Interpersonal Skills	Participating as a Member of a Team	Teaching Others	Serving Clients/ Customers	Exercising Leadership	Negotiating to Arrive at a Decision	Working with Cultural Diversity
Systems	Understanding Systems	Monitoring and Correcting Performance	Improving and Designing Systems			
Technology	Selecting Technology	Applying Technology to Task	Maintaining and TroubleshootingTechnology			

Internet Extension

Activity: Have students use the Internet to research the price of a home in your area. Allow them to present the price of the home and its features to the class.

Keywords: real estate, home price, etc. Searches can be conducted through a local newspaper with online classifieds, by using the name of a real estate agency that sells property in your area, or by using Web sites such as **buyowner.com** or **realtor.com**.

Enrichment/Application Activity

Guest Speaker: Invite an auctioneer to class to talk about the antiques, collectibles, and property he or she has sold during his or her career. Ask the auctioneer to discuss what makes things valuable and how auctions work.

Topic Spotlight

Government: Discuss why interest charges on mortgages and property taxes are deductions on income taxes. Explain that the federal government uses deductions on income tax as incentives to buy homes.

Ethics: Ask students how collectors know they are buying from reputable dealers. How can collectors find out who is reputable and who is not?

Money: Have students calculate the following: Josephine owns a rental house. She makes mortgage payments of $600 per month, which include insurance, and pays $1,800 per year in property taxes and maintenance. Utilities are paid by the renter. How much should Josephine charge for monthly rent to cover her costs? To earn $1,000 profit each year? [ANSWER: $750 per month ($1,800 ÷ 12 = $150; $600 + $150 = $750); $833.33 per month ($1,000 ÷ 12 = $83.33; $750 + $83.33 = $833.33)]

Additional Resources

Books

The Beginner's Guide to Real Estate Investing by Gary W. Eldred (paperback: Wiley, ©2004). This guide presents case studies of people who used the simple strategies outlined in this book to earn big returns. This practical guide also shows you how to find below-market deals; how to invest using little or none of your own cash; use low or no down payment seller financing; and flip properties for fast profit.

Collectibles Price Guide 2005 by Judith Miller (paperback: DK Publishing, ©2004). This includes information on more than 5,000 collectibles—from Native American artifacts and folk art to familiar and collectible items such as Depression glass and decoy ducks. This guide is handy for shopping at a local thrift shop, at a garage sale, or on the Internet.

Internet

realestatepromo.com This site is a real estate resource center for investors. It provides resources for real estate products, services, and a place to find local real estate investment clubs.

nareit.com This is the Web site for the National Association of Real Estate Investment Trusts, which offers information on topics such as how to invest in REITs, government relations, research and statistics, and tax-reporting information.

ebay.com and **icollector.com** These are two popular auction Web sites. On eBay, the Internet's most successful auction Web site, a collector can buy or sell everything from cars to books. Icollector is home to more than 200 auction houses, dealers, and galleries.

gia.org This Web site of the Gemological Institute of America offers a wealth of information on gems. Topics include GIA education, gem trade laboratory, gems and gemology, and how to buy a diamond.

Note: Web-site addresses may change.

Section 11.1

Focus

Motivation

Remind students of all the expenses homeowners have to pay: mortgages, insurance, taxes, and repair and maintenance expenses. Point out that owners of other properties—apartment buildings, office buildings, and industrial properties—have the same basic expenses. Ask students, then, why they think real estate investments are so popular.

Prereading

1. Have students skim the section, looking at the pictures, reading the captions, and reading the headings.
2. Ask a student to read aloud Read to Learn on page 352.
3. Have students list the Key Terms in their notebooks, and remind them to enter the definitions as they learn them.

Teach

Guided Practice

1. Ask students to read aloud In the Real World on page 351 and ask them to discuss why collectibles are risky investments.
2. Ask students to read aloud Ask Standard and Poor's on page 351, and discuss it briefly with them.
3. Have students silently read the rest of the section, noting and mentally answering the Predict, Relate, Question, and caption questions and reading the features such as Document Detective.

Independent Practice

Ask students to research the median home price in 1950, 1960, 1970, 1980, 1990, and 2000 and create graphs of the changes. Ask them also to research the inflation rates in those years and determine if buying a home was a good investment in each year.

Assess

Reteaching

1. Have the students write sentences using each term in the Key Terms list.
2. Divide the class in half, and ask them to debate the pros and cons of real estate investments.
3. Discuss with students the Reading Strategies and the pictures and figures with their caption questions. Assign features questions to students and go over responses.

Enrichment

Invite a financial expert who specializes in real estate investment to discuss with the students direct and indirect real estate investments. Have students prepare questions.

Assessment

1. Have students complete the Section 11.1 Assessment.
2. Give students a vocabulary quiz based on the Key Terms.
3. Assign an activity from Chapter 11 of the *Student Activity Workbook.*

Close

Invite a commercial property manager to class to talk about this career option.

Section 11.2

Focus

Motivation

Ask students: "What might be some risk factors involved in investing in precious metals or gems?"

Teacher Manual

Prereading

1. Have students skim the section, looking at the pictures, reading the captions, and reading the headings.
2. Ask a student to read aloud Read to Learn on page 361.
3. Write the three terms *precious metals, precious gems,* and *collectibles* on the board, and have students brainstorm examples of each term.

Teach

Guided Practice

1. Ask students to read aloud the section titled Gold on page 361, and ask them if such an investment appeals to them and why.
2. Ask students to read aloud Silver, Platinum, Palladium, and Rhodium on pages 361–363. Ask them what they know about palladium or rhodium before.
3. Have students silently read the rest of the section, noting and mentally answering the Predict, Relate, Question, React, and caption questions and reading the features such as Global Financial Landscape.

Independent Practice

Have the students select a collectible and research how much it is currently selling for online and how much it sold for a year ago. Ask students whether they think this collectible would be a good investment.

Assess

Reteaching

1. Ask students what they think are the most important aspects of this section and why.
2. Ask students to compare the investments in this section to other investments they have studied and start thinking about which investments appeal to them.
3. Discuss with students the Reading Strategies and the pictures and figures with their caption questions. Assign features questions to students and go over responses.

Enrichment

Invite a jeweler to class to discuss how gems are guarded, cut, and priced.

Assessment

1. Have students complete the Section 11.2 Assessment.
2. Assign Chapter 11 Review and Activities.
3. Administer the test for Chapter 11 from the Reproducible Tests in the *Lesson Planner Plus* supplement.

Close

Ask the students to write a paragraph explaining why it is important to understand both the risks and rewards of investing in precious metals, gems, and collectibles.

ANSWERS

Document Detective

1. 30-05655
2. 2,251 sq. ft.
3. Colonial frame
4. $1,330
5. 20,000 sq. ft. This was calculated by multiplying 100 ft. by 200 ft. as listed in the land description.

Careers in Finance

A commercial property manager can increase the value of a property by making improvements, making the property desirable to tenants and thereby driving up demand. A property manager can decrease the value of a property by failing to maintain or improve it.

Academic Connection

Student maps should identify the places where these metals and gems are mined and include an accurate color key.

STANDARD &POOR'S Global Financial Landscape

Students' answers will differ but should include the students' reasoning.

STANDARD &POOR'S Put on Your Financial Planner's Cap

Student answers will differ: Some may suggest that they divide their investment amount between precious metals, which is a relatively high-risk investment, and real estate, which is a safer investment.

Section 11.1 Assessment

Quick Check

1. Direct real estate investments include single-family houses, duplexes, apartments, land, and commercial property. Indirect real estate investments include real estate syndicates or limited partnerships, real estate investment trusts (REITs), high-risk mortgages, and participation certificates.
2. a hedge against inflation, easy entry, possible profit, limited financial liability, and possible financial leverage
3. Disadvantages of direct and indirect real estate investment include real estate's illiquidity, declining property values, lack of diversification, lack of a tax shelter, and management problems.

Think Critically

4. The similarity is that groups of people combine their money to make real estate investments. Differences include: In a limited partnership, a general partner forms the partnership and sells shares to other investors. Liability is amount invested. Shares in REITs are traded on stock exchanges or in the over-the-counter market. The federal government regulates REITs, unlike limited partnerships. Investors purchase participation certificates from government agencies. PCs are risk-free, guaranteed by agencies with close ties to the federal or state governments.

Use Communication Skills

5. Advertisements will vary but should stress the limited financial commitment and the guaranteed nature of the investment.

Solve Money Problems

6. Advice will vary, but students may suggest indirect investments, such as syndicates, REITs, and participation certificates.

Section 11.2 Assessment

Quick Check

1. Precious metals can lose value when the political situation, international relations, and the economy are stable. Whether your investment increases in value depends upon your making the correct predictions of market behavior.
2. Gems appeal to investors because of their small size, ease of storage, great durability, and potential as protection against inflation.
3. Buying an item on the Internet does not allow you to deal with a person face-to-face or examine the item for flaws. The possibility of fraud is a danger.

Think Critically

4. The value of diamonds generally rises during periods of inflation and political unrest, especially in diamond-producing countries. Prices fall during times of economic prosperity and stability.

Use Math Skills

5. Raul sold 25 ounces of gold at $800 an ounce in 1980; his profit was $19,125. [ANSWER: $800 − $35 = $765 × 25 = $19,125]

He sold 25 ounces in 1982; his profit was \$9,125. [ANSWER: \$400 − \$35 = \$365 × 25 = \$9,125] If he had sold all his gold in 1980, his profit would have been \$38,250. [ANSWER: \$765 × 50 = \$38,250]

Solve Money Problems

6. Answers may include: Samantha should have the stones evaluated by an independent geological laboratory to determine their worth. If the stones are very valuable, she might sell them and invest the money in a financial instrument that pays interest or dividends. If the stones have historical value, Samantha should hold on to them, as they are likely to increase in value. If the stones are of minimal financial but great sentimental value, she could have them reset and wear them.

Chapter 11 Review & Activities

Communicating Key Terms

Answers should indicate students' understanding of the meanings of the terms used and the concept of the variability of collectibles' value.

Reviewing Key Concepts

1. Student answers may include: with direct real estate investments, you hold the title and are responsible for the property. With indirect investments, you may invest with a smaller amount of money, a trustee or fund manager holds the title, and your involvement is minimal.
2. Advantages of real estate investments may include: a hedge against inflation, easy entry, limited financial liability, and financial leverage. Disadvantages include: illiquidity, declining property values, lack of diversification, lack of a tax shelter, and management problems.
3. Precious metals and gems, such as gold or diamonds, have decorative, sentimental, and other qualitative values beyond financial value.
4. Collectibles include art, antiques, coins, stamps, memorabilia, rugs, and other items that appeal to collectors. Examples will vary.
5. Because the Internet does not allow the purchaser to evaluate the dealer face to face or closely examine the item for sale, it is difficult to determine whether you will actually receive what the seller says he or she is selling. There is great potential for fraud.

ACADEMIC SKILLS

Answers will differ but should demonstrate students' understanding that the jewelry's value fluctuates widely, so its sale may not be as profitable as the parents may expect.

YOUR FINANCIAL FIGURES

1. (a) Answers will depend on the mutual fund selected and the current value of gold. (b) Students should use current bank interest rates.
2. Students should show their calculations using the software described.

REAL-WORLD Application

Positives include: tax advantages, tax deductions, greater control, and growth of equity. Negatives relate to lifestyle and time and expense involved in manteinance.

Internet CONNECTION

Answers will vary depending on the area selected but should demonstrate that students have read stories online and done research.

BusinessWeek ONLINE

Accept all paragraphs that demonstrate students have read the online article and understand the concepts.

Protecting Your Finances

Chapter 12
Planning Your Tax Strategy

Chapter 13
Home and Motor Vehicle Insurance

Chapter 14
Health, Disability, and Life Insurance

Chapter 15
Retirement and Estate Planning

Unit Overview

This unit introduces students to basic information about protecting financial resources. In Chapter 12, they will learn about preparing a federal income tax return and selecting the best tax strategies for current and future financial and personal needs. Chapter 13 explains and discusses home and motor vehicle insurance, and Chapter 14 describes health, disability, and life insurance. The unit concludes with Chapter 15, which discusses protecting students' future financial resources for retirement and explains the importance of estate planning.

Introductory Activity

Divide the class into small groups and have each group brainstorm a list of their most valuable possessions. As a class, create a master list of valuable possessions on the board and discuss the list. Does it include one's health or a loved one's security? Are all the possessions material? Then have each group write and present a commercial for a product or service that protects the valuables on their lists.

Explain that this unit describes how planning and insurance products can help a person protect his or her valuable possessions. Have the students consider how the products and services advertised in their commercials are similar to or different from those presented throughout this unit.

BusinessWeek
FINANCE FILE

So What's the Plan?

Answer Accept all reasonable answers that demonstrate student effort. Answers might include having enough money to retire, live comfortably, and get the necessary medical care.

Get a Financial Life!

Making Retirement Plans

STEP A **The Process**
Make sure students have access to all the necessary materials. Explain that this unit lab will lead them to better understand how it feels to get older.

1. Suggest students think about an older person whom they admire and use that person's life as an example for thinking about their own lives when they get older. Ask students to consider why they admire this person. In what ways would they like their life to be similar and different?
2. Give students the names of the Web sites listed in the Chapter 14 Planning Guide, such as the Life and Health Insurance Foundation for Education Web site, **life-line.org** and **insweb.com.**
3. If time permits, show the 1985 movie *Cocoon*, directed by Ron Howard. Allow students to discuss the issues of the retirees in the film.
4. Invite the recreation director of a seniors' community center or assisted-living facility to discuss activities for seniors.

STEP B **Create Your Portfolio**
Evaluate students' portfolios based on whether all four steps of the process are completed, the information seems reasonably well researched, and the contents are neat and in order. Make sure the short story covers a person's basic needs, and references are cited for the long-term care insurance research. Find out if students were able to implement their activities.

STEP C **Mathematics**
If necessary, organize the class into groups of three. Evaluate the students' word problems using the following criteria:

1. Participation from all team members is evident. Each member should contribute about ten problems.
2. Each member has the opportunity to solve another member's set of problems.
3. Word problems should be understandable by most students, even if difficult to solve.

Unit Closure

Have students outline the steps they would now take to protect their most valuable possessions. Have them describe what insurance they would buy and when and how they would plan for taxes, retirement, and death.

Evaluation

Administer the Unit 4 test from the **Exam***View*® Pro Testmaker CD-ROM.

CHAPTER 12 Planning Your Tax Strategy

pages 378–409

SECTION	LEARNING OBJECTIVES	FEATURES	TEXT RESOURCES	TECHNOLOGY RESOURCES
12.1	**After completing this section, students will have learned to:** Discuss the importance of tax planning. Identify taxable income. Explain deductions and tax credits. Explain the W-4 form.	**S&P's Global Financial Landscape,** p. 382 **TechByte,** p. 383 **Academic Connection,** p. 385	**Section Assessment,** p. 388 Quick Check Think Critically Use Math Skills Solve Money Problems **Student Activity Workbook**	Lesson Planner Plus Online Learning Center Interactive Student Edition *Presentation Plus!* **Exam***View*® Pro Test Generator Financial Planner Software
12.2	**After completing this section, students will have learned to:** Describe the types of federal income tax forms.	**Careers in Finance,** p. 390 **Savvy Saver,** p. 391 **WebQuest,** p. 392 **S&P Put on Your Financial Planner's Cap,** p. 396 **Go Figure**—1040EZ Tax Due, p. 396	**Section Assessment,** p. 400 Quick Check Think Critically Use Math Skills Solve Money Problems **Student Activity Workbook**	Lesson Planner Plus Online Learning Center Interactive Student Edition *Presentation Plus!* **Exam***View*® Pro Test Generator Financial Planner Software
12.3	**After completing this section, students will have learned to:** Identify tax strategies.	**Common Cents,** p. 403 **Document Detective,** p. 404	**Section Assessment,** p. 405 Quick Check Think Critically Use Math Skills Solve Money Problems **Student Activity Workbook**	Lesson Planner Plus Online Learning Center Interactive Student Edition *Presentation Plus!* **Exam***View*® Pro Test Generator Financial Planner Software

Meeting National Standards for Business Education		
Section 12.1	**Section 12.2**	**Section 12.3**
Economics I. Allocation of Resources II. Economic Systems III. Economic Institutions and Incentives VII. The Role of Government **Personal Finance** I. Personal Decision Making II. Earning a Living	**Economics** VII. The Role of Government **Personal Finance** II. Earning a Living V. Buying Goods and Services	**Economics** I. Allocation of Resources II. Economic Systems III. Economic Institutions and Incentives VII. The Role of Government VIII. International Economic Concepts **Personal Finance** I. Personal Decision Making II. Earning a Living IV. Saving and Investing V. Buying Goods and Services

Teaching Connection

No Taxation without Representation!

Explain to students that the Boston Tea Party—which was a starting point for the American Revolution against Great Britain—occurred because people in Boston were angry at having to pay a tax on the tea they bought from Great Britain. They had no say in being taxed, even though, at the time, they viewed themselves as full citizens of Great Britain.

Ask students to make a list of what they receive in return for paying federal, state, and local taxes. Ask whether they currently have representation among the governing bodies that impose taxes. Have students share their lists in a discussion. Use this discussion as a starting point for the lesson on taxes.

Visual Guide

Chapter 12 Opener

Discussion: Have the students study the chapter opening photo and describe what they see. Then lead a discussion about how civic activities, such as parades, Fourth of July celebrations, and town fairs, are funded.

Follow-Up: Ask students to brainstorm the different types of taxes, such as federal and state income tax, sales tax, and inheritance tax. Write these on the board. Then ask: "How might you influence the amount of taxes you have to pay?"

Workplace Skills and Chapter Correlations

FOUNDATION SKILLS						
Basic Skills	Reading	Writing	Math	Listening	Speaking	
Thinking Skills	Creative Thinking	Decision Making	Problem Solving	Seeing Things in the Mind's Eye	Knowing How to Learn	Reasoning
Personal Qualities	Responsibility	Self-Esteem	Sociability	Self-Management	Integrity/ Honesty	

WORKPLACE COMPETENCIES						
Resources	Allocating Time	Allocating Money	Allocating Material and Facility Resources	Allocating Human Resources		
Information	Acquiring and Evaluating Information	Organizing and Maintaining Information	Interpreting and Communicating Information	Using Computers to Process Information		
Interpersonal Skills	Participating as a Member of a Team	Teaching Others	Serving Clients/ Customers	Exercising Leadership	Negotiating to Arrive at a Decision	Working with Cultural Diversity
Systems	Understanding Systems	Monitoring and Correcting Performance	Improving and Designing Systems			
Technology	Selecting Technology	Applying Technology to Task	Maintaining and TroubleshootingTechnology			

Internet Extension

Activity: Have students use the Internet to research the price of a home in your area. Allow them to present the price of the home and its features to the class.

Keywords: home prices, real estate. Searches can be conducted through a local newspaper with online classifieds, by using the name of a real estate agency that sells property in your area, or by using Web sites such as **buyowner.com** or **realtor.com**.

Enrichment/Application Activity

Guest Speaker: Contact your local IRS Taxpayer Assistance Center to arrange for a speaker and tax forms for students to view or fill out.

Topic Spotlight

Marketing: Ask students how they would look for someone who could give tax assistance. How and where do these professionals advertise their businesses?

Government: Tell students that some U.S. legislators and citizens want to eliminate income taxes and collect taxes solely through sales tax. Discuss whether this form of tax collection would be more or less fair.

Money: Explain to students that, in some states, sales tax is collected on used cars sold by used car dealers but not on those sold by private owners. If the sales tax in such a state were 7 percent and the price of the car $12,000, how much would be saved by purchasing the car from the private owner? [ANSWER: $12,000 × 7% or .07 = $840]

Additional Resources

Books

J.K. Lasser's Year-Round Tax Strategies 2004 by David S. DeJong, Ann Gray Jakabcin (paperback: Wiley, ©2003) A complete guide to proactive tax planning, this book includes detailed coverage of new tax legislation and IRS rules; income-reporting rules, tax deductions, and tax credits; and tax-filing and tax-planning techniques.

The Ernst & Young Tax Guide 2004 by Peter W. Bernstein (paperback: Wiley, ©2003) An annual guide from one of the big five tax and accounting firms, the guide includes coverage of new tax law changes, easy-to-use explanations and tax-saving tips; and the 50 most commonly overlooked deductions.

Internet

irs.gov The IRS Web site provides federal tax forms and tax tips. It also gives a state-by-state list of local IRS offices. These offices can be contacted for free curriculum kits for high school educators, under a program called "Understanding Taxes."

ey.com and **hrblock.com** These two sites offer tax planning suggestions and guides from Ernst & Young and H & R Block, respectively.

1040.com This site offers downloadable federal tax forms and tax tips.

taxadmin.org State tax information and forms are available through this site.

Note: Web site addresses may change.

Section 12.1

Focus

Motivation

Tell the students that the first income tax in the United States was imposed in 1864 to help finance the Civil War. Ask the students how the federal government uses the tax money it currently collects.

Prereading

1. Have students skim the section, looking at the pictures, reading the captions, and reading the headings.
2. Ask a student to read aloud Read to Learn on page 380.
3. Have students list the Key Terms in their notebooks, and remind them to enter the definitions as they learn them.

Teach

Guided Practice

1. Ask students to read aloud In the Real World on page 379, and ask them what they think the term *tax strategies* means.
2. Ask students to read aloud Ask Standard and Poor's on page 379 and discuss it briefly with them.
3. Have students silently read the rest of the section, noting and mentally answering the Predict, Relate, Question, and caption questions and reading the features such as Academic Connection.

Independent Practice

Direct students to reread the four major categories of taxes. Ask students: "Of these, what tax do all people pay? What tax do most people pay? Who pays the other taxes?" Have the students research, list, and define all the taxes payable in their state, county, and city.

Assess

Reteaching

1. Have the students form two teams for a Key Terms bee.
2. Ask students what they think are the most important aspects of this section and why.
3. Discuss with students the Reading Strategies and the pictures and figures with their caption questions. Assign features questions to students and go over responses.

Enrichment

Invite a CPA to speak to the class about their responsibilities regarding taxation.

Assessment

1. Have students complete the Section 12.1 Assessment.
2. Give students a vocabulary quiz based on the Key Terms.
3. Assign an activity from the *Student Activity Workbook.*

Close

Discuss with students why it is so important to understand taxes when setting financial goals and planning your financial future.

Section 12.2

Focus

Motivation

Ask the students if they would like to pay the absolute maximum to the government in taxes. Undoubtedly, none of them will say "yes." Then ask them how much they know about filing their tax returns. Discuss with them the idea that, if they are ignorant about how to file taxes, they might overpay.

Prereading

1. Have students skim the section, looking at the pictures, reading the captions, and reading the headings.
2. Ask a student to read aloud Read to Learn and Main Idea on page 389.
3. Ask the students what they think is the purpose for studying this section.

Teach

Guided Practice

1. Read aloud to the students the section The W-2 Form on page 389.
2. Ask students to read aloud Understanding the Federal Income Tax Return on page 389 through the section Who Must File, and discuss it briefly with them.
3. Have students silently read the rest of the section, noting and mentally answering the Predict, Relate, Question, and caption questions and reading the features such as Careers in Finance.

Independent Practice

1. Have students imagine themselves 15 years from now: Are they married? Do they have children? What are their careers, and how much do they earn? Do they own homes, property, investments? Students should write down the details as they imagine them.
2. Next, have students write reports detailing the information they would need to gather to prepare their taxes.

Assess

Reteaching

1. Have students close their books, and then ask them to name the five tax-filing status categories.
2. Ask students to look at Figure 12.4 and judge how much of it they understand after studying this section.
3. Discuss with students the Reading Strategies and the pictures and figures with their caption questions. Assign features questions to students and go over responses.

Enrichment

Have students write a paragraph explaining specifically how and where they will file, store, and keep track of the information they will need to file tax returns.

Assessment

1. Have students complete the Section 12.2 Assessment.
2. Assign an activity from the *Student Activity Workbook*.

Close

Ask the students how many of them are considering careers as tax accountants, and discuss what they will need to learn.

Section 12.3

Focus

Motivation

Ask the students if they needed help learning to drive; did they know all the rules just because they had a class? They may think preparing their own tax returns will be difficult. Tell them that, in the same way they needed help to learn to drive and got that help from qualified people, there will be help available when they do their taxes.

Prereading

1. Have students skim the section, looking at the pictures, reading the captions, and reading the headings.
2. Ask a student to read aloud Read to Learn and Main Idea on page 401.

3. Tell the students that, although there is only one Key Term listed, they should add any new or unfamiliar words to their notebook lists and be sure to learn them.

Teach

Guided Practice

1. Ask students to read aloud Tax Assistance on page 401, and make sure they understand there are many sources for assistance.
2. Ask students to read aloud Tax Audits on page 401, and discuss it briefly with them.
3. Have students silently read the rest of the section, noting and mentally answering the Predict, Relate, Question, and caption questions and reading the features such as Document Detective.

Independent Practice

Have students consider this sentence from the text: "Smart taxpayers know how to legally minimize the amount of tax they have to pay." Ask them to read the paragraph they wrote about themselves 15 years from now (Section 12.2) and, based on that, write three strategies that will help them lower their taxes.

Assess

Reteaching

1. Ask students what they think are the most important aspects of this section and why.
2. Tell students that tax laws constantly change, as will their personal financial situations. Have students write a paragraph explaining how they will keep current on changes in tax laws in order to plan their tax strategies.
3. Discuss with students the Reading Strategies and the pictures and figures with their caption questions. Assign features questions to students and go over responses.

Enrichment

Ask the students to research and describe the structure and functions of the IRS as a part of the Department of the Treasury down to its district offices.

Assessment

1. Have students complete the Section 12.3 Assessment.
2. Assign Chapter 12 Review and Activities.
3. Administer the test for Chapter 12 from the Reproducible Tests in the *Lesson Planner Plus* supplement.

Close

Discuss with students the best ways to avoid IRS audits and what to do if they are selected for an audit.

ANSWERS

STANDARD & POOR'S Global Financial Landscape

Students might answer that some people in the United States support abolishing the income tax altogether; others support replacing the current system with a flat tax. Also, replacing the current system with a religious tax would not be possible because the U.S. encompasses diverse religious beliefs.

Academic Connection

$7.81 ($125 × .0625 = $7.81)

Careers in Finance

Tax preparers need retraining because tax laws and regulations usually change every year.

Teacher Manual

Put on Your Financial Planner's Cap

Students might say "yes," if affordable, because most people do not have the time to keep up with the tax laws that might affect them.

Document Detective

1. $86,411.75
2. $5,449.80
3. $5,326.50
4. 26-8310024
5. $87,900

Section 12.1 Assessment

Quick Check

1. Effective tax planning can help to avoid having no money left after paying taxes and living expenses.
2. Your taxable income is your adjusted gross income less any allowable tax deductions and exemptions.
3. To complete a W-4 form, fill in your name and address, your Social Security number, your marital status, whether your last name differs from the name on your Social Security card, the number of allowances you are claiming, how much additional money (if any) you wish to have withheld from each paycheck, whether you are exempt from paying income tax, your signature, and the date.

Think Critically

4. A tax deduction is an expense that you are allowed to subtract from your adjusted gross income to arrive at your taxable income. A tax credit is an amount subtracted directly from the amount of taxes you owe.

Use Math Skills

5. Accept all answers that compare and contrast the different options and offer a reasonable recommendation.

Solve Money Problems

6. Because Eric will claim fewer allowances, he will have the greater amount of money withheld from his paycheck.

Section 12.2 Assessment

Quick Check

1. File if you are a citizen or resident of the United States or a U.S. citizen who resides in Puerto Rico and if your income is above a certain amount. That amount is based on your filing status and other factors, such as your age.
2. Form 1040EZ, Form 1040A, and Form 1040
3. the most current tax forms and instructions, copies of tax returns from previous years, W-2 form, and (if applicable) Form 1099-INT and Form 1099-DIV

Think Critically

4. It is advantageous to use Form 1040A if you are able to claim tax deductions and tax credits. You may use Form 1040EZ if you are single or married (filing a joint tax return), under age 65, and claiming no dependents; your income consisted of only wages, salaries, tips, and not more than $1,500 of taxable interest; your taxable income is less than $100,000; and you do not itemize deductions, claim any adjustments to income, or claim tax credits.

Use Math Skills

5. Shirley will receive a refund of $737. (taxable income = $4,609; refund = $1,200 − $463 = $737)

Solve Money Problems

6. Students should suggest that Fred needs to make sure that he has the most current tax forms and instructions; copies of his tax returns from previous years (unless he is filing for the first time); his W-2 form; and, if applicable, his Form 1099-INT and 1099-DIV.

If he needs additional forms, he can find them at post offices, libraries, banks, and the local IRS office or download them from the IRS Web site. If Fred lives in a state that has an income tax, he must file a state income tax return.

Section 12.3 Assessment

Quick Check

1. Students may name any three of the following: the IRS Web site and local IRS offices, books and personal finance magazines, tax preparation software, and tax professionals.
2. If you purchase a house, both the interest you pay on your mortgage and the real estate property taxes you pay are deductible. You can also deduct the interest on a home equity loan. Some job-related expenses may also be deductible. These include union dues, some travel and education expenses, business tools, and certain job search expenses.
3. Investments that improve your tax situation include: a house, municipal bonds, and investments that are tax deferred.

Think Critically

4. Taxpayers should check their math for accuracy, fill out all forms completely, and make sure that they are taking the appropriate type and amount of deductions. If they have a complicated tax situation, they might consult a tax professional.

Use Math Skills

5. Students playing the role of the tax professional should suggest deducting mortgage interest, interest on home equity loans, and job-related expenses. They should also mention the impact of investment and retirement planning decisions on tax liability.

Solve Money Problems

6. Action plans might include: (1) She should locate and bring all paperwork related to the tax years to be audited. (2) If a professional prepared her taxes, Felicia should ask him or her to accompany her. (3) At the audit, Felicia should remain calm and composed. She should answer all questions directly and truthfully, and not offer any unsolicited information.

Chapter 12 Review & Activities

Communicating Key Terms

Student answers should demonstrate an understanding of the terms used and reflect the material presented in the chapter.

Reviewing Key Concepts

1. All types of taxes reduce the amount of income you have available to cover your expenses and to invest for your future. When you plan your finances, you should make decisions that reduce your tax liability and remember the impact of taxes on the amount you have available.
2. Adjusted gross income is total income minus specific reductions, such as IRA contributions and student loan interest. Taxable income is the amount taxed after exemptions and deductions are subtracted from the adjusted gross income.
3. You itemize deductions when their total is greater than the standard deduction.
4. On the W-4 form, you can claim allowances that reduce the amount of money withheld from your paycheck to cover your income taxes. Allowances are based on marital status and dependents.
5. Form 1040EZ is the simplest to complete. Qualifications for using this form include income of less than $100,000 consisting of wages, salaries, tips, and $1,500 or less of taxable interest. This form does not allow you to claim such tax advantages as itemized deductions, adjustments, or tax credits. Form 1040A allows you to claim a limited number of deductions, which will reduce your taxable income. Form 1040 is an expanded form of Form 1040A; this form allows you to itemize your deductions.

6. Many retirement investments are tax deferred, that is, you do not pay taxes on this money until you start withdrawing it from the retirement account; this is how IRAs and 401(k)s are set up. Other retirement investments are tax-exempt.

ACADEMIC SKILLS

Answers should demonstrate research on the procedure used to determine U.S. income tax brackets and tax rates. The U.S. income tax is a graduated tax: People pay a higher percentage rate as their income rises through various tax brackets. Tax brackets are adjusted each year.

YOUR FINANCIAL FIGURES

1. All earnings = \$33,435 + \$486 + \$3,766 = \$37,687 − \$512 = \$37,175. Tax owed: \$37,175 × 25% or .25 = \$9,293.75. You should use Form 1040EZ because the standard deduction is probably your best bet.
2. Students should show the above calculations using an appropriate software.

REAL-WORLD Application

1. Accept all answers that demonstrate research into the estate laws of your state.
2. Accept all reasonable answers.

Internet CONNECTION

1. Checks and written receipts are needed for charitable contributions to any one charity more than \$250.
2. You have to itemize deductions—that is, use Form 1040—to receive this deduction to your taxable income.

BusinessWeek ONLINE

Accept all answers that demonstrate students have read the online article and understand the concepts.

CHAPTER 13 Home and Motor Vehicle Insurance

pages 410–441

SECTION	LEARNING OBJECTIVES	FEATURES	TEXT RESOURCES	TECHNOLOGY RESOURCES
13.1	**After completing this section, students will have learned to:** Identify types of risks and risk management methods. Explain how an insurance program can help manage risks. Describe the importance of property and liability insurance.	**Savvy Saver,** p. 416 **S&P's Put on Your Financial Planner's Cap,** p. 417	**Section Assessment,** p. 418 Quick Check Think Critically Use Communication Skills Solve Money Problems **Student Activity Workbook**	Lesson Planner Plus Online Learning Center Interactive Student Edition *Presentation Plus!* **Exam***View*® Pro Test Generator Financial Planner Software
13.2	**After completing this section, students will have learned to:** Identify the types of insurance coverage and policies available to homeowners and renters. Analyze the factors that influence the amount of coverage and cost of home insurance.	**S&P's Global Financial Landscape,** p. 423 **Academic Connection,** p. 424 **Careers in Finance,** p. 428	**Section Assessment,** p. 429 Quick Check Think Critically Use Math Skills Solve Money Problems **Student Activity Workbook**	Lesson Planner Plus Online Learning Center Interactive Student Edition *Presentation Plus!* **Exam***View*® Pro Test Generator Financial Planner Software
13.3	**After completing this section, students will have learned to:** Identify the important types of motor vehicle insurance coverage. Explain factors that affect the cost of motor vehicle insurance.	**WebQuest,** p. 432 **TechByte,** p. 433 **Document Detective,** p. 435 **Common Cents,** p. 437	**Section Assessment,** p. 437 Quick Check Think Critically Use Communication Skills Solve Money Problems **Student Activity Workbook**	Lesson Planner Plus Online Learning Center Interactive Student Edition *Presentation Plus!* **Exam***View*® Pro Test Generator Financial Planner Software

CHAPTER 13 Planning Guide

Meeting National Standards for Business Education		
Section 13.1	**Section 13.2**	**Section 13.3**
Personal Finance I. Personal Decision Making VIII. Protecting Against Risk	**Economics** I. Allocation of Resources **Personal Finance** VIII. Protecting Against Risk	**Economics** III. Economic Institutions and Incentives VIII. International Economic Concepts **Personal Finance** I. Personal Decision Making VIII. Protecting Against Risk

Teaching Connection

Minimum Coverage Discussion

Write on the board a list of major automobile insurance companies and the annual premium for standard insurance for a teen driver. This information can be obtained online or from an automobile club. In many states automobile liability insurance is required; you cannot obtain a driver's license and/or register your car unless you show proof of insurance. Ask students their opinions of this requirement. Why do they think this requirement was instituted? How does/will it affect their plans for owning cars and/or driving a family car? Why do some insurance companies offer a discount if the student has better grades?

Visual Guide

Chapter 13 Opener

Discussion: Have the students study the chapter opening photo and describe what they see. Then lead a discussion about the different costs and expenses involved with an automobile accident—for people and for cars. Ask students if they think mandatory automobile insurance is fair and necessary. Have them explain their answers.

Follow-Up: Ask students to make a list of risks that should be covered by automobile insurance. Write them on the board. Have a student copy the list, and then review the list again after studying the chapter.

Teacher Manual

Workplace Skills and Chapter Correlations

FOUNDATION SKILLS						
Basic Skills	Reading	Writing	Math	Listening	Speaking	
Thinking Skills	Creative Thinking	Decision Making	Problem Solving	Seeing Things in the Mind's Eye	Knowing How to Learn	Reasoning
Personal Qualities	Responsibility	Self-Esteem	Sociability	Self-Management	Integrity/ Honesty	

WORKPLACE COMPETENCIES						
Resources	Allocating Time	Allocating Money	Allocating Material and Facility Resources	Allocating Human Resources		
Information	Acquiring and Evaluating Information	Organizing and Maintaining Information	Interpreting and Communicating Information	Using Computers to Process Information		
Interpersonal Skills	Participating as a Member of a Team	Teaching Others	Serving Clients/ Customers	Exercising Leadership	Negotiating to Arrive at a Decision	Working with Cultural Diversity
Systems	Understanding Systems	Monitoring and Correcting Performance	Improving and Designing Systems			
Technology	Selecting Technology	Applying Technology to Task	Maintaining and TroubleshootingTechnology			

Internet Extension

Activity: Have students research the car insurance rates for a specific car. Give them an automobile make and model, a rating territory or residence area, and driver classification, and see who can find the lowest rate.

Keywords: automobile insurance rates

Enrichment/Application Activity

Guest Speaker: Invite a fire fighter from your community to talk to the class about fire safety in the home and how it can reduce the cost of homeowners insurance.

Topic Spotlight

Technology: Have students explain how technology can have an impact on the cost of homeowners insurance.

Government: Discuss the laws in your state regarding uninsured drivers and no-fault insurance.

Marketing: Have students bring to class copies of printed advertisements or written descriptions of a radio or television commercial for motor vehicle insurance. Discuss the differences in marketing techniques among different insurance companies

Additional Resources

Books

Car Insurance Secrets by Ron Alford (paperback: The Plan, ©2002) This book provides advice on how to handle a repair in the event of a car accident, ensuring the insurance company pays what the respective parties are due. Other details are included about what insurance companies do not freely reveal.

Internet

www.jumpstartcoalition.org The Jump$tart Coalition for Personal Financial Literacy (see Additional Resources in Chapter 1) lists the following free publication: *InVEST Automobile Insurance Manual for Teachers*. This manual accompanies the student workbook and provides tools to teach basic business management skills with a focus on automobile insurance.

ircweb.org The Web site for the Insurance Research Council offers current information on various insurance research studies, public policy issues, and IRC publications, as well as links to related Web sites.

insure.com This Web site provides answers to questions regarding basic information and current developments in auto and home insurance.

insweb.com Insurance rate information and quotes for a variety of insurance needs can be found at the Quicken insurance Web site. Links to over 20 major insurance companies are also provided at this site.

Note: Web-site addresses may change.

Section 13.1

Focus

Motivation

Ask the students questions about how they think insurance works: How does it benefit the insured? How does it benefit the insurers? What do they think is the purpose of insurance?

Prereading

1. Have students skim the section, looking at the pictures, reading the captions, and reading the headings.
2. Ask a student to read aloud Read to Learn on page 412.
3. Have students list the key terms in their notebooks, and ask them to make flashcards for each term as they use it.

Teach

Guided Practice

1. Ask students to read aloud In the Real World on page 411 and ask them if they can understand why it is important to have insurance.
2. Ask students to read aloud Ask Standard and Poor's on page 411 and discuss it briefly with them.
3. Have students silently read the rest of the section, noting and mentally answering the Predict, Relate, Question, and caption questions and reading the features such as Savvy Saver.

Independent Practice

Ask the students to interview their parents or other family members about their insurance coverage. They should ask them: (1) Do you have an insurance plan? How did you decide what kind of insurance to carry? (2) Do you think you have enough insurance? Too much? (3) Do your policies have deductibles? Are they too high or just right? (4) How did you decide what insurance company to use?

Assess

Reteaching

1. Have the students practice in pairs with their flashcards until they know all the Key Terms.
2. To clarify the terms *risk avoidance, risk reduction, risk assumption*, and *risk shifting*, divide the students into groups of four and have them come up with examples of the terms.
3. Discuss with students the Reading Strategies and the pictures and figures with their caption questions. Assign features questions to students and go over responses.

Enrichment

Have a representative of the Independent Insurance Agents Association (IIAA) speak to the class about the program for students called InVEST and to discuss possible careers in the insurance industry.

Assessment

1. Have students complete the Section 13.1 Assessment.
2. Give students a vocabulary quiz based on the Key Terms.
3. Assign an activity from Chapter 13 of the *Student Activity Workbook*.

Close

Discuss with the students what the following people in the insurance industry actually do: sales agents, underwriters, actuaries, and marketing specialists.

Section 13.2

Focus

Motivation

Have the students imagine themselves as homeowners. Ask them what risks they think homeowners might have that require insurance.

Prereading

1. Have students skim the section, looking at the pictures, reading the captions, and reading the headings.
2. Ask a student to read aloud Read to Learn and Main Idea on page 419.
3. Have students list the key terms in their notebooks, and remind them to enter the definitions as they learn them.

Teach

Guided Practice

1. Ask students to read aloud the paragraph under Homeowners Insurance Coverage on page 419 and go over the bulleted list with them, clarifying terms as necessary.
2. Ask students to read aloud Buildings and Other Structures and Additional Living Expenses on page 419 and discuss those paragraphs briefly with them.
3. Have students silently read the rest of the section, noting and mentally answering the Predict, Relate, Question, and caption questions and reading the features such as Global Financial Landscape.

Independent Practice

1. Divide the students into groups of four, and have each group prepare a list of things that could damage a home and/or cause financial loss.
2. Have the groups verify that the items on their lists would be covered by homeowners insurance.
3. The groups should prepare a poster or other graphic, using the items on the list, demonstrating why homeowners insurance is so vital.

Assess

Reteaching

1. Have the students write sentences using each term in the Key Terms list.
2. To demonstrate why personal property is such a major portion of homeowners insurance, have students take an inventory of just their personal possessions and assign dollar values to the listed items.
3. Discuss with students the Reading Strategies and the pictures and figures with their caption questions. Assign features questions to students and go over responses.

Enrichment

Invite an appraiser to class to speak to the students about how appraisals are done. Encourage the students to ask questions.

Assessment

1. Have students complete the Section 13.2 Assessment.
2. Give students a vocabulary quiz based on the Key Terms.
3. Assign an activity from Chapter 13 of the *Student Activity Workbook.*

Close

Tell the students about FEMA, the Federal Emergency Management Agency, and the assistance they provide for natural disaster relief.

Section 13.3

Focus

Motivation

Ask students how many of them have ever been involved in any type of motor vehicle accident. Then say that those who have will understand the importance of having vehicle insurance. Emphasize that, although insurance cannot prevent accidents or damage, it can alleviate the problems accidents can cause, including medical bills and vehicle repair bills.

Prereading

1. Have students skim the section, looking at the pictures, reading the captions, and reading the headings.
2. Ask a student to read aloud Read to Learn and Main Idea on page 430.
3. Have students list the key terms in their notebooks, and remind them to enter the definitions as they learn them.

Teach

Guided Practice

1. Ask students to read aloud the introductory paragraphs under Motor Vehicle Insurance on page 430. Have them explain why they think states require people to carry motor vehicle insurance, and if they think that requirement is a good idea and why or why not.
2. Have students silently read the rest of the section, noting and mentally answering the Predict, Relate, Question, and caption questions and reading the features such as Document Detective.

Independent Practice

Take the students on a field trip to an auto body repair shop, and ask the owner to give them a tour, telling about the accidents that created the damage. At the same time, have the owner detail the costs of repairs.

Assess

Reteaching

1. Have the students write sentences using each term in the Key Terms list.
2. Have the students create a chart with two columns: "Bodily Injury Coverage" and "Property Damage Coverage." Ask them to list the types of coverage in each category, and then to use their charts as study guides.
3. Discuss with students the Reading Strategies and the pictures and figures with their caption questions. Assign features questions to students and go over responses.

Enrichment

Have the students clip articles from the newspaper about traffic accidents and share the articles with the class. Ask: "What caused the accident? Were people injured? Do you think the accident could have been prevented? How? What do you think insurance might cover?"

Assessment

1. Have students complete the Section 13.3 Assessment.
2. Assign the Chapter 13 Review and Activities.
3. Administer the test for Chapter 13 from the Reproducible Tests in the *Lesson Planner Plus* supplement.

Close

Have your students each write a paragraph explaining why they think insurance is a necessary cost of being a vehicle owner.

ANSWERS

Put on Your Financial Planner's Cap

Answers will vary, but most students will say their cars and personal property at this time.

Global Financial Landscape

Answers will vary, but many would believe it is fair because of the higher risk of accidents and the higher repair costs.

Careers in Finance

Accidents can occur at any time, and many occur on nights, weekends, and holidays; insurance claims adjusters may have to respond quickly.

Document Detective

1. A02 0076215
2. $1,000,000
3. $20 per day with a maximum payment of $600
4. two
5. $1,411 per year

Academic Connection

Accept all reasonable answers that demonstrate student effort and an understanding of the concepts.

Section 13.1 Assessment

Quick Check

1. personal risks, property risks, and liability risks
2. When you buy an insurance policy, you shift your risk to the insurance company. In return for the fees paid by policyholders, the insurance company agrees to pay for their losses.
3. Property and liability insurance can protect a homeowner by covering damage to or loss of the homeowner's property or the property of others as well as expenses related to injuries to other people.

Think Critically

4. Students who argue in favor of insurance may say that it enables money to be available if disaster strikes. Students who argue against insurance may say that the cost is too high and that they can protect themselves against many forms of risk.

Use Communication Skills

5. Accept all responses that demonstrate an understanding that having insurance will lessen the consequences of loss or damage to property.

Solve Money Problems

6. Most students may agree that it is worth paying to protect the valuable car.

Section 13.2 Assessment

Quick Check

1. basic form (HO-1), broad form (HO-2), special form (HO-3), tenants' form (HO-4), comprehensive form (HO-5), and condominium owner's insurance (HO-6)
2. A personal property floater is additional insurance that covers the loss or damage of a specific item of high value, such as jewelry, electronic equipment, or expensive musical instruments.
3. Insurance companies charge lower rates to insure homes near fire hydrants or other water supply or located in an area with a good fire department. They charge higher rates for homes in high-crime areas or severe-weather regions.

Think Critically

4. Answers might include: A neighbor or guest slips on your driveway and is seriously injured, or a member of your family accidentally breaks an expensive glass statue while at another person's house.

Use Math Skills

5. Multiply the insured value of the house ($80,000) by the percentage of coverage (55%). [ANSWER: $80,000 × .55 = $44,000] Because the value of the lost items was $25,000, Carolina will receive payment for all of them.

Solve Money Problems

6. A house located in an area where flooding occurs will cost more to insure. In addition, an older house may be more difficult to restore to its original condition, which means that it will cost more to insure. The more economical choice, therefore, is the newer house that is located farther from the river.

Section 13.3 Assessment

Quick Check

1. The three main types of motor vehicle insurance for bodily injuries are bodily injury liability, medical payments coverage, and uninsured motorist's protection.
2. Collision insurance covers damage to your vehicle when it is involved in an accident. Comprehensive physical damage coverage protects you if your vehicle is damaged in a non-accident situation.
3. Insurance companies offer discounts for vehicles with security devices because the devices reduce the risk of theft.

Think Critically

4. Answers may include: Maintain a good driving record; get good grades in school; comparison shop; take advantage of discounts; increase your deductible; and do not smoke.

Use Communication Skills

5. Accept all presentations that demonstrate student effort and an understanding of the concepts.

Solve Money Problems

6. Depending on the insurance company, Malcolm will probably pay more for insurance because he wants a vehicle that will be costly to repair, and he has recently received a traffic ticket. Ishiro's good driving record and the type of vehicle that he wants to insure will probably make his rate lower than Malcolm's.

Chapter 13 Review & Activities

Communicating Key Terms

Accept all paragraphs that reflect an understanding of the Key Terms and chapter topics.

Reviewing Key Concepts

1. Risk is the chance of loss or injury. Perils are anything that may cause a loss. Hazards are anything that increases the possibility of a loss through a peril. The four methods of managing risk include: (1) risk avoidance, (2) risk reduction, (3) risk assumption, and (4) risk shifting.
2. By buying insurance, you transfer most of your risk to an insurance company, an example of risk shifting. The deductible you pay is an example of your assumption of part of the risk.
3. Property insurance protects your home, business property, and vehicles from damage due to natural causes and criminal behavior. It also provides you with funds to cover expenses you incur while the property is being repaired or replaced. Liability insurance protects you from claims if people are injured on or by your property. It covers your legal responsibilities.
4. Financial institutions that lend money for home mortgages require homeowners insurance because this transfers the financial institution's risk of loss if anything damages the home.
5. Actual cash value reduces the replacement value by the cost of depreciation. So, you receive only the current value of the insured property when you claim a loss.

This value is usually less than its replacement value. The replacement value is the cost of buying a new item to replace the item that was lost or damaged.

6. Advantages of no-fault insurance system include: reduced time, cost, and effort involved in settling vehicle injury cases. Disadvantages include: Even if you are not at fault and you experience injury or property damage, you will submit a claim to your insurance company. Depending on your history, these claims can result in increased premiums.
7. They require it to cover cost of car in case of loss and to protect against lawsuits for personal injury damages.

ACADEMIC SKILLS

Answers will vary, but should indicate students' understanding that driver classification is a significant factor in insurance cost because of the statistics and trends related to each classification.

YOUR FINANCIAL FIGURES

1. $555 and $2,370
2. Accept all reasonable answers.

REAL-WORLD Application

Answers will vary but should reflect students' understanding of risk in the broad sense. In other words, an individual may drive safely and never have an accident. DUI penalties are stringent as a deterrent—a way of preventing people from driving when they are impaired.

Internet CONNECTION

Answers will vary, but students may include factors such as the location of a home. Homes close to water may have flooding in their basements or may, as in California, be destroyed by mudslides. Homes in certain parts of the country can be damaged by hurricanes, tornadoes, or earthquakes. Homeowners' premiums can be reduced by avoiding flood plains.

BusinessWeek ONLINE

Accept all answers that demonstrate students have read the online article and understand the concepts.

CHAPTER 14 Health, Disability, and Life Insurance

pages 442–475

SECTION	LEARNING OBJECTIVES	FEATURES	TEXT RESOURCES	TECHNOLOGY RESOURCES
14.1	**After completing this section, students will have learned to:** Explain the importance of health insurance in financial planning. Analyze costs and benefits of various health insurance.	**Common Cents,** p. 447 **S&P's Global Financial Landscape,** p. 448 **Academic Connection,** p. 449	**Section Assessment,** p. 452 Quick Check Think Critically Use Communication Skills Solve Money Problems **Student Activity Workbook**	Lesson Planner Plus Online Learning Center Interactive Student Edition *Presentation Plus!* **Exam***View*® Pro Test Generator Financial Planner Software
14.2	**After completing this section, students will have learned to:** Differentiate between private and government health care plans.	**S&P's Put on Your Financial Cap,** p. 455 **Savvy Saver,** p. 456 **Careers in Finance,** p. 458	**Section Assessment,** p. 459 Quick Check Think Critically Use Math Skills Solve Money Problems **Student Activity Workbook**	Lesson Planner Plus Online Learning Center Interactive Student Edition *Presentation Plus!* **Exam***View*® Pro Test Generator Financial Planner Software
14.3	**After completing this section, students will have learned to:** Explain the importance of disability insurance in financial planning. Describe different sources of disability income.	**TechByte,** p. 462	**Section Assessment,** p. 471 Quick Check Think Critically Use Communication Skills Solve Money Problems **Student Activity Workbook**	Lesson Planner Plus Online Learning Center Interactive Student Edition *Presentation Plus!* **Exam***View*® Pro Test Generator Financial Planner Software
14.4	**After completing this section, students will have learned to:** Describe various types of life insurance coverage. Identify the key provisions of a life insurance policy.	**WebQuest,** p. 467 **Document Detective,** p. 469	**Section Assessment,** p. 471 Quick Check Think Critically Use Math Skills Solve Money Problems **Student Activity Workbook**	Lesson Planner Plus Online Learning Center Interactive Student Edition Presentation Plus! **Exam***View*® Pro Test Generator Financial Planner Software

Meeting National Standards for Business Education	
Section 14.1	**Section 14.2**
Economics I. Allocation of Resources II. Economic Systems **Personal Finance** I. Personal Decision Making II. Earning a Living VIII. Protecting Against Risk	**Economics** VII. The Role of Government **Personal Finance** I. Personal Decision Making V. Buying Goods and Services VIII. Protecting Against Risk
Section 14.3	**Section 14.4**
Economics VII. The Role of Government **Personal Finance** VIII. Protecting Against Risk	**Economics** III. Economic Institutions and Incentives VIII. International Economic Concepts **Personal Finance** I. Personal Decision Making III. Managing Finances and Budgeting IV. Saving and Investing VIII. Protecting Against Risk

Teaching Connection

Prereading and Writing

Before the class begins to study this chapter, ask the students to skim over the main headings in the first section of the chapter. Have them create a list, or outline, of all the paragraph headings in the section. Then ask students to write a short paragraph explaining the topics that will be covered. Have students do the same exercise for each of the remaining sections of the chapter. Then ask them to write a short paragraph describing the most important idea of the chapter.

Visual Guide

Chapter 14 Opener

Discussion: Have the students study the chapter opening photo and describe what they see. Then lead a discussion about accidents. Ask for volunteers to describe an injury accident each of them might have had. Accidents can be sports related or otherwise. Ask if they went to the doctor or hospital or had to spend money to get help.

Follow-Up: Ask students to discuss whether health insurance was a necessity under those circumstances. What would an injured person do without health insurance? What are the alternatives?

Workplace Skills and Chapter Correlations

FOUNDATION SKILLS						
Basic Skills	Reading	Writing	Math	Listening	Speaking	
Thinking Skills	Creative Thinking	Decision Making	Problem Solving	Seeing Things in the Mind's Eye	Knowing How to Learn	Reasoning
Personal Qualities	Responsibility	Self-Esteem	Sociability	Self-Management	Integrity/ Honesty	

WORKPLACE COMPETENCIES						
Resources	Allocating Time	Allocating Money	Allocating Material and Facility Resources	Allocating Human Resources		
Information	Acquiring and Evaluating Information	Organizing and Maintaining Information	Interpreting and Communicating Information	Using Computers to Process Information		
Interpersonal Skills	Participating as a Member of a Team	Teaching Others	Serving Clients/ Customers	Exercising Leadership	Negotiating to Arrive at a Decision	Working with Cultural Diversity
Systems	Understanding Systems	Monitoring and Correcting Performance	Improving and Designing Systems			
Technology	Selecting Technology	Applying Technology to Task	Maintaining and TroubleshootingTechnology			

Internet Extension

Activity: Have each student choose a health topic to research on the Internet using at least one of the Web sites given in the text. Then have them write a short report on their findings and present it to the class.

Keywords: Healthfinder, Medline, and National Institute of Health

Enrichment/Application Activity

Guest Speaker: Invite a physical therapist or occupational therapist to class to explain how physical therapy or occupational therapy helps people who have had disabling accidents. Have the speaker note the differences between the two types of therapy.

Topic Spotlight

Ethics: Ask students how they would respond to a doctor who charges more for services to someone who has physician's insurance versus someone who does not have physician's insurance.

Marketing: Discuss how hospitals in your region market their services. Ask: "Do your families prefer a particular hospital? If so, why?"

Technology: With the class, create a list of the new technologies used in health care today, such as CT scans and laser surgery. Discuss how these applied technologies might affect health care costs.

Additional Resources

Books

Insurance for Dummies by Jack Hungelmann (paperback: For Dummies, ©2001) Author Hungelmann has 25 years of experience in the insurance industry and wrote this book to make buying insurance as simple as possible. Among the most popular topics covered: managing risk, reducing liability, insuring a home business, buying an umbrella policy, dealing with insurers and filing claims, assessing your life insurance needs, and deciding between group and individual policies.

Making Them Pay: How to Get the Most from Health Insurance and Managed Care by Rhonda Orin (paperback: St. Martin's Griffin, ©2001) This consumer guide to health insurance and managed care programs explains how to read and understand a health plan and how to get all of your benefits. The book outlines the components of typical plans, the services covered, and the limits and exclusions insurance companies and managed care systems may apply to deny coverage.

Internet

life-line.org LIFE, the Life and Health Insurance Foundation for Education, offers a free educational program designed to teach young people about life, health, and disability income insurance. The Life and Health Insurance Foundation for Education Web site, provides information, such as types of insurance, choosing an agent, and needs analysis, for life, health, and disability insurance.

insurance.yahoo.com/lh/life.html This comprehensive site covers life insurance basics, cost calculators, and life insurance quotes and news.

bankrate.com/brm/insurance_home.asp?link=2 This Web site provides helpful articles, quotes, surveys, quizzes, and statistics on life, health, and auto insurance.

healthseek.com Access links to various health Web sites through this site.

ssa.gov/mediinfo.htm Information on Medicare can be found at the Social Security Administration Web site.

Note: Web addresses may change.

Section 14.1

Focus

Motivation

Tell the students that health insurance is crucial in financial planning. Ask them if they agree. Then ask why they think this is so, and then write their responses on the board.

Prereading

1. Have students skim the section, looking at the pictures, reading the captions, and reading the headings.
2. Ask a student to read aloud Read to Learn on page 444.
3. Have students list the key terms in their notebooks and remind them to enter the definitions as they learn them.

Teach

Guided Practice

1. Ask students to read aloud In the Real World on page 443 and ask them if they think the character's experience is common or uncommon. Do the students think they are immune from illnesses or accidents because they are young?
2. Ask students to read aloud Ask Standard and Poor's on page 443 and discuss briefly what good habits they can develop now.
3. Have students silently read the rest of the section, noting and mentally answering the Predict, Relate, Question, and caption questions and reading the features such as Global Financial Landscape.

Independent Practice

Have the students research two individual health insurance plans and compare them for the following: benefits, co-payments, deductibles, cost, and coverage for psychotherapy and alternative treatments, such as acupuncture. Then have them compare a group health insurance policy to the individual ones. Ask them to write up the results of their surveys, including any conclusions they may draw.

Assess

Reteaching

1. Have the students write sentences using each term in the Key Terms list.
2. Ask students what they think are the most important aspects of this section and why.
3. Discuss with students the Reading Strategies and the pictures and figures with their caption questions. Assign features questions to students and go over responses.

Enrichment

Ask the students to research the controversy surrounding the national health care issue in the United States. Tell them to be sure to look at how national coverage works in one or two other countries.

Assessment

1. Have students complete the Section 14.1 Assessment.
2. Give students a vocabulary quiz based on the Key Terms.
3. Assign an activity from Chapter 14 of the *Student Activity Workbook*.

Close

Ask your students to write a paragraph discussing how not having health insurance could affect their goals.

Section 14.2

Focus

Motivation

Ask the students if they know about any health care plans offered by the government, both federal and state. Having elicited Medicare and Medicaid, ask them if they think these programs work, if they are worth the cost to the government, and who they benefit.

Prereading

1. Have students skim the section, looking at the pictures, reading the captions, and reading the headings.
2. Ask a student to read aloud Read to Learn and Main Idea on page 453.
3. Have students list the key terms in their notebooks, and remind them to enter the definitions as they learn them.

Teach

Guided Practice

1. Ask students to read aloud the paragraphs on page 453 through Managed Care. Discuss paragraphs as they are read to ensure understanding.
2. Have students silently read the rest of the section, noting and mentally answering the Predict, Relate, Question, and caption questions and reading the features such as Careers in Finance.

Independent Practice

1. Divide the students into groups of three. Have each group research home health agencies, home-care aid organizations, and hospices in your state and one other state (assign states to avoid duplication).
2. Each group is to prepare a graphic representation that compares these agencies in the two states.
3. Each group will present their work to the class which will vote on the three best renderings. Display the three favorites on bulletin boards.

Assess

Reteaching

1. Have the students participate in a Key Terms bee.
2. Have students find a Web site providing health insurance information that will help people evaluate health care plans.
3. Discuss with students the Reading Strategies and the pictures and figures with their caption questions. Assign features questions to students and go over responses.

Enrichment

1. Have the students download a publication from the Medicare Web site (**medicare.gov**) and read it carefully.
2. Have the students write imaginary letters to elderly relatives explaining how Medicare works. Then ask them if they experienced any specific difficulties in understanding the publications they downloaded or in trying to explain to someone else.
3. Ask if they think Medicare is easy or difficult to understand.

Assessment

1. Have students complete the Section 14.2 Assessment.
2. Give students a vocabulary quiz based on the Key Terms.
3. Assign an activity from Chapter 14 of the *Student Activity Workbook.*

Close

Invite to class an insurance agent who works with HMO, PPO, and managed care health insurance plans to speak to the class and answer questions.

Section 14.3

Focus

Motivation

Have the students discuss their dreams for the future and ask if they think money is important for fulfilling those dreams. Ask how many of them expect to work to finance their dreams. Then ask them what might happen if, for some reason, they are unable to work for an extended period of time. How long do they think their emergency savings would last? What would they do after that?

Prereading

1. Have students skim the section, looking at the pictures, reading the captions, and reading the headings.
2. Ask a student to read aloud Read to Learn and Main Idea on page 460.
3. Ask the students to explain the purpose of this section in their views.

Teach

Guided Practice

1. Ask students to read aloud Disability Income on page 460 and ask them if they know anyone who has collected disability insurance or anyone with a disability who does not have that insurance. Have them share one or two stories with the class.
2. Have students silently read the rest of the section, noting and mentally answering the Predict, Relate, Question, and caption questions and reading the features such as TechByte.
3. Assign an activity from Chapter 14 of the *Student Activity Workbook.*

Independent Practice

Have the students choose two companies that offer disability insurance and find out what they cover, what kinds of disability qualify, and how much it costs. Then students are to report their findings and state conclusions they draw.

Assess

Reteaching

Discuss with students the Reading Strategies and the pictures and figures with their caption questions. Assign features questions to students and go over responses.

Enrichment

Have the students work in pairs. Ask them to select a disability that might occur through an accident or illness. Have them write a paragraph about the problems a person with this disability would encounter.

Assessment

1. Have students complete the Section 14.3 Assessment.
2. Assign an activity from Chapter 14 of the *Student Activity Workbook.*

Close

Ask students to identify the most important thing they learned in this section.

Section 14.4

Focus

Motivation

Ask the students if they think talking about life insurance is morbid (most students will say "yes"). Then ask if only old people should have life insurance and why life insurance might be important for younger people. Write their answers on the board.

Prereading

1. Have students skim the section, looking at the pictures, reading the captions, and reading the headings.
2. Ask a student to read aloud Read to Learn and Main Idea on page 464.
3. Have students list the key terms in their notebooks and remind them to enter the definitions as they learn them.

Teach

Guided Practice

1. Read aloud to students the introductory paragraph on page 464.
2. Ask students to read aloud The Purpose of Life Insurance on page 464 and discuss it briefly with them.
3. Have students silently read the rest of the section, noting and mentally answering the Predict, Relate, Question, and caption questions and reading the features such as Document Detective.

Independent Practice

Ask the students to select at least two life insurance companies that are stock companies and to track the stocks for one week. Have them answer these questions: How do the stocks compare in terms of value? Are the two (or more) stocks performing similarly or are there major differences between them?

Assess

Reteaching

1. Have the students write sentences using each term in the Key Terms list.
2. Clarify the types of term insurance and whole life policies discussed in this section. Have students note characteristics of each and use that information as a study guide.
3. Discuss with students the Reading Strategies and the pictures and figures with their caption questions. Assign features questions to students and go over responses.

Enrichment

Invite someone from an insurance company to class to explain the variety of policies available and the riders that are offered. Encourage students to ask questions.

Assessment

1. Have students complete the Section 14.4 Assessment.
2. Assign Chapter 14 Review and Activities.
3. Administer the test for Chapter 14 from the Reproducible Tests in the *Lesson Planner Plus* supplement.

Close

Ask your students to react to this statement: "Life insurance protects the standard of living of a policyholder's survivors."

ANSWERS

STANDARD &POOR'S Global Financial Landscape

Answers will vary, but one important fact is the aging of the baby-boom generation. Also, as medical technology has increased, so has the cost for treatment.

Academic Connection

Accept all reasonable answers that reflect student effort and understanding of the concept.

STANDARD &POOR'S Put on Your Financial Planner's Cap

Accept all reasonable answers that reflect student effort and understanding of the concept.

Careers in Finance

Answers might include that the more people an insurance agent meets, the more opportunities there are to make sales. Additionally, the people an agent would meet in those ways are often family people with sufficient means to effectively include insurance in their financial planning.

Document Detective

1. $502.44
2. June 23, 2003
3. $100,000
4. June 23, 2016
5. $4,260.82

Section 14.1 Assessment

Quick Check

1. Health insurance eases the financial burden people might experience as a result of illness or injury. A health insurance plan may reimburse you for hospital stays, doctors' visits, medications, and sometimes vision and dental care.
2. Hospital expense coverage pays for some or all of the daily costs of room and board during a hospital stay. Routine nursing care, minor medical supplies, and the use of other hospital facilities are covered as well. Surgical expense coverage pays all or part of the surgeon's fees for an operation. Physician expense coverage meets some or all of the costs of physician care that do not involve surgery.
3. Trade-offs include reimbursement versus indemnity, internal limits versus aggregate limits, deductibles and coinsurance, out-of-pocket limits, and benefits based on reasonable and customary charges.

Think Critically

4. Answers will vary, but students may state that limits are necessary to ensure that hospitals and doctors charge reasonable rates. The limits may discourage some individuals from seeking medical tests or treatments that they do not need.

Use Communication Skills

5. Answers will vary but may include the fact that a healthy lifestyle is no guarantee against illness, or the chance that she could experience extreme financial loss if she suffered a serious accident.

Solve Money Problems

6. Answers will vary, but students may argue that Richard should choose the third plan with the $250 deductible. It has no additional monthly premium, a reasonable lifetime limit, and a low deductible.

Section 14.2 Assessment

Quick Check

1. Blue Cross provides hospital care benefits. Blue Shield provides benefits for surgical procedures and medical services performed by physicians.
2. The premiums for PPOs are slightly higher than the premiums for HMOs. HMOs require members to receive care from HMO providers only, while PPOs allow members greater flexibility. Members can either visit a preferred provider (a physician whom you select from a list, as in an HMO) or go to their own physicians. Patients who decide to use their own doctors do not lose coverage as they would with an HMO. Instead, they must pay deductibles and larger copayments.
3. Medicare is a federally funded health insurance program available to people over 65 and to people with certain disabilities. Medicaid is a state and federally funded medical program offered to certain low-income individuals and families.

Think Critically

4. Benefits: HMOs typically cover routine immunizations and checkups, screening programs, and diagnostic tests. They also provide customers with coverage for surgery, hospitalization, and emergency care. If you have an HMO, you will usually pay a small copayment for each covered service. Drawbacks: You must receive care through your plan physician; if you do not, you are responsible for the cost of the service. The only exception to this rule is in the case of a medical emergency.

Use Math Skills

5. Rose had to pay a total of $410. [ANSWER: $850 − $300 = $550; $550 × .20 = $110; $300 + $110 = $410]. The PPO had to pay $440. [ANSWER: $550 × .80 = $440]

Solve Money Problems

6. Students might advise her to drop the HMO or switch to another because she does not like the plan. Others might point out that Medicare is not designed to cover all medical expenses, and therefore, she should keep the HMO coverage.

Section 14.3 Assessment

Quick Check

1. Disability can cause great financial problems. Disabled persons lose their earning power but still have to meet their living expenses. They often face huge costs for medical treatment and special care that their disabilities require.
2. Worker's compensation, a group insurance plan through your employer, Social Security, and private income insurance programs
3. Answers will vary but should include two of the following: Weigh the length of the elimination period against the amount of the premium; consider the duration of benefits as compared to your needs; make a trade-off between the benefit amount and the cost of the insurance; determine whether a policy that pays for accidents only is acceptable or whether you need a policy that also pays for sickness; and weigh guaranteed coverage against the higher premiums that you would pay for this coverage.

Think Critically

4. Situations might include suffering a repetitive stress injury. This could apply to people who work on an assembly line in a manufacturing plant or those who work with computers in almost any setting. Other situations might include contracting a sudden disease, forcing a person to stay in the hospital or at home, and becoming pregnant.

Use Communication Skills

5. Students should mention the possibility of an entertainer being unable to perform because of a disability and the financial dangers of becoming disabled without insurance.

Solve Money Problems

6. Answers will vary but may include: He should have a policy that pays benefits for at least seven years; he should not rely on Social Security; or he can probably choose a plan with a long elimination period because he has enough saved to get him through that period.

Section 14.4 Assessment

Quick Check

1. Most people buy life insurance to protect the people who depend upon them from financial losses caused by their death. Life insurance benefits may be used to pay off a home mortgage or other debts at time of death; provide lump-sum payments through an endowment for children when they reach a certain age; and provide education or income for children.

Benefits may also provide charitable donations after death; a retirement income; savings; a regular income for survivors; an estate plan; or estate and death tax payments.

2. Term insurance provides protection against loss of life for only a specified term, or period of time. If you stop paying the premiums, your coverage stops. If you have a renewable term policy, the premium will increase each time you renew your insurance. Whole life policies have higher annual premiums. You will pay a specified premium each year for the rest of your life. The insurance company pays your beneficiary a stated sum when you die, regardless of your age. Whole life insurance can also serve as an investment.
3. naming your beneficiary, the incontestability clause, and the suicide clause

Think Critically

4. Students who agree may say that it provides flexibility, allowing you to buy insurance coverage for the time when you most need it. Students who disagree may say that it is restrictive because it pays a benefit only if you die during the period covered by the policy. Also, the premium may increase over time, depending on the type of term insurance that you buy.

Use Math Skills

5. Students' graphs should show a line that gradually rises.

Solve Money Problems

6. Issues may include whether his sister will need help (whether his parents have provided for her through their insurance or wills); how wealthy his parents are; and how soon he can pay off the loans. He may need only a short-term policy, a decreasing term policy, or none at all.

Chapter 14 Review & Activities

Communicating Key Terms

Accept all paragraphs that reflect an understanding of the Key Terms and chapter topics.

Reviewing Key Concepts

1. A copayment is a flat fee, usually between $5 and $25, paid each time healthcare services are provided. Coinsurance is the proportion of medical costs paid by the person insured, usually up to a certain total amount. For example, a policy may call for a $1,000 deductible and 20 percent coinsurance up to $3,000. In other words, the insured has at most $3,000 in out-of-pocket expenses.
2. An HMO directly employs or contracts with physicians and other healthcare providers, and covers a great deal of preventative care. In a PPO, a group of doctors and hospitals agree to provide services to PPO members at prearranged fees. Private insurance has the fewest restrictions on the physicians and hospitals the patient chooses, but it is significantly more expensive than HMOs and PPOs.
3. Government healthcare programs are limited to certain population groups that meet certain qualifications, such as age and/or income level. Private plans are offered by private insurers, HMOs, and other organizations.
4. It is important if you are single, in a one-income household, or if your income is essential to the well-being of others.
5. Workers compensation is paid if you become disabled as a result of job-related accidents or illnesses. Receiving Social Security benefits for disabilities depends on your meeting Social Security requirements. These sources of funds are usually not immediately available. Private disability insurance can be designed with greater flexibility but at greater cost.

6. Term life insurance pays a benefit only if you die during the period it covers and during the period you pay the premiums. So, it can be the best value while you are raising your children, for example. Once they are grown and self-supporting, your need for life insurance is reduced. With whole life insurance, you pay an annual premium until you die. Then a specified benefit is paid to your beneficiary. If you cancel the policy, you receive its cash value.
7. Provisions include naming a beneficiary, an incontestability clause, a suicide clause, and policy riders.

ACADEMIC SKILLS

Answers will vary but should indicate an understanding that unless the credit life insurance is very inexpensive, it is probably unnecessary if you have emergency funds and not much credit card debt.

YOUR FINANCIAL FIGURES

1) $2,316 nine years ago, $3,224 today; 2) 39 percent; and 3) 4.4 percent

REAL-WORLD Application

Students may find the "one-stop shop" to be convenient. Also, this situation may mean that the financial advisor can develop a closer relationship with the client, and thus, provide more individual attention and advice. However, a stockbroker is probably more knowledgeable about securities investments.

Internet CONNECTION

Accept all reasonable answers that demonstrate student effort.

BusinessWeek ONLINE

Accept all answers that demonstrate students have read the online article and understand the concepts.

CHAPTER 15 Retirement and Estate Planning

pages 476–517

SECTION	LEARNING OBJECTIVES	FEATURES	TEXT RESOURCES	TECHNOLOGY RESOURCES
15.1	**After completing this section, students will have learned to:** Explain the importance of retirement planning. Identify retirement living costs and housing needs.	**Careers in Finance,** p. 483	**Section Assessment,** p. 485 Quick Check Think Critically Use Communication Skills Solve Money Problems **Student Activity Workbook**	Lesson Planner Plus Online Learning Center Interactive Student Edition *Presentation Plus!* **Exam***View*® Pro Test Generator Financial Planner Software
15.2	**After completing this section, students will have learned to:** Describe the role of Social Security in planning for retirement. Discuss the benefits offered by employer pension plans. Explain various personal retirement plans.	**TechByte,** p. 488 **Savvy Saver,** p. 489 **S&P's Global Financial Landscape,** p. 491 **Document Detective,** p. 494 **Academic Connection,** p. 495 **Common Cents,** p. 496	**Section Assessment,** p. 498 Quick Check Think Critically Use Math Skills Solve Money Problems **Student Activity Workbook**	Lesson Planner Plus Online Learning Center Interactive Student Edition *Presentation Plus!* **Exam***View*® Pro Test Generator Financial Planner Software
15.3	**After completing this section, students will have learned to:** Identify various types of wills. Discuss several types of trusts. Describe common characteristics of estates. Identify the types of taxes that affect estates.	**S&P's Put on Your Financial Planner's Cap,** p. 509 **WebQuest,** p. 510	**Section Assessment,** p. 513 Quick Check Think Critically Use Math Skills Solve Money Problems **Student Activity Workbook**	Lesson Planner Plus Online Learning Center Interactive Student Edition *Presentation Plus!* **Exam***View*® Pro Test Generator Financial Planner Software

Meeting National Standards for Business Education		
Section 15.1	**Section 15.2**	**Section 15.3**
Economics III. Economic Institutions and Incentives VII. The Role of Government **Personal Finance** I. Personal Decision Making III. Managing Finances and Budgeting IV. Saving and Investing	**Economics** III. Economic Institutions and Incentives VII. The Role of Government **Personal Finance** I. Personal Decision Making II. Earning a Living III. Managing Finances and Budgeting IV. Saving and Investing	**Economics** III. Economic Institutions and Incentives VII. The Role of Government VIII. International Economic Concepts **Personal Finance** I. Personal Decision Making II. Earning a Living III. Managing Finances and Budgeting

Teaching Connection

Gross Pay versus Net Pay

Have a recent college graduate who is now working come to your class to talk about decisions he or she made regarding payroll deductions for insurance choices and pension savings. Ask the speaker in advance to address the following issues:

- Why did he or she decide to choose specific types of insurance at this time in his or her career?
- What percentage of pre-tax income is being saved in a 401(k) retirement plan and why?
- What is the speaker's opinion of private accounts for Social Security income?
- How is the speaker managing on the reduced pay resulting from these and other deductions?

Engage the students in a discussion about the importance of starting retirement savings early, reminding them of the impact of compounding on interest earnings.

Visual Guide

Chapter 15 Opener

Discussion: Have students study the chapter opening photo and describe what they see. Then lead a discussion about why it is important for people to plan for retirement.

Follow-Up: Ask students how their financial needs might change as they get older (e.g., inability to earn an income, increasing medical costs). How might they plan now to meet those future needs?

Workplace Skills and Chapter Correlations

FOUNDATION SKILLS						
Basic Skills	Reading	Writing	Math	Listening	Speaking	
Thinking Skills	Creative Thinking	Decision Making	Problem Solving	Seeing Things in the Mind's Eye	Knowing How to Learn	Reasoning
Personal Qualities	Responsibility	Self-Esteem	Sociability	Self-Management	Integrity/ Honesty	

WORKPLACE COMPETENCIES						
Resources	Allocating Time	Allocating Money	Allocating Material and Facility Resources	Allocating Human Resources		
Information	Acquiring and Evaluating Information	Organizing and Maintaining Information	Interpreting and Communicating Information	Using Computers to Process Information		
Interpersonal Skills	Participating as a Member of a Team	Teaching Others	Serving Clients/ Customers	Exercising Leadership	Negotiating to Arrive at a Decision	Working with Cultural Diversity
Systems	Understanding Systems	Monitoring and Correcting Performance	Improving and Designing Systems			
Technology	Selecting Technology	Applying Technology to Task	Maintaining and TroubleshootingTechnology			

Internet Extension

Activity: Have students access the Web site for Aging with Dignity at **agingwithdignity.org** and report on the organization's mission statement.

Keywords: Aging with Dignity

Enrichment/Application Activity

Field Trip: Arrange for the class to visit a seniors' community center or an assisted-living facility. Arrange for students to talk with several retired people about their retirement lifestyle and what activities they pursue.

Topic Spotlight

Ethics: Tell your students: "Greg and Beth's grandmother died but left no letter of last instructions. Greg wants to have a big funeral, but Beth believes their grandmother would not have wanted it." Ask: "How should they deal with this situation? Is there a 'right' or 'wrong' thing to do?"

Money: How much would a retired couple spend on medical care if medical care accounted for 11.3 percent of their income and their annual income was $24,000? [ANSWER: .113 × $24,000 = $2,712]

Government: Review with students why there are taxes—to pay for services such as police and fire protection; public schools; road maintenance; parks; libraries; and safety inspection of foods, drugs, and other products.

Additional Resources

Books

WealthBuilding: Investment Strategies for Retirement and Estate Planning by David R. Reiser, Robert L. DiColo (paperback: Wiley, ©2002). *WealthBuilding* features real-life stories of 31 investors—from young professionals to retired seniors—and shows how these investors are managing their wealth successfully. In addition, it offers investment strategies including how to pick financial advisors and form effective partnerships.

New IRAs and How to Make Them Work for You by Neil Downing (paperback: Dearborn Trade, ©2002). This book offers advice on how to take advantage of the new tax breaks for IRAs and discover the most favorable tax terms from a personal finance columnist.

Internet

ssa.gov The Social Security Administration Web site offers a directory of their publications and a page called "Youthlink," which provides educational information for kids, teens, and teachers.

investorguide.com This site offers a basic primer on financial planning, which includes 401(k) and IRA investment information, Social Security, estate planning, calculators, discussion groups, and organization.

estateplanninglinks.com This site provides one-stop shopping for estate planning needs: links to estate planning forms, calculators, examples of living wills, legal resources, and a free seven-part e-mail minicourse on estate planning, wills, and living trusts.

motleyfool.com/landing/newsletters The Motley Fool Web publication *Eight Ways to Rule Your Retirement* can be found at this site. This free, comprehensive newsletter is filled with ways to take control of your investments.

Note: Web addresses may change.

Section 15.1

Focus

Motivation

Ask the students to brainstorm a list of activities in which retired people participate; write their responses on the board. Tell students that, because people are living longer, retirement does not mean the end of life for many people, but to enjoy retirement fully requires good financial planning.

Prereading

1. Have students skim the section, looking at the pictures, reading the captions, and reading the headings.
2. Ask a student to read aloud Read to Learn and Main Idea on page 478.
3. Ask students why people their age should start planning for retirement.

Teach

Guided Practice

1. Ask students to read aloud In the Real World on page 477, and ask them to share stories about retired people they know.
2. Ask students to read aloud Ask Standard and Poor's on page 477, and discuss it briefly with them.
3. Have students silently read the rest of the section, noting and mentally answering the Predict, Relate, Question, and caption questions and reading the features such as Careers in Finance.

Independent Practice

Have students research three different types of retirement communities in your area and assess: Are all retirement communities the same? If not, in what ways do they differ? Do they serve different populations?

Assess

Reteaching

1. Have the students write additions to the Key Terms list that identify various types of retirement communities.
2. Ask students what expenses should be considered when planning retirement.
3. Discuss with students the Reading Strategies and the pictures and figures with their caption questions. Assign features questions to students and go over responses.

Enrichment

Ask students to interview someone who is retired to learn how that person prepared for retirement. Students should ask the retirees whether they think they planned effectively for retirement. They should also ask what advice the retirees would offer regarding retirement planning.

Assessment

1. Have students complete the Section 15.1 Assessment.
2. Assign an activity from Chaper 15 of the *Student Activity Workbook.*

Close

Have the students complete this statement: "It is important to plan early and carefully for retirement because...."

Section 15.2

Focus

Motivation

Tell the students the class is now going to start their retirement planning. Ask them how they think they will fund their retirement. Write their responses on the board.

Prereading

1. Have students skim the section, looking at the pictures, reading the captions, and reading the headings.
2. Ask a student to read aloud Read to Learn on page 486.
3. Have students list the Key Terms in their notebooks, and prepare flash cards for later use. Suggest they write the definitions on the flash cards and in their notebooks as they learn them.

Teach

Guided Practice

1. Ask a student to read aloud the introductory paragraph Public Pension Plans on page 486, and ask another student to paraphrase it.
2. Ask another student to read aloud the first paragraph under Social Security on page 486, and discuss it briefly with them. Ask: "Did you know that Social Security is not designed to cover 100 percent of retirement income?"
3. Have students silently read the rest of the section, noting and mentally answering the Predict, Relate, Question, and caption questions and reading the features such as Document Detective.

Independent Practice

Divide the students into three groups. Have group one research the history of Social Security to determine how it has changed over the years. They should determine what it provides to retirees, the terms or regulations, who is eligible, and whether benefits are taxable. Have group two research retirement plans offered to teachers, firemen, or police officers and determine what such retirement plans offer, on what terms, and whether they are taxable. Have group three research independent retirement accounts and find out the same things as group one. Have each group report findings to the class.

Assess

Reteaching

1. Have the students write sentences using each term in the Key Terms list.
2. Review the meanings of defined-contribution plan and defined-benefit plan, and ensure students understand the difference.
3. Discuss with students the Reading Strategies and the pictures and figures with their caption questions. Assign features questions to students and go over responses.

Enrichment

Have the students research free and low-cost recreation opportunities for retirees in your community, including senior discounted theaters, concerts, and sporting activities.

Assessment

1. Have students complete the Section 15.2 Assessment.
2. Give students a vocabulary quiz based on the Key Terms.
3. Assign an activity from Chapter 15 of the *Student Activity Workbook*.

Close

Discuss with the students whether their study in this section has opened their eyes to both the opportunities and difficulties retirement can bring.

Section 15.3

Focus

Motivation

Ask students and discuss with them the following questions: "When do you think people should write wills? Should everyone have a will or just people with a lot of money? What does estate planning involve?"

Prereading

1. Have students skim the section, looking at the pictures, reading the captions, and reading the headings.
2. Ask a student to read aloud Read to Learn on page 499.
3. Have students list the Key Terms in their notebooks and remind them to enter the definitions as they learn them.

Teach

Guided Practice

1. Ask students to read aloud The Importance of Estate Planning on page 499, and ask if they can think of reasons why people with no children should plan their estates.
2. Ask students to read silently What Is Estate Planning? on pages 499–500; then ask students to read aloud the section Legal Documents on page 500, and ask them where they should store these documents.
3. Have students silently read the rest of the section, noting and mentally answering the Predict, Relate, Question, React, and caption questions and reading the features such as Common Cents.

Independent Practice

Tell students to imagine they are 35 years old, working, and married with two children; they are homeowners and own other assets (they may decide what those assets are). They are financially comfortable, but not rich. Have students determine whether they will write wills and what kind or if they will set up trusts. Tell them they must consider executors and/or trustees. Have them write reports detailing their plans.

Assess

Reteaching

1. Have the students write sentences using each term in the Key Terms list.
2. Ask students what they think are the most important aspects of this section and why.
3. Discuss with students the Reading Strategies and the pictures and figures with their caption questions. Assign features questions to students and go over responses.

Enrichment

Invite an attorney specializing in trusts and wills to speak to the class about estate planning. Encourage the students to prepare specific questions for the attorney.

Assessment

1. Have students complete the Section 15.3 Assessment.
2. Assign Chapter 15 Review and Activities.
3. Administer the test for Chapter 15 from the Reproducible Tests in the *Lesson Planner Plus* supplement.

Close

Have the students write an essay discussing why it is important to carefully create estate plans.

ANSWERS

Careers in Finance

Answers may include: If you have planned well for retirement, you have reviewed your assets and made sure you have enough income to cover your expenses during retirement. This will help when you write your will because your paperwork will be in order and you can determine how your assets will be divided.

STANDARD &POOR'S Global Financial Landscape

Language and cultural differences may make obtaining services such as medical care and legal help difficult; or those services may be different than those in the United States.

Document Detective

1. $85,200
2. They probably plan to pay off their house mortgage before they retire.
3. They might currently be raising children who will probably not be living with them during retirement. They may currently be commuting by car to work and will not have that expense after they retire.
4. They might determine that they no longer need the insurance policy and choose to cancel it to receive the cash value.
5. Yes. Their projections provide a yearly income surplus of $6,010.

Academic Connection

Answers will vary but should note that if retirement plans are beneficial to employers, they have an incentive to provide them.

STANDARD &POOR'S Put on Your Financial Planner's Cap

Answers might include that this means that your part of the property does not pass automatically to your spouse; it allows you to designate your heir. If you designate your spouse, there are no gift or estate taxes.

Section 15.1 Assessment

Quick Check

1. It may help you cope with any unforeseen changes that occur in your life. It can give you a sense of control over your future. It will help you make your retirement a happy and comfortable time in your life.
2. You will probably spend more money on recreation, health insurance, and medical care and less on transportation and clothing. Your taxes will probably be lower. You will need to put money into an emergency fund and plan for inflation.
3. Assisted-living facilities (ALFs) offer personal and medical services for elderly retirees who might not be able to live alone and care for themselves. ALFs provide minimal to full and continuous nursing care.

Think Critically

4. The house could become a valuable financial asset. When you are ready to retire, you could sell it or leave it to your heirs. However, there is risk, and the money you spend is not invested in retirement savings plans.

Use Communication Skills

5. Accept all reasonable answers.

Solve Money Problems

6. Answers might include: Move to a less expensive home to reduce living expenses, or move closer to family in California to reduce travel expenses.

Section 15.2 Assessment

Quick Check

1. You must have earned a certain number of credits. These are based on the length of time you have paid into the system. People born after 1928 need 40 quarters of credit. Most people can begin collecting benefits at age 62.
2. Defined-contribution plans specify how much money your employer will contribute annually, but do not guarantee any particular benefit. Defined-benefit plans specify the benefits you will receive at retirement but not how much the employer must contribute.

3. A regular IRA lets you contribute an annual amount up to $4,000 ($5,000 in 2008 and after) until age 70½. These contributions may have tax benefits. You must begin to withdraw minimum distributions by age 70½ or pay a penalty. A Roth IRA lets you contribute the same amount as a regular IRA, provided your adjusted gross income is less than a certain amount. Contributions are not tax deductible, but earnings are tax free. You can make annual contributions to a Roth IRA after age 70½ with no penalty.

Think Critically

4. You might continue to work during retirement but have less leisure time. You could cut back on expenses and take advantage of senior discounts. You could sell some of your assets, but that might affect your heirs and your financial stability.

Use Math Skills

5. The answer is $2,839.44 as shown below.

Year 1	$1,110.00	Year 6	$1,870.42
Year 2	$1,232.10	Year 7	$2,076.17
Year 3	$1,367.63	Year 8	$2,304.55
Year 4	$1,518.07	Year 9	$2,558.05
Year 5	$1,685.06	Year 10	$2,839.44

Solve Money Problems

6. Answers will vary but may include the use of a rollover IRA or an annuity. A rollover IRA would allow Mike to continue to earn tax-deferred income from his money. An annuity would also produce tax-deferred interest, and Mike could arrange to receive payments from the annuity.

Section 15.3 Assessment

Quick Check

1. simple will, traditional marital share will, exemption trust will, and stated dollar amount will
2. A credit-shelter trust enables the spouse/heir of a deceased person to avoid federal taxes on a certain amount of assets. With a disclaimer trust, the surviving spouse receives everything but has the right to disclaim, or deny, a portion of the estate. Anything disclaimed goes into a credit-shelter trust. A living trust allows the trustor to receive benefits during his or her lifetime and avoids fees and delays in settling an estate.
3. Options include: purchasing a life insurance policy; saving cash; selling assets; borrowing money; and arranging with the IRS to make deferred payments.

Think Critically

4. A formal will is best from a legal point of view because some states do not recognize holographic, or handwritten, wills.

Use Math Skills

5. The surviving spouse will pay $192,000. ($400,000 × .48 = $192,000)

Solve Money Problems

6. (1) A simple will leaves everything to a spouse. It is not suited for a large or complex estate. It may also result in higher taxation, since everything will be taxed as part of the spouse's estate. (2) A traditional marital share will leaves half of the estate to the spouse; the other half may go to children, other heirs, or a trust. In this type of will, half the estate will be taxed at your death and half at your spouse's death. This results in the lowest federal taxes on estates above a certain size; but state taxes may be higher. (3) An exemption trust will passes everything to the surviving spouse except for an amount equal to the marital exemption, which goes into a trust. There are fewer taxes. (4) With a stated dollar amount will, you can pass on to a spouse any amount. Tax benefits may be significant, but this type of will is not good for estates in which the assets may decrease in value. Irving and Irma should have a traditional marital share will or exemption trust will.

Chapter 15 Review & Activities

Communicating Key Terms

Accept all reasonable responses that demonstrate an understanding of the key term definitions.

Reviewing Key Concepts

1. Expenses that may decrease include transportation, clothing, income taxes, and housing.
2. Alternative living arrangements in retirement include remaining in one's home, living with adult children; moving to smaller quarters; living in a home designed for older people; and living in assisted-living facilities.
3. Social Security is not likely to be enough to cover all your expenses; you cannot begin to collect Social Security until you are a certain age; and future revisions to the program may reduce benefits.
4. Defined-contribution plans specify how much money your employer will contribute annually, but do not guarantee any particular benefit. Defined-benefit plans specify the benefits you will receive at retirement but not how much the employer must contribute.
5. With the Roth IRA, you pay taxes on money when you invest it in the IRA, but none on the income it makes. Withdrawals from the Roth IRA are tax-free.
6. A living will gives instructions to your family and physicians on how you want your care to be managed in case you become physically or mentally disabled. It saves your family from having to make difficult decisions with major emotional, financial, and legal consequences.
7. Trusts may reduce estate taxes, avoid probate, make asset management easier, quickly transfer assets to beneficiaries, and ensure that your wishes are carried out.
8. The executor carries out the wishes presented in the deceased's will, including taking inventory of the estate, paying debts, preparing income taxes, and distributing the estate.
9. Answers might include reducing the size of the estate by giving portions of it as gifts while you are still alive.

ACADEMIC SKILLS

Student answers should demonstrate research on the average life expectancy during each decade mentioned. A table showing this information can be found at **cdc.gov/nchs/fastats/lifexpec.htm**.

YOUR FINANCIAL FIGURES

1. Answers will vary, depending on the cities chosen, but should demonstrate research into the cost of living.
2. Students should use appropriate software to show research in number one.

REAL-WORLD Application

1. Answers will differ but should indicate that the AARP advocates that the Social Security system be strengthened.
2. Accept all reasonable answers that are supported by students' logic.

Internet CONNECTION

1. Trusts are recommended in certain circumstances because they make asset management easier, lower estate taxes, and provide a source of income.
2. Answers will vary, depending on the state of residence.

BusinessWeek ONLINE

Accept all paragraphs that demonstrate students have read the online article and understand the concepts. Accept all reasonable lists.

Business Ownership and Planning

Chapter 16
Types of Business Ownership

Chapter 17
Developing a Business Plan

Chapter 18
Developing a Financial Plan

Unit Overview

In previous units students learned about planning and managing personal finances. In this unit and Unit 6, students will be reading about business finances. Unit 5 focuses on how businesses develop a plan to start and then manage their finances. Chapter 16 explains three types of business ownership—sole proprietorships, partnerships, and corporations—and how choice of ownership affects a business financially. Chapter 17 introduces the concept of a business plan and the financial management of a business. Chapter 18 describes in detail how to develop a financial plan and provides step-by-step guidelines.

Introductory Activity

Write the definition for *entrepreneur* on the board: one who organizes, manages, and assumes the risks of a business or enterprise (from the Old French *entreprendre*, to undertake). Then ask if any of your students have ever thought about opening their own business one day. What kind of business would it be? Where would they get the money to start it? How would they know how much money would be needed? Allow students time to write the answers to these questions, and encourage them to use their imaginations. Then explain that the answers to these questions are addressed in a business plan, and that a business plan is the first step in managing the finances of a business.

BusinessWeek
FINANCE FILE

Good Works—with a Business Plan

Answer Accept all reasonable answers that show an understanding of the concept. Answers might include public daycare centers, recycling businesses, ecologically-minded landscape businesses, construction businesses that build low-income housing, and health clinics for low-income patients.

Get a Financial Life!

A Business Is Born

STEP A **The Process** Make sure students have access to all necessary materials.

1. Remind students that the Careers in Finance feature in Chapter 17 describes a bookkeeper. Students can use the information in this feature to help them write their newspaper ad.
2. The business plans will vary but should include two of the three main sections: the strategic plan and the marketing plan. The strategic plan should include short-term goals and long-term goals as well as steps to achieve those goals. The marketing plan should include competition, advertising outlets, and ideas for promotional activities as well as a preliminary budget for advertising and promotion.
3. Outlines should include a list of the six required financial statements to be completed for the financial plan.
4. Resources will vary. Give students the names of the Additional Resources listed in the chapter planning guides for Chapters 16, 17, and 18 of this unit.

STEP B **Create Your Portfolio** Evaluate students' portfolios based on whether all four steps of the process are completed, the information seems reasonably well researched, and the contents are neat and in order.

STEP C **Applying Technology** Evaluate students' research and papers based on the following criteria:

- Research should be thorough but need not be exhaustive
- If vendors for a particular technology are not readily available, accept material from catalogs or the Internet.
- Visual aids should be attractive and informative.
- Papers should cite references found through research.

Unit Closure

Have students write a one-page paper defending why they would or would not like to start and run their own businesses. Make sure they address the responsibilities of writing a business plan and developing a financial plan.

Evaluation

Administer the Unit 5 test from the **Exam***View*® Pro Testmaker CD-ROM.

CHAPTER 16 Types of Business Ownership

pages 522–547

SECTION	LEARNING OBJECTIVES	FEATURES	TEXT RESOURCES	TECHNOLOGY RESOURCES
16.1	**After completing this section, students will have learned to:** Identify the advantages and disadvantages of a sole proprietorship. Explain the differences between general and limited partners. Identify the advantages and disadvantages of a partnership.	**Careers in Finance,** p. 526 **Savvy Saver,** p. 527 **Document Detective,** p. 531 **S&P's Put on Your Financial Planner's Cap,** p. 532	**Section Assessment,** p. 533 Quick Check Think Critically Use Communication Skills Solve Money Problems **Student Activity Workbook**	Lesson Planner Plus Online Learning Center Interactive Student Edition *Presentation Plus!* **Exam***View*® Pro Test Generator Financial Planner Software
16.2	**After completing this section, students will have learned to:** Describe two types of corporations. Summarize the process of forming a corporation. Discuss the advantages and disadvantages of a corporation.	**TechByte,** p. 535 **S&P's Global Financial Landscape,** p. 537 **WebQuest,** p. 539 **Common Cents,** p. 539 **Academic Connection,** p. 542	**Section Assessment,** p. 543 Quick Check Think Critically Use Math Skills Solve Money Problems **Student Activity Workbook**	Lesson Planner Plus Online Learning Center Interactive Student Edition *Presentation Plus!* **Exam***View*® Pro Test Generator Financial Planner Software

Meeting National Standards for Business Education	
Section 16.1	**Section 16.2**
Personal Finance I. Personal Decision Making II. Earning a Living VI. Banking	**Economics** VII. The Role of Government VIII. International Economic Concepts **Personal Finance** I. Personal Decision Making II. Earning a Living IV. Saving and Investing

Teaching Connection

Discussion: On Your Own

Ask students whether they would like to have their own businesses someday. Many will answer positively. Ask them to list the reasons they would to do this. What advantages do they see in owning one's own business? Ask them to also list the characteristics a business owner needs to have to succeed. Have them share their lists and categorize their responses on the board. Ask them whether anything is missing from the lists. It is likely that self-discipline, willingness to work very hard for more than 40 hours a week, and risk-taking are not there. Ask students whether they see any disadvantages to owning a business. List those answers on the board as well. Refer to these lists as you discuss business ownership.

You may also ask a small business owner to address the class and the advantages and disadvantages the students have listed.

Visual Guide

Chapter 16 Opener

Discussion: Have the students study the chapter opening photo and describe what they see. Then lead a discussion introducing the different types of business ownership, such as sole proprietorship, partnership, and corporation, and how the size of the business might affect the type of business organization.

Follow-Up: Tell students to imagine that they are about to open their own business. Ask: "What type of business is it?" "What type of business ownership did you choose?" "Why?"

Workplace Skills and Chapter Correlations

FOUNDATION SKILLS						
Basic Skills	Reading	Writing	Math	Listening	Speaking	
Thinking Skills	Creative Thinking	Decision Making	Problem Solving	Seeing Things in the Mind's Eye	Knowing How to Learn	Reasoning
Personal Qualities	Responsibility	Self-Esteem	Sociability	Self-Management	Integrity/ Honesty	

WORKPLACE COMPETENCIES						
Resources	Allocating Time	Allocating Money	Allocating Material and Facility Resources	Allocating Human Resources		
Information	Acquiring and Evaluating Information	Organizing and Maintaining Information	Interpreting and Communicating Information	Using Computers to Process Information		
Interpersonal Skills	Participating as a Member of a Team	Teaching Others	Serving Clients/ Customers	Exercising Leadership	Negotiating to Arrive at a Decision	Working with Cultural Diversity
Systems	Understanding Systems	Monitoring and Correcting Performance	Improving and Designing Systems			
Technology	Selecting Technology	Applying Technology to Task	Maintaining and TroubleshootingTechnology			

Internet Extension

Activity: Have students use the Internet to research businesses for sale online. Students should find out what good or service the business offers, the business's form of ownership, and the cost of the business.

Keywords: businesses for sale, business opportunities

Enrichment/Application Activity

Corporate Activity: Divide the class into three groups, and have each group research one of the following forms of ownership: corporation, partnership, and franchise. Have the groups present their findings, and have the class vote on which form of ownership is best.

Topic Spotlight

Technology: Discuss the impact technology has on a sole proprietorship. Have students consider the cost of equipment versus the need that a sole proprietor has for help on the job.

Ethics: Ask students whether trust is an important element in a successful partnership. Have them explain why or why not.

Marketing: Explain that assistance with advertising is one of the advantages of owning a franchise. Have students brainstorm other ways the parent company assists a franchise with marketing.

Additional Resources

Books

Let's Go Into Business Together by Azriela Jaffe (paperback: Career Press, ©2001). This book profiles more than 100 individuals with experience in business partnerships. They provide insight into what makes a business successful, what being a business partner entails, and the obstacles partners may face.

Buy-Sell Agreement Handbook: Plan Ahead for Changes in the Ownership of Your Business by Anthony Mancuso, Bethany K. Laurence (paperback: Nolo.com, ©2003). What if your partner wants out of the business? This book offers a detailed description of the buy-sell agreement, the legal document designed to ensure a smooth transition after a co-owner departs. The document outlines when co-owners can sell their interest, circumstances when someone must sell, who can buy into the business, and what price will be paid.

Internet

nolo.com/article.cfm/objectID/2C1A52D5-9364-4F92-AD191B56DF9D4CE6/111/182/ART/ This site provides a useful guide to choosing a form of business ownership: corporation, LLC, partnership, or sole proprietorship. It explains the key terms and concepts in plain English and includes links to state law, checklists for forming a corporation and an LLC, and related articles.

toolkit.cch.com/text/P07_4445.asp This site offers a wide range of practical information for small business owners. In addition to advice and news items related to small businesses, it provides a small business guide, business tools, downloadable material, and an online newsletter.

Note: Web addresses may change.

Section 16.1

Focus

Motivation

Ask the students how many prefer working on their own and how many prefer working in groups and, why. Then tell them that working on your own compares, in business, to a sole proprietorship while working on teams is similar to working in partnerships.

Prereading

1. Have students skim the section, looking at the pictures, reading the captions, and reading the headings.
2. Ask a student to read aloud Read to Learn on page 524.
3. Have students list the Key Terms in their notebooks, and remind them to enter the definitions as they learn them.

Teach

Guided Practice

1. Ask students to read aloud In the Real World on page 523, and ask them whether any of them have ever had similar business experiences.
2. Ask students to read aloud Ask Standard and Poor's on page 523, and discuss it briefly with them.
3. Have students silently read the rest of the section, noting and mentally answering the Predict, Relate, Question, and caption questions and reading the features such as Careers in Finance.

Independent Practice

To help students understand sole proprietorship, ask them to do the following:

1. Research the local requirements for starting a sole proprietorship, including licenses and fees.
2. Interview a local sole proprietor or a small business partner and ask about the advantages and disadvantages of that type of business ownership. They are also to ask what skills are critical in a sole proprietorship or how the partners divide up responsibilities.
3. Write their findings as a newspaper article.

Assess

Reteaching

1. Have the students write sentences using each term in the Key Terms list.
2. Ask students to recall the advantages versus the disadvantages of sole proprietorships and partnerships. Which did they find more compelling? Why?
3. Discuss with students the Reading Strategies and the pictures and figures with their caption questions. Assign features questions to students and go over responses.

Enrichment

Invite someone from the Small Business Administration (SBA) to speak to the class about how the SBA helps entrepreneurs.

Assessment

1. Have students complete the Section 16.1 Assessment.
2. Give students a vocabulary quiz based on the Key Terms.
3. Assign an activity from Chapter 16 of the *Student Activity Workbook.*

Close

Ask the students if they can think of businesses that started small, as sole proprietorships or partnerships, and later became big businesses.

Section 16.2

Focus

Motivation

Ask the students what they know, about corporations, and list their responses on the board. Tell them that they will find out in this section what a corporation is, how it is formed, and how it differs from other forms of business ownership.

Prereading

1. Have students skim the section, looking at the pictures, reading the captions, and reading the headings.
2. Ask a student to read aloud Read to Learn on page 534.
3. Have students list the Key Terms in their notebooks and prepare flash cards, filling in the definitions as they learn them.

Teach

Guided Practice

1. Ask a student to read aloud What Is a Corporation? on page 534.
2. Ask another student to read aloud Starting a Corporation through Paperwork and Documents on page 534, and discuss it briefly with them.
3. Have students silently read the rest of the section, noting and mentally answering the Predict, Relate, Question, React, and caption questions and reading the features such as Global Financial Landscape.

Independent Practice

Assign each student a business type (shoe store, Web design, fast food restaurant, bank, for example). Have students then determine which type of business ownership would be best for that type of business. Have students present their answers to the class for discussion.

Assess

Reteaching

1. Have the students practice the terms in the Key Terms list with a partner using flash cards.
2. To emphasize a disadvantage in corporations, discuss the problems that could occur because decisions are not made quickly.
3. Discuss with students the Reading Strategies and the pictures and figures with their caption questions. Assign features questions to students and go over responses.

Enrichment

Have the students create a bulletin board showing the advantages and disadvantages of the various forms of business ownership.

Assessment

1. Have students complete the Section 16.2 Assessment.
2. Assign Chapter 16 Review and Activities.
3. Administer the test for Chapter 16 from the Reproducible Tests in the *Lesson Planner Plus* supplement.

Close

Discuss with students what it means to say that corporations are a driving force in the American economy.

ANSWERS

Careers in Finance

Contractors often have to build teams of subcontractors, such as electricians, plumbers, painters; he or she needs to be able to pay these subcontractors what is due them and still make a profit. Contractors also need money-management skills to bid successfully.

Teacher Manual

Document Detective

1. Businesses that intend to hire one or more employees to work for them should use this form.
2. The purpose of the form is to assign a federal identification number to a business in order to monitor the business's taxes.
3. The business was started March 3, 20--.
4. The business is not incorporated.
5. cutting and trimming trees

STANDARD &POOR'S Put on Your Financial Planner's Cap

Student charts should include the information specified and demonstrate an understanding of what is needed for each type of ownership.

STANDARD &POOR'S Global Financial Landscape

Answers might include that stockholders will reward a company that uses alternative sources of energy if they think the company will get a competitive edge and improve its earnings.

Academic Connection

Answers might include that advertising media are determined based on the advertising budget (corporations will have bigger budgets and can buy more expensive media, such as television) and how best to reach the business's target market.

Section 16.1 Assessment

Quick Check

1. Answers might include any one of the following: A sole proprietorship is easy to set up, you make your own decisions, you keep all the profits, and there are few government regulations.
2. General partners have decision-making authority, take an active role in the operation of the business, and sign contracts. They also have unlimited liability for the losses or debts of the partnership. A limited partner does not take an active role in running the business, and the partner's liability is limited to the amount of his or her investment.
3. Disadvantages include unlimited liability for the general partners, possible disagreements, the requirement to share profits, and limited life of the partnership.

Think Critically

4. Answers might be the duties, rights, and responsibilities of each partner; procedures for sharing profits and losses; or how assets will be divided when the partnership is dissolved.

Use Communication Skills

5. Answers might recommend that the partners redefine their duties, rights, and responsibilities. If the conflict cannot be resolved, the partnership may dissolve.

Solve Money Problems

6. Answers should demonstrate an understanding of the advantages and disadvantages of sole proprietorships and partnerships and how a business might be expanded.

Section 16.2 Assessment

Quick Check

1. The articles of incorporation are the application you file with the state in order to operate as a corporation. A corporate charter is the license to operate a corporation. The corporate bylaws are the rules by which your corporation will operate.
2. A closely held corporation is a corporation whose shares are owned by a small group of people and are not traded openly in stock markets.
3. Advantages of a corporation include: ease of raising capital, limited liability, continued life of the business if an owner dies or leaves, and separation of ownership and management.

Think Critically

4. Answers might include that the corporation would have a greater amount of money available for growth and other purposes. However, an increase in the number of stockholders might also increase costs.

Use Math Skills

5. They will have to sell 33,899 shares. (ANSWER: $1,000,000 ÷ $29.50 = 33,898.3)

Solve Money Problems

6. The sole proprietorship poses the greater financial risk to Beverly because she could lose the $35,000 she invested and any assets pledged as collateral. If the corporation fails, her loss is limited to $33,000.

Chapter 16 Review & Activities

Communicating Key Terms

Answers should indicate students' understanding of the terms used and the advantages and disadvantages of each form of business ownership.

Reviewing Key Concepts

1. Most new businesses begin as sole proprietorships because they are easy to set up and involve little government regulation.
2. In partnerships, general partners have decision-making authority, are active in the business, and have unlimited liability for all losses and debts of the partnership. Limited partners rarely take an active role in the business, and their liability is limited to the extent of their investment.
3. In a partnership, more skills, knowledge, and capital are available to start the business than in a sole proprietorship.
4. In a closely held corporation, shares are owned by a small group of people. This gives that group greater control than they would have in a publicly held corporation. However, each investor is liable for a larger share of any debt that is incurred. Advantages of a publicly held corporation include being able to raise capital quickly by issuing more stock and, often, of the company being run by professionally trained corporate officers.
5. company name and type of business
6. Issuing more stock dilutes the value of the stock currently held. The "pie," i.e., corporation, will be cut into more and smaller "pieces" if more stock is issued.

ACADEMIC SKILLS

Student answers should indicate research into growing cities in the United States and student understanding of the advantages and disadvantages of the types of business ownership.

YOUR FINANCIAL FIGURES

1. The total worth of stock that must be sold will depend on the costs associated with issuing the stock.
2. Factors may include the costs of issuing the stock, the price of similar stocks, etc.

REAL-WORLD Application

1. Answers might be, initially, sole proprietorship may be more convenient, because of ease of setup.
2. The role play should demonstrate students' understanding of the concepts.

Internet CONNECTION

Answers should indicate students' understanding that entrepreneurship requires risk tolerance, decision-making ability, and the willingness to work long hours.

BusinessWeek ONLINE

Accept all paragraphs that demonstrate students have read the online article and understand the steps involved in starting your own business.

CHAPTER 17 Developing a Business Plan

pages 548–571

SECTION	LEARNING OBJECTIVES	FEATURES	TEXT RESOURCES	TECHNOLOGY RESOURCES
17.1	**After completing this section, students will have learned to:** Discuss the importance of financial management for a business. Explain the components of a business plan. Describe the aspects of a financial plan.	**S&P's Global Financial Landscape,** p. 555 **Common Cents,** p. 556 **TechByte,** p. 558 **WebQuest,** p. 559 **Academic Connection,** p. 560	**Section Assessment,** p. 560 Quick Check Think Critically Use Communication Skills Solve Money Problems **Student Activity Workbook**	Lesson Planner Plus Online Learning Center Interactive Student Edition *Presentation Plus!* **Exam***View*® Pro Test Generator Financial Planner Software
17.2	**After completing this section, students will have learned to:** Explain the importance of accounting in financial management. Identify the primary functions of accounting.	**Document Detective,** p. 562 **S&P's Put on Your Financial Planner's Cap,** p. 563 **Savvy Saver,** p. 565 **Careers in Finance,** p. 566	**Section Assessment,** p. 567 Quick Check Think Critically Use Math Skills Solve Money Problems **Student Activity Workbook**	Lesson Planner Plus Online Learning Center Interactive Student Edition *Presentation Plus!* **Exam***View*® Pro Test Generator Financial Planner Software

Meeting National Standards for Business Education	
Section 17.1	**Section 17.2**
Economics III. Economic Institutions and Incentives **Personal Finance** I. Personal Decision Making II. Earning a Living VII. Using Credit	**Economics** III. Economic Institutions and Incentives VI. Productivity VIII. International Economic Concepts **Personal Finance** I. Personal Decision Making II. Earning a Living IV. Saving and Investing

Teaching Connection

Discussion: Integrating Economics

Discuss with students the characteristics of the free enterprise system and capitalism. Ask them to contrast it to socialist and communist economies. Try to draw out the primary differences between the economic systems, such as choice of products and choice of careers. Ask the students to think of advantages and disadvantages of free enterprise versus the other economic systems.

Consider: Discuss competition and its place in free enterprise. Is it an advantage, a disadvantage, or both—and how? Consider the dissolution of Russian communism and the attempts in China to mesh a market economy for small business with a state-run communist economy for large-scale business, such as steel production and electrical utilities.

Visual Guide

Chapter 17 Opener

Discussion: Have the students study the chapter opening photo and describe what they see. Then lead a discussion about how an interest in sports might lead to a business opportunity.

Follow-Up: Ask students what merchandise related to sports events might have value. Then ask: "What steps would you have to take to create a business based on trading that merchandise?"

Workplace Skills and Chapter Correlations

FOUNDATION SKILLS						
Basic Skills	Reading	Writing	Math	Listening	Speaking	
Thinking Skills	Creative Thinking	Decision Making	Problem Solving	Seeing Things in the Mind's Eye	Knowing How to Learn	Reasoning
Personal Qualities	Responsibility	Self-Esteem	Sociability	Self-Management	Integrity/ Honesty	

WORKPLACE COMPETENCIES						
Resources	Allocating Time	Allocating Money	Allocating Material and Facility Resources	Allocating Human Resources		
Information	Acquiring and Evaluating Information	Organizing and Maintaining Information	Interpreting and Communicating Information	Using Computers to Process Information		
Interpersonal Skills	Participating as a Member of a Team	Teaching Others	Serving Clients/ Customers	Exercising Leadership	Negotiating to Arrive at a Decision	Working with Cultural Diversity
Systems	Understanding Systems	Monitoring and Correcting Performance	Improving and Designing Systems			
Technology	Selecting Technology	Applying Technology to Task	Maintaining and TroubleshootingTechnology			

Internet Extension

Activity: Have students use the Internet to research financial plans for business start-ups.

Keywords: financial plan and start-ups

Enrichment/Application Activity

Cooperative Activity: Have students choose a type of business the class would like to start. Write a list of the possible items or services needed to start the business on the board. Assign each student one item from the list to research. Have students report their findings and, as a class, develop a statement of required start-up capital.

Topic Spotlight

Money: Have students research the prices of different assets commonly needed by businesses. Where do students think they can get the best buys on these items?

Technology: Have students research the latest trends in business technology. Allow them to share their findings with the class and discuss whether new businesses need the newest or best.

Marketing: Ask volunteers to describe a new business they would like to start, and ask what marketing strategies they would use to promote their new businesses.

Additional Resources

Books

Capital Campaigns from the Ground Up: How Nonprofits Can Have the Buildings of Their Dreams by Stanley Weinstein (Wiley, ©2003). This handbook will guide you through a campaign to fund and complete a significant building project. It will help you think strategically in the early preparation stage, build a committed team, and determine what has worked in past successful campaigns.

Internet

bplans.com This Web site offers a wide range of information to help you start and build your business. Included are expert advice on business start-ups, sample business plans, articles, and interactive tools, such as a starting costs calculator.

sba.gov The Web site of the Small Business Administration provides a wealth of information about starting and operating a small business. Included are a checklist for business start-ups, an online business planning workshop, and business plan basics.

Note: Web-site addresses may change.

Section 17.1

Focus

Motivation

Ask students to imagine they are opening a store to sell custom T-shirts and tennis shoes. Ask them to list, as you write on the board, things they need to plan before opening the shop. (Elicit: location, store design, stock, employees, capital, etc.)

Prereading

1. Have students skim the section, looking at the pictures, reading the captions, and reading the headings.
2. Ask a student to read aloud Read to Learn on page 550.
3. Have students list the Key Terms in their notebooks, and remind them to enter the definitions as they learn them.

Teach

Guided Practice

1. Ask students to read aloud In the Real World on page 549, and ask them whether they can see themselves in the same situation as John Irvin.
2. Ask students to read aloud Ask Standard and Poor's on page 549, and discuss it briefly with them.
3. Have students silently read the rest of the section, noting and mentally answering the Predict, Relate, Question, and caption questions and reading the features such as Global Financial Landscape.

Independent Practice

1. Divide students into groups of four, and have each group decide on a shop they want to open. The groups are to establish goals for their businesses, following the guidelines in the text.
2. One student in each group will be in charge of location and store design; one student will be in charge of store inventory (source, quantity, and cost); one student will be in charge of a marketing plan; and one in charge of staffing and day-to-day operations.
3. Have each group research to find what they need. Then have the groups graphically display the results of their efforts to the class.

Assess

Reteaching

1. Have the students write sentences using each term in the Key Terms list.
2. Ask students what they think is the most difficult aspect of preparing a businessplan.
3. Discuss with students the Reading Strategies and the pictures and figures with their caption questions. Assign features questions to students and go over responses.

Enrichment

With the students, develop a definition of a mission statement. Then have each group from the Independent Practice activity write a mission statement for its shop.

Assessment

1. Have students complete the Section 17.1 Assessment.
2. Have students write sentences using each of the Key Terms.
3. Assign an activity from Chapter 17 of the *Student Activity Workbook.*

Close

Remind the students that the planning they have done for their shops is only the tip of the iceberg. Have them name aspects of planning still to be achieved.

Section 17.2

Focus

Motivation

Ask the students how many have taken accounting courses. Ask them to list advantages of understanding accounting for small business owners, and write them on the board. Then ask if there is any disadvantage to understanding accounting, and elicit "no."

Prereading

1. Have students skim the section, looking at the pictures, reading the captions, and reading the headings.
2. Ask a student to read aloud Read to Learn and Main Idea on page 561.
3. Have students list the Key Terms in their notebooks, and remind them to enter the definitions as they learn them.

Teach

Guided Practice

1. Read aloud Aspects of Financial Management on page 561.
2. Ask students to read aloud Accounting: The Backbone of Financial Management on page 561, and discuss it with them.
3. Have students silently read the rest of the section, noting and mentally answering the Predict, Relate, Question, React, and caption questions and reading the features such as Document Detective.

Independent Practice

Have students continue in the same groups they were in for Section 17.1. Ask them to prepare a one-month operations budget for their shops. Explain that, while they cannot know the amount of revenue they will make, they need to make expenses conform to a projected income figure.

Assess

Reteaching

1. Have the students write sentences using each term in the Key Terms list.
2. Ask students what they think are the most important aspects of this section and why.
3. Discuss with students the Reading Strategies and the pictures and figures with their caption questions. Assign features questions to students and go over responses.

Enrichment

Invite three local small business owners to provide a panel for the students, and have the students prepare questions to ask. Encourage questions about the owners' business planning.

Assessment

1. Have students complete the Section 17.2 Assessment.
2. Assign Chapter 17 Review and Activities.
3. Administer the test for Chapter 17 from the Reproducible Tests in the *Lesson Planner Plus* supplement.

Close

Many entrepreneurs fail many times before they are successful. Ask students if they believe they would be that persistent, and then explain why or why not.

ANSWERS

STANDARD &POOR'S Global Financial Landscape

Accept all reasonable answers that demonstrate student effort. Possible answers might include hotels, restaurants, tours of historic sites, or any business that would have tourists and students as a target market.

Academic Connection

Accept all research that reflects student effort and an understanding of the concepts.

Document Detective

1. The owner will receive 20 percent of sales as compensation.
2. The accountant should have excellent verbal and written communication skills, the ability to work with others, at least two years experience in construction or a related service or manufacturing industry, and certification as a CPA.
3. The director of operations will develop operational procedures in conjunction with owner; implement all policies, procedures, and guidelines of operations; manage all operations and assist owner with hiring and employee evaluation functions; and troubleshoot all problems.
4. The accountant job is not a full-time position, so the hourly wages are spread out over the year.
5. The director of operations needs four years of experience in the construction industry or a two-year degree in construction management, plus two years of management experience.

STANDARD &POOR'S Put on Your Financial Planner's Cap

Answers will vary but may include reinvest the money into business expansion, use the money to pay down debt, and launch a new advertising campaign.

Careers in Finance

Someone has to do such things as deposit and keep records of receipts, monitor inventories, and do reporting required by government agencies.

Section 17.1 Assessment

Quick Check

1. The basic parts of a business plan are: 1) a strategic plan, which outlines your business goals and the steps you will take to achieve them; 2) a marketing plan, which outlines how you will promote your business to increase sales and make a profit; and 3) a financial plan, which outlines how you will fund the start-up and operations of your business and maintain your financial operations and business records.
2. Good financial management provides the opportunity for sales to rise, expenses to fall, profits to increase, assets to be acquired, liabilities to be paid, credit to expand, customers to increase, and new products to be developed. It is the backbone of a business.
3. Aspects of a financial plan include identifying needed assets, determining the method to purchase needed assets, and daily financial operations.

Think Critically

4. Answers mght include: The business owner or operator might make a decision to purchase assets without realizing the extent of outstanding debts of the business. As a result, the business might not be able to pay its debts on time, jeopardizing its ability to obtain funding (loans) for its operations.

Use Communication Skills

5. Flyers will vary but should send a message that persuades customers to purchase the jewelry.

Solve Money Problems

6. Santiago's list should include the merchandise he will be selling—doughnuts and hot chocolate mix—as well as materials for advertising and selling the merchandise. Students may suggest that he borrow the table and other reusable supplies.

Section 17.2 Assessment

Quick Check

1. Accounting is a systematic process of recording and reporting the financial position of a business.
2. Five of the most essential functions of accounting are budgeting, inventory, payroll, cash flow, and investments.
3. Businesses can determine the amount of merchandise sold, what merchandise is selling well, when they need to reorder merchandise, and what merchandise to reorder. The wrong level of inventory can cause a business to lose sales.

Think Critically

4. Without enough cash reserves, a business may not be able to pay for emergencies or other unexpected costs that might arise.

Use Math Skills

5. The toy store had a positive cash flow of \$21,500 [\$62,500 – (\$16,000 + \$25,000) = \$21,500]

Solve Money Problems

6. Examine the budget to determine ways to decrease spending; increase customer base; and improve inventory.

Chapter 17 Review & Activities

Communicating Key Terms

Points might indicate that students understand the purpose of the meeting is to secure a loan.

Reviewing Key Concepts

1. Good financial management enables the goals outlined in the strategic plan and marketing plan to be met so sales rise, expenses fall, profits increase, assets are acquired, liabilities are paid, credit expands, customers increase, and new products are developed.
2. A strategic plan includes an executive summary, a mission statement, a company description, a product and service plan, and a management team plan. A marketing plan includes an industry overview, market analysis, competitive analysis, operational plan, and organization plan; a financial plan identifies the assets needed, purchasing methods, and daily financial operations.
3. assets needed, purchasing methods, and daily financial operations
4. buying supplies, selling merchandise, and/or paying utility bills
5. The GAAP enable people to compare the financial reports of different companies.

ACADEMIC SKILLS

Profit is a goal written in many businesses' strategic plans; their ability to profit is a measure of their success.

YOUR FINANCIAL FIGURES

1. \$0. [(\$17,500 + 93,000 + 87,455 + 162,000 + 147,000) – (\$114,000 + 216,000 + 176,955) = 0]
2. Students should show the above calculation using appropriate software.

REAL-WORLD Application

1. Accept all answers that demonstrate research into these illegal practices.
2. Student opinions will differ. The Sarbanes-Oxley Act established strict rules concerning accounting procedures and standards and mandated oversight, internal audits, and other measures.

Internet CONNECTION

Accept all answers that demonstrate research into e-businesses.

BusinessWeek ONLINE

Accept answers that demonstrate students have read the online article and understand the concepts. Accept reasonable business plans.

Teacher Manual

CHAPTER 18 Developing a Financial Plan

pages 572–603

SECTION	LEARNING OBJECTIVES	FEATURES	TEXT RESOURCES	TECHNOLOGY RESOURCES
18.1	**After completing this section, students will have learned to:** Explain start-up capital. Identify start-up costs. Describe operating capital. Explain projected income statements. Discuss the role of reserve capital.	**Savvy Saver,** p. 575 **TechByte,** p. 579 **S&P's Put on Your Financial Planner's Cap,** p. 585 **S&P's Global Financial Landscape,** p. 586 **Document Detective,** p. 587 **WebQuest,** p. 588	**Section Assessment,** p. 588 Quick Check Think Critically Use Communication Skills Solve Money Problems **Student Activity Workbook**	Lesson Planner Plus Online Learning Center Interactive Student Edition *Presentation Plus!* **Exam***View*® Pro Test Generator Financial Planner Software
18.2	**After completing this section, students will have learned to:** Identify the elements of a financial plan.	**Academic Connection,** p. 591 **Common Cents,** p. 593 **Careers in Finance,** p. 593	**Section Assessment,** p. 599 Quick Check Think Critically Use Math Skills Solve Money Problems **Student Activity Workbook**	Lesson Planner Plus Online Learning Center Interactive Student Edition *Presentation Plus!* **Exam***View*® Pro Test Generator Financial Planner Software

Meeting National Standards for Business Education	
Section 18.1	**Section 18.2**
Economics II. Economic Systems VI. Productivity **Personal Finance** VI. Banking VIII. Protecting Against Risk	**Economics** VIII. International Economic Concepts **Personal Finance** II. Earning a Living VII. Using Credit

Teaching Connection

Brainstorming a Start-Up

Have the students brainstorm a list of start-up costs involved in a new business. Let the students come to consensus on the type of business to start. They do not have to estimate amounts for these costs but rather compile a thorough list of the types of costs that must be met in starting a business. During the course of this unit, students might investigate the actual price of the various services, permits, and products that comprise start-up costs. At the end of the unit, you can revisit this exercise and ask students if they would want to start this business.

Visual Guide

Chapter 18 Opener

Discussion: Have the students study the chapter opening photo and describe what they see. Then lead a discussion about the kinds of things you might need to start your own business (for example, a store, a computer, shelves, inventory). How might students pay for such items?

Follow-Up: Ask students if they ever borrowed money to purchase something or to begin a project. Ask: "How did they convince the lender the money would be repaid?" Then ask: "How might this process be different if the lender were a bank?"

Workplace Skills and Chapter Correlations

FOUNDATION SKILLS						
Basic Skills	Reading	Writing	Math	Listening	Speaking	
Thinking Skills	Creative Thinking	Decision Making	Problem Solving	Seeing Things in the Mind's Eye	Knowing How to Learn	Reasoning
Personal Qualities	Responsibility	Self-Esteem	Sociability	Self-Management	Integrity/ Honesty	

WORKPLACE COMPETENCIES						
Resources	Allocating Time	Allocating Money	Allocating Material and Facility Resources	Allocating Human Resources		
Information	Acquiring and Evaluating Information	Organizing and Maintaining Information	Interpreting and Communicating Information	Using Computers to Process Information		
Interpersonal Skills	Participating as a Member of a Team	Teaching Others	Serving Clients/ Customers	Exercising Leadership	Negotiating to Arrive at a Decision	Working with Cultural Diversity
Systems	Understanding Systems	Monitoring and Correcting Performance	Improving and Designing Systems			
Technology	Selecting Technology	Applying Technology to Task	Maintaining and TroubleshootingTechnology			

Internet Extension

Activity: Have students access the Small Business Administration (SBA) Web site at **sba.gov**. Ask them how the information presented on the Web site can help with financial planning for a new business.

Keywords: Small Business Administration

Enrichment/Application Activity

Guest Speaker: Invite a representative from your local SBA office to talk to the class about starting a new business. Also ask him or her to bring a copy of the Small Business Resource Guide or Start-Up Kit for the class to review. (Local SBA offices are listed on the SBA Web site, **sba.gov**.)

Topic Spotlight

Government: Explain to students that in a free enterprise economic system, individuals have the freedom to organize and operate a business for profit with little government interference. Ask students in what ways government regulates businesses in this country and why.

Marketing: Choose a local business with which the students are familiar, and ask them to describe the services offered, local real estate prices, potential customers, and advertising and promotions. Allow students to discuss whether that business's marketing is helping the business grow.

Money: Give students the following math word problem: The costs to promote the opening of your retail business were \$5,000. Operating expenses for the first week, including payroll, inventory, and utilities, were \$10,000. If you brought in \$3,000 a day that week, how many days was it before you recovered your first week's costs? [ANSWER: 5 days; \$15,000 ÷ 3,000 = 5]

Additional Resources

Books

The Entrepreneur's Guide to Preparing a Winning Business Plan and Raising Venture Capital, by W. Keith Schilit (Financial Times Prentice Hall, ©2004). This book focuses on selling your business plan to investors to raise capital. In addition to guidance on preparing a sound plan, it offers advice on communicating the value of your business to an investor.

Streetwise Complete Business Plan With Software: Interactive Software to Quickly Create a Powerful Business Plan Plus a Comprehensive Book, by Bob Adams (CD-ROM and paperback: Adams Media Corporation, ©2002) This book and software will help you write an effective business plan containing: budgeting and financials, competitive analysis, management, marketing, sales and marketing, and strategic planning.

Internet

sba.gov The Web site of the Small Business Administration provides information about starting and operating a small business. Included are a checklist for business start-ups, an online business planning workshop, and business plan basics.

sba.gov/starting_business This page on the SBA site offers a business plan outline, a tutorial, as well as a Small Business Start-up Kit.

sba.gov/young/indexyoung.html At this page on the SBA site, students can find Discover Business! and learn about starting a business. Teachers can find curriculum guides designed to augment a semester course in entrepreneurship or small business ownership.

bplans.com This Web site offers a wide range of information to help you start and build your business. Included are expert advice on business start-ups, sample business plans, articles, and interactive tools, such as a starting costs calculator.

planware.org/strategy.htm This site offers tutorials and links for writing business plans, including a free sample template and software.

Note: Web-site addresses may change.

Section 18.1

Focus

Motivation

Ask the students if they perform well at school or work when they are ill. Then explain that a business performs best when it is healthy too. The financial plan of a business, much like a doctor's directive, shows what a business must do to be healthy so that it can achieve its goals.

Prereading

1. Have students skim the section, looking at the pictures, reading the captions, and reading the headings.
2. Ask a student to read aloud Read to Learn on page 574.
3. Have students list the Key Terms in their notebooks, and remind them to enter the definitions as they learn them.

Teach

Guided Practice

1. Ask a student to read aloud In the Real World on page 573, and ask students to try answering the question now and revisit it later when they have read the chapter.
2. Ask a student to read aloud Ask Standard and Poor's on page 573, and discuss it briefly with the class.
3. Have students silently read the rest of the section, noting and mentally answering the Predict, Relate, Question, and caption questions and reading the features such as Document Detective.

Independent Practice

1. Have students form the same groups they did in Chapter 17 and work on the same business.
2. Assign start-up capital to one student, operating capital to the second, and reserve capital to the third.
3. Have the students research to determine roughly how much capital they will need to start their businesses. The student working on reserve capital can assist the other two.

Assess

Reteaching

1. Have the students close their books, and divide them into four teams. Hand each team a list of the Key Terms, and tell them that the team that correctly writes the definitions first will get a prize. (Note: Have small prizes ready.)
2. Ask students if they see any difference between personal and business income statements.
3. Discuss with students the Reading Strategies and the pictures and figures with their caption questions. Assign feature questions to students and go over responses.

Enrichment

Have students brainstorm a list of uses for reserve capital in a small business. Write their responses on the board and discuss.

Assessment

1. Have students complete the Section 18.1 Assessment.
2. Give students a vocabulary quiz based on the Key Terms.
3. Assign an activity from Chapter 18 of the *Student Activity Workbook*.

Close

Tell the students that a good financial plan does not guarantee success. Ask them if they think a bad financial plan necessarily leads to failure, and have them explain their answers.

Section 18.2

Focus

Motivation

Tell the students that many people think the financial plan is the most important part of a business plan. Ask them why they think this is so. Then tell them that what they learn in this section may be critical to any plans they may have to start their own businesses. This is where they will learn to establish the financial basis for a healthy business.

Prereading

1. Have students skim the section, looking at the pictures, reading the captions, and reading the headings.
2. Ask a student to read aloud Read to Learn and Main Idea on page 589.

Teach

Guided Practice

1. Ask students to read aloud Starting a Business on page 589, and discuss it with them.
2. Ask students to look at the photo on page 590; lead students in discussing the caption question.
3. Have students silently read the rest of the section, noting and mentally answering the Predict, Relate, Question, React, and caption questions and reading the features such as Careers in Finance.

Independent Practice

Have students remain with the groups they formed in Chapter 17. Ask students to write strategic and marketing plans for their businesses. They might try writing a projected 12-month income statement.

Assess

Reteaching

1. Ask students to define the Key Term *chart of accounts* and explain its importance.
2. Ask students what they think are the most important aspects of this section and why.
3. Discuss with students the Reading Strategies and the pictures and figures with their caption questions. Assign feature questions to students and go over responses.

Enrichment

Invite an accountant to the class to speak to the students about raising capital for a new business.

Assessment

1. Have students complete the Section 18.2 Assessment.
2. Assign Chapter 18 Review and Activities.
3. Administer the test for Chapter 18 from the Reproducible Tests in the *Lesson Planner Plus* supplement.

Close

Ask the students to recall what they have done regarding starting a new business. After completing the activities in the last two or three chapters, ask them if they think they are ready to start their own businesses.

ANSWERS

STANDARD &POOR'S **Put on Your Financial Planner's Cap**

Answers might include: What are the incomes of similar businesses? What will be the cost of your merchandise? What other expenses can you project?

Global Financial Landscape

Answer might be students may opt to go to a foreign country, largely because they believe a person cannot earn a good living and move ahead in Russia.

Document Detective

1. The purpose of a personal financial statement is to show the financial health of an individual applying for a loan.
2. Sarah's net worth is $29,000.
3. Net worth is calculated by subtracting total liabilities from total assets.
4. Her salary is $55,000.
5. The SBA might want to contact the banks and other people to verify the information or to see if Sarah's loan payments are made on schedule.

Academic Connection

Answers will vary but should indicate that research must be done on the types and amount of business promotions done by rivals.

Careers in Finance

A controller coordinates all the accounting and financial aspects of a business, from accounts payable to investment strategies, and works with people at all levels of a company.

Section 18.1 Assessment

Quick Check

1. The two categories are: capital required to purchase the assets needed to start a business (equipment, inventory, etc.) and start-up costs (permits, fees, etc.).
2. You can estimate operating capital through financial forecasting, which involves preparing projected income statements, balance sheets, and statements of cash flow.
3. You can analyze financial information for other similar businesses, which can be obtained from trade associations, business organizations, and government agencies, such as the Small Business Administration and the Bureau of the Census.

Think Critically

4. Answers should reflect the idea that a financial plan allows a potential business owner to determine the amount of capital needed to start and operate the business. Without a financial plan and adequate funding, a business may not succeed.

Use Communication Skills

5. A written financial plan is essential because it is needed to determine the amount of start-up capital needed, to obtain funding from institutional lenders, and to determine the amount of capital available for growth.

Solve Money Problems

6. Assets might include supplies, a computer system, a telephone, and basketballs. Start-up costs might include insurance, gym rental deposits, professional association fees, business permits, and advertising.

Section 18.2 Assessment

Quick Check

1. Her financial plan included the following: Statement of Required Start-Up Capital, Projected 12-Month Income Statement, Projected 12-Month Statement of Cash Flows, Projected 3-Year Income Statement, Projected 3-Year Statement of Cash Flows, and Projected 3-Year Balance Sheet.
2. She projects she will show a positive net income during the ninth month.
3. Molly estimated her cash receipts and her cash payments (purchase of merchandise, operating expenses, interest expense, and taxes) for her first 12 months in business. Her total estimated cash payments were greater than her total estimated cash receipts, resulting in a negative cash flow.

Think Critically

4. Answers might include: She has taken business courses and seminars; researched locations and potential markets for her shop; and written a strategic plan and a marketing plan. She has saved money and established a good credit history. She has also consulted with an attorney and an accountant.

Use Math Skills

5. Year 2: $275,670 ($204,200 × 135% = $275,670)
   Year 3: $372,154.50 ($275,670 × 135% = $372,154.50)
   Molly might use the increased revenue to hire more employees, extend store hours, or increase advertising expenses.

Solve Money Problems

6. Answers may include that Molly postpone the purchase of office furniture and a photocopier until she can afford them. She might also consider using her own vehicle to deliver orders and cut back on merchandise she wants to purchase.

Chapter 18 Review & Activities

Communicating Key Terms

Answers should demonstrate an understanding of the terms used and the idea that banks need assurances that the company seeking a commercial loan is likely to make a profit.

Reviewing Key Concepts

1. Identify required assets; identify start-up costs; and assign costs to identified items.
2. Students' answers will vary but should demonstrate an understanding that start-up costs are costs or fees associated with starting a business, such as license fees.
3. If you estimate operating capital on the high side, you are likely to have enough to cover unexpected expenses.
4. The information needed for projected income statements can be estimated by using information for similar businesses. This can be obtained from trade associations, vendors, local business organizations, and government agencies such as the Small Business Administration.
5. Reserve capital is money set aside for unexpected costs or opportunities, much like cash in a savings account.
6. It determines how much cash may be available to pay bills, meet payroll, and do other necessary business functions.

ACADEMIC SKILLS

Answers should demonstrate an understanding that variable expenses are expenses that fluctuate. Molly might purchase fewer supplies or find a better deal on phone service.

YOUR FINANCIAL FIGURES

1. She is paying 25.9 percent. ($30,000 ÷ $116,000 = .2586)
2. Students should show the above calculation using appropriate software.

REAL-WORLD Application

1. Students should review the chapter information.
2. Answers may include: Risks include the possibility that her home will decrease in value, causing the equity in her home to decrease; her business will fail; and her family members will need their loans to be repaid quickly. Lenders may want to know what additional collateral she has.

Internet CONNECTION

1. Internet research but will depend on what is available locally.
2. Internet research but will depend on what is available locally.

BusinessWeek ONLINE

Accept all answers that demonstrate students have read the online article and understand the consequences of lacking capital.

Business Finance Basics

Chapter 19
Sources of Funding

Chapter 20
Financial Accounting

Chapter 21
Managing Payroll and Inventory

Chapter 22
Pricing, Costing, and Growth

Unit Overview

In Unit 5, students learned that a good business plan and financial plan are necessary to successfully start a new business. In Unit 6, students will learn how good financial management is necessary to keep a business operating. Chapter 19 discusses the various business costs and identifies different sources of funding. In Chapter 20, students will learn about basic aspects of accounting, including analyzing business transactions and the accounting cycle. Chapter 21 discusses a business's two greatest expenses—payroll and inventory. Chapter 22 discusses financial decisions that relate to pricing products and growth of a business.

Introductory Activity

Discuss with students the similarities between a person and a business being financially successful. Have students review the money management strategies from Chapter 3 and ask how these same strategies could be used by businesses. Point out how calculating a personal net cash flow is like calculating a business's net income. Show students that the equation for a personal balance sheet is the same one used for a business's balance sheet; it is just written differently. Both net worth and owner's equity measure the difference between what is owned (assets) and what is owed (liabilities). Then have students predict how planning for a business's financial success is like planning for personal financial success.

BusinessWeek
FINANCE FILE

Cycling Back to the Future

Answer Accept all reasonable answers that show student effort. Answers might include that Gaansari did not compete with the large bicycle companies, but carried specialized merchandise for a niche market. Once customers were loyal, Gaansari capitalized on his brand and expanded his product lines.

Get a Financial Life!

Growing a Business

STEP A The Process

Make sure students have access to all necessary materials.

1. Have students explain how their recommended new product or line will increase Party Town's market share.
2. If possible, arrange for a field trip to a local mall or shopping center that has several businesses which students could research.
3. If a business owner from your community is scheduled as a guest speaker, allow students time to ask him or her questions about running a successful business and expansion strategies.
4. The selling price per bouquet is \$21.78. [ANSWER: \$5.25 + \$6 + \$0.85 = \$12.10; \$12.10 × .80 = \$9.68; \$12.10 + \$9.68 = \$21.78] The break-even point is 31 (30.99) bouquets. [ANSWER: \$21.78n = \$12.10n + \$300; \$9.68n = \$300]
5. Answers will vary depending on the target profit students choose. To calculate the number of bouquets that must be sold to achieve the target profit, students must use the following formula:

   \$21.78n = \$12.10n + \$300 + target profit

   n = number of bouquets they must sell to reach target profit. To calculate margin of safety, students must use this formula:

   Target sales − break-even sales = margin of safety
6. Research should include a list of costs for starting a Web site with e-tail capability.

STEP B Create Your Portfolio

Evaluate students' portfolios based on whether all steps of the process are completed, the calculations are accurate, the information seems well researched, and the contents are in order.

STEP C Applying Technology

Evaluate students' research and policy based on the following criteria:

1. The definition for *ethics* is accurate. Have students cite the dictionary they used.
2. Students should explain how they arrived at their policies.
3. Research should be thorough but need not be exhaustive.
4. If possible, cite examples of information accessed that was not accurate.

Unit Closure

Ask students: "Why will good planning usually result in growth for a business?" Ask them if they think this is true and why. Then ask what they have learned in this unit that would help a business to plan and grow.

Evaluation

Administer the Unit 6 test from the **Exam***View*® Pro Testmaker CD-ROM.

CHAPTER 19 Sources of Funding

pages 608–633

SECTION	LEARNING OBJECTIVES	FEATURES	TEXT RESOURCES	TECHNOLOGY RESOURCES
19.1	**After completing this section, students will have learned to:** Explain the role of entrepreneurs. Differentiate between start-up costs, operating costs, and reserve funds. Identify sources of personal and private financing. Discuss the options available through bank funding. Identify the factors banks consider to approve commercial loans.	**Careers in Finance,** p. 613 **WebQuest,** p. 614 **Document Detective,** p. 615 **Savvy Saver,** p. 616 **Go Figure**—A Home Equity Loan, p. 618 **S&P's Global Financial Landscape,** p. 619 **TechByte,** p. 621 **Academic Connection,** p. 622 **Common Cents,** p. 623	**Section Assessment,** p. 624 Quick Check Think Critically Use Math Skills Solve Money Problems **Student Activity Workbook**	Lesson Planner Plus Online Learning Center Interactive Student Edition *Presentation Plus!* **Exam***View*® Pro Test Generator Financial Planner Software
19.2	**After completing this section, students will have learned to:** Describe the function of the Small Business Administration. Identify alternative sources of funding for a business.	**S&P's Put on Your Financial Planner's Cap,** p. 628	**Section Assessment,** p. 629 Quick Check Think Critically Use Communication Skills Solve Money Problems **Student Activity Workbook**	Lesson Planner Plus Online Learning Center Interactive Student Edition *Presentation Plus!* **Exam***View*® Pro Test Generator Financial Planner Software

CHAPTER 19 Planning Guide

Meeting National Standards for Business Education	
Section 19.1	**Section 19.2**
Economics II. Economic Systems III. Economic Institutions and Incentives **Personal Finance** I. Personal Decision Making II. Earning a Living IV. Saving and Investing VII. Using Credit VIII. Protecting Against Risk	**Economics** III. Economic Institutions and Incentives VIII. International Economic Concepts **Personal Finance** II. Earning a Living VII. Using Credit

Teaching Connection

Funding Discussion

Based on the business the students brainstormed about at the beginning of Chapter 18, ask them about sources of the funds they will need to start their business. This may be a good place to bring up the concept of sources and uses of funds, which is the starting point for organizing financial statements. If the students appear to believe that they can easily obtain a bank loan to start their business, remind them of the concept of *risk* that they learned about earlier in this course. Ask them whether they think banks will view them as good credit risks for commercial loans. What might improve their credit-worthiness in the bank's eyes? How might their willingness to risk their personal funds and use other sources affect the bank's decision? What are some things they might do to improve the bank's estimation of their chances of success?

Visual Guide

Chapter 19 Opener

Discussion: Have students study the chapter opening photo and describe what they see. Then lead a discussion about ways to fund a new business (for example, personal savings, loans from family and friends, loans from a bank, loans from private investors).

Follow-Up: Ask students if they were starting a business, where they would look for funding. Ask: "Would it be a good idea to put your expenses on a credit card? Why or why not?"

Teacher Manual

Workplace Skills and Chapter Correlations

FOUNDATION SKILLS						
Basic Skills	Reading	Writing	Math	Listening	Speaking	
Thinking Skills	Creative Thinking	Decision Making	Problem Solving	Seeing Things in the Mind's Eye	Knowing How to Learn	Reasoning
Personal Qualities	Responsibility	Self-Esteem	Sociability	Self-Management	Integrity/ Honesty	

WORKPLACE COMPETENCIES						
Resources	Allocating Time	Allocating Money	Allocating Material and Facility Resources	Allocating Human Resources		
Information	Acquiring and Evaluating Information	Organizing and Maintaining Information	Interpreting and Communicating Information	Using Computers to Process Information		
Interpersonal Skills	Participating as a Member of a Team	Teaching Others	Serving Clients/ Customers	Exercising Leadership	Negotiating to Arrive at a Decision	Working with Cultural Diversity
Systems	Understanding Systems	Monitoring and Correcting Performance	Improving and Designing Systems			
Technology	Selecting Technology	Applying Technology to Task	Maintaining and TroubleshootingTechnology			

Internet Extension

Activity: Have students access one of the ACE-Net Web sites and print out the page that tells who maintains the site (this may be found under "About Us"). Ask: "What university maintains the ACE-Net Web site?" Ask: "What does that say about the reliability of the information." [ANSWER: Different Web sites are maintained by different universities, e.g., University of New Hampshire and California State University at San Bernardino]

Keywords: ACE-Net

Enrichment/Application Activity

Guest Speaker: Invite a commercial loan officer to class to talk about his or her job: the career path that led to the position, what the speaker likes and dislikes about the job. Have each student write a question to ask the guest speaker.

Topic Spotlight

Government: Ask students: "Do you think the government should be in the business of providing or guaranteeing loans to business? Why or why not? How might this affect our economy?"

Ethics: Write the term *usury* on the board, and ask volunteers for a definition. [ANSWER: the lending of money at exorbitant interest rates or in excess of a legal rate.] Ask: "What kind of lender would practice usury? Why might a business owner be willing to tolerate usury?"

Money: Ask students if they charge interest when they lend friends money. Why or why not? Does the loan amount affect whether or not interest is charged? If so, how?

Additional Resources

Books

The Small Business Bible: Everything You Need to Know to Succeed in Your Small Business by Steven D. Strauss (paperback: Wiley, ©2004). This is a comprehensive, A–Z guide to everything you need to know to establish and operate a small business. Topics include developing your business idea, buying an existing business or franchise, and operating and growing on a shoestring budget.

Six-Week Start-Up: A Step-By-Step Program for Starting Your Business, Making Money, and Achieving Your Goals! by Rhonda Abrams (paperback: The Planning Shop, ©2004). This book offers entrepreneurs a guide to getting a new business started fast. In six weeks, readers learn to identify their competitive edge, determine how much money they will need and where to get it, choose effective marketing techniques, and more.

Internet

eonetwork.org This is the Web site of the Entrepreneurs' Organization (EO), a membership organization for entrepreneurs. It provides entrepreneurs the opportunity to learn from each other through features such as Direct Peer-to-Peer Learning, Once-in-a-Lifetime Experiences, and Connections to Experts.

morebusiness.com This is the Web site for the Business Resource Center, which offers articles on starting and running your own business and downloadable templates for business plans and contracts.

sba.gov To find out about the lending programs available from the Small Business Administration, log on to its Web site, then click on Financing Your Business. There you will find links to Financing Eligibility Topics, SBA Loan Topics, Surety Bond Topics, and other useful information.

businessfinance.com Search a base of more than 4,000 sources for information on business loans, venture capital, equipment leasing, and commercial real estate financing.

Note: Web-site addresses may change.

Section 19.1

Focus

Motivation

Ask students if they have thought about where they would get the money to open a business, and tell them this chapter may help them figure that out.

Prereading

1. Have students skim the section, looking at the pictures, reading the captions, and reading the headings.
2. Ask a student to read aloud Read to Learn on page 610.
3. Have students list the Key Terms in their notebooks and begin making flash cards, and remind them to enter the definitions as they learn them.

Teach

Guided Practice

1. Ask a student to read aloud In the Real World on page 609, and ask students why a lender would want to see a business plan before lending money.
2. Ask a student to read aloud Ask Standard and Poor's on page 609, and discuss it briefly with them.
3. Have students silently read the rest of the section, noting and mentally answering the Predict, Relate, Question, and caption questions and reading the features such as Document Detective.

Independent Practice

Ask students to search newspapers and magazines for ads from banks and other institutions offering home equity and personal loans. Have each student bring three ads to class. Ask students to compare interest rates and terms, and write a one-page report.

Assess

Reteaching

1. Have the students learn the Key Terms by practicing with partners using flash cards.
2. Reinforce the five C's of credit by having students, with books closed, name and define them.
3. Discuss with students the Reading Strategies and the pictures and figures with their caption questions. Assign features questions to students and go over responses.

Enrichment

Give students copies of a commercial loan application, and ask the students to correlate the information required with the five C's of credit.

Assessment

1. Have students complete the Section 19.1 Assessment.
2. Give students a vocabulary quiz based on the Key Terms.
3. Assign an activity from Chapter 19 of the *Student Activity Workbook*.

Close

Talk to students about why a degree in economics, accounting, or business might be required for a commercial loan officer.

Section 19.2

Focus

Motivation

Inform the students that the federal government has a variety of plans to help small businesses, and ask them why they think the government is so interested in small business development.

Prereading

1. Have students skim the section, looking at the pictures, reading the captions, and reading the headings.
2. Ask a student to read aloud Read to Learn and Main Idea on page 625.
3. Have students list the Key Terms in their notebooks, and remind them to enter the definitions as they learn them.

Teach

Guided Practice

1. Ask students to read aloud Small Business Administration on page 625 and ask them if they think they would consider using this agency.
2. Have students look at the picture Federal Assistance on page 626 and have them find the answer to the caption question.
3. Have students silently read the rest of the section, noting and mentally answering the Predict, Relate, Question, React, and caption questions and reading the features such as Put on Your Financial Planner's Cap.

Independent Practice

Tell the students that the Small Business Administration has 15 different guaranteed loan programs. Assign programs to the students, and have them research them. Students are to write summaries or make graphic displays of their findings.

Assess

Reteaching

1. Have the students write sentences using each term in the Key Terms list.
2. To reinforce the concept, ask students to define venture capital and explain why venture capital firms lend money.
3. Discuss with students the Reading Strategies and the pictures and figures with their caption questions. Assign features questions to students and go over responses.

Enrichment

Invite a local small businessperson to class to speak to students about funding a new business and continued funding for growth. Have students prepare questions before the guest arrives.

Assessment

1. Have students complete the Section 19.2 Assessment.
2. Assign Chapter 19 Review and Activities.
3. Administer the test for Chapter 19 from the Reproducible Tests in the *Lesson Planner Plus* supplement.

Close

Review the process of start-up financing by creating with students a list on the board of "Do's and Don'ts for Start-Up Financing."

ANSWERS

Careers in Finance

Answers might include that commercial loans frequently deal with larger amounts of money, a business's revenue history is more irregular than most personal incomes, and commercial loans may be for growth.

Document Detective

1. It will have 22 employees.
2. The company will purchase land and construct a new building.
3. $400,000
4. It owes $12,500.
5. The term is ten years.

Global Financial Landscape

It enables people to take advantage of educational opportunities, to connect to the world, and to learn about economic opportunities, which will help build the Estonian economy.

Academic Connection

Answers should demonstrate student understanding of the kinds of information that convince a lender to loan money to a business (mainly that the business is likely to make a profit and repay the loan).

Put on Your Financial Planner's Cap

A loan from a commercial finance company may offer the best terms, and because the business has shown a profit, it should qualify for a loan.

Section 19.1 Assessment

Quick Check

1. Start-up costs are the costs or expenses of setting up your business. Operating costs are the ongoing expenses for operating your business.
2. You can use your personal savings or investments, such as stocks or bonds, or get a consumer or home equity loan.
3. A small business might use a line of credit for unexpected costs or routine expenses that it cannot handle in the short term, such as fixing the plumbing or re-roofing the building.

Think Critically

4. Answers will vary, but students should recognize that a home equity loan may be risky. Private financing may be the best idea because friends and family are more likely to provide funds to an unproven business, may not charge interest, and may be flexible about repayment.

Use Math Skills

5. Mario will need to borrow $5,200. [ANSWER: $8,900 + $6,300 + $10,000 = $25,200; $25,200 − $20,000 = $5,200] He will borrow 20.6 percent of his total costs. [ANSWER: $5,200 ÷ $25,200 = 0.206 or 20.6%]

Solve Money Problems

6. Answers should identify the primary sources of funding and present logical reasoning to explain choices. She should avoid accumulating debt on a credit card.

Section 19.2 Assessment

Quick Check

1. The SBA offers assistance to people who are starting small businesses and to those who want to expand existing businesses.
2. business credit cards, private investors, commercial finance companies, venture capital firms, and state and local government programs
3. One way you can get venture capital is through SBICs, which are venture capital firms regulated by the SBA.

Think Critically

4. Answers will vary, but students should recognize that a business credit card charges high interest and should be used for expenses that can be paid off every month.

Use Communication Skills

5. Answers will vary, but students should advise Ashley that the SBA can help her to receive a loan under the Guaranteed Loan Program.

Solve Money Problems

6. Answers will vary, but the best choices for Kimo would be a bank loan guaranteed by the SBA or a loan from a private investor in his community, provided the terms are good. Kimo might not be able to get a loan from a venture capital firm because his loan is under $500,000.

Chapter 19 Review & Activities

Communicating Key Terms

Answers should demonstrate an understanding of the terms used and the process of applying for an SBA approved loan.

Reviewing Key Concepts

1. Small businesses contribute significantly to the American economy in terms of providing jobs, paying taxes, and producing goods and services.
2. Start-up costs are the costs or expenses of setting up your business. Operating costs are the ongoing expenses for operating your business. A reserve fund is money set aside for future growth or other needs.
3. Pros include they are fairly easy to get if you have a lot of equity in your home. Cons include if your business fails, you may lose your house.
4. Answers may include: 1) secured loan advantage, if you provide collateral you are more likely to have your loan funded; disadvantage, if you fail to repay the loan, you lose your collateral; 2) unsecured loan advantage, you do not risk losing any assets; disadvantage, the interest rate is higher; 3) line of credit advantage, you have immediate access to money; disadvantage, once you borrow money, the bank charges you interest.
5. The five C's of credit are character, capacity, capital, collateral, and credit history. These are the criteria loan officers use to evaluate applications for commercial loans.
6. The SBA, an agency of the federal government, guarantees part of SBA-approved loans. Under this arrangement, the lender wins, because its risk is lowered. The entrepreneur wins because the business loan is usually funded.
7. A venture capital firm is a company that provides private funding for small businesses that need a substantial amount of immediate cash, usually $500,000 or more.

ACADEMIC SKILLS

Answers will vary, but start-up costs may include office supplies, a computer, Internet service, advertising, and a deposit for rental space; operating costs may include utilities, office supplies, Internet service, and travel costs to visit clients.

YOUR FINANCIAL FIGURES

1. $2,500 ($1,200 + $700 + $100 + $500 = $2,500); the computer accounts for 48 percent of start-up costs.
2. Students should show the above calculation using appropriate software.

REAL-WORLD Application

1. Answers will differ depending on current home equity loan rates.
2. A home equity loan might be a good choice if the entrepreneur cannot obtain a consumer loan, if the value of the property is likely to remain the same or rise, and if the business is likely to succeed.

Internet CONNECTION

1. SBA advantages include the services it provides, such as training, organization guidance, and assistance obtaining funding.
2. Answers may include: A bank that participates in the SBA Guaranteed Loan Program will be more likely to fund your loan, and venture capital firms known as SBICs are regulated by the SBA.

BusinessWeek ONLINE

Accept all paragraphs that demonstrate students have read the online article and understand the concepts.

Teacher Manual

CHAPTER 20 Financial Accounting

pages 634–663

SECTION	LEARNING OBJECTIVES	FEATURES	TEXT RESOURCES	TECHNOLOGY RESOURCES
20.1	**After completing this section, students will have learned to:** Describe the accounting system. Identify the first five steps of the accounting cycle. Discuss the role of the general journal. Explain the purpose of posting. Summarize the purpose of a trial balance.	**Savvy Saver,** p. 637 **WebQuest,** p. 639 **Careers in Finance,** p. 639 **Common Cents,** p. 640 **S&P's Put on Your Financial Planner's Cap,** p. 641 **Document Detective,** p. 643	**Section Assessment,** p. 649 Quick Check Think Critically Use Communication Skills Solve Money Problems **Student Activity Workbook**	Lesson Planner Plus Online Learning Center Interactive Student Edition *Presentation Plus!* **Exam***View*® Pro Test Generator Financial Planner Software
20.2	**After completing this section, students will have learned to:** Identify items included on an income statement. Explain the purpose of a balance sheet. Define and explain the role of a statement of cash flows.	**Academic Connection,** p. 652 **TechByte,** p. 656 **S&P's Global Financial Landscape,** p. 658	**Section Assessment,** p. 659 Quick Check Think Critically Use Math Skills Solve Money Problems **Student Activity Workbook**	Lesson Planner Plus Online Learning Center Interactive Student Edition *Presentation Plus!* **Exam***View*® Pro Test Generator Financial Planner Software

Meeting National Standards for Business Education	
Section 20.1	**Section 20.2**
Economics VII. The Role of Government **Personal Finance** II. Earning a Living IV. Saving and Investing	**Economics** VIII. International Economic Concepts **Personal Finance** II. Earning a Living VIII. Protecting Against Risk

Teaching Connection

Accounting in the News

Write the following names on the board:

- Sarbanes-Oxley Act
- Enron Corporation
- Worldcom Corporation
- Arthur Andersen Company

Ask the students to write down a few words that these names bring to mind and call on them to share what they wrote. Based on the students' responses, discuss the ramifications of inaccurate or misrepresented accounting information. Ask the students how such information might affect them. If they seem to think the stock market is too far afield from their lives, bring up their parents' investments for retirement or their children's college educations. Ask the students how falsified financial statements might affect their ability to get a car loan (prime lending rates—which affect vehicle and residential loan rates—are affected by the money supply and general economic conditions—which are closely related to stock market conditions). A goal here is to help students realize that while they may perceive accounting as dull, accurate accounting, done according to Generally Accepted Accounting Principles (GAAP), is actually is the first line of defense in protecting consumers' investments.

Visual Guide

Chapter 20 Opener

Discussion: Have the students study the chapter opening photo and describe what they see. Then lead a discussion about how finances might influence business decisions. Ask: "What kinds of financial information might help you improve your business and make a better profit?"

Follow-Up: Ask students if they have ever sold anything—at a garage sale, a lemonade stand, or over the Internet. How did they determine what to sell and how much to charge?

Teacher Manual

Workplace Skills and Chapter Correlations

FOUNDATION SKILLS

Basic Skills	Reading	Writing	Math	Listening	Speaking	
Thinking Skills	Creative Thinking	Decision Making	Problem Solving	Seeing Things in the Mind's Eye	Knowing How to Learn	Reasoning
Personal Qualities	Responsibility	Self-Esteem	Sociability	Self-Management	Integrity/ Honesty	

WORKPLACE COMPETENCIES

Resources	Allocating Time	Allocating Money	Allocating Material and Facility Resources	Allocating Human Resources		
Information	Acquiring and Evaluating Information	Organizing and Maintaining Information	Interpreting and Communicating Information	Using Computers to Process Information		
Interpersonal Skills	Participating as a Member of a Team	Teaching Others	Serving Clients/ Customers	Exercising Leadership	Negotiating to Arrive at a Decision	Working with Cultural Diversity
Systems	Understanding Systems	Monitoring and Correcting Performance	Improving and Designing Systems			
Technology	Selecting Technology	Applying Technology to Task	Maintaining and TroubleshootingTechnology			

Internet Extension

Activity: Have students use the Internet to find out what accounting services are available to small business owners.

Keywords: small business and accounting

Enrichment/Application Activity

Field Trip: Arrange for students to visit a bookstore and computer software store to review a variety of accounting books and software products. Have students write a report about either software or a book that tells the title, what is covered (book), what it does (software), and who wrote it or produced it.

Topic Spotlight

Technology: Discuss with students whether they would prefer to use a computer or accounting paper to keep accounting records for a small service business, if they had one.

Money: What is the price of one can of soda when a 6-pack of 12-oz. cans sells two for $5? [ANSWER: 42 cents: $5.00 ÷ 2 = $2.50; $2.50 ÷ 6 = $.417, or 42 cents] If one can of soda sells for $1.00 in a vending machine, how much money can you save by bringing a can from home 5 days a week for a year? [ANSWER: $150.80: $1.00 − .42 = .58; 5 days × 52 weeks = 260 days; .58 × 260 days = $150.80]

Marketing: Have students create an advertisement for a bookkeeping or accounting firm to be placed in a financial magazine.

Additional Resources

Books

Financial Accounting: Tools for Business Decision Making, 3rd edition, by Paul D. Kimmel, Jerry J. Weygandt, Donald E. Kieso (Wiley, ©2003). This book provides readers with an understanding of basic accounting concepts. It includes both a large-scale view of accounting and an introduction to real financial statements and accounting activities.

Financial Accounting, Study Guide by Jerry Weygandt, Donald E. Kieso, Paul D. Kimmel (paperback: Wiley, ©2002) Each chapter of the guide includes study objectives, and a chapter review with 20–30 key points. True/false, multiple-choice, and matching questions provide additional practice. Solutions for the exercises are detailed to provide substantial feedback.

Internet

bambooweb.com/articles/a/c/Accountancy.html This Web site provides encyclopedic information on the topic of accounting as well as news articles and information about accounting services.

hoovers.com/free Hoover's provides access to company profiles of more than 40,000 companies, public and private, and worldwide. Readers can view company financial statements, annual reports, stock quotes, company history, and more.

quicken.com/small_business This Web site provides valuable information for small businesses on topics such as managing your finances. It includes tools to help you find the right financial management software and get advice from CPAs and other financial professionals.

Note: Web-site addresses may change.

Section 20.1

Focus

Motivation

Have the students imagine they want to sell their businesses. Ask them what a potential buyer might want to know about the business; remind them the business's financial statements are the windows into the business. Then tell them that in this chapter, they will learn about a standardized accounting system that helps people such as buyers and lenders evaluate the financial health of a company and compare companies.

Prereading

1. Have students skim the section, looking at the pictures, reading the captions, and reading the headings.
2. Ask a student to read aloud Read to Learn on page 636.
3. Have students list the Key Terms in their notebooks and remind them to enter the definitions as they learn them.

Teach

Guided Practice

1. Ask students to read aloud In the Real World on page 635 and discuss the question with them.
2. Ask a student to read aloud Ask Standard & Poor's on page 635 and discuss it briefly with them.
3. Have students silently read the rest of the section, noting and mentally answering the Predict, Relate, Question, and caption questions and reading the features such as Document Detective.

Independent Practice

Ask the students to research three available computer accounting systems and compare and contrast their features. Ask the students to assess whether the users of the systems need to understand accounting. Finally, ask which one of the three systems they would recommend and why. Have the students report their findings in writing.

Assess

Reteaching

1. Have students create crossword puzzles using the terms in the Key Terms list.
2. To reinforce the first five steps in the accounting cycle, have students create posters illustrating the cycle.
3. Discuss with students the Reading Strategies and the pictures and figures with their caption questions. Assign features questions to students and go over responses.

Enrichment

Ask the students to prepare a list of books, magazines, and Internet sites that would be useful to a business owner with little accounting experience.

Assessment

1. Have students complete the Section 20.1 Assessment.
2. Give students a vocabulary quiz based on the Key Terms.
3. Assign an activity from Chapter 20 of the *Student Activity Workbook.*

Close

Ask students to identify the advantages of a standardized accounting system, and ask if there are any disadvantages.

Section 20.2

Focus

Motivation

Ask students how they will know if their businesses are doing well; if some say by the amount of money in the bank, counter with the notion they may not have paid their bills yet. Follow up with the idea that, to have an accurate picture, they need to have good financial reports.

Prereading

1. Have students skim the section, looking at the pictures, reading the captions, and reading the headings.
2. Ask a student to read aloud Read to Learn and Main Idea on page 650.
3. Have students list the Key Terms in their notebooks and prepare flash cards, and remind them to enter the definitions as they learn them.

Teach

Guided Practice

1. Ask students to read aloud Financial Statements on page 650, and ask them if they can see why such reports are essential.
2. Have students silently read the rest of the section, noting and mentally answering the Predict, Relate, Question, React, and caption questions and reading the features such as Academic Connection.

Independent Practice

Take a field trip to the accounting department of a medium-sized local business. The students are to determine how the records are kept, job duties, the departmental structure (managers, supervisors, clerks, specialists, etc.), statements produced, how the statements are verified, and technology used. Have students write a report.

Assess

Reteaching

1. Have the students practice with flash cards each term in the Key Terms list.
2. Ask students which report they think is easiest to prepare and easiest to understand: the income statement, balance sheet, or statement of cash flows, and why. Have them name two characteristics of each report.
3. Discuss with students the Reading Strategies and the pictures and figures with their caption questions. Assign features questions to students and go over responses.

Enrichment

Have students analyze the kinds and amounts of information each financial report offers. Ask them whether the reports duplicate each other or describe different aspects of the financial picture.

Assessment

1. Have students complete the Section 20.2 Assessment.
2. Assign Chapter 20 Review and Activities.
3. Administer the test for Chapter 20 from the Reproducible Tests in the *Lesson Planner Plus* supplement.

Close

Discuss with the students if they think business owners should prepare these financial statements for themselves or have someone do it for them. Have them justify their answers.

ANSWERS

Careers in Finance

Answers might include communication skills, patience, and a sense of humor.

STANDARD &POOR'S Put on Your Financial Planner's Cap

Advantages might include the ability to offer a fuller range of services, and your financial records will be in order; one disadvantage might be differing approaches.

Document Detective

1. Gross profit is calculated by subtracting the cost of goods sold from sales.
2. The statement covers the year ending December 31, 2007.
3. 50 percent
4. $250,000
5. The company can try to increase its sales revenue or cut its expenses.

Academic Connection

Answers vary from day to day. Accept all answers that show that the research was done.

STANDARD &POOR'S Global Financial Landscape

Answers may include enter the transaction and post the amounts as well as other functions.

Section 20.1 Assessment

Quick Check

1. (1) Collect and verify source documents; (2) analyze each transaction; (3) journalize each transaction; (4) post to the general ledger; and (5) prepare a trial balance.
2. All of the transactions of the business are recorded in a general journal.
3. A general ledger contains a page for each account. The accounts are grouped, and this allows for easy access to information.

Think Critically

4. Answers might include: You may have made a mistake in addition, reversed two digits within an amount, omitted an account balance from the general ledger, or put a number in the wrong column.

Use Communication Skills

5. Accept paragraphs that explain the first five steps in the accounting cycle.

Solve Money Problems

6. Answers might include cash in bank, merchandise, equipment, accounts payable, rent, utilities, telephone, and payroll.

Section 20.2 Assessment

Quick Check

1. revenue, cost of merchandise sold, gross profit on sales, operating expenses, and net income (or loss)
2. A balance sheet shows the current financial position of the business by reporting its assets and the claims against those assets.
3. A statement of cash flows can determine if there is enough cash to pay bills, buy merchandise, or pay for emergencies. It can help you get a loan.

Think Critically

4. Answers may include: A business may show a profit for the most recent accounting period but still have more cash outflows than inflows during a time period. If so, the business may not have enough money available to pay its employees.

Use Math Skills

5. Fall semester: $5,420 − 3,500 = $1,920 gross profit on sales; percentage of gross profit to sales: $1,920 ÷ 5,420 = 0.3542 or 35%. Spring semester: $4,890 − 3,060 = $1,830 gross profit on sales; percentage of gross profit to sales: $1,830 ÷ 4,890 = 0.3742 or 37%. Profits did not improve.

Solve Money Problems

6. Accept all reasonable answers, such as cash inflow and outflow and value of assets.

Chapter 20 Review & Activities

Communicating Key Terms

Presentations should demonstrate an understanding of the terms used and of accounting and financial statements and their importance to business decision making.

Reviewing Key Concepts

1. The accounting equation is Assets − Liabilities = Owner's Equity. This means that the assets of the business minus the liabilities equals the owner's equity.
2. (1) Collect and verify source documents; (2) analyze each transaction; (3) journalize each transaction; (4) post to the general ledger; and (5) prepare a trial balance.
3. (1) An asset account increases on the debit side and decreases on the credit side; and (2) liability and owner's equity accounts increase on the credit side and decrease on the debit side.
4. The figures posted to the general ledger—and then checked in the trial balance—are done by category, so that the information can be presented as well-organized reports.
5. It is a list of all the account names for a business and their current balances.
6. An income statement reports net income or net loss for an accounting period. An income statement for a merchandising business has five sections: revenue, cost of merchandise sold, gross profit on sales, operating expenses, net income (or loss).
7. Answers may include: A business may have a reasonable balance sheet but a poor cash flow situation if too much of its assets are inventory and/or fixed assets, neither of which contribute to cash flow until they are sold, and neither of which can be sold quickly under normal circumstances.
8. A statement of cash flows is a financial statement that reports how much cash a business took in and where the cash went. It explains changes in the Cash in Bank account during the accounting period.

ACADEMIC SKILLS

Accept all articles that explain that preparing a trial balance is similar to balancing your personal checkbook.

YOUR FINANCIAL FIGURES

1.

Assets	**2003**	**2004**	**%change**
Cash	17,500	24,300	+39%
Marketable securities	93,000	88,000	–5.4%
Accounts receivable	87,455	68,600	–22%
Inventories	162,000	169,000	+4.3%
Fixed assets	147,000	138,000	–6.1%
Liabilities			
Current liabilities	114,000	122,000	+7.0%
Long-term debt	216,000	214,000	–1.0%
Partnership equity	176,955	151,900	–14.2%

2. Students should show the calculations.

REAL-WORLD Application

Accept all role plays that demonstrate an understanding that accounting systems differ for different types of business.

Internet CONNECTION

Answers and presentations should show that types of software were researched and should indicate students' understanding of the features that differentiate the software.

BusinessWeek ONLINE

Accept all answers that demonstrate students have read the online material and understand the concepts.

Teacher Manual

CHAPTER 21 Managing Payroll and Inventory

pages 664–695

SECTION	LEARNING OBJECTIVES	FEATURES	TEXT RESOURCES	TECHNOLOGY RESOURCES
21.1	**After completing this section, students will have learned to:** Identify six steps in managing a payroll system. Describe the common methods of paying employees. Discuss required and voluntary payroll deductions. Identify the accounts used in recording payroll.	**Careers in Finance,** p. 667 **Go Figure**—Gross Earnings and Overtime, p. 668 **Academic Connection,** p. 671 **Go Figure**—FICA Deduction, p. 671 **TechByte,** p. 672 **S&P's Global Financial Landscape,** p. 676 **Go Figure**—Unemployment Taxes, p. 678	**Section Assessment,** p. 679 Quick Check Think Critically Use Math Skills Solve Money Problems **Student Activity Workbook**	Lesson Planner Plus Online Learning Center Interactive Student Edition *Presentation Plus!* **Exam***View*® Pro Test Generator Financial Planner Software
21.2	**After completing this section, students will have learned to:** Identify information needed for an inventory control system. Summarize methods of determining inventory quantity. Explain methods used to calculate cost of inventory. Discuss how to analyze inventory turnover.	**WebQuest,** p. 682 **Common Cents,** p. 684 **Document Detective,** p. 685 **S&P's Put on Your Financial Planner's Cap,** p. 688 **Go Figure**—Average Inventory, p. 689 **Go Figure**—Inventory Turnover, p. 689 **Go Figure**—Number of Days in Stock, p. 690	**Section Assessment,** p. 691 Quick Check Think Critically Use Communication Skills Solve Money Problems **Student Activity Workbook**	Lesson Planner Plus Online Learning Center Interactive Student Edition *Presentation Plus!* **Exam***View*® Pro Test Generator Financial Planner Software

Meeting National Standards for Business Education	
Section 21.1	**Section 21.2**
Economics I. Allocation of Resources III. Economic Institutions and Incentives **Personal Finance** VI. Banking	**Economics** VI. Productivity VIII. International Economic Concepts **Personal Finance** II. Earning a Living

Teaching Connection

Business and Math Connection

Explain to students that many manufacturing companies store their inventory—products ready to be shipped to buyers (e.g., stores, mail orders)—in warehouses, and usually pay rent based on the volume of storage space used. Ask students to figure out the volume (length × width × height) of specific pieces of furniture in the classroom. Then determine the volume of the classroom itself. If the classroom were a warehouse, how many of each piece of furniture measured could be stored in that space? If an 8 × 10 × 8 foot storage space rents for $400 per month, how many specific pieces of furniture could be stored for how much rent for seven months? If you have time, do the same exercise using the metric system of measurement and base the rent on the current value of $400 in euros.

Visual Guide

Chapter 21 Opener

Discussion: Have the students study the chapter opening photo and describe what they see. Then lead a discussion about the type of merchandise a vendor such as this would need. Ask: "How might a vendor keep track of inventory of that merchandise?"

Follow-Up: Ask students if their family has a system for keeping track of items they need from the grocery store—or office supply store. Have them describe the system.

Workplace Skills and Chapter Correlations

FOUNDATION SKILLS

Basic Skills	Reading	Writing	Math	Listening	Speaking	
Thinking Skills	Creative Thinking	Decision Making	Problem Solving	Seeing Things in the Mind's Eye	Knowing How to Learn	Reasoning
Personal Qualities	Responsibility	Self-Esteem	Sociability	Self-Management	Integrity/ Honesty	

WORKPLACE COMPETENCIES

Resources	Allocating Time	Allocating Money	Allocating Material and Facility Resources	Allocating Human Resources		
Information	Acquiring and Evaluating Information	Organizing and Maintaining Information	Interpreting and Communicating Information	Using Computers to Process Information		
Interpersonal Skills	Participating as a Member of a Team	Teaching Others	Serving Clients/ Customers	Exercising Leadership	Negotiating to Arrive at a Decision	Working with Cultural Diversity
Systems	Understanding Systems	Monitoring and Correcting Performance	Improving and Designing Systems			
Technology	Selecting Technology	Applying Technology to Task	Maintaining and TroubleshootingTechnology			

Internet Extension

Activity: Have students use the Internet to find out about job opportunities in payroll accounting. Suggest they access the online classified ads of a local newspaper. List the different job titles on the board.

Keywords: accounting, payroll

Enrichment/Application Activity

Cooperative Activity: As a class, choose a small business and assign each student a job in this business. Have each student research to find out the average pay rate for people in his or her job. To get an idea of payroll costs, estimate on the board the total gross earnings of your employees for a one-week pay period.

Topic Spotlight

Ethics: Ask students what kind of personal information is necessary to calculate an employee's earnings and deductions. [EXAMPLES: marital status, dependents, amount earned] Discuss who should have access to this information, who should not, and why.

Government: Ask students to research the income taxes in other countries. Ask: "How do they compare with U.S. income taxes?"

Money: Give students the following math word problem. Jamie earns a salary of $3,700 per month. Last month he worked 235 hours. The month before, he worked 212 hours. On average, how much does Jamie earn per hour? [ANSWER: $16.55. 235 + 212 = 447 hours; $3,700 × 2 = $7,400; $7,400 ÷ 447 = $16.55]

Additional Resources

Books

Essentials of Inventory Management by Max Muller (American Management Association, ©2002). This manual addresses key issues in inventory management, from physical control and layout to problem identification and resolution. Also, the book covers theft prevention, legal obligations, and handling emergencies.

Inventory Accuracy: People, Processes, and Technology by David J. Piasecki (Ops Publishing, ©2003). This book offers comprehensive treatment of inventory accuracy in distribution, fulfillment, and manufacturing. In addition to documenting the standard tools and techniques, it provides insights into why many of the standard solutions do not provide the best results and suggests alternative methods.

Internet

ISM.ws This is the Web site of the Institute for Supply Management™, whose mission is to lead supply management. The site offers links to ISM publications and other industry-related articles as well as information about seminars and online learning opportunities.

apics.org The Association for Operations Management (APICS) is a trade association for professionals in production and inventory management. Its Web site provides information about educational opportunities, an online bookstore, and online tools, such as a dictionary of industry terms and professional guidelines.

Note: Web-site addresses may change.

Section 21.1

Focus

Motivation

Ask the students how many of them work or have worked for a store or company. Then ask if they read the pay stubs they receive showing gross pay, deductions, and net pay amounts. Ask: "How many understand what those numbers mean?" Explain that in this section they will learn about those numbers and that anyone who regularly hires one other person is responsible for correctly computing, paying, and reporting payroll.

Prereading

1. Have students skim the section, looking at the pictures, reading the captions, and reading the headings.
2. Ask a student to read aloud Read to Learn on page 666.
3. Have students list the Key Terms in their notebooks and remind them to enter the definitions as they learn them.

Teach

Guided Practice

1. Ask a student to read aloud In the Real World on page 665 and ask the students what Wendy can do to avoid running out of the items she sells.
2. Ask a student to read aloud Ask Standard and Poor's on page 665 and discuss it briefly with the students.
3. Have students silently read the rest of the section, noting and mentally answering the Predict, Relate, Question, and caption questions and reading the features such as Careers in Finance.

Independent Practice

1. Have your students contact the Social Security Administration, the IRS, and any applicable state agencies and request copies of the forms employers use to report payroll taxes.
2. Tell students most agencies require that these reports be filed quarterly. Read the reports and instructions with your students and clarify any confusing parts.
3. Put students in small groups and ask them to try filling out the reports, using their own or made up pay stubs.

Assess

Reteaching

1. Have students make up crossword puzzles using each term in the Key Terms list.
2. To reinforce the nature of payroll taxes, ask students to write lists of the taxes employees pay (deductions) and lists of the taxes employers pay. Ask them to identify the purpose of each tax (e.g., funding government, providing retirement income).
3. Discuss with students the Reading Strategies and the pictures and figures with their caption questions. Assign features questions to students and go over responses.

Enrichment

Have someone from a payroll service company speak to the class about what such companies do and how much they charge. Ask the students afterwards under what circumstances they think it would be a good idea to use such a service.

Assessment

1. Have students complete the Section 21.1 Assessment.
2. Give students a vocabulary quiz based on the Key Terms.
3. Assign an activity from Chapter 21 of the *Student Activity Workbook*.

Close

Ask students to consider the various types of pay: salaries, hourly pay, and commissions. Rank them in order of the difficulty of preparing payroll, with the easiest first. Ask them what determines whether payroll is easy or hard to prepare.

Section 21.2

Focus

Motivation

Ask students to think about their favorite sporting goods store and list, as completely as possible, all the items the store sells. Tell them this is the store's inventory. Then ask: "How many put on their lists 'tennis rackets' or 'running shoes'?" Explain that for a complete inventory, they would need to list each brand and style separately. Ask if they think it might be difficult to keep track of so many items.

Prereading

1. Have students skim the section, looking at the pictures, reading the captions, and reading the headings.
2. Ask a student to read aloud Read to Learn on page 680.
3. Have students list the Key Terms in their notebooks and remind them to enter the definitions as they learn them.

Teach

Guided Practice

1. Ask a student to read aloud Establishing an Inventory System on page 680, and ask students if they would rather manage inventory by a manual system or a computerized one.
2. Have students silently read the rest of the section, noting and mentally answering the Predict, Relate, Question, React, and caption questions and reading the features such as Document Detective.

Independent Practice

Have your students select and write down they best type of inventory system for the following businesses: a video rental store, a fast food restaurant, and a boutique selling fashion accessories. Have students interview local owners of such stores and find out what kinds of inventory systems they use. Students should then compare their recommendations to the systems used and suggest reasons for any differences.

Assess

Reteaching

1. Have the students write sentences using each term in the Key Terms list.
2. To reinforce the math of inventory control, divide students into four to six teams. Each team should write one math problem (and its solution) for each of the following: average inventory, inventory turnover, and number of days in stock. Have the teams exchange and solve the math problems.
3. Discuss with students the Reading Strategies and the pictures and figures with their caption questions. Assign features questions to students and go over responses.

Enrichment

Have students research three different commercial inventory systems and write a brief report comparing their features, advantages, and disadvantages. They should recommend one and justify their recommendation.

Assessment

1. Have students complete the Section 21.2 Assessment.
2. Assign Chapter 21 Review and Activities.
3. Administer the test for Chapter 21 from the Reproducible Tests in the *Lesson Planner Plus* supplement.

Close

Ask students what they think is the importance of maintaining accurate inventory counts as well as developing and consistently using sound inventory control systems.

ANSWERS

Careers in Finance

Answers may include: Payroll is one of the main cash flows through a business. Good payroll management is necessary in order for the business to know how much cash is available for purchasing.

Academic Connection

Student answers should demonstrate an understanding of how such factors as type of work, number of hours worked, and business cash flow patterns would affect payment method.

STANDARD &POOR'S Global Financial Landscape

Answers may include that too much government control can stifle competition and inhibit creativity by lowering rewards for it or mandating too much standardization.

Document Detective

1. She makes $6.75 per hour.
2. No, she makes the same rate.
3. January 11, 20--
4. $12.93
5. $100.14

STANDARD &POOR'S Put on Your Financial Planner's Cap

Most students will answer FIFO, but other answers are acceptable if students can justify their answers.

Section 21.1 Assessment

Quick Check

1. The steps of a payroll system are calculating gross earnings, calculating payroll deductions, preparing payroll records, preparing paychecks, recording payroll information in accounting records, and reporting payroll information to the government.
2. Common ways to pay employees are salary, hourly wage, and salary plus commission.
3. Required deductions include federal income tax, FICA taxes (Social Security and Medicare), and state and local income tax (depending on where you work or live). Voluntary deductions include health and/or life insurance, union dues, charitable contributions, retirement plans, and direct deposits.

Think Critically

4. Answers may include: Advantages of paying someone a salary include: you do not have to pay overtime and the amount does not vary from pay period to pay period, making payroll easy. A disadvantage is that the employee is guaranteed the same pay each week, whether there are sales to support the pay or not.

Use Math Skills

5. Shari: \$310.50 (\$6.75 × 40 = \$270 regular pay; \$6.75 × 1.5 = \$40.50 overtime pay; \$270 + \$40.50 = \$310.50 gross earnings)
Rolf: \$294 (\$7.35 × 40 = \$294 gross earnings)
Litisha: \$231 (\$185 weekly salary; \$1,150 × 4% = \$46 commission; \$185 + \$46 = \$231 gross earnings)
Shari earned the most money this week.

Solve Money Problems

6. Alicia is paying her current employees \$1,350 in overtime each week. (\$7.50 × 1.5 × 8 hours × 15 employees = \$1,350.) Answers may include: The total amount of overtime is 120 hours. It would be less expense to hire three employees at 40 hours of straight time each (\$7.50 × 40 × 3 = \$900) than to pay \$1,350 in overtime.

Section 21.2 Assessment

Quick Check

1. The perpetual inventory system keeps a constant, up-to-date record of merchandise on hand. In a periodic inventory system, inventory records are updated only after someone makes a physical count of the merchandise on hand.
2. Costing methods include the specific identification method; first-in, first-out method (FIFO); and last-in, first-out method (LIFO).
3. Positive cash flow is necessary for a business to meet its financial commitments. Since payroll is one of the main cash flows through a business, it is important that this be kept within reason so that the business maintains a positive cash flow.

Think Critically

4. Even if a business uses a perpetual inventory system, it should conduct a physical inventory at least once a year to verify the accuracy of inventory records. Errors can be made in various ways, such as when entering inventory data or at point-of-sale terminals. A physical inventory ensures that accounting records are accurate and agree with what your business actually has in stock.

Use Communication Skills

5. Students may identify the following causes: stocking the wrong auto parts or slower sales for this year. Suggestions might include: Analyze the current inventory based on last year's inventory and change purchasing practices; do additional advertising to increase sales.

Solve Money Problems

6. Because it is a small gallery and she can easily identify each item, Aurora should use a perpetual inventory system. She should use the specific identification costing method. She can identify the cost per item because she has so few items to sell and their prices differ according to the value of the artwork.

Chapter 21 Review & Activities

Communicating Key Terms

Answers should indicate students' understanding of the terms used and of payment methods, deductions, and the impact of payroll and inventory on business operations.

Reviewing Key Concepts

1. Payroll deductions are consistent from pay period to pay period for most employees (an exception may be employees paid by commission) and are often a percentage of income. Therefore, calculations of gross and net pay and deduction amounts can be done easily and efficiently by computer, as can net paycheck printing.
2. Types of pay by type of job include: salary: professional, supervisory, and management hourly wages: most full-time non-managerial jobs, temporary jobs, and part-time jobs, except sales; commission: usually sales positions (commission is often combined with salary).
3. Required deductions include federal income tax, FICA taxes (Social Security and Medicare), and state and local income tax (depending on where you work or live).
4. Employee deductions are liabilities (payables) of the business until they are paid.
5. The following information is needed for an inventory control system: 1) the amount of merchandise sold in each accounting period, 2) information about which items are selling well, and 3) information about which items are not selling well.
6. The perpetual inventory system immediately reduces inventory as it is sold, thereby enabling greater control of when new inventory is ordered; plus it provides an immediate picture of how inventory is moving and the costs of items at any time.
7. In first in, first out (FIFO) costing, the first items sold are the first items that the business bought. In last in, first out (LIFO) costing, the first items sold are the last items that the business bought.
8. Low inventory turnover indicates low sales for the item, which may mean it should no longer be carried.

ACADEMIC SKILLS

Students' ads will vary but should indicate an understanding that the reduced prices will encourage people to buy the advertised item; pricing should reflect research into current prices for the item.

YOUR FINANCIAL FIGURES

1. For these six months, Marika's gross pay is \$28,424 [\$13,500 salary + \$14,924 commission = \$28,424 gross pay]
   Salary: \$13,500 [\$2,250/month]
   Sales Commission: \$14,924 [(\$10,300 + \$17,000 + \$35,300 + \$42,000 + \$53,000 + \$72,000) × 6.5% commission = \$14,924]

Monthly Sales Reported		Marika's commission	Marika's gross pay/mo
January	\$10,300	669.50	2,919.50
February	\$17,000	1,105	3,355
March	\$35,300	2,294.50	4,544.50
April	\$42,000	2,730	4,980
May	\$53,000	3,445	5,695
June	\$72,000	4,680	6,930
		Total	\$28,424

2. Students should show the calculations, such as those above, used to arrive at Marika's gross pay of \$28,424.

REAL-WORLD Application

1. Student answers should demonstrate research into the official views on this issue of various groups. The AARP opposes private accounts, which would take money out of the Social Security system.
2. Accept all reasonable opinions that demonstrate research and an understanding of the issues.

Internet CONNECTION

1. Student answers should demonstrate research into just-in-time inventory management, which is designed to make the production cycle more efficient. Numerous industries are experimenting with this management concept, although it has been applied most successfully in manufacturing industries.
2. Answers will vary but should indicate students' understanding that JIT promises to help businesses avoid tying up large amounts of cash in inventories.

BusinessWeek ONLINE

Accept all answers that demonstrate students have read the online article and understand the concepts.

CHAPTER 22 Pricing, Costing, and Growth

pages 696–719

SECTION	LEARNING OBJECTIVES	FEATURES	TEXT RESOURCES	TECHNOLOGY RESOURCES
22.1	**After completing this section, students will have learned to:** Explain how to calculate selling price. Identify variable and fixed costs. Discuss effective pricing.	**Careers in Finance,** p. 701 **S&P's Global Financial Landscape,** p. 702 **Common Cents,** p. 703 **Academic Connection,** p. 704 **WebQuest,** p. 705 **Document Detective,** p. 706 **TechByte,** p. 707 **Go Figure**—Break-Even Point, p. 707	**Section Assessment,** p. 708 Quick Check Think Critically Use Math Skills Solve Money Problems **Student Activity Workbook**	Lesson Planner Plus Online Learning Center Interactive Student Edition *Presentation Plus!* **Exam***View*® Pro Test Generator Financial Planner Software
22.2	**After completing this section, students will have learned to:** Describe different forms of business growth. Discuss profit planning. Explain how to calculate target sales and margin of safety. Explain the importance of planning for growth.	**Savvy Saver,** p. 710 **Go Figure**—Target Sales, p. 712 **S&P's Put on Your Financial Planner's Cap,** p. 713	**Section Assessment,** p. 715 Quick Check Think Critically Use Communication Skills Solve Money Problems **Student Activity Workbook**	Lesson Planner Plus Online Learning Center Interactive Student Edition *Presentation Plus!* **Exam***View*® Pro Test Generator Financial Planner Software

Teacher Manual

Meeting National Standards for Business Education	
Section 22.1	**Section 22.2**
Economics IV. Markets and Prices VI. Productivity **Personal Finance** II. Earning a Living	**Economics** III. Economic Institutions and Incentives VIII. International Economic Concepts **Personal Finance** I. Personal Decision Making II. Earning a Living

Teaching Connection

Charting the Right Price

Draw a chart in the shape of a lowercase "T" on the board. Label the upper left side "Fixed Costs" and the upper right side "Variable Costs." Show the students a common item of interest, such as an iPod or article of clothing. Ask the students to list the fixed and variable costs that went into producing and marketing the item. You may have to explain the difference between fixed and variable costs. Make sure the students include the less visible components of production, such as transportation, taxes, and salaries and wages. After listing all the elements, ask students: "What about profit?" Then ask: "What would be a fair profit?"

Visual Guide

Chapter 22 Opener

Discussion: Have students study the chapter opening photo and describe what they see. Then lead a discussion about how the price of merchandise is determined. Ask students: "What factors do you think are considered when determining price?" Then ask: "Do you think businesses can charge what they like for an item? Why or why not?"

Follow-Up: Ask students how they determine where, and when, to buy certain items, such as tennis shoes or school supplies. Ask: "If one store was having a sale on the item they wanted and the other was not, where would they choose to buy the item?"

Teacher Manual

Workplace Skills and Chapter Correlations

FOUNDATION SKILLS

Basic Skills	Reading	Writing	Math	Listening	Speaking	
Thinking Skills	Creative Thinking	Decision Making	Problem Solving	Seeing Things in the Mind's Eye	Knowing How to Learn	Reasoning
Personal Qualities	Responsibility	Self-Esteem	Sociability	Self-Management	Integrity/ Honesty	

WORKPLACE COMPETENCIES

Resources	Allocating Time	Allocating Money	Allocating Material and Facility Resources	Allocating Human Resources		
Information	Acquiring and Evaluating Information	Organizing and Maintaining Information	Interpreting and Communicating Information	Using Computers to Process Information		
Interpersonal Skills	Participating as a Member of a Team	Teaching Others	Serving Clients/ Customers	Exercising Leadership	Negotiating to Arrive at a Decision	Working with Cultural Diversity
Systems	Understanding Systems	Monitoring and Correcting Performance	Improving and Designing Systems			
Technology	Selecting Technology	Applying Technology to Task	Maintaining and TroubleshootingTechnology			

Internet Extension

Activity: Have students use the Internet to research and find articles and information on growing a business.

Keywords: business growth, business development

Enrichment/Application Activity

Guest Speaker: Invite a store manager or a manufacturing company manager to speak to the class about pricing strategies used in his or her store or company.

Topic Spotlight

Money: Ask students if they have ever witnessed price wars between or among competitors in a given industry. Ask a volunteer to explain what that means. Explain that they are common among car dealers, for example, when a dealer is trying to attract customers.

Marketing: Explain that the largest retailers can pay much less for their merchandise than smaller stores because the larger stores buy much greater quantities. Discuss how smaller, locally owned stores could compete against larger, national chains.

Technology: Discuss how technology affects a business's ability to stay competitive.

Additional Resources

Books

Pricing for Profitability: Activity-Based Pricing for Competitive Advantage by John L. Daly (Wiley, ©2001). This book teaches the reader activity-based pricing, which is establishing prices based on solid knowledge of customer demand and product cost. It will help readers stop unintentionally pricing products at a loss, determine how much of a price is profit, and use financial knowledge to yield high financial returns.

The Strategy and Tactics of Pricing: A Guide to Profitable Decision Making, 3rd Edition, by Thomas T. Nagle, Reed K. Holden (Prentice Hall, ©2002). The authors help readers understand the downfall of pursuing market share at all costs, and mistakes businesses and salespeople make when determining or negotiating price. This book offers a better way to attract the right buyers. It explains strategic pricing, and covers market place competition, pricing and the marketing mix for industrial and consumer goods, and the psychology of pricing.

Internet

Deloitte.com/US Deloitte and Touche, LLP, is a consulting firm offering audit, tax, consulting, and financial advisory services. Its Web site offers information about pricing via a Q&A page and links to related articles and publications.

sba.gov The Small Business Administration offers information on growing a business, including news, online tools, and several publications in their Emerging Business Series. There is also a publication on pricing, *Pricing Your Products and Services Profitably*, in the SBA's Financial Management Series.

onlinewbc.gov/docs/growing/busrisk.com The U.S. Small Business Administration has a site devoted to helping women entrepreneurs. This page specifically targets risk taking when it comes to business growth. A quiz follows which helps assess your own attitude toward business growth, and determining how you feel about taking risks.

Note: Web-site addresses may change.

Section 22.1

Focus

Motivation

Ask students how many times they have seen an item at one store for one price, then seen the same item somewhere else for a different price. Ask them why they think that happens; then ask why a retailer might lower the price on goods for sale. List their responses on the board.

Prereading

1. Have students skim the section, looking at the pictures, reading the captions, and reading the headings.
2. Ask a student to read aloud Read to Learn and Main Idea on page 698.
3. Have students list the Key Terms in their notebooks, and remind them to enter the definitions as they learn them.

Teach

Guided Practice

1. Ask a student to read aloud In the Real World on page 697 and discuss with students the suggested question.
2. Ask students to read aloud Ask Standard and Poor's on page 697 and discuss it briefly with them.
3. Have students silently read the rest of the section, noting and mentally answering the Predict, Relate, Question, and caption questions and reading the features such as Document Detective.

Independent Practice

1. Have students imagine they have decided to make and sell brownies to markets that sell to the public.
2. Each student is to find a recipe and use that to create a list of the materials needed.
3. Have students determine the cost of each batch of brownies; this involves finding the prices for the supplies and computing *cost* per batch and adding in labor and packaging. (Ignore other costs, such as rent and utilities.)
4. Each student then must set a price per batch of brownies, being sure to add in the desired profit.

Assess

Reteaching

1. Have the students participate in a Key Terms bee.
2. To reinforce the difference between "product cost-plus" pricing and "product costing" (retail versus manufacturing), have students create a word problem for each, then exchange with a partner to solve.
3. Discuss with students the Reading Strategies and the pictures and figures with their caption questions. Assign features questions to students and go over responses.

Enrichment

Have each student research a product to identify significant price variations; ask students to speculate about the reasons for these differences; ask if they think the businesses may have different pricing goals.

Assessment

1. Have students complete the Section 22.1 Assessment.
2. Give students a vocabulary quiz based on the Key Terms.
3. Assign an activity from Chapter 22 of the *Student Activity Workbook*.

Close

Discuss with students how one might go about establishing a price for a service that uses no or very minimal supplies.

Section 22.2

Focus

Motivation

Ask the students to consider their own growth. Ask: "How many different ways can you measure your growth?" and list their answers on the board. Then ask: "How many of these might also be ways to measure a business's growth?" Have students name additional ways to measure business growth.

Prereading

1. Have students skim the section, looking at the pictures, reading the captions, and reading the headings.
2. Ask a student to read aloud Read to Learn on page 709.
3. Have students list the Key Terms in their notebooks and remind them to enter the definitions as they learn them.

Teach

Guided Practice

1. Ask a student to read aloud Sources of Business Growth on page 709, and discuss it with them.
2. Have a student read aloud each source of growth listed on pages 709–710, and discuss each briefly with them.
3. Have students silently read the rest of the section, noting and mentally answering the Predict, Relate, Question, React, and caption questions and reading the features such as Go Figure.

Independent Practice

1. Have students work on the same business they did in Section 22.1. Their goal now will be to investigate growing the business.
2. Students are to assess how they would grow the business in each of the seven growth areas (pages 709–710).
3. Students should write up their results in a two-page report.

Assess

Reteaching

1. Have the students write sentences using each term in the Key Terms list.
2. To reinforce the formulas in this section, have students create word problems for "target sales" and "margin of safety"; have them exchange problems with a partner and solve.
3. Discuss with students the Reading Strategies and the pictures and figures with their caption questions. Assign features questions to students and go over responses.

Enrichment

Invite to class a business owner whose business has noticeably grown over the years to discuss ways to successfully grow a business. Have students prepare questions for him or her.

Assessment

1. Have students complete the Section 22.2 Assessment.
2. Assign Chapter 22 Review and Activities.
3. Administer the test for Chapter 22 from the Reproducible Tests in the *Lesson Planner Plus* supplement.

Close

Discuss with the students ways to determine if their businesses are ready to grow.

ANSWERS

Careers in Finance

Answers will vary but may include that the CFO makes decisions about pricing, and goods must be priced so the business succeeds.

STANDARD &POOR'S Global Financial Landscape

Answers may include that the relatively low cost of materials in Vietnam and the inexpensive price of vacationing there will make it an attractive option for travelers from the United States and other more developed nations.

Academic Connection

widget: \$1.32 × 1.70 = \$2.24; doodads: \$4.80 × 1.70 + \$8.16; thingamabobs: \$8.74 × 1.70 = \$14.86

Document Detective

1. Total fixed costs are \$10,000.
2. The break-even point for necklaces is 40 necklaces.
3. The necklace has the highest markup, \$50.45.
4. The number of units needed to be sold in order to break even would decrease.
5. \$90.00

STANDARD &POOR'S Put on Your Financial Planner's Cap

Answers will vary; some students may suggest selling other items to the teen market because they know that market.

Section 22.1 Assessment

Quick Check

1. to obtain a given share of the market, to generate sales that produce a specific profit, and to meet competitors' prices
2. Variable costs vary in direct proportion to the activity level of production. If the business operation increases, the variable costs will increase and vice versa. Fixed costs remain constant even if the activity or production level changes
3. Calculating the break-even point allows a business owner to determine the sales the business must achieve to break even, or cover all costs.

Think Critically

4. Student answers should indicate that a business would lose money because there would be nothing left to pay fixed and variable expenses or provide a profit.

Use Math Skills

5. Her break-even point is 20 mirrors: Unit Sales Price × n = (Unit Variable Costs × n) + Fixed Costs

$$\$75n = \$25n + \$1{,}000$$
$$\$75n - \$25n = \$1{,}000$$
$$\$50n = \$1{,}000$$
$$n = 1000 \div 50$$
$$n = 20 \text{ mirrors}$$

Solve Money Problems

6. The selling price is \$118.80. (\$72 × 65% = \$46.80 markup; \$72 + 46.80 = \$118.80)

Section 22.2 Assessment

Quick Check

1. increases in the number of customers, sales, share of the market, market development, employees, product development, and profit
2. Target Sales = Variable Costs + Fixed Costs + Target Profit
3. Target Sales − Break-Even Sales = Margin of Safety

Think Critically

4. Students should indicate an understanding that growth must be analyzed, planned, and controlled. If a business grows too rapidly or in the wrong area, serious financial problems can result.

Use Communcation Skills

5. Students might suggest that Lil carefully consider the new areas of merchandise or services that she plans to offer. She should make sure a market for new items exists.

Solve Money Problems

6. Refer students to pages 712–713. Windy River will need to sell 165 bracelets: Unit Sales Price × n = (Unit Variable Costs × n) + Fixed Costs + Target Profit

$$\$13n = \$7.65n + \$280 + \$600$$
$$\$13n - \$7.65n = \$880$$
$$\$5.35n = \$880$$
$$n = \$880 \div \$5.35$$
$$n = 164.49, \text{ or } 165 \text{ bracelets}$$

Chapter 22 Review & Activities

Communicating Key Terms

Lists of questions should demonstrate an understanding of the terms used and of pricing.

Review Key Concepts

1. Manufacturing businesses buy raw materials to process into finished products, not finished products to sell. Product cost-plus pricing is based on the cost of a product to the business.
2. Variable costs depend on the number of items produced or sold. Therefore, if sales are low, these costs are similarly reduced. It is best to keep fixed costs to a minimum, because they do not vary with sales; when sales are low, you must still pay the same fixed costs.
3. The contribution margin is total sales minus total variable costs. It is an indicator of how much of the price of the product is available to pay fixed costs and to keep as profit.
4. Expanding into new lines of merchandise may cause the company to spread its ability to invest in growth or its expertise too thinly, thereby leading to opportunity costs and other problems.
5. A major use of profits is reinvestment in the company to enable growth. Setting target profits helps achieve profit goals, producing profit needed for growth.
6. The margin of safety is target sales minus break-even sales. It is the amount that sales can drop before the business experiences an actual loss.
7. The reserve fund is designed to meet unexpected costs or unexpected opportunities. The larger the fund—that is, the larger the target profits—the more you are able to respond to growth opportunities.

ACADEMIC SKILLS

Answers might include: Clothing marked up more than 100 percent means you pay more than twice as much as the item cost the retailer. The markup has to cover the costs of transporting, storing, merchandising, promoting, and selling the clothing, as well as provide a profit to the store's owner.

YOUR FINANCIAL FIGURES

1. The margin of safety is \$49,000. (\$338,000 − \$289,000 = \$49,000) This is the amount sales could go down before Cricket Lane would experience a loss.
2. Students should show the above calculation using appropriate software.

REAL-WORLD Application

1. Answers will vary, but should indicate that students understand different people's tolerance for risk.
2. Student scripts should indicate the opinions of the owner and the investor.

Internet CONNECTION

Answers might include ways the new company will differentiate itself from the competition. To increase market share, you may have to provide assurances to potential customers that you guarantee your work as much as a plumbing contractor does.

BusinessWeek ONLINE

Accept all lists that show students have read the online article and understand concepts.

GLENCOE

Business and Personal FINANCE

Jack R. Kapoor
Professor of Business and Economics
Business and Services Division
College of DuPage
Glen Ellyn, Illinois

Les R. Dlabay
Professor of Business
Department of Economics and Business
Lake Forest College
Lake Forest, Illinois

Robert J. Hughes
Professor of Business
Dallas County Community Colleges
Dallas, Texas

William B. Hoyt
Contributing Editor
Wilton High School
Wilton, Connecticut

McGraw Hill Glencoe

About the Authors

Jack R. Kapoor
Jack R. Kapoor is professor of business and economics in the Business and Services Division at College of DuPage, where he has taught since 1969. He received his Bachelor of Arts in Business Administration and Master of Science in International Business from San Francisco State College. He received his Doctor of Education from Northern Illinois University. Dr. Kapoor was awarded the Business and Services Division's Outstanding Professor Award for 1999–2000.

Les R. Dlabay
Les R. Dlabay teaches in the Department of Economics and Business at Lake Forest College. He received his Bachelor of Science in Accounting from University of Illinois, his Master of Business Administration in Business Management from DePaul University, and his Doctor of Education in Business and Economic Education from Northern Illinois University. He is a founding member of the Illinois Consumer Education Association.

Robert J. Hughes
Robert J. Hughes teaches business, management, and finance courses at Dallas County Community Colleges. He received his Bachelor of Arts in Business Administration from Southern Nazarene University and his Master of Business Administration and Doctor of Education from the University of North Texas. Dr. Hughes has taught at the high school, community college, and four-year university levels for 36 years. He received the Excellence in Teaching Award at Richland College and has 15 years of experience teaching personal finance courses.

NOTICE: Information on featured companies, organizations, and their products and services is included for educational purposes only, and it does not present or imply endorsement of the *Business and Personal Finance* program.

McGraw Hill Glencoe

The McGraw-Hill Companies

Printed in the United States of America.

Send all inquiries to:

Glencoe/McGraw-Hill
4400 Easton Commons
Columbus, OH 43219

ISBN-13: 978-0-07-868712-9 (Student Text)
ISBN-10: 0-07-868712-8 (Student Text)

ISBN-13: 978-0-07-869846-0 (Teacher Annotated Edition)
ISBN-10: 0-07-869846-4 (Teacher Annotated Edition)

5 6 7 8 9 DOW 12 11 10 09 08

Reviewers

Rosella Bannister
Jump$tart Personal Finance Clearinghouse
Ann Arbor, Michigan

Janet Barnes
Hazelwood West High School
Hazelwood, Missouri

Thelma Brooks
Educational Consultant
Columbus, Ohio

Edlena Carmon
Marion Franklin High School
Columbus, Ohio

Sharon Clemons
Thomas Worthington High School
Worthington, Ohio

John E. Clow, Ph.D.
State University of New York
Oneonta, New York

Joe Cook
Southeast Career Center
Columbus, Ohio

Diane W. Culpepper
Winter Park Tech
Winter Park, Florida

Joy Davis
Delaware Area Career Center
Delaware, Ohio

Laneita Dunphy
Montclair High School
Montclair, New Jersey

Ernestine Gordon
Montclair High School
Montclair, New Jersey

Georgia Hoover
Dublin Scioto High School
Dublin, Ohio

Paul Jussila
South Windsor High School
South Windsor, Connecticut

Mike Kelly
Hazelwood East High School
St. Louis, Missouri

Jason Lee
Olympia High School
Orlando, Florida

Diane Manley
St. Louis, Missouri

Greg Moore
Columbus, Ohio

Jeff Noyes
Minnetonka High School
Minnetonka, Minnesota

Verta Parks
Marion Franklin High School
Columbus, Ohio

Kevin Richberg
Montclair High School
Montclair, New Jersey

Verlin Samples
Hamilton Local
Columbus, Ohio

James C. Scharer
Fremont Ross High School
Fremont, Ohio

Natalie Schaublin
Westerville North High School
Westerville, Ohio

Ken Schnitzer
Montclair High School
Montclair, New Jersey

Julie Smith
Southeast Career Center
Columbus, Ohio

Betty Tobler
St. Louis Public Schools
St. Louis, Missouri

Mark Van Hoy
Hazelwood West High School
Hazelwood, Missouri

Patty Wamble
Cape Central High School
Cape Girardeau, Missouri

Elizabeth Watt
North Education Center
Columbus, Ohio

Ken Watts
Montclair High School
Montclair, New Jersey

Polly White
Wawasee High School
Syracuse, Indiana

Tamara Wickline
Dublin Coffman High School
Dublin, Ohio

Susie Wright
Walnut Ridge High School
Columbus, Ohio

Glenn Zipfel
Christian Brothers High School
St. Louis, Missouri

Welcome to *Business and Personal Finance*

Each day you are surrounded by new choices for shopping, watching television, and other activities. You also have many choices about how to spend your money. *Business and Personal Finance* can help you make the right decisions. You will develop financial literacy through integrated academics, real-world examples, and practical advice. By learning how to make informed decisions related to spending, saving, borrowing, and investing, you can build a solid foundation for your financial security now and in the future.

Brief Table of Contents

Table of Contents

UNIT 2 Banking and Credit 118

UNIT 5 Business Ownership and Planning 520

Understanding the Unit

The 22 chapters of *Business and Personal Finance* are divided into six units. Each unit opens with a *BusinessWeek* Finance File feature and WebQuest activity and concludes with a finance simulation application that gives you a chance to apply what you have learned.

Previewing the Unit

Unit 1

Planning Personal Finances

WebQuest Internet Project

One Life to Plan

Financial planners help people plan for paying for college or retirement, and then show them how to save to reach those goals. Life planners assist clients to pinpoint what they want out of life, and then use financial planning to help people achieve it. In this project, you will weigh the pros and cons of each career and decide which one might best suit you.

Log on to finance07.glencoe.com. Begin your WebQuest by reading Task 1. Then continue working on your WebQuest as you study Unit 1.

Section	1.2	2.2	3.2	4.1
Page	25	52	71	108

2 finance07.glencoe.com

BusinessWeek FINANCE FILE

Which Adviser Knows the Way?

Almost anyone can claim to be a financial planner or investment adviser. If you're looking for an adviser for the first time—you need to figure out how much and what kind of advice you need. If all you want are some suggestions for your IRA or your investment portfolio, you could get that through Charles Schwab or Fidelity Brokerage Services for a fee of about $250.

But there's more to your financial well-being than stocks and bonds. Do you have a debt-management problem? Do you have enough insurance, and is your estate in order?

And what about credentials? Certified Financial Planner (CFP) is the most recognized designation. CFPs have comprehensive education and must pass a ten-hour certification exam and have at least three years' experience before qualifying.

The irony is that most people seek advisers to relieve the burden of managing their finances themselves. But it's a burden in itself to make sure you've got the right adviser.

— By Lewis Braham with Amy Borrus

Write About It Why should you know how to plan your personal finances even if you can hire a financial planner?

Log On To read the complete BusinessWeek article and do the BusinessWeek Extension activity to help you learn more about financial and life planning, go to finance07.glencoe.com.

finance07.glencoe.com 3

Unit-Opener Photo
The unit-opener photo illustrates a concept that is related to the unit. Ask yourself: "How does the photo relate to the content of the unit?"

WebQuest This unit activity is continued in each chapter in the unit as it introduces you to a unit topic and directs you to the Online Learning Center to research and complete this Web-based project.

***BusinessWeek* Finance File** Each unit opens with an excerpt from a real *BusinessWeek* article about an aspect of the unit material. The feature directs you to the Online Learning Center to read the complete article and do an application activity.

Closing the Unit

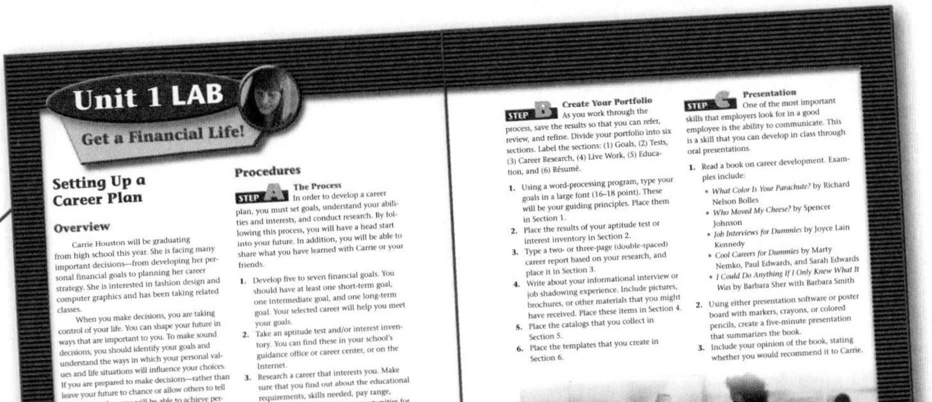
Unit 1 LAB

Get a Financial Life!

Setting Up a Career Plan

Overview

Carrie Houston will be graduating from high school this year. She is facing many important decisions—from developing her personal financial goals to planning her career strategy. She is interested in fashion design and computer graphics and has been taking related classes.

When you make decisions, you are taking control of your life. You can shape your future in ways that are important to you. To make sound decisions, you should identify your goals and understand the ways in which your personal values and life situations will influence your choices. If you are prepared to make decisions—rather than leave your future to chance or allow others to tell you what to do—you will be able to achieve personal satisfaction and financial security.

Develop a process to help plan your own career; then share it with Carrie so that she can plan her future career.

Resources & Tools

- Career center/guidance office at school
- Career-development book
- Crayons, markers, colored pencils
- Internet
- Portfolio (ring binder or file folder)
- Poster board
- Presentation software (optional)
- Public or school library
- Word-processing software

Procedures

STEP A The Process

In order to develop a career plan, you must set goals, understand your abilities and interests, and conduct research. By following this process, you will have a head start into your future. In addition, you will be able to share what you have learned with Carrie or your friends.

1. Develop five to seven financial goals. You should have at least one short-term goal, one intermediate goal, and one long-term goal. Your selected career will help you meet your goals.
2. Take an aptitude test and/or interest inventory. You can find these in your school's guidance office or career center, or on the Internet.
3. Research a career that interests you. Make sure that you find out about the educational requirements, skills needed, pay range, duties and responsibilities, opportunities for advancement, and future trends in the field.
4. Conduct an informational interview with someone who is working in your area of interest to gather practical information, or arrange to "job shadow" someone in your selected field. (To *job shadow* means to follow a person on the job for a day to learn about a particular career.)
5. Obtain catalogs from colleges or other post-secondary institutions where training is offered in the field you are researching. Try to locate at least one institution in your community, one in your state, and one out of state.
6. Using a word-processing program, create templates for a résumé and cover letter.

116 Unit 1 Planning Personal Finances

STEP B Create Your Portfolio

As you work through the process, save the results so that you can refer, review, and refine. Divide your portfolio into six sections. Label the sections: (1) Goals, (2) Tests, (3) Career Research, (4) Live Work, (5) Education, and (6) Résumé.

1. Using a word-processing program, type your goals in a large font (16–18 point). These will be your guiding principles. Place them in Section 1.
2. Place the results of your aptitude test or interest inventory in Section 2.
3. Type a two- or three-page (double-spaced) career report based on your research, and place it in Section 3.
4. Write about your informational interview or job shadowing experience. Include pictures, brochures, or other materials that you might have received. Place these items in Section 4.
5. Place the catalogs that you collect in Section 5.
6. Place the templates that you create in Section 6.

STEP C Presentation

One of the most important skills that employers look for in a good employee is the ability to communicate. This is a skill that you can develop in class through oral presentations.

1. Read a book on career development. Examples include:
   - *What Color Is Your Parachute?* by Richard Nelson Bolles
   - *Who Moved My Cheese?* by Spencer Johnson
   - *Job Interviews for Dummies* by Joyce Lain Kennedy
   - *Cool Careers for Dummies* by Marty Nemko, Paul Edwards, and Sarah Edwards
   - *I Could Do Anything If I Only Knew What It Was* by Barbara Sher with Barbara Smith
2. Using either presentation software or poster board with markers, crayons, or colored pencils, create a five-minute presentation that summarizes the book.
3. Include your opinion of the book, stating whether you would recommend it to Carrie.

117

Get a Financial Life! Unit Lab Simulation
This unit simulation provides hands-on experience that expands your understanding of finance as you apply what you have learned to a real-world project.

Understanding the Chapter

Each unit of *Business and Personal Finance* includes three to four chapters. Each chapter focuses on an aspect of finance that will apply to your everyday financial management.

Previewing the Chapter

Chapter-Opener Photo The chapter-opener photo focuses on the chapter topic as you get ready to read. You might ask yourself: "How does this photo relate to the chapter title?"

In the Real World A brief scenario introduces a chapter concept so you can relate it to the real world as you get ready to begin the chapter.

Chapter Objectives The objectives help you preview the most important things you will learn as you study the chapter.

Ask Standard & Poor's Get expert financial advice from Standard & Poor's as this feature answers real-world questions about everyday business and personal finance.

Reading Strategies The reading strategies listed in the Reading Strategies box at the beginning of each chapter can help you to read actively. Also, notice them in the margins as you read.

Using the Section

Each chapter of *Business and Personal Finance* is divided into two to four sections. Each section introduces and develops material in organized segments.

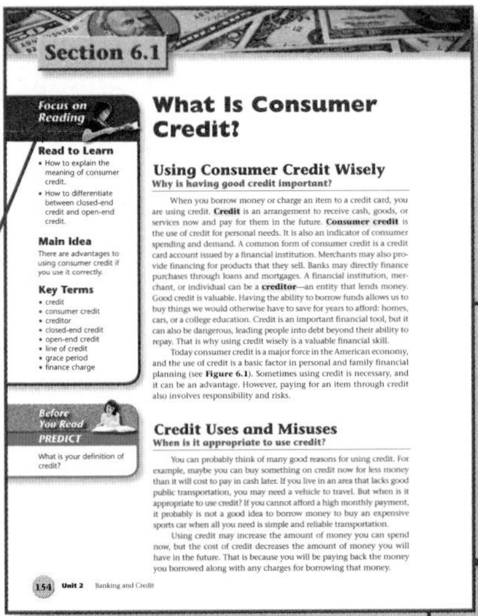

Photographs and Figures Throughout each section, relevant photographs, and useful charts and graphs illustrate and reinforce the content. Captions with questions guide you.

Focus on Reading
- **Read to Learn** lists the concept you will learn in the section.
- **Main Idea** explains the main concepts that you will learn.
- **Key Terms** list the major terms presented in each section. You will also see them highlighted as you read each chapter.

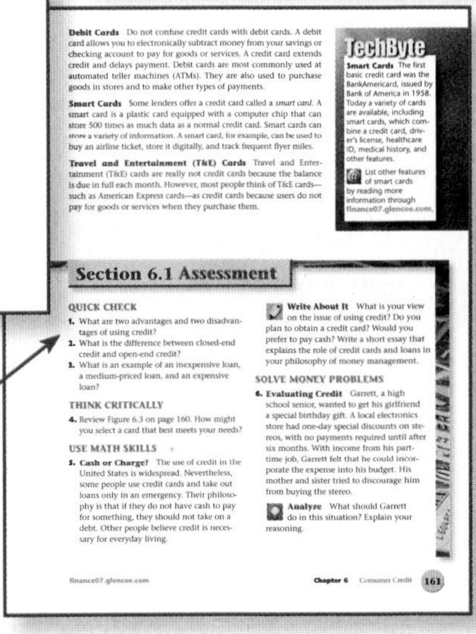

Section Assessment The section-ending assessments help you review, apply, and respond to what you have read.

Understanding the Features

Special features in each chapter are designed to interest you and to promote your understanding of the chapter topics. Features incorporate activities, such as critical-thinking questions, that help you to integrate what you have learned and apply it.

STANDARD &POOR'S

Global Financial Landscape

Standard and Poor's publishes the globally recognized S&P 500® financial index. It also gathers financial statistics, information, and news, and analyzes this data for international businesses, governments, and individuals to help them guide their financial decisions.

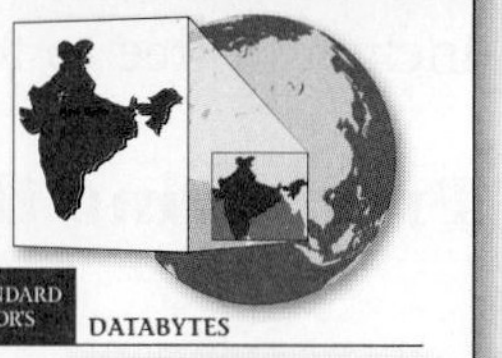

INDIA

Most travelers to India expect to see a country carved out of 5,000-year-old traditions, but they also find modern-day landmarks that look like home. Driven by a booming economy and growing incomes in large cities, Indians have become avid consumers of Western culture. Fast-food chains and sprawling malls dot the ancient landscape. Teenagers wear the latest fashions. In fact, India also boasts a growing fashion design industry. Imported cosmetics are popular, and beauty pageants are national events. On a one-mile stretch of a typical city, construction takes place to accommodate more than 40,000 multinational software and service workers.

A decade ago, when India opened its doors to the world, critics labeled this kind of expansion as corruptive. But as foreign businesses pour billions into the country, some say the modernization is too slow. One young Indian laments, "Night life is nonexistent."

STANDARD &POOR'S DATABYTES

Capital	New Delhi
Population	1,086,572,000
Language	Hindi, English, and 14 other official languages
Currency	Indian rupee
Gross Domestic Product (GDP)	$3.02 trillion (2003 est.)
GDP per capita	$2,900

Industry: Textiles, chemicals, food processing, steel, transportation equipment, cement, and mining

Agriculture: Rice, wheat, oilseed, cotton, cattle, and fish

Exports: Textile goods, gems and jewelry, engineering goods, chemicals, and leather

Natural Resources: Coal, iron ore, manganese, mica, and bauxite

Think Globally

Working Indian teens spend money to keep up with the times. Many of them like the same things American ... Create a budget for a typical Indian teen.

Global Financial Landscape
The S&P's Global Financial Landscape feature presents interesting financial profiles of different countries with a DataByte snapshot of the country's statistics by Standard and Poor's.

Document Detective

Learn to identify and understand the standard financial documents you will use in the real world.

Investigate: A Monthly Budget Worksheet
A monthly budget worksheet contains the following information:

- Income
- Payroll deductions
- Take-home pay
- Other income
- Expenses
- Income less expenses

Your Motive: A monthly budget worksheet helps you analyze and compare your monthly expenses to the income you receive each month. This analysis helps you plan your spending.

Janet Lopez's Monthly Budget Worksheet

Variable Monthly Expenses

Document Detective This feature is a guide to understanding the financial documents you will use in everyday finance. Questions reinforce your understanding.

Careers in Finance The *Careers in Finance* feature provides insight through profiles of real people working in the world of finance. Information on the education and skills needed for the career is provided. A chapter-related, critical-thinking question follows.

Careers in Finance

PERSONAL BANKER **Jason Lee**
National Bank

Working as a personal banker for National Bank, Jason develops, manages, and expands customer relationships. His challenge is to recognize the needs of the customers and match them to the services offered by his branch. His clients range from high school students, who are opening their first savings and checking accounts, to businesspeople, who are seeking very precise financial products and services. Jason enjoys working with a wide variety of customers and gains satisfaction from helping them reach their financial goals.

SKILLS: Communication, customer-service, computer, interpersonal, math, sales, cross-selling, and second language skills

PERSONAL TRAITS: Good judgment, likes working with people, tactful, detail oriented, ability to adapt to a flexible schedule in a high-volume environment

GO FIGURE FINANCIAL MATH

UNIT PRICING

Synopsis: Knowing the unit price of an item can help you determine the best buy.

Example: The brand of peppermint mouthwash that Claudia likes is offered in two sizes, 12 ounces for $2.89 and 16 ounces for $3.39. Which is the better buy?

Formula: $\frac{\text{Total Price}}{\text{Unit of Measurement}} = \text{Unit Price}$

Solution: $\frac{\$2.89}{12 \text{ oz.}} = \$0.24/\text{oz.}$

$\frac{\$3.39}{16 \text{ oz.}} = \$0.21/\text{oz.}$

The 16-ounce size is the better buy at 21 cents per ounce.

YOU FIGURE

You are considering buying soft drinks for your sister's birthday party. The market is offering a six-pack of 12-ounces for $2.99 and a liter bottle for $1.29. Which is the better buy? (Hint: One liter equals 33.8 ounces.)

Go Figure This feature provides a financial math formula related to chapter discussions, and then gives you a chance to use it in the *You Figure* application.

TechByte

Using Software There are many software products on the market today designed to help you keep track of your personal finances. One of the first and most popular is Quicken®. Features allow you to track and pay bills and see if you have enough money to cover upcoming bills. You can also schedule bill payments and deposits.

@ Describe the information given on the Quicken monthly view screen by reading information through **finance07.glencoe.com**.

TechByte Technology is today's number-one trend. This feature highlights the wide range of technological applications that enhance business and personal finance today. An exercise directs you to the book's Online Learning Center at **finance07.glencoe.com**.

S&P's Put on Your Financial Planner's Cap Real scenarios provide problems you can solve as you think like a financial planner.

STANDARD & POOR'S

Put on Your Financial Planner's Cap

If you were planning an investment for yourself, would you choose an annuity? Why or why not?

Savvy Saver Lists of interesting tips and facts about business and personal finance help you save money.

$avvy Saver

Get a Good Credit Rating

1. Open a savings account and make regular deposits.
2. Apply for a department store or gasoline credit card and use it responsibly.
3. Pay all loans and credit card bills on time.
4. Open a checking account and do not bounce checks.
5. Never let anyone use your credit card.

Common CENTS

One Is Enough

When you turn 18, you may start receiving applications for credit cards. Be a smart consumer and compare interest rates, annual fees, and any other fees. Decide which credit card best suits your needs and apply for that one. Toss any other applications you get into the trash. *Why should you get the best (or lowest) interest rate for a credit card?*

Academic Connection

HISTORY

The first credit card, a travel and entertainment card, was issued in 1950 by Diners Club. Card holders could charge meals in 27 restaurants in New York City. Eight years later, the first bank credit card was issued. By 1965, about 5 million credit cards were in circulation. Fast forward to 2004, and U.S. consumers held more than 1.8 billion credit cards. Credit cards make buying easier—but give less incentive to save. *Do you think that credit cards have caused people to have more debt? Explain why or why not in two sentences.*

Academic Connection Integrate finance with your academic subjects as you complete brief activities.

Common Cents Quick finance facts related to the chapter topics are reinforced with a critical-thinking application.

Understanding Assessments

At the end of each chapter, *Review and Activities* presents a chapter summary with a key terms activity, recall and review questions, real-world applications, and activities that help you integrate a variety of academics with finance.

Chapter Summary The Chapter Summary is a list of chapter highlights to help you review and remember. Each highlight is related to a chapter objective.

Communicating Key Terms Review the financial key terms you learn throughout the chapter by applying them in written context.

Academic Skills Reinforce the connection between a variety of academic subjects as you relate and apply them to finance.

Your Financial Figures Solve a financial problem presented as a real-life scenario as you calculate the answer and use software.

Real-World Application Make the connection with real-world finance as you solve a problem.

Internet Connection This activity helps you develop your Internet research skills. Resources can be found through the book's Online Learning Center at **finance07.glencoe.com**.

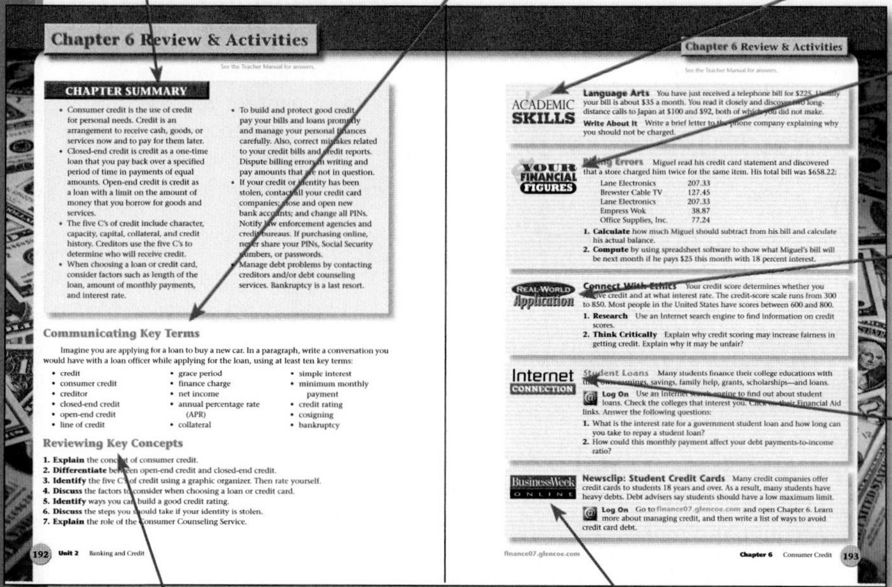

Chapter 6 Review & Activities

See the Teacher Manual for answers.

CHAPTER SUMMARY

- Consumer credit is the use of credit for personal needs. Credit is an arrangement to receive cash, goods, or services now and to pay for them later.
- Closed-end credit is credit as a one-time loan that you pay back over a specified period of time in payments of equal amounts. Open-end credit is credit as a loan with a limit on the amount of money that you borrow for goods and services.
- The five C's of credit include character, capacity, capital, collateral, and credit history. Creditors use the five C's to determine who will receive credit.
- When choosing a loan or credit card, consider factors such as length of the loan, amount of monthly payments, and interest rate.
- To build and protect good credit, pay your bills and loans promptly and manage your personal finances carefully. Also, correct mistakes related to your credit bills and credit reports. Dispute billing errors in writing and pay amounts that are not in question.
- If your credit or identity has been stolen, contact all your credit card companies; close and open new bank accounts; and change all PINs. Notify law enforcement agencies and credit bureaus. If purchasing online, never share your PINs, Social Security numbers, or passwords.
- Manage debt problems by contacting creditors and/or debt counseling services. Bankruptcy is a last resort.

Communicating Key Terms

Imagine you are applying for a loan to buy a new car. In a paragraph, write a conversation you would have with a loan officer while applying for the loan, using at least ten key terms:

- credit
- consumer credit
- creditor
- closed-end credit
- open-end credit
- line of credit
- grace period
- finance charge
- net income
- annual percentage rate (APR)
- collateral
- simple interest
- minimum monthly payment
- credit rating
- cosigning
- bankruptcy

Reviewing Key Concepts

1. **Explain** the concept of consumer credit.
2. **Differentiate** between open-end credit and closed-end credit.
3. **Identify** the five C's of credit using a graphic organizer. Then rate yourself.
4. **Discuss** the factors to consider when choosing a loan or credit card.
5. **Identify** ways you can build a good credit rating.
6. **Discuss** the steps you should take if your identity is stolen.
7. **Explain** the role of the Consumer Counseling Service.

192 Unit 2 Banking and Credit

Chapter 6 Review & Activities

See the Teacher Manual for answers.

ACADEMIC SKILLS

Language Arts You have just received a telephone bill for $225. Usually your bill is about $35 a month. You read it closely and discover two long-distance calls to Japan at $100 and $92, both of which you did not make.

Write About It Write a brief letter to the phone company explaining why you should not be charged.

YOUR FINANCIAL FIGURES

Billing Errors Miguel read his credit card statement and discovered that a store charged him twice for the same item. His total bill was $658.22:

Lane Electronics	207.33
Brewster Cable TV	127.45
Lane Electronics	207.33
Empress Wok	38.87
Office Supplies, Inc.	77.24

1. **Calculate** how much Miguel should subtract from his bill and calculate his actual balance.
2. **Compute** by using spreadsheet software to show what Miguel's bill will be next month if he pays $25 this month with 18 percent interest.

REAL-WORLD Application

Connect With Ethics Your credit score determines whether you receive credit and at what interest rate. The credit-score scale runs from 300 to 850. Most people in the United States have scores between 600 and 800.

1. **Research** Use an Internet search engine to find information on credit scores.
2. **Think Critically** Explain why credit scoring may increase fairness in getting credit. Explain why it may be unfair?

Internet CONNECTION

Student Loans Many students finance their college educations with their own earnings, savings, family help, grants, scholarships—and loans.

Log On Use an Internet search engine to find out about student loans. Check the colleges that interest you. Click on their Financial Aid links. Answer the following questions:

1. What is the interest rate for a government student loan and how long can you take to repay a student loan?
2. How could this monthly payment affect your debt payments-to-income ratio?

BusinessWeek ONLINE

Newsclip: Student Credit Cards Many credit companies offer credit cards to students 18 years and over. As a result, many students have heavy debts. Debt advisers say students should have a low maximum limit.

Log On Go to finance07.glencoe.com and open Chapter 6. Learn more about managing credit, and then write a list of ways to avoid credit card debt.

finance07.glencoe.com Chapter 6 Consumer Credit 193

Reviewing Key Concepts Review questions are correlated to the chapter objectives to help you check your understanding of the text through defining terms, describing processes, and explaining concepts.

***BusinessWeek* Online** Go to the Student Center of the book's Online Learning Center, and you will find a complete chapter-related article to read.

Application Activity and Portfolio

At the end of each chapter's text, *What's Your Financial ID?* provides a special self-assessment, quiz, or other profile activity.

Your Financial Portfolio ends each chapter with an exercise to demonstrate your knowledge of business and personal finance topics.

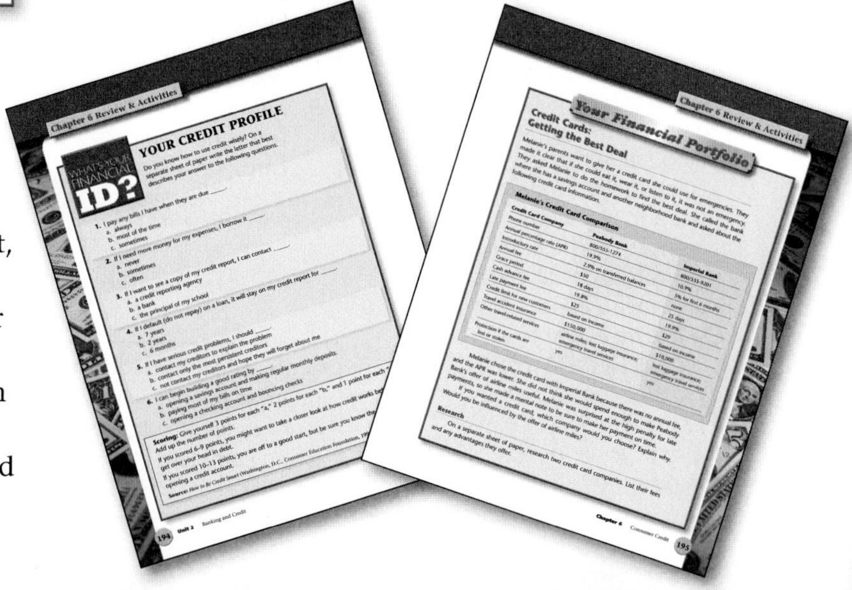

Chapter 6 Review & Activities

WHAT'S YOUR FINANCIAL ID?

YOUR CREDIT PROFILE

Chapter 6 Review & Activities

Your Financial Portfolio

Credit Cards: Getting the Best Deal

Melanie's Credit Card Comparison

Focus on Reading

Top 10 Reasons to Become a Better Reader

10. **Give yourself more choices in life.** Reading well opens the door to a wider variety of interesting career options.

9. **Empower yourself through the written word.** Teach yourself sailing, computer skills, the latest techniques in skateboarding. Discover how to create your own Web site.

8. **Improve your chances of getting into and graduating from an institution of higher learning.** On average, a person who gets a postsecondary education makes three times more money than a high school dropout!

7. **Increase your chances of getting a job when you look for one.** That is important, considering that the average person will hold 11 different jobs over his or her lifetime.

6. **Advance more quickly in your chosen career.** In many positions, people with strong reading skills are ten times as likely to receive training from their employer as those with limited reading skills.

5. **Make the country economically stronger.** More people reading well means more people contributing to the progress and prosperity of the country.

4. **Save money and gain confidence in many real-life situations.** For example, you will be able to pass your driver's test and read the lease for your first apartment.

3. **Be more civic minded.** People who read well are more likely to vote and to participate in democratic elections and in civic life.

2. **Once learned, never forgotten.** Reading is a lifelong skill, like riding a bicycle—once you learn, you will never forget!

1. **Enjoy life more!** Reading well can not only help you get ahead and stay ahead in life—it's fun!

Reading Strategies

Reading Strategies

How can you get the most from your reading?
Effective readers are active readers. Get involved with the text. Think of your textbook as a tool that helps you learn more about the world around you. The material is a form of nonfiction writing—it describes real-life ideas, people, events, and places. Use the reading strategies listed in the *Reading Strategies* box at the beginning of each chapter along with strategies in the margins to help you read actively.

Before You Read

PREDICT

Make educated guesses about what the section is about by combining clues in the text with what you already know. Predicting helps you anticipate questions and stay alert to new information.

Ask yourself:
- What does this section heading mean?
- What is this section about?
- How does this section tie in with what I have read so far?
- Why is this information important in understanding the subject?

As You Read

RELATE

Draw parallels between what you are reading and the events and circumstances in your own life.

Ask yourself:
- What do I know about the topic?
- How do my experiences compare to the information in the text?
- How could I apply this information to my own life?
- Why is this information important in understanding the subject?

As You Read

QUESTION

Ask yourself questions to help clarify the reading as you go along.

Ask yourself:
- Do I understand what I have read so far?
- What is this section about?
- What does this mean?
- Why is this information important in understanding the subject?

After You Read

REACT

React to what you are reading. Form opinions and make judgments about the section while you are reading—not just after you have finished.

Ask yourself:
- Does this information make sense?
- What can I learn from this section?
- How can I use this information to start planning for my financial future?
- Why is this information important in understanding the subject?

To the Student

More Reading Strategies

Use this menu for more reading strategies to help you get the most from your reading.

Before You Read

Set a purpose
- Why are you reading the textbook?
- How does the subject relate to your life?
- How might you be able to use what you learn in your own life?

Preview
- Read the chapter title to preview the topic.
- Read the subtitles to see what you will learn about the topic.
- Skim the photos, charts, graphs, or maps. How do they support the topic?
- Look for key terms that are boldfaced. How are they defined?

Draw from your background
- What have you read or heard concerning new information on the topic?
- How is the new information different from what you already know?
- How will the information that you already know help you understand the new information?

As You Read

Predict
- Predict events or outcomes by using clues and information that you already know.
- Change your predictions as you read and gather new information.

Connect
- Think about people, places, and events in your own life. Are there any similarities with those in your textbook?
- Can you relate the textbook information to other areas of your life?

Question
- What is the main idea?
- How do the photos, charts, graphs, and maps support the main idea?

Visualize
- Pay careful attention to details and descriptions.
- Create graphic organizers to show relationships that you find in the information.

Notice Comparison and Contrast Sentences
- Look for clue words and phrases that signal comparison, such as *similarly, just as, both, in common, also,* and *too.*
- Look for clue words and phrases that signal contrast, such as *on the other hand, in contrast to, however, different, instead of, rather than, but,* and *unlike.*

Notice Cause-and-Effect Sentences
- Look for clue words and phrases, such as *because, as a result, therefore, that is why, since, so, for this reason,* and *consequently.*

Notice Chronological Sentences
- Look for clue words and phrases, such as *after, before, first, next, last, during, finally, earlier, later, since,* and *then.*

After You Read

Summarize
- Describe the main idea and how the details support it.
- Use your own words to explain what you have read.

Assess
- What was the main idea?
- Did the text clearly support the main idea?
- Did you learn anything new from the material?
- Can you use this new information in other school subjects or at home?
- What other sources could you use to find more information about the topic?

Unit 1

Planning Personal Finances

WebQuest Internet Project

One Life to Plan

Financial planners help people plan for paying for college or retirement, and then show them how to save to reach those goals. Life planners assist clients to pinpoint what they want out of life, and then use financial planning to help people achieve it. In this project, you will weigh the pros and cons of each career and decide which one might best suit you.

Log on to finance07.glencoe.com. Begin your WebQuest by reading Task 1. Then continue working on your WebQuest as you study Unit 1.

Section	1.2	2.2	3.2	4.1
Page	25	52	71	96

BusinessWeek

FINANCE FILE

Which Adviser Knows the Way?

Almost anyone can claim to be a financial planner or investment adviser. If you're looking for an adviser for the first time—you need to figure out how much and what kind of advice you need. If all you want are some suggestions for your IRA or your investment portfolio, you could get that through Charles Schwab or Fidelity Brokerage Services for a fee of about $250.

But there's more to your financial well-being than stocks and bonds. Do you have a debt-management problem? Do you have enough insurance, and is your estate in order?

And what about credentials? Certified Financial Planner (CFP) is the most recognized designation. CFPs have comprehensive education and must pass a ten-hour certification exam and have at least three years' experience before qualifying.

The irony is that most people seek advisers to relieve the burden of managing their finances themselves. But it's a burden in itself to make sure you've got the right adviser.

— By Lewis Braham with Amy Borrus

Write About It Why should you know how to plan your personal finances even if you can hire a financial planner?

See the Teacher Manual for answer.

Log On To read the complete *BusinessWeek* article and do the *BusinessWeek* Extension activity to help you learn more about financial and life planning, go to **finance07.glencoe.com**.

CHAPTER 1

Personal Financial Planning

$ What You'll Learn

When you have completed this chapter, you will be able to:

Section 1.1

- Define personal financial planning.
- Name the six steps of financial planning.
- Identify factors that affect personal financial decisions.

Section 1.2

- Explain opportunity costs associated with personal financial decisions.
- Identify eight strategies for achieving financial goals at different stages of life.

Reading Strategies

To get the most out of your reading:

Predict what you will learn in this chapter.
Relate what you read to your own life.
Question what you are reading to be sure you understand.
React to what you have read.

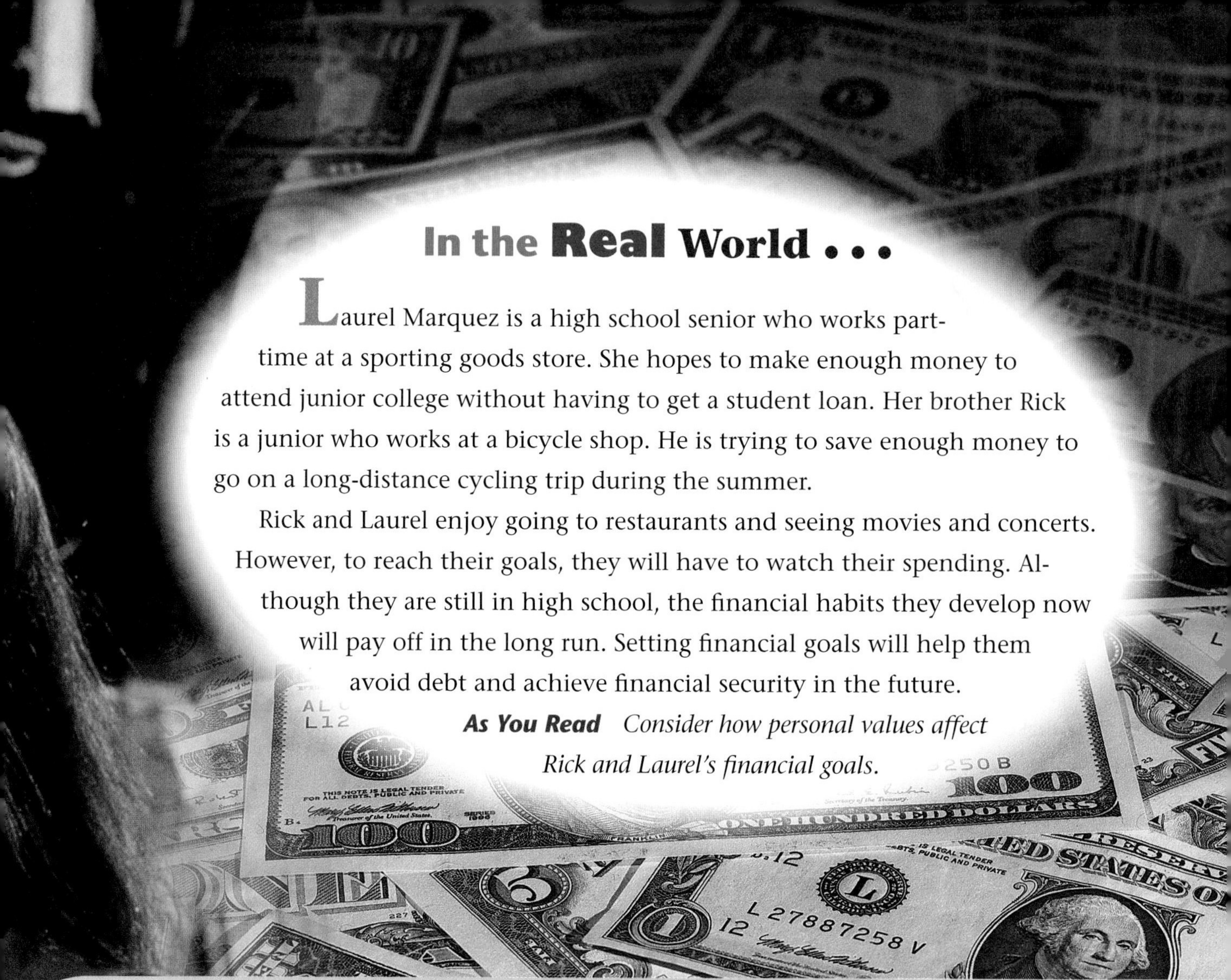

In the **Real** World . . .

Laurel Marquez is a high school senior who works part-time at a sporting goods store. She hopes to make enough money to attend junior college without having to get a student loan. Her brother Rick is a junior who works at a bicycle shop. He is trying to save enough money to go on a long-distance cycling trip during the summer.

Rick and Laurel enjoy going to restaurants and seeing movies and concerts. However, to reach their goals, they will have to watch their spending. Although they are still in high school, the financial habits they develop now will pay off in the long run. Setting financial goals will help them avoid debt and achieve financial security in the future.

As You Read *Consider how personal values affect Rick and Laurel's financial goals.*

Lesson Plan See the Teacher Manual for the Chapter 1 planning guide and lesson plan.

ASK STANDARD & POOR'S

The Money Plan

Q: I am a high school student. I do not have money for investments or buying property. So what difference does it make how I spend my money now?

A: You will not always be a student. Learning to save and use money wisely now will help you know how to achieve financial security in the future. While you are in high school, financial planning can help you decide how to spend, save, and invest your money for special purchases or activities that matter to you. You may even be able to buy stock!

Ask Yourself What item do you think you could buy if you saved some money for several months? Explain why this would be financial planning.

@ Go to **finance07.glencoe.com** to complete the Standard & Poor's Financial Focus activity.

Section 1.1

Financial Decisions and Goals

Focus on Reading

Read to Learn

- How to define personal financial planning.
- How to name the six steps of financial planning.
- How to identify factors that affect personal financial decisions.

Main Idea

The financial planning process can help you reach your financial goals.

Key Terms

- personal financial planning
- goals
- values
- opportunity cost
- liquidity
- service
- good
- economics
- economy
- supply
- demand
- Federal Reserve System
- inflation
- consumer
- interest

Before You Read

PREDICT

List three of your financial goals.

Personal Financial Decisions

What are the benefits of financial planning?

What is personal finance? It is everything in your life that involves money. **Personal financial planning** is arranging to spend, save, and invest money to live comfortably, have financial security, and achieve goals. Everyone has different financial goals. **Goals** are the things you want to accomplish. For example, getting a college education, buying a car, and starting a business are goals. Planning your personal finances is important because it will help you to reach your goals, no matter what they are. It is up to you to make and follow a financial plan.

Some of the benefits of planning are:

- You have more money and financial security.
- You know how to use money to achieve your goals.
- You have less chance of going into debt you cannot handle.
- You can help your partner and support your children, if you have a family.

Whether you are spending, saving, or investing money, planning can help you to make big or small financial decisions. The financial planning process has six steps to help you reach your goals.

STEP 1: Determine Your Current Financial Situation

To figure out your current financial situation, make a list of items that relate to your finances:

- Savings
- Monthly income (job earnings, allowance, gifts, and interest on bank accounts)
- Monthly expenses (money you spend)
- Debts (money you owe to others)

A good way to estimate your expenses is to keep a careful record of everything you buy for one month. You can use a small notebook to track your expenses. When you have determined your financial situation, you will be able to start planning.

STEP 2: Develop Your Financial Goals

To develop clear financial goals, think about your attitude toward money and ask yourself some questions: Is it more important to spend your money now or to save for the future? Would you rather get a job right after high school or continue your education? Do your personal values affect your financial decisions? **Values** are the beliefs and principles you consider important, correct, and desirable. Different people value different things.

Needs and Wants Another important aspect of developing financial goals is knowing the difference between your needs and your wants. A *need* is something you must have to survive, such as food, shelter, and clothing. A *want* is something you desire or would like to have or do. For example, if you live in an area where the winter is cold, you need a coat. So you may want a leather jacket, but other less expensive coats would also keep you warm.

Only you can decide what specific goals to pursue. For example, you might want to save money. So, you could save $50 every month or 15 percent of every paycheck.

STEP 3: Identify Your Options

It is impossible to make a good decision unless you know all your options. Generally, you have several possible courses of action. Suppose that you are saving $50 a month. You might have these options:

- **Expand the current situation.** You may decide to increase the amount of money you save every month to $60.
- **Change the current situation.** You could invest in stocks instead of putting your money into a savings account.
- **Start something new.** You could use the $50 to pay off your debts.
- **Continue the same course of action.** You may choose not to change anything.

However, in each case, be aware that the costs of your decision may outweigh the benefits.

TechByte

Using Software There are many software products on the market today designed to help you keep track of your personal finances. One of the first and most popular is Quicken®. Features allow you to track and pay bills and see if you have enough money to cover upcoming bills. You can also schedule bill payments and deposits.

@ Describe the information given on the Quicken monthly view screen by reading information through **finance07.glencoe.com**.

Springboard Ask the students if they feel confident about their ability to make personal financial decisions. Have them explain why or why not.

Caption Answer Answers may include to find bargains, find collectibles, for fun.

▶ **MONEY MATTERS** Your values affect your spending habits. *Why might people shop at vintage clothing stores or swap meets?*

Motivating Students Have students name aloud some personal financial goals they have; list them on the board.

STEP 4: Evaluate Your Alternatives

In this step, you evaluate your alternatives as part of the financial planning process. Use the many sources of financial information that are available. (See **Figure 1.1.**) Look at your situation in life, your present financial situation, and your personal values. Consider the consequences and risks of each decision you make.

Sources of Financial Information It is important to keep up-to-date with social and economic conditions because they can affect your financial situation. For example, a company that manufactures the latest technology or designs the trendiest clothes may be a good investment. On the other hand, if you learn that the company is being sued, would you invest in it?

Critical Thinking Have students think and write briefly about possible advantages of each of the five listed sources of financial information.

Consequences of Choices When you choose one option, you eliminate other possibilities. You cannot choose all options. Suppose that you want to become a full-time college student. You also want the income you would earn at a full-time job. In choosing to pursue your education, you give up the opportunity to work full time, at least for the moment. An **opportunity cost**, or a trade-off, is what is given up when making one choice instead of another. The opportunity cost of going to college would be the benefit of having a full-time job.

Figure 1.1 Get the Facts

Information on financial planning can come from many sources:

1 **Financial Specialists:** accountants, bankers, financial planners, insurance agents, tax attorneys, and tax preparers

2 **Technology:** computer software and the Internet

However, choosing involves more than knowing what you might give up. It also involves knowing what you would gain. For example, by going to college, you could gain a higher-paying job.

Understanding Risks If you decide to ride your bicycle on a very busy city street, you are taking a risk of having an accident. When you make a financial decision, you also accept certain financial risks. Some types of financial risks include:

- **Inflation Risk**—If you wait to buy a car until next year, you accept the possibility that the price may increase.
- **Interest Rate Risk**—Interest rates go up or down, which may affect the cost of borrowing or the profits you earn when you save or invest.
- **Income Risk**—You may lose your job due to unexpected health problems, family problems, an accident, or changes in your field of work.
- **Personal Risk**—Driving for eight hours on icy mountain roads may be hazardous. The risk may not be worth the money you would save on airfare.
- **Liquidity Risk**—**Liquidity** is the ability to easily convert financial assets into cash without loss in value. Some long-term investments, such as a house, can be difficult to convert quickly.

As You Read

RELATE

What are your financial goals? Which goals are needs and which goals are wants?

Teaching Activity Divide students into groups of four. Assign a "financial goal" to each group, as much as possible according to the group's preference. Have each group take its goal through Steps 3 and 4 of the goal process and devise a chart illustrating their thinking.

3 **The Media:** books, magazines, newsletters, newspapers, radio, and television

4 **Financial Institutions:** banks, credit unions, insurance and investment companies, and savings and loan associations

5 **Education:** high school and college courses and seminars

STEP 5: Create and Use Your Financial Plan of Action

A plan of action is a list of ways to achieve your financial goals. If your goal is to increase your savings, a plan of action could be to cut back on spending. If you want to increase your income, you might get a part-time job or work more hours at your present job. You could use the extra money you earn to pay off debts, save money, purchase stocks, or make other investments.

STEP 6: Review and Revise Your Plan

Financial planning continues as you follow your plan. As you get older, your finances and needs will change. That means that your financial plan will have to change too. You should reevaluate and revise it every year.

Developing Personal Financial Goals

What should you consider to set financial goals for yourself?

Why do so many people have money problems? The main reason is that they do not plan how they will use their money. You can avoid money problems by planning with some clear financial goals in mind.

Types of Financial Goals

Two factors will influence your planning for financial goals. The first factor is the time frame in which you would like to achieve your goals. The second factor is the type of financial need that inspires your goals.

Time Frame of Goals Goals can be defined by the time it takes to achieve them:

- **Short-term goals** take one year or less to achieve (such as saving to buy a computer).
- **Intermediate goals** take two to five years to achieve (such as saving for a down payment on a house).
- **Long-term goals** take more than five years to achieve (such as planning for retirement).

Start with short-term goals that may lead to long-term ones. Some goals, such as having money for the holidays or other special occasions, occur every year. Other goals, such as buying a car, may come up only occasionally. What are some of your short-term, intermediate, and long-term financial goals?

Common Cents $670.80 ($860 x .01 = $8.60; $860 x .02 = $17.20, etc. Then add $8.60 + $17.20, etc. = $670.80)

Common CENTS

Pay Yourself First
When you receive your paycheck, pay yourself first. This means that before you pay bills or buy anything, you should put something into your savings account—even a small amount. Think of it as paying yourself. Try saving a percentage of your take-home pay or allowance—1 percent the first month, 2 percent the second month, and so forth. Then sit back and watch your money grow. *If your take-home pay is $860 a month and you save the percentages listed above for 12 months, how much would you have?*

Careers in Finance

PERSONAL BANKER **Jason Lee**
National Bank

Working as a personal banker for National Bank, Jason develops, manages, and expands customer relationships. His challenge is to recognize the needs of the customers and match them to the services offered by his branch. His clients range from high school students, who are opening their first savings and checking accounts, to businesspeople, who are seeking very precise financial products and services. Jason enjoys working with a wide variety of customers and gains satisfaction from helping them reach their financial goals.

SKILLS: Communication, customer-service, computer, interpersonal, math, sales, cross-selling, and second language skills

PERSONAL TRAITS: Good judgment, likes working with people, tactful, detail oriented, ability to adapt to a flexible schedule in a high-volume environment

EDUCATION: Associate degree or bachelor's degree with a major in business administration or economics

ANALYZE Banking services are increasingly offered via ATMs, the telephone, or online. Explain why personal bankers are still in demand.

See the Teacher Manual for answer.

@ To learn more about career paths for personal bankers, visit **finance07.glencoe.com**.

Goals for Different Needs The need to have your hair cut at a salon is different from the need to buy a new car. A haircut is a **service**, or a task that a person or a machine performs for you. A new car is a **good**, or a physical item that is produced and can be weighed or measured. You might buy a soda every day. You might buy a new car every five or six years. How you establish and reach your financial goals will depend on whether a goal involves the need for consumable goods (such as a soda), durable goods (such as a car), or intangible items (such as an education):

- **Consumable goods** are purchases that you make often and use up quickly. Food and products, such as shampoo and conditioner, are in this category. Although the cost of such items may not equal the cost of a car, the costs of consumable goods add up.
- **Durable goods** are expensive items that you do not purchase often. Most durable goods, such as cars and large appliances, will last three years or more when used on a regular basis.
- **Intangible items** cannot be touched but are often important to your well-being and happiness. Examples of intangibles include your personal relationships, health, education, and free time. Intangibles are often overlooked but can be expensive.

Pay as you go; small increments

Question Answer consumable goods.

As You Read

QUESTION

Think about consumable goods, durable goods, and intangibles. Over the long term (ten years or more), which category do you think has the highest cost?

Document Detective

Learn to identify and understand the standard financial documents you will use in the real world.

See the Teacher Manual for answers.

Investigate: A Monthly Budget Worksheet

A monthly budget worksheet contains the following information:

- Income
- Payroll deductions
- Take-home pay
- Other income
- Expenses
- Income less expenses

Your Motive: A monthly budget worksheet helps you analyze and compare your monthly expenses to the income you receive each month. This analysis helps you plan your spending.

Janet Lopez's Monthly Budget Worksheet

Monthly Income	Amount
Wages (before taxes)	$3,500
Allowance	0
Other income	35
Payroll Deductions	
Federal tax	$ 700
Social Security tax	268
State tax	175
Local tax	35
Other	0
Total Take-Home Income	$ 2,357
Fixed Monthly Expenses	
Savings	$ 100
Rent/Mortgage	750
Car loan	425
Vehicle and apartment or house insurance	125
Life and health insurance	55
Cable TV/Internet access	95

Variable Monthly Expenses	Amount
Utilities (gas, electric)	$75
Telephone/Cell phone	65
Groceries	135
Clothing	75
Credit card	150
Donations	25
Gasoline	85
Personal items	45
Discretionary Monthly Expenses	
Movies	$ 15
Hobbies	35
Restaurants	55
Other	155
Total Expenses	$ 2,465
Income Less Expenses	- $ 108

Key Points: You create a budget by determining your take-home income. Take-home income is the difference between your wages and deductions. Taxes, union dues, and health insurance are wage deductions. Expenses are also listed. Some expenses are fixed. They do not change. Variable expenses change each month. Discretionary expenses do not include expenses for basic needs.

Find the Solutions

1. Explain the difference between fixed expenses and variable expenses.
2. List other possible expenses that are not listed on this worksheet.
3. Decide if Janet has enough monthly income for monthly expenses.
4. Explain why utilities are a variable expense.
5. Suggest ways this budget can be balanced.

Guidelines for Setting Goals

How can you make good financial decisions? You must identify your goals. Then identify the time frame for achieving each goal and the type of need. However, these factors will change as you go through life. The financial goals you set as a student will be different from the goals you may have if you marry or have children. **Figure 1.2** shows examples of financial goals and activities related to various life situations.

When setting your financial goals, follow these guidelines:

1. Your financial goals should be realistic.
2. Your financial goals should be specific.
3. Your financial goals should have a clear time frame.
4. Your financial goals should help you decide what type of action to take.

Academic Connection

LANGUAGE ARTS

Look at Figure 1.2 and consider setting some financial goals for yourself. *Think of three goals. Write them down, explaining how each meets the four guidelines.*

See the Teacher Manual for answer.

Figure 1.2 **Financial Goals and Activities for Various Life Situations**

Life Situation	Financial Goals and Activities
Young single adult	• Obtain career training. • Become financially independent. • Obtain health insurance. • Develop a savings plan. • Carefully manage your use of credit.
Young couple with no children	• Create an effective financial record-keeping system. • Obtain adequate health and life insurance. • Implement a budget. • Carefully manage your use of credit. • Develop a savings and investment program.
Couple with young children	• Purchase a home. • Obtain adequate health and life insurance. • Start a college fund. • Make a will and name a guardian for your children.
Single parent with young children	• Obtain adequate health, life, and disability insurance. • Make a will and name a guardian for your children. • Establish an emergency fund.
Middle-aged, single adult	• Contribute to a tax-deferred retirement plan. • Evaluate and select appropriate investments. • Accumulate an adequate emergency fund. • Review will and estate plans.
Older couple with no children at home	• Plan retirement housing, living expenses, and activities. • Obtain health insurance for retirement. • Review will and estate plans.

Economic Conditions Your financial needs and goals change at different stages of life.

What are some goals you will have ten years from now that you do not have today?

Caption Answer Answers might include buying a house, owning a business, and saving for college.

$avvy Saver

Good Financial Habits

1. Save money every time you get paid.
2. Spend less than you make.
3. Work out a budget and stick to it.
4. Pay your bills and taxes on time.
5. Balance your checkbook every month.

Influences on Personal Financial Planning

What factors can influence your personal financial planning?

Many factors will influence your day-to-day decisions about finances. The three most important factors are:

- Life situations
- Personal values
- Economic factors

Life Situations and Personal Values

As you enter adulthood, you will experience many changes. You may go to college, start a new career, get married, have children, or move to a new city. These new life situations will affect your financial planning. Your personal values also influence your financial decisions.

For example, Angela just graduated from high school and will be going to college in the fall. She will move out of her parents' house and live in the college dorm. Angela is beginning a new and exciting stage in her life. She values independence, and so she plans to move to an apartment with a roommate in her sophomore year. She will experience more personal freedom, but with her independence will also come more financial responsibility.

Economic Factors

Economic factors across the country and around the world can affect personal finances. They play a role in day-to-day financial planning and decision making for most people. **Economics** is the study of the decisions that go into making, distributing, and using goods and services. The **economy** consists of the ways in which people make, distribute, and use their goods and services. To understand economics and the economy, you need to be aware of the market forces, financial institutions, global influences, and economic conditions that affect global as well as personal decisions.

Market Forces The forces of supply and demand determine the prices of products, or goods and services, you purchase. **Supply** is the amount of goods and services available for sale. **Demand** is the amount of goods and services people are willing to buy. When there is a high demand for an item, such as a popular toy, or when a company cannot manufacture enough of a certain product to keep up with the demand, the price of the product rises. When there is little demand for a product, or when a company produces more than it can sell, the price of the product drops.

Financial Institutions Most people do business with financial institutions, which include banks, credit unions, savings and loan associations, insurance companies, and investment companies. Financial institutions provide services that increase financial activity in the economy. For example, they handle savings and checking accounts, provide loans, sell insurance, and make investments for their clients.

STANDARD & POOR'S

Global Financial Landscape

Standard and Poor's publishes the globally recognized S&P 500® financial index. It also gathers financial statistics, information, and news, and analyzes this data for international businesses, governments, and individuals to help them guide their financial decisions.

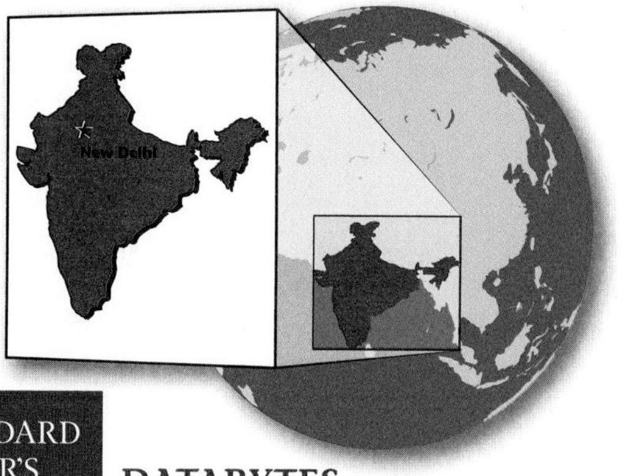

INDIA

Most travelers to India expect to see a country carved out of 5,000-year-old traditions, but they also find modern-day landmarks that look like home. Driven by a booming economy and growing incomes in large cities, Indians have become avid consumers of Western culture. Fast-food chains and sprawling malls dot the ancient landscape. Teenagers wear the latest fashions. In fact, India also boasts a growing fashion design industry. Imported cosmetics are popular, and beauty pageants are national events. On a one-mile stretch of a typical city of India, construction takes place to accommodate more than 40,000 multinational technology and service workers.

A decade ago, when India opened its doors to the world, critics labeled this kind of expansion as corruptive. But as foreign businesses pour billions into the country, some say the modernization is too slow. One young Indian laments, "Night life is nonexistent."

STANDARD & POOR'S **DATABYTES**

Capital	New Delhi
Population	1,086,572,000
Language	Hindi, English, and 14 other official languages
Currency	Indian rupee
Gross Domestic Product (GDP)	$3.02 trillion (2003 est.)
GDP per capita	$2,900

Industry: Textiles, chemicals, food processing, steel, transportation equipment, cement, and mining

Agriculture: Rice, wheat, oilseed, cotton, cattle, and fish

Exports: Textile goods, gems and jewelry, engineering goods, chemicals, and leather

Natural Resources: Coal, iron ore, manganese, mica, and bauxite

Think Globally

Working Indian teens spend money to keep up with the times. Many of them like the same things American teens like. Create a budget for a typical Indian teen.

See the Teacher Manual for answer.

Research Have students look up the Federal Reserve System and the Consumer Price Index on the Internet. Ask them to research the figures, under the current economy, the following: (a) interest rates, (b) inflation rate, (c) consumer spending/saving rates, and (c) the U.S. gross domestic product (GDP).

Among the various government agencies that regulate the financial activities of financial institutions, the Federal Reserve System has a significant responsibility in the U.S. economy. The **Federal Reserve System**, or the Fed, is the central banking organization of the United States. Its primary role in the U.S. economy is the regulation of the money supply. The Fed controls the money supply by determining interest rates and by buying or selling government securities. Its decisions affect the interest rate you earn on your savings, the interest rate you pay when you borrow money, and to some extent the prices of the products you buy.

Global Influences You and the money you spend are part of the global marketplace, which is another economic factor that can affect financial planning. Look at the items in your home or classroom and you will discover that many of the products were made in other countries.

The economy of every nation is affected by competition with other nations. Each country wants consumers in other countries to buy their products. When other countries sell more goods to the United States than U.S. companies can sell in those markets, more money leaves the United States than enters it. Then less money is available for spending and investing, and interest rates may rise. These global influences also affect financial decisions.

Economic Conditions Current economic conditions also affect your personal financial decisions. **Figure 1.3** shows how economic conditions can influence financial planning. There are three important economic conditions:

1. Consumer prices
2. Consumer spending
3. Interest rates

- **Consumer Prices** Over time the prices of most products go up. This rise in the level of prices for goods and services is called **inflation**. During times of rapid inflation, it takes more money to buy the same amount of goods and services. For example, if the rate of inflation is 5 percent, then a computer that cost $1,000 a year ago would now cost $1,050 if the computer price increased at the inflationary rate.

  The main cause of inflation is an increase in demand without an increase in supply. For example, if people have more money to spend because of pay increases or borrowing, but the same amounts of goods and services are available, then prices will rise.

  Inflation can be especially hard on certain groups, such as retired people whose income may not increase. The inflation rate affects consumer prices and varies from year to year. In the early 1960s, the annual inflation rate was between 1 and 3 percent. In the late 1970s and early 1980s, the inflation rate climbed to 10–12 percent each year. More recently it slowed to 2–4 percent each year.

- **Consumer Spending** A **consumer** is a person who purchases and uses goods or services. You are a consumer whenever you buy anything—a CD, books, clothes, lunch, or even a haircut. Consumer spending affects the economy by helping to create and maintain jobs. When people buy more goods or services, companies have to hire extra employees to meet the demand. This situation leads to a higher rate of employment, making more jobs available. More people work, and they have more money to spend. However, when consumers buy fewer goods and services, companies have to produce less and lay off workers. Then unemployment rises, making jobs harder to find.

Figure 1.3 **Economic Conditions and Financial Planning**

Economic Condition	What It Measures	How It Influences Financial Planning
Consumer prices	The value of a dollar; changes in inflation	If consumer prices increase faster than wages, the value of the dollar decreases—a dollar buys less than it did before. Consumers tend to buy fewer goods and services. Lenders charge higher interest rates.
Consumer spending	Demand for goods and services by individuals and households	Increased consumer spending usually creates more jobs and higher wages. Reduced consumer spending causes unemployment to increase.
Interest rates	Cost of money, cost of credit when you borrow, and the return on your money when you save or invest	Higher interest rates make borrowing money more expensive and make saving more attractive. When interest rates increase, consumer prices tend to increase.
Money supply	The dollars available for spending in our economy	The Federal Reserve System (Fed) sometimes adjusts interest rates in order to increase or decrease the amount of money circulating in the economy. If the Fed lowers interest rates, the money supply increases. If the Fed raises interest rates, the money supply decreases.
Unemployment	The number of people without jobs who are willing and able to work	Low unemployment increases consumer spending. High unemployment reduces consumer spending.
Gross domestic product (GDP)	Total dollar value of all the goods and services produced in a country in one year	The GDP provides an indication of how well people are living in a country.

Economic Conditions Economic conditions you cannot control will affect your financial planning.

Choose an economic condition listed above, and explain how it affects your life today.

Caption Answer Accept all reasonable answers that demonstrate an understanding of the economic condition.

- **Interest Rates** Like everything else, money has a price, and this price is called interest. **Interest** is the price that is paid for the use of another's money. Interest rates also affect the economy. When you deposit your paycheck in a savings account, the interest you receive is money the bank or another financial institution pays you for the use of your money. The bank, in turn, uses your money to make loans to people who want to purchase items such as houses, automobiles, and new businesses. Borrowers who receive the loans must pay a fee, or interest to the bank or lending institution.

Interest rates represent the cost of money. When consumers increase their savings and investments, the supply of money that is available for others to borrow grows, and interest rates go down. When consumers borrow more money, the demand for money increases, and interest rates go up.

Interest rates on loans also rise during times of inflation. Interest rates will affect your financial planning, whether you save, invest, or obtain loans. The amount of earnings you receive from your savings account or the interest you pay on a loan depend on the current interest rates. Interest rates are just one facet of the economic factors that influence your personal financial planning.

Section 1.1 Assessment

See the Teacher Manual for answers.

QUICK CHECK

1. What are the six steps used to create a financial plan?
2. What is the relationship between the timing of your goals and the type of good or service that you want?
3. What are two economic factors that affect financial decisions? How might these factors influence your financial planning?

THINK CRITICALLY

4. Why is it important to distinguish between your needs and your wants?

USE COMMUNICATION SKILLS

5. **Left to Chance?** You are talking to a friend who says that she never sets any financial goals and that her financial success or failure happens by luck.

Role-Play With a partner, role-play a response to your friend's philosophy. Explain how planning, more than luck, determines financial success or failure.

SOLVE MONEY PROBLEMS

6. **Financial Planning Process** Rosa and her best friend, Linda, live in Chicago and want to drive cross-country next year. Both work part-time and earn $97 a week after taxes. They need to save at least $500 each to pay for the trip. They plan to visit Rosa's aunt, who lives in Albuquerque, and Linda's brother in Los Angeles.

Write About It Help Rosa and Linda apply the six steps of the financial planning process to reach their goal. Write a six-step plan for them.

Section 1.2

Opportunity Costs and Strategies

Personal and Financial Opportunity Costs

What are personal and financial opportunity costs?

As discussed in Section 1.1, whenever you make a choice, you have to give up, or trade off, some of your other options. When making your financial decisions and plans, consider both the personal and financial opportunity costs carefully.

Personal Opportunity Costs

Like financial resources, your personal resources—your health, knowledge, skills, and time—require management. Do you eat a lot of junk food and avoid exercise? Do you get enough sleep each night? The decisions you make about your health now can have consequences as you get older.

In much the same way, the financial decisions you make today will affect your financial health in the future. For example, suppose that you and your friends have tickets to a sold-out concert this Thursday night. On Thursday afternoon your algebra teacher announces an important test for Friday. You must decide whether you will go to the concert, study for the test, or somehow do both. The opportunity cost of going to the concert might be getting a good grade on the test. You have to decide how to use your time to meet your needs, to achieve your goals, and to satisfy your values.

Financial Opportunity Costs

You also must make choices about how you spend money. For example, would you buy the $129 pair of sneakers you saw at the mall or save that money? You cannot do both, because most people have a limited amount of money. To help make choices, consider the **time value of money**, which is the increase of an amount of money due to earned interest or dividends. If you decide to save or invest the $129 instead of buying the sneakers, that money could be worth more later because you would earn interest or dividends on it.

Focus on Reading

Read to Learn

- How to explain opportunity costs associated with personal financial decisions.
- How to identify eight strategies for achieving financial goals at different stages of life.

Main Idea

By recognizing the trade-offs of financial decisions and learning to use your money wisely now, you will be able to live according to your values and meet your financial needs and goals throughout your life.

Key Terms

- time value of money
- principal
- future value
- annuity
- present value

Before You Read

PREDICT

Why do you think you may have to make trade-offs to meet your financial goals?

Springboard Ask the students if making choices (such as which CD, stereo, or sports equipment to buy) is ever difficult for them. Have volunteer students relate such incidents from the past.

▲ **TIMING YOUR FUN** Managing your time by making trade-offs is as important as managing your money. *How can you use your time more efficiently when studying so you will also have time to do things you enjoy?*

Caption Answer Answers might include: Start your homework during free time in school; finish your homework as soon as you get home.

Motivating Students Have the students list trade-offs they are considering now or may have to make in the future, using the following format:

1. Decision: Buy Car Accessory vs. Save Money
   Benefits:
   Costs:
2. Decision:
   Benefits:
   Costs:

On the other hand, perhaps your sneakers are worn out. In that case, your current needs would determine that trading off interest earnings is worthwhile.

Every time you spend, save, or invest money, think about the time value of that money as an opportunity cost. For example, if you start early in life to save money for retirement, you will probably be able to live comfortably in the future.

Calculating Interest You can calculate the time value of your savings by figuring out how much interest you will earn. To do this, you need to know the principal, the annual interest rate, and the length of time your money will be in an account.

For a savings account, the **principal** is the original amount of money on deposit. (For a loan, the principal is the amount that you borrow.) When you open a savings account, the bank or financial institution identifies the interest rate for your account. This is usually given as an annual percentage so that you know how much you will earn each year. By comparing interest rates at several financial institutions, you can figure out which one will make your money grow the fastest.

You can figure out how much interest your money will earn in the first year by multiplying the principal by the annual interest rate.

As You Read
RELATE

Is it important to start planning your financial future and monitoring your costs at your age now? Why or why not?

GO FIGURE — FINANCIAL MATH

ANNUAL INTEREST

Synopsis: Interest is extra money earned from money in an account.

Example: You just deposited $1,000 in a savings account. The bank will pay you 3 percent annual interest. How much interest will you earn if you keep your money in the bank for one year?

Formula: Principal × Annual Interest Rate = Interest Earned for One Year

Solution: $1,000 × .03 = $30

You will earn $30 in interest.

YOU FIGURE

What if your sister deposited $50 for one year at the same interest? How much would she have?

Future Value of a Single Deposit **Future value** is the amount your original deposit will be worth in the future based on earning a specific interest rate over a specific period of time. Figure out how much your savings will earn and grow by multiplying the principal by the annual interest rate and then adding that interest amount to the principal.

You can determine the future value for two years, three years, and so on. Each year, interest is earned on your principal and on previously earned interest.

To calculate the interest earned for the second year, add interest earned in the first year to the principal. Then take that amount and multiply it by the annual interest rate.

Future value computations are also called *compounding*. With compounding, your money increases faster over time. If you make deposits now, your money will have more time to increase.

Answer $50 + $1.50 interest = $51.50

Answer $1,639.09 ($1,500 × .03 = $45; $1,500 + $45 = $1,545 × .03 = $46.35; $1,545 + $46.35 = $1,591.35 × .03 = $47.74; $1,591 + $47.74 = $1,639.09)

GO FIGURE — FINANCIAL MATH

THE FUTURE VALUE OF A SINGLE DEPOSIT

Synopsis: When you earn interest from money you deposit in the bank, your balance increases over time.

Example: You just deposited $1,000 in a savings account that will pay you 3 percent (.03) annual interest. You earned $30 in interest after the first year. How much will you earn after two years?

Formula: (Principal + Previously Earned Interest) × Annual Interest Rate = Interest Earned for the Second Year

Solution: ($1,000 + $30) × .03 = $30.90

You will earn $30.90 in interest. Add this earned interest to your previous amount ($1,030 + $30.90 = $1,060.90). The future value of your original $1,000 deposit will be $1,060.90 after two years.

YOU FIGURE

What if you decided to deposit more money, say, $1,500? With 3 percent annual interest, how much would you have after three years?

As You Read

QUESTION

Why should you know the future value of a deposit when making financial plans?

Question Answer It can help you determine the opportunity costs of spending now or saving for the future.

Teaching Activity Divide students into groups of four or five. Tell them that each group has $10,000 to do with as they please. Ask them to discuss options, opportunity costs, interest rates, or any other relevant matters they can come up with. The group is then to determine how they will use the money and prepare a presentation discussing their decisions and how they arrived at them.

Critical Thinking Ask students to individually work out the following: Starting next year, you plan to take $1,000 out of your savings account each year for five years. Your account earns 9 percent interest. How much will you need to deposit to make this plan succeed? Use part D of Figure 1.4. (Answer: $1,000 × 3.890 = $3,890).

STANDARD &POOR'S

Put on Your Financial Planner's Cap

If you were planning an investment for yourself, would you choose an annuity? Why or why not?

See the Teacher Manual for answer.

Future value tables simplify the process of figuring out the effect of compounding. Many online future value calculators are available. The table in Part A of **Figure 1.4** shows the future value of a single deposit of $1. To use the table, find the annual interest rate that your money is earning. Then see what the future value is at Year 5, Year 6, and so on. Multiply the future value figure by the amount of your deposit. For example, if you deposit $1 in a 7 percent account, at the end of Year 7, you would have $1.61:

$$\$1 \times 1.606 = \$1.606$$

Future Value of a Series of Deposits Some savers and investors like to make regular deposits into their savings. A series of equal regular deposits is sometimes called an **annuity**. Use Part B of the chart in Figure 1.4 (future value of a series of equal yearly deposits) to find out the future value of $1,000 a year at 5 percent annual interest for six years. At the end of the six years, you would have $6,802:

$$\$1{,}000 \times 6.802 = \$6{,}802$$

Present Value of a Single Deposit You can also calculate the **present value**, which is the amount of money you would need to deposit now in order to have a desired amount in the future. For example, if you want to have $1,000 in five years for a down payment on a car, and your savings account pays 5 percent annual interest, how much money will you need to deposit now to accumulate $1,000? Part C of Figure 1.4 will help you find the answer. Find Year 5 in the left column, and look across to the 5 percent interest-rate column. The value given is 0.784. Multiply this value by the amount of money you want to have in five years:

$$\$1{,}000 \times 0.784 = \$784$$

You need to deposit $784 now to have $1,000 in five years.

Present Value of a Series of Deposits You can also use present value calculations to determine how much you would need to deposit so you can take a specific amount of money out of your savings account for a certain number of years. If you want to take $400 out of your account each year for nine years, and your money is earning interest at 8 percent a year, how much money would you need to deposit now? Part D of Figure 1.4 will help you find the answer. Find Year 9 in the left column and look across to the 8 percent interest-rate column. The value given is 6.247. Multiply this value by the amount of money that you want to take out every year:

$$\$400 \times 6.247 = \$2{,}498.80$$

You need to deposit $2,498.80 now to be able to take out $400 each year for nine years. This calculation is used for retirement.

Figure 1.4 Future and Present Value Tables

A. Future Value of a Single Deposit of $1

	Annual Interest Rate				
Year	**5%**	**6%**	**7%**	**8%**	**9%**
5	1.276	1.338	1.403	1.469	1.539
6	1.340	1.419	1.501	1.587	1.677
7	1.407	1.504	1.606	1.714	1.828
8	1.477	1.594	1.718	1.851	1.993
9	1.551	1.689	1.838	1.999	2.172
10	1.629	1.791	1.967	2.159	2.367

B. Future Value of a Series of Equal Annual Deposits

Year	5%	6%	7%	8%	9%
5	5.526	5.637	5.751	5.867	5.985
6	6.802	6.975	7.153	7.336	7.523
7	8.142	8.394	8.654	8.923	9.200
8	9.549	9.897	10.260	10.637	11.028
9	11.027	11.491	11.978	12.488	13.021
10	12.578	13.181	13.816	14.487	15.193

C. Present Value of a Single Deposit

Year	5%	6%	7%	8%	9%
5	0.784	0.747	0.713	0.681	0.650
6	0.746	0.705	0.666	0.630	0.596
7	0.711	0.665	0.623	0.583	0.547
8	0.677	0.627	0.582	0.540	0.502
9	0.645	0.592	0.544	0.500	0.460
10	0.614	0.558	0.508	0.463	0.422

D. Present Value of a Series of Equal Annual Deposits

Year	5%	6%	7%	8%	9%
5	4.329	4.212	4.100	3.993	3.890
6	5.076	4.917	4.767	4.623	4.486
7	5.786	5.582	5.389	5.206	5.033
8	6.463	6.210	5.971	5.747	5.535
9	7.108	6.802	6.515	6.247	5.995
10	7.722	7.360	7.024	6.710	6.418

Time Is Money Future value tables can save you time and reduce errors when you compute interest over a long period of time. Present value tables can help you figure out how much you need to deposit now in order to have a certain amount of money in the future.

How much money will you have if you save $2,000 a year for ten years at 9 percent interest?

Caption Answer $2,000 × 15.193 = $30,386

After You Read

REACT

Do you think financial planning and the strategies provided in this book can help you to achieve your goals? If yes, in what ways? If no, why not?

React Answer Some students may say "yes" because they will learn how to manage their money to make it grow, thereby enabling them to better reach financial goals.

Achieving Your Financial Goals

What strategies can you use to reach your financial goals?

Throughout your life you will have many different financial needs and goals. By learning to use your money wisely now, you will be able to achieve many of those goals.

Financial planning involves choosing a career, and then learning how to protect and manage the money you earn. By using eight strategies, you can avoid many common money mistakes:

1. **Obtain**—Obtain financial resources by working, making investments, or owning property. Obtaining money is the foundation of financial planning because you will use that money for all other financial activities.
2. **Plan**—The key to achieving your financial goals and financial security is to plan how you will spend your money.
3. **Spend Wisely**—Many people spend more than they can afford. Other people buy things they can afford but do not need. Spending less than you earn is the only way to achieve financial security.
4. **Save**—Long-term financial security starts with a savings plan. If you save on a regular basis, you will have money to pay your bills, make major purchases, and cope with emergencies.
5. **Borrow Wisely**—When you use a credit card or take out another type of a loan, you are borrowing money. Borrowing wisely—and only when necessary—will help you achieve your financial goals and avoid money problems.
6. **Invest**—People invest for two main reasons: to increase their current income and to achieve long-term growth. To increase current income, you can choose investments that pay regular dividends or interest. To achieve long-term growth, you might choose stocks, mutual funds, real estate, and other investments that have the potential to increase in value in the future.

Caption Answer Answers may include: insurance, a cash emergency fund, warming up before playing, wearing protective gear, and being careful.

◀ **RISKY BUSINESS** Accidents can happen when you least expect them. *What are some ways to manage the financial risks associated with sports accidents?*

7. **Manage Risk**—To protect your resources in case you are ever seriously injured, get sick, or die, you will need insurance coverage. Insurance will protect you and those who depend on you.
8. **Plan for Retirement**—When you start to plan for retirement, consider the age at which you would like to stop working full time. You should also think about where you will want to live and how you will want to spend your time: at a part-time job, doing volunteer work, or enjoying hobbies or sports.

WebQuest

One Life to Plan
Learn about how financial counselors help people get out of debt and plan for the future—just one aspect of a financial planner's job.

To continue with Task 2 of your WebQuest project, visit **finance07.glencoe.com**.

Extension Have the students contact local banks to learn what the interest rates are on savings accounts. If the rates differ, ask the students why.

Developing and Using a Financial Plan

A good personal financial plan includes assessing your present financial situation, making a list of your current needs, and deciding how to plan for future needs. You can design a plan on your own, hire a financial planner, or use a good money-management software program. Making your financial plan work takes time, effort, and patience, but you will develop habits that will give you a lifetime of satisfaction and security.

Section 1.2 Assessment

See the Teacher Manual for answers.

QUICK CHECK

1. What are the opportunity costs associated with financial decisions?
2. What is the time value of money?
3. What are the eight strategies you can apply to achieve your financial goals?

THINK CRITICALLY

4. Using the concept of the time value of money, write an argument in favor of shopping for a good interest rate.

USE MATH SKILLS

5. **Saving Strategies** Tanya wants to open her own pet-grooming business after she graduates from high school. However, after doing research, she realizes that she needs to save $18,000 for the start-up capital for her business. Tanya plans to make a series of deposits of $3,000 every year for five years. She estimates that she will earn an annual interest rate of 5 percent on her savings.

Calculate Using the tables in Figure 1.4, calculate what amount Tanya will have available in five years to start her business. How much more money will she need to save?

SOLVE MONEY PROBLEMS

6. **Saving Versus Spending** Omar received $1,525 in gifts when he graduated from high school. His parents want him to save the money for college, but Omar wants to buy new clothes, a watch, some CDs, and a video game. He also needs new tires because the ones on his car are badly worn. Omar asks you for advice. How should he spend his graduation money?

Analyze Working in a small group, discuss what Omar should do with his money. Consider the various financial opportunity costs and the time value of money.

Chapter 1 Review & Activities

See the Teacher Manual for answers.

CHAPTER SUMMARY

- Personal financial planning means managing your money (spending, saving, and investing) so that you can achieve financial independence and security.
- The six steps of financial planning are: (1) Determine your current financial situation; (2) develop financial goals; (3) identify alternative courses of action; (4) evaluate alternatives; 5) create and use your financial plan of action; and (6) review and revise your plan.
- The most important factors that influence personal financial planning are your life situations, your personal values, and outside economic factors.
- For all your financial decisions, you must make choices and give up something. These opportunity costs, or trade-offs, can be personal or financial.
- The eight strategies for achieving your financial goals and avoiding money problems are: Obtain, plan, spend, save wisely, borrow wisely, invest, manage risk, and plan for retirement.

Communicating Key Terms

Find an article on unemployment, inflation, interest rates, or the value of the U.S. dollar. Use 8 to 12 of the terms below and write three paragraphs relating the information in the article to personal financial planning.

- personal financial planning
- goals
- values
- opportunity cost
- liquidity
- service
- good
- economics
- economy
- supply
- demand
- Federal Reserve System
- inflation
- consumer
- interest
- time value of money
- principal
- future value
- annuity
- present value

Reviewing Key Concepts

1. **Explain** personal financial planning and its importance.
2. **Describe** the six strategies of financial planning.
3. **Describe** the factors that affect personal financial decisions.
4. **Explain** opportunity costs and how they might affect your personal financial decisions.
5. **List** eight strategies for achieving financial goals.

See the Teacher Manual for answers.

ACADEMIC SKILLS

Language Arts The prices of new electronic gadgets usually come down over time.

Write About It Write a paragraph explaining why this might occur. Also explain how those prices might affect your financial planning if you want to buy certain items.

YOUR FINANCIAL FIGURES

Current Interest Rates Find out from a bank or other financial institution the current interest rate on a standard savings account. Find out what other savings plans are available and their interest rates.

1. **Calculate** by using the interest rate on regular savings accounts to find out the future value of your account after eight years if you deposit $1,600 in it every year.
2. **Compute** by using spreadsheet software to calculate and compare the future values of your series of deposits based on the different interest rates offered for other savings plans.

REAL-WORLD Application

Connect with Global Economics Your brother works for a company that makes components for DVD players. The company has started to outsource some of its component assembly work to a country where employees' wages are much lower than in the United States. As a result, the company can sell components at lower prices. However, your brother's employer has started to lay off employees at its U.S. plants. Your brother believes he will have a job for two more years, but after that, he is not sure.

1. **Research** Use the Internet or library to research the trend to outsource manufacturing of electronic products in countries such as China.
2. **Think Critically** Your brother comes to you and asks if you think he should look for another job now. What would you say to him?

Internet CONNECTION

Interest Rates and Inflation Inflation (how much your money will buy) and interest rates (how much your money will earn if saved) are connected—and both of these economic factors should be considered in your financial planning, particularly for long-term goals.

@ **Log On** Use an Internet search engine. Type "inflation and interest rates." Answer the following questions:

1. If inflation is low, how does that affect interest rates?
2. If inflation is high, how does that affect interest rates?

BusinessWeek ONLINE

Newsclip: Internet Planning If your knowledge about personal finance is limited, being Web and tech savvy will help you learn more. Finance is a frequent topic on the news and is easy to research.

@ **Log On** Go to **finance07.glencoe.com** and open Chapter 1. Learn more about financial decisions and strategies. Write a list of ways you can learn more about finance.

WHAT'S YOUR FINANCIAL ID?

YOUR SPENDING PROFILE

Being a saver or a spender is part of your personality. Here is a chance to test your financial personality.

If someone gave you $200, what would you do with it? Read the options below and choose three. Write the number of points for each of the three choices on a separate piece of paper. Then add up your points.

_____ Take my closest friends out to eat and to the movies (5 points)

_____ Spend $50 on fun items and save the rest (3 points)

_____ Put the money toward my next car payment (1 point)

_____ Buy new clothes for school (3 points)

_____ Hit the nearest record store and buy several CDs (5 points)

_____ Buy a CD player (3 points)

_____ Get a cell phone (5 points)

_____ Buy a savings bond (1 point)

_____ Put it in a savings account for future education (1 point)

_____ Buy the hottest new concert tickets (5 points)

What do your choices say about you?

Big saver: If you scored 3–5, you are willing to give up things today so you can buy something you want more tomorrow.

Middle of the roader: If you scored 7–11, you know how to use your money for current needs while keeping an eye on the future.

Big spender: If you scored 13–15, you like to spend money!

Accept all reasonable answers that show student effort and an understanding of the concept.

Your Financial Portfolio

Getting Your Own Wheels

Are you dreaming of buying your own car? Olivia Johnson is. So far she has saved $3,000. Olivia has her eye on a used car that costs $9,000. Olivia figures she can afford a monthly car payment of no more than $200. Using the interest-rate table below, Olivia calculates the monthly payment needed to repay her car loan by multiplying the amount of the loan by the interest factor. She wants to pay off her loan in three years.

Olivia's Loan Story

Cost of car	$9,000.00
Less the down payment	– 3,000.00
Amount of loan	$6,000.00
Interest Rate of 8%	
Months	**Interest Factor**
12 (one year)	0.08698
24 (two years)	0.04522
36 (three years)	**0.03133**
48 (four years)	0.02441
Multiply loan amount by interest factor (0.03133) for 36 months	
$6,000 X 0.03133 = $187.98	

Olivia will pay $187.98 a month if she decides to borrow $6,000 for three years.

Calculate

Now look in your local newspaper for a car you would like to buy. How much will it cost? Suppose you can afford 25 percent of the total price for a down payment. How much money will you need to borrow to pay the complete cost of the car you want? On a separate sheet of paper, calculate how much money you will need for your monthly car payment. Calculate what your monthly payment will be if you paid off your loan in 1, 2, 3, or 4 years. (1) What is the total amount you will pay for your car if you pay it off in 1, 2, 3, or 4 years? (2) How much interest will you pay on your loan? (3) Which payment plan would enable you to pay the least amount of money for your car? (4) Which payment plan would have the lowest payments?

(1) (2) Answers will vary. (3) The lowest total cost would be over one year. (4) The lowest payments would be over four years.

CHAPTER 2
Finances and Career Planning

$ What You'll Learn

When you have completed this chapter, you will be able to:

Section 2.1

- Identify the personal issues to consider when choosing and planning your career.
- Explain how education and training affect career advancement.
- Discuss the factors that influence employment.

Section 2.2

- Describe effective strategies to obtain employment.
- Identify sources of career opportunities.
- Identify the financial and legal issues to consider when looking for employment.

Reading Strategies

To get the most out of your reading:

Predict what you will learn in this chapter.
Relate what you read to your own life.
Question what you are reading to be sure you understand.
React to what you have read.

In the **Real** World . . .

George Leonard is not sure what career to pursue. Since graduating from high school, he has held jobs at a sandwich shop, a bookstore, and an animal park. George learned about small businesses while he was working. As a result, he has decided that he would like to run his own business one day—perhaps a pet store.

Jessica Rodriguez, a high school junior, loves movies. She watches classic films and edits her own short features on the computer. She hopes to work in the film industry.

George and Jessica are not exactly sure what their careers will be, but they realize they will need to make informed decisions.

As You Read *Consider how education and training might affect careers and job opportunities.*

Lesson Plan See the Teacher Manual for the Chapter 2 planning guide and lesson plan.

ASK STANDARD & POOR'S

Planning for Life

Q: Career plans are for people who do not know what they want. I know already that I want a high-paying job. So why should I bother thinking about career planning?

A: Money is just one motivation for work. You need to consider many other factors as well. Career planning considers your personal values, goals, and interests—the basics for any career decision. Since you will probably spend the majority of your life working, consider the old adage: "Choose a career you love, and the money will follow."

Ask Yourself What job would you love to do?

@ Go to **finance07.glencoe.com** to complete the Standard & Poor's Financial Focus activity.

Section 2.1

Focus on Reading

Read to Learn

- How to identify the personal issues to consider when choosing and planning your career.
- How to explain how education and training affect career advancement.
- How to discuss the factors that influence employment.

Main Idea

Choosing and planning for the right career will help you find fulfillment both personally and financially.

Key Terms

- job
- career
- standard of living
- trends
- potential earning power
- aptitudes
- interest inventories
- demographic trends
- geographic trends
- service industries

Before You Read

PREDICT

Why will choosing the right career help you find both personal satisfaction and financial security?

Planning Your Career

Choosing a Career

What is the difference between a job and a career?

Some people find true satisfaction in their work, while others work just to make money. Like many people, you may decide to get a **job**—work that you do mainly to earn money. On the other hand, you may decide to prepare for a career. A **career** is a commitment to work in a field that you find interesting and fulfilling. Ensuring that your career will fulfill your personal and financial goals requires planning.

Career Decision Trade-Offs

Your choice of career will affect the amount of money you make, the people you meet, and how much spare time you have. Some people work just to maintain a **standard of living**, a measure of quality of life based on the amounts and kinds of goods and services a person can buy. They also work to pay for the hobbies and activities they enjoy. Others pursue careers that provide them with both money and personal fulfillment. They select careers that reflect their interests, values, and goals.

Choosing a career will involve trade-offs, or opportunity costs. Many people devote most of their time and energy to their work. As a result, their family lives and personal satisfaction may suffer. Recent **trends**—developments that mark changes in a particular area—indicate that some people are making career decisions, such as declining a promotion, that allow them to spend more time with their families or to enjoy their hobbies and interests.

You may select a career that is challenging and offers you the chance to grow, even if it does not earn you a large salary. On the other hand, you may choose to work in a job that is less satisfying but offers more money. You may look for part-time work or work situations with flexible hours so that you will have more time to spend with your family. You could also decide to give up the security of working for someone else to take on the challenge of running your own business.

The more you know about your own interests, values, needs, and goals, the better you will be able to choose a career that will provide a balance between personal satisfaction and financial rewards.

◀ **WEIGHING YOUR OPTIONS** Choosing a career involves trade-offs. Some parents will decline a job with a higher salary for a job that offers a flexible schedule. *What other trade-offs might a parent have to make?*

Caption Answer Answers might include declining jobs with long commutes or jobs with no dependent health care benefits.

Career Training and Skill Development

Springboard Ask the students if they have considered what careers they may want to follow. If so, have they found out what they need to do to prepare for such careers?

Obtaining as much education as possible will help you meet your financial goals. The more you know, the greater your chances are for success. Having a college degree does not guarantee that you will reach your goals and make a lot of money. However, acquiring more education increases your **potential earning power**, which is the amount of money you may earn over time. Your field of study will also affect your salary. Some careers, such as law and medicine, generally offer higher salaries than others, such as education and the fine arts.

Education is not the only ingredient for success in your job or career. By developing certain habits, you will become an asset to any employer. For example, most successful people are able to work well with others. They always strive to do their best. They do not allow conflict with other employees or changes in their duties to affect the quality of their work. They are creative when it comes to solving problems. They communicate well. They understand themselves and other people. These basic qualities and skills make success more likely in most job situations. How do you measure up to this checklist for success? If you think that you might fall short in some areas, what might you do to improve?

Motivating Students Have students look on the Internet to discover what preparation their career choices require; then discuss with the class what this means for them.

As You Read

RELATE

Imagine yourself 15 years from now. Will you have a career or a job? Would that career or job fulfill personal and financial goals?

Critical Thinking Have students brainstorm with a partner to determine what type of career interests them, considering the following: balance between financial rewards and personal satisfaction, time commitments, their personalities. Students are then to write brief essays reporting on the outcome of these brainstorming sessions.

Teaching Activity Give students an interest inventory test. Work with them to interpret the results and relate them to possible careers.

Personal Factors

You can take special tests to learn more about your own abilities, interests, and personal qualities. These tests—called *aptitude tests* and *interest inventories*—may give you an edge in choosing a career. You can usually find out more about such tests in your school's guidance office. If you would rather test yourself, you can find test materials in public libraries, bookstores, and on the Internet.

What Do You Do Best? **Aptitudes** are the natural abilities that people possess. For example, you may have a beautiful singing voice, excel at math, or be able to solve puzzles easily. These are all natural aptitudes. Try taking an aptitude test to find out what you do best.

What Do You Enjoy? **Interest inventories** are tests that help you identify the activities you enjoy the most. They match your interests, likes, and dislikes with various kinds of work. For example, someone who enjoys nature and the outdoors could become a science teacher, nature photographer, or landscape designer. A person who likes to make things could study to become a carpenter, clothes designer, architect, or engineer. List some of your interests. What types of careers can you think of that would match your interests?

The Right Fit Aptitude tests and interest inventories may not lead you to the ideal career. They can only point you in the right direction. Another important issue to consider is your personality. For example, do you enjoy large parties, or would you rather stay at home and read a book? Do you like to take chances, or do you prefer to play it safe? Do you work well under pressure, or do you need time to do a job?

The goal is to find a job or career that gives you the right balance between financial rewards and personal satisfaction. Some people adapt easily to any work environment. Others are always looking for something better. Because your work situation will never stop changing, the key to success is to remain flexible.

Academic Connection

SCIENCE

The world around us is constantly changing, and the field of science is expanding to keep up with it. There are many careers in the science field, such as cancer research, environmental science, pharmaceutical research, and genetic engineering. *Choose three careers, one science-related, and find out the educational requirements and average salaries for them. Which of the three jobs pays more? Do you think salary should affect your choice of career?*

See the Teacher Manual for answer.

Stages of Career Planning

Before you make any decisions about your career, you should review your situation. Changes in your personal life and in society will affect your work life, and the reverse is also true. **Figure 2.1** shows the stages of career planning, changes, and advancement. If you are getting ready to enter the workforce, you will probably start at Stage 1. That stage will involve determining your personal and career interests.

The diagram in Figure 2.1 is only one plan of action. Your progress will depend on your opportunity costs, the choices that are available to you, and your career area. If you are unsure about your direction, talk to people in your field of interest. Ask them what they like and dislike about their work and how they got into the field. Answers to these questions can help you with your career planning.

Figure 2.1 **Stages of Career Planning, Changes, and Advancement**

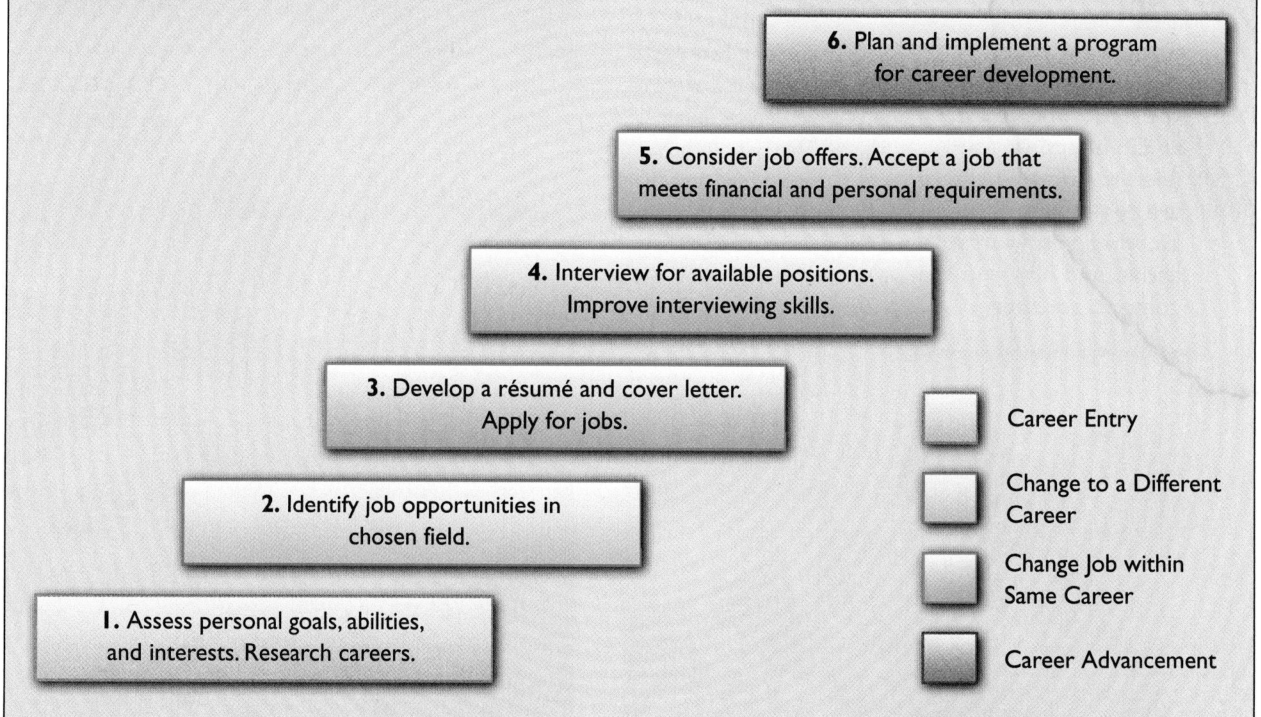

Source: Federal Reserve Bank of Minneapolis

Starting Over If you choose a career and are dissatisified with the work that you are doing, you have the option of changing to a different career.

What are some ways to make a wise choice?

Caption Answer Answers might include reassessing interests and abilities.

External Factors and Opportunities

Why should you consider external influences when thinking about your career?

Before you begin your job search, you should think about how external factors such as social influences, economic factors, and trends might affect your career. These factors directly affect the job market and the opportunities that are available to you. When you consider your career options, you not only need to focus on your skills, training, and experience, you also need to view the "big picture" on a national and global scale. You may have no control over these particular factors, but you can make some personal decisions based on real-world influences.

Social influences include factors such as demographic trends and geographic trends. Economic conditions include factors such as interest rates, inflation, and consumer demand. Industry trends are affected by factors such as foreign competition and the changing and expanding uses of technology.

Research Have students research a city where they would like to live with regard to its demographics (population statistics, industries, per capita income) as well as job opportunities in fields they are interested in, submitting their results as charts or graphs.

Figure 2.2 Developing a Career Plan of Action

If you want your career to start off on the right foot, you need a plan of action. You need to know where you are, where you want to go, when you want to arrive, and how you are going to get there.

1 **Personal and Career Interests** Make a list of things you enjoy doing. Think about how you could turn an activity like that into a career.

2 **Career Skills** Think about work experiences you have already had. Which ones did you like? Which ones did not go so well? What skills did you learn?

3 **Career Training and Education** What kind of education or training do you need for the career you want?

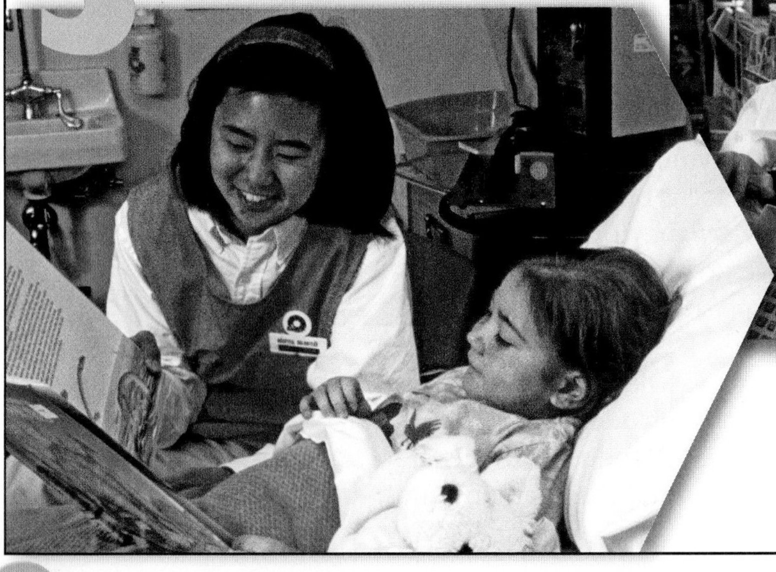

4 **Employment Position** Now begin to focus. Pinpoint the particular work situation that you would like.

Social Influences

Demographic trends are tendencies of people grouped by age, gender, ethnicity, education, or income that change over time. These developments can affect your employment opportunities. Several demographic trends have affected the job market:

- More working parents, which expands the supply of jobs in child care and food services
- More leisure time, which boosts interest in health, physical fitness, and recreational products
- More elderly people in the overall population, which produces a greater need for workers in retirement facilities, health care, and travel services
- Greater demand for ongoing employment training, which increases career opportunities for teachers and trainers

Geographic trends are tendencies of people moving from one area of the country to another as financial centers shift location. In recent years, some of the fastest-growing job markets have included cities in Florida, Nevada, Arizona, Arkansas, New Jersey, and California.

Geographic location also influences earning level. Remember to consider differences in earning levels as you decide where to look for employment. Big cities, such as San Francisco, New York, and Chicago, usually offer higher salaries, but the cost of living (the cost of food, housing, transportation, and other expenses) is also higher in such areas. If you accept a high-paying position in a big city, you may actually have a lower standard of living than you would in an area where income levels and the cost of living are lower.

Economic Factors

High interest rates, price increases, or decreased demand for certain goods and services can reduce career opportunities. The job market changes as the economy does, and so the demand for certain types of jobs changes. For example, in the 1990s many companies were looking for people to work in the computer and technology fields. As a result, there were a lot of jobs from which to choose, and salaries were high. As we moved into the 21st century, however, the demand for workers in those industries decreased, and salaries either stayed the same or came down. You cannot control the effects of economic factors on employment trends, so be aware of what jobs are currently in high demand.

In addition, economic factors affect some businesses more than others. For example, high interest rates may reduce employment in housing-related industries, such as construction and real estate, because people are less likely to buy houses when interest rates are high. Being aware of current economic trends will help you to choose a career so that you can achieve your financial goals.

Common CENTS

Career Center
At your school's career center, you will find a variety of free information that can help you with college choices, résumé preparation, job opportunities, and career counseling. *How can researching different careers that interest you help your financial planning for the future?*

Common Cents Answers might include research may help you understand job availabilities and pay ranges.

Question Answer Answers might include a "baby boom," producing more jobs in toy manufacture, preschools and child care, schools, children's clothing, etc.

As You Read
QUESTION

What other employment opportunities might be influenced by demographic and geographic trends?

Trends in Industry and Technology

Changes in industry and technology also affect the job market. In recent years, the need for workers in manufacturing has decreased as a result of several trends. First, increased competition from other countries has reduced demand for American-made products. Second, automation has taken over many tasks that used to be done by factory workers.

Perhaps you would like a career in the field of electronics technology. You know that your skills are valuable, but you also know that constant technological advances can quickly outdate products and jobs. As a result, you must accept some financial uncertainty.

STANDARD & POOR'S

Global Financial Landscape

Standard and Poor's publishes the globally recognized S&P 500® financial index. It also gathers financial statistics, information, and news, and analyzes this data for international businesses, governments, and individuals to help them guide their financial decisions.

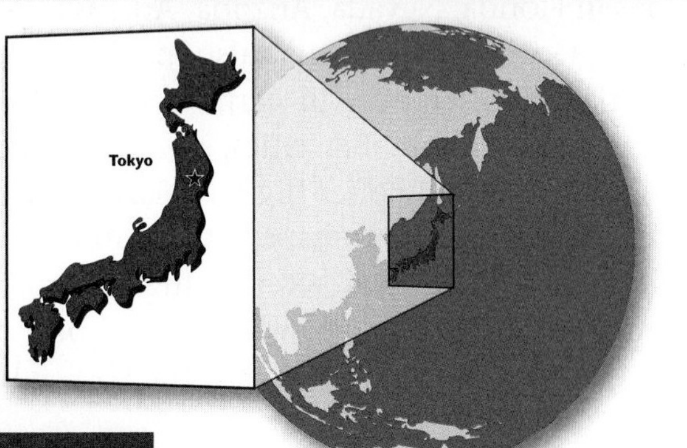

JAPAN

Traditionally, the domain of Japanese women has been the home and children. However, when the first equal-opportunity law was passed in Japan in the mid-1980s, many women began to shun marriage for the workplace. In fact, in the past decade, the number of unmarried women ages 25 to 29 has grown from 40 to 54 percent. As a result, the birthrate in Japan dropped steadily during that time. Japanese leaders fear that there will be a decrease in population and consequent labor shortages in the future. In response to this potential problem, policymakers have suggested that companies provide better job opportunities *and* child-care programs to the female workforce. That way Japanese women can opt for marriage and having children as well as successful careers.

STANDARD & POOR'S **DATABYTES**

Capital	Tokyo
Population	127,508,000
Language	Japanese
Currency	yen
Gross Domestic Product (GDP)	$3.567 trillion (2003 est.)
GDP per capita	$28,000

Industry: Motor vehicles, electronic equipment, machine tools, steel, and non-ferrous metals

Agriculture: Rice, sugar, beets, vegetables, fruit, pork, and fish

Exports: Motor vehicles, semiconductors, office machinery, and chemicals

Natural Resources: Mineral resources and fish

Think Globally

What trend in Japan might affect job opportunities there? Why?

See the Teacher Manual for answer.

While opportunities have dwindled in some areas of the economy, opportunities in other areas have grown. **Service industries**, which are businesses that provide services for a fee, offer employment potential in coming years. There are numerous careers in these industries:

- Computer or telecommunications technology—systems analysts, Web-site developers, service technicians
- Health care—medical assistants, physical therapists, home-health workers
- Business services—employee benefit managers, trainers
- Social services—child-care workers, elder-care coordinators
- Hospitality services—travel agents, food service managers
- Management—employment service workers, recruiters
- Education—elementary, secondary, postsecondary, and adult education teachers
- Financial services—insurance agents, investment brokers

Whatever career area you choose, having knowledge of a variety of computer programs and the Internet will be essential.

Section 2.1 Assessment

See the Teacher Manual for answer.

QUICK CHECK

1. What are three characteristics of successful people? Describe how each characteristic might be an asset at school or work.

2. How can you learn more about your own abilities, interests, and personal qualities as they relate to career planning?

3. What are three factors that influence employment opportunities?

THINK CRITICALLY

4. Why do you think that the increase in the number of working parents has contributed to a higher demand for food services?

USE COMMUNICATION SKILLS

5. New Career Choices Service industries will offer some of the greatest potential for jobs in coming years.

Analyze With a partner, conduct a survey of five students and identify their most popular career choices.

SOLVE MONEY PROBLEMS

6. Geographic Influences Tyrell has worked his way up from sales associate to department supervisor for a large suburban discount store. Now he has been offered a higher position in Atlanta. Currently, Tyrell earns about $18,000 annually, which covers the cost of food, housing, transportation, and other living expenses. With the new job, his salary would increase 20 percent, but the cost of living in Atlanta is much higher than it is in the suburbs. By doing some research, he found that the rent for a one-bedroom apartment averages $800 per month, and the round-trip train ride to work will cost about $4 per day. Food will probably cost $65 per week.

Calculate Assuming Tyrell works five days a week and 52 weeks a year, help him calculate what his living expenses would total per year if he moved to Atlanta.

Section 2.2

Focus on Reading

Read to Learn

- How to describe effective strategies to obtain employment.
- How to identify sources of career opportunities.
- How to identify the financial and legal issues to consider when looking for employment.

Main Idea

Learn effective strategies to help you get the job or career that meets your personal and financial goals.

Key Terms

- internship
- cooperative education
- networking
- informational interview
- résumé
- cover letter
- cafeteria-style employee benefits
- pension plan
- mentor

Before You Read

PREDICT

What are some strategies you think might be effective in obtaining employment experience?

Employment and Career Development

Employment Search Strategies

What are steps to take when searching for a job?

Meg filled out dozens of job applications but never received a call for an interview. Douglas went to many interviews and found a challenging and satisfying job. What were the differences between these two people? The answer has to do with how well they communicated the value of the experience they already had and how effectively they used proven employment strategies.

Obtaining Employment Experience

Many young people who are entering the world of work worry that they do not have enough experience. They may be overlooking the importance of various kinds of work-related training:

- Part-time work
- Volunteer work
- Internships and cooperative education
- Class projects or after-school activities

Part-Time Work Summer and part-time jobs can provide valuable experience. If you have been a camp counselor during the summer, you may decide that you really enjoy working with children and would like to get a job in a day-care center. Perhaps you are a cashier at a drugstore after school and on weekends. You may want to pursue a career in pharmacology or business administration.

Many companies use temporary workers to fill various positions. Working as a "temp" is a good way to gain experience and learn more about a particular field. For the same reasons, part-time and temporary work can be worthwhile for people who are changing careers.

Volunteer Work You can learn new skills, develop good work habits, and make professional contacts by volunteering. Many nonprofit community organizations and some government agencies include volunteers on their staffs. You might collect funds for a disaster relief project or build houses with Habitat for Humanity. Volunteering can help you develop skills that you can apply to other work situations. Where could you volunteer in your community?

Internships and Cooperative Education An internship may give you the experience you need to obtain employment. An **internship** is a position in which a person receives training by working with people who are experienced in a particular field. Sometimes it can lead to permanent employment. You also get a chance to practice your application and interviewing skills.

Cooperative education programs allow students to enhance classroom learning with part-time work related to their majors and interests. For example, you would take your high school classes in the morning, and in the afternoon you would work at a local business to apply the workplace skills you learned in class.

Class Projects or After-School Activities Class assignments and school activities can be sources of work-related experience. They can help you gain valuable career skills such as:

- Managing, organizing, and coordinating people
- Public speaking
- Goal setting, planning, and supervising
- Financial planning and budgeting
- Conducting research

Career Information Sources

You need up-to-date information to make the best career decisions. Many sources of information are available to you.

Libraries Most school and public libraries offer a variety of references on careers. Start with such guides as the *Occupational Outlook Handbook*, the *O*NET Dictionary of Occupational Titles*, and Occupational Outlook Quarterly Online.

◀ **VOLUNTEER** Volunteering for a local or national nonprofit organization can provide work-related experience. *What types of skills might you gain by helping to clean up a city park?*

$avvy Saver

Money for College

1. Ask your school counselor about student loans, grants, and scholarships.
2. Check the Internet, using the keywords *college scholarships*.
3. Ask for money for college instead of gifts.
4. Apply for scholarships offered by your parents' employers.
5. Get a part-time job and save as much money as possible.

Springboard Ask the students for a show of hands: How many have had part-time jobs? How many have done volunteer work? Have any ever had full-time jobs?

Motivating Students Have the students list any jobs of any kind that they have had. Underneath each, have them brainstorm in pairs to list as many job skills as they can that they have learned.

Caption Answer Accept all reasonable answers that demonstrate an understanding of the concept.

Document Detective

Learn to identify and understand the standard financial documents you will use in the real world.

See the Teacher Manual for answers.

Investigate: An IRS Form W-4

A Form W-4 asks you for the following

- Your name and address
- Your marital status
- Number of allowances
- Additional withholdings
- Signature and date

Your Motive: By properly filling out a Form W-4, you will ensure that the appropriate amount of tax is deducted from your paychecks. Withholding too little from your pay can result in penalties when you file your yearly income tax return.

Personal Allowances Worksheet (Keep for your records.)

A Enter "1" for **yourself** if no one else can claim you as a dependent . . . . A ______

B Enter "1" if: { • You are single and have only one job; or • You are married, have only one job, and your spouse does not work; or • Your wages from a second job or your spouse's wages (or the total of both) are $1,000 or less. } . . B ______

C Enter "1" for your **spouse.** But, you may choose to enter "-0-" if you are married and have either a working spouse or more than one job. (Entering "-0-" may help you avoid having too little tax withheld.) . . . . C ______

D Enter number of **dependents** (other than your spouse or yourself) you will claim on your tax return . . . . . . D ______

E Enter "1" if you will file as **head of household** on your tax return (see conditions under **Head of household** above) . E ______

F Enter "1" if you have at least $1,500 of **child or dependent care expenses** for which you plan to claim a credit . . F ______
(**Note.** Do **not** include child support payments. See **Pub. 503,** Child and Dependent Care Expenses, for details.)

G **Child Tax Credit** (including additional child tax credit):
• If your total income will be less than $54,000 ($79,000 if married), enter "2" for each eligible child.
• If your total income will be between $54,000 and $84,000 ($79,000 and $119,000 if married), enter "1" for each eligible child plus "1" **additional** if you have four or more eligible children. G ______

H Add lines A through G and enter total here. (**Note.** This may be different from the number of exemptions you claim on your tax return.) ▶ H ______

For accuracy, complete all worksheets that apply. {
• If you plan to **itemize or claim adjustments to income** and want to reduce your withholding, see the **Deductions and Adjustments Worksheet** on page 2.
• If you have **more than one job** or are **married and you and your spouse both work** and the combined earnings from all jobs exceed $35,000 ($25,000 if married) see the **Two-Earner/Two-Job Worksheet** on page 2 to avoid having too little tax withheld.
• If **neither** of the above situations applies, **stop here** and enter the number from line H on line 5 of Form W-4 below.

Cut here and give Form W-4 to your employer. Keep the top part for your records.

Form **W-4** — Department of the Treasury, Internal Revenue Service

Employee's Withholding Allowance Certificate

▶ **Whether you are entitled to claim a certain number of allowances or exemption from withholding is subject to review by the IRS. Your employer may be required to send a copy of this form to the IRS.**

OMB No. 1545-0010 — **20--**

1 Type or print your first name and middle initial | Last name | 2 Your social security number

Home address (number and street or rural route) | 3 ☐ Single ☐ Married ☐ Married, but withhold at higher Single rate.
Note. If married, but legally separated, or spouse is a nonresident alien, check the "Single" box.

City or town, state, and ZIP code | 4 **If your last name differs from that shown on your social security card, check here. You must call 1-800-772-1213 for a new card.** ▶ ☐

5 Total number of allowances you are claiming (from line **H** above **or** from the applicable worksheet on page 2) 5 ______
6 Additional amount, if any, you want withheld from each paycheck . . . . 6 $ ______
7 I claim exemption from withholding for 2005, and I certify that I meet **both** of the following conditions for exemption.
• Last year I had a right to a refund of **all** federal income tax withheld because I had **no** tax liability **and**
• This year I expect a refund of **all** federal income tax withheld because I expect to have **no** tax liability.
If you meet both conditions, write "Exempt" here . . . . ▶ 7 ______

Under penalties of perjury, I declare that I have examined this certificate and to the best of my knowledge and belief, it is true, correct, and complete.
Employee's signature
(Form is not valid unless you sign it.) ▶ **Date** ▶

8 Employer's name and address (Employer: Complete lines 8 and 10 only if sending to the IRS.) | 9 Office code (optional) | 10 Employer identification number (EIN)

For Privacy Act and Paperwork Reduction Act Notice, see page 2. Cat. No. 10220Q Form **W-4** (20--)

Key Points: Employers are required to have each employee complete an IRS Form W-4 to determine the tax withholding. The number of dependents (people you are financially responsible for) you claim on Form W-4 determines the amount of tax withheld from your paychecks. The tax rate varies by the number of dependents you claim. The more dependents, the less you pay in taxes. Because your tax situation may change, review your withholdings each year.

Find the Solutions

1. What is the purpose of the Form W-4?
2. On line 6, you may elect to withhold additional money from your pay. Why would someone choose to do this?
3. How could a person be exempt from having withholdings taken from his or her pay?
4. Why is it necessary for the employee to sign the form?
5. Can a married person withhold at the same rate as a single person?

Mass Media Most newspapers feature business and employment sections with articles on job hunting and career trends.

The Internet Log on to the Internet for a wealth of information about jobs and employment. You will find tips and suggestions on everything from filling out applications to job interviewing.

School Guidance Offices Visit your school guidance office for materials and advice on career planning. Take advantage of any placement services your school may offer.

Community Organizations Almost every community has business and civic groups that can help you in your career search. Attending their meetings gives you an opportunity to meet local businesspeople.

Professional Organizations Many professions have organizations dedicated to sharing information. The *Encyclopedia of Associations* can help you find organizations representing careers that interest you.

Contacts Family, friends, coworkers, teachers, professors, and former employers are the people you already know who can help you to prepare for your career. Even people whom you do not know can assist you in a job search. That is why it is never too late to begin networking. **Networking** is a way of making and using contacts to get job information and advice. The contacts you make may not be people who can hire you, but they may know someone who can.

They may be able to arrange an **informational interview**, which is a meeting with someone who works in your area of interest who can provide you with practical information about the career or company you are considering.

Identifying Job Opportunities

What sources can you use to find an employment opportunity?

If you are going to find employment that is right for you, you need to know where to look for job openings. Explore sources such as job advertisements, job fairs, and employment agencies.

Job Advertisements

All newspapers have classified ads that include job listings. Although most advertise only jobs that are available locally, some major newspapers, such as *The Wall Street Journal,* list jobs from a wide geographic area.

The Internet is a valuable source for job opportunities. If you are interested in working for a particular company, you can use a search engine to find its Web site and learn more about it. Sometimes you can also find that company's list of current job openings. In addition to company Web sites, the Internet offers job-search Web sites with job advertisements, advice, and résumé services.

As You Read

RELATE

Make a list of people you already know who may be able to offer you help as you prepare for a career.

Discussion Discuss with the students the various career information sources available to them at their school and in their nearby community. Emphasize internship programs and cooperative education as well as the possibilities of after-school activities.

TechByte

Job Hunting Online

A wide selection of online resources awaits job seekers interested in any career. Many Web sites have listings of current job openings. Some sites offer additional features, such as tips on résumé writing and interviewing. These online tools allow job seekers to discover job opportunities locally and nationally.

@ Find and list two jobs you are interested in pursuing in your city or town through **finance07.glencoe.com**.

Research Have students search a local newspaper and find two jobs for which they would qualify based on the job skills they have identified. Then have them search the Internet for two more such job openings. They should be prepared to discuss which source (a) was easier to use and (b) offered more choices.

Job Fairs

At a job fair, recruiters from local and national companies set up tables or booths where you can discuss job opportunities and submit your résumé. To make the most of a job fair, be prepared to make your best impression on several recruiters in a short amount of time. They may call you for an in-depth interview at a later date.

Employment Agencies

Employment agencies are businesses that match job hunters with employers. Most often the company that hires you pays the employment agency fee. In some cases, you pay the fee, or you and your new employer share the cost. Do not get involved with agencies that ask you to pay a fee without promising you a job in return. The government also supports employment services. To find out more about them, contact your state's employment service or department of labor.

Other Ways to Find a Job

Your ability to find a job is limited only by your imagination and energy. Remember that finding a job is a job in itself. There are also other ways to find a job:

- **Visit**—Visit specific companies where you would like to work and ask to speak to someone who might help you.
- **Call**—Check your local telephone directories for the names of businesses in your field of interest, and contact them.
- **Network**—Talk to people with similar interests who have already graduated from your school. They may be able to help you focus your career search.

▶ **ANOTHER APPROACH**
One way to find a job is to write a letter to a company that interests you. *What might be some of the benefits of contacting companies even if they are not advertising a job opening?*

Caption Answer Answers might include companies may not yet have advertised for available jobs, or they may have a sudden need.

Applying for a Job

What are the steps involved in the job application process?

This morning the personnel director of a company to whom Christopher had sent his résumé and cover letter many weeks ago called him. In two days, he has an appointment for a job interview. He is excited, but he knows that he has a lot to do to prepare.

Making the best possible presentation of your skills and experience is the key to landing a job. Your résumé is your most important tool. A **résumé** is a one- or two-page summary of your education, training, experience, and qualifications. It provides prospective employers with an overview of the special contribution you may be able to make to their companies.

The two basic types of résumés are the chronological résumé and the skills résumé. The chronological résumé provides a year-by-year (or longer periods) outline of your education, work experience, and related information. This format is useful for job hunters who have continuous work experience. A skills résumé highlights your skills and abilities in specific categories, such as communications, supervision, or research. If you are a recent graduate or are changing careers, a skills résumé might be the better choice for you.

When you send your résumé to an employer by regular mail, e-mail, or fax, you will want to include a cover letter. A **cover letter** is the personal letter that you present along with your résumé. While the résumé serves as an overall summary of your qualifications, a cover letter tells a potential employer why you are interested in a particular job and why you think that it would be worthwhile for him or her to interview you. See **Figure 2.3** on page 46 for examples of a chronological résumé and a skills résumé, and **Figure 2.4** on page 47 for a sample cover letter.

The interview is a formal meeting with your potential employer that allows you to express why you think you are the best person for the job. If you are granted an interview, you should obtain as much information as you can about the company or industry before your interview. Possible resources include the library, the Internet, and informal interviews with people who are familiar with that company or industry. Here are some typical questions an employer might ask:

- What education and training qualify you for this job?
- Why are you interested in working for this company?
- Other than past jobs, what experiences have helped prepare you for this job?
- What are your major strengths? Major weaknesses?
- What do you plan to be doing five or ten years from now?

Most interviewers will end the interview by telling you when you can expect a response. While you are waiting, send that person a note reiterating your interest and expressing your thanks for the opportunity to interview. You may also want to recall your performance during the interview and think about how you might improve.

As You Read

QUESTION

Why would a skills résumé be a better choice for a recent high school graduate?

Question Answer A skills résumé highlights skills and abilities instead of experience.

Teaching Activity Have each student prepare a list of questions he or she would ask a job applicant. Tell students they will interview and be interviewed the next day in class, so they should dress appropriately. The next day, with students in pairs, have them interview each other. After all students have played both roles, discuss as a class their impressions of the process.

Figure 2.3 Types of Résumés

Chronological Résumé

CHAD BOSTWICK
2348 University Drive
Apartment 212
Jasper, Missouri 54321

Phone: 315-555-7659
E-mail: chbos@internet.com

CAREER OBJECTIVE: Seeking an entry-level position in medical or healthcare administration.

EXPERIENCE:

November 20-–Present
PATIENT ACCOUNT CLERK
University Hospital,
Jasper, Missouri
- Researched overdue accounts.
- Created collection method for faster accounts receivable turnover.
- Assisted in training billing clerks.

January–August 20--
SALES DATA CLERK
Jones Medical Supply Company,
Benton, Kansas
- Maintained inventory records.
- Processed customer records.

EDUCATION: B.S. in business administration and healthcare marketing, 20--
University of Western Missouri, Jasper, Missouri.

CAMPUS ACTIVITIES: Newsletter editor, University of Western Missouri chapter of Financial Management Association, 20--.

HONORS: College of Business Community Service Award, University of Western Missouri, May 20--.

COMPUTER SKILLS: Microsoft® Windows®, Microsoft Office®, Peachtree Complete® Accounting.

Skills Résumé

NANCY FRANK
670 Dove Circle
Apartment 5B
Reston, Maine 01267

Phone: 203-555-6710
E-mail: nanfrank@internet.com

CAREER OBJECTIVE: Seeking a human resources position in which supervisory, communication, and research experience can be used to train new and existing company employees.

ACHIEVEMENTS:

SUPERVISORY EXPERIENCE
- Developed and implemented training programs.
- Coordinated conference committees.

COMMUNICATION EXPERIENCE
- Created training manuals.
- Wrote press releases.

RESEARCH EXPERIENCE
- Investigated training problems of large industrial organizations.

COMPUTER SKILLS
- Mastered Microsoft® Windows®, Microsoft Office®.

EMPLOYMENT HISTORY:
- Assistant to director of human resources, Arkond Incorporated, Harper, Maine, June 20-- – Present.
- Copy writer, Ashton Marketing Services, Benton, Maine, January 20-- – May 20--.
- Research associate for Representative Henry Lake, Benton, Maine, June 20-- – December 20--.

EDUCATION: High School Diploma (College Preparatory Program), James Madison High School, Reston, Maine

Getting to Know You Your résumé should give a clear overview of your education, training, experience, and qualifications.

What are some experiences that you would describe in your résumé?

Caption Answer
Answers might include babysitting, volunteer work, part-time work, and after-school activities.

Figure 2.4 **Cover Letter**

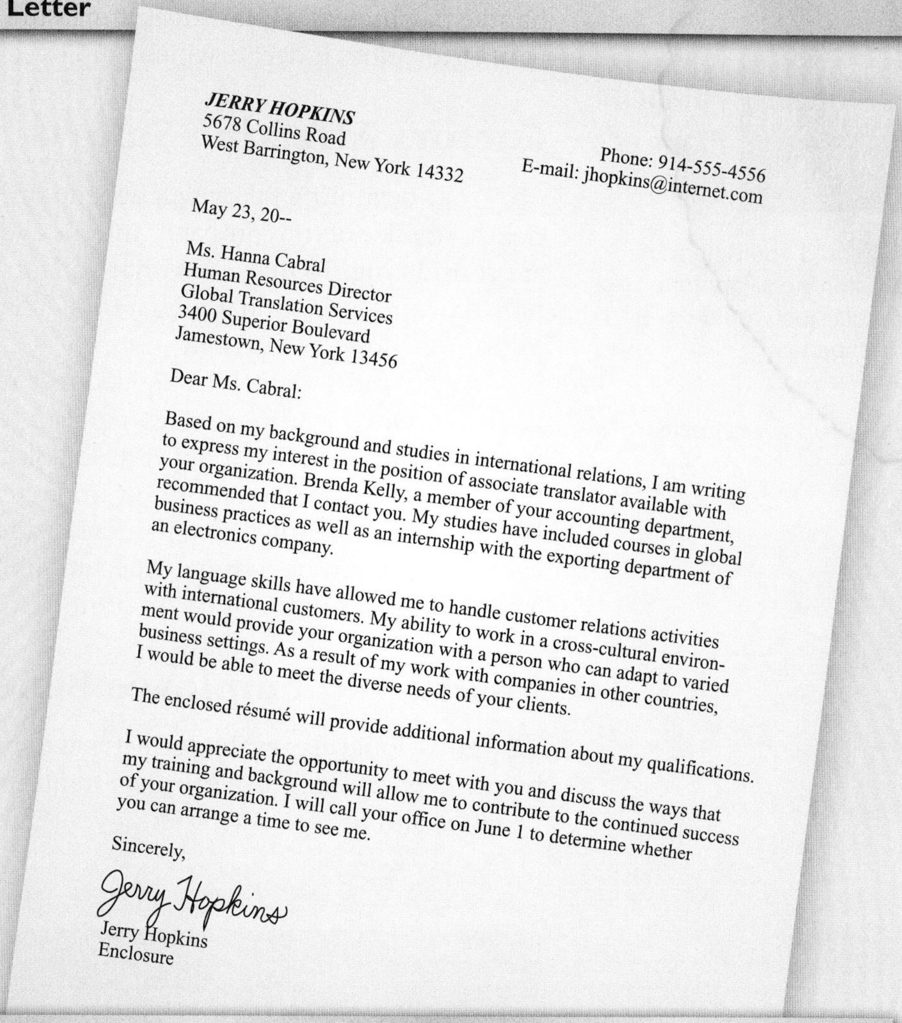

JERRY HOPKINS
5678 Collins Road
West Barrington, New York 14332

Phone: 914-555-4556
E-mail: jhopkins@internet.com

May 23, 20--

Ms. Hanna Cabral
Human Resources Director
Global Translation Services
3400 Superior Boulevard
Jamestown, New York 13456

Dear Ms. Cabral:

Based on my background and studies in international relations, I am writing to express my interest in the position of associate translator available with your organization. Brenda Kelly, a member of your accounting department, recommended that I contact you. My studies have included courses in global business practices as well as an internship with the exporting department of an electronics company.

My language skills have allowed me to handle customer relations activities with international customers. My ability to work in a cross-cultural environment would provide your organization with a person who can adapt to varied business settings. As a result of my work with companies in other countries, I would be able to meet the diverse needs of your clients.

The enclosed résumé will provide additional information about my qualifications.

I would appreciate the opportunity to meet with you and discuss the ways that my training and background will allow me to contribute to the continued success of your organization. I will call your office on June 1 to determine whether you can arrange a time to see me.

Sincerely,

Jerry Hopkins

Jerry Hopkins
Enclosure

The Introduction Your cover letter should be simple, informative, and free of errors.

What information could you include in your letter that would set you apart from other applicants?

Caption Answer
Answers will vary but could include personal attributes or specific experiences.

Considering a Job Offer

What factor would be most important to you when considering a job offer?

You may go on several interviews and experience disappointment. Sooner or later, however, someone will say, "We'd like you to work for us." But before you accept an offer, you have to consider several factors. Find out all you can about the company, the job itself, the working environment, the salary, and any other benefits.

The Work Environment

As you go on interviews, you will notice differences in workplaces. The pace and pressure will vary. Even the way people behave when they are at work will depend on the company.

Put on Your Financial Planner's Cap

STANDARD & POOR'S

How would you determine if the starting salary for a particular job would cover your expenses?

See the Teacher Manual for answers.

Ask about official company policies. How does the company handle pay increases? How does it measure the quality of employees' work? How does it decide which employees to promote?

Factors Affecting Salary

Your beginning salary will depend on your education and experience, the size of the company, and the average salary for the job you are considering. To make sure that you are starting with a fair salary, talk to people with similar jobs at other companies or look for related information on the Internet.

Raises and promotions are a direct result of how well you do your job. Once you have accepted a job offer and started to work, meet regularly with your supervisor. Ask for feedback on your performance and any suggestions for improvement. Let your supervisor know that you are interested in increased responsibility. Meeting—or exceeding—your supervisor's expectations should bring the reward of a raise. If it does not, you might want to look for another job.

Measuring Employee Benefits

You should also evaluate the types of benefits the company offers besides a paycheck. Pay particular attention to health care, retirement benefits, and the specific needs of your family.

▲ **WORK CULTURE** The pace and pressure of work differ from company to company. *What type of pace might be most appropriate for your personality and work habits?*

Caption Answer Answers will vary but should match personality to type of work.

Careers in Finance

CASHIER

Mark Leeds
Burlington Coat Factory

Mark has always wanted a job that balances his attention to detail with his ability to work with customers. Working as a cashier for Burlington Coat Factory, Mark is responsible for providing outstanding service and a friendly environment to each customer. His duties include handling money, totaling bills, making change, and giving receipts. He also handles returns, exchanges, and gift certificates. Mark likes interacting with people and also appreciates that his schedule is flexible. If something comes up, he can usually trade shifts with another cashier. Sales, holidays, and a varied work schedule provide diversity in the activity and intensity of a cashier's job.

SKILLS: Communication, dexterity, computer, and math

PERSONAL TRAITS: Detail oriented, honest, likes working with people, tactful, neat, and able to work weekends, holidays, and evenings

EDUCATION: High school diploma or equivalent, on-the-job training

ANALYZE What types of factors might a cashier examine before accepting a job?
See the Teacher Manual for answer.

@ To learn more about career paths for cashiers, visit **finance07.glencoe.com**.

Meeting Employee Needs Changes in society have brought about changes in the types of benefits that employees receive. Today single-parent families and households in which both parents work are common. Businesses have responded to these changes in a variety of ways.

Cafeteria-style employee benefits are programs that allow workers to choose the benefits that best meet their personal needs. A married employee with children may want more life and health insurance, whereas a single parent may also be interested in child-care services.

Because people today live longer, retirement programs are more important than ever. In addition to Social Security benefits, some companies contribute to a **pension plan**, which is a retirement plan that is funded at least in part by an employer. The features of pension plans vary among several basic types. Some plans provide you with a fixed amount of money at retirement. If a business uses a profit-sharing plan, it makes an annual contribution to a retirement fund each year. The money in this fund builds up until you reach retirement age. A third type of pension plan is a 401(k). You set aside a portion of your salary from each paycheck to go into your 401(k) fund. Your employer may match a percentage of your contribution.

Comparing Benefits You can compare the dollar value of employee benefits in several ways. The market value of a benefit is what the benefit would cost if you had to pay for it yourself. For example, the market value of free health insurance is what it would cost you to buy the same insurance. Also, the market value of one week's (five days') paid vacation is one week's salary.

Taxes should also play a part in your decisions about employment benefits. There are two types of employment benefits: tax-exempt and tax-deferred. A tax-exempt benefit is a benefit that is not taxable. For example, medical insurance paid by an employer is tax exempt. For example, if your employer pays $2,000 for your medical insurance, it equals $2,500 before taxes (for the 25 percent tax bracket). A free life insurance policy for an employee is an example of a tax-exempt benefit.

A tax-deferred benefit is a benefit for which you will have to pay income tax sometime in the future, most likely after you retire. A 401(k) plan is an example of a tax-deferred benefit.

Your Rights as an Employee

Why should you know your legal rights as an employee?

As an employee, you have certain legal rights, which can also affect your financial situation. You also have certain legal rights during the hiring process:

- An employer cannot refuse to hire a woman or terminate her employment because she is pregnant. A female employee who stops working because she is pregnant must be given full credit for previous service and for any retirement benefits.
- An employer cannot discriminate against a person for any reason related to age, race, color, religion, gender, marital status, national origin, or any mental or physical disabilities.
- In some cases, an employer must pay the minimum wage set by the government as well as a certain amount for overtime work.
- An employer must pay for unemployment insurance, contribute to Social Security, and provide for workers' compensation funds in case of a work-related injury or illness.

Long-Term Career Development

What steps can you take to help make your career a success?

A job is for today, but a career can last a lifetime. As you enter the world of work, ask yourself: Will you always enjoy the work that you do today? Will you be successful in the career you select? You cannot predict the future, but you can develop skills and attitudes that will increase your chances of being satisfied with your work in years to come. Here are some basic guidelines to follow for career success:

◀ **YOUR RIGHTS** An employer cannot discriminate against a person during the hiring process for any reason related to age, race, color, religion, gender, marital status, national origin, or any mental or physical disabilities. *What would you do if your legal rights were not honored?*

Caption Answer Answers should include talk to someone in authority or report the problem to an appropriate government agency.

- Make a point of improving your communication skills—both written and oral.
- Do your best to get along with your coworkers.
- Remain flexible and open to new ideas.
- Develop good work habits.
- Use lists, short-term and long-term goals, note cards, and other time-management techniques. When you have a task to complete, do it as well as you can.
- Be aware that problems may arise, and be ready to take action when they do.
- Be creative in solving your own problems.
- Be willing to learn new techniques and technologies.

Training Opportunities

Advances in technology are changing the world of work at a rapid pace. Many careers that people have today did not exist just a few years ago. These changes will surely continue. A key to your ongoing success will be your ability to keep up with changes in technology and to adapt to the global economy. Remember that you will always be learning new skills and ideas.

How can you make sure that your skills remain up to date? Many companies offer regular training programs, encourage attendance at professional seminars, or help pay for college courses. Read as much as possible on your own. Take advantage of the wealth of information on business, economic, and social trends on the Internet and in newspapers, magazines, and professional journals. Talk with others in your field. Informal meetings with coworkers and associates from other companies can be a valuable source of new information.

Figure 2.5 Stages of Career Development

Stage	Tasks	Concerns
Pre-entry and career exploration	• Assess personal interests. • Obtain necessary training. • Find an entry-level job.	• Matching interests and abilities to job • Dealing with disappointment
Career growth	• Obtain experience, develop skills. • Concentrate on an area of specialization. • Gain respect of colleagues.	• Developing career contacts • Avoiding career burnout
Advancement and mid-career adjustment	• Continue to gain experience and knowledge. • Seek new challenges and expanded responsibility.	• Finding continued satisfaction • Maintaining sensitivity toward colleagues and subordinates
Late career and preretirement	• Make financial and personal plans for retirement.	• Determining professional involvement after retirement • Planning participation in community activities

New Horizons Each stage of career development brings new tasks and new concerns.

Why might you decide to seek new challenges and responsibilities during the mid-career adjustment stage?

Caption Answer Answers might include to earn more money, to re-motivate and re-invigorate yourself, or to learn something new.

Career Paths and Advancement

As time goes by, you will experience changes in your personal interests, values, and goals. Outside factors, such as economic conditions and social trends, will also affect you. These changes will influence your career choices and other financial decisions that you make. You will probably go through a series of career stages, such as those shown in **Figure 2.5,** and experience specific tasks and concerns with each one.

One way to make sure that your career develops in the right direction is to gain support from someone with more experience and knowledge. A **mentor** is an experienced employee who serves as a teacher and counselor for a less-experienced person. A mentor can give you one-on-one training and help you to meet other knowledgeable people. He or she can also provide you with emotional support during difficult times at work. Many organizations have formal mentoring programs. Some of the best mentors are retired people who are eager to share a lifetime of knowledge and experience.

In addition, you may know a small number of people who can provide opportunities and guidance on a personal basis. Mentors can be role models, or they can be professionals outside your career area who take an interest in your career. They can make suggestions, inform you of opportunities, introduce you to key people, and help guide you through your career. Besides mentors, you probably know other people, friends and/or family, who can serve as role models and supporters as you travel your career path.

WebQuest

One Life to Plan
Learn more about life planners and how you can apply what they do for people to your own life right now.

@ To continue with Task 3 of your WebQuest project, visit **finance07.glencoe.com**.

Changing Careers

Most workers change jobs several times over the course of their lives. Some seek a better position within the same field. Others move to new careers. There are various signs that it is time to move on:

- You feel bored or depressed at work.
- Your job adversely affects you physically or emotionally.
- You receive a series of poor performance evaluations.
- You have little opportunity to obtain a raise or promotion.
- You have a poor relationship with your supervisor or coworkers.

At some point you may find yourself out of a job through no fault of your own. This situation can cause emotional and financial stress. While you are looking for another job, continue to eat, sleep, and exercise as usual. Stay involved in family and community activities. You may find new career contacts anywhere. Improve your skills through personal study, classes, or volunteer work. Think about opportunities with nonprofit or government organizations.

Whether looking for a new job or your first job, always consider how the financial and personal costs and benefits of your career choice will affect your needs and goals.

After You Read

REACT

Do you think the skills needed to embark on a career are the same as those needed to simply get a job? How are they the same? How are they different?

React Answer Embarking on a career requires different skills than simply getting a job. Career employment means you understand the business or field you are entering, and you choose to enter it and learn more; you need specific skills. A job usually requires general skills. They are the same in that both require good performance in an interview.

Section 2.2 Assessment

See the Teacher Manual for answers.

QUICK CHECK

1. What are three ways through which you might obtain employment experience?

2. What factors will affect your salary?

3. What are two methods that you might use to grow and develop your career?

THINK CRITICALLY

4. Compare the advantages and disadvantages of using the career information sources discussed in this section.

USE MATH SKILLS

5. Employee Benefits Gustavo has received a promising job offer from XYZ Company. He would earn $25,000 a year. In addition, he would receive two weeks of paid vacation, five paid personal days, and five sick days. He would also receive a free health insurance plan that has an equivalent market value of approximately $5,000.

Calculate If you consider the dollar value of employee benefits, how much will Gustavo's employment package be worth if he accepts this job offer?

SOLVE MONEY PROBLEMS

6. Measuring Employee Benefits Suzanne is a single mother who works full time and pays a sitter to take care of her two children. She recently moved to another state and found a new job. The company offers a variety of employee benefit plans. Suzanne needs to determine which benefits will be best for her family.

Write About It Based on the information in the section on measuring employee benefits, what possibilities might Suzanne have? What will she have to consider in making her decision? Write a one-page report to help Suzanne make her decision.

Chapter 2 Review & Activities

See the Teacher Manual for answers.

CHAPTER SUMMARY

- Personal issues to consider when choosing a career include your aptitudes, interests, personality, and current personal situation.
- The more education and training you have, the greater your potential earning power will be. Also, the field of study you select will affect your salary.
- Employment opportunities are affected by social influences, such as demographic trends, geographic trends, and economic factors, as well as industry and technology trends.
- Gain experience through part-time work, volunteer work, internships, cooperative education, and class projects.
- To evaluate career opportunities, use sources such as the Internet, libraries, newspapers, school guidance offices, community organizations, and networking with people working in the field you choose.
- Financial issues to consider when looking for employment are your starting salary, opportunities for promotions and raises, benefits, and the cost of living. Legal issues to consider relate to the work environment of the company, its adherence to laws regarding discrimination, minimum wage unemployment insurance, Social Security, and workers' compensation.

Communicating Key Terms

Using 8 to 12 of the terms below, write an article for a class or school newspaper on the primary influences that will affect your personal career choice.

- job
- career
- standard of living
- trends
- potential earning power
- aptitudes
- interest inventories
- demographic trends
- geographic trends
- service industries
- internship
- cooperative education
- networking
- informational interview
- résumé
- cover letter
- cafeteria-style employee benefits
- pension plan
- mentor

Reviewing Key Concepts

1. **List** some of the personal issues you will need to consider when planning your career.
2. **Describe** factors that affect your potential earning power.
3. **Explain** how current demographic trends might influence your choice of career.
4. **List** some ways you might obtain job-related experience.
5. **Identify** sources of information to find out more about the career in which you are interested.
6. **Explain** your rights as an employee.

See the Teacher Manual for answers.

ACADEMIC SKILLS

Language Arts Review the information about the factors involved in choosing a career. Choose a career you would be interested in pursuing.

Write About It Write a short essay about why you chose this career. Be sure to discuss some of the personal issues that influenced you.

YOUR FINANCIAL FIGURES

Cost of Living Use an Internet search engine to find a Web site that compares the cost of living in cities in the United States. If you were offered a salary of $35,000 in Columbus, Ohio, what salary would you need to maintain the same standard of living in Chicago, Illinois? In Richmond, Virginia? In San Diego, California?

1. **Analyze and Calculate** (a) What are the differences among the cities in percent increases and decreases? (b) Use the cost of living information and real estate Web sites to find out the reason for the difference in costs of housing, insurance, and utilities.
2. **Compute** by using spreadsheet software to calculate and compare the proportional differences in costs of living among the cities.

REAL-WORLD Application

Connect with Communication Skills You are applying for summer jobs. Look through the sources described in this chapter and prepare a list of employers to whom you will submit your résumé and cover letter.

1. **Write About It** For each job, prepare a résumé and cover letter. Next, work with a partner to role-play an interview. Interview each other using the résumés and cover letters as a basis.
2. **Think Critically** How will you change your résumé and cover letter to emphasize your specific skills?

Internet CONNECTION

Career Information Updates Forecasts about careers with the greatest potential can help you narrow your choices.

Log On Go to **finance07.glencoe.com** for a link to a Web site for nationwide career information developed by the U.S. Department of Labor. Click on Résumé Tutorial to find directions about what to include in your résumé. Answer the following questions:

1. What are most employers looking for when they read your résumé?
2. What can you do to make your résumé stand out from other résumés?

BusinessWeek ONLINE

Newsclip: Career Edge Students who develop strong job-search skills have a career advantage. They develop clear career direction. They also communicate and promote their competitive edge to employers.

Log On Go to **finance07.glencoe.com** and open Chapter 2. Learn more about career strategies. Write a paragraph about how you can boost your chances of getting hired.

WHAT'S YOUR FINANCIAL ID?

FIND YOUR PERSONALITY TRAITS

Learning more about your own personality will help you choose the best career for you. Read the characteristics below that describe people's personalities. On a separate piece of paper, write down the five traits that best describe you, then answer the question that follows the list of characteristics.

Personality Traits

outgoing	ambitious	patient
studious	kind	thoughtful
neat	strong	intelligent
quiet	trustworthy	respectful
playful	warm	happy
energetic	persistent	spontaneous
serious	organized	worried
easygoing	rebellious	sensitive
caring	stubborn	sociable
loyal	responsible	creative
confident	fair	talkative
cheerful	calm	inquisitive
dependable	brave	funny
generous	helpful	athletic
shy	imaginative	competitive

Activity

Keeping in mind the five traits that best describe your personality, what kind of work do you think would suit you? For example, if you are persistent, outgoing, assertive, energetic, and confident you might enjoy working in sales. If you are inquisitive, creative, imaginative, inquisitive, and intelligent you might enjoy a career in writing. List the jobs or careers that you think fit best with your personality.

Accept all reasonable answers that show student effort and an understanding of the concept.

Your Financial Portfolio

Applying for a Job

Mark Cortez was interested in working at his neighborhood grocery store as a clerk. He wanted to work part-time after school and on weekends to earn money for his personal expenses. He filled out the application at the store and was called back for an interview. Mark interviewed with the store manager and got the job.

Complete

Before you interview for a job, you will probably have to fill out an application. Take time to practice "the art" of completing application forms. Always fill out a job application as neatly and accurately as possible. Write "N/A" in any blank for which an answer is not required. N/A means "Not Applicable" and tells the employer that you saw the question, but it does not apply to you. Fill out the application on a separate sheet of paper, being sure to fill it out completely. Use a pencil before you complete the application in ink, or use a rough copy. Were there any questions that you could not answer? If so, list those questions and see if you can find answers to them elsewhere.

APPLICATION FOR EMPLOYMENT

SUPERIOR MARKETS

DIRECTIONS: Please use a pen and print.
Answer all sections completely and accurately.

NAME			SOCIAL SECURITY NUMBER
LAST	FIRST	MIDDLE	
Cortez	Mark	A.	032 -XX-XXXX

HOME ADDRESS				
NUMBER	STREET	CITY	STATE	ZIP
134	North Avenue	Indianapolis	IN	46268

TELEPHONE #	ALTERNATE #
(317) 555-2492	

POSITION APPLIED FOR	SPECIFY DAYS AND HOURS AVAILABLE	PAY DESIRED
Clerk	evenings and weekends	negotiable

EDUCATION	NAME AND ADDRESS OF SCHOOL	COURSE	DATE LEFT
MIDDLE SCHOOL	Valley Middle School Indianapolis, IN 46266	N/A	June 6, 20--
HIGH SCHOOL	Northwest High School Indianapolis, IN 46244	N/A	N/A
VOCATIONAL SCHOOL	N/A	N/A	N/A
COLLEGE OR UNIVERSITY	N/A	N/A	N/A
OTHER	N/A	N/A	N/A

LAST EMPLOYMENT				
NAME OF COMPANY	ADDRESS	SUPERVISOR	JOB	PAY
Cameron's Business Supply	1217 Sheldon Ave Indianapolis, IN 46244	Jill Lambert	Clerk	$6.50/hr
DATE BEGAN	DATE LEFT	REASON FOR LEAVING		
June 20--	September 20--	Summer position only		

Additional qualifications applicant has to offer for consideration. These may include job-related interests, experiences, or volunteer activities.

Volunteer one night a week to help deliver meals-on-wheels, on weight-lifting team, and run track at school.

The facts set forth on my application are true and complete.

DATE October 8, 20-- SIGNATURE *Mark A. Cortez*

Analyze

What would a neatly prepared application tell a prospective employer about you?

Accept all reasonable answers that show student effort and an understanding of the concept.

CHAPTER 3
Money Management Strategy

$ What You'll Learn

When you have completed this chapter, you will be able to:

Section 3.1
- Discuss the relationship between opportunity costs and money management.
- Explain the benefits of keeping financial records and documents.
- Describe a system to maintain personal financial documents.

Section 3.2
- Describe a personal balance sheet and cash flow statement.
- Develop a personal balance sheet and cash flow statement.

Section 3.3
- Identify the steps of creating a personal budget.
- Discuss the advantage of increasing your savings.

Reading Strategies

To get the most out of your reading:

Predict what you will learn in this chapter.
Relate what you read to your own life.
Question what you are reading to be sure you understand.
React to what you have read.

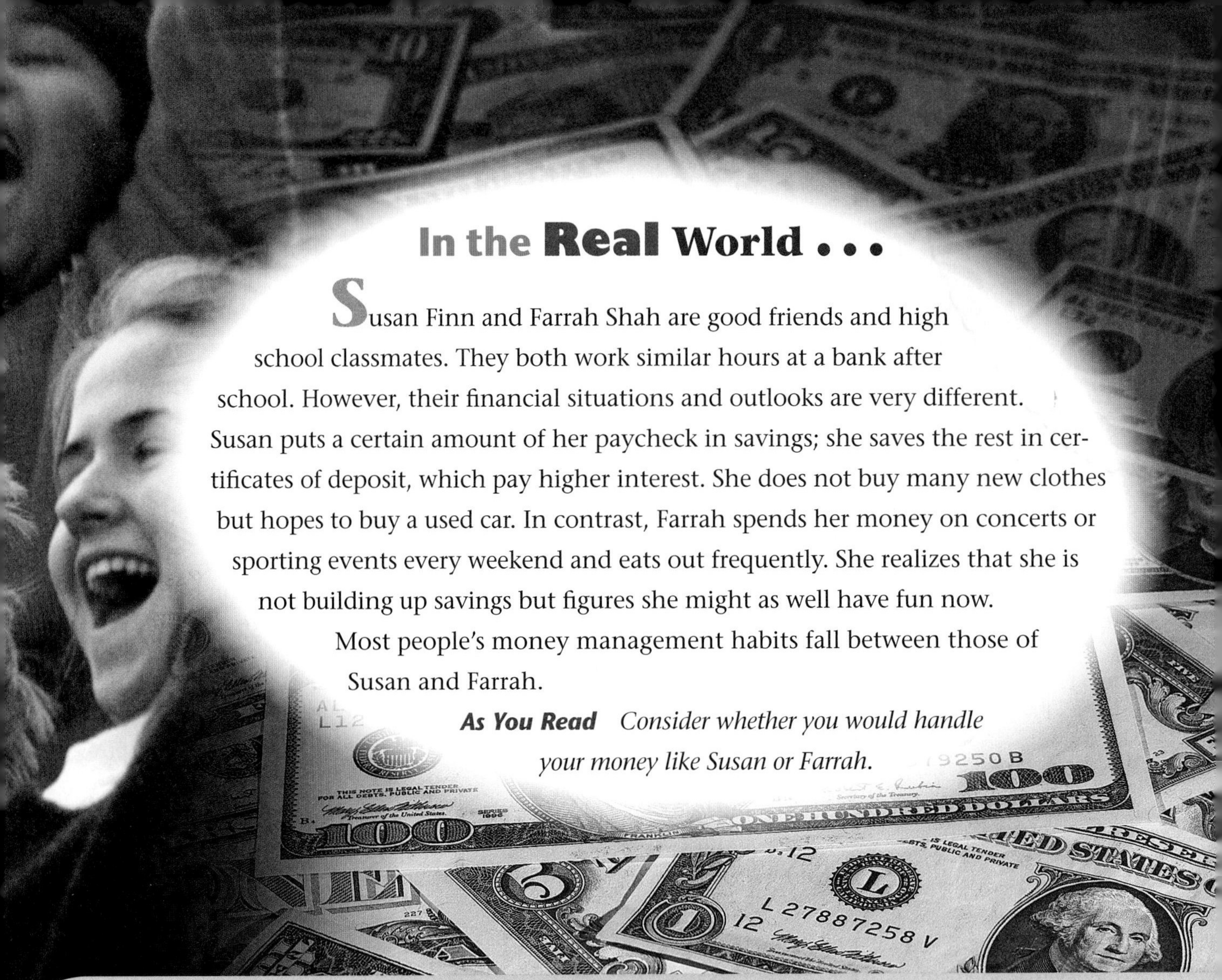

In the Real World . . .

Susan Finn and Farrah Shah are good friends and high school classmates. They both work similar hours at a bank after school. However, their financial situations and outlooks are very different. Susan puts a certain amount of her paycheck in savings; she saves the rest in certificates of deposit, which pay higher interest. She does not buy many new clothes but hopes to buy a used car. In contrast, Farrah spends her money on concerts or sporting events every weekend and eats out frequently. She realizes that she is not building up savings but figures she might as well have fun now.

Most people's money management habits fall between those of Susan and Farrah.

As You Read *Consider whether you would handle your money like Susan or Farrah.*

Lesson Plan See the Teacher Manual for the Chapter 3 planning guide and lesson plan.

ASK STANDARD & POOR'S

Money When You Need It

Q: Do I need an emergency fund even though I work part time, live at home, and have no bills?

A: There is no guarantee that your job will always be there for you. If you become sick or injured, you may have to take time off from work. Even if you have disability insurance, it may pay only a fraction of what you earn. If you own a car, you may have unexpected repair bills. Emergency funds are for those unexpected things.

Ask Yourself How much of your monthly income do you think you should put into your emergency fund?

@ Go to **finance07.glencoe.com** to complete the Standard & Poor's Financial Focus activity.

Section 3.1

Focus on Reading

Read to Learn

- How to discuss the relationship between opportunity costs and money management.
- How to explain the benefits of keeping financial records and documents.
- How to describe a system to maintain personal financial documents.

Main Idea

Organizing your personal financial records can help you make informed decisions about your spending.

Key Terms

- money management
- safe-deposit box

Before You Read

PREDICT

Do you think it is necessary to keep organized copies of your financial records? Why or why not?

Springboard Ask the students if they know and can define the phrase "getting the most for your money." List responses on the board, suggesting students consider as they study the chapter.

Organizing Financial Records

Opportunity Costs and Money Management

How do opportunity costs affect managing your money?

Every time you make a decision, you choose one thing and reject another. This is true no matter how major or minor the decision may be. Perhaps you decide to go to the movies instead of reading a book for your English homework assignment. On a Saturday afternoon, you may choose to play with the neighbor's dog instead of watching television or playing with your Xbox. Every decision you make represents a trade-off, or opportunity cost.

Trade-offs are especially common when it comes to making decisions about money management. **Money management** is planning how to get the most from your money. Good money management can help you keep track of where your money goes so that you can make it go farther. In order to manage your money well, you probably consider financial trade-offs. For example, you may consider whether you should spend your paycheck on clothes or put some of it in the bank to earn interest. You might also wonder if you should shop around for a CD or MP3 player at a lower price or if doing that is a waste of time.

Trade-offs can be very hard to resolve because you might think of good reasons for making either choice. In the first example, the first option would increase the amount you can spend now. However, depositing some money would contribute to your long-term financial security. In the second example, you might be able to save some money by checking prices at other stores downtown or at a different mall, but you would also be using up something you can never replace—your time.

How can you be sure of making the right decisions when you are faced with tough opportunity costs? You may never be sure, but you can become a better judge of your options. Consider the factors that influence your decision making by compiling a mental list of your options. Then consider how those options fit your values, your current financial situation, and your goal of effective money management.

By considering your values, your goals, and the state of your bank account, you can make better spending decisions. For example, if your goal is to save as much money as you can for college, then you might borrow a book from a library rather than buy it from a bookstore. On the other hand, if your goal is to put aside only a certain amount of your paycheck each month, you might be able to buy the book with the money you have left.

As You Read

RELATE

Have you ever wondered what happened to a sum of money you had? Explain the circumstances.

Motivating Students Ask for a show of hands responding to: "How many of you sometimes feel like there is never enough money for your needs?" Then discuss with students how better money management makes mon...

Benefits of Organizing Your Financial Documents

Why is it important to have a system to organize your financial documents?

The first step in effective money management is to organize your personal financial documents. The category of "perso documents" includes a variety of materials, such as ban and paycheck stubs. (The receipt for the shirt you bou document.) These documents tell you how much mone

Personal financial documents also include records directly related to your day-to-day use of money. Autom ship titles, birth certificates, and tax forms are personal fin ments. Together, these records present a clear picture of yo

Creating an organized system for handling your per cial documents has several advantages. Most obviously, a s you quickly find any document you may need in a hurry. your documents also helps you:

Relate to Katrina video

- Plan and measure your financial progress.
- Handle routine money matters, such as paying bills
- Determine how much money you will have now and in the future.
- Make effective decisions about how to save money.

Where to Keep Your Financial Documents

Why should you keep your financial documents in a specific place?

You can keep your financial documents in different places—in a home file, in a safe-deposit box, or on a computer. See **Figure 3.1** on page 62 for a list of the types of financial documents you might keep in these places. To organize your documents as effectively as possible, you may want to use all three. Each method has advantages and disadvantages, depending on the types of documents being kept.

Figure 3.1 Where to Keep Your Financial Records

Home File

1. Personal and Employment Records (Social Security number, employee benefit information, current résumé)
2. Money Management Records (current budget, balance sheet, cash flow statement, list of financial goals, copies of documents in safe-deposit box)
3. Financial Services Records (checkbook, canceled checks, bank statements, location and number of safe-deposit box)
4. Tax Records (W-2 forms, paycheck stubs, copies of income tax returns)
5. Consumer Records (receipts for major purchases, automobile service and repair records, owner's manuals for cars and major appliances, warranties)
6. Housing Records (lease, if renting; property tax records; home repair and improvement receipts)
7. Insurance Records (original insurance policies; list of insurance premium amounts and due dates; medical information, such as health history, prescription drug information)
8. Investment Records (records of stock, bond, and mutual fund purchases and sales, list of investment certificate numbers, brokerage statements, dividend records)
9. Estate Planning and Retirement Records (will, pension plan information, IRA statements, Social Security information)

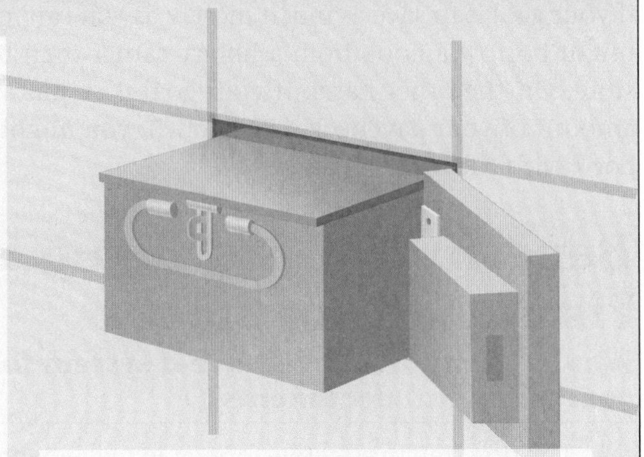

Safe-Deposit Box

Birth certificates, mortgage loan papers, title deeds, copy of will, certificates of deposit, checking and savings account numbers, automobile title(s), insurance policy numbers, valuable collectibles

Home Computer

Current and past budgets, summaries of checks written and other banking transactions, tax records, résumé

Safe and Sound A home file, safe-deposit box, or personal computer will enable you to organize your financial documents.

Name at least three personal financial documents that you might store in a home file.

Caption Answer
Answers may include a desk drawer or file cabinet; personal financial documents may include paycheck stubs, receipts for major purchases, guarantees, etc.

Home Files

A home file is one place to keep financial documents. This type of file is simple to set up and does not take up much space. You can use a file drawer, several folders, or even a cardboard box. Whatever method you use, your home file should be simple so that you have quick access to your documents.

You may already have the beginnings of a home filing system. For example, you may have been keeping a savings account passbook in the back of a bureau drawer since you were ten years old, or maybe you have an accordion file folder where you store all your receipts. To make good use of a home filing system, sort through all your personal financial records and arrange them according to the type of each document. Next, label all folders or boxes. Train yourself to file your receipts and other financial papers as soon as possible after receiving them.

What types of financial documents should you keep in a home file? If you have a checking account, keep your bank statements so that you can determine how much money you have in your account or verify your checkbook against the statements. However, do not keep hard-to-replace documents, such as a car title or paperwork related to a mortgage loan, in a home file. A cardboard box does not protect against fire, water, or theft.

Safe-Deposit Boxes

You should keep important documents such as car titles and mortgage loan papers locked away in a **safe-deposit box**—a small, secure storage compartment that you can rent in a bank, usually for $100 a year or less. Other items commonly kept in safe-deposit boxes include rental agreements, birth certificates, adoption papers, a list of insurance policies, stock certificates, and valuable collectibles, such as coins or stamps.

Safe-deposit boxes are usually kept in a locked, fireproof room that is accessible only while the bank is open for business. Each box has two individual locks. You, the holder of the box, have one key; the bank keeps the other key. The box can be opened only when both keys are used together.

Safe-deposit boxes offer more security for your valuables than your home file because at a bank loss from fire and other disasters is extremely rare. Moreover, the financial institution that owns the box usually (though not always) has insurance to cover such losses. Nevertheless, it is probably a wise idea to keep copies at home of all the financial records in your safe-deposit box.

As an alternative, some people use home fire-safe boxes that lock. These "safes" are an inexpensive way to protect against loss due to fire but not due to theft.

As You Read

QUESTION

Why might it be necessary to have easy access to auto repair records, bank statements, and receipts for purchases such as clothes or video games?

Question Answer (a) You need to know when auto repairs were done and when they will need to be done again; also, you need to know when guarantees expire. (b) Bank statements are useful to resolve disputes if someone claims you have not paid a bill; also, you need bank statements to pinpoint your financial situation. (c) Purchase receipts are necessary if you need to return an item; additionally, some may be useful when doing tax returns.

Discussion Ask students what kinds of financial records they keep; list their responses on the board. For each item listed, discuss why, how long, and with what security it should be kept.

TechByte

Net Worth Calculator

Your net worth is the difference between your assets (the things you own that have value) and your liabilities (short-term and long-term debts you are working to pay off). Figuring out your net worth from time to time will help you evaluate the progress you are making toward your financial goals.

@ Calculate your net worth through **finance07.glencoe.com**.

Research Divide the class into three groups. Group 1 is to research what one would need and how much it would cost to set up a good home filing system. Group 2 is to research safe-deposit boxes, finding rates in a variety of banking institutions and learning about the requirements and restrictions. Group 3 is to research the computer security systems available to protect computerized financial records and back-ups that might be necessary. Each group is to report back to the class.

Home Computers

Rental agreements and canceled checks cannot be stored on a home computer. However, if you have a personal computer, it can be a great place to keep certain types of financial records. It is also a good tool to use for planning your financial future.

You can use a software program specifically designed to keep a running summary of checks you have written. You enter any checks, and the program automatically calculates the new balance in your account. Some programs also facilitate payments online. By tracking your monthly spending on a computer, you can see at a glance how much money you are spending, and you can easily compare your expenses from one month to the next. You can also generate personal financial documents and statements from the information you have organized by using software.

Section 3.1 Assessment

See the Teacher Manual for answers.

QUICK CHECK

1. How will organizing your financial documents help you manage your money?
2. What steps would you take to create a home filing system?
3. What are the advantages of using a safe-deposit box to store your personal financial documents?

THINK CRITICALLY

4. List three examples of money-related opportunity costs you have faced in the last two months. Write a sentence explaining what decision you made for each one and why.

USE COMMUNICATION SKILLS

5. **Organizing Financial Records** To become a member of an Internet DVD library, Maritza has to put down a deposit of $100, using her credit card. When and if Maritza chooses to discontinue her membership, the library will refund her deposit only if she has returned all her rented DVDs, has paid the annual membership fee, and has presented her membership agreement.

Write About It Write a list of some places Maritza might store the agreement to ensure her claim to the deposit.

SOLVE MONEY PROBLEMS

6. **Financial Documents** Martin is sitting in his bedroom surrounded by dozens of papers—gas receipts for his car, a checkbook, a couple of unopened and unpaid bills, paycheck stubs from his work at a day-care center, and much more. He wants to organize his financial documents in a shoebox, but he is completely overwhelmed by the amount of paper.

Analyze Help Martin prioritize this job. Give him some suggestions about breaking it down into parts, starting with the most important tasks. For example, tell Martin to begin by categorizing his documents by the type of each document.

Section 3.2

Personal Financial Statements

Personal Balance Sheet

How can a personal balance sheet help you find out your current worth?

Most of the documents mentioned in the previous section are issued by banks, federal and state governments, and businesses. However, such documents reveal only part of your financial picture. For a complete look at your financial situation, you should create a personal balance sheet and a cash flow statement. These reports are known as personal financial statements. A **personal financial statement** is a document that provides information about an individual's current financial position and presents a summary of income and spending.

Personal financial statements can help you:

- Determine what you own and what you owe.
- Measure your progress toward your financial goals.
- Track your financial activities.
- Organize information that you can use when you file your tax return or apply for credit.

To evaluate your financial situation, you first need to create a balance sheet. A **personal balance sheet**, also called a net worth statement, is a financial statement that lists items of value owned, debts owed, and a person's net worth. Your **net worth** is the difference between the amount that you own and the debts that you owe. Net worth is a measure of your current financial position. To create a personal balance sheet, follow these steps. **Figure 3.2** on page 66 shows an example of a personal balance sheet.

STEP 1: Determine Your Assets

Assets are any items of value that an individual or company owns, including cash, property, personal possessions, and investments. To determine your assets, you need to consider four categories of wealth. **Wealth** is an abundance of valuable material possessions or resources. The categories include: liquid assets, real estate, personal possessions, and investment assets.

Focus on Reading

Read to Learn

- How to describe a personal balance sheet and cash flow statement.
- How to develop a personal balance sheet and cash flow statement.

Main Idea

A personal balance sheet and cash flow statement can help you to analyze your financial situation.

Key Terms

- personal financial statement
- personal balance sheet
- net worth
- assets
- wealth
- liquid assets
- real estate
- market value
- liabilities
- insolvency
- cash flow
- income
- take-home pay
- discretionary income
- surplus
- deficit

Before You Read

PREDICT

What information do you think might be on a cash flow statement?

Figure 3.2 A Personal Balance Sheet

Melinda and Carroll Durbin
Personal Balance Sheet as of October 31, 20--

Assets		
Liquid Assets		
Checking account balance	$1,450	
Savings account balance	550	
Total liquid assets		$2,000
Real Estate		
Market value of house		105,000
Personal Possessions		
Market value of car	$4,250	
Furniture and appliances	2,500	
Electronic equipment	2,000	
Collectibles	750	
Total personal possessions		9,500
Investment Assets		
Retirement accounts	$15,000	
Stock investments	3,300	
Total investment assets		18,300
Total Assets		$134,800
Liabilities		
Current Liabilities		
Medical bills	$1,250	
Credit card balances	2,300	
Total current liabilities		$3,550
Long-Term Liabilities		
Mortgage	$92,500	
Student loan	3,500	
Car loan	2,500	
Total long-term liabilities		98,500
Total Liabilities		$102,050
Net Worth (assets minus liabilities)		$32,750

True or False? The Durbins' personal balance sheet indicates that they have a positive net worth of $32,750.

Does this net worth figure reflect their true financial situation? Explain your answer.

Caption Answer No. Most of their assets are not liquid (real estate and investments) and not easily convertible to cash.

Liquid Assets The first category is called liquid assets. **Liquid assets** are cash and items that can be quickly converted to cash. The money in your savings and checking accounts is a liquid asset. For example, if Bharat has $500 in his savings account and $35 in cash, his liquid assets are worth $535 ($500 + $35 = $535). This money is immediately available for Bharat to spend. He may be able to convert other assets into cash, but the process is not quite as easy or as fast.

Springboard Ask the students how many of the key terms they have heard of; then ask them how many they understand. Explain that the difference is because we hear terms that no one ever seems to interpret for us, and we usually do not want to ask. Telll them that by the end of this section, these words will be clear.

Real Estate The second category of wealth is **real estate**, land and any structures that are on it, such as a house or any other building that a person or family owns. The amount recorded on the real estate portion of your balance sheet is the property's **market value**, or the price at which property would sell. Suppose that the Louis family owns a house and a cottage with market values at $135,000 and $84,000, respectively. They would list the sum of those figures—$219,000—under the heading "Real Estate" on their balance sheet.

▼ **PLAY TIME** Many people save favorite toys or other items from childhood. *Which items do you have that might be valuable? How can you find out?*

Personal Possessions Personal possessions—cars and any other valuable belongings that are not real estate—make up the third category. For example, Joyce might choose to list her new $800 electric guitar, her television, her skis, and several pieces of fine jewelry. Note that the emphasis is on "valuable"; old clothes and used CDs do not count.

You may list personal possessions on the balance sheet at their original cost, but you will get a better idea of your financial situation by recording their current market value. For example, Joyce's television is worth less now than it was when she purchased it five years ago. In contrast, collectible items, such as old baseball cards and comic books, may increase in value over time. Although determining current values for some items may be difficult, doing so will give you a more accurate picture of your net worth. You may have to look up comparable items in newspaper classified ads or visit thrift stores. You can also check Web sites where people buy and sell such items.

Caption Answer Items might be baseball cards or dolls. They can find value by looking on the Internet, in thrift stores, or newspaper ads to see what comparable items are worth.

GO FIGURE — FINANCIAL MATH

NET WORTH

Synopsis: Calculating your net worth will help you get an accurate measure of your current financial situation.

Example: What is Janine's net worth if her assets are worth $3,000 and her liabilities total $700?

Formula: Assets − Liabilities = Net Worth

Solution: $3,000 − $700 = $2,300

Janine's net worth is $2,300.

YOU FIGURE

You own a bike that is worth $250, a watch that is worth $60, and a stereo that is worth $400. You owe your older brother $70 for some concert tickets he bought for you, and you owe $120 to a department store. What is your net worth?

Answer $710 − $190 = $520

Motivating Students Have students consider the terms "assets" and "liabilities" as they might be used when discussing a new classmate. What might be some of his/her assets? Liabilities? List on the board. Ask what they think those same terms might mean when discussing finance.

Investment Assets The fourth category of wealth is investment assets. Investment assets include retirement accounts and securities such as stocks and bonds. Set aside such assets for long-term financial needs, such as paying for college, buying a house, or retirement.

STEP 2: Determine Your Liabilities

When you prepare a personal balance sheet, you must also record your **liabilities**, or the debts that you owe. Suppose that Marlene borrows $200 from her mother to buy a new printer for her computer. She would record the printer as an asset, but she would also have to record $200 as a liability on her personal balance sheet.

Current Liabilities Current liabilities are short-term debts that have to be paid within one year. Most medical bills, cash loans, and taxes fall under this heading.

Discussion Ask the students what assets they currently own, and then list their responses on the board. Encourage them to broaden their thinking about assets to include not only money, but also stamp collections, vehicles, sports equipment, computers, etc. Then ask them what their liabilities might be and list on the board.

Long-Term Liabilities Long-term liabilities are debts that do not have to be fully repaid for at least a year. Car loans, student loans, and mortgage loans are examples of long-term liabilities. Note that the term "liabilities" includes only money that you will owe for longer than a month. For example, a telephone bill does not qualify as a liability.

STEP 3: Calculate Your Net Worth

Once you know the amounts of your assets and liabilities, you can calculate your net worth. To determine your net worth, subtract your liabilities from your assets; the difference is your net worth.

It is important to understand the meaning of net worth. If the Romano family has a net worth of $62,300, that does not mean they have $62,300 to spend. Much of their wealth may be in stocks, real estate, and personal possessions, which cannot be easily converted to cash. Net worth is only an indication of your general financial situation.

As You Read

RELATE

Using the formula in the Go Figure box, calculate your net worth.

Although you may have a high net worth, you can still have trouble paying your bills. This is especially true when most of your assets are not liquid and you do not have enough cash to meet your expenses. That can happen if you purchase a more expensive car than you can afford or spend all of your savings to buy a house.

If you are unable to pay all your debts, you may experience insolvency. **Insolvency** is a financial state that occurs if liabilities are greater than assets. Suppose that Brad owes $4,000 and that his assets—a ten-year-old car and an old computer—are worth $1,800. Even if Brad sold all his assets and put his whole $1,500 paycheck toward paying his debts, he would still be insolvent.

Critical Thinking Remind students that people often complain about the taxes they pay to local, state, and federal agencies. Have students write an essay entitled "Are Taxpayers Getting Their Money's Worth?" in which they discuss what services these governments provide for the taxes they receive. At the end of the essay, they are to answer the title question.

STEP 4: Evaluate Your Financial Situation

You can use a balance sheet to track your financial progress. Update your balance sheet, or make a new one, every few months to chart changes over time. Is your net worth increasing? Good! Keep doing what you are doing to make that happen. Is it decreasing or just holding steady? Then you might make changes. As a rule, you can increase your net worth by increasing your savings, increasing your investments, reducing your expenses, and/or reducing your debts.

Careers in Finance

FINANCIAL ADVISOR **Elaine Hawkins**
AXA Financial, Inc.

Elaine has always been good at coming up with solutions to difficult or complicated problems, so handling finances comes naturally to her. In her capacity as a financial advisor, Elaine visits with a wide variety of clients and helps them understand their financial needs. She also helps them create a plan for reaching their goals through financial planning, investment services, and risk management. At a time when people are unsure of the soundness of Social Security and may be financially unprepared for retirement, Elaine is able to provide them with options and comfort. Elaine gains work through word of mouth and enjoys building and assisting a network of friends and acquaintances.

SKILLS: Finance, math, communication, business, and problem-solving skills

PERSONAL TRAITS: Entrepreneurial, social, tactful, and goal oriented

EDUCATION: Bachelor's degree or higher in law, accounting, banking, or management; certification as a Certified Financial Planner or Chartered Financial Consultant

ANALYZE What are some financial goals that a financial advisor could help you reach?
See the Teacher Manual for answer.

@ To learn more about career paths for financial advisors, visit **finance07.glencoe.com**.

As You Read

QUESTION

What is the difference between net worth and cash flow?

Question Answer Net worth tells you your general financial situation; cash flow tells you how much money you have to spend or save in a given time period.

Teaching Activity Have students maintain a cash journal for one week in which they record all money coming in and all money spent. At the end of the week, have them bring those journals to class and prepare a cash flow statement, including their net cash flow, based on the entries.

Cash Flow Statement: Income Versus Expenses

What kind of information do you get from creating a cash flow statement?

The money that actually goes into and out of your wallet and bank accounts is called **cash flow**. It is divided into two parts: cash inflow and cash outflow. Cash inflow is the money you receive, or your **income**. That may include a paycheck from a job, an allowance from your parents, or interest earned in your savings account. Cash outflow includes all of the money you spend.

A cash flow statement is simply a summary of your cash flow during a particular period, usually a month or a year. This summary gives you important information and feedback on your income and spending patterns. To create a cash flow statement, such as the one shown in **Figure 3.3,** follow these steps:

1. Record your income.
2. Record your expenses.
3. Determine your net cash flow.

Figure 3.3 Cash Flow Statement

Amy Grossman	Cash Flow Statement for Month Ending July 31, 20--
Income (Cash Inflow)	
Take-home pay	$450
Allowance	100
Savings account interest	12
Total income	$562
Expenses (Cash Outflow)	
Fixed expenses (cable TV, train commuter tickets, etc.)	$ 80
Variable expenses (recreation, clothing, take-out food)	320
Total expenses	$400
Net Cash Flow	**$162**

Money Supply Amy's cash flow statement indicates that her net cash flow is $162.

How might she increase her net cash flow?

Caption Answer She can cancel cable TV or reduce variable expenses.

STEP 1: Record Your Income

List all of your sources of income during a given month, and record the amounts as your cash inflow. Make sure that you record the exact amount. Most paychecks include various deductions for federal and state taxes. These taxes are withheld from the total amount of money you have earned, or your gross pay. Your **take-home pay**, or net pay, is the amount of income left after taxes and other deductions are taken out of your gross pay. For example, Joshua earns $1,000 a month, but he does not receive the entire amount. After taxes, his take-home pay is $700. Your take-home pay plus your interest earnings on investments and savings is your cash *inflow*.

Some financial experts evaluate the strength of a person's income by measuring **discretionary income**—the money left over after paying for the essentials, such as food, clothing, shelter, transportation, and medication. You can spend this amount at your discretion, or according to your wants. The higher your discretionary income, the better off you are.

WebQuest

One Life to Plan
Learn about different kinds of investments that a financial planner would suggest for a young person planning for college and then beginning a career.

@ To continue with Task 4 of your WebQuest project, visit **finance07.glencoe.com**.

STEP 2: Record Your Expenses

Expenses can be fixed or variable. Fixed expenses are those that are more or less the same each month. Cable television charges, rent, and bus fare for commuting to work or school are all examples of fixed expenses. Variable expenses may change from month to month. Food and clothing are variable expenses. During some months you may need to buy new sweaters and pants, but during other months, you may not buy any clothing. Electricity, medical costs, and recreation are also examples of variable expenses. The total of your fixed and variable expenses is your cash *outflow*.

Answer $384 − $125 = $259. You have a positive cash flow of $259.

GO FIGURE FINANCIAL MATH

NET CASH FLOW

Synopsis: Computing your net cash flow will help you determine your financial health.

Example: What is Jason's net cash flow if his income for the month is $1,500 and his expenses add up to $1,350?

Formula: Income − Expenses = Net Cash Flow

Solution: $1,500 − $1,350 = $150.

Jason has a positive net cash flow of $150.

YOU FIGURE

You work 12 hours a week, 3 weeks a month, at a part-time job after school. You get $8 an hour. You pay $40 a month for gas, $60 a month for entertainment (CDs, movies, etc.), and $25 a month toward paying off your new skis. What is your net cash flow?

Critical Thinking Have students prepare graphic demonstrations as follows: Students who had a negative net cash flow are to graphically plan to change that; students who had a positive net cash flow are to graphically demonstrate how they achieved it. Students may use graphs, charts, pictures, or any graphic device they choose.

STEP 3: Determine Your Net Cash Flow

You can determine your net cash flow by subtracting your expenses from your income.

Because Jason's net cash flow is positive, he has a **surplus**—extra money that can be spent or saved, depending on a person's financial goals and values. A cash surplus can be placed in an emergency fund savings account for unexpected expenses or to pay living costs if you do not receive a salary. You might also place cash surplus in savings and investment plans.

If Jason's net cash flow were negative, however, he would have a deficit. A **deficit** is the financial situation that occurs when more money is spent than is earned or received.

A current and accurate cash flow statement can provide the foundation for preparing and implementing your spending, savings, and investment plans.

Figure 3.4 Evaluating Your Financial Progress

Ratio	Calculation	Example	Meaning
Debt ratio	Liabilities divided by net worth	$25,000 ÷ $50,000 = 0.5	Compares your liabilities to your net worth. A low debt ratio is desirable.
Liquidity ratio	Liquid assets divided by monthly expenses	$10,000 ÷ $4,000 = 2.5	Indicates number of months you would be able to pay your living expenses in case of a financial emergency, such as the loss of your job. The higher the liquidity ratio, the better.
Debt-payments ratio	Monthly credit payments divided by take-home pay	$540 ÷ $3,600 = 0.15 = 15%	Indicates how much of a person's earnings goes to pay debts (excluding a home mortgage). Most financial experts recommend a debt-payments ratio of less than 20 percent.
Savings ratio	Amount saved each month divided by gross monthly income	$600 ÷ $5,000 = 0.12 = 12%	Most financial experts recommend a savings ratio of at least 10 percent.

Expert Advice You can check your financial progress by figuring different ratios.

Suppose that you earned $2,200 gross monthly income and you were paid twice a month. What would be your savings ratio if you saved approximately $60 from each paycheck? Would you be saving enough?

Caption Answer Your savings ratio would be .05, or 5%. No, you should be saving 10% or more.

Your Financial Position

How do you calculate your net worth by using personal financial statements?

When your net cash flow changes, so does your net worth. Every time you create a deficit by spending more than you earn, your net worth decreases. To make up for the deficit, you can either borrow money (increasing your liabilities) or draw from your savings (decreasing your assets). In either case, your net worth declines.

On the other hand, if you end a month with a surplus, your net worth will probably go up. You can choose to save the money, adding to your assets, or you can use it to pay off previous debts and reduce your liabilities. Whichever path you select, your net worth will increase. As a general rule, if you have a surplus cash flow, your net worth increases; if you have a deficit, your net worth decreases.

However, net worth does not give you a completely accurate picture of your finances. You can use your balance sheet and cash flow statement to determine your financial situation in other ways as well. See **Figure 3.4** for details.

Section 3.2 Assessment

See the Teacher Manual for answers.

QUICK CHECK

1. How do you calculate your net worth when preparing a balance sheet?
2. How should you record your income on a cash flow statement?
3. If your personal financial statements indicate that you have a deficit, what might you do to change your financial situation?

THINK CRITICALLY

4. List the three most valuable items that you own that would fall into the category of personal possessions.

USE MATH SKILLS

5. **Finding the Net** Tameka's income for the month of January was $2,375. Her fixed expenses during that same month were $750, and her variable expenses totaled $1,750.

Calculate What was Tameka's net cash flow during the month of January? Be sure to indicate whether she had a surplus or a deficit.

SOLVE MONEY PROBLEMS

6. **Spending Wisely** Larry's personal balance sheet shows $1,200 in credit card debts; a savings account of $550; and personal property amounting to $3,700 in rare stamps. Recently he was promoted at his part-time job. Because of that and because he made an effort to reduce his expenses, he had a positive cash flow of $600 last month. He asks what you think he should do with the surplus cash.

Present Evaluate Larry's possible choices and come up with a specific plan of action for his use of the surplus.

Section 3.3

Focus on Reading

Read to Learn

- How to identify the steps of creating a personal budget.
- How to discuss the advantage of increasing your savings.

Main Idea

Learn to budget and achieve financial goals by increasing your savings.

Key Terms

- budget
- consumer price index (CPI)
- budget variance

Before You Read

PREDICT

What is your definition of a budget, and what are the advantages of using one?

Springboard Ask the students if any of them currently use a budget (most will say "no"). Then ask if their parents have ever turned down a request to buy something by saying, "It's not in our budget." Discuss when they began to understand what that meant.

Budgeting for Financial Goals

Preparing a Practical Budget

What is so important about having a budget?

A **budget** is a plan for using money to meet wants and needs. Having a budget is necessary for successful financial planning. By using a budget, you will learn how to live within your income and how to spend your money wisely. You will also develop good money management skills that will help you reach your financial goals.

STEP 1: Set Your Financial Goals

As discussed in Chapter 1, your financial goals are the things you want to accomplish with your money. What you do with your money today will affect your ability to achieve your financial goals in the future. To meet those financial goals, you will need to plan your savings, your spending, and your investments.

How should you set your financial goals? That depends on your lifestyle, your values, and your hopes for the future. The type of job you choose will determine your income and your ability to save to reach your financial goals. For example, perhaps you would like to get a pilot's license after you graduate from college. When setting your financial goals, you will need to take into account the cost of the lessons and the amount of time it will take to obtain the license.

It is important to make your financial goals as specific as possible. Having a definite time frame can also help you achieve your goals. You can separate your goals into short-term, intermediate, and long-term goals.

STEP 2: Estimate Your Income

When you have set your goals, you can begin working on a budget that is practical for you. Start by recording your estimated income for the next month. Include all sources of income that you know you will be receiving, such as your take-home pay and income on investments and savings. Do not include money you may or may not get, such as bonuses and gifts.

Estimating income is easier in some cases than in others. For example, because Ryan always works 12 hours each week, he gets paid the same amount every month. In contrast, Rachel works irregular hours at two part-time jobs. During some weeks, she earns only $75, but there are weeks when her earnings are more. Rachel should estimate her income based on her best guess about what will happen in the coming month. She might make her estimate a little lower than she thinks it will actually be. That will help her avoid overspending.

In another example, in **Figure 3.5** on page 76, the Thompsons have estimated that their income for next month will be $3,550. Estimate your income and record that amount, using a similar budget form. Remember that a budget should always be a written document.

STEP 3: Budget for Unexpected Expenses

The Thompsons have decided to put aside a little money each month for unexpected expenses and savings to reach their financial goals. Every month they place $100 in an emergency fund. One of their financial goals is to save three to six months' worth of living expenses in case someone in the family becomes unemployed, needs medical attention, or encounters some other financial problem. They keep their emergency fund in a separate savings account that will earn interest.

The Thompsons are also trying to meet three other financial goals, some short-term, others long-term. They deposit money in their vacation fund each month, hoping that they will soon have enough to take a trip to Jamaica. They also have a college fund for their young children and an investment fund to buy stocks. They put $150 into these other special savings accounts each month, bringing their total monthly savings to $250.

STEP 4: Budget for Fixed Expenses

The Thompsons then list all their monthly expenses. They start by listing their fixed expenses, or those that do not change from month to month. That includes their mortgage, automobile and student loan payments, and insurance premiums. Their budgeted total for fixed payments totals $1,200.

STEP 5: Budget for Variable Expenses

Planning for variable expenses—those that vary from month to month—is not as easy as budgeting for fixed expenses. Such items as medical costs are often unexpected. Heating and cooling costs can vary with the season. You should make your best guesses based on costs from previous months. When in doubt, guess high. The Thompsons budgeted $2,100 for these variable expenses.

Academic Connection

HISTORY

By 1865, approximately one-third of all circulating currency was counterfeit. As a result, the Department of the Treasury established the United States Secret Service in an effort to control counterfeiting. Just as it is important that the government manages the distribution of currency and tracks down counterfeiters, it is important that you properly manage your money. *Why is setting financial goals such an essential part of good money management?*

See the Teacher Manual for answer.

Motivating Students Ask students if they would like to know how to make their money go further and last longer. Discuss with them how budgeting makes their money more available to them and easier to manage; hence, they can better achieve their financial goals.

As You Read

RELATE

Do you think you should have an emergency fund? How large do you think your fund should be?

Figure 3.5 The Monthly Budget

Step 1: Set Financial Goals — **Financial Goals:** Pay off car loan, save for college, take vacation trip, and increase investments

Step 6: Record What You Spend

	Budgeted Amounts	Actual Amounts	Variance
Step 2: Estimate Your Income — **Income:**			
Salary and interest income	$3,550	$3,550	–
Outflows:			
Step 3: Budget for Unexpected Expenses and Savings — **Unexpected Expenses and Savings**			
Emergency fund savings	100	100	–
Vacation savings	30	30	–
College savings	70	70	–
Investment savings	50	50	–
Total savings	250	250	–
Step 4: Budget for Fixed Expenses — **Fixed Expenses**			
Mortgage	700	700	–
Automobile loan	200	200	–
Student loan	150	150	–
Insurance premiums	150	150	–
Total fixed expenses	1,200	1,200	–
Step 5: Budget for Variable Expenses — **Variable Expenses**			
Food	500	600	−100
Clothing	250	250	–
Utilities	250	250	–
Entertainment	200	150	+50
Medical	250	250	–
Transportation	450	450	–
Personal allowances	200	225	−25
Total variable expenses	2,100	2,175	−75
Total outflow	**$3,550**	**$3,625**	**−$75**

Step 7: Review Spending and Saving Patterns

Keeping Track You can use this sample monthly budget form to keep track of your own income and expenses so you can manage your finances and reach goals.

In this sample, how might the Thompsons' budget be affected if they had to buy a second automobile?

Caption Answer
They would need to revise their budget to allow for another car payment, and their total outflow would increase.

How can you determine reasonable expense levels? Financial experts publish guidelines that tell what percentage of income should go for various expenses. The U.S. Department of Labor produces the **consumer price index (CPI),** which is a measure of the changes in prices for commonly purchased goods and services in the United States. Comparing the CPI to your actual budget can indicate when you are spending too much on various items. A third source of information is your friends and relatives. If you eat out more often than your friends do or buy more clothes than your siblings buy, your budget may be in trouble.

STEP 6: Record What You Spend

Your budget is prepared, but your work is still incomplete. You must begin to keep track of your actual income and expenses. Remember, many budgeted items are only guesses. Your old car may continue to run through the month. However, maybe it will break down next week and need $400 worth of repairs. To find out how practical your budget is, you will need to keep track of your expenses during an entire month and then revise your budget if necessary.

In **Figure 3.5,** the Thompsons have used a second column to record the actual amounts they spent. Some of their expenses were what they had expected, and some were not. Your spending will not always work out as planned. The **budget variance** is the difference between the budgeted amount and the actual amount that you spend. This figure can be either a surplus or a deficit. It is a surplus if you spend less money than you had expected, and it is a deficit if you spend more. Budget variances can also occur in the income category. Earning more than you anticipated creates a surplus, whereas earning less results in a deficit.

Although the Thompsons have no budget variance on the income side, they have a surplus in their expense section. They spent $50 less than they had expected they would spend on entertainment. However, they spent more than they had budgeted in the other variable expense categories, creating a deficit in those categories. The overall result was a total monthly deficit of $75.

STEP 7: Review Spending and Saving Patterns

Budgeting is a continual process. You may need to review your budget each month and consider making changes based on the nature of your expenses.

Reviewing Financial Progress If you fall behind on bill payments, or if you are left with a lot of money at the end of the month, you may need to revise your budget. Even if your budget generally seems to be on target, it is a good idea to prepare an occasional budget summary to review your progress. (See **Figure 3.6** on page 78.)

$avvy Saver

Have Fun for Less

1. Rent movie videos or DVDs or go to a matinee with friends.
2. Call a museum; many offer free admission one day a month.
3. Check with your local parks for free music concerts.
4. Volunteer as an usher at a theater to see plays and concerts for free.
5. Look in your newspaper's calendar section for free events.

Critical Thinking Have the students discuss, in groups of four, situations that might occur today in which they would need an emergency fund. For each situation, they should try to assess how large a fund they would require. Then they are to discuss emergency situations that could occur in ten years, and how much money they would require. Ask them to assess what is different between now and then.

Question Answer Accept all reasonable answers that demonstrate an understanding of the concept.

As You Read

QUESTION

Prepare a written monthly budget according to Steps 1 to 7. How well does your budget match your financial goals?

Figure 3.6 A Budget Summary

You can prepare an annual budget summary to compare your actual spending with the amounts that you have budgeted. Completing an annual budget summary will be vital to both successful short-term money management and long-term financial security.

1 **Create** your own monthly budget document.

2 **Record** what you spend in each category of your budget during a period of several months.

3 **Highlight** areas where your spending consistently goes over your budget. Also highlight areas where you have spent less than you budgeted. This will help you identify the changes you need to make in your budget.

Revising Goals and Adjusting Your Budget If you always have deficits, ask yourself where you can cut your expenses. Review your spending patterns carefully to see where the shortfalls occur. Could you rent videos instead of going to the movie theater every week? Could you take a bag lunch to school instead of buying cafeteria food? Perhaps you do not really need a car to get around. Doing without it might sometimes be inconvenient, but it certainly would be cheaper.

To decide which expenses to cut, you might take another look at your financial goals. Which purchases fit into your overall plan for the future? The answer can help you in deciding what to cut. How quickly are you progressing toward your objectives? Are your goals changing or outdated? It may be necessary to revise your goals to meet your needs.

Teaching Activity Tell the students that in order to set meaningful financial goals, they need to predict where they think they will be in ten years. Have them write scenarios detailing where they hope to be regarding their jobs and lifestyles. They are to conclude by establishing financial goals to reach this status. Have students share their scenarios and goals with the class.

How to Budget Successfully

How can you plan a good budget?

Simply preparing a budget will not solve your financial problems, nor will keeping track of every expense down to the last penny. You have to follow a practical spending plan to make it work.

Money management experts agree that a budget should have several important characteristics:

1. **A good budget is carefully planned.** Your estimates cannot be wild guesses, and your spending categories must cover all expenses.
2. **A good budget is practical.** If your first full-time job pays you $1,500 a month, do not expect to buy an expensive sports car soon.
3. **A good budget is flexible.** As you experience changes in your life—marriage, children, or retirement—you will need to adapt your budget accordingly. You will also encounter unexpected expenses and unexpected shifts in income. Your budget should be easy to revise when life changes such as these occur.
4. **A good budget must be written and easily accessible.** Use a notebook, folder, or computer to store your budget. Do not try to keep the information in your head or on loose scraps of paper. The odds are you will forget or lose the information.

See the Teacher Manual for answer.

STANDARD &POOR'S

Put on Your Financial Planner's Cap

Your client has just started his first full-time job and needs to revise his budget to reflect the new income. What expense categories will you suggest to change?

Ways to Increase Your Savings

Why is it important to have a savings plan?

Increasing your savings is the key to establishing a sound financial future. The more you save, the better you will be able to handle unexpected emergencies and the sooner you will be able to meet your financial goals. If you save large amounts, it may be possible for you to retire comfortably and to send your children to college. Best of all, money that is saved earns interest income.

Teaching Activity Have the students prepare personal budgets for today's use.

However, learning to save is not easy. Many people are tempted to buy whatever they want, whenever they want it. Moreover, when income is low, saving anything at all can be especially hard. From 1996 to 2001, Americans saved an average of only 31 cents for every ten dollars they earned. Fortunately, you can improve your savings rate by using several savings strategies.

STANDARD &POOR'S

Global Financial Landscape

Standard and Poor's publishes the globally recognized S&P 500® financial index. It also gathers financial statistics, information, and news, and analyzes this data for international businesses, governments, and individuals to help them guide their financial decisions.

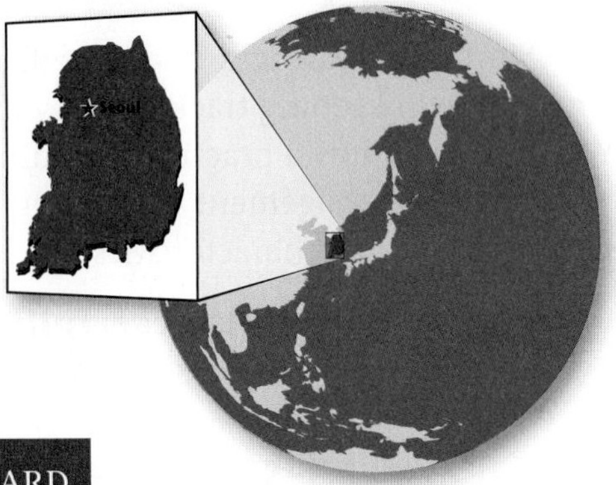

SOUTH KOREA

In the last half-century, South Korea has grown into one of the world's leading high-tech economies. This success is due in large part to the Korean peoples' willingness to spend great amounts of time and money on education. Fierce competition to attend the country's best colleges and universities has developed. As a result, there is an extremely high demand for private tutoring, "cram schools," pre-testing services for college entrance exams, and educational sites on the Internet. Children as young as two can receive 20 minutes of weekly instruction in Korean, English, and math. This type of extra schooling does not come cheap. In a single year, Koreans pay more than $25 billion for after-school instruction. Parents may spend as much as $36,000 on each child per year, as Koreans compete for a position in the global landscape.

STANDARD &POOR'S **DATABYTES**

Capital	Seoul
Population	47,939,000
Languages	Korean, English
Currency	South Korean won
Gross Domestic Product (GDP)	$855.3 billion (2003 est.)
GDP per capita	$17,700

Industry: Electronics, automobile production, chemicals, shipbuilding, steel, and textiles

Agriculture: Rice, root crops, barley, vegetables, cattle, and fish

Exports: Electronic products, machinery and equipment, motor vehicles, steel, ships, and textiles

Natural Resources: Coal, tungsten, graphite, and molybdenum

Think Globally
Why do you think education has been such an important part in South Korea's growth into a high-tech economic leader?

See the Teacher Manual for answer.

Document Detective

Learn to identify and understand the standard financial documents you will use in the real world.

See the Teacher Manual for answers.

Investigate: A Personal Balance Sheet
A personal balance sheet contains the following information:

- Your assets with a value for each
- Your liabilities with a value for each
- Amount of your net worth

Your Motive: A balance sheet shows your financial health at a given point in time. Updating your personal balance sheet from time to time will help you keep track of your financial situation.

Tanisha Brigg's Personal Balance Sheet

Assets	Amount
Cash/Checking & Savings	$3,000
Securities (stocks, bonds, etc.)	15,000
Real estate/home	125,000
Other real estate	0
Automobiles	18,000
Personal property	23,000
Personal loans	5,000
Insurance cash values	15,000
Total Assets	$204,000
Liabilities	
Loans	$ 3,500
Credit card debt	6,500
Current monthly bills	2,500
Mortgage	145,000
Unpaid taxes	4,500
Other debt	2,300
Total Liabilities	$164,300
NET WORTH	$39,700

Key Points: A balance sheet lists the items of value that you own, the debts that you owe, and your net worth. Personal financial statements such as a personal balance sheet can help you determine what you own and what you owe; measure your progress toward your financial goals; track your financial activities; and organize information for taxes and credit applications.

Find the Solutions

1. What are Tanisha's assets?
2. What are Tanisha's liabilities?
3. According to the balance sheet, what is Tanisha's current net worth?
4. Why might a bank be interested in a person's net worth?
5. How do you figure net worth?

▶ **SAVE** Bringing your lunch to school or work is one way to spend less money than you would by eating out. *On an average day, how much money do you spend on food? How might you save in this area?*

Caption Answer Answers will vary. Buying larger quantities of snacks at the grocery store and packing some each day is less expensive than buying from vending machines. Eat meals prepared at home instead of eating out at least one more day per week.

Common Cents The interest rate is always printed on the statement from the credit card company, Alternatively, you can call the company's customer service number (usually found on the back of the credit card) and inquire.

Common CENTS

Pay or Save?

Be a smart consumer and pay off your credit card bills before you put money away in a savings account. The interest rate charged on credit cards is usually higher than the interest you can earn from your savings account. *How do you determine the interest rate on your credit card?*

Pay Yourself First

One method you can adopt is to set aside a fixed amount as savings before you sit down to pay your bills. For example, Tyronne considers his savings as a fixed expense. He writes himself a check for $75 before he pays his bills; then he sends the check for immediate deposit into his savings account. As an alternative to writing a check each month, many banks will automatically deduct a certain amount from your checking account each month and deposit that in your savings account. Tyronne has set a specific dollar amount, but you can also set aside a percentage of your monthly income.

Payroll Savings

Your employer may offer a similar option called a payroll savings deduction. A payroll savings deduction is a portion of your earnings that is automatically taken out of your paycheck and put into your savings or retirement account.

For example, Teresa has authorized her employer to deduct $50 from each paycheck. Although that arrangement reduces her take-home pay to $750, she knows she is on her way to meeting her financial goals.

Spending Less to Save

A third way to save is to start small. Make an effort to spend less each day. If you read a magazine in the library rather than buying it in a store, count out the purchase price of the magazine and place it in a jar. If you go to the $4.50 matinee movie instead of the $7.75 evening show, pat yourself on the back and pay the jar the $3.25 difference. Before long you will have enough cash to start a savings account or make a substantial deposit into an existing one.

How you save, though, is less important than the action of saving. The earlier you start, the better. Even small amounts of savings can grow quickly and help you reach your financial goals.

After You Read

REACT

With the information provided in this chapter, would you be able to create a budget and stick to it? Why or why not?

React Answer Accept all reasonable answers that show an understanding of the concept.

Research Divide the students into groups of four, and assign a foreign country to each group. Groups are to research the spending and saving habits of people in that country as well as their use of credit cards and how they make large purchases, such as houses or cars.

Section 3.3 Assessment

See the Teacher Manual for answers.

QUICK CHECK

1. What are some practical ways to budget for variable expenses?
2. If you continually experience budget deficits, how can you decide which expenses to cut?
3. What are three methods you might use to increase your savings?

THINK CRITICALLY

4. List three of your variable expenses. Estimate the amounts for each of these expenses for one month.

USE COMMUNICATION SKILLS

5. **No Cuts!** Tara complains that she cannot seem to get ahead financially. Every time she receives a paycheck, it seems to disappear. She also points out that all her expenses, such as her phone bill, car payment, and subscriptions to several magazines, are absolutely necessary.

Write About It Write a paragraph persuading Tara that cutting some of her expenses is not only possible but is also necessary if she wants to meet her financial goals.

SOLVE MONEY PROBLEMS

6. **Budgets** Hiroko earns $2,000 a month. Her monthly expenses are about $1,850, leaving $150 for savings. She now has $1,000 in her emergency savings account and another $300 in an account for a new computer. Hiroko has been offered a job that will pay her an extra $200 a month, but she will need to buy a car to travel to the new job.

Analyze What financial factors should Hiroko consider as she decides whether to accept the job?

Chapter 3 Review & Activities

See the Teacher Manual for answers.

CHAPTER SUMMARY

- There are opportunity costs, or trade-offs, in all decisions. When you make a decision about how to manage your money, you remove the option to use the money in a different way.
- Organizing your financial documents makes it easier to plan and measure progress, handle routine money matters, know how much money is available, and make effective decisions.
- You can organize financial documents in home files, a safe-deposit box, and on a computer.
- A personal balance sheet helps determine your net worth, so you can manage your money to meet your financial goals. A personal cash flow statement helps determine the amount of cash you receive and how you spend it.
- On a personal balance sheet, list the value of all your assets, along with all your liabilities. On a personal cash flow statement, record your income and expenses. Then subtract your expenses from your income to determine your net cash flow.
- To create a budget: (1) Set financial goals; (2) estimate your income; 3) budget for unexpected expenses and savings; 4) budget for fixed expenses; (5) budget for variable expenses; (6) record what you spend; and (7) review your spending and saving patterns.
- Savings are the key to a sound financial future. Savings enable you to handle unexpected emergencies.

Communicating Key Terms

Your best friend has asked you to explain how much he needs to save from each paycheck to buy a digital camera that costs $350. Use 8 to 12 of the terms below to write an explanation.

- money management
- safe-deposit box
- personal financial statement
- personal balance sheet
- net worth
- assets
- wealth
- liquid assets
- real estate
- market value
- liabilities
- insolvency
- cash flow
- income
- take-home pay
- discretionary income
- surplus
- deficit
- budget
- consumer price index (CPI)
- budget variance

Reviewing Key Concepts

1. **List** at least three examples from your own experience of opportunity costs.
2. **Explain** the benefits of keeping and organizing financial records and documents.
3. **Identify** documents to store in home files, safe-deposit boxes, or on a computer.
4. **Describe** what you learn from a balance sheet and personal cash flow statement.
5. **List** the steps in preparing a personal balance sheet and a personal cash flow statement.
6. **Identify** the steps in preparing a personal budget.
7. **Explain** how you can use your budget to identify ways to increase your savings.

See the Teacher Manual for answers.

ACADEMIC SKILLS

Social Studies Many people have difficulty saving money for a variety of reasons. Research some typical roadblocks to saving money.

Write About It Write a paragraph explaining at least three reasons and how you would counsel them if they asked you for help.

YOUR FINANCIAL FIGURES

Saving for a Club Trip The school Spanish Club is sponsoring a trip to Mexico that will cost $1,000 per student. Your parents will contribute $300, but you need to save the remaining $700 over the next four months. You currently work seven hours a week babysitting for $10 per hour. The following are your monthly expenses:

Variable Expenses (clothes, CDs, movie tickets, etc.)	$180
Fixed Expenses (school fees, bus pass)	$65

1. **Calculate** your total monthly earnings and expenses.
2. **Compute** by using spreadsheet software to calculate how much you need to earn and/or reduce your expenses to meet your goal.

REAL-WORLD Application

Connect with Mathematics You want to save $2,000 for college by working over the summer. You can find a job that will pay you for 40 hours per week at regular rates plus an average of 10 hours per week at overtime rates at 1.5 times. You can work for 10 weeks. You figure that you need $150 per week to pay miscellaneous variable expenses.

1. **Calculate** How much will you need to earn per hour to save at least $2,000 in addition to meeting your weekly expenses?
2. **Think Critically** Is $150 in weekly expenses a realistic estimate? What are you not including?

Internet CONNECTION

How Much Is Enough? You have started a job at an annual salary of $32,000. Your take-home pay is about 2/3 of your gross salary.

Log On Use an Internet search engine to find Web sites that discuss what proportion of your salary you should spend on fixed expenses. Answer the following questions:

1. What percentage of your take-home pay should be fixed expenses?
2. What percentage of your take-home pay should be discretionary income?

BusinessWeek ONLINE

Newsclip: Ways to Save Best-selling personal finance authors advise finding ways to save by cutting small luxuries and saving money from summer jobs.

Log On Go to **finance07.glencoe.com** and open Chapter 3. Read the article. Then make a record of expenses. Ask yourself: What are your spending and saving habits?

Accept all reasonable answers that show student effort and an understanding of the concept.

WHAT'S YOUR FINANCIAL ID?

MONEY MANAGEMENT QUIZ

Imagine you were living on your own. How would you handle your money? On a separate sheet of paper, take this money management quiz.

1. I would create a budget for my income and expenses.
   a. Always
   b. Sometimes
   c. Never

2. I would pay the rent or mortgage payment and utility bills on time.
   a. Always
   b. Sometimes
   c. Never

3. I would keep three months of my living expenses in reserve for emergencies.
   a. Always
   b. Sometimes
   c. Never

4. I would save 10 percent of my take-home pay.
   a. Always
   b. Sometimes
   c. Never

5. I would set money aside for large expenses.
   a. Always
   b. Sometimes
   c. Never

6. I would save to buy what I want.
   a. Always
   b. Sometimes
   c. Never

7. I would use credit only when I have money to cover the charge.
   a. Always
   b. Sometimes
   c. Never

8. I would balance my checkbook every month.
   a. Always
   b. Sometimes
   c. Never

How did you score? Give yourself 2 points for each "Always," 1 point for each "Sometimes," and 0 points for each "Never."
If you scored 12–16, you are practicing good money management skills.
If you scored 6–11, with a little more effort you could improve your money management skills.
If you scored 0–5, it is time to start developing money management skills.

Your Financial Portfolio

What Is Your Net Worth?

Roberto plans to go to Europe next summer with the school band. He probably will be able to save enough money by working all year at his part-time job. However, he is prepared to sell some of his possessions if he needs to, so he made a list of his assets and liabilities to determine his net worth.

Roberto's Balance Sheet as of December 31, 20--

Liquid Assets	
Checking account balance	$150
Savings accounts	635
Total liquid assets	$785
Personal Possessions	
Market value of automobile	$2,300
Stereo, TV, and video equipment	1,600
Computer	1,350
Watch	330
Total personal possessions	$5,580
Investment Assets	
Savings bonds	$ 600
Total investment assets	600
Total Assets	**$6,965**
Liabilities	
Balance due on car loan	$1,527
Total Liabilities	**$1,527**
Net Worth	**$5,438**

Calculate

Determine your net worth. In your workbook or on a separate sheet of paper, list your assets, personal possessions, and liabilities (what you owe). Are you surprised that your net worth is as much (or as little) as it is? How much would you like your net worth to be in ten years? When you retire? Accept all reasonable answers that show student effort and an understanding of the concept.

CHAPTER 4

Consumer Purchasing and Protection

$ What You'll Learn

When you have completed this chapter, you will be able to:

Section 4.1
- Determine the factors that influence buying decisions.
- Explain a research-based approach to buying goods and services.
- Identify strategies for making wise buying decisions.

Section 4.2
- Identify ways to solve consumer problems.
- Describe the legal alternatives for consumers.

Reading Strategies

To get the most out of your reading:

Predict what you will learn in this chapter.
Relate what you read to your own life.
Question what you are reading to be sure you understand.
React to what you have read.

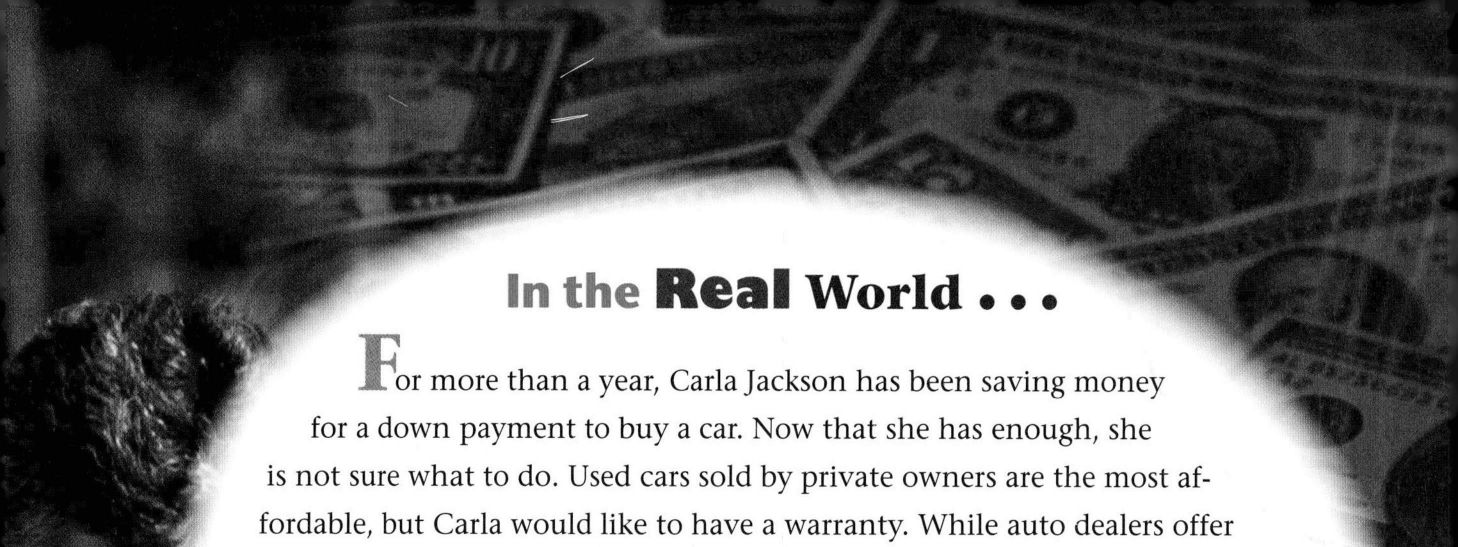

In the Real World . . .

For more than a year, Carla Jackson has been saving money for a down payment to buy a car. Now that she has enough, she is not sure what to do. Used cars sold by private owners are the most affordable, but Carla would like to have a warranty. While auto dealers offer financing, they do not sell the model that she wants. Everyone seems to have a different opinion about where to buy a car, and Carla is unsure about what to believe. In addition, when she decides where to buy the car, Carla is faced with other dilemmas: How much money should she put down? If the car ends up being a "lemon," how can she protect her investment?

As You Read *Consider the safest strategy for a consumer who is making a major purchase and what protection he or she can expect.*

Lesson Plan See the Teacher Manual for the Chapter 4 planning guide and lesson plan.

ASK STANDARD & POOR'S

Comparison Shopping

Q: I would like to purchase a new stereo. Is it really that important for me to comparison shop?

A: Prices and quality can be very different from one store to another. Particularly with expensive items, it is worthwhile to compare prices on similar items to see if one store has a lower price than the others. If you write down the manufacturer and style information, you can do a lot of this "legwork" by phone or by looking at store advertisements or by doing research on the Internet.

Ask Yourself What is the benefit of comparison shopping?

@ Go to **finance07.glencoe.com** to complete the Standard & Poor's Financial Focus activity.

Section 4.1

Consumer Purchasing

Focus on Reading

Read to Learn

- How to determine the factors that influence buying decisions.
- How to explain a research-based approach to buying goods and services.
- How to identify strategies for making wise buying decisions.

Main Idea

Understanding the factors that influence your buying decisions will help you get the best value for your money.

Key Terms

- down payment
- cooperative
- impulse buying
- open dating
- unit pricing
- rebate
- warranty
- service contract

Before You Read

PREDICT

How could learning about consumer purchasing benefit you now and in the future?

Factors That Influence Buying Decisions

What influences you to make a purchase?

You may enjoy shopping and do it often, or you might go to the mall only if you need to buy something. In either case, wise buying decisions will help you get the most out of the products you buy now and will enable you to meet your long-term financial goals. To get the most for your money, you need to recognize the factors that affect your buying habits. **Figure 4.1** shows some of the economic, social, and personal factors that influence the purchases you make.

The following example shows several of these factors at work. Jessica is thinking about buying a new backpack. Economic factors will play an important role in her decision. She will be more likely to spend her money on a backpack that is well made but not too expensive and can be repaired easily if it rips. Social factors may also affect Jessica's choice. She may be more likely to buy a certain brand if it is in style and if she could use it for her hobby, painting. In addition, personal factors may be at work. Jessica will have to determine how much of her income she can spend on the backpack.

Trade-Offs and Buying Decisions

To make the most of your buying power, consider trade-offs. Suppose that you buy a sound system with a credit card instead of waiting until you have saved enough money to pay cash for it. You get the pleasure of having the sound system now. However, you may pay a higher price in the long run because of fees and interest the credit card company charges for use of the card.

Perhaps you choose a jacket because it is the cheapest one available. Within a few days, you may discover that it is poorly made or difficult to repair. You may save time by ordering a sweater from a catalog or online. However, if you decide that you do not want it, you may have to pay postage to return it to the mail-order company. You might not get your money back for the initial shipping and handling charges. Keep in mind that buying decisions always involve trade-offs, so you will be prepared to make wise choices.

Researching Consumer Purchases

How do you research a product you want to buy?

By taking time to do research and evaluating products you want to buy, you can get more value for your money. By following a research-based approach to buying goods and services, you can buy a high-priced item, such as a treadmill or a gym membership, more intelligently. In addition, you will gain useful practice in making ordinary purchasing decisions about low-cost items, such as toothpaste. A research-based approach to buying has four phases:

1. Before you shop
2. Weighing alternatives
3. Making the purchase
4. After the purchase

PHASE 1: Before You Shop

Before you can begin to construct the walls of a house, you need to lay its foundation. In the same way, before you begin to shop, you need to do some background work. A good start to successful shopping involves three steps: identifying your needs, gathering information, and becoming aware of the marketplace. Completing these steps will enable you to get what you really want.

As You Read

RELATE

What are the economic, social, and personal factors that would influence you if you were going to buy a car?

Springboard Ask the students if they think they most frequently overpay for goods and services, find bargain rates, or pay average prices. Discuss their buying patterns with them, including whether they get value for the money if they buy apparent bargains.

Motivating Students
Have the students list their purchases for the last two weeks and the approximate amount they paid. Have them ask themselves these questions: "Did I get value for the money spent? Could I have done without this purchase?" Then have them calculate the amount of money they could have saved.

Figure 4.1 **Influences on Consumer Buying Decisions**

Economic Factors	Social Factors	Personal Factors
• Prices • Interest rates • Product quality • Supply and demand • Convenience • Product safety • Brand name • Maintenance costs • Warranty	• Lifestyle • Interests • Hobbies • Friends • Culture • Advertisements • Media (magazines, radio, television, newspapers)	• Gender • Age • Occupation • Income • Education • Family size • Geographic region • Ethnic background • Religion

Making a Difference Economic, social, and personal factors influence consumer buying decisions.

How might a family's size and income affect the type of house the family buys?

Caption Answer A family with children may need more bedrooms, access to good schools, recreation, and shopping; poorer families may have to compromise size and/or location to keep prices down. The wealthy may prefer custom houses in excellent areas.

Critical Thinking Ask the students to carefully consider what motivates them to make purchases. Are they influenced by advertising? Their friends? Their parents? Have them write brief essays explaining and evaluating the influences on them, determining whether these influences lead them to make wise purchasing decisions.

Identify Your Needs Suppose that your VeryKool jeans are worn out, and you would like to buy a new pair. You think that your problem is a "need for a new pair of VeryKool jeans," when the actual problem is a "need for new jeans." Some people always buy Brand A when Brand B sells for the same price. They may not even consider Brand C, which is cheaper than either A or B, and which also serves their needs. If you define your needs clearly, you will be more likely to make the best buying decisions.

Gather Information For example, suppose that Sarah loses her watch on a white-water rafting trip. She might be able to borrow a watch from a friend for a day or two, but eventually she will need to buy a new watch. To begin her research, she should gather information on the different models and prices of watches.

Information for buying decisions usually falls into three categories: costs, options, and consequences. Sarah might ask questions related to cost, such as "What do watches cost at different stores?" Her options will depend on the brands that the manufacturers produce and on where those brands are available. Sarah will also have to consider consequences—how the purchase will affect her budget.

Figure 4.2 **Sources of Consumer Information**

You can gather information to help with purchasing decisions from a number of different sources. Make sure they are reliable, complete, relevant, and impartial.

1 **People** you know might be able to provide insight on a product's performance, quality, and average price.

2 **Ads and packaging** can tell you a lot about a product, so be sure to read the labels.

Some people do not spend enough time gathering and evaluating information. Others do so much research that they become confused and frustrated. Simple, routine purchases probably do not require much more research than your own experience can provide. For more expensive items, ask people you know for recommendations.

Other resources include product advertising and labeling, media sources, consumer publications, such as *Consumer Reports*, government agencies, or the Internet. **Figure 4.2** illustrates some of these resources. As you research and gather information, take notes on what you learn. Having a written record of the information you collect can be helpful in making comparisons later.

Be Aware of the Marketplace Knowledge is power. Research provides sources for the item you want to buy. In addition, you will be able to identify the brands and features from which you can choose, average prices for an item, and where you can obtain reliable information about similar products. Also, familiarize yourself with some common myths about sales, returns, and credits in **Figure 4.3** on page 94.

Teaching Activity Divide students into groups of four, assigning a major purchase to each group: a car, a computer, a music system, a DVD player, a racing bicycle, etc. Have the group thoroughly research a variety of ways to make the purchase and determine the best. The group will then prepare a graphic display of their research results and present it to the class.

3 **Reports** issued by the media and independent testing organizations on the quality of products and services are usually valuable, easily available, and inexpensive.

4 **Web sites** for companies, magazines, newspapers, and government agencies have product information and shopping suggestions.

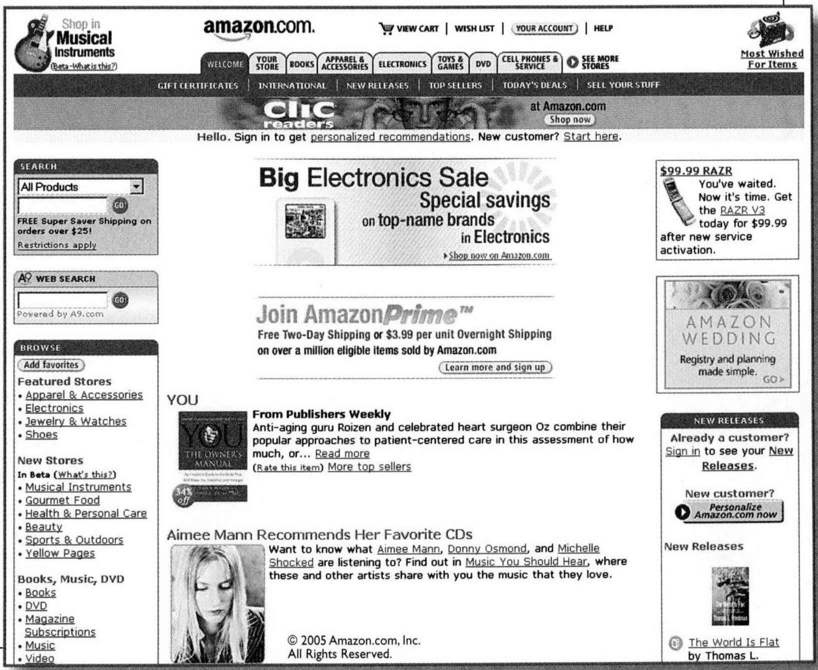

Figure 4.3 Common Consumer Myths

The National Association of Consumer Agency Administrators recently identified a list of common consumer myths. These include:

"I can return my car within three days of purchase." While many people would say that this statement is true, there is no such time period.

"It says right here that I've won; it must be true." Fake prize notifications continue to become more convincing. Some consumers actually go to company offices to try to pick up their prizes.

"If I lose my credit cards, I'm liable for purchases." Federal laws limit charges on lost or stolen cards to $50. Most major credit card companies will not even charge you the $50 if you make a reasonable effort to notify the company quickly of lost or stolen cards.

"An auto lease is just like a rental; if I have problems with the car or problems paying, I can just bring it back." Most leases require payments for the duration of the contract. Early termination of the contract can often result in various additional charges.

"You can't repossess my car; it's on private property." While state laws vary, the general rule is that repossession cannot occur if it involves force or entry into a dwelling. However, vehicles in driveways and unlocked garages are usually fair game.

Source: "Ten Top Consumer Law 'Urban Myths,'" National Association of Consumer Agency Administrators, Two Brentwood Commons, Suite 150, 750 Old Hickory Blvd, TN 37207; (615) 371-6125 or 866-SAY-NACAA; Web site: www.nacaa.net.

Fact or Fiction? There are some typical myths that consumers believe about sales, returns, and credit.

How do such myths affect you as a consumer?

Caption Answer
Such myths may lead to unwise purchasing decisions.

PHASE 2: Weighing the Alternatives

Every consumer decision may be approached in several effective ways. Instead of buying an item, for example, you might decide to rent it, borrow it, or do without it. You also have alternatives to spending cash for a product. You might take advantage of special deals that allow you to delay payment, or you might choose to pay with a credit card.

Identify What Is Important to You As you evaluate alternatives, decide which characteristics of the product—such as features, performance, or design—are important to you. As you research the available brands, you will recognize the characteristics that most closely match your needs. You can judge a potential purchase by considering the following factors:

- Your personal values
- Available time for research
- Amount of money you have to spend
- Convenience of buying the item immediately
- Pros and cons of a particular brand

For example, as Sarah considers the selection of watches in a department store, she decides that a light-up dial and an alarm are two features that she would use. In terms of performance, she prefers a model that can withstand rugged outdoor activities. She wants a watch that has big numbers and a stainless steel wristband.

Compare Prices The price of an item is an important consideration. Prices can vary for all types of products. For example, Sarah's watch may cost as little as $15 or as much as $500. Differences in price may be related to quality, but price does not always equal quality. When the quality and quantity are basically the same for an item such as aspirin, sugar, or salt, the lowest-priced item is probably the wisest choice.

When prices and quality vary, you have two options. If you can afford all choices, you can buy the highest-quality item. If you cannot afford all choices, you should consider buying the item that gives you the best value per dollar.

Do Comparison Shopping Comparison shopping means you compare prices and features of similar items at different stores. Many people consider comparison shopping a waste of time. However, it can be very useful under certain circumstances:

- You are buying complex or expensive items, such as a computer or a mountain bike.
- You are buying items you purchase often, such as shampoo or school supplies.
- You are using the Internet, print advertisements, or mail-order catalogs.
- Different sellers are offering different prices and services.
- Product quality or price varies greatly.

$avvy Saver

Shopping for Clothes

1. Look at the sale items first.
2. Choose clothes that you can mix and match or wear over several seasons.
3. Shop at outlet malls and discount stores, from sale catalogs, and on the Internet.
4. Wait for end-of-season clearance sales.
5. Buy only items you are sure you will wear.

Extension Have the students find advertising in a newspaper, magazine, on the Internet, and on television for a product they are considering buying. They are to write a report discussing what the advertising does (appeal to needs? appeal to wants? provide valuable information on the product? understate problems?), comparing the different media and evaluating usefulness.

▶ **BEST BUYS** Timing your purchases to get the best buys is not limited to clothes. *Why do you think that September, October, and November are the best months to buy apples?*

Caption Answer Apples are in season, so supply is high, driving prices down.

PHASE 3: Making the Purchase

After you have completed the research and evaluation process, some other activities and decisions may be appropriate. These include negotiating the price (if possible), deciding whether to use credit or cash, and determining the real price of the product.

Negotiate the Price Certain purchases, such as real estate or cars, may involve price negotiation. To negotiate, research information about the product and the buying situation. Be sure that you are dealing with the person, such as the owner or store manager, who has authority to give you a lower price or additional features.

Decide on Credit or Cash When making a purchase, you usually have two options—pay credit or cash. You need to consider the costs and benefits of each one.

Credit is an arrangement to buy something now and pay for it later. It is a type of loan. To repay the loan, you make monthly payments that often include additional fees or interest. The advantage of paying cash is that you do not have to pay these extra fees or make continuing payments. However, because the cash is no longer in your bank account, you lose the opportunity to earn interest on it. In addition, the money is no longer available for emergencies.

Before deciding to use credit, evaluate its costs, such as interest rates and fees. These costs will differ depending on various factors:

- Source of the loan (e.g., parents, bank, or credit card company)
- Type of credit account
- Payment period
- Amount of **down payment**—a portion of the total cost of an item that must be paid at the time of purchase

WebQuest

One Life to Plan
Learn about personal inventories and how you can use them to match yourself to the right job, which will be part of your financial plan.

@ To continue with Task 3 of your WebQuest project, visit **finance07.glencoe.com**.

Know the Real Price Sometimes you may discover that what appears to be a bargain is not such a good deal after extra costs are added to the price. Stores may charge you a fee for installation or delivery. Find out exactly what the purchase price includes and get all costs and conditions in writing.

PHASE 4: After the Purchase

After making a purchase, you may have other costs or tasks. A car, for example, will require additional maintenance and ownership costs, such as gasoline and insurance. You may have to learn how to operate it correctly to improve its performance and to avoid major repairs. If your car requires repair service, you should follow a process similar to the one you used when you bought the car—investigate, evaluate, and negotiate a variety of servicing options.

In some cases, you may be dissatisfied with a purchase and want to return or replace it. When that happens, you need to know how to handle your complaints effectively. The next section of this chapter explains how to resolve consumer complaints.

Remember that the purchasing process is an ongoing activity. You should rethink and reevaluate your decisions. The information that you gather before you shop, along with your previous buying experiences, will help you make decisions in the future. Also, be sure to consider changes in your needs, lifestyle, values, goals, and financial resources.

Smart Buying Strategies

How can you make an informed purchase decision?

People have a variety of buying styles. For example, Gordon looks for ways to save on the brands he buys regularly. Anita and Roger buy the lowest-priced brands or look for bargains.

Caption Answer Time your purchases, compare brands and prices, choose the best purchase method and place, and evaluate warranties.

▶ **SMART SHOPPING** To get the best buys, do research about products and do comparison shopping. *What is comparison shopping?*

Whatever your style, several strategies can help you get the most value for your dollar—timing of purchases, store selection, brand comparison, information research, price comparison, and warranty evaluation.

Timing Purchases

You are more likely to find a bargain at certain times of the year. Stores traditionally offer reduced prices for seasonal clothing, such as swimsuits, overcoats, and other items, about midway through a particular season. You can also find reduced prices at back-to-school sales, spring sales, and other special sales. Timing your purchases to take advantage of sales can result in big savings.

The law of supply and demand can also affect the timing of purchases. For example, if you wait a few months before buying a popular new CD or DVD, the price may be lower than it was when it first came out because the demand for the item has decreased. When businesses want to reduce the supply of a product, they have clearance sales.

Figure 4.4 Types of Retailers

	Benefits	Limitations
Traditional Stores		
Department stores	• Wide variety of products grouped by department	• Possible inexperience or limited knowledge of sales staff
Specialty stores	• Wide selection of a specific product line; knowledgeable sales staff	• Prices generally higher; location and shopping hours may not be convenient
Discount stores	• Convenient parking; low prices	• Self-service format; minimal assistance from sales staff
Contemporary Retailers		
Convenience stores	• Convenient location; long hours; fast service	• Prices generally higher than those of other types of retail outlets
Factory outlet	• Brand-name items; low prices	• May offer only "seconds" or "irregulars"; few services; returns may not be allowed
Hypermarket	• Full supermarket combined with general merchandise discount store	• Clerks not likely to offer specialized service or product information
Warehouse, Superstore	• Large quantities of items at discount prices	• May require membership fee; limited services; inventory items may vary

Shop Around Consumers have a choice of many different types of stores, each of which has pros and cons.

How can competition among stores benefit consumers?

Caption Answer Competition results in more choices, better prices, and better service for consumers.

Store Selection

The quality and variety of goods as well as the price at a store may influence your decision to shop there. Store selection may affect the value of the products you purchase. You may also choose a retail store because of its hours, location, reputation, policies, and services such as parking and delivery. **Figure 4.4** provides an overview of the major types of retailers—businesses that sell directly to consumers.

Over the years, several alternatives to store shopping have emerged. One alternative is the **cooperative**, a nonprofit organization owned and operated by its members for the purpose of saving money on the purchase of goods and services. Because a cooperative buys large amounts of goods, it can lower prices for its members. The main drawback to cooperatives is that they offer few customer services.

Another alternative to store shopping is direct selling, which includes mail order, TV home shopping, and online shopping. An advantage of these types of shopping is the convenience of not having to leave home. Online shopping sometimes offers lower prices, and you may find excellent product information on the Internet. The possible disadvantages of online direct selling are paying for shipping and handling, and difficulty in returning purchases.

STANDARD & POOR'S

Put on Your Financial Planner's Cap

Many people prefer the convenience of doing their shopping online. If you were advising a client about buying a car, what would you say are some trade-offs of buying online?

See the Teacher Manual for the answers.

Brand Comparison

Most items are sold under a number of well-known brand names that identify the products and their manufacturers. National-brand products are widely advertised and available in many stores. Although they are usually more expensive than non-brand products, national brands usually offer consistent quality or value for your money.

A store-brand, or generic, product is usually sold by one chain of stores and carries the name of that chain on its label. Examples of these products include paper, canned goods, and dairy foods. Because store-brand products are often made by the same companies that make national-brand products, their quality is good. However, because they do not carry a brand-name label, they are less expensive.

When you compare brands, remember to consider price and quality. Plan what you are going to buy before you shop and take a list of what you need. Displays may attract your attention and lead to **impulse buying**, which is purchasing items on the spur of the moment. Impulse buying may be fun, but it can cost you more. Also, you may buy products that you do not really need.

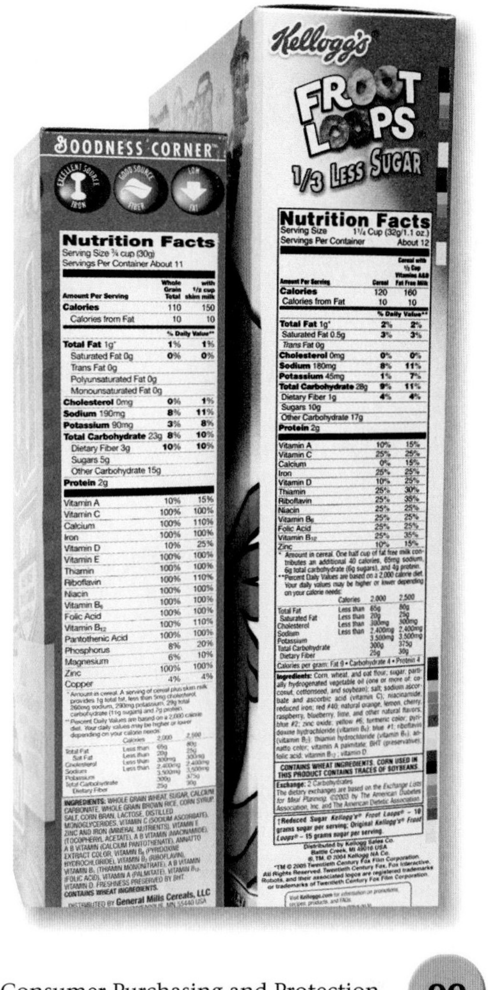

▶ **HONEST BRANDING** Some food labels claim that the product is considered "low in fat" or "light." Foods must meet government criteria to be labeled with such terms. *Why do you think this type of regulation is necessary?*

Caption Answer "Low in Fat" may be accurate only if compared to a high-fat product; "light" or "lite" are vague if not regulated.

Common CENTS

Impulse Buying
Too much impulse buying can ruin a budget. When you are tempted to buy clothes, cool sneakers, CDs, or anything else that you really do not need, give yourself a two-day cool-down period. If you decide you really want it, you can go back to the store and buy it. However, chances are that most things will not seem as necessary a few days later. *How would you plan your budget to allow for some impulse buying?*

Common Cents Some impulse buying can be budgeted for entertainment or recreation; in the same way, the entertainment budget can be lowered and another category created for impulse buying.

Label Information Research

Labels on product packages typically include a great deal of advertising. However, federal laws also require labels to present factual information. For example, food labels must indicate the common name of the product, the name and address of the manufacturer or distributor, the net weight of the product, and a list of the ingredients in decreasing order of weight.

In addition, labels on almost all processed foods must have nutritional information, such as the number of calories in one serving and the specific amounts of nutrients and food substances in the product. Some foods are advertised as being "low in fat" or "light," "low in sodium," or "high in fiber." Foods must meet government criteria to be labeled with such terms. Manufacturers can include health claims on product packages only if they have scientific evidence to support the claims.

To help consumers determine the freshness of some foods, manufacturers print dates on the labels. **Open dating** is a labeling method that indicates the freshness, or shelf life, of a perishable product, such as milk or bread. Labels indicate open dating with phrases such as "Use before May 25, 2008" or "Not to be sold after October 8."

Product labels for appliances, such as refrigerators and washing machines, include information about operating costs, which identify the most energy-efficient models.

Price Comparison

Unit pricing is the use of a standard unit of measurement to compare the prices of packages that are different sizes. For example, Claudia went to the drugstore to buy a bottle of mouthwash and noticed that her favorite brand comes in two sizes at different prices. The best way for her to determine which one is the better buy is to use unit pricing. Most grocery stores and drugstores display the unit pricing information for the products they sell. If a store does not provide this information, you can calculate the unit price by dividing the price of the item by the unit of measurement (weight, volume, or quantity). For example, an 8-ounce can of frozen orange juice that costs $1.60 has a unit price of 20 cents per ounce.

When you know how to calculate the unit price, you can compare the unit prices for various sizes, brands, and stores. Keep in mind that the package with the lowest unit price may not be the best buy for your situation. For example, a 10-pound bag of potatoes might have the lowest unit price; but if you do not eat potatoes often, they may spoil before you can use them.

Two common ways to save money are to take advantage of discount coupons and manufacturers' rebates. By using discount coupons, you save money on products at the time you purchase them. A **rebate** is a partial refund of the price of a product. To obtain a rebate, you usually have to submit a form, the original receipt, and the package's UPC symbol, or bar code.

GO FIGURE — FINANCIAL MATH

UNIT PRICING

Synopsis: Knowing the unit price of an item can help you determine the best buy.

Example: The brand of peppermint mouthwash that Claudia likes is offered in two sizes, 12 ounces for \$2.89 and 16 ounces for \$3.39. Which is the better buy?

Formula: $\frac{\text{Total Price}}{\text{Unit of Measurement}} = \text{Unit Price}$

Solution: $\frac{\$2.89}{12 \text{ oz.}} = \$0.24/\text{oz.}$

$\frac{\$3.39}{16 \text{ oz.}} = \$0.21/\text{oz.}$

The 16-ounce size is the better buy at 21 cents per ounce.

YOU FIGURE

You are considering buying soft drinks for your sister's birthday party. The market is offering a six-pack of 12-ounces for \$2.99 and a liter bottle for \$1.29. Which is the better buy? (Hint: One liter equals 33.8 ounces.)

Answer $6 \times 12 = 72$ ounces; $\$2.99 \div 72 = \$0.042$; $\$1.29 \div 33.8 = \$0.038$. The liter of soda is the better buy.

When comparing prices, the following guidelines can be very helpful:

- More convenience (location, hours, sales staff) usually means higher prices.
- Ready-to-use products (frozen prepared dinners, preassembled toys) usually have higher prices.
- Large packages are usually the best buy; use unit pricing to compare brands, sizes, and stores.
- Buying items "on sale" may not always mean that you save money; the sale price at one store may be higher than the regular price at another store.

Warranty Evaluation

Many products come with a guarantee of quality called a warranty. A **warranty** is a written guarantee from the manufacturer or distributor that states the conditions under which the product can be returned, replaced, or repaired. Federal law requires sellers of products that cost more than \$15 (and that have a warranty) to make the warranty available to customers before purchase. The warranty is often printed directly on the package.

Types of Warranties Warranties are divided into two basic types: implied and express. *Implied warranties* are unwritten guarantees that cover certain aspects of a product or its use. An implied warranty of merchantability guarantees that a product is fit for its intended use. For example, a toaster will toast bread, or a CD player will play CDs.

Document Detective

Learn to identify and understand the standard financial documents you will use in the real world.

See the Teacher Manual for the answers.

Investigate: A Warranty

A warranty for a product contains the following information:

- Name of the seller or manufacturer
- Name of product
- Terms of the warranty
- Instructions for how to get service

Your Motive: Before making a purchase, you should read the product's warranty to understand exactly what protections the manufacturer offers you. A warranty is an assurance from the seller to the buyer that a product will perform as promised, or it will be replaced or repaired.

FREE FLOW® ONE-YEAR LIMITED WARRANTY

FREE FLOW® plumbing fixture, faucets, and fittings are warranted to be free of defects in material and workmanship for one year from date of installation.

Free Flow will, at its election, repair, replace, or make appropriate adjustments where Free Flow inspection discloses any such defects occurring in normal usage within one year after installation. Free Flow is not responsible for removal or installation costs.

To obtain warranty service, contact Free Flow either through your dealer, plumbing contractor, home center or e-tailer, or by writing to Free Flow, Attn: Customer Service Department, 2525 Highland Drive, Glenview, WI 53044, USA.

IMPLIED WARRANTIES INCLUDING THAT OF MERCHANTABILITY AND FITNESS FOR A PARTICULAR PURPOSE ARE EXPRESSLY LIMITED IN DURATION TO THE DURATION OF THIS WARRANTY. FREE FLOW DISCLAIMS ANY LIABILITY FOR SPECIAL, INCIDENTAL, OR CONSEQUENTIAL DAMAGES. Some states/provinces do not allow limitations on how long an implied warranty lasts, or the exclusion or limitation of special, incidental, or consequential damages so these limitations and exclusions may not apply to you. This warranty gives you specific legal rights. You may also have other rights, which vary from state/province to state/province.

This is our exclusive written warranty.

Notes:
1. There may be variation in color fidelity between catalog images and actual plumbing fixtures.
2. Free Flow reserves the right to make changes in product characteristics, packaging, or availability at any time without notice.

Copyright © 2006.

Key Points: A warranty usually covers defects in materials and workmanship, and promises that the product will work properly under normal circumstances. It does not usually cover defects that occur due to the user's carelessness or inappropriate use of the product. It also explains how a buyer can resolve any problems.

Find the Solutions

1. For how many years are Free Flow fixtures covered by this warranty?
2. If you purchased a Free Flow faucet in November of 2006 and installed it in August of 2007, when would the warranty expire?
3. What will Free Flow do if a product is defective?
4. Who is responsible for the cost of removing a defective faucet and replacing it?
5. If a faucet is replaced under this warranty, will it be the same model faucet?

Express warranties, which are usually written, come in two forms. A full warranty states that a defective product will be fixed or replaced at no charge during a reasonable amount of time. A limited warranty covers only certain aspects of the product, such as parts. This type may also require the buyer to pay a portion of the shipping or repair charges.

When you buy a product, you may be offered a **service contract**, which is a separately purchased agreement by the manufacturer or distributor to cover the costs of repairing the item. Service contracts are sometimes called *extended warranties,* but they are not really warranties. You have to pay extra to obtain a service contract. Such contracts are generally offered on large, expensive items, such as cars and home appliances. Sometimes service contracts are not worth the cost.

Smart shoppers know when to buy, where to buy, what to buy, how much to pay, and how to make sure that the products they buy will perform as advertised. In the next section, you will learn some additional rules for smart shoppers: how to resolve consumer complaints and how to use the law to ensure that your rights as a consumer are protected.

As You Read

QUESTION

What research should you do if you are considering buying a used car with a limited warranty? What do you need to consider if a service contract is offered?

Question Answer You need to know what *is* covered and what *is not* covered, so you must research the costs to repair or replace unwarrantied items. You need to know what services the service contract offers and determine if you can have them done for less money than the contract costs.

Section 4.1 Assessment

See the Teacher Manual for answers.

QUICK CHECK

1. What are three economic factors that influence what people buy?
2. Suppose that you are considering buying a pair of in-line skates. What steps might you take before you shop and as you weigh your alternatives?
3. What are at least five strategies followed by smart shoppers.

THINK CRITICALLY

4. Create a scenario in which someone is considering a purchase. Discuss the economic, social, and personal factors that will affect this buying decision.

USE MATH SKILLS

5. **Cat Food Costs** Gilda would do anything for Luna, her 11-year-old cat. Until recently, she had been paying an animal hospital \$22.50 every two weeks for a 10-pound bag of vitamin-enriched organic cat food designed for older cats. On Wednesday, Gilda called a local pet store. The store stocks food similar to the one she buys at the animal hospital, but it is not organic. The store sells 25-pound bags for \$59.55 and 50-pound bags for \$99.50.

Calculate Using the formula for unit pricing, calculate the best buy among the three different-sized bags of cat food. Would the lowest-priced cat food be the best choice? Why or why not?

SOLVE MONEY PROBLEMS

6. **Getting the Best Buy** Marta loves shopping for holiday gifts for her friends and family. This year she started looking for gifts early, in June. She hopes that the extra time will allow her to find the perfect gift for everyone on her shopping list. By shopping early, she might get some good buys.

Write About It Using the information in the section on smart buying strategies, explain how Marta can shop wisely to make the best choices for gifts and get good bargains.

Section 4.2

Focus on Reading

Read to Learn

- How to identify ways to solve consumer problems.
- How to describe the legal alternatives for consumers.

Main Idea

Various methods can solve consumer problems. Legal alternatives are available to consumers.

Key Terms

- fraud
- mediation
- arbitration
- small claims court
- class-action suit
- legal aid society

Before You Read

PREDICT

What would you do if you received a bill for an item you did not buy?

Resolving Consumer Complaints

Sources of Consumer Complaints

What are some examples of consumer complaints?

When you purchase a product, you do not expect to have any problems with it, especially if you have done research and considered the alternatives. Unfortunately, every purchase involves some degree of risk.

Most customer dissatisfaction results from products that are defective or of poor quality. Consumers also complain about unexpected costs, deceptive pricing, and unsatisfactory repair service. Another source of consumer complaints is **fraud**—dishonest business practices that are meant to deceive, trick, or gain an unfair advantage.

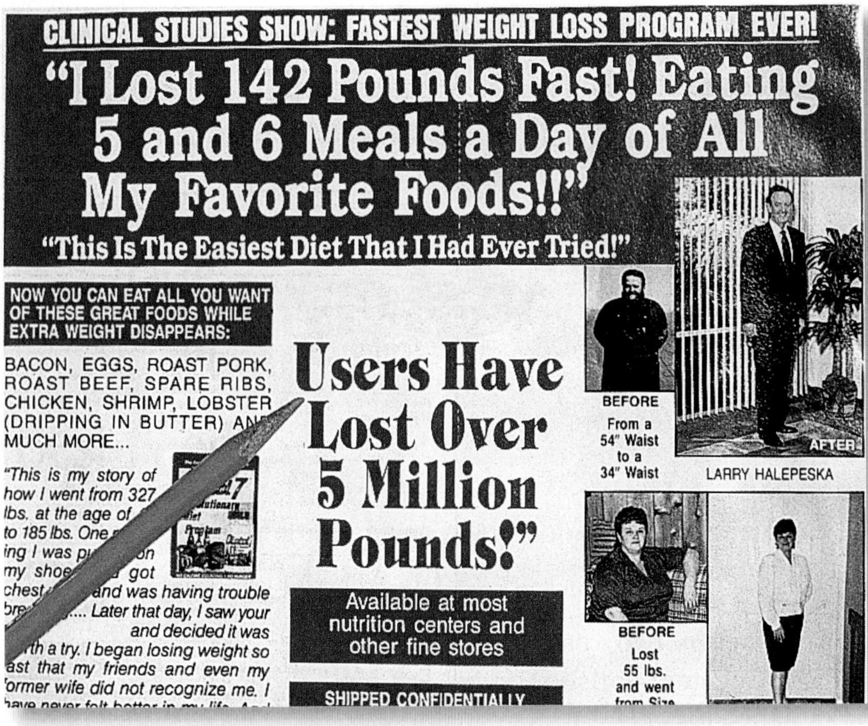

▲ **BUYER BEWARE** Many advertisements appeal to the emotions of consumers. *How might this ad influence someone to buy the product?*

Caption Answer Answers will vary but may address that such ads prey on gullible consumers through emotions.

Common Types of Fraud

Every year millions of consumers become victims of unethical people who use dishonest business practices to trick or cheat buyers. Experts estimate that fraud costs consumers tens of billions of dollars annually.

As a consumer, you must be aware of various types of fraud. Telephone and mail scams may offer you phony free prizes, travel packages, work-at-home schemes, and investment opportunities. Fraudulent diet products and other remedies attract consumers with phrases such as "scientific breakthrough" or "miraculous cure." The best way to protect yourself from consumer fraud is to recognize it before you become a victim—and to report it if you see it happening.

Springboard Ask the students if they have ever purchased products that turned out to be unacceptable and what they were able to do about it.

Motivating Students Have student volunteers tell stories about "worst-case scenarios" either they or members of their families experienced regarding unacceptable purchases. Have the class vote on which situation was worst and which situation(s) could have been resolved.

Resolving Differences Between Buyers and Sellers

What is the best way to resolve a dispute over goods or services?

If you are dissatisfied with a product or service and decide to make a complaint, remember to document the process. Keep a file of receipts, names of people you talk to, dates of attempted repairs, copies of letters you write, and any fees that you have had to pay. Resolving complaints with a business can be handled in five different ways.

Caption Answer Answers should include receipts, names and dates of people you talk to, and copies of letters you write.

▼ BACK TO THE STORE If you have a problem with a product and want to resolve it, remember to document each step you take. *What types of records should you keep?*

As You Read

RELATE

Have you ever been dissatisfied with a purchase? What did you do?

Return to the Place of Purchase

Most consumers can resolve their complaints at the original place of purchase. Most businesses care about having a reputation for honesty and fairness and will usually do what is necessary to settle reasonable complaints. Remember to bring sales receipts and other relevant information. Also, keep calm and avoid yelling or threatening the salespeople or managers. Explain the problem as clearly as possible, and ask them to help you resolve it.

STANDARD & POOR'S

Global Financial Landscape

Standard and Poor's publishes the globally recognized S&P 500® financial index. It also gathers financial statistics, information, and news, and analyzes this data for international businesses, governments, and individuals to help them guide their financial decisions.

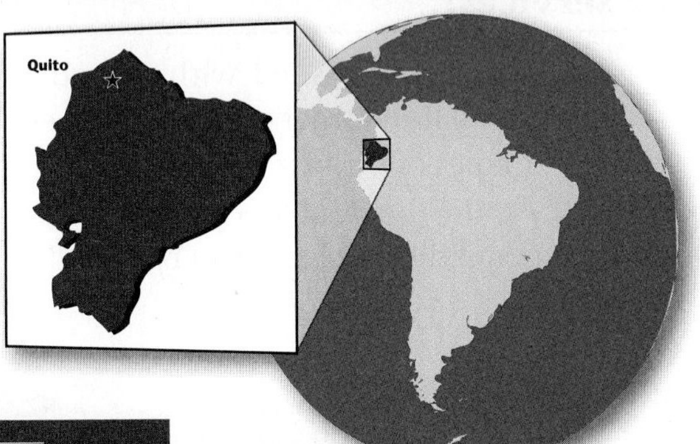

ECUADOR

In 2000, Ecuador became the first country in Latin America to adopt U.S. currency and discontinue using its own—a practice called *dollarization.* Although most nations have their own money, dollarization in Ecuador's case was a last-ditch effort to save the country's collapsing economy. It was hoped that trading Ecuadorian money for the American dollar would improve the country's financial situation. It has—but to greater and lesser degrees. For example, the exchange has lowered inflation but has spurred wage increases only slightly. (Ecuador's minimum wage has grown from $50 to $120 a month.) For now dollarization has set up a stable economic foundation for growth. It was "a life raft," sums up one Ecuadorian economist. "We didn't have many options."

STANDARD & POOR'S **DATABYTES**

Capital	Quito
Population	12,558,000
Languages	Spanish and Quechua
Currency	U.S. dollar
Gross Domestic Product (GDP)	$45.4 billion (2003 est.)
GDP per capita	$3,200

Industry: petroleum, food processing, textiles, and metal work

Agriculture: *bananas, coffee, cacao, rice; cattle; balsa wood; and fish*

Exports: petroleum, bananas, shrimp, coffee, and cacao

Natural Resources: petroleum, fish, and timber

Think Globally

Do you think consumers in Ecuador can resolve purchase complaints as suggested in this chapter? Why or why not?

See the Teacher Manual for answer.

Contact Company Headquarters

If you cannot resolve your problem at the local store or business, contact the company's headquarters. Sending a complaint letter such as the one shown in **Figure 4.5** can be effective. To find a company's address, check the *Consumer's Resource Handbook*. Your library may have other useful references as well. Company Web sites are also good sources. If you would rather talk to someone in the company's customer service department but do not know the telephone number, call 1-800-555-1212, the information number. Your library may also carry a directory of toll-free numbers. Some companies print their toll-free customer-service numbers on their packages.

Figure 4.5 **Sample Complaint Letter**

Your Name
Your Address
Your City, State, ZIP Code

Note: Keep copies of your letter and all related documents and information.

Date

Appropriate Person
Company Name
Street Address
City, State, ZIP Code

Describe your purchase

Dear ______(Appropriate Name)______:

Last week I purchased (or had repaired) a (name of product with model number or service performed). I made this purchase at (location and other important details of the transaction).

State problem

Unfortunately, your product (or service) has not performed satisfactorily (or the service was inadequate) because ____________. Therefore, to solve the problem I would appreciate your (here state the specific action you want). Enclosed are copies (copies—NOT originals) of my records (receipts, guarantees, warranties, cancelled checks, contracts, model and serial numbers, and any other documents).

Give history of problem

I am looking forward to your reply and resolution of my problem, and will wait three weeks before seeking third-party assistance. Contact me at the above address or by phone at (home and office numbers here).

State reasonable time for action

Sincerely yours,

Your Name

Enclosure

Source: *Consumer's Resource Handbook,* reprinted by permission of Diana Publishing Co., Collingdale, PA.

In Writing Sending a letter to a company's headquarters can produce results when you want to resolve a consumer complaint.

When should you take this step to resolve a problem?

Caption Answer Write a letter when you are unable to resolve a situation at the store where you made the purchase.

Academic Connection

LANGUAGE ARTS

In 2003, the U.S. Better Business Bureau system handled over 773,000 written consumer complaints. Some of the products and businesses that had the highest number of complaints against them included automobile dealers and cellular phone dealers. If you have a complaint, you should always approach the company first. *With a partner, prepare a script you could use when approaching a company with a complaint. Rehearse your script together and then present it to the class.*

See the Teacher Manual for the answer.

Consumer Agency Assistance

If the company is not providing the answers you seek, get help from various consumer, business, and government organizations. These groups include national organizations that deal with issues such as nutrition and automobile safety. Local organizations also handle complaints, do surveys, and provide legal assistance.

Among the best-known consumer agencies is the Better Business Bureau, a network of offices around the country sponsored by local business organizations. These bureaus deal with complaints against local merchants. However, the merchants are under no obligation to respond to those complaints. Therefore, the bureaus are most useful before you buy a product. They can tell you about the experiences other consumers have had with a certain store or company.

Government Agencies A large network of local, state, and federal government agencies is also available. These agencies handle all types of problems, from false advertising to illegal business activities. One federal agency is the Food and Drug Administration, which sets safety standards for food, drugs, chemicals, cosmetics, and household and medical devices. The Consumer Product Safety Commission, another federal agency, helps protect consumers against unsafe products. If you do not know which consumer protection agency to choose, contact your U.S. representative locally or in Washington, D.C.

Dispute Resolution

Dispute resolution programs offer other ways to settle disagreements about a product. Working out a complaint may involve **mediation**—the attempt by a neutral third party to resolve a conflict between a customer and a business through discussion and negotiation. However, a decision made in mediation is not legally binding. Sometimes manufacturers and industry organizations use the arbitration process to resolve consumer complaints. **Arbitration** is a process whereby a conflict between a customer and a business is resolved by an impartial third party whose decision is legally binding.

Settling a dispute through one of these methods can be quicker, less expensive, and less stressful than going to court. Sources for dispute resolution programs in your area include:

- Local or state consumer protection agencies
- State attorney general's office
- Small claims courts
- Better Business Bureau
- trade associations
- local bar associations.

If these dispute resolution methods do not produce the results you want, you may choose to take legal action.

Critical Thinking Divide the students into five sections, two to be "pro," two to be "con," and the last to be judges. The four teams will each research, prepare, and debate this question: Should government be active in consumer protection? Have the judging team determine the outcome of the debate.

Legal Options for Consumers

What are your legal rights?

First, try to settle your dispute by going to the place of business, contacting the company's headquarters, or getting help from a consumer agency. However, if you are still unhappy with the outcome, your final alternative is the legal system.

Small Claims Court

Every state has a court system to settle minor disagreements. A **small claims court** is a court that deals with legal disputes that involve amounts below a certain limit. The amount varies from state to state, ranging from about $500 to $10,000. Cases usually do not involve juries or lawyers, so the cost of this type of legal action is relatively low. The decision of the judge is final.

When you present your case, you should be calm and polite and stick to the point. Submit your own evidence, such as receipts, contracts, and photographs. You may use witnesses who can testify on your behalf and support your claim. The process takes a few weeks.

As You Read

QUESTION

What are the alternative measures available to consumers before they resort to the legal system?

Question Answer (1) Return to the place of purchase and talk to a manager; (2) contact the company headquarters; (3) go to a consumer agency for assistance; and (4) have the dispute mediated or arbitrated.

Teaching Activity Set up mock mediation or arbitration processes. Divide students into groups of five. In each group, one student will be the mediator or arbitrator; another will be the consumer bringing the action with one witness; the business will be represented by another student with one witness.

Careers in Finance

RETAIL SALES ASSOCIATE

Jamie Jefferson
Patagonia

Before Jamie worked at Patagonia, she was a frequent customer. As a participant of outdoor sports, Jamie was happy to land a sales associate position at a Patagonia store, a company that specializes in outdoor gear. She appreciates being surrounded by merchandise that she actually uses. She enjoys working with others and tending to customers who share similar interests. Jamie also finds value in working with a company that shares her enthusiasm for the environment. Patagonia employees are expected to educate themselves about environmental campaigns, and the workplace recycles all paper, glass, and plastic items. Retail sales associates often work for stores that reflect their interests.

SKILLS: Sales, communication, cooperation

PERSONAL TRAITS: Positive, neat, detail-oriented, shares company's vision for outdoor activities and responsibilities, able to lift heavy objects and stand for long periods of time

EDUCATION: High school diploma or equivalent, sales experience

ANALYZE How do you think a company such as Patagonia trains employees to respond to customer complaints?

See the Teacher Manual for answer.

@ To learn more about career paths for retail sales associates, visit **finance07.glencoe.com**.

Research Divide the class into four groups. One group will research how to take a case to small claims court. Group two will research how class action suits work. Group three will research legal aid societies to see how lawyers would represent consumers in disputes. Group four will research government consumer agency assistance. All groups are to consider costs, procedures, requirements, and restrictions. Each group will report its findings to the class.

Caption Answer Small claims court does not involve juries or lawyers, and the amounts you can sue for are strictly limited.

▲ **FORMAL COMPLAINTS** To resolve a consumer complaint, sometimes you must take your case to small claims court. *How is a small claims court different from a trial court?*

Class-Action Suits

Sometimes many people have the same complaint. For example, several people may have been injured by a defective product or overcharged by a utility company. Such a group may qualify for a class-action suit. A **class-action suit** is a legal action on behalf of all the people who have suffered the same injustice. These people are called a "class" and are represented by one lawyer or a group of lawyers working together.

If a situation qualifies for a class-action suit, all parties must be notified of the suit. An individual may decide to file a separate lawsuit instead. If the court rules in favor of the class action, the money awarded is divided among the claimants or put into public funds.

TechByte

Lawyering Up If you have not been able to resolve a consumer complaint by talking with the company's customer service representative, you can take some legal steps on your own without the help of a lawyer. But if you still cannot resolve the issue, you may need to search for a lawyer to help you.

@ List two things you can do to resolve a complaint. Then list steps for finding a good lawyer after reading information through **finance07.glencoe.com**.

Other Legal Alternatives

If you do not want to go to small claims court or join in a class-action suit, you may seek the services of a lawyer. Get a referral for a lawyer from someone you know. You can also find the names of lawyers in newspapers, in the yellow pages of the phone book, or by calling a local branch of the American Bar Association (ABA), a professional organization of lawyers. It is important to make sure that the lawyer you choose has experience in handling your type of case. You should also ask about fees and payment policies. Lawyers can be expensive. You may decide that your problem is not worth the time and expense.

If the cost of lawyers and other legal services is too high for you, you may seek help from a **legal aid society**, a network of community law offices that provide free or low-cost legal assistance. Supported by public funds, these offices provide a variety of legal services. Not everyone is eligible for help from a legal aid society. Your income must fall below a certain amount to qualify, which varies from state to state.

If you do not qualify to use the legal aid society, and hiring a private attorney is out of your budget, you might visit a legal clinic. In many cases, such businesses can offer basic assistance with advice and filing paperwork. In addition, some private attorneys offer their services at reduced rates and work part time in legal clinics.

Many tools are available to protect your rights. However, they will not be valuable, unless you use them. You will have fewer consumer problems if you do business only with companies that have good reputations. You should avoid signing contracts and other documents you do not understand, and watch out for offers that seem too good to be true.

After You Read

REACT

What legal remedies are available for settling consumer disputes?

React Answer Legal remedies include small claims court, class action lawsuits, or seeking a lawyer to represent you.

Section 4.2 Assessment

See the Teacher Manual for answers.

QUICK CHECK

1. What are some typical consumer complaints?
2. What are five methods of resolving consumer complaints?
3. What are some of the advantages and disadvantages of taking a consumer dispute to small claims court?

THINK CRITICALLY

4. Write a brief paragraph describing a product or service with which you were dissatisfied, and explain what the problem was. Did you complain? If so, what specific steps did you take, and what was the outcome?

USE COMMUNICATION SKILLS

5. **Too Good to Be True?** You recently received a letter offering a four-day vacation trip to Hawaii for only $350. The price includes transportation, a hotel room, and meals. To reserve a space, you must send $175. The offer sounds too good to be true, and you suspect that it is fraudulent.

Discuss With your classmates, brainstorm various types of fraud. Discuss ways to avoid becoming a victim of fraud.

SOLVE MONEY PROBLEMS

6. **Resolving Consumer Complaints** Eduardo and Ana recently bought a new dining room table that they saw advertised on a furniture manufacturer's Web site. When the table arrived and they opened the box, they discovered long, deep scratches on the top of the table. The manufacturer is located thousands of miles from where they live. The box had no directions about how they could return the product.

Write About It Describe the steps Eduardo and Ana should take to resolve their situation and get either a refund or a new table.

Chapter 4 Review & Activities

See the Teacher Manual for answers.

CHAPTER SUMMARY

- Buying decisions are influenced by several factors: economic factors, such as prices, brand names, quality, and maintenance costs; social factors, such as lifestyle and culture; and personal factors, such as age, occupation, and family size.
- A research-based approach to buying involves identifying needs, gathering information, becoming aware of the marketplace, weighing alternatives, and making the purchase. The purchase may involve negotiation, plus you will need to determine whether to pay cash or use credit.
- Make buying decisions by using the following strategies: time your purchases, select stores, compare brands, check labels, compare prices, and evaluate warranties.
- To solve consumer problems, return to the place of purchase, contact the company that manufactured the disputed product, obtain help from a consumer agency or dispute resolution program, or initiate legal action.
- Legal alternatives available to consumers include lawsuits in small claims court, joining in a class-action suit, hiring a lawyer, and obtaining assistance from a legal aid society.

Communicating Key Terms

A neighbor who has just moved to the United States is buying several large appliances. He is having some difficulty understanding some of the advertising information on the products. Write simple explanations of eight of the terms below that you think he may be having trouble understanding.

- down payment
- cooperative
- impulse buying
- open dating
- unit pricing
- rebate
- warranty
- service contract
- fraud
- mediation
- arbitration
- small claims court
- class-action suit
- legal aid society

Reviewing Key Concepts

1. **List** the economic, social, and personal factors that influence a decision to buy an article of clothing.
2. **Describe** the research-based steps for buying a personal computer.
3. **Explain** why some of the strategies for making wise purchases may be more important than others, depending on the item being purchased.
4. **Identify** methods to resolve consumer complaints.
5. **Describe** the advantages and disadvantages of small claims court and joining a class-action suit.

See the Teacher Manual for answers.

ACADEMIC SKILLS

Language Arts Many consumers are attracted to name brands because they are recognized through advertising. However, generic or store brands have become popular alternatives.

Write About It Write a paragraph explaining three reasons for buying a brand-name product and three reasons for buying a store brand instead.

YOUR FINANCIAL FIGURES

Back to School You have $130 to spend at August "back-to-school" sales. The tennis shoes you really want cost $105 plus 7 percent sales tax. Online, the shoes cost $95.99, with 11 percent shipping charges but no sales tax. Based on experience, you think the shoes' price will be one-third less by mid-October.

1. **Calculate** (a) How much will the shoes cost in October? Compare that total price to the current store and online prices. (b) What trade-offs do you incur by waiting to buy the shoes? (c) How do those trade-offs compare to having more money now for other purchases?
2. **Compute** by using spreadsheet software the total costs of the shoes in stores now, online now, and in stores in October.

REAL-WORLD Application

Connect with Social Studies In late 2004, a pain medication called Vioxx was removed voluntarily from the market by its manufacturer, Merck, Inc., due to a risk of heart-related problems. Merck lost a great deal of income and its stock price went down significantly.

Research Use library and Internet sources to find out about Merck's voluntary removal of Vioxx and the potential for class-action lawsuits against the company. Investigate the Federal Food and Drug Act and other laws aimed at protecting citizens and summarize your findings

Internet CONNECTION

Shopping Online Many people limit their online purchases to books, CDs, and airplane tickets. Based on this chapter, explain why you would or would not buy the following items online:

@ **Log On** Use an Internet search engine to find Web sites selling the items listed:

1. Expensive tennis shoes
2. An iPod
3. A dress or suit for the prom
4. Flowers for your mother
5. The latest CD from your favorite band
6. Four CDs from your favorite bands

BusinessWeek ONLINE

Newsclip: Continuous Shopping Consumer spending has been on the rise since 2001. Despite unemployment rates, higher oil prices, and terrorist threats, Americans continue to shop.

@ **Log On** Go to **finance07.glencoe.com** and open Chapter 4. List reasons consumers continue to spend. Ask your teenage friends what they buy and want. Make a list.

WHAT'S YOUR FINANCIAL ID?

ARE YOU A SMART SHOPPER?

With so many places to shop and a wide variety of products to buy, it takes skill and practice to get the most from your money. On a separate sheet of paper, test your shopping know-how.

1. When I want something, I
 a. go to the nearest store that has it and buy it. (1 point)
 b. locate where I can buy it at the lowest cost today and buy it. (2 points)
 c. wait for the item to go on sale. (3 points)

2. I like to
 a. buy what looks good to me at the time. (1 point)
 b. look at consumer guides to help me choose the best buy. (2 points)
 c. compare all the brands and decide which offers the most value. (3 points)

3. When buying an item in the drugstore, I
 a. always buy name brands. (1 point)
 b. always buy generic brands. (2 points)
 c. calculate the best price per weight or unit and buy accordingly. (3 points)

4. When shopping for clothes, I
 a. buy what strikes my fancy. (1 point)
 b. only buy what's on sale. (2 points)
 c. only buy what I know I will wear. (3 points)

5. I use coupons whenever I can.
 a. Never (1 point)
 b. Sometimes (2 points)
 c. Always (3 points)

6. When eating out, I
 a. order what I want, regardless of cost. (1 point)
 b. sometimes am more concerned about cost but sometimes order expensive dishes. (2 points)
 c. always look at prices and order accordingly. (3 points)

7. Whenever I can, I borrow books and DVDs from the library.
 a. Never (1 point)
 b. Sometimes (2 points)
 c. Always (3 points)

8. When buying CDs or DVDs, I
 a. get what I want as soon as it comes out. (1 point)
 b. try to wait for a sale but get what I want if I really want it. (2 points)
 c. wait for a sale. (3 points)

If you scored:

21–24: You are a smart shopper. However, be sure you treat yourself occasionally.
16–20: You sometimes make choices that cost more, but you are usually aware of them.
Less than 16: Try to practice a few more smart shopping skills and see how much you save.

Accept all reasonable answers that show student effort and an understanding of the concept.

Your Financial Portfolio

Your Budget

David wants a $2,500 laptop computer. At his part-time job at Computer Warehouse, he earns $7 an hour and works an average of 16 hours a week. For ten weeks in the summer, he works 40 hours a week. He also makes money on the side by setting up and troubleshooting computers. By keeping track of his expenses, he has figured his monthly budget.

If David sticks to his budget, in a year's time he can save $3,630 ($302.50 × 12 = $3,630). That would be more than enough to buy the computer he wants.

Average Monthly Income	
Income:	
Monthly take-home pay from Computer Warehouse	$502.50
Income from setting up and troubleshooting computers	50.00
Other income	20.00
Total Income	**$572.50**
Average Monthly Expenses	
Expenses:	
Fixed Expenses	
Online services	$ 20.00
Car loan and insurance	135.00
Variable Expenses	
Entertainment and personal	90.00
Gifts and contributions	25.00
Total Expenses	**$270.00**

(Total Income − Total Expenses = Savings)
($572.50 − 270.00 = $302.50)
David can save $302.50 a month.

Calculate

What is your budget? A budget can help you see where you are spending your money and assist you in determining how long it will take to save for a special purchase. In your workbook or on a separate sheet of paper, calculate your income and expenses for one month. How much can you save in one month? What is the cost of your desired purchase? How long will it take you to save for what you want?

Accept all reasonable answers that show student effort and an understanding of the concept.

Unit 1 LAB

Get a Financial Life!

See the Teacher Manual for Unit Lab teaching guide.

Setting Up a Career Plan

Overview

Carrie Houston will be graduating from high school this year. She is facing many important decisions—from developing her personal financial goals to planning her career strategy. She is interested in fashion design and computer graphics and has been taking related classes.

When you make decisions, you are taking control of your life. You can shape your future in ways that are important to you. To make sound decisions, you should identify your goals and understand the ways in which your personal values and life situations will influence your choices. If you are prepared to make decisions—rather than leave your future to chance or allow others to tell you what to do—you will be able to achieve personal satisfaction and financial security.

Develop a process to help plan your own career; then share it with Carrie so that she can plan her future career.

Resources & Tools

- Career center/guidance office at school
- Career-development book
- Crayons, markers, colored pencils
- Internet
- Portfolio (ring binder or file folder)
- Poster board
- Presentation software (optional)
- Public or school library
- Word-processing software

Procedures

STEP A **The Process**

In order to develop a career plan, you must set goals, understand your abilities and interests, and conduct research. By following this process, you will have a head start into your future. In addition, you will be able to share what you have learned with Carrie or your friends.

1. Develop five to seven financial goals. You should have at least one short-term goal, one intermediate goal, and one long-term goal. Your selected career will help you meet your goals.
2. Take an aptitude test and/or interest inventory. You can find these in your school's guidance office or career center, or on the Internet.
3. Research a career that interests you. Make sure that you find out about the educational requirements, skills needed, pay range, duties and responsibilities, opportunities for advancement, and future trends in the field.
4. Conduct an informational interview with someone who is working in your area of interest to gather practical information, or arrange to "job shadow" someone in your selected field. (To *job shadow* means to follow a person on the job for a day to learn about a particular career.)
5. Obtain catalogs from colleges or other post-secondary institutions where training is offered in the field you are researching. Try to locate at least one institution in your community, one in your state, and one out of state.
6. Using a word-processing program, create templates for a résumé and cover letter.

STEP B Create Your Portfolio

As you work through the process, save the results so that you can refer, review, and refine. Divide your portfolio into six sections. Label the sections: (1) Goals, (2) Tests, (3) Career Research, (4) Live Work, (5) Education, and (6) Résumé.

1. Using a word-processing program, type your goals in a large font (16–18 point). These will be your guiding principles. Place them in Section 1.
2. Place the results of your aptitude test or interest inventory in Section 2.
3. Type a two- or three-page (double-spaced) career report based on your research, and place it in Section 3.
4. Write about your informational interview or job shadowing experience. Include pictures, brochures, or other materials that you might have received. Place these items in Section 4.
5. Place the catalogs that you collect in Section 5.
6. Place the templates that you create in Section 6.

STEP C Presentation

One of the most important skills that employers look for in a good employee is the ability to communicate. This is a skill that you can develop in class through oral presentations.

1. Read a book on career development. Examples include:
   - *What Color Is Your Parachute?* by Richard Nelson Bolles
   - *Who Moved My Cheese?* by Spencer Johnson
   - *Job Interviews for Dummies* by Joyce Lain Kennedy
   - *Cool Careers for Dummies* by Marty Nemko, Paul Edwards, and Sarah Edwards
   - *I Could Do Anything If I Only Knew What It Was* by Barbara Sher with Barbara Smith
2. Using either presentation software or poster board with markers, crayons, or colored pencils, create a five-minute presentation that summarizes the book.
3. Include your opinion of the book, stating whether you would recommend it to Carrie.

Unit 2

Banking and Credit

WebQuest Internet Project

Your Own Home

Buying your first home takes a lot of planning and preparation. In this project, you will write a plan designed to help you to purchase your first home when you are an adult. Since you have several years to accomplish this goal, you have time to save some money for a down payment, establish a good credit rating, choose a home, apply for a mortgage, and negotiate a price.

Log on to **finance07.glencoe.com**. Begin by reading Task 1. Then continue on your WebQuest as you study Unit 2.

Section	5.1	6.2	7.3
Page	135	170	223

BusinessWeek

FINANCE FILE

Consumer Debt: The Deeper the Hole, the Better for Business

When is bad debt good business? Public collection agencies that specialize in the purchase of unpaid credit-card obligations and other bills are expected to get a lift as the consumer starts to show signs of overload.

Consumers have borrowed a bundle in recent years—over $2 trillion in credit card and auto debt, according to the Federal Reserve. Add mortgages and the figure jumps to nearly $10 trillion. The average U.S. household is deeper in the hole than it was four years ago, carrying debt of about $9,200, up from $7,200.

Since household income isn't keeping pace with debt growth, more consumers are getting close to the edge. Credit card charge-offs, or the bad debt that banks write off the books, were expected to hit a record $65 billion in 2004, up from $57.3 billion in 2003, according to the *Nilson Report*. Such debts will increase to $2.8 trillion by 2010.

Ultimately, collection companies make their money from bad-debt portfolios by working out reasonable solutions with borrowers. Zaro [CEO of Cavalry Investments] says: "If you don't help them, you don't help yourself."

—By Mara Der Hovanesian

Write About It How do you think consumers can reduce their credit debt?

See the Teacher Manual for answer.

Log On To read the complete *BusinessWeek* article and do the *BusinessWeek* Extension activity to help you learn more about handling credit and avoiding debt, go to **finance07.glencoe.com**.

CHAPTER 5
Banking

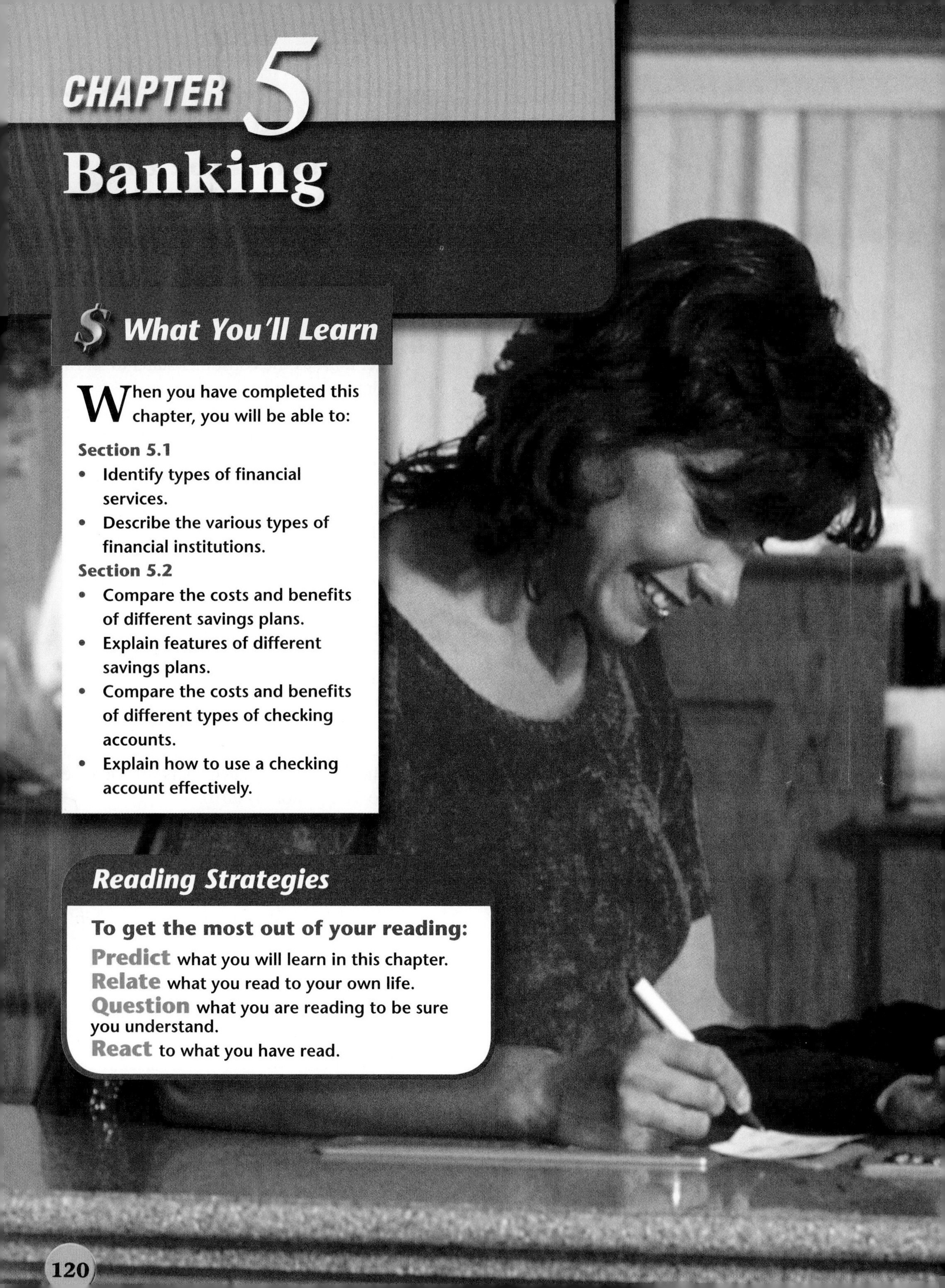

$ What You'll Learn

When you have completed this chapter, you will be able to:

Section 5.1

- Identify types of financial services.
- Describe the various types of financial institutions.

Section 5.2

- Compare the costs and benefits of different savings plans.
- Explain features of different savings plans.
- Compare the costs and benefits of different types of checking accounts.
- Explain how to use a checking account effectively.

Reading Strategies

To get the most out of your reading:

Predict what you will learn in this chapter.
Relate what you read to your own life.
Question what you are reading to be sure you understand.
React to what you have read.

In the Real World . . .

When Lynn Podesta was hired for her first job, she decided to open a bank account. She went to local branches and picked up brochures that explained interest rates, fees for services, locations of ATMs, and online services. Lynn was surprised to find out that each bank had different benefits and costs. Some banks charged for ATM usage and teller services. She also found a bank that offered a free checking account if her paychecks were deposited directly.

Lynn felt that it was important to start an account. Using a debit card would allow her to shop without carrying cash, and having an account would help her establish credit. Getting to know banking would not be too difficult, and she would have advantages.

As You Read *Consider how you can use basic banking services to your advantage.*

Lesson Plan See the Teacher Manual for the Chapter 5 planning guide and lesson plan.

ASK STANDARD & POOR'S

Savings Account

Q: I make only $75 a week at my part-time job and use most of it for movies, food, and CDs. Because I make so little, do I really need to put my money in a bank?

A: Since you have a small amount of money to take care of, you may not need a bank. However, $75 a week is a large sum to spend on entertainment. You should open a savings account and try to save at least $10 a week. After three months you would have $130, and after a year you would have more than $500.

Ask Yourself Why is it a good idea to start a savings account now?

Go to **finance07.glencoe.com** to complete the Standard & Poor's Financial Focus activity.

Section 5.1

Focus on Reading

Read to Learn

- How to identify types of financial services.
- How to describe the various types of financial institutions.

Main Idea

Understanding the features of financial services and institutions will help you choose options that best meet your needs.

Key Terms

- direct deposit
- automated teller machine (ATM)
- debit card
- point-of-sale transaction
- commercial bank
- savings and loan association (S&L)
- credit union

Before You Read

PREDICT

What might be the differences between commercial banks, savings and loans, and credit unions?

Springboard Ask the students to predict what banks will be like in 15 years, and then write their predictions on the board.

Financial Services and Institutions

How to Manage Your Cash

What are your cash needs?

Banking in America began in 1791, soon after the United States declared independence. Congress established the nation's first central bank with eight branches. Today, with more than 11,000 banks, 2,000 savings and loan associations, and 12,000 credit unions in the United States, you have a wide array of financial services from which to choose. A trip to the bank may be a visit to an automated teller machine (ATM) in the mall or a quick look at your savings account balance on the Internet. Your choice of financial services will depend on your daily cash needs and your savings goals. (See **Figure 5.1.**)

Daily Cash Needs

Your daily cash needs may include buying lunch, going to the movies with friends, filling the car with gasoline, or paying for other routine activities. Of course, you can carry cash, or currency—bills and coins—to pay for these items. You can also use a credit card or go to an ATM, also known as a cash machine.

As you decide which method to use for your everyday cash needs, consider the pros and cons of each one. For example, ATMs may charge a fee for each use. If you pay a $1 fee each time you take out cash, say, twice a week, you will spend $104 on fees each year.

In addition to your short-term cash needs, you need to consider your long-term financial goals. Resist the temptation to overspend and avoid buying on impulse or overusing credit cards. Try not to dip into your savings to pay current bills. Put extra money you have to work for you—in a savings account or an investment plan.

Sources of Quick Cash

Regardless of how well you plan, you may sometimes need more cash than you have available. You have two options: Use your savings or borrow the money. Remember that either choice requires a trade-off. Although you will have immediate access to the funds you need, long-term financial goals—such as paying for college, buying a car, or starting a business—may be delayed.

Types of Financial Services

Which financial services would benefit you?

In order to stay competitive in today's marketplace, banks and other financial institutions have expanded the range of services that they offer. These services can be divided into three main categories:

- Savings
- Payment services
- Borrowing

Motivating Students Ask students what types of financial services they use now and tabulate their responses in categories: banks, savings & loans, credit unions; savings accounts, checking accounts, and credit cards.

Savings

Safe storage of funds for future use is a basic need for everyone. Money that is going to be left in a financial institution for months or years is called a *time deposit.* Some examples of time deposit funds include money that you keep in any type of savings account and certificates of deposit or CDs. Having a savings acount is essential for any personal finance plan.

Discussion Discuss with students the advantages and disadvantages of carrying cash, using ATMs, using debit cards, and using credit cards.

Figure 5.1 **Financial Services**

Financial Services for Short-Term Needs			
• Daily purchases • Living expenses • Emergency fund			
Daily Cash Needs • Check cashing • Automated teller machines (ATMs) • Prepaid cards	**Savings** • Regular savings account • Money market account	**Checking** • Regular checking account • Online payments • Automatic preauthorized payments • Payment by phone • Cashier's checks • Money orders	**Credit Cards**
Financial Services for Long-Term Needs			
• Major purchases • Long-term financial security			
Savings • Certificates of deposit (CDs) • U.S. Savings Bonds	**Credit Services** • Cash loans for cars, education • Home loans	**Investment Services** • Mutual funds • Financial advice	**Other Services** • Tax preparation • Insurance • Budgeting

Planning Ahead You may think that you need only cash and checking services at this time in your life.

Why would it be a good idea to save a small amount regularly?

Caption Answer Answers might include to establish useful habits, to have an emergency fund, to have money for major purchases.

Careers in Finance

BANK TELLER

Brandon Lewis
American Bank and Trust

Brandon has always been good at handling money. Brandon's job is to process customer transactions in a timely, accurate manner according to established policies and procedures. His tasks may include tending to checking and savings accounts, ATM/debit cards, telephone and Internet banking, bill payment, certificates of deposit, IRAs, safe deposit, discount brokerage, credit cards, and merchant processing. A bank teller is expected to uphold the positive image of his or her bank by providing the best possible customer service in a responsible and professional manner.

SKILLS:	Communication, problem-solving, decision-making, retail sales, and cash-handling skills, as well as proficiency with office machines
PERSONAL TRAITS:	Personable, courteous, outgoing, team oriented, and able to remain calm under pressure
EDUCATION:	High school diploma or equivalent; associate degree or higher degree

ANALYZE Why would a bank teller's job require selling skills? Provide examples.
See the Teacher Manual for answer.

@ To learn more about career paths for bank tellers, visit **finance07.glencoe.com**.

Payment Services

Transferring money from a personal account to businesses or individuals for payments is a basic function of day-to-day financial activity at a bank. The most commonly used payment service is a checking account. Money that you place in a checking account is called a *demand deposit* because you can withdraw the money at any time, or on demand.

Borrowing

Most people use credit at some time during their lives. If you need to borrow money, financial institutions offer many options. You can borrow money for a short term by using a credit card or taking out a personal cash loan. If you need to borrow for a longer term, say, for the purpose of buying a house or car, you may apply for a mortgage or auto loan. Chapter 6 discusses the types and costs of credit.

Other Financial Services

Financial institutions may also offer a variety of services, such as insurance protection; stock, bond, and mutual fund investment accounts; income tax assistance; and financial planning services.

Electronic Banking Services

How can you use electronic banking services?

When Jeff's older brother was in high school, he had to get to his bank by 3 P.M. on Friday, or he would have to wait until 9 A.M. on Monday to cash his paycheck. Today Jeff's bank is open for longer periods on weekdays as well as on Saturdays. For more convenience, Jeff can use the bank's electronic services 24 hours a day. He can check the status of his account or make a transaction from an ATM, by telephone, or online. Other online services allow customers to get up-to-date account information with personal financial management software to view details about a home loan or a line of credit and to check the amount of interest paid.

Security is the number one issue for online customers. The way to ensure online security is to use a security code, or password, and a customer identification name or number.

Direct Deposit

Many businesses offer their employees **direct deposit**, an automatic deposit of net pay to an employee's designated bank account. Instead of a paper paycheck, employees receive a printed statement that lists deductions and information about their earnings. Direct deposit saves time, money, and effort—and offers a safe way to transfer funds.

As You Read

RELATE

Would you use electronic banking services? Why or why not?

Caption Answer You should give others privacy and protect your own security.

▼ **CASH AT HAND** Follow simple rules of ATM etiquette when using this banking convenience. If you are in line, stand at least a few feet away from the person who is using the machine. When you are at the machine, protect the screen as you enter your PIN and other information. *Why are these practices important?*

Critical Thinking Have students write an essay or prepare a presentation in which they consider: the advantages, disadvantages, and security issues of online banking, and how to best protect themselves from risks.

Automatic Payments

Utility companies, lenders, and other businesses allow customers to use an automatic payment system. With your authorization, your bank will withdraw the amount of your monthly payment or bill from your bank account. Make sure you have enough money in your account for the payment. Arrange your payments according to when you receive your paycheck. Check your bank statements each month to make sure the payments were made correctly.

Automated Teller Machines (ATMs)

A cash machine, or **automated teller machine (ATM)**, is a computer terminal that allows a withdrawal of cash from an account. You can also make deposits and transfer money from one account to another. ATMs are located in banks, shopping malls, grocery stores, and even sports arenas.

To use an ATM for banking, you must apply for a card from your financial institution. This card is called a **debit card**, which is a cash card that allows you to withdraw money or pay for purchases from your checking or savings account. The card also allows you to access the machine for other purposes. Some financial institutions may charge a small fee for the use of the card. Unlike a credit card, a debit card enables you to spend only the money that you have in your account.

When you use your debit card, the ATM computer will ask you to enter your personal identification number (PIN). Never give this number to any business or individual, or for online transactions. Memorize it and keep a written record in a safe place. Never keep your PIN with your debit card. If your card is lost or stolen along with your PIN, anyone could withdraw money from your account.

ATM Fees The fees that some financial institutions charge for the convenience of using an ATM can add up over time. You may feel that the benefit is worth the cost. However, you might consider these suggestions:

Caption Answer Answers may include not all businesses accept them; you have to ensure you have enough in your account and remember to subtract the debited amount.

▶ **PLASTIC PAYMENT** Debit cards are convenient, cashless ways to make purchases. *What might be one drawback of using a debit card?*

- Compare ATM fees before opening an account. Get a list of fees in writing.
- Use your bank's ATM machines to avoid the additional fees that other banks charge when you use their machines.
- Consider using traveler's checks, credit cards, personal checks, and prepaid cash cards when you are away from home.

Lost Debit Cards If you lose your debit card, or if it is stolen, notify your bank immediately. Most card issuers will not hold you responsible for stolen funds. Check with your card issuer. However, some institutions require you to notify them within two days of losing your card. If you wait longer, you may be held responsible for up to $500 for its unauthorized use for up to 60 days. Beyond that time, your liability may be unlimited.

Plastic Payments

Although cash and checks are very common methods of paying for goods and services, various access cards are also available.

Point-of-Sale Transactions A **point-of-sale transaction** is a purchase by a debit card of a good or service at a retail store, a restaurant, or elsewhere. Financial institutions offer two types of cards for these transactions—online and offline. An online card works like an ATM card. You have to use your PIN to authorize the payment, and the money is transferred from your account instantly. Charges made with an offline card do not require a PIN, and the funds to cover the payment are deducted from your account within a day or two.

Stored-Value Cards Prepaid cards that you can use for bus or subway fares, school lunches, long-distance phone calls, or library fees are popular. Some of these cards, such as phone cards, are disposable. Others, called *stored-value cards*, are reloadable or rechargeable, which means that money can be added to the card.

Electronic Cash Some companies are working to develop electronic money. They plan to create electronic versions of all existing payment systems—paper money, coins, credit cards, and checks. The day may come when you will not handle currency at all.

Opportunity Costs of Financial Services

What are the trade-offs when you choose financial services?

When you are making decisions about saving and spending, try to find a balance between your short-term needs and your future financial security. Also, consider the opportunity costs, or trade-offs, of each choice you make as you select financial services. Ask several questions.

TechByte

Paperless Banking
In October 2004, the Check Clearing for the 21st Century Act took effect. Known as Check 21, this law made check processing and clearing easier for financial institutions. Now, if you write a check to pay for an item, you may never see that check again. Instead, you may receive a copy of the check from your bank.

@ Write a paragraph comparing the old system of clearing checks with the new system after reading more information through **finance07.glencoe.com**.

- Is a higher interest rate on a certificate of deposit worth giving up liquidity, which is the ability to easily convert your resources into cash without a loss in value?
- Would you trade the convenience of getting cash from the ATM near your office for lower ATM fees?
- Is it worth opening a checking account that has no fees—but does not earn interest—if you have to keep a minimum balance of $500?

Remember to consider the value of your time in addition to the money you are saving. Reevaluate your choices occasionally. You may find a new financial institution that offers you more of the services you need or offers less expensive services.

Types of Financial Institutions

What are the differences between financial institutions?

After you have identified the services you want, you can choose from among many types of financial institutions. You may select an institution that offers a wide range of services or one that specializes in certain services. **Figure 5.2** provides some tips for selecting a financial institution. Many institutions provide the option of cyberbanking, or banking via the Internet. Some banks operate exclusively on the Internet.

Figure 5.2 Selecting a Financial Institution

When you are ready to choose a financial institution, plan so that you will have the services you need and will not have to pay for those you will not use. Do your banking homework.

1 **Stop by the bank.** Pick up brochures about the bank's services. While there, speak to a customer service representative about the bank's services.

2 **Take the brochures home.** Study them and discuss the features with your parents.

Federal Deposit Insurance Corporation

When you consider a financial institution consider its safety record. During the Great Depression of the 1930s, many banks failed. The people and businesses that had made deposits in these institutions lost their money. In 1933, the federal government created the Federal Deposit Insurance Corporation (FDIC) to protect deposits in banks. The FDIC insures each account in a federally chartered bank up to $100,000 per account. The FDIC also administers the Savings Association Insurance Fund (SAIF) for savings and loan associations. Like the FDIC, the SAIF insures deposits up to $100,000. All federally chartered banks must participate in the FDIC program. Banks that are not federally chartered may choose to enroll in the program.

Deposit Institutions

Most people use deposit-type institutions to handle their banking needs. These institutions include commercial banks, savings and loan associations, mutual savings banks, and credit unions.

Commercial Banks A **commercial bank** is a for-profit institution that offers a full range of financial services, including checking, savings, and lending. Commercial banks serve individuals and businesses. These banks are authorized to conduct business through a charter, or license, granted by either the federal government or a state government.

Research Divide the class into four groups, and assign a deposit institution type to each group: commercial banks, savings and loan associations, mutual savings banks, and credit unions. Each group is to research the assigned institution type to determine: services offered, organization, advantages, and disadvantages. Each group will present its findings to the class.

▲ CONVENIENCE Many people use commercial banks because these banks offer a full range of financial services. *What might be some benefits of using a large commercial bank?*

Caption Answer Answers may include the ability to use an ATM, electronic banking, or deal with tellers; and having more than one branch location available.

Savings and Loan Associations A **savings and loan association (S&L)** is a financial institution that traditionally specialized in savings accounts and mortgage loans but now offers many of the same services as commercial banks. Services include checking accounts, business loans, and investment services. S&Ls have either a federal or a state charter.

Mutual Savings Banks Mutual savings banks specialize in savings accounts and mortgage loans. Some offer personal and automobile loans as well. The interest rates on loans from a mutual savings bank may be lower than those that a commercial bank charges. In addition, mutual savings banks sometimes pay a higher interest rate on savings accounts.

Credit Unions A **credit union** is a nonprofit financial institution that is owned by its members and organized for their benefit. Traditionally, its members have some common bond, such as membership in a labor union, college alumni association, or employment by the same company. Most credit unions offer a full range of services, including checking accounts, loans, credit cards, ATMs, and investment services. Credit union fees and loan rates may be lower than those at commercial banks.

Non-Deposit Institutions

Financial services are also available at institutions such as life insurance companies, investment companies, finance companies, and mortgage companies.

Life Insurance Companies Though the main purpose of life insurance companies is to provide financial security for dependents, many insurance policies also contain savings and investment features. In addition, some insurance companies offer retirement planning services. You will learn more about life insurance in Chapter 14.

Investment Companies These firms combine your money with funds from other investors in order to buy stocks, bonds, and other securities. The investment company then manages these combined investments, which are called *mutual funds*. Chapter 10 discusses more about mutual funds.

Finance Companies Finance companies make higher-interest loans to consumers and small businesses that cannot borrow elsewhere because they have below-average credit ratings.

Teaching Activity Divide the students into groups of four and assign to each group a deposit or non-deposit financial institution. Have each group prepare a poster advertisement for an institution of that type, promoting what will best sell that institution to the general public. Display completed ads around the room.

Mortgage Companies Mortgage companies specialize in loans for the purchase of homes. Chapter 7 discusses the finances of housing.

Comparing Financial Institutions

What should you know to choose a financial institution?

When you compare banks and other financial institutions, you should ask these questions to help choose the best one:

- Where can you get the highest rate of interest on your savings?
- Where can you obtain a checking account with low (or no) fees?
- Will you be able to borrow money from the institution—with a credit card or another type of loan—when you need it?
- Do you need an institution that offers free financial advice?
- Is the institution FDIC- or SAIF-insured?
- Does the institution have convenient locations?
- Does it have online banking services?
- Does it have any special banking services that you might need?

As You Read

QUESTION

Under what circumstances might you be better off with each of these institutions: a commercial bank, a savings and loan association, a mutual savings bank, or a credit union?

Question Answer Commercial banks are best if you need a wide range of services. Savings and loans now provide many of the same services but may have better lending rates/policies. Mutual savings banks may have lower interest rates on loans and higher rates on savings accounts. Credit unions also offer a full range of services and may have lower rates/fees.

Section 5.1 Assessment

See the Teacher Manual for answers.

QUICK CHECK

1. What are three main categories of services offered by financial institutions?
2. What are the types of electronic banking services that are available?
3. Which institutions fall under the category of deposit institutions? Which are classified as non-deposit institutions?

THINK CRITICALLY

4. Name some financial services you use now. How might your needs for services change in the next five years?

USE MATH SKILLS

5. **Wise Use of ATMs** Margaret uses an ATM three times a week. It is not her bank's machine, but it is convenient to the store where she works. For every transaction, Margaret pays a fee of $1.50.

Calculate What is Margaret's annual expense for the use of this ATM?

SOLVE MONEY PROBLEMS

6. **Choosing a Financial Institution** Dakota is thinking about changing banks. He has a part-time job at a supermarket. Sometimes he works late hours, and he would like the convenience of being able to make deposits and withdrawals at any time. He needs cash for food and gas, and he writes only two checks a month—to his music CD club account and to his credit card company. Soon he will need to take out a loan to buy a car. He also wants to put aside some money to pay for technical school.

Write About It Help Dakota select the type of financial institution that offers the features that would be most useful to him and write a list for him.

Section 5.2

Focus on Reading

Read to Learn

- How to compare the costs and benefits of different savings plans.
- How to explain features of different savings plans.
- How to compare the costs and benefits of different types of checking accounts.
- How to use a checking account effectively.

Main Idea

Recognizing the types of savings plans and payment methods that financial institutions offer can help you use money wisely.

Key Terms

- certificate of deposit (CD)
- money market account
- rate of return
- compounding
- annual percentage yield (APY)
- overdraft protection
- stop-payment order
- endorsement
- bank reconciliation

Before You Read

PREDICT

What is the difference between a CD and a money market account?

Savings Plans and Payment Methods

Types of Savings Plans

What are some savings program options?

To achieve your financial goals, you will need a savings program. Various types of savings programs include regular savings accounts, certificates of deposit, money market accounts, and U.S. Savings Bonds. (See **Figure 5.3.**)

Regular Savings Accounts

Regular savings accounts, traditionally called *passbook accounts*, are ideal if you plan to make frequent deposits and withdrawals. They require little or no minimum balance and allow you to withdraw money on demand. The trade-off for this convenience is that the interest you earn will be low compared with other savings plans.

You may receive a passbook that records deposits and withdrawals, but typically, you will get a monthly or quarterly statement in the mail. Commercial banks, savings and loan associations, and other financial institutions offer regular savings accounts. At credit unions they may be called *share accounts*.

Certificates of Deposit

A **certificate of deposit (CD)** is a savings alternative in which money is left on deposit for a stated period of time to earn a specific rate of return. This period of time is called the *term*. The date when the money becomes available to you is called the *maturity date*. This savings plan is a relatively low-risk way to invest your money. It offers a higher interest rate than a regular savings account pays, but you will have to accept a few trade-offs.

To earn the higher interest rate paid by CDs, you must accept three key limitations. First, you may have to leave your money on deposit for one month to five or more years. Second, you probably will pay a penalty if you take the money out before the maturity date. Third, financial institutions require that you deposit a minimum amount to buy a certificate of deposit. This amount is usually larger than the balance a regular savings account requires.

CD Investment Strategies Here are some tips for investing in CDs:

- Find out where you can get the best rate. You can put your savings in a bank anywhere in the United States. You can use the Internet to find out what rates banks offer all over the country.
- Consider the economy as you decide what maturity date to choose. You may want to buy a long-term CD if interest rates are relatively high. Then, if interest rates go down because of changes in the economy, your money will continue to earn the higher rate.
- Never let a financial institution "roll over" a CD. For example, if your one-year CD matures, and you do nothing, the bank will redeposit that money in another one-year CD. You may decide to roll over, however, if you know that you will get the best rate possible.
- Consider when you will need the money. If you plan to use the money in two years to help pay for college, then buy a CD with a term of two years or less.
- If you have enough funds to have several accounts, you might consider creating a CD portfolio, which includes CDs that mature at different times. For example, you could have $1,000 in a three-month CD, $1,000 in a six-month CD, and $1,000 in a one-year CD. This way, you would be able to withdraw money at different times and still get better interest rates than you would with a passbook savings account.

Springboard Ask students to outline on paper a savings plan for themselves and to set two goals that will make their programs successful.

Motivating Students Ask the students why they think people often put some money into various savings plans rather than investing everything in the stock market or real estate.

Figure 5.3 **Savings Alternatives**

Type of Account	Benefits	Drawbacks
Regular savings accounts	• Low minimum balance • Ease of withdrawal • Insured	• Low rate of return
Certificates of deposit (CDs)	• Guaranteed rate of return for time of CD • Insured	• Possible penalty for early withdrawal • Minimum deposit
Money market accounts	• Good rate of return • Some check writing • Insured	• Minimum balance • No interest and possible service charge if below a certain balance
U.S. Savings Bonds	• Low minimum deposit • Guaranteed by the government • Free from state and local taxes	• Lower rate of return when cashed in before bond reaches maturity date

So Many Choices Each type of savings plan has pros and cons that you should consider.

Which type(s) would be best for a person who wants to save frequently but with small amounts?

Caption Answer regular savings accounts and savings bonds

Critical Thinking Have the students research both certificates of deposit and money market accounts to learn what each offers savers. Then have students write an essay comparing and contrasting the two account types.

Money Market Accounts

A **money market account** is a savings account that requires a minimum balance and earns interest that varies from month to month. The rates float, or go up and down, as market rates change. Although the interest rate of a money market account is usually higher than that of a regular savings account, a money market account also requires a higher minimum balance, typically $1,000. You may have to pay a penalty if your balance goes below the minimum amount. You can write a limited number of checks to make large payments or to transfer money to other accounts. The FDIC insures money market accounts up to $100,000.

U.S. Savings Bonds

Another savings option is purchasing a U.S. Savings Bond (also called a *Patriot Bond*). For example, when Meagan graduated high school in 2005, her aunt gave her a U.S. Savings Bond as a gift. Her aunt paid $250 for the bond, but it has a face value of $500. This means that if Meagan keeps the bond long enough until the designated maturity date, it will eventually earn enough interest to be worth $500 or even more.

▲ **MEETING GOALS** Most people save for many years to go to college. *Why might certificates of deposit and U.S. Savings Bonds be good investments for someone who is saving for a long-term goal such as college?*

Caption Answer They are sold in varying amounts and periods of time, and offer better interest than regular savings accounts, and you can stagger maturity dates.

You can purchase Series EE Savings Bonds from the federal government in amounts that range from $25 to $5,000 (face values of $50 to $10,000, respectively). The government limits total purchases per year to $15,000 ($30,000 face value) per person. You may buy savings bonds from banks or through the governments' Web site. The Federal Reserve sends bond certificates within 15 business days.

The maturity date, or the date a bond reaches its face value, depends on the date it was bought and the interest rate the bond is earning. For some bonds, the rate changes every six months. Because interest rates vary, no official maturity date exists for Series EE Savings Bonds. Bonds purchased after April 1997 and cashed after less than five years are subject to a three-month penalty—that is, you will not receive any interest for the last three months before you cash it. For example, if you cash a bond after 18 months, you receive only 15 months' worth of interest.

A Series EE Savings Bond continues to earn interest for 30 years if you do not cash it in. The longer you hold it, the more it is worth. Its value may be more than the face value if it is held past maturity.

Meagan kept her bond for ten years. In 2004, she decided to cash it in to help her make a down payment on a condominium. She found out that it was worth a little more than $450. Your bond's worth will depend on current interest rates and on the month and year in which the bond was issued.

Taxes on Savings Bonds The interest you earn on Series EE Bonds is exempt from, or free of, state and local taxes. You do not pay federal taxes on the interest earnings until you cash in the bond. Once a Series EE Bond has reached maturity, you can choose to defer federal taxes further by exchanging it for a Series HH Bond. Low- and middle-income families who use the money from redeemed Series EE Bonds to pay for higher education pay no taxes on the interest.

WebQuest

Your Own Home
Learn about saving for a down payment on your first home and how to choose a bank that fits your needs.

To continue with Task 2 of your WebQuest project, visit **finance07.glencoe.com**.

Discussion Discuss with students the advantages of buying series EE U.S. Savings Bonds; include in the discussion where bonds can be purchased.

Evaluating Savings Plans

How should you evaluate a savings plan?

Your selection of a savings plan will be influenced by several factors. You should consider the rate of return, inflation, tax considerations, liquidity, restrictions, and fees.

Rate of Return

Earnings on savings can be measured by the rate of return, or yield. The **rate of return** is the percentage of increase in the value of your savings from earned interest. For example, when Emisha put the $75 she earned from babysitting on New Year's Eve into a regular savings account last year, she earned $3 in interest. Therefore, her rate of return was 4 percent. To calculate the rate of return, she divided the total interest by the amount of her deposit ($3 ÷ $75 = .04 or 4 percent).

Teaching Activity Tell students three bankers representing three different types of banking institutions will be coming to class to talk about various savings plans at their banks. Have the students each prepare three questions they want to ask.

As You Read

RELATE

Do you currently have a savings account? Do you know if your interest is compounded daily, monthly, or annually? What difference does it make?

Compounding The yield on your savings will usually be greater than the stated interest rate. **Compounding** is the process in which interest is earned on both the principal—the original amount you deposited—and on any previously earned interest. It is a multistep process for computing interest. First, the interest on the principal is computed. That interest is added to the principal. The next time interest is computed, the new, larger balance is used. Compounding may take place every year, every quarter, every month, or even every day.

How much interest would your account earn in one year if the interest were compounded monthly? To make this calculation, first multiply the principal by the annual interest rate. Divide that figure by 12, the number of months in a year. This is the interest you would earn after the first month. To calculate the interest earned for the second month, add any interest earned in the first month to the principal. Then take that amount and multiply it by the annual interest rate. Next divide that number by 12. This is your interest earned in the second month. After you have repeated this calculation for all 12 months, add the monthly interest totals. The sum of the monthly interest amounts is the interest your account would earn in one year if the interest were compounded monthly.

GO FIGURE FINANCIAL MATH

INTEREST COMPOUNDED MONTHLY

Synopsis: Savings accounts that pay interest monthly can end up earning more interest than an account that pays once a year.

Example: You deposit $100 in a savings account. The bank is paying you 4 percent annually, which is compounded monthly. How much interest will you earn for the year?

Formula: Find the interest earned for the first month:

A. $$\frac{\text{Principal} \times \text{Annual Interest Rate}}{12} = \text{Interest Earned for First Month}$$

B. $$\frac{(\text{Principal} + \text{Previously Earned Interest}) \times \text{Annual Interest Rate}}{12} = \text{Interest Earned for a Given Month}$$

Solution:

Month	Calculation
1	(\$100.00 × 4%) ÷ 12 = \$0.33
2	(\$100.33 × 4%) ÷ 12 = \$0.33
3	(\$100.66 × 4%) ÷ 12 = \$0.34
4	(\$101.00 × 4%) ÷ 12 = \$0.34
5	(\$101.34 × 4%) ÷ 12 = \$0.34
6	(\$101.68 × 4%) ÷ 12 = \$0.34
7	(\$102.02 × 4%) ÷ 12 = \$0.34
8	(\$102.36 × 4%) ÷ 12 = \$0.34
9	(\$102.70 × 4%) ÷ 12 = \$0.34
10	(\$103.04 × 4%) ÷ 12 = \$0.34
11	(\$103.38 × 4%) ÷ 12 = \$0.34
12	(\$103.72 × 4%) ÷ 12 = \$0.35

At the end of the year, you will have $104.07 ($100.00 + $4.07 = $104.07). You earned $4.07 in compounded interest for the year.

YOU FIGURE

How much interest would this account earn if interest was paid once for the whole year?

Answer $4.00 ($100 x .04 = $4)

GO FIGURE — FINANCIAL MATH

RATE OF RETURN

Synopsis: A compounded rate of return (percentage) is more than the stated year's rate.

Example: You deposit $100 in a savings account. The bank is paying you 4 percent annually, compounded monthly. After one year, the account has earned $4.07 in interest. What would your rate of return be for one year?

Formula: $\frac{\text{Total Interest Earned}}{\text{Original Deposit}} = \text{Rate of Return}$

Solution: $\frac{\$4.07}{\$100} = 0.0407 = 4.07\%$

Your rate of return is 4.07 percent.

YOU FIGURE

What would be your rate of return for one year if the account earned $5.14 in interest on a deposit of $100?

Answer $5.14 ÷ 100 = 5.14%

The more frequently your balance is compounded, the greater your yield, or rate of return, will be. For example, if you deposited $100 in an account with a 4 percent annual interest rate that is compounded annually (once a year), after one year you will earn $4 ($100 × .04 or 4% = $4). Your rate of return is 4 percent. If you put that same $100 in an account that is compounded monthly at an annual interest rate of 4 percent, your rate of return will be higher.

Remember, your rate of return is the total interest earned divided by the amount of your original deposit. The difference may not seem like much, but compounding can have a great impact on large amounts of money that are held in savings accounts for long periods.

Truth in Savings According to the Truth in Savings law (Federal Reserve Regulation DD), financial institutions have to inform you of the following information:

- Fees on deposit accounts
- Interest rate
- Annual percentage yield (APY)
- Terms and conditions of the savings plan

The **annual percentage yield (APY)** is the amount of interest that a $100 deposit would earn, after compounding, for one year. The interest is based on the annual stated interest rate and the frequency of compounding for a 365-day period. In the previous **Go Figure** example, the APY is 4.07 percent. The higher the APY is, the better the return. The APY helps you determine the amount you can expect to earn on your money. Because the APY is stated as a percentage and as an annual rate, it you can compare savings plans that have different rates and compounding frequencies.

Document Detective

Learn to identify and understand the standard financial documents you will use in the real world.

See the Teacher Manual for answers.

Investigate: A Checking Account Bank Statement

A checking account bank statement contains the following information:

- Balance, or amount, in the account at the beginning of a time period
- Deposits made to the account
- Deductions made from the account
- Ending balance at the end of the time period

Your Motive: You need to keep track of deductions and deposits in your check register as you write checks and deposit money. The monthly statement is the bank's record of that activity. It is important that your records and the bank's records are the same so your account will not get overdrawn.

SMITHVILLE BANK N.A.

Tom Jones
21 First Street
Smithville, Florida 55523

ACCOUNT SUMMARY	***Statement Date: 02/24/05***
Balance forwarded from 01/23/05	$41,452.80
Checks	6,310.00
Interest added	50.59
Ending balance	**$35,193.39**

ELECTRONIC CREDITS

Date	Description	
2/24/05	INTEREST PAID	$50.59

CHECKS AND OTHER DEBITS

Date	Check#	Amount
01/27/05	1043	$70.00
02/18/05	1044	100.00
02/12/05	1045	3,600.00
02/10/05	1046	2,440.00
02/19/05	1047	100.00

DAILY BALANCE SUMMARY

Date	Balance
1/27/05	$41,382.80
02/10/05	38,942.80
02/12/05	35,342.80
02/18/05	35,242.80
02/19/05	35,142.80
02/24/05	35,193.39

Key Points: If there is a difference between your records and the bank's records, you need to resolve the problem with your bank. If the bank thinks you have less money than you do, your checks may "bounce," or be rejected and go unpaid, causing the bank to charge you penalty fees.

Find the Solutions

1. What time period does this statement cover?
2. From this statement, what do you think is the meaning of the word *credits*?
3. From this statement, what do you think is the meaning of the word *debits*?
4. On 02/10/05, the balance in this account changed. Why?
5. There is a line on this statement that reads "Checks 6,310.00." What does this mean?

Inflation

You should compare the rate of interest you earn on your savings with the rate of inflation. If you open a savings account that offers 3 percent interest, and the inflation rate rises to 6 percent, your money will lose value and buying power. Usually, however, the interest rates offered on savings accounts increase if the rate of inflation increases. The biggest problem with inflation occurs if you are locked into a lower interest rate for a long period.

Tax Considerations

Like inflation, taxes reduce the interest earned on savings. For example, Karim was glad to find a savings account that would pay 5 percent interest. However, he was not happy when he filled out his tax return and had to pay taxes on that interest. He decided to look into tax-exempt and tax-deferred savings plans for some of his money.

Liquidity

Check the savings plans you are considering to determine whether they charge a penalty or pay a lower rate of interest if you withdraw your funds early. If you need to be able to withdraw your money easily, put your money in a liquid account—even if it earns lower interest. On the other hand, if you are saving for long-term goals, a high interest rate is more important than liquidity.

Restrictions and Fees

Be aware of any restrictions on savings plans, such as a delay between the time when interest is earned and when it is actually paid into your account. Also check for fees for making deposits and withdrawals. Find out about any service charges you may have to pay if your balance drops below a certain amount, or if you do not use your account for a certain period. These fees and service charges can add up.

STANDARD & POOR'S — Put on Your Financial Planner's Cap

A previously unknown relative has died and left your friend $50,000. Would you recommend that she open a checking account, a savings account, or another type of account? Why or why not?

See the Teacher Manual for answers.

Types of Checking Accounts

What are the different kinds of checking accounts?

Checking accounts can be divided into three main categories: regular, activity, and interest-earning accounts.

Regular Checking Accounts

Regular checking accounts usually do not require a minimum balance. However, if the account does require a minimum balance, and your account drops below that amount, you will have to pay a monthly service charge. A $10 charge every month can take a bite out of your funds. Some institutions will waive a service charge if you keep a certain balance in your savings account.

STANDARD
&POOR'S

Global Financial Landscape

Standard and Poor's publishes the globally recognized S&P 500® financial index. It also gathers financial statistics, information, and news, and analyzes this data for international businesses, governments, and individuals to help them guide their financial decisions.

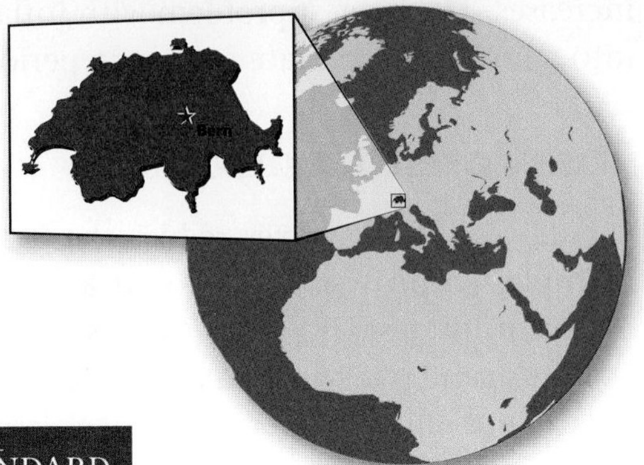

SWITZERLAND

Say "Switzerland," and people often think of rich chocolate, cozy alpine villages, and cuckoo clocks. Switzerland also boasts its most famous industry—banking. Once called the crossroads of Europe, the country of Switzerland has been one of the world's most important financial centers for centuries. Its government's neutrality during times of war and the skill of its bankers attract depositors by the millions. Above all, clients—from the ordinary to the rich—appreciate the banks' secrecy. Numbers, not names, identify each customer. "Serious money is safe and private in a Swiss bank in Switzerland," promises one ad. However, a new Swiss federal law now prohibits complete secrecy. Deposits of questionable or criminal origin must be reported to the authorities.

STANDARD
&POOR'S **DATABYTES**

Capital	Bern
Population	7,341,000
Languages	German, French, Italian, and Romanisch
Currency	Swiss franc
Gross Domestic Product (GDP)	$239.8 billion (2003 est.)
GDP per capita	$32,800

Industry: Banking, machinery, chemicals, watches, textiles, and precision instruments

Agriculture: Grains, fruits and vegetables, and meat

Exports: Machinery, chemicals, metals, watches, and agricultural products

Natural Resources: Hydropower potential, timber, and salt

Think Globally

If you were planning to open a checking or savings account in Switzerland or the United States what three types of accounts would you consider?

See the Teacher Manual for answer.

Activity Accounts

If you write only a few checks each month and are unable to maintain a minimum balance, this type of checking account may be right for you. The financial institution will charge a fee for each check you write and sometimes a fee for each deposit. In addition, a monthly service fee will be charged. However, you do not need to maintain a minimum balance.

Interest-Earning Checking Accounts

Interest-earning checking accounts are a combination of checking and savings accounts. These accounts pay interest if you maintain a minimum balance. If your account balance goes below the limit, you may not earn any interest, and you may also have to pay a service charge.

Evaluating Checking Accounts

What factors should you consider when choosing a checking account?

How do you decide which type of checking account will meet your needs? You will need to weigh several factors: restrictions, fees and charges, interest, and special services.

Restrictions

The most common restriction is the requirement that you keep a minimum balance. Other restrictions may include the number of transactions allowed and the number of checks you may write in a month.

Fees and Charges

You may pay a monthly service charge as well as fees for check printing, overdrafts, and stop-payment orders.

Interest

Interest rates, frequency of compounding, and the way in which interest is calculated all affect an interest-bearing checking account.

Special Services

Checking account services include ATMs and banking by telephone and online. As a checking account customer, you may also receive **overdraft protection**—an automatic loan made to an account if the balance will not cover checks written. The institution will charge interest on that loan, but the amount may be less than the fee for overdrawing your account. Your bank may also offer an overdraft protection service that transfers money from your savings to your checking account.

The Check Clearing for the 21st Century Act, or "Check 21," took effect as of October 28, 2004. The Act allows banks to dispense with original paper checks. Banks can now transmit electronic images of checks through the check-clearing process. If you want to receive your cancelled paper check, the bank will provide a substitute check, such as a printout of an electronic image, for a fee.

Academic Connection

HISTORY

In response to financial hardship caused by the Great Depression, the Emergency Banking Act of 1933 called for a four-day bank holiday during which time all banks were assessed by federal inspectors. Within those four days, roughly two-thirds of the nation's banks were declared financially secure and were reopened, restoring Americans' faith in banking institutions. *Research the Great Depression and write a short paragraph explaining why you think the Emergency Banking Act helped restore faith in banking institutions.*

See the Teacher Manual for answer.

$avvy Saver

Finding the Best Savings Account

1. Shop around to find the bank that offers the highest interest rates.
2. Ask if you must deposit a minimum amount.
3. Find out if the bank pays less on small accounts.
4. Ask the bank how often it credits interest to your account.
5. Ask if you will receive simple interest or compound interest.

Using a Checking Account

How do you open and use a checking account?

After you select the type of checking account that best fits your needs, you need to know how to use it effectively.

Opening a Checking Account

Before you open a checking account, decide whether you want an individual or joint account. An individual account has one owner; a joint account has two or more. Personal joint accounts are usually "or" accounts, which means that only one of the owners needs to sign a check. You sign a signature card at the bank so that your signature on a check can be verified.

Writing Checks

Before you write a check, write the date, the number of the check, the name of the party who will receive the payment, and the exact amount in your check register. A check register is a small booklet that you use to record activity in your account. You receive it with your supply of blank checks. Record all checks that you write, deposits, ATM withdrawals, debit card charges, interest earned (if any), any fees, and other transactions. Be sure to keep a current balance of the money you have by deducting from or adding to your balance the amount of any check transaction. **Figure 5.4** shows a sample check register.

Figure 5.4 Check Register

NUMBER	DATE	DESCRIPTION OF TRANSACTION	PAYMENT/DEBIT (-)		√ T	FEE (IF ANY) (-)	DEPOSIT/CREDIT (+)		BALANCE	
									$ 418	00
106	7/15	Bob's Service Station	$ 25	00		$	$		-25	00
		oil change							393	00
107	7/15	Cutler Enterprises	14	00					-14	00
		magazine subscription							379	00
108	7/16	Motor Vehicles Department	160	00					-160	00
		renewal							219	00
109	7/18	Jack's Music	34	00					-34	00
		gift							185	00

Keeping Track This sample check register shows how to keep track of checks as you write them.

What other amounts should you record in your check register?

Caption Answer deposits, fees, interest earned (if any), debits made with a debit card

Figure 5.5 Sample Personal Check

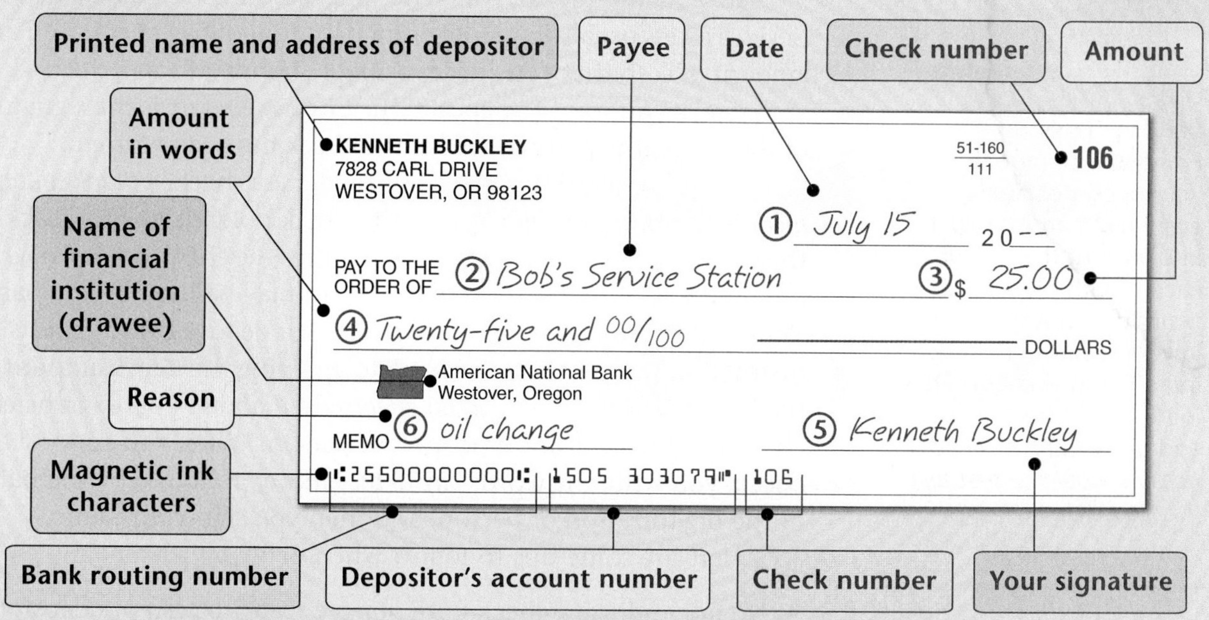

Personal Check Never write a check in pencil and always write legibly.

Why do you have to write the amount in words and in numerals?

Caption Answer There will be no confusion about the amount of the check.

Figure 5.5 illustrates the correct way to write a check. Follow these steps when you write a check:

1. Write the current date.
2. Write the name of the party (payee) who will receive the check.
3. Record the amount of the payment in numerals.
4. Write the amount in words.
5. Sign the check in the same way you signed your signature card at the bank.
6. Make a note of the reason for the payment. This is a good place to record an account number if the payment is for a credit card or service, such as electricity or cable television.

If you make a mistake when writing a check, do not erase the error. Write a new check, tear up the old check, and write the word *Void* in your check register. If the mistake is small, you may be able to correct the check and write your initials next to the correction.

If a check is lost or stolen, or if you want to take back your payment for a business transaction, you may ask the bank to issue a stop-payment order. A **stop-payment order** is a request that a bank or other financial institution not cash a particular check. Fees for this service can range from $10 to $20 or more.

Extension Provide each student with a mock-up check register and three mock-up checks. In class, have the students practice writing checks. Ask the students to begin their check registers with the amount of money they have. Then have the students fill in the check register, over a three-day period, with all their cash outgo and "deposits" representing cash income. At the end of the period, the balance in the register should be the same as the money they then have.

Common CENTS

Money Toss
Empty the change from your pocket or wallet every night and throw it into a jar. At the end of each month, deposit all your "throwaway" money in your savings or checking account account. That loose change can really add up. *What type of bank account would be best for your loose change? Why?*

Common Cents A regular savings account because you can add to it in small increments.

Making Deposits

To add money to your checking account, fill out a deposit ticket. Tickets usually include room to list four or five checks and any amount of cash that you are depositing. Endorse, or sign, the back of each check you want to deposit. The **endorsement** is the signature of the payee, the party to whom the check has been written.

There are also different ways to endorse a check. A *blank endorsement* is the most simple. You or the check holder signs the back of the check. A *restrictive endorsement* requires the check holder's signature and a restriction on how the paper may be used by the bank. The most common expression used is "For deposit only." This is an instruction that restricts the bank to applying the check amount to the holder's account. A *special endorsement* allows you to transfer a check to an organization or another person. When you endorse the check, you write the words *pay to the order of,* followed by the name of the organization or person, and then you sign your name.

Here are some tips to follow when endorsing a check:

- Do not endorse a check until you are ready to cash or deposit it.
- Write your signature on the back of the check at the top left end.
- Sign your name exactly as it appears on the front of the check.
- Use a pen so that your signature cannot be erased.
- If depositing a check by mail, write "For deposit only" above your signature.

Check Clearing

Check clearing is a system that ensures that the money you deposited in the account is available for withdrawal. For example, if you deposit a check for $50 into your account, your bank usually holds that $50 until it clears with the bank on which it was drawn. During this time you cannot withdraw that money. By law, institutions are limited to holding funds from checks drawn on local banks to no more than two business days, and from checks drawn on nonlocal banks to no more than five business days. Check-clearing rules vary by bank, so ask your bank about its rules.

Keeping Track of a Checking Account

Each month your bank will send you a statement that shows your checking account activity for the month.

Your bank statement will list:

- Deposits
- Checks you have written (charged against your account)
- ATM withdrawals
- Debit card charges (identified by the business or organization to whom you made the payment)
- Interest earned
- Fees

Reconciliation The balance reported on the bank statement may be different from the balance in your check register. You might have written checks that have not yet cleared your bank, or maybe you deposited money into your account after the bank prepared your statement.

To determine your true balance, you can fill out a bank reconciliation form. A **bank reconciliation** is a report that accounts for the differences between the bank statement and a checkbook balance. This process is called *balancing your checkbook*. To balance, or reconcile, your account, follow several steps (a simplified version of a reconciliation form is shown in **Figure 5.6**).

Figure 5.6 **Bank Account Reconciliation**

American National Bank
WESTOVER, OREGON

Kenneth Buckley
7828 Carl Drive
Westover, OR 98123

FDIC

Account Number: 303079
Statement Date: 7/15/--

Balance Last Statement	Deposits & Other Credits		Checks & Other Debits		Balance This Statement
	No.	Amount	No.	Amount	
00.00	2	700.00	5	482.00	218.00

Description	Checks & Other Debits	Deposits & Other Credits	Date	Balance
Balance Forward				00.00
Deposit		500.00	7/01	500.00
Check 101	273.00		7/04	227.00
Check 102	27.00		7/07	200.00
Check 103	50.00		7/08	150.00
Deposit		200.00	7/10	350.00
Check 104	100.00		7/14	250.00
Check 105	32.00		7/14	218.00

PLEASE EXAMINE YOUR STATEMENT AT ONCE. IF NO ERROR IS REPORTED IN 10 DAYS THE ACCOUNT WILL BE CONSIDERED CORRECT AND VOUCHERS GENUINE. ALL ITEMS ARE CREDITED SUBJECT TO FINAL PAYMENT.

BANK RECONCILIATION FORM

PLEASE EXAMINE YOUR STATEMENT AT ONCE. ANY DISCREPANCY SHOULD BE REPORTED TO THE BANK IMMEDIATELY.

1. In your checkbook, record any transactions appearing on this statement but not yet listed.		
2. List any checks still outstanding in the space provided to the right.		
3. Enter the balance shown on this statement here.	218	00
4. Enter deposits recorded in your checkbook but not shown on this statement.	——	—
5. Total lines 3 and 4 and enter here.	218	00
6. Enter total checks outstanding here.	69	00
7. Subtract line 6 from line 5. This adjusted bank balance should agree with your checkbook balance.	149	00

CHECKS OUTSTANDING		
Number	Amount	
106	25	00
107	14	00
108	30	00
TOTAL	69	00

Balancing Your Checkbook The adjusted bank balance should agree with your checkbook register.

Why should you reconcile your checking account with each new statement?

Caption Answer So you will avoid overdrawing your account, for you will know the exact balance. Another reason is to spot any bank errors.

As You Read
QUESTION

When you receive your checking account bank statement each month, what items might be on it that you do not show in your account register? Why is it important to enter these each month on your account register?

Question Answer Fees for various items might be on the statement; these should be entered so you will have the correct balance and avoid overdrawing your account.

1. Compare the checks you have written during the month with those that are listed on the bank statement as paid, or cleared. List all outstanding checks—checks you wrote but have not cleared. Subtract the total amount of outstanding checks from the balance on the bank statement.
2. Determine whether any recent deposits are not on the bank statement. If so, add the amounts of those deposits to the bank statement balance.
3. Subtract fees and charges listed on the statement from your checkbook balance.
4. Add interest earned to your checkbook balance.

Then compare the balance in your check register and the adjusted bank balance on the reconciliation form. They should be the same. If the balances do not match, check your math, and make sure all checks and deposits are entered in your check register and on the statement. If there is a bank error, report it.

Other Payment Methods

You may make payments by other methods besides using a personal check. A certified check is a personal check with a guaranteed payment. The financial institution deducts the amount from your account when it certifies the check. You can also purchase a cashier's check or money order from a financial institution. You pay the amount of the check or money order plus a fee. Travelers checks allow you to obtain cash in a country's currency when you are away from home.

Caption Answer Travelers checks are safer to carry than cash, because they can be replaced if lost or stolen.

▶ **TRAVELING MONEY** Travelers checks are one option for students who need to carry money while traveling in foreign countries. Most banks, hotels, and stores will accept this currency. *Why are travelers checks preferred over regular cash when traveling?*

You sign each check once when you purchase the checks and a second time when you cash them. If you lose a check or it is stolen, it can be replaced with proof of purchase. Prepaid travelers cards allow travelers to get local currency from ATMs throughout the world.

After You Read

REACT

What is a bank reconciliation? Why is it important?

React Answer A bank reconciliation allows you to balance your checkbook to the bank's figures. It is important so that you know your exact balance and catch any bank errors.

Financial Institutions and Your Money

How Do Banks Make Money?

The amount of deposits held by a bank affects its ability to loan money. Banks make money by making loans. The amount of money that banks can lend is affected by the reserve requirement set by the Federal Reserve. The reserve requirement is 3 percent to 10 percent of a bank's total deposits, including your deposit. For example, when a bank gets a deposit of $100, the bank can then lend out $90. That $90 goes back into the economy, paying for goods or services, and may end up deposited in another bank. That bank can then lend out $81 of that $90 deposit, and that $81 goes into the economy to pay for goods or services, and is then deposited into another bank that proceeds to lend out a percentage of it. Thus, banking your money benefits you as well as others in the economic system.

Section 5.2 Assessment

See the Teacher Manual for answers.

QUICK CHECK

1. What are some of the costs and benefits of a certificate of deposit?
2. What factors can you use to evaluate a savings plan?
3. What are regular, activity, and interest-earning checking accounts?

THINK CRITICALLY

4. Why do you think a law was passed to standardize the ways in which financial institutions inform consumers of the terms and conditions of savings plans?

USE COMMUNICATION SKILLS

5. **The Banking Business** Banks advertise to attract customers.

Present a Poster Choose one or more features of savings or checking accounts and create a poster advertising those features in a way that will inform people and invite them to become customers.

SOLVE MONEY PROBLEMS

6. **Checking Account Choices** Matthew Delarosa has just moved to a new town and is about to open a checking account. He pays for all his monthly expenses—rent, phone, car payment, credit card bills, dry cleaning, and insurance—by check.

Write About It With a partner, examine the features of the different types of checking accounts and write a paragraph to help Matthew decide which type would be best for him.

Chapter 5 Review & Activities

See the Teacher Manual for answers.

CHAPTER SUMMARY

- The three primary types of financial services are savings; payment services; and borrowing.
- Commercial banks, savings and loan associations, mutual savings banks, and credit unions are financial institutions that accept secure deposits and provide transfer and lending services. Life insurance companies and investment companies accept customers' funds, provide financial security for dependents, and invest and manage funds. Finance companies and mortgage companies offer loans.
- Bank savings plans offer the lowest interest rates with the greatest liquidity. Higher interest rates are available on certificates of deposit (CDs); money must be on deposit for a specified time. Money market accounts and U.S. Savings Bonds are less liquid than bank savings accounts, but may provide greater returns.
- To evaluate a savings plan, look at its features, such as its rate of return compared with inflation, tax considerations, liquidity, and restrictions and fees.
- Regular, activity, and interest-earning are the three categories of checking accounts. Some of these require minimum balances and/or fees for transactions. Some pay interest on deposits.
- To use a checking account, write checks carefully, endorse checks you deposit, and reconcile your checkbook against bank statements.

Communicating Key Terms

Write the copy for a promotional brochure for a commercial bank, explaining what the bank offers its customers. Use at least eight of the terms below in your brochure copy.

- direct deposit
- automated teller machine (ATM)
- debit card
- point-of-sale transaction
- commercial bank
- savings and loan association (S&L)
- credit union
- certificate of deposit (CD)
- money market account
- rate of return
- compounding
- annual percentage yield (APY)
- overdraft protection
- stop-payment order
- endorsement
- bank reconciliation

Reviewing Key Concepts

1. **Explain** two advantages and two disadvantages of online banking.
2. **Identify** the services offered by the different financial institutions.
3. **Explain** why a large, nationally chartered bank may be the safest place to deposit your money.
4. **Discuss** how you benefit when interest is compounded monthly as opposed to annually.
5. **Explain** the circumstances under which a person should choose a regular checking account, activity checking account, or interest-bearing checking account.
6. **List** the steps to take to use a checking account effectively.

See the Teacher Manual for answers.

ACADEMIC SKILLS

Economics Explain at least three ways to reduce ATM fees charged to your account. Also describe the trade-offs involved in each action.

Write About It Create a list with your explanations.

YOUR FINANCIAL FIGURES

Checking Account Minimum Balances Bank X offers a checking account with a minimum balance of $300, but does not charge fees nor give interest. Bank Y's minimum balance is $50, but it charges a fee of $25 if you have more than 35 transactions per month, including deposits. Both banks pay 2 percent interest on regular savings accounts and 3 percent on certificates of deposit with terms of 24 months.

1. **Describe** (a) Someone for whom Bank A's offer is the best deal. (b) Someone for whom Bank B's offer is the best deal.
2. **Compute** by using spreadsheet software bank statements that compare returns from Bank A and Bank B for the people profiled.

REAL-WORLD Application

Connect with Business and Government Check 21 is a federal law that lets banks handle more checks electronically, which should make check processing faster, more efficient, and less expensive. Before Check 21 became effective in late 2004, banks physically moved paper checks from one bank to another. If you used to receive your cancelled checks after they cleared your bank, you now receive a picture of the front and back of your checks instead.

1. **Research** Use library and online sources to find out more about Check 21.
2. **Think Critically** Who do you think benefits the most from this change? The least?

Internet CONNECTION

Banking Online Many banks offer online banking, but it does not appeal to everyone.

Log On Go to the Web site of a bank that you or your family uses and find out if it offers Internet banking. Answer the following questions:

1. How can you be sure the site is secure?
2. What transactions can you perform with an online account?

BusinessWeek ONLINE

Newsclip: Teen Savings Banks offer many savings options to teenagers. A teen can open a savings/passbook account or a CD (certificate of deposit).

Log On Go to **finance07.glencoe.com** and open Chapter 5. Read about the different types of available savings options. Then answer this question: When is it the right time to save, and what types of savings accounts are available?

WHAT'S YOUR FINANCIAL ID?

BASIC BANKING QUIZ

How much do you know about basic bank services and terms? Take this quiz before you read the chapter and retake it after studying the chapter to see how much you have learned. Write your answers on a separate sheet of paper.

1. A bank CD is a ____c____ .

a. cash deposit c. certificate of deposit
b. compact disc d. compact deposit

2. To borrow money from the bank, you need to ask for a ____a____ .

a. loan c. safe-deposit box
b. money market account d. transfer

3. You can store valuables in the bank's vault if you have ____c____ .

a. permission c. a safe-deposit box
b. a money market account d. an ATM card

4. You keep money in a bank account to ____d____ .

a. keep it safe c. learn financial responsibility
b. earn interest d. all of the above

5. The total amount of money in your bank account is called ____c____ .

a. the statement c. the balance
b. the interest d. peanuts

6. The amount of money your bank account earns depends on the ____d____ .

a. type of account you have c. interest rate
b. balance in your account d. all of the above

7. When you make a purchase and have the funds taken directly from your checking account, you use a ____c____ .

a. credit card c. debit card
b. note from your mother d. driver's license

8. To set up a savings plan that requires a low minimum balance and allows you to withdraw funds at any time, you would ____d____ .

a. buy a CD c. put the money under your mattress
b. buy a U.S. Savings Bond d. open a savings account

Your Financial Portfolio

Comparison Shopping for Banking Services

Sean is ready to open some bank accounts and is looking for the bank that best suits his needs. He is deciding between the local bank and the credit union where he works.

Sean's Savings Search

Name of Institution	Kensington Bank	Acme Credit Union
Savings		
Annual interest rate	1.8%	2.5%
Minimum balance required	$100	none
Certificate of Deposit (CD) interest rate for 6 months	5.20%	5.40%
Checking		
Monthly service charge	$8.50	$6.00
Minimum balance for "free" checking	$3,000	$1,000
Fees for ATM	Free	no ATMs
Cost of checks	$10.00	$8.75
Overdraft protection	yes	none
Banking hours	Mon.–Sat. 9–6, Closed Sun.	Mon.–Fri. 9–6, Closed Sat. and Sun.

Sean decided to open a checking account at the bank because he needs the convenience of using the ATM. He opened a savings account at the credit union because it pays higher interest. When he has enough money, he will also purchase a CD at the credit union.

Compare

In your workbook or on a separate sheet of paper, list the banking services that are important to you. Then call or visit several banks in your area and compare services, costs, and interest rates that are available to you. What services are most important to you? Which bank would you choose? Explain why.

Accept all reasonable answers that show student effort and an understanding of the concept.

CHAPTER 6

Consumer Credit

$ What You'll Learn

When you have completed this chapter, you will be able to:

Section 6.1

- Explain the meaning of consumer credit.
- Differentiate between closed-end credit and open-end credit.

Section 6.2

- Name the five C's of credit.
- Identify factors to consider when choosing a loan or credit card.
- Explain how to build and protect your credit rating.

Section 6.3

- Discuss how to protect yourself from fraud and identity theft.

Section 6.4

- Identify ways to manage debt problems.

Reading Strategies

To get the most out of your reading:

Predict what you will learn in this chapter.
Relate what you read to your own life.
Question what you are reading to be sure you understand.
React to what you have read.

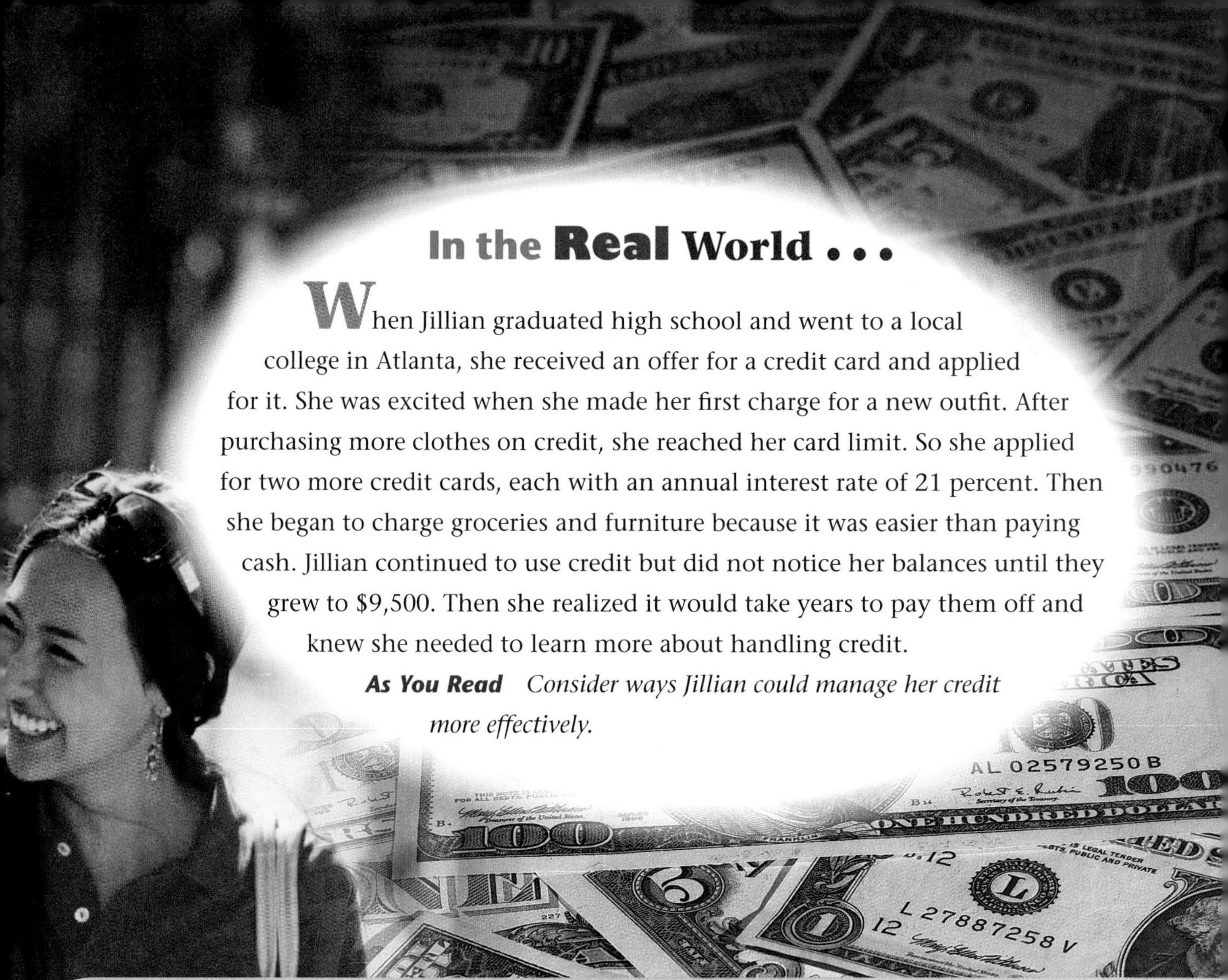

In the **Real** World . . .

When Jillian graduated high school and went to a local college in Atlanta, she received an offer for a credit card and applied for it. She was excited when she made her first charge for a new outfit. After purchasing more clothes on credit, she reached her card limit. So she applied for two more credit cards, each with an annual interest rate of 21 percent. Then she began to charge groceries and furniture because it was easier than paying cash. Jillian continued to use credit but did not notice her balances until they grew to $9,500. Then she realized it would take years to pay them off and knew she needed to learn more about handling credit.

As You Read *Consider ways Jillian could manage her credit more effectively.*

Lesson Plan See the Teacher Manual for the Chapter 6 planning guide and lesson plan.

ASK STANDARD & POOR'S

Credit Payments

Q: My brother is going to college and has three credit cards with balances totaling $5,000. He is having trouble paying the minimum monthly payments. What should I tell him?

A: He needs a plan to pay down these debts. Have him contact the credit card companies and tell them that he wants to pay the debt and maintain good credit. They may accept payments of interest only for a few months while he finds ways to increase his income or cut spending.

Ask Yourself Why would communicating with a debtor (the credit card company) benefit someone who is behind in payments?

@ Go to **finance07.glencoe.com** to complete the Standard & Poor's Financial Focus activity.

Section 6.1

Focus on Reading

Read to Learn

- How to explain the meaning of consumer credit.
- How to differentiate between closed-end credit and open-end credit.

Main Idea

There are advantages to using consumer credit if you use it correctly.

Key Terms

- credit
- consumer credit
- creditor
- closed-end credit
- open-end credit
- line of credit
- grace period
- finance charge

Before You Read

PREDICT

What is your definition of credit?

Springboard Ask the students how many of them have credit cards and what they use them for. Then ask and lead discussion on whether high school students should be permitted to have credit cards.

What Is Consumer Credit?

Using Consumer Credit Wisely

Why is having good credit important?

When you borrow money or charge an item to a credit card, you are using credit. **Credit** is an arrangement to receive cash, goods, or services now and pay for them in the future. **Consumer credit** is the use of credit for personal needs. It is also an indicator of consumer spending and demand. A common form of consumer credit is a credit card account issued by a financial institution. Merchants may also provide financing for products that they sell. Banks may directly finance purchases through loans and mortgages. A financial institution, merchant, or individual can be a **creditor**—an entity that lends money. Good credit is valuable. Having the ability to borrow funds allows us to buy things we would otherwise have to save for years to afford: homes, cars, or a college education. Credit is an important financial tool, but it can also be dangerous, leading people into debt beyond their ability to repay. That is why using credit wisely is a valuable financial skill.

Today consumer credit is a major force in the American economy, and the use of credit is a basic factor in personal and family financial planning (see **Figure 6.1**). Sometimes using credit is necessary, and it can be an advantage. However, paying for an item through credit also involves responsibility and risks.

Credit Uses and Misuses

When is it appropriate to use credit?

You can probably think of many good reasons for using credit. For example, maybe you can buy something on credit now for less money than it will cost to pay in cash later. If you live in an area that lacks good public transportation, you may need a vehicle to travel. But when is it appropriate to use credit? If you cannot afford a high monthly payment, it probably is not a good idea to borrow money to buy an expensive sports car when all you need is simple and reliable transportation.

Using credit may increase the amount of money you can spend now, but the cost of credit decreases the amount of money you will have in the future. That is because you will be paying back the money you borrowed along with any charges for borrowing that money.

Figure 6.1 Consumer Installment Credit

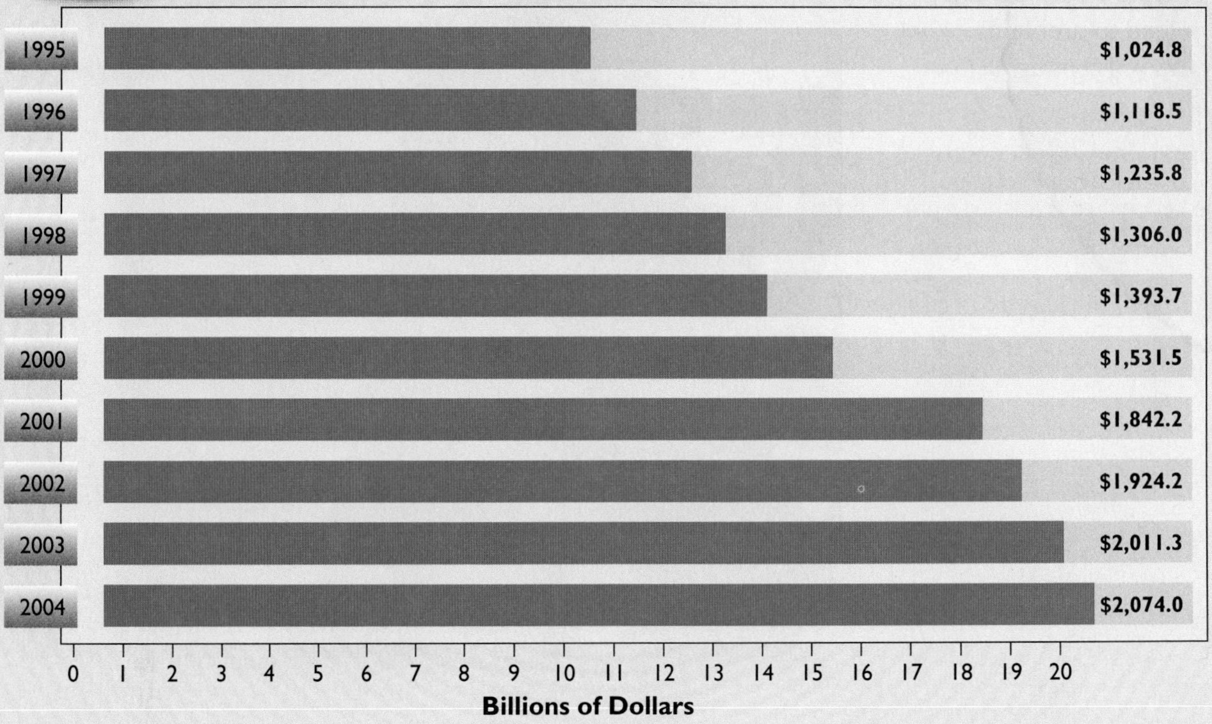

Source: *Statistical Abstract of the United States 2004*, G.19.

Colossal Credit Economists recognize consumer credit as a major force in the U.S. economy.

What is one disadvantage of using credit?

Caption Answer
Answers may include:
Credit costs money; using credit tempts people to buy more than they can afford; if you fail to repay credit loans, you will lose your credit reputation; or you can lose money or property to repay credit debt.

Factors to Consider Before Using Credit

What should you know before using credit?

Imagine you want to finance—give or get money for—a used vehicle. Before you decide to finance a major purchase by using credit, consider:

- Do you have the cash you need for the down payment?
- Do you want to use your savings instead of credit?
- Can you afford the item?
- Could you use the credit in some better way?
- Could you put off buying the item for a while?
- What are the costs of using credit?

When you buy something on credit, you also agree to pay the fee that a creditor adds to the purchase price. For example, if you do not pay your credit card bill in full every month, you will be charged interest on the amount that you have not paid. Interest is the price that is paid for the use of another's money. It can be a periodic charge for the use of credit. Think carefully before you decide to use credit. Make sure the benefits of making the purchase now outweigh the costs of credit.

As You Read

RELATE

Did you ever use credit to buy something you could not afford?

Motivating Students Have students write down one costly item that they would buy if they had enough credit. Then explain that this was a trap because, although they might be able to make the purchase on credit, they probably would not be able to make the monthly payments. Discuss the list of Factors to Consider.

▶ **THINK FIRST** Everyone likes to have nice things, but using credit unwisely can lead to problems. *What should you consider before using credit?*

Caption Answer Consider if you can really afford to buy the items when it is time to pay for them.

Advantages of Credit

Discussion Discuss with students whether they think loans between family members are a good or a bad idea.

The main advantage of using consumer credit is that it lets you enjoy goods and services now, perhaps when your funds are low, and pay for them later. Credit cards allow you to combine several purchases, making just one monthly payment.

If you are making hotel reservations, renting a car, or shopping by phone or online, you will probably need a credit card. Using credit gives you a record of your expenses. Shopping and traveling without carrying a lot of cash is safer.

Finally, if you use credit wisely, other lenders will view you as a responsible person.

As You Read

QUESTION

Why is it important to protect your good reputation as a borrower?

Question Answer Lenders will view you as responsible and a good risk for future loans.

Disadvantages of Credit

Always remember that credit costs money. Perhaps the greatest disadvantage of using credit is the temptation to buy more than you can afford. Using credit to buy goods or services you cannot afford can lead to serious trouble. If you fail to repay a loan, or a credit card balance, you can lose your good credit reputation. You may also lose some of your income and property, which may be taken from you in order to repay your debts.

Using credit does not increase your total purchasing power, nor does it mean that you have more money. It just allows you buy things now for which you must pay later. If your income does not increase, you may have difficulty paying your bills. Therefore, you should always approach credit with caution and avoid using it for more than your budget allows.

Types of Credit

Why will you need more than one type of credit?

There are two basic types of consumer credit: closed-end credit and open-end credit. You may use both types during your lifetime because each has advantages and disadvantages.

Closed-End Credit

Closed-end credit is credit as a one-time loan that you will pay back over a specified period of time in payments of equal amounts. Closed-end credit is used for a specific purpose and involves a definite amount of money.

A mortgage—a long-term loan extended to someone who buys property—is a common use of closed-end credit. Vehicle loans and installment loans for purchasing furniture or large appliances are also examples of closed-end credit. These types of loans usually carry lower interest rates than open-end credit carries.

For example, when the Petersons were ready to move out of their apartment, they decided to buy a three-bedroom house and apply for a mortgage from a bank. They signed a written agreement that indicated how much their monthly payments would be, how many payments they would make, and the cost of the credit over the life of the loan. The bank will hold the title to the house until the Petersons have completed their payments.

Suppose that you want to buy a sofa and loveseat to furnish your living room. You might apply for an installment loan from a furniture company. You would sign a contract promising to repay the balance, plus interest, in equal installments over a specified period.

Open-End Credit

What does open-end credit mean? **Open-end credit** is credit as a loan with a certain limit on the amount of money you can borrow for a variety of goods and services. A **line of credit** is the maximum amount of money a creditor will allow a credit user to borrow. Department store credit cards and bank credit cards, such as Visa or MasterCard, are examples of open-end credit. After a credit card company has approved your application for credit and you have received the card, you can use it to make as many purchases as you wish, as long as you do not exceed your line of credit. You are then billed periodically for at least partial payment of the total amount you owe.

Sources of Consumer Credit

What are some sources of consumer credit?

Many sources of consumer credit are available, including commercial banks and credit unions. **Figure 6.2** summarizes the major sources of consumer credit. Study and compare the differences to determine which source might best meet your needs and requirements.

Critical Thinking Write these three statements on the board: "It's fine to use credit for necessities, but you should always pay cash for luxuries." "Overusing credit cards indicates money problems." "Credit cards should only be given to people with steady income." Students are to choose one statement and write an essay in which they discuss the statement, either supporting it or opposing it.

$avvy Saver

Get a Good Credit Rating

1. Open a savings account and make regular deposits.
2. Apply for a department store or gasoline credit card and use it responsibly.
3. Pay all loans and credit card bills on time.
4. Open a checking account and do not bounce checks.
5. Never let anyone use your credit card.

Figure 6.2 Sources of Consumer Credit

Credit Source	Type of Loan	Lending Policies
Commercial Banks	Single-payment loan Personal installment loans Passbook loans Check-credit loans Credit card loans Second mortgages	• Seek customers with established credit history • Often require collateral or security • Prefer to deal in large loans, such as vehicle, home improvement, and home modernization, with the exception of credit card and check-credit plans • Determine repayment schedules according to the purpose of the loan • Vary credit rates according to the type of credit, time period, customer's credit history, and the security offered • May require several days to process a new credit application
Consumer Finance Companies	Personal installment loans Second mortgages	• Often lend to consumers without established credit history • Often make unsecured loans • Often vary rates according to the size of the loan balance • Offer a variety of repayment schedules • Make a higher percentage of small loans than other lenders • Maximum loan size limited by law • Process applications quickly, frequently on the same day the application is made
Credit Unions	Personal installment loans Share draft-credit plans Credit card loans Second mortgages	• Lend to members only • Make unsecured loans • May require collateral or cosigner for loans over a specified amount • May require payroll deductions to pay off loan • May submit large loan applications to a committee of members for approval • Offer a variety of repayment schedules
Life Insurance Companies	Single-payment or partial payment loans	• Lend on cash value of life insurance policy • No date or penalty on repayment • Deduct amount owed from the value of the policy benefit if death or other maturity occurs before repayment
Federal Savings Banks (Savings and Loan Associations)	Personal installment loans (generally permitted by state-chartered savings associations) Home improvement loans Education loans Savings account loans Second mortgages	• Will lend to all creditworthy individuals • Often require collateral • Loan rates vary depending on size of loan, length of payment, and security involved

Seeking Customers Consumer credit is available from several types of sources.

Which sources seem to offer the widest variety of loans?

Caption Answer
commercial banks and federal savings banks (savings and loan associations)

Loans

A loan is borrowed money with an agreement to repay it with interest within a certain amount of time. If you were considering taking out a loan, your immediate thought might be to go to your local bank. However, you might want to explore some other options first.

Inexpensive Loans Parents or other family members are often the source of the least expensive loans—loans with low interest. They may charge only the interest they would have earned on the money if they had deposited it in a savings account. They may even give you a loan without interest. Be aware, however, that loans can complicate family relationships.

Medium-Priced Loans Often you can obtain medium-priced loans—loans with moderate interest—from commercial banks, savings and loan associations, and credit unions. Borrowing from credit unions has several advantages. Credit unions provide personalized service, and they are usually willing to be patient with borrowers who can provide good reasons for late or missed payments. As you learned in Chapter 5, you must be a member of a credit union in order to get a loan from one.

Caption Answer A debit card subtracts money you have from your account; a credit card spends someone else's money (the card company's) and defers your payment for the purchase.

Expensive Loans The easiest loans to obtain are also the most expensive. Finance companies and retail stores that lend to consumers will frequently charge high interest rates, ranging from 12 to 25 percent. Banks also lend money to their credit card holders through cash advances—loans that are billed to the customer's credit card account. Most cards charge higher interest for a cash advance and charge interest from the day the cash advance is made. As a result, it is much more expensive to take out a cash advance than to charge a purchase to a credit card.

▼ **QUICK CASH** Using a debit card can be a convenient way to get cash any time you need it. *How is a debit card different from a credit card?*

Home Equity Loans A home equity loan is a loan based on your home equity—the difference between the current market value of your home and the amount you still owe on the mortgage. Unlike interest on most other types of credit, the interest you pay on a home equity loan is tax-deductible. Use these loans only for major items such as education, home improvements, or medical bills. If you miss payments on a home equity loan, the lender can take your home. For more information about home equity loans, see Chapters 7 and 17.

Credit Cards

Credit cards are extremely popular. The average cardholder has more than nine credit cards, including bank, retail, gasoline, and telephone cards. Cardholders who pay off their balances in full each month are often known as convenience users. Cardholders who do not pay off their balances every month are known as borrowers.

Teaching Activity Divide the students into groups of four. Each group is to research four different credit cards (bank cards, store cards, gas cards) to determine their interest rates, any restrictions, and payment policies. The group is to graphically display the material they gather.

Most credit card companies offer a **grace period**, a time period during which no finance charges will be added to your account. A **finance charge** is the total dollar amount you pay to use credit. Generally, if you pay your balance before the due date stated on your monthly bill, you do not have to pay a finance charge. Borrowers who carry balances beyond the grace period pay finance charges.

The cost of a credit card depends on the type of credit card you have and the terms set forth by the lender. As a cardholder, you may have to pay interest or other finance charges. Some credit card companies charge cardholders an annual fee, usually about $20. However, many companies have eliminated annual fees. If you are looking for a credit card, be sure to shop around for one with no annual fee. **Figure 6.3** gives some other helpful hints for choosing a credit card.

Figure 6.3 Choosing and Using a Credit Card

When you choose a credit card, it pays to shop around. Follow these suggestions to find the card that best meets your needs and to use it wisely:

1. Department stores and gasoline companies are good places to obtain your first credit card.
2. Bank credit cards are offered through banks and savings and loan associations. Annual fees and finance charges vary widely, so shop around.
3. If you plan on paying off your balance every month, look for a card that has a grace period and carries no annual fee or a low annual fee. You might have a higher interest rate, but you plan to pay little or no interest anyway.
4. Watch out for creditors that offer low or no annual fees but instead charge a transaction fee every time you use the card.
5. If you plan to carry a balance, look for a card with a low monthly finance charge. Be sure that you understand how the finance charge is calculated.
6. To avoid delays that may result in finance charges, follow the card issuer's instructions as to where, how, and when to make bill payments.
7. Beware of offers of easy credit. No one can guarantee to get you credit.
8. If your card offers a grace period, take advantage of it by paying off your balance in full each month. With a grace period of 25 days, you actually get a free loan when you pay bills in full each month.
9. If you have a bad credit history and have trouble getting a credit card, look for a savings institution that will give you a secured credit card. With this type of card, your line of credit depends on how much money you keep in a savings account that you open at the same time.
10. Travel and entertainment cards often charge higher annual fees than most credit cards. Usually, you must make payment in full within 30 days of receiving your bill, or no further purchases will be approved on the account.
11. Be aware that debit cards are not credit cards but simply a substitute for a check or cash. The amount of the sale is subtracted from your checking account.
12. Think twice before you make a telephone call to a 900 number to request a credit card. You will pay from $2 to $50 for the 900 call and may never receive a credit card.

Sources: American Institute of Certified Public Accountants; U.S. Office of Consumer Affairs; Federal Trade Commission.

Critical Thinking Before you enter the world of credit, you need to understand the various options that are available to you.

Which of these factors would be most important in your choice of a credit card?

Caption Answer Accept all reasonable answers that demonstrate an understanding of the concepts.

Debit Cards Do not confuse credit cards with debit cards. A debit card allows you to electronically subtract money from your savings or checking account to pay for goods or services. A credit card extends credit and delays payment. Debit cards are most commonly used at automated teller machines (ATMs). They are also used to purchase goods in stores and to make other types of payments.

Smart Cards Some lenders offer a credit card called a *smart card.* A smart card is a plastic card equipped with a computer chip that can store 500 times as much data as a normal credit card. Smart cards can store a variety of information. A smart card, for example, can be used to buy an airline ticket, store it digitally, and track frequent flyer miles.

Travel and Entertainment (T&E) Cards Travel and Entertainment (T&E) cards are really not credit cards because the balance is due in full each month. However, most people think of T&E cards—such as American Express cards—as credit cards because users do not pay for goods or services when they purchase them.

TechByte

Smart Cards The first basic credit card was the BankAmericard, issued by Bank of America in 1958. Today a variety of cards are available, including smart cards, which combine a credit card, driver's license, healthcare ID, medical history, and other features.

List other features of smart cards by reading more information through **finance07.glencoe.com**.

Section 6.1 Assessment

See the Teacher Manual for answers.

QUICK CHECK

1. What are two advantages and two disadvantages of using credit?
2. What is the difference between closed-end credit and open-end credit?
3. What is an example of an inexpensive loan, a medium-priced loan, and an expensive loan?

THINK CRITICALLY

4. Review Figure 6.3 on page 160. How might you select a card that best meets your needs?

USE MATH SKILLS

5. **Cash or Charge?** The use of credit in the United States is widespread. Nevertheless, some people use credit cards and take out loans only in an emergency. Their philosophy is that if they do not have cash to pay for something, they should not take on a debt. Other people believe credit is necessary for everyday living.

Write About It What is your view on the issue of using credit? Do you plan to obtain a credit card? Would you prefer to pay cash? Write a short essay that explains the role of credit cards and loans in your philosophy of money management.

SOLVE MONEY PROBLEMS

6. **Evaluating Credit** Garrett, a high school senior, wanted to get his girlfriend a special birthday gift. A local electronics store had one-day special discounts on stereos, with no payments required until after six months. With income from his part-time job, Garrett felt that he could incorporate the expense into his budget. His mother and sister tried to discourage him from buying the stereo.

Analyze What should Garrett do in this situation? Explain your reasoning.

Section 6.2

Focus on Reading

Read to Learn

- How to name the five C's of credit.
- How to identify factors to consider when choosing a loan or credit card.
- How to explain how to build and protect your credit rating.

Main Idea

You should consider the costs of credit and your own credit standing when applying for credit.

Key Terms

- net income
- annual percentage rate (APR)
- collateral
- simple interest
- minimum monthly payment
- credit rating

Before You Read

PREDICT

What is your definition of credit?

Springboard Ask the students if they have ever borrowed money from a friend or family member. Ask if they paid interest. If not, explain that the cost of borrowing was zero, but in the real world, borrowing has costs.

The Costs and Methods of Obtaining Credit

Can You Afford a Loan?

What is a loan?

A loan is money that you borrow and must repay. Loans cost money to the borrower in the form of interest. Taking out a loan can be a substantial financial burden. Before you take out a loan, you need to be sure that you can afford it. Will you be able to meet all your usual expenses plus the monthly loan payments you will have to make? You can answer this question in several ways.

One way is to add up all your basic monthly expenses and then subtract the total from your take-home pay. If the difference is not enough to make a monthly loan payment and still have a little left over, you cannot afford the loan.

A second way is to consider what you might give up to make the monthly loan payment. For example, perhaps you are putting some of your monthly income into a savings account. Would you be willing to use that money to make loan payments instead? If not, would you consider cutting back on unnecessary but fun activities, such as going to movies or eating out? Are you prepared to make this trade-off?

Although you cannot measure your credit capacity exactly, you can use the debt payments-to-income ratio formula to decide whether you can safely take on the responsibility of credit.

Debt Payments-to-Income Ratio

The debt payments-to-income ratio is the percentage of debt you have in relation to your net income. **Net income** is the income you receive (take-home pay, allowance, gifts, and interest). Experts suggest that you spend no more than 20 percent of your net income on debt payments. For example, if your net income is $1,000 per month, your monthly debt payments should total no more than $200. Monthly debt payments include credit card and loan payments. You can calculate your debt payments-to-income ratio by dividing your total monthly debt payments (not including housing payments) by your monthly net income.

GO FIGURE — FINANCIAL MATH

DEBT PAYMENTS-TO-INCOME RATIO (DPR)

Synopsis: Computing your monthly net income will help you calculate how much to spend on debt payments. Your debt payments-to-income ratio (DPR) will also determine your monthly budget.

Example: Suppose that your monthly net income is \$1,200. Your monthly debt payments include your student loan payment and a gas credit card, and they total \$180. What is your debt payments-to-income ratio?

Formula:

$$\frac{\text{Monthly Debt Payments}}{\text{Monthly Net Income}} = \text{Debt Payments-to-Income Ratio (DPR)}$$

Solution:

$$\frac{\$180}{\$1{,}200} = 0.15 = 15\%$$

YOU FIGURE

What is your debt payments-to-income ratio if your debt payments total \$342 and your net income is \$1,000 per month?

Answer 34.2% (\$342 ÷ \$1,000 = .342 = 34.2%)

Twenty percent is the most you should spend on debt payments, but 15 percent is much better. The higher figure does not take into account emergency expenses, and it is based on an average family's average expenses. If you are a young adult who is just beginning to experiment with credit, play it safe and stay below the 20 percent limit.

Motivating Students Ask students if they know what collateral is, and assist them to arrive at a definition. Then ask them what they own that could be used as collateral. List answers on board.

The Cost of Credit

What does it cost to apply for credit?

If you are thinking of taking out a loan or applying for a credit card, your first step should be to figure out how much the loan will cost you and whether you can afford it. Then you should shop for the best credit terms. Two key factors will be the finance charge and the annual percentage rate (APR).

The Finance Charge and the Annual Percentage Rate (APR)

The finance charge is the total dollar amount you pay to use credit. In most cases, you will have to pay finance charges to a creditor on any unpaid balance.

The finance charge is calculated using the annual percentage rate. The **annual percentage rate (APR)** is the cost of credit on a yearly basis, expressed as a percentage. For example, an APR of 18 percent means that you pay \$18 per year on each \$100 you owe. Every organization that extends credit of any kind must state the true APR that it charges its customers. This makes it easy to compare the cost of credit at several businesses or among several different credit cards.

STANDARD & POOR'S — Put on Your Financial Planner's Cap

If you were a financial planner, what is the first thing you would say to a client who was in serious credit card debt?

See the Teacher Manual for answers.

STANDARD &POOR'S

Global Financial Landscape

Standard and Poor's publishes the globally recognized S&P 500® financial index. It also gathers financial statistics, information, and news, and analyzes this data for international businesses, governments, and individuals to help them guide their financial decisions.

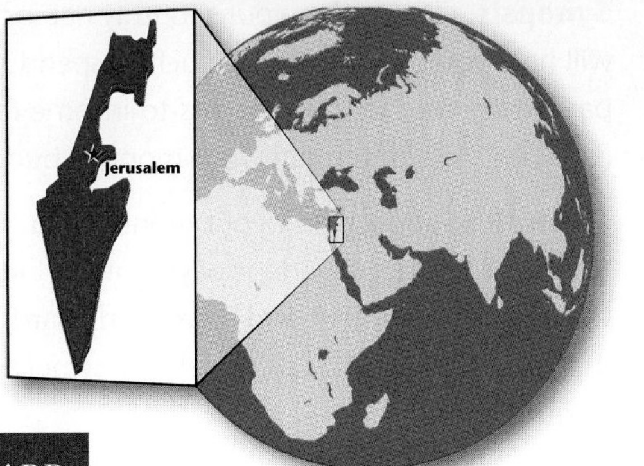

ISRAEL

Israel's economy operates on borrowed money from institutions such as the World Bank and the International Monetary Exchange or from foreign nations. However, because of ongoing political conflicts and an economic slump, the country's credit rating dropped. When countries or individuals carry excessive debt, lenders view them as credit risks. However, tight security and an upbeat global market set the stage for Israel's financial recovery. Israeli exports grew by 20 percent. Incentives such as tax-free "holidays" encouraged the development of new companies. Even tourism has grown. In fact, the country made its biggest economic gain in 2004. One news headline described the country and its turnaround: "Israel: A Bunch of Blooms in the Desert."

STANDARD &POOR'S

DATABYTES

Capital	Jerusalem
Population	6,707,000
Languages	Hebrew, Arabic, and English
Currency	new Israeli shekel
Gross Domestic Product (GDP)	$120.6 billion
GDP per capita	$19,700

Industry: High-technology projects, wood and paper products, potash and phosphates, and food

Agriculture: Citrus, vegetables, cotton, and beef

Exports: machinery and equipment, software, cut diamonds, agricultural products, and chemicals

Natural Resources: Copper, phosphates, bromide, potash, and clay

Think Globally

Would you invest in an international stock from Israel? Why or why not?

See the Teacher Manual for answer.

Discussion Discuss with students how they can safely build credit.

To determine the total amount of finance charges that you will pay on $100 borrowed, look at **Figure 6.4.** Find the APR at the top of the chart and the number of payments at the left side of the chart. The point at which they meet is the total amount you will pay in finance charges for each $100 borrowed.

For example, find the column showing an APR of 8 percent. Follow it down until it meets the row showing 24 monthly payments. You will see that if you borrow $100 at an APR of 8 percent for two years (24 months), you will pay $8.55 in finance charges. Under the Truth in Lending Act, the creditor must inform you, in writing and before you sign any agreement, of the finance charge and the APR.

Figure 6.4 **Annual Percentage Rate Table for Monthly Payments**

	Annual Percentage Rate—APR (Finance Charge per $100 Borrowed)				
Number of Monthly Payments	7.0%	7.5%	8.0%	8.5%	9.0%
6	$2.05	$2.20	$ 2.35	$ 2.49	$ 2.64
12	$3.83	$4.11	$ 4.39	$ 4.66	$ 4.94
18	$5.63	$6.04	$ 6.45	$ 6.86	$ 7.28
24	$7.45	$8.00	$ 8.55	$ 9.09	$ 9.64
30	$9.30	$9.98	$10.66	$11.35	$12.04

Finding the Finance Charge If you borrow money and do not pay it back right away, you will probably have to pay a finance charge.

What is the finance charge that you would pay if you borrowed $100 for 18 months at an APR of 9 percent?

Caption Answer
You would pay $7.28.

Tackling the Trade-Offs

When you select your financing, you will have to make trade-offs. You will have to choose among various features, including the length of the loan, the size of monthly payments, and the interest rate. Here are some of the major trade-offs you should consider.

Term Versus Interest Costs Many people choose longer-term financing because they want smaller monthly payments. However, the longer the term (the period of time) of a loan at a given interest rate, the greater the amount you will pay in interest charges. Compare the following credit arrangements on a $6,000 loan:

	APR	Term of Loan	Monthly Payment	Total Finance Charge	Total Cost
Creditor A	14%	3 years	$205.07	$1,382.52	$7,382.52
Creditor B	14%	4 years	163.96	1,870.08	7,870.08

How do these choices compare? The answer depends partly on what you need. The lower-cost loan is available from Creditor A. If you are looking for lower monthly payments, you could repay the loan over a longer period of time. However, you would have to pay more in total costs. A loan from Creditor B provides smaller monthly payments but adds about $488 to your total finance charge.

Lender Risk Versus Interest Rate You may prefer financing that requires a minimum down payment, a portion of the total cost of an item that is required at the time of purchase. Another option is to take out a loan that features low fixed payments with a large final payment. Keep in mind that the lender's goal is to minimize risk, or make sure that you pay back the loan in full. Consumers who want these types of features have to accept the trade-off of a more expensive loan.

GO FIGURE — FINANCIAL MATH

SIMPLE INTEREST ON A LOAN

Synopsis: Simple interest, compounded annually, is a percentage of the amount borrowed. The amount borrowed is called principal. Compound interest may be computed daily, monthly, or yearly.

Example: Janelle's cousin agreed to lend her $1,000 to purchase a used laptop computer. She has agreed to charge only 5 percent simple interest, and Janelle has agreed to repay the loan at the end of one year. How much interest will she pay for the year? Use the formula below to help compute Janelle's loan interest.

Formula: Principal × Interest Rate × Amount of Time = Simple Interest

Solution: $1,000 × .05 or 5% × 1 = $50 interest

YOU FIGURE

You just bought a used car for $3,500 from your aunt. She agreed to let you make payments for 3 years with simple interest at 6 percent. How much interest will you pay?

Answer $630 ($3,500 × .06 × 3 = $630)

Teaching Activity Have students create a "borrowing chain": Using paper filled out to represent sums of money, student number 1 lends money to number 2 who lends money to number 3, etc., until the last student lends money to the first. Students may determine loan amounts and interest rates as well as fees (negotiable), loan term, and repayment requirements. All borrowers are to specifically spend the amount borrowed. After the exercise, discuss with students what they learned and whether they preferred being the lender or the borrower and why.

To reduce lender risk and increase your chance of getting a loan at a lower interest rate, consider the following options:

- **Variable Interest Rate** A variable interest rate is based on changing rates in the banking system. This means that the interest rate you pay on your loan will vary from time to time. If you have a loan with a variable interest rate and overall interest rates rise, the rate on your loan is adjusted accordingly. Therefore, the lender may offer you a lower beginning interest rate than you would have with a fixed-rate loan.
- **A Secured Loan** You will probably receive a lower interest rate on your loan if you pledge collateral. **Collateral** is a form of security to help guarantee that the creditor will be repaid. It indicates that if you lost your source of income, you could repay your loan with the collateral, such as your savings, or by selling some of your property. If you do not pay back the loan, the lender may have the legal right to take whatever you pledged as collateral.
- **Up-Front Cash** Many lenders believe that you have a higher stake in repaying a loan if you make a large down payment. Thus, you may have a better chance of getting the other loan features you want.
- **A Shorter Term** The shorter the period of time (or term) for which you borrow, the smaller the chance that something will prevent you from repaying your loan. This lowers the risk to the lender. Therefore, you may be able to borrow at a lower interest rate if you accept a shorter-term loan, but your monthly payments will be higher.

Careers in Finance

CREDIT ANALYST **Michelle Molyneux**
3Com Corporation

Before joining 3Com Corporation, a global company specializing in computer networks, Michelle worked for a credit department at a bank where she evaluated business loans. She explains that a credit analyst considers a company's credit by evaluating financial statements, company statistics, and its managers. Credit analysts evaluate the worthiness of corporate customers, credit risk, and then set credit lines. They also advise whether to extend credit to a company.

SKILLS: Time-management, accounting, judgment, investigative, analytical, communication, some foreign language, and interpersonal skills

PERSONAL TRAITS: Curiosity, a desire to know the big picture, and an international perspective

EDUCATION: High school diploma or equivalent; bachelor's degree in accounting or finance

ANALYZE People can get into debt by mistaking needs and wants. List your needs, such as clothing and food. Then list your wants, such as luxury items or recreation. Describe how a credit analyst might rate your credit worthiness, based on your needs and wants.
See the Teacher Manual for answer.

@ To learn more about career paths for credit analysts visit **finance07.glencoe.com**.

Calculating the Cost of Credit

To assess your trade-offs, you can also compare loans and credit cards by calculating the interest to find the cost of credit. The most common method of calculating interest is the simple interest formula. Other methods, such as simple interest on the declining balance and add-on interest, are variations of this formula.

Simple Interest **Simple interest** is the interest computed only on the principal, the amount that you borrow. It is based on three factors: the principal, the interest rate, and the amount of time for which the principal is borrowed. To calculate the simple interest on a loan, multiply the principal by the interest rate and by the amount of time (in years) for which the money is borrowed. (See the Go Figure box on page 166.)

Simple Interest on the Declining Balance When a simple interest loan is paid back in more than one payment, the method of computing interest is known as the declining balance method. You pay interest only on the amount of principal that you have not yet repaid. The more often you make payments, the lower the interest you will pay. Most credit unions use this method.

As You Read

RELATE

Why should you pay more than the monthly minimum balance on a credit card debt?

Add-On Interest With the add-on interest method, interest is calculated on the full amount of the original principal, no matter how often you make payments. When you pay off the loan with one payment, this method produces the same APR as the simple interest method. However, if you pay in installments, your actual rate of interest will be higher than the stated rate. Interest payments on this type of loan do not decrease as the loan is repaid. The longer you take to repay the loan, the more interest you will pay.

Extension Help students to obtain a copy of the Truth in Lending Act and rewrite it in words a teenager can understand.

Cost of Open-End Credit The Truth in Lending Act requires that open-end creditors inform consumers as to how the finance charge and the APR will affect their costs. For example, they must explain how they calculate the finance charge. They must also inform you when finance charges on your credit account begin to accrue so that you know how much time you have to pay your bills before a finance charge is added.

Cost of Credit and Expected Inflation Inflation reduces the buying power of money. Each percentage point increase in inflation means a decrease of about 1 percent in the quantity of goods and services you can buy with the same amount of money. Because of this, lenders incorporate the expected rate of inflation when deciding how much interest to charge.

Remember the earlier example in which Damon borrowed $1,000 from his aunt at the bargain rate of 5 percent for one year? If the inflation rate was 4 percent that year, his aunt's actual rate of return on the loan would have been only about 1 percent (5 percent stated interest minus 4 percent inflation rate). A professional lender that wanted to receive 5 percent interest on Damon's loan might have charged him 9 percent interest (5 percent interest plus 4 percent—anticipated inflation rate).

The Minimum Monthly Payment Trap On credit card bills and for other forms of credit, the **minimum monthly payment** is the smallest amount you can pay and remain a borrower in good standing. Lenders often encourage you to make the minimum payment because it will then take you longer to pay off the loan. However, if you are paying only the minimum amount on your monthly statement, you need to plan your budget more carefully. The longer it takes for you to pay off a bill, the more interest you pay. The finance charges you pay on an item could end up being more than the item is worth.

For example, suppose that Natasha is buying new books for college. She spends $500 on textbooks, using a credit card that charges 19.8 percent interest per year, and she makes only the minimum monthly payment of $21.67. Based on that payment amount, it will take Natasha approximately two and one-half years to pay off the loan. Interest charges of $150 will be added to the cost of her purchase.

Applying for Credit

Why does a lender need to know about your credit history to extend credit?

When you are ready to apply for a loan or a credit card, you should understand the factors that determine whether a lender will extend credit to you.

The Five C's of Credit

When a lender extends credit to consumers, it takes for granted that some people will be unable or unwilling to pay their debts. Therefore, lenders establish policies for determining who will receive credit. Most lenders build such policies around the "five C's of credit": character, capacity, capital, collateral, and credit history.

Character: Will You Repay the Loan? Creditors want to know what kind of person to whom they will be lending money. They want to know that you are trustworthy and stable. They may ask for personal or professional references, and they may check to see whether you have a history of trouble with the law. Some questions a lender might ask to determine your character are:

- Have you used credit before?
- How long have you lived at your present address?
- How long have you held your current job?

Capacity: Can You Repay the Loan? Your income and the debts you already have will affect your ability to pay additional debts. If you already have a large amount of debt in proportion to your income, lenders probably will not extend more credit to you.

Common CENTS

One Is Enough
When you turn 18, you may start receiving applications for credit cards. Be a smart consumer and compare interest rates, annual fees, and any other fees. Decide which credit card best suits your needs and apply for that one. Toss any other applications you get into the trash. *Why should you get the best (or lowest) interest rate for a credit card?*

Common Cents The lowest interest rate means that your repayment amount will be lower.

◀ **LOOK BEFORE YOU LEAP** Before taking out a loan, you should sit down and figure out your finances. *What is perhaps the most important point you should consider?*

Caption Answer Consider if you can afford the monthly payments.

A creditor may ask several questions about your income and expenses:

- What is your job, and how much is your salary?
- Do you have other sources of income?
- What are your current debts?

WebQuest

Your Own Home
Learn how to establish and maintain good credit so you can get a mortgage when the time comes to buy your first home.

@ To continue with Task 3 of your WebQuest project, visit **finance07.glencoe.com**.

Capital: What Are Your Assets and Net Worth? You may recall from Chapter 3 that assets are any items of value that you own, including cash, property, personal possessions, and investments. Your capital is the amount of your assets that exceed your liabilities, or the debts you owe. Lenders want to be sure that you have enough capital to pay back a loan. That way, if you lost your source of income, you could repay your loan from your savings or by selling some of your assets. A lender might ask:

- What are your assets?
- What are your liabilities?

Collateral: What If You Do Not Repay the Loan? Creditors look at what kinds of property or savings you already have, because these can be offered as collateral to secure the loan. If you fail to repay the loan, the creditor may take whatever you pledged as collateral. A creditor might ask:

- What assets do you have to secure the loan (a vehicle, your home, or furniture)?
- Do you have any other assets (bonds or savings)?

Teaching Activity Divide the students into five groups, assigning one of the "five C's of credit" to each group. Have each group prepare a skit, a song, or other light presentation about its "C" and present it to the class.

Credit History: What Is Your Credit History? Lenders will review your credit history to find out whether you have used credit responsibly in the past. They will probably obtain a copy of your credit report from a credit bureau. Some questions a creditor might ask about your credit history are:

- Do you pay your bills on time?
- Have you ever filed for bankruptcy?

The information gathered from your application and the credit bureau establishes your credit rating.

As You Read
QUESTION
Why does a lender need to know about your credit history to extend credit?

Question Answer The lender wants to know if you are a good credit risk.

A **credit rating** is a measure of a person's ability and willingness to make credit payments on time. The factors that determine a person's credit rating are income, current debt, information about character, and how debts have been repaid in the past. If you always make your payments on time, you will probably have an excellent credit rating. If not, your credit rating will be poor, and a lender probably will not extend credit to you. A good credit rating is a valuable asset that you should protect.

Creditors use different combinations of the five C's to reach their decisions. Some creditors set unusually high standards, and others simply do not offer certain types of loans. Creditors also use various rating systems. Some rely strictly on their own instincts and experience. Others use a credit scoring or statistical system to predict whether an applicant is a good credit risk. When you apply for a loan, the lender is likely to evaluate your application by asking questions such as those included in the checklist in **Figure 6.5** on page 172.

Document Detective

Learn to identify and understand the standard financial documents you will use in the real world.

See the Teacher Manual for answers.

Investigate: A Credit Card Statement
A credit card statement lists this information:

- Payments made
- New balance
- Your available credit
- Transactions for the month
- Minimum payment due

Your Motive: Understanding how to read your credit card statement is important so you can track where you spend your money each month. You can also verify that the transactions on the statement are accurate.

BANK CENTER VISA

CREDIT CARD STATEMENT

Previous Balance	Payments and Credits	New Charges	New Balance	Credit Line
$100	$100	$40.60	$40.60	$5,000

Statement Date 02/03/--
Payment Date 02/28/--

FOR CUSTOMER SERVICE CALL OR WRITE 1-800-555-4553 P.O. BOX 23 SIOUX FALLS, SD

SEND PAYMENTS TO: BANKCENTER P.O. BOX 6575 GOLDEN, NEVADA 88777

6593-5800-0086-1905	Cash Advance Limit	Available Credit Line	Available Cash Line*
	$500	$4,900	$500

Sale Date	Post Date	Reference Number	Type of Activity	Location	Amount
01/05	01/07	24036215006661	Daisy Market	Clover, IL	4.30
01/08	01/10	24692165008000	Chloe's Coffee	Fielding, CT	2.30
01/13	01/13	74046585013013	PAYMENT RECEIVED--THANK YOU		100.00
01/18	01/20	24036215019664	Real Music	Clover, IL	15.50
02/02	02/03	242753050337531	Books 'n' News	Montclair, MO	13.90
02/01	02/03	242753950329000	Nick's Candy	Montclair, MO	4.60

DAYS IN BILLING PERIOD: 40

		Purchases	Cash Advance
Balance Subject to Interest Charge	>	0.00	.00
Periodic Rate	>	.0000%	.0000%
ANNUAL PERCENTAGE RATE	>	0.00%	0.00%

Payment Due:	20.00
Amount Over Credit Limit:	.00
Amount Past Due	.00
MINIMUM AMOUNT DUE:	20.00

Key Points: A credit card statement is sent to you each month. It lists all the purchases you have made using your credit card and the amount of each purchase. It also lists the payments you made during the month. In addition, it indicates how much money you can still borrow from the credit card.

Find the Solutions

1. How many charges or transactions were completed on this statement?
2. How much more can you charge on the credit card?
3. What is the new balance listed on the statement?
4. What is the minimum payment to be paid?
5. What is the due date of the next payment?

Figure 6.5 Credit Application Information

- Amount of loan requested
- Proposed use of the loan
- Your name and birth date
- Social Security and driver's license numbers
- Present and previous street addresses
- Present and previous employers and their addresses
- Present salary
- Number and ages of dependents
- Other income and sources of other income
- Have you ever received credit from us?
- If so, when and at which office?
- Checking account number, institution, and branch
- Savings account number, institution, and branch
- Name of nearest relative not living with you
- Relative's address and telephone number
- Your marital status

Who Are You? A potential lender will require you to answer a number of specific questions on a credit application.

Why do you think that a creditor would want to know the names and addresses of your present and previous employers?

Caption Answer
Answers may vary but may include to determine if you are stable and to ensure you make enough money to repay debts.

Credit and Equal Opportunity

You should also know what factors a lender cannot consider, according to the law. The Equal Credit Opportunity Act (ECOA) gives all credit applicants the same basic rights. It states that a lender may not use race, nationality, age, sex, marital status, and certain other factors to discriminate against you.

Age The Equal Credit Opportunity Act (ECOA) is very specific about how a person's age may be used as a factor in credit decisions. A creditor may request that you state your age on an application, but if you are old enough to sign a legal contract (usually 18 or 21 years old, depending on state law), a creditor may not turn you down or decrease your credit because of your age. Creditors may not close your credit account because you reach a certain age or retire.

Public Assistance You may not be denied credit because you receive Social Security or public assistance. However, certain information related to this source of income can be considered in determining your creditworthiness.

Housing Loans The ECOA also covers applications for mortgages or home improvement loans. In particular, it bans discrimination against you based on the race or nationality of the people in the neighborhood where you live or want to buy your home, a practice that is called *redlining*.

What If Your Application Is Denied?

If your credit application is denied, the ECOA gives you the right to know the reasons. If the denial is based on a credit report from a credit bureau, you are entitled to know what specific information in the report led to the denial. After you receive this information, you can contact the credit bureau and ask for a copy of your credit report. The bureau cannot charge a fee for this service as long as you ask to see your files within 60 days of notification that your credit application has been denied. You are entitled to ask the bureau to investigate any inaccurate or incomplete information and correct its records. (See **Figure 6.6.**)

Figure 6.6 **What If You Are Denied Credit?**

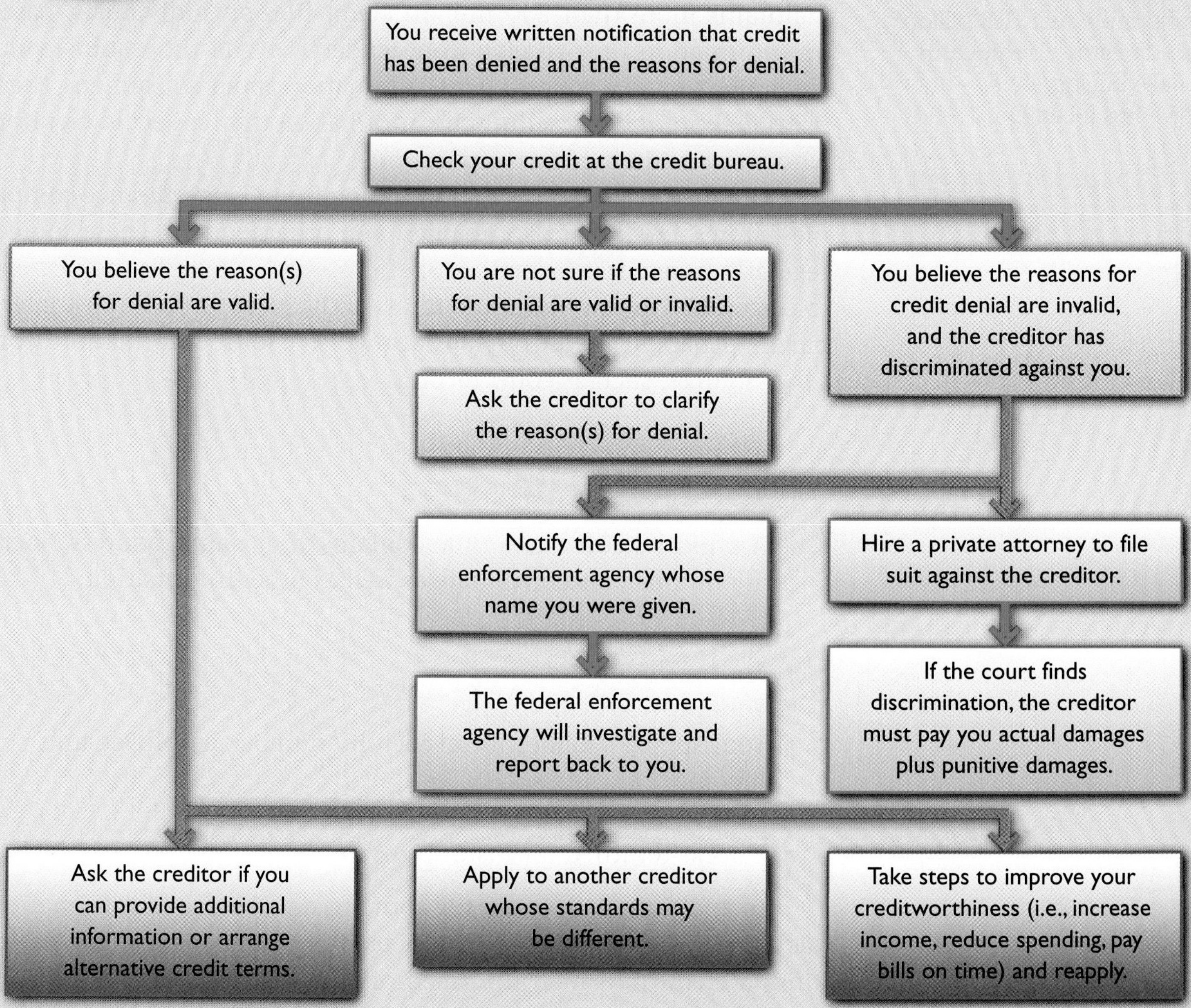

Source: Federal Reserve Bank of Minneapolis

Right the Wrong The law requires credit card companies to correct inaccurate or incomplete information in your credit report.

Why is it best to request changes of incorrect information by letter rather than by phone?

Caption Answer
A letter is written documentation of your request.

Your Credit Report

Why is your credit report important?

Academic Connection

HISTORY

The first credit card, a travel and entertainment card, was issued in 1950 by Diners Club. Card holders could charge meals in 27 restaurants in New York City. Eight years later, the first bank credit card was issued. By 1965, about 5 million credit cards were in circulation. Fast forward to 2004, and U.S. consumers held more than 1.8 billion credit cards. Credit cards make buying easier—but give less incentive to save. *Do you think that credit cards have caused people to have more debt? Explain why or why not in two sentences.*

See the Teacher Manual for answer.

When you apply for a loan, the lender will review your credit history closely. The record of your complete credit history is called your credit report, or credit file. Your credit records are collected and maintained by credit bureaus. Most lenders rely heavily on credit reports when they consider loan applications. **Figure 6.7** provides information on building and protecting your credit history.

Credit Bureaus

A credit bureau is an agency that collects information on how promptly people and businesses pay their bills. The three major credit bureaus are Experian, Trans Union, and Equifax. Each of these bureaus maintains more than 200 million credit files on individuals, based on information they receive from lenders. Several thousand smaller credit bureaus also collect credit information about consumers. These firms make money by selling the information they collect to creditors who are considering loan applications.

Credit bureaus get their information from banks, finance companies, stores, credit card companies, and other lenders. These sources regularly transmit information about the types of credit they extend to customers, the amounts and terms of the loans, and the customers' payment habits. Credit bureaus also collect some information from other sources, such as court records.

Your Credit File

A typical credit bureau file contains your name, address, Social Security number, and birth date as well as other information:

- Your employer, position, and income
- Your previous address
- Your previous employer
- Your spouse's name, Social Security number, employer, and income
- Homeowner or renter status
- Checks returned for insufficient funds

In addition, your credit file contains detailed credit information. Each time you use credit to make a purchase or take out a loan of any kind, a credit bureau is informed of your account number and the date, amount, terms, and type of credit.

Your file is updated regularly to show how many payments you have made, how many payments were late or missed, and how much you owe. Any lawsuits or judgments against you may appear as well. Federal law protects your rights if the information in your credit file is incorrect.

Figure 6.7 Ways to Build and Protect Your Credit

- ☑ Open a checking or savings account, or both.
- ☑ Apply for a local department store credit card.
- ☑ Take out a small loan from your bank.
- ☑ Make payments on time.

Be aware that a creditor must:

1. Evaluate all applicants on the same basis.
2. Consider income from part-time employment.
3. Consider the payment history of all joint accounts, if this accurately reflects your credit history.
4. Disregard information on accounts if you can prove that it does not affect your ability or willingness to repay.

Be aware that a creditor cannot:

1. Refuse you individual credit in your own name if your are creditworthy.
2. Require your spouse to cosign a loan. Any creditworthy person can be your cosigner if one is required.
3. Ask about your family plans or assume that your income will be interrupted to have children.
4. Consider whether you have a telephone listing in your name.

Source: Reprinted by permission of the Federal Reserve Bank of Minneapolis.

Firm Foundation If you want a good credit rating, you must use credit wisely.

Why is it a good idea to apply for a local department credit card or a small loan from your bank?

Caption Answer
It is a way to begin to build a credit history to prove to other creditors that you are worth the risk.

Fair Credit Reporting

Fair and accurate credit reporting is vital to both creditors and consumers. In 1971, the U.S. Congress enacted the Fair Credit Reporting Act, which regulates the use of credit reports. This law requires the deletion of out-of-date information and gives consumers access to their files as well as the right to correct any misinformation that the files may include. The act also places limits on who can obtain your credit report.

Who Can Obtain a Credit Report?

Your credit report may be issued only to properly identified persons for approved purposes. It may be supplied in response to a court order or by your own written request. A credit report may also be provided for use in connection with a credit transaction, underwriting of insurance, or some other legitimate business need. Friends, neighbors, and other individuals cannot be given access to credit information about you. In fact, if they even request such information, they may be subject to a fine, imprisonment, or both.

The credit bureaus contend that current laws protect a consumer's privacy, but many consumer organizations believe that anyone with a personal computer and a modem can easily access credit bureau files.

You may obtain a copy of your credit report free of charge if you have been denied credit. Current law also allows anyone using credit to obtain one free credit report per year.

▲ **EQUAL PLAYING FIELD**
Part of the American dream is to own a home. *What federal law ensures that all applicants for mortgages or home improvement loans will be treated equally?*

Caption Answer The Equal Credit Opportunity Act

Time Limits on Unfavorable Data

Most of the information in your credit file may be reported for only seven years. However, if you have declared personal bankruptcy, that fact may be reported for ten years. A credit reporting agency cannot disclose information in your credit file that is more than seven or ten years old unless you are being reviewed for a credit application of $75,000 or more, or unless you apply to purchase life insurance of $150,000 or more.

Incorrect Information

Credit bureaus are required to follow reasonable procedures to make sure that the information in their files is correct. Mistakes can and do occur, however. If you think that a credit bureau may be reporting incorrect data from your file, contact the bureau to dispute the information. The credit bureau must check its records and change or remove the incorrect items. If you challenge the accuracy of an item on your credit report, the bureau must remove the item unless the lender can verify that the information is accurate.

If you are denied credit, insurance, employment, or rental housing based on the information in a credit report, you can get a free copy of your report. Request it within 60 days of the denial.

Legal Action

You have a legal right to sue a credit bureau or creditor that has caused you harm by not following the rules established by the Fair Credit Reporting Act. If the agency or the user is found guilty, the consumer may be awarded actual damages, court costs, and attorneys' fees. In the case of willful noncompliance, punitive damages in the form of money may also be awarded by the court. The action must be brought within two years of the occurrence or within two years after the discovery of material and willful misrepresentation of the information.

An unauthorized person who obtains a credit report under false pretences may be fined up to $5,000, imprisoned for one year, or both. The same penalties apply to anyone who willfully provides credit information to someone not authorized to receive it.

Section 6.2 Assessment

See the Teacher Manual for answers.

QUICK CHECK

1. What are some ways to determine whether you can afford a loan?
2. What are the five C's of credit?
3. What are at least three steps you can take to maintain a good credit rating?

THINK CRITICALLY

4. Summarize ways you can lower lender risk to increase your chances of getting a loan at a lower interest rate?

USE MATH SKILLS

5. **Debt Payments-to-Income Ratio** Kim Lee is trying to decide whether she can afford a loan she needs so she can go to chiropractic school. Right now, Kim lives at home and works in a shoe store earning a gross income of $820 per month. Kim also pays $95 on several credit card debts each month. The loan she needs for chiropractic school will cost her an additional $120 per month.

Calculate Help Kim make her decision by calculating her debt payments-to-income ratio with and without the college loan. (Remember the 20 percent rule.)

SOLVE MONEY PROBLEMS

6. **Equal Credit Opportunity Act** Eleanor Davis is a single woman. Although she has a good income and uses credit wisely, she has been denied a loan to buy a house and does not know why. She believes that she may have been discriminated against or that there may be some incorrect information on her credit report.

Write About It Using the information in this section on applying for credit, discuss Eleanor's rights and options for finding out why she was denied credit.

Section 6.3

Focus on Reading

Read to Learn

- How to protect yourself from fraud and identity theft.

Main Idea

You must take action to protect your credit if you discover billing errors, have purchase disputes, or experience identity theft.

Key Term

- cosigning

Before You Read

PREDICT

How could you protect you credit?

Springboard Ask the students: "Imagine you open your credit card bill and see you have been billed for something you never bought. What should you do?"

Protecting Your Credit

Billing Errors and Disputes

What can you do to correct billing errors?

Have you ever received a bill for something you did not buy? Have you ever made a payment that was not credited to your account? If so, you are not alone. You may be a responsible consumer who pays bills promptly and manages personal finances carefully. Even so, mistakes can happen. If you want to protect your credit rating, your time, and your money, you need to know how to correct mistakes that may pop up in your credit dealings.

What can you do to dispute billing errors? Follow these steps if you think that a bill is wrong or want more information about it. First, notify your creditor in writing, and include any information that might support your case. (A telephone call is not sufficient and will not protect your rights.) Then pay the portion of the bill that is not in question.

Your creditor must acknowledge your letter within 30 days. Then within two billing periods (but not longer than 90 days), the creditor must either adjust your account or tell you why the bill is correct. If the creditor made a mistake, you do not have to pay any finance charges on the disputed amount. If no mistake is found, the creditor must promptly send you an explanation of the situation and a statement of what you owe, including any finance charges that accumulated and any minimum payments you missed while you were questioning the bill.

Protecting Your Credit Rating

According to law, a creditor may not threaten your credit rating or do anything to damage your credit reputation while you are negotiating a billing dispute. In addition, the creditor may not take any action to collect the amount in question until your complaint has been answered.

Defective Goods and Services

According to the Fair Credit Billing Act, if you purchase a defective item and the store will not accept a return, you may tell your credit card company to stop payment because you made a sincere attempt to resolve the problem.

▲ **PLAYING FAIR** Suppose that you buy something with your credit card, and it turns out to be defective. *If you try to get your money back and the store refuses your request, what might you do?*

Caption Answer You can ask your credit card company to stop payment because you have made a sincere effort to resolve the dispute directly with the store.

Credit and Stolen Identity

How can someone steal your identity?

Motivating Students Have students relate incidents in which they have been billed incorrectly or a payment was not credited to an account.

Imagine yourself saying: "I don't remember charging those items. I've never been in that store." Maybe you never charged those goods and services, but someone else did—someone who used your name and personal information to commit fraud. When impostors use your personal information for their own purposes, they are committing a crime, sometimes called "identity theft."

You may not even know that your identity has been stolen until you notice that something is wrong: You may get bills for a credit card account you never opened, or you may see charges to your account for things that you did not purchase. In addition, a thief may access your bank account and withdraw your money using your ATM information.

If you think that your identity has been stolen and that someone is using it to charge purchases or obtain credit in some other way, you can take action. See **Figure 6.8** on page 181 for information on what to do if your identity is stolen.

Protecting Your Credit from Theft or Loss

What should you do when you realize your credit has been stolen?

Some thieves will pick through your trash in the hope of coming across your personal information. You can prevent this from happening by tearing or shredding any papers that contain personal information before you throw them out.

If you believe that an identity thief has accessed your bank accounts, close the accounts immediately. If your checks have been stolen or misused, stop payment on them. If your debit card has been lost or stolen, cancel it and get another with a new Personal Identification Number (PIN). You may also need to close your account and open a new one as a precaution.

Lost credit cards are a key element in credit card fraud. To protect your card, you should take the following actions:

- Be sure that your card is returned to you after you make a purchase. Unreturned cards can sometimes find their way into the wrong hands.
- Keep a record of your credit card number. You should keep this record separate from your card.

Extension Invite a police officer to class to discuss credit card scams and identity theft so that students can learn how to avoid becoming victims.

Notify the credit card company immediately if your card is lost or stolen. Under the Consumer Credit Protection Act, the maximum amount that you must pay if someone uses your card illegally is $50. If you manage to inform the company before the card is used illegally, you have no obligation to pay at all. However, many credit card companies do not require the cardholder to pay even the maximum amount if the card is used.

Keeping Track of Your Credit

A big problem with credit or identity theft is that you may not know your credit has been stolen until you notice that something is wrong. As discussed in Section 6.2, you might get bills for a credit card account you never opened. Your credit report may include debts you never knew you had; a billing cycle may pass without you receiving a statement; or you may see charges on your bills for which you did not sign or did not authorize.

Steps to Protect Other Accounts If you believe an identity thief has accessed your bank accounts, checking account, or ATM card, close those accounts immediately. When you open new accounts, insist on password-only access. If your checks have been stolen or misused, stop payment on them. If your ATM card has been lost, stolen, or otherwise compromised, cancel the card and get another one with a new PIN. Stay alert to new instances of identity theft. Notify the company or creditor immediately, and follow up in writing.

Figure 6.8 Dealing With Stolen Identity

If someone has stolen your identity, the Federal Trade Commission recommends that you take three actions immediately:

1 **Contact the Credit Bureaus** Tell them to flag your file with a fraud or security alert, including a statement that creditors should call you for permission before they open any new accounts in your name.

2 **Contact the Creditors** Contact the creditors for any accounts that have been tampered with or opened fraudulently. Follow up in writing.

3 **File a Police Report** Keep a copy of the police report in case your creditors need proof of the crime. If you are still having identity problems, stay alert to new instances of identity theft. You can also contact the Privacy Rights Clearinghouse.

Government Agency Protection If you continue to experience identity-theft problems after taking these steps, contact the Privacy Rights Clearinghouse of the Federal Trade Commission (FTC), which provides information on how to network with other victims.

The U.S. Secret Service has jurisdiction over financial fraud cases. Although the service generally investigates cases that involve substantial monetary loss, your information may provide evidence of a larger pattern of fraud that requires its attention.

The Social Security Administration may issue you a new Social Security number if you are still having difficulties after trying to resolve problems resulting from identity theft. Unfortunately, however, there is no guarantee that a new number will resolve the problem.

The Federal Trade Commission cannot resolve individual problems for consumers, but it can act against a company if it sees a pattern of possible law violations. You can file a complaint with the FTC through a toll-free consumer help line; by mail; or at its Web site, using the online complaint from.

As You Read

RELATE

Do you, your friends, or family members shop online? How do you or they make sure all transactions are secure?

Protecting Your Credit Information on the Internet

The Internet is becoming almost as important to daily life as the telephone and television. Increasing numbers of consumers use the Internet for financial activities, such as investing, banking, and shopping.

When you make purchases online, make sure that your transactions are secure, that your personal information is protected, and that your "fraud sensors" are sharpened. Although you cannot control fraud or deception on the Internet, you can take steps to recognize it, avoid it, and report it. Here's how:

- Use a secure browser.
- Keep records of your online transactions.
- Review your monthly bank and credit card statements.
- Read the privacy and security policies of Web sites you visit.
- Keep your personal information private.
- Never give your password to anyone online.
- Do not download files sent to you by strangers.

Research Have students research methods and mechanisms to help them safeguard their identities on the Internet.

Cosigning a Loan

Why would someone ask a friend or relative to cosign a loan?

Discussion Discuss with students problems that can arise through co-signing a loan for a friend. As a class, devise a fair policy for dealing with such requests.

If a friend or relative ever asks you to cosign a loan, think twice. **Cosigning** a loan means that you agree to be responsible for the loan payments if the other person fails to make them. When you cosign, you are taking a chance that a professional lender will not take. The lender would not require a cosigner if the borrower were considered a good risk.

If you cosign a loan and the borrower does not pay the debt, you may have to pay up to the full amount of the debt as well as any late fees or collection costs. The creditor can even collect the debt from you without first trying to collect from the borrower. The creditor can use the same collection methods against you that can be used against the borrower. If the debt is not repaid, that fact will appear on your credit record.

Complaining About Consumer Credit

When should you complain about a lender?

If you believe that a lender is not following the consumer credit protection laws, first try to solve the problem directly with the lender. If that fails, then you should use more formal complaint procedures. This section describes how to file a complaint with the federal agencies that administer consumer credit protection laws.

Teaching Activity Divide the students into five groups, assigning one of the listed consumer credit protection laws to each group (pages 183–184). Have students research to discover what the specifc act does to protect consumers and the history of the law: What led up to it being written and passed? Each group will present its findings to the class.

Consumer Credit Protection Laws

If you have a particular problem with a bank in connection with any of the consumer credit protection laws, you can get advice and help from the Federal Reserve System. You do not need to have an account at the bank to file a complaint. You may also take legal action against a creditor. If you decide to file a lawsuit, you should be aware of the various consumer credit protection laws described below.

As You Read

QUESTION

What is the Truth in Lending Act?

Question Answer The Truth in Lending Act requires that creditors accurately disclose information, follow rules regarding credit cards, and permits class action lawsuits.

Truth in Lending and Consumer Leasing Acts If a creditor fails to disclose information as required under the Truth in Lending Act or the Consumer Leasing Act, or gives inaccurate information, you can sue for any money loss you suffer. You can also sue a creditor that does not follow rules regarding credit cards. In addition, the Truth in Lending Act and the Consumer Leasing Act permit class-action lawsuits. A class-action suit is a legal action on behalf of all of the people who have suffered the same injustice.

Equal Credit Opportunity Act (ECOA) If you think that you can prove that a creditor has discriminated against you for any reason prohibited by the ECOA, you may sue for actual damages plus punitive damages—a payment used to punish the creditor who has violated the law—up to $10,000.

Fair Credit Opportunity Act A creditor that fails to follow the rules that apply to correcting any billing errors will automatically give up the amount owed on the item in question and any finance charges on it, up to a combined total of $50. This is true even if the bill was correct. You may also sue for actual damages plus twice the amount of any finance charges.

Figure 6.9 Federal Agencies that Enforce Consumer Credit Laws

If you think you've been discriminated against by:	You may file a complaint with the following agency:
A retailer, nonbank credit card issuer, consumer finance company, state-chartered credit union or bank, and noninsured savings and loan institution	Consumer Response Center Federal Trade Commission (FTC) Washington, DC 20580
A national bank	Comptroller of the Currency Compliance Management Mail Stop 7–5 Washington, DC 20219
A Federal Reserve member bank	Board of Governors of the Federal Reserve System Director, Division of Consumer and Community Affairs Washington, DC 20551
Other insured banks	Federal Deposit Insurance Corporation Consumer Affairs Division Washington, DC 20429
Insured savings and loan institutions and federally chartered state banks	Office of Thrift Supervision Consumer Affairs Program Washington, DC 20552
The FHA mortgage program	Housing and Urban Development (HUD) Department of Health, Education and Welfare Washington, DC 20410
A federal credit union	National Credit Union Administration Consumer Affairs Division Washington, DC 20456

Protecting Your Rights The law gives you certain rights as a consumer of credit.

What types of complaints about a creditor might you report to these government agencies?

Caption Answer Answers will vary but should reflect an understanding of consumer credit laws.

Fair Credit Reporting Act You may sue any credit bureau or creditor that violates the rules regarding access to your credit records or that fails to correct errors in your credit file. You are entitled to actual damages plus any punitive damages the court allows if the violation is proven to have been intentional.

Research Have the students research credit bureaus to find out how they acquire and record information, how they get paid, and how collections are pursued.

Consumer Credit Reporting Reform Act The Consumer Credit Reporting Reform Act of 1997 places the burden of proof for accurate credit information on the credit bureau rather than on you. Under this law, the creditor must prove that disputed information is accurate. If a creditor or the credit bureau verifies incorrect data, you can sue for damages.

The Federal Reserve System has set up a separate office, the Division of Consumer and Community Affairs, in Washington to handle consumer complaints. This division also writes regulations to carry out the consumer credit laws, enforces these laws, and helps banks comply with these laws.

Your Rights Under Consumer Credit Laws

If you believe that you have been refused credit because of discrimination, you can take one or more of the following steps:

1. Complain to the creditor. Let the creditor know that you are aware of the law.
2. File a complaint with the government. You can report any violations to the appropriate government enforcement agency, as shown in **Figure 6.9.**
3. If all else fails, sue the creditor. You have the right to bring a case in a federal district court. If you win, you can receive actual damages and punitive damages of up to $10,000. You can also recover reasonable attorneys' fees and court costs.

Section 6.3 Assessment

See the Teacher Manual for answers.

QUICK CHECK

1. What should you do if you think that a bill is wrong or want more information about it? How should your creditor respond to your attempt to resolve the situation?
2. How can you protect yourself against credit card theft or loss?
3. How does the Fair Credit Reporting Act protect you?

THINK CRITICALLY

4. Recall the suggestions for protecting your credit information on the Internet. Predict the problems that could result from not following the guidelines.

USE COMMUNICATION SKILLS

5. **Cosigning a Loan** Suppose that a close friend has asked you to cosign a loan she needs to start up a children's clothing store. You would like to help if you can. However, your friend is currently unemployed, and you are concerned that she will not be able to repay the loan. After much thought, you decide not to cosign the loan.

Write About It Write a letter to your friend explaining why you have decided not to cosign her loan. In the letter, point out what the consequences to you will be if she is unable to repay the loan.

SOLVE MONEY PROBLEMS

6. **Putting a Stop to Fraud** Joel went to the ATM the other day to withdraw some cash. When he checked his receipt, he noticed that the balance on his savings account was $500 less than it should have been. After discussing the matter with a customer service representative at his bank, he realized that someone else had gained access to his account number and Personal Identification Number (PIN).

Role-Play Using what you have learned about protecting yourself from fraud, explain to Joel the steps he should take to stop any further damage from being done. Partner with another student to role-play the conversation.

Section 6.4

Focus on Reading

Read to Learn

- How to identify ways to manage debt problems.

Main Idea

If you experience the warning signs of debt problems, there are several options available to manage your finances.

Key Term

- bankruptcy

Before You Read

PREDICT

What corrective steps would you take if you were experiencing the debt troubles listed here?

Springboard Ask the students how they plan to ensure they will not get seriously into debt.

Managing Your Debts

Signs of Debt Problems

How do you know when you are getting in financial trouble?

Carl Reynolds is in his early 20s. A recent college graduate, he has a steady job and earns an annual income of $40,000. With the latest model sports car parked in the driveway of his new home, it would appear that Carl has the ideal life.

However, Carl is deeply in debt. He is drowning in a sea of bills. Almost all of his income is tied up in debt payments. The bank has already begun foreclosure proceedings on his home, and several stores have court orders to repossess practically all of his new furniture and electronic gadgets. His current car payment is overdue, and he is behind in payments on all of his credit cards. If he does not come up with a plan of action, he will lose everything.

Carl's situation is all too common. Some people who seem to be wealthy are just barely keeping their heads above water financially. They may lack self-discipline and do not control their impulses. They use poor judgment or fail to accept responsibility for managing their money. Carl and others like him are not necessarily bad people. They simply have not thought about their long-term financial goals.

The Warning Signs

There are some warning signs of being in financial trouble. If you are experiencing two or more of these warning signs, it is time for you to rethink your priorities.

- You make only the minimum monthly payment on credit cards.
- You are having trouble making even the minimum monthly payment on your credit card bills.
- The total balance on your credit cards increases every month.
- You miss loan payments or often pay late.
- You use savings to pay for necessities such as food and utilities.
- You receive second or third payment due notices from creditors.
- You borrow money to pay off old debts.
- You exceed the credit limits on your credit cards.
- You have been denied credit because of a bad credit report.

▲ **LIVING IT UP** Some people use credit to finance a comfortable lifestyle. *How might this approach create problems in the future?*

Caption Answer People can lose money, property, and their good credit ratings.

Debt Collection Practices

Are debt collection practices regulated by laws?

When people are in debt and getting behind in payments, they may worry about debt collection agencies. Creditors will often turn their bad debts over to such companies. However, a federal agency protects certain legal rights of debtors in their dealings with these types of agencies.

The Federal Trade Commission enforces the Fair Debt Collection Practices Act (FDCPA). This act prohibits certain practices by debt collectors—businesses that collect debts for creditors. The act does not erase the legitimate debts that consumers owe, but it does control the ways in which debt collection agencies do business and deal with consumers in debt.

Financial Counseling Services

What are sources of financial counseling?

If you are having trouble paying your bills and need help, you have several options. You can contact your creditors and try to work out an adjusted repayment plan. In addition, you can contact a nonprofit financial counseling program, such as the Consumer Credit Counseling Service, which operates nationwide.

Motivating Students Have students relate incidents in which they or someone they know have gotten into serious debt and how the situation was resolved.

Consumer Credit Counseling Service

The Consumer Credit Counseling Service (CCCS) is a nonprofit organization affiliated with the National Foundation for Consumer Credit (NFCC). Local branches of the CCCS provide debt counseling services for families and individuals with serious financial problems. The CCCS is not a charity, a lending institution, or a government agency. CCCS counseling is usually free. However, when the organization supervises a debt repayment plan, it sometimes charges a small fee to help pay administrative costs.

According to the NFCC, millions of consumers contact CCCS offices each year for help with their personal financial problems. To find an office near you, check the white pages of your local telephone directory under Consumer Credit Counseling Service, or call 1-800-388-CCCS. All information is kept confidential.

Credit counselors know that most individuals who are overwhelmed with debt are basically honest people who want to clear up their unmanageable indebtedness, the condition of being deeply in debt. Too often, such problems arise from a lack of planning or a miscalculation of earnings. The CCCS is concerned with preventing problems as much as it is with solving them. As a result, its activities are divided into two parts:

Extension Have someone from a financial counseling service come to class to discuss how they function in order to help people who are seriously in debt.

- Aiding families with serious debt problems by helping them manage their money better and setting up a realistic budget
- Helping people prevent indebtedness by teaching them the importance of budget planning, educating them about the pitfalls of unwise credit buying, and encouraging credit institutions to withhold credit from people who cannot afford it

Other Counseling Services

In addition to the CCCS, universities, credit unions, military bases, and state and federal housing authorities sometimes provide nonprofit credit counseling services. These organizations usually charge little to nothing for their assistance. You can also check with your bank or local consumer protection office to see whether it has a listing of reputable financial counseling services.

Declaring Personal Bankruptcy

Why do people declare personal bankruptcy?

What if an individual suffers from an extreme case of debt problems? Is there any relief? As a last resort, an individual can declare bankruptcy. **Bankruptcy** is a legal process in which some or all of the assets of a debtor are distributed among the creditors because the debtor is unable to pay his or her debts. Bankruptcy may also include a plan for the debtor to repay creditors on an installment basis. Declaring bankruptcy is a last resort because it severely damages your credit rating.

Prakrit Singh illustrates the new face of bankruptcy. A 43-year-old freelance photographer from California, she was never in serious financial trouble until she began running up big medical costs. She reached for her credit cards to pay the bills. Because Prakrit did not have health insurance, her debt quickly mounted and soon reached $17,000—too much to pay off with her $25,000-a-year income. Her solution was to declare personal bankruptcy and enjoy the immediate freedom it would bring from creditors' demands.

In 1994, the U.S. Senate passed a bill that reduced the time and cost of bankruptcy proceedings. The bill strengthened creditor rights and enabled more individuals to get through bankruptcy proceedings without selling their assets. Today legislators have enacted new tougher bankruptcy law reforms that are intended to end perceived abuses of the current bankruptcy system.

As You Read

RELATE

What might cause you or someone you know to declare personal bankruptcy?

Figure 6.10 **U.S. Bankruptcies 1970–2003**

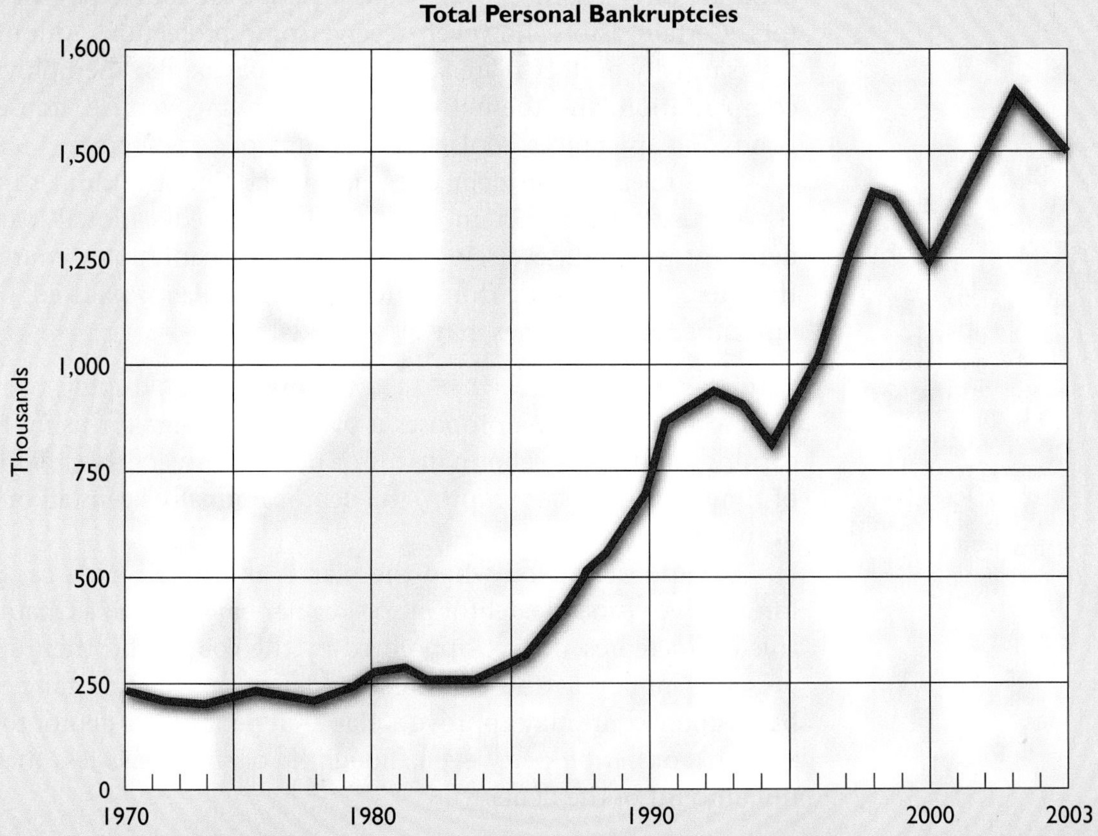

Source: Administrative Office of the United States Courts, May 2004.

Bankruptcy Boom The total number of personal bankruptcies has risen sharply in the last few decades.

Why do you think the number of personal bankruptcies in the United States was relatively low in the early 1960s as compared to the late 1990s?

Caption Answer The likeliest answer is because people had far fewer credit cards in the early 1960s. Other answers are possible.

As You Read
QUESTION

How would filing for bankruptcy negatively impact a person's future?

Question Answer It stays on a credit report up to ten years and can affect future loans for a car, education, or a home.

Critical Thinking Divide the students into teams to research, prepare, and debate the question: Is declaring bankruptcy ethical? Ask one team of students to judge the debates. This team should do its own research on the question to ensure the debating teams are using correct information. Note: Depending on class size, set up three or six teams.

The U.S. Bankruptcy Act of 1978

Figure 6.10 on page 189 illustrates the rate of personal bankruptcy in the United States. The vast majority of bankruptcies in the United States, like Prakrit Singh's, are filed under a part of the U.S. bankruptcy code known as Chapter 7. You have two choices in declaring personal bankruptcy:

- Chapter 7 (a straight bankruptcy)
- Chapter 13 (a wage-earner plan bankruptcy)

Both choices are undesirable, and neither should be considered an easy way to get out of debt.

Chapter 7 Bankruptcy In a Chapter 7 bankruptcy, an individual is required to draw up a petition listing his or her assets and liabilities. A person who files for relief under the bankruptcy code is called a debtor. The debtor submits the petition to a U.S. district court and pays a filing fee.

Chapter 7 is a straight bankruptcy in which many, but not all, debts are forgiven. Most of the debtor's assets are sold to pay off creditors. Certain assets, however, receive some protection. Among the assets usually protected are Social Security payments, unemployment compensation, and the net value of your home, vehicle, household goods and appliances, tools used in your work, and books.

The release from debt does not affect alimony, child support, certain taxes, fines, certain debts arising from educational loans, or debts that you fail to disclose properly to the bankruptcy court. Furthermore, debts arising from fraud, driving while intoxicated, or certain other acts or crimes may also be excluded.

Chapter 13 Bankruptcy In a Chapter 13 bankruptcy, a debtor with a regular income proposes a plan to the court for using future earnings or assets to eliminate his or her debts over a specific period of time. In such a bankruptcy, the debtor normally keeps all or most of his or her property.

During the period when the plan is in effect, which can be as long as five years, the debtor makes regular payments to a Chapter 13 trustee, or representative appointed by the court, who then distributes the money to the creditors. Under certain circumstances, the bankruptcy court may approve a plan that permits the debtor to keep all of his or her property even though he or she repays less than the full amount of the debts.

Using a Lawyer

Choosing a bankruptcy lawyer may be difficult. Some of the least reputable lawyers make easy money by handling hundreds of bankruptcy cases without considering individual needs. Recommendations from friends, family, or employee assistance programs are most useful.

Effects of Bankruptcy

People have varying experiences in obtaining credit after they file for bankruptcy. Some find the process more difficult, whereas others find it easier because they have removed the burden of prior debts or because creditors know that they cannot file another bankruptcy case for a certain period of time. Obtaining credit may be easier for people who file a Chapter 13 bankruptcy and repay some of their debts than for those who file a Chapter 7 bankruptcy and make no effort to repay any of their debts. Bankruptcy reports are kept on file in credit bureaus for ten years, a fact that is likely to make getting credit more difficult during that time. Therefore, you should take the extreme step of declaring bankruptcy only when you have no other options. Of course, the best way to solve your financial problems is to avoid them by maintaining good credit.

After You Read

REACT

What would be the best way to avoid credit problems and bankruptcy?

React Answer Answers may vary, but the best answer is to avoid buying more than you can afford and avoid excessive use of credit cards.

Section 6.4 Assessment

See the Teacher Manual for answers.

QUICK CHECK

1. What are some of the warning signs of debt problems?
2. What consumer credit counseling services are available?
3. What are the differences between declaring Chapter 7 and Chapter 13 bankruptcy?

THINK CRITICALLY

4. Consider your own financial situation and determine whether any of the warning signs of debt problems might apply to you or to someone you know. Analyze what you might do to correct them or how you might advise someone else.

USE MATH SKILLS

5. **Declaring Bankruptcy** Unfortunately, bankruptcy has increased.

   Calculate Using the graph in Figure 6.10 on page 189, determine the percent increase of total personal bankruptcies from 1990 to 2003. Do you think this figure will rise? Why?

SOLVE MONEY PROBLEMS

6. **Making Financial Decisions** Deanne is a customer service representative for a popular fitness club. Her income is modest, but that does not stop her from satisfying her most important desire—to travel. Deanne takes two vacations a year, and she has been all over the world. She has paid for most of her trips to faraway places with her credit card. However, when she received the bills for her last trip to India, reality hit hard. Her monthly debt payments are actually greater than her monthly net income.

   Write About It According to what you have learned in this section, what can Deanne do to solve her problem? Consider the options she might have, and write a plan.

Chapter 6 Review & Activities

See the Teacher Manual for answers.

CHAPTER SUMMARY

- Consumer credit is the use of credit for personal needs. Credit is an arrangement to receive cash, goods, or services now and to pay for them later.
- Closed-end credit is credit as a one-time loan that you pay back over a specified period of time in payments of equal amounts. Open-end credit is credit as a loan with a limit on the amount of money that you borrow for goods and services.
- The five C's of credit include character, capacity, capital, collateral, and credit history. Creditors use the five C's to determine who will receive credit.
- When choosing a loan or credit card, consider factors such as length of the loan, amount of monthly payments, and interest rate.
- To build and protect good credit, pay your bills and loans promptly and manage your personal finances carefully. Also, correct mistakes related to your credit bills and credit reports. Dispute billing errors in writing and pay amounts that are not in question.
- If your credit or identity has been stolen, contact all your credit card companies; close and open new bank accounts; and change all PINs. Notify law enforcement agencies and credit bureaus. If purchasing online, never share your PINs, Social Security numbers, or passwords.
- Manage debt problems by contacting creditors and/or debt counseling services. Bankruptcy is a last resort.

Communicating Key Terms

Imagine you are applying for a loan to buy a new car. In a paragraph, write a conversation you would have with a loan officer while applying for the loan, using at least ten key terms:

- credit
- consumer credit
- creditor
- closed-end credit
- open-end credit
- line of credit
- grace period
- finance charge
- net income
- annual percentage rate (APR)
- collateral
- simple interest
- minimum monthly payment
- credit rating
- cosigning
- bankruptcy

Reviewing Key Concepts

1. **Explain** the concept of consumer credit.
2. **Differentiate** between open-end credit and closed-end credit.
3. **Identify** the five C's of credit using a graphic organizer. Then rate yourself.
4. **Discuss** the factors to consider when choosing a loan or credit card.
5. **Identify** ways you can build a good credit rating.
6. **Discuss** the steps you should take if your identity is stolen.
7. **Explain** the role of consumer counseling services.

See the Teacher Manual for answers.

ACADEMIC SKILLS

Language Arts You have just received a telephone bill for $225. Usually your bill is about $35 a month. You read it closely and discover two long-distance calls to Japan at $100 and $92, both of which you did not make.

Write About It Write a brief letter to the phone company explaining why you should not be charged.

YOUR FINANCIAL FIGURES

Billing Errors Miguel read his credit card statement and discovered that a store charged him twice for the same item. His total bill was $658.22:

Lane Electronics	207.33
Brewster Cable TV	127.45
Lane Electronics	207.33
Empress Wok	38.87
Office Supplies, Inc.	77.24

1. **Calculate** how much Miguel should subtract from his bill and calculate his actual balance.
2. **Compute** by using spreadsheet software to show what Miguel's bill will be next month if he pays $25 this month with 18 percent interest.

REAL-WORLD Application

Connect With Ethics Your credit score determines whether you receive credit and at what interest rate. The credit-score scale runs from 300 to 850. Most people in the United States have scores between 600 and 800.

1. **Research** Use an Internet search engine to find information on credit scores.
2. **Think Critically** Explain why credit scoring may increase fairness in getting credit. Explain why it may be unfair.

Internet CONNECTION

Student Loans Many students finance their college educations with their own earnings, savings, family help, grants, scholarships—and loans.

Log On Use an Internet search engine to find out about student loans. Check the colleges that interest you. Click on their Financial Aid links. Answer the following questions:

1. What is the interest rate for a government student loan and how long can you take to repay a student loan?
2. How could this monthly payment affect your debt payments-to-income ratio?

BusinessWeek ONLINE

Newsclip: Student Credit Cards Many credit companies offer credit cards to students 18 years and over. As a result, many students have heavy debts. Debt advisers say students should have a low maximum limit.

Log On Go to **finance07.glencoe.com** and open Chapter 6. Learn more about managing credit, and then write a list of ways to avoid credit card debt.

WHAT'S YOUR FINANCIAL ID?

YOUR CREDIT PROFILE

Do you know how to use credit wisely? On a separate sheet of paper write the letter that best describes your answer to the following questions.

1. I pay any bills I have when they are due _____.
   a. always
   b. most of the time
   c. sometimes

2. If I need more money for my expenses, I borrow it _____.
   a. never
   b. sometimes
   c. often

3. If I want to see a copy of my credit report, I can contact _____.
   a. a credit reporting agency
   b. a bank
   c. the principal of my school

4. If I default (do not repay) on a loan, it will stay on my credit report for _____.
   a. 7 years
   b. 2 years
   c. 6 months

5. If I have serious credit problems, I should _____.
   a. contact my creditors to explain the problem
   b. contact only the most persistent creditors
   c. not contact my creditors and hope they will forget about me

6. I can begin building a good rating by _____.
   a. opening a savings account and making regular monthly deposits.
   b. paying most of my bills on time
   c. opening a checking account and bouncing checks

Scoring: Give yourself 3 points for each "a," 2 points for each "b," and 1 point for each "c." Add up the number of points.

If you scored 6–9 points, you might want to take a closer look at how credit works before you get over your head in debt.

If you scored 10–13 points, you are off to a good start, but be sure you know the pitfalls of opening a credit account.

Source: *How to Be Credit Smart* (Washington, D.C., Consumer Education Foundation, 1994).

Accept all reasonable answers that show student effort.

Your Financial Portfolio

Credit Cards: Getting the Best Deal

Melanie's parents want to give her a credit card she could use for emergencies. They made it clear that if she could eat it, wear it, or listen to it, it was not an emergency. They asked Melanie to do the homework to find the best deal. She called the bank where she has a savings account and another neighborhood bank and asked about the following credit card information.

Melanie's Credit Card Comparison

Credit Card Company	Peabody Bank	Imperial Bank
Phone number	800/555-1274	800/555-9201
Annual percentage rate (APR)	19.9%	10.9%
Introductory rate	2.9% on transferred balances	5% for first 6 months
Annual fee	$50	none
Grace period	18 days	25 days
Cash advance fee	19.8%	19.9%
Late payment fee	$25	$29
Credit limit for new customers	based on income	based on income
Travel accident insurance	$150,000	$10,000
Other travel-related services	airline miles; lost luggage insurance; emergency travel services	lost luggage insurance; emergency travel services
Protection if the cards are lost or stolen	yes	yes

Melanie chose the credit card with Imperial Bank because there was no annual fee, and the APR was lower. She did not think she would spend enough to make Peabody Bank's offer of airline miles useful. Melanie was surprised at the high penalty for late payments, so she made a mental note to be sure to make her payment on time.

If you wanted a credit card, which company would you choose? Explain why. Would you be influenced by the offer of airline miles?

Research

On a separate sheet of paper, research two credit card companies. List their fees and any advantages they offer.

Accept all research information that shows student effort and an understanding of the concept.

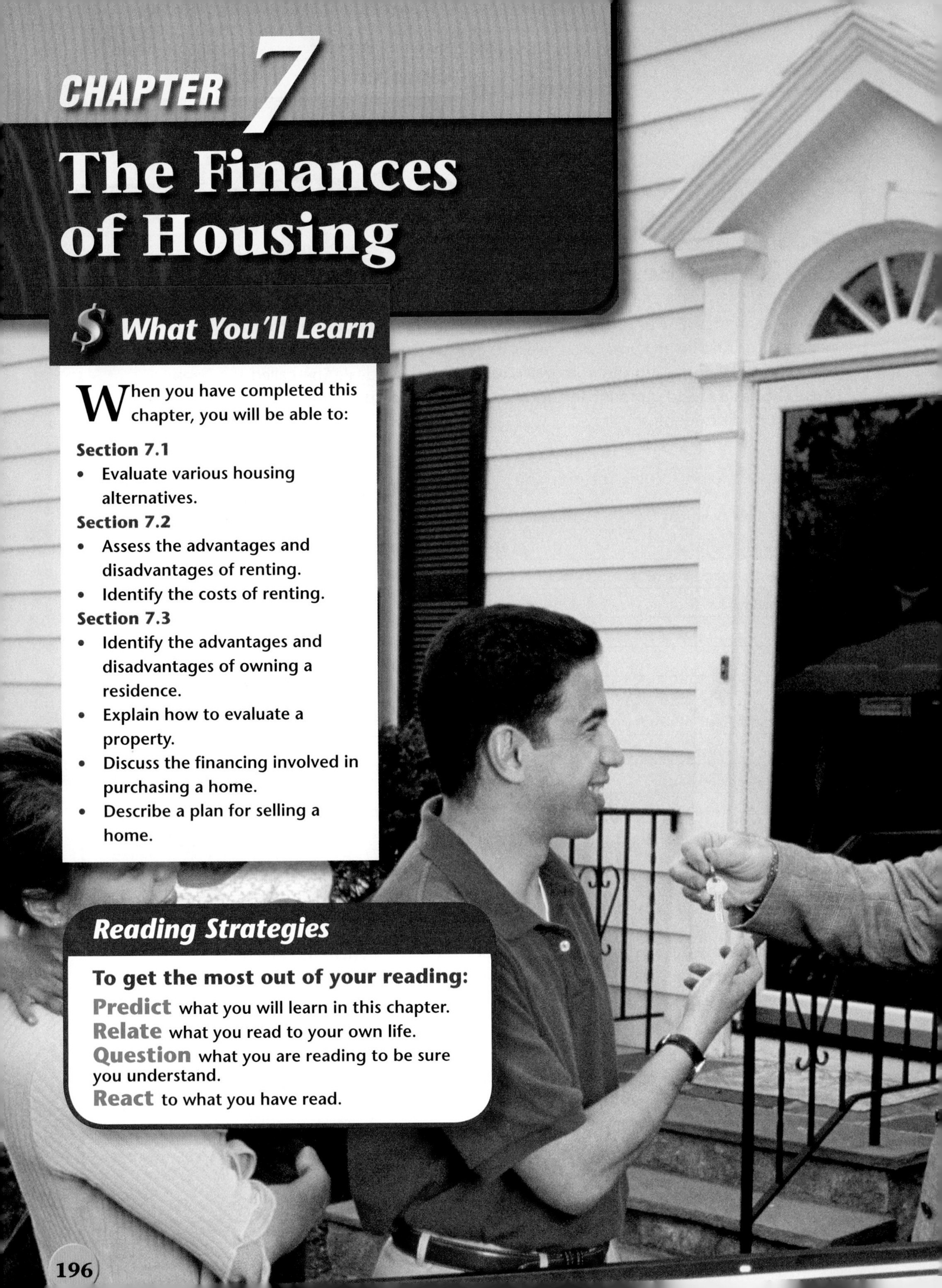

CHAPTER 7
The Finances of Housing

$ What You'll Learn

When you have completed this chapter, you will be able to:

Section 7.1
- Evaluate various housing alternatives.

Section 7.2
- Assess the advantages and disadvantages of renting.
- Identify the costs of renting.

Section 7.3
- Identify the advantages and disadvantages of owning a residence.
- Explain how to evaluate a property.
- Discuss the financing involved in purchasing a home.
- Describe a plan for selling a home.

Reading Strategies

To get the most out of your reading:

Predict what you will learn in this chapter.
Relate what you read to your own life.
Question what you are reading to be sure you understand.
React to what you have read.

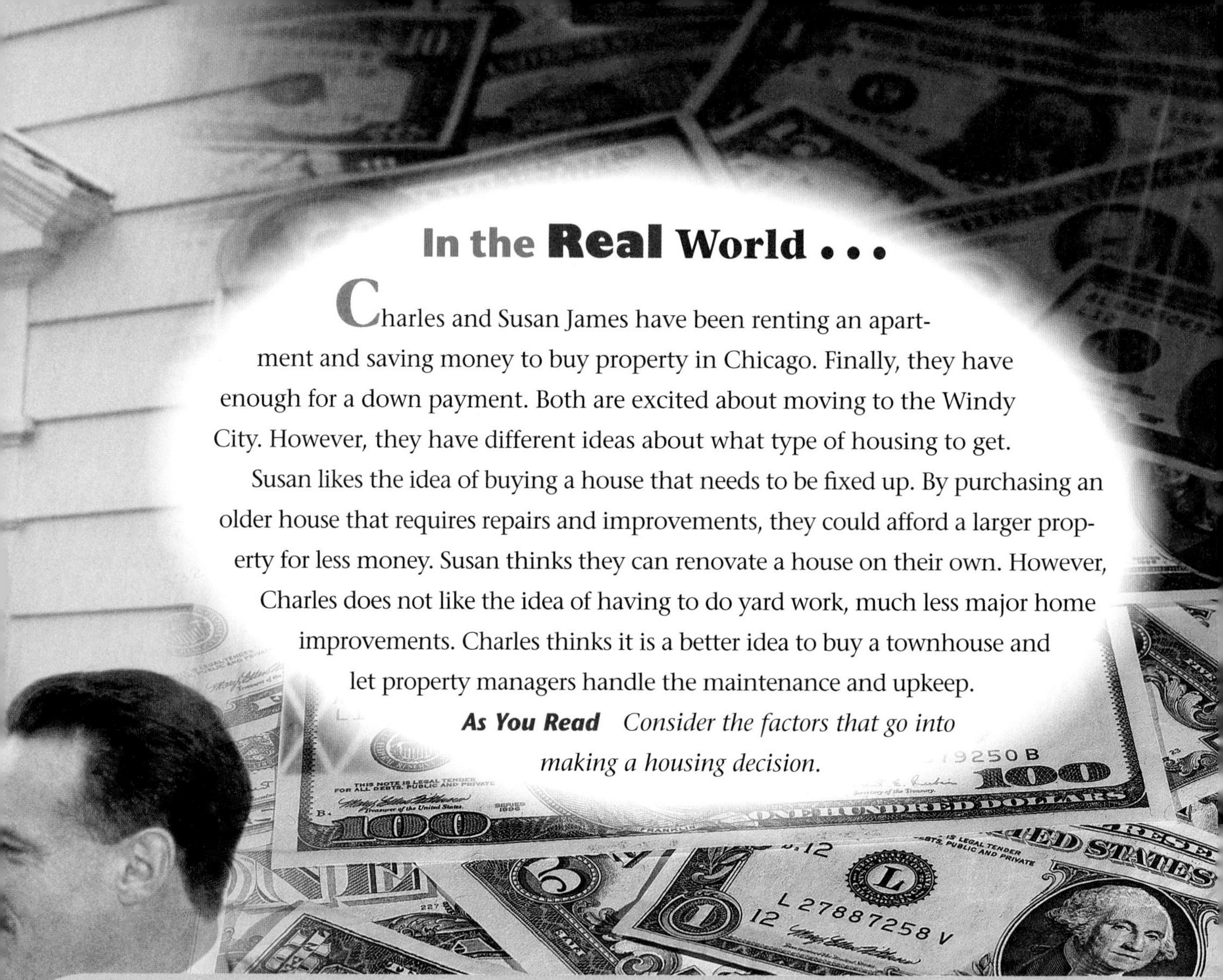

In the Real World . . .

Charles and Susan James have been renting an apartment and saving money to buy property in Chicago. Finally, they have enough for a down payment. Both are excited about moving to the Windy City. However, they have different ideas about what type of housing to get.

Susan likes the idea of buying a house that needs to be fixed up. By purchasing an older house that requires repairs and improvements, they could afford a larger property for less money. Susan thinks they can renovate a house on their own. However, Charles does not like the idea of having to do yard work, much less major home improvements. Charles thinks it is a better idea to buy a townhouse and let property managers handle the maintenance and upkeep.

As You Read *Consider the factors that go into making a housing decision.*

Lesson Plan See the Teacher Manual for the Chapter 7 planning guide and lesson plan.

ASK STANDARD & POOR'S

Housing Options

Q: My older sister loves her new job and has decided that she would like to work for her company at least five years. Is this a good time for her to buy a house, or should she continue renting?

A: A home can be an excellent investment, but your sister will need to take some things into consideration before she makes this decision. For example, she will need to assess her finances to determine if she can afford to buy a house. She must also consider whether she wants to spend time maintaining a house; if not, it may be best for her to continue renting.

Ask Yourself What could be some advantages of owning a house?

@ Go to **finance07.glencoe.com** to complete the Standard & Poor's Financial Focus activity.

Section 7.1

Focus on Reading

Read to Learn

- How to evaluate various housing alternatives.

Main Idea

Knowing about housing options will help you spend your money wisely now and in the future.

Key Term

- mobility

Housing Options

Your Lifestyle and Choice of Housing

How does your lifestyle affect your choice of housing?

Finances play an important role in housing decisions. Whether you are renting a small apartment in a city or buying a house in the country, you will have to consider your financial situation. You can use your budget and the other personal financial statements discussed in Chapter 3 to determine how much you should spend for housing.

One major factor you will need to consider when making housing decisions is your lifestyle, which is the way you choose to spend your time and money. For example, when looking at your housing choices, you might consider if you like hosting big family gatherings. If so, you would probably want a large living room or family room. **Figure 7.1** lists types of housing for people in different life situations. Your lifestyle will determine several housing decisions:

- How close to work you want to live
- How long you plan to stay in one place
- How much privacy you would like to have

Before You Read

PREDICT

Do you plan to own or rent a residence? Explain your choice.

Opportunity Costs of Housing Choices

What are some opportunity costs to consider when purchasing a home?

A housing decision requires many trade-offs, or opportunity costs. For example, buying a handyman's special—a home that is priced lower because it needs repairs and improvements—may allow you to purchase a larger property for less money, but it also means that you will have to work on the house. Renting an apartment may give you more **mobility**, which is the ability to move easily from place to place. However, you will give up the tax advantages that homeowners enjoy. When you make choices about housing, you cannot look at only the benefits. You also have to consider what you will be giving up in terms of time, effort, or money.

Springboard Ask the students to name housing features they think are desirable (fireplace, two bathrooms, etc.). List answers on the board. Then ask what one feature students consider to be essential and why.

Figure 7.1 **Housing for Different Life Situations**

Life Situation	Possible Types of Housing
Young single	• Rent an apartment or house because mobility is important and finances are low. • Buy a small home for tax advantages and possible increase in value.
Single parent	• Rent an apartment or house because time for maintenance is at a premium, playmates for children may be nearby, and finances are low. • Buy a home to build long-term financial security.
Young couple, no children	• Rent an apartment or house because mobility is important and finances are low • Buy a home to build long-term financial security.
Couple with children	• Rent an apartment or house because time for maintenance is at a premium and playmates for children may be nearby. • Buy a house to build long-term financial security and to provide more space and privacy.
Retired person	• Rent an apartment or house to meet financial, social, and physical needs. • Buy a home that needs little maintenance, offers convenience, and provides different services.

Rent or Buy? Different life situations will require different housing choices.

What might be a wise housing choice for a single parent? Explain your reasoning.

Caption Answer Answers might include renting because funds may be low, other families with children would be near, or buying to provide financial security.

Renting versus Buying

Why would you rent a home if you could buy one?

One of the most basic considerations about housing is whether to rent or buy. Your decision will depend on your lifestyle and on financial factors.

Renting is a good choice for young adults who are beginning their careers. It also appeals to people who want or need mobility. Renting is also a good choice for people who do not want to devote time or money to maintenance. Because renting is often—though not always—cheaper than owning a home, it appeals to people whose funds are limited.

In contrast, owning property also has advantages. It is a wise choice for people who want a certain amount of stability in their lives. Buying a home also gives the owner privacy and some freedoms that may not be available to a renter. For example, you may not be allowed to have pets or large parties in an apartment, but you can do so in a house that you own. While ownership can be costly—at least in the short run—it offers financial benefits, such as tax advantages. In addition, the value of a house may increase, making the purchase of a home a good long-term investment. See **Figure 7.2** on page 200 for more information about renting and buying.

As You Read

RELATE

What opportunity costs are you willing to pay to obtain the home you would like?

Motivating Students Refer students to the earlier list of desirable housing features from the Springboard activity. For each feature, ask if it would be found in a house or apartment; then discuss which features they would forego to bring the price down.

Discussion Ask how many students live in apartments. Then discuss with students reasons apartments may restrict pets, pianos, waterbeds, loud noise, etc.

Figure 7.2 Evaluating Housing Alternatives

	Advantages	Disadvantages
Renting an Apartment 	• easy to move • low maintenance responsibility • low financial commitment	• no tax advantage • limitations on activities • less privacy
Renting a House 	• easy to move • low maintenance responsibility • low financial commitment • more space	• higher utility expenses • some limitations on activities • no tax advantage
Owning a House 	• pride of ownership • plenty of space • tax benefits	• financial commitment • high living expenses • limited mobility
Owning a Condominium 	• pride of ownership • fewer maintenance costs or responsibilities than a house • tax benefits • access to recreation and businesses	• financial commitment • less privacy than in a house • need to get along with others • typically small and limited space • may be hard to sell
Owning a Mobile Home 	• less expensive than other ownership options	• may be hard to sell • possible poor construction quality

On the Other Hand Choosing a type of housing is a decision that involves many trade-offs.

Find the three advantages or disadvantages on this list that seem most important to you now.

Caption Answer Accept all reasonable answers.

Housing Information Sources

Where can you research housing options?

Housing information is plentiful and often free. You can begin researching on your own, using a variety of sources:

- **Libraries**—The public library will probably have books and other basic resources on the subject.
- **Newspapers**—You can find articles on renting, buying, and other housing topics in the real estate section of a newspaper.
- **Internet**—The Internet can provide home buying tips, the latest mortgage rates, and information on available housing in your area and in other parts of the United States.

Research Have students choose cities where they would like to live. Ask them to research housing costs and availability in their cities. Post their results on a large map in the front of the room.

- **Friends and Family**—Friends and family can also be good sources of information on housing. They can share some of their own housing choices.
- **Real Estate Agents**—You might seek the services of an experienced real estate agent who is familiar with the local housing market.
- **Government Agencies**—You can also write to government agencies, such as the U.S. Department of Housing and Urban Development (HUD).

Any combination of these sources will provide the information you need to make wise housing decisions, whether you decide to rent or buy your home.

As You Read

QUESTION

What are some sources of housing information?

Question Answer Answers may include libraries, newspapers, the Internet, friends and family, realtors, and government agencies.

Section 7.1 Assessment

See the Teacher Manual for answers.

QUICK CHECK

1. What should you consider when you evaluate available housing alternatives?
2. When would buying a residence be a better choice than renting one?
3. What are at least three sources of housing information?

THINK CRITICALLY

4. Write a short paragraph explaining the probable housing needs of a family that consists of two working adults and three school-age children. Decide whether this family should rent or buy, and explain why you think so.

USE COMMUNICATION SKILLS

5. **Housing Options** Your uncle Manny's company has transferred him to your area, and he and his wife, Karen, will be moving within the next two months. Because Manny's work requires fairly frequent moves, he and Karen are not interested in purchasing a home at this time. Manny and Karen are both busy with their jobs, so they have little time to research a place to live. You have offered to do some background work to get them started.

Present Review the classified section of your local newspaper. Choose several houses and apartments for Manny and Karen that are about the same size and for rent, and prepare a chart that compares the prices, locations, and features of each option. Display it in class.

SOLVE MONEY PROBLEMS

6. **Housing and Lifestyle** Your cousin Lavani, who is 25 years old and single, tells you that she is thinking of buying a house. She has been at her job for eight months and loves it so far, but she has not made many friends yet. The house she is looking at is 10 miles from her workplace. Lavani says that the house needs a new roof, and the basement sometimes floods, but otherwise it is in good shape. She thinks that she will be able to afford it when she gets her first raise.

Analyze Help Lavani determine the opportunity costs of this potential purchase. Would buying the house be a good decision for Lavani? Explain your answer.

Section 7.2

Focus on Reading

Read to Learn

- How to assess the advantages and disadvantages of renting.
- How to identify the costs of renting.

Main Idea

Knowing more about the advantages, disadvantages, and costs of renting will help you make the right choice.

Key Terms

- tenant
- landlord
- lease
- security deposit
- renters insurance

Before You Read

PREDICT

How would you begin a search for an apartment?

Springboard Ask the students when they plan to rent their first apartment. Discuss how much they think they will have to pay for rent and if they may need a roommate.

Caption Answer Answers might include: There are many ads; looking is free; you can compare costs. For disadvantages: You may need more information; not all rentals are listed; and ads may paint a false picture.

Renting a Residence

Selecting a Rental Unit

What should you know before signing a lease?

Are you interested in a "3-bdrm apt., a/c, w/w carpet, pvt back ent, $800 + utils, ref reqd"? This is not a secret code. It is just a short way of describing an apartment for rent listed in the classified ads of a newspaper. Decoded, the message reads: "Three-bedroom apartment for rent. It has air conditioning, wall-to-wall carpeting, and a private back entrance. The rent is $800, and the renter must also pay for utilities. The renter must provide references." The ability to read and understand such ads is one of the skills you will need if you are going to look for some type of rental housing.

When you rent the place where you live, you become a **tenant**—a person who pays for the right to live in a residence owned by someone else. Your **landlord** is the person who owns the property that is rented. You should consider the differences in the size, cost, and location of rental units when making a selection.

Size and Cost

Most people who rent live in apartments. These units may be located in a two-story house, in a high-rise building, or in an apartment complex. An apartment building contains a number of separate living units that can range in size from one room (an efficiency or studio) to three-bedroom or larger units.

HAMILTON TWP—2 bdrm 1 bath, off str prkg. quiet nghborhd. Use of cellar. $800 mo. 602-989-7767.

PRINCETON—Close to campus. Pvt 1st flr, 1 bdrm. apt., wood flr., lndry. & prkg. No smkg/pets. $925/mo + utils. Avail 7/1 or 8/1. 1 yr lse. 616-433-8756.

TRENTON—Historic dist. Attractive apt. Refinished wood fire, 1 large bdrm, lg liv rm, lg kit, yard. $850/mo. 677-547-6400.

SIERRAS—2 bdrm 1 bath, beautiful view, quiet nghborhd. $700 mo. 612-999-7647.

AUSTIN—Close to stores. 1 bdrm. apt., wood flr., lndry. & prkg. No smkg/pets. $825/mo + 1st and last. Avail 10/2 or 11/2. 788-997-8211.

UPSTATE—Affordable rental. Spacious apt. Refinished wood floor, 2 large bdrm, lg kit, din rm, bsmnt storage. $950/mo. 565-989-5466.

▲ **MEET THE PRESS** Newspaper ads are one way to find out about available rental units. *What information is usually included in an ad for a rental unit?*

If a unit features a patio and a bit of lawn, it may be called a *garden apartment.* Some apartments are located in complexes with on-site conveniences such as swimming pools, tennis courts, and laundry facilities.

A family or individual who needs more space than an apartment provides may prefer to rent a house. The trade-off for the extra space is usually higher rent. A single person with very few possessions might choose to rent a private room in a house. He or she may have to share common areas, such as the kitchen and bathroom.

Motivating Students Discuss with students the advantages of remaining in their parents' homes as long as possible versus the advantages of renting a home.

Sources of Information

To find a rental unit, you can check the classified section of the local newspaper. Friends and coworkers are good sources of suggestions, too. You can also check with real estate and rental offices. **Figure 7.3** describes what to look for when selecting an apartment.

Research Have the students research the laws in your state regarding renting. They are to find out both tenants' and landlords' rights and responsibilities. Have them submit their research in the form of an essay or a graphic depiction.

Figure 7.3 **Selecting an Apartment**

Location	Finances	Building	Layout and Facilities
• Near school or work • Near place of worship • Near shopping • Near public transportation • Near recreation: parks and museums	• Amount of monthly rent • Amount of security deposit • Cost of utilities • Length of lease	• Condition of building and grounds • Parking facilities • Recreation on premises • Security system • Condition of hallways, stairs, and elevators • Access to mailboxes	• Size and condition of unit • Type and controls of heating and cooling systems • Plumbing and water pressure • Type and condition of appliances • Condition of doors, locks, windows, closets, and floors

On Your Own Many considerations go into renting an apartment.

Which of the four broad categories above would be most important to you right now?

Caption Answer Accept all reasonable answers.

▶ **ON THE MOVE** Many people like to rent because it allows them to move easily to different places. *What types of individuals might find such mobility most attractive?*

Caption Answer Answers will vary but may include young people just starting out, people who have few possessions, and young couples without children.

As You Read
RELATE

How would you begin a search for an apartment?

Advantages of Renting

What are some of the advantages of renting?

The three main advantages of renting over buying a home are greater mobility, fewer responsibilities, and lower initial costs.

Mobility and Fewer Responsibilities

For many people, the appeal of renting is the mobility it offers. If you want to move, you can usually notify your landlord 30 days before you plan to leave, and he or she can find a new tenant. If you are offered a job in another town, you can move quickly and simply. This is also an advantage for growing families who need more space. If your landlord increases your rent beyond the amount you have budgeted, or if you decide that you want to live in a different community, making a change will be fairly easy if you rent an apartment.

Tenants do not have many of the responsibilities that homeowners have. Making major repairs and maintaining the property are the landlord's concern. Tenants do not have to worry about property taxes or property insurance. Of course, they must pay the rent and any utility bills on time, and keep their homes clean.

Teaching Activity Divide the students into groups of four. Assign and have each group research a different rental property in the area. They are to research rents on different sizes of apartments, amenities of the apartment and the building, security deposit amounts, restrictions, and whether the tenancy is month-to-month or lease. Then have students compare all the properties and decide which one appeals to them most, and then explain why.

Low Initial Costs

A third advantage to renting is cost. Buying a house typically requires many thousands of dollars for the down payment and other costs. In contrast, you usually pay the equivalent of only one or two months' rent to move into a rental unit.

Disadvantages of Renting

What are some of the disadvantages of renting?

Renting is a good option for many people, but it has some disadvantages. Renting offers few financial benefits, and it can contribute to a more restrictive lifestyle. In addition, renting may involve various legal issues for tenants.

Financial and Lifestyle Restrictions

Although it has lower initial costs, renting may actually be more expensive than owning property in some cases. Certain financial benefits are available to homeowners but not to tenants. Homeowners, for example, are eligible for various tax deductions. They also benefit as the value of their property increases. Over time, homeowners pay back the money they borrowed to buy their home, eventually eliminating their monthly housing payments after many years. Tenants, on the other hand, must continue to pay housing costs each month for as long as they continue to rent. They are also subject to rent increases.

Tenants must accept certain limitations regarding their activities in the places they rent. For example, you might not be allowed to paint your walls without first getting permission from your landlord. Homeowners have more freedom to do what they want on their own property.

TechByte

Virtual Tour Software Online virtual tours are making selling a home easier than ever. Virtual tour software allows you to create, with a digital camera, rotating, 360-degree photographs that show all the features of a home. Virtual tours can be uploaded to Web sites or distributed to potential buyers on CDs.

@ See example tours, list the features and build into a virtual tour, and download some free software to create a virtual tour of your home through **finance07.glencoe.com**.

Legal Issues

If you decide to rent, you will probably have to sign a **lease**, a legal document that defines the conditions of the rental agreement between the tenant and the landlord (see **Figure 7.4** on page 206 for an example of a lease).

Never sign a lease without making sure that you understand and agree with what it says. Pay special attention to the amount and due date of the monthly rent and the length of the rental period. Also, check to see whether you have the right to sublet the property if you want to move out before the lease expires. To sublet is to have a person other than the original tenant take over the rental unit and payments for the remaining term of the lease. If you disagree with any of the terms of the lease, discuss those issues with the landlord before you sign the lease—not afterward. Sometimes landlords are willing to negotiate changes to the document.

A lease is designed to protect the rights of both the landlord and the tenant. The tenant is usually protected from rent increases during the lease term. In most states, the tenant cannot be locked out or forced to move without a court hearing. However, the lease gives the landlord the right to take legal action against a tenant who does not pay his or her rent or who damages the property.

Discussion Ask the students: "What would you do if something in your apartment needed repairs, but the manager would not respond to your requests?"

Figure 7.4 A Typical Lease Agreement

- Description of the property, including its address
- Names of owners and tenants
- Dates during which the lease is valid
- Amount of the security deposit
- Amount and due date of monthly rent and penalties for late payment
- List of restrictions regarding pets, remodeling, activities, and so on
- Tenant's right to sublet the rental unit
- Conditions under which the landlord may enter the apartment
- Charges to the tenant for damage or for moving out of the unit early or refusing to pay rent

RENTAL AGREEMENT OF PROPERTY
AT 4744 LEMONA STREET, EAST TROY, WISCONSIN 53120

Parties in agreement are Blanca Romero and April Shullman. Blanca Romero has rented the second floor apartment to be used as a private residence, for his or her (one person) use only and for no other purpose, for a term of six months.

The term of this agreement will be from June 1, 20--, to November 30, 20--, at which time another six-month agreement will be drawn.

The rent will be $650 per month. There will be a security deposit of one and one-half months' rent, for a total of $975. The monies held as security will be held until such time that the tenant desires to move or until he/she is asked to vacate the premises. The security deposit along with any interest it accrues will be returned to the tenant, minus any monies held for repair of damages, rubbish removal, or cleaning to be done.

Rent will be due from the tenant on the first of each month and not later than five days after the first of each month. A late penalty of 5% of the monthly rent will be assessed for any rent not paid by the end of the five-day grace period.

The tenant is personally responsible for paying the monthly expenses, including electric, telephone, and cable service. These expenses are not included in any monthly rent payment.

The tenant was advised that there is to be NO SMOKING in the apartment, while he/she is in residence at this address.

There will be no pets allowed at any time in the apartment while he/she resides here.

If the tenant or landlord decides that the tenant must vacate the apartment, a thirty (30) day notice must be given before the first of the month.

The tenant may not sublease (rent to another person) this property without the landlord's written permission.

The tenant must provide his/her own insurance on the contents of the apartment, such as furniture, jewelry, clothes, etc. The tenant will not hold the landlord or landlord's agent responsible in the event of a loss.

The tenant agrees to let landlord enter property at reasonable hours to inspect or repair the property. Landlord will notify the tenant 24 hours in advance and give the time and reason for the visit.

This place of residence shall be occupied by no more than one (1) person.

At the expiration of tenancy, the tenant will surrender the premises to the landlord in as good condition as when received. The tenant will remove all rubbish from the premises. Failing to do so, the tenant will forfeit part of the security deposit in order for the landlord to pay for removal. If tenant breaks the lease for any reason, the landlord may keep the security deposit.

This agreement is between Blanca Romero and April Shullman. On this day, this agreement is signed by both parties.

Tenant *Blanca Romero* Date *6/1/--* Landlord ________ Date *6/1/--*

Making a Deal A lease is a legal document extending protection to both tenant and landlord.
Which components of a lease are likely to be most negotiable?

Caption Answer
Answers will vary but may include lease dates, restrictions, and the right to sublet.

The Cost of Renting

What are the factors affecting the cost of renting besides basic rent?

Several factors affect and determine the price of renting a home: location, living space, utilities, security deposit, and insurance.

Location

The amount of your monthly rent will depend on the location, or neighborhood, in which you choose to live (see **Figure 7.5**). You may decide that you are willing to live near the freeway if it costs less than living elsewhere. However, you may be willing to pay more for an apartment that is close to a park or work.

Living Space

The price of a rental unit will also depend on the amount of living space that you require. The least expensive choice might be a private room in a house, but you have to be willing to share common areas. Apartments, which are more expensive, often feature one to four bedrooms. Your most costly option might be to rent a townhouse or single-family house. You might consider living with one or more roommates to share expenses.

Common CENTS

On Your Own
Sharing an apartment or a house with a roommate is a great way to cut costs and can be fun. It is a good idea to have a trial period to make sure you get along before making a long-term commitment. *Why do you think sharing an apartment or a house will help you cut costs?*

Common Cents Roommates can divide or share all expenses.

Figure 7.5 Finding and Living in Rental Housing

Step 1: The Search
- Choose a location and a price that fits your needs.
- Compare costs and features among possible rental units.
- Talk to people who live in the apartment complex or the neighborhood where the units are located.

Step 2: Before Signing a Lease
- Be sure that you understand and agree with all aspects of the lease.
- Note the condition of the rental unit in writing; have the unit's owner sign it.

Step 3: Living in Rental Property
- Notify the owner of any necessary repairs.
- Respect the rights of neighbors.
- Obtain renters insurance to protect personal belongings.

Step 4: At the End of the Lease
- Leave the unit in good condition.
- Tell your landlord where to send your refunded security deposit.
- Ask that any deductions from your deposit be explained in writing.

Seeing Eye to Eye Renting involves more than just finding a desirable apartment.

How do these steps protect the rights of both tenant and landlord?

Caption Answer The lease clearly states each party's specific rights and responsibilities.

As You Read QUESTION

What factors affect the cost of renting?

Question Answer Some factors are location, size and amenities of apartments, competition, availability of schools/services, and accessibility to employment as well as factors such as inflation.

Extension Ask each student to imagine he or she has just signed a lease for a first apartment in one of the apartment buildings researched earlier. Have students do the following: (1) decide if they will have roommates, (2) determine what they need to buy for the apartment and the cost of each item, (3) determine total move-in costs, including utilities, and (4) set up a system for keeping necessary papers and data accessible.

Utilities

You may also have to pay for utilities, such as electricity, gas, water, and trash. Before you sign a lease, be sure to ask your landlord if the rent payment includes any utilities.

Security Deposits

When you sign a lease, you may have to pay a **security deposit**, an amount of money paid to the owner of the property by a tenant to guard against any financial loss or damage that the tenant might cause. Security deposits usually equal one or two months' rent.

When you move out, your landlord must return the security deposit, minus any charges for damage you may have caused or for any unpaid rent. Most states require landlords to return the security deposit within one month. In California, however, it must be returned within three weeks.

Renters Insurance

Another expense is **renters insurance**, a type of insurance that covers the loss of a tenant's personal property as a result of damage or theft. Many tenants neglect to buy renters insurance, wrongly assuming that their possessions are covered by their landlord's insurance. Most tenants who buy it find the cost worth the peace of mind it brings.

Section 7.2 Assessment

See the Teacher Manual for answers.

QUICK CHECK

1. What are the three main advantages of renting a residence?
2. What are the disadvantages of renting a residence.
3. What are the costs of renting a residence?

THINK CRITICALLY

4. Explain which types of apartments would best suit two friends who plan to become roommates.

USE MATH SKILLS

5. **Sharing Costs** Raji is currently paying $675 a month to rent a one-bedroom apartment. The cost of all utilities is included in the rent. However, he is thinking about renting a house with his friend Jon. The monthly rent on the house is $900. Utilities will be $300 a month. Raji and Jon have agreed to split all costs evenly.

   Calculate How much would the move save or cost Raji each month and over the course of a year?

SOLVE MONEY PROBLEMS

6. **Lease Terms** Jaycee is a college student who has a small apartment for which she pays $450 a month in rent. The lease she signed in August specified that no pets were allowed. However, while visiting her parents over winter break, Jaycee found a stray cat, and she would like to keep it.

   Analyze What options does Jaycee have? Consider all possibilities and rank them from most to least desirable.

Buying and Selling a Home

The Home-Buying Process

How do you buy a home?

Many people dream of owning a home. Buying a home, however, is a huge financial commitment. It will probably be the most costly purchase you will ever make. There are a number of steps that you will need to take to purchase a home. You will need to determine your home ownership needs, find and evaluate a property to purchase, price the property, obtain financing, and close the transaction.

STEP 1: Determine Your Home Ownership Needs

What are some of the benefits and drawbacks of owning a home?

To make an informed decision about whether to buy a home, you will need to consider the benefits and drawbacks of ownership. You will also need to consider the types of homes that are available and how much you can afford to spend.

Owning Your Residence: Benefits

While renters may be attracted to the idea of mobility, homeowners may enjoy a sense of stability and permanence. Home ownership also allows individual expression. You have more freedom to decorate and change your own home and to have pets. Many people find this type of flexibility very appealing.

As a homeowner, you will also gain financial benefits. You can deduct the interest charges on your loan payments from your federal income taxes each year. Your property taxes are also deductible. Moreover, the value of many homes rises steadily. Therefore, homeowners can usually sell their homes for a profit, depending on their **equity**, which is the value of the home less the amount still owed on the money borrowed to purchase it. In addition, once the borrowed money is paid off, homeowners have no further payments to make other than property taxes, homeowners insurance, and maintenance costs.

Focus on Reading

Read to Learn

- How to identify the advantages and disadvantages of owning a residence.
- How to explain how to evaluate a property.
- How to discuss the financing involved in purchasing a home.
- How to describe a plan for selling a home.

Main Idea

Understanding the processes involved with homeownership is necessary when you buy or sell a home.

Key Terms

- equity
- escrow account
- private mortgage insurance (PMI)
- mortgage
- points
- amortization
- fixed-rate mortgage
- adjustable-rate mortgage (ARM)
- home equity loan
- refinance
- closing
- title insurance
- deed
- appraisal

Springboard "Owning a home is a major component of the American Dream." Ask the students what this means, and if it is part of their dreams.

▶ FREEDOM OF EXPRESSION For many people, one of the most appealing advantages of home ownership is the ability to decorate or remodel freely. *Can you think of any situations in which homeowners are not completely free to change the look of their homes?*

Caption Answer Answers will vary but may include that some people cannot afford to remodel; homeowners' associations may restrict choices; and zoning may forbid some changes.

Before You Read

PREDICT

If you plan to own a house one day, how do you think you begin the process?

Owning Your Residence: Drawbacks

Of course, buying a home does not guarantee happiness. Home ownership can involve financial risk. Saving money for a down payment to buy a home is very difficult for many people. Moreover, the tax deductions may not make up for high loan payments. Property values do not always go up; in some cases, they may even decline.

A second drawback is limited mobility. A homeowner who wants to move must either sell his or her property or arrange to rent it to tenants. These processes can be slow and may result in financial loss.

Owning a home can involve high expenses. Homeowners must pay for all maintenance and repairs, such as fixing a leaky roof, cleaning out a flooded basement, putting up new wallpaper, and replacing or repairing broken appliances. The cost of taking good care of a home can be quite high, even if homeowners do most of the work themselves.

Motivating Students Relate this scenario to students: You have a choice—you can rent a beautiful new townhouse, 2 bedrooms and 2½ baths, built-in stove, new refrigerator, space for washer and dryer, and many other amenities in an excellent location for $1,300 per month. Or you can buy a small, older house, 2 bedrooms and 1 bath, small yard, in a fair location with mortgage payments of $1,300 per month. Which home would you choose? Why?

Types of Housing

Homes come in all shapes and sizes, providing housing alternatives for a range of budgets and lifestyles.

Single-Family Dwellings The most popular type of housing in the United States is the single-family house. A single-family house usually stands on a separate lot with a lawn and some outdoor living space. The home is not attached to any other buildings. Because a single-family dwelling provides the most privacy of any type of housing, it is often the most expensive.

Multiunit Dwellings This category of housing includes duplexes and townhouses. A duplex is a single building divided into living spaces for two families—or two units. A building divided into three units is a triplex. A townhouse is one of many single-family units attached to other units. For these types of housing, each unit has its own outside entrance.

Teaching Activity Divide the class into five groups. Assign one of the housing alternatives (pages 210–212) to each group. Have each group prepare and make a convincing presentation as to why someone should purchase its housing alternative.

Condominiums A condominium is one of a group of apartments or townhouses that people own instead of rent. Condominium owners pay a monthly fee to cover the cost of maintenance, repairs, improvements, and insurance for the building and its common spaces. The unit owners form a condominium association, which manages the housing complex. Common spaces, such as hallways, lawns, elevators, and recreational areas, belong to the association, not to individual owners.

Cooperative Housing Cooperative housing is another apartment-style living arrangement in which a building that contains a number of units is owned by a nonprofit organization. Members of the organization do not actually own the property. Members pay a monthly fee which covers their rent and the operating expenses of the organization.

Prefabricated Homes Prefabricated houses are manufactured and partially assembled at a factory. The pieces are then transported to a building site and put together there. Prefabricated homes are often cheaper than other single-family houses because the mass production of their pieces and partial assembly at the factory help keep costs down.

Caption Answer Answers will vary but may include younger adults starting out or retirees who need less expensive residences.

◀ **OPTIONS TO BUY**
Attractively designed prefabricated homes are a less costly alternative for housing. *Who might be interested in purchasing these homes? Why?*

$avvy Saver

Furnishing Your First Apartment

1. Buy large items such as sofas and tables at thrift shops.
2. Shop for items such as kitchen-ware at discount stores.
3. Browse garage or moving sales to find great buys.
4. Ask friends and relatives if they want to get rid of household items they do not use.
5. Be creative: Make curtains from colorful sheets.

Discussion Tell students: "When you rent, after the move-in expenses, all you pay every month is rent. When you buy, you pay the mortgage, homeowners insurance, property taxes, all utilities including water, and any repair and maintenance costs. What kinds of sacrifices might you have to make to buy a home?"

Mobile Homes Another type of manufactured home is known as a *mobile home*. Most mobile homes are not truly mobile because they are rarely moved from their original sites. Mobile homes are fully assembled in factories. They contain many of the features of larger houses, such as fully equipped kitchens, bathrooms, and even fireplaces. Some mobile-home owners purchase the land on which their houses are located. Spaces can also be rented in mobile-home parks where access to community recreation facilities is often included.

Compared with other housing choices, mobile homes are relatively inexpensive. However, they are not as well constructed or as safe as many other types of housing, and they usually do not increase in value at the same rate as single-family houses do.

Affordability and Your Needs

Selecting a type of dwelling is only one part of determining your home ownership needs. You will also need to consider the price of a home, its size, and its quality.

Price and Down Payment To determine how much you can afford to spend on a home, you will need to examine your income, your savings, and your current living expenses. Can you afford to make a large down payment when you buy a home? A down payment is a portion of the total cost of an item that is required at the time of purchase. You will need to make monthly payments on a loan, pay property taxes, and buy homeowners insurance. The exact amounts will depend on interest rates and local economic conditions. Is your income enough to cover these costs as well as other current expenses?

Before you look for the home of your dreams, it is smart to know exactly what you can afford to pay. To determine how much you can afford to spend on a home and if you will be approved for a loan, talk to a loan officer at a mortgage company or other financial institution. Many companies and banks will prequalify loan applicants so that prospective home buyers will know in advance if they can get a mortgage loan. This service is usually provided without charge.

Size and Quality Ideally, the home you buy will be big enough for your needs and will be in good condition. If you are a first-time buyer, though, you may not be able to get everything you want.

Trading Up Most financial experts recommend buying what you can afford, even if you have to sacrifice the size and features you would love to have. As you advance in your career and your income increases, you may be able to "trade up" and purchase a home with some extra comforts. For example, eight years ago, Kanya bought a condominium that had only a tiny garden and one small bathroom. Last week she sold it, made a profit, and moved into a larger house, where she will be able to plant a vegetable and flower garden and enjoy the convenience of two full baths.

STEP 2: Find and Evaluate a Property to Purchase

Why is the location of your home important?

When you know what type of residence you would prefer and what you can afford, you will be able to start searching for a property to purchase.

Critical Thinking Ask each student to select an area of your town or city in which he/she would like to live, and then research the average price of a two-bedroom, single-family dwelling, condominium, and townhouse in that area. Then have students select any one of the three choices, determine the down payment (at 20 percent), and list and consider other costs to move in. Each student will write a brief report outlining this information. Finally, the students are to estimate how much income they believe someone would need to buy that dwelling.

Selecting a Location

The location of your home is very important. Ask yourself if you would rather live in a city, in the suburbs, or in a small-town or country setting. Perhaps you want a neighborhood with parks and trails that accommodate cyclists and runners. If you commute to work by bus, you will have to make sure that your house is close to the bus lines. The distance between home and work, the quality of the local school system, your interests and lifestyle, and other factors all help determine where you will want to live.

Careers in Finance

REAL ESTATE AGENT **Carlos Garza**
RealTime Real Estate, Inc.

Carlos has always had a knack for putting people at ease. This ability has proven very useful in his job as a real estate sales agent. Carlos is also very good at handling the complicated procedures involved in selling real estate. He sees his job as being a matchmaker between buyers and sellers.He works well with both sides, advising sellers on how to make homes more appealing to potential buyers and advising buyers on the suitability and value of the homes they visit. As a real estate agent, he relishes the challenge of making his clients happy and the satisfaction of closing a deal.

SKILLS: Sales, marketing, administration, time-management, communication, negotiation, math, and legal skills

PERSONAL TRAITS: Personable, highly disciplined, persistent, trustworthy, and self-starting

EDUCATION: High school diploma or equivalent; training through a real estate company or organization; and state license

ANALYZE If you were looking for a home to buy, what qualities, in addition to trustworthiness, would you look for in a real estate agent?

See the Teacher Manual for answer.

@ To learn more about career paths for real estate agents, visit **finance07.glencoe.com**.

Document Detective

Learn to identify and understand the standard financial documents you will use in the real world.

See the Teacher Manual for answers.

Investigate: Calculating a Mortgage Payment

A worksheet to calculate an affordable mortgage payment contains the following information:

- Your monthly income
- Your monthly expenses
- Difference between your monthly income and expenses

Your Motive: You may not realize all of the expenses you incur each month. Therefore, when considering purchasing a home, you must carefully calculate your cash flow to be sure you are not overestimating your ability to pay for expenses.

Name: LeBron	
Monthly Income (cash flow)	
Wages and salary	$5,500
Investment income	300
Other income	0
Total Monthly Income	**$5,800**
Monthly Expenses	
Groceries	$300
Car payments	350
Car maintenance	50
Gasoline	75
Clothing	125
Student loan payments	200
Medical expenses not covered by insurance	55
Automatic deposit, savings account	200
Retirement account	200
Credit card payments	350
Insurance payments (car, life, health, etc.)	550
Income taxes, including Social Security	1,925
Restaurants	50
Charitable contributions	25
Vacations	150
Entertainment	75
Other expenses	0
Total Monthly Expenses	**$4,680**
Affordable Mortgage Payment (Monthly Income – Expenses)	**$1,120**

Key Points: A mortgage payment for a house is usually the single largest monthly expense you will incur. It is important that you are able to pay it each month. By determining your monthly income and expenses, you will be able to calculate how much you can afford to pay each month for a mortgage.

Find the Solutions

1. What are some other possible expenses?
2. Why are income taxes monthly expenses?
3. Does LeBron have enough money to cover monthly mortgage payments and closing and other costs?
4. Should LeBron spend all of the money he has left after paying his monthly expenses on a mortgage payment?
5. What expenses would you be willing to cut if your mortgage payment was $1,500 per month? Why?

Local Zoning Laws Some communities have strict zoning laws, which are regulations that limit how property in a given area can be used. The existence of such laws may also affect your housing decisions. William wanted to live in an all-residential area, so he bought a duplex in a neighborhood where local zoning laws ban any commercial construction of stores or business buildings. In contrast, Alicia bought a condominium in a much less restrictive community because she wanted to be able to walk to nearby restaurants and businesses.

Hiring a Real Estate Agent

Real estate agents are people who arrange the sale and purchase of homes as well as other buildings and land. They are good sources of information about the location, availability, prices, and quality of homes. Potential home buyers often use real estate agents to help them find housing. The agents can also negotiate the purchase price between buyer and seller. They help buyers arrange financing for the purchase, and they can recommend lawyers, insurance agents, and home inspectors to serve the buyers' needs.

Real estate services are usually free to the buyer. The agents may represent the sellers, who pay them a commission of 3 to 6 percent when the property is sold. Some real estate agents also represent buyers. In this case, the agent may be paid by either the buyer or the seller.

As You Read

RELATE

How would you go about finding a real estate agent who suits you?

Conducting a Home Inspection

Before you make a final decision to buy property, it is important to get an evaluation of the house and land by a qualified home inspector. (See **Figure 7.6** on page 216.) When Josh Samuels called in a home inspector to check the house he wanted to buy, the inspector found cracks in the foundation, an overloaded electrical system, and problems with the water quality. Josh still wanted the house, and he was able to negotiate a lower price because he had the inspector's report. A home inspection costs money, but it can save you from problems and unplanned expenses in the future.

Some states, cities, and lenders require inspection documents. The mortgage company will usually conduct an appraisal to determine the fair market value of the property. An appraisal is not a detailed inspection. It is an estimation of the value of the property usually in comparison with other similar properties that have recently sold in the particular area.

Critical Thinking You have chosen your first house, and the price is manageable. Now you want the house to be evaluated by a qualified home inspector. Write a list of all the things you believe the inspection should check.

STEP 3: Price the Property

What price should you offer to pay?

After you have checked out the property as thoroughly as possible, it is time to consider making an offer to the current owner. This is usually done through a real estate agent, unless the owner is acting as his or her own agent.

Figure 7.6 Conducting a Home Inspection

Taking steps to evaluate a home before you buy it may save you unplanned expenses and disappointments later.

1 **The Exterior** The buyer does a "walk-through" of the neighborhood to check the condition of streets and sidewalks. It is also important to check the exterior features of the home.

2 **The Interior** The buyer looks at the interior design of the home to be sure that it will meet his or her needs.

3 **Professional Home Inspection** The buyer hires a home inspector who checks the exterior: windows, foundation, chimney, and roof. The home inspector will also look at the interior construction: wiring, plumbing, heating system, walls, and floors.

Apple Pie Home Inspection Service
21044 Manitowoc Avenue
Woodland Hills, CA 91364

Inspection No: 099422909
Inspection Date: 09/29/--
Inspector: Michelle Cabalu
Client: Peggie Thompson
Address: 6301 Glade Rd. Carlsbad, CA 91335

The house is a single-family dwelling, one-story structure built on a flat lot. Estimated age is approximately 35 to 40 years old. Weather at time of inspection was sunny.

100 EXTERIOR

101 Driveway: Concrete with cracks noted.
102 Walks: Concrete and brick with cracks noted. Missing bricks noted.
103 Fence/Gates: Wood and chain links. Detached wood fence noted.
104 Siding: Stucco and wood with cracks noted.
105 Trim: Wood.
106 Window Frames: Metal and wood.
107 Elec. Fixtures: S
108 Gutters/Downspouts: S

4 **Inspection Report** The buyer reviews the home inspector's report to decide whether this is the right home to buy.

Determining the Price of the Home

Every home that is for sale has a listing price—the price that the owner is asking for it. That price is not necessarily the price you will pay, however. You are free to make a lower offer. What should you offer? Here are some questions to consider:

- How long has the home been on the market? If a home is on the market for a while, the owner may accept a lower price.
- What have similar homes in the neighborhood sold for recently? If a listing price is too high, you should offer less.
- How tight is the housing market? In a "seller's market," homes are in high demand, and sellers can get the highest prices. In a "buyer's market," there is an abundant supply of homes for sale, and buyers can pay lower prices.
- Do the current owners need to sell in a hurry? If so, they may be willing to accept less than they feel the home is worth.
- How well does the home meet your needs? If a home fits your needs, you may be willing to pay more.
- How easily can you arrange financing? If interest rates are high, your payment will be higher.

Teaching Activity (Part 1)
Ask half of the class to select pictures of houses (from magazines, newspaper real-estate sections, or your sources) to represent homes they are selling. Meanwhile, have the other half of the class assess how much they are willing to spend to buy a house. Ask sellers to display their photos along with asking prices. Have the buyers circulate and select the houses they want. When all buyers and sellers are paired, have them begin negotiations for the house.

Negotiating the Purchase Price

Once you have decided on a reasonable amount to offer, the real estate agent will communicate it to the seller, who may either accept or reject it. If your offer is accepted, congratulations! You will soon have a new home—and at a price you are willing to pay.

Sometimes the seller will not accept your offer if it is below the listing price. In that case, you will have to make a second, higher offer, or start looking for a different home. A seller may also make a counteroffer in response to your bid. Making a counteroffer means dropping the asking price. For example, Jian Wang offered $178,900 for a condominium that was listed at $186,000. The sellers rejected his offer but made a counteroffer of $184,500. Jian thought that the price was still too high, so he submitted a bid of $182,000. They eventually settled on a purchase price of $183,000.

When the buyer and seller agree on a price, they must sign a purchase agreement, or purchase contract, that states their intention to complete the sale. Most purchase contracts are conditional; that is, they take effect only if certain other events occur. For example, the contract may be valid only if the buyers can obtain financing, or only if they can sell their current home in a specified period of time.

At this point in the process, the buyer sometimes must pay the seller a portion of the purchase price, called *earnest money.* This money shows that the offer is serious. It is held in an escrow account until the sale is completed. An **escrow account** is an account where money is held in trust until it can be delivered to a designated party. The earnest money is applied toward the down payment.

Academic Connection
MATH

An average homeowner stays in a home for about six years. With an 8 percent mortgage, the homeowner will sell the home, still owing over 90 percent of the mortgage. If this trend continued, the homeowner would *never* pay off a mortgage in his or her lifetime. *Imagine you have purchased a house for $97,000, with $9,700 down and a simple interest rate of 8 percent. How long would it take to pay off your mortgage if you paid $700 a month?*

See the Teacher Manual for answer.

STEP 4: Obtain Financing

What are the costs involved in purchasing property?

After you have decided to purchase a specific home and have agreed on a price, you will have to think about how you will pay for your purchase. First, you will have to come up with money for the down payment. Next, you will probably have to get a loan to help pay for the remainder of the purchase price. Finally, you will be responsible for fees and other expenses related to the settlement of the real estate transaction.

Determining Amount of Down Payment

As a general rule, the greater the portion of the total purchase price you can pay up front, the easier it will be to obtain a loan. Many lenders suggest that you put 20 percent or more of the purchase price as a down payment. For example, if the purchase price of the house is $100,000, you would need to make a down payment of $20,000. The most common sources of funds for down payments are personal savings accounts, sales of investments or other assets, or gifts or loans from relatives.

Private Mortgage Insurance Lenders might accept lower down payments. However, if the down payment is less than 20 percent of the purchase price, some lenders will require you to obtain private mortgage insurance. **Private mortgage insurance (PMI)** is a special policy that protects the lender in case the buyer cannot make payments or cannot make them on time. Sometimes buyers will pay the cost of PMI up front, and sometimes they will agree to spread the cost over the life of the loan. When the borrower has paid between 20 to 25 percent of the purchase price, the insurance can be dropped.

Qualifying for a Mortgage

A **mortgage** is a long-term loan extended to someone who buys property. The buyer borrows money from a bank, credit union, savings and loan association, or mortgage company, which pays the full amount of the loan to the seller. In return, the buyer makes monthly payments to the lender. These monthly payments are usually made over a period of 15, 20, or 30 years. The home you buy serves as collateral, a type of guarantee that the loan will be repaid. If you fail to repay the mortgage or make regular payments, the lender can foreclose, or take possession of the property.

Financial Qualifications To take out a mortgage, you need to meet certain criteria, just as you would to qualify for any other type of loan. Lenders look at your income, your debts, and your savings to decide whether you are a good risk. These figures are put into a formula to determine how much you can afford to pay.

Question Answer They will need to know your income, assets, credit history, and savings history.

As You Read

QUESTION

Lenders want to know how much money you owe. What other information do they look for?

▲ **THE TEST** Applying for a loan requires paperwork that will be examined by the lender to determine your eligibility for the loan. *Why is this process so important to the lender?*

Interest Rate Factors The size of your mortgage will also depend on the current interest rate. The higher the rate, the more you will need to pay in interest each month. That means that less of your money will be available to pay off the purchase price. When interest rates rise, fewer people are able to afford the cost of an average-priced home. In contrast, low rates increase the size of the loan that you can receive.

For example, Bernadette qualifies for a monthly mortgage payment of $700. If interest rates are 7 percent, she will be able to take out a 30-year loan of $105,215. However, if interest rates increase to 12 percent, she will qualify for a 30-year loan of only $68,053. Both of these loans will carry the same monthly payment of $700. The differences can be quite surprising.

Caption Answer Answers may vary but should include that the paperwork helps the lender determine whether the loan applicant has enough income and assets to make the payments; it will also help the lender learn the applicant's credit history.

Paying Points

Different lenders may offer slightly different interest rates for mortgages. In addition, when you compare the cost of doing business with various lenders, you will have to consider other factors. If you want a lower interest rate, you may have to pay a higher down payment and **points**—extra charges that must be paid by the buyer to the lender in order to get a lower interest rate. Each point equals 1 percent of the loan amount. For example, suppose that a bank offers you a $100,000 mortgage with two points, or 2 percent. Since 2 percent of $100,000 is $2,000, you will have to pay an extra $2,000 when you get the loan to purchase your home.

Teaching Activity (Part 2) Ask the home sellers in Part 1 to become lenders. Have the buyers determine how much down payment they are willing or able to pay for their houses. Lenders should decide how much down payment they will require. Lenders will establish all the terms of the loan they will give, and the buyers will decide what they are willing to do. Have lenders and buyers go through the process of qualifying for loans. (You may want to provide copies of loan applications.)

STANDARD & POOR'S

Global Financial Landscape

Standard and Poor's publishes the globally recognized S&P 500® financial index. It also gathers financial statistics, information, and news, and analyzes this data for international businesses, governments, and individuals to help them guide their financial decisions.

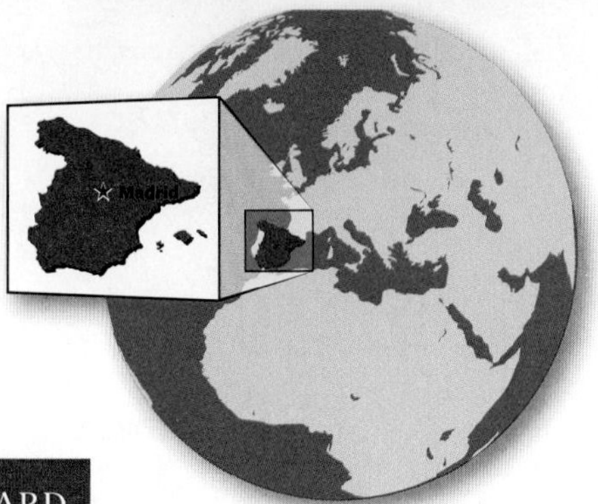

SPAIN

Each year thousands of people from Britain make their way to Spain, seeking what their homeland does not offer—affordable housing. The average house in England costs more than 150,000 pounds (US $278,000). In comparison, a three-bedroom home not far from the beautiful Spanish coast costs less than 100,000 pounds (US $185,000). A roomy handyman's special can be found for under 20,000 pounds (US $37,000). Many of the British house-hunters may purchase a house to fit their pocketbooks, but there may be other motivations as well. Some buy Spanish property as an investment, and then lease the homes to renters. Others simply prefer the more stress-free life and agreeable climate of sunny Spain.

STANDARD & POOR'S

DATABYTES

Capital	Madrid
Population	41,334,000
Languages	Castilian Spanish, Catalan, Galician, and Basque
Currency	euro
Gross Domestic Product (GDP)	$885.5 billion (2003 est.)
GDP per capita	$22,000

Industry: Textiles and apparel, food and beverages, metal manufacturing, and chemicals

Agriculture: Grain, vegetables, olives, wine grapes, beef, and fish

Exports: Machinery, motor vehicles, foodstuffs, and other consumer goods

Natural Resources: Coal, lignite, iron ore, and uranium

Think Globally
Would you buy a home in another country? Why or why not?

Research Using newspapers or any sources they choose, have students research the mortgage rates in your community, including both 15-year and 30-year mortgages. Have each student create a chart displaying these rates.

Comparing Points How does a high interest rate with no points compare to a low interest rate with points? A lower interest rate results in a lower monthly payment, but you pay more money up front.

If you keep your home for only a short time, you may lose money with the lower rate because the monthly savings will not add up to what you had to pay in points. If you keep the home for several years, however, your monthly savings will eventually make up for what you paid in points. As a rule, the longer you keep the home, the better off you are when paying the points in exchange for a lower interest rate.

The Loan Application Process

Most lenders charge home buyers a fee of between $100 and $300 to apply for a mortgage, which is added into the loan amount. To apply, the buyer must fill out forms, giving details of his or her income, employment, debts, and other information. The lender will verify this information by obtaining a buyer's credit report.

After a careful examination of the buyer's financial history and the size, location, and condition of the property, the lender decides to approve or deny the application. If it is approved, the purchase contract between seller and buyer becomes legally binding.

STANDARD &POOR'S

Put on Your Financial Planner's Cap

A client has $27,000 in savings and an excellent credit history. Assuming 20 percent down, what price should your client pay for a house?

See the Teacher Manual for answers.

Types of Mortgages

How do the various types of mortgages differ?

For most people, a mortgage is the greatest financial obligation of their lives. There are several types of mortgages. Depending on the terms of the loan, a homeowner will have to make monthly payments for many years.

The monthly payments on a mortgage are set at a level that allows amortization of the loan. **Amortization** is the reduction of a loan balance through payments made over a period of time. So the balance is reduced every time you make a payment. The amount of your payment is applied first to the interest owed and then to the principal, which is the original amount you borrowed. In the first years of the loan, only a small part of each monthly payment goes to reduce the principal. Most goes toward paying off the interest. Near the end of the loan period, almost all of each payment goes toward reducing the principal. By the end of the loan period, both the interest and the principal will be completely paid off.

It is possible to pay off a mortgage early. Paying a little extra each month and applying that amount to the principal will save interest charges over the long run. For example, paying $25 extra a month on a 30-year, 10 percent mortgage of $75,000 will save more than $34,000 in interest charges—and will repay the loan in about 25 years. Some lenders charge an extra fee for prepaying.

Fixed-Rate Mortgages

A **fixed-rate mortgage**, or conventional mortgage, is a mortgage with a fixed interest rate and a fixed schedule of payments. A fixed rate is an interest rate that does not change. For example, if the interest rate is 8.75 percent when the loan is granted, the homeowner will continue to pay 8.75 percent throughout the life of the loan, even if interest rates for new loans rise. Conventional mortgages typically run for a period of 15, 20, or 30 years. They offer peace of mind because monthly payments always remain the same.

Adjustable-Rate Mortgages

Fixed-rate loans guarantee a particular interest rate for the life of the loan. An **adjustable-rate mortgage (ARM)**, also known as a variable-payment mortgage, is a mortgage with an interest rate that increases or decreases during the life of the loan. The rate changes according to economic indicators, such as rates on U.S. Treasury securities, the Federal Home Loan Bank Board's mortgage rate index, or the lender's own cost-of-funds index. As a result, your loan payments may go up or down.

Your rates will change according to the terms of your agreement with the lender. Generally, if interest rates decline and stay low, an ARM will save you substantial amounts of money. However, if rates increase and stay high, an ARM may cost you a lot of money because your monthly payment will go up.

Evaluating Adjustable-Rate Mortgages Consider several factors when you evaluate adjustable-rate mortgages:

1. Determine the frequency of and restrictions on allowed changes in interest rates.
2. Consider the frequency of and restrictions on changes in the monthly payment.
3. Find out what index the lender will use to set the mortgage interest rate over the term of the loan.

Discussion In a classroom discussion, converse with the students about the advantages and disadvantages of fixed-rate and variable-rate mortgages as well as ARMs and rate caps.

Rate Caps Most adjustable-rate mortgages have a rate cap, which limits the amount the interest rate can rise or fall. Rate caps generally limit increases (or decreases) of the interest rate to one or two percentage points in a year—or no more than five points over the life of the loan.

Some ARMs also carry payment caps, which limit the size of monthly payments. That may seem like good protection for the buyer, but it has drawbacks. When interest rates rise while monthly payments remain the same, the payments will not cover the interest. As a result, the loan balance increases, and payments may have to be extended over a longer time.

Convertible ARMs Some lenders also offer convertible ARMs. Convertible ARMs permit a borrower to convert, or change, an adjustable-rate mortgage to a fixed-rate mortgage during a certain period of time. If you decide to make the change, your interest rate will be 0.25 to 0.50 percent higher than current rates for conventional 30-year mortgages. You will also have to pay a conversion fee, which is usually $500 or less.

Government Financing Programs The Federal Housing Administration (FHA) and the Veterans Administration (VA) help home buyers obtain low-interest, low-down-payment loans. VA loans are available to eligible veterans of the armed services. These government agencies do not actually lend the money. Instead, they help qualified buyers arrange for loans from regular lenders.

Typically, an agency guarantees repayment to the lender if the borrower defaults, or is unable to make payments. As a result, many government-guaranteed loans have lower interest rates. Although extra insurance fees may be added on to these loans, government-backed mortgages are a good deal for those who qualify for them.

Home Equity Loans

A second mortgage is also called a **home equity loan**, which is a loan based on the difference between the current market value of a home and the amount the borrower owes on the mortgage. To determine the amount of this type of loan, the financial institution will find out the current market value of a home and how much equity is in the property. Such loans can provide money for education, home improvements, or other purposes. However, some states limit the ways in which the money may be used.

Second mortgages are one source of extra cash for homeowners. However, taking out additional loans can keep a homeowner continually in debt. Also, if the borrower cannot make the payments on a second mortgage, the lender can take the home. For more information on home equity loans, see Chapter 19.

Refinancing

Many homeowners need extra money or want to reduce their monthly payments. These options are possible when they **refinance**, which is obtaining a new mortgage to replace an existing one. For example, Esther Aquino originally took out a fixed-rate mortgage at 11 percent interest, and then watched interest rates fall to 6 percent. Fortunately, she was able to refinance her home, and take out a new mortgage at the lower 6 percent interest rate. In Esther's case, her monthly payment decreased considerably.

Refinancing is not always a good choice. To refinance, a homeowner usually pays extra fees, which may reduce any savings from a small drop in interest rates. Moreover, refinancing may extend the life of a loan. In general, refinancing is an advantage when the interest rate drops two or more points below the current rate and when the owner plans to stay in his or her present home for at least two or more years.

WebQuest

Your Own Home
Learn about different kinds of mortgages and how to qualify for one. Then learn how to negotiate the purchase of your first home.

@ To continue with Tasks 4 and 5 of your WebQuest project, visit **finance07.glencoe.com**.

STEP 5: Close the Transaction

What are closing costs?

The final step in the home-buying process is the **closing**, a meeting of the seller, the buyer, and the lender of funds, or representatives of each party, to complete the transaction. At the closing, documents are signed, last-minute details are settled, and money is paid. The seller and buyer must also pay a number of fees and charges, which are *closing costs*.

Extension Ask students to interview people (by phone) who work at title companies to learn what is involved in doing a title search and what kinds of problems can be revealed from the search.

Closing Costs

Most closing costs involve the legal details related to purchasing a home. For example, a title company researches the property to make sure that no disputes exist over its ownership or that there are no unpaid real estate taxes for the property. The title company also offers **title insurance**, a type of insurance that protects the buyer if problems with the title are found later.

Another typical closing cost is a fee for recording the **deed**, which is the official document transferring ownership from seller to buyer. Buyers also pay for private mortgage insurance, which protects the lender from any loss resulting from default on the loan. See **Figure 7.7** for a list of other common closing costs.

Escrow Account

After the closing, your lender might require that you deposit money into an escrow account. The money, usually held by the lender, is set aside to pay for taxes and insurance. The lender does not have to worry whether the borrower is paying these obligations because the money is available. See **Figure 7.8** for a list of home-buying issues.

Taxes and Insurance Homeowners must pay property taxes and homeowners insurance in addition to their mortgage payments. In most states, property taxes generally cover the cost of public services, such as police and fire protection, schools, and street repair. Homeowners insurance protects the lender's investment in case of damage to the home from fire or other hazards.

Figure 7.7 Closing Costs

Item	Cost Range: Buyer	Cost Range: Seller
Title search fee	$ 50 – $ 100	$ 300 – $ 900
Title insurance	$ 300 – $ 900	$ 50 – $1000
Attorney's fee	$ 50 – $1000	$ 100 – $ 500
Property survey	–	–
Appraisal fee	$ 100 – $ 350	–
Recording fees	$ 30 – $ 65	$ 35 – $ 65
Credit report	$ 35 – $ 75	–
Termite inspection	$ 100 – $ 250	–
Lender's origination fee	1–5% of loan	–
Real estate agent's commission	–	5–7% of purchase price
Insurance, taxes, and interest	varies	–

Costs Add Up Closing costs add to the expense of buying a home.

For a loan amount of $100,000 with $3,500 in insurance, taxes, and interest, what could a buyer pay in closing costs, based on the figures in this chart?

Caption Answer $4,890 to $8,805

Figure 7.8 The Elements of Buying a Home

It is important to consider these factors when making a home purchase:

- **Location** Consider both the surrounding community and the geographic region. The same home may vary greatly in cost depending on where it is located: in Kansas or California, on a busy highway or a quiet street, in a landscaped suburb or an urban neighborhood.
- **Down Payment** A large down payment reduces your mortgage costs, but how much can you afford to pay up front?
- **Mortgage Rates and Points** You will have to choose between a lower mortgage rate with points and a higher mortgage rate without points. You will also need to consider what type of mortgage to arrange. When you apply for the loan, be prepared to provide the lender with copies of your financial records and other relevant information.
- **Closing Costs** Settlement costs may range anywhere from 2 to 6 percent of the total amount you borrow. That is in addition to the down payment.
- **Monthly Payments** Your monthly payment for interest, principal, insurance, and taxes will be among your largest, most enduring expenses. Beware of buying a home that costs more than you can afford.
- **Maintenance Costs** Homes require a lot of repair and maintenance. Be sure to set aside funds for these necessities.

Think It Over Buying a home is a complicated process.

What are some possible results of not thinking through all the elements listed above?

Caption Answer Answers might include buying a home in an area you do not like, paying more than you can afford or more than the house is worth, and/or choosing the wrong mortgage.

Selling a Home

What can an owner do to his or her home to get the best selling price?

As your needs change, you may decide to sell your home. You will have to get it ready for the market, set a price, and decide whether to sell it on your own or get professional help from a real estate agent.

Teaching Activity Divide the class into groups of four. Have each group determine what repairs or redecoration to consider before selling a home. Next have the students get quotes for the costs to do these things (they will have to determine sizes of rooms, etc.). Finally, have the groups estimate the amount they would spend and weigh it against the increased price they could get for the house.

Preparing a Home for Selling

The nicer your home looks, the faster it will sell at the price you want. Real estate salespeople recommend that homeowners make needed repairs and paint worn exterior and interior areas when preparing a home for selling. For example, Dora and Dennis Muldoon repainted several rooms, replaced some light fixtures, and changed the living room carpet before they put their house on the market. They kept the house as clean, neat, bright, and airy as possible while prospective buyers were visiting. They also made sure that the lawn was cut regularly and that their children did not leave toys in the yard. Their work paid off: They sold their home within a few months of listing their home.

▶ LENDING A HAND
A real estate agent will suggest to a seller ways to improve the "curb appeal" of a home, such as landscaping, to attract buyers. *What is the biggest disadvantage of using a real estate agent?*

Caption Answer The best answer is that real estate agents charge a commission, which can be quite high. Other answers may be possible.

Determining the Selling Price

Setting a price on a home can be difficult. A price that is too high may scare off potential buyers. Setting the price too low will result in lost profit. Some sellers will pay for an **appraisal**—an estimate of the current value of the property—and use that as a basis for a listing price. If you ever sell a home, find out whether the current market and demand for housing favors buyers or sellers. Then decide how quickly you need to sell your home and evaluate any improvements you have made to the property. Adding certain features—such as a deck or an extra bathroom—can increase a home's value.

Choosing a Real Estate Agent

Many sellers put the sale of their home into the hands of a licensed real estate agent who is affiliated with an agency. There is a wide choice of firms, from small local real estate agencies to nationally known companies. When choosing an agent, pick someone who knows your neighborhood and is eager to sell your home.

Real Estate Agent Services Real estate agents provide various services. They can help determine a selling price, attract buyers, show your home, and handle the financial aspects of the sale.

They are paid a commission, or fee, upon the sale of a home—usually 5 to 7 percent of the purchase price.

Sale by Owner

Each year about 10 percent of home sales are made directly by homeowners without the help of real estate agents. Selling your home yourself can save you thousands of dollars, but it will cost you time and energy. Advertising the home will be up to you. Showing the home to prospective buyers will also be your responsibility. Be sure to use the services of a lawyer or a title company to help you with the contract, closing, and other legal matters.

After You Read

REACT

With the information provided in this chapter, do you feel that you could make a wise decision about whether to rent or buy a home? Why or why not?

React Answer Accept all reasonable answers that show student effort.

Making Choices

Your housing decisions will be affected by many factors, including your lifestyle and financial situation. By carefully reviewing your options, making educated decisions, and following the appropriate processes, you will make the best housing choice to suit your needs.

Section 7.3 Assessment

See the Teacher Manual for answers.

QUICK CHECK

1. What are five steps that make up the process of buying a home?
2. What costs are associated with buying a home?
3. What activities are associated with selling a home?

THINK CRITICALLY

4. State three reasons you should carefully inspect the property you plan to purchase.

USE COMMUNICATION SKILLS

5. **Owner Obligations** Imagine that you are a condominium owner attending a meeting of the condominium association. What should the association do about a homeowner who leaves garbage in the hallway? Should the association limit the use of the pool and tennis courts to owners?

Write About It Write a paragraph answering one of the questions.

SOLVE MONEY PROBLEMS

6. **Making an Offer** After several weeks of searching for a new home, Renée has found a house that seems to be in good shape and is located in a nice neighborhood. The listing price is $125,000, which is about $15,000 more than she wants to pay. She would like to make a lower bid, but the housing market is tight, and she worries that someone else may buy the house at the listing price. Renée wonders what she should do.

Analyze Working in a small group, brainstorm some ideas about what factors Renée should consider in making a decision.

Chapter 7 Review & Activities

See the Teacher Manual for answers.

CHAPTER SUMMARY

- Renting tends to be less expensive than buying and offers more flexibility. Home ownership offers stability, financial benefits, and increased value over time.
- Renting a residence has the advantages of mobility, few maintenance responsibilities, and relatively low initial costs. Disadvantages include rent increases, few tax benefits, and restricted activities.
- The cost of renting is affected by the neighborhood, space, monthly rent, security deposit, and renters insurance.
- Advantages of owning a residence include stability, individual expression, tax benefits, and increased value. Disadvantages include financial risk, the possibility of value not increasing, limited mobility, and high expenses.
- When evaluating property, walk through the neighborhood, check the home exterior and interior, and get a home inspection.
- A down payment is needed to purchase a home. Then a buyer must get a long-term loan, or mortgage, to pay for the remaining purchase price. Closing costs must also be paid.
- To sell a home, decide whether to use a real estate agent, prepare the home, set a fair price, and keep the home neat and clean.

Communicating Key Terms

With a partner, role-play a real estate agent and a client discussing preparations for closing on a house. Write a script of the conversation you would have, using most of the terms below.

- mobility
- tenant
- landlord
- lease
- security deposit
- renters insurance
- equity
- escrow account
- private mortgage insurance (PMI)
- mortgage
- points
- amortization
- fixed-rate mortgage
- adjustable-rate mortgage (ARM)
- home equity loan
- refinance
- closing
- title insurance
- deed
- appraisal

Reviewing Key Concepts

1. **Evaluate** the various housing alternatives that are available.
2. **List** the advantages and disadvantages of renting.
3. **Identify** the costs of renting.
4. **List** the advantages and disadvantages of owning a residence.
5. **Explain** how to evaluate a property.
6. **Discuss** the financing involved in purchasing a home.
7. **Describe** a plan for selling a home.

See the Teacher Manual for answers.

ACADEMIC SKILLS

Language Arts Different life circumstances affect housing needs for people at different stage of their lives.

Write About It Write a paragraph describing the housing needs of a 28-year-old married couple expecting a baby in six months, who have a combined annual income of $62,000. Compare their needs with those of a 23-year-old single person who is earning $36,000 a year.

YOUR FINANCIAL FIGURES

Choosing Prices Imagine that you want to purchase a home and you have narrowed your choice down to three different houses. The prices for the houses are: House #1—$165,000; House #2—$151,000; House #3—$172,000.

1. **Calculate** the monthly mortgage payment for each home, assuming that there will be a 10 percent down payment and a 30-year mortgage with a simple interest rate of 5.2 percent.
2. **Compute** by going to the Web site of a real estate company or bank to find current interest rates and monthly payments.

REAL-WORLD Application

Connect with Math Today it is possible to buy a home without making a down payment. This is called a 100 percent mortgage. It is available to people with good credit scores and usually requires private mortgage insurance and slightly higher interest on the overall loan.

1. **Research** Use an Internet search engine to find a financial institution that offers 100 percent mortgages.
2. **Think Critically** For whom would a 100 percent mortgage be a good deal?

Internet CONNECTION

Selling a Home Your neighbors are thinking of selling their two-bedroom home in the suburbs and moving to a two-bedroom condominium. Help them make this decision.

@ **Log On** Use an Internet search engine to find local real estate Web sites. Answer these questions:

1. What is the average asking price of a two-bedroom home in your neighborhood or nearby?
2. Based on the prices you find, would you advise a neighbor to sell this type of home? Why or why not?

BusinessWeek ONLINE

Newsclip: Low Interest Rates Home prices have been on the rise since 2000, driven by low interest rates that make mortgages affordable.

@ **Log On** Go to **finance07.glencoe.com** and open Chapter 7. Learn more about the different types of mortgages available. How is buying a home different today? Write a list of answers.

WHAT'S YOUR FINANCIAL **ID?**

WHERE WOULD YOU LIKE TO LIVE?

There are many factors that will help you decide where to live. These factors may change over the next few years. As you look into your housing options, you will need to consider your lifestyle, family situation, finances, and future plans. Here is a quick quiz to test your preferences. Write your answers on a separate sheet of paper.

1. I do not care about having a yard.

True False

2. My income varies right now.

True False

3. I never want to own a house or a condominium.

True False

4. I need to be able to move at any time.

True False

5. I want to keep my expenses as low as possible.

True False

6. I do not want to be responsible for repairs and upkeep.

True False

7. I do not plan to have a family for a while.

True False

Scoring: The more "true" answers you have, the better it is for you to rent an apartment and postpone house hunting until you are ready.

Accept all reasonable answers that show student effort and an understanding of the concept.

Your Financial Portfolio

Renting or Buying Your Home

Atul and Elena have saved enough money to buy a townhouse and have found one they like, but they need to consider how much it will actually cost to live there. The rent on their apartment is $700 a month ($8,400 a year), and the townhouse costs $85,000. They will need to consider any additional costs.

Atul and Elena's Dilemma

Rental Costs	
Annual rent payments	$8,400
Renters insurance	170
Total annual cost of renting	**$8,570**
Buying Costs	
Down payment (at 10%)	8,500
Annual mortgage payments	8,060
Property taxes (annual costs)	1,275
Mortgage insurance (annual premium)	536
Homeowners insurance (annual premium)	400
Estimated maintenance costs	850
Financial Benefits of Home Ownership	
Less: Tax savings for mortgage interest	–1,820
Less: Tax savings for property taxes	–357
Total cost of buying first year	**$17,444**
Less: one-time down payment	–8,500
Estimated annual appreciation (4%)*	–3,400
Total long-term annual cost of buying	**$5,544**

*Nationwide average; actual appreciation varies by geographic area and economic conditions.

Atul and Elena compared the annual costs of renting ($8,570) and buying ($5,544) and decided that it would be a good investment to buy the townhouse.

Compare

On a separate sheet of paper, compare renting versus buying your place of residence. Check a newspaper for a rental price for a two-bedroom apartment and a selling price for a two-bedroom house. Use those figures to complete your comparison.

Accept all reasonable answers that show student effort and an understanding of the concept.

Unit 2 LAB

Get a Financial Life!

Home Ownership

Overview

Carrie Houston finished her associate in arts science degree at the local community college and is now working as a fashion designer for Outside Box Designs. Last year she married David Lanier, a high school computer science teacher and basketball coach. Carrie and David have many decisions to make as a married couple. One of their goals is to purchase a home within the next two years. Recently, Carrie and David met with a real estate agent and a banker. The real estate agent helped them think about the features and location they want for their future residence. The banker discussed mortgages and budgeting with the young couple. Both Carrie and David realize that they have a lot of research and planning ahead of them.

Resources & Tools

- Crayons, markers, colored pencils
- Internet (optional)
- Newspapers and real estate magazines
- Portfolio (ring binder or file folder)
- Public or school library
- Spreadsheet software (optional)
- Word processor

Procedures

STEP A **The Process**

Carrie and David's combined income is $85,000 a year. Their banker told them that the most they should spend for a home is 2.5 times their annual income.

1. Determine the maximum amount that Carrie and David should spend on their future home.
2. Write a list of the features in the home. Then write a two-paragraph description of their future home and draw a picture of it.
3. Using the newspaper, real estate magazines, or the Internet, find an ad or listing for a home in their price range. You might look in different regions of the country to find different price ranges. Clip or print the ad or listing.
4. Request an amortization table from a local bank, or find one on the Internet. Determine Carrie and David's monthly mortgage payment based on current interest rates.
5. Contact a homeowners insurance company and find out the cost of insuring the home.
6. Contact companies that provide electricity, gas, water, cable television, telephone, and trash pickup. Determine the installation fees, deposits, and monthly cost of each service for the home.
7. Using newspapers, catalogs, garage sale ads, the Internet, or other sources, furnish their home for $15,000. Provide a picture or a drawing of the items bought.
8. Prepare a budget for Carrie and David for their first year as homeowners. If possible, use a spreadsheet program.

STEP B Create Your Portfolio

As you work through the process, save the results so that you can refer, review, and refine. Use a ring binder or a file folder to create a portfolio of your work.

1. The title of the binder or folder should be "Home Ownership." Decorate the front of the binder or folder—and be creative.
2. Organize the results of Step A (2–8) in your binder or folder. If possible, use a word processor to ensure that your work is neat and easy to read.
3. Read a magazine article on one of the following topics: (1) buying your first home, (2) making home repairs, (3) decorating a home, or (4) landscaping a home. Present a summary of the article to the class.

STEP C Technical Writing and Reading

Many workplaces need employees who are skilled in technical writing and reading. Technical writing is the process of communicating technical information in writing, clearly and accurately. To practice technical writing, complete activity 1 or activity 2 (below). Activity 3 will allow you to practice technical reading.

1. When Carrie and David are ready to purchase their home, they will have to decide which lender to use to obtain a mortgage. Write a technical paper (one or two pages) outlining the steps Carrie and David must take to choose a mortgage.
2. Carrie and David have decided to acquire a credit card. Write a technical paper (one or two pages) outlining the steps Carrie and David must take to choose a credit card.
3. Exchange technical writing papers with another student. Read your classmate's paper and critique it for accuracy, completeness, punctuation, and grammar. Return each other's papers.

Unit 3

Investing Financial Resources

WebQuest Internet Project

Nest Egg

Everyone wants to look forward to the future with confidence. Knowing you can be financially secure helps to build that confidence. Savings and investments are keys to financial security. If you do not have the resources right now to save and invest, you can begin planning to start your nest egg. In this project, you will find investment experts and get their advice about how a young person can get ready to save and invest.

Log on to **finance07.glencoe.com**. Begin by reading Task 1. Then continue on your WebQuest as you study Unit 3.

Section	8.1	9.3	10.4	11.1
Page	241	286	337	358

BusinessWeek

FINANCE FILE

The Best Homes for Rollover IRAs

When you go to work for an employer, you are not just getting a job but a retirement account as well. You will be stuck with the 401(k) that is offered, and you get no opportunity to shop around for more attractive investment options or services.

But when you leave your job—for another one or to retire—the situation changes. Chances are you will want to roll over the money in the 401(k) to an IRA that will probably become the most important source of your income throughout retirement.

"Anyone who is shopping to move a 401(k) should identify three or four options, and do a thorough analysis so they understand the fees," Doland [a financial advisor] recommends. One cost is fees for services, such as opening or closing an account, or account maintenance.

When you retire, you'll be making regular withdrawals from your IRA, so easy access to information and good service may be more important than before. Online account management is a great tool for keeping track of balances and withdrawals.

—By Ellen Hoffman

Write About It Why might having a 401(k) retirement account be important to someone who already has Social Security?

See the Teacher Manual for answer.

Log On To read the complete *BusinessWeek* article and do the *BusinessWeek* Extension activity to help you learn more about IRAs and other investment options, go to **finance07.glencoe.com**.

CHAPTER 8

Saving and Investing

$ What You'll Learn

When you have completed this chapter, you will be able to:

Section 8.1

- Explain how to establish goals for a savings or investment program.
- Discuss ways to obtain funds for investing.
- Identify the factors that affect your investment choices.

Section 8.2

- Identify the main types of savings and investment alternatives.
- Explain the steps involved in developing a personal investment plan.

Section 8.3

- Describe your role in a personal investment program.
- Identify sources of financial information.

Reading Strategies

To get the most out of your reading:

Predict what you will learn in this chapter.
Relate what you read to your own life.
Question what you are reading to be sure you understand.
React to what you have read.

In the **Real** World . . .

Nellie Magdaleno has been working as a part-time florist. She opened a checking account for her regular expenses as well as a savings account to earn interest. However, she earns only pennies for each dollar she saves. So Nellie has been researching stocks, bonds, and mutual funds. She has found investment plans that will earn her more interest than a savings account. She is excited about finding a way to make her money work for her and hopes to save enough to invest in real estate one day.

Different types of investments are suitable for different personalities, situations, and stages of life.

As You Read *Consider how your personality and goals will affect your choices for investment and savings plans.*

Lesson Plan See the Teacher Manual for the Chapter 8 planning guide and lesson plan.

ASK STANDARD & POOR'S

Investments

Q: After paying my bills, I do not have much money left over. I save any extra that I get. Since I do not have a lot of money, why should I even consider investing?

A: If inflation increases at a higher rate than your savings account return, you can lose purchasing power. To stay ahead of inflation and taxes, the money you set aside for long-term goals will need to earn more than the rates usually paid on savings accounts. Consider other investments that can earn a higher return.

Ask Yourself Besides investing some of your money, what are some other things that you could do to help you reach your long-term financial goals?

@ Go to **finance07.glencoe.com** to complete the Standard & Poor's Financial Focus activity.

Section 8.1

Focus on Reading

Read to Learn

- How to establish goals for a savings or investment program.
- How to discuss ways to obtain funds for investing.
- How to identify the factors that affect your investment choices.

Main Idea

Laying a foundation for your savings or investment program will help ensure that you meet your future financial goals.

Key Terms

- emergency fund
- speculative investment
- dividends
- retained earnings
- investment liquidity

Before You Read

PREDICT

Can you think of any reasons to risk putting money in investments instead of a savings account?

Springboard Ask the students what they dream of achieving in their lives. Then ask how they think they will make those dreams come true. Do they think working hard is enough?

Preparing for a Savings or Investment Program

Establishing Your Financial Goals

Why are financial goals important to your future?

When you think about the future, do you picture yourself owning your own home, being the president of your own company, or retiring at age 50? You might want to travel or start a family. No matter how much you may want to have something, you will not acquire it if you cannot pay for it.

To gather the funds, you need to plan carefully—and have self-discipline along the way. If you are saving or investing to meet a goal that will make you happy and financially secure, the sacrifices you make will be worth it.

A savings or investment plan starts with a specific, measurable goal. For example, you may want to save $15,000 to make a down payment on a house five years after graduating from school. To reach that goal, a savings account provides safety but does not increase in value quickly. An investment may be safe or risky and increase in value slowly or quickly—or it may lose value.

You might also decide that you should begin saving money in an **emergency fund**—a savings account that you can access quickly to pay for unexpected expenses or emergencies. For example, if you had to pay for an unexpected car repair or if you lost your job, you could use the money you put away in your emergency fund.

Your Goals and Values

Your goals should correspond with your values. At one extreme, some people save or invest as much of each paycheck as possible. The satisfaction they get from fulfilling long-term financial goals is more important to them than spending a lot of money on something temporary, such as a weekend trip. At the other extreme, some people spend every cent they earn, and then run out of money before they receive their next paycheck.

Outlining Goals

It is probably wise to take a middle-of-the-road approach. You can spend money on some things you enjoy and still save enough for a savings or investment program. As you will learn, even a small amount of money saved or invested on a regular basis can add up to a large amount over time.

As you outline your financial goals, ask yourself these questions:

- How do I want to spend my money?
- How much money do I need to satisfy my goals?
- How will I get the money?
- How long will it take to save the money?
- How much risk am I willing to take when I invest?
- What conditions in the economy or in my life could change my investment goals?
- Are my goals reasonable, considering my circumstances or future circumstances?
- Am I willing to make sacrifices to save?
- What will happen if I do not meet my goals?

Motivating Students Have the students write down their definitions of the word *discipline*; have several students share their definitions. Ask if they think the word has positive or negative connotations. Ask them if they think it can benefit them.

Performing a Financial Check-Up

How can you assess the health of your finances?

Before you think about investing for the future, you must take steps to be sure your personal finances are in good shape. Then you will be ready to move ahead with your financial plan. See **Figure 8.1** on page 240 for tips on how to perform your own financial check-up.

Teaching Activity Have the students write down three financial goals. Then direct them to the list of questions at the top of page 239, and have them answer the questions, in writing, to the best of their ability.

Money to Get Started

What are some sources of money to invest?

After you have set your goals and completed your financial check-up, you are almost ready to start saving or investing. But first you have to get the money. Here are a few ways to do that.

Pay Yourself First

People often save or invest money that is left over after they have paid all their other expenses, from monthly bills to video games. As you might guess, in many cases, nothing is left over. Here is a better approach:

1. Include the amount you want to save in your monthly expenses. Pay that amount first. Consider it as a bill that you owe to yourself.
2. Pay your monthly living expenses, such as rent and food.
3. Use money that is left over for personal pleasures, such as going to the movies or buying a new CD.

As You Read

RELATE

If you used the pay-yourself-first plan, how much would you be able to save each month?

Figure 8.1 Your Financial Checkup

Keeping your personal finances in order is an important step in meeting your long-term financial goals.

1 **Balance your budget.** Spend less money than you make; stay out of debt; and limit your credit card use. Eventually, the amount of cash remaining after you pay your bills will increase. You will be able to use that money to start a savings program.

2 **Have insurance.** When you are on your own, you should have enough insurance to cover losses from events such as a car accident, a medical emergency, or theft.

3 **Start an emergency fund.** Save money that you can access quickly to help you pay for unexpected situations, such as not being able to work. You should have enough money to cover living expenses for three to nine months.

4 **Have other sources of cash.** A source might be a line of credit with a financial institution or cash advance capability from a credit card company. Use it only for serious emergencies.

Employer-Sponsored Retirement Plans

If your employer offers a retirement plan, usually a 401(k) or 403(b) plan, you can take advantage of a ready-made investment program. Saving is simple because an amount you choose is deducted automatically from each paycheck. Many employers match part or all of the money you save. For example, for every dollar you contribute, your employer may put in 25 cents, 50 cents, or even a dollar, which would double your savings. In addition, money put in a retirement fund is not taxed until you withdraw it—usually at retirement age.

Starting an employer-sponsored or private retirement plan is an important step toward having financial security when you are older. Most people will need this retirement income in addition to Social Security as the Social Security system is revised. To learn more about retirement plans, read Chapter 15.

WebQuest

Nest Egg
Before you can save and invest, you have to pay your bills—every month! That means sticking to a budget. Learn about budgeting—why it is important, how to do it, and how to maintain it—and create a budget that reflects your needs today.

To continue with Task 2 of your WebQuest project, visit **finance07.glencoe.com**.

Elective Savings Programs

Some employers provide the option of having money automatically withheld from your paycheck and deposited in a standard savings account. On your own, you can also arrange with a mutual fund or brokerage firm to take a certain amount from your bank account every month and invest it. This is an easy way to save because you do not have to think about it. You may be less tempted to use the money if you never see it. An elective savings program is an excellent way to fund a traditional IRA or Roth IRA account.

Special Savings Effort

Another way to save is to set aside a specific time each year when you cut back sharply on what you spend and put the money you save in an investment fund.

Discussion Ask students if they see themselves as savers or spenders. Ask the spenders if they are concerned about reaching their financial goals. Ask the savers how they go about saving and why they do it. Suggest all students try at least one of the savings methods in the text.

Gifts, Inheritances, and Windfalls

During your lifetime, you might receive gifts of money, or you might inherit some money. You may also receive bonuses at work, tax refunds, and salary raises.

What would you do with that money? Often people choose to spend this extra money on something they could not afford under normal circumstances. Consider Jihwan's plan and whether you would make the same choice.

When Jihwan received his income tax refund, his friends suggested that this would be the perfect time to buy a big-screen television. Jihwan's friends were disappointed when he decided to put the money in a certificate of deposit that earned 6 percent interest. Jihwan did not mind watching television on his parents' 19-inch TV screen because his savings deposit was increasing. No one can make you save money to finance a savings or investment program. You have to choose to do it.

The Value of Long-Term Investment Programs

Why should you invest in a long-term program?

Many people do not start investing because they have only a small amount of money. Others believe that they are too young to invest. However, having a small amount of money in a bank account should not stop you.

Remember that small amounts of money add up because of the *time value of money*. As you read in Chapter 1, the time value of money is the increase in an amount of money due to interest earned over time.

Figure 8.2 shows the growth of $2,000 during different time periods and at different rates of return. A rate of return is the percentage of increase in the value of your savings due to earned interest. Remember that you must continue to add money to your investments to see the growth that is represented in Figure 8.2.

Figure 8.2 **Long-Term Investing and Growth**

	Balance at End of Year					
Rate of Return	**1**	**5**	**10**	**20**	**30**	**40**
4%	$2,000	$10,832	$24,012	$59,556	$112,170	$190,052
5%	2,000	11,052	25,156	66,132	132,878	241,600
6%	2,000	11,274	26,362	73,572	158,116	309,520
7%	2,000	11,502	27,632	81,990	188,922	399,280
8%	2,000	11,734	28,974	91,524	226,560	518,120
9%	2,000	11,970	30,386	102,320	272,620	675,780
10%	2,000	12,210	31,874	114,550	328,980	885,180
11%	2,000	12,456	33,444	128,406	398,040	1,163,660
12%	2,000	12,706	35,098	144,104	482,660	1,534,180

Growing Wild The growth shown in this table at different rates of return assumes that you will invest $2,000 at the end of each year.

Why would you be willing to invest $2,000 a year for a long term?

Caption Answer
Answers will vary, but some may say the benefit is greater than the sacrifice.

Making Investment Decisions

What are the factors you should consider when choosing investments?

Once you know how much money you need to meet your goals, you then have to think about where to invest it. To make that decision, you need to understand the different risk factors. Also, you should consider each investment's potential for income and growth as well as its liquidity.

Safety and Risk

Critical Thinking Have students write a brief essay in which they explore whether they are risk takers. They are to discuss what kinds of risks they are and are not willing to take, and why. They should conclude by determining if there is a pattern to their risk behavior.

In the financial world, the words *safety* and *risk* have specific meanings. Safety means that the chance of losing your money in an investment is fairly small. Risk indicates that you cannot be certain about the profit of your investment. You can select investments that are very safe or very risky, or in between these extremes.

Generally, if you choose a safe investment, your rate of return will be low. On the other hand, a **speculative investment** is considered a high-risk investment that might earn a large profit in a short time. The disadvantage of a speculative investment is the possibility that at any time you could lose most or all of the money you invest. **Figure 8.3** categorizes each type of investment according to its safety record.

Figure 8.3 Typical Investment Risks

Safe	Can Vary	High Risk
• Government bonds and debt securities: Treasury bills, Treasury notes, Treasury bonds, Municipal bonds, U.S. Savings Bonds • Savings accounts • Certificates of deposit (CDs)	• Stocks • Corporate bonds • Mutual funds • Real estate	• Commodities • Options • Precious metals and gems • Collectibles, such as coins, stamps, and comic books

Investment Spectrum Only you can decide how much risk you are willing to take.

Why do you think savings accounts and certificates of deposit are considered safe investments?

Caption Answer In most financial institutions, FDIC insures accounts up to $100,000.

TechByte

From Ticker Tape to PDAs In 1870, Thomas Edison invented the first practical ticker-tape machine. With a printing speed of one character per second, it enabled people to track changes in the prices of stocks and bonds. Information was printed on long thin strips of paper called *ticker tape*. Used ticker tape was cut into a form of confetti and tossed in ticker-tape parades. Today you can have data from the world's markets, streaming charts, and analysis downloaded to your Smart Phone or Personal Digital Assistant (PDA) through a service called QuoTrek.

@ Read more about how to get financial information on the go and make a list of the features available with QuoTrek through **finance07.glencoe.com**.

Teaching Activity Divide the class into five groups and assign one risk component to each group. Each group is to research its risk factor, determine how it can affect investments, what kinds of investments (if any) are safest from this risk, and how big a risk it is. Have each group write up its results and present them to the class.

One basic rule sums up the relationship between the factors of safety and risk: The potential return on any investment should be directly related to the risk you, the investor, take. Your attitude toward risk will vary according to your circumstances. For example, when you are young, you may be more willing to take risks because you have long-term investment goals. When you are older and close to retirement, you may decide to shift your investments from speculative to conservative investments to be sure that you will not lose your life savings.

Beginning investors may be afraid of the risk associated with some investments. However, it helps to remember that without risk, it is impossible to obtain returns that make investments grow. The key is to determine how much risk you are willing to take. Then choose quality investments that offer higher returns without an extremely high risk.

Five Components of Risk

Evaluate the overall risk factor of an investment by examining five different components of risk:

1. Inflation
2. Interest rate
3. Business failure
4. Financial market
5. Global investment

Inflation Risk Inflation is a persistent economic condition that affects everyone. For example, when Harry Majors opened his deli in 1985, he framed the first dollar he earned and hung it on the wall. Twenty years later, one of his customers reminded him that his 1985 dollar could now buy less than 50 cents' worth of salami. The loss of value to Harry's dollar was a result of inflation, which is a general rise in prices that affects everybody.

Investing your money can help you stay ahead of inflation. However, during periods of rapid inflation, the return from your investments might not keep up with the inflation rate. When that happens, you lose buying power, and your money will buy less.

You can calculate the effect of inflation on your investments. First, subtract your rate of interest from the inflation rate. This is your loss of buying power converted to a percentage. Then multiply that percentage by the original amount of your investment. The result is your loss of buying power in dollars. (See the **Go Figure** box.)

In addition, you can find out the current price of your investment, based on the rate of inflation during the period that you held the investment. Multiply the original price of the investment by the rate of inflation. Add that figure to the original price of the investment. The result is how much it would cost you to purchase the same investment today.

Some investments will protect you from inflation better than others. For example, over the period from 1926 to 2002, the compounded rate of return on common stocks adjusted for inflation was 7 percent. Concurrently, U.S. Treasury bills (T-bills) had an inflation-adjusted compounded rate of return of only 0.6 percent. During that time, common stocks provided a better protection against inflation than did T-bills.

Teaching Activity Divide the class into groups of four and have each group research how interest rates are set. The groups are to prepare graphic presentations of the research results and vote on the best graphic. This work then will be displayed on a bulletin board.

Interest Rate Risk If you put money in an investment that gives you a fixed rate of return (stable rate), such as government or corporate bonds, the value of your investment will go down if interest rates go up. If you have to sell your bonds, you will get less than you originally paid.

To figure out the market price of a $1,000 bond if interest rates go up, divide one year of interest at a fixed rate of 8 percent by the new higher interest rate of 10 percent. (See the **Go Figure** box on page 246.) If you hold onto the bond until maturity, you will get your full $1,000 back, but you will receive only 8 percent annual interest.

GO FIGURE FINANCIAL MATH

INFLATION RATE AND INVESTMENTS

Synopsis: When prices and the cost of living rise in one year, your money will buy less and be worth less than it was during the prior year. For example, $500 this year will buy less than it did last year.

Example: Nina put $500 in a certificate of deposit for one year at 3 percent interest. The inflation rate during that year was 5 percent. How much of her buying power did she lose? How much money would she need at the end of the year to buy what she bought a year ago with $500?

A. Calculate the percentage of the loss of buying power:

Formula: Inflation Rate − Interest Rate = Loss-of-Buying-Power Percentage

Solution: 5% − 3% = 2% Loss of Buying Power

B. Calculate the loss of buying power in dollars:

Formula: Original Price of Investment × Loss of Buying Power Percentage = Loss of Buying Power in Dollars

Solution: $500 × 2% or .02 = $10

Nina lost $10.

C. Calculate how much it would cost to buy the same investment today:

Formula: (Original Price of Investment × Inflation Rate) + Original Price of Investment = Current Price of Investment

Solution: ($500 × 5% or .05) + $500 = $525

Nina would need $525 at the end of the year to buy what she bought a year ago with $500.

YOU FIGURE

A year ago, you worked part-time and put $1,000 in a savings account. The interest rate for one year was 6 percent. The inflation rate during that year was 4 percent. How much money would you need at the end of the year to buy what you bought a year ago with $1,000?

Answer ($1,000 × 4% or .04) + $1,000 = $1,040

GO FIGURE — FINANCIAL MATH

A BOND'S MARKET PRICE WHEN INTEREST RATES GO UP

Synopsis: A bond's interest earnings can be reduced if you sell it before the maturity date when bond rates are higher than those at time of purchase.

Example: You buy a $1,000 corporate bond that pays a fixed rate of 8 percent interest. You earn $80 a year ($1,000 × 8% or .08 = $80) until maturity. What price would you get if you sold it before the maturity date when bond rates were 10 percent?

Formula: $\frac{\text{Annual Interest Earned}}{\text{New Interest Rate}} = \text{Market Price}$

Solution: $\frac{\$80}{10\% \text{ or } .10} = \$800$

You would get $800, which equals a loss of $200. ($1,000 − $800 = $200).

YOU FIGURE

You buy a $1,500 corporate bond that pays a fixed rate of 8.5 percent interest. You earn $127.50 a year ($1,500 × .085 or 8.5% = $127.50) until maturity. What price would you get if you sold it before the maturity date when bond rates were 11 percent?

Answer $127.50 ÷ 11% or .11 = $1,159.09

Research Divide students into groups of no more than four. Each group is to research a foreign stock or bond to determine and present the company's earnings, its product(s), and whether its product(s) is exported to the United States.

Academic Connection

LANGUAGE ARTS

It is commonly thought that choosing a foreign investment is more complicated than choosing a domestic one. In actuality, however, the process is much the same. When searching for a foreign mutual fund, for example, you should look for the characteristics you would look for in a domestic one, such as strong relative performance over time and reasonable expenses. *Research foreign investments and write a paragraph describing its benefits and its drawbacks.*

See the Teacher Manual for answer.

Business Failure Risk This type of risk applies to common stock, preferred stock, and corporate bonds. When you buy stocks or corporate bonds, you are investing in a particular company. You are betting that the company will succeed. However, it could fail, especially if the company is managed poorly. Even if the company offers a valuable product or service, positive response from customers is not guaranteed. Lower profits usually mean lower **dividends**, which are distributions of money, stock, or other property that a corporation pays to stockholders. If the company declares bankruptcy, your investment may become worthless. Your best protection is to do careful research on companies in which you might invest. Another good idea is to invest your money in more than one company.

Financial Market Risk Sometimes the prices of stocks, bonds, mutual funds, and other investments go up or down because of the overall state of financial markets. The value of a stock may decrease, even though a company is financially healthy. Factors that affect financial markets include social and political conditions. For example, the price of oil stocks may be affected by the political situation in the Middle East, where much of the world's oil supply is produced.

Global Investment Risk Today many investors are investing their money in stocks and bonds issued by companies in other countries. Because these types of investments may be risky, financial analysts advise small investors to invest in global mutual funds, instead of individual international stocks. Global mutual funds are offered by U.S. firms. These mutual funds specialize in companies that operate in another nation or region of the world. A mutual fund includes stocks or bonds from many companies and may offer more safety than one company's stocks or bonds.

GO FIGURE — FINANCIAL MATH

A BOND'S MARKET PRICE WHEN INTEREST RATES GO DOWN

Synopsis: You may profit from selling a bond before maturity when bond interest rates are lower than those at time of purchase.

Example: Your $1,000 corporate bond pays a fixed rate of 8 percent interest, or $80 a year ($1,000 × 8% or .08 = $80). What price would you get if you sold it before maturity when bond rates were 6 percent?

Formula: $\frac{\text{Annual Interest Earned}}{\text{New Interest Rate}} = \text{Market Price}$

Solution: $\frac{\$80}{6\% \text{ or } .06} = \$1{,}333.33$

You would receive $1,333.33, which equals a profit of $333.33 ($1,333.33 − $1,000 = $333.33).

YOU FIGURE

Your $1,200 corporate bond pays a fixed rate of 8.5 percent interest, or $102 a year ($1,200 × 8.5% or .085 = $102). What price would you get if you sold it before maturity when bond rates were 6 percent?

Answer $102 ÷ 6% or .06 = $1,700

If you plan to invest in companies outside the United States, take these steps:

1. **Evaluate international investments as if they were U.S. investments:** Be aware that because of different accounting standards in other countries, it may be hard to discover the true financial condition of foreign companies.
2. **Consider the currency exchange rate:** This rate may affect the return on your investment, favorably or unfavorably. For example, if you buy stock in a French company, stock dividends will be paid to you in euros and then converted to dollars.

Also, keep in mind that the economic and political stability of a country can affect the value of your investment. It is risky to invest in stocks and bonds issued by individual companies in other countries. Only experienced investors should consider this option.

Caption Answer An international investment is paid in the currency of its country. Even if your investment earns the same percentage every month, the cash you receive will go up or down depending upon the exchange rate between the United States and that country at the time the money is issued.

▼ **EXPLORING NEW WORLDS** When investing in global mutual funds, evaluate the choices carefully. *How does the currency exchange rate affect the return on an international investment?*

Investment Income

There are a variety of other types of investments for income. If you want a dependable source of income, you have several choices. The safest and most predictable investments include: savings accounts, certificates of deposit (CDs), U.S. Savings Bonds, and U.S. Treasury bills. With these programs, you know the interest rate and how much interest income you will receive on a specific date.

▲ **TAKING CHANCES** Only experts may be able to handle the risk of speculative investments. *Can you afford to lose money on a speculative investment?*

Caption Answer Speculative investments can offer high rewards but also equally high losses.

Other sources of investment income include government bonds, corporate bonds, preferred stocks, utility stocks, certain common stocks, annuities, and stable mutual funds. Before investing in stocks or corporate bonds, obtain information about the company's overall profits, its history of dividend payments, and its outlook for the future. Be sure to check out the costs associated with annuities before investing. See Chapters 9 and 10 for more information on stocks, bonds, and mutual funds.

Real estate rental property also offers income, but it is not guaranteed. For example, your profits from a rental property may be lower than expected if you have vacancies or expensive repairs. In addition, Real Estate Investment Trusts, or REITs, also offer income that is not guaranteed. These trusts are similar to mutual funds. See Chapter 11 for more information on real estate and other investments.

Speculative investments, such as commodities, options, precious metals and gems, and collectibles, offer little potential for income and are risky. These types of investments are more appropriate for investors who have expertise and experience in these markets.

Discussion In a discussion with the students, generate two lists: investments that would be easy to liquidate and investments that provide a safe income. Ask the students why so many of the items on one list also appear on the other list.

Investment Growth

To investors, growth means that their investments will increase in value. The best opportunities for growth usually come from common stocks and growth stocks. A growth stock is a common stock issued by a corporation. This type of stock has the potential to earn above-average profits in comparison to other corporate stocks.

Growth companies usually reinvest their profits rather than pay dividends. **Retained earnings** are profits that a company reinvests, usually for expansion or to conduct research and development. Growth that is financed by retained earnings usually contributes to increasing the stock's value. Therefore, if you buy stock in a growth company, you may not receive immediate cash dividends, but you will benefit because your stock may increase in value.

As You Read

QUESTION

If you want to buy a house in ten years, should you put your money in a CD or invest it in growth stocks? Why?

Question Answer Some students will answer "in a CD" because it is safe, but others will answer "in growth stocks" because they may have more potential for increased value.

Investment Liquidity

A final factor to consider when choosing investments is **investment liquidity**—the ability to buy or sell an investment quickly without substantially reducing its value. You may be able to sell some investments quickly, but market conditions or other factors may prevent you from regaining your original investment.

A passbook savings account is an example of a high-liquidity investment, because you can withdraw all your money immediately. A low-liquidity investment requires more time to sell your investment. An investment in real estate is usually a low-liquidity investment because finding a buyer takes time.

Section 8.1 Assessment

See the Teacher Manual for answers.

QUICK CHECK

1. What steps should you take when preparing to establish an investment program?
2. How can you obtain the money you need to start investing?
3. What factors might affect your investment choices?

THINK CRITICALLY

4. A friend wants to invest a $500 bonus she received. What would you advise?

USE COMMUNICATION SKILLS

5. **Risk Tolerance** Everyone has a different tolerance for risk. Some people will try anything once, including skydiving and white-water rafting. Others take every precaution to avoid danger.

Analyze With a small group of classmates, discuss the five components of risk. Decide which components of risk might affect every investor.

SOLVE MONEY PROBLEMS

6. **Preparing for Emergencies** Roya and Sashi are performing a financial check-up. They are trying to decide how much money to put into an emergency fund and what type of account to open. The couple has $3,000 in take-home pay a month and monthly living expenses of $2,600. They have a young child and a limited health insurance plan. They are worried about unexpected expenses.

Write About It Write a plan describing how much money Roya and Sashi should have in their emergency fund and what type of account they should choose for the fund.

Section 8.2

Focus on Reading

Read to Learn

- How to identify the main types of savings and investment alternatives.
- How to explain the steps involved in developing a personal investment plan.

Main Idea

The more you know about different investment opportunities and the planning process, the better able you will be to select a savings or investment program that meets your needs.

Key Terms

- equity capital
- common stock
- preferred stock
- corporate bond
- government bond
- mutual fund
- diversification

Before You Read

PREDICT

Since stock investments can be risky, why do you think people choose them?

Springboard Write the words "saving" and "investing" on the board. Ask the class to identify the similarities and differences between the two words.

Savings and Investment Options

Types of Investments

How would you invest your money?

When you have your personal finances in order, an emergency fund, and money for investments, and you know how much risk you can take, you can begin to research different types of investment alternatives: stocks, bonds, mutual funds, and real estate.

Stocks

A business that is owned by one person gets operating money from that one owner, who is the sole proprietor. In a partnership, the partners provide the money, or equity capital. **Equity capital** is money that a business gets from its owners in order to operate. A corporation gets its equity capital from its stockholders, who become owners when they buy shares of stock in the company. The two basic types of stock are common and preferred.

Common Stock **Common stock** is a unit of ownership of a company, and it entitles the owner, or stockholder, to voting privileges. Common stock can sometimes provide a source of income if the company pays dividends. Stock can provide growth profits if the dollar value of the stock increases. In addition, if the company "splits" its stock, or divides shares into a larger number of shares, the stockholder gains because he or she will get more shares. Most large corporations generate money they need by selling common stock.

Preferred Stock A corporation may also issue preferred stock. **Preferred stock** is a type of stock that gives the owner the advantage of receiving cash dividends before common stockholders receive cash dividends. This is important if a company is having financial problems. If a company fails, preferred stockholders receive dividends first and any assets that are left before common stockholders receive anything. Chapter 9 discusses other factors you should consider when buying common or preferred stock.

Stock can be an attractive investment because, as owners, stockholders share in the success of the company. However, you should consider several facts before you invest in stock.

1. A corporation does not have to repay you what you paid for the stock. If you want to sell your stock, another investor must buy your shares through a stockbroker.
2. The current value of your stock is partially determined by how much another investor is willing to pay for your shares.
3. The corporation does not have to pay dividends. If the company has a bad year or decides to reinvest earnings, the board of directors can vote to eliminate dividend payments.

As You Read

RELATE

Are you willing to invest your money in stock, or would you prefer to keep your money in a CD?

Corporate and Government Bonds

You may also consider investing in bonds. There are two types of bonds an investor can consider: a corporate bond and a government bond. A **corporate bond** is a corporation's written pledge to repay a specific amount of money, along with interest. A **government bond** is the written pledge of a government or a municipality, such as a city, to repay a specific sum of money with interest. When you buy a bond, you are lending money to a corporation or government entity for a period of time.

Motivating Students Ask the students to show hands for how many would like to invest in stocks, how many in bonds, how many in CDs, and how many in real estate. Have them explain their answers.

The Value of a Bond Two key factors affect the value of a bond: (1) whether the bond will be repaid at maturity and (2) whether the corporation or government entity will be able to pay interest until maturity. Maturity dates range from 1 to 30 years, and interest on bonds is usually paid every six months. You can keep a bond until maturity and then redeem it, or you can sell it to another investor. In either case, the value of the bond is closely tied to the ability of the corporation or government agency to repay the bond at maturity. If a corporation or government agency cannot pay the interest on its bonds, the value of those bonds will decrease. Some investors also make money on bonds by receiving regular interest payments until maturity.

Caption Answer Investors should consider whether the bond will be repaid at maturity and whether the government agency will be able to pay interest until maturity.

▶ **PAYING UP** Government bonds offer a fixed rate of interest. *What are two key considerations for buying a government bond?*

Teaching Activity Divide the class into groups of four and assign a public company to each. Have groups research the company to determine if they believe the company is a good investment. The group should look at annual reports, financial statements, or news articles, and follow the stock for a week. Each group will present its results to the class.

Mutual Funds

A **mutual fund** is an investment in which investors pool their money to buy stocks, bonds, and other securities selected by professional managers who work for an investment company. Their knowledge is an advantage for inexperienced investors. If one of the fund stocks or other securities performs poorly, the loss can be offset by gains in another stock or security within the mutual fund. Chapter 10 provides information on types of funds.

Real Estate

The goal of real estate investing is to own property that increases in value so that you can sell it at a profit—or to receive rental income. When you invest in real estate, you need to find out if the property is priced as similar properties. You also need to know what financing is available and the cost of property taxes.

Before making a decision to purchase any property, ask the following questions: Why are the present owners selling? Is the property in good condition? What is the condition of other properties in the area? Is there a chance that the property will decrease in value?

When you sell real estate, consider these questions: Can you find an interested buyer? Can the buyer get financing to buy the property? Chapter 11 provides more information on real estate investments.

Careers in Finance

INVESTMENT ANALYST

Michelle Bondi
Robert Half Finance & Accounting

Michelle Bondi is fascinated with the world of finance. She studies and tracks the performance of financial market sectors, such as finance or construction. In addition to tracking the performance of individual stocks, Michelle studies the factors that affect them and compares the stocks' results with other similar stocks. She prepares internal and external reports on a stock's financial health on a daily basis or as requested. Investment analysts enjoy making connections between the news and economics, as well as finding patterns in the unpredictable world of finance.

SKILLS: Math, statistics, economics, and teamwork skills

PERSONAL TRAITS: Analytical, methodical, rigorous, self-starting, and up-to-date in current events

EDUCATION: High school diploma or equivalent; bachelor's degree in finance, accounting, economics, or business

ANALYZE Why would an investment analyst need to be aware of news and current events?
See the Teacher Manual for answers.

@ To learn more about career paths for investment analysts, visit **finance07.glencoe.com**.

Document Detective

Learn to identify and understand the standard financial documents you will use in the real world.

See the Teacher Manual for answers.

Investigate: A Savings Goals Worksheet
A savings goals worksheet contains this information:
- Your savings goal
- Amount you have
- Amount you need to achieve your goal
- Target date to goal

Your Motive: In order to make large purchases or achieve lofty financial goals, you need a savings plan. A savings plan will help you determine how much you need to reach your goals and how long it will take to achieve them.

Savings Goals Worksheet

Name: Susan Sharpe

Goals	Target Dates	Cost	Current Assets	Amount Still Needed	Years to Target Date	Amount to Save This Year
Down payment to purchase a house	2010	$30,000	$5,000	$25,000	5 years	$5,000
Buy a new car	2008	$22,000	$7,000	$15,000	3 years	$5,000
Save for retirement	2035	$500,000	$10,000	$490,000	30 years	$10,000

Key Points: A savings plan should be ambitious but not unrealistic. Do not try to set goals that you know you cannot reach. You should also reevaluate your savings plan at least once each year to make sure your savings plan is on track with your goals.

Find the Solutions
1. How much should Susan save to reach her goal?
2. What should Susan save this year to be on track to achieve her goals?
3. What assets other than savings might Susan use to help pay for a new car?
4. Why might Susan need to adjust her plan each year?
5. Susan's retirement savings plan calls for saving $10,000 each year for 30 years to save $300,000. However, she needs $490,000. What missing factor will enable Susan to achieve her savings goal?

Figure 8.4 Possible Investments

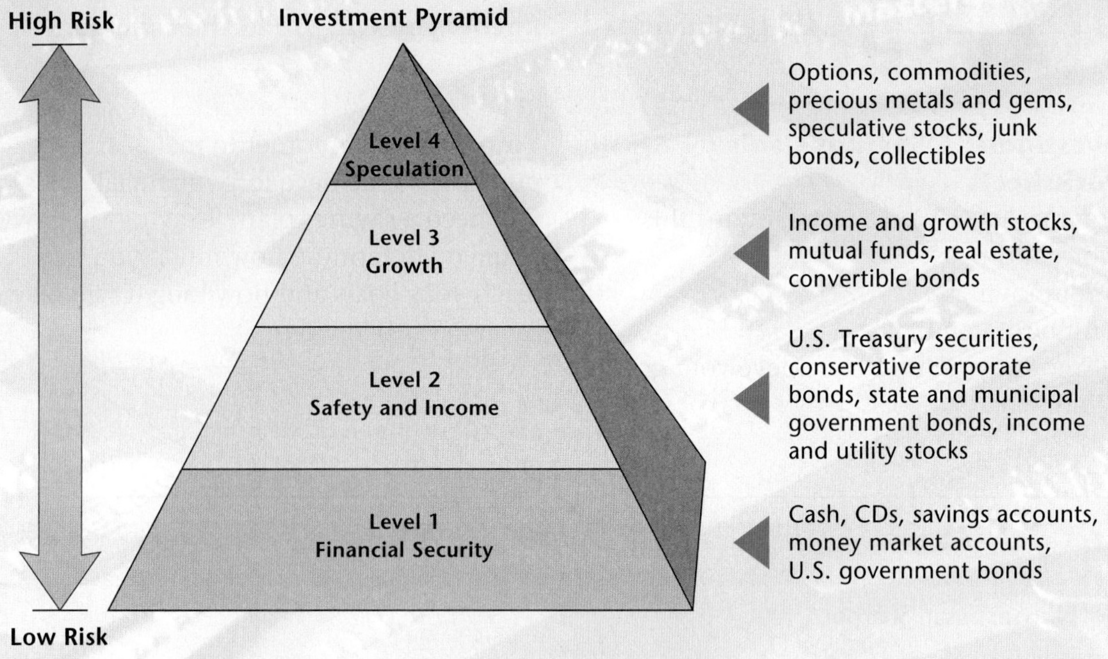

Building for the Future Without a solid foundation, you risk losing your investment.

Should a good investment plan include investments from all four levels?

Caption Answer
Speculative investments at the top level are optional for those who can handle the risk.

Evaluating Investment Alternatives

How would you diversify your investments?

As You Read
QUESTION

Why is diversification important?

Question Answer
It reduces risk.

You have learned how safety, risk, income, growth, and liquidity affect investment choices. You have also examined different investment possibilities. Which ones would you choose?

As you make your choices, remember it is wise to diversify. **Diversification** is the process of spreading your assets among several different types of investments to reduce risk. You should avoid "putting all your eggs in one basket." Some financial advisers suggest that you think of your investment program as a pyramid, as illustrated in **Figure 8.4**. This strategy provides both financial growth and protection no matter what your age, circumstances, or level of financial knowledge. Level 1 provides a solid foundation with safe investments. Once that foundation is built, you may choose from the alternatives listed in Levels 2 and 3, which carry moderate risk. Because the investments in Level 4 are highly speculative, you may want to skip that level entirely.

Critical Thinking Have the students select four investments, one for each of the levels on the Investment Pyramid. Have them explain in writing why each investment is suitable for that level.

Developing a Personal Investment Plan

How do you create an investment plan?

Teaching Activity Have the students decide which of the companies in Part 1 they would, as a class, like to "invest" in. When they decide, tell them they are making a $1,000 investment today. Have them determine how many shares they are purchasing. Tell students to monitor the stock for the next three weeks. Have them calculate the gain or loss that would result from selling at the end of three weeks.

To be a successful investor, develop a plan and put it into action. Each person has different ideas and goals. Establish your investment goals first, and then continue to follow through. Often the follow-through is the most important component of a successful, long-range, personal investment plan. Follow a series of steps and begin earning money through investment.

Consider this case: Ginny is single and has recently started her first full-time job after graduation. Her monthly take-home pay (after deductions for taxes and other items) is $1,600. Her monthly expenses are $1,200. She has a surplus of $400 a month. She is using her surplus to set up an emergency fund. She recently received an inheritance of $5,000 when her grandfather died. She plans to use this money to fund her investments.

Figure 8.5 illustrates how Ginny developed her individual investment plan. Your plan may be quite different, but the steps will be the same.

Figure 8.5 Ginny's Personal Investment Plan

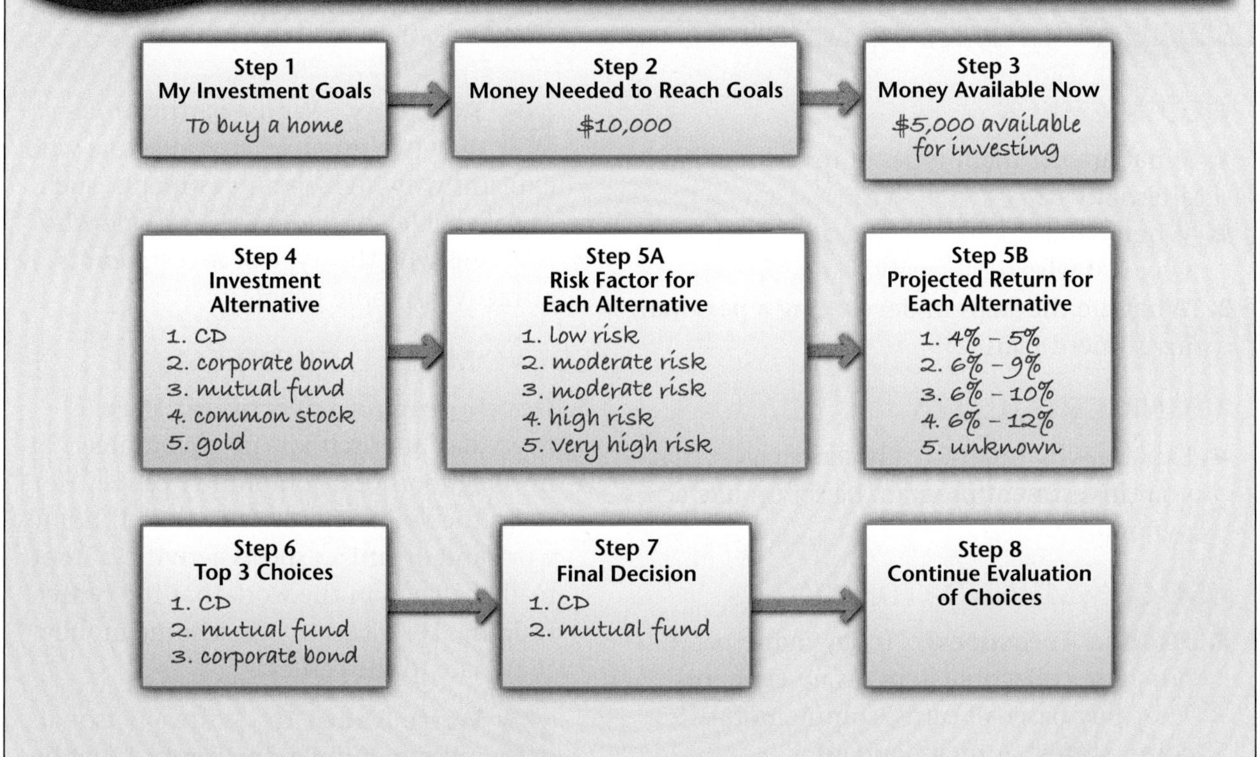

Master Plan Ginny decided to choose low-risk and moderate-risk investments.

Why do you think she made this decision?

Caption Answer Answers will vary but may include that Ginny wants an overall good return on her investments but does not want to risk losing her inheritance money, a one-time gift.

STANDARD &POOR'S

Put on Your Financial Planner's Cap

Your client is young and nervous, making a first time investment of $5,000. Would you advise investing in a savings account or CD, mutual fund, growth stock, or real estate? Explain why.

See the Teacher Manual for answers.

You may find these steps helpful to get started:

1. Establish investment goals.
2. Decide how much money you will need to reach those goals by a particular date.
3. Determine the amount of money you have to invest.
4. List all the investments you want to evaluate.
5. Evaluate the risks and potential return for each investment on your list.
6. Reduce your list of possible investments to a reasonable number.
7. Choose at least two investments so that you have some diversity. You may want to add more investments as the value of your holdings grows.
8. Because your investment goals may change as you go through life, recheck your investment program regularly. Remember that changes in the economy can affect your investments. For example, if interest rates on certificates of deposit are high, you might invest some of your money in a CD.

To develop your personal investment plan, establish your goals, and then follow through. If your goals are important to you, you will be willing to work to attain them.

Section 8.2 Assessment

See the Teacher Manual for answers.

QUICK CHECK

1. What are the main types of investment alternatives?
2. When choosing investment alternatives, why is it wise to diversify?
3. What are the steps in developing a personal investment plan?

THINK CRITICALLY

4. Explain why financial advisers suggest that your investment program be set up like a pyramid.

USE COMMUNICATION SKILLS

5. **Hidden Treasures?** Today many people purchase collectible items as investments. They buy baseball cards, commemorative coins, stuffed animals, and art.

Role-Play With a partner, role-play two financial advisors: one who explains why high-risk investments, such as collectibles, are not wise; and one who discusses why this type of investment is attractive to some people.

SOLVE MONEY PROBLEMS

6. **Developing an Investment Plan** Every day after school, Trent volunteers at his neighborhood community center. He helps the young children with their homework and organizes sports activities. Trent really believes in the work that the center is doing. He wants to invest some money to donate to the center.

Write About It Write a personal investment plan for Trent so that he can reach his goal.

Section 8.3

Reducing Risk and Sources of Information

Financial Planners

What is the role of a financial planner?

When making your investment decisions, you may want to consult a **financial planner**, a specialist who is trained to offer specific financial help and advice.

There are two main factors to consider when deciding if you need a financial planner: (1) your income level and (2) your willingness to make your own financial decisions. If you make less than $45,000 a year, you may not need a planner's services.

Types of Financial Planners

Financial planners work for various insurance companies, investment companies, real estate agencies, and law firms. Some are self-employed. There are four main types of financial planners:

1. **Fee-only planners** charge an hourly rate from $75 to $200 or a flat fee, ranging from about $500 to several thousand dollars. They may also charge an annual fee ranging from 0.04 percent to 1 percent of the value of the investments they manage.
2. **Fee-offset planners** charge an hourly or annual fee, but they reduce, or offset, it with the commissions, or earnings, they make by buying or selling investments.
3. **Fee-and-commission planners** charge a fixed fee for a financial plan and earn commissions from the products they sell.
4. **Commission-only planners** earn all their money through the commissions they make on sales of insurance, mutual funds, and other investments.

When hiring a financial planner, find out the exact fees for specific services. Also discuss how and when the fees will be collected from you. There should be no hidden commission charges if the financial planner provides "fee only" services.

Focus on Reading

Read to Learn

- How to describe your role in a personal investment program.
- How to identify sources of financial information.

Main Idea

By becoming an informed investor, you will be able to reach your investment goals.

Key Terms

- financial planner
- tax-exempt income
- tax-deferred income
- capital gain
- capital loss
- prospectus

Before You Read

PREDICT

How might investing change your income tax reporting?

Springboard Ask students what they think is the right age to begin investing, and why. Then ask if both younger and older people should use the same investment strategies. Why or why not?

Motivating Students Ask the students if they think they would prefer (a) to manage their investments alone, (b) to have a stockbroker account executive assist them, or (c) use a financial planner's services.

$avvy Saver

Giving Is Fun

1. Give whatever you can afford to your favorite charity.
2. Donate old clothes, toys, books, or eyeglasses instead of money.
3. Cash in your bottles and cans at a recycling center and give the money to charity.
4. Volunteer at a hospital, nursing home, animal shelter, or favorite charity.
5. Save $1 a week for a year, and make a donation to your favorite charity.

Selecting a Financial Planner

Look for a financial planner who will provide these basic services:

- Assess your current financial situation
- Offer a clearly written plan with investment recommendations
- Discuss the plan with you and answer questions
- Help you keep track of your progress
- Guide you to other financial experts and services as needed

You can find a financial planner by looking in the yellow pages, by contacting financial institutions, and by getting recommendations from friends, coworkers, or professional contacts. **Figure 8.6** suggests questions that you might ask a financial planner to help you make a decision.

Certification of Financial Planners

The requirements for becoming a financial planner vary from state to state. Some states require that financial planners pass an exam. Other states issue licenses to individual planners and planning companies. Some states have no regulations at all. The federal government requires that the Securities and Exchange Commission (SEC) monitor the largest financial planning companies.

A financial planner may have credentials, such as Certified Financial Planner (CFP) or Chartered Financial Consultant (ChFC). Not all planners are licensed, however. You should research and investigate any financial planner you might be considering.

Figure 8.6 **Selecting a Financial Planner**

When evaluating a financial planner, ask the following questions:

- What are your areas of expertise?
- Are you affiliated with a major financial services company, or do you work independently?
- Are you licensed or certified?
- What is your education and training?
- How is your fee determined? (Is this amount something I can afford?)
- Am I allowed a free initial consultation?
- May I see a sample of a written financial plan?
- May I contact some of your clients as references?
- Is financial planning your primary activity?

Research, Research This type of investigation takes time and effort.

Why do you think it is worthwhile?

Caption Answer
Answers might include that because you are considering placing your financial future in this person's hands, you need to know if he or she is capable of carrying out this task.

STANDARD &POOR'S

Global Financial Landscape

Standard and Poor's publishes the globally recognized S&P 500® financial index. It also gathers financial statistics, information, and news, and analyzes this data for international businesses, governments, and individuals to help guide their financial decisions.

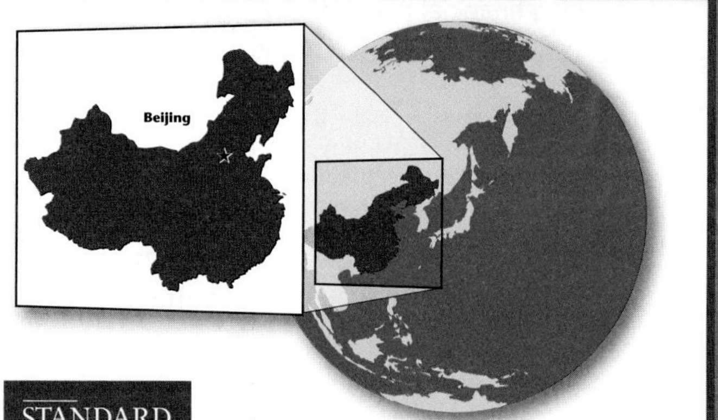

CHINA

Though lagging behind the United States, China is catching up as the number one consumer of oil. The United States uses 20.5 million barrels of oil per day; China uses 6.3 barrels. By 2010, that number may double. The country's swelling population—the world's largest—and increasing affluence has stimulated a fuel-driven economy. Thousands of factories stretch across the country; car sales are up by 55 percent; and China's electric power grids are on overdrive. Once energy independent, the country imports half of its oil. Soon China will be in serious competition with other oil-consuming nations for a dwindling supply of oil. Meanwhile, the country copes. In one city, shopping malls lowered their thermostats. In another, electricity was cut off four days a week to save on oil consumption.

STANDARD &POOR'S **DATABYTES**

Capital	Beijing
Population	1,288,679,000
Languages	Chinese (Mandarin), Cantonese, and other dialects and languages
Currency	yuan, or Renminbi
Gross Domestic Product (GDP)	$6.4 trillion (2003 est.)
GDP per capita	$5,000

Industry: Iron, steel, coal, machinery, armaments, textiles and apparel, petroleum, and cement

Agriculture: Rice, wheat, potatoes, sorghum, pork, and fish.

Exports: Machinery and equipment, textiles, apparel, footwear, toys, sporting goods, and mineral fuels

Natural Resources: Coal, iron ore, crude oil, mercury, tin, and hydropower

Think Globally
Would you buy stock in a Chinese electricity company? Why or why not?

See the Teacher Manual for answer.

Managing Your Investments

What should you do to manage your investments?

Most people do not have professional financial planners and need to learn how to manage their own finances. Managing your savings and investments requires ongoing attention. You can take an active role by taking these steps: Evaluate investments; monitor investments; keep accurate records; and consider tax consequences.

Research Have students research financial planners' certification requirements in your state. Have them write a one-page report of their findings.

As You Read

RELATE

Would you want to manage your own investments or hire a financial planner?

Teaching Activity Have the students set up systems they can use for performing the four steps in managing investments. These systems are to have step-by-step procedures to follow, and students should also create any forms they think might be useful.

Evaluating Investments

Always research and evaluate before you invest so that you can make an informed decision. Suppose that you invest $2,000. With a 5 percent return the first year, you will earn $100. While your money is earning, you also need to continue to evaluate your current investment. Evaluate future investment opportunities as well.

Monitoring Your Investments

Many people forget to keep track of or monitor the value of their investments. Always keep track of the value of your stocks, bonds, or mutual funds by checking price quotations reported on the Internet, in newspapers, and on financial news programs. Keep a chart of the value of your investments to check their progress over time.

Northern Trust Corporation Member FDIC

Caption Answer You should keep records of sources of evaluation information, purchase records including fees paid, records of earnings, and records tracking your investment's value.

▶ **LOOKING AHEAD** Even if an investment company handles your money, always track and evaluate your investments on a regular basis. They will pay off for years to come. *What investment records should you keep?*

Keeping Accurate Records

Accurate recordkeeping helps you notice opportunities to increase your profits or reduce losses. It can also help you decide whether to put more money in a stock, bond, or other investment—or to sell a particular investment. Keep purchase records that list the cost of the investment and commissions or fees you have paid. Also keep the sources of information you used to evaluate an investment. With these records, you will know where to begin your research when it is time to reevaluate the investments you own.

Tax Considerations

It is your responsibility to determine how taxes may affect your investments. The city, state, and federal governments charge various amounts of tax to individuals and businesses for income they earn.

In general, investment income falls into three categories: tax-exempt, tax-deferred, and taxable. **Tax-exempt income** is income that is not taxed. For example, the interest you can receive from most state and municipal bonds is exempt from federal income tax. **Tax-deferred income** is income that is taxed at a later date. The most common type of tax-deferred income is earned from a traditional individual retirement account (IRA). When you withdraw earnings from your IRA, you must pay federal income tax. The 401(k) and 403(b) retirement plans offered by your employer or privately are also tax-deferred. Income from most other investments is taxable.

Dividends, Interest Income, and Rental Income You must report cash dividends on your tax return as ordinary income. You also have to pay tax on the interest from banks, credit unions, and savings and loan associations. In addition, interest you receive from bonds (unless tax-exempt), promissory notes, loans, and U.S. securities must be reported as income. Income from rental property is also taxable.

Capital Gains and Capital Losses A **capital gain** is the profit from the sale of assets such as stocks, bonds, or real estate. Capital gains are taxed according to how long you own an asset—over a short term or a long term.

Under current law, a short-term capital gain is profit you make when you sell an asset owned for 12 months or less. It is taxed as ordinary income. For example, if you are in the 15 percent tax bracket for general income taxes, you will also pay 15 percent tax on your short-term capital gains.

The profit from selling investments owned for more than 12 months is considered a long-term capital gain. Long-term capital gains are usually taxed at the rate of 5 to 15 percent. Investors in low tax brackets are taxed at only 5 percent. As of 2008, these investors pay no tax on long-term capital gains. Some personal property, such as collectibles, is taxed at a higher rate. Examples of collectible assets include rare books and stamp collections. You will learn more about collectibles in Chapter 11.

Common CENTS

A Dollar a Day
Do you know that if you save a dollar a day—less than what you would spend on a soda and a candy bar—and save or invest it at 5 percent interest, in five years you will have more than $2,000? In ten years you will have $4,600! *How much would you have in 40 years?*

Common Cents approximately $45,000

Critical Thinking Ask the students to answer the following question in writing: Why do you think you have to pay taxes on interest and dividends you earn from savings account and investments?

A **capital loss** is the sale of an investment for less than its purchase price. You can subtract up to $3,000 a year in capital losses from your ordinary income. If your losses are greater than $3,000, you can subtract the rest of the loss in later tax years.

Sources of Investment Information

Where can you find information about investments?

Because there is so much investment information available, both complex and basic, you need to be selective. The important thing is to be sure that the source of advice and information that you receive is accurate and reliable.

The Internet and Online Services

As You Read

QUESTION

How can you ensure that online sources of investment information are accurate and reliable?

Question Answer Double check the information using another source, such as *The Wall Street Journal,* perhaps, or a television program dealing specifically with financial data (CNBC, for example). Access only reputable and well-established company Web sites.

The Internet offers a wealth of information on investments with the click of a button. One of the best ways to find what you need is to use a search engine. Search engines are available through many Internet service providers (ISPs), including commercial Internet companies. Just type the key words for your topic into a search engine, and you will get a list of Web sites that provide information on that topic. Most large investment firms have Web sites where you can obtain a variety of information and services:

- Interest rates for certificates of deposit
- Prices of stocks, bonds, and other securities
- Advice on starting an investment program
- Trading of securities through online brokers

Newspapers and News Programs

The financial page of your metropolitan newspaper or *The Wall Street Journal* is another source of investment information that is easy to access. In addition, many radio and television stations broadcast investment market summaries and economic information as part of their regular news programs. Several television channels, such as CNN Fn (Financial), are also dedicated to financial news.

Business and Publications

Teaching Activity Have the students select an article from one of the investment information sources mentioned in this section, write a review of it, and be prepared to share it with the class.

Barron's, BusinessWeek, Forbes, Fortune, Harvard Business Review, and similar business publications provide general news about the economy as well as information about individual companies. Other publications cover specific industries. In addition, magazines, such as *Money*, *Consumer Reports*, *Smart Money*, and *Kiplinger's Personal Finance,* provide information and advice designed to improve your investment skills. In addition, national news magazines often feature stories on the economy and finance.

▲ **IN THE KNOW** Keeping up with financial news helps you track your investments and may help you reach your goals. *Name at least three publications that could help you become a smart investor.*

Caption Answer Answers will vary but may include *Barron's, BusinessWeek, Kiplinger's Personal Finance* among several others.

Government Publications

The United States federal government is also an excellent resource of information—and much of it is free. *The Federal Reserve Bulletin,* published by the Federal Reserve System, and the *Survey of Current Business,* published by the Department of Commerce, are just two sources of useful financial information. You can read articles from both of these publications on the Internet.

Discussion Ask students: Why might it be important to have information from a variety of sources in addition to a company's prospectus when considering an investment.

Corporate Reports

As required by the federal government, any corporation selling new issues of securities must provide investors with a prospectus. A **prospectus** is a document that discloses information about a company's earnings, assets and liabilities, its products or services, a particular stock, and the qualifications of its management. All publicly owned corporations also send investors quarterly reports and annual reports that contain detailed financial data.

Teaching Activity Divide the class into groups of four, and assign one statistical average (see Figure 8.7) to each group. Tell them that for the next month, they are to graph the average and find out if it is increasing or decreasing. At the end of the month, have the groups compare their graphs.

Statistical Averages

You can keep track of the value of your investments by following one or more recognized statistical averages, such as the Standard & Poor's 500 Stock Index or the Dow Jones Industrial Average. These averages are reported daily online and in newspapers. The average indicates whether the category it measures is increasing or decreasing in value. It will not pinpoint the value of a specific investment, but it will show the general direction of stocks, bonds, mutual funds, and other investments. **Figure 8.7** lists some of the most widely used statistical averages.

Figure 8.7 **Statistical Averages for Evaluating Investments**

Statistical Average	Type of Investment
Dow Jones Industrial Average	Stocks
Standard & Poor's 500 Stock Index	Stocks
Value Line Stock Index	Stocks
New York Stock Exchange Index	Stocks on New York Stock Exchange
American Stock Exchange Index	Stocks on American Stock Exchange
NASDAQ Composite Stock Index	Over-the-counter stocks
Lipper Mutual Funds Index	Mutual funds
Dow Jones Bond Average	Corporate bonds
The Wall Street Journal Consumer Rates Index	Interest and finance rates
New Residential Sales Index	Real estate
Dow Jones Spot Market Index	Commodities
Sotheby's Art Sales Index	Art/paintings
Linn's Trends of Stamp Values	Stamps

Trend Watchers You can locate these statistical averages in the newspaper and on the Internet.

How do these averages affect investments?

Caption Answer They indicate if value is increasing or decreasing. These averages are valuable for showing trends, not for specific information about a company.

Investor Services

Many stockbrokers and financial planners mail free newsletters to their clients. In addition, investor services, such as Moody's Investors Service, sell subscription newsletters that are available in print and on the Internet.

Five widely used and useful publications are:

- *Standard & Poor's Stock and Bond Guide*
- *Value Line Investment Survey®*
- *Handbook of Common Stocks* (information on companies)
- *Morningstar Mutual Funds™*
- *Wiesenberger Investment Companies Yearbook* (information on mutual funds)

In addition to these publications, securities exchanges provide information in print and on the Internet. They include the American Stock Exchange, the Chicago Mercantile Exchange, the New York Stock Exchange, and the NASDAQ market. All of these sources of financial information are most often used by professionals. Many individual private investors also refer to them to become well-informed when making investment decisions.

After You Read

REACT

Would it be useful to follow the Dow Jones Industrial Average and/or the Standard and Poor's 500 Stock Index before making investments? Why or why not?

React Answer Yes. Watching these indices will give you the overall trend of the markets in which you will be investing.

Section 8.3 Assessment

See the Teacher Manual for answers.

QUICK CHECK

1. What is a financial planner's role in a personal financial program?
2. What is your role in your personal financial program?
3. What are some sources of financial information?

THINK CRITICALLY

4. Why do you think some people do not keep track of their investments? Give reasons why they should.

USE COMMUNICATION SKILLS

5. **Tax Considerations** Elliott is going to receive capital gains on some stock he just sold. He owned the stock for less than a year and made a profit of $200. He is in the 15 percent tax bracket.

Calculate How much will Elliott pay in capital gains tax on the profits from his stock sale?

SOLVE MONEY PROBLEMS

6. **Finding a Financial Planner** Helene has decided to hire a financial planner. She has to rely on ads and the yellow pages for names because she is new in town. She wants to meet with several people before choosing one.

Write About It Compile a list of specific questions that Helene should ask candidates when she interviews them.

Chapter 8 Review & Activities

See the Teacher Manual for answers.

CHAPTER SUMMARY

- Before investing, set financial goals that are compatible with your values.
- Obtain money to start investing by setting aside funds before you buy other things; by contributing to employer-sponsored retirement plans and savings programs; and by saving gifts of money and unexpected windfalls.
- An investment's safety or degree of risk, income potential, and liquidity are factors to consider before choosing an investment. Also, diversifying your investments is wise.
- Saving and investment alternatives include savings accounts, certificates of deposit, stocks, bonds, some annuities, mutual funds, and real estate.
- Steps in developing a personal investment plan include establishing goals, determining funds needed and funds available, evaluating investments in terms of risk and return, and choosing at least two investments.
- Check your investments for yourself, keep track of them, keep accurate records, and consider the tax consequences of buying and selling.
- A great deal of investment information is available on the Internet, in books, magazines, newspapers, government publications, as well as from individual corporations and investment companies.

Communicating Key Terms

You are a financial planner. One of your clients, who owns a medium-sized company with 75 employees, asks you to speak to her employees to encourage them to participate in the company 401(k) retirement savings plan. Use as many of the terms below as possible in writing your speech.

- emergency fund
- speculative investment
- dividends
- retained earnings
- investment liquidity
- equity capital
- common stock
- preferred stock
- corporate bond
- government bond
- mutual fund
- diversification
- financial planner
- tax-exempt income
- tax-deferred income
- capital gain
- capital loss
- prospectus

Reviewing Key Concepts

1. **Explain** why it is important to have a goal before making investments.
2. **Describe** sources of funds for investing.
3. **Describe** a demographic group that may not prefer investment risk. Describe another demographic group that may be more comfortable with a greater degree of risk.
4. **Compare** the main types of investment alternatives in terms of their risk and liquidity.
5. **Write** an investment plan for yourself.
6. **Describe** the role of the investor in the investment process.
7. **List** four specific sources of financial information.

See the Teacher Manual for answers.

ACADEMIC SKILLS

Economics You should buy insurance and establish an emergency fund before you invest, and you should invest early.

Write About It Write several paragraphs explaining why you should take these steps before investing and how you can do both.

YOUR FINANCIAL FIGURES

Investing Your Money You are evaluating two investments that each require $1,000. One is a municipal bond that pays 9 percent interest annually. The interest is exempt from federal and state taxes. The other is a corporate bond that pays 11 percent interest, but its earnings are subject to 20 percent capital gains tax if kept for less than 12 months, and 15 percent capital gains tax if kept for more than 12 months.

1. **Calculate** (a) Which bond provides the largest return? (b) Does the situation change if you need to sell the bond before 12 months?
2. **Compute** by using spreadsheet software to create scenarios about the circumstances under which each investment gives a bigger return.

REAL-WORLD Application

Connect with Economics Risk associated with investments can be categorized as diversifiable risk and undiversifiable risk. This is one reason mutual funds are so popular—many investors' money is pooled and numerous stocks are purchased. Some of the risk is reduced because you buy a piece of so many different companies. Undiversifiable risks are those over which you have no control, such as the risks described in Section 8.1.

1. **Research** Use an Internet search engine or look in the newspaper or magazine to find descriptions of three mutual funds.
2. **Think Critically** Select one mutual fund of interest to you. Why did you select it?

Internet CONNECTION

401(k) Retirement Savings Many employers offer 401(k) retirement savings plans as an employee benefit. Many companies match a certain percentage of each employee's deposits in the plan.

Log On Use an Internet search engine to find Web sites of two companies you might be interested in working for in the future.

Answer the following questions:

1. Do they offer 401(k) plans profit-sharing or other savings programs?
2. Do your relatives, neighbors, or friends participate in such plans? Why?

BusinessWeek ONLINE

Newsclip: Less Savings Americans do not save as they once did. Weak savings mean fewer investments in the economy, and that contributes to slower economic growth.

Log On Go to **finance07.glencoe.com** and open Chapter 8. Learn more about the different types of investments. Write down what type of investment you would buy and explain why.

WHAT'S YOUR FINANCIAL ID?

ARE YOU A RISK TAKER?

As a general rule, the greater the promised return on an investment, the greater the risk involved. Risk tolerance is your ability to ride the ups and downs of the market without panicking when the value of your investment goes down. This quiz will help you gauge your own risk tolerance. Answer the following questions on a separate sheet of paper:

1. Which best describes your feelings about investing?
   a. Better safe than sorry
   b. Moderation in all things
   c. Nothing ventured, nothing gained

2. Which is most important to you as an investor?
   a. You receive a steady income.
   b. You receive a steady income and growth.
   c. The price of your investments rises rapidly.

3. You won! Which prize would you pick?
   a. $4,000 in cash
   b. A 50 percent chance to win $10,000
   c. A 20 percent chance to win $100,000

4. The stocks you own have dropped 20 percent since the last quarter. What would you do?
   a. Sell the stocks to avoid losing more
   b. Keep the stocks and wait for their value to rebound
   c. Buy more stocks because they are cheaper now

5. The stocks you own have gone up 20 percent since the last quarter. What would you do?
   a. Sell the stocks and take the gains
   b. Keep the stocks and hope the price goes up higher
   c. Buy more stocks because the price may go up higher

6. Would you borrow money to take advantage of a good investment opportunity?
   a. Never   b. Maybe   c. Yes

7. How would you characterize yourself?
   a. I do not like to take risks.
   b. I am a moderate risk taker.
   c. I enjoy taking risks.

Give yourself one point for each question that you answered with "a."
Give yourself two points for each question that you answered with "b."
Give yourself three points for each question that you answered with "c."
If you scored 7–11 points, you're a conservative investor who prefers to minimize financial risks.
If you scored 12–16 points, you're a moderate risk taker.
If you scored 17–21 points, you're comfortable taking risks in pursuit of greater returns.

Source: "Five-Minute Quiz" from *Standard & Poor's Your Financial Future,* ©1996 by The McGraw-Hill Companies.

Accept all reasonable answers that show student effort and an understanding of the concept.

Your Financial Portfolio

Avoiding Future Shock

Mackenzie is already showing signs of being a great scholar at age three. At least that is what her dad, Jasper, thinks. He wants Mackenzie to be able to continue her education, so he has decided to start a college fund for her now. Jasper has $2,000 to start and has decided to invest $175 a month. He has developed an investment plan to reach his goal.

Jasper figures he has 15 years to invest and will invest in an aggressive stock mutual fund. He feels that the diversity of a mutual fund will be safer and give greater returns. Jasper has plenty of time to take a fair amount of risk and is comfortable that he will have Mackenzie's college money when she needs it.

Goal Tending

Established goal:	College	
Amount of money needed:	$50,000	
Initial amount to invest:	$2,000	
Possible investment alternatives:	(1) savings account (2) CD (3) money market account	(4) mutual fund (5) stock
Risk factor for each alternative:	(1) low risk (2) low risk (3) low risk	(4) moderate risk (5) high risk
Expected return on each alternative:	(1) 1%–3% (2) 4%–5% (3) 4%–6%	(4) 6%–10% (5) 6%–12%
Top 3 choices:	(1) mutual fund (2) stock	(3) CD
Final choice:	**mutual fund**	

Prepare

Choose a short-term or long-term financial goal you would like to reach. On a separate sheet of paper, prepare an investment plan for yourself using the same guidelines as shown above. Research some of the available investments and come up with your own investment alternatives. Explain the reasons for your final choice.

Accept all reasonable answers that show student effort and an understanding of the concept.

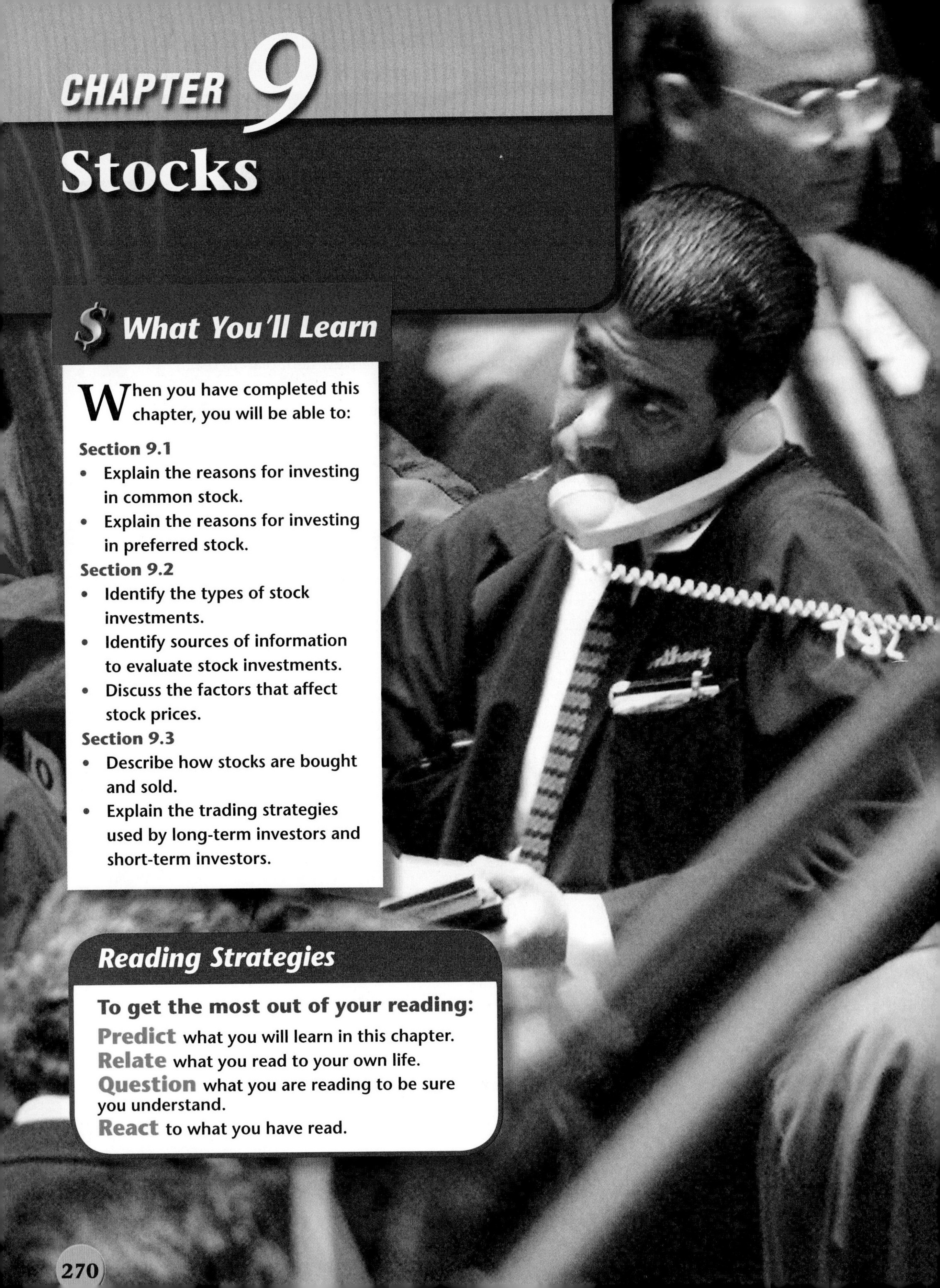

CHAPTER 9
Stocks

$ What You'll Learn

When you have completed this chapter, you will be able to:

Section 9.1
- Explain the reasons for investing in common stock.
- Explain the reasons for investing in preferred stock.

Section 9.2
- Identify the types of stock investments.
- Identify sources of information to evaluate stock investments.
- Discuss the factors that affect stock prices.

Section 9.3
- Describe how stocks are bought and sold.
- Explain the trading strategies used by long-term investors and short-term investors.

Reading Strategies

To get the most out of your reading:

Predict what you will learn in this chapter.
Relate what you read to your own life.
Question what you are reading to be sure you understand.
React to what you have read.

In the **Real** World . . .

Shari Rogers thought investing in stocks was something only older or wealthy people did. However, thanks to the Internet, she has discovered that anyone can have access to stock information. She has been considering opening an account with an online broker. She feels she understands the risks involved, but she is still unsure of how to pick a stock. Before Shari can begin to successfully trade stocks, she will learn how to evaluate a stock's chances for profit. She also needs to determine if she believes in the products and policies of the companies in which she would like to invest. Then Shari can choose a stock and start building a balanced portfolio.

As You Read *Consider why you should research stocks before you buy them.*

Lesson Plan See the Teacher Manual for the Chapter 9 planning guide and lesson plan.

ASK STANDARD & POOR'S

Stock Certificates

Q: My parents gave me stock certificates for a graduation present. Is it a good idea to put them in a safe-deposit box and save them for retirement?

A: A safe-deposit box is a good way to store important documents, but a better option for stock certificates would be to place them in a brokerage account with a bank or brokerage firm. This will make it easier for you to buy or sell shares of these or other stocks. Also, you will receive statements showing the value of your shares and dividends.

Ask Yourself Why do you think it is easier to buy and sell shares of stock if you have a brokerage account?

@ Go to **finance07.glencoe.com** to complete the Standard & Poor's Financial Focus activity.

Section 9.1

Focus on Reading

Read to Learn

- How to explain the reasons for investing in common stock.
- How to explain the reasons for investing in preferred stock.

Main Idea

Recognizing the reasons for investing in common and preferred stock will enable you to make the best investments for your financial situation.

Key Terms

- securities
- private corporation
- public corporation
- par value

Before You Read

PREDICT

What do you think it means to own stock in a company?

Springboard Ask the students why they think many people are reluctant to invest in stocks. Then ask what they might need to know to make sound stock investment decisions.

Common and Preferred Stocks

Common Stock

Why do companies offer common stock?

Investors have a choice of **securities**, which are all of the investments—stocks, bonds, mutual funds, options, and commodities—that are bought and sold on the stock market.

When investors buy shares of stock in a company, the company uses that money to make and sell its products, fund its operations, and expand. If the company earns a profit, the stockholders (owners of shares of stock in the company) earn a return, or gain, on their investment. People buy and sell stocks for one reason: They want larger returns than they can get from more conservative investments, such as savings accounts or government bonds.

Before you invest your money in stock, it might help you to understand why corporations issue common stock.

Why Corporations Issue Common Stock

Companies issue common stock to raise money to start up their businesses and then to help pay for ongoing activities. A **private corporation**, or a closely held corporation, is a company that issues stock to a small group of people. A private corporation's stocks are not traded openly in stock markets. On the other hand, a **public corporation**, or publicly held corporation, is one that sells its shares openly in stock markets, where anyone can buy them. Some large corporations, such as AT&T, General Electric, Procter & Gamble, and General Motors, have thousands or even millions of stockholders.

A Form of Equity Because corporations do not have to repay the money a stockholder pays for stock, they are able to use that money to fund their ongoing activities. For the stockholder to make money on the stock, he or she sells the stock to another investor. The price is set according to how much the buyer is willing to pay. As the demand for a certain company's stock increases or decreases, the price goes up or down accordingly. News on expected sales revenues, earnings, company expansions, or mergers with other companies can make demand for the stock go up or down.

Dividends Not Mandatory It is up to the corporate board of directors, a group of individuals elected to make the major decisions for the corporation, to decide whether any profits will be paid to stockholders as dividends. Companies that are growing quickly might pay low or no dividends. They may decide to use profits to expand the company even further. Of course, any company's board of directors can reduce or even stop dividend payments when a corporation has a bad year.

▲ **UNDERSTANDING STOCKS** Investors buy stocks in the hopes of earning a large return on their investments. *What causes the demand for stock to change?*

Caption Answer News about expected revenues, earnings, company expansions, and mergers cause stock values to change.

Why Investors Purchase Common Stock

Most investors purchase common stock to make money in three different ways: They profit when they receive dividends, when the dollar value of their stock appreciates (increases), and when the stock splits and increases in dollar value.

Income from Dividends A corporation's board members do not have to pay dividends, but they do want to keep stockholders happy because those same stockholders are funding the corporation's business. As a result, board members often vote to pay dividends if possible, unless they decide to place the profits back into the company.

With a cash dividend, each common stockholder receives an equal amount per share. Most dividends are paid quarterly, or every three months. Some companies that have large increases in earnings might declare a special cash dividend at the end of the year. You might also receive a dividend of company stock—or of company products, though this is very unusual.

Appreciation of Stock Value If the market value of the stock increases, or appreciates, you must decide whether to sell your stock at the higher price or continue to hold on to it. If you sell, the difference between the price that you paid and the price at which you sell is your profit. Of course, if the value of the stock falls, then your return will be less than your original investment. **Figure 9.1** on page 274 provides tips for tracking your stock investment. If a company's board decides to place profits back into the company, it might reward its stockholders through dollar appreciation of stock value instead of dividends.

Motivating Students Have the students look at the stock pages of a newspaper. Ask them if they have any idea what these pages say. Then ask if they would like to understand if understanding is step one in learning to invest.

Increased Value from Stock Splits Your profits can also increase through a stock split. A stock split occurs when the shares of stock owned by existing stockholders are divided into a larger number of shares.

Teaching Activity Have students select from the newspaper a stock to track for two weeks, graphing the last trade price each day. Students are to see if they can discover, through research or reading the paper, reasons for any major changes in the stock price.

For example, in a two-for-one stock split, the corporation doubles the number of outstanding shares. Suppose that a corporation has 10,000 shares of stock valued at $50 a share. If the corporation splits its stock, the value of each share decreases to $25, but the number of outstanding shares increases to 20,000. If you owned 200 shares before the split, you would own 400 shares after it.

	Before	After
Shares issued	$10,000	$20,000
Value	50	25
Your shares	200	400
Your value	$10,000	$10,000

Research Assign specific stocks to students and have them research how many times they have split since the companies went public. The students are to determine if the stock's market value increased after the stock split. They should also decide when would have been a good time to purchase this stock.

Why do corporations split their stock? Often the management believes that the stock should be trading within an ideal price range. If the market value is a lot higher than this range, a stock split brings the market value back into line. The lower price of stocks after they are split often attracts more investors. As a result, the price starts to rise again. The public wants to buy because of the belief that most corporations split their stock only when the company's financial future looks very good. Be aware that a stock's market value is not guaranteed to go up after a stock split.

Figure 9.1 **Tracking Your Stock Investments**

1. **Monitor.**
   Graph the dollar value of your stock on a daily or weekly basis.

2. **Watch the financials.**
   Continually evaluate the company's current sales and profits and those projected for the future. Compare its progress to the performance of other companies in the same industry. If it can not compete, sell.

3. **Track the products.**
   Poor-quality products or a lack of new or up-to-date products can make the value of a company's stock drop.

4. **Watch the economy.**
   The inflation rate, the state of the overall economy, and other economic factors can affect your company's stock price.

5. **Be patient.**
   If you think that you have bought into a good company, hang on. Over time, your investment will usually increase in value.

Evaluating Stocks By keeping up with information about the companies that issue stock you own, you are more likely to increase the return on your investment.

Why is patience important in investing?

Caption Answer Answers may include: (1) You can see the market value increase over time; and (2) you will earn greater dividends over time.

Voting Rights and Control of the Company In addition to the profit that stockholders may make on their investments, they are also given certain rights in return for the money they invest. For example, a corporation is required by law to hold a yearly meeting at which stockholders can vote on company business. Stockholders usually get one vote for each share they own.

Some states require that corporations offer existing stockholders a preemptive right. A preemptive right gives current stockholders the right to buy any new stock a corporation issues before its stock is offered to the public. By buying more shares, a stockholder can keep the same proportion of ownership in the company. This can be important when a corporation is small and control is critical.

As You Read

RELATE

Imagine that you own stock in a small Web design firm. Describe a situation where preemptive rights would benefit you.

Discussion Discuss with the class the value of stockholder voting rights. As a stockholder, do your votes matter? Do you think stockholders vote on important things or just to re-elect the board of directors per company advice?

Preferred Stock

Is preferred stock preferable?

You could buy preferred stock in addition to, or instead of, common stock. Remember from Chapter 8 that preferred stock gives the owner the advantage of receiving cash dividends before common stockholders receive any cash dividends. If a company is struggling financially, then the preferred stockholder might get the dividends.

Preferred stockholders should know the amount of the dividend they will receive. It is either a specific amount of money or a percentage of the par value of the stock. The **par value** is an assigned dollar value that is printed on a stock certificate. If the par value of a stock is $30 and the dividend rate is 5 percent, then the dollar amount of the dividend is $1.50 per share ($30 X 5% or .05 = $1.50). Unlike market value, par value does not change.

Why Corporations Issue Preferred Stock

Few corporations use preferred stock as a way of raising money. However, for some companies, it is another method of financing which may attract more conservative investors who do not want to buy common stock. Preferred stockholders receive limited voting rights, and they usually vote only if the corporation issuing the stock is in financial trouble.

Why Investors Purchase Preferred Stock

Preferred stock is considered a "middle investment." The yield on preferred stock is generally lower than the yield on corporate bonds but higher than the yield on common stock. Preferred stock is considered a safer investment than common stock, but not as safe as bonds. People who want a steady source of income often buy preferred stock. However, preferred stocks lack the potential for growth that common stocks offer. As a result, preferred stocks are not considered a good investment for most people.

TechByte

Playing Games One of the best ways to learn about how the stock market works without risking any of your money is to play a stock market simulation game. In a simulation game, players work in teams and create a stock portfolio using virtual money. Based on their research of market trends, economic conditions, and business news, the teams select and trade common or preferred stocks. Portfolios "earn" interest and "pay" commissions—and make and lose virtual money.

@ Read a review of stock market simulation games and list those you would like to play through **finance07.glencoe.com**.

As You Read

QUESTION

Why might it be rare for corporations to offer a participation feature to their stockholders?

Question Answer Accept all reasonable answers.

To make preferred stocks more attractive to investors, some corporations may offer cumulative preferred stock, convertible preferred stock, or a participation feature.

Cumulative Preferred Stock Cumulative preferred stock is stock whose unpaid dividends build up and must be paid before any cash dividend is paid to the common stockholders. This means that if a corporation decides to omit one or more dividend payments to preferred stockholders, people who hold cumulative preferred stock will still receive those dividend payments during a later payment period.

Convertible Preferred Stock Convertible preferred stock is stock that can be exchanged for a specific number of shares of common stock. This feature provides an investor with the safety of preferred stock and the possibility of greater returns through conversion to common stock.

Participation Feature Some corporations offer a participation feature, which allows preferred stockholders to share in the corporation's earnings with the common stockholders. After a required dividend is paid to preferred stockholders and a stated dividend is paid to common stockholders, the remainder of earnings is shared by preferred and common stockholders. This feature is rare.

Critical Thinking Ask students to write a short essay discussing whether they would be more likely to buy preferred or common stock, and why.

Section 9.1 Assessment

See the Teacher Manual for answers.

QUICK CHECK

1. Why do corporations issue common stock?
2. Why do investors purchase common stock?
3. Why do investors purchase preferred stock?

THINK CRITICALLY

4. Justify a corporation's decision to split its stock when the stock price has risen significantly.

USE COMMUNICATION SKILLS

5. **Part Owners** Investors purchase common stock as a way to increase their income. As stockholders, they earn the right to vote on company business.

   Write About It Write a paragraph that tells why a stockholder might wish to exercise his or her voting rights.

SOLVE MONEY PROBLEMS

6. **Perks of Preferred Stock** Kwame's grandmother recently gave him 25 shares of preferred stock. Kwame would like to figure out the actual dollar amount of the dividend, which is a percentage of the par value of the stock.

   Calculate According to the stock certificates that Kwame's grandmother gave to him, the par value of each share is $45 and the dividend rate is 6 percent. What is the total dollar amount that Kwame should receive each year?

Section 9.2

Evaluating Stocks

Types of Stock Investments

How are stocks classified?

Financial professionals classify most stocks into the following categories: blue-chip stocks, income stocks, growth stocks, cyclical stocks, defensive stocks, large-cap stocks, small-cap stocks, and penny stocks.

Blue-Chip Stocks

A **blue-chip stock** is considered a safe investment that generally attracts conservative investors. These stocks are issued by the strongest and most respected companies, such as AT&T, General Electric, and Kellogg. If you are interested in a blue-chip stock, look for a company that shows leadership in an industry, a history of stable earnings, and consistency in the payment of dividends.

Income Stocks

An **income stock** pays higher-than-average dividends compared to other stock issues. The buyers of preferred stock are also attracted to this type of common stock because the dividends are predictable. Stocks issued by companies such as Bristol-Myers Squibb and Dow Chemical are classified as income stocks. This is also the type of stock issued by gas and electric companies.

Focus on Reading

Read to Learn

- How to identify the types of stock investments.
- How to identify sources of information to evaluate stock investments.
- How to discuss the factors that affect stock prices.

Main Idea

Knowing how to evaluate, buy, and sell stocks helps you increase the value of your investments.

Key Terms

- blue-chip stock
- income stock
- growth stock
- cyclical stock
- defensive stock
- large-cap stock
- capitalization
- small-cap stock
- penny stock
- bull market
- bear market
- current yield
- total return
- earnings per share
- price-earnings (PE) ratio

Caption Answer Blue-chip stocks are considered safe investments: Those companies are very large industry leaders with steady earnings.

◀ **CLASSIFYING STOCKS** This corporation issues blue-chip stocks. *Why do conservative investors like blue-chip stocks?*

▶ ECONOMY DEPENDENT When the economy is doing well, people have more money to spend, which allows the economy to grow even more. *What kind of stock is most closely linked with the state of the economy?*

Caption Answer cyclical stock

Before You Read

PREDICT

What type of stock do you think would be best for a person who is just beginning to make investments?

Springboard Have the students name ways they can research stock to make wise buying decisions. Write their suggestions on the board.

Motivating Students Write column headings on the board: Income Stock, Growth Stock, Cyclical Stock, and Defensive Stock. Ask the students what types of investors would buy each of these, and write their answers on the board.

Growth Stocks

A **growth stock** is issued by a corporation whose potential earnings may be higher than the average earnings predicted for all the corporations in the country. Stocks issued by these corporations generally do not pay dividends. Look for signs that the company is engaged in activities that produce higher earnings and sales revenues: building new facilities; introducing new, high-quality products; or conducting recognized research and development. Growth companies in the early 2000s included Home Depot and Southwest Airlines.

Cyclical Stocks

A **cyclical stock** has a market value that tends to reflect the state of the economy. When the economy is improving, the market value of a cyclical stock usually goes up. During an economic decline, the market value of a cyclical stock may decrease. This is because the products and services of these companies are linked directly to the activities of a strong economy. Investors try to buy these stocks when they are still inexpensive, just before the economy starts to improve. Then they seek to sell them just before the economy declines. Stocks issued by Ford and Centex (a construction firm) are considered cyclical stocks.

Defensive Stocks

A **defensive stock** is a stock that remains stable during declines in the economy. The companies that issue such stocks have steady earnings and can continue dividend payments even in periods of economic decline. Many blue-chip stocks and income stocks, such as those issued by Procter & Gamble, are defensive stocks.

Large-Cap and Small-Cap Stocks

A **large-cap stock** is stock from a corporation that has issued a large number of shares of stock and has a large amount of *cap*italization. **Capitalization** is the total amount of stocks and bonds issued by a corporation. The stocks listed in the Dow Jones Industrial Averages, a stock indicator which measures the overall condition of the stock market, are typically large-cap stocks. These stocks appeal to conservative investors because they are considered secure.

Teaching Activity Divide the students into groups of four. Have each group make a poster which graphically displays large-cap, small-cap, and penny stocks, and delineates the differences between them. Have the students vote on the best posters, and display two or three in the room.

STANDARD & POOR'S

Global Financial Landscape

Standard and Poor's publishes the globally recognized S&P 500® financial index. It also gathers financial statistics, information, and news, and analyzes this data for international businesses, governments, and individuals to help them guide their financial decisions.

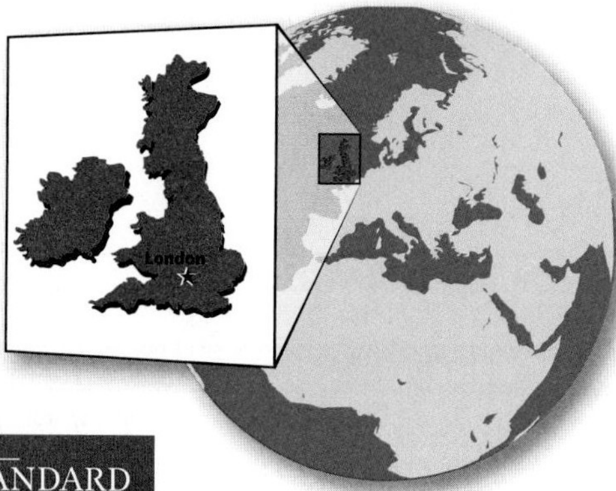

UNITED KINGDOM

In 1698, the London Stock Exchange (LSE) got its start at Jonathan's Coffee House, located in London's bustling Change Alley. The founders created a simple list entitled "The Course of the Exchange and Other Things," which announced stock and commodity prices to the local traders. Today, more than 300 years later, the LSE lists more than 2,700 companies—from high profile to high tech—that are worth a total of over $2.7 billion. The LSE has become Europe's largest stock exchange and one of the world's most famous. It is headquartered close to where it originated, at the heart of London's financial district. Displayed on the stock exchange building's exterior is the LSE's coat of arms, which boasts the Latin motto *Dictum Meum Pactum,* which means "My Word is My Bond."

STANDARD & POOR'S

DATABYTES

Capital	London
Population	59,200,000
Languages	English, Welsh, and Scottish form of Gaelic
Currency	British pound
Gross Domestic Product (GDP)	$1.66 trillion (2003 est.)
GDP per capita	$27,700

Industry: Tools, electric power equipment, automated equipment, railroad equipment, and shipbuilding

Agriculture: Cereals, oilseed, potatoes, vegetables, cattle, and fish

Exports: Manufactured goods, fuels, chemicals, food, beverages, and tobacco

Natural Resources: Coal, crude oil, natural gas, tin, limestone

Think Globally

Do you think the LSE lists large-cap stocks? Why or why not?

See the Teacher Manual for answer.

As You Read

RELATE

What type of stock would you buy? Why?

Research Have students use the newspaper or the Internet to select penny stocks. Ask them to find as much information about the company as possible, and then track the stock's activity for a week. They are to write up the results of their work, creating a graph to show the stock's activity, and assessing whether they would invest in that stock.

A **small-cap stock** is a stock issued by a company with a capitalization of $500 million or less. Since these stocks are issued by smaller, less-established companies, they are considered to be a higher investment risk.

Penny Stocks

A **penny stock** typically sells for less than $1 a share, although it can sell for as much as $10 a share. These stocks are issued by new companies or companies whose sales are very unsteady. The prices of these stocks can go up and down wildly. It is difficult to keep track of a penny stock's performance because information about them is hard to find. Penny stocks should be purchased only by investors who understand the risks.

Sources for Evaluating Stocks

How do you assess a stock investment?

There are many sources where you can find information about stocks before making investment decisions. Some sources include: newspapers, the Internet, stock advisory services, and corporate news publications.

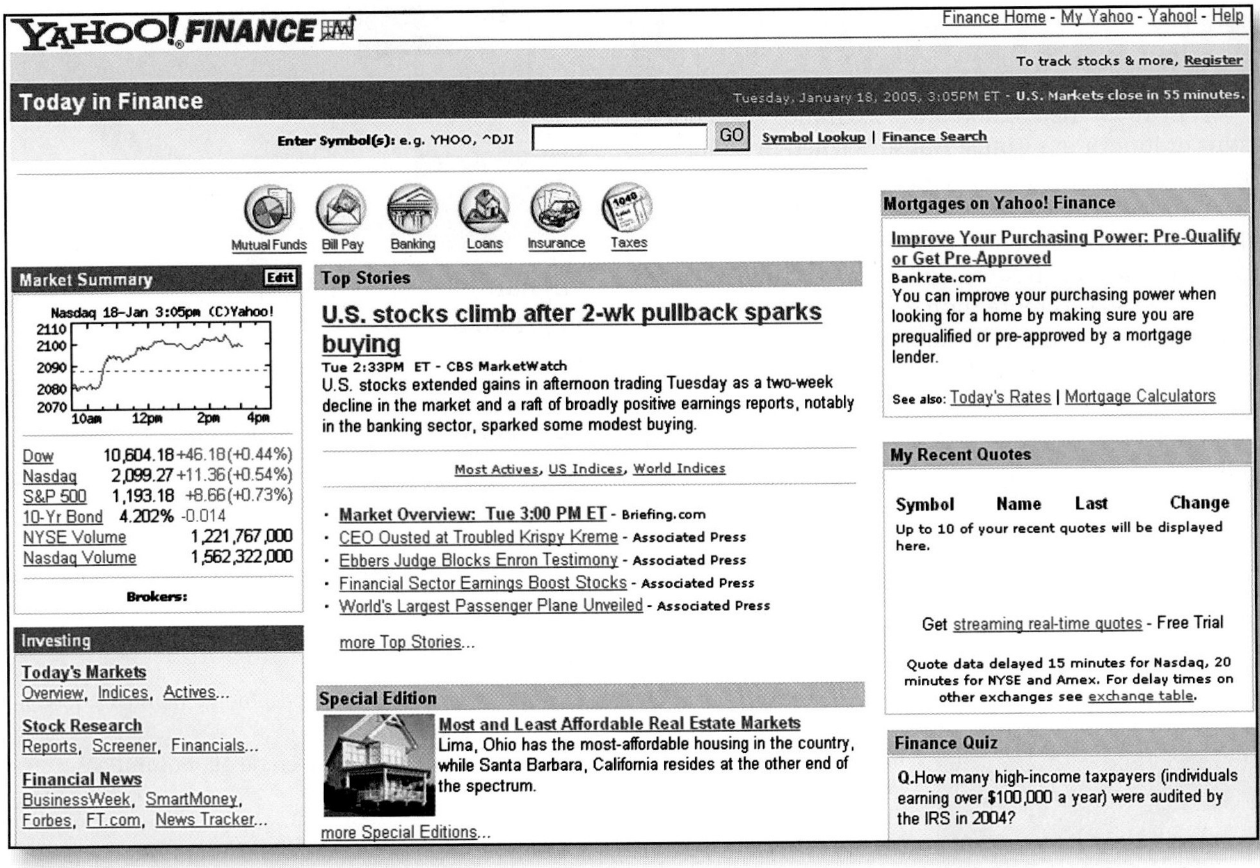

▲ **UTILIZING THE INTERNET** This search engine is one example of the many Web sites that can be used to find financial information. *What Web sites would help you find up-to-date information about a corporation's financial status?* **Caption Answer** Answers will vary but should mention the corporation's home page.

Newspapers

Most major newspapers have financial sections that contain information about stocks that are listed on major stock exchanges, such as the New York Stock Exchange (NYSE) and the American Stock Exchange (AMEX). Newspapers may also cover stocks of local interest. **Figure 9.2** illustrates the detailed information provided in *The Wall Street Journal* about common stock.

Critical Thinking In a brief essay, have students answer the following questions: Where would you research a stock before buying? Would you use more than one source? What kind of stock will you look for (i.e., income, growth, etc.)? Should you track and graph a stock's activity before buying? Why or why not? If so, for how long? What would make you consider selling it?

The Internet

Today most corporations have their own Web sites. The information may be more up to date and detailed than material from the corporation's printed publications.

You can also use search engines to find information about investing in stocks. Sites provide general financial news and specific information about a company and its stock's performance.

Figure 9.2 Common Stock Information in *The Wall Street Journal*

Highest price paid for one share of Mattel during the past 52 weeks: $19.79

Lowest price paid for one share of Mattel in the past 52 weeks: $15.94

Name of the company: Mattel

Ticker symbol or letter that identifies a stock for trading: **MAT**

Number of shares of Mattel traded during the day, expressed in hundreds of shares: 1,056,700

Ytd % Chg	52-Week Hi	Lo	Stock (Sym)	Div	Yld %	PE	Vol 100s	Close	Net Chg
–3.1	19.79	15.94	Mattel **MAT**	.45f	2.4	16	10567	18.88	–0.01
–3.3	32.24	16.95	Mavrck Tube **MVK**			7	4641	29.31	.56
.04	41.24	26.35	Maximus **MMS**			18	958	31.01	

YTD % change reflects the stock price change for the calendar year to date: Mattel's stock price has decreased 3.1% since January 1.

Projected annual dividend for next year based on the amount of the firm's last dividend: $0.45

Price-earnings (PE) ratio: 16

Price paid in the close transaction of the day: $18.88

Difference between the price paid for the last share traded today and for the last share traded on the previous day: –$0.01

Yield percentage, or the percentage of return based on the dividend and current price of the stock: $0.45 ÷ 18.88 = 2.4%

Source: Republished with permission of Dow Jones, Inc., from *The Wall Street Journal*, January 7, 2005; permission conveyed through Copyright Clearance Center, Inc.

Reading Financial News Many major newspapers offer a wealth of financial information.

What is represented in the column "Net Chg"?

Caption Answer "Net Change" is the difference between the price paid for the last share traded today and the price of the last share traded yesterday.

Document Detective

Learn to identify and understand the standard financial documents you will use in the real world.

See the Teacher Manual for answers.

Investigate: A Stock Confirmation Report

A stock confirmation report contains the following information:

- Name and address of the stock owner
- Account number
- Name of the stock purchased or sold
- Price of the stock
- Number of shares held
- Commission and fees

Your Motive: When you buy or sell stock, you will receive a confirmation report that the purchase or sale has occurred. Be sure to check that the transaction was completed correctly. Check to see that the correct number of shares were purchased or sold, and that the fees for completing the transaction are reasonable.

Taylor Financial Services

175 Montrose Avenue
Cincinnati, OH 52549

Account Number: DR 199704

Hector Gonzales
3482 Mayfair Lane
Cincinnati, OH 52546

Trade date:	04/29/20--
Date processed:	04/29/20--
Payment Date:	05/04/20--

SOLD:

Quantity	Description	Price	Gross Amount	Commission	Fees	Total Amount
160	Analog Devices	$43.90	$7,024.00	$159.20	$5.42	$6,859.38

Key Points: When you own stock, there will be times when you want to sell or buy more. You may also want to purchase stocks from other companies as well. When you make these transactions, you will receive a stock confirmation report that will help you keep track of all your stock transactions.

Find the Solutions

1. Who performed the stock transaction?
2. Did Hector purchase or sell stock?
3. How many shares were involved in the transaction?
4. Why is there a difference between the gross amount and the total amount Hector received?
5. When will Hector be sent his money?

Stock Advisory Services

In addition to newspapers and the Internet, you can use stock advisory services to evaluate potential stock investments. Many stock advisory services, such as Moody's Investors Service, charge fees for their information, which can vary from simple alphabetic listings to detailed financial reports. As mentioned in Chapter 8, three widely used sources for information on companies' stock are *Standard & Poor's Stock and Bond Guide, Value Line Investment Survey,* and Mergent's *Handbook of Common Stocks.*

As shown in **Figure 9.3** on page 284, basic financial report from *Mergent's Handbook of Common Stocks* consists of six sections. One section contains information about stock prices and capitalization, earnings, and dividends. A background section, "Business," provides a detailed description of the company's major operations, such as the products they produce. A third section, "Recent Developments," offers current information about net income and sales revenue. A "Prospects" section describes the company's outlook, or prospects for the future. The "Annual Financial Data" section provides important statistics on the company for a specific length of time in the past. A final section lists information such as important officers in the corporation and the location of its headquarters.

As You Read

QUESTION

What are some sources for evaulating stock?

Question Answer newspapers, the Internet, stock advisory services, and corporate news publications

Teaching Activity Divide students into groups of four. Give them copies of reports from three stock advisory services. Have each group prepare a brochure to promote one of the companies; the brochure should highlight the quality information the service offers and tell potential investors why it is a good idea to use such a service.

▲ **ONCE A YEAR** An annual report can provide a great deal of information for investors. *How can you get a copy of an annual report?*

Caption Answer Call, write, or e-mail the company's headquarters. Some companies post the reports on their home pages.

Figure 9.3 A Basic Financial Report

REEBOK INTERNATIONAL, LTD.

EXCH.	SYM.	REC. PRICE	P/E RATIO	YLD.	MKT. CAP.	RANGE (52-WK.)	'01 Y/E PR.
NYSE	RBK	27.68 (2/28/02)	16.6	...	$1.59 bill.	35.75 - 18.50	26.50

LOWER MEDIUM GRADE. THE COMPANY EXPECTS IMPROVED MARKET CONDITIONS TO OCCUR IN THE SECOND HALF OF 2002.

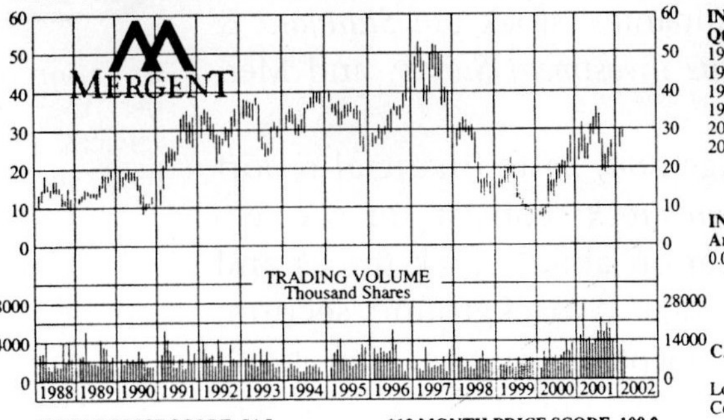

*7 YEAR PRICE SCORE 84.5 *12 MONTH PRICE SCORE 109.0

*NYSE COMPOSITE INDEX=100

INTERIM EARNINGS (Per Share):

Qtr.	Mar.	June	Sept.	Dec.
1996	0.64	0.27	0.75	0.35
1997	0.69	0.35	1.26	0.01
1998	d0.06	0.11	0.50	d0.13
1999	0.32	0.08	0.06	d0.26
2000	0.56	0.19	0.56	0.11
2001	0.68	0.24	0.66	0.09

INTERIM DIVIDENDS (Per Share):

Amt.	Decl.	Ex.	Rec.	Pay.
0.075Q	7/25/96	9/09/96	9/11/96	10/02/96

Dividend Payment Suspended

CAPITALIZATION (12/31/00):

	($000)	(%)
Long-Term Debt	345,015	36.2
Common & Surplus	607,863	63.8
Total	952,878	100.0

BUSINESS:

Reebok International, Ltd. is a worldwide company engaged primarily in the design and marketing of sports and fitness products, including footwear and apparel, as well as the design and marketing of footwear and apparel for casual use. The Company has four major brand groups. The Reebok Division designs, produces and markets sports, fitness and casual footwear, apparel and accessories under the REEBOK® brand. The Rockport Company designs, produces and distributes specially-engineered comfort footwear for men and women worldwide under the ROCKPORT® brand. Ralph Lauren Footwear Co., Inc., a subsidiary of the Company, is responsible for footwear and certain apparel sold under the RALPH LAUREN® and POLO SPORT® brands. The Greg Norman Division produces a range of men's apparel and accessories marketed under the GREG NORMAN name and logo.

RECENT DEVELOPMENTS:

For the year ended 12/31/01, net income grew 26.9% to $102.7 million from $80.9 million in the previous year. Net sales increased 4.5% to $2.99 billion versus $2.87 billion in the prior year. U.S. footwear sales rose to $930.5 million from $925.1 million a year earlier, while U.S. apparel sales climbed 68.1% to $395.1 million. International sales declined slightly to $1.17 billion versus $1.18 billion in 2000. Sales from the Rockport division fell 5.4% to $399.6 million. For the quarter ended 12/31/01, net income dropped 17.7% to $5.1 million from $6.2 million in the year-earlier period. Net sales rose 6.8% to $664.6 million versus $622.5 million the year before.

PROSPECTS:

RBK continues to experience weakness in footwear sales in the United States as retailers ordered less replacement inventory. However, U.S. apparel sales are being fueled by licensing deals with the NBA and the NFL. Looking ahead, RBK will introduce a new group of street-inspired products called Rbk. The new collection will be aimed at young male consumers. In addition, RBK intends to continue its focus on the young women's market and its Classic print campaign. Going forward, RBK expects earnings to rise in 2002, with the majority of the increase occurring in the second half as general economic and market conditions improve.

ANNUAL FINANCIAL DATA:

FISCAL YEAR	TOT. REVS. ($mill.)	NET INC. ($mill.)	TOT. ASSETS ($mill.)	OPER. PROFIT %	NET PROFIT %	RET. ON EQUITY %	RET. ON ASSETS %	CURR. RATIO	EARN. PER SH. $	CASH FL. PER SH. $	TANG. BK. VAL. $	DIV. PER SH. $	PRICE RANGE	AVG. P/E RATIO	AVG. YIELD %
p12/31/01	**2,992.9**	**102.7**							**1.66**			...	**35.75 - 18.50**	**16.3**	...
12/31/00	2,865.2	80.9	1,463.0	5.9	2.8	13.3	5.5	2.5	1.40	2.20	9.45	...	28.33 - 6.94	12.6	...
12/31/99	2,891.2	[1] 11.0	1,564.1	4.5	0.4	2.1	0.7	2.0	[1] 0.20	1.06	8.17	...	22.75 - 7.81	76.4	...
12/31/98	3,205.4	[1] 23.9	1,739.6	3.8	0.7	4.6	1.4	2.2	[1] 0.42	1.26	8.05	...	33.19 - 12.56	54.5	...
12/31/97	3,637.4	[1] 135.1	1,756.1	7.4	3.7	26.6	7.7	2.5	[1] 2.32	3.13	8.27	...	52.88 - 27.63	17.3	...
12/31/96	3,482.9	139.0	1,786.2	7.7	4.0	36.4	7.8	2.8	2.00	2.65	5.58	0.30	45.25 - 25.38	17.7	0.8
12/31/95	3,484.6	[1] 164.8	1,656.2	10.5	4.7	18.4	10.0	3.1	[1] 2.07	2.57	11.11	0.30	39.63 - 24.13	15.4	0.9
12/31/94	3,287.6	254.5	1,649.5	13.0	7.7	25.7	15.4	2.6	3.02	3.46	11.05	0.30	40.25 - 28.38	11.4	0.9
12/31/93	2,893.9	[1] 223.4	1,391.7	13.6	7.7	26.4	16.1	2.8	[1] 2.53	2.93	8.99	0.30	38.63 - 23.00	12.2	1.0
12/31/92	3,060.6	[1] 114.8	1,345.3	14.0	3.8	13.7	8.5	2.7	[1] 1.24	1.72	8.23	0.30	35.63 - 21.38	23.0	1.1

Statistics are as originally reported. [1] Incl. non-recurr. chrg. 1999, $61.6 mill.; 1998, $35.0 mill.; 1997, $58.2 mill.; 1995, $72.1 mill.; 1993, $8.4 mill.; 1992, $155.0 mill.

OFFICERS:
P. B. Fireman, Chmn., C.E.O.
J. Margolis, Pres., C.O.O.
K. I. Watchmaker, Exec. V.P., C.F.O.
INVESTOR CONTACT: Neil Kerman, V.P., Finance, (781) 401-7152
PRINCIPAL OFFICE: 1895 J.W. Foster Boulevard, Canton, MA 02021

TELEPHONE NUMBER: (781) 401-5000
FAX: (781) 401-7402
WEB: www.reebok.com
NO. OF EMPLOYEES: 6,000 (approx.)
SHAREHOLDERS: 6,335
ANNUAL MEETING: In May
INCORPORATED: MA, July, 1979

INSTITUTIONAL HOLDINGS:
No. of Institutions: 204
Shares Held: 39,908,808
% Held: 67.8
INDUSTRY: Rubber and plastics footwear (SIC: 3021)
TRANSFER AGENT(S): American Stock Transfer & Trust Company, New York, NY

Source: *Handbook of Common Stocks,* © 2002 by Mergent, Inc. Reprinted by permission.

Up and Down This financial report from Mergent's *Handbook of Common Stocks* provides information about Reebock International, Ltd.

What is reported in the lower section of the graph?

Caption Answer The "Trading Volume" section shows how many shares of Reebok were traded over 15 years.

▲ **BULL AND BEAR MARKETS** Knowing the current market is important when you make decisions as an investor *How does a bull market affect stocks?*

Caption Answer A bull market increases the value of many stocks and the stock market as a whole.

Corporate News Publications

Annual and quarterly reports offer a summary of a corporation's activities as well as detailed financial information. You do not have to be a stockholder to get an annual report. Simply call, write, or e-mail to request a copy from the company's headquarters. Financial publications such as *Barron's, BusinessWeek, Fortune, Kiplinger's Personal Finance, Money,* and *Smart Money* also provide information about specific companies.

Factors that Influence the Price of Stock

How would you determine whether your investment is increasing or decreasing in dollar value?

Discussion Discuss with students the kind of news they might be reading if the market is bearish, and what they might be reading if the market is bullish.

When you are deciding whether it is the right time to buy or sell a particular stock, you must first consider the overall condition of the stock market. A **bull market** is a market condition that occurs when investors are optimistic about the economy and buy stocks. Because of the greater demand for stock, the value of many stocks and the value of the stock market as a whole increases. A **bear market** is a market condition that occurs when investors are pessimistic about the economy and sell stocks. As a result of this decline in demand, the value of individual stocks and the stock market as a whole decreases.

Next you should consider the company's profits, losses, and other numerical measures of its financial situation.

WebQuest

Nest Egg
How do you tell where stocks are headed? When is the best time to buy or sell a stock? Making good decisions about when to buy and when to sell is difficult because it involves predicting the future of stock prices. Learn about how investors make these crucial financial decisions.

@ To continue with Task 3 of your WebQuest project, visit **finance07.glencoe.com**.

Numerical Measures for a Corporation

Using numerical measures such as current yield, total return, earnings per share, and the price-earnings ratio is a good way to find out about the health of a corporation.

Current Yield One of the most common calculations investors use to track the value of their investments is the current yield. **Current yield** is the annual dividend of an investment divided by the current market value. The current yield is expressed as a percentage. As a general rule, an increase in current yield is a healthy sign for any investment.

Total Return The current yield calculation is useful, but you also need to know whether your investment is increasing or decreasing in dollar value. **Total return** is a calculation that includes the annual dividend as well as any increase or decrease in the original purchase price of the investment.

To calculate total return, add the current return on your investment to its capital gain. The current return is the total amount of dividends paid to you, based on the number of shares you own and how long you have held them. To figure out your current return, multiply your dividend amount per share by the number of shares and the length of time that you have held the shares.

Next determine your capital gain. As you learned in Chapter 8, capital gain is the profit you make from the sale of an asset, or the difference between the selling price and the purchase price. To compute capital gain, subtract the purchase price per share from the selling price per share. Then multiply that number by the number of shares held.

GO FIGURE — FINANCIAL MATH

CURRENT YIELD OF A STOCK INVESTMENT

Synopsis: Computing the current yield of your stocks will help you to determine the value of your investment.

Example: Suppose that Tanika purchases stock in EatGrapes.com. Assume that EatGrapes.com pays an annual dividend of $1.20 and is currently selling for $24 a share. What is Tanika's current yield?

Formula: $\frac{\text{Annual Dividend}}{\text{Current Market Value}} = \text{Current Yield}$

Solution: $\frac{\$1.20}{\$24.00} = 0.05 = 5\% \text{ or } .05$

Tanika's current yield would be 5 percent.

YOU FIGURE

If your stock pays an annual dividend of $.80 and is currently selling for $18 a share, what is your current yield?

Answer $.80 ÷ $18 = .04 or 4%

GO FIGURE FINANCIAL MATH

TOTAL RETURN

Synopsis: Calculating the total return of your investment will let you know whether your investment is increasing or decreasing in value.

Example: Two years ago Mark bought 40 shares of Ferguson's Motor Company for $70 a share. The stock pays an annual dividend of $1.50. Mark is going to sell his stock at the current price of $120 a share. What would be the total return on his investment?

Formula:
Current Return + Capital Gain = Total Return

Solution:

A. Find the current return:

Dividend × Number of Shares × Years Held = Current Return

$1.50 × 40 × 2 = $120

The current return is $120.

B. Calculate the capital gain:

(Selling Price per Share − Purchase Price per Share) × Number of Shares Held = Capital Gain

($120 - $70) × 40 = $2,000

The capital gain is $2,000

C. Find the total return:

Current return + Capital Gain = Total Return

$120 + $2,000 = $2,120

The total return on Mark's investment would be $2,120.

YOU FIGURE

If your current return on a stock is $60 and your capital gain is $1,280, what is your total return?

Answer $60 + $1,280 = $1,340

Once you have determined your current return and your capital gain, add those two figures to arrive at your total return.

In the **Go Figure** example, Mark's investment in Ferguson's Motor Company increased in value, so the total return was greater than the current return. For an investment that decreases in value, the total return will be less than the current return. The larger the dollar amount of the total return, the better.

Earnings Per Share Another measurement of a company's performance is **earnings per share**. Earnings per share are a corporation's net, or after-tax, earnings divided by the number of outstanding shares of common stock. This calculation measures the amount of corporate profit assigned to each share of common stock. This figure gives a stockholder an idea of a company's profitability. In general, an increase in earnings per share is a good sign for any corporation and its stockholders.

Price-Earnings Ratio The **price-earnings (PE) ratio** is the price of one share of stock divided by the corporation's earnings per share of stock over the last 12 months. This measurement is commonly used to compare the corporate earnings to the market price of a corporation's stock.

GO FIGURE — FINANCIAL MATH

EARNINGS PER SHARE

Synopsis: Figuring out the earnings per share can help you find out a company's profits. This information can help you determine the general health of the company in which you are investing.

Example: EFG Corporation had net earnings of \$800,000 last year. EFG had 100,000 outstanding shares of common stock. What were EFG's earnings per share?

Formula: $\frac{\text{Net Earnings}}{\text{Common Stock Outstanding}} = \text{Earnings Per Share}$

Solution: $\frac{\$800{,}000}{100{,}000} = \$8$

The corporation's earnings per share were \$8.

YOU FIGURE

You recently invested in an up-and-coming home improvement company and you want to know about the company's health. If the company had net earnings of \$400,000 last year and had 80,000 outstanding shares of common stock, what were the company's net earnings per share?

Answer \$400,000 ÷ 80,000 = \$5

The PE ratio is a key factor that serious investors as well as beginners can use to decide whether to invest in a stock. A low PE ratio indicates that a stock may be a good investment: The company has a lot of earnings when compared to the price of the stock. A high PE ratio tells you that it might be a poor investment. The company has little earnings when compared to the price of the stock.

Generally, you should study the PE ratio for a corporation over a period of time so that you can see a range. Although PE ratios vary by industry, they range between 5 and 35 for most corporations.

GO FIGURE — FINANCIAL MATH

PRICE-EARNINGS RATIO

Synopsis: The price-earnings ratio is the most common measure of how expensive a stock is. Determining the price-earnings ratio can help you decide whether a stock is worth purchasing.

Example: EFG's stock is selling for \$96 a share. EFG's earnings per share are \$8. What is EFG's price-earnings ratio?

Formula: $\frac{\text{Market Price Per Share}}{\text{Earnings Per Share}} = \text{Price-Earnings Ratio}$

Solution: $\frac{\$96}{\$8} = 12$

The corporation's price-earnings ratio is 12.

YOU FIGURE

If a company's market price per share is \$67 and its earnings per share is \$6, what is the company's price-earning ratio?

Answer \$67 ÷ \$6 = 11.17

Careers in Finance

STOCKBROKER **Wendy Ross**
Scottrade

Wendy loves the process of observing the stock market, making speculations, and turning a profit. As a stockbroker, Wendy serves as an agent between her company's clients and the stock exchange. She assists clients with trades, quotes, and account inquiries via telephone and e-mail. Simply put, she helps people buy and sell stocks. Like most stockbrokers, Wendy enjoys the challenge of working with the unpredictable stock market and likes to introduce new customers to Wall Street.

SKILLS: Communication, math, customer-service, computer and data-entry, and multitasking skills

PERSONAL TRAITS: Organized, people oriented, able to travel 4 to 6 weeks per year, discreet, and positive

EDUCATION: Bachelor's degree in finance, business, or a related area or equivalent experience; current Series 7 and Series 63 licenses

ANALYZE The Internet enables individuals to trade their own stocks. What advantages might come from hiring a stockbroker instead of handling your stock trades yourself?
See the Teacher Manual for answer.

To learn more about career paths for stockbrokers, visit **finance07.glencoe.com**.

Investment Theories

Which investment theory do you think makes the most sense?

Teaching Activity Divide the class into triads; assign one investment theory to each person in each triad. Have the groups discuss/debate the theories until they can agree on an answer to this question: Which investment theory do you think makes the most sense? Why?

Over the years theories have developed about ways to evaluate possible investments. Three investment theories dominate:

- The fundamental theory
- The technical theory
- The efficient market theory

The Fundamental Theory

The *fundamental theory* assumes that a stock's real value is determined by looking at the company's future earnings. If earnings are expected to increase in the future, then the stock's price should go up, too. People who believe in the fundamental theory also look at the financial strength of the company, the type of industry the company is in, its new products, and the state of the economy.

The Technical Theory

The *technical theory* is based on the idea that a stock's value is really determined by forces in the stock market itself. Technical theorists look at factors such as the number of stocks bought or sold over a certain period or the total number of shares traded.

The Efficient Market Theory

In the *efficient market theory,* sometimes called the random walk theory, the argument is that stock price movements are purely random. This theory declares that all investors have considered all of the available information on a stock as they make their decisions. Therefore, according to the efficient market theory, it is impossible for an investor to outperform the stock market average over a long period of time.

STANDARD & POOR'S — Put on Your Financial Planner's Cap

Your clients, Mayra and Bob, have $25,000 they want to invest. Bob is enthusiastic about investing in something that will make a quick return. Mayra does not want to jeopardize their savings. How should this couple invest their money?

See the Teacher Manual for the answer.

Section 9.2 Assessment

See the Teacher Manual for answers

QUICK CHECK

1. What are the different types of stock investments?
2. What are the sources that you might use to evaluate stock investments?
3. What numerical measures of corporations can be used to evaluate stock investments?

THINK CRITICALLY

4. Explain how the calculations that involve a company's earnings might help you to make a decision about buying or selling a particular stock.

USE MATH SKILLS

5. **Total Return** Two years ago, Andrei bought 100 shares of Snowland, a ski apparel company. The price of the stock is up $10 from the $20-a-share purchase price, and the stock even paid a dividend of $0.50 per share each year. Andrei wants to determine his total return on the stock.

Calculate Use the formula from this section to determine the total return on Andrei's shares in Snowland.

SOLVE MONEY PROBLEMS

6. **Finding Stock Information** Sandy's mother works for Arf, a nationwide chain of dog kennels. She is receiving company stock as part of her employee retirement plan. She wants to track the stock's performance to see how her retirement nest egg is doing.

Write About It List two items in the stock reports in the financial section of the newspaper for Sandy's mother to review every week to get an idea of how the company's stock is doing. Write a paragraph explaining to Sandy why this information is useful and important to monitor.

Section 9.3

Buying and Selling Stocks

Markets for Stocks

What are the markets for stocks?

To buy common or preferred stock, you usually have to go through a brokerage firm. In turn, the brokerage firm must buy the stock in the primary or secondary markets.

The Primary Markets

The primary market is a market in which investors purchase new security issues from a corporation through an investment bank or some other representative of the corporation. An investment bank is a financial firm that helps corporations to raise funds, usually by helping to sell new securities. The investors are commercial banks, insurance companies, pension funds, mutual funds, and the general public.

An initial public offering (IPO) occurs when a company sells stock to the general public for the first time. Companies use IPOs to fund new business start-ups or to finance new corporate growth and expansion. IPOs are considered a high-risk investment.

A corporation can also get financing through the primary market by selling directly to its current stockholders. By doing so, the corporation bypasses the investment bank, avoids any fees it might have had to pay, and therefore obtains financing at a lower cost.

The Secondary Markets

Once a company's stocks have been sold on the primary market, they can then be sold in the secondary market. The secondary market is a market for existing financial securities currently traded among investors.

Securities Exchanges A **securities exchange** is a marketplace where brokers who represent investors meet to buy and sell securities. Many securities issued by national corporations are first registered and then traded at either the NYSE or AMEX. There are also regional exchanges in San Francisco, Boston, Chicago, and other cities that trade stocks of companies in their respective regions. For example, American firms that do business abroad may also trade on the Tokyo, London, or Paris exchanges.

Focus on Reading

Read to Learn

- How to describe how stocks are bought and sold.
- How to explain the trading strategies used by long-term investors and short-term investors.

Main Idea

By understanding the stock markets and buying and selling techniques, you can cut costs and increase your profit.

Key Terms

- securities exchange
- over-the-counter (OTC) market
- portfolio

Before You Read

PREDICT

How would you go about buying stock?

Springboard Say to the class: "When you buy or sell real estate or jewelry, you're dealing with something tangible, something you can touch and measure. But what are you dealing with when you buy stocks?" Lead a discussion about buying and selling stocks.

Academic Connection

ECONOMICS

On October 19, 1987, the United States stock market plunged 508 points—the largest one-day stock market crash in history. So how did the nation avoid an economic depression such as the Great Depression that followed the 1929 crash? The Fed reacted quickly and lowered short-term interest rates to prevent a banking crisis. This allowed the market time to recover from its losses. *Create a timeline of the events that helped to trigger the 1987 stock market crash.*

See the Teacher Manual for the answer.

Motivate Have the students explore the concept of the stock market as somewhere to "get rich quick."

The NYSE is one of the largest securities exchanges in the world, listing more than 3,000 corporations with a total market value of about $16 trillion. Most of its 1,366 members, or seats, represent brokerage firms. In addition to meeting other requirements, a corporation must have a very large capitalization and trade many shares in order to be listed on the NYSE. Companies that cannot meet the NYSE requirements can use AMEX or regional exchanges.

Over-the-Counter Market Not all stocks are traded on organized exchanges. Several thousand companies trade their stock in the over-the-counter market. The **over-the-counter (OTC) market** is a network of dealers who buy and sell the stocks of corporations that are not listed on a securities exchange.

Most over-the-counter stocks are traded through NASDAQ (pronounced "NAZZ-dack"), an electronic marketplace for more than 4,000 different stocks. NASDAQ stands for the National Association of Securities Dealers Automated Quotation System. The association was established in 1939 to regulate the OTC. When you want to buy or sell a stock that trades on NASDAQ, such as Microsoft®, your brokerage firm sends your order in to the NASDAQ computer system. It shows up on a screen with all the other orders from people who want to buy or sell Microsoft. Then a NASDAQ dealer matches the orders of those who want to buy and those who want to sell Microsoft. Once a match is found, your order is completed.

Typically, NASDAQ handles trades for many forward-looking companies, many of which are fairly small. However, some very large companies such as Microsoft, Intel, and MCI are also traded on NASDAQ.

▲ **THE BIG BOARD** The New York Stock Exchange (NYSE) is one of the largest securities exchanges in the world. *What qualifications must a corporation have to be traded on the NYSE?*

Caption Answer It must have large capitalization and trade many shares, among other requirements.

How to Buy and Sell Stock

Why is it important to be directly involved in your investment program?

There are many decisions that you need to make before beginning to buy and sell stock. You must decide on a brokerage firm, an account executive, and on what type of order—market order, limit order, or stop order—you want to use to make your transaction.

As You Read

RELATE

If you had $5,000 to invest in the stock market right now, what type of brokerage firm would you choose? Explain your reasoning.

Brokerage Firms

Today you can choose a full-service or discount brokerage firm or trade stocks online. The biggest difference is the amount of the commissions you will be charged when you buy or sell securities. A commission is a fee charged to an investor by a brokerage firm for the buying and/or selling of a security. Generally, full-service and discount brokerage firms charge higher commissions than online brokerage firms. Full-service firms usually charge the highest commissions in exchange for personalized service and free research information. However, there may be other differences among the types of firms.

Research Have the students research a stock that is an IPO. They are to report the type of company, the product or service sold, and the price of the stock when it was first sold. Have them track and graph its trading price for the next two weeks.

First, consider the amount of research information that will be available to you and how much it costs. All of these firms offer excellent research materials, but you are more likely to pay extra for information if you choose a discount brokerage or online firm. Although most discount brokerage firms do not charge a lot of money for research reports, the fees can add up. Second, consider how much help you will need in order to make an investment decision. The full-service account executive may not have a lot of time to spend with each client, but you can expect him or her to answer questions and make recommendations.

Discount and online firms generally believe that you alone are in charge of your investment plan and that the most successful investors are totally involved in their programs. They usually have printed material or information on their Web sites to help you become a better investor.

Caption Answer the over-the-counter (OTC) market

▶ **ANOTHER WAY** More than 4,000 different stocks are traded on NASDAQ. *What market does NASDAQ serve?*

▲ **YOUR BROKER** One of the biggest advantages of a full-service brokerage firm is personal attention from an account executive. *How can you protect your portfolio from a dishonest or incompetent account executive?*

Caption Answer Make sure you understand your account executive's recommendations and make all final decisions yourself.

Account Executives

An account executive, or stockbroker, is a licensed individual who buys or sells securities, or stocks, for clients. Account executives usually work for brokerages.

Whether he or she is called an account executive or stockbroker, this person deals with all types of securities, not just stocks, and can handle your entire portfolio. A **portfolio** is a collection of all the securities held by an investor. Some account executives will take risks, while others are more conservative. When you are choosing an account executive, be sure that you can clearly describe your short- and long-term financial goals so that you will receive the best service for your needs.

Remember that account executives can make errors, so be sure to stay actively involved in decisions concerning your investments. Never let the stockbroker take action on your account without your permission. Brokerage firms are usually not responsible for financial losses that are the result of a recommendation by your account executive.

Be aware of a practice known as "churning." Churning occurs when an account executive does a lot of buying and selling of stocks within your portfolio to generate more commissions. Although churning is illegal, it is difficult to prove. Note that the value of your portfolio does not increase through churning; rather, it stays about the same.

Most traditional brokerage firms have a minimum commission that ranges from $25 to $55 for buying and selling stocks. However, commissions for online brokerage firms can be as low as $10. Additional fees based on the number of shares and the value of the stock can also be charged. On the floors of the exchanges, stocks are traded in round lots, which are 100 shares or multiples of 100 shares of a particular stock. An odd lot contains fewer than 100 shares of a stock.

Types of Orders

When you are ready to trade a stock, you will execute an order to buy or sell. Most investors do this either over the telephone or on the Internet. You can also go to a brokerage firm and place your order in person. The types of orders used to trade stocks include market orders, limit orders, and stop orders.

Market Orders A market order is a request to buy or sell a stock at the current market value. Because the stock market is essentially an auction, the account executive's representative will try to get the best price possible and make the transaction as soon as possible. **Figure 9.4** illustrates how a typical market order on the NYSE would be executed.

Teaching Activity Divide the class into groups of four. Explain that each group wants to select an account executive, and suggest that the process is a lot like hiring an employee: You need to "interview" several before making a decision. Have each group brainstorm questions and topics for discussion with the account executive candidates.

Figure 9.4 **Trading Stock**

Several steps are involved in trading stock on the New York Stock Exchange (NYSE).

1 Receiving an Order Your account executive receives your order to sell stock and relays the order electronically to the brokerage firm's representative at the stock exchange.

2 Signal to Floor Broker A clerk for the firm signals the transaction to a floor broker on the stock exchange floor.

3 Trading The floor broker goes to the trading post at which this stock is traded and trades with a floor broker (from another firm) who has an order to buy.

4 To the Ticker System The floor broker signals the transaction back to the clerk. Then a floor reporter—an employee of the NYSE—collects the information about the transaction and inputs it into the ticker system.

5 On the Board The sale appears on the price board, and a confirmation is relayed to your account executive, who notifies you of the completed transaction.

$avvy Saver

Stock Research

1. Choose a few companies whose products interest you.
2. Look up the stocks in the newspaper or on the Internet.
3. Watch how their prices change and graph their progress weekly.
4. Request and study an annual report from each company.
5. Research the companies in *Value Line Investment Survey*.

Note that every stock listed on the NYSE is traded at a computer-equipped trading post on the floor of the exchange. A computer monitor above the trading post indicates current price information for all stocks traded at each post.

Then each transaction is recorded, and the necessary information—the ticker symbol (the letters that identify a stock for trading), number of shares, and price—is transmitted through a communications network called the *ticker system*. The NYSE also uses the SuperDot system, which transmits orders electronically and can handle daily trading volumes of more than 2 billion shares.

Payment for stocks is generally required within three business days of the sale. About four to six weeks later, the broker sends a stock certificate (proof of ownership) to the purchaser. **Figure 9.5** shows a sample of a common stock certificate. However, the investor's brokerage firm can receive the certificate and hold it, which is convenient when it comes time to sell the stock. The phrase *left in the street name* is used to describe investor-owned securities held by a brokerage firm.

Limit Orders A limit order is a request to buy or sell a stock at a specified price. You agree to buy the stock at the best price up to a certain dollar amount. When you are selling, the limit order ensures that you will sell at the best price and not below a certain price.

Figure 9.5 A Common Stock Certificate

Paper Trail This common stock certificate is valuable because it serves as proof of ownership.

Who handles the purchase of these stock certificates?

Caption Answer account executives, also called stockbrokers.

For example, if you place a limit order to buy Kellogg common stock for $34 a share, the stock will not be purchased until the price drops to $34 or lower. If you place a limit order to sell a stock, the Kellogg stock will not be sold until the price rises to $34 or higher.

However, a limit order does not guarantee that the purchase or sale will be made when the desired price is reached. Limit orders are filled in the order in which they are received, so other investors may get orders filled before you do. If the price of Kellogg, for example, continues to rise while purchase orders ahead of yours are being filled, then when your turn comes, the price may reach $36, and you will miss the chance to buy the stock at $34.

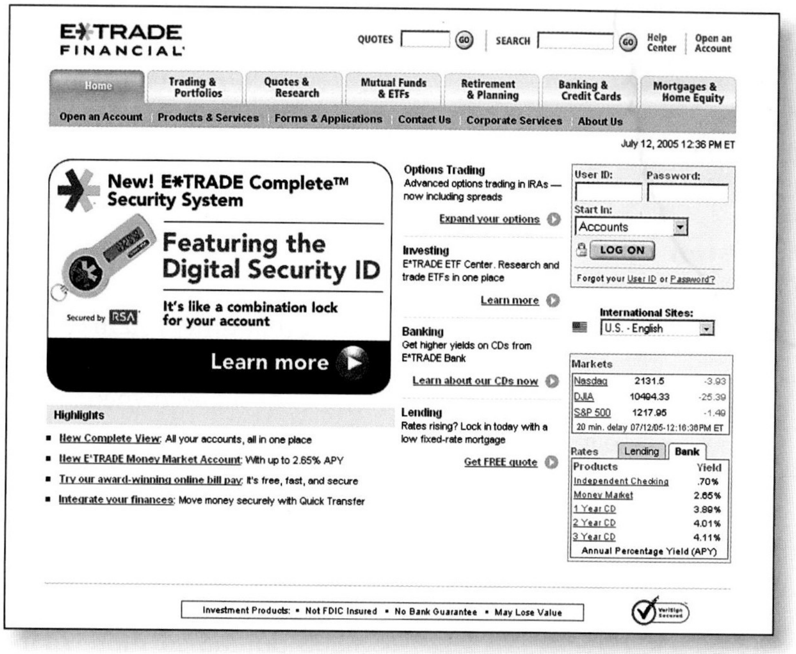

▲ **COMPUTERIZED TRANSACTIONS** Internet brokerage companies offer instant access to your account information and the ability to buy and sell online. *Why would having this be beneficial?*

Caption Answer Stock prices can change very rapidly, so instant access is useful when buying or selling.

Stop Orders You can also place a stop order, which is used for selling stock. A stop order is a type of limit order to sell a particular stock at the next available opportunity when the market price reaches a specified amount. A stop order does not guarantee that your stock will be sold at the price you want, but it does guarantee that it will be sold at the next available opportunity. Both stop and limit orders can be good for a day, a week, a month, or until you cancel them.

Computerized Transactions

More and more people are using their computers to make securities transactions. To meet the demand for this service, discount brokerage firms and some full-service firms allow investors to trade online. You can use a software package or the brokerage's Web site to help you evaluate stocks, track your portfolio and monitor its value, and buy and sell securities online. Of course, you are still responsible for doing research and analyzing the information you get.

Investment Strategies

Which type of investment strategy would you use: long term or short term?

Once you purchase stock, the investment may be categorized as long term (held for ten years or more), or short term (held for one year or less). Generally, if you hold investments for at least a year, you are considered an investor. If you buy and sell investments within short periods of time, you are a speculator or a trader.

Long-Term Techniques

Long-term techniques such as the buy-and-hold technique, dollar cost averaging, direct investment, and dividend reinvestment are used by all investors who are interested in avoiding losses in their investments.

Buy-and-Hold Technique A typical long-term investing method is to buy stock and hold on to it for a number of years, often ten or more. During that time, you may get dividends, and the price of the stock may go up. The stock may also be split, which increases its value as well as number of shares owned.

Dollar Cost Averaging With this method, you buy an equal dollar amount of the same stock at equal intervals. For example, suppose that you invested $2,000 in Johnson & Johnson common stock each year for a period of three years. When the price of the stock went up, your $2,000 purchased fewer shares, and when it went down, your $2,000 purchased more shares. This system protects investors from buying at high prices and selling at low prices. The price you pay for the stock averages out over time.

Direct Investment and Dividend Reinvestment Plans A large number of companies sell their stock directly to investors. This plan lets you buy stock without going through your account executive at a brokerage firm and paying commissions. You have the same advantage of not paying fees with a dividend reinvestment plan, which automatically reinvests any dividends you earn by buying more shares of that stock with those earnings.

Short-Term Techniques

Investors sometimes use more speculative, short-term techniques. These methods are quite risky. Only investors who fully understand the risks should use techniques such as buying on margin and selling short.

Buying on Margin When buying stock on margin, an investor borrows through a brokerage firm part of the money needed to purchase a stock. The Federal Reserve Board currently limits the margin requirement to 50 percent and $2,000, which means that you can borrow up to half of the purchase price as long as you have at least $2,000 in your brokerage account. Investors buy stock on margin in order to purchase more shares. If the shares go up in value, the investor makes more money. However, if the shares go down in value, the investor loses more money.

Selling Short Your ability to make money buying and selling securities is related to how well you can predict what the stock is going to do—whether it will rise or fall in value. Normally you want to buy a stock that will go up in value, and this is called buying long. Of course, the value of stocks can decrease, too.

Common CENTS

Listen Up
It is smart to shop at music stores that let you listen to CDs before you purchase them. You can also check out your friends' music to see if you like it. You will save money by not buying CDs you will not use.

What are some other types of purchases to which you could apply this method?

Common Cents Answer Answers might include test driving cars before you buy them, trying out pianos or other instruments, testing computer keyboards, sampling foods, or trying on clothes and shoes.

As You Read QUESTION

What is the advantage of a dividend reinvestment plan?

Question Answer It allows you to acquire more stock without paying more commissions. This is attractive if you do not need investment income and believe the stock will continue to rise.

Teaching Activity Divide the class into five groups and assign each group one of the long- or short-term investment strategies. Have each group make a poster illustrating the strategy. When the posters are presented to the class, have students vote on the best one or two; display those on bulletin boards.

You can actually make money by selling short when the value of a stock appears as if it may go down. Selling short is selling a stock that has been borrowed from a brokerage firm and that must be replaced at a later date. You sell the stock you have borrowed today, knowing that you will have to buy the stock again at a later date. Here is how it is done:

1. Arrange to borrow a certain number of shares of a particular stock from a brokerage firm.
2. Sell the borrowed stock, assuming that it will drop in value in a reasonably short period of time.
3. Buy the stock at a lower price than the price it sold for in Step 2.
4. Use the stock you purchased in Step 3 to replace the stock that you borrowed from the brokerage firm in Step 1.

Remember that when you borrow the stock, it really belongs to someone else, so if a dividend is due, you must pay it. Eventually these dividends may absorb all the profits you make on the transaction. To make money, you have to predict correctly that the value of the stock will go down. If the value increases, you lose money.

After You Read

REACT

Using the information provided in this chapter, do you think you could develop an investment plan for yourself?

React Answer Accept all reasonable answers.

Discussion After viewing the posters made earlier, discuss with the students the advantages and disadvantages of the five investment strategies.

Section 9.3 Assessment

See the Teacher Manual for answers.

QUICK CHECK

1. What is the difference between the primary and secondary stock markets?
2. What are characteristics of full-service, discount, and online brokerage firms in terms of service and cost?
3. What are the trading techniques that are used by investors and speculators?

THINK CRITICALLY

4. Design a handout for students that explains the various long-term investment strategies.

USE COMMUNICATION SKILLS

5. **Short-Term Trading** Some of your classmates are boasting that they can make a killing by trading stocks over a short period of time.

Present Choose one of your favorite songs and create song lyrics for it that warn of the dangers of short-term trading methods. Be as specific about the methods as you can, noting why beginning investors could get "burned."

SOLVE MONEY PROBLEMS

6. **Using a Broker** Bruce is a high school senior with a busy fall schedule. He saved enough money to start investing, but he has no time to monitor his investments or make decisions. He wants to let his account executive buy or sell stocks without bothering him.

Analyze List and explain the dangers of Bruce's plan to let his account executive act without consulting him.

Chapter 9 Review & Activities

See the Teacher Manual for answers.

CHAPTER SUMMARY

- Investors choose common stock because stocks provide a greater potential return than bank savings accounts and government bonds.
- Investors choose preferred stocks because they are less risky than common stocks and because they provide a steady income in the form of dividends.
- Types of stock investments include blue-chip stocks, income stocks, growth stocks, cyclical stocks, defensive stocks, large- and small-cap stocks, and penny stocks.
- Information about stocks' risk can be found in newspapers, stock advisory services, corporate reports, and on the Internet.
- Factors affecting stock prices include general attitudes about current economic conditions and corporate performance.
- Stocks are bought and sold in primary markets, such as in an initial public offering (IPO), and in secondary markets, such as securities exchanges and the over-the-counter (OTC) market.
- Long-term investors buy and hold stocks, use dollar-cost averaging to smooth out the prices they pay for stocks they buy regularly, and reinvest their dividends and buy more stock directly from companies in which they have already invested to avoid stockbroker commissions. Short-term speculators use techniques such as buying stock on margin and selling short.

Communicating Key Terms

You have a client who owns a company with 75 employees. She asks you to describe the stock option offered to employees in the company's 401(k) retirement savings plan. Use as many of the terms below as possible to develop a presentation for these employees.

- securities
- private corporation
- public corporation
- par value
- blue-chip stock
- income stock
- growth stock
- cyclical stock
- defensive stock
- large-cap stock
- capitalization
- small-cap stock
- penny stock
- bull market
- bear market
- current yield
- total return
- earnings per share
- price-earnings (PE) ratio
- securities exchange
- over-the-counter (OTC) market
- portfolio

Reviewing Key Concepts

1. **Explain** why corporations prefer to issue common stock to raise funds for their operations.
2. **Explain** how cumulative preferred and convertible preferred stock offer advantages to investors.
3. **Describe** why a small-cap stock is more likely to be a growth stock rather than an income stock.
4. **Identify** the advantages and disadvantages of a stock advisory service to evaluate a stock.
5. **Describe** why the price-earnings ratio is a good measure of a stock investment.
6. **List** the differences among market order, limit order, and stop order.
7. **Identify** the tax advantages of long-term investment strategies.

See the Teacher Manual for answers.

ACADEMIC SKILLS

Language Arts Sometimes the best career information comes from informational interviews with people working in the real world.

Write About It Interview a stockbroker and ask him or her questions about the background, education, training, and experience needed to work in that profession. Then write an article based on the interview for your school or class newsletter.

YOUR FINANCIAL FIGURES

Buying and Selling Stocks You bought 200 shares of a stock at $17 per share in 2001. After 12 months, the stock doubled in value, and you sold 100 shares. Eighteen months later, the stock reached $60 and split. After another year, the stock is now selling at $52 a share.

1. **Calculate** (a) how much you received when you sold 100 shares in 2002; (b) your capital gain; (c) how many shares of this stock you own today; and (d) your gain on these shares.
2. **Compute** by using spreadsheet software to make these calculations.

REAL-WORLD Application

Connect with Government The capital gains received on stock sales is considered income, and you have to pay taxes on it. To encourage people to invest and to hold on to those investments, the U.S. government taxes capital gains on investments held less than 12 months at the investor's regular tax rate, but capital gains on investments held longer are taxed at 15 percent—which for most people is less than the regular tax rate.

1. **Research** Use the Internet to find out more about why the government wants to encourage investors to hold on to their investments.
2. **Think Critically** How does the tax difference (15 percent tax rate versus regular tax rate) provide an incentive to people to invest in corporations, as opposed to corporate bonds or government bonds?

Internet CONNECTION

Institutional Investors Many investors buying stocks are not individuals, but institutions, such as retirement plans and mutual funds, which have extremely large amounts of money to buy and sell large blocks of stock.

@ **Log On** Use an Internet search engine to find Web sites of companies that manage such funds. One is TIAA-CREF, which manages the retirement funds of teachers in many states. Answer the following questions:

1. What types of investments do institutional investors make?
2. What can you say about their tolerance for risk?

BusinessWeek ONLINE

Newsclip: Investor Concern Despite a growing economy, investor concern has decreased the popularity of stocks. However, quality stocks are usually sound even in shaky times.

@ **Log On** Go to **finance07.glencoe.com** and open Chapter 9. Learn more about what affects stock prices and make a list of safe stocks.

WHAT'S YOUR FINANCIAL ID?

TAKING STOCK

Test your knowledge of stocks after you read the chapter. Write your answers on a separate sheet of paper. If you had the money, would you be ready to invest in stocks?

1. All stocks pay dividends.

True False

2. Blue-chip stocks are generally a safe investment that attracts conservative investors.

True False

3. A bull market occurs when ranchers take their cattle to the stockyards.

True False

4. An initial public offering (IPO) occurs when a company first sells its products or services to the public.

True False

5. The price-earnings (PE) ratio is the price of one share of stock divided by the stock's earnings per share.

True False

6. A good way to learn about the financial health of a company is by reading its annual report.

True False

7. An income statement shows a company's profits and losses.

True False

8. The appeal of investing in high-risk stocks is the possibility of large returns.

True False

Accept all reasonable answers that show student effort and an understanding of the concept.

Your Financial Portfolio

Investing in Stock

Rick would like to invest in the stock market. Before he invests any money, Rick is researching a company he thinks has potential. He picked eSongz, an online music store that lets you rent or purchase MP3 players and buy songs for them directly from its site. Along with the price of stock, he watches for any announcements or industry changes that may affect the stock.

Rick's Research

eSongz

Highest price paid per share during the past 52 weeks	$41.80
Lowest price paid per share in the past 52 weeks	$19.89
Current price paid per share	$35.35
Price-earnings (PE) ratio	20
Earnings per share	$1.78

Rick has studied eSongz' financial reports and also keeps tabs on its financial news reports. He believes eSongz will continue to be successful, but he plans to watch the stock a little longer before he makes his decision to invest.

Research

In your workbook or on a separate sheet of paper, choose a stock you would like to buy and research it. You can get information about a company in the financial section of major newspapers, the Internet, and from the companies themselves. You can also find information from *Standard & Poor's Stock and Bond Guide, Mergent's Handbook of Common Stocks,* or *Value Line Investment Survey.* What type of stock would you be interested in purchasing? Explain why. Do you think the company you chose to research would be a wise investment choice? Explain your answer.

Accept all reasonable answers that show student effort and an understanding of the concept.

CHAPTER 10

Bonds and Mutual Funds

What You'll Learn

When you have completed this chapter, you will be able to:

Section 10.1

- Describe the characteristics of corporate bonds.
- Identify the reasons corporations sell bonds.
- Explain why investors buy corporate bonds.
- Discuss the reasons governments issue bonds.
- Identify the types of government bonds.

Section 10.2

- Identify sources of information for selecting bond investments.

Section 10.3

- Identify types of mutual funds.

Section 10.4

- Discuss sources of information for selecting mutual funds.
- Describe the methods of buying and selling mutual funds.

Reading Strategies

To get the most out of your reading:

Predict what you will learn in this chapter.
Relate what you read to your own life.
Question what you are reading to be sure you understand.
React to what you have read.

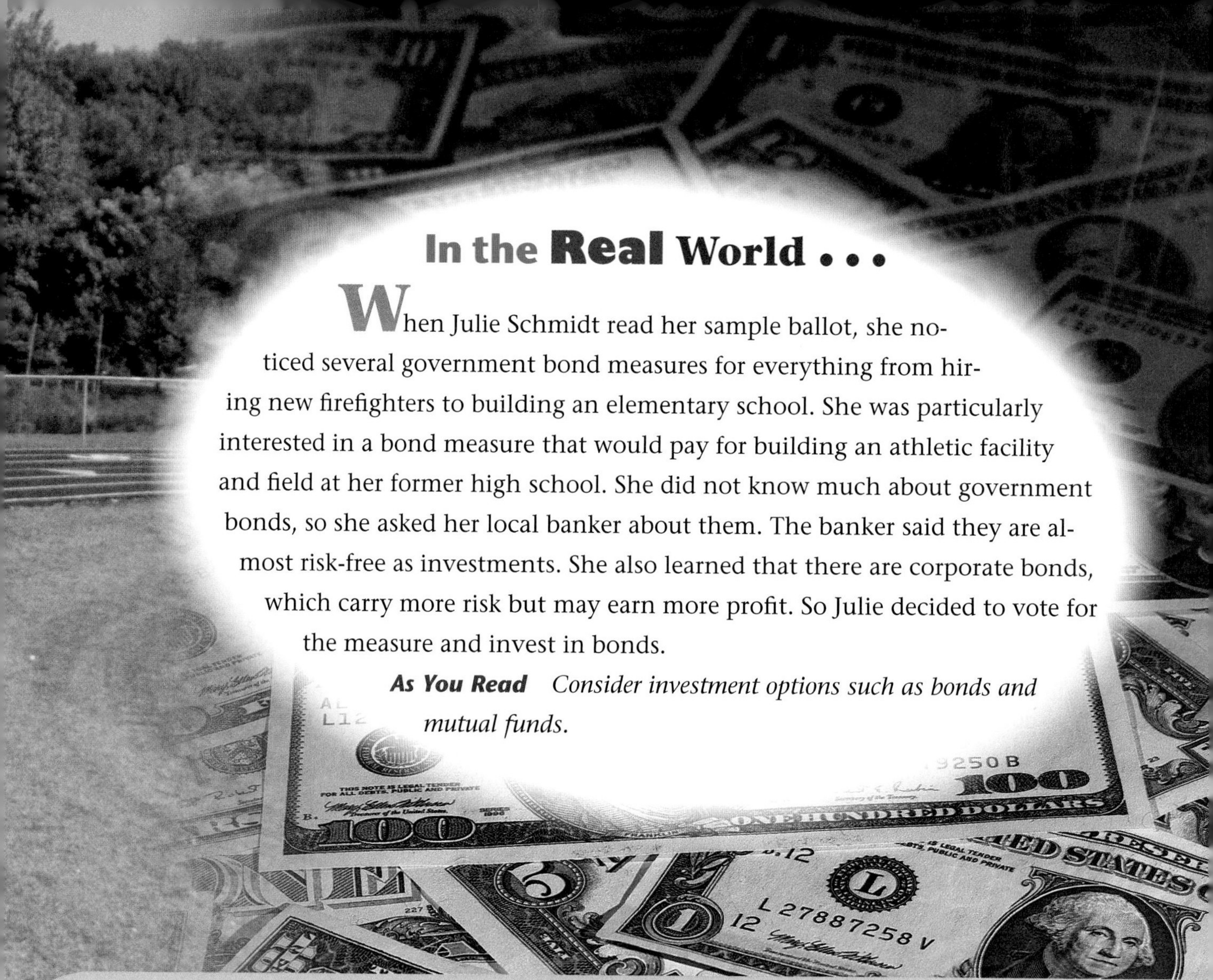

In the Real World . . .

When Julie Schmidt read her sample ballot, she noticed several government bond measures for everything from hiring new firefighters to building an elementary school. She was particularly interested in a bond measure that would pay for building an athletic facility and field at her former high school. She did not know much about government bonds, so she asked her local banker about them. The banker said they are almost risk-free as investments. She also learned that there are corporate bonds, which carry more risk but may earn more profit. So Julie decided to vote for the measure and invest in bonds.

As You Read *Consider investment options such as bonds and mutual funds.*

Lesson Plan See the Teacher Manual for the Chapter 10 planning guide and lesson plan.

ASK STANDARD & POOR'S

Mutual Funds

Q: I have about $50 a month to invest. What is a good investment choice for me?

A: Many mutual fund companies offer systematic investment programs in which you invest the same amount each month regardless of changes in the share price. As a result, your money buys more shares when prices are low and fewer shares when prices are high. Over time, this strategy can result in a lower average cost per share; however, it does not guarantee a profit or protect against a loss.

Ask Yourself Why is it a good idea to invest even a small amount of money each month?

Go to **finance07.glencoe.com** to complete the Standard & Poor's Financial Focus activity.

Section 10.1

Focus on Reading

Read to Learn

- How to describe the characteristics of corporate bonds.
- How to identify the reasons corporations sell bonds.
- How to explain why investors buy corporate bonds.
- How to discuss the reasons governments issue bonds.
- How to identify the types of government bonds.

Main Idea

Understanding bonds and why they are bought and sold will give you more choices to consider when investing your money.

Key Terms

- maturity date
- face value
- debenture
- mortgage bond
- convertible bond
- sinking fund
- serial bonds
- registered bond
- coupon bond
- bearer bond
- zero-coupon bond
- municipal bond

Springboard Ask the students if they can explain the difference between stocks and bonds. If some can, write their answers on the board. If no one can, tell them this is one of the things they will learn in this chapter.

Corporate and Government Bonds

Corporate Bonds

What is a corporate bond?

When you buy a corporate bond, you are basically loaning money to a corporation. As discussed in Chapter 8, a corporate bond is a corporation's written pledge to repay a bondholder (the person who bought the bond) a specified amount of money with interest. **Figure 10.1** on page 313 shows an example of a typical corporate bond. The bond's interest rate, maturity date, and face value are stated on the bond. The **maturity date** is the date when a bond will be repaid. The **face value** is the dollar amount that the bondholder will receive at the bond's maturity. Typically, the face value of a corporate bond is $1,000. However, corporate bonds can have face values as high as $50,000.

Between the date when you buy a bond and the maturity date, the corporation pays you annual interest at the rate stated on the bond. Interest is usually paid semiannually (twice a year). By multiplying the face value by the interest rate, you can calculate how much interest you would earn each year.

At the maturity date, you cash in the bond and receive a check in the amount of the bond's face value. Maturity dates for bonds can range from 1 to 30 years. Maturities for corporate bonds are classified as short term (less than 5 years), intermediate term (5 to 15 years), and long term (more than 15 years).

Types of Corporate Bonds

There are several types of corporate bonds. These types include debentures, mortgage bonds, subordinated debentures, and convertible bonds.

Debentures Most corporate bonds are debentures. A **debenture** is a bond that is backed only by the reputation of the issuing corporation, rather than by its assets. Investors buy this type of bond because they believe that the company, or corporation, that issues them is on solid financial ground. Investors expect the company to repay the face value of the bond and make interest payments until the bond matures.

GO FIGURE — FINANCIAL MATH

A BOND'S ANNUAL INTEREST

Synopsis: The interest on a bond is paid twice a year. By calculating the annual interest on your bond, you will be able to determine how much money you will earn on the bond each year.

Example: Suppose that you purchase a $1,000 Mobil Corporation bond. The interest rate for the bond is 8.5 percent (8.5%). How much annual interest would you earn on this bond?

Formula:
Face Value × Interest Rate = Annual Interest

Solution:
$1,000 × 8.5% or .085 = $85

You would receive interest of $85 a year from Mobil, paid in two installments of $42.50.

YOU FIGURE

If you purchased two $2,000 bonds that had an interest rate of 7 percent, how much annual interest would you earn?

Answer $2,000 × 7% or .07 = $140 × 2 = $280

Mortgage Bonds A bond issue occurs when a company makes available a quantity of bonds at one time. To make these bonds more appealing to conservative investors, a corporation may also issue mortgage bonds. A **mortgage bond,** sometimes referred to as a secured bond, is a bond that is backed by assets of a corporation. A mortgage bond is a safer investment than a debenture because it is backed by corporate assets. These assets, such as real estate or equipment, can be sold to repay the mortgage bondholders if the corporation fails to make good on its bonds. Though safer, mortgage bonds usually earn less interest than debentures because their risk to the investor is lower.

Motivating Students Ask the students if they think bonds are safer than stocks. Have them explain why or why not.

Subordinated Debentures A subordinated debenture is a type of unsecured bond that gives bondholders a claim to interest payments and assets of the corporation only after all other bondholders have been paid. Because subordinated debentures are more risky than other bonds, investors who buy them usually receive higher interest rates than other bondholders.

Critical Thinking Have students write a brief essay in which they cite the advantages and disadvantages of each type of corporate bond and decide which they would be most likely to invest in, justifying their decisions.

Convertible Bonds A **convertible bond** is a bond that an investor can trade for shares of the corporation's common stock. Because of the unique flexibility that it offers investors, the interest rate on a convertible bond is often 1 to 2 percent lower than interest rates on other types of corporate bonds.

Many bondholders choose not to convert their bonds into stock even when stock values are high. The reason for this is simple: As the market value of a company's common stock increases, the market value of the company's convertible bonds also increases. Bondholders benefit from this increase in value while keeping the relative safety of a bond and its interest income.

Before You Read

PREDICT

What do you think government bonds are?

▲ **A CORPORATE BOND**
Mobil Corporation issued this bond with an interest rate of 8.5 percent. *What is the face value of this bond?*

Caption Answer $1,000

Methods Corporations Use to Repay Bonds

Today most corporate bonds are "callable," which means they have a call feature that allows a corporation to buy back bonds from bondholders before the maturity date. Corporations may get the money to call a bond by selling stock, by using profits, or by selling new bonds at a lower interest rate.

For example, suppose that Mobil Corporation issued bonds at 8.5 percent, but later, interest rates on comparable bonds dropped to 4.5 percent. Mobil Corporation might decide to call the bonds it had issued at 8.5 percent. By buying back those bonds early, Mobil would not have to pay bondholders interest at that high rate.

Premiums Usually, companies agree not to call their bonds for the first five to ten years after the bonds are issued. When they do call their bonds, they may have to pay bondholders a premium. A premium is an additional amount above the face value of the bond. The amount of the premium is stated in a *bond indenture,* which details all the conditions pertaining to a particular bond issue.

Sinking Funds A corporation may use one of two methods to make sure that it has enough funds to pay off a bond issue. First, the corporation may set up a sinking fund. A **sinking fund** is a fund to which a corporation makes deposits for the purpose of paying back a bond issue. If the bond indenture states that the corporation will deposit money in a sinking fund, the company will be able to repay its bonds.

Discussion Discuss with the students the ways corporations repay bonds, asking them why each method might appeal to a particular corporation.

Serial Bonds Second, a corporation may issue serial bonds. **Serial bonds** are bonds issued at the same time but which mature on different dates. For example, Seaside Productions issued $100 million of serial bonds for a 20-year period. None of the bonds matured during the first ten years. Therefore, during that time the company did not have to pay anything but the interest owed on the outstanding bonds. Instead, Seaside Productions used the funds raised by selling the bonds to grow its business. After that, only 10 percent of the bonds matured each year until all the bonds were retired at the end of 20 years. That allowed Seaside Productions to repay its bonds a few at a time instead of having to repay all $100 million at once.

As You Read

RELATE

Do you think that investing in corporate bonds would be a good way to reach your financial goals? Why?

Why Corporations Sell Bonds

What are a corporation's responsibilities to its stockholders and to its bondholders?

Corporations sell bonds to raise money when it is difficult or impossible to sell stock. Companies also often use bonds simply to finance regular business activities. Selling bonds can also reduce the amount of tax a corporation must pay because the interest paid to bondholders is tax-deductible.

A corporation may sell both bonds and stocks to help pay for its activities. However, the corporation's responsibility to investors is different for bonds and for stocks. Bondholders must be repaid at a future date for their investments. Stockholders do not have to be repaid. Companies are required to pay interest on bonds. They can choose whether to pay dividends to their stockholders. Finally, if a corporation files for bankruptcy, bondholders' claims to assets are paid before the claims of stockholders.

Teaching Activity Divide students into groups of three. Have each team prepare two graphic displays, one showing the different types of bonds and their features, the other showing the ways corporations repay bonds. Display all posters around the room and have students vote to decide which poster of each type is the best.

Caption Answer Investors can be fairly sure these bonds will be repaid whether or not the company is successful, for they are backed by the company's assets.

◀ **SECURE FOOTING** Mortgage bonds may be backed by a company's real estate, stock, or machinery and equipment. *Why would an investor want to buy a mortgage bond?*

Common CENTS

Savings Mind-Set
It is exciting when you get a raise or finally pay off a loan. You know you have more money available. Be a smart saver—stick to your current budget and stash that newfound money in your savings or investment account.
If you received a $30 per week raise in net pay and were paid four times per month, how much "extra" money would you have in ten months from February to November? Would you save or invest that money? Why or why not?

Common Cents $30 × 4 = $120 × 10 = $1,200

Research Have students find on the Internet two corporations that have issued bonds in the last year or so. Have them research further to determine: (1) what kind of bonds (debentures, etc.) were sold; (2) were the bonds registered, coupon, bearer, or zero-coupon; and (3) for what time periods have the companies agreed not to call their bonds.

Why Investors Buy Corporate Bonds

Why are bonds considered safe investments?

Historically, stocks have resulted in greater profits than bonds. Why, then, should you consider investing in bonds? Many corporate and government bonds are safe investments. Some investors use corporate and government bonds to diversify their investment portfolios (all the securities held by an investor). Bonds offer you three other benefits:

- Most bonds provide interest income.
- Bonds may increase in value, depending on the bond market, overall interest rates in the economy, and the reputation and assets of the issuer.
- The face value of a bond is repaid when it reaches maturity.

Interest Income

Bondholders usually receive interest payments every six months. The dollar amount of annual interest is determined by multiplying the interest rate by the face value of the bond. The method used by a company to pay you interest depends on the type of corporate bond you purchase:

- Registered bond
- Coupon bond
- Bearer bond
- Zero-coupon bond

Registered Bonds A **registered bond** is a bond registered in the owner's name by the company that issues the bond. This ensures that only the owner can collect money from the bond. Interest checks for registered bonds are mailed directly to the bondholder.

Coupon Bonds A registered **coupon bond** is a bond that is registered in the owner's name for only the face value and not for interest. This type of bond comes with detachable coupons. Because the face value of the bond is registered, only the bond's owner can collect the face value. However, anyone who holds the coupons can collect the interest. To collect an interest payment on a registered coupon bond, you simply present one of the detachable coupons to the issuing corporation or to the appropriate bank or broker.

Bearer Bonds A **bearer bond** is a bond that is not registered in the investor's name. As with registered coupon bonds, the owner of a bearer bond must present coupons in order to collect interest payments. Anyone who has physical possession of the bonds or their coupons can collect on them. A few bearer bonds are still in circulation, but they are no longer issued by corporations.

Zero-Coupon Bond A **zero-coupon bond** is a bond that does not produce interest payments. It is sold at a price far below its face value, but it is redeemed for its full face value at maturity. Because you buy it for less than its face value, you automatically make a profit when your zero-coupon bond is repaid.

As You Read
QUESTION
What type of investor would be interested in a zero-coupon bond?

Question Answer The zero-coupon bond investor does not need the interest income. The investor could be someone who wants to invest a relatively small amount of money now to secure funds for retirement.

Market Value of a Bond

Many beginning investors think that a $1,000 bond is always worth $1,000. Actually, the market value of a corporate bond may fluctuate before its maturity date. Usually, shifts in bond prices result from changes in overall interest rates in the economy.

For example, suppose that Vanessa has a bond with a 7.5 percent interest rate. If overall interest rates fall below 7.5 percent, Vanessa's bond will go up in market value because it earns more interest than bonds issued at the new lower rate. If overall interest rates rise above 7.5 percent, the market value of Vanessa's bond will fall because it earns less interest than bonds issued at the new, higher rate.

When a bond is selling for less than its face value, it is said to be selling at a *discount.* When a bond is selling for more than its face value, it is said to be selling at a *premium.* You can calculate a bond's approximate market value by using a formula that compares the bond's interest rate to that of similar new corporate bonds. (See **Go Figure** on page 312.) Find the dollar amount of the bond's annual interest by multiplying the face value by the annual interest rate. Then, compute the bond's approximate market value by dividing the dollar amount of annual interest by the interest rate of comparable new corporate bonds.

The market value of a bond may also be affected by the financial condition of the company that issues it. In addition, the law of supply and demand changes in the economy and can affect a bond's value.

Discussion Go over the information regarding market value of a bond with the students, asking them to invent situations in which bonds would be selling at a discount and selling at a premium.

Caption Answer They are used to collect interest on the bond. The coupon holder only needs to present the coupon to the company or its banker or broker.

◀ **REDEEMABLE COUPONS** Registered coupon bonds come with detachable coupons. *How are the coupons used?*

GO FIGURE FINANCIAL MATH

APPROXIMATE MARKET VALUE OF A BOND

Synopsis: The market value of a bond can change many times before its maturity date. Calculating the approximate market value of a bond can help you determine what your bond will be worth at its maturity date.

Example: Shawn purchased a New York Telephone bond that pays 4.5 percent interest based on a face value of $1,000. Comparable new corporate bond issues are paying 7 percent. How much is Shawn's bond worth?

Formula:

$$\frac{\text{Dollar Amount of Annual Interest}}{\text{Interest Rate of Comparable New Corporate Bonds}} = \text{Approximate Market Value}$$

Solution:

A. Find the dollar amount of annual interest.

Face Value of Bond × Annual Interest Rate = Dollar Amount of Annual Interest

$1,000 × 4.5% or .045 = $45

The dollar amount of annual interest is $45.

B. Solve for approximate market value.

$$\frac{\text{Dollar Amount of Annual Interest}}{\text{Interest Rate of Comparable New Corporate Bonds}} = \text{Approximate Market Value}$$

$$\frac{\$45}{7\% \text{ or } .07} = \$642.86$$

The approximate market value of Shawn's New York Telephone bond is $642.86.

YOU FIGURE

You bought two $1,000 bonds, each with an interest rate of 5.5 percent. New corporate bonds being issued are paying 8 percent interest. What is the approximate market value of your bonds?

Answer $1,000 × 5.5% or .055 = $55; $55 ÷ 8% or .08 = $687.50 × 2 = $1,375.00

Repayment at Maturity

Corporate bonds are repaid at maturity. After you purchase a bond, you have two choices. You can keep the bond until its maturity date and then cash it in. You can also sell the bond at any time to another investor. In either case, the value of the bond is closely tied to the corporation's ability to repay it. Other investors will pay more money to get a quality bond that has solid prospects of repayment.

A Typical Bond Transaction

Where can you purchase corporate bonds?

Most bonds are sold through full-service brokerage firms, discount brokerage firms, or online. If you use a full-service brokerage firm, your account executive should provide information and advice about bond investments. If you use a discount brokerage firm or buy bonds online, you must do your own research and make your own decisions. However, you will probably pay a lower commission.

You can also buy corporate bonds directly from account executives or brokerage firms. If you buy or sell a bond through an account executive or brokerage firm, you should expect to pay a commission.

Purchasing in Primary and Secondary Markets

Bonds are purchased in the same way as stocks. Corporate bonds may be purchased in the primary or secondary markets. In the primary market, you purchase financial securities from an investment banker representing the corporation or government agency that issued them. In the secondary market, you trade financial securities with other investors. Corporate bonds issued by large companies are traded on the New York Bond Exchange and American Bond Exchange.

Sample Bond Transaction

Figure 10.1 shows an example of a bond transaction—Ms. Mansfield's Borden bond transaction. On October 8, 1995, Ms. Mansfield purchased an 8.375 percent corporate bond issued by Borden, Inc. She paid $680 for the bond plus a $10 commission ($680 + $10 = $690). On October 8, 2006, she sold it at its current market value of $1,030 minus a $10 commission ($1,030 − $10 = $1,020).

After paying commissions for buying and selling her Borden bond, Ms. Mansfield had a capital gain of $330 ($1,020 − $690 = $330). The market value of the bond increased because overall interest rates in the economy declined during the time she owned the bond. Borden also established a good business reputation during this period, making the bond more secure and, therefore, more valuable.

Figure 10.1 **Ms. Mansfield's Borden, Inc., Bond Transaction**

Interest, 8.375 percent; maturity date, 2019; purchased October 8, 1995; sold October 8, 2006.

Costs when purchased	
1 bond @ $680	$680
Plus commission	+ 10
Total investment	$690

Return when sold	
1 bond @ $1,030	$1,030
Minus commission	− 10
Dollar return	$1,020

Transaction summary	
Dollar return	$1,020.00
Minus total investment	− 690.00
Profit from bond sale	$ 330.00
Plus interest ($83.75 for 11 years)	+ 921.25
Total return on the transaction	$1,251.25

Transaction Fees Ms. Mansfield paid a commission fee when she bought her bond and again when she sold it.

How did these fees affect the cost of her investment and the profit she made from selling the bond?

Caption Answer Fees add to the cost of the bond and reduce the profit on the bond's sale.

Ms. Mansfield also made money on her Borden bond by collecting interest payments. For each of the 11 years she owned the bond, Borden paid her \$83.75 (\$1,000 × 8.375% = \$83.75) in interest. By the time she sold the bond, she had received interest payments totaling \$921.25. These earnings, together with her \$330 capital gain, added up to a total return of \$1,251.25.

$avvy Saver

Savvy Savings Bonds

1. President Franklin D. Roosevelt bought the first \$500 Series EE Savings Bond in a radio broadcast on April 30, 1941.
2. Savings bonds can earn interest tax-free for your college education.
3. Over 55 million people own savings bonds.
4. If your savings bond is accidentally destroyed, it can be replaced.
5. You can buy paperless savings bonds online through the Department of Treasury's Web site.

Government Bonds and Securities

Why does the government issue bonds and securities?

Like private corporations, the federal government as well as state and local governments issue bonds to help raise the money they need to operate.

The federal government sells bonds and other securities to help fund its regular activities and services, and to finance the national debt. U.S. government securities are considered to be almost risk-free. They are backed by the full faith and credit of the United States government. However, because they have a low risk of default, which means failure to pay debts, government bonds offer lower interest rates than corporate bonds.

Treasury Bills, Notes, and Bonds

The U.S. Department of the Treasury issues three basic types of securities: Treasury bills (T-bills), Treasury notes, and U.S. government savings bonds. Treasury bonds, another type of security, were sold by the Treasury Department until October 2001.

You can buy Treasury bills and Treasury notes online through Treasury Direct, which is a Web site operated by the Department of the Treasury. When you buy through Treasury Direct, you do not have to pay a commission. You can also buy these securities through banks or brokers, which charge a commission for their services. U.S. government savings bonds can also be purchased through Treasury Direct, commercial banks, savings and loan associations, or other financial institutions.

You can hold U.S. government securities until maturity or cash before the maturity date. You must pay federal income tax on interest you receive from these investments. However, state and local governments do not tax this income.

Treasury Bills Treasury bills are sold in units of \$1,000. They may reach maturity in 4 weeks, 13 weeks, 26 weeks, or 52 weeks. T-bills are discounted securities. That means that the actual purchase price you pay when you buy a T-bill is less than the face value of the T-bill. On the maturity date, you receive the full face value of the T-bill. A T-bill held until maturity can be reinvested in another bill or can be paid to the owner.

GO FIGURE FINANCIAL MATH

DOLLAR AMOUNT OF RETURN ON A T-BILL

Synopsis: The purchase price of a Treasury bill is less than its full face value. By calculating the return you will receive at the T-bill's maturity date, you will be able to determine how much money you earned on your investment.

Example: Suppose that you buy a 52-week T-bill for $950. On the maturity date, you receive $1,000. What is the dollar amount of return on the T-bill?

Formula:

Face Value − Purchase Price = Dollar Amount of Return

Solution: $1,000 − $950 = $50

The dollar amount of return on your T-bill would be $50.

YOU FIGURE

The maturity date of your 13-week T-bill is coming up. If you paid $1,500 for a T-bill with a face value of $2,000, what is the dollar amount of your return?

Answer $2,000 - $1,500 = $500

To figure out the dollar amount of return on a T-bill, just subtract the purchase price of the T-bill from the face value.

After you have determined the dollar amount of return on your T-bill, you can calculate the rate of return by dividing the dollar amount of return by the purchase price. (See **Go Figure** on page 316.)

Treasury Notes Treasury notes are issued in $1,000 units with a maturity of between one and ten years. Interest rates for Treasury notes are slightly higher than those for Treasury bills because investors must wait longer to get their money back.

Treasury Bonds As mentioned earlier, the Treasury Department no longer issues Treasury bonds. However, many are still in existence and may be purchased in the secondary market through a broker or other financial institution.

Treasury bonds were issued in minimum units of $1,000 with maturities that ranged from 10 to 30 years. The most common maturity is 30 years. Because of the length of time to maturity, interest rates for Treasury bonds are usually higher than those for Treasury bills or Treasury notes.

Series EE Savings Bonds As you learned in Chapter 5, the federal government also offers savings bonds called Series EE Savings Bonds. The purchase price for a Series EE bond is one-half of its face value. For example, a $100 bond costs $50. You can redeem a savings bond anytime from 6 months to 30 years after you purchase it. You receive the amount that you paid for it plus interest. Series EE bonds can accumulate interest for up to 30 years. The interest on Series EE bonds is not taxed by state or local governments. You do not pay federal taxes on the interest until you cash in the bond.

Teaching Activity Divide the students into groups of four. Ask groups to research the interest rates and any other pertinent facts about: treasury bills, treasury notes, Series EE savings bonds, or Series I savings bonds. Have each group debate the advantages and disadvantages of each and determine which investment they, as a group, prefer and why.

GO FIGURE — FINANCIAL MATH

RATE OF RETURN ON A T-BILL

Synopsis: Calculating the rate of return on your T-bill will help you determine whether the T-bill is a good addition to your investment portfolio.

Example: The dollar amount of return on your T-bill is $50. What is the rate of return on the T-bill?

Formula:
Dollar Amount of Return ÷ Purchase Price = Rate of Return

Solution: $50 ÷ $950 = .0526 or 5.26%

The rate of return on your T-bill is 5.26 percent.

YOU FIGURE

If the dollar amount of return on your T-bill is $500 and you paid $1,500 for it, what is the rate of return on your T-bill?

Answer $500 ÷ $1,500 = .33 or 33%

TechByte

Security in an Uncertain Time Just like paper money, stock certificates, corporate bonds, and U.S. Treasury bills have value and can be counterfeited. Since 1877, the Bureau of Engraving and Printing (BEP) has been the sole maker of U.S. currency and other financial instruments, including U.S. Treasury bills, notes, and savings bonds. The BEP has been committed to advanced security for more than a century.

@ Read about how the Bureau of Engraving and Printing maintains a secure environment and describe the technology through **finance07.glencoe.com**.

Series I Savings Bonds The federal government offers other types of savings bonds, too. The most popular bonds, Series I bonds, are inflation-indexed. This means that Series I bonds pay a fixed interest rate that is lower than the rate of traditional savings bonds, but they also pay a variable rate that increases with inflation.

The inflation rate is measured by the Consumer Price Index, which measures the change in cost of a fixed group of products and services such as gasoline, food, and automobiles. The inflation rate for Series I bonds is recalculated twice a year. Series I bonds pay interest for up to 30 years. If you redeem the bond less than five years from the date purchased, there is a penalty of three months of earnings.

Bonds Issued by Federal Agencies

What are agency bonds?

In addition to the securities issued by the Department of the Treasury, bonds are issued by other federal agencies as well. Agency bonds, such as the participation certificates issued by the Federal National Mortgage Association (sometimes referred to as *Fannie Mae*) and the Government National Mortgage Association (sometimes referred to as *GinnieMae),* are almost completely risk-free. However, they offer a slightly higher interest rate than securities issued by the treasury department and have an average maturity of about 12 years. Generally, their minimum denomination is $25,000. Securities issues by federal agencies have maturities ranging from 1 year to 30 years, with an average life of about 12 years. You will learn more about these types of investments in Chapter 11, which discusses real estate and other investments.

▲ **TEAM EFFORT** State and local governments often finance major projects, such as schools, airports, and highways, by selling municipal bonds. *Where can you buy municipal bonds?*

Caption Answer You can buy them directly from the government that issues them or through an account executive.

Bonds Issued by State and Local Governments

What are the two classifications of municipal bonds?

A **municipal bond**, sometimes called a *muni,* is a security issued by a state or local government (town, city, or county) to pay for its ongoing activities. These bonds may also pay for major projects, such as the building of airports, schools, and highways. You can buy municipal bonds directly from the government that issues them or through an account executive.

State and local government securities are classified as either general obligation bonds or revenue bonds. A general obligation bond is a bond that is backed by the full faith and credit of the government that issued it. A revenue bond is a bond that is repaid from the income generated by the project it is designed to finance. For example, a municipal sports arena would generate profits that would repay the investors who bought the bond to build the arena.

Although these bonds are relatively safe, on rare occasions, governments have defaulted, or failed to repay, their bonds. If a government defaults, investors could lose millions of dollars.

Research In groups of four or five, have students research a municipal bond issued by their city or county, determining when it was issued, what the money was used for, and its interest rate.

Insured Municipal Bonds

If the risk of default worries you, you might consider buying insured municipal bonds. Some states offer to guarantee payments on these selected securities. Also, three large private insurers guarantee such bonds: MBIA, Inc.; the Financial Security Assurance Corporation; and the American Municipal Bond Assurance Corporation. Because of the reduced risk of default, insured municipal securities usually carry a slightly lower interest rate than uninsured bonds.

The interest on municipal bonds may be exempt from federal taxes. Tax-exempt status depends on how the funds generated by the bonds are used. Before you invest in a particular municipal bond, find out whether the interest that you will receive from it is taxable.

Like a corporate bond, a municipal bond may be callable by the government that issued it. In most cases, the municipality that issues the bond agrees not to call it for the first ten years. If your municipal bond is not called, you can hold the bond until the maturity date or sell it to another investor.

Section 10.1 Assessment

See the Teacher Manual for answers.

QUICK CHECK

1. What are three characteristics of bonds?
2. Why might the government or a company decide to issue bonds?
3. What are reasons investors buy bonds?

THINK CRITICALLY

4. Discuss ways in which securities issued by state and local governments are similar to corporate bonds.

USE COMMUNICATION SKILLS

5. **Comparing Bonds** You have decided to diversify your investment portfolio. To research, compare a type of corporate bond with a type of government security.

Write About It Write one or two paragraphs making a case for both bonds. Then write a one-paragraph summary describing which investment you think would be best for diversifying your portfolio.

SOLVE MONEY PROBLEMS

6. **Personal and Financial Goals** The county in which Marie Kilbane lives is selling bonds to finance a new storm sewer system. Marie knows that the storm sewers need replacing because her street was flooded last week. At the same time, she knows that her county is not very stable financially. She is not sure that the bonds are a good investment.

Analyze Use what you have learned about personal satisfaction and financial goals in previous chapters to help Marie decide what to do. Should she buy the bonds to help improve her community and her own personal living conditions, or should she invest her money in another way that has a better chance of helping her meet her financial goals? Explain your reasoning.

Section 10.2

Investing in Bonds

Determining Investment Value

How do you determine the investment value of a bond?

Before you make a decision to include bonds in your investment portfolio, you must learn how to accurately determine the investment value of a bond. By understanding bond price quotations, researching various sources of information on bonds, checking bond ratings, and calculating the yield of your bond investment, you will be able to determine whether a bond is a good investment.

Bond Price Quotations

Before you buy or sell bonds, you should become familiar with bond price quotations. Not all local newspapers contain bond price quotations, but many metropolitan newspapers publish complete information on the subject. Two other valuable sources for bond information are *The Wall Street Journal* and *Barron's*.

In a bond price quotation, the price of a bond is given as a percentage of its face value. Remember that a bond's face value is usually $1,000. To find the current market value, or price, for a bond, you must multiply the face value ($1,000) by the price quotation given in the newspaper. For example, a price quoted as "84" means that the current market value is 84 percent of the face value. Therefore, the selling price is $840 ($1,000 × 84% = $840). Purchases and sales of bonds are reported in tables. (See **Figure 10.2** on page 320.)

For government bonds, most financial publications include two price quotations: the bid price and the asked price. The bid price is the amount a seller could receive for the bond. The asked price represents the amount a buyer could pay to purchase the bond. Newspaper bond sections also provide information about interest rates, maturity dates, and yields.

Sources of Information on Bonds

As a bondholder, you should always be aware of the financial stability of the issuer of your bonds. The most important questions are:

- Will the bond be repaid at maturity?
- Will you receive interest payments until maturity?

To help answer these questions, annual reports, the Internet, business magazines, and government reports are good resources.

Focus on Reading

Read to Learn

- How to identify sources of information for selecting bond investments.

Main Idea

Knowing how to read, analyze, and calculate bond information in newspapers and annual reports can help you make wise investments.

Key Terms

- investment-grade bonds
- yield

Before You Read

PREDICT

Do you think buying government bonds would free you from watching your investments?

Springboard Ask the students if they think investing in bonds is a good way to diversify their investment portfolios. If the answer is "no," ask why not; if "yes," ask them why.

Figure 10.2 Corporate Bond Information

Corporate Bonds

Monday, January 10, 2005
Forty most active fixed-coupon corporate bonds

COMPANY (TICKER)	COUPON	MATURITY	LAST PRICE	LAST YIELD	*EST SPREAD	UST	EST $ VOL (000's)
General Motors Acceptance (GM)	6.750	Dec 01, 2014	97.856	7.053	278	10	245,352
General Motors (GM)	8.375	Jul 15, 2033	101.029	8.280	346	30	242,397
General Motors Acceptance (GM)	5.625	May 15, 2009	98.754	5.953	222	5	111,727
Ford Motor Credit (F)	7.000	Oct 01, 2013	103.380	6.484	221	10	104,831
Encana Holdings Finance (ECACN)	5.800	May 01, 2014	106.151	4.965	67	10	96,000
Target (TGT)	5.875	Mar 01, 2012	109.037	4.385	10	10	95,148
General Motors Acceptance (GM)	6.875	Sep 15, 2011	100.858	6.711	298	5	94,355
General Electric (GE)	5.000	Feb 01, 2013	102.338	4.648	37	10	93,211

Look at the bond quotation highlighted above. Each column includes information about this bond. Reading from left to right:

Column 1: Company (Ticker)—The name of the issuing firm is Target. Its abbreviated name is TGT.
Column 2: Coupon—This bond's current yield, or return, based on today's market price is 5.875 percent.
Column 3: Maturity—The date this bond matures is March 1, 2012.
Column 4: Last Price—The current market price of this bond at the close of trading on this day was 109.037 percent of the bond's face value.
Column 8: Estimated $ Volume—On this day, 95,148,000 bonds of this issue were traded.

Source: Reprinted by permission of *The Wall Street Journal*, January 12, 2005; permission conveyed through Copyright Clearance Center, Inc.

Bond Values Newspaper bond quotations indicate a bond's interest, yield, and price.

What was the last price of the Target (TGT) bond?

Caption Answer 109.037 percent of the bond's face value

Annual Reports Annual reports provide detailed financial information about a company and its products, services, activities, goals, and future plans. You will also find news about the company's position in its industry and the industry's major trends. A typical annual report contains the following sections:

Motivating Students Ask students why they might invest in bonds instead of stocks.

- Letter to stockholders from the chief executive officer
- Company highlights for the year
- Detailed company review for the year
- Financial statements
- Notes to financial statements
- Independent auditors' report
- List of directors and officers
- Investor information

To receive an annual report, call, e-mail, or write to the corporation's headquarters and request one. Many large companies have toll-free telephone numbers for customers. You may also find annual reports for major corporations on the Internet or in the reference section of some large libraries.

As you read an annual report, look for signs of financial strength or weakness and ask:

- Is the firm profitable?
- Are sales increasing?
- Are long-term liabilities increasing?
- How might the company's current activities and future plans affect its ability to repay bonds?

The Internet You can access a wealth of information about bond investments on the Internet. You will find answers to many of your questions on corporate Web sites, which typically offer information about the particular company's financial performance. Some sites even include financial information from past years, which allows you to compare one year's performance with another's.

Other sites are devoted to general information about bonds. However, some bond Web sites charge a fee for their research and recommendations.

When investing in bonds, you can use the Internet to obtain price information on specific bond issues to track investments. If you live in a small town or rural area without access to newspapers that provide bond coverage, the Internet can be a good source of current bond prices. You also might visit Web sites operated by Standard & Poor's or Moody's to obtain detailed information about both corporate and government bonds.

Once your research is completed, you can even use the Internet to purchase bonds, to monitor the value of your bonds, and to manage your investments. If you trade bonds online, you might pay lower commissions than you would if you used a full-service or discount brokerage firm.

Business Magazines Another way to research possible bond investments is by reading business magazines. They provide information about the overall economy and give detailed financial data about companies that issue bonds.

Government Reports and Research You can also consult reports and research published by the government to track the nation's economy. This information is available in printed form and on the Internet. If you want to buy U.S. Treasury bills or notes, or U.S. savings bonds, check Web sites run by the Federal Reserve System. In addition, you can review information from the Securities and Exchange Commission by accessing its Web site. State and local governments will also give you information about specific municipal bond issues upon request.

As You Read

RELATE

What section of an annual report would be most important for you to read? Why?

Teaching Activity Divide students into groups of four; either provide or help each group obtain an annual report, a business magazine, and a government report. In addition, they are to use the Internet for this activity. Ask the students to assess each source for its ability to answer the four bulleted questions posed on this page and to assist in making bond investment decisions. Groups are to submit their results in writing.

Academic Connection

GOVERNMENT

Federal, state, and local governments issue bonds to help raise money for various activities and to relieve debt. It is the job of the Bureau of the Public Debt, a division of the U.S. Department of the Treasury, to promote the sale of U.S. Savings Bonds. *Research the Bureau of the Public Debt and write a paragraph about its origins and duties.*

See the Teacher Manual for answer.

Figure 10.3 **Bond Ratings**

Quality	Moody's	Standard & Poor's	Description
High-grade	Aaa	AAA	Bonds that are judged to be of the best quality. They have the lowest risk and the most secure interest and principal payments.
	Aa	AA	Bonds that are judged to be of high quality by all standards. Protection of principal and interest payments is only slightly less than the best.
Medium-grade	A	A	Bonds that have many favorable investment attributes and adequate security.
	Baa	BBB	Bonds that are neither highly protected nor poorly secured.
Speculative	Ba	BB	Bonds that have some risky elements. Often their protection of principal and interest payment is very moderate.
	B	B	Bonds that lack the characteristics of a desirable investment. Investors cannot be sure that interest and principal will be paid in the future.
Default	Caa	CCC	Bonds that are of poor standing. They are currently unlikely to be repaid.
	Ca	CC	Bonds that are highly risky.
	C		Moody's lowest-rated class of bonds, considered the poorest investments.
		C	Standard & Poor's rating given to bonds whose issuers have filed for bankruptcy.
		D	Bond issues that are in default, or are failing to make payments.

Source: "Ratings Defintions," standardandpoors.com, March 18, 2003.

Know Your AAABC's Smart investors check a bond's rating before they buy.

Why are these ratings important to investors?

Caption Answer They tell investors how secure or risky a bond investment is likely to be.

Bond Ratings

Before you invest in a particular corporate or municipal bond, you should check its rating. This rating will give you a good idea of the quality and risk associated with that bond. Bond issues are rated or evaluated by independent rating companies. These companies assign to each bond a rating based on the financial stability of its issuer.

Two of the best-known sources of bond ratings are *Moody's Bond Survey*, published by Moody's Investors Service, Inc., and *Standard & Poor's Stock and Bond Guide*, published by Standard & Poor's. Investors rely on this information when making investment decisions. You can also find bond ratings on the Internet, in financial magazines, and at your public library.

Research Have the students use Standard & Poor's Stock and Bond Guide or Moody's Bond Survey to locate companies with bond ratings in each rating category.

As you can see in **Figure 10.3,** bond ratings are generally categorized from AAA (the highest—the best) to D (the lowest—the worst). The top four categories (Moody's Aaa, Aa, A, and Baa and Standard & Poor's AAA, AA, A, and BBB) include investment-grade bonds. **Investment-grade bonds** are bonds that are issued by financially stable companies or municipalities. They are considered safe investments that will provide a predictable source of income.

Bonds in the next two categories (Moody's Ba and B and Standard & Poor's BB and B) are considered riskier, or speculative. Bonds in the C and D categories may be in default or cannot continue interest payments to bondholders.

U.S. government securities are usually not rated because they are basically risk-free. Long-term municipal bonds are rated in much the same way as corporate bonds. However, short-term municipal bonds are rated differently. Standard & Poor's rates municipal bonds that have maturity dates of three years or less with the following system:

- SP-1: Strong ability to pay face value and interest (Bonds with very safe characteristics get a plus (+) sign.)
- SP-2: Satisfactory ability to pay face value and interest
- SP-3: Doubtful ability to pay face value and interest

Critical Thinking Pose this question to the class: "Is there any reason for an investor to purchase bonds with C or D ratings?" Divide the class in half. Have the first half assume the "yes" position and support it. Have the other half assume the "no" position and support it. Then have the two sides debate.

Yield of a Bond Investment

To determine the return that a particular bond may produce, investors calculate and track its yield. The **yield** is the rate of return, usually stated as a percentage, earned by an investor who holds a bond for a certain period of time.

GO FIGURE **FINANCIAL MATH**

CURRENT YIELD OF A BOND INVESTMENT

Synopsis: Yield is the rate of return an investor earns. By calculating the current yield of a bond, you can determine the return on a bond.

Example: Suppose that you own a $1,000 AT&T corporate bond that pays 7.5 percent interest per year. This means that each year you will receive $75 in interest ($1,000 × 7.5% = $75). Assume that the current market value of the AT&T bond is $960. What is the current yield of your bond investment?

Formula:

$$\frac{\text{Dollar Amount of Annual Interest Income}}{\text{Current Market Value}} = \text{Current Yield of a Bond}$$

Solution: $\frac{\$75}{\$960} = 0.078 \text{ or } 7.8\%$

The current yield is 7.8 percent.

YOU FIGURE

You receive $120 in interest each year on your $2,000 corporate bond. What is the current yield of your bond?

Answer $120 ÷ $2,000 = .06 or 6%

Document Detective

Learn to identify and understand the standard financial documents you will use in the real world.

See the Teacher Manual for answers.

Investigate: A Mutual Fund Account Statement

A mutual fund account statement contains the following information:

- Name of the fund
- Account number
- Beginning and ending share balance
- Activity since the last statement

Your Motive: When you invest in a mutual fund, you need to monitor how effectively your investment is growing. Periodically, you may find it necessary to sell a mutual fund and place your money in another mutual fund that has a potential to grow faster.

President's Group
P.O. Box 605, Springfield, NY 12345

Tanya Sawyer
5744 Pioneer Trail, Harrison, UT 54321

Account number: 6875430001 Account statement: DECEMBER 31, 2005

JEFFERSON MUTUAL INVESTORS FUND

Trade Date	Description	Dollar Amount	Share Price	Shares This Transaction	Share Balance
10/1/05	Beginning share balance		$34.20		721.273
10/19/05	Income dividend	$104.58	$34.20	3.058	724.331
11/11/05	Income dividend	$105.03	$33.45	3.140	727.471
11/28/05	Direct investment	$1,000.00	$34.70	28.818	756.289
12/05/05	Direct investment	$700.00	$32.26	21.699	777.988
Ending share balance					777.988

Ending value as of 12/31/05 was $25,097.89

Key Points: An account statement for a mutual fund will list your contributions and any dividends your account has earned. It will also tell you how many shares of the mutual fund you own and what the value of each is on a given day.

Find the Solutions

1. How many shares did Tanya have at the beginning of the period?
2. How is the *Shares This Transaction* amount calculated?
3. Why is the share price different for each transaction?
4. How is the ending value calculated?
5. Did the value of Tanya's account grow or decline during this time period?

The simplest way to measure a bond's yield is to calculate its current yield. To find the current yield of a bond, divide the dollar amount of annual interest income by its current market value. (See **Go Figure** on page 323 for an example.)

This calculation lets you compare the yield on a bond investment with the yields of other investment alternatives such as savings accounts, certificates of deposit, common stocks, preferred stocks, and mutual funds. If the current market value is higher than the bond's face value, the current yield decreases. If the current market value is less than the bond's face value, the current yield increases. The higher the current yield, the better the return is for the investor.

Investors may also consider the yield to maturity of a bond. This calculation takes into account the relationship between a bond's maturity value, the time to maturity, the current price, and the dollar amount of interest. Like the current yield, the yield to maturity allows you to compare returns on a bond investment with other investments, which is another strategy to track and evaluate your investment finances.

As You Read

QUESTION

Why might an investor consider purchasing Ba, B, or BB bonds?

Question Answer An investor with a secure portfolio may speculate on a riskier bond because it offers a potentially high yield.

Section 10.2 Assessment

See the Teacher Manual for answers.

QUICK CHECK

1. What are three pieces of information about corporate bonds that you could find in the bond section of a newspaper?
2. What information in a company's annual report would be important to an investor who is interested in its corporate bonds?
3. How could you use the Internet to help you learn about investing in bonds?

THINK CRITICALLY

4. Identify two sources for bond ratings, and explain what a bond rating tells you about a bond.

USE MATH SKILLS

5. **Bond Quotations** Every day Elise looks at the bond section of The Wall Street Journal to see if she can get a good deal on a $1,000 bond and add it to her portfolio. This morning a price quotation of 98 for TechnoWiz, a telecommunications firm, caught her interest.

Calculate Figure out the current market value of that bond.

SOLVE MONEY PROBLEMS

6. **Calculating Bond Yields** Tom and Rika Nagata plan to retire in ten years. In 2004, they purchased three bonds:

- Two 20-year AT&T corporate bonds, each with a face value of $1,000 and 7 percent annual interest. The purchase price was $830 each. The current market value is $910 each.
- A 30-year Coca-Cola corporate bond, with a face value of $1,000 and 8.5 percent annual interest. The purchase price was $1,050. The current market value is $1,020.

Calculate To plan ahead, Tom and Rika need to know the current yield on their bonds. Use the formula in this section to calculate the current yield on their bond investments.

Section 10.3

Focus on Reading

Read to Learn

- How to identify types of mutual funds.

Main Idea

Understanding the many kinds of mutual funds will help you decide which funds might be smart investments for you.

Key Terms

- closed-end fund
- open-end fund
- net asset value (NAV)
- load fund
- no-load fund

Before You Read

PREDICT

Based on its name, what do you think is the definition of a mutual fund?

Springboard Write the word *mutual* on the board and ask the students to define it, honing the definition as it emerges. Then ask them to define *fund,* following the same procedure. Then ask: "So what do you think a mutual fund is?" Write the answers on the board.

Mutual Funds

Defining Mutual Funds

What are mutual funds?

Mutual funds are an excellent choice for many investors. A mutual fund is an investment alternative in which investors pool their money to buy stocks, bonds, and other securities based on the selections of professional managers who work for an investment company. By buying shares in a mutual fund, even an investor with limited resources can own part of an entire portfolio of diverse securities. These funds can also be used for retirement accounts, such as 401(k) and 403(b) plans, individual retirement accounts (IRAs), and Roth IRAs, which are discussed in Chapter 15.

Why Investors Buy Mutual Funds

What is a key benefit of purchasing a mutual fund?

One major reason for purchasing a mutual fund is professional management. Investment companies employ professional fund managers who try to pick the best securities for their mutual fund portfolios. However, this can lead some investors to become careless. Many mutual fund investors assume that their investments will increase in value. They might not research and evaluate funds carefully before they buy. They may also neglect to keep track of the performance of the funds they own. Even the best portfolio managers make mistakes. Therefore, wise investors should monitor and review their mutual funds regularly.

Another key reason for buying a mutual fund is diversification. Mutual funds include a variety of securities, which reduces the shareholders' risk. An occasional loss from one investment in a mutual fund is usually offset by gains from other investments in the same fund. Researching and tracking the right mutual fund can provide great results with less effort than it would take to maintain such a diverse portfolio on your own.

Because of these advantages, mutual funds have become extremely popular investments. In 1970, there were 361 mutual funds. By 2003, there were more than 8,300 mutual funds, and the combined assets owned by mutual funds in the United States were worth more than $6 trillion. In the month of April 2003 alone, investors poured more than $16.1 billion into mutual fund investments. Read the material in this section to see if mutual funds are right for you.

◀ **GREAT TIP** Mutual funds can be wise investments for people who have limited time and limited funds to invest. *Why might a mutual fund be a good choice for such an investor?*

Caption Answer They are professionally managed and diverse. Researching and tracking a mutual fund can give good results and take up less time and effort than maintaining a diverse portfolio on your own.

Types of Mutual Funds

What is the difference between a closed-end and an open-end fund?

Motivating Students Have the students read this page, and then ask if they would be interested in investing in mutual funds; most will say "yes." Ask them what it is about mutual funds that appeals to them.

An investment company is a firm that invests the pooled funds of many investors in various securities. The firm receives fee for this service. Mutual funds managed by investment companies are classified as either closed-end funds or open-end funds.

Closed-End Funds

About 6 percent of all mutual funds are closed-end funds offered by investment companies. A **closed-end fund** is a mutual fund with a fixed number of shares that are issued by an investment company when the fund is first organized. After all the original shares have been sold, an investor can buy shares only from another investor. Shares of closed-end funds are traded (bought and sold) on the floors of stock exchanges or in the over-the-counter market. A special section of *The Wall Street Journal* provides information about closed-end funds.

Open-End Funds

Most mutual funds are open-end funds. An **open-end fund** is a mutual fund with an unlimited number of shares that are issued and redeemed by an investment company at the investors' request. Shares of open-end funds are bought and sold on any business day by contacting the investment company that manages the mutual fund.

Extension Using *The Wall Street Journal,* have the students locate one closed-end and one open-end fund.

GO FIGURE — FINANCIAL MATH

NET ASSET VALUE

Synopsis: Investors can buy and sell shares in an open-end mutual fund at the net asset value (NAV). The net asset value is the amount that one share of a mutual fund is worth. Investors use the net asset value formula to assess the real worth of their portfolios and make buying decisions.

Example: Beth owns shares in the New American Frontiers Mutual Fund. The value of the fund's portfolio is $124 million, and its liabilities total $4 million. If this mutual fund has 6 million shares outstanding, what is the net asset value of each of Beth's shares?

Formula:

$$\frac{\text{Value of the Fund's Portfolio} - \text{Liabilities}}{\text{Number of Shares Outstanding}} = \text{Net Asset Value}$$

Solution:

$$\frac{\$124 \text{ million} - \$4 \text{ million}}{6 \text{ million shares}} = \$20 \text{ per share}$$

The net asset value of each of Beth's shares is $20.

YOU FIGURE

You own shares in an open-end mutual fund that has a portfolio value of $220 million. Its liabilities are $6 million, and it has 8 million shares outstanding. What is the net asset value of your shares?

Answer ($220 million − $6 million) ÷ 8 million = $26.75

Teaching Activity Invite a professional mutual fund salesperson or manager to speak to the class. Ask him or her to describe the characteristics of mutual funds and explain the differences for the investor between closed-end and open-end funds and load and no-load funds.

Net Asset Value Investors are free to buy and sell shares at the net asset value. The **net asset value (NAV)** is the amount that one share of a mutual fund is worth. To calculate the net asset value of a mutual fund, subtract the fund's liabilities from the value of the fund's portfolio, and divide the result by the number of shares outstanding. Shares outstanding are the number of shares held by all the investors.

Services If you buy shares of an open-end fund from an investment company, you gain access to a wide variety of services. These services include payroll deduction programs, automatic reinvestment programs, and automatic withdrawal programs.

Load Funds

Before investing in any mutual fund, compare its cost or fees with the cost of other types of investments. Mutual funds are classified as either load funds or no-load funds. A **load fund** (sometimes referred to as an "A" fund) is a mutual fund for which you pay a commission every time you buy or sell shares. The commission, or sales charge, can be as high as 8.5 percent. The average load charge for mutual funds is between 3 and 5 percent. The supposed advantage of a load fund is that the fund's representatives, such as account executives and financial planners, will offer advice and guidance about when shares of the fund should be bought or sold.

No-Load Funds

A **no-load fund** is a mutual fund that has no commission fee. No-load funds do not charge commissions when you buy shares because they have no salespeople. No-load funds offer the same investment opportunities as load funds. If you have a choice between a load fund and a no-load fund, and both offer the same investment opportunities, choose the no-load fund.

Critical Thinking Ask students to think about the fees mutual funds charge, and look at them from both the perspective of the investor and the perspective of the fund managers. Have students write a brief essay addressing these questions: Why would funds charge such fees? Are they justified? Should an investor try to avoid such fees? Is it reasonable for mutual fund investors not to expect to pay fees?

Management Fees and Other Charges

The investment companies that sponsor mutual funds also charge management fees. This fee is a fixed percentage of the fund's asset value. The fees generally range from 0.5 to 1.25 percent of the fund's assets.

Instead of charging investors a fee when they purchase shares, some mutual funds charge a back-end load, which is a fee that is charged for withdrawing money from the fund. Fees range from 1 to 5 percent and are based on how long you own shares of the mutual fund. A back-end load is designed to discourage early withdrawals. A 12b-1 fee is a fee that an investment company charges to help pay for the marketing and advertising of a mutual fund. It is approximately 1 percent of a fund's assets per year.

Careers in Finance

CERTIFIED FINANCIAL PLANNER

Matt Tucker
Self-Employed

Matt enjoys helping people reach their goals in life. He advises individuals and companies about managing their money wisely and effectively. He interviews his clients to determine their assets, liabilities, cash flow, insurance coverage, tax status, and financial objectives. Then he identifies and analyzes their income, spending, and investment patterns to develop a customized financial plan. Plans may include investment strategies, securities, insurance, pension plans, real estate, and tax strategies. Matt is self-employed, but certified financial planners may work for credit unions, banks, and other companies.

SKILLS: Communication, math, economic, financial, and customer-service skills

PERSONAL TRAITS: Good listener, people-oriented, detail-oriented, trustworthy, discreet, honest, and tactful

EDUCATION: Bachelor's degree; Certified Financial Planner (CFP) or Chartered Financial Consultant (ChFC) designation

ANALYZE What sort of company might need help from a certified financial planner?
See the Teacher Manual for answer.

To learn more about career paths for certified financial planners, visit **finance07.glencoe.com**.

▶ **WORLD-CLASS OPPORTUNITIES** Investment firms that create international and global mutual funds are always looking for stocks in countries that are experiencing growth. *Why would an investor choose a fund that includes stocks from India or another such country?*

Caption Answer As these countries experience growth, the value of such investments will rise.

As You Read

RELATE

Have you seen advertisements for mutual funds on television or the Internet? What information do these ads give you?

Categories of Mutual Funds

What are the three main groups of mutual funds?

The managers of mutual funds match their investment portfolios to the investment objectives of their customers. Usually a fund's objectives are clearly explained in its prospectus—a report that provides potential investors with detailed information about a company and its products, such as a particular mutual fund. It can be helpful to sort mutual funds into three main groups: stock mutual funds, bond mutual funds, and mixed mutual funds. Within each group, mutual funds may fall into one of many categories. Note that different sources of investment information may use different categories for the same mutual fund.

Stock Mutual Funds

Most mutual funds are part of the stock mutual funds group. Stock mutual funds are made up of stocks. These funds fall into 14 categories, which describe the fund objectives and types of stock.

Aggressive Growth Funds Aggressive growth funds (sometimes called *capital appreciation funds*) seek to grow money rapidly by investing in stocks whose prices will increase greatly in a short period of time. Because the stocks are often risky, the market value of shares in this type of fund frequently swings between low and high.

Equity Income Funds Equity income funds include stocks issued by companies with a long history of paying dividends. The major objective of these funds is to provide steady income. These funds are investment choices for conservative or retired investors.

Global Stock Funds Global stock funds invest in stocks of companies throughout the world, including the United States. The managers of global funds are not restricted by national boundaries.

Growth Funds Growth funds buy shares of companies expecting higher-than-average revenue and earnings growth. Growth funds tend to invest in larger, less risky companies that may pay some dividends. As a result, the market value of shares in a growth fund is more stable when compared to aggressive growth funds.

Growth and Income Funds Growth and income funds purchase stocks that provide both a steady source of dividend income and the potential for growth. These funds are considered conservative because they invest in large, established companies.

Index Funds Index funds include stocks of companies that are listed in an index such as Standard & Poor's 500 Stock Index. Fund managers select stocks issued by the companies that are included in the index. Thus, an index fund should provide about the same performance as the index. Index funds may have lower management fees.

International Funds International funds include foreign stocks that are sold in securities markets throughout the world. That way, if the economy in one region or nation is in a decline, profits can still be earned in others. Such funds invest outside of the United States.

Large-Cap Funds Large-cap funds generally invest in companies with market values greater than $8 billion. For most investors, a large-cap fund is a long-term holding used for retirement savings.

Mid-Cap Funds Mid-cap funds include stocks of companies with total assets of at least $500 million. Mid-cap funds offer more security than small-cap funds and more growth potential.

Small-Cap Funds Small-cap funds include shares of small, innovative companies with total assets of less than $500 million. They offer high growth potential but are riskier.

Teaching Activity Put the students into pairs. Ask the students to carefully read the 14 different types of stock mutual funds. Students are to determine what kind of investor should or would invest in each type of fund. They may report either in writing or in a graphic display.

Put on Your Financial Planner's Cap

If your client wanted to expand his or her investment portfolio by purchasing a mutual fund, what type of mutual fund would you suggest?

See the Teacher Manual for answers.

Micro-Cap Funds As the name suggests, micro-cap funds invest in the smallest companies. Micro-cap funds buy shares of companies with market values below $250 million. These funds tend to include start-up companies, takeover companies, or companies about to exploit new growing markets. With stocks this small, the risk is always extremely high, but the growth potential is exceptional.

Regional Funds Regional funds include stocks that are traded within one region of the world. Examples include the European region, the Latin American region, and the Pacific region.

Sector Funds Sector funds invest in companies within the same industry. Examples of sectors include health and biotechnology, science and technology, computers, and natural resources.

Utility Funds Utility funds include stocks of companies that provide utility services to their customers. Because these funds are generally safe and stable investments, they are often chosen by conservative investors, such as retired people.

Bond Mutual Funds

Mutual funds in the bond mutual funds group invest only in bonds. The bond fund categories are based on the type of bond the mutual funds purchase.

High-Yield (Junk) Bond Funds High-yield (junk) bond funds invest in high-yield, high-risk corporate bonds.

Research Divide the students into nine groups, and assign one bond mutual fund category to each group. Have each group research its fund type and gather as much information as they can. Have the groups share their findings with the class.

Insured Municipal Bond Funds Insured municipal bond funds include municipal bonds that provide tax-exempt income. An outside company insures them against the risk of default, or nonpayment.

Intermediate Corporate Bond Funds Intermediate corporate bond funds invest in investment-grade corporate bonds that have maturities between five and ten years.

Intermediate U.S. Bond Funds Intermediate U.S. bond funds include U.S. Treasury notes that have maturities between five and ten years.

Long-Term Corporate Bond Funds Long-term corporate bond funds buy investment-grade corporate bonds that have maturities of more than ten years.

Long-Term U.S. Bond Funds Long-term U.S. bond funds include U.S. Treasury bonds and zero-coupon bonds that have maturities of longer than ten years.

Municipal Bond Funds Municipal bond funds invest in municipal bonds that provide investors with tax-exempt interest income.

Short-Term Corporate Bond Funds Short-term corporate bond funds include investment-grade corporate bond issues that have maturities of between one and five years.

Short-Term U.S. Bond Funds Short-term U.S. bond funds invest in U.S. Treasury bills and some Treasury notes that have maturities of between one and five years.

Mixed Mutual Funds

Other mutual funds are part of a third group—mixed mutual funds. These funds invest in a mix of stocks and bonds or in various other types of securities. The funds fall into three categories: balanced funds, money-market funds, and stock/bond blend funds.

STANDARD & POOR'S

Global Financial Landscape

Standard and Poor's publishes the globally recognized S&P 500® financial index. It also gathers financial statistics, information, and news, and analyzes this data for international businesses, governments, and individuals to help them guide their financial decisions.

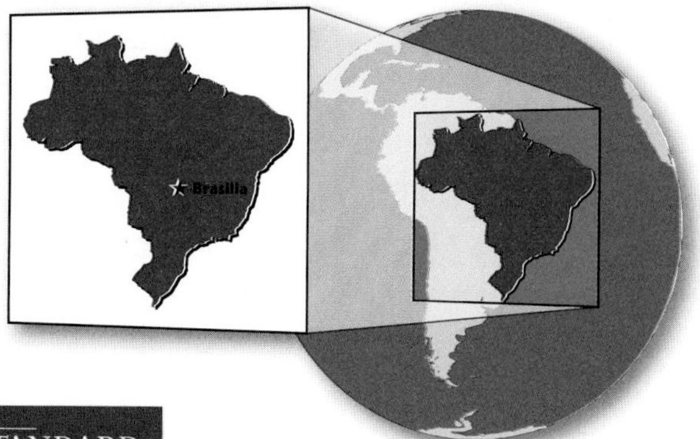

BRAZIL

Latin America is "Hot, hot, hot!" but it is not due to the climate. This enthusiastic description refers to the region's financial markets. Although stocks in a number of Latin countries have been riding high, Brazil has been the "darling of the investing public." Since the Brazilian president made a number of economic reforms in 2003, the stock market has soared. The easy money—over 100 percent return—may have been made already. Some stocks, however, still show promise. Brazil's Petrobras, a state-run oil giant, is a favorite, especially with the increasing cost of fuel. AmBev, the country's only Pepsi distributor, is another popular stock. For the more conservative investors, advisors suggest mutual funds as the safest way to go.

STANDARD & POOR'S **DATABYTES**

Capital	Brasilia
Population	176,464,000
Languages	Portuguese, Spanish, English, and French
Currency	real
Gross Domestic Product (GDP)	$1.38 trillion (2003 est.)
GDP per capita	$7,600

Industry: Textiles, shoes, chemicals, cement, lumber, and iron ore

Agriculture: Coffee, soybeans, wheat, rice, and beef

Exports: Transport equipment, iron ore, soybeans, footwear, and coffee

Natural Resources: Bauxite, gold, iron ore, manganese, and nickel

Think Globally

What type of mutual fund would include stocks from Brazilian companies? Would that fund be a good investment choice? Why or why not?

See the Teacher Manual for the answer.

As You Read

QUESTION

Which of these investments, stock, bond, or mixed mutual funds, do you think would be a good investment? Why?

Question Answer Accept all reasonable answers that show student effort and an understanding of the concept.

Balanced Funds Balanced funds include both stocks and bonds to provide income while avoiding excessive risk. Often the percentage of stocks and bonds is stated in the fund's prospectus.

Money-Market Funds Money-market funds invest in certificates of deposit, government securities, and other safe investments. It is relatively easy to withdraw money from a money-market fund.

Stock/Bond Blend Funds Stock/bond blend funds invest in both stocks and bonds, enabling investors to diversify their holdings with a single fund.

Variety of Funds A variety of mutual funds managed by one investment company is called a *family of funds*. Each mutual fund within the family has a different financial objective. For instance, one fund may be a short-term U.S. bond fund and a growth stock fund. Most investment companies make it easy for shareholders to switch among the mutual funds within a family. This allows investors to adjust their investments conveniently to suit their changing needs or to maximize their profits over time.

Section 10.3 Assessment

See the Teacher Manual for answers.

QUICK CHECK

1. What are the characteristics of closed-end mutual funds?
2. What is an open-end mutual fund?
3. What are three categories of funds that fall under the bond mutual fund group?

THINK CRITICALLY

4. Choose three categories of stock or bond funds in which you think you might like to invest. Explain why you think they are good investments.

USE MATH SKILLS

5. **Load Fund** Noah is thinking about investing $1,000 in a global mutual fund. However, the fund is a load fund, which charges a commission of 8.5 percent. The investment company would deduct this fee from Noah's $1,000 before his money is invested in the fund.

Calculate and Advise What is the dollar amount of the commission that Noah must pay the investment company to invest in this fund? Should he look for a no-load fund? Why or why not?

SOLVE MONEY PROBLEMS

6. **Fund Objectives** Hilda wants to invest her savings in a mutual fund, but she is concerned about the risk of investing. She wants a fund that is stable and safe. Her friend Ana recommends that she consider utility funds and money-market funds. Her friend Jack says she should explore aggressive growth funds and high-yield (junk) bond funds.

Write About It Review the characteristics of utility funds, money-market funds, aggressive growth funds, and high-yield (junk) bond funds. Write down a list of the objectives for these funds. Whose advice is best? Why?

Section 10.4

Investing in Mutual Funds

Making an Informed Decision

What steps can you take to decide on mutual fund investments?

Which mutual funds are best for you? When should you buy or sell your shares? You will have to answer these questions for yourself. However, by considering your financial goals and consulting various sources of information on mutual funds, you will be able to determine the best approach for investing in mutual funds.

Considering Your Financial Goals

You can consider several questions when you are in the process of identifying your investment goals:

- How old are you?
- What is your family situation?
- How much risk do you want to take?
- How much money do you make now?
- How much money are you likely to make in the future?

After you have considered these factors and answered these questions, you can set your investment goals. Once you know your goals, find a mutual fund with investment objectives that match your own.

Information on Mutual Funds

You will find a great deal of information that can guide you through the decision-making process of buying or selling shares in a mutual fund. The main sources of information on mutual funds include:

- Newspapers
- Quotations
- Prospectuses
- Annual reports
- Financial publications
- Professional advice
- Internet

Newspapers Metropolitan newspapers and financial newspapers, such as *The Wall Street Journal* and *Barron's*, provide a wealth of information.

Focus on Reading

Read to Learn

- How to discuss sources of information for selecting mutual funds.
- How to describe the methods of buying and selling mutual funds.

Main Idea

Knowing how to evaluate, buy, and sell mutual funds will enable you to invest wisely.

Key Terms

- income dividends

Before You Read

PREDICT

What would be your definition of capital gain?

Springboard Ask students what they may also need to think about when making decisions about investing. Elicit their financial goals and information on specific mutual funds.

Motivating Students Students may feel overwhelmed by investment choices. Discuss with them the fact that researching different investments and investment strategies is worth the effort. Ask them to quickly jot down a list of investments that they think might be interesting; they should save their jottings and revisit them in a month's time.

Figure 10.4 Mutual Fund Information in *The Wall Street Journal*

How to Read the Monthly Performance Tables

Performance tables are provided by Lipper, Inc. These tables include all primary funds listed by NASDAQ. Bond performance numbers are preliminary. Though verified, the data cannot be guaranteed by Lipper or its data sources. Double-check with funds before investing.

Performance calculations assume reinvestment of all distributions and are after subtracting annual expenses. But figures do not reflect sales charges ("loads") or redemption fees.

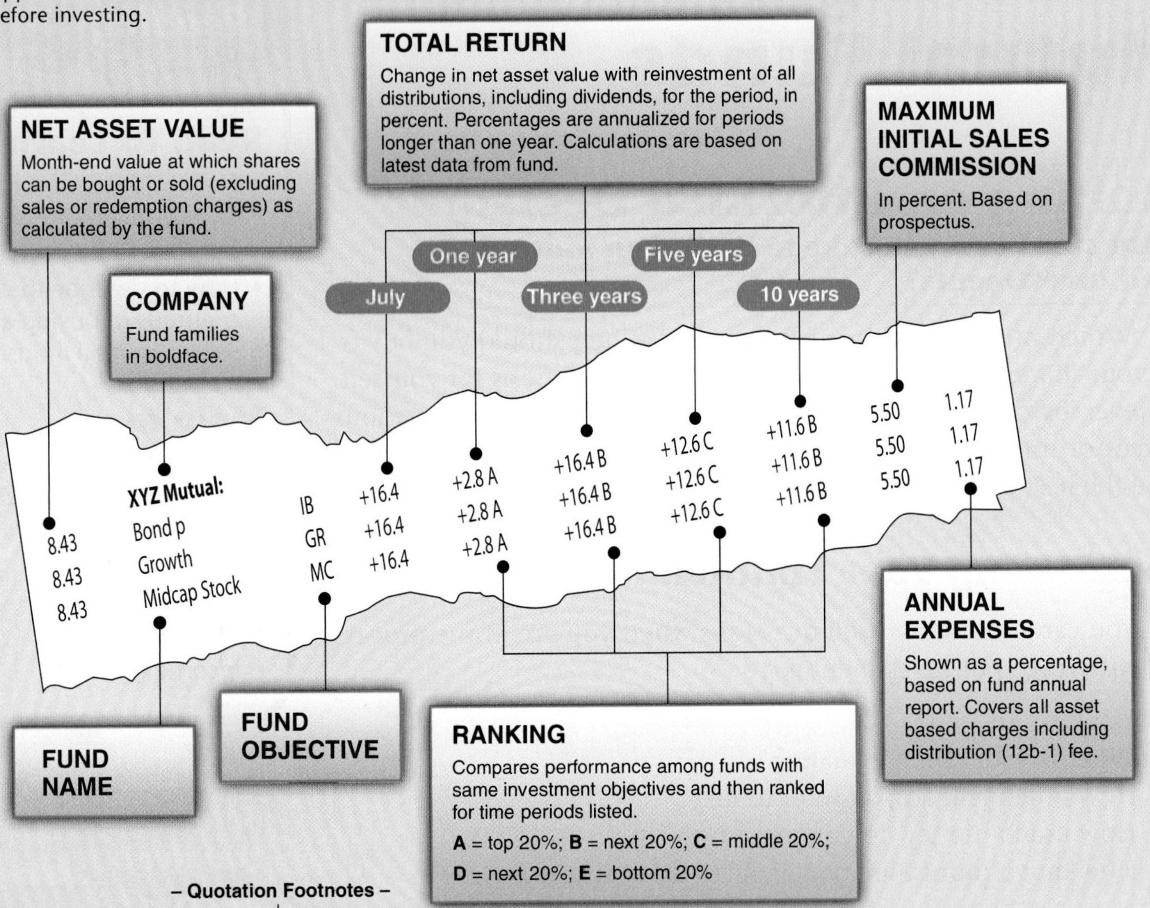

– Quotation Footnotes –

e–Ex-distribution, **f**–Previous day's quotation. **g**–Footnotes x and s apply. **j**–Footnotes e and s apply. **p**–Distribution costs apply, 12b-1. **r**–Redemption charge may apply. **s**–Stock split or dividend. **t**–Footnotes p and r apply. **v**–Footnotes x and e apply. **x**–Ex-dividend. **z**–Footnotes x, e, and s apply.

NA–Not available due to incomplete price performance or cost data. **NE**–Not released by Lipper; data under review. **NN**–Fund not tracked. **NS**–Fund didn't exist at start of period.

Decoding Quotations When you read newspaper quotations, notice the letter(s) beside the name of a specific fund and refer to the quotations footnotes.

What does the letter "p" indicate about a fund?

Caption Answer It indicates that distribution costs apply: The mutual fund has a 12b-1 fee that the investment company charges to help pay for marketing and advertising.

Quotations As shown in **Figure 10.4,** mutual fund quotations contain information about a fund's net asset value, objective, performance, and cost. When you read mutual fund quotations, remember to note any letters beside the name of a specific fund. Then look up their meanings in the quotation footnotes.

Mutual Fund Prospectuses After you have narrowed your search, check out the prospectuses of the mutual funds that most interest you. To get a copy of a prospectus, call, write, or e-mail the investment company that manages the mutual fund. Many investment companies have toll-free telephone numbers that you can find by calling the toll-free information number (1-800-555-1212). An investment company sponsoring a mutual fund must give a potential investor a prospectus when requested.

Read the prospectus completely before you invest. The prospectus summarizes the fund and lists any fees you will have to pay. The prospectus usually provides the following information:

- A description of the fund's objective
- The risk factor associated with the fund
- A fee table
- A description of the fund's past performance
- A description of the type of investments contained in the fund's portfolio
- Information about dividends, distributions, and taxes
- Information about the fund's management
- Information on limitations or requirements the fund must honor when choosing investments
- The process by which investors can buy or sell shares of the mutual fund
- A description of services provided to investors
- Fees for services
- Information about how often the fund's investment portfolio changes (sometimes referred to as *turnover ratio*)
- Information about how to open a mutual fund account

WebQuest

Nest Egg
Have you ever pooled your money with friends or family to buy party supplies or donate to a charity? If you have, then you know something about mutual funds. In the world of investing and finance, a mutual fund contains a group of stocks, and you can buy a small piece of all of them by investing in the fund. Choosing a mutual fund that is right for you usually involves some careful research.

@ To continue with Task 4 of your WebQuest project, visit **finance07.glencoe.com**.

Mutual Fund Annual Reports If you are a potential investor, you may request an annual report by mail, telephone, or e-mail. When you become a shareholder, the investment company will automatically send you an annual report. Annual reports may also be posted on a company's Web site. A fund's annual report contains a letter from the president of the investment company, the fund manager, or both.

Teaching Activity Have each student obtain a mutual fund prospectus. Have students write a brief statement regarding each of the bulleted items on this page as it relates to the mutual fund prospectus each has.

Do not forget the role of the fund manager in determining a fund's success. If a fund's present manager has been doing a good job for five years or longer, chances are that he or she will continue to perform well in the future.

The annual report contains detailed financial information about the fund's assets and liabilities. It also includes a statement of operations that describes expenses and day-to-day operating costs of the fund, a statement of changes in net assets, and a schedule of investments.

Finally, most annual reports include a letter from the fund's independent auditors. This letter backs up the accuracy of the information contained in the report.

Figure 10.5 Mutual Fund Survey

Equity Funds

MUTUAL FUND SCOREBOARD

How to use the tables

BUSINESSWEEK RATINGS Overall ratings are based on five-year, risk-adjusted returns. They are calculated by subtracting a fund's risk-of-loss factor (see RISK) from pretax total return. Category ratings are based on risk-adjusted returns of the funds in that category. The ratings;

A SUPERIOR
B+ VERY GOOD
B ABOVE AVERAGE
C AVERAGE
C– BELOW AVERAGE
D POOR
F VERY POOR

These tables list A-rated funds. For others go to http://bwnt.businessweek.com/mutual_fund
MANAGEMENT CHANGES indicates the fund's manager has held the job at least 10 years; a indicates a change since Dec. 31, 2003.
S&P 500 COMPARISON The pretax total returns for the Standard & Poor's 500-stock index are as follows: 2004, 10.9%; three-year average (2002-2004), 3.6%; five-year average (2000-2004), –2.3%; 10-year average (1995-2004), 12.1%.
CATEGORY U.S. diversified funds are classified by market capitalization of the stocks in the portfolio and by the nature of those stocks. If the average market cap is greater than $10 billion, the fund is large-cap; from $2 billion to $10 billion, mid-cap; less than $2 billion, small-cap. All-cap funds are those that don't follow a fixed-capitalization policy. Value funds are those whose stocks have price-to-earnings and price-to-book ratios lower than average for their market capitalizations. Growth funds have higher than average p-e and p-b ratios. Blend funds are those in which the ratios are about average. Hybrids mix stocks and bonds, and possibly other assets. World funds generally include U.S. stocks, foreign funds do not. Sector and regional funds are as indicated.

FUND/SYMBOL	OVERALL RATING (COMPARES RISK-ADJUSTED PERFORMANCE OF EACH FUND AGAINST ALL FUNDS)	CATEGORY (COMPARES RISK-ADJUSTED PERFORMANCE OF EACH FUND AGAINST ALL FUNDS)	RATING	SIZE: ASSETS $MIL	SIZE: % CHG. 2003-2004	FEES: SALES CHARGE($)	FEES: EXPENSE RATIO(%)	2004 RETURNS(%): PRE TAX	2004 RETURNS(%): AFTER-TAX	2004 RETURNS(%): YEILD
ABN AMRO MID CAP N CHTTX	B+	**Mid-cap Blend**	A	423.9	130	No load	1.34	18.9	18.3	0.0
ABN AMRO REAL ESTATE N ARFCX	A	**Real Estate**	C	76.6	51	0.00*	1.37	33.4	32.2	1.9
ABA FIVE STAR LARGE CAP INSTITUTIONAL AFBEX	C	**Large-cap Growth**	A	20.3	–1	No load	1.08	7.8	7.7.8	0.1
AFBA FIVE STAR USA GLOBAL INSTITUTIONAL AFGLX	C	**Large-cap Growth**	A	40.0	1	No load	1.08	6.6	6.6	0.4
AIM ENERGY INV. FSTEX **(A)**	A	**Natural Resources**	B	311.1	52	No load	1.76	36.6	36.6	0.0
AIM GOLD & PRECIOUS METALS INV. FGLDX **(b)**	A	**Precious Metals**	C	117.8	–18	No load	1.93	–4.9	–5.0	1.1
AIM REAL ESTATE A IARAX	A	**Real Estate**	B+	625.3	147	4.75	1.65	36.0	35.1	1.4
AEGIS VALUE AVALX	A	**Small-cap Value**	B+	815.2	92	No load	1.50	13.5	12.7	0.0
AL FRANK VALUX	A	**Mid-cap Value**	B+	244.0	103	0.00*	1.79	15.8	15.8	0.0
ALLIANCE BERNSTEIN REAL ESTATE INV. ADV. ARSYX	A	**Real Estate**	B	159.3	56	No load	1.44	35.2	34.5	2.9

SALES CHARGE Many funds take this "load" out of the initial investment, and for ratings purposes, returns are reduced by these charges. Loads may be levied on withdrawls.

EXPENSE RATIO This counts expenses as a percentage of average net assets. Footnotes indicate a 12(b)-1 plan, which uses shareholder money for marketing. The average is 1.38%.

PRETAX TOTAL RETURN A fund's net gain to investors, including reinvestment of dividends and capital gains at month-end prices.

AFTERTAX TOAL RETURN Returns adjusted for U.S. taxes; treats all capital gains and long-term.

YIELD Income as a percent of net asset value.

TOP 10 STOCKS The percentage of fund assets that represents the 10 largest holdings. The higher the number, the more concentrated the fund, and the more dependent on the performance of a relatively small number of stocks.

Source: Reprinted from the January 24, 2005, issue of *BusinessWeek* by permission. © 2005 McGraw-Hill Companies, Inc.

Fund Scores Every year *BusinessWeek* magazine publishes and rates equity funds based on performance and risk.

Besides ratings, what other types of information does this survey provide?

Caption Answer It includes information about each fund's size, fees, and returns for the past year.

Critical Thinking Have students track the mutual fund for which each has a prospectus for two weeks. They are to track the NAV and fund quotation. At the end of that period, students are to write up the results of their tracking and decide whether they would invest.

Financial Publications Financial magazines such as *BusinessWeek, Forbes, Kiplinger's Personal Finance,* and *Money* are sources of information about mutual funds. These publications provide annual surveys and rankings of mutual funds, such as the example from *BusinessWeek* magazine shown in **Figure 10.5.**

In addition to annual surveys, a number of mutual fund guidebooks are available at bookstores or your local public library.

Figure 10.6 Morningstar Mutual Fund Research

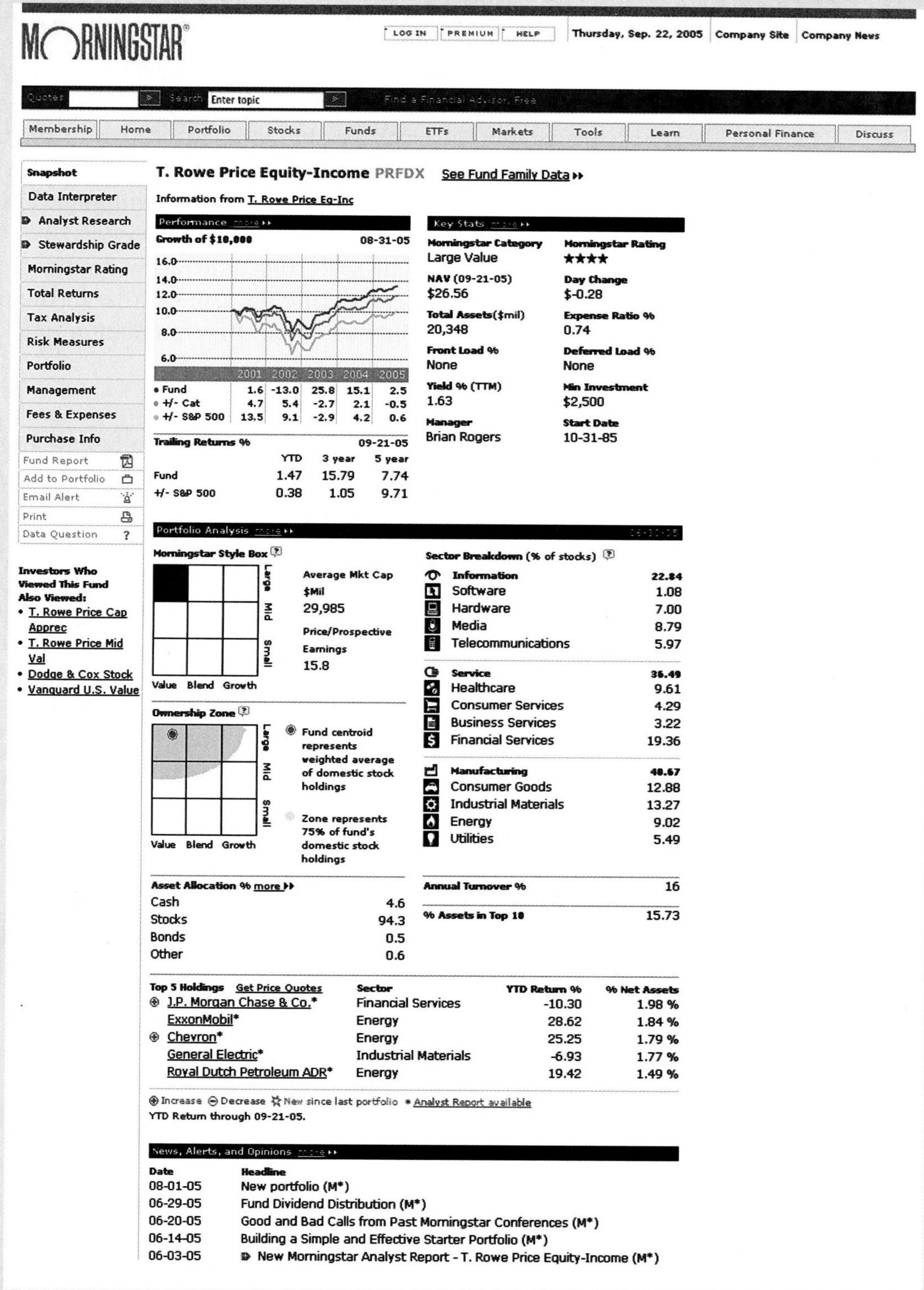

MORNINGSTAR

LOG IN | PREMIUM | HELP | Thursday, Sep. 22, 2005 | Company Site | Company News

Quotes | Search Enter topic | Find a Financial Advisor, Free

Membership | Home | Portfolio | Stocks | Funds | ETFs | Markets | Tools | Learn | Personal Finance | Discuss

Snapshot
Data Interpreter
Analyst Research
Stewardship Grade
Morningstar Rating
Total Returns
Tax Analysis
Risk Measures
Portfolio
Management
Fees & Expenses
Purchase Info
Fund Report
Add to Portfolio
Email Alert
Print
Data Question

T. Rowe Price Equity-Income PRFDX See Fund Family Data

Information from T. Rowe Price Eq-Inc

Performance more

Growth of $10,000 08-31-05

	2001	2002	2003	2004	2005
Fund	1.6	-13.0	25.8	15.1	2.5
+/- Cat	4.7	5.4	-2.7	2.1	-0.5
+/- S&P 500	13.5	9.1	-2.9	4.2	0.6

Trailing Returns % 09-21-05

	YTD	3 year	5 year
Fund	1.47	15.79	7.74
+/- S&P 500	0.38	1.05	9.71

Key Stats more

Morningstar Category: Large Value	Morningstar Rating: ★★★★
NAV (09-21-05): $26.56	Day Change: $-0.28
Total Assets($mil): 20,348	Expense Ratio %: 0.74
Front Load %: None	Deferred Load %: None
Yield % (TTM): 1.63	Min Investment: $2,500
Manager: Brian Rogers	Start Date: 10-31-85

Portfolio Analysis more 06-30-05

Morningstar Style Box

Average Mkt Cap $Mil 29,985

Price/Prospective Earnings 15.8

Ownership Zone

Fund centroid represents weighted average of domestic stock holdings

Zone represents 75% of fund's domestic stock holdings

Sector Breakdown (% of stocks)

Information	**22.84**
Software	1.08
Hardware	7.00
Media	8.79
Telecommunications	5.97
Service	**36.49**
Healthcare	9.61
Consumer Services	4.29
Business Services	3.22
Financial Services	19.36
Manufacturing	**40.67**
Consumer Goods	12.88
Industrial Materials	13.27
Energy	9.02
Utilities	5.49

Asset Allocation % more

Cash	4.6
Stocks	94.3
Bonds	0.5
Other	0.6

Annual Turnover % 16

% Assets in Top 10 15.73

Top 5 Holdings (Get Price Quotes)	Sector	YTD Return %	% Net Assets
⊕ J.P. Morgan Chase & Co.*	Financial Services	-10.30	1.98 %
ExxonMobil*	Energy	28.62	1.84 %
⊕ Chevron*	Energy	25.25	1.79 %
General Electric*	Industrial Materials	-6.93	1.77 %
Royal Dutch Petroleum ADR*	Energy	19.42	1.49 %

⊕ Increase ⊖ Decrease ☆ New since last portfolio * Analyst Report available

YTD Return through 09-21-05.

Investors Who Viewed This Fund Also Viewed:
- T. Rowe Price Cap Apprec
- T. Rowe Price Mid Val
- Dodge & Cox Stock
- Vanguard U.S. Value

News, Alerts, and Opinions more

Date	Headline
08-01-05	New portfolio (M*)
06-29-05	Fund Dividend Distribution (M*)
06-20-05	Good and Bad Calls from Past Morningstar Conferences (M*)
06-14-05	Building a Simple and Effective Starter Portfolio (M*)
06-03-05	New Morningstar Analyst Report - T. Rowe Price Equity-Income (M*)

Source: Morningstar.com, © 2005. Morningstar, Inc., 225 W. Wacker Dr., Chicago, IL 60606.

Online Information This report shows the type of information that Morningstar.com provides to an investor who is interested in the T. Rowe Price Equity Income Fund.

What can you learn by reading the section titled "Performance" at the top of the Web page?

Caption Answer Morningstar, Inc., rates the T. Rowe Price Equity-Income Fund as having an above-average return and below-average risk, and gives the fund a four-star rating.

As You Read

RELATE

Of the several listed resources available to research mutual funds, which two seem most important to you? Why?

Professional Advice Professional advisory services also provide detailed information on mutual funds (see **Figure 10.6**). Popular sources include Standard & Poor's, Lipper Analytical Services, Morningstar, Inc., Value Line, and Wiesenberger Investment Companies. In addition, various mutual fund newsletters provide financial information to subscribers for a fee. These publications are expensive, but you may be able to obtain copies of them from brokerage firms or public libraries.

Professional advisory services, such as Morningstar, also offer online research reports for mutual funds. Many investors find that the research reports provided by such companies are worth the fees they charge. The information is basically the same as that in the printed reports. However, the ability to obtain the information quickly can be a real advantage.

Research Have the students use the Internet to find information about the mutual fund they are tracking. They can use this information to expand their results to write their paper.

Internet Many investors research mutual fund investments on the Internet. You may access this information online by one of several methods. If you know the name or the four- or five-letter symbol for a fund, you may obtain current market values by using Web sites such as Yahoo! Finance. You can also get a price history and a profile.

Most investment companies that sponsor mutual funds have Web sites. These sites are another source of useful information. To obtain information, use a search engine, such as Google, and type in the name of the fund. You will find information regarding statistics about individual funds, procedures for opening an account, promotional literature, and investor services. However, investment companies want you to become a shareholder, and therefore, their Web-site material may read like a sales pitch. Look at the facts before you invest your money.

GO FIGURE — FINANCIAL MATH

CAPITAL GAIN

Synopsis: Capital gain is the amount by which a share's selling price exceeds its purchase price. Determining the capital gain that you will receive when you sell the shares of your mutual fund will tell you how much the return on your investment will be.

Example: Sani purchased shares in the Fidelity Stock Selector Fund at $17 per share. Two years later, Sani sold the shares at $19.50 per share. What was the capital gain per share on Sani's mutual fund?

Formula:

Sales Price − Purchase Price = Capital Gain per Share

Solution: $19.50 − $17.00 = $2.50

The capital gain per share on Sani's mutual fund was $2.50.

YOU FIGURE

If you purchased mutual fund shares at $8.50 each and sold them for $11 per share, what would be your capital gain?

Answer $11 − $8.50 = $2.50

Return on Investment

What is the difference between a capital gain distribution and a capital gain?

Whether you choose a closed-end fund or an open-end fund, the purpose of investing in a mutual fund is to receive income. As a mutual fund shareholder, you may gain income in one of three ways.

First, you may receive income dividends. **Income dividends** are the earnings a fund pays to shareholders. Second, you may earn capital gain distributions. Capital gain distributions are payments made to shareholders that result from the sale of securities in the fund's portfolio. Third, you may make a good return by buying shares at a low price and then selling them after the price increases.

When you sell shares in a mutual fund, the profit that results from an increase in value is referred to as a capital gain. As discussed in Chapter 8, a capital gain is the profit from the sale of an asset such as stocks, bonds, or real estate. Of course, if the price of a fund's shares goes down between the time of purchase and the time of sale, you lose money. Note the difference between a capital gain distribution and a capital gain. A capital gain distribution occurs when the fund sells securities within the fund's portfolio and distributes profits to shareholders. A capital gain occurs when the shareholder sells some of his or her shares in the mutual fund.

As You Read

QUESTION

What factors influence the price of a fund's shares?

Question Answer Factors include the law of supply and demand, the fund manager's track record, anticipated future profits, and the overall state of the stock and bond markets.

Discussion Discuss with students the tax implications of money earned from mutual funds; ask students the difference between mutual funds and other securities as regards capital gains.

Taxes and Mutual Funds

How are mutual fund earnings taxed?

Income dividends, capital gain distributions, and capital gains are all taxable earnings. At the end of every year, investment companies and brokerage firms send each shareholder a statement detailing the income dividends and capital gain distributions he or she received. Usually, this information is provided on the IRS Form 1099DIV. However, the investor is responsible for maintaining clear and accurate records of the purchase and sale prices. The following are some general guidelines on how mutual fund transactions are taxed:

- Income dividends are reported along with all other dividend amounts you have received. They are taxed as regular income.
- Capital gain distributions are reported on your federal income tax return.
- Capital gains or losses that result from your selling shares in a mutual fund are reported on your federal income tax return.

You should be aware of two factors when you pay taxes on your mutual funds. First, almost all investment companies allow you to reinvest the capital gains distributions and income dividends you earn instead of receiving cash. These distributions are taxable and must be reported on your income tax return. Second, you decide when to sell your stocks or bonds.

Caption Answer Mutual funds can be used to invest money that is contributed to tax-deferred 401(k) and 403(b) plans or individual retirement accounts. Also, investments will grow larger over time.

▲ **THE GOLDEN YEARS** Many people use mutual funds to save for their retirement. *What is the advantage of starting to invest in a mutual fund at a young age?*

Thus, you can pick the tax year when you pay tax or deduct losses on these investments. Mutual funds, on the other hand, buy and sell securities on a regular basis during any 12-month period. Unlike investments that you manage, you have no control over when the mutual fund sells securities. Therefore, you have no control over when you are taxed on capital gain distributions.

Buying and Selling Mutual Funds

How do you buy and sell mutual funds to help you meet your financial goals?

The main reason for investing is the opportunity to make money on your investment. Mutual funds can provide investors with income dividends, capital gain distributions, and profits that result from their decision to sell their shares. Various purchase options and withdrawal options allow you to manage your mutual fund investments and profits to help you meet your financial goals.

Purchase Options

Before you buy shares in a fund, you will need to consider several different purchase options. As discussed earlier in this chapter, different types of funds are sold by different means. Closed-end funds are traded through stock exchanges, such as the New York Stock Exchange or in the over-the-counter market. You can purchase shares of an open-end fund from a brokerage firm or by contacting the investment company that sponsors the fund.

A wide variety of both no-load and load funds can also be bought from mutual fund supermarkets that are available through brokerage firms such as Charles Schwab and E*Trade. Mutual fund supermarkets offer at least two advantages. First, instead of dealing with several investment companies, you can make one toll-free phone call to buy or sell a large number of mutual funds. Second, you receive one statement from the brokerage firm instead of receiving a statement from each investment company. This statement provides the information that you need to monitor all of your investments in one place and in the same format.

When you buy shares in an open-end mutual fund from an investment company, you have several purchase options. You can choose a regular account transaction, a voluntary savings plan, a payroll deduction plan, a contractual savings plan, or a reinvestment plan.

Regular Account Transactions A regular account transaction is the most popular and least complicated way to buy shares. With this method you decide how much money to invest and when to invest it. Then you simply buy as many shares as possible.

Voluntary Savings Plans A voluntary savings plan lets you make smaller purchases than the minimum required by the regular account transaction. However, when you make your first purchase, you also must commit to making regular minimum purchases of the fund's shares. Such small monthly investments can be a great way to save for long-term objectives. For most voluntary savings plans, the minimum purchase ranges from $25 to $100.

Payroll Deduction Plans Most voluntary savings plans also offer payroll deduction plans. This means that with your approval, the investment company will deduct a certain amount from your paycheck each month and invest it in your mutual fund. Mutual fund savings plans can also be used to invest money that is contributed to tax-deferred 401(k) and 403(b) retirement plans or individual retirement accounts (IRAs).

Contractual Savings Plans Contractual savings plans require you to make regular purchases of shares over a specific period of time, usually 10 to 20 years. You will pay penalty fees if you do not make the required purchases. Financial experts and government agencies disapprove of contractual savings plans because many investors lose money with these plans.

Teaching Activity Divide students into groups of four. Have students reread the purchase options (this page) to thoroughly understand them. Then have each group prepare a demonstration of these options; these demonstrations may be skits, puppet shows, posters, songs, or any form of graphic or creative presentation the students choose (subject to approval).

After You Read

REACT

Which mutual fund purchasing plan do you think would be best for a young investor and for a retired investor? Why?

React Answer Answers will vary, but the voluntary savings plan or the reinvestment plan would be good for a young person investing for the future. A retired investor may do best with regular account transactions which give the freedom to buy when it suits the investor to do so.

Reinvestment Plans You can also buy shares in an open-end fund by using the fund's reinvestment plan. With a reinvestment plan, your income dividends and capital gain distributions are automatically reinvested to buy additional shares of the fund. Most reinvestment plans allow shareholders to reinvest without having to pay additional sales charges or commissions. Reinvestment is a great way to add to your portfolio.

Withdrawal Options

If you choose to invest in mutual funds, you will also need to know how you can take your money out of a fund. You can sell shares of closed-end funds to another investor anytime you want on the stock exchange or in the over-the-counter market. Shares in an open-end fund can be sold to the investment company that sponsors the fund. In this case, provide proper notification, and the fund will send you a check for the net asset value of your shares. With some funds, you can write checks to withdraw money. If you have at least $5,000 worth of shares in a mutual fund, most funds will offer you four additional ways of withdrawing money.

Critical Thinking Have the students, in writing, assess the withdrawal options and determine what type of investor would most benefit from each option.

Investment Period Withdrawal First, you may withdraw a certain amount each investment period until your fund has been exhausted. Typically, an investment period is three months, and most funds require investors to withdraw a minimum amount, usually $50, if the investor chooses to withdraw funds.

GO FIGURE **FINANCIAL MATH**

PERCENTAGE OF ASSET GROWTH WITHDRAWAL

Synopsis: Most mutual funds will allow an investor to withdraw a prearranged percentage of his or her investment's asset growth—or the amount that the investment has grown during a period.

Example: Marco invested $1,500 in a green energy mutual fund. This first period, his investment was reported to be worth $1,800. He is allowed to withdraw 60 percent of the asset growth per period. How much can he withdraw?

Formula:
Current Portfolio Value − Original Portfolio Value = Asset Growth

Asset Growth × Prearranged Percentage = Withdrawal Amount

Solution: $1,800 − $1,500 = $300

$300 × 60% or .60 = $180

Marco can withdraw $180.

YOU FIGURE

You invested $1,000 in a mutual fund specializing in cell-phone technology. During the first period, your portfolio has a value of $1,235. Your prearranged withdrawal percentage is 40 percent of net asset growth. How much can you withdraw?

Answer $1,235 − $1,000 = $235; $235 × .40 = $94

Investment Period Liquidation A second option is to liquidate or "sell off" a certain number of shares each investment period. Of course the net asset value of shares in a fund varies from one period to the next. Therefore, the amount of money you receive will also vary.

Asset Growth Withdrawal A third choice lets you withdraw a prearranged percentage of your investment's asset growth, which is the amount by which your portfolio has increased in value. For example, suppose that you arrange to receive 60 percent of the asset growth of your portfolio. The asset growth of your portfolio was $800 in a particular investment period. For that period you will receive a check for $480 ($800 × 60% = $480). If the value of your portfolio does not increase, you receive no payment. Under this option, your principal (the amount of your original investment) remains untouched.

Dividend and Distribution Withdrawal A final option allows you to withdraw all income that results from income dividends and capital gains distributions earned during an investment period. Under this option, too, your principal remains untouched.

Section 10.4 Assessment

See the Teacher Manual for answers.

QUICK CHECK

1. What type of information does a mutual fund quotation provide to help you evaluate a fund?
2. What are three ways in which you can receive income from your mutual fund investments?
3. What are the withdrawal options that are available when selling shares in a mutual fund?

THINK CRITICALLY

4. Newspaper mutual fund quotations, financial magazines, and the Internet are three sources you might use to research a mutual fund that matches your financial goals. Decide which source you would use first, and explain why.

USE COMMUNICATION SKILLS

5. **Sales Pitch** Imagine that you are the professional manager of a large mutual fund. You are looking for investors to buy shares in your fund.

Present Prepare a flyer that will convince people to invest in your fund. Name your fund, and give as many reasons as possible why it would be a solid investment. Make your flyer appealing by using exciting language and by including pictures, charts, and graphs.

SOLVE MONEY PROBLEMS

6. **Purchase Options** Malia has invested in a mutual fund. She wants to add to her investment on a regular basis and is trying to decide which purchase option to use. Her mutual fund offers a voluntary savings plan, a contractual savings plan, and a reinvestment plan.

Analyze Analyze the advantages and disadvantages of the three purchase options available to Malia. Which purchase option would you suggest to her? Why?

Chapter 10 Review & Activities

See the Teacher Manual for answers.

CHAPTER SUMMARY

- Corporate bonds have the following characteristics: interest rates, maturity dates, and face values.
- Corporations sell bonds to raise funds for operations, expansions, or purchases.
- Investors buy bonds because they provide regular income, plus the principal must be repaid by maturity.
- Governments sell bonds for reasons similar to corporations: to fund regular activities and finance the national debt.
- Government bonds include Treasury bills, Treasury notes, and U.S. savings bonds (Series EE).
- Information on bonds is available in the financial press, corporate annual reports, bond rating reports, and online.
- Types of mutual funds include closed-end mutual funds, open-end mutual funds, load funds, and no-load funds.
- Mutual fund information is found in newspapers, annual reports, and financial publications, and through Web sites and advisors.
- Methods of buying and selling include regular account transactions, voluntary savings plans, payroll deduction plans, contractual savings plans, reinvestment plans, and withdrawal options.

Communicating Key Terms

You meet with employees who will retire in five years to discuss adding bonds to their 401(k) plans. Explain the benefits of bond investments, using as many of these key terms as possible.

- maturity date
- face value
- debenture
- mortgage bond
- convertible bond
- sinking fund
- serial bonds
- registered bond
- coupon bond
- bearer bond
- zero-coupon bond
- municipal bond
- investment-grade bonds
- yield
- closed-end fund
- open-end fund
- net asset value (NAV)
- load fund
- no-load fund
- income dividends

Reviewing Key Concepts

1. **Explain** the advantages of the call feature on bonds to corporations and to investors.
2. **Explain** why corporations may prefer to issue bonds to raise funds for their operations.
3. **Explain** how the market value of a bond is determined.
4. **List** three examples of reasons state and local governments might issue bonds.
5. **Describe** the characteristics of a municipal bond, including tax factors.
6. **Explain** the meaning of bond ratings and their impact on buying decisions.
7. **Describe** the characteristics of a closed-end, open-end, load, and no-load mutual fund.
8. **Describe** a mutual fund prospectus.
9. **Compare** the three ways you can purchase mutual funds.

See the Teacher Manual for answers.

ACADEMIC SKILLS

History Today mutual funds are very popular investment options. However, since their origin in 1924, they have fallen in and out of favor.

Write About It Research and write a one-page essay on the history of mutual funds in the United States.

YOUR FINANCIAL FIGURES

Bond Market Value You own 12 20-year General Electric Capital Services corporate bonds with face values of $1,000. Their coupon rate is 7.5%. Their current yield is 5.2%.

1. **Calculate** (a) What is the current market value of one of these bonds? (b) Of the total investment? (c) If you do not have an immediate need for the cash, what would be your best course of action, sell and reinvest in some other security or hold?
2. **Compute** by using spreadsheet software to make and present these calculations.

REAL-WORLD Application

Connect with Economics You just inherited $4,000. You need to decide whether to invest this money in a mutual fund, pay down your credit card debt, or simply hold the money in an interest-bearing checking account to pay upcoming bills.

1. **Think Critically** What is your current financial situation, and do you foresee a legitimate need for extra funds in the short term?
2. **Analyze** What is the "health" of your emergency fund?

Internet CONNECTION

Mutual Fund Prospectus The prospectus of a mutual fund is where you find out about the structure, fees, and "rules" of investing in the fund.

Log On Use an Internet search engine and find Web sites of mutual fund companies, such as Fidelity and T. Rowe. Review at least one mutual fund's prospectus. Answer the following questions:

1. What are the investment orientation, risk tolerance, and goals of the managers of this fund?
2. Would you recommend this fund? Why or why not?

BusinessWeek ONLINE

Newsclip: Reliable Bonds? A bond fund is a mutual fund comprised mainly of bonds. These types of funds are usually safe investments with greater opportunity for returns.

Log On Go to **finance07.glencoe.com** and open Chapter 10. Learn more about the different types of bond funds. Write a list of points you have learned about bond funds. Would you invest in a bond fund? Why or why not?

WHAT'S YOUR FINANCIAL ID?

WHAT'S YOUR INVESTING IQ?

The more you know about investing, the greater your chance for higher returns. Before you read this chapter, answer the questions below on a separate sheet of paper. After you have studied the chapter in class, take the quiz again to see how much you have learned.

1. Liquidity is the ability to ___________.
   a. easily convert your financial resources into cash without a loss in value
   b. invest in any liquid substance
   c. transfer funds electronically

2. The least speculative investment listed below is ___________.
   a. municipal bonds
   b. treasury bonds
   c. zero-coupon bonds

3. A mutual fund prospectus is ___________.
   a. a possible date for Saturday night
   b. a report that provides potential investors with information about the fund
   c. a statement of your earnings

4. Federally tax-exempt interest can be earned on ___________.
   a. an annuity
   b. a convertible bond
   c. a municipal bond

5. Investors buy junk bond funds because ___________.
   a. of the possibility of a high yield
   b. municipalities always need to remove junk
   c. they usually resist fluctuations in the stock market

6. Mutual funds are popular because ___________.
   a. they generally receive the highest (AAA) rating
   b. investors can choose which stocks are in their portfolio
   c. investors can acquire a diversified portfolio

Accept all reasonable answers that show student effort and an understanding of the concept.

Your Financial Portfolio

Evaluating Mutual Funds

Eric is looking at a mutual fund because it might earn a greater return than a CD. He used the following checklist as a way to evaluate the Pacific Sun Growth Fund, a stock mutual fund.

After evaluating Pacific Sun Growth Fund, Eric has decided that he likes the potential for a high return. He may go with the fund, even though he needs $1,000 to make his initial investment.

	Pacific Sun Growth Fund
1. Name of mutual fund	1. Pacific Sun Growth Fund
2. Mutual fund group and category	2. Stock mutual fund/aggressive growth
3. Mutual fund's objective (Aggressive growth, moderate growth, income and safety, and income)	3. Aggressive growth of capital
4. Yield in the last twelve months	4. 15%
5. Average return or yield for last five years	5. 11%
6. Average return or yield for last ten years	6. 18%
7. Load fees or redemption fees	7. no fees
8. What is the minimum investment?	8. $1,000
9. Is the fund closed to new investors?	9. No
10. Morningstar rating (in stars and risk)	10. Three-star rating and moderate risk

Research

Call an investment company for a prospectus of a mutual fund. You can also visit your local library and look in *Morningstar Mutual Funds* or the *Weisenberger Investment Companies Yearbook*. On a separate sheet of paper, fill in the information on the checklist to evaluate the fund.

Accept all reasonable answers that show student effort and an understanding of the concept.

CHAPTER 11

Real Estate and Other Investments

What You'll Learn

When you have completed this chapter, you will be able to:

Section 11.1

- Explain the different types of real estate investments.
- Discuss the advantages and disadvantages of real estate investments.

Section 11.2

- Identify the different types of precious metal and gem investments.
- Describe collectibles investments.
- Analyze the risks of investing in precious metals, gems, and collectibles.

Reading Strategies

To get the most out of your reading:

Predict what you will learn in this chapter.
Relate what you read to your own life.
Question what you are reading to be sure you understand.
React to what you have read.

In the Real World . . .

Erica Sato loves to visit thrift shops, where she looks for rare books and records that cannot be found on CDs. She has a knack for knowing what items are in demand and supplements her income by selling those things through online auctions. Erica also knows that old Disney® and Coca-Cola® items are coveted by collectors around the world. The Internet makes it easy for her to sell to people near and far, and she has built an excellent online reputation by sending items on time and in protective boxes. Collectibles can be a good investment, but Erica realizes they are more risky than other investments, so she wants to diversify her investments to include real estate and other alternatives.

As You Read *Why do you think collectibles are considered a risky investment?*

Lesson Plan See the Teacher Manual for the Chapter 11 planning guide and lesson plan.

ASK STANDARD &POOR'S

Collecting

Q: Are collectible action figures a smart investment for retirement?

A: Although collecting can be an enjoyable and sometimes profitable pursuit, collectibles are not a mainstay of retirement planning. It would be best if you focused your retirement planning efforts on building a diversified portfolio that may include stock and bond investments. You could still use collectibles as a small part of your portfolio, but their returns are very unpredictable.

Ask Yourself Why are the returns on collectibles so unpredictable?

@ Go to **finance07.glencoe.com** to complete the Standard & Poor's Financial Focus activity.

Section 11.1

Focus on Reading

Read to Learn

- How to explain the different types of real estate investments.
- How to discuss the advantages and disadvantages of real estate investments.

Main Idea

Real estate investment opportunities vary widely. Consider the advantages and disadvantages of each type of investment opportunity.

Key Terms

- direct investment
- commercial property
- indirect investment
- syndicate
- participation certificate (PC)
- financial leverage

Before You Read

PREDICT

Why do you think so many Americans invest in real estate?

Springboard Ask the students to imagine that a relative owns a 16-unit apartment complex and has offered them free rent in return for managing it. How will they manage the building?

Real Estate Investment

Real Estate Investments

What is the difference between direct and indirect investment in real estate?

Real estate has always been a favorite investment for Americans. Unlike stocks and bonds, a piece of property is something you can see and touch and take pride in. However, if you are new to the real estate market, you may be confused by all the different choices you have.

Direct Real Estate Investments

Real estate investments can be direct or indirect. The owner of a **direct investment** holds legal title to the property he or she has purchased. Direct investments include single-family houses, duplexes, apartments, land, and commercial property.

A Home as an Investment What is a home? Obviously, it is the place where you and your family live. However, owning a home can also be a good investment.

According to Mortgage Bankers Association of America, home ownership is most Americans' largest financial asset. In 2003, the market value of homes in the United States was nearly $12 trillion, which was 50 percent higher than five years earlier. Homeowners' equity, the value of a home less the amount owed on the money borrowed to purchase it, accounted for 30 percent of household wealth.

As discussed in Chapter 8, during periods of inflation, the purchasing power of your money declines. Investing your money can help you stay ahead of inflation. Owning a home is a good investment because, generally, home prices have risen steadily over the years, as shown in **Figure 11.1.** In fact, during the past 150 years, owning a home produced an average rate of return after inflation of about 2.5 percent. That is about the same rate of return you would expect from a bond.

Most homeowners have mortgages, which can provide certain tax benefits. Homeowners can report the interest charges on mortgage payments as well as property taxes as deductions on their income tax returns.

Vacation Homes Second-home mortgages also provide tax benefits. For example, Kevin's parents own a vacation home on Fox Lake. It is a good investment because the family uses it year-round and never rents it out to others. According to the federal government, that qualifies it as a second home. Therefore, Kevin's parents can take advantage of certain tax deductions. If the parents rented out the home for more than 14 days each year, the government would consider it a rental property. As a result, any tax deductions would depend on whether Kevin's parents managed the property and on the size of their income.

Motivating Students Have students consider the homes they would like to buy one day. Do they see the homes as places to live or as investments? Ask them why it makes a difference.

Commercial Property In addition to the vacation home on the lake, Kevin's parents also own commercial property. **Commercial property** is land and buildings that produce rental income. Kevin's parents own an apartment building that adds to their income. Other examples of commercial property include duplexes, hotels, office buildings, and stores. Most small investors favor duplexes, four-plexes, or small apartment buildings. Many investors start by purchasing a small commercial property. Then they buy larger properties as the equity in their original investment increases.

Figure 11.1 Average Sales Prices of New Single-Family Homes

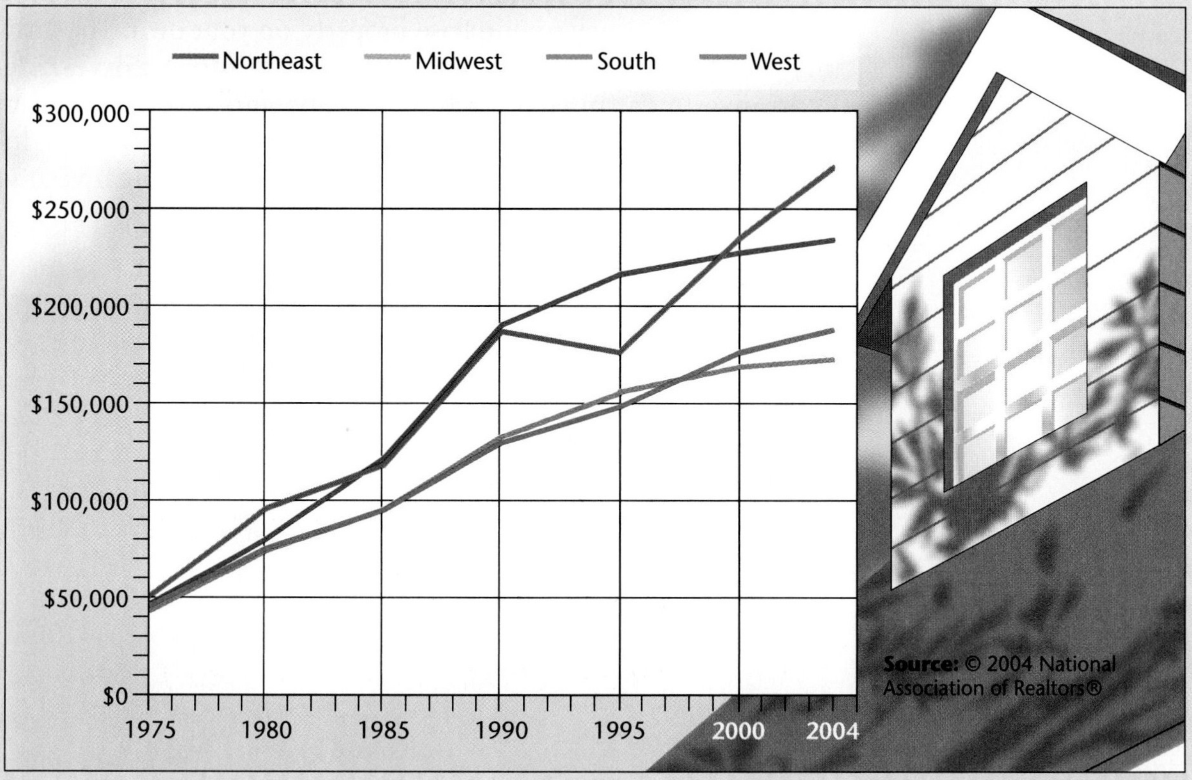

Up and Away The average selling price of homes in the United States has risen steadily since 1970.

Which region experienced the greatest gain? The lowest?

Caption Answer greatest: West; lowest: Midwest

$avvy Saver

Utility Savers

1. Use fluorescent lamps to save 30 to 38 percent of lighting bills.
2. Seal and weather-strip doors and windows.
3. Repair all leaky faucets.
4. Unplug refrigerators when not in use.
5. Plant shade trees to block heat from buildings.

Land In 1986, Kevin's parents received quite a shock. Tax laws in the United States were rewritten so that many popular real estate investments, such as apartment buildings, lost some of their tax advantages. Owning commercial property became less appealing to some real estate investors. Many of these investors began investing in land that was ready to be developed.

Kevin's parents talked to an investment banker before they purchased land. She told them that while land investments often promise tremendous gains, they also pose enormous risks. If construction in general slowed or business activity declined, Kevin's parents might not be able to sell their property at a profit. Even worse, they might not be able to get the price that they had paid for it. Furthermore, the banker reminded them that unlike an apartment building, land in urban areas usually does not produce any income.

The banker also cautioned Kevin's parents about buying land and then dividing it into smaller lots to build single-family houses. They must be certain that water, sewers, and other utilities would be available. Otherwise, they would have to supply those services. The most common and least expensive way to obtain water and sewer service is to connect to existing services in a nearby city or town.

Indirect Real Estate Investments

Research Have students research the rates of return during the last ten years in your state for the following: homes, duplexes, small apartment buildings (16 units or under), and undeveloped land. Have students chart or graph their findings.

Suppose that you want to invest in real estate, but you do not have enough money to purchase property on your own. The answer may be an indirect real estate investment. An **indirect investment** is an investment in which a trustee is appointed to hold legal title to the property on behalf of an investor or group of investors. Indirect investments include real estate syndicates, real estate investment trusts, high-risk mortgages, and participation certificates.

Caption Answer Under certain circumstances, owners can deduct mortgage interest and property taxes from their income taxes.

▶ INVESTMENT IN LEISURE
A family vacation home can be part of a sensible investment strategy. *Why are vacation homes smart investments?*

Real Estate Syndicates or Limited Partnerships A **syndicate** is a temporary association of individuals or business firms organized to perform a task that requires a large amount of funds. A real estate syndicate invests in real estate. A syndicate may be organized as a corporation or as a trust. Most commonly, however, a syndicate is organized as a limited partnership.

Here is how a limited partnership works: A general partner, who takes complete responsibility for all of the partnership's liabilities, forms the partnership. The general partner then sells participation units, or shares, to a number of limited partners, or investors. Suppose that you decide to join the syndicate. As a limited partner, you are liable for only the amount of money you have invested, perhaps $5,000 or $10,000. This limited liability is an important condition of a real estate syndicate because the syndicate's mortgage debt may be more than your personal net worth or that of the other limited partners.

A real estate syndicate offers you and the other partners a variety of benefits. For example, if the syndicate purchases several types of property, your investment will be diversified. That is, you will be part owner of different types of property. In addition, the property owned by the syndicate is professionally managed. You do not need to care for it yourself.

At one time, people would join a real estate syndicate to create a tax shelter, which is a legal arrangement to take advantage of income tax deductions. However, the Tax Reform Act of 1986 limits the tax advantages available to syndicate investors. For example, investors can no longer use losses from their syndicate investments to offset, or reduce, their income from other sources. The 1986 law limits deductions for interest and for depreciation, which is the cost of general wear and tear. It also raised the tax on capital gains.

As You Read

RELATE

Do you know anyone who owns a home or invests in real estate?

Real Estate Investment Trusts (REITs) Joshua's grandfather gave him $3,000 for graduation. Joshua would like to invest that money in real estate, but realizes that he cannot buy an apartment building or condominium for that much money. One real estate investment choice Joshua could consider is a real estate investment trust (REIT). A REIT works much like a mutual fund. Like mutual funds, REITs combine money from many investors. However, while mutual funds are investments in stocks, bonds, and other securities, REITs are investments of the investors' money in real estate or in construction or mortgage loans. Shares in REITs are traded on stock exchanges or on the over-the-counter market.

There are three types of REITs: equity, mortgage, and hybrid. If you choose an equity REIT, your money will be invested in properties. Choosing a mortgage REIT will put your money to work financing construction loans and mortgages on developed properties. If you want to combine the investment goals of equity and mortgage REITs, you can choose a hybrid REIT.

Discussion Discuss with students what they think is the primary appeal of investing in real estate syndicates; would they be interested? How about REITs? Ask if they think the Tax Reform Act of 1986 would discourage people from investing in real estate syndicates.

Document Detective

Learn to identify and understand the standard financial documents you will use in the real world.

See the Teacher Manual for answers.

Investigate: A County Real Estate Valuation
A county real estate valuation contains the following information:

- Property parcel ID number
- Description of the property
- Appraised value
- Assessed value

Your Motive: Real estate property, such as a house or land, is taxed based on its value. The higher the value, the more taxes you pay to the local government. You will need to make sure that your property is valued correctly so that you do not pay excessive taxes.

Parcel Number:	30-05655				
Owner:	Milo Lucky				
Property Address:	6731 Williamsburg Circle				
Legal Description:	Williamsburg Colony Phase C Lot 73				
Land Description:	100 ft. by 200 ft.				
Description of Primary Building(s)					
Colonial frame 2.0 story 2,251 sq. ft. built about 1988 with 8 total rooms with 4 bedrooms with 2 bathrooms with 1 half bath with full basement with no attic with 0 car basement garage with 1 fireplace.					
Description OBY Building(s)	**Value**	**Proposed 2007 Appraised Value**		**2007 Assessed Value**	
WD1: Wood Deck	$1,330	Land:	$42,900	Total:	$205,770
		Building(s):	$162,870	Land:	$15,020
		Total:	$205,770	Building(s):	$57,010
				Total:	$72,020

Key Points: The county government assesses the value of real estate property to determine how much tax should be paid for the property. County auditors review the value of recent real estate purchases and any improvements made to the property. The auditors then determine an appraised value for the property and an assessed value. The assessed value determines the amount of tax. Then a statement is sent to the property owner explaining the valuation.

Find the Solutions

1. What is the parcel ID number?
2. How many square feet of interior space does the building have?
3. What style is the building?
4. What is the appraised value of the wood deck?
5. What is the total square footage of the lot?

According to federal government regulations, REITs are required to:

- Distribute at least 90 percent of their net annual earnings to shareholders.
- Avoid investing in risky, short-term real estate holdings in the hope of selling them for quick profits.
- Hire independent real estate professionals to carry out certain management activities.
- Have at least 100 shareholders, with no more than half the shares owned by five or fewer people.

If you are interested in finding out more about REITs, you can contact the National Association of Real Estate Investment Trusts.

▲ **PART OF SOMETHING BIG** Giant corporate complexes can cost millions of dollars to build and maintain. *Do you need to be extremely wealthy to invest in large commercial properties? Why or why not?*

Caption Answer No. Through REITs and real estate syndicates, small investors can become part owners of otherwise unattainable real estate.

High-Risk Mortgages Some investors accept high risk in exchange for possible profits. For example, Mr. Moy is a wealthy investor who purchases high-risk mortgages and other debt contracts. Because he is wealthy, Mr. Moy is willing to take risks that financial institutions, such as banks and savings and loan associations, will not. For example, Mr. Moy might purchase the mortgage on a property that is not in demand because the title to the property may not be legally clear or insurable. Because of such risks, Mr. Moy and other similar investors might receive a high rate of return on their investments. Even though Mr. Moy is not guaranteed a high rate of return, he hopes that the demand for his property will increase so he will make a handsome profit in the future. On the other hand, if the demand does not increase, Mr. Moy may lose most or all of his investment.

Participation Certificates Unlike Mr. Moy, investors cannot afford to take such risks with their money. If you are looking for a risk-free real estate investment, then participation certificates might be a good choice for you. A **participation certificate (PC)** is an investment in a group of mortgages that have been purchased by a government agency. Because the investment is made in a group of mortgages, it is considered a mutual fund. You can buy participation certificates from these federal agencies:

- Government National Mortgage Association (Ginnie Mae)
- Federal Home Loan Mortgage Corporation (Freddie Mac)
- Federal National Mortgage Association (Fannie Mae)
- Student Loan Marketing Association (Sallie Mae)

Teaching Activity Divide students into groups of four. Each group wants to invest in an apartment complex. The groups need to decide whether to invest in a real estate syndicate, an equity REIT, a mortgage REIT, or a hybrid REIT. Next they are to design the complex, including its size, location, name, logo, and amenities. Groups will share their work with the class.

As You Read

QUESTION

Why do people join limited partnerships and/or REITs?

Question Answer People can invest relatively small amounts without the difficulties of property management while getting benefits from ownership. Also, their liability is limited, and returns can be good.

A few states also issue participation certificates. You can purchase PCs from the State of New York Mortgage Agency (Sonny Mae) and the New England Education Loan Marketing Corporation (Nellie Mae).

Agencies with close ties to the federal government guarantee Maes and Macs. The PCs they issue are as secure as U.S. Treasury bonds and notes. You can invest as little as $1,000 to buy shares. Each month, you can receive a check for the principal and interest or reinvest the profits.

Real Estate Investment: Pros and Cons

What should you know when considering real estate investment?

Before you invest in real estate, you will want to weigh the advantages and disadvantages.

Advantages of Real Estate Investments

There are several advantages enjoyed by certain types of real estate investments:

Hedge Against Inflation When inflation rises, your purchasing power decreases. Both direct and indirect investments in areas such as real estate are wise because they provide some protection against inflation. Historically, real estate continues to increase in value or at least hold its value, thus protecting investors from declining purchasing power.

Easy Entry By making an indirect investment in a real estate syndicate, you can easily become a part owner of an apartment building or a shopping center. By combining your money with that of other investors, you can purchase commercial property.

Limited Financial Liability An indirect investment in a real estate syndicate allows you to be a limited partner. That means you are not liable, or responsible, for losses beyond your original investment. This advantage is important if the syndicate is investing in a risky venture.

Financial Leverage **Financial leverage** is the use of borrowed funds for direct investment purposes. By using borrowed money, you can purchase more expensive property. If property values and incomes are rising, this can be an advantage.

For example, suppose that Deborah buys a building for $100,000 with no borrowed funds. She then sells the building for $120,000. Deborah's $20,000 profit equals a 20 percent return on her $100,000 investment ($20,000 ÷ $100,000 = 0.20 or 20%).

On the other hand, suppose that Deborah invested just $10,000 of her own money and had a $90,000 mortgage with an interest rate of 8.5 percent. After three years, she sells the property for $120,000, with a profit of $7,721 ($20,000 profit − $12,279 in interest = $7,721). Her profit would represent a 77 percent return on her $10,000 investment ($7,721 ÷ $10,000 = 0.7721 or 77.21%).

WebQuest

Nest Egg

Is it a waste of time for a young person to think about investing in real estate? Buying a home is just for married couples, right? Not necessarily. You can make owning real estate a part of your plan for the future starting right now. Learn about the basic steps for investing in real estate.

To continue with Task 5 of your WebQuest project, visit **finance07.glencoe.com**.

Disadvantages of Real Estate Investments

Unfortunately, investors such as Deborah cannot be certain that their real estate investments will pay off. There are several possible disadvantages to real estate investments:

Illiquidity Real estate is an illiquid investment, which means that it cannot be easily converted into cash without a loss in value. It may take months or even years to sell commercial property or shares in a limited partnership.

Declining Property Values As discussed earlier, real estate investments usually offer some protection against inflation. However, when interest rates fall, or if the economy is in a decline, the value of real estate investments may decrease. If you own property, you may have to make the difficult decision to sell your property for less than you paid for it and accept a loss.

Lack of Diversification Because real estate is expensive, many investors can afford only one or two properties. Subsequently, it may be difficult to build a diversified real estate investment portfolio. Keep in mind, however, that REITs, PCs, and syndicates do offer various levels of diversification.

Critical Thinking Divide the students into four groups. The first group is to "sell" investment in real estate syndicates. The second group is to discourage such investment. The third group is to "sell" investment in REITs. The fourth group is to discourage such investment. Groups are to research and plan. Then have the groups debate their positions.

Careers in Finance

COMMERCIAL PROPERTY MANAGER

Yvonne Inger
Hartman Management

Yvonne has always been able to manage many tasks at once. As the commercial property manager for three retail buildings, this skill comes in handy. Yvonne monitors and maintains the building systems, vendor contracts, tenant relations, and profit and loss responsibilities for all three buildings. To keep in touch with her tenants, she visits the retail sites regularly and attends weekly and monthly tenant meetings. In addition to handling her tenants' concerns, she takes care of the properties' bills, licenses, and any emergencies that may arise. As a commercial property manager, Yvonne is able to work independently and acts as her own boss.

SKILLS: Communication, math, management, customer-service, organization, and time-management skills

PERSONAL TRAITS: Discretion, good judgment, and tactfulness

EDUCATION: Bachelor's degree or master's degree in business administration, finance, administration, or related fields

ANALYZE How might a skilled commercial property manager affect the value of the property?
See the Teacher Manual for answer.

To learn more about career paths for commercial property managers, visit **finance07.glencoe.com**.

Discussion Discuss with students why they think the Tax Reform Act of 1986 was passed.

Lack of a Tax Shelter In the past, real estate syndicates were tax shelters for investors. However, the Tax Reform Act of 1986 eliminated that advantage. Syndicate investors cannot deduct real estate losses from the income they receive through other sources, such as wages, dividends, and interest.

Management Problems When you invest in REITs, syndicates, or PCs, property management is provided as a part of your investment. When you invest in mortgages, property management is not an issue. However, when you buy your own properties, you must manage them. That means that you are responsible for such things as finding reliable tenants, replacing worn carpeting, and fixing the furnace. Property management can be a full-time job, and many investors are not willing to take on that much responsibility.

Investment Options

If you consider all the advantages and disadvantages of investing in real estate and you believe it is too risky or too complicated, you might consider other tangible investments. Gold and other precious metals, gems, and collectibles are options that some investors choose. However, these investments carry risk with the reward, as discussed in the next section.

Section 11.1 Assessment

See the Teacher Manual for answers.

QUICK CHECK

1. What are examples of direct and indirect real estate investments?
2. What are the advantages of indirect real estate investments?
3. What are the disadvantages of direct and indirect real estate investments?

THINK CRITICALLY

4. Identify some similarities and differences among syndicates, REITs, and PCs.

USE COMMUNICATION SKILLS

5. **Selling Participation Certificates** PCs are considered risk-free investments. This makes them appealing to investors who are looking for protection against inflation but who do not have a lot of money to invest. How would you interest potential investors in these certificates?

Write About It Write a persuasive ad that points out the advantages of participation certificates. Be sure to include information that highlights the risk-free nature of these investments.

SOLVE MONEY PROBLEMS

6. **Diversification** Teresa has been working as an advertising copywriter for five years. She has been saving money and now has $10,000 to invest in real estate. Teresa wants to make sure that her real estate investments will be diversified, not too risky, and easy for her to manage.

Analyze Give Teresa some advice about the different types of real estate investments that would best meet her investment goals.

Section 11.2

Precious Metals, Gems, and Collectibles

Gold

Why do people invest in gold and other precious metals?

Precious metals include such valuable ores as gold, platinum, and silver. Many people invest their money in precious metals as a hedge, or protection, against inflation.

When Mark graduated from high school, his grandfather gave him a gold pocket watch. Ever since, Mark has been fascinated by gold and has wanted to own more of it. If you are interested in purchasing gold, you have several choices, as shown in **Figure 11.2** on page 362.

The price of gold rises when people believe that war, political unrest, or inflation may be just around the corner. As international tensions ease or the political situation stabilizes, the price of gold falls. In January 2005, the price of gold was about $425 per ounce. **Figure 11.3** on page 363 shows how the price of gold rose and fell from 1979 to 2003.

Silver, Platinum, Palladium, and Rhodium

What is one disadvantage of investing in a precious metal such as platinum?

Other precious metals that rise in value during times of political or economic trouble are silver, platinum, palladium, and rhodium. Silver prices have ranged from a historic low of 24.25 cents an ounce in 1932 to more than $50 an ounce in early 1980. In January 2005, the price of silver was about $6.80 an ounce.

Platinum, palladium, and rhodium, which are three lesser-known precious metals, are also popular investments. All of these metals have industrial uses, particularly in automobile production. In January 2005, platinum sold for about $877 an ounce, palladium for about $200 an ounce, and rhodium for about $1,300 an ounce.

Focus on Reading

Read to Learn

- How to identify the different types of precious metal and gem investments.
- How to describe collectibles investments.
- How to analyze the risks of investing in precious metals, gems, and collectibles.

Main Idea

Understanding the risks and rewards of investing in precious metals, gems, and collectibles will help you build a sound, diversified portfolio.

Key Terms

- precious metals
- precious gems
- collectibles

Before You Read

PREDICT

Do you think investments in precious metals, gems, or collectibles are risky or safe?

Springboard Have students brainstorm lists of precious metals and gems. Write the lists on the board. Ask which ones they think are most valuable and if they think these are good investments.

Figure 11.2 Investing in Gold

When the economy weakens or political unrest develops, some people believe that gold is the safest investment they can make. Investments in gold can take many forms.

1 **Bullion** You can purchase gold bullion, which is offered in bars and wafers, from dealers of precious metals and from banks. The seller's commission can range from 1 to 8 percent. If you do not store the gold with the dealer, you must have it reassayed (tested for quality) before you can resell it.

2 **Coins** Gold coins represent a simple way to invest in this precious metal. Most coin dealers require a minimum order of ten coins and will charge you a seller's commission of at least 2 percent.

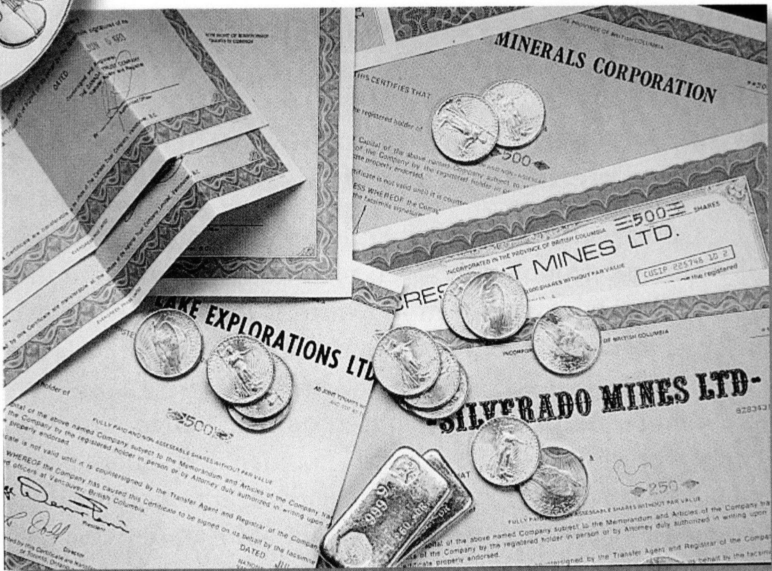

3 **Stocks** You can diversify your investment portfolio by purchasing common stock in gold mining companies. When the economy is healthy, the price of gold stocks tends to fall while the value of other investments rises. When the economy falters so that traditional investments lose value, gold stocks tend to rise in value.

Storing precious metals can be tricky. Twenty thousand dollars' worth of gold, for example, is about the size of a thick paperback book. That same amount in silver weighs more than 200 pounds and could require several safe-deposit boxes for storage space.

In addition, remember that while stocks, bonds, and other interest-bearing investments are earning money for you, precious metals sit in vaults, earning nothing. In order to make a profit when you sell precious metals, you must correctly predict the behavior of the market and sell the metals when their value is higher than what you paid for them.

TechByte

Collectibles Are you interested in antiques or other collectibles? In order to make sure your initial investment grows, you have to buy items at the right price. To better understand what objects sell for and what makes something valuable, you can visit the Web site of an auction house and view collectible objects and their suggested prices.

@ Select a type of antique or work of art that interests you and create a list of sale prices for these items through **finance07.glencoe.com**.

Motivating Students Ask students if they own any jewelry made from precious metals and gems. Ask if they consider these to be ornaments or investments.

Precious Gems

What is one of the advantages of investing in precious gems?

When the Queen of England opens the British Parliament, she wears a crown and carries a scepter, both of which are covered with diamonds, rubies, sapphires, and other glittering gems. As soon as the ceremony is over, the royal ornaments are quickly locked up again in the Jewel House at the Tower of London.

Throughout world history people have valued the precious gems that lie below the earth's surface. **Precious gems** are rough mineral deposits (usually crystals) that are dug from the earth by miners and then cut and shaped into brilliant jewels. These gems include diamonds, sapphires, rubies, and emeralds. They appeal to investors because of their small size, ease of storage, great durability, and their potential as a protection against inflation.

Figure 11.3 Changing Price of Gold Since 1980

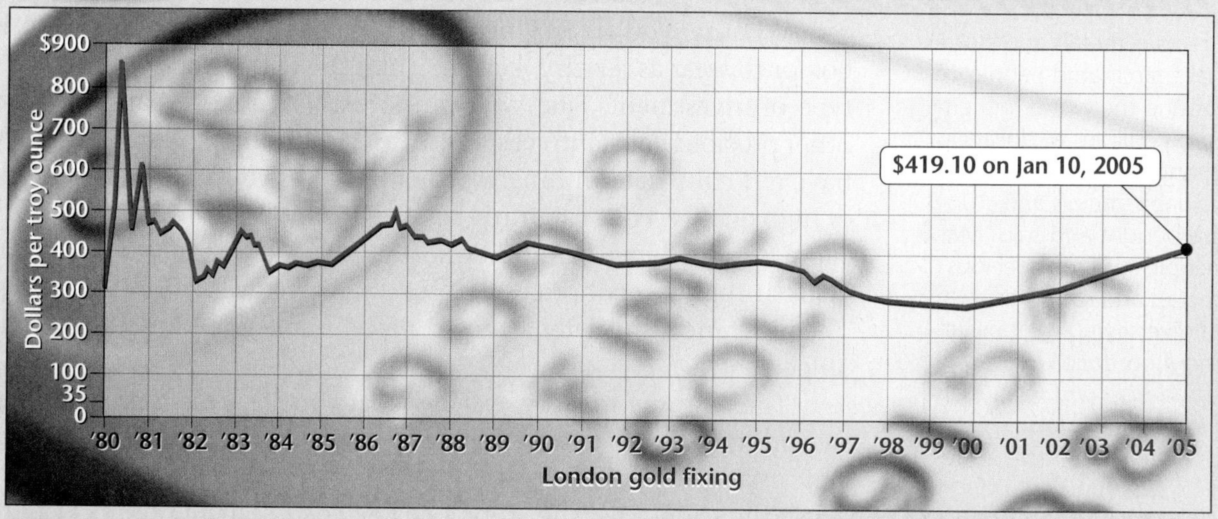

Gold's Wild Ride The value of gold fluctuated widely during the last quarter of the 1900s.

What might explain the spike in gold prices during 1980?

Caption Answer This was a period of inflation, political tension, and fears about the economy's stability.

▶ CROWN JEWELS

Throughout history, precious gems have been associated with royalty. *Why do you think diamonds, rubies, and other precious stones fascinate people?*

Caption Answer Answers will vary, though many will cite their rarity and beauty.

Teaching Activity Divide the students into groups of four. Assign each group a precious metal or gem. Have the groups find out the value of these and create posters stating their value and illustrating their uses as well as their beauty.

Research Have students research the industrial uses of gold, silver, platinum, palladium, and rhodium, and write up their findings.

Academic Connection

GEOGRAPHY

Precious metals and stones have fascinated people around the world for centuries. Billions of dollars change hands each year as valuable metals and stones are bought and sold. Many people invest in precious metals and stones as a way of diversifying their investment portfolios. *Print a world map and mark the places where gold, silver, platinum, diamonds, emeralds, and rubies are found. Use a color key to identify each precious metal and gem on the map.*

See the Teacher Manual for answer.

The inflation that occurred in the United States during the 1970s prompted investors to put more of their money into tangible assets such as gemstones. The result was a 40-fold increase in the price of diamonds. A few lucky investors made fortunes during that time.

Whether you are buying precious gems to store in a safe-deposit box or to wear as jewelry, keep in mind the risks associated with this type of investment. First, you cannot easily convert diamonds and other precious gems into cash. Also, as a beginning investor, you may have difficulty determining whether the gems you are purchasing are of high quality. Political unrest in gem-producing countries can affect supply and pricing. In addition, you will likely have to buy your gems at higher retail prices and sell them at lower wholesale prices. The difference is usually 10 to 15 percent and sometimes as high as 50 percent.

The best way to know exactly what you are getting in an expensive precious gem is to have the stone certified by an independent geological laboratory, such as the Gemological Institute of America. The certificate should list the stone's characteristics, including its weight, color, clarity, and quality of cut. The grading of gems, however, is not an exact science. Experiments have shown that the same stone submitted twice to the same laboratory may get two different ratings.

Despite the attraction of precious metals and gems, the investment risks are sizable. The primary risk is the great fluctuation in prices, which can be influenced by global, economic, financial, and political factors. For example, in 1980, world events caused the prices of precious metals and gems to shoot up. Investors bought gold for as much as $850 an ounce, and a one-carat diamond for $62,000.

As You Read

RELATE

Would you purchase precious metals? Why or why not?

STANDARD & POOR'S

Global Financial Landscape

Standard and Poor's publishes the globally recognized S&P 500® financial index. It also gathers financial statistics, information, and news, and analyzes this data for international businesses, governments, and individuals to help them guide their financial decisions.

SOUTH AFRICA

Diamonds, one of the oldest substances on Earth, are today's most popular gem. They were once used to guard against "evil spirits" but have since become a token of everlasting love. They are used to commemorate engagements, April birthdays, and 75th wedding anniversaries. Diamonds are mined in about 25 countries and on every continent but Europe and Antarctica.

One country that is well-known for its diamond mining is South Africa. Diamonds were discovered there in 1867. News spread quickly, and thousands of prospectors staked their claims and began to mine South Africa's diamond fields. This spurred economic growth in South Africa. Some of the world's most beautiful and famous diamonds were found in South Africa. In fact, the world's largest diamond was found in 1905 among the rich deposits of South Africa. It weighed 3,106.75 carats. When cut, the stone produced 105 gems, including the famous 530.20-carat "Star of Africa."

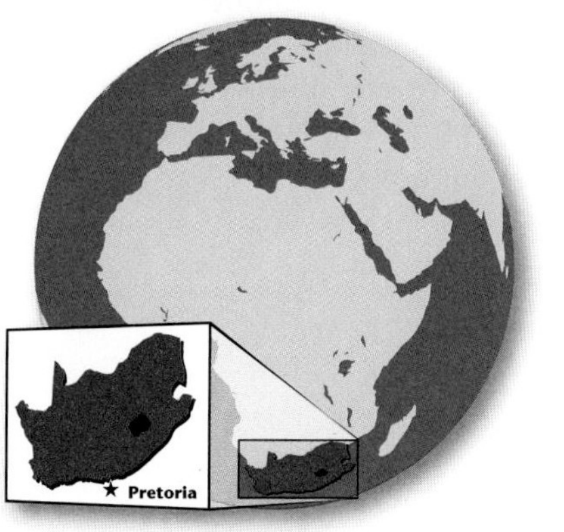

STANDARD & POOR'S **DATABYTES**

Capital	Pretoria (administrative capital), Bloemfontein (judicial capital), and Capetown (legislative capital)
Population	44,024,000
Languages	Afrikaans, English, Ndebele, Pedi, Sotho, Swazi, Tsonga, Tswana, Venda, Xhosa, and Zulu
Currency	rand
Gross Domestic Product (GDP)	$456.7 billion (2003 est.)
GDP per capita	$10,700 (2003 est.)

Industry: Mining, automobile assembly, metalworking, and machinery

Agriculture: Corn, wheat, sugarcane, fruits, and beef

Exports: Gold, diamonds, platinum, other metals and minerals, and machinery and equipment

Natural Resources: Gold, diamonds, chromium, antimony, coal, and iron ore

Think Globally

With technology making it possible to manufacture imitation diamonds, do you think real diamonds will continue to be valued highly? Why or why not?

See the Teacher Manual for answer.

Collectibles

What are collectibles?

Collectibles are another type of investment. **Collectibles** include rare coins, works of art, antiques, stamps, rare books, comic books, sports memorabilia, rugs, ceramics, paintings, and other items that appeal to collectors and investors. Each of these items offers the knowledgeable collector or investor both pleasure and an opportunity for profit. Many collectors have been surprised to discover that items they bought for their own enjoyment have increased greatly in value while they owned them.

For example, when Hannah was a little girl, her Aunt Sylvia bought her two collectible dolls. As she grew up, Hannah received more dolls as gifts and also bought some of her own. She now has an extensive collection of over 100 different dolls. Although Hannah never really thought of her dolls as an investment, she recently discovered that several of them are worth $500 each, which is more than three times what she paid for them.

STANDARD &POOR'S **Put on Your Financial Planner's Cap**

Julius and Martha are a middle-aged couple who have asked your advice. All of their investments are in CDs, but you have recommended that they diversify their investments. They have $25,000 to invest, and Julius wants to put $15,000 into precious metals. Martha wants to put all the money into undeveloped land. What is your advice?

See the Teacher Manual for answer.

Research Ask how many students have collections of what might be considered collectibles. Have them go online to research the value of these items, their history, and whether and how they are traded. For students without collections, assign each a collectible item and have them do the same research. Students will present their findings to the class.

▲ **UNEXPECTED RICHES** Collecting can be an enjoyable and sometimes profitable pastime. *Are collectibles a wise investment?*

Caption Answer Answers may include that they can be, but they should not be the sole component of an investment plan.

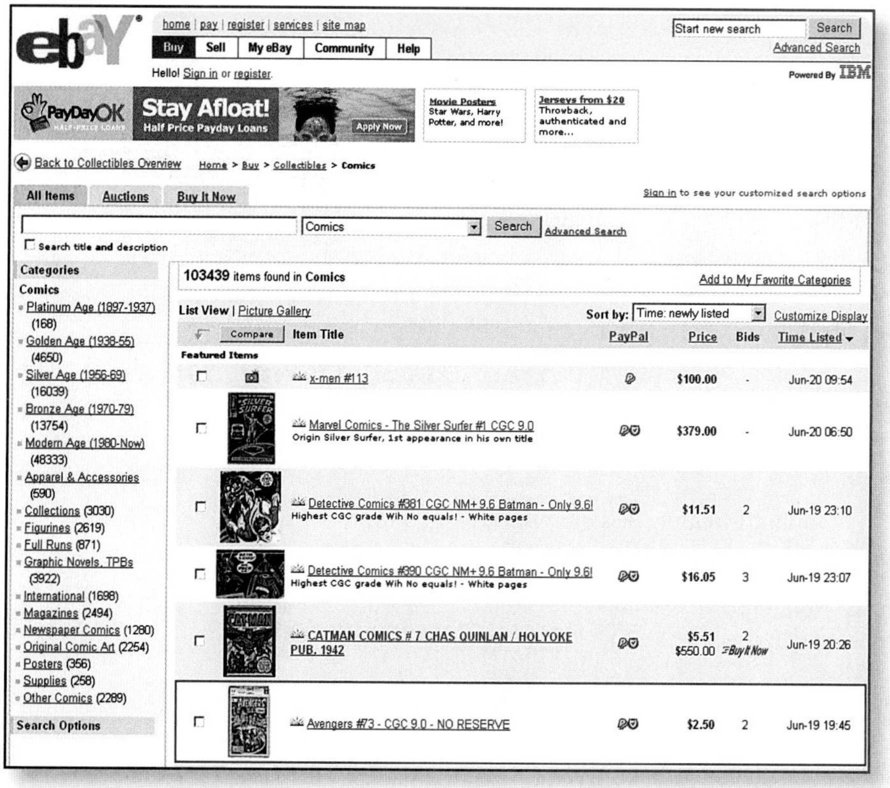

▲ **CYBER AUCTIONS** When buying or selling collectibles through online auction sites, do your research on quality and current values. *What are some advantages and disadvantages of collecting via the Internet?*

Critical Thinking Have the students brainstorm ways to protect against fraud when investing in collectibles. List ideas on the board and discuss.

Caption Answer Advantages include ease of searching for items, ability to reach a wide market, ability to comparison shop, and no buyer commissions. Disadvantages include no face-to-face interaction with dealer, inability to handle items, and danger of fraud.

Collectibles on the Internet

Before the era of the World Wide Web, finding items to add to your collections could be very time-consuming. You would have to pore over collectors' trade magazines to research the value of items you wished to buy. Then you would have to go to shows, sometimes far away, where collectors met to buy and sell their merchandise.

That process has changed. The Internet has made buying and selling collectibles efficient and convenient, and the number of Web sites for collectors has exploded. In 1999, when Guernsey's Auction House offered Mark McGwire's 70th home run baseball to bidders, they opened the bidding process to online buyers as well. Although the baseball went to an anonymous telephone bidder (later known to be the famed comic book artist Todd McFarlane) for $3 million, the use of the Internet as an auction site was firmly established.

It is easy to see why the Internet appeals to collectors. As a buyer, you can search for items to add to your collection with a few keystrokes, and sellers can reach people all around the world. Prices are not necessarily lower on the Internet, but comparison shopping is easier, and most sites do not charge a buyer's commission.

Of course, collecting through the Internet has its drawbacks. As an online buyer, you cannot assess a dealer face-to-face or examine the objects for flaws or trademarks. Furthermore, fraud is an ever-present danger.

Common CENTS

Collectible Gifts

Suggest to your family and friends that you make gifts for each other instead of buying them for special days and holidays. You will all save money, and your gifts may become family heirlooms. *How much money do you think you could save each year by making gifts instead of buying them?*

Common Cents Answer Accept all reasonable answers.

Figure 11.4 Stocks for the Long Term

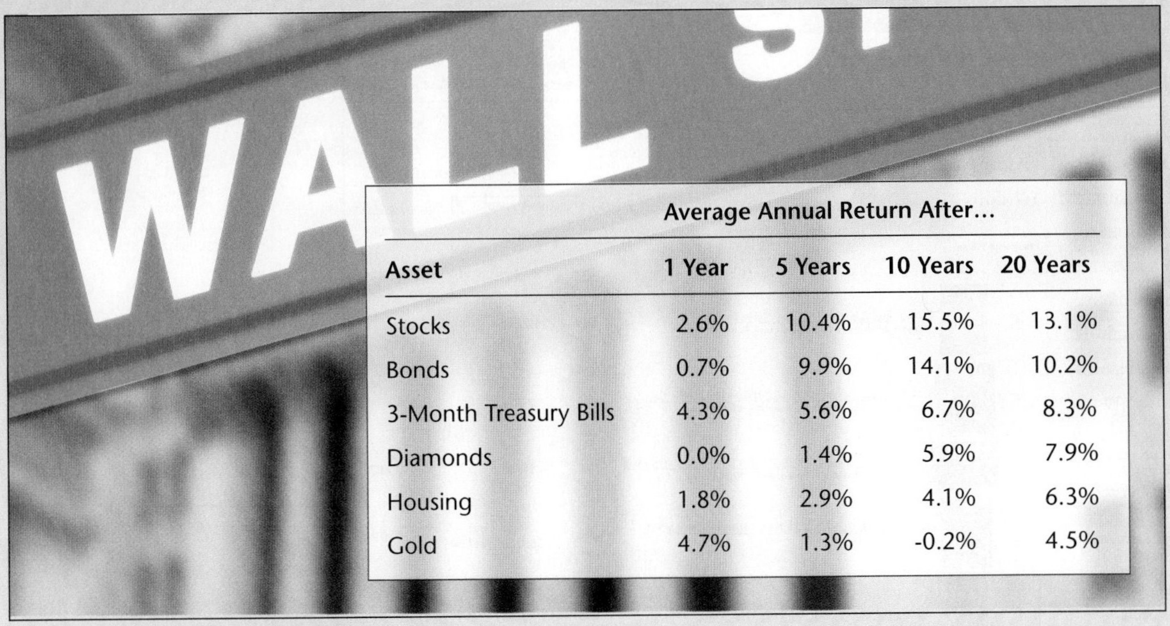

	Average Annual Return After...			
Asset	**1 Year**	**5 Years**	**10 Years**	**20 Years**
Stocks	2.6%	10.4%	15.5%	13.1%
Bonds	0.7%	9.9%	14.1%	10.2%
3-Month Treasury Bills	4.3%	5.6%	6.7%	8.3%
Diamonds	0.0%	1.4%	5.9%	7.9%
Housing	1.8%	2.9%	4.1%	6.3%
Gold	4.7%	1.3%	-0.2%	4.5%

Source: Sumner N. Levine, ed., *Business and Investment Almanac*, 1995 (Burr Ridge, IL: Richard D. Irwin, 1996), p. 249.
© Sumner N. Levine, 1995.

Best Investments According to this table, stocks and bonds offered investors the highest average annual return over the long term.

After one year, which asset provided the highest average annual return? After five years?

Caption Answer one year: gold; five years: stocks.

Let the Collector Beware

Collecting can be a satisfying hobby and a good investment. Nevertheless, a wise collector must always be alert for scams—on or off the Internet. For example, how do you know that the fielder's glove you bought was actually signed by Mickey Mantle? Could your Civil War–era postage stamps be counterfeit? Is that Barbie® doll, Lionel® locomotive, or Darth Vader™ action figure really as rare and valuable as you have been told?

When you trade collectibles, be aware that some online auction and exchange sites are more reliable than others. According to figures from Internet Fraud Watch, which is sponsored by the National Consumers League (NCL), 76 percent of the fraud complaints it received during the period between January and June of 2004 were related to online auctions. Consumers can report suspected Internet fraud by calling the NCL Fraud Hotline.

The safest way to steer clear of collectibles-related fraud is to learn everything you can about the items you collect and to buy and sell only with reputable dealers and auction Web sites.

As You Read

QUESTION

Take a mental inventory of your keepsakes and favorite possessions. Do you own any items that might be considered collectibles in the future?

Question Answer Accept all reasonable answers that demonstrate an understanding of the concept.

Remember that collectibles do not offer interest or dividends. Also, you may have a hard time selling items at a good price on short notice. If your collection grows significantly in value, you will have to purchase insurance against damage and theft.

After You Read

REACT

With the information provided in this chapter, do you think that you could make a wise investment in precious metals, gems, or collectibles?

React Answer Answers will vary, but most will say "yes."

Planning Investments

How do you choose the best types of investments?

Investments such as stocks and bonds may not be very interesting or exciting, but as you can see in **Figure 11.4,** they have proven to be the most stable types of investments in the long run. Investing in collectibles may seem interesting, but it may not be the best way for you to achieve your financial goals.

Wise planning is the best way to get the most out of your investments. Be sure to research the types of investments that are available so you can make an informed decision. Weigh the advantages and disadvantages of each type of investment. Ask yourself how much risk and responsibility you are willing to assume. By taking these steps, you will be able to make a decision that is best for your financial future.

Section 11.2 Assessment

See the Teacher Manual for answers.

QUICK CHECK

1. What are the risks of investing in precious metals?
2. Why do precious gems appeal to investors?
3. How has the Internet increased the risks of investing in collectibles?

THINK CRITICALLY

4. Describe two different scenarios: one that causes the price of diamonds to rise and one that causes the price to fall.

USE MATH SKILLS

5. **Golden Investment** In 1978, Raul bought 50 ounces of gold for $1,750 as protection against rising inflation. He sold half the gold in 1980 at a price of $800 an ounce. Raul sold the other half in 1982 when the price was $400 an ounce.

Calculate What was Raul's profit in 1980 and in 1982? What would Raul's profit have been if he had sold all of his gold in 1980?

SOLVE MONEY PROBLEMS

6. **Evaluating an Inheritance** Samantha inherited a diamond-and-ruby necklace from her grandmother's estate. Unfortunately, the settings for the stones are damaged beyond repair. Samantha is trying to decide what to do with her inheritance.

Analyze Create a strategy that will help Samantha determine the value of her inheritance and how she might increase that value.

Chapter 11 Review & Activities

See the Teacher Manual for answers.

CHAPTER SUMMARY

- The owner of a direct investment in real estate directly holds the legal title to the residential or commercial property and is responsible for its maintenance and management. An indirect investment is similar to investing in mutual funds. A group of investors buys property, and legal title is held by a trustee. Real estate syndicates, limited partnerships, and real estate investment trusts (REITs) are examples of indirect investments.
- The advantages of investments (syndicates and REITs) in real estate are: use as a hedge against inflation, ease of entering the market, and limited liability. Lack of liquidity and diversification, risk of declining property values, fewer tax incentives, and potential management problems are disadvantages.
- Precious metals include gold, silver, platinum, palladium, and rhodium. Precious gems include diamonds, sapphires, rubies, and emeralds.
- Collectibles include rare coins, works of art, antiques, stamps, rare books, comic books, sports memorabilia, rugs, ceramics, and other items.
- The value of precious metals and gems can fluctuate greatly, making them a risky investment. It is also difficult to predict the value of collectibles.

Communicating Key Terms

Your friend, Jeremiah, is the sole heir of a recently deceased relative. Jeremiah has discovered that his relative had invested in several REITs and Ginnie Mae certificates. Plus, Jeremiah found two diamond rings, as well as a collection of 40 Hummels, which are ceramic figurines made in Germany. Jeremiah asks your advice in determining which investments to keep and which to sell. Use the terms below to prepare your recommendations.

- direct investment
- commercial property
- indirect investment
- syndicate
- participation certificate (PC)
- financial leverage
- precious metals
- precious gems
- collectibles

Reviewing Key Concepts

1. **Compare and contrast** direct and indirect real estate investments.
2. **List** two advantages and two disadvantages of real estate investments.
3. **Describe** precious metal and gem investments and why they remain popular despite their speculative nature.
4. **Explain** what is meant by the term *collectible,* and give some examples of collectible items you or your family may own.
5. **Explain** why so many fraud complaints are related to online auctions.

See the Teacher Manual for answers.

ACADEMIC SKILLS

Communication Skills A friend of yours tells you that his parents plan to pay for his college education by selling some family jewelry.
Write About It Write a paragraph explaining why you might question this plan.

YOUR FINANCIAL FIGURES

Comparative Return Imagine that you have $10,000 to invest. Use a newspaper, the Internet, or other source to select a mutual fund. Use the same source to find out how much gold you could buy for $10,000. Track the performance of these two investments for 30 days.

1. **Calculate** (a) the rate of return if you invested the $10,000 and sold the investment 30 days later. Disregard tax consequences or mutual fund withdrawal penalties. (b) How much return would you receive if you had put the money in a savings account with 4 percent interest?
2. **Compute** by using graphics or presentation software to show the two investments' performance.

REAL-WORLD Application

Connect with Economics Your brother recently graduated from college and started his first job. He rents half a duplex, but the owner has put the building up for sale. Your brother thinks that purchasing the building would be a good investment for him. He asks for your opinion.

1. **Research** Use the newspaper or search the Internet to find current prices for duplexes.
2. **Think Critically** What are the positives and negatives of your brother buying the building? What factors need to be considered?

Internet CONNECTION

PBS Antiques Roadshow The PBS television program, *Antiques Roadshow*, has generated enormous interest among viewers to find out the value of the furniture, art, jewelry, and collectibles they own.

@ **Log On** Go to **finance07.glencoe.com** for a link to the Web site of the *Antiques Roadshow* television program.

1. Click on "Follow the Stories" and select an area of interest and at least three stories from the *Antiques Roadshow*.
2. Summarize the stories you selected in one or two paragraphs. Add more information by using an Internet search engine to find out more about the area of interest you selected.

BusinessWeek ONLINE

Newsclip: A Piece of Childhood Animation art, hand-painted images from which cartoons used to be made, is a popular collectible.

@ **Log On** Go to **finance07.glencoe.com** and open Chapter 11. Learn more about the different types of alternative investments, such as collectibles. Write a paragraph about the kinds of things you like to collect. Could any of them be valuable?

WHAT'S YOUR FINANCIAL **ID?**

ALL THAT GLITTERS

Whether you want to buy precious stones and metals as an investment, a gift, or for yourself, you will have the edge when you know what you are buying. Test your knowledge of gems and precious metals. Write your answers on a separate sheet of paper.

1. Precious stones generally have more commercial value than semiprecious stones. Some precious stones are (choose all that apply):

_____ garnet
__X__ diamond
_____ turquoise
_____ pearl
__X__ ruby
__X__ sapphire
_____ black onyx
_____ amethyst
_____ opal
_____ topaz
__X__ emerald

2. Rank these precious metals from 1 (most valuable per ounce) to 4 (least valuable):

__3__ silver
__2__ gold
__1__ platinum
__4__ copper

3. The word *brilliant* describes a diamond's __________.

_____ color
__X__ cut
_____ clarity

4. When it comes to diamonds, the word *flawless* refers to __________.

_____ cut
_____ color
__X__ clarity

5. All diamonds have a cubic crystal structure and are made primarily of __________.

_____ boron
__X__ carbon
_____ nitrogen

Your Financial Portfolio

Collecting Treasures

Russell inherited three diamonds from his grandmother and needs to decide whether to keep them or sell them. He already had them evaluated for the "4 Cs"—clarity, color, cut, and carat weight—but not their actual dollar value. He took the diamonds and the evaluation papers to the Diamond Mart downtown.

A sales representative at the Diamond Mart appraised them. The four-carat diamond was the most valuable because it was beautifully cut in a marquise shape, and it also had good clarity, meaning it had few microscopic bits of other elements embedded in it. Its color, which was very close to the whitest end of the scale, also added to its value. The other two diamonds, a matched set of one-carat gems cut as round brilliants, were of a higher quality in clarity but more yellow. The appraiser told Russell that the three diamonds could be worth $5,000, but gem dealers would probably offer him about half that. He also told him that the Diamond Mart would not be interested in buying them.

Russell went to another store that had a sign, "We Buy Diamonds," but the most the store could offer was $2,350. Rather than settling for a price well below the actual worth of the diamonds, Russell decided to keep them in a safe-deposit box. By keeping them, he had the option of turning them into cash in the future, possibly selling them for more money. He also liked the idea of making them into jewelry someday. After researching his grandmother's diamonds, Russell is now interested in finding out more about other gems. One day he would like to start a gem collection.

Apply

On a separate sheet of paper, list five things you might enjoy collecting that will keep their value or possibly be worth more in the future. Choose one and describe why it appeals to you. Describe how an expert could appraise its value, using such criteria as age, quality, rarity, and popular demand. Why would this collectible be interesting for you to keep?

Do you think it would be a good or bad long-term investment? Explain why.

Accept all reasonable answers that show student effort and an understanding of the concept.

Unit 3 LAB

Get a Financial Life!

See the Teacher Manual for Unit Lab teaching guide.

Investment Strategies

Overview

Carrie and David are about to celebrate their 36th birthdays. Carrie recently accepted a new position as a fashion design supervisor at a sportswear company. David is now an assistant principal at a high school specializing in technology and Internet applications. Through the years, they have saved money in traditional savings accounts and certificates of deposit. In addition, Carrie has invested money in a 401(k) plan at work. Because David has been working for the public school system, he has been investing in a 403(b) plan. Besides saving for retirement, Carrie and David realize that they will have to accumulate enough money to put their children, Eva and Jack, through college someday. Therefore, they would like to expand their investment strategies.

Resources & Tools

- Career development book
- Crayons, markers, colored pencils
- Internet (optional)
- Multimedia tools (videos, music, and so on)
- Portfolio (ring binder or file folder)
- Poster board
- Presentation software (optional)
- Public or school library
- Word processor

Procedures

STEP A **The Process**

Imagine that you are a financial planner. Carrie and David have hired you to help them make investment decisions for their future. They have $25,000 in savings that they want to invest in stocks, bonds, mutual funds, and/or real estate.

1. Prepare a mock résumé for yourself as a financial planner. Showcase your experiences and qualifications so that Carrie and David will feel confident that they have hired an expert.
2. Recommend appropriate investment options for Carrie and David. To ensure a diverse portfolio, you must make at least three different recommendations.
3. Using the various sources of investment information (the financial section of a newspaper, business magazines, the Internet, investor services, and corporate reports), collect articles and other relevant information about the investment options that you will recommend. Your research should demonstrate to Carrie and David that your recommendations are sensible.
4. Contact a financial planner, investment counselor, banker, or accountant. Arrange for a time when you can either meet or speak on the phone to discuss the investment decisions you have made for Carrie and David. Prepare a report of your conversation.

STEP B Create Your Portfolio

As you work through the process, save the results so that you can refer, review, and refine. Create a professional-looking portfolio of investment recommendations that you will present to Carrie and David.

1. The first page should be a title page with the following information centered:
   - Investment Options
   - Presented to Carrie and David Lanier
   - By (Your Name)
2. Next include the résumé that you prepared.
3. Prepare a section in the portfolio for each investment option that you recommend. Include the recommendation and the research that supports your suggestion.
4. In the last section, include the report of the conversation you had with the financial expert you interviewed in Step A (4) on the previous page.

STEP C Teamwork

Teamwork is essential in today's workplace. Many companies are replacing the traditional management with self-managed work teams. Team members must be able to accept more responsibility, communicate effectively, and get along well with others.

Create a team of at least four classmates. Prepare a 15-minute seminar and present it to other members of your class or to other classes in the school. Organize your team in order to accomplish the following tasks in the best and most efficient way possible.

1. Choose one topic from Chapters 8–11 for your seminar.
2. Prepare an oral presentation, using presentation software, multimedia tools, posters, or other visuals.
3. Draft a written outline and relate the topics to financial planning for Carrie and David in the presentation.
4. Create handouts for the audience.
5. Prepare a pre-test and post-test for the audience. Compile the results in a graph.
6. Present the seminar to your class or to other classes in the school.

Unit 4

Protecting Your Finances

WebQuest Internet Project

Avoiding Financial Fraud

You might experience financial trouble if you trust the wrong person or buy financial products from a disreputable company. You should plan for unforeseen problems. In this project, you will learn how to spot financial fraud and scams, and write a plan designed to help you protect your finances.

Log on to **finance07.glencoe.com**. Begin by reading Task 1. Then continue on your WebQuest as you study Unit 4.

Section	12.3	13.3	14.4	15.3
Page	392	432	467	510

BusinessWeek

FINANCE FILE

So What's the Plan?

Once you know how much you will need to retire, crafting a detailed map of your future financial moves is the next step. If you think you're too young to bother with a plan, remember that when it comes to building savings, time is on your side.

When I asked several financial planners how they work with clients who have figured out the amount of money they'll need in retirement, they said they start by compiling information on the client's financial status and potential retirement resources. Brewster [a planner] asks clients to provide up to 26 different types of documents, including investment- and retirement-account statements, tax returns, mortgage statement, insurance policies, and wills.

He raises such issues as whether the client has a realistic idea of future pension income. If the client were to switch jobs ten years before retirement, the final pension could end up being less than anticipated.

One of the findings [of the Retirement Confidence Survey was]: More than a quarter of those who feel "very confident" about their retirement prospects owe that peace of mind to "doing a good job of preparing financially."

— By Ellen Hoffman

Write About It How might financial planning protect you?

See the Teacher Manual for answer.

Log On To read the complete *BusinessWeek* article and do the *BusinessWeek* Extension activity to help you learn more about planning your finances for the present and future, go to **finance07.glencoe.com**.

CHAPTER 12

Planning Your Tax Strategy

$ What You'll Learn

When you have completed this chapter, you will be able to:

Section 12.1

- Discuss the importance of tax planning.
- Identify your taxable income.
- Explain deductions and tax credits.
- Explain the W-4 form.

Section 12.2

- Describe the types of federal income tax forms.

Section 12.3

- Identify tax strategies.

Reading Strategies

To get the most out of your reading:

Predict what you will learn in this chapter.
Relate what you read to your own life.
Question what you are reading to be sure you understand.
React to what you have read.

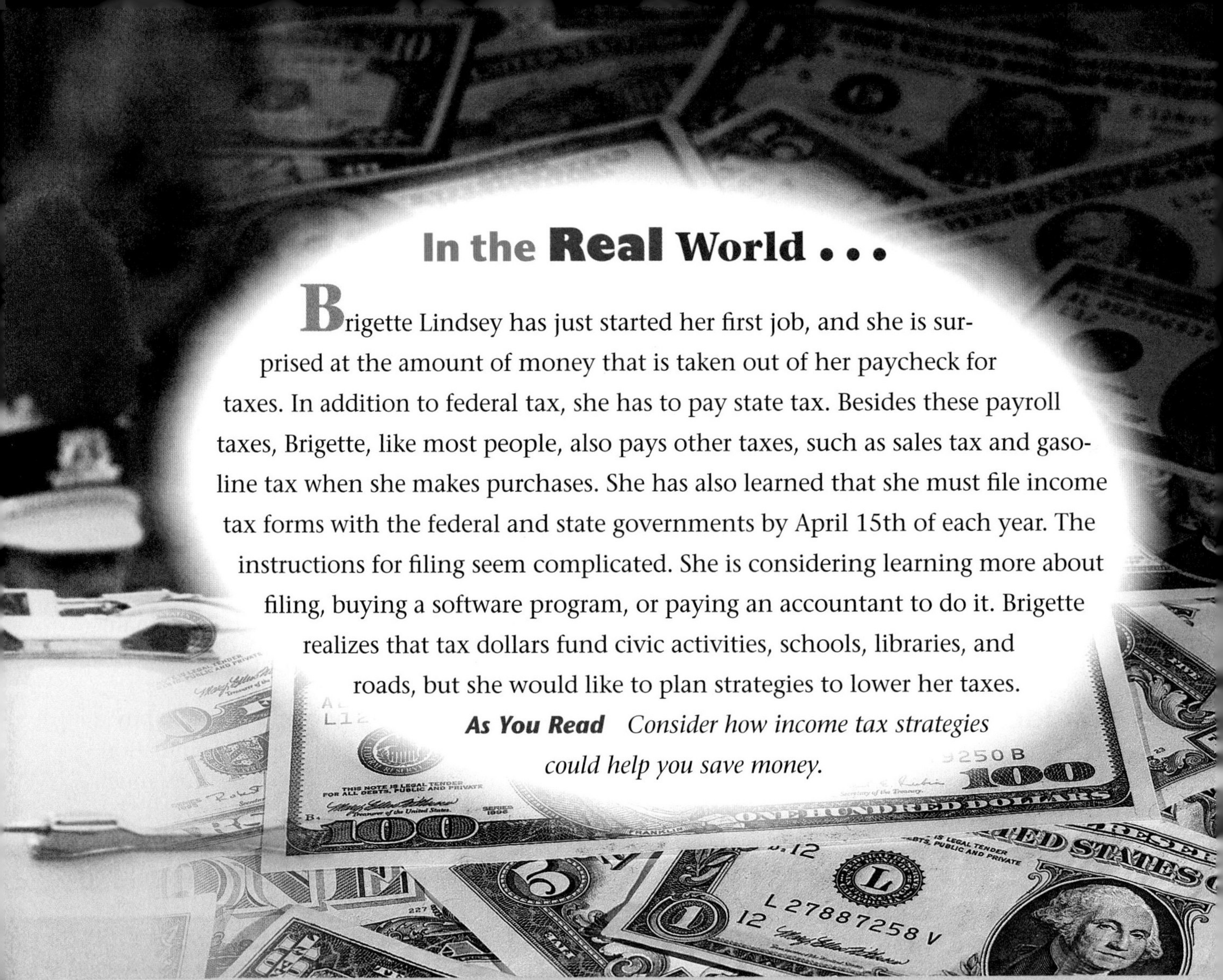

In the Real World . . .

Brigette Lindsey has just started her first job, and she is surprised at the amount of money that is taken out of her paycheck for taxes. In addition to federal tax, she has to pay state tax. Besides these payroll taxes, Brigette, like most people, also pays other taxes, such as sales tax and gasoline tax when she makes purchases. She has also learned that she must file income tax forms with the federal and state governments by April 15th of each year. The instructions for filing seem complicated. She is considering learning more about filing, buying a software program, or paying an accountant to do it. Brigette realizes that tax dollars fund civic activities, schools, libraries, and roads, but she would like to plan strategies to lower her taxes.

As You Read *Consider how income tax strategies could help you save money.*

Lesson Plan See the Teacher Manual for the Chapter 12 planning guide and lesson plan.

ASK STANDARD & POOR'S

Electronic Taxes

Q: I would like to file my income tax form electronically. Is it risky to file through the Internet?

A: If you are concerned about being charged late penalties if your tax return is not received by the IRS via the Internet, you can protect yourself by using filing services that offer a receipt, such as a confirmation number or e-mail confirmation.

Ask Yourself What would be the advantage of filing income tax forms electronically instead of by mail?

@ Go to **finance07.glencoe.com** to complete the Standard & Poor's Financial Focus activity.

Section 12.1

Focus on Reading

Read to Learn

- How to discuss the importance of tax planning.
- How to identify your taxable income.
- How to explain deductions and tax credits.
- How to explain the W-4 form.

Main Idea

Taxes are an important part of financial planning. There are several types of taxes and terms to know for preparing your tax return.

Key Terms

- tax liability
- estate tax
- inheritance tax
- income tax
- income tax return
- exclusion
- adjusted gross income
- taxable income
- tax deduction
- standard deduction
- itemized deduction
- exemption
- tax credit
- allowance

Springboard Ask the students what they think about taxes: Are they positive or negative? Why should we pay taxes?

Income Tax Fundamentals

Taxes and You

Why are taxes so important?

Taxes are an everyday expense of life that allow your local, state, and federal governments to provide important services. Taxes pay the bills for those services such as Medicare, Medicaid, the military, the national debt, police and fire protection, public schools, road maintenance, parks, libraries, and safety inspection of foods, drugs, and other products.

You pay some type of tax every time you get a paycheck, buy a new CD, or fill up your car's gas tank. Each year the Tax Foundation, an independent public policy research group, determines how much of the year the average person works to pay taxes. In recent years, "Tax Freedom Day" came in early May. This means that from January 1 until early May, all the money you earn goes toward paying taxes.

Effective tax planning can help you to have money left after paying taxes and living expenses. Use several strategies to plan for taxes. First, find out how the current tax laws and regulations affect you. Second, maintain complete and accurate tax records. Third, learn how to make decisions that can reduce your **tax liability**, which is the total amount of taxes owed. If you follow these strategies, you will pay a fair share of taxes while taking advantage of tax benefits that allow you to owe less money.

Types of Taxes

What are the different types of taxes?

Throughout your life, you will pay different types of taxes in four major categories: purchases, property, wealth, and earnings.

Taxes on Purchases

You probably already pay sales tax each time you buy a product. These taxes are added to the prices of most products you purchase and are collected by state and local governments. Many states do not charge sales tax on food and medicine. Another type of sales tax is an *excise tax,* a tax on specific goods and services (such as gasoline, air travel, and telephone service) collected by federal and state governments.

Taxes on Property

Real estate property tax is a major source of income for local governments. This tax is based on the value of land and buildings. As the value of any real estate, such as a home, goes up, the amount of property tax may increase as well. In some areas of the country, state and local governments may assess taxes on the value of property, such as automobiles, boats, furniture, and farm equipment.

Before You Read
PREDICT
Why would planning a tax strategy be a good idea?

Motivating Students Have students brainstorm the various kinds of taxes we have; list them on the board. Then ask students if people should pay whatever is requested, try to minimize their taxes, or evade them altogether. Have them justify their answers.

Research Have the students research the taxes charged on gasoline, cigarettes, alcohol, and telephones; ask them to identify these types of taxes. Have them write up their results.

Taxes on Wealth

An **estate tax** is a federal tax collected on the value of a person's property at the time of his or her death. Unfortunately, that is not always the end of tax liability. States may collect an inheritance tax. An **inheritance tax** is a state tax collected on the property left by a person to his or her heir(s) in a will. Therefore, before heirs can claim their inheritance, they have to pay the inheritance tax.

Another type of federal tax on wealth is the gift tax. A gift tax is a tax collected on money or property valued at more than $11,000, given by one person to another in a single year. However, gifts of any amount that are designated for educational or medical expenses are not subject to gift taxes.

▲ **YOUR TAX DOLLARS** Public museums, parks, and roads are built and maintained with your taxes. *What other expenses are paid with tax funds?*

Caption Answer Answers will vary but may include police, fire protection, schools, and libraries.

Teaching Activity Have students who are working bring in their pay stubs; those who are not are to partner with those who are. Have the students determine: the tax deductions, the percentage of gross income for each deduction, and for what that tax pays. Individuals or pairs are to write up their responses.

Taxes on Earnings

Income tax is the tax on wages, salaries, and self-employed earnings. Wages are payments received for hourly work, but salaries are payments received for weekly or monthly work, regardless of the number of hours worked. The personal income tax, or tax you pay on the income you receive, is the federal government's main source of revenue (money). Social Security funds are also collected as a tax. These funds finance retirement, disability, and life insurance benefits of the federal government's Social Security program. Current and future revisions to the Social Security program may affect amount of benefits.

STANDARD &POOR'S

Global Financial Landscape

Standard and Poor's publishes the globally recognized S&P 500® financial index. It also gathers financial statistics, information, and news, and analyzes this data for international businesses, governments, and individuals to help them guide their financial decisions.

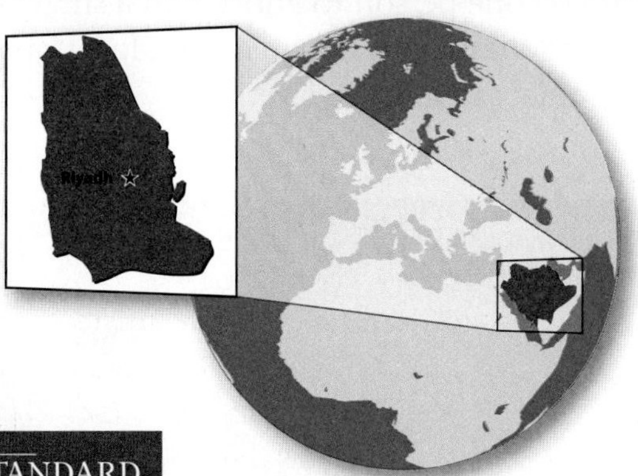

SAUDI ARABIA

Unlike U.S. citizens, Saudis are not required to pay income tax. They also do not pay local, regional, property, or most sales taxes. There is one exception. Saudi citizens must pay a religious tax called the *zagat*. The zagat amounts to an annual 2.5 percent of an individual's net worth. Before oil was discovered, when Saudi Arabia was a land of desert dwellers, the government survived with small taxes on religious pilgrims and on tobacco. Although many people think that Saudi Arabia's oil wealth is responsible for its low tax status, scholars point to the independent nature of the population. The national attitude toward taxation might be summed up by the 1920s decree of the country's leaders: "Taxes, we have ruled, are completely illegal."

STANDARD &POOR'S DATABYTES

Capital	Riyadh
Population	24,070,000
Languages	Arabic
Currency	Saudi riyal
Gross Domestic Product (GDP)	$286.2 billion (2003 est.)
GDP per capita	$10,500

Industry: Crude oil, petroleum, basic petrochemicals, and cement

Agriculture: Wheat, barley, tomatoes, melons, and mutton

Exports: Petroleum and petroleum products

Natural Resources: Crude oil, natural gas, iron ore, gold, and copper

Think Globally
Do you think the United States could operate under a similar taxation system? Why or why not?

See the Teacher Manual for answer.

The Internal Revenue Service (IRS) The Internal Revenue Service (IRS) is the federal agency that collects these taxes, or tax revenues. Headquartered in Washington, D.C., the IRS is an agency of the Department of the Treasury. The two primary missions of the IRS are to collect federal income taxes and to enforce the nation's tax laws.

Taxes on earnings are collected on a pay-as-you-earn basis. Your employer must withhold, or take out, Social Security and income tax payments from your paycheck and send the money to the IRS. If you are self-employed, own your own business, or are retired, you could be required to make your own estimated tax payments. When you complete your federal income tax return forms each year, you determine if you have paid too much or too little income tax. At that time you either pay more tax or you receive a refund from the IRS.

As You Read

RELATE

What kinds of taxes do you already pay?

Discussion Talk to students about how the federal government knows if they are earning money and have to file tax returns.

Understanding Income Taxes

How do you determine how much tax you owe?

Every year millions of taxpayers in the United States prepare income tax returns and send their completed forms to the IRS by mail or through the Internet. An **income tax return** is a form, such as 1040 or 1040EZ, on which a taxpayer reports how much money he or she received from working and other sources and the exact taxes that are owed.

You determine the amount of tax you owe when filling out the returns. Then you compare that amount to the total income tax your employer withheld from your paychecks during the year. If the income tax you paid through your employer was greater than your tax liability, you will receive a refund. However, if your tax liability is greater than the tax you paid, you will need to pay the difference to the U.S. Treasury because you owe more taxes than were withheld.

TechByte

Collecting Taxes
Helping federal, state, and local governments collect taxes is a growing market. Microsoft has partnered with several companies who have used Microsoft's technology to create tax collection software and integrated systems designed to be used by various government entities. For example, some programs help local municipalities collect property taxes, and others help government agencies distribute unemployment benefits and collect taxes from those employers who fund this program.

@ Read more about Microsoft's partnerships with tax collection software makers through **finance07.glencoe.com**.

Gross and Adjusted Gross Income

Most but not all income is subject to taxation. Gross income, or total income, can include one, two, or three main components:

1. **Earned income**—the money you receive for working, including wages, salary, commissions, fees, tips, bonuses, and self-employed earnings
2. **Interest income**—the interest that you receive from banks, credit unions, and savings and loan associations
3. **Dividend income**—the cash dividends that you receive from investments

Your gross income can also be affected by exclusions—amounts of income that do not have to be included in your gross income. An **exclusion** is also called tax-exempt income, or income that is not subject to taxes. For example, interest earned on most municipal bonds is exempt from federal income tax.

Another kind of income is tax-deferred income, or income that will be taxed at a later date. The earnings on an individual retirement account (IRA) are tax-deferred income. Although these earnings are credited to your account now, you do not have to pay tax on this money until you withdraw it from the account, usually at retirement.

You pay income tax on your adjusted gross income, not on your gross income. Your **adjusted gross income** is your gross income after calculating certain reductions. These reductions are called *adjustments* to income. They include items such as contributions to an IRA or student loan interest. The correct amount of your adjusted gross income is important because it is the basis for other tax calculations. (Note: If you have adjustments to income, you cannot use Form 1040EZ.)

Your Taxable Income

When you determine your adjusted gross income, you can figure out your **taxable income**. Your taxable income is your adjusted gross income less any allowable tax deductions and exemptions. Your income tax is calculated based on the amount of your taxable income.

Tax Deductions A **tax deduction** is an expense that you can subtract from your adjusted gross income to figure your taxable income. Every taxpayer receives at least the **standard deduction**, an amount of money set by the IRS that is not taxed. In 2004, a single person's standard deduction was $4,850. A married couple filing a joint tax return could deduct $9,700. People over age 65 or people who are blind are entitled to higher standard deductions.

You may qualify for other deductions that can reduce your taxable income. An **itemized deduction** is a specific expense, such as a medical expense, that you deduct from your adjusted gross income. You can take the standard deduction or itemize your deductions, but you cannot take both. You would take the standard deduction if it were greater than your total itemized deductions.

A few of the most common itemized deductions include:

- **Medical and Dental Expenses** These include doctors' fees, prescription medications, hospital expenses, medical insurance premiums, eyeglasses, hearing aids, and medical travel that has not been reimbursed or paid by others, such as a health insurance provider. You can deduct only the amount of your medical and dental expenses that is more than 7.5 percent of your adjusted gross income (as of 2004). Therefore, if your adjusted gross income is $10,000, you can deduct only the amount of non-reimbursed medical and dental expenses that exceeds $750.

Caption Answer Expenses include doctors' fees, prescription medicine, hospital expenses, medical insurance premiums, eyeglasses, hearing aids, and travel related to medical care.

▼ **MEDICAL DEDUCTIONS** Medical expenses can help reduce the taxes you owe. *What are medical expenses?*

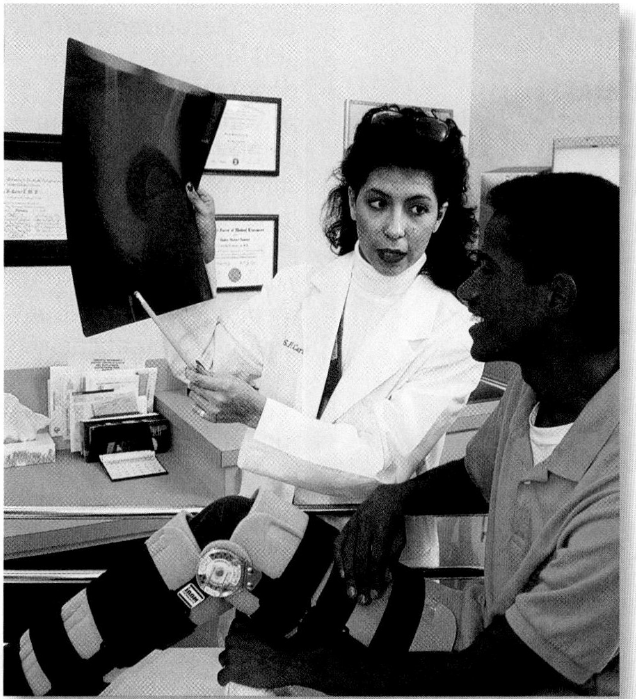

Figure 12.1 **The Six-Rate System for Federal Income Taxes**

Rate on Taxable Income	Single Taxpayers	Married Taxpayers
10%	Up to $7,000	Up to $14,000
15%	$7,000 – $28,400	$14,000 – $56,800
25%	$28,400 – $68,800	$56,800 – $114,650
28%	$68,800 – $143,500	$114,650 – $174,700
33%	$143,500 – $311,950	$174,700 – $311,950
35%	$311,950 and up	$311,950 and up

Tax Rates The six-rate system is an example of a progressive tax.

What do you think is meant by "progressive tax"?

Caption Answer The tax rate increases as the amount of taxable income increases.

- **Taxes** You can deduct state and local income tax, real estate property tax, and state and local personal property tax.
- **Interest** You can deduct home mortgage interest and home equity loan interest.
- **Contributions** You can deduct contributions of cash or property to qualified charities. If your contribution is more than 20 percent of your adjusted gross income, the deduction is subject to certain limitations.

You must keep records to document tax deductions. For more information about financial records, review Chapter 3.

Exemptions An **exemption** is a deduction from adjusted gross income for the taxpayer, the spouse, and qualified dependents. A dependent is someone you support financially, such as a child. To qualify as a dependent, a person must meet all of the following requirements:

1. A dependent must not earn more than a set amount unless he or she is under age 19 or is a full-time student under age 24.
2. He or she must be a specified relative or live in the home of the taxpayer who claims him or her on the tax return.
3. More than half of a dependent's support must be provided by the taxpayer who claims him or her on the tax return.
4. A dependent must meet certain citizenship requirements.

Academic Connection

MATH

In states that charge sales tax, even people who live outside the state have to pay taxes on purchases they make within the state. This means that tourists who purchase items in a state that collects sales tax are helping to pay for the upkeep of the state. *If you live in a state that collects a sales tax of 6.25 percent, how much sales tax do you owe on a $125 purchase?*

See the Teacher Manual for answer.

Calculating Your Tax

Once you know your taxable income, you can calculate how much income tax you owe. Most taxpayers use either a Tax Table or a Tax Rate Schedule to figure income tax. The Tax Rate Schedules are based on the six rates shown in **Figure 12.1.** The examples in this book use a Tax Table instead of Tax Rate Schedules.

Teaching Activity Divide the class in half. Have half the students take the position that progressive taxes are fair; have the other half take the position that they are not fair. Have them research material that supports their position. Have each group write summaries.

As You Read

QUESTION

Why is it important for you to keep accurate and organized tax records?

Question Answer When the tax deadline comes, you need to have accurate information easily available to avoid paying unnecessary taxes or penalties.

Tax Credits Your income tax may be reduced by a **tax credit**, which is an amount of money that can be subtracted directly from taxes you owe. A tax credit is different than a deduction. A tax deduction is an expense that you can subtract from your adjusted gross income. However, a tax credit results in a dollar-for-dollar reduction in the amount of taxes you owe. For example, suppose you owe $300 in taxes. If you can get a $100 tax credit, you can subtract that and owe only $200 ($300 – $100 = $200).

Lower-income workers can benefit from a tax credit called *earned income credit* (EIC). This federal tax credit is for people who work and whose taxable income is less than a certain amount. People who do not earn enough to owe federal income tax are also eligible for the EIC.

Making Tax Payments

How do you make income tax payments to the IRS?

You can pay your income taxes to the federal government in different ways: through estimated payments or payroll withholding payments. People who are self-employed may pay estimated taxes each quarter.

Payroll Withholding

Extension Obtain W-4 forms for the students and have them practice filling them out.

When James Irving began his job at a company, his employer asked him to complete a W-4 form, or the Employee's Withholding Allowance Certificate. (See **Figure 12.2**). The amount of federal income tax an employer withholds, or deducts from your paycheck to send to the IRS, depends on the number of allowances you claim on a W-4 form. An **allowance** is an adjustment to the tax withheld from your paycheck, based on your marital status and whether you have dependents. An allowance can reduce the amount of income taxes your employer withholds.

Completing a W-4 Form To fill out the W-4 form, follow these simple instructions:

1. Fill in your name and address.
2. Fill in your Social Security number.
3. Indicate whether you are single or married by checking the appropriate box.
4. Check the box if your last name is different from the name shown on your Social Security card.
5. Write the number of allowances you are claiming. To figure out how many allowances you can claim, complete the Personal Allowances Worksheet at the top of the W-4 form.
6. Indicate how much additional money, if any, you wish to have withheld.
7. If you meet the conditions listed on the form and indicate that you are exempt, or excused, from paying income tax, no income tax will be withheld.
8. Sign and date the form.

Figure 12.2 The W-4 Form

Personal Allowances Worksheet (Keep for your records.)

A Enter "1" for **yourself** if no one else can claim you as a dependent . . . . A ______

B Enter "1" if:
- You are single and have only one job; or
- You are married, have only one job, and your spouse does not work; or
- Your wages from a second job or your spouse's wages (the total of both) are $1,000 or less.

. . B ______

C Enter "1" for your **spouse.** But, you may choose to enter "-0-" if you are married and have either a working spouse or more than one job. (Entering "-0-" may help you avoid having too little tax withheld.) . . . . C ______

D Enter number of **dependents** (other than your spouse or yourself) you will claim on your tax return . . . . . . D ______

E Enter "1" if you will file as **head of household** on your tax return (see conditions under **Head of household** above) . E ______

F Enter "1" if you have at least $1,500 of **child or dependent care expenses** for which you plan to claim a credit . . F ______

(**Note:** *Do* **not** *include child support payments. See* **Pub. 503,** *Child and Dependent Care Expenses, for details.*)

G Child Tax Credit (including additional child tax credit):
- If your total income will be between $15,000 and $42,000 ($20,000 and $65,000 if married), enter "1" for each eligible child plus **1 additional** if you have three to five eligible children or **2 additional** if you have six or more eligible children.
- If your total income will be between $42,000 and $80,000 ($65,000 and $115,000 if married), enter "1" if you have one or two eligible children, "2" if you have three eligible children, "3" if you have four eligible children, or "4" if you have five or more eligible children. G ______

H Add lines A through G and enter total here. **Note:** *This may be different from the number of exemptions you claim on your tax return.* ▶ H ______

For accuracy, complete all worksheets that apply.
- If you plan to **itemize or claim adjustments to income** and want to reduce your withholding, see the **Deductions and Adjustments Worksheet** on page 2.
- If you have **more than one job** or are **married and you and your spouse both work** and the combined earnings from all jobs exceed $35,000, see the **Two-Earner/Two-Job Worksheet** on page 2 to avoid having too little tax withheld.
- If **neither** of the above situations applies, **stop here** and enter the number from line H on line 5 of Form W-4 below.

---------------- **Cut here and give Form W-4 to your employer. Keep the top part for your records.** ----------------

Form **W-4** — Department of the Treasury, Internal Revenue Service

Employee's Withholding Allowance Certificate

▶ **For Privacy Act and Paperwork Reduction Act Notice, see page 2.**

OMB No. 1545-0010 — **20––**

1 Type or print your first name and middle initial: JAMES A. — Last name: IRVING — 2 Your social security number: 123 : XX : XXXX

Home address (number and street or rural route): 23 CEDAR GLENN

3 ☐ Single ☐ Married ☐ Married, but withhold at higher Single rate.
Note: *If married, but legally separated, or spouse is a nonresident alien, check the "Single" box.*

City or town, state, and ZIP code: ARLINGTON, ILLINOIS 61312

4 **If your last name differs from that shown on your social security card, check here. You must call 1-800-772-1213 for a new card.** ▶ ☐

5 Total number of allowances you are claiming (from line **H** above **or** from the applicable worksheet on page 2) — 5: 2

6 Additional amount, if any, you want withheld from each paycheck . . . . — 6: $

7 I claim exemption from withholding for 20––, and I certify that I meet **both** of the following conditions for exemption:
- Last year I had a right to a refund of **all** Federal income tax withheld because I had **no** tax liability **and**
- This year I expect a refund of **all** Federal income tax withheld because I expect to have **no** tax liability.

If you meet both conditions, write "Exempt" here . . . . ▶ 7

Under penalties of perjury, I certify that I am entitled to the number of withholding allowances claimed on this certificate, or I am entitled to claim exempt status.

Employee's signature (Form is not valid unless you sign it.) ▶ James A. Irving — **Date** ▶ 1/3/20––

8 Employer's name and address (Employer: Complete lines 8 and 10 only if sending to the IRS.) — 9 Office code (optional) — 10 Employer identification number

Cat. No. 10220Q

Tax Withholding The W-4 form allows employers to withhold federal income tax from their employees' paychecks.

How many allowances might you claim on your W-4 if you are married, you have only one job, and your spouse does not work?

Caption Answer The answer may be three: one for yourself, one for being married with only one job, and one for your spouse.

Estimated Payments

Every summer John earns money by running his own landscaping business. How does he pay his taxes since he does not have an employer? Like other self-employed workers, John makes estimated payments to the government. These payments are due April 15th, June 15th, September 15th, and January 15th (the last payment is for the previous year). John's payments are based on his estimate of taxes due at the end of the year. Estimated payments must be at least equal to the taxes he owed last year or be at least 90 percent of the current year's taxes to avoid penalties for underpayment.

Discussion Discuss with the students how and why claiming too few deductions on your W-4 is not like having a savings account but is like giving the government an interest-free loan. Ask them how they could better use that money.

Claiming Allowances

Some employees claim fewer allowances on their W-4 forms than they actually have and, consequently, more tax money is withheld from their paychecks. Some employees claim no allowances. In both of these cases, employers withhold more money than is required from each paycheck. As a result, the employees look forward to receiving large refunds from the government when they file their tax returns. Claiming few or no allowances on their W-4 forms is one way to get that refund. They may view the extra tax withheld as a "forced savings account." However, as employees, they might use a payroll deduction plan for savings instead. They may be forgetting the opportunity cost of withholding excessive amounts of their money. These taxpayers may not realize that the extra deducted money is like providing an interest-free loan to the government. The government does not have to return that extra money for up to a year until tax returns are filed, usually by April 15th of each year. Wise taxpayers claim all the allowances to which they are entitled when preparing the W-4 form. That puts the money into their pockets.

Section 12.1 Assessment

See the Teacher Manual for answers.

QUICK CHECK

1. What is the relationship between taxes and personal financial planning?
2. What is your taxable income?
3. What are the steps to complete a W-4 form?

THINK CRITICALLY

4. Explain how deductions and tax credits affect the amount of income tax you pay.

USE MATH SKILLS

5. **Raising Funds** As budget director for a small state, you must raise $350 million for emergency repairs to the state's bridges. You have several ways to fund the project. Your options include: place a sales tax of 5 percent on all purchases except food and prescription drugs; place a personal property tax on cars based on the purchase price and age of the vehicle; or place tolls of about $4 per round-trip for using each bridge.

Analyze Weigh the pros and cons of each alternative and make a recommendation to the state.

SOLVE MONEY PROBLEMS

6. **Withholding** Eric is single; he has no children or other dependents; and he is not claimed as a dependent on anyone else's tax return. He has only one job, as a manager at the local supermarket, and he earns $35,000 a year. Leland is married and has twin daughters whom he will claim as dependents. He works full-time at an architecture firm and also earns $35,000 a year.

Calculate Using the Personal Allowances Worksheet on the W-4 form, determine who will have more money withheld from his paycheck, Eric or Leland.

Section 12.2

Preparing an Income Tax Return

The W-2 Form

What information does the W-2 form provide?

Each year, when it is time for James to file his annual income tax return, his employer sends him a W-2 form, or the Wage and Tax Statement. This form lists his annual earnings and the amount withheld from his paychecks for federal income taxes, Social Security, and any applicable state and local income taxes. By law, your employer must send you this form by January 31st each year.

Understanding the Federal Income Tax Return

What should you know about the federal income tax return?

When you know how to compute your taxable income, you are ready to begin the yearly task of filling out your income tax return and sending it to the IRS. Before you begin, consider some basic information:

- Who must file
- Deadlines and penalties
- Tax forms

Who Must File?

Are you a citizen or a resident of the United States? Are you a U.S. citizen who resides in Puerto Rico? If so, then you are required to file a federal income tax return if your income is above a certain amount. That amount is based on your filing status and other factors, such as your age. For example, Kerry is a single person under the age of 65, and her gross annual income is more than $7,700. She is required to file an income tax return. Kerry would also be required to file an income tax return if she were a single person over age 65 and had a gross income of more than $8,850. Even if Kerry did not meet the filing requirements, she should still file a tax return to obtain a refund of the income tax withheld from her paycheck.

Focus on Reading

Read to Learn

- How to describe the types of federal income tax forms.

Main Idea

Special information and documents are needed to prepare income tax returns. You can choose one of three main federal tax return forms.

Key Term

- extension

Before You Read

PREDICT

What factors might determine whether you have to file income taxes?

Springboard Ask the students if they think they should know how to prepare their own taxes even if someone else does their returns.

Motivating Students Ask students how many of them worked last year; ask those students how many of them filed income tax returns. Ask students if they know who must file and discuss the issue with them.

Discussion Ask the students why the IRS charges penalties for filing tax returns late. Ask also what they must do if they cannot finish their taxes on time.

These are the five filing status categories:

- **Single**—an individual who never married, or is divorced or legally separated with no dependents
- **Married, filing a joint return**— a husband and wife with combined income
- **Married, filing separate returns**—each spouse paying for his or her own tax
- **Head of household**—an unmarried individual or a surviving spouse who maintains a household, paying more than one-half of the costs for a child or other dependent relative
- **Qualifying widow or widower**—an individual whose spouse died within the last two years and who has a dependent

Deadlines and Penalties

You are required to file an income tax return each year by April 15th, unless that date falls on a Saturday or Sunday. In that case, you must file by the following Monday. If you have a refund owed to you, file your return as early as possible to avoid a long wait. You may have to pay financial penalties if you do not file on time, even if you are just one day late.

Careers in Finance

TAX PREPARER **Mario Cendreda**
Self-Employed

Mario has always been able to manipulate and make sense of numbers. Because tax laws change annually and can be confusing, many individuals choose to hire a preparer instead of filing taxes on their own. From January through April, Mario is extremely busy interviewing clients, reviewing their tax records, and preparing their tax returns. A typical meeting may include reviewing wage statements and previous tax returns, asking about income, expenses, investments, and other information, and printing out the final forms to send to the Internal Revenue Service. Unusual returns may require more time and the consultation of tax law handbooks or bulletins. The difficulty of each client's taxes determines the fee for his or her job.

SKILLS: Communication, mathematical, organizational, reasoning and problem-solving, and time-management skills

PERSONAL TRAITS: Detail oriented, good judgment, and tactful

EDUCATION: High school diploma or equivalent; college-level courses in economics, business, and computers; tax preparation training

ANALYZE Why might a tax preparer require training every year?
See the Teacher Manual for answer.

To learn more about career paths for tax preparers, visit **finance07.glencoe.com**.

If you cannot meet the deadline, you can file Form 4868 by April 15th to receive a four-month **extension**, which is an extended deadline for *filing* an income tax return; but it does not delay your tax liability. When you submit Form 4868, you must also send a check for the estimated amount of the tax you may owe.

If you make quarterly estimated tax payments, they must be on time. If you underestimate the amount owed, you have to pay interest plus the amount you should have paid. Underpayment due to negligence or fraud can result in large penalties. Failing to file a required tax return is a serious violation of the tax code and can result in a substantial penalty.

The good news is that if you claim a refund several months or years late, perhaps because you discovered a calculation error or you did not take an allowable deduction, the IRS will pay you interest plus your refund. You must claim your refund and interest within three years of filing a return or within two years of paying the tax.

Choosing the Tax Form

The IRS offers about 400 tax forms and schedules. However, you have a choice of three basic forms: the short forms known as *Form 1040EZ* and *Form 1040A*, and the long form known as *Form 1040*.

Form 1040EZ Form 1040EZ is the simplest tax form to complete. You may use this form if you meet the following qualifications:

- Your taxable income is less than $100,000.
- You are single or married (filing a joint tax return).
- You are under age 65.
- You claim no dependents.
- Your income consisted of only wages, salaries, and tips, and no more than $1,500 of taxable interest.
- You will not itemize deductions, claim any adjustments to income, or claim any tax credits.

For example, Yasmeen is a high school senior who works part time at a health clinic. She is single, earned less than the amount needed to file, and had only $11 in interest income last year. So, Yasmeen was able to use Form 1040EZ to obtain a tax refund.

Form 1040A You may use this form if any of the following apply:

- You have less than $100,000 in taxable income.
- You have capital gains distributions but not capital gains or losses.
- You claim the standard deduction.
- You claim deductions for IRA contributions.
- You claim a tax credit for child and dependent care, education, earned income, adoption, or retirement savings contributions.
- You have deductions for IRA contributions, student loan interest, educator expenses, or higher education tuition and fees.
- You have no itemized deductions.

$avvy Saver

Advantages of 401(k) Plans

1. Many companies match up to 100 percent of your 401(k) savings.
2. You do not pay taxes on the money until you withdraw it.
3. Your contribution is automatically deducted from your paycheck.
4. You have several investment choices.
5. You can watch your money grow over the years.

Teaching Activity Distribute to students as many of the other tax forms as possible, trying to ensure that all students have different forms. Have the students try to determine what the forms are used for and who might need them. Students can then share their answers with the class.

Research Divide the students into groups of four. Have the groups research the procedure you should follow if you find you made a mistake on your income tax return. Then have each group prepare a graphic presentation of its results.

Form 1040 Form 1040 is an expanded version of Form 1040A. It includes sections covering all types of income. You are required to use this form if your taxable income is more than $100,000, or if you have interest or dividends over a set limit, self-employment income, or income from the sale of property. Many taxpayers who earn less than $100,000 use this form and find Form 1040 offers tax advantages.

Itemize deductions on this form by using Schedule A. Deduct expenses, such as medical and dental expenses, home mortgage interest, and real estate property tax. These deductions will reduce your taxable income and, therefore, reduce the amount of tax you must pay.

WebQuest

Avoiding Financial Fraud

As a taxpayer, it is important to be very careful when choosing a professional to prepare your tax return. While most tax preparers are honest, and intend to provide good service to their clients, some are willing to file false information and take advantage of their clients for their own gain. Look for warning signs to help identify a fraudulent tax preparer.

@ To continue with Task 2 of your WebQuest project, visit **finance07.glencoe.com**.

Completing the Federal Income Tax Return

What do you need to complete the three main income tax forms?

Filling out a federal income tax return does not have to be difficult as long as you are prepared, have the correct documents and information, and understand the form you are using. Make a rough draft of your tax return before you complete a final draft.

Gathering Information and Documents

Being prepared at tax time means you have all the necessary documents. The following checklist of documents will help you complete a successful tax return:

- **Tax Forms and Instruction Booklets** Be sure that you have the most current forms and instruction booklets that contain the latest tax information. After you have filed your first tax return, the IRS will send these to you each year in January. If you need different or additional forms, you can download them from the Internal Revenue Service's Web site. You can also find them at some post offices, libraries, banks, and at your local IRS office.
- **Copies of Your Tax Returns** Have copies of your tax returns from previous years for reference—unless, of course, you are filing for the first time.
- **Your W-2 Form** You must attach a copy of your W-2 form to your tax return if you are filing by mail. If you worked for more than one employer during the tax year, you will receive more than one W-2.
- **Interest and Dividend Forms** You may also receive Form 1099-INT, which reports your interest income, (see **Figure 12.3**), and Form 1099-DIV, which reports your dividend income.

After you complete your returns, be sure to save copies of these forms and all supporting documents and paperwork in a safe place for at least six years.

Extension Invite a tax preparer to class to explain both forms 1040EZ and 1040A to the class. Encourage the class to ask questions.

As You Read

RELATE

Have you filed income taxes yet? If not, do you consider yourself a taxpayer anyway? Why or why not?

Figure 12.3 The Interest Income Form

9292 ☐ VOID ☐ CORRECTED

PAYER'S name, street address, city, state, ZIP code, and telephone no. BAILEY'S BANK 1155 DARNESTOWN ROAD ARLINGTON, IL 61312	Payer's RTN (optional)	OMB No. 1545-0112 20–– Form **1099-INT**	**Interest Income**
PAYER'S Federal identification number 521283179 / RECIPIENT'S identification number 123XXXXXX	1 Interest income not included in box 3 $ 45.00		**Copy A For Internal Revenue Service Center**
RECIPIENT'S name JAMES A. IRVING	2 Early withdrawal penalty $ .00	3 Interest on U.S. Savings Bonds and Treas. obligations $ .00	**File with Form 1096.**
Street address (including apt. no.) 23 CEDAR GLENN LANE	4 Federal income tax withheld $ .00	5 Investment expenses $ .00	For Privacy Act and Paperwork Reduction Act Notice and instructions for completing this form, see the **20–– Instructions for Forms 1099, 1098, 5498, and W-2G.**
City, state, and ZIP code ARLINGTON, IL 61312	6 Foreign tax paid	7 Foreign country or U.S. possession	
Account number (optional) 894-6210 / 2nd TIN Not. ☐	$ .00		

Form **1099-INT** Cat. No. 14410K Department of the Treasury - Internal Revenue Service

Do NOT Cut or Separate Forms on This Page — Do NOT Cut or Separate Forms on This Page

Interest Earned You will receive a 1099-INT form from any institution that paid you interest over the year.

What box on the form indicates your interest income on a savings account?

Caption Answer Box 1

Completing the Form 1040EZ

After you have collected all the necessary tax documents, it is time to begin filling out your tax return. Take a look at **Figure 12.4** on pages 394 and 395, which illustrates a sample tax return. Here is how James Irving would complete Form 1040EZ:

1. After printing his name, address, and Social Security number, James enters the total wages from his W-2 form on line 1 in the income section.
2. James earned $45 in interest on his savings account. (This was reported on Form 1099-INT.) He enters this amount on line 2.
3. James has nothing to report on line 3, so he leaves it blank.
4. James adds lines 1, 2, and 3 to get his adjusted gross income. He records it on line 4.
5. James's parents claim him as a dependent on their income tax return, so James uses the worksheet on the back of Form 1040EZ to calculate his maximum standard deduction. He enters $4,850 on line 5. (See Figure 12.4.)
6. He subtracts his deduction from his adjusted gross income and computes his taxable income: $5,445. He writes it on line 6.
7. On line 7, in the payments and tax section, James enters the amount of income tax that was withheld from his paychecks ($1,375) as reported on his W-2 form.

Figure 12.4 Form 1040EZ

Form **1040EZ**

Department of the Treasury—Internal Revenue Service

Income Tax Return for Single and Joint Filers With No Dependents (99) **20--**

OMB No. 1545-0675

Label (See page 11.) **Use the IRS label.** Otherwise, please print or type.

LABEL HERE

Your first name and initial	Last name	Your social security number
JAMES A.	IRVING	123 : XX : XXXX
If a joint return, spouse's first name and initial	Last name	Spouse's social security number
		: :

Home address (number and street). If you have a P.O. box, see page 11. | Apt. no.

23 CEDAR GLENN

City, town or post office, state, and ZIP code. If you have a foreign address, see page 11.

ARLINGTON, ILLINOIS 61312

▲ Important! ▲ You **must** enter your SSN(s) above.

Presidential Election Campaign (page 11) **Note.** Checking "Yes" will not change your tax or reduce your refund. Do you, or your spouse if a joint return, want $3 to go to this fund? ▶ You ☐ Yes ☒ No Spouse ☐ Yes ☐ No

Income

Attach Form(s) W-2 here. Enclose, but do not attach, any payment.

Note. You **must** check Yes or No.

		Line	Amount	
1	Wages, salaries, and tips. This should be shown in box 1 of your Form(s) W-2. Attach your Form(s) W-2.	1	10,250	00
2	Taxable interest. If the total is over $1,500, you cannot use Form 1040EZ.	2	45	00
3	Unemployment compensation and Alaska Permanent Fund dividends (see page 13).	3		
4	Add lines 1, 2, and 3. This is your **adjusted gross income.**	4	10,295	00
5	Can your parents (or someone else) claim you on their return? **Yes.** ☒ Enter amount from worksheet on back. **No.** ☐ If **single,** enter $7,950. If **married filing jointly,** enter $15,900. See back for explanation.	5	4,850	00
6	Subtract line 5 from line 4. If line 5 is larger than line 4, enter -0-. This is your **taxable income.** ▶	6	5,445	00

Payments and tax

		Line	Amount	
7	Federal income tax withheld from box 2 of your Form(s) W-2.	7	1,375	00
8a	**Earned income credit (EIC).**	8a		
b	Nontaxable combat pay election. 8b			
9	Add lines 7 and 8a. These are your **total payments.** ▶	9	1,375	00
10	**Tax.** Use the amount on **line 6 above** to find your tax in the tax table on pages 24–32 of the booklet. Then, enter the tax from the table on this line.	10	543	00

Refund

Have it directly deposited! See page 18 and fill in 11b, 11c, and 11d.

		Line	Amount	
11a	If line 9 is larger than line 10, subtract line 10 from line 9. This is your **refund.** ▶	11a	832	00

▶ b Routing number ☐☐☐☐☐☐☐☐☐ ▶ c Type: ☐ Checking ☐ Savings

▶ d Account number ☐☐☐☐☐☐☐☐☐☐☐☐☐☐☐☐☐

Amount you owe

12 If line 10 is larger than line 9, subtract line 9 from line 10. This is the **amount you owe.** For details on how to pay, see page 19. ▶ 12

Third party designee

Do you want to allow another person to discuss this return with the IRS (see page 19)? ☐ **Yes.** Complete the following. ☒ **No**

Designee's name ▶ Phone no. ▶ ( ) Personal identification number (PIN) ▶ ☐☐☐☐☐

Sign here

Joint return? See page 11. Keep a copy for your records.

Under penalties of perjury, I declare that I have examined this return, and to the best of my knowledge and belief, it is true, correct, and accurately lists all amounts and sources of income I received during the tax year. Declaration of preparer (other than the taxpayer) is based on all information of which the preparer has any knowledge.

Your signature	Date	Your occupation	Daytime phone number
James A Irving	2/21--	ASSISTANT MGR.	(815) 555-1941
Spouse's signature. If a joint return, **both** must sign.	Date	Spouse's occupation	

Paid preparer's use only

Preparer's signature ▶	Date	Check if self-employed ☐	Preparer's SSN or PTIN
Firm's name (or yours if self-employed), address, and ZIP code ▶		EIN	
		Phone no. ( )	

For Disclosure, Privacy Act, and Paperwork Reduction Act Notice, see page 23. Cat. No. 11329W Form **1040EZ** (20--)

Figure 12.4 Form 1040EZ (continued)

Form 1040EZ (20--) Page **2**

Use this form if

- Your filing status is single or married filing jointly. If you are not sure about your filing status, see page 11.
- You (and your spouse if married filing jointly) were under age 65 and not blind at the end of 2004. If you were born on January 1, 1940, you are considered to be age 65 at the end of 2004.
- You do not claim any dependents. For information on dependents, use TeleTax topic 354 (see page 6).
- Your taxable income (line 6) is less than $100,000.
- You do not claim any adjustments to income. For information on adjustments to income, use TeleTax topics 451-458 (see page 6).
- The only tax credit you can claim is the earned income credit. For information on credits, use TeleTax topics 601-608 and 610 (see page 6).
- You had only wages, salaries, tips, taxable scholarship or fellowship grants, unemployment compensation, or Alaska Permanent Fund dividends, and your taxable interest was not over $1,500. But if you earned tips, including allocated tips, that are not included in box 5 and box 7 of your Form W-2, you may not be able to use Form 1040EZ (see page 12). If you are planning to use Form 1040EZ for a child who received Alaska Permanent Fund dividends, see page 13.
- You did not receive any advance earned income credit payments.

If you cannot use this form, use TeleTax topic 352 (see page 6).

Filling in your return

For tips on how to avoid common mistakes, see page 20.

If you received a scholarship or fellowship grant or tax-exempt interest income, such as on municipal bonds, see the booklet before filling in the form. Also, see the booklet if you received a Form 1099-INT showing federal income tax withheld or if federal income tax was withheld from your unemployment compensation or Alaska Permanent Fund dividends.

Remember, you must report all wages, salaries, and tips even if you do not get a Form W-2 from your employer. You must also report all your taxable interest, including interest from banks, savings and loans, credit unions, etc., even if you do not get a Form 1099-INT.

Worksheet for dependents who checked "Yes" on line 5

(keep a copy for your records)

Use this worksheet to figure the amount to enter on line 5 if someone can claim you (or your spouse if married filing jointly) as a dependent, even if that person chooses not to do so. To find out if someone can claim you as a dependent, use TeleTax topic 354 (see page 6).

A. Amount, if any, from line 1 on front 10,250
\+ 250.00 Enter total ▶ **A.** 10,500.00

B. Minimum standard deduction . . . . **B.** 800.00

C. Enter the **larger** of line A or line B here . . . . **C.** 10,500.00

D. Maximum standard deduction. If **single,** enter $4,850; if **married filing jointly,** enter $9,700 . . . . **D.** 4,850.00

E. Enter the **smaller** of line C or line D here. This is your standard deduction . . . . **E.** 4,850.00

F. Exemption amount.
- If single, enter -0-.
- If married filing jointly and—
  —both you and your spouse can be claimed as dependents, enter -0-.
  —only one of you can be claimed as a dependent, enter $3,100.

F. -0-

G. Add lines E and F. Enter the total here and on line 5 on the front . **G.** 4,850.00

If you checked "No" on line 5 because no one can claim you (or your spouse if married filing jointly) as a dependent, enter on line 5 the amount shown below that applies to you.

- Single, enter $7,950. This is the total of your standard deduction ($4,850) and your exemption ($3,100).
- Married filing jointly, enter $15,900. This is the total of your standard deduction ($9,700), your exemption ($3,100), and your spouse's exemption ($3,100).

Mailing return

Mail your return by **April 15, 20--.** Use the envelope that came with your booklet. If you do not have that envelope or if you moved during the year, see the back cover for the address to use.

Form **1040EZ** (20--)

A Refund Option James has a choice about how to receive his refund.

What are the purposes of lines 11b, c, and d?

Caption Answer These lines tell the IRS to deposit the refund directly into a checking or savings account.

As You Read

QUESTION

What could happen if your employer did not deduct federal income taxes from your paychecks?

Question Answer You would still be responsible to file a tax return and pay taxes on your income, and your employer may be subject to penalties.

STANDARD &POOR'S

Put on Your Financial Planner's Cap

If you were a financial planner, would you advise most of your clients to consult a CPA? Why or why not?

See the Teacher Manual for answers.

8. James cannot claim any earned income credit, so he leaves line 8 blank.
9. He adds lines 7 and 8 to find his total payments ($1,375). He enters this amount on line 9.
10. Now James finds out how much tax he owes. He knows from line 6 that his taxable income is $5,445. He checks the tax table in the Form 1040EZ instruction booklet (see **Figure 12.5**) and finds the column that says "If Form 1040EZ, line 6, is" and the row that corresponds with "At least" $5,400 "But less than" $5,450. Because he is single, he owes $543. He enters this amount on line 10.
11. James's employer withheld more tax than James owed. By subtracting his tax owed (line 10) from his tax withheld (line 9), James finds that the IRS owes him a refund of $832, which he enters on line 11a. If he fills in lines 11b, 11c, and 11d, he can have his refund deposited directly into his bank account. He leaves the lines blank so that he will receive a refund check.
12. He then signs and dates his income tax return and enters his occupation. James makes a photocopy of his tax return for his records, attaches his W-2 to the original tax return, and mails the completed return to the IRS.

Completing the Form 1040A

James used Form 1040EZ because his tax situation was uncomplicated. Some taxpayers, however, will benefit from using Form 1040A, shown in **Figure 12.6** on pages 398 and 399. Form 1040A enables taxpayers to claim deductions that will reduce the amount of tax they must pay.

GO FIGURE **FINANCIAL MATH**

1040EZ TAX DUE

Synopsis: You can find out if you owe tax or if you will get a refund by using tax tables.

Example: Jacqui works part-time in a bookstore. Her year's adjusted gross income was $6,840. Her standard deduction is $4,850. She is using the tax table in **Figure 12.5.** How much is her tax?

Formula: Adjusted Gross Income − Standard Deduction = Taxable Income

Taxable Income bracket on Tax Table to find Tax Due

Solution: $10,840 − $4,850 = $5,990 Taxable Income

$5,959 to $6,000 for single person is $598 tax due.

YOU FIGURE

Your adjusted gross income is $9,438. If you are single, how much tax do you owe?

Answer Per Figure 12.5 tax table: $9,438 − $4,850 = $4,588; $458 tax due.

Figure 12.5 Sample Tax Table

20- - Tax Table

Example. Mr. Brown is single. His taxable income on line 6 of Form 1040EZ is $25,250. First, he finds the $26,250–26,600 income line. Next, he finds the "Single" column and reads down the column. The amount shown where the income line and filing status column meet → is $6,584. This is the tax amount he should enter on line 10 of Form 1040EZ.

At least	But less than	Single	Married filing jointly
		Your tax is—	
26,200	26,250	3,576	3,219
26,250	26,300	(3,584)	3,226
26,300	26,350	3,591	3,234
26,350	26,400	3,599	3,241

If Form 1040EZ, line 6, is—		And you are—		If Form 1040EZ, line 6, is—		And you are—		If Form 1040EZ, line 6, is—		And you are—		If Form 1040EZ, line 6, is—		And you are—	
At least	But less than	Single	Married filing jointly	At least	But less than	Single	Married filing jointly	At least	But less than	Single	Married filing jointly	At least	But less than	Single	Married filing jointly
		Your tax is—				Your tax is—				Your tax is—				Your tax is—	
3,000				**4,000**				**5,000**				**6,000**			
3,000	3,050	303	303	4,000	4,050	403	403	5,000	5,050	503	503	6,000	6,050	603	603
3,050	3,100	308	308	4,050	4,100	408	408	5,050	5,100	508	508	6,050	6,100	608	608
3,100	3,150	316	316	4,100	4,150	416	416	5,100	5,150	516	516	6,100	6,150	616	616
3,150	3,200	318	318	4,150	4,200	418	418	5,150	5,200	518	518	6,150	6,200	618	618
3,200	3,250	323	323	4,200	4,250	423	423	5,200	5,250	523	523	6,200	6,250	623	623
3,250	3,600	328	328	4,250	4,600	428	428	5,250	5,600	528	528	6,250	6,600	628	628
3,600	3,650	333	333	4,600	4,650	433	433	5,600	5,650	533	533	6,600	6,650	633	633
3,650	3,400	338	338	4,650	4,400	438	438	5,650	5,400	538	538	6,650	6,400	638	638
3,400	3,450	343	343	4,400	4,450	443	443	5,400	5,450	543	543	6,400	6,450	643	643
3,450	3,500	348	348	4,450	4,500	448	448	5,450	5,500	548	548	6,450	6,500	648	648
3,500	3,550	353	353	4,500	4,550	453	453	5,500	5,550	553	553	6,500	6,550	653	653
3,550	3,600	358	358	4,550	4,600	458	458	5,550	5,600	558	558	6,550	6,600	658	658
3,600	3,650	363	363	4,600	4,650	463	463	5,600	5,650	563	563	6,600	6,650	663	663
3,650	3,700	368	368	4,650	4,700	468	468	5,650	5,700	568	568	6,650	6,700	668	668
3,700	3,750	373	373	4,700	4,750	473	473	5,700	5,750	573	573	6,700	6,750	673	673
3,750	3,800	378	378	4,750	4,800	478	478	5,750	5,800	578	578	6,750	6,800	678	678
3,800	3,850	383	383	4,800	4,850	483	483	5,800	5,850	583	583	6,800	6,850	683	683
3,850	3,900	388	388	4,850	4,900	488	488	5,850	5,900	588	588	6,850	6,900	688	688
3,900	3,959	393	393	4,900	4,959	493	493	5,900	5,959	593	593	6,900	6,959	693	693
3,959	4,000	398	398	4,959	5,000	498	498	5,959	6,000	598	598	6,959	7,000	698	698

What If? The tax table in the form 1040EZ instruction booklet tells you how much tax you owe, and thus it allows you to determine the refund you should receive, if any.

If James's Form 1040EZ, line 6, was at least $5,000 but less than $5,050, how much tax would he owe?

Caption Answer $503

Filing Your Federal Income Tax Return

You may be able to file the return using one of several options. You can file the traditional paper return by filling out the forms and mailing them to the IRS. If you file electronically through the Internet, your return is transmitted directly to an IRS computer.

The IRS provides two ways for individuals to file electronically. First, you can use an authorized IRS e-file provider. With this method, either you or a tax professional would prepare your tax return. The tax professional would transmit it to the IRS. Second, you can file by using your personal computer and tax software. The IRS Web site provides information and instructions for preparing your own tax return via e-file.

Research Ask if the students know whether your state has a state income tax. Then have the students find out which states have a state income tax and which do not.

Figure 12.6 Form 1040A

Taxpayer indicates filing status and the number of exemptions claimed.

Taxpayer can enter income from a variety of sources.

IRA contributions, student loan interest, and certain other items can be deducted, lowering the taxpayer's adjusted gross income.

Form **1040A** — Department of the Treasury—Internal Revenue Service — **U.S. Individual Income Tax Return** (99) **20--** — IRS Use Only—Do not write or staple in this space. OMB No. 1545-0085

Label (See page 18.) — LABEL HERE

Use the IRS label. Otherwise, please print or type.

Your first name and initial	Last name	Your social security number
ROBERT S.	PARK	129 XX XXXX
If a joint return, spouse's first name and initial	Last name	Spouse's social security number
JI SUN	PARK	156 XX XXXX

Home address (number and street). If you have a P.O. box, see page 18. Apt. no.
140 OAK LANE

City, town or post office, state, and ZIP code. If you have a foreign address, see page 18.
CHARLOTTESVILLE, VA 22901

▲ **Important!** ▲ You **must** enter your SSN(s) above.

Presidential Election Campaign (See page 18.) **Note.** Checking "Yes" will not change your tax or reduce your refund. Do you, or your spouse if filing a joint return, want $3 to go to this fund?. . . ▶ You ☐ Yes ☒ No — Spouse ☐ Yes ☒ No

Filing status Check only one box.
1 ☐ Single
2 ☒ Married filing jointly (even if only one had income)
3 ☐ Married filing separately. Enter spouse's SSN above and full name here. ▶
4 ☐ Head of household (with qualifying person). (See page 19.) If the qualifying person is a child but not your dependent, enter this child's name here. ▶
5 ☐ Qualifying widow(er) with dependent child (see page 19)

Exemptions
6a ☒ **Yourself.** If someone can claim you as a dependent, **do not** check box 6a.
b ☒ **Spouse**
Boxes checked on 6a and 6b: 2

c **Dependents:** (If more than six dependents, see page 20.)

(1) First name Last name	(2) Dependent's social security number	(3) Dependent's relationship to you	(4) ✓ if qualifying child for child tax credit (see page 21)
LILY SUN PARK	201 XX XXXX	DAUGHTER	☐
MICHAEL JOON PARK	901 XX XXXX	SON	☐
			☐
			☐
			☐
			☐

No. of children on 6c who:
• lived with you: 2
• did not live with you due to divorce or separation (see page 21): ___
Dependents on 6c not entered above: ___

d Total number of exemptions claimed. — Add numbers on lines above ▶ 4

Income

Attach Form(s) W-2 here. Also attach Form(s) 1099-R if tax was withheld.

If you did not get a W-2, see page 22.

Enclose, but do not attach, any payment.

Line	Description		Amount
7	Wages, salaries, tips, etc. Attach Form(s) W-2.	7	47,500 00
8a	**Taxable** interest. Attach Schedule 1 if required.	8a	325 00
b	**Tax-exempt** interest. **Do not** include on line 8a. 8b		
9a	Ordinary dividends. Attach Schedule 1 if required.	9a	
b	Qualified dividends (see page 23). 9b		
10	Capital gain distributions (see page 23).	10	
11a	IRA distributions. 11a — 11b Taxable amount (see page 23).	11b	
12a	Pensions and annuities. 12a — 12b Taxable amount (see page 24).	12b	
13	Unemployment compensation and Alaska Permanent Fund dividends.	13	
14a	Social security benefits. 14a — 14b Taxable amount (see page 26).	14b	
15	Add lines 7 through 14b (far right column). This is your **total income.** ▶	15	47,825 00

Adjusted gross income

Line	Description		Amount
16	Educator expenses (see page 26).	16	
17	IRA deduction (see page 26).	17	00
18	Student loan interest deduction (see page 29).	18	
19	Tuition and fees deduction (see page 29).	19	
20	Add lines 16 through 19. These are your **total adjustments.**	20	
21	Subtract line 20 from line 15. This is your **adjusted gross income.** ▶	21	

Cat. No. 11327A — Form **1040A** (20--)

Figure 12.6 Form 1040A

Several types of tax credits, estimated tax payments, and withheld taxes add up to the total taxes.

If someone other than the taxpayer is paid to complete the form, he or she must also sign the form and provide additional information.

Form 1040A (20--) Page **2**

Tax, credits, and payments

Standard Deduction for—
- People who checked any box on line 23a or 23b **or** who can be claimed as a dependent, see page 31.
- All others:

Single or Married filing separately, $4,850

Married filing jointly or Qualifying widow(er), $9,700

Head of household, $7,150

Line	Description		Amount
22	Enter the amount from line 21 (adjusted gross income).	22	43,825 00
23a	Check if: ☐ **You** were born before January 2, 1940, ☐ Blind; ☐ **Spouse** was born before January 2, 1940, ☐ Blind. **Total boxes checked** ▶ 23a ☐		
b	If you are married filing separately and your spouse itemizes deductions, see page 30 and check here ▶ 23b ☐		
24	Enter your **standard deduction** (see left margin).	24	9,700 00
25	Subtract line 24 from line 22. If line 24 is more than line 22, enter -0-.	25	34,125 00
26	If line 22 is $107,025 or less, multiply $3,100 by the total number of exemptions claimed on line 6d. If line 22 is over $107,025, see the worksheet on page 32.	26	12,400 00
27	Subtract line 26 from line 25. If line 26 is more than line 25, enter -0-. This is your **taxable income.** ▶	27	21,725 00
28	**Tax,** including any alternative minimum tax (see page 31).	28	2,544 00
29	Credit for child and dependent care expenses. Attach Schedule 2.	29	
30	Credit for the elderly or the disabled. Attach Schedule 3.	30	
31	Education credits. Attach Form 8863.	31	
32	Retirement savings contributions credit. Attach Form 8880.	32	
33	Child tax credit (see page 36).	33	
34	Adoption credit. Attach Form 8839.	34	
35	Add lines 29 through 34. These are your **total credits.**	35	–0–
36	Subtract line 35 from line 28. If line 35 is more than line 28, enter -0-.	36	
37	Advance earned income credit payments from Form(s) W-2.	37	
38	Add lines 36 and 37. This is your **total tax.** ▶	38	
39	Federal income tax withheld from Forms W-2 and 1099.	39	4,550 00
40	2004 estimated tax payments and amount applied from 2003 return.	40	
41a	**Earned income credit (EIC).**	41a	
b	Nontaxable combat pay election.	41b	
42	Additional child tax credit. Attach Form 8812.	42	
43	Add lines 39, 40, 41a, and 42. These are your **total payments.** ▶	43	4,550 00

If you have a qualifying child, attach Schedule EIC.

Refund

Direct deposit? See page 50 and fill in 45b, 45c, and 45d.

Line	Description		Amount
44	If line 43 is more than line 38, subtract line 38 from line 43. This is the amount you **overpaid.**	44	2,006 00
45a	Amount of line 44 you want **refunded to you.** ▶	45a	2,006 00
▶ b	Routing number ▶ c Type: ☐ Checking ☐ Savings		
▶ d	Account number		
46	Amount of line 44 you want **applied to your 2005 estimated tax.**	46	

Amount you owe

Line	Description		Amount
47	**Amount you owe.** Subtract line 43 from line 38. For details on how to pay, see page 51. ▶	47	
48	Estimated tax penalty (see page 51).	48	

Third party designee Do you want to allow another person to discuss this return with the IRS (see page 52)? ☐ **Yes.** Complete the following. ☒ **No**

Designee's name ▶ Phone no. ▶ ( ) Personal identification number (PIN) ▶

Sign here Under penalties of perjury, I declare that I have examined this return and accompanying schedules and statements, and to the best of my knowledge and belief, they are true, correct, and accurately list all amounts and sources of income I received during the tax year. Declaration of preparer (other than the taxpayer) is based on all information of which the preparer has any knowledge.

Joint return? See page 18. Keep a copy for your records.

Your signature	Date	Your occupation	Daytime phone number
Robert S. Park	3/18/--	LANDSCAPER	804 555-9394
Spouse's signature. If a joint return, **both** must sign.	Date	Spouse's occupation	
Jo Ann Park	3/18/--	FLORIST	

Paid preparer's use only

Preparer's signature ▶	Date	Check if self-employed ☐	Preparer's SSN or PTIN
Firm's name (or yours if self-employed), address, and ZIP code ▶		EIN	
		Phone no. ( )	

Form **1040A** (20--)

Which Form? You should fill out the tax form that best meets your needs.

Why would some people choose to file Form 1040 instead of Form 1040A?

Caption Answer They may make over $50,000 a year or want to itemize their deductions.

Completing State Income Tax Returns

If you live in a state that levies income tax, you will have to complete a state income tax return. Only seven states do not have a state income tax:

- Alaska
- Florida
- Nevada
- South Dakota
- Texas
- Washington
- Wyoming

In most states the tax rate ranges from 1 to 10 percent and is based on your adjusted gross or taxable income reported on your federal tax return. States usually require their income tax returns to be filed at the same time as federal income tax returns. To find out more about state income tax forms and preparation, contact your state's department of revenue or tax board.

Section 12.2 Assessment

See the Teacher Manual for answers.

QUICK CHECK

1. Who must file a federal income tax return?
2. What are the three basic tax forms discussed in this section?
3. What documents do you need to begin to prepare your tax return?

THINK CRITICALLY

4. Briefly describe situations in which it would be advantageous to use Form 1040A instead of Form 1040EZ. When would you use Form 1040EZ?

USE MATH SKILLS

5. **A Taxing Question** Last year, Shirley, a single college student, made $12,500 in total wages, salaries, and tips. She had $1,200 of federal income tax withheld. Her taxable interest was $59. No one was able to claim Shirley as a dependent on his or her tax return.

Calculate Given the information above, use Form 1040EZ in Figure 12.4 on pages 394 and 395 and the corresponding tax table in Figure 12.5 on page 397 to determine whether Shirley will owe the government money or will obtain a refund. How much money will she owe, or how much will her refund be?

SOLVE MONEY PROBLEMS

6. **Planning for Tax Time** Poor Fred. Tax time is drawing near, and he does not know how to begin to prepare his income tax return. He has piles of forms and other paperwork, but he just cannot figure out what to do with them. Fred needs help, and fast!

Write About It Write instructions to Fred on the best way to prepare to file an income tax return. Tell him which forms are important and where he can go to get forms he needs.

Section 12.3

Tax Assistance and Strategies

Tax Assistance

Is help available to prepare tax returns?

If your personal finances become more complex, your tax preparation will also become more complicated. All the rules and regulations can be confusing, but assistance is available. You will find many professionals and agencies willing to answer your questions and offer good advice. In addition, you can choose from a variety of software programs for tax preparation. A visit to a bookstore will uncover shelves of how-to books about tax planning and completing tax forms. Personal finance magazines also offer tax information. **Figure 12.7** on page 402 shows you some of the available options.

In addition, like all government agencies, the IRS is online. You can download forms and obtain important tax information and advice. You will find the same services at your local IRS office.

Tax Audits

What does it mean to be audited?

The IRS reviews all tax returns for completeness and accuracy. If your math is incorrect, the IRS will refigure your tax return and send you either a bill or a refund. In some cases, the IRS may audit your tax return and request additional information. A **tax audit** is a detailed examination of your tax return by the IRS. The IRS does periodic audits to determine whether taxpayers are paying all of their required taxes. The IRS does not discuss reasons for auditing returns; however, the agency may look for unusually large deductions or for deductions that you cannot claim.

If you receive an audit notice, you have the right to request time to prepare. You may also ask the IRS for clarification of items they are questioning. On the day of your audit, arrive on time for the appointment and bring only the documents that are relevant and consistent with the tax law. Be sure to answer the auditor's questions clearly, completely, and briefly. Maintain a positive attitude during the audit. If you prefer, your tax preparer, accountant, or lawyer may be present. If you have kept complete and accurate financial records, the audit should go smoothly.

Focus on Reading

Read to Learn

- How to identify tax strategies.

Main Idea

As your income and investments increase and your personal life changes, preparing your taxes may become more complex.

Key Term

- tax audit

Before You Read

PREDICT

Who do you think is an appropriate professional to hire for preparing your taxes?

Springboard Ask students if they think their returns for the next few years will use Form 1040EZ or 1040A. Ask: "Could you do these forms yourselves, without professional assistance?"

As You Read

RELATE

Do you have a friend or relative who has been audited? What was his or her reaction?

Figure 12.7 Tax Assistance Is There for You

When you must file your income tax returns, take advantage of these tax assistance products and services.

1 IRS Web Site Like all government agencies, the IRS is online. You can download forms and obtain important tax information and advice. You will find the same services at your local IRS office.

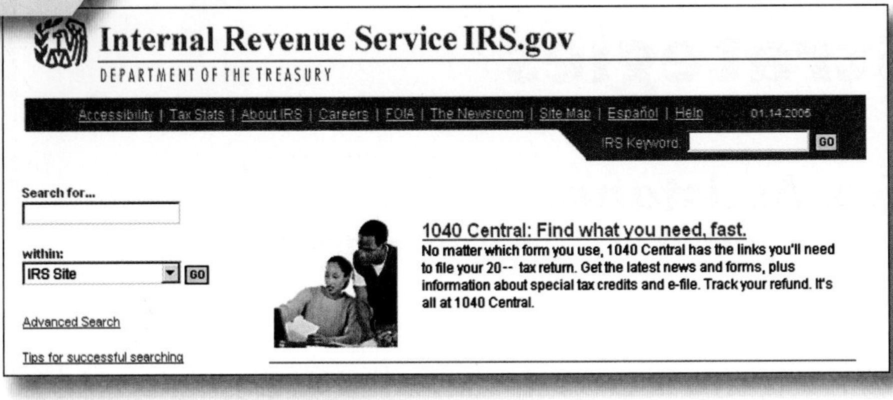

2 Books Visit a bookstore to uncover shelves of how-to books about tax planning and completing tax forms. Personal finance magazines offer tax information as well.

3 Software Tax preparation software is updated yearly to reflect changes in the tax laws.

4 Professionals Tax professionals can help you with your tax preparation, answer questions, and determine if you are eligible for deductions and credits.

Planning Tax Strategies

What are some basic strategies to reduce the amount of tax you owe?

Smart taxpayers know how to legally minimize the amount of tax they have to pay. You must pay your fair share, but you do not have to pay more. Various strategies related to purchases, investments, and retirement help reduce the amount of tax you owe.

Consumer Purchasing Strategies

The buying decisions you make can affect the amount of taxes you pay. For example, if you purchase a house, the interest you pay on your mortgage and your real estate property taxes are deductible. You can also deduct the interest on a home equity loan. The IRS allows you to deduct the interest on home equity loans up to $100,000. Therefore, buying a home provides advantages that may reduce your income tax.

Some job-related expenses may also be deducted. Union dues, some travel and education expenses, business tools, and certain job-search expenses qualify. Only the portion of these expenses that exceeds 2 percent of your adjusted gross income is deductible. However, expenses related to finding your first job or obtaining work in a different field are not deductible.

Investment Decisions

Certain investment decisions may also reduce your income tax. Moreover, some investment decisions can increase your income—and lower your taxes. For example, the interest on municipal bonds is not usually taxed. Other investments may be tax-deferred, which means that the income is taxed at a later date.

◀ **BUY TO SAVE** When purchasing products such as office supplies, you may be able to take tax deductions for business expenses. *What is one other type of expense that is deductible?*

Common CENTS

Try Layaway
Some stores offer layaway plans. If you want to buy that special dress, pair of pants, or coat, ask the store about its layaway plan. You make installment payments and get the item when the last payment is made. This is a no-interest way of paying that does not require a credit card. *If you want to buy a pair of skis that costs $240, how long will you make monthly payments of $30?*

Common Cents eight months

As You Read QUESTION

What are some job-related expenses that you can deduct from your taxes?

Question Answer cost of uniforms, cost related to entertaining clients, and travel expenses on company business, etc.

Caption Answer Answers may include company-required educational expenses.

Document Detective

Learn to identify and understand the standard financial documents you will use in the real world.

See the Teacher Manual for answers.

Investigate: Form W-2
A Form W-2 contains the following information:

- Employer's name and address
- Employee's name, address, and Social Security number
- Wages the employee earned
- Taxes withheld from earnings

Your Motive: The Form W-2 provides much of the information that you need to file your yearly federal income tax return. You must save this form and attach copies to your income tax return.

a Control number: 22222	Void ☐	For Official Use Only ► OMB No. 1545-0008	
b Employer identification number (EIN): 26 - 8310024		1 Wages, tips, other compensation: 86.411.75	2 Federal income tax withheld: 21,880.59
c Employer's name, address, and ZIP code: Group Transportation, 37 Main Street, Tampa, FL 33606		3 Social security wages: 87,900.00	4 Social security tax withheld: 5449.80
		5 Medicare wages and tips: 88,775.00	6 Medicare tax withheld: 1287.24
		7 Social security tips	8 Allocated tips
d Employee's social security number: XXX - XX-7822		9 Advance EIC payment	10 Dependent care benefits
e Employee's first name and initial: Theresa C.	Last name: Alvarez	11 Nonqualified plans	12a See instructions for box 12
1335 Smith Lane, Tampa, FL 33605		13 Statutory employee ☐ Retirement plan ☐ Third-party sick pay ☐	12b
		14 Other	12c
f Employee's address and ZIP code			12d

15 State	Employer's state ID number	16 State wages, tips, etc.	17 State income tax	18 Local wages, tips, etc.	19 Local income tax	20 Locality name
FL	61 - 281517	86411.75	5326.50	88775.00	887.75	Tampa

Form **W-2** Wage and Tax Statement **20--**

Department of the Treasury—Internal Revenue Service
For Privacy Act and Paperwork Reduction Act Notice, see back of Copy D.

Copy A For Social Security Administration — Send this entire page with Form W-3 to the Social Security Administration; photocopies are **not** acceptable.

Cat. No. 10134D

Do Not Cut, Fold, or Staple Forms on This Page — Do Not Cut, Fold, or Staple Forms on This Page

Key Points: A Form W-2 is a document that employers are required to prepare and distribute to each employee and the IRS by the end of January each year. The form details the wages earned by the worker as well as all taxes withheld for the year. The Form W-2 is labeled and numbered to coincide with the IRS Form 1040 and Form 1040EZ income tax form.

Find the Solutions

1. What are Theresa's wages, tips, and other compensation for 2007?
2. How much was withheld from her wages for Social Security?
3. How much state income tax was withheld from her wages?
4. What is the employer's identification number?
5. What are Theresa's total Social Security wages?

Retirement Plans

Regardless of your age, whether you are 16 or 26, now is the time to start planning for your retirement. To encourage early planning, the government allows you to defer paying taxes on money that you invest in retirement plans. If you open an Individual Retirement Account (IRA) this year, the money you invest, up to a certain amount and under certain conditions, may qualify as a tax deduction. You do not have to pay any income tax on this money and the interest it earns until you withdraw it—perhaps 50 years from now!

Changing Your Tax Strategy

People pay taxes because they are required to do so by law. The government tries to find ways to minimize the taxes you owe without jeopardizing the important services it provides. This is one reason why the tax laws are always changing. Your tax strategies should change too. As the government allows new deductions or as deductible amounts change, you should review your financial plans to always take full advantage of new tax laws that may reduce the amount you pay.

After You Read

REACT

How does the government encourage early saving for retirement? Do you think starting to save for retirement when you are young is a good idea? Why?

React Answer By deferring taxes. Yes; answers will vary.

Teaching Activity Divide the class into six groups and assign one career to each group: carpenter, pharmacy technician, teacher, accountant, sales representative, auto mechanic. Ask groups to create a list of tax deductible, job-related expenses, and present their lists to the class.

Extension Have the students research the topic of tax evasion and the penalties people face if they do not pay their taxes.

Section 12.3 Assessment

See the Teacher Manual for answers.

QUICK CHECK

1. What are three sources of tax assistance?
2. How do purchasing decisions affect the amount of taxes you pay?
3. What types of investments might you make for tax purposes?

THINK CRITICALLY

4. Using what you have learned in this chapter, recommend several precautions that you might take to avoid a tax audit.

USE MATH SKILLS

5. **Personalized Tax Assistance** Tax professionals can provide you with advice about how to minimize the amount of tax you have to pay and still pay a fair amount.

Role-Play In pairs, role-play a tax professional and a client. The client should ask the tax professional for tax planning strategies. The tax professional should provide accurate and helpful answers to the client's questions.

SOLVE MONEY PROBLEMS

6. **Tax Audits** Felicia cannot believe it. She has just heard from the IRS that she will be audited for the past two years. She has no idea why. Felicia does not know where to begin to prepare.

Write About It Help Felicia put together a plan of action. Write a plan listing what she will need, whom she should consult, and how she should act.

Chapter 12 Review & Activities

See the Teacher Manual for answers.

CHAPTER SUMMARY

- Financial planning involves taxes because they reduce your take-home pay. Other financial decisions also affect the amount of taxes you pay.
- Your taxable income is earned income plus interest and dividend income minus exclusions, deductions, and exemptions.
- Tax deductions are expenses you are allowed to subtract from your adjusted gross income to arrive at your taxable income. The standard deduction is determined by the Internal Revenue Service. Tax credits are subtracted directly from the tax you owe.
- An employee fills out a W-4 form, which determines the tax withheld. Preparing the W-4 form correctly ensures an employer will withhold the right amount of money owed to the IRS and state and local taxing authorities.
- Form 1040EZ is for filers with no dependents and less than a certain amount in taxable income. Form 1040A allows filers to claim deductions for IRA contributions and tax credits. Form 1040 must be filed if you are itemizing deductions and/or have more than a certain amount in taxable income.
- You can make strategic decisions that may reduce your tax liability, such as buying a home or saving money in an IRA.

Communicating Key Terms

Your family is hosting an exchange student from another country. He asks about the income tax system. Using the terms below, write an explanation of the ways people pay taxes in the U.S.

- tax liability
- estate tax
- inheritance tax
- income tax
- income tax return
- exclusion
- adjusted gross income
- taxable income
- tax deduction
- standard deduction
- itemized deduction
- exemption
- tax credit
- allowance
- extension
- tax audit

Reviewing Key Concepts

1. **Describe** how taxes have an impact on financial planning.
2. **Explain** how you determine your adjusted gross income and taxable income.
3. **Describe** why you should itemize deductions as opposed to taking the standard deduction.
4. **Identify** the factors to consider when filling out the W-4 form for your employer.
5. **Describe** the 1040EZ, 1040A, and 1040 income tax forms.
6. **List** some tax advantages of retirement investing.

See the Teacher Manual for answers.

ACADEMIC SKILLS

Civics/Government The rate or percentage at which the federal government taxes your income is determined by your tax bracket, which is your level of income. Each year, the tax brackets can change.

Write About It Research and write a paragraph explaining how the government decides the income tax rates and tax brackets for taxpayers.

YOUR FINANCIAL FIGURES

How Much Tax Do You Owe? Your gross earnings last year were $33,435, and your taxable interest income was $486. You also earned $3,766 on freelance projects, on which you have not paid any income tax. Last year, you contributed $512 to your company 401(k) retirement plan.

1. **Calculate** the tax you owe by using the six-rate system shown in Figure 12.1 on page 385.
2. **Compute** by using financial planning or tax software to determine your tax liability.

REAL-WORLD Application

Connect with Social Studies The U.S. government now excludes up to $1.5 million of an estate from tax. However, states vary in how they tax estates, whether they tax inheritances, and how much is excluded. New Jersey, for example, does not tax the inheritances of a deceased person's spouse and children but does tax other people who inherit.

1. **Research** Find out how your state taxes estates and inheritances.
2. **Write About It** Why do federal and state governments exclude parts of estates from taxation? What is your opinion about the variation in estate and inheritance taxes depending on the state where you die?

Internet CONNECTION

Charitable Contributions The IRS categorizes non-governmental organizations into various types. Organizations that qualify for 501c3 status are charitable, educational, and beneficial. Contributions to these organizations, including travel expenses in volunteering (but not time) are deductible.

Log On Go to **finance07.glencoe.com** for a link to the IRS Web site. Click on Charities and Non-Profits and find out about the rules and limits on the deductibility of contributions and answer these questions:

1. What records do you need to keep?
2. Where on your income tax return do you indicate these deductions?

BusinessWeek ONLINE

Newsclip: Tax Checkup Tax laws can change each year. Knowing the new rules can help you save money.

Log On Go to **finance07.glencoe.com** and open Chapter 12. Learn about the laws or tax updates during 2004. What do you need to know before filing your tax return from your summer job?

WHAT'S YOUR FINANCIAL ID?

TEST YOUR TAX FACTS

The more you know about the way tax laws relate to your personal finances, the easier it is to file your taxes. To test your knowledge of tax strategy, write the answer to these questions on a separate sheet of paper.

1. The tax-reporting requirement for cash tips is ___a___.
- a. you need to report tips and pay taxes on them
- b. you do not need to report cash tips on your tax return
- c. your employer takes care of it

2. Besides saving your tax returns you need to keep all necessary paperwork and receipts for at least ___b___.
- a. 1 year b. 6 years c. 20 years

3. Tax-deferred income is ___c___.
- a. income that is not subject to tax
- b. income that has had all its fur removed
- c. income that will be taxed at a later date

4. Tax-exempt income is ___a___.
- a. income that is not subject to tax
- b. income that you invest
- c. income that will be taxed at a later date

5. You would use the standard deduction instead of itemizing your deductions when ___b___.
- a. itemized deductions are more than the standard deduction
- b. itemized deductions are less than the standard deduction
- c. line 32 on Schedule C exceeds the allowable limit of line 12 on Schedule E on Form 1040A

6. Estate tax is a ___c___.
- a. tax on capital gains from selling a house
- b. tax on money withdrawn from a retirement account
- c. tax on the value of a person's property at the time of death

7. The person responsible for the contents of your tax return is ___c___.
- a. your tax preparer
- b. your mom and dad
- c. you

8. If you itemize your deductions, you can deduct interest on ___b___.
- a. credit cards
- b. mortgages, home equity, and student loans
- c. car loans

Your Financial Portfolio

Take It EZ

Using a photocopy of this form, complete your income tax return. Assume that your wages for the year were $13,220 and you earned $137 in interest. Your W-2 form shows that you had $1,003 in federal income tax withheld. Your parents cannot claim you on their income tax return. Find your tax using the tax table on page 397, and then calculate your refund or the amount you owe.

Accept all reasonable answers that show student effort and an understanding of the concept.

Form **1040EZ** Department of the Treasury—Internal Revenue Service
Income Tax Return for Single and Joint Filers With No Dependents (99) **20--** OMB No. 1545-0675

Label (See page 11.) **Use the IRS label.** Otherwise, please print or type. LABEL HERE

Your first name and initial | Last name | **Your social security number**

If a joint return, spouse's first name and initial | Last name | **Spouse's social security number**

Home address (number and street). If you have a P.O. box, see page 11. | Apt. no.

City, town or post office, state, and ZIP code. If you have a foreign address, see page 11.

▲ Important! ▲ You **must** enter your SSN(s) above.

Presidential Election Campaign (page 11)
Note. Checking "Yes" will not change your tax or reduce your refund.
Do you, or your spouse if a joint return, want $3 to go to this fund? . . . . . . ► You ☐ Yes ☐ No Spouse ☐ Yes ☐ No

Income
Attach Form(s) W-2 here. Enclose, but do not attach, any payment.

1 Wages, salaries, and tips. This should be shown in box 1 of your Form(s) W-2. Attach your Form(s) W-2. — 1

2 Taxable interest. If the total is over $1,500, you cannot use Form 1040EZ. — 2

3 Unemployment compensation and Alaska Permanent Fund dividends (see page 13). — 3

4 Add lines 1, 2, and 3. This is your **adjusted gross income.** — 4

Note. You **must** check Yes or No.

5 Can your parents (or someone else) claim you on their return?
Yes. Enter amount from worksheet on back. ☐
No. If **single,** enter $7,950. If **married filing jointly,** enter $15,900. See back for explanation. ☐ — 5

6 Subtract line 5 from line 4. If line 5 is larger than line 4, enter -0-. This is your **taxable income.** ► 6

Payments and tax

7 Federal income tax withheld from box 2 of your Form(s) W-2. — 7

8a **Earned income credit (EIC).** — 8a

b Nontaxable combat pay election. — 8b

9 Add lines 7 and 8a. These are your **total payments.** ► 9

10 **Tax.** Use the amount on **line 6 above** to find your tax in the tax table on pages 24–32 of the booklet. Then, enter the tax from the table on this line. — 10

Refund
Have it directly deposited! See page 18 and fill in 11b, 11c, and 11d.

11a If line 9 is larger than line 10, subtract line 10 from line 9. This is your **refund.** ► 11a

► b Routing number ☐☐☐☐☐☐☐☐☐ ► c Type: ☐ Checking ☐ Savings

► d Account number ☐☐☐☐☐☐☐☐☐☐☐☐☐☐☐☐☐

Amount you owe
12 If line 10 is larger than line 9, subtract line 9 from line 10. This is the **amount you owe.** For details on how to pay, see page 19. ► 12

Third party designee
Do you want to allow another person to discuss this return with the IRS (see page 19)? ☐ **Yes.** Complete the following. ☐ **No**
Designee's name ► Phone no. ► ( ) Personal identification number (PIN) ► ☐☐☐☐☐

Sign here
Joint return? See page 11. Keep a copy for your records.
Under penalties of perjury, I declare that I have examined this return, and to the best of my knowledge and belief, it is true, correct, and accurately lists all amounts and sources of income I received during the tax year. Declaration of preparer (other than the taxpayer) is based on all information of which the preparer has any knowledge.
Your signature | Date | Your occupation | Daytime phone number ( )
Spouse's signature. If a joint return, **both** must sign. | Date | Spouse's occupation

Paid preparer's use only
Preparer's signature ► | Date | Check if self-employed ☐ | Preparer's SSN or PTIN
Firm's name (or yours if self-employed), address, and ZIP code ► | EIN | Phone no. ( )

For Disclosure, Privacy Act, and Paperwork Reduction Act Notice, see page 23. Cat. No. 11329W Form **1040EZ** (20--)

CHAPTER 13

Home and Motor Vehicle Insurance

$ What You'll Learn

When you have completed this chapter, you will be able to:

Section 13.1

- Identify types of risks and risk management methods.
- Explain how an insurance program can help manage risks.
- Describe the importance of property and liability insurance.

Section 13.2

- Identify the types of insurance coverage and policies available to homeowners and renters.
- Analyze the factors that influence the amount of coverage and cost of home insurance.

Section 13.3

- Identify the important types of motor vehicle insurance coverage.
- Explain factors that affect the cost of motor vehicle insurance.

Reading Strategies

To get the most out of your reading:

Predict what you will learn in this chapter.
Relate what you read to your own life.
Question what you are reading to be sure you understand.
React to what you have read.

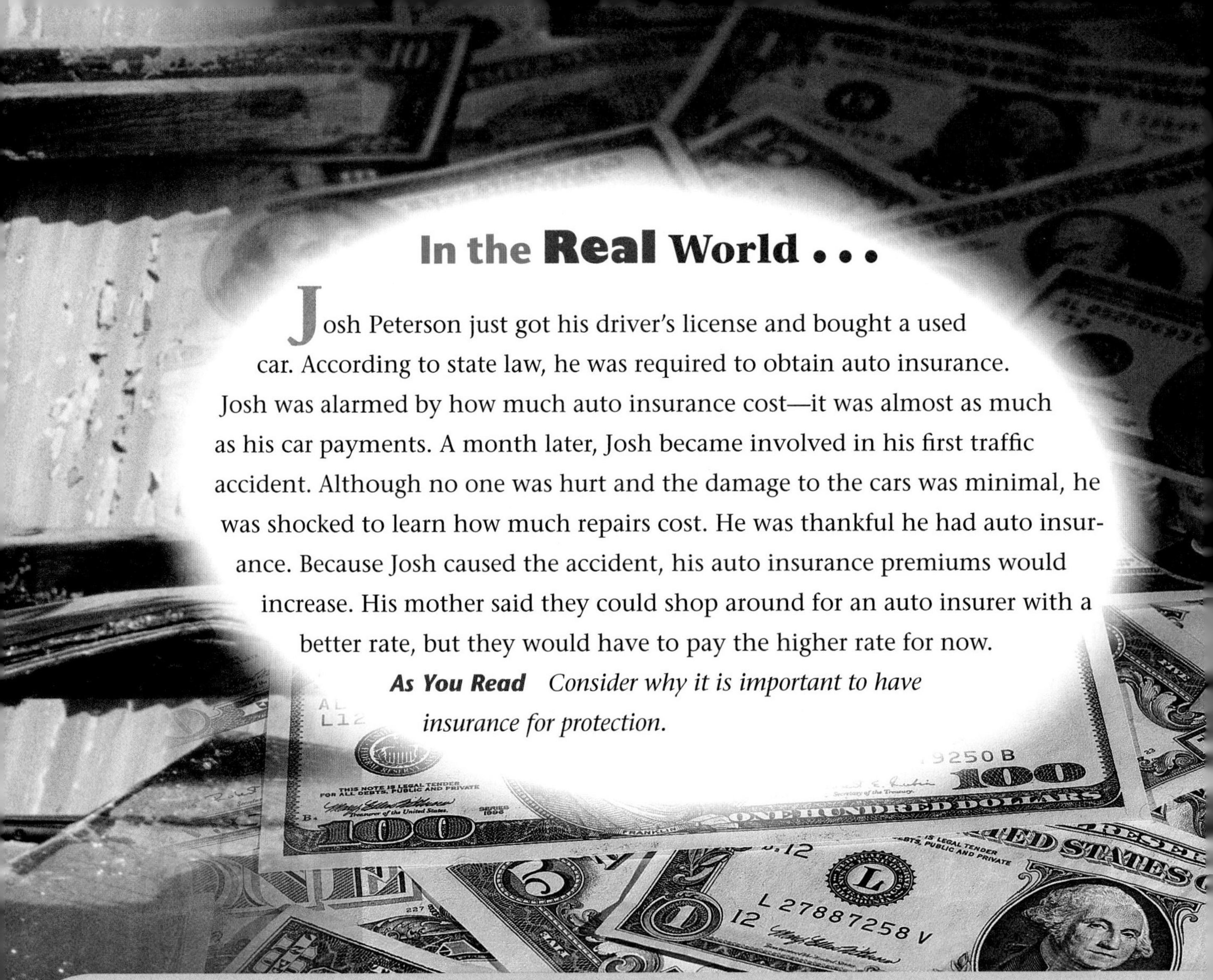

In the **Real** World . . .

Josh Peterson just got his driver's license and bought a used car. According to state law, he was required to obtain auto insurance. Josh was alarmed by how much auto insurance cost—it was almost as much as his car payments. A month later, Josh became involved in his first traffic accident. Although no one was hurt and the damage to the cars was minimal, he was shocked to learn how much repairs cost. He was thankful he had auto insurance. Because Josh caused the accident, his auto insurance premiums would increase. His mother said they could shop around for an auto insurer with a better rate, but they would have to pay the higher rate for now.

As You Read *Consider why it is important to have insurance for protection.*

Lesson Plan See the Teacher Manual for the Chapter 13 planning guide and lesson plan.

ASK STANDARD & POOR'S

Insurance Rates

Q: My brother is 17 and has an excellent driving record. Why are his motor vehicle insurance rates higher than rates for females in his same age group?

A: Insurance rates are based on an analysis of accident statistics for all types of drivers. Since young men have a higher incidence of being involved in accidents than young women have, insurance rates for young men are more expensive. Some insurance companies offer discounts for young adults covered on a parent's policy.

Ask Yourself What can you do to ensure that your insurance rate stays as low as possible?

@ Go to **finance07.glencoe.com** to complete the Standard & Poor's Financial Focus activity.

Section 13.1

Focus on Reading

Read to Learn

- How to identify types of risks and risk management methods.
- How to explain how an insurance program can help manage risks.
- How to describe the importance of property and liability insurance.

Main Idea

Recognizing the importance of insurance and knowing how to develop an insurance program can protect you from financial loss.

Key Terms

- insurance
- policy
- premium
- risk
- peril
- hazard
- negligence
- deductible
- liability

Before You Read

PREDICT

What do you think are the benefits of having a good insurance program?

Insurance and Risk Management

What Is Insurance?

Why is it important to have insurance?

Insurance is protection against possible financial loss. Since you cannot predict the future, you never know when something bad might happen to you or your property. Insurance allows you to be prepared for the worst. It provides protection against many risks, such as unexpected property loss, illness, and injury. Although many kinds of insurance exist, they all have several characteristics in common. For example, they give you peace of mind, and they protect you from financial loss when trouble strikes.

An insurance company, or insurer, is a risk-sharing business that agrees to pay for losses that may happen to someone it insures. A person joins the risk-sharing group by purchasing a contract known as a **policy**. The purchaser of the policy is called a policyholder. Under the policy, the insurance company agrees to take on the risk of the policyholder. In return, the policyholder pays the company a **premium**, which is a fee for insurance. The protection provided by the terms of an insurance policy is known as *coverage,* and the person protected by the policy is known as the *insured.*

Types of Risks

What are the most common types of risks?

Risk, peril, and *hazard* are important terms in insurance. In everyday use, these terms have almost the same meanings. In the insurance business, however, each word has a distinct and special meaning.

Risk is the chance of loss or injury. You face risks every day. For example, if you cross the street, there is some danger that a motor vehicle might hit you. If you own property, there is risk that it will be lost, stolen, damaged, or destroyed.

In the insurance business, risk refers to the fact that no one can predict trouble. This means that an insurance company is taking a chance every time it issues a policy. Insurance companies frequently refer to the insured person or property as *the risk.*

Peril is anything that may possibly cause a loss. It is the reason that someone takes out insurance. People buy policies for protection against a wide range of perils, including fire, windstorms, explosions, robbery, and accidents.

Hazard is anything that increases the likelihood of loss through peril. For example, defective electrical wiring in a house is a hazard that increases the chance that a fire will start.

The most common risks are personal risks, property risks, and liability risks. Personal risks involve loss of income or life due to illness, disability, old age, or unemployment. Property risks include losses to property caused by perils, such as fire or theft, and hazards. Liability risks involve losses caused by negligence that leads to injury or property damage. **Negligence** is the failure to take ordinary or reasonable care to prevent accidents from happening. If a homeowner does not clear the ice from the front steps of her house, for example, he or she creates a liability risk because visitors could fall on the ice.

Personal risks, property risks, and liability risks are types of pure, or insurable, risk. The insurance company will have to pay only if some event that the insurance covers actually happens. Pure risks are accidental and unintentional. Although no one can predict whether a pure risk will occur, it is possible to predict how much it will cost if it does.

A speculative risk is a risk that carries a chance of either loss or gain. Starting a small business that may or may not succeed is an example of speculative risk. Speculative risks are not insurable.

As You Read

RELATE

Do you have any insurance now? If so, what kind?

Springboard Ask the students to define insurance. Ask if they think insurance companies take advantage of people; or if people should have the right to insure anything, e.g., hands, legs, etc.

Risk-Management Methods

Why is risk management important?

Risk management is an organized plan for protecting yourself, your family, and your property. It helps reduce financial losses caused by destructive events. Risk management is a long-range planning process. Your risk-management needs will change at various points in your life. If you understand how to manage risks, you can provide better protection for yourself and your family. **Figure 13.1** on page 415 summarizes various risks and effective ways of managing them.

Most people think of risk management as buying insurance. However, insurance is not the only way of dealing with risk.

Motivating Students Have students try to differentiate between risks, perils, and hazards, explaining that, to insurance companies, the terms are very distinct.

Risk Avoidance

You can avoid the risk of a traffic accident by not driving to work. A car manufacturer can avoid the risk of product failure by not introducing new cars. These are both examples of risk avoidance. They are ways to avoid risks, but they involve serious trade-offs. You might have to give up your job if you cannot get there by driving a car. The car manufacturer might lose business to competitors who take the risk of producing exciting new cars.

Teaching Activity Have the class generate a list of examples of negligence. Then divide the class into groups and assign items on the list to each group. They are to come up with a way the accidents could be prevented, and then create a graphic representation of the method(s).

▲ **REDUCING RISKS** Taking steps to protect yourself and your property from harm can reduce your risk of financial loss. *Besides wearing your seat belt, what are some other ways of reducing risks when you are driving?*

Caption Answer Answers might include carrying a fire extinguisher, locking doors when the car is parked, carrying flares, and ensuring that signal lights function.

In some cases, though, risk avoidance is practical. For example, by taking precautions in high-crime areas, you might avoid the risk of being robbed. By installing a security system in your car, you might avoid the risk of having it stolen.

Risk Reduction

You cannot avoid risks completely. However, you can decrease the likelihood that they will cause you harm. For example, you can reduce the risk of injury in a car accident by wearing a seat belt. You can reduce the risk of developing lung cancer by not smoking. By installing fire extinguishers in your home, you can reduce the damage that could be caused by a fire. In addition, you can lower your risk of illness by eating properly and exercising regularly.

Risk Assumption

Risk assumption means taking on responsibility for the negative results of a risk. It makes sense to assume a risk if you know that the possible loss will be small. It also makes sense when you have taken all the precautions you can to avoid or reduce the risk.

When insurance coverage for a particular item is expensive, it may not be worth insuring. For instance, older cars are generally worth less than new cars. So even if an accident happens and the car is wrecked, you may be better off financially by not paying for the insurance coverage since the car was not worth much anyway.

Self-insurance is another option for risk assumption. By setting up your own special fund, perhaps from savings, you can cover the cost of loss. Self-insurance does not eliminate risks, but it does provide a way of covering losses as an alternative to an insurance policy. Some people self-insure because they cannot obtain insurance from an insurance company.

Risk Shifting

The most common method of dealing with risk is to shift it, which means to transfer it to an insurance company. In exchange for the fee you pay, the insurance company agrees to pay for your losses.

Most types of insurance policies include deductibles. Deductibles are a combination of risk assumption and risk shifting. A **deductible** is the set amount that the policyholder must pay per loss on an insurance policy. For example, if a falling tree damages your car, you may have to pay $200 toward the repairs. Your insurance company will pay the rest.

Planning an Insurance Program

What factors will affect your insurance goals?

Research Ask students what kinds of insurance they, as high school students, should have; elicit health and auto. Then have the students research rates their parents would have to pay to provide this for them. Tell them to consider policies with higher and lower deductibles.

Your personal insurance program should change along with your needs and goals. For example, Kirk and Luanne are a young married couple. The following four steps outline how they will plan their insurance program to meet their needs and goals.

STEP 1: Set Insurance Goals

Kirk and Luanne's main goal should be to minimize personal, property, and liability risks. They also need to decide how they will cover costs resulting from a potential loss. Income, age, family size, lifestyle, experience, and responsibilities are important factors in determining the goals they set. The insurance that they buy must reflect those goals.

Kirk and Luanne should try to come up with a basic risk-management plan that achieves the following goals:

- Reduces possible loss of income caused by premature death, illness, accident, or unemployment
- Reduces possible loss of property caused by perils, such as fire or theft, or hazards
- Reduces possible loss of income, savings, and property caused by personal negligence

Figure 13.1 **Risks and Risk Management Strategies**

Risks		Strategies for Reducing Financial Impact
Personal Events	**Financial Impact**	
Disability	• Loss of income • Increased expenses	• Savings and investments • Disability insurance
Death	• Loss of income	• Life insurance • Estate planning
Property Loss	• Catastrophic storm damage to property • Repair or replacement • Cost of theft	• Property repair and upkeep • Motor vehicle insurance • Homeowners insurance • Flood or earthquake insurance
Liability	• Claims and settlement costs • Lawsuits and legal expenses • Loss of personal assets and income	• Maintaining property • Homeowners insurance • Auto insurance

Risky Business Risk management strategies help reduce the financial impact of various risks. **Can you think of other strategies that would apply to the risks mentioned in the chart?**

Caption Answer Answers will vary but might include observing safety precautions to prevent disability or death and keeping valuables secure to prevent loss.

Step 2: Develop a Plan

Planning is a way of taking control of your life instead of just letting life happen to you. Kirk and Luanne need to determine what risks they face and what risks they can afford to take. They also have to determine what resources can help them reduce the damage that could be caused by serious risks.

Furthermore, they need to know what kind of insurance is available. The cost of different kinds of insurance and the way the costs vary among companies will be key factors in their plan. Finally, this couple needs to research the record of reliability of different insurance companies.

Kirk and Luanne must ask four questions as they develop their risk-management plan:

- What do they need to insure?
- For how much should they insure it?
- What kind of insurance should they buy?
- Which insurance company should they choose?

$avvy Saver

Saving Gas—and Money

1. Use the correct grade of gas for your car and save as much as 20 cents per gallon.
2. Buy non-brand name gasoline at lower prices.
3. Drive at the speed limit and not above. Speed wastes gas.
4. Inflate your tires at the recommended pressure and save as much as $180 a year.
5. Tune up your engine and change the oil and filter regularly.

Step 3: Put Your Plan into Action

After they have developed their plan, Kirk and Luanne need to follow through by putting it into action. During this process they might discover that they do not have enough insurance protection. If that is the case, they could purchase additional coverage or change the kind of coverage they have. Another alternative would be to adjust their budget to cover the cost of additional insurance. Finally, Kirk and Luanne might expand their savings or investment programs and use those funds in the case of an emergency.

The best risk-management plans will be flexible enough to allow Kirk and Luanne to respond to changing life situations. Their goal should be to create an insurance program that can grow or shrink as their protection needs change.

Step 4: Review Your Results

Discussion Discuss with the students the four steps in planning an insurance program. Ask them to analyze the steps and decide which is the most difficult to achieve and explain why.

You should take time to review a risk-management plan every two or three years, or whenever family circumstances change.

For example, Kirk and Luanne have been satisfied with the coverage provided by their insurance policies. However, when the couple bought a house six months ago, it was time for them to review their insurance plan. With the new house, the risks became much greater. After all, what would happen if a fire destroyed part of their home?

The needs of a couple who rent an apartment differ from the needs of a couple who own a house. Both couples face similar risks, but their financial responsibilities differ greatly. When you are developing or reviewing a risk-management plan, ask yourself if you are providing the financial resources you will need to protect yourself, your family, if you have one, and your property.

Property and Liability Insurance in Your Financial Plan

Why is it important to include property and liability insurance in a financial plan?

Major natural disasters have caused catastrophic amounts of property loss in the United States and other parts of the world. In 2004, the damage caused by Hurricane Charley resulted in $6.8 billion in insurance claims in the state of Florida alone. Insurance claims are requests for payment to cover financial losses. Without the money they received from their insurance, the people affected by the hurricane may not have been able to make repairs to their homes.

Most people spend a great deal of money on their houses, vehicles, furniture, clothing, and other personal property. Therefore, protecting these items from loss is extremely important. Each year homeowners and renters in the United States lose billions of dollars from more than 3 million burglaries, 500,000 fires, and 200,000 cases of damage from other perils. The cost of injuries and property damage caused by vehicles is also enormous. By including property and liability insurance in your financial plan, you can help protect yourself from such financial loss.

Think of the price you pay for insurance as an investment in the protection of your most valuable possessions. Although the cost of such insurance may seem high, the financial losses against which it protects could be much higher.

There are two main types of risks related to your home and your car or other vehicle. One is the risk of damage to or loss of your property. The second type of risk involves your responsibility for injuries to other people or damage to their property.

Property Damage or Loss

Property owners face two basic types of risks. The first is physical damage caused by perils such as fire, wind, and flooding. These perils can damage or destroy your property. For example, a windstorm might cause a large tree branch to smash the windshield of your car. As a result, you would have to find another way to get around while it was being repaired.

The second type of risk that property owners face is loss or damage caused by criminal behavior, such as robbery, burglary, vandalism, and arson. Insurance can help you protect yourself from loss of or damage to your property.

STANDARD & POOR'S **Put on Your Financial Planner's Cap**

If you were planning an insurance program for a client, what types of things would you insure?

See the Teacher Manual for answers.

Caption Answer Be aware of natural disasters common to our area; follow guidelines issued by local authorities; and have an emergency plan in place for you and your family.

▼ **DISASTROUS RESULTS** Events such as hurricanes and tornados can cause widespread devastation. *What can you do to protect your property against natural disasters?*

As You Read

QUESTION

Why do most people want to have their cars, homes, and personal property insured?

Question Answer to minimze financial loss from accidents, injuries, and theft

Discussion Discuss with the class if they think Terry's family should be allowed to sue Lisa's parents or if Ed should be allowed to sue Sanjay.

Liability

Liability is legal responsibility for the financial cost of another person's losses or injuries. You can be judged legally responsible even if the injury or damage was not your fault. For example, suppose that Terry falls and gets hurt while playing in her friend Lisa's yard. Terry's family may be able to sue Lisa's parents even though Lisa's parents did nothing wrong. Similarly, suppose that Sanjay accidentally damages a valuable painting while helping Ed move some of his furniture. Ed may take legal action against Sanjay to pay for the cost of the painting.

Usually, if you are found liable (or legally responsible) in a situation, it is because negligence on your part caused the mishap. Examples of such negligence include letting young children swim in a pool without supervision or cluttering a staircase with things that could cause someone to slip and fall, and become injured.

Section 13.1 Assessment

See the Teacher Manual for answers.

QUICK CHECK

1. What are the three main types of insurable risks?
2. How can developing an insurance program help you manage risk?
3. Why are property and liability insurance necessary to protect a homeowner from financial loss?

THINK CRITICALLY

4. "Insurance is a waste of money. If and when you suffer a financial loss because of an accident or some other event, you can pay for it from your savings account." Do you agree or disagree with this statement? Explain your position.

USE COMMUNICATION SKILLS

5. **My Favorite Things** Make a list of your most valuable possessions. Consider new and used items that may have collectible value. Also consider how much it would cost to replace your valuable possessions.

Write About It Write a paragraph discussing the personal and financial consequences of having the items on your list lost, stolen, damaged, or destroyed. Also explain the effect of having the items insured in the event of loss.

SOLVE MONEY PROBLEMS

6. **Paying for Insurance Protection** Hans has recently purchased a fully restored 1957 Chevy. The car cost $35,000, but for Hans, the price was worth it. The best price he can find for insurance is $2,500 per year. He is thinking about cutting corners on his insurance coverage to save money. However, he knows he would be taking a risk by doing so.

Calculate Help Hans solve his problem by comparing the cost of his insurance with the cost of his vehicle. Is it worth the insurance expense to protect his prized vehicle, or is it too much to spend to insure what is, after all, just a car?

Section 13.2

Home and Property Insurance

Homeowners Insurance Coverage

What does a homeowners insurance policy cover?

Insuring your residence and its contents is absolutely necessary to protect your investment. **Homeowners insurance** is coverage that provides protection for your residence and its associated financial risks, such as damage to personal property and injuries to others.

A homeowners policy provides coverage for the following:

- The home, building, or any other structures on the property
- Additional living expenses
- Personal property
- Personal liability and related coverages
- Specialized coverages

Buildings and Other Structures

The main purpose of homeowners insurance is to protect you against financial loss in case your home is damaged or destroyed. Detached structures on your property, such as a garage and tool shed, are also covered under a homeowners insurance policy. In fact, the insurance coverage even includes trees, shrubs, and other plants, which are landscaping.

Additional Living Expenses

If a fire or other event damages your home, additional living expense coverage pays for you to stay somewhere else. For example, you may need to stay in a motel or rent an apartment while your home is being repaired or rebuilt. These extra living expenses will be paid for by your insurance. Some policies limit additional living expense coverage to 10 to 20 percent of the home's total coverage amount. They may also limit the payment period to a maximum of six to nine months. Other policies may pay additional living expenses for up to a year.

Focus on Reading

Read to Learn

- How to identify the types of insurance coverage and policies available to homeowners and renters.
- How to analyze the factors that influence the amount of coverage and cost of home insurance.

Main Idea

You need an effective risk management plan for your home or apartment and your personal belongings. When purchasing insurance, your goal is to get the best protection at the lowest cost.

Key Terms

- homeowners insurance
- personal property floater
- medical payments coverage
- actual cash value
- replacement value

Before You Read

PREDICT

Why would it be important to have homeowners insurance?

Springboard Tell your students when they take out a mortgage to buy a home, lenders will require them to buy homeowners insurance. Ask the students if they can explain why.

Personal Property

Household belongings, such as furniture, appliances, and clothing, are covered by the personal property portion of a homeowners insurance policy up to a portion of the insured value of the home. That portion is usually 55, 70, or 75 percent. For example, a home insured for $80,000 might have $56,000 (70 percent) worth of coverage for household belongings.

Personal property coverage typically includes limits for the theft of certain items, such as $1,000 for jewelry. It also provides protection against the loss or damage of articles that you take with you when you are away from home. For example, items you take on vacation or use at school are usually covered up to the policy limit. Personal property coverage even extends to property that you rent, such as a rug cleaner, while it is in your possession.

Most homeowners policies also include optional coverage for personal computers, including stored data, up to a certain limit. Your insurance agent can determine whether the computer equipment is covered against data loss as well as damage from spilled drinks or power surges.

As You Read

RELATE

Do you own something you think should be insured separately from your parents' homeowners insurance?

Household Inventories If something does happen to your personal property, you must prove how much it was worth and that it belonged to you. To make the process easier, you can create a household inventory. A household inventory is a list or other documentation of personal belongings, with purchase dates and cost information. You can get a form for an inventory from an insurance agent. **Figure 13.2** provides a list of items you might include if you decide to compile your own household inventory. For items of special value, you should have receipts, serial numbers, brand names, model names, and proof of value.

In addition, keep a video recording or photographs of your home and its contents with your inventory list. Make sure that closet and storage area doors are photographed open. On the backs of the photographs, indicate the date and the value of the objects pictured. Update your inventory, photos, and related documents on a regular basis. Keep a copy of each document in a secure location, such as a safe-deposit box.

Motivating Students Have the students name (and write on the board) five or six benefits of having homeowners insurance. Then ask them if they can name any disadvantages. If cost is the only one, ask them whether it would cost more to buy insurance or deal with possible losses.

Additional Property Insurance If you own valuable items, such as expensive musical instruments, or need added protection for computers and related equipment, you can purchase a personal property floater. A **personal property floater** is additional property insurance that covers the damage or loss of a specific item of high value. The insurance company will require a detailed description of the item and its worth. You will also need to have the item appraised, or evaluated, by an expert from time to time to make sure that its value has not changed. In addition, keep photographs of valuable items as well as descriptions, receipts, and appraisals.

Figure 13.2 Household Inventory

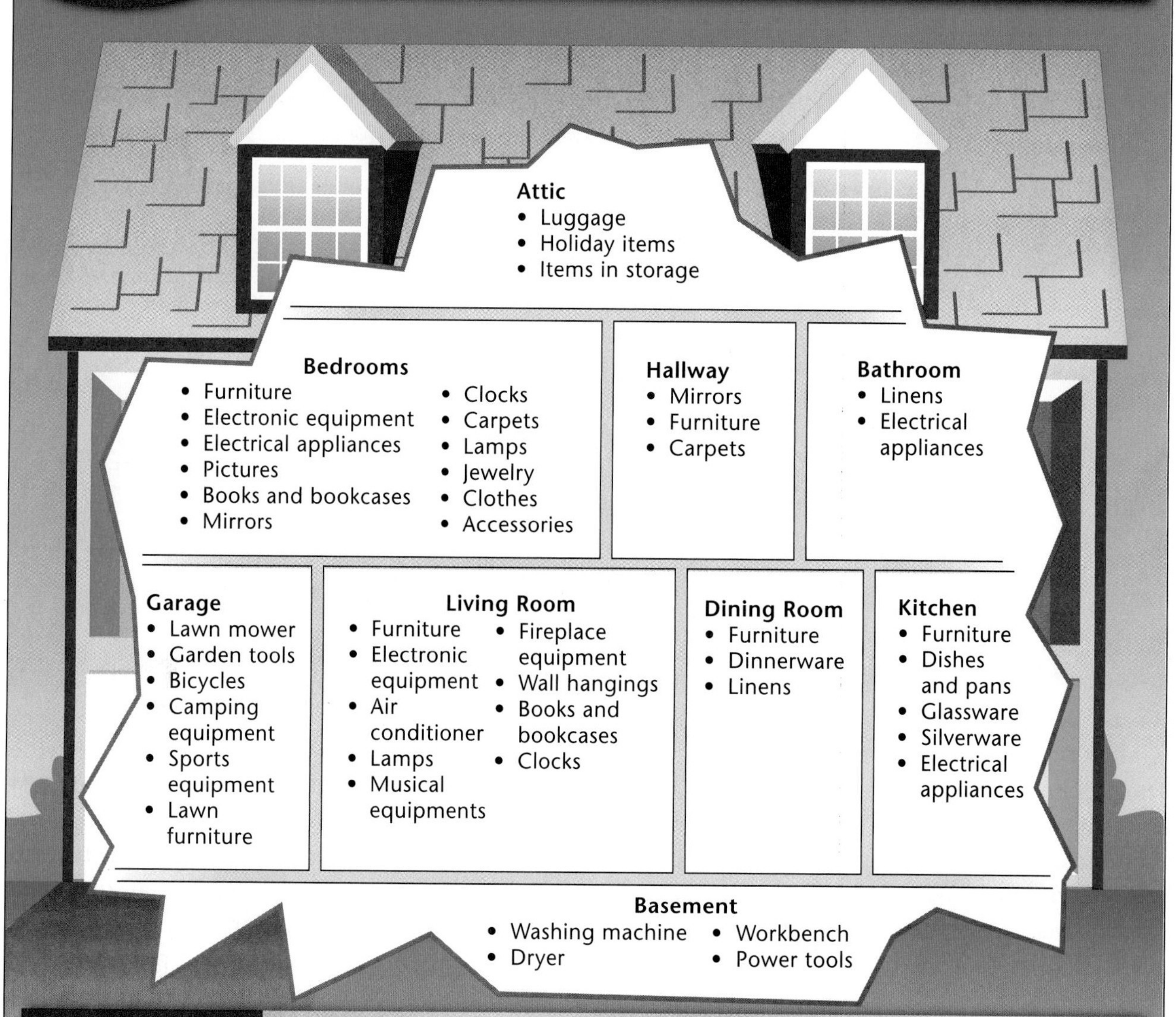

Full House A household inventory should list the items in each room of your home.

Why is it important to create a household inventory?

Caption Answer to prove ownership and to value items if they are stolen, damaged, or destroyed

Personal Liability and Related Coverages

Every day people face the risk of financial loss due to injuries to other people or their property. For example, a guest could fall on a patch of ice on the steps to your home and break his arm. A spark from the barbecue in your backyard could start a fire that damages a neighbor's roof, or your son or daughter could accidentally break an antique lamp while playing at a neighbor's house.

In these situations, you could be held responsible for paying for the damage. The personal liability portion of a homeowners policy protects you and members of your family if others, except regular employees, sue you for injuries they suffer or for damage to their property. This coverage includes the cost of legal defense.

Discussion Have the students identify (and write on the board) the expenses they might be liable for in any of the three circumstances cited on pages 420–421. In discussion, help them estimate the costs, and then compare those with the cost of liability insurance.

▲ **ADDITIONAL PROTECTION** The purchase of a valuable item such as a high-quality musical instrument is a major investment. *Why would a person who buys an expensive piano get a personal property floater for it?*

Caption Answer Homeowners insurance might not cover the full price if the item were seriously damaged or lost.

Amounts of Coverage Most homeowners policies provide basic personal liability coverage of $100,000, but often that is not enough. An umbrella policy, also called a *personal catastrophe policy*, supplements basic personal liability coverage. This added protection covers all kinds of personal injury claims. For example, an umbrella policy will cover you if someone sues you for saying or writing something negative or untrue, damaging his or her reputation.

Extended liability policies are useful for wealthy people and for businesses. The policies are sold in amounts of $1 million or more. If you are a business owner, you may need other types of liability coverage as well.

Medical payments coverage pays the costs of minor accidental injuries to visitors on your property. It also covers minor injuries caused by you, members of your family, or even your pets, away from home. Settlements under medical payments coverage are made without determining who was at fault. This makes it fast and easy for the insurance company to process small claims, generally up to $5,000. If the injury is more serious, the personal liability portion of the homeowners policy covers it. Medical payments coverage does not cover injury to you or the other people who live in your home.

If you or a family member should accidentally damage another person's property, the supplementary coverage of homeowners insurance will pay for it. This protection is usually limited to $500 or $1,000. Again, payments are made regardless of fault. If the damage is more expensive, however, it is handled under the personal liability coverage.

Extension Invite an insurance agent to speak to the class about how insurance works and career possibilities in the insurance industry. Have students prepare questions before he or she arrives.

Specialized Coverages

Homeowners insurance usually does not cover losses from floods and earthquakes. If you lived in an area that had frequent floods or earthquakes, you would need to purchase special coverage. In some places the National Flood Insurance Program, run by the federal government, makes flood insurance available. This protection is separate from a homeowners policy. An insurance agent or the Federal Emergency Management Agency (FEMA) of the Federal Insurance Administration can give you additional information about this coverage.

Teaching Activity Divide the students into five groups and assign one of these disasters to each group: floods, earthquakes, tornados, hurricanes, and wildfires. Each group should: (1) discover which states/areas are most susceptible to the disaster; (2) find out what aid FEMA will provide;(3) find out what typical homeowners insurance would pay (if anything). Groups are to prepare graphic displays and present them to the class.

STANDARD &POOR'S

Global Financial Landscape

Standard and Poor's publishes the globally recognized S&P 500® financial index. It also gathers financial statistics, information, and news, and analyzes this data for international businesses, governments, and individuals to help them guide their financial decisions.

GERMANY

Sometimes called the "Motherland of the Automotive Industry," Germany is one of the world's leading car manufacturers. From the luxurious Mercedes-Benz to the sleek and sporty Porsche to the unique and practical Volkswagen Beetle, Germans design cars that turn heads. In fact, the German-made Volkswagen Beetle has been called the "most popular vehicle of all time."

The German economy has experienced ups and downs, but car manufacturing has remained one of its cornerstones. The industry pulls in over $90 million in sales within the country and over $145 billion from other countries. The United States, with its fondness for status cars, is Germany's number one foreign market.

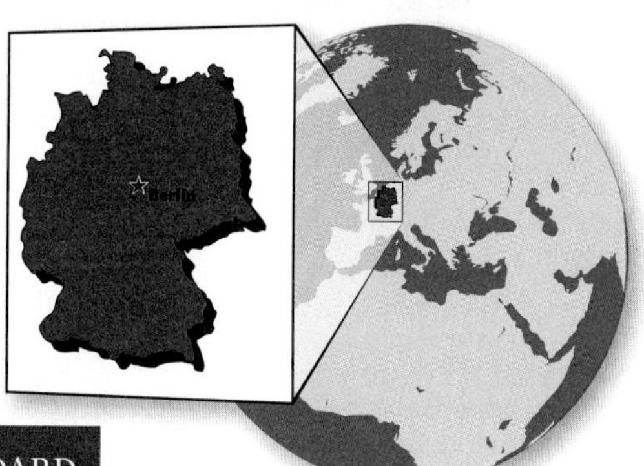

STANDARD &POOR'S **DATABYTES**

Capital	Berlin
Population	82,621,000
Languages	German
Currency	euro
Gross Domestic Product (GDP)	$2.27 trillion (2003 est.)
GDP per capita	$27,600

Industry: Iron, steel, coal, cement, chemicals, machinery, vehicles, machine tools, and electronics

Agriculture: Potatoes, wheat, barley, sugar beets, and cattle

Exports: Machinery, vehicles, chemicals, metals, foodstuffs, and textiles

Natural Resources: Iron ore, coal, potash, and timber

Think Globally

Automobile insurance is higher for someone who owns a sports car such as a Porsche. Why?

See the Teacher Manual for answer.

Academic Connection

LANGUAGE ARTS

The property belonging to most renters is not covered under a landlord's insurance. Therefore, without renters insurance, a renter must pay for replacing possessions if they are stolen from his or her apartment or destroyed by a fire or some other unexpected event. *Choose three companies offering renters insurance and compare what each company covers and the costs of coverage. Then choose the company you believe offers the best deal and write a paragraph explaining why.*

See the Teacher Manual for answer.

Research Have the students imagine they are about to rent an apartment, and they will have personal property worth $10,000. Have them research, using the Internet and other resources, to find out the cost of renters insurance.

You may be able to get earthquake or flood insurance as an endorsement (addition of coverage) to a homeowners policy or through a state-run insurance program. The most serious earthquakes occur in the Pacific Coast region. However, earthquakes can happen in other regions, too. If you purchase a home in an area that has a high risk of earthquakes or floods, you may have to buy insurance for those risks.

Renters Insurance

Why is it important for a renter to get renters insurance?

For people who rent, home insurance coverages include personal property protection, additional living expenses coverage, and personal liability and related coverages. Renters insurance does not provide coverage on the building or other structures.

The most important part of renters insurance is the protection it provides for personal property. Many renters believe that they are covered under their landlords' policies. However, that is true only when the landlord is liable for damage. For example, if bad wiring causes a fire and damages a tenant's property, the tenant may be able to collect money from the landlord. Renters insurance is relatively inexpensive and provides protection similar to homeowners insurance.

Home Insurance Policy Forms

What coverage is offered by each type of policy form?

Home insurance policies are available in several forms. The forms provide different combinations of coverage. Some forms are not available in all areas.

The basic form (HO-1) protects against perils such as fire, lightning, windstorms, hail, volcanic eruptions, explosions, smoke, theft, vandalism, glass breakage, and riots. The broad form (HO-2) covers an even wider range of perils, including falling objects and damage from ice, snow, or sleet.

The special form (HO-3) covers all basic- and broad-form risks, plus any other risks except those specifically excluded from the policy. Common exclusions are flood, earthquake, war, and nuclear accidents. Personal property is covered for the risks listed in the policy.

The tenants' form (HO-4) protects the personal property of renters against the risks listed in the policy. It does not include coverage on the building or other structures.

The comprehensive form (HO-5) expands the coverage of the HO-3. The HO-5 includes endorsements for replacement-cost coverage on contents and guaranteed replacement-cost coverage on buildings.

Condominium owners insurance (HO-6) protects personal property and any additions or improvements made to the living unit. These might include bookshelves, electrical fixtures, wallpaper, or carpeting. The condominium association purchases insurance on the building and other structures.

Manufactured housing units and mobile homes usually qualify for insurance coverage with conventional policies. However, some mobile homes may need special policies with higher rates that are dependent on the home's location and the way it is attached to the ground. Mobile home insurance is quite expensive: A $50,000 mobile home can cost as much to insure as a $150,000 house.

Though some risks are not covered by home insurance (see **Figure 13.3**), home insurance policies do include coverage for addtional costs:

- Credit card fraud, check forgery, and counterfeit money
- Removal of damaged property
- Emergency removal of property to protect it from damage
- Temporary repairs after a loss to prevent further damage
- Fire department charges in areas with such fees

How Much Coverage Do You Need?

What is the actual cash value method?

You can get the best insurance value by choosing the right amount of coverage and knowing the factors that affect insurance costs. Your insurance should be based on the amount of money you would need to rebuild or repair your house, not the amount you paid for it. As construction costs rise, you should increase the amount of coverage. In fact, today most insurance policies automatically increase coverage each year as construction costs rise.

Figure 13.3 **Not Everything Is Covered**

Certain personal property is not covered by homeowners insurance:

- Items insured separately, such as jewelry, furs, boats, or expensive electronic equipment
- Animals or fish
- Motorized vehicles not licensed for road use, except those used for home maintenance
- Sound devices used in motor vehicles, such as radios and CD players
- Aircraft and parts
- Property belonging to tenants
- Property contained in a rental apartment
- Property rented by the homeowner to other people
- Business property

Coverage Exclusions Separate coverage may be available for personal property that is not covered by a homeowners insurance policy.

Give an example of another type of policy that would cover one of the items listed here.

Caption Answer Answers will vary but may include personal property floaters covering items such as jewelry; renters insurance covering tenants' property.

▶ CLAIM SETTLEMENTS Insurance companies use two different methods for settling insurance claims. *If your television is damaged in a fire, how will you be reimbursed for the television under the actual cash value method? Under the replacement value method?*

Caption Answer actual cash value: the replacement cost of the TV minus depreciation; replacement value: full cost of repairing or replacing the TV

In the past, many homeowners' policies insured a building for only 80 percent of the replacement value. If the building were destroyed, the homeowner would have to pay for part of the cost of replacing it, which could be expensive. Today most companies recommend full coverage.

If you are borrowing money to buy a home, the lender will require that you have property insurance. The amount of insurance on your home determines the coverage on your personal belongings. Coverage for personal belongings is usually between 55 and 75 percent of the amount of insurance you have on your home.

Insurance companies base claim settlements on one of two methods. Under the **actual cash value** method, the payment you receive is based on the replacement cost of an item minus depreciation. Depreciation is the loss of value of an item as it gets older. This means you would receive less for a five-year-old bicycle than what you originally paid for it.

Under the **replacement value** method for settling claims, you receive the full cost of repairing or replacing an item. Depreciation is not considered. Many companies limit the replacement cost to 400 percent of the item's actual cash value. Replacement value coverage is more expensive than actual cash value coverage.

As You Read

QUESTION

Which policy would most likely pay you more if your home burned down?

Question Answer replacement value coverage

Home Insurance Cost Factors

Why do the location and type of construction of your home affect your home insurance costs?

The cost of your home insurance will depend on several factors, such as the location of the home and the type of structure and construction materials used. The amount of coverage and type of policy you choose will also affect the cost of your home insurance. Furthermore, different insurance companies offer different rates.

Location of Home

The location of your home affects your insurance rates. Insurance companies offer lower rates to people whose homes are close to a water supply or fire hydrant—or are located in an area that has a good fire department. Rates are higher in areas where crime is common. People living in regions that experience severe weather, such as tornadoes and hurricanes, may pay more for insurance.

Research Divide the students into three groups and assign either location, type of structure, or price of house to each group. Have the students individually research the effect their factor has on the price of insurance in your town.

Type of Structure

The type of structure and its construction influence the price of insurance coverage. A brick house, for example, will usually cost less to insure than a similar structure made of wood. However, earthquake coverage is more expensive for a brick house than for a wooden dwelling because a wooden house is more likely to survive an earthquake. Also, an older house may be more expensive to restore to its original condition. That means that it will cost more to insure.

Price, Coverage Amount, Policy Type

The purchase price of a house directly affects how much you pay for insurance. Therefore, it costs more to insure a $300,000 home than a $100,000 home. Also, the type of policy you choose and the amount of coverage you select affect the amount of premium you pay.

Caption Answer They reduce the risk of damage, thereby lowering the amount insurance companies will have to pay for losses.

◀ **LOWER YOUR PREMIUM** Fires can cause costly damage to property and personal possessions. *Why might insurance companies offer discounts to people who have homes with composite roofs instead of wood roofs?*

Careers in Finance

INSURANCE CLAIMS ADJUSTER

Rita Young
21st Century Insurance

Rita likes to help people when disasters strike. As an insurance claims adjuster, she is responsible for investigating complex homeowner claims by interviewing, inspecting, and securing documentation from insured clients, claimants, and witnesses. She evaluates the extent of damage to property and determines the value of claims. Helping clients is one of her favorite parts of her job. She provides a high level of customer service when she reviews policies with her clients and investigates claims-coverage questions.

SKILLS: Interpersonal, problem-solving, negotiating; mathematical skills; comprehensive knowledge of codes, home construction, repair techniques, and legal terminology

PERSONAL TRAITS: Organizational ability and tactfulness

EDUCATION: High school diploma or equivalent; bachelor's degree in business, insurance, or related area; certified Associate of Claims

ANALYZE Why might an insurance claims adjuster be expected to work on weekends or holidays?
See the Teacher Manual for answer.

@ To learn more about career paths for insurance claims adjusters, visit **finance07.glencoe.com**.

Critical Thinking Tell the students that most insurance companies will not want to sell homeowners policies to everyone in the same neighborhood. Have the students write a brief paper explaining that stance.

The deductible amount listed on the policy also affects the cost of insurance. If you increase the amount of the deductible, the premium will be lower because the company will pay out less in claims. The most common deductible amount is $250. Raising the deductible from $250 to $500 or $1,000 can reduce the premium you pay by 15 percent or more.

Home Insurance Discounts

Most companies offer discounts if a homeowner takes action to reduce risks to a home. Your premium may be lower if you have smoke detectors or a fire extinguisher. If your home has dead-bolt locks and alarm systems, which make it harder for thieves to get in, insurance costs may be lower.

Company Differences

A homeowner can save up to 25 percent on homeowners insurance by comparing rates from several companies. Some insurance agents work for only one company. Others are independent agents who represent several different companies.

Do not select a company on the basis of price alone. Also consider service and coverage. Not all companies settle claims in the same way.

For example, suppose that all of the homes on Evergreen Terrace are hit on one side by large hailstones. They all have the same kind of siding. Unfortunately, the homeowners discover that this type of siding is no longer available. So all the siding on all the houses will need to be replaced. Some insurance companies will pay to replace all the siding. Others will pay only to replace the damaged parts.

State insurance commissions and consumer organizations can give you information about different insurance companies. *Consumer Reports*, a magazine that provides unbiased information on a variety of goods and services, rates insurance companies on a regular basis.

Research Have the students look up *Consumer Reports'* most recent insurance company ratings and find out the ranking of three large homeowners insurance companies.

Section 13.2 Assessment

See the Teacher Manual for answers.

QUICK CHECK

1. What are six home insurance policy forms and their coverages?

2. What type of coverage does a personal property floater provide?

3. How can the location of a home affect insurance costs?

THINK CRITICALLY

4. Describe at least two situations in which personal liability coverage might be required.

USE MATH SKILLS

5. Insurance Coverage Homeowners insurance covers your personal possessions up to a percentage of the insured value of your home. When Carolina's house burned down, she lost household items worth a total of $25,000. Her house was insured for $80,000, and her homeowners policy provided coverage for personal belongings up to 55 percent of the insured value of the house.

Calculate Determine how much insurance coverage Carolina's policy provides for her personal possessions and whether she will receive payment for all the items destroyed in the fire.

SOLVE MONEY PROBLEMS

6. Analyzing Insurance Costs Kara and Adam Gottlieb are in the process of buying their first home. After months of shopping, they have narrowed down their choices to two. One is an older house near a river, where flooding occurs occasionally. The other is a newer house that is located farther from the river. They need to know how much homeowners insurance will cost for each house before making a final decision.

Analyze Given this information, make your best educated guess about which house would be less expensive to insure.

Section 13.3

Focus on Reading

Read to Learn

- How to identify important types of motor vehicle insurance coverage.
- How to explain factors that affect the cost of motor vehicle insurance.

Main Idea

Various types of motor vehicle insurance offer different coverages. A variety of factors affect the cost of insurance.

Key Terms

- bodily injury liability
- uninsured motorist's protection
- property damage liability
- collision
- no-fault system
- assigned risk pool

Before You Read

PREDICT

Do you think your driving record affects your car insurance rates? Why?

Springboard Ask the students to share their experiences with motor vehicle accidents and estimate what costs were involved (property damage, medical, etc), if any.

Motor Vehicle Insurance

Motor vehicle accidents cost more than $150 billion in lost wages and medical bills every year. They can destroy people's lives physically, financially, and emotionally. Buying insurance cannot eliminate the pain and suffering that vehicle accidents cause. However, insurance can reduce the financial impact.

Every state in the United States has a financial responsibility law, which is a law that requires a driver to prove he or she can pay for damage or injury caused by an automobile accident if he or she is at fault. As of 2003, more than 45 states had laws requiring people to carry motor vehicle insurance. When injuries and property damage occur in an accident, the driver(s) is required to file a report with the state. In the remaining states, most people buy motor vehicle insurance by choice. Very few people have the money they would need to meet the financial responsibility requirements on their own.

The coverage provided by motor vehicle insurance falls into two categories: protection for bodily injury and protection for property damage. (See **Figure 13.4.**)

Motor Vehicle Bodily Injury Coverages

Who is covered by bodily injury liability insurance?

Most of the money that motor vehicle insurance companies pay out in claims goes for legal expenses, medical expenses, and other costs that arise when someone is injured. The main types of bodily injury coverages are:

- Bodily injury liability
- Medical payments
- Uninsured motorist's protection

Bodily Injury Liability

Bodily injury liability is insurance that covers physical injuries caused by a vehicle accident for which you are responsible. If pedestrians, people in other vehicles, or passengers in your vehicle are injured or killed, bodily injury liability coverage pays for expenses related to the crash.

Figure 13.4 **Motor Vehicle Insurance Coverage**

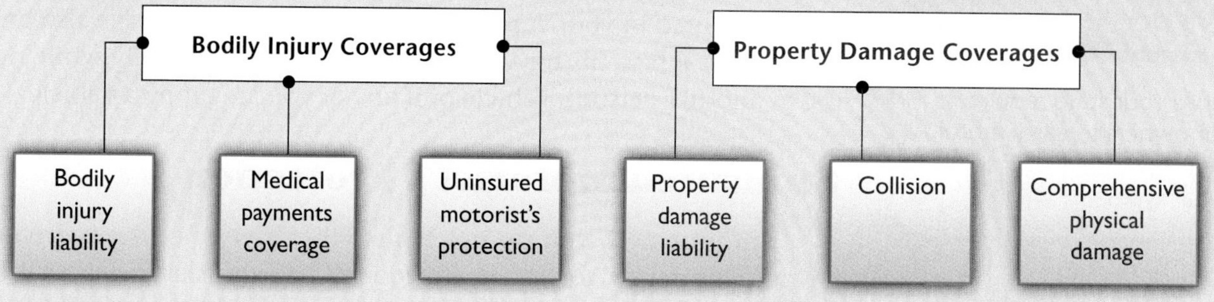

Protect Yourself Buying bodily injury and property damage coverage can reduce the financial impact of an accident.

What type of expenses would be paid for by bodily injury liability coverage?

Caption Answer injuries from an accident for which the driver was responsible

Liability coverage is usually expressed by three numbers, such as 100/300/50. These amounts represent thousands of dollars of coverage. The first two numbers refer to bodily injury coverage. In the 100/300/50 example, $100,000 is the maximum amount that the insurance company will pay for the injuries of any one person in any one accident. The second number, $300,000, is the maximum amount the company will pay for all injured parties (two or more) in any one accident. The third number, $50,000, indicates the limit for payment for damage to the property of others. (See **Figure 13.5.**)

Motivating Students Ask students if they think states should require motor vehicle coverage of all drivers, and why or why not.

Figure 13.5 **Motor Vehicle Insurance Coverage**

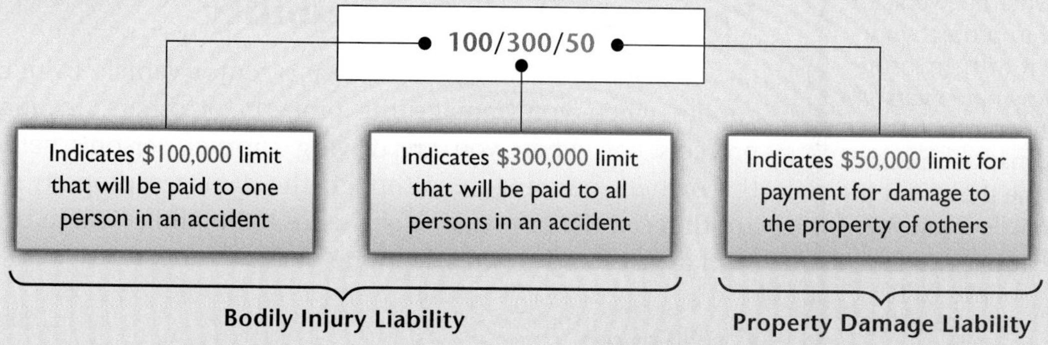

Liability Coverage The three numbers used to describe liability coverage refers to the limits on different types of payments.

Why do you think the middle number of the liability coverage amounts is the highest?

Caption Answer It is the maximum amount the company will pay for all injured parties (two or more) in any one accident.

As You Read

RELATE

Does your state require car owners to carry motor vehicle insurance? If so, what type?

Medical Payments Coverage

Medical payments coverage is insurance for medical expenses of anyone injured in your vehicle, including you. This coverage also provides medical benefits for you and members of your family while riding in another person's vehicle or if any of you are hit by a vehicle.

Uninsured Motorist's Protection

Unfortunately, you cannot assume that everyone who is driving has auto insurance. You can guard yourself and your passengers against the risk of getting into an accident with someone who has no insurance by having uninsured motorist's protection.

Uninsured motorist's protection is insurance that covers you and your family members if you are involved in an accident with an uninsured or hit-and-run driver. In most states it does not cover damage to the vehicle itself. Penalties for driving without insurance vary by state, but they generally include stiff fines and the suspension of driving privileges.

Critical Thinking Divide the students into groups of four and have them discuss what they think should happen if someone does not carry motor vehicle insurance, and he or she causes an accident. Have them consider this in a state that requires vehicle insurance and in one that does not. Have the groups share their results with the class.

Motor Vehicle Property Damage Coverages

What does comprehensive physical insurance cover?

One afternoon, during a summer storm, Carrie was driving home from her job as a hostess at a pancake house. The rain was torrential, and she could not see very well. As a result, she did not realize that the car in front of her had stopped to make a left turn, and she hit the car. The crash totaled Carrie's new car. Fortunately, she had purchased insurance with property damage coverage. Property damage coverage protects you from financial loss if you damage someone else's property or if your vehicle is damaged. It includes property damage liability, collision, and comprehensive physical damage.

WebQuest

Avoiding Financial Fraud

As the owner of a vehicle, you need to protect your investment with an insurance policy that covers the variety of risks that vehicle owners face. But if you become the victim of an automobile insurance fraud scheme, you may pay dearly—even with your life. Be aware of the different types of automobile insurance scams.

@ To continue with Task 3 of your WebQuest project, visit **finance07.glencoe.com**.

Property Damage Liability

Property damage liability is motor vehicle insurance that applies when you damage the property of others. In addition, it protects you when you are driving another person's vehicle with the owner's permission. Although the damaged property is usually another car, the coverage also extends to buildings and to equipment such as street signs and telephone poles.

Collision

Collision insurance is insurance that covers damage to your vehicle when it is involved in an accident. You collect money no matter who is at fault. However, the amount that you can collect is limited to the actual cash value of your vehicle at the time of the accident. So keep a record of your car's condition and value.

Comprehensive Physical Damage

Comprehensive physical damage insurance protects you if your vehicle is damaged in a non-accident situation. It covers your vehicle against risks such as fire, theft, falling objects, vandalism, hail, floods, tornadoes, earthquakes, and avalanches.

No-Fault Insurance

Why are some states adopting the no-fault system?

To reduce the time and cost of settling vehicle injury cases, some states are trying a number of alternatives, including the no-fault system. The **no-fault system** is an arrangement whereby drivers who are involved in accidents collect money from their own insurance companies. It does not matter who caused the accident. Each company pays the insured up to the limits of his or her coverage. No-fault systems and coverages vary by state.

Other Coverages

When is wage loss insurance required?

Several other kinds of motor vehicle insurance are available. For example, rental reimbursement coverage pays for a rental car if your vehicle is stolen or is being repaired. Wage-loss insurance pays for any salary or income you might have lost due to being injured in a vehicle accident. States that have adopted a no-fault insurance system usually require auto owners to carry wage-loss insurance. It is available by choice in other states.

Emergency road service coverage pays for mechanical assistance in the event that your vehicle breaks down. This can be helpful on long trips or during bad weather. If necessary, you can get your vehicle towed to a service station. However, once your vehicle arrives at the repair shop, you are responsible for paying the bill. If you belong to an automobile club, your membership may include towing coverage. If that is the case, paying for emergency road service coverage could be a waste of money.

Motor Vehicle Insurance Costs

Why is bodily injury liability coverage of 100/300 recommended?

Motor vehicle insurance is not cheap. The average household spends more than $1,000 for motor vehicle insurance yearly. The premiums are related to the amount of claims that insurance companies pay out each year.

Frank is a high school junior who recently got his license. At his part-time job, he earns minimum wage. Frank's situation provides an example of what to consider to get the best insurance value—amount of coverage, insurance premium factors, and ways to reduce insurance premiums.

As You Read

QUESTION

What kind(s) of vehicle insurance would you need if you knocked over your neighbor's mailbox with your car *and* the neighbor was injured by the falling mailbox?

Question Answer bodily injury liability and property damage liability

Teaching Activity Have the students find a state that has no-fault insurance and one that does not (one should be your state). In writing, have them compare the two states' systems and determine if they think no-fault insurance is a good idea.

TechByte

Reducing Car Insurance Costs High auto-theft rates lead to high auto insurance rates. Australia has one of the highest auto-theft rates in the world—twice that of the United States. Scientists there have developed a high-tech solution to keep insurance rates down. Tiny microdots called "DataDots" are laser-etched with vehicle identification numbers and spray-glued on engines and most other parts. This makes it difficult to resell stolen cars and parts.

@ Read more about DataDot technology and list other uses for this technological advance through **finance07.glencoe.com**.

Amount of Coverage

The amount that Frank will pay for insurance depends on the amount of coverage he requires. He needs enough coverage to protect himself legally and financially.

Legal Concerns As discussed earlier, most people who are involved in motor vehicle accidents cannot afford to pay an expensive court settlement with their own money. For this reason, most drivers buy liability insurance.

Many basic insurance policies provide 10/20 coverage for bodily injury liability. However, some accident victims have been awarded millions of dollars in bodily injury cases; therefore, coverage of 100/300 is usually recommended.

Property Values Just as medical expenses amounts of and legal settlements have increased, so has the cost of vehicles. Therefore, Frank should consider a policy with a limit of $50,000 or even $100,000 for property damage liability.

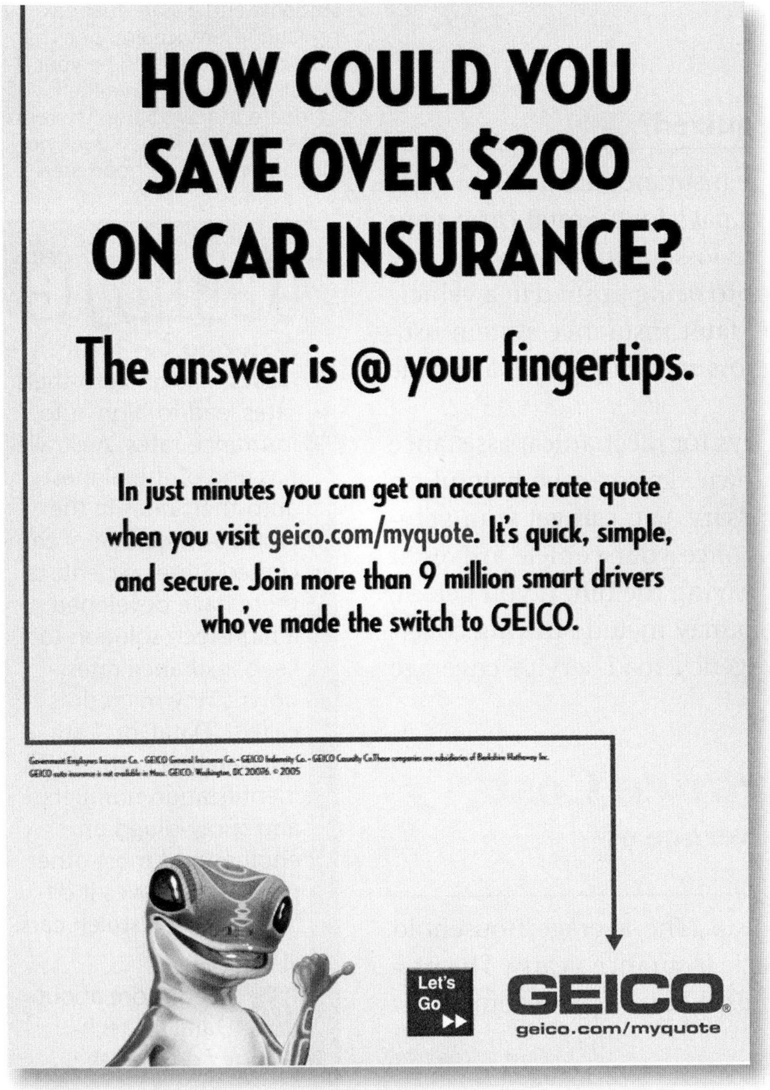

▲ **RATE QUOTES** Shopping around for the best auto insurance rate can save you money in the long run. *What are some factors that may affect the rates offered by different companies?*

Caption Answer vehicle type, residence area, age, sex, marital status, driving record, and occupation

Motor Vehicle Insurance Premium Factors

Vehicle type, rating territory, and driver classification are three other factors that influence insurance costs.

Vehicle Type The year, make, and model of a vehicle affect insurance costs. High-priced vehicles and vehicles that have expensive replacement parts and complicated repairs cost more to insure. Also, premiums can be higher for those vehicle makes and models that are frequently stolen.

Rating Territory In most states the rating territory, or owner's place of residence, is used to determine the vehicle insurance premium. Different locations have different costs. For example, accidents and incidents of theft occur less frequently in rural areas. Your insurance would probably cost less than if you lived in a large city.

Document Detective

Learn to identify and understand the standard financial documents you will use in the real world.

See the Teacher Manual for answers.

Investigate: An Auto Insurance Declaration

The declaration lists this information:

- Policy identification number
- Time period of insurance policy
- Amount of insurance coverage
- Premium amount

Your Motive: In most states the law requires that you insure your automobile. To protect yourself from financial loss, it is important to know exactly what your auto insurance covers and how much it will cost.

The Premier Global Insurance Company Auto Declarations

Policy Number A02 0076215
Policy Period: From 12/27/2007 To 12/27/2008
12:01 Standard Time at the Address of the Named Injured

Coverages and Limits of Liability

Coverages	Vehicle 1		Vehicle 2	
	Limit	Premium	Limit	Premium
A Bodily Injury and Property Damage		$265.00		$339.00
Each Accident	$1,000,000		$1,000,000	
B Medical Payments	$5,000	$9.00	$5,000	$11.00
C Uninsured Motorists Bodily Injury		$76.00		$76.00
Each Accident	$1,000,000		$1,000,000	
D Damage to Your Auto Other Than Collision		$63.00		$126.00
Actual Cash Value Less Deductible	$500.00		$500.00	
Collision		$155.00		$271.00
Actual Cash Value Less Deductible	$500.00		$500.00	
Additional Coverages				
Transportation Expense		Included		Included
Per Day/Maximum	$20/$600		$20/$600	
Towing and Labor Costs		$10.00		$10.00
Each Disablement	$50		$50	
Theft Coverage - Electronic				
Tapes, Records & Discs				
GAP Coverage				
Total		**$578.00**		**$833.00**

Key Points: An auto insurance declaration details what is covered by the policy. It states what the policy will pay in the event of an accident. This includes damage to the car(s) and injury to people. The declaration also explains how the premium is determined.

Find the Solutions

1. What is the policy identification number?
2. What is the bodily injury payment limit?
3. How much will the policy pay for transportation expenses, such as renting a car?
4. How many vehicles are covered by this policy?
5. What is the cost of this policy?

After You Read

REACT

The first Predict question in this chapter asked what you thought the benefits of a good insurance program might be. How would you revise your answer after reading the chapter?

React Answer Accept all reasonable answers.

Driver Classification Driver classification is based on age, sex, marital status, driving record, and driving habits. In general, young drivers (under 25) and elderly drivers (over 70) have more frequent and more serious accidents. As a result, these groups pay higher premiums. Because Frank is under 25, he may have to pay a standard higher rate. Your driving record will also influence how much you pay for insurance premiums. If you have accidents or receive traffic tickets, your rates will increase.

The cost and number of claims that you file with your insurance company also affect your premium. If you file expensive claims, your rates will increase. If you have too many claims, your insurance company may cancel your policy, and it will be difficult to get coverage from another company. To deal with this problem, every state has an **assigned risk pool**, which is a group of people who cannot get motor vehicle insurance who are assigned to each insurance company operating in the state. These policyholders pay several times the normal rates. If they establish a good driving record, they can reapply for insurance at regular rates.

Reducing Vehicle Insurance Premiums

Two ways in which Frank can reduce his vehicle insurance costs are by comparing companies and by taking advantage of discounts.

Teaching Activity Divide the class into groups and assign one of the following discounts to each group: good driver; security device installation; nonsmoker; for under 25, maintaining good grades or taking a driver training course; and teacher. Have the groups contact three insurance companies and compare discounts.

Comparing Companies Rates and services vary among motor vehicle insurance companies. Even among companies in the same area, premiums can vary by as much as 100 percent. Frank should compare the services and rates of local insurance agents. Most states publish this type of information. Furthermore, Frank can check a company's reputation with sources such as *Consumer Reports* or his state insurance department.

Caption Answer The answer is the teenager because drivers under 25 have more frequent and more serious accidents.

▶ **DRIVER CLASSIFICATION**
A driver's age affects the price of insurance premiums. *Who is likely to pay more for insurance—teenagers or parents? Why?*

Premium Discounts The best way for Frank to keep his rates down is to maintain a good driving record by avoiding accidents and traffic tickets. In addition, most insurance companies offer various types of discounts.

Because Frank is under 25, he can qualify for reduced rates by taking a driver training program or maintaining good grades in school. In addition, installing security devices in his vehicle will decrease the chance of theft and lower Frank's insurance costs. Being a nonsmoker can qualify him for lower motor vehicle insurance premiums as well. Discounts are also offered for insuring two or more vehicles with the same company. Increasing the amounts of deductibles will also lead to a lower premium. For example, an older car may not be worth the cost of carrying collision and comprehensive coverage.

No matter what coverage you choose, motor vehicle insurance is a valuable and mandatory protection to include in any personal finance plan.

Common CENTS

Student Discounts
Many places, such as theaters, zoos, and museums, offer discount prices to students. You can also get discounts for buses and subways, movies, and cultural and sporting events. Be sure to ask before paying full price. *Why do you think businesses offer discounts to students?*

Common Cents Answer Accept all reasonable answers that demonstrate an understanding of the concept.

Section 13.3 Assessment

See the Teacher Manual for answers.

QUICK CHECK

1. What are three main types of motor vehicle insurance that cover bodily injuries?
2. What is the difference between collision and comprehensive physical damage coverages?
3. Why do some insurance companies offer discounts to drivers who install security devices in their vehicles?

THINK CRITICALLY

4. Explain some ways you might reduce motor vehicle insurance premiums.

USE COMMUNICATION SKILLS

5. **Drinking and Driving** Alcohol use is a factor in more than 60 percent of all traffic accidents. Interview classmates, parents, and others to get their views on what can be done to reduce alcohol-related traffic incidents. Consider contacting an organization such as MADD (Mothers Against Drunk Driving) for information.

Present You have probably seen or heard public service announcements urging people not to drink and drive. Use what you have learned to create your own public service announcement. It may be in the form of a radio or television script. If possible, get some friends to help you produce your spot, using audio or video recording equipment.

SOLVE MONEY PROBLEMS

6. **Cost of Motor Vehicle Insurance** Malcolm wants to buy an expensive sport-utility vehicle. However, his mechanic has warned him that the replacement parts for the vehicle that he wants are costly. His friend Ishiro is on a tight budget and does not have a car. He is considering buying a car that has low maintenance costs. Malcolm and Ishiro live in the same neighborhood. Malcolm has never had a traffic accident, but he received one traffic ticket last year. Ishiro's driving record is perfect.

Analyze Who will have a lower car insurance rate? Why?

Chapter 13 Review & Activities

See the Teacher Manual for answers.

CHAPTER SUMMARY

- Risk is the probability of loss or injury; peril is something that may cause a loss; hazards increase the probability of loss; and negligence is failing to take reasonable care to prevent accidents. Risk avoidance, risk reduction, risk assumption, and risk shifting are ways of managing risk.
- Insurance involves the risk management method of shifting risk: In exchange for fees, the insurance pays for losses.
- Property insurance protects from losses resulting from natural causes, fire, and criminal activity. Liability insurance covers legal responsibility for the cost of losses to others.
- Homeowners insurance covers the building, living expenses, personal property, and personal liability. Renters insurance covers personal possessions, living expenses, and personal liability.
- Factors affecting the cost of home-owners insurance are home location, structural type, coverage amount and policy type, discounts, and differences among insurance companies.
- The types of motor vehicle insurance include bodily injury liability, medical payments coverage, uninsured motorist's protection, property damage liability, collision, and comprehensive physical damage coverage.
- Factors affecting the cost of motor vehicle insurance include the amount of coverage, type of vehicle, rating territory, and driver classification.

Communicating Key Terms

Your older brother is preparing to take the state test for an insurance license. Help him review the following terms by making up fill-in-the-blank sentences that define each term.

- insurance
- policy
- premium
- risk
- peril
- hazard
- negligence
- deductible
- liability
- homeowners insurance
- personal property floater
- medical payments coverage
- actual cash value
- replacement value
- bodily injury liability
- uninsured motorist's protection
- property damage liability
- collision
- no-fault system
- assigned risk pool

Reviewing Key Concepts

1. **Identify** each type of risk and list the four methods of managing risk.
2. **Describe** how insurance uses different risk management methods to reduce risk.
3. **Explain** how property and liability insurance protect.
4. **Identify** reasons that home mortgage lenders require homeowners insurance.
5. **Explain** the difference between actual cash value and replacement value.
6. **List** advantages and disadvantages of the no-fault insurance system.
7. **Discuss** why lenders require drivers to carry bodily injury and property damage coverage.

See the Teacher Manual for answers.

ACADEMIC SKILLS

Geography Prices for insurance vary in different areas of the United States. For example, auto insurance may be less expensive in rural areas.
Research Look at a map of the United States. Find your town or city, Los Angeles, Chicago, Dallas, and Orlando. Research the population and average cost of auto insurance in each of these cities. Compare the cost to the population of each city. Is there a connection? If so, explain.

YOUR FINANCIAL FIGURES

Insurance Deductibles The annual premium for a 2,500 square foot home in a medium-sized Midwestern city was $628 in 2005—with discounts for a home security system, a good claims record, and the combination of home and auto insurance policies. Replacement cost for the dwelling is estimated at $237,000, and the current deductible is $1,000. The insurance company offered to reduce the premium by $73 if the policyholder agreed to increase the deductible to 1 percent of the replacement cost.

1. **Calculate** the new premium amount and new deductible amount.
2. **Compute** by using the Internet to locate and compare homeowners premium and coverage information from five insurance companies.

REAL-WORLD Application

Connect with Ethics and Social Studies Laws and penalties for driving under the influence (DUI) are extremely strict in many states. Furthermore, the number of motor vehicle accidents involving young drivers has increased and become more serious, resulting in more deaths and injuries.

1. **Research** Access the Web site of your state's department of motor vehicles for the laws and penalties for DUI. Also check in your local newspaper for recent accidents involving young drivers.
2. **Think Critically** Why are DUI penalties so stringent? Do you think the higher insurance premiums charged to younger drivers are "fair"? Why?

Internet CONNECTION

Risk Assessment Actuaries determine the costs and risks involved with insuring people's property. Actuaries are experts in evaluating the likelihood of future events. They design creative ways to reduce the likelihood of undesirable events and decrease the impact of undesirable events that occur.

@ **Log On** Go to the Web sites of insurance companies and the Society of Actuaries to find out factors that affect the cost of homeowners insurance. Answer the following questions:

1. Should any of these factors influence decisions when buying a home?
2. How can homeowners premiums be reduced?

BusinessWeek ONLINE

Newsclip: Higher Rates Car insurance companies charge higher rates for male teenagers than female teenagers.

@ **Log On** Go to **finance07.glencoe.com** and open Chapter 13. Learn about why insurance companies raise rates for males and not females. Write a list of reasons for this practice.

WHAT'S YOUR FINANCIAL ID?

VEHICLE INSURANCE QUIZ

When you insure your vehicle, you will need to make decisions about the insurance you carry. Test your knowledge about motor vehicle insurance by answering questions on a separate sheet of paper.

1. Liability coverage pays for _____c_____.
   a. theft, fire, vandalism, or other damages not related to an accident
   b. the accident-related cost of repairing or replacing your vehicle
   c. damage or injury for which you are responsible

2. Collision coverage pays for _____b_____.
   a. theft, fire, vandalism, or other damages not related to an accident
   b. the accident-related cost of repairing or replacing your vehicle
   c. damage or injury for which you are responsible

3. Comprehensive coverage pays for _____a_____.
   a. theft, fire, vandalism, or other damages not related to an accident
   b. the accident-related cost of repairing or replacing your vehicle
   c. all the items that passengers lose in the backseat of your vehicle

4. If you are in an accident, your vehicle insurance medical coverage handles _____a_____.
   a. only people injured in your vehicle
   b. anyone injured
   c. only people injured who were not in your vehicle

5. A higher deductible results in _____b_____.
   a. a higher premium
   b. a lower premium
   c. tax savings

6. Speeding tickets or accidents may result in _____a_____.
   a. a higher premium
   b. a lower premium
   c. migraine headaches

7. Safety features such as antitheft devices and automatic seat belts may result in a _____b_____.
   a. higher premium
   b. lower premium
   c. higher resale value

8. Taking driver education classes may result in a _____b_____.
   a. higher premium
   b. lower premium
   c. later curfew

Your Financial Portfolio

The Price of Car Insurance

Before Mario bought the car he wanted, he needed to be sure he could afford the insurance for it. In this example he chose low liability, uninsured motorist coverage, and high deductibles to keep his insurance payments as low as possible. Clearly, Insurer B offered a lower price for the same coverage.

Investigating Insurance Companies

	Insurer A	Insurer B
Bodily Injury Coverage:		
Bodily injury liability $50,000 each person; $100,000 each accident	$472	$358
Uninsured motorist's protection	208	84
Medical payments coverage $2,000 each person	48	46
Property Damage Coverage:		
Property damage liability $50,000 each accident	182	178
Collision with $500 deductible	562	372
Comprehensive physical damage with $500 deductible	263	202
Car Rental:	40	32
Discounts: good driver, air bags, garage parking	(165)	
Annual Total	**$1,610**	**$1,272**

Research

Identify a make, model, and year of a vehicle you might like to own. Research two insurance companies and get prices using this example. You can get their rates by telephone. Many companies also have Web sites. On a separate sheet of paper, record your findings. How do they compare? Which company would you choose and why?

Accept all reasonable answers that show student effort and an understanding of the concept.

CHAPTER 14

Health, Disability, and Life Insurance

$ What You'll Learn

When you have completed this chapter, you will be able to:

Section 14.1

- Explain the importance of health insurance in financial planning.
- Analyze costs and benefits of various health insurance.

Section 14.2

- Differentiate between private and government health care plans.

Section 14.3

- Explain the importance of disability insurance in financial planning.
- Describe different sources of disability income.

Section 14.4

- Describe various types of life insurance coverage.
- Identify the key provisions in a life insurance policy.

Reading Strategies

To get the most out of your reading:

Predict what you will learn in this chapter.
Relate what you read to your own life.
Question what you are reading to be sure you understand.
React to what you have read.

In the **Real** World . . .

Upon graduating from college, Sharon Lewis discovered that she was no longer covered by her parents' health insurance. When she found out what the monthly premium would be if she purchased her own policy, she decided to do without one. She said, "I'm healthy, and I get plenty of exercise skiing. I haven't needed to visit the doctor in years." Then she got in an accident. Rushing out of her apartment one morning, she tripped and fell, injuring her ankle. When she went to the emergency room, she was shocked to learn how much the visit would cost. A follow-up visit would be an additional expense. Health, disability, and life insurance are important for even the healthiest person.

As You Read *Consider the importance of having health insurance when you need it.*

Lesson Plan See the Teacher Manual for the Chapter 14 planning guide and lesson plan.

ASK STANDARD & POOR'S

Health Care Costs

Q: I am a high school student. Why should I be concerned about my future health care costs now?

A: Your health care costs, now and in the future, can be affected by your personal health habits. Many health problems result from poor habits, such as lack of exercise or inadequate diet, and may take years to develop. By establishing good habits now, you can reduce the likelihood of future health problems and related expenses.

Ask Yourself What good habits can you establish now that will help you ensure that your health care costs will stay low in the future?

@ Go to **finance07.glencoe.com** to complete the Standard & Poor's Financial Focus activity.

Section 14.1

Focus on Reading

Read to Learn

- How to explain the importance of health insurance in financial planning.
- How to analyze costs and benefits of various health insurance.

Main Idea

Knowing how to determine the type of health insurance plan that you need can help you meet your financial goals even when dealing with unexpected medical costs.

Key Terms

- health insurance
- coinsurance
- stop-loss
- co-payment

Before You Read

PREDICT

What does major medical expense insurance cover?

Springboard Ask the students how many times they went to the doctor or hospital this year; discuss with them how important it is to have health insurance.

Health Insurance and Financial Planning

What Is Health Insurance?

Why is it important for healthy people to have health insurance?

Health insurance is a form of protection that eases the financial burden people may experience as a result of illness or injury. You pay a premium, or fee, to the insurer. In return, the company pays most of your medical costs. Plans vary, but some of the things that they might cover are hospital stays, doctors' visits, medications, and sometimes vision and dental care.

Health insurance includes both medical expense insurance and disability income insurance. *Medical expense insurance* typically pays only the actual medical costs. *Disability income insurance* provides payments to make up for some of the income of a person who cannot work as a result of injury or illness. In this chapter the term "health insurance" generally refers to medical expense insurance.

Health insurance plans can be purchased as several different plans: group health insurance, individual health insurance, and COBRA.

Group Health Insurance

Most people who have health insurance are covered under group plans. Typically, these plans are employer sponsored. This means that an employer offers the plans and usually pays some or all of the premiums. Other organizations, such as labor unions and professional associations, also offer group plans. Group insurance plans cover you and your immediate family. The Health Insurance Portability and Accountability Act of 1996 set new federal standards to ensure that workers will not lose their health insurance if they change jobs. For example, a parent with a sick child can move from one group health plan to another plan without a lapse in coverage. Moreover, the parent will not have to pay more for coverage than other employees do.

The cost of group insurance is fairly low because many people are insured under the same policy, which is a contract with a risk-sharing group or insurance company. However, group insurance plans vary in the amount of protection that they provide. For example, some plans limit the amount that they will pay for hospital stays and surgical procedures.

Coordination of Benefits If your plan does not cover all your health insurance needs, you have some options. If you are married, you may be able to take advantage of a coordination of benefits (COB) provision, which is included in most group insurance plans. This provision allows you to combine the benefits from more than one insurance plan. The benefits received from all plans are limited to 100 percent of all allowable medical expenses. For example, a couple could use benefits from the wife's group plan and from the husband's group plan up to 100 percent. If this type of provision is not available to you, or if you are single, you can get added protection by buying individual health insurance.

Motivating Students Have the students name the various types of health insurance or assistance they know about, and list them on the board. Tell them this chapter will teach about the various types.

Individual Health Insurance

Some people may not be offered an employer-sponsored group insurance plan. Some may not have access to one because they are self-employed. Others are simply dissatisfied with the coverage that their group plans provide. In these cases, individual health insurance may be the answer. You can buy individual health insurance directly from the company of your choice. Plans usually cover you as an individual or as a family. Individual plans can be adapted to meet your own needs. You should comparison shop, however, because rates can vary between companies.

Research Have the students research the group health insurance plans offered to your school district's employees. Have them find out what the plan(s) cover and the cost to employees, and briefly write up their results.

COBRA

The Consolidated Omnibus Budget Reconciliation Act of 1986, known as *COBRA*, allows an employee who loses his or her job to keep the former employer's group coverage for a set period of time. For example, Hakeem had a group insurance plan through his employer, but he was laid off. He wondered how he would be able to get medical coverage until he found a new job. Fortunately for Hakeem, COBRA allowed him to keep coverage for a while. He had to pay the premiums himself, but the coverage was not canceled. When he found a new job, he was then able to switch to the new employer's group plan with no break in coverage.

Not everyone qualifies for COBRA. You have to work for a private company or a state or local government to be eligible for the benefits.

Types of Health Insurance Coverage

Why do you think basic health insurance and major medical insurance are often offered together?

Several types of health insurance coverage are available, either through a group plan or through individual purchase. Some benefits are included in nearly every health insurance plan; other benefits are less common.

As You Read

RELATE

Imagine and describe a situation in which a young, healthy person would need health insurance.

Teaching Activity Divide the students into five groups and assign the following reasons for hospitalization to the groups: a heart attack, having a baby, an appendix surgery, an ulcer surgery, and a broken leg. Have each group check three hospitals and find out the average length of stay in the hospital and the cost for someone who is uninsured. Have the groups prepare graphic illustrations comparing their results and present them to the class.

Caption Answer Some or all of room and board for mother and baby, routine nursing care, minor medical supplies, anesthesia, lab tests, and use of a delivery or operating room.

▼ **MATERNITY WARD** The medical costs of childbirth can be high. *What related costs might be paid by hospital expense coverage?*

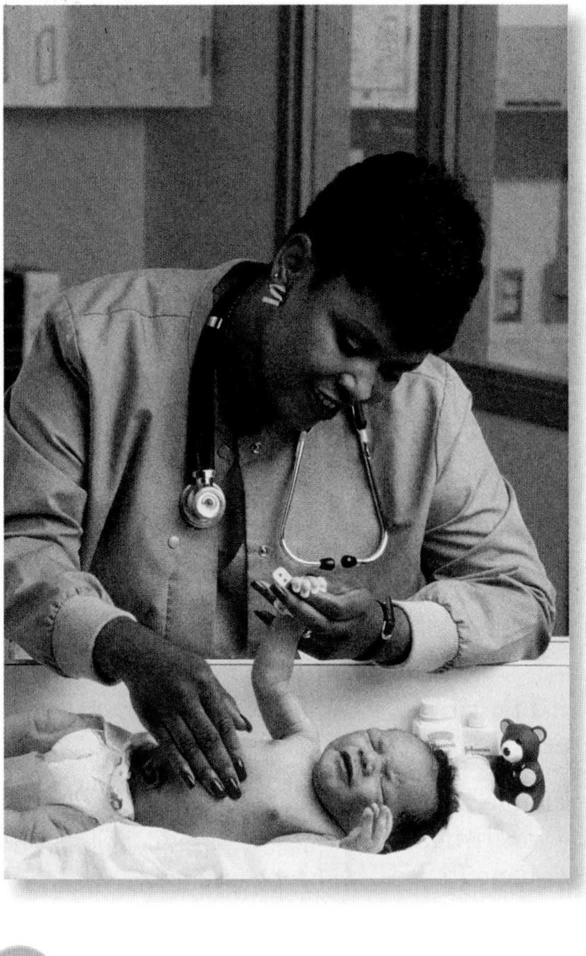

Basic Health Insurance Coverage

Basic health insurance coverage includes hospital expense coverage, surgical expense coverage, and physician expense coverage.

Hospital Expense Hospital expense coverage pays for some or all of the daily costs of room and board during a hospital stay. Routine nursing care, minor medical supplies, and the use of other hospital facilities are covered as well. For example, covered expenses would include anesthesia, dressings, related X-rays, and the use of an operating room.

Most policies set a maximum amount they will pay for each day you are in the hospital. They may also limit the number of days they will cover. As you may remember from Chapter 13, many policies may also require a deductible.

Surgical Expense Surgical expense coverage pays all or part of the surgeon's fees for an operation, whether it is done in the hospital or in the doctor's office. Policies often have a list of the services that they cover, which specifies the maximum payment for each type of operation. For example, a policy might allow $500 for an appendectomy. If the entire surgeon's bill is not covered, the policyholder has to pay the difference. People often buy surgical expense coverage in combination with hospital expense coverage.

Physician Expense Physician expense coverage meets some or all of the costs of physician care that do not involve surgery. It covers treatment by a physician in a hospital, a doctor's office, or even the patient's home. Plans may cover routine doctor visits, X-rays, and lab tests. Like surgical expense, physician expense includes maximum benefits for specific services. Physician expense coverage is usually combined with surgical and hospital coverage in a basic health insurance package.

Major Medical Expense Insurance

Most people find that basic health insurance meets their usual needs. The cost of a serious illness or accident, however, can quickly go beyond the amounts that basic health insurance will pay. For example, Chen had to have emergency surgery, which meant an operation, a two-week hospital stay, a number of lab tests, and several follow-up visits. He was shocked to discover that his basic health insurance paid less than half of the total bill, leaving him with debts of more than $10,000.

Major medical expense insurance would have better protected Chen. This coverage pays the large costs involved in long hospital stays and multiple surgeries. In other words, it takes up where basic health insurance coverage leaves off. Almost every type of care and treatment prescribed by a physician, in or out of a hospital, is covered by this type of plan. Maximum benefits can range from $5,000 to over $1 million per illness per year.

Coinsurance Of course, this type of coverage is not inexpensive. To keep premiums lower, most major medical plans require a deductible. Some plans also include a coinsurance provision. **Coinsurance** is the percentage of the medical expenses the policyholder must pay in addition to the deductible amount. Many policies require policyholders to pay 20 or 25 percent of expenses after they have paid the deductible.

For example, Ariana's policy includes an $800 deductible and a coinsurance provision requiring her to pay 20 percent of all bills. If her bills total $3,800, the insurance company will first exclude $800 from coverage, which is Ariana's deductible. It will then pay 80 percent of the remaining $3,000, which would total $2,400. Therefore, Ariana's total costs are $1,400 ($800 for the deductible and $600 for the coinsurance).

Stop-Loss Provisions Some major medical policies contain a stop-loss provision. **Stop-loss** is a provision that requires the policyholder to pay all costs up to a certain amount, after which the insurance company pays 100 percent of the remaining expenses covered in the policy. Typically, the policyholder will pay between $3,000 and $5,000 in out-of-pocket expenses before the coverage begins.

Comprehensive Major Medical Major medical expense insurance may be offered as part of a single policy that includes basic health insurance coverage, or it can be bought separately. *Comprehensive major medical insurance* is a type of complete health insurance that helps pay hospital, surgical, medical, and other bills. It has a very low deductible, usually $200 to $300. Many major medical policies set limits on the benefits they will pay for certain expenses, such as surgery and hospital room and board.

Hospital Indemnity Policies

A hospital indemnity policy pays benefits when you are hospitalized. Unlike most of the other plans mentioned, however, these policies do not directly cover medical costs. Instead, you are paid in cash, which you can spend on medical or nonmedical expenses as you choose. Hospital indemnity policies are used as a supplement to—not a replacement for—basic health insurance or major medical insurance policies. The average person who buys such a policy, however, usually pays much more in premiums than he or she receives in payments.

As You Read

QUESTION

Why do you think major medical expense insurance is expensive?

Question Answer Major medical insurance picks up where other insurance stops; it provides for lengthy and expensive hospital stays.

Critical Thinking Have the students find out the costs for several different types of insurance from different insurance companies. Have them report their findings in writing, and then answer this question: Why is there so much variation in insurance rates?

Common CENTS

Fitness Fun

Expensive exercise clothes may look good, but they usually do not improve your workout. If you cannot afford to pay to join a health club, you can get your exercise by walking or jogging in your neighborhood or at your school's track. All you need is a good pair of athletic shoes. *How can staying fit save you money?*

Common Cents Staying fit can help you avoid some health problems that a weakened physical condition might cause.

Dental Expense Insurance

Dental expense insurance provides policyholders reimbursement for the expenses of dental services and supplies. It encourages preventive dental care because it pays for maintenance care. The coverage normally provides for oral examinations, X-rays, cleanings, fillings, extractions, oral surgery, dentures, and braces. However, some dental expense policies do not cover X-rays and cleanings. As with other insurance plans, dental insurance may have a deductible and a coinsurance provision, stating that the policyholder pays from 20 to 50 percent of the dental expenses after the deductible.

STANDARD &POOR'S

Global Financial Landscape

Standard and Poor's publishes the globally recognized S&P 500® financial index. It also gathers financial statistics, information, and news, and analyzes this data for international businesses, governments, and individuals to help them guide their financial decisions.

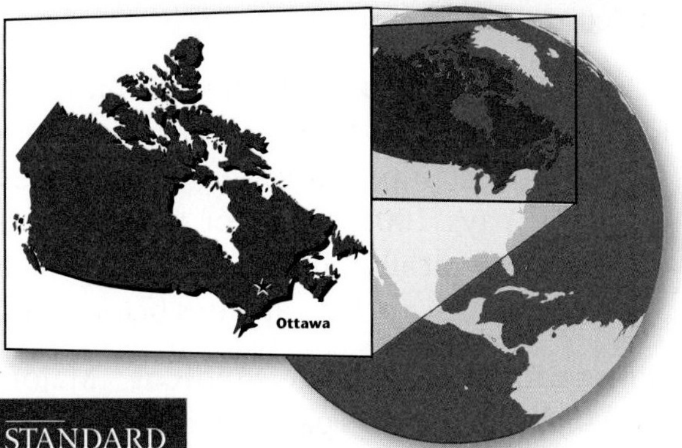

CANADA

When faced with the frustrations of finding affordable health care and insurance, Americans often think Canadians have the solution. Canada offers its citizens free doctor's visits, free hospital care, and free surgery. Children receive some dental work for free, and people over the age of 65 receive free prescription drugs. Taxes, which make up about 9 percent of the country's gross domestic product (GDP), cover these health care costs.

Though the Canadian health care system provides many benefits, it has a down side. Some Canadian patients complain of overcrowding, a shortage of medical staff, outdated equipment, and long waits for treatment. Citizens are prohibited from hiring private health services in Canada, but they can travel outside the country for care. Ironically, many Canadians have come to the United States for health care.

STANDARD &POOR'S **DATABYTES**

Capital	Ottawa
Population	31,630,000
Language	English and French
Currency	Canadian dollar
Gross Domestic Product (GDP)	$957.7 billion (2003 est.)
GDP per capita	$29,700

Industry: Transportation equipment, chemicals, processed and unprocessed minerals, and food products

Agriculture: Wheat, barley, oilseed, tobacco, dairy products, forest products, and fish

Exports: Motor vehicles and parts, industrial machinery, aircraft, telecommunications equipment, chemicals, timber, and crude petroleum

Think Globally
Why do you think medical costs have increased?

See the Teacher Manual for answer.

Vision Care Insurance

Many insurance companies offer vision care insurance as part of group plans. Vision care insurance may cover eye examinations, glasses, contact lenses, eye surgery, and the treatment of eye diseases.

Dread Disease Policies

Dread disease, trip accident, death insurance, and cancer policies are usually sold through the mail, in newspapers, and magazines. These policies play upon unrealistic fears, and they are illegal in many states. They only cover very specific conditions, which are already fully covered under a major medical plan.

Long-Term Care Insurance

Long-term care insurance provides coverage for the expense of daily help that you may need if you become seriously ill or disabled and are unable to care for yourself. It covers a lengthy stay in a nursing home and help at home with daily activities such as dressing, bathing, and household chores. Annual premiums range from $900 up to $15,000, depending on age and the amount of coverage.

Academic Connection

ART

It is vitally important to have health insurance that covers such things as hospital expenses. For example, the average hospital cost for someone injured in a motor vehicle accident is more than $14,000. Without hospital expense coverage you would have to pay the full amount of those costs. *Create a collage of pictures from magazines and/or newspapers to represent some situations that are covered by health insurance.*

See the Teacher Manual for answer.

Major Provisions in a Health Insurance Policy

What are the benefits and limits of the major provisions in a health insurance policy?

Although all health insurance policies have certain provisions in common, you must be sure that you understand what your own policy covers. What are the benefits? What are the limits? The following provisions are included in most health insurance policies:

- **Eligibility** This provision defines the people covered by the policy. That usually includes the policyholder, a spouse, and children up to a certain age.
- **Assigned Benefits** You are reimbursed for payments when you submit your bills and claim forms. When you assign benefits, you let your insurer make direct payments to your doctor or hospital.
- **Internal Limits** A policy with internal limits sets specific levels of repayment for certain services. Even if your hospital room costs $400 a day, you will not be able to get more than $250 if an internal limit specifies that maximum.
- **Co-payment** A **co-payment** is a flat fee that you pay every time you receive a covered service. The fee is usually between $5 and $20, and the insurer pays the balance of the cost of the service. This is different from coinsurance, which is the percentage of your medical costs for which you are responsible after paying your deductible.

Critical Thinking Tell the students that in 2001, 7.8 million children did not have health care insurance. Have them explore medical coverage in at least two other developed countries and describe what is available. Have them write an essay describing their results and answering this question: What role, if any, should our federal government have in providing health care to all children? To all citizens? To all residents?

Discussion Discuss with the students the nine major provisions listed on pages 449-450, explaining to them how these affect both the costs of the policies and the compensation policyholders receive. Ensure students understand what these points mean and how they vary.

- **Service Benefits** Policies with this provision list coverage in terms of services, not dollar amounts. For example, you are entitled to X-rays, instead of $40 worth of X-rays per visit. Service benefits provisions are always preferable to dollar amount coverage because the insurer pays all of the costs for a particular service.
- **Benefit Limits** This provision defines a maximum benefit, either in terms of a dollar amount or in terms of number of days spent in the hospital.
- **Exclusions and Limitations** This provision specifies services that the policy does not cover. That may include preexisting conditions (conditions diagnosed before the insurance plan took effect), cosmetic surgery, and more.
- **Guaranteed Renewable** With this provision, the insurer cannot cancel the policy unless you fail to pay the premiums. It also forbids insurers from raising your premiums unless they raise all premiums for all members of your group.
- **Cancellation and Termination** This provision explains the circumstances under which the insurer can cancel your coverage. It also explains how you can convert your group insurance policy into an individual insurance policy.

Caption Answer It is a flat fee, usually between $5 and $15, that you must pay whenever you receive a covered service while the insurer pays the balance of the cost.

Choosing Coverage

What type of health insurance coverage should you choose?

Now that you are familiar with the available types of health insurance and some of their major provisions, how do you choose one? The type of coverage you choose will be affected by the amount you can afford to spend on the premiums and the level of benefits that you feel you want and need. It may also be affected by the kind of coverage your employer offers, if you are covered through your employer.

▼ SHARING THE COST
All health insurance policies have certain provisions in common.
What is a co-payment?

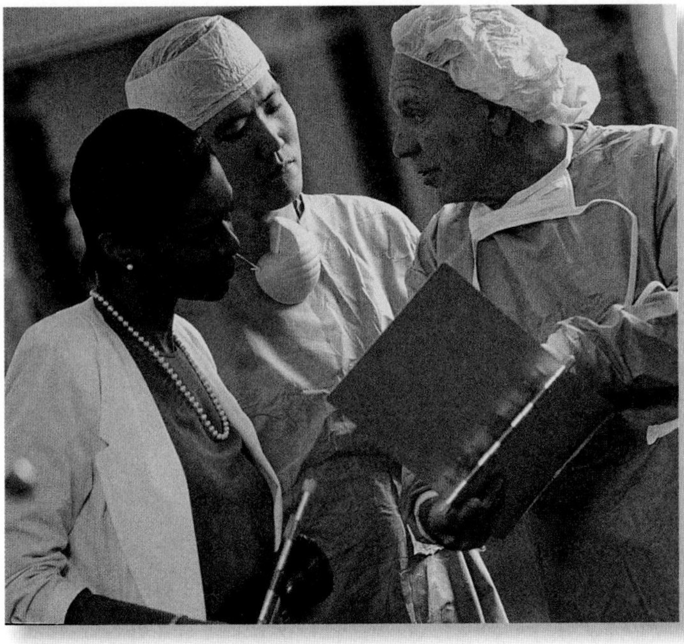

You can buy basic health coverage, major medical coverage, or both basic and major medical coverage. Any of these three choices will take care of at least some of your medical expenses. Ideally, you should get a basic plan and a major medical supplement. Another option is to purchase a comprehensive major medical policy that combines the value of both plans in a single policy. See **Figure 14.1** for a description of the basic features you should look for in a health insurance plan. You should also consider the trade-offs of the various benefits.

Health Insurance Trade-Offs

Different health insurance policies may offer very different benefits. As you decide which insurance plan to buy, you should consider the following trade-offs.

Reimbursement Versus Indemnity A reimbursement policy pays you back for actual expenses. An indemnity policy pays specified amounts, regardless of how much the actual expenses may cost.

For example, Katie and Seth were both charged $200 for an office visit to the same specialist. Katie's reimbursement policy has a deductible of $300. Once she has met the deductible, the policy will cover the full cost of subsequent visits. Seth's indemnity policy will pay him only $125, which is what his plan provides for each visit to any specialist.

Internal Limits Versus Aggregate Limits A policy with internal limits covers only a fixed amount for an expense, such as the daily cost of room and board during a hospital stay. A policy with aggregate limits may limit only the total amount of coverage (the maximum dollar amount paid for all benefits in a year), such as $1 million in major expense benefits, or it may have no limits.

Deductibles and Coinsurance The cost of a health insurance policy is affected by the size of the deductible, which is the set amount that the policyholder must pay toward medical expenses before the insurance company pays benefits. It can also be affected by the terms of the coinsurance provision.

Figure 14.1 Health Insurance Must-Haves

A health insurance plan should:

- Offer basic coverage for hospital and doctor bills.
- Provide at least 120 days' hospital room and board in full.
- Provide at least a $1 million lifetime maximum for each family member.
- Pay at least 80 percent for out-of-hospital expenses after a yearly deductible of $500 per person or $1,000 per family.
- Impose no unreasonable exclusions.
- Limit your out-of-pocket expenses to no more than $3,000 to $5,000 a year, excluding dental, vision care, and prescription costs.

Essential Coverage Health insurance plans vary greatly, but all plans should have some basic features.

Would you add anything to this list of must-haves?

Caption Answer Accept all reasonable answers.

Teaching Activity Draw students' attention to the list of trade-offs on pages 451–452. Have students choose between the two opposing items and justify their choices in writing. Explain that there are no right or wrong answers, just opinions.

Out-of-Pocket Limits Some policies limit the amount of money you must pay for the deductible and coinsurance. After you have reached that limit, the insurance company covers 100 percent of any additional expenses. Having out-of-pocket limits may help you lower your financial risk, but those limits may also increase the price of your premiums.

Benefits Based on Reasonable and Customary Charges Some policies consider the average fee for a service in a particular geographical area. They then use that average amount to set a limit on payments to policyholders. If the standard cost of a certain procedure is $1,500 in your part of the country, then your policy will not pay more than that amount.

Section 14.1 Assessment

See the Teacher Manual for answers

QUICK CHECK

1. Why is it important to include health insurance in your financial planning?
2. What are benefits provided by hospital expense coverage, surgical expense coverage, and physician expense coverage?
3. What are the trade-offs between reimbursement and indemnity?

THINK CRITICALLY

4. Explain why it is necessary for insurance companies to place limits on the amount of costs they will cover.

USE COMMUNICATION SKILLS

5. **Benefits of Insurance** Your 25-year-old sister never gets sick and leads an active, healthy life. She sees no reason to buy health insurance and calls the premiums a waste of money.

   Role-Play With a partner, role-play a response to your sister's argument. Explain why she might benefit from health insurance regardless of her current situation.

SOLVE MONEY PROBLEMS

6. **Choosing an Insurance Plan** Richard is 35, single, and in reasonably good health. He works for a construction company that offers three health insurance plans. The first has a lifetime benefit of $1 million for all covered expenses, an annual deductible of $500, and a 15 percent coinsurance provision up to the first $2,000 in covered charges. The second requires a monthly premium of $50 and sets a $500,000 lifetime limit on benefits, has no annual deductible, and requires a $15 co-payment per office visit. The third has an annual deductible of $250 and a 25 percent coinsurance provision up to the first $1,500 in covered charges, with a lifetime limit on benefits of $700,000.

   Analyze Help Richard determine which of these three plans makes the most sense for his particular situation. Be prepared to defend your reasoning.

Section 14.2

Private and Government Plans

Private Health Care Plans

What is the difference between an HMO and a PPO?

Most health insurance in the United States is provided by private organizations rather than by the government. Private health care plans may be offered by a number of sources: private insurance companies; hospital and medical service plans; health maintenance organizations; preferred provider organizations; home health care agencies; and employer self-funded health plans.

Private Insurance Companies

Several hundred private insurance companies are in the health insurance business. They provide mostly group health plans to employers, who in turn offer them to their employees as an employment benefit. Premiums may be fully or partially paid by the employer, with the employee paying any remainder. These policies typically pay for medical costs by sending payments directly to the doctor, hospital, or lab that provides the services.

Hospital and Medical Service Plans

Blue Cross and Blue Shield are statewide organizations similar to private health insurance companies. Each state has Blue Cross and Blue Shield. **Blue Cross** is an insurance company that provides hospital care benefits. **Blue Shield** is an insurance company that provides benefits for surgical and medical services performed by physicians. The "Blues" provide health insurance to millions of Americans.

Managed Care

According to a recent industry survey, 23 percent of employed Americans are enrolled in some form of managed care, due to rising health care costs. **Managed care** refers to prepaid health plans that provide comprehensive health care to their members. Managed care is designed to control the cost of health care services by controlling how they are used. Managed care is offered by health maintenance organizations, preferred provider organizations, and point-of-service plans.

Focus on Reading

Read to Learn

- How to differentiate between private and government health care plans.

Main Idea

Understanding plans offered by private companies and by the government will help you choose the plan that best meets your physical and financial needs now and as you get older.

Key Terms

- Blue Cross
- Blue Shield
- managed care
- health maintenance organization (HMO)
- preferred provider organization (PPO)
- point-of-service (POS) plan
- Medicare
- Medicaid

Before You Read

PREDICT

What is the difference between insurance provided by private organizations and insurance provided by the government?

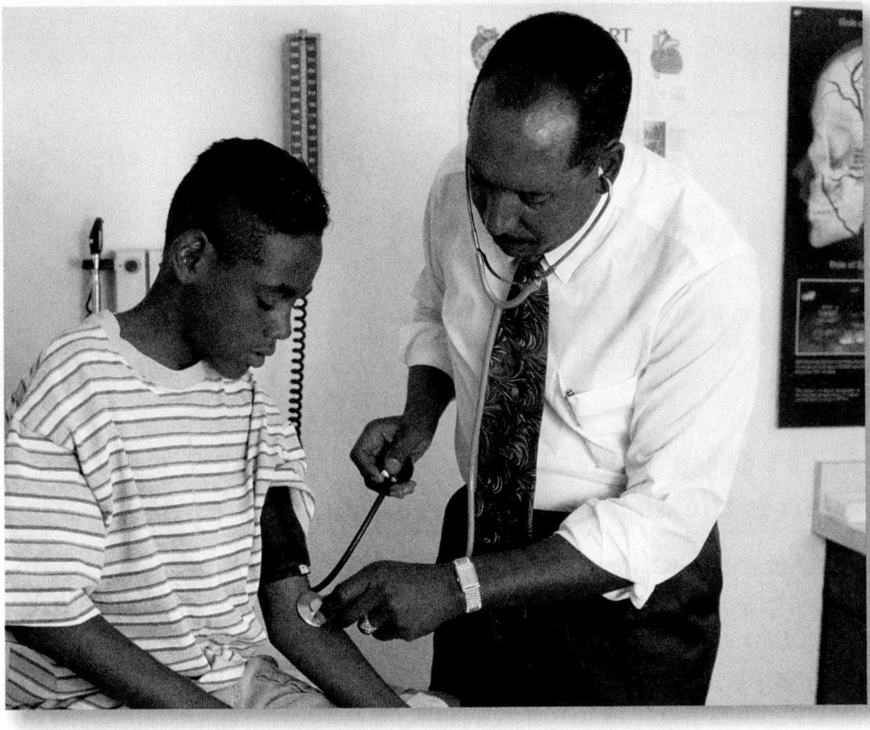

▲ **PROMOTING HEALTH** HMOs are based on the idea that preventive services will minimize future medical problems. *What kinds of preventive services do HMOs cover?*

Caption Answer routine immunizations and checkups, screening programs, and diagnostic tests

Springboard Ask the students to develop criteria they would use when selecting their own health plan.

Health Maintenance Organizations One managed-care option is a **health maintenance organization (HMO)**, which is a health insurance plan that directly employs or contracts with selected, or preapproved, physicians and other medical professionals to provide health care services in exchange for a fixed, prepaid monthly premium. HMOs are an alternative to basic health insurance and major medical expense insurance.

HMOs are based on the idea that preventive services will minimize future medical problems. Therefore, these plans typically cover routine immunizations and checkups, screening programs, and diagnostic tests. They also provide customers with coverage for surgery, hospitalization, and emergency care. If you have an HMO, you usually pay a small co-payment for each covered service, such as a doctor's office visit. Supplemental services may include vision care and prescription services, which are typically available for an additional fee.

When you first enroll in an HMO, you must choose a plan physician from a list of doctors provided by the HMO. This physician provides or arranges for all your health care services. If you receive care from a physician outside your HMO's approved physician list, you are responsible for the cost of the service. The only exception to this rule is in the case of a medical emergency. If you experience a sudden illness or injury that would threaten your life or health if not treated immediately, you may go to the nearest emergency room. All other care must be provided by hospitals and doctors under contract with the HMO.

Motivating Students Ask the students if they think health insurance needs change as people get older; then ask at what ages they might have to consider changes in their health care coverage, and why.

HMOs are not for everyone. Many HMO customers complain that their HMO denies them necessary care. Others feel restricted by the limited choice of doctors.

Here are some tips on using and choosing an HMO. Because HMOs require you to use only certain doctors, you should make sure that those doctors are near your home or place of work. You should also be able to change doctors easily if you do not like your first choice. Second opinions should always be available at the HMO's expense, and you should be able to appeal any case in which the HMO denies care. Finally, look at the costs and benefits—whether you will incur out-of-pocket expenses or co-payments and what services the plan will provide.

STANDARD & POOR'S **Put on Your Financial Planner's Cap**

You just started your first full-time job, working for a company that provides both an HMO and a POS plan. Which health insurance plan would best fit your financial situation?

See the Teacher Manual for answer.

Preferred Provider Organizations A variation on the HMO is a **preferred provider organization (PPO)**, which is a group of doctors and hospitals that agree to provide specified medical services to members at prearranged fees. PPOs offer these discounted services to employees either directly or indirectly through an insurance company. The premiums for PPOs are slightly higher than the premiums for HMOs.

PPO plan members often pay no deductibles but may have minimal co-payments. While HMOs require members to receive care from HMO providers only, PPOs allow members greater flexibility. Members can either visit a preferred provider (a physician selected from a pre-approved list) or go to their own physicians. Patients who decide to use their own doctors do not lose coverage as they would with an HMO. However, they must pay deductibles and larger co-payments.

Point-of-Service (POS) Plan A **point-of-service (POS) plan** combines features of both HMOs and PPOs. POS plans use a network of participating physicians and medical professionals who have contracted to provide services for certain fees. As with an HMO, you choose a plan physician who manages your care and controls referrals to specialists. As long as you receive care from a pre-approved provider, you pay little or nothing, just as you would with an HMO. However, you are allowed to seek care outside the network at a higher charge, as with a PPO.

As You Read

RELATE

Would you choose an HMO, PPO, or POS? Why?

Home Health Care Agencies

Rising hospital costs, new medical technology, and the increasing number of elderly people have helped make home care one of the fastest-growing areas of the health care industry. Home health care consists of home health care agencies; home care aide organizations; and hospices, which are facilities and organizations that provide care for the terminally ill. These providers offer medical care in a home setting in agreement with a medical order, often at a fraction of the cost charged by hospitals for similar services.

Teaching Activity Have the students find out what home health care agencies exist in your community, what they offer, what they charge, and what money they receive other than fees from patients (i.e., grants, donations, state or federal funding). You may choose to divide the class into three groups to research home health agencies, home care aide organizations, and hospices. Have students report their findings in class discussion.

$avvy Saver

Non-Smokers Save

1. A pack of cigarettes each day for 15 years can cost about $15,000.
2. Smokers miss more work than non-smokers do.
3. Smokers spend more money on medical treatment.
4. Non-smokers pay less for health insurance.
5. Non-smokers pay almost half as much for life insurance.

Employer Self-Funded Health Plans

Some companies choose to self-insure. The company runs its own insurance plan, collecting premiums from employees and paying medical benefits as needed. However, these companies must cover any costs that exceed the income from premiums. Unfortunately, some corporations do not have the financial assets necessary to cover these situations, which can cause a financial disaster for the company and its employees.

Government Health Care Programs

Who benefits most from government health care programs?

The health insurance coverages discussed so far are normally purchased through private companies. Some consumers, however, are eligible for health insurance coverage under programs offered by federal and state governments. The federal program is Medicare, and the federal and state program is Medicaid.

Medicare

Research Have the students research the Medicare program, discovering under which president it began and what changes have occurred in the program since then and under which presidents. Have students create a timeline that charts this information.

Perhaps the best-known government program is Medicare. **Medicare** is a federally funded health insurance program available mainly to people over 65 and to people with certain disabilities. Medicare has two parts: hospital insurance (Part A) and medical insurance (Part B).

Medicare Part A is funded by part of the Social Security payroll tax. Part A helps pay for inpatient hospital care, inpatient care in a skilled nursing facility, home health care, and hospice care. Program participants pay a single annual deductible.

Part B helps pay for doctors' services and a variety of other medical services and supplies not covered, or not fully covered, by Part A. Part B has a deductible and a 20 percent coinsurance provision. Medicare medical insurance is a supplemental program paid for by individuals who feel that they need additional coverage. A regular monthly premium is charged. The federal government matches this amount.

Medicare Finances Medicare is at risk financially. Health care costs continue to grow, and the population of senior citizens in the United States is increasing. This situation puts Medicare in danger of running out of funds. According to projections made in 2004, the program will be bankrupt by the year 2019 if no changes are made.

The Balanced Budget Act of 1997 created the additional program, Medicare 1 Choice. This program allows many Medicare members to choose a managed care plan in addition to their Medicare coverage. For some additional costs, members can receive greater benefits.

As You Read

QUESTION

How might the projected shortfall in Medicare funds affect the future of government health care programs?

Question Answer Answers will vary but may include that the programs will be scaled back or that taxes to support the programs will rise.

▲ **LIVING WELL** The Medicare health program covers more people over the age of 65 than ever because of the increasing population of senior citizens. *What services do Medicare Parts A and B cover?*

Caption Answer Part A helps pay for inpatient hospital care, inpatient care in a skilled nursing facility, home health care, and hospice care. Part B helps pay for doctors' services and a variety of other medical services and supplies not covered by Part A.

What Is Not Covered by Medicare? Medicare effectively covers many medical costs, but there are some medical expenses that Medicare will not cover at all. These expenses include certain types of skilled or long-term nursing care, out-of-hospital prescription drugs, routine checkups, dental care, and most immunizations. Medicare also limits the types of services it will cover and the amount it will pay for those services. If a doctor does not accept Medicare's approved amount as payment in full, the patient is responsible for paying the difference.

Medigap People who are eligible for Medicare and who would like to have more coverage may buy Medigap insurance. Medigap insurance supplements Medicare by filling the gap between Medicare payments and medical costs not covered by Medicare. It is offered by private companies.

Critical Thinking Set up a class debate in which students research, prepare for, and address this question: Do you think people over 65 who can afford private health insurance should be allowed to use Medicare?

Teaching Activity Divide the class into groups of three and have each group look up one of the 60 Web sites operated by the Department of Health and Human Services (you may obtain a list and assign sites). Each group is to report back to the class the type of information its site provides.

Medicaid

The other well-known government health program is **Medicaid**, a medical assistance program offered to certain low-income individuals and families. Medicaid is administered by the individual states, but it is financed by a combination of state and federal funds. Unlike Medicare, Medicaid coverage is so comprehensive that people with Medicaid do not need supplemental insurance. Typical Medicaid benefits include:

- Physicians' services
- Inpatient hospital services
- Outpatient hospital services
- Lab services
- Skilled nursing and home health services
- Prescription drugs
- Eyeglasses
- Preventive care for people under 21

Careers in Finance

INSURANCE AGENT **Alicia Hopkins**
Farmer's Insurance

Alicia is an excellent salesperson who cares about her clients. She sells insurance policies to individuals, families, business firms, and other groups to protect them from future financial loss due to injury, illness, death, property damage, or theft. Alicia interviews prospective clients to obtain data about their financial resources and needs, as well as the physical condition of the person or property to be insured. She then works out an insurance program suited to that customer, explains the program's costs and benefits, and writes a policy. Alicia follows up regularly with her client so she can handle any changes and renewals to his or her policy. Alicia, like all insurance agents, is always on the lookout for new clients.

SKILLS: Sales, communication, legal and financial awareness, mathematical, and time-management skills

PERSONAL TRAITS: Diligent, self-confident, outgoing, tactful, and good judgment

EDUCATION: High school diploma or equivalent; a license from the State Department of Insurance; pre-licensing and continuing education

ANALYZE Why might it be helpful for an insurance agent to be active in civic or social organizations?
See the Teacher Manual for answer.

To learn more about career paths for insurance agents, visit **finance07.glencoe.com**.

Government Consumer Health Information Web Sites

The Department of Health and Human Services operates more than 60 Web sites that contain a wealth of reliable information related to health and medicine.

Healthfinder Healthfinder includes links to over a thousand Web pages operated by government and nonprofit organizations. It lists topics according to subject.

MedlinePlus MedlinePlus is the world's largest Internet collection of published medical information. It was originally designed for health professionals and researchers, but it is also valuable for students and others who are interested in health care and medical issues.

NIH Health Information The National Institutes of Health (NIH) operates a Web site that can direct you to the consumer health information in NIH publications and on the Internet.

FDA The Food and Drug Administration (FDA), a federal consumer protection agency, provides a Web site with information about the safety of various foods, drugs, cosmetics, and medical devices.

Section 14.2 Assessment

See the Teacher Manual for answers.

QUICK CHECK

1. What types of coverage are provided by Blue Cross and Blue Shield?
2. What are the differences between an HMO and a PPO?
3. What is the difference between Medicare and Medicaid?

THINK CRITICALLY

4. Identify the benefits and drawbacks to membership in an HMO.

USE MATH SKILLS

5. **PPOs** Last month Rose was involved in a car accident and was rushed to the emergency room. After receiving stitches for a facial wound and treatment for a broken finger, she was released from the hospital.

Calculate Under Rose's PPO, emergency room care at a network hospital is 80 percent covered after the member has met a $300 annual deductible. Assume that Rose went to a hospital within her PPO network. Her total emergency room bill was $850. What amount did Rose have to pay? What amount did the PPO cover?

SOLVE MONEY PROBLEMS

6. **HMOs** Your Aunt Alice will be 65. She pays $200 a month for an HMO she does not like. She will be eligible for Medicare and is wondering if she should drop the HMO coverage at that time.

Analyze With a partner, discuss Aunt Alice's alternative and if she should drop her HMO coverage.

Section 14.3

Focus on Reading

Read to Learn

- How to explain the importance of disability insurance in financial planning.
- How to describe different sources of disability income.

Main Idea

Disability income insurance is important if you become unable to work.

Key Term

- disability income insurance

Before You Read

PREDICT

What might disability insurance cover?

Springboard Ask the students if and/or when they should start planning for the possibility of becoming disabled. Have them justify their answers.

Disability Insurance

Disability Income

Why is it important to have disability insurance?

Before disability insurance existed, people who were ill often lost more money from missed paychecks than from paying medical bills. Disability income insurance was set up to protect against such loss of income. **Disability income insurance** provides regular cash income when an employee is unable to work due to pregnancy, a non-work-related accident, or an illness. It protects your earning power, which is your most valuable resource. This kind of coverage is very common today, and several hundred insurance companies offer it.

The exact definition of the word *disability* varies from insurer to insurer. Some insurers will pay you when you are unable to work at your regular job. Other insurers will pay only if you are so ill or badly hurt that you cannot work at any job. A violinist with a hand injury, for example, might have trouble doing his or her regular work but might be able to perform a range of other jobs. A good disability income insurance plan pays you if you cannot work at your regular job. A good plan will also pay partial benefits if you are able to work only part-time.

Many people make the mistake of ignoring disability insurance, not realizing that it is very important to have. A disability can cause even greater financial problems than death because disabled persons lose their earning power but still have to pay for their living expenses. In addition, they often face huge costs for the medical treatment and special care that their disabilities require.

Sources of Disability Income

Before you buy disability income insurance from a private insurance company, remember that you may already have some form of this insurance. This coverage may be available through worker's compensation if you are injured on the job. Disability benefits may also be available through your employer or through Social Security in case of a long-term disability.

Worker's Compensation If your disability is the result of an accident or illness that occurred on the job, you may be eligible to receive worker's compensation benefits. The amount of benefits will depend on your salary and your work history.

Employer Many employers provide disability income insurance through group insurance plans. In most cases, your employer will pay part or all of the cost of such insurance. Some policies may only provide continued wages for several months, while others will provide long-term protection.

Social Security Social Security may be best known as a source of retirement income, but it also provides disability benefits. If you are a worker who pays into the Social Security system, you are eligible for Social Security funds if you become disabled. How much you get depends on your salary and the number of years you have been paying into Social Security. Your dependents also qualify for certain benefits. However, Social Security has very strict rules. Workers are considered disabled if they have a physical or mental condition that prevents them from working for at least 12 months, or if they have a condition that may result in death. Benefits start at the sixth full month the person is disabled. They stay in effect as long as the disability lasts.

Private Income Insurance Programs Privately owned insurance companies offer many policies to protect people from loss of income resulting from illness or disability. Disability income insurance gives weekly or monthly cash payments to people who cannot work due to illness or accident. The amount paid is usually 40 to 60 percent of a person's normal income. Some plans pay as much as 75 percent.

As You Read

RELATE

Do Social Security disability benefits provide enough coverage for you to feel comfortable about your financial future if you were to become disabled? Why or why not?

Motivating Students Ask students if they have ever known someone who was disabled, either temporarily or permanently, from an accident. Have them recount their stories, including whether these people had any income.

Caption Answer It could provide a dancer with regular cash income while he or she is unable to work.

◀ **ACCIDENTS HAPPEN** Disability income insurance can be very important because it provides funds if you are unable to work due to illness or injury. *How would disability income insurance help a dancer who broke a leg in a surfing accident?*

TechByte

Transferable Skills
If you have a disability claim due to illness or an accident, your disability insurance carrier will require you to take a test called a Transferable Skills Analysis (TSA). The TSA determines if a disabled person has the potential to work at a job that uses his or her skills. Several software programs can perform a TSA. Insurance companies also use TSAs to detect fraudulent claims.

@ Look at a sample TSA and write a description of its information through **finance07.glencoe.com**.

Disability Insurance Trade-Offs

When you purchase health or disability insurance, you must make certain trade-offs when you decide among different private disability insurance policies. You should consider several factors as you look for a plan.

Waiting or Elimination Period Your benefits will not begin the day you become disabled. You will have to wait between one and six months before you can begin collecting. This span of time is called a waiting, or elimination, period. Usually a policy with a longer elimination period charges lower premiums.

Duration of Benefits Every policy names a specified period during which benefits will be paid. Some policies are valid for only a few years. Others are automatically canceled when you turn 65. Still others continue to make payments for life. You should look for a policy that pays benefits for life. If a policy stops payments when the policyholder is age 65, then having a permanent disability could be a major financial burden.

Amount of Benefits You should aim for a benefit amount that, when added to other sources of income, will equal 70 to 80 percent of your take-home pay. Of course, greater benefits cost more money.

Critical Thinking Ask students to research and respond in writing to this question: Why do you think the federal government provides disability insurance?

Caption Answer Worker's Compensation

▶ **HIGH RISK** Your chances of becoming disabled are greater in professions that involve physical risk. *What program would provide disability income for a construction worker who is injured on the job?*

Accident and Sickness Coverage Some disability policies pay only for accidents. However, accidents are not the only cause of disability, so coverage for sickness is also important.

Guaranteed Renewability If your health becomes poor, your disability insurer may try to cancel your coverage. Look for a plan that guarantees coverage as long as you continue to pay your premiums. Some plans may even suspend premiums if you become disabled.

As You Read

QUESTION

What are the disability insurance trade-offs?

Question Answer waiting or elimination period, duration of benefits, amount of benefits, accident and sickness coverage, and guaranteed renewability

Your Disability Income Needs

How do you determine your disability income needs?

After you find out what your benefits would be from the numerous public and private sources, you should determine whether those benefits would meet your disability income needs. Ideally, you want to replace all the income you otherwise would have earned. This money should enable you to pay your day-to-day expenses while you are recovering. You will not have work-related expenses, and your taxes will be lower during the time that you are disabled. In some cases, you may not have to pay various taxes at all.

Teaching Activity Ask an agent who sells disability insurance to speak to the class about the benefits and costs of available policies.

Section 14.3 Assessment

See the Teacher Manual for answers.

QUICK CHECK

1. Why is disability income insurance important in personal financial planning?
2. What are the four main sources of disability income?
3. What are two trade-offs that you might have to make when choosing among different private disability insurance policies.

THINK CRITICALLY

4. Describe at least two situations for which a person might need disability income insurance.

USE COMMUNICATION SKILLS

5. **Earning Power** Many people who insure their houses, cars, and other property fail to insure their most valuable resource—their earning power.

Write About It Imagine that you are a health columnist for a newsletter aimed at people in the entertainment industry, such as dancers, actors, writers, and musicians. Explain why these artists should make sure that they are adequately covered by disability insurance.

SOLVE MONEY PROBLEMS

6. **Choosing Plans** Your next-door neighbor has about nine months' salary saved up. He is 58, has no dependents, and plans to retire in seven years. He has just changed jobs. He now works in the office of a road-building company where he has a choice of disability insurance plans.

Analyze What features should your neighbor be looking for in a disability income insurance plan?

Section 14.4

Life Insurance

Focus on Reading

Read to Learn

- How to describe various types of life insurance coverage.
- How to identify the key provisions in a life insurance policy.

Main Idea

Making decisions about life insurance and choosing the right policy takes time, research, and careful thought.

Key Terms

- beneficiary (insurance)
- term insurance
- whole life insurance
- cash value
- endowment

Before You Read

PREDICT

Who do you think would need life insurance most, a 65-year-old widower with grown children or a single mother with three young children?

Springboard Discuss with students what they think is the right age to buy life insurance.

What Is Life Insurance?

Why is it important to include life insurance in your financial planning?

When you buy life insurance, you are making a contract with the company issuing the policy. You agree to pay a certain amount of money—the premium—periodically. In return, the company agrees to pay a death benefit, or a stated sum of money upon your death, to your beneficiary. A **beneficiary** is a person named to receive the benefits from an insurance policy.

The Purpose of Life Insurance

Buying life insurance can help you protect the people who depend upon you from financial losses caused by your death. Those people could include a spouse, children, an aging parent, or a business partner. Life insurance benefits may be used to:

- Pay off a home mortgage or other debts at the time of death.
- Provide lump-sum payments as an endowment for children when they reach a certain age.
- Provide an education or income for children.
- Make charitable donations after death.
- Provide a retirement income.
- Accumulate savings.
- Establish a regular income for survivors.
- Set up an estate plan.
- Pay estate and death taxes.

The Principle of Life Insurance

No one can say with any certainty how long a particular person will live. However, insurance companies are able to make some educated guesses. Over the years they have compiled tables that show an estimate of how long people live. Using these tables, the companies make a rough guess about a person's life span and set the price of insurance premiums for him or her accordingly. The sooner a person is likely to die, the higher the premium he or she will pay to have life insurance. For example, life insurance will cost more for a 65-year-old woman than for a 25-year-old woman.

How Long Will You Live?

If history is any guide, you will live longer than your ancestors lived. In 1900, the life expectancy of an American male was 46.3 years, and it was 48.3 years for an American female. In contrast, by the year 2000, the life expectancy increased to 74 years for men and 80 years for women. **Figure 14.2** shows an estimate of how many years a person can be expected to live today. This type of table guides insurance companies when they set prices. For example, a 30-year-old woman can be expected to live another 50.6 years. That does not mean that she has a high probability of dying at age 80.6. This just means that 50.6 is the average number of additional years a 30-year-old woman may expect to live.

Motivating Students Ask students why they think someone should buy life insurance. Does everyone need it? If so, why? If not, who does?

Do You Need Life Insurance?

Before you buy life insurance, you will have to decide whether you need it at all. Generally, if your death would cause financial hardship for somebody, then life insurance is a wise purchase. Households with children usually have the greatest need for life insurance. Single people who live alone or with their parents, however, usually have little or no need for life insurance unless they have a great deal of debt or want to provide for their parents or a friend, relative, or charity.

Figure 14.2 Life Expectancy Table

Age	Both Sexes	Male	Female	Age	Both Sexes	Male	Female
0	76.9	74.1	79.5	**45**	34.4	32.2	36.3
1	76.4	73.7	79.0	**50**	30.0	27.9	31.8
5	72.5	69.8	75.1	**55**	25.7	23.8	27.4
10	67.6	64.9	70.1	**60**	21.6	19.9	23.1
15	62.6	59.9	65.2	**65**	17.9	16.3	19.2
20	57.8	55.2	60.3	**70**	14.4	13.0	15.5
25	53.1	50.6	55.4	**75**	11.3	10.1	12.1
30	48.3	45.9	50.6	**80**	8.6	7.6	9.1
35	43.6	41.3	45.8	**85**	6.3	5.6	6.7
40	38.9	36.7	41.0				

The Average Life This type of table helps insurance companies determine insurance premiums.

Use the table to find the average number of additional years a 15-year-old male and female were expected to live, based on the statistics gathered by the U.S. government as of 2000.

Caption Answer
59.9 years; 65.2 years

As You Read
RELATE

Imagine your life 5, 10, and 15 years from now. At what point would you want a good life insurance policy?

Discussion Discuss with the students how lifestyle choices might affect their life expectancy. Ask the students: "Do you think they could affect your insurance rates? Why or why not?"

Types of Life Insurance Policies

When do you think it is most important to have life insurance?

You can purchase life insurance from two types of life insurance companies: stock life insurance companies, which are owned by shareholders, and mutual life insurance companies, which are owned by their policyholders. About 95 percent of life insurance companies in the United States are stock companies. Insurance policies can be divided into two types: term insurance and whole life insurance.

Term Insurance

Term insurance, which is sometimes called *temporary life insurance,* is insurance that provides protection against loss of life for only a specified term, or period of time. A term insurance policy pays a benefit only if you die during the period it covers, which may be 1, 5, 10, or 20 years, or up to age 70. If you stop paying the premiums, your coverage stops. Term insurance is often the best value for most consumers. You need life insurance coverage most while you are raising children. As your children become independent and your assets increase, you can reduce your coverage. Term insurance comes in many different forms.

Renewable Term The coverage of term insurance ends at the conclusion of the term, but you can continue it for another term, such as five years, if you have a renewable option. However, the premium will increase because you will be older. It also usually has an age limit, which means you cannot renew your coverage after you reach a certain age.

Multiyear Level Term A multiyear level term, or straight term, policy guarantees that you will pay the same premium for the duration of your policy.

Caption Answer renewable term, multiyear level term, conversion term, and decreasing term

◀ **COMING TO TERMS** Many experts say that term insurance is best for most people—especially growing families. *Name the types of term insurance policies that are available.*

Conversion Term This type of policy allows you to change from term to permanent coverage. This change will require a higher premium.

Decreasing Term Term insurance is also available in a form that pays less to the beneficiary as time passes. The premiums are usually the same over the entire period of coverage. The insurance period you select might depend on your age or on how long you want to be covered. For example, if you have a mortgage on a house, you might buy a 25-year decreasing term policy as a way to make sure that the debt could be paid if you died. The coverage would decrease as the balance on the loan decreased.

WebQuest

Avoiding Financial Fraud
Choosing the right type of life insurance policy can be complicated. There are many options available, and it can be difficult to sort out the details to decide what is best. Another complicating factor is that con artists may try to defraud you. Learn some of the do's and don'ts of choosing life insurance and avoiding fraud.

@ To continue with Task 4 of your WebQuest project, visit **finance07.glencoe.com**.

Whole Life Insurance

The other major type of life insurance is known as whole life insurance (also called a straight life policy, a cash value policy, or an ordinary life policy). **Whole life insurance** is a permanent policy for which you pay a specified premium each year for the rest of your life. The insurance company pays your beneficiary a stated sum when you die. The amount of your premium depends mostly on the age at which you purchase the insurance.

Whole life insurance can also serve as an investment. Part of each premium you pay is set aside in a savings account. When and if you cancel the policy, you are entitled to the accumulated savings, which is known as the **cash value**. Whole life policies are popular because they provide both a death benefit and a savings component. You can also borrow from your cash value if necessary, although you must pay interest on the loan. Cash value policies may make sense for people who intend to keep the policies for the long term or for people who want a more structured way to save. However, the Consumer Federation of America Insurance Group suggests that you explore other savings and investment strategies before investing your money in a permanent policy.

Teaching Activity Divide students into groups of three and assign a different type of term or whole life insurance to each group. Groups are to research their assigned insurance and present their findings to the class.

The premium on a term insurance policy will increase each time you renew your insurance. In contrast, whole life policies have higher annual premiums at first, but the payment amount remains the same for the rest of your life. Several types of whole life policies have been developed to meet the needs of different customers. These include the limited payment policy, the variable life policy, the adjustable life policy, and universal life insurance.

Limited Payment Policy Limited payment policies charge premiums for only a certain length of time, usually 20 or 30 years or until the insured reaches a certain age. At the end of this time, the policy is "paid up" and the policyholder remains insured for life. When the policyholder dies, the beneficiary receives the full death benefit. The annual premiums are higher for limited payment policies because the premiums have to be paid within a shorter period of time.

As You Read

QUESTION

What are the risks and benefits associated with variable life insurance?

Question Answer Benefits include: fixed payments; possibility of increasing cash value through stock, bond, or money markets. Risks include: drop in cash value if stock, bond, or money markets crash.

Critical Thinking Have the students write brief essays discussing why age would impact the purchase price of whole life insurance; they should also address whether age affects term life insurance and why or why not.

Extension Have students interview an insurance salesperson and ask about the advantages and disadvantages of whole life insurance.

Variable Life Policy With a variable life policy, premium payments are fixed. As with a cash value policy, part of the premium is placed into a separate account; this money is invested in a stock, bond, or money market fund. The death benefit is guaranteed, but the cash value of the benefit can vary considerably according to the ups and downs of the stock market. Your death benefit can also increase if the earnings of that separate fund increase.

Adjustable Life Policy An adjustable life policy allows you to change your coverage as your needs change. For example, if you want to increase or decrease your death benefit, you can change either the premium payments or the period of coverage.

Universal Life Universal life insurance is essentially a term policy with a cash value. Part of your premium goes into an investment account that grows and earns interest. You are able to borrow or withdraw your cash value.

Other Types of Life Insurance Policies

Other types of life insurance policies include group life insurance, credit life insurance, and endowment life insurance.

Group Life Insurance Group life insurance is a variation of term insurance. It covers a large number of people under a single policy. The people included in the group do not need medical examinations to get coverage. Group insurance is usually offered by employers, who pay part or all of the costs for their employees. It may also be offered by professional organizations, which allow members to obtain coverage. However, it can be more expensive than similar term policies.

Credit Life Insurance Credit life insurance pays off debts, such as auto loans or mortgages, in the event that you die before they are paid in full. These types of policies are not the best buy for the protection they offer. Decreasing term insurance is a better option.

Endowment Life Insurance **Endowment** is life insurance that provides coverage for a specific period of time and pays a sum of money to the policyholder if he or she is living at the end of the endowment period. If the policyholder dies before that time, the beneficiary receives the money.

Key Provisions in a Life Insurance Policy

Why should you consider adding provisions to your life insurance policy?

Study the provisions in your policy carefully and be sure to update the necessary information as changes in your life occur. The following features are the most common provisions found in life insurance policies.

Document Detective

Learn to identify and understand the standard financial documents you will use in the real world.

See the Teacher Manual for answers.

Investigate: A Life Insurance Policy Statement

A life insurance policy statement contains the following information:

- Policy identification number
- Name of insured
- Death benefit amount
- Cash value
- Cost of the premium

Your Motive: If a person who holds a life insurance policy dies, the people who depended upon that policyholder can be protected from financial losses by the life insurance policy. By obtaining a life insurance policy, you are ensuring that your loved ones, who are your beneficiaries, will not be stuck with your debts.

GENERAL HOME LIFE

Policy Anniversary Statement

Juan Ramirez
21 First Street
Smithville, Florida 55523

Policy number:	2–615–879
Date prepared:	May 18, 20--
Insured:	Juan Ramirez
Plan name:	Whole Life
Face amount:	$36,364
Premium:	$41.87 monthly
Issued:	June 23, 2003
Paid to:	June 23, 2016

This policy will provide the following benefits up to June 23, 2016, assuming premiums are paid to that date and no other changes occur.

	DEATH BENEFIT	CASH VALUE
Basic policy	$36,364.00	$4,253
Paid-up additions	$81.39	$7.82
Option term	$63,554.61	0.00
TOTAL	**$100,000.00**	**$4,260.82**

Key Points: A life insurance policy provides a predetermined payment that the insurance company will make in the event of the death of the policy owner. This amount is called the death benefit. In addition, the policy also accumulates a cash value over time as the holder of the policy pays premiums. If the owner chooses to cancel the policy before death, he or she will receive the policy's cash value.

Find the Solutions

1. What is the yearly cost of this policy?
2. When was this policy issued or started?
3. How much will the policy pay upon Juan's death?
4. When does Juan's insurance coverage expire?
5. If Juan decides to cancel this policy, how much will the insurance company pay him?

Beneficiary Designation

You decide who receives the benefits of your life insurance policy. The beneficiary could be your spouse, your child, or your business partner, for example. You can also name *contingent beneficiaries*, those who will receive the money if your primary beneficiary dies before or at the same time as you do. You will need to update your list of beneficiaries as your needs change.

Incontestability Clause

The incontestability clause says that the insurer cannot cancel the policy if it has been in force for a specified period, usually two years. After that time the policy is considered valid during the lifetime of the insured. The incontestability clause protects the beneficiaries from financial loss in the event that the insurance company refuses to meet the terms of the policy.

Critical Thinking Ask the students why they think the suicide clause exists. Do they think it puts undue hardship on the survivors? Then ask what they think about the incontestability clause, especially that it holds even if the policy was gained by fraud. Pose these questions in open discussion.

Suicide Clause

Many insurance policies state that in the first two years of coverage, beneficiaries of someone who dies by suicide receive only the amount of the premiums paid. After two years from the date of death, beneficiaries may receive the full value of death benefits. However, some insurance policies will not provide benefits at all if a policyholder dies by suicide.

Riders to Life Insurance Policies

An insurance company can change the conditions of an insurance policy by adding a rider to it. A rider is a document attached to a policy that changes its terms by adding or excluding specified conditions or altering its benefits. Examples of riders include a waiver of premium disability benefit, an accidental death benefit, and a guaranteed insurability option.

Discussion Discuss with the class why they think insurance companies require physical exams. Does it imply that people with certain illnesses cannot be insured? Do they think this is fair?

Waiver of Premium Disability Benefit One type of rider is a waiver of premium disability benefit. This clause allows a policyholder to stop paying premiums if he or she is totally and permanently disabled before reaching a certain age, usually 60. The insurance company will continue to pay the premiums at its own expense so that the policy remains in force.

Accidental Death Benefit Another typical rider to life insurance policies is an accidental death benefit, sometimes called *double indemnity*. Double indemnity pays twice the value of the policy if the insured is killed in an accident. Again, the accident must occur before a certain age, generally 60 or 65. Experts counsel against adding this rider to your coverage. The benefit is expensive, and your chances of dying in an accident are slim.

Guaranteed Insurability Option A third important rider is a guaranteed insurability option. This rider allows you to buy a specified additional amount of life insurance at certain intervals without undergoing medical exams. This is a good option for people who anticipate needing more life insurance in the future.

Cost of Living Protection This special rider is designed to help prevent inflation from eroding, or reducing, the purchasing power of the protection that your policy provides. A *loss, reduction,* or *erosion of purchasing power* refers to the effect that inflation has on a fixed amount of money. As inflation increases the costs of goods and services, that fixed amount of money will not buy as much in the future as it does today.

After You Read

REACT

Using the information provided in this chapter, what insurance plans would you choose to meet both your health and financial needs?

React Answer Accept all reasonable answers that show an understanding of the concepts.

Insurance Needs

Before you buy any type of insurance, you should always consider a number of factors, such as your source of income, financial responsibilities, savings, and net worth. As your life situation and goals change, you need to regularly evaluate your insurance needs to determine if you have the right kind of coverage to support your personal financial plan.

Section 14.4 Assessment

See the Teacher Manual for answers.

QUICK CHECK

1. What is the purpose of life insurance?
2. What are the differences between term and whole life insurance?
3. What are the key provisions in a life insurance policy?

THINK CRITICALLY

4. "Term insurance is often the best value for most consumers." Do you agree or disagree with this statement? Support your argument.

USE MATH SKILLS

5. **Life Expectancy** Review the life expectancy tables in Figure 14.2 on page 465.

   Present Show the life expectancy at various ages for both genders on a line graph. Add number of years lived to number of years expected to remain. For example, at age 50, life expectancy for males and females is 80 years (50 + 30 = 80). What trends do you notice in your line graph?

SOLVE MONEY PROBLEMS

6. **Life Insurance Comparisons** Jon is a 27-year-old single man with no children. He has a younger sister who has a developmental disability. Both his parents are living, though neither parent is in good health. Jon has an auto loan, a $50,000 mortgage on his condominium, and no consumer debt.

   Analyze Is Jon a good candidate for life insurance? If so, what kind and how much life insurance should he buy? In a small group, discuss Jon's situation and his needs to determine his ideal life insurance policy.

Chapter 14 Review & Activities

See the Teacher Manual for answers.

CHAPTER SUMMARY

- Health insurance is important for financial planning because it can help protect against the financial burden of illness or injury.
- Health insurance policies have certain similarities but can differ in terms of reimbursement versus indemnity, internal limits versus aggregate limits, deductibles and coinsurance, and out-of-pocket limits.
- Private health care plans are offered by private insurance companies, hospital and medical service plans, health maintenance organizations, preferred provider organizations, home health care agencies, and employer self-funded health plans. Government health care programs are Medicare and Medicaid.
- Disability insurance provides regular cash income for people who are unable to work due to pregnancy, a non-work-related accident, or illness.
- Sources of disability income are workers' compensation, an employer, Social Security, and private disability insurance.
- Types of life insurance policies include term insurance, whole life insurance, group life insurance, credit life insurance, and endowment life insurance.
- The key provisions in a life insurance policy include naming a beneficiary, an incontestability clause, a suicide clause, and policy riders.

Communicating Key Terms

Choose your ideal benefits package for a job and include health and life insurance. Using the terms below, write instructions for what insurance you want your employer to buy for you.

- health insurance
- coinsurance
- stop-loss
- co-payment
- Blue Cross
- Blue Shield
- managed care
- health maintenance organization (HMO)
- preferred provider organization (PPO)
- point-of-service (POS) plan
- Medicare
- Medicaid
- disability income insurance
- beneficiary (insurance)
- term insurance
- whole life insurance
- cash value
- endowment

Reviewing Key Concepts

1. **Explain** how increasing co-payments and deductibles affects premium rates.
2. **Discuss** basic health insurance coverage and major medical expense insurance.
3. **Compare** government health care programs and those offered by private companies.
4. **Explain** the importance of disability insurance in financial planning.
5. **Describe** the advantages of worker's compensation.
6. **Identify** the types of term and whole life insurance.
7. **Explain** the key provisions of life insurance.

See the Teacher Manual for answers.

ACADEMIC SKILLS

Social Studies Hector Ramirez and Walter Chan are both shopping for life insurance policies. Hector and his wife just bought a car. Walter, his wife, and four children just moved into a new $150,000 home. Hector and Walter have narrowed their choices to either decreasing term insurance or credit life insurance.

Write About It Which type of insurance should each person choose? Provide a list of reasons for each of your choices.

YOUR FINANCIAL FIGURES

Heath Insurance Premiums Because you are self-employed, you started buying individual health insurance nine years ago at a cost of $579 per quarter. Now the quarterly premium is $806.

1. **Calculate** what your annual premium was nine years ago and what it is today. What was the percentage increase over those nine years?
2. **Compute** by using an Internet search engine to locate information on health insurance premiums and coverage from five insurance companies. Compare and contrast the offers using spreadsheet software.

REAL-WORLD Application

Connect with Economics and Law Many companies that once sold just life insurance have "reinvented" themselves as financial services companies. Many of these firms promote themselves as "one-stop shops" for all your financial service needs.

1. **Research** Access the Web site of your state's insurance regulatory agency and find out what requirements insurance agents must meet to be able to sell other financial products, such as mutual funds.
2. **Think Critically** What are the pros and cons of buying financial products from an insurance company versus a stockbroker?

Internet CONNECTION

Buying Insurance on the Internet You may not need to purchase life insurance right now, but it is a good idea to know how much a policy will cost so that you will be able to plan your finances accordingly.

@ **Log On** Use an Internet search engine to find the Web sites of three insurance companies. Obtain quotes for a term life insurance policy from the three companies. Answer the following questions:

1. What forms of term life insurance do these companies offer?
2. Choose one form of term life insurance offered by all three companies and determine which company's policy you feel is the best deal for you. Explain why you would choose that policy.

BusinessWeek ONLINE

Newsclip: More Choices A health savings account (HSA) is a plan that allows employees to save for medical expenses in a tax-free account.

@ **Log On** Go to finance07.glencoe.com and open Chapter 14. Learn more about HSAs. Write a paragraph about how HSAs might affect your future. Would you sign up for an HSA?

WHAT'S YOUR FINANCIAL ID?

INSURANCE FACTS AND FICTION

Insurance may not be a big issue for you now, but when you are no longer covered under your parents' or guardian's policies or you start full-time employment, you will need to know your options. Here is an opportunity to test your knowledge. Write your answers to the following questions on a separate sheet of paper.

1. Health insurance is only available as a benefit from an employer.

True　　False (circled)

2. You can continue your health insurance even if you leave a job.

True (circled)　　False

3. A co-payment is the small amount you pay for a doctor's visit or a prescription.

True (circled)　　False

4. In general the younger you are, the less expensive life insurance is.

True (circled)　　False

5. Life insurance can also be used as an investment for retirement.

True (circled)　　False

6. Life insurance companies can cancel policies if you develop a serious illness after you are insured.

True　　False (circled)

7. You can collect life insurance benefits before you die.

True (circled)　　False

8. The amount of disability insurance you can buy is based on a percentage of your total income.

True (circled)　　False

Your Financial Portfolio

Comparing Life Insurance

Sean Richards is investigating the cost of life insurance. He is 28 years old, married, and has two children. Sean contacted two reputable insurance companies and based his comparison on $100,000 worth of insurance.

Type of Policy	Company A	Company B
20-year decreasing term insurance $100,000		
Monthly premium	$14.00	$8.25
Total premiums for 20 years	$3,360.00	$1,980.00
Cash value in 20 years	none	none
Whole life insurance (limited payment) $100,000		
Monthly premium	$82.00	$62.60
Total premiums for 20 years	$19,280.00	$15,024.00
Cash value in 20 years	$25,000.00	$21,243.00

Sean chose the 20-year decreasing term insurance because of the low cost, even though he cannot convert it into cash at a future date. He purchased his policy with Company B.

Compare

On a separate sheet of paper, follow Sean's chart to compare life insurance rates. Using the Internet, or by visiting, calling, or writing, get quotes from two different insurance companies. Base the quote on (1) a 20-year decreasing term insurance policy for $100,000 and (2) a whole life (limited payment) insurance policy for $100,000. Use your own age.

Accept all reasonable answers that show student effort and an understanding of the concept.

CHAPTER 15

Retirement and Estate Planning

$ What You'll Learn

When you have completed this chapter, you will be able to:

Section 15.1
- Explain the importance of retirement planning.
- Identify retirement living costs and housing needs.

Section 15.2
- Describe the role of Social Security in planning for retirement.
- Discuss the benefits offered by employer pension plans.
- Explain various personal retirement plans.

Section 15.3
- Identify various types of wills.
- Discuss several types of trusts.
- Describe common characteristics of estates.
- Identify the types of taxes that affect estates.

Reading Strategies

To get the most out of your reading:

Predict what you will learn in this chapter.
Relate what you read to your own life.
Question what you are reading to be sure you understand.
React to what you have read.

In the **Real** World . . .

Every summer, Shelly Garfield visits her grandparents, who live in a retirement community designed with swimming pools and recreation rooms. Her grandparents decided to move there after Shelly's grandmother broke her hip. They liked the idea of having a full medical staff on duty. Shelly's grandparents had saved enough money so they could afford to move there. As the elderly population increases, Social Security, Medicare, and pensions will be stretched, and may not cover many retirees' total expenses. Shelly is a high school senior, but it is not too early for her to start thinking about retirement. By estimating retirement costs and housing needs now, she can save for retirement on her own terms.

As You Read *Consider why it is wise to begin a retirement plan early.*

Lesson Plan See the Teacher Manual for the Chapter 15 planning guide and lesson plan.

ASK STANDARD & POOR'S

Will Power

Q: My parents do not have a lot of money, so is it really that important for them to write up a will?

A: Even if your parents do not have a lot of money, they should have a will. If they die without a will, their state of residence will step in and control how their estate is distributed. It costs somewhere between $200 and $350 to have an attorney draft a will. The peace of mind it will provide your parents will be worth the cost.

Ask Yourself If you had to write up a will right now, how would you want your possessions and money distributed?

@ Go to **finance07.glencoe.com** to complete the Standard & Poor's Financial Focus activity.

Section 15.1

Focus on Reading

Read to Learn

- How to explain the importance of retirement planning.
- How to identify retirement living costs and housing needs.

Main Idea

Estimating your retirement living costs and housing needs will enable you to save or invest enough money to live comfortably during retirement.

Key Term

- assisted-living facility (ALF)

Before You Read

PREDICT

When do you think you should begin planning for your retirement?

Springboard Ask the students if they know people who are retired—grandparents, friends, etc. What kinds of lifestyles do they have? Do you know how they planned for their retirement?

Retirement Planning

Planning for Retirement

What factors should you consider when planning for retirement?

A recent poll from Harris Interactive reported that 95 percent of people ages 55 to 64 years old plan to do at least some work after they have retired. Another survey reported that future retirees expected to continue to learn, try news things, and pursue new hobbies and interests. Someday, when you retire, you too may desire an active life.

Your retirement years may seem a long way off right now. You are still in high school, and after you graduate, you will probably work for many years. However, it is never too early to start planning for retirement. Planning can help you cope with sudden changes that may occur in your life, and it can give you a sense of control over your future. Planning can also help make the retirement years more comfortable.

If you have not done any research on the subject of retirement, you may have some misconceptions about the "golden years." Here are some myths about retirement:

- You have plenty of time to start saving for retirement.
- Saving a small amount of money will not help.
- You will spend less money when you retire.
- Your retirement will last about 15 years.
- You can depend on Social Security and a company pension plan to pay your basic living expenses.
- Your pension benefits will increase to keep pace with inflation.
- Your employer's health insurance plan and Medicare will cover all your medical expenses.

Some of these statements may have been true in the past, but they are no longer true today. You may live for many years after you retire. If you want your retirement to be a happy and comfortable time of your life, you will need enough money to suit your lifestyle. That is why you should start planning and saving as early as possible. It is never too late to start saving for retirement, but the sooner you start, the better off you will be.

Suppose that you want to have at least $1 million when you retire at age 65. If you start saving at age 25, you can meet that goal by putting about $127 per month into investment funds that grow at a rate of about 11 percent each year. If you wait to begin saving until age 50, the monthly amount to achieve that goal skyrockets to $2,244.

Setting Long-Range Goals

As you think about your retirement years, consider your long-range goals. What does retirement mean to you? Maybe it will be a time to stop working and to relax. Perhaps you imagine traveling the world, developing a hobby, or starting a second career. Ask yourself: Where do you want to live after you retire? What type of lifestyle would you like to have? Then analyze your current financial situation to determine what you need to do to reach your long-range goals.

As You Read

RELATE

Imagine what you would like to do when you retire. What are three financial goals for that time?

Motivating Students Ask the students to take a giant imaginative leap to try to picture themselves at 65. Ask how they would like to live, if they want to be still working or if they would rather be traveling, playing golf, and riding motorcycles. Tell them planning when they are young will help them reach their goals.

Conducting a Financial Analysis

The checklist in **Figure 15.1** is an example of how you might analyze your financial assets and liabilities. As you learned in Chapter 3, an asset is any item of value that you own, including cash, property, personal possessions, and investments. This includes cash in checking and savings accounts, a house, a car, a television, and so on. It also includes the current value of any stocks, bonds, other investments, life insurance policies, and pension funds.

Your liabilities are the debts you owe, including the balance on an automobile loan, credit card balances, other loans, and unpaid taxes. If you subtract your liabilities from your assets, you get your net worth. Ideally, your net worth should increase each year.

Figure 15.1 **Assets, Liabilities, and Net Worth**

Assets:	
Cash:	
Checking account	$ 800
Savings account	4,500
Investments:	
U.S. Savings Bonds (current cash-in value)	5,000
Stocks, mutual funds	4,500
Life insurance:	
Cash value, accumulated dividends	10,000
Company pension rights:	
Accrued pension benefit	20,000
Property:	
House (resale value)	50,000
Furniture and appliances	8,000
Collections and jewelry	2,000
Automobile	3,000
Other:	
Loan to brother	1,000
Gross assets	$108,800

Liabilities:	
Current unpaid bills	$ 600
Home mortgage (remaining balance)	9,700
Auto loan	1,200
Property taxes	1,100
Home improvement loan	3,700
Total liabilities	$16,300

Net worth:

Assets	–	Liabilities	=	Net Worth
$108,800	–	$16,300	=	$92,500

Calculating Net Worth Assets are everything that you own, while liabilities are everything you owe.

How can you determine your net worth?

Caption Answer Your assets minus your liabilities equal your net worth.

▲ **LIVING THE GOOD LIFE** When you retire you may not be able to afford to take lavish vacations or buy many expensive items. *What are some of the decisions you will have to make now to ensure a comfortable retirement?* **Caption Answer** You will have to make decisions about the trade-offs between spending and saving: Spend less, save more, or spend now and do not think about tomorrow.

Critical Thinking Have the students answer this question: "How can a teenager plan for retirement, so far in the future?" Then have the students explain what retirement means to them now. Students are to respond in a well-organized short essay.

As You Read

QUESTION

Does planning for your retirement alter today's investment strategies?

Question Answer Planning can mean that you keep a foundation of conservative investments. If riskier investments fail, you will have a nest egg.

Reviewing Assets

Review your assets on a regular basis. You may need to make adjustments in your saving, spending, and investments to stay on track with your goal. As you review your assets, consider the following factors: housing, life insurance, savings, and investments. Each asset will have an important effect on your retirement income.

Housing A house can be your most valuable asset. However, if you buy a home with large mortgage payments, you may be unable to save money for retirement. In that case, you might consider buying a smaller, less expensive place to live. A smaller house is usually easier and less expensive to maintain. You can use the money you save by having lower payments to increase your retirement fund.

Life Insurance At some point in the future, you might buy life insurance to provide for your loved ones. If you have children, life insurance can provide financial support in case you die while they are still young. As you near retirement, though, your children will probably be self-sufficient. When that time comes, you might reduce your premium payments by decreasing your life insurance coverage. This would give you extra money for living expenses or investments.

Other Investments When you review your assets, also evaluate any other investments you have. When you originally chose those investments, you may have been more interested in making your money grow over time than in getting a quick return. When you are ready to retire, you may want to use the income from those investments to cover living expenses.

Teaching Activity Draw students' attention to Figure 15.2. Have students create a similar graph showing their spending at age 20 or 21, assuming themselves to be completely self-supporting. Then have students compare the two graphs on a T-page to see what areas show the most change. Finally, they are to write a paragraph stating their conclusions.

Retirement Living Expenses

What living expenses should you consider when planning for retirement?

When planning for retirement, estimate how much money you will need to live comfortably during your retirement years. You cannot predict exactly how much money you will need, but you can estimate the expense of your basic needs. To do this, think about how your spending patterns and living situation might change.

For example, when you are retired, you may spend more money on recreation, health insurance, and medical care than you will as a young adult. At the same time, you may spend less money on transportation and clothing. Your federal income taxes may be lower as well. Also, some income from various retirement plans may be taxed at a lower rate or not at all. **Figure 15.2** provides an example of retirement expenses.

Figure 15.2 Expenses for Older Households (65+ years)

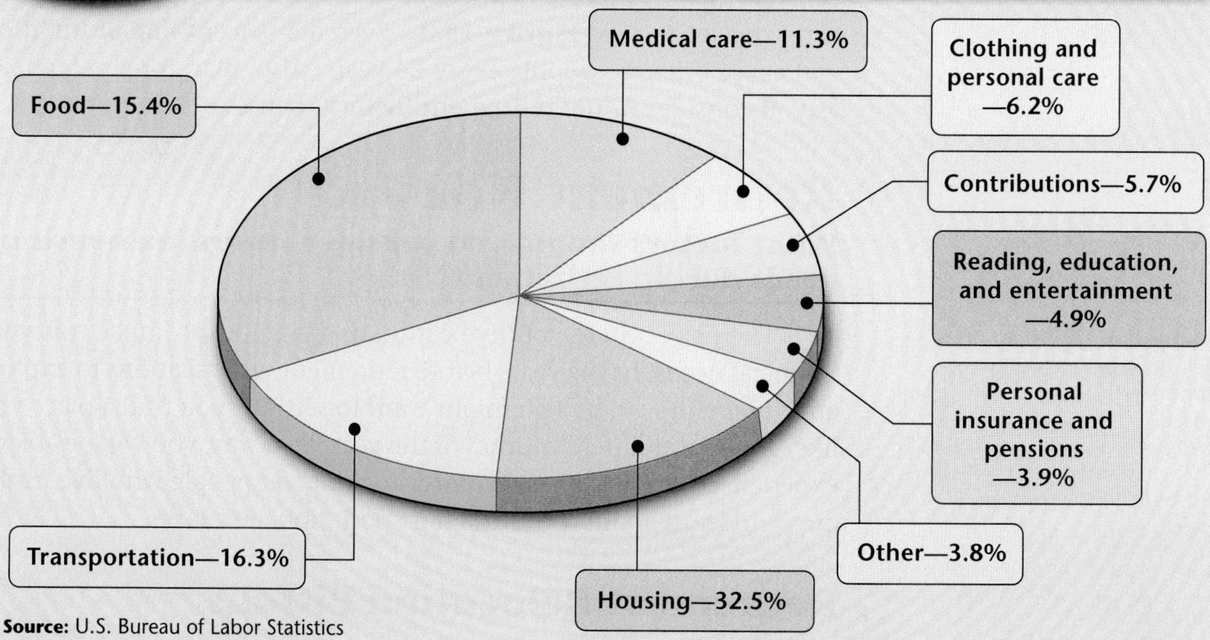

Source: U.S. Bureau of Labor Statistics

Spending More or Less? The amount of money you spend during retirement will vary, depending on many different factors.

Calculate how much money an older household with an annual income of $16,000 spends on food each year.

Caption Answer $2,464 ($16,000 × .154 = $2,464)

Figure 15.3 Inflation Over Time

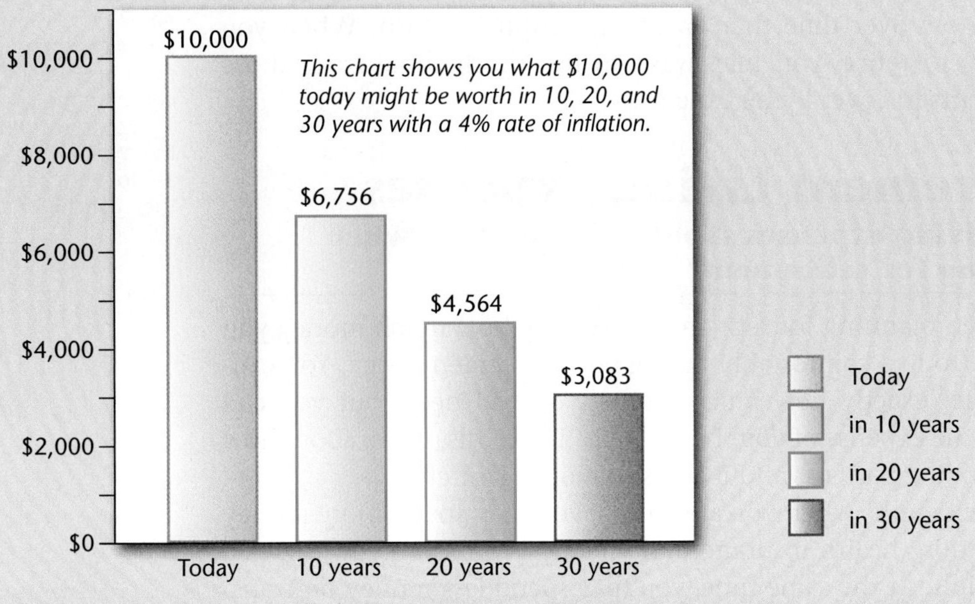

Rising Prices The prices of goods and services rarely remain the same for any period of time because of inflation.

How much will $10,000 be worth in 30 years, assuming a 4 percent rate of inflation? What can you do to counteract the effects of inflation?

Caption Answer $3,083; Choose investments that outpace inflation.

Remember to take inflation into account. Estimate high when calculating how much the prices of goods and services will rise by the time you retire. (See **Figure 15.3.**) Even a 3 percent rate of inflation will cause prices to double every 24 years. Also, plan for emergencies as you consider future retirement living expenses.

Retirement Housing

What factors should you consider regarding housing needs during retirement?

Discussion Ask students if their grandparents or great-grandparents moved when they retired. Discuss how they may have decided where to live and what they may have gained and/or lost in making their choice.

The place where you live can have a significant impact on your financial needs. In the years before retirement, use vacations to explore areas and cities where you might want to settle. If you find a place you like, go there at different times of the year. That way, you will be able to experience the climate and environment. Meet people who live in the area and learn about activities, transportation, and taxes.

Retirement Relocation Pitfalls

Consider the downside of moving to a new location. People sometimes find themselves stuck in a place they really do not like. Some retirees find they miss their children, grandchildren, and friends and relatives left behind. Other retired people move to the location of their dreams and discover they have made a mistake financially.

Researching Locations Here are some tips from specialists on how to research taxes and other costs before moving to a new area:

- Contact the local chamber of commerce for details on area property taxes and the local economy.
- Contact the state tax department to research income, sales, inheritance taxes, and exemptions for retirees.
- Read the Sunday edition of the local newspaper of the town or city you are considering.
- Check with local utility companies to estimate energy costs.
- Visit the area in different seasons and talk to local residents about the cost of living there.
- If you plan to buy a home, take time and rent a home first.

Critical Thinking Have the students assess the list of six things one can do to avoid retirement pitfalls. Have them write down how each item on the list will help and what someone would gain from doing this?

Types of Housing

Even if you do not move to a new location, housing needs may change during retirement. Many retirees want a home that is easy and inexpensive to maintain, such as a smaller house, a condominium, or an apartment. Having access to public transportation, stores, and recreation areas is also important. **Figure 15.4** presents several housing options.

Careers in Finance

ESTATE ADMINISTRATOR

Paul Francisco
Choate, Hall & Stewart

Paul has very strong organizational and communication skills, which are essential in his work as an estate administrator. Under the direction of the attorney responsible for estate administration, Paul handles all phases of estate execution. He determines and informs the parties of procedural and tax deadlines and ensures compliance with the deadlines. He also calculates debts, expenses, taxes, and cash needs. In his role as an estate administrator, Paul may need to develop and implement steps to uncover and reconcile conflicts between beneficiaries or family members.

SKILLS: Writing, communication, organizational, problem-solving, analytical, and multitasking skills

PERSONAL TRAITS: Discreet, good judgment, likes working with people and numbers, tactful, and quick thinking

EDUCATION: High school diploma or equivalent; bachelor's degree in finance or related field or equivalent work experience

ANALYZE How might planning for retirement affect your will?
See the Teacher Manual for answer.

@ To learn more about career paths for estate administrators, visit **finance07.glencoe.com**.

Figure 15.4 Retirement Housing Options

Housing options for retirement are based on personal, financial, and medical factors. The goal of most retirees is to have comfortable and affordable housing that meets their particular needs.

1 **Most retired people** decide to remain where they are and continue living in their own homes.

2 **Living with grown children** and young grandchildren can be a choice for some elderly retired people and their families.

3 **For retired people with disabilities,** a universal design home built with special features, such as extra-wide doors, lower appliances, and automatic faucets, can be both appealing and practical. These homes help people with disabilities to maintain their independence.

A great majority of people prefer to grow old in their own homes in their own communities. Recognizing this trend, building suppliers offer everything from lever door handles to faucets that turn on automatically when you put your hand beneath the spout. Remodeling to accommodate aging homeowners is creating a demand for these products. In addition, contractors are building universal design homes from scratch that can accommodate people who use wheelchairs and walkers or those who simply want more convenience.

Many elderly people move into assisted-living facilities during their retirement years. An **assisted-living facility (ALF)** is a residence complex that provides personal and medical services for the elderly. Assisted-living facilities offer everything from minimal services to full, continuous nursing care. They may vary greatly in quality, but ALFs are increasingly popular with elderly retirees, some of whom are no longer able to live alone and care for themselves.

Extension Take the students on a tour of a local assisted-living facility.

Section 15.1 Assessment

See the Teacher Manual for answers.

QUICK CHECK

1. What are several reasons that early retirement planning is important?
2. What factors should you consider when estimating your retirement living expenses?
3. What are some features and benefits of an assisted-living facility?

THINK CRITICALLY

4. Imagine that you are 20 years away from retirement and you are thinking of spending a large portion of your income to purchase an expensive home. Discuss the advantages and disadvantages of this plan.

USE COMMUNICATION SKILLS

5. **Free at Last!** Enrique and his wife, Maribel, have both been working at the same company for almost 35 years and are nearing retirement. They have been looking forward to the time when they will be free to do almost anything they want. They already have a long list of places they would like to visit, things they would like to do, and ways they would like to spend their time after they retire.

Present Imagine the type of life you would like to have when you retire. Combine pictures and words to create a collage that expresses your thoughts and feelings about your retirement dreams.

SOLVE MONEY PROBLEMS

6. **Changing Lifestyles** Jeff and Maureen McBride have been retired for a couple of years. Although their income is lower than when they were working, they continue to live as they did before retirement. They have a three-bedroom house in New Jersey. Twice a year, they travel to California to visit their children and grandchildren. Unfortunately, they now find themselves in a financial pinch. They need to cut back on their expenses and have a plan to live more economically without giving up many of the activities they enjoy.

Analyze Help Jeff and Maureen by discussing various options they might have for saving money.

Section 15.2

Focus on Reading

Read to Learn

- How to describe the role of Social Security in planning for retirement.
- How to discuss the benefits offered by employer pension plans.
- How to explain various personal retirement plans.

Main Idea

Various types of retirement plans are suited to different financial situations and personal needs.

Key Terms

- defined-contribution plan
- 401(k) plan
- vesting
- defined-benefit plan
- individual retirement account (IRA)
- Keogh plan
- annuity (insurance)
- heirs

Before You Read

PREDICT

Besides Social Security, what other retirement plans might be available?

Springboard Some people believe Social Security will not be available when this generation retires. Ask your students to respond to this.

Planning Retirement Income

Public Pension Plans

Who receives benefits under Social Security?

You learned in Chapter 2 that a pension plan is a retirement plan that is funded, at least in part, by an employer. Public pension plans are established by states and municipalities. Social Security is a public pension plan established by the United States government in 1935. The government agency that manages the program is called the Social Security Administration.

Social Security

Social Security is an important source of retirement income for many Americans. The program covers 97 percent of all workers, and almost one out of every six Americans currently collects some form of Social Security benefit. Social Security is a package of protection that provides benefits to retirees, survivors, and disabled persons. You should not rely on Social Security to cover all of your retirement expenses. Social Security was not designed to provide 100 percent of retirement income. In addition, current and future revisions to the program may reduce retirement benefits in years to come.

Who Is Eligible The amount of Social Security retirement benefits you receive is based on your earnings over the years. The more you earn, the greater your benefits will be, up to a maximum amount.

Each year the Social Security Administration will send you a history of your earnings and an estimate of your future monthly benefits. The statement includes an estimate, in today's dollars, of how much you would get each month if you retired at different ages. For example, your statement might list benefits for retirement at age 62, 67, and 70, based on the year you were born, your earnings to date, and your projected future earnings.

To qualify for retirement benefits, you must earn a certain number of credits. These credits are based on the length of time you work and pay Social Security tax, or contributions, on your earnings. Your credits are calculated on a quarterly basis. The number of quarters needed to qualify depends on your year of birth. For example, people born after 1928 need at least 40 quarters to qualify for benefits.

Dependent Eligibility Certain dependents of a worker may also receive benefits under the Social Security program. They include a spouse age 62 or older; unmarried children under 18 (or under 19 if they are full-time students no higher than grade 12); and unmarried individuals with disabilities aged 18 or older. Widows and widowers can receive Social Security benefits before age 62.

Social Security Retirement Benefits Most people can begin collecting Social Security retirement benefits at age 62. However, the monthly amount at age 62 is less than it would be if the person waited until full retirement age. This initial amount becomes the permanent base amount.

In the past people could receive full retirement benefits at age 65. However, the full retirement age is being increased in gradual steps. For people born in 1960 and later, the full retirement age is 67. If you postpone applying for benefits when you are eligible, your monthly payment amount will increase slightly for each year you wait, but only up to age 70.

Social Security Information For more information about Social Security, you can visit the Social Security Web site. It provides access to forms and publications and gives links to other valuable information. To learn more about the taxability of Social Security benefits, contact the Internal Revenue Service (IRS) and ask for Publication 554, Older Americans' Tax Guide, and Publication 915, Social Security and Equivalent Railroad Retirement Benefits. These publications can also be found on the IRS Web site.

▲ **SOCIAL SECURITY BENEFITS** Social Security is an important source of income for many retired people. *How are Social Security benefits calculated?*

As You Read

RELATE

If you currently hold a job, look at a recent paycheck stub. Are you paying into Social Security?

Motivating Students Ask students to imagine how they will pay for their retirement years.

Teaching Activity Divide the students into four teams. Two of the teams will debate this question: Should the federal government be responsible for taking care of its citizens when they retire? The other two teams will debate this question: Should federal government employees be covered by Social Security? All teams are to research and prepare their arguments as well as participate in the debates.

Caption Answer Your Social Security benefit amount is based on past earnings: The more you earned, the more you receive in benefits, up to a certain limit.

Other Public Pension Plans

Besides Social Security, the federal government provides other special retirement plans for federal government workers and railroad employees. These employees are not covered by Social Security. The Veterans Administration provides pensions for survivors of people who died while serving in the armed forces. It also offers disability pensions for eligible veterans. In addition, many state and local governments provide retirement plans for their employees.

Employer Pension Plans

What is one of the benefits of having an employer pension plan?

Another possible source of retirement income is an employer pension plan offered by the company for which you work. With this type of plan, your employer contributes to your retirement benefits, and sometimes you contribute, too. These contributions and their earnings remain tax-deferred until you withdraw them during retirement.

Private employer pension plans vary. If the company you work for offers one, find out what benefits you will receive and when you will become eligible to receive those benefits. Most employer plans are one of two basic types: defined-contribution plans or defined-benefit plans.

Defined-Contribution Plan

A **defined-contribution plan**, sometimes called an individual account plan, is an individual account for each employee. The employer contributes a specific amount to the account annually. This type of retirement plan does not guarantee any particular benefit. When you retire and become eligible for benefits, you receive the total amount of funds (including investment earnings) that is in your account. Several types of defined-contribution plans exist.

Money-Purchase Plans With a money-purchase plan, your employer promises to set aside a certain amount of money for you each year. That amount may be a percentage of your earnings.

Stock Bonus Plans Under a stock bonus plan, your employer's contribution is used to buy stock in the company for you. The stock is held in trust until you retire. Then you can keep your shares or sell them.

Profit-Sharing Plans Under a profit-sharing plan, your employer's contribution depends on the company's profits each year.

401(k) Plans A **401(k) plan**, or salary-reduction plan, is a type of retirement savings plan funded by a portion of your salary that is deducted from your gross paycheck and placed in a special account. Many employers match their employees' 401(k) contributions up to a specific dollar amount or percentage of salary.

TechByte

Calculate Your Benefits It is never too early to start thinking about how you will fund your retirement. One source of retirement income will probably be your Social Security benefits. The Social Security administration will help you calculate how much your Social Security benefits will be. A good way to start planning for your retirement is to make some reasonable guesses about what your yearly earnings will be when you are in your mid-20s.

@ Use the Social Security Administration's special calculator to plug in your best guesses and see how much you could receive upon your retirement through **finance07.glencoe.com**.

Discussion Have the students imagine they have graduated from high school or college and are job hunting. Would an employer-provided 401(k) plan be an attractive benefit? Why or why not?

Teaching Activity Have students research the retirement plan offered to employees of your school system, a local major hospital, and your police department. They should find out the types of plans, how many years it takes before an employee is fully vested, and any other critical information. Then they are to illustrate the results as a recruitment poster for the employer who is offering the best plan.

The funds in 401(k) plans can be invested in stocks, bonds, and mutual funds. As a result, you can accumulate a significant amount of money in this type of account if you begin contributing to it early in your career. In addition, the money that accumulates in your 401(k) plan is tax-deferred, which means that you do not have to pay taxes on it until you withdraw it.

403(b) Plans If you are employed by a tax-exempt institution, such as a hospital or a nonprofit organization, the salary-reduction plan is called a Section 403(b) plan. The funds in this plan are also tax-deferred. The 401(k) and 403(b) plans are known as tax-sheltered annuity (TSA) plans. The amount that can be contributed each year to 401(k) and 403(b) plans is limited by law, as is the amount of contributions to other types of defined-contribution plans.

Vesting Employee contributions to a pension plan belong to you, the employee, regardless of the amount of time that you are with a particular employer. But what happens to the contributions that the employer has made to your account if you change jobs and move to another company? One of the most important aspects of these plans is vesting. **Vesting** is the right of an employee to keep the company's contributions from company-sponsored plans, such as pensions, even if the employee no longer works for that employer. Vesting occurs at different points in time, depending on company policy. After a certain number of years with a company, you become fully vested, or entitled to receive 100 percent of the company's contributions to the plan on your behalf. Under some plans, vesting may occur in stages. For example, you might become eligible to receive 20 percent of your benefits after three years and gain another 20 percent each year until you are fully vested.

$avvy Saver

Making the Most of a 401(k) Plan

1. Begin contributing as soon as your company allows.
2. Contribute the maximum amount.
3. Learn as much as you can about the investment options offered.
4. Review your investments periodically.
5. Make adjustments to your investments as needed.

Defined-Benefit Plan

A **defined-benefit plan** is a retirement plan that specifies the benefits an employee will receive at retirement age, based on total earnings and years on the job. The plan does not specify how much the employer must contribute each year. Instead, your employer's contributions are based on how much money the fund will need for each participant in the plan who retires. If the fund is inadequate, the employer will have to make additional contributions.

Moving to Another Plan

Some pension plans allow "portability," which means that you can carry earned benefits from one pension plan to another when you change jobs. Workers are also protected by the Employee Retirement Income Security Act of 1974 (ERISA), which sets minimum standards for pension plans. Under this act, the federal government insures part of the payments promised by defined-benefit plans.

Research Have students research ERISA and write a paper discussing its history and contents: Was it designed to correct a specific problem or set of problems? How well has it worked? What does it provide?

As You Read

QUESTION

What type of IRA seems more flexible—traditional or Roth?

Question Answer Roth IRA

Personal Retirement Plans

What is the biggest benefit of an IRA?

In addition to public and employer retirement plans, many people choose to set up personal retirement plans. Such plans are especially important to self-employed people and other workers who are not covered by employer pension plans. Among the most popular personal retirement plans are individual retirement accounts (IRAs) and Keogh accounts.

Individual Retirement Accounts

An **individual retirement account (IRA)** is a special account in which a person saves a portion of income for retirement. **Figure 15.5** on page 492 summarizes the various types of IRAs.

Regular IRA A regular IRA, which is a traditional or classic IRA, allows you to make annual contributions until age 70½. In the year 2004, you could contribute up to $3,000 per year. From 2005 to 2007, the limit was set at $4,000. From 2008 and on, you can contribute up to $5,000 per year. Depending on your tax filing status and income, the contribution may be fully or partially tax-deductible. The tax deductibility of a traditional IRA also depends on whether you belong to an employer-provided retirement plan.

Discussion Discuss with students the various types of individual retirement accounts, determining who they are designed for, i.e., on what basis someone would choose one plan over another.

Roth IRA Annual contributions to a Roth IRA are not tax-deductible, but the earnings are tax-free. You may contribute the same amounts as allowed for a regular IRA if you are a single taxpayer with an adjusted gross income (AGI) of less than $95,000. For married couples, the combined AGI must be less than $150,000.

You can continue to make annual contributions to a Roth IRA even after age 70½. If you have a Roth IRA, you can withdraw money from the account without paying taxes or penalities after five years if you are at least 59½ years old or if you are using the money to help buy your first home. You may convert a regular IRA to a Roth IRA. Depending on your situation, one type of account may be better for you than the other.

Simplified Employee Pension (SEP) Plan A Simplified Employee Pension (SEP) plan, also known as a *SEP-IRA,* is an individual retirement account that is ideal for small businesses or for self-employed individuals. For a small-business SEP-IRA, each employee sets up an IRA account at a bank or other financial institution. Then the employer makes an annual contribution up to a maximum set by law. The employees' contributions, which can vary from year to year, are fully tax-deductible, and earnings are tax-deferred. The SEP-IRA for a self-employed individual works much the same way. An individual could contribute up to $42,000 a year in 2005. The limits increase yearly until 2010.

Spousal IRA You can make contributions to a Spousal IRA on behalf of your nonworking spouse if you file a joint tax return. The contributions are the same as for the traditional and Roth IRAs. This contribution may be fully or partially tax-deductible.

Rollover IRA A rollover IRA is a traditional IRA that allows roll over, or transfer of, all or a portion of your taxable distribution from one retirement plan to another IRA without paying taxes on it.

STANDARD & POOR'S

Global Financial Landscape

Standard and Poor's publishes the globally recognized S&P 500® financial index. It also gathers financial statistics, information, and news, and analyzes this data for international businesses, governments, and individuals to help them guide their financial decisions.

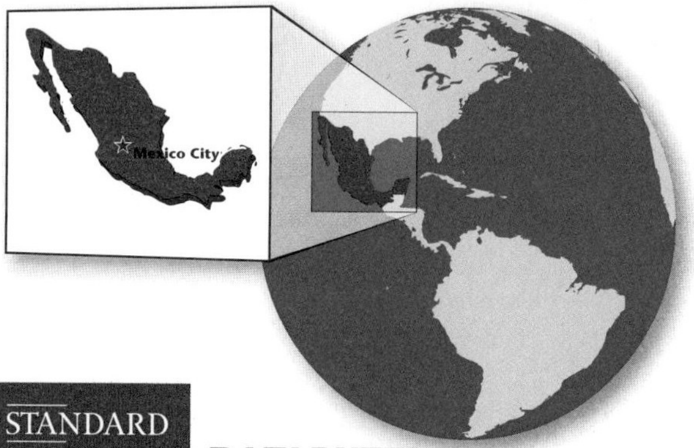

MEXICO

According to the U.S. Embassy, a growing number of American citizens are finding Mexico an attractive place to spend their golden years. Americans are drawn to Mexico's warm climate, easygoing lifestyle, and lower cost of living. Since the average Social Security benefit is only about $1,000 a month, many retirees cannot afford to stay in the United States. In Mexico, however, they can live comfortably. San Miguel is a favorite place for many of the older generation. The city is designated as a national monument and offers culture, fine restaurants, and an easy drive to the warm waters of the Gulf of Mexico.

STANDARD & POOR'S **DATABYTES**

Capital	Mexico City
Population	106,202,903
Languages	Spanish, Mayan, and Nahuatl
Currency	Mexican peso
Gross Domestic Product (GDP)	$1.006 trillion
GDP per capita	$9,600

Industry: Food and beverages, tobacco, chemicals, iron and steel, petroleum, mining, textiles, clothing, motor vehicles, consumer durables, and tourism

Agriculture: Corn, wheat, soybeans, rice, beans, cotton, coffee, fruit, tomatoes, beef, poultry, dairy products, and wood products

Exports: Manufactured goods, oil and oil products, silver, fruits, vegetables, coffee, and cotton

Natural Resources: Petroleum, silver, copper, gold, lead, zinc, natural gas, and timber

Think Globally
What services needed by retirees might be lacking in a foreign country?

See the Teacher Manual for answer.

Figure 15.5 Types of IRAs

Type of IRA	IRA Features
Regular IRA	• Tax-deferred interest and earnings • Annual limit on individual contributions • Limited eligibility for tax-deductible contributions • Contributions do not reduce current taxes
Roth IRA	• Tax-deferred interest and earnings • Annual limit on individual contributions • Withdrawals are tax-free in specific cases • Contributions do not reduce current taxes
Simplified Employee Pension Plan (SEP-IRA)	• "Pay yourself first" payroll reduction contributions • Pre-tax contributions • Tax-deferred interest and earnings
Spousal IRA	• Tax-deferred interest and earnings • Both working spouse and nonworking spouse can contribute up to the annual limit • Limited eligibility for tax-deductible contributions • Contributions do not reduce current taxes
Rollover IRA	• Traditional IRA that accepts rollovers of all or a portion of your taxable distribution from a retirement plan • You can roll over to a Roth IRA
Education IRA	• Tax-deferred interest and earnings • 10% early withdrawal penalty is waived when money is used for higher-education expenses • Annual limit on individual contributions • Contributions do not reduce current taxes

Planning Ahead IRAs can be a good way to save money for retirement.

What are the features of the Education IRA?

Caption Answer Answer includes tax-deferred interest and earnings, no early withdrawal penalty when money is used for higher education expenses, $500 annual limit on individual contributions, and no reduction of current taxes for contributions.

Teaching Activity Divide the class into six groups, and assign one type of IRA to each. Groups are to research their assigned plans to find out when they started and their advantages and disadvantages. Each group is to prepare an illustration of the results and present it to the class.

Education IRA An Education IRA, also known as a *Coverdell Education Savings Account,* is a special IRA with certain restrictions. It allows individuals to contribute up to $2,000 per year toward the education of any individual under age 18. The contributions are not tax-deductible, but they do provide tax-free distributions for education expenses.

Even if you are covered by another type of pension plan, you can make IRA contributions that are not tax-deductible. All of the income your IRA earns will compound, tax-deferred, until you begin making withdrawals. Remember, the biggest benefit of an IRA lies in its tax-deferred earnings growth. (See **Figure 15.6.**)

IRA Withdrawals When you retire, you can withdraw the money from your IRA by one of several methods. You can take out all of the money at one time, but the entire amount will be taxed as income. If you decide to withdraw the money from your IRA in installments, you will have to pay tax only on the amount that you withdraw. You might also place the money that you withdraw in an annuity that guarantees payments over your lifetime. See the discussion on annuities later in this section for further information about this option.

Discussion Draw students' attention to Figure 15.6, saying this should prove to them the advantage of planning early for retirement. Ask if they can think of other advantages; write them on the board and discuss.

Keogh Plans

A **Keogh plan**, which is also an H.R.10 plan or a self-employed retirement plan, is a retirement plan specially designed for self-employed people and their employees. Keogh plans have various restrictions, including limits on the amount of annual tax-deductible contributions you can make. You should get professional tax advice before using this type of personal retirement plan.

Limits on Retirement Plans

When must you begin to withdraw your money?

With the exception of Roth IRAs, you cannot keep money in most tax-deferred retirement plans forever. When you retire, or by age 70½ at the latest, you must begin to receive "minimum lifetime distributions." These are withdrawals from the funds you have accumulated through your plan. The amount of the distributions, or withdrawals, is based on your life expectancy at the time the distributions begin. If you do not withdraw the minimum distributions from a retirement account, the IRS will charge you a penalty.

Figure 15.6 Benefits of Starting a Retirement Plan Early

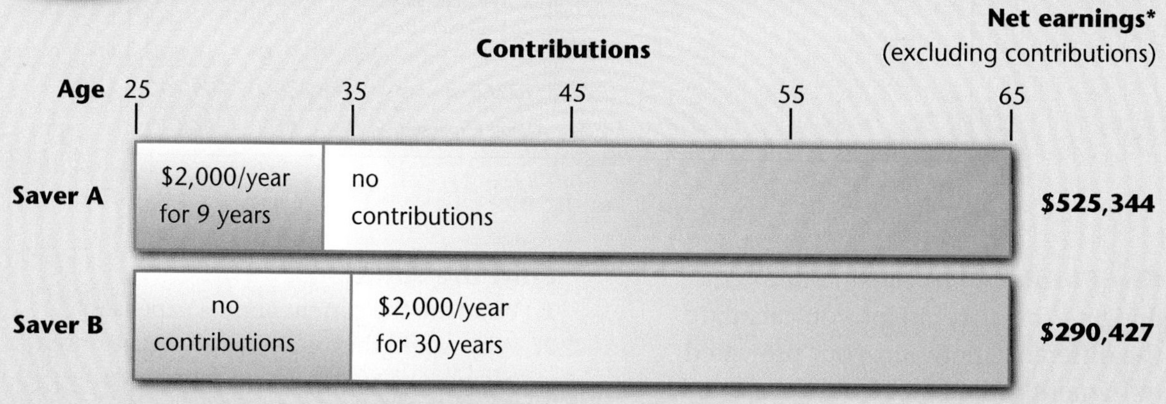

*Assumes 9 percent fixed rate of return, compounded monthly, with no change in the principle.

Start Early If you start investing in them early, tax-deferred investments, such as IRAs, can grow considerably by the time you retire.

In this figure, which person contributed more money to the retirement plan? Which one earned more by age 65? Why?

Caption Answer Saver B contributed more money, but Saver A earned more by age 65 because the contributions had more time to grow.

Document Detective

Learn to identify and understand the standard financial documents you will use in the real world.

See the Teacher Manual for answers.

Investigate: A Projected Retirement Budget Worksheet

A projected retirement budget worksheet contains the following information:

- Your current annual income and projected income
- Your current annual expenses and projected expenses

Your Motive: The best time to plan for your retirement is when you are young. You will need to save money each month during your working career to provide you with enough money to live on when you stop working.

Projected Retirement Budget Worksheet —Robert & Emily Rathcliff

Annual Income	Current	Retirement
Wages	$85,000	$0
Pension	0	12,000
Social Security	0	19,200
Rental income	0	0
IRAs	0	14,000
Annuities	0	5,000
Bond interest	0	0
Stock dividends	0	2,300
Mutual fund dividends	0	3,210
Money market interest	250	0
Other	0	0
Total Income	**$85,250**	**$55,710**

Annual Expenses	Current	Retirement
Mortgage/rent	$27,600	$0
Real estate taxes	4,500	7,500
Homeowner's insurance	1,200	2,000
Income and Social Security taxes	29,750	13,750
Contributions to savings	5,000	1,000
Utilities	450	750
Food	1,000	650
Medical expenses insurance	750	3,500
Life insurance	850	0
Vehicle payments	1,500	750
Vehicle insurance	1,400	800
Vehicle maintenance and gasoline	2,500	1,500
Charitable contributions	1,000	1,000
Gifts	1,500	1,000
Travel/entertainment	5,000	15,000
Loans/credit cards	1,200	500
Other	0	0
Total Expenses	**$85,200**	**$49,700**
Total Income Minus Expenses	**$50**	**$6,010**

Key Points: A Projected Retirement Budget Worksheet helps you calculate the difference between your projected retirement income and your projected expenses. This worksheet will help you determine how much money you will need to save for retirement years.

Find the Solutions

1. What are the current annual expenses?
2. Why would they not list a mortgage or rent payment as an expense in retirement?
3. Why might food and vehicle expenses go down when they retire?
4. Why might the Rathcliffs not have a life insurance expense in retirement?
5. Do they have enough projected income?

Annuities

Why do people purchase annuities in addition to other retirement plans?

What do you do if you have funded your 401(k), 403(b), Keogh, or profit-sharing plans up to the allowable limits and you want to put away more money for retirement? The answer may be an annuity. An **annuity** is a contract purchased from an insurance company that guarantees a future fixed or variable payment to the purchaser for a certain number of years or for life.

You might also want to purchase an annuity with the money you receive from an IRA or company pension. You can buy an annuity to supplement the income you will receive from these other types of retirement plans. You can choose to purchase an annuity that has a single payment or installment payments. You will also need to decide whether you want the insurance company to send the income from your annuity to you immediately or begin sending it to you at a later date. The payments you receive from an annuity are taxed as ordinary income. However, the interest you earn from the annuity accumulates tax-free until payments begin.

Academic Connection

LANGUAGE ARTS

Employer pension plans can be beneficial not only to employees but to employers as well. For example, employers may receive a tax credit for part of the costs of starting up a retirement plan. They may also receive a tax deduction for any plan contributions they make. *Write an essay explaining why a retirement plan is beneficial to employers and how that benefits employees.*

See the Teacher Manual for answer.

Caption Answer Annuities provide supplemental income during retirement. Also, the interest earned is tax-free until payments begin.

◀ **GOLDEN TIME** With continuing revisions in the Social Security system, many people are thinking ahead and making arrangements for supplemental income in their golden years. *What advantage does an annuity offer?*

Extension Ask the students if they have seen senior citizens working at fast-food restaurants, grocery stores, or other retail establishments. Have the students speculate on why they may be working.

Types of Annuities

Annuities may be fixed or variable. Fixed annuities provide a certain amount of income for life. Variable annuities provide payments guaranteed above a minimum amount, depending on the rate of return on your investment. Either way, the rate of return on an annuity is usually tied to overall interest rates.

Immediate Annuities People approaching retirement age can purchase immediate annuities. These annuities provide income payments at once. They are usually purchased with a lump-sum payment. When you are 65, you may no longer need all of your life insurance coverage—especially if you have grown children. You may decide to convert the cash value of your insurance policy into a lump-sum payment for an immediate annuity.

Deferred Annuities With deferred annuities, income payments start at some future date. Meanwhile, interest accumulates on the money you deposit. Younger people often buy such annuities to save money toward retirement. A deferred annuity purchased with a lump-sum payment is known as a *single-premium deferred annuity*. A "premium" is the payment you make. These annuities are popular because of the greater potential for tax-free growth. If you are buying a deferred annuity on an installment basis, you may want one that allows flexible premiums, or payments. That means that your contributions can vary from year to year.

Costs of Annuities

There are various choices regarding the type of annuity and the annuity income it will generate. The costs, fees, and other features of annuities differ from policy to policy, so you should discuss all of the possible options with an insurance agent. Ask about charges, fees, and interest-rate guarantees. Also, be sure to check the financial health of the insurance company that offers the annuity.

Living on Retirement Income

What are some things you can do to stretch retirement income farther?

As you plan for retirement, you will estimate a budget or spending plan. When the time to retire arrives, however, you may find that your expenses are higher than you had expected. If that is the case, you will have to make some adjustments.

First, make sure that you are getting all the income to which you are entitled. Are there other programs or benefits for which you might qualify? You will also need to think about any assets or valuables you might be able to convert to cash or into other sources of income.

Common CENTS

Time to Save
Saving money in a savings or retirement account is the simplest way to build assets for retirement. Starting to save while you are young may even allow early retirement. However, if you have 30 or 40 years until retirement, every year without saving can subtract from one to five years off retirement. *At what age will you want to retire?*

Common Cents Accept all reasonable answers that show student effort and an undestanding of the concepts.

In addition, retirees can re-examine the trade-off between spending and saving. For example, instead of taking an expensive vacation, they can take advantage of free and low-cost recreation opportunities, such as public parks, museums, libraries, and fairs, which are enjoyable options. Retirees can also receive special discounts at movie theaters, restaurants, stores, and more.

Working During Retirement

Retirees can use their skills and time instead of spending money. Some people decide to work part-time after they retire. Some even take new full-time jobs. Many people prefer to keep active and pursue new careers. Work can provide a person with a greater sense of usefulness, involvement, and self-worth. It is also a good source of supplementary retirement income.

▲ **RETIREMENT INCOME** The income needed during retirement can come from various sources. *What are some possible sources of income you might find?*

Caption Answer Social Security, employer retirement plans, IRAs, Keogh plans, annuities, and work

Using Your Nest Egg

When should you take money out of your "nest egg," or savings, during retirement? The answer depends on your financial circumstances, your age, and how much you want to leave to your heirs. Your **heirs** are the people who will have the legal right to your assets when you die. Your savings may be large enough to allow you to live comfortably on just the interest earned by your savings. On the other hand, you may need to make regular withdrawals to help finance your retirement. However, do so with caution.

If you dip into your retirement funds, you should consider: how long your savings will last if you make regular withdrawals? For example, if you have $10,000 in savings that earns 5.5 percent interest, compounded quarterly, you could take out $68 every month for 20 years before reducing those savings to zero. Whatever your situation, you should try to conserve your retirement fund to make it last.

Section 15.2 Assessment

See the Teacher Manual for answers.

QUICK CHECK

1. What are the eligibility requirements to receive Social Security retirement benefits?
2. What is the difference between defined-contribution plans and defined-benefit plans?
3. What is the difference between regular IRAs and Roth IRAs?

THINK CRITICALLY

4. Describe the trade-offs that you would need to consider if you reached retirement age and realized that your expenses were higher than you could afford.

USE MATH SKILLS

5. **Growing a Nest Egg** When Jamal graduated from college recently, his parents gave him $1,000 and told him to use it wisely. Jamal decided to use the money to start a retirement account. After doing some research about different options, he put the entire amount into a tax-deferred IRA that pays 11 percent interest, compounded annually.

Calculate How much money will Jamal have in his IRA at the end of ten years, assuming that the interest rate remains the same and that he does not deposit any additional money? Show your calculations in the form of a chart.

SOLVE MONEY PROBLEMS

6. **Making Decisions** Mike Johnson has worked for the same company for 45 years. Now, at age 67, he is about to retire. When he does, he will be entitled to receive the $600,000 that has accumulated in his 401(k) plan. Now Mike has to decide what to do with the money. If he manages it wisely, it can help make his retirement years comfortable and rewarding.

Analyze Use what you have learned in this section to help Mike decide what to do with his 401(k) funds. Consider the options available to him, such as rollover IRAs and annuities. Explain why your recommendation would make the best use of Mike's money.

Section 15.3

Estate Planning and Taxes

The Importance of Estate Planning

Why is it important to have an estate plan?

Many people think of estates as belonging only to the rich or elderly. However, the fact is that everyone has an estate. An **estate** is all property and assets owned by an individual or group. During your working years, your financial goal is to build your estate by acquiring and accumulating money for your current and future needs. However, as you grow older, your point of view will change. Instead of working to acquire assets, you will start to think about what will happen to your hard-earned wealth after you die. In most cases, people want to pass that wealth along to their loved ones. That is why estate planning becomes important.

What Is Estate Planning?

Estate planning is the process of creating a detailed plan for managing personal assets to make the most of them while you are alive and to ensure that they are distributed wisely after your death. It is not pleasant to think about your own death, but doing so is a necessary part of estate planning. Without a good estate plan, the assets you accumulate during your lifetime might be greatly reduced by various taxes when you die.

Estate planning is an essential part of retirement planning and financial planning. It has two stages. The first stage involves building your estate through savings, investments, and insurance. The second stage consists of making sure that your estate will be distributed as you wish at the time of your death. If you get married, your estate planning should take into account the needs of your spouse and children, if you have any. If you are single, your financial affairs should be in order for your beneficiaries. A **beneficiary (estate)** is a person who is named to receive a portion of someone's estate.

When you die, your surviving spouse, children, relatives, and/or friends will face a period of grief. One or more of these people will probably be responsible for settling your affairs. This will be a difficult time, and so your estate plan should be clear and well-organized.

Focus on Reading

Read to Learn

- How to identify various types of wills.
- How to discuss several types of trusts.
- How to describe common characteristics of estates.
- How to identify the types of taxes that affect estates.

Main Idea

Different types of wills and trusts protect your financial interests and those of your family. Applying strategies for paying estate taxes can help limit expenses for your heirs.

Key Terms

- estate
- estate planning
- beneficiary (estate)
- will
- intestate
- trust
- probate
- executor
- guardian
- codicil
- living will
- power of attorney

Before You Read

PREDICT

What is your definition of a will?

▲ **ASSETS AND POSSESSIONS** Most people have various assets and possessions that make up their estate. *What does your estate consist of at this point in your life?*

Caption Answer Answers will vary but should include personal possessions and savings accounts or other financial assets.

Otherwise, the people you have left behind may encounter problems settling your estate, and your intentions may not be carried out according to your wishes. One way to avoid these problems is to make sure that important documents are accessible, understandable, and legal.

Legal Documents

An estate plan involves various legal documents such as a **will**, which is a legal declaration of a person's wishes regarding disposal of his or her estate after death. When you die, the person who is responsible for handling your affairs will need access to your will and other important documents. The documents must be reviewed and verified before your heirs can receive the money and other assets to which they are entitled. If no one can find the necessary documents, your heirs may experience difficult delays. They could even lose a portion of their inheritance as a result. You should collect and organize various important papers:

- Birth certificates for you, your spouse, and your children
- Marriage certificates and divorce papers
- Legal name changes (especially important for protecting adopted children)
- Military service records
- Social Security documents
- Veteran's documents
- Insurance policies
- Transfer records of joint bank accounts
- Safe-deposit box records
- Automobile registrations
- Titles to stock and bond certificates

Springboard Ask students if they have ever seen a movie in which people fight over a deceased person's estate. Then ask how this scenario can be avoided in real life.

Have several copies of the documents needed for processing insurance claims and settling your estate. In some cases, children whose parents have died may need to have documents proving their parents' births and marriage and/or divorce. Surviving spouses, children, and other heirs may also be required to show proof of death in the form of a death certificate.

Wills

Why is a will such an important document?

One of the most important documents that every adult should have is a written will. If you die **intestate**—which is the status of not having a valid will—your legal state of residence will step in and control the distribution of your estate without regard for your wishes. Make sure that you have a written will. An attorney with estate planning experience can draft a will, which can help your heirs avoid many difficulties. Legal fees for drafting a will vary with the size of an estate and particular family situation. A standard will costs between $200 and $500.

Motivating Students Ask students: At what age should people consider making a will? Most will answer 50s or 60s. Then ask if they can think of any reasons someone in his or her 20s should make a will. List their responses on the board.

Types of Wills

You have several options in preparing a will. The four basic types of wills are the simple will, the traditional marital share will, the exemption trust will, and the stated dollar amount will. The differences among the types of wills can affect how your estate will be taxed.

All types of wills usually designate a beneficiary, the person who is named to receive a portion or all of an estate after your death. A beneficiary can be a spouse, relative, friend, or organization. In the following discussions, the beneficiary will be referred to as the *spouse*.

Teaching Activity Provide for students copies of will forms available at stationery and office supply stores. Ask them to identify the type. Explain to students that these forms are not actually the best way to prepare a will and tell them why (page 503). Have students read the form carefully and fill it out based on their current "estates."

Simple Will A simple will leaves everything to the spouse. Such a will is generally sufficient for people with small estates. However, for a large or complex estate, a simple will may not meet objectives. This type of will may also result in higher overall taxation, since everything left to the spouse will be taxed as part of his or her estate.

Traditional Marital Share Will The traditional marital share will leaves one-half of the adjusted gross estate (the total value of the estate minus debts and costs) to the spouse. The other half of the estate may go to children or other heirs. It can also be held in trust for the family. A **trust** is an arrangement in which a designated person known as a *trustee* manages assets for the benefit of someone else. A trust can provide a spouse with a lifelong income and would not be taxed at his or her death.

Exemption Trust Will With an exemption trust will, all assets go to the spouse except for a certain amount, which goes into a trust. This amount, plus any interest it earns, can provide the spouse with lifelong income that will not be taxed. In 2004 and 2005, the tax exemption amount was $1.5 million. That amount increased to $2 million for the years 2006 through 2008. In 2009, the amount increases to $3.5 million. The tax-free aspect of this type of will may become important if property values increase considerably. This type of will is beneficial for large estates.

Extension Invite an attorney who handles trusts and wills to speak to students about the legal aspects of preparing a will. Give students an opportunity to ask questions they may have developed when reading the will forms and preparing their wills.

Stated Dollar Amount Will The stated dollar amount will allows you to pass on to your spouse any amount that satisfies your family's financial goals. For tax purposes, you could pass on the exempted amount of $1.5 million (in 2004 and 2005). However, you might decide to pass on a stated amount related to your family's future income needs or related to the value of personal items.

State law may dictate how much you must leave to your spouse. Most states require that the spouse receive a certain amount, usually one-half or one-third of the value of an estate. States also have laws regarding when and how portions of an estate must pass to beneficiaries.

The stated dollar amount will has one major drawback. Suppose that you leave specific dollar amounts to your listed heirs and the balance to your spouse. Although these amounts may be fair and reasonable when the will is drafted, they can soon become outdated. What if the value of the estate decreases because of a business problem or a drop in the stock market? That decrease will not affect heirs who are left specific dollar amounts, but it will affect the value of your spouse's inheritance. For this reason, most experts recommend using percentages rather than specific amounts.

▲ **PEACE OF MIND** Preparing a will can make things easier for your family and can ensure that your estate is distributed according to your wishes. *What would happen if an adult were to die without preparing a will?*

Caption Answer The state in which the person lived would take over distributing the estate without considering the deceased's wishes.

Wills and Probate

The type of will that is best for your particular needs depends on many factors, including the size of your estate, inflation, your age, and your objectives. No matter what type of will you choose, it is best to avoid probate. **Probate** is the legal procedure of proving that a will is valid or invalid. It is also the process by which your estate is managed and distributed after your death, according to the provisions of your will. A special probate court validates wills and makes sure that your debts are paid. You should avoid probate because it is expensive, lengthy, and public. As you will read later in this chapter, a living trust avoids probate and is also less expensive, quicker, and private.

As You Read

RELATE

What situations might motivate you to change your will?

Formats of Wills

Wills may be either holographic or formal. A *holographic will* is a handwritten will that you prepare yourself. It should be written, dated, and signed entirely in your own handwriting. No printed or typed information should appear on its pages. Some states do not recognize holographic wills as legal.

A *formal will* is usually prepared with the help of an attorney. It may be typed, or it may be a preprinted form that you fill out. You must sign the will in front of two witnesses; neither witness can be a beneficiary named in the will. Witnesses must sign in front of you.

A *statutory will* is prepared on a preprinted form, which is available from lawyers, office-supply stores, and some stationery stores. There are serious risks in using preprinted forms to prepare your will. The form may include provisions that are not in the best interests of your heirs. If you change the preprinted wording, part or all of the will may be declared invalid. Furthermore, the form may not remain up-to-date with current laws regarding wills. For these reasons, it is best to seek a lawyer's advice when you prepare your will.

Critical Thinking Students are to research and respond in an essay to the following questions: If probate courts validate wills and ensure your debts are paid, why should they be avoided? Do you think probate is ever necessary or desirable? If so, under what circumstances? If not, then why does it exist?

Writing Your Will

Writing a will allows you to express exactly how you want your property to be distributed to your heirs. It is the only way to make sure that all of your property will end up where you want it. Some guidelines for writing a will include:

1. Work closely with your spouse or partner to prepare your will.
2. Write your will to conform to your current wishes.
3. Do not choose a beneficiary as a witness.
4. Consider signing prenuptial agreement if you are remarrying.
5. Consider using percentages instead of dollar amounts.
6. If you are married, your spouse should also write a will.
7. Be flexible.
8. Keep your original will in a safe place and a copy at home.
9. If you alter your will, prepare a new one or add a codicil.
10. Select an executor who is willing to do the needed tasks.

Teaching Activity Say to students: "Because selecting executors and guardians is so important, we should think carefully about how we select them." Have the students choose partners. Each pair is to come up with criteria for selecting executors and guardians and prepare a poster displaying both lists.

Selecting an Executor An **executor** is a person who is willing and able to perform the tasks involved in carrying out a will. These tasks include preparing an inventory of assets, collecting any money due, and paying off debts. An executor must also prepare and file all income and estate tax returns. In addition, he or she will be responsible for making decisions about selling or reinvesting assets to pay off debts and provide income for your family while the estate is being settled. Finally, an executor must distribute the estate and make a final accounting to beneficiaries and to the probate court. An executor can be a family member, a friend, an attorney, an accountant, or the trust department of a bank. You may also name a beneficiary as the executor. State law sets fees for executors. If you do not name an executor in your will, the court will appoint one. Naming your own executor eliminates that possibility and helps prevent unnecessary delay in the distribution of your property. It will also minimize estate taxes and settlement costs.

Selecting a Guardian If you have children, your will should name a guardian to care for them in the event that you and your spouse die at the same time and the children cannot care for themselves. A **guardian** is the person who accepts the responsibility of caring for the children of the deceased and managing an estate for the children until they reach a certain age. Many states require a guardian to post a bond (several hundred dollars) with the probate court. The bonding company will reimburse the minor's estate the amount of the bond if the guardian uses the minor's property for his or her own gain. When you name a guardian for your children, choose someone you know who loves them and shares your beliefs about raising children. Of course, the person must also be capable and willing to accept the responsibilities associated with the role of being a parent.

Altering or Rewriting Your Will There may be times when you wish to change the provisions of your will because of changes in your life or in the law. After you have made a will, review it frequently so that it remains current. Here are some reasons to review your will:

- You have moved to a new state that has different laws.
- You have sold property that is mentioned in the will.
- The size and composition of your estate have changed.
- You have married, divorced, or remarried.
- Potential heirs have died, or new ones have been born.

Do not make any written changes on the pages of an existing will. Additions, deletions, or erasures on a will that has been signed and witnessed can invalidate the will. If you want to make only a few minor changes, adding a codicil may be the best choice. A **codicil** is a document that explains, adds, or deletes provisions in an existing will. To be valid, it must meet the legal requirements for a will. If you want to make major changes in your will, or if you have already added a codicil, it is best to prepare a new will. In the new will, be sure to include a clause that revokes, or cancels, all earlier wills and codicils.

A Living Will

Why is it important to have a living will?

At some point in your life, you may become physically or mentally disabled and unable to act on your own behalf. If that happens, a living will can help ensure that you will be cared for according to your wishes. A **living will** is a legal document in which you state if you want to be kept alive by artificial means if you become terminally ill and are unable to make such a decision. Many states recognize living wills. **Figure 15.7** illustrates a typical living will. Sign and date the document before two witnesses. Review your living will from time to time to update your decisions.

Teaching Activity Divide the class into groups of four and give each group a copy of the form for creating a living will. Ask each group to evaluate the form's ease of use. Have groups prepare lists of information needed to complete the form.

Figure 15.7 A Living Will

Living Will Declaration

Declaration made this _____ day of ______ (month, year)

I, _________________________, being of sound mind, willfully and voluntarily make known my desire that my dying shall not be artificially prolonged under the circumstances set forth below, do hereby declare: if at any time I should have an incurable injury, disease, or illness regarded as a terminal condition by my physician and if my physician has determined that the application of life-sustaining procedures would serve only to artificially prolong the dying process and that my death will occur whether or not life-sustaining procedures are utilized, I direct that such procedures be withheld or withdrawn and that I be permitted to die with only the administration of medication or the performance of any medical procedure deemed necessary to provide me with comfort care.

In the absence of my ability to give directions regarding the use of such life-sustaining procedures, it is my intention that this declaration shall be honored by my family and physician as the final expression of my legal right to refuse medical or surgical treatment and accept the consequences from such refusal. I understand the full import of this declaration, and I am emotionally and mentally competent to make this declaration.

Signed ___________________________

City, County, and State of Residence___________________________

The declarant has been personally known to me, and I believe him or her to be of sound mind.

Witness___________________________

Witness___________________________

Making Choices A living will ensures that a person's preference about medical care is honored if he or she becomes terminally ill or falls into a coma.

What is the basic purpose of a living wills?

Caption Answer A living will expresses your wishes about whether your life should be prolonged artificially if you become terminally ill.

You might consider writing a living will when you draw up a traditional will. Most lawyers will prepare a living will at no cost if they are already preparing a traditional will or your estate plan. You can also get the necessary forms for a living will from nonprofit groups such as Aging With Dignity.

Power of Attorney

A **power of attorney** is a legal document that authorizes someone to act on your behalf. If you become seriously ill or injured, you will probably need someone to take care of your needs and personal affairs. This can be done through a power of attorney.

You can assign a power of attorney to anyone you choose. You can give that person power to carry out only certain actions or transactions, or you may allow the person to act on your behalf in all matters, including your living will.

Letter of Last Instruction

In addition to a traditional will and a living will, it is a good idea to prepare a letter of last instruction. This document is not legally binding, but it can provide heirs with important information. It should contain preferences for funeral arrangements as well as the names of the people who are to be informed of the death. With a letter of last instruction, you can also let people know the locations of your bank accounts, safe-deposit box, and other important items.

Trusts

Why is it important that trusts avoid probate?

Discussion Discuss with students whether they think a letter of last instruction is important. Ask: Where should such a letter be kept? Should it be given to someone, sealed? Should it be kept with your will?

Basically, a trust is a legal arrangement that helps manage the assets of your estate for your benefit or that of your beneficiaries. The creator of the trust is called the *trustor,* or *grantor.* The trust is administered by the trustee, which can be a person or an institution, such as a bank. A bank charges a small fee for its services in administering a trust. The fee is usually based on the value of the assets in the trust.

Individual circumstances determine whether it makes sense to establish a trust. Some of the common reasons for setting up a trust are to:

- Reduce or provide for payment of estate taxes.
- Avoid probate and transfer your assets immediately to your beneficiaries.
- Free yourself from managing your assets while you receive a regular income from the trust.
- Provide income for a surviving spouse or other beneficiary.
- Ensure that your property serves a desired purpose after your death.

▲ **IN WHOM WE TRUST** For some people, setting up a trust is an effective way to organize and manage an estate. *What are some of the main reasons to establish a trust?*

Caption Answer Reasons may include: to reduce or provide payment of estate taxes; to avoid probate and transfer assets immediately to beneficiaries; to provide income for beneficiaries; and to ensure your property serves a desired purpose after your death.

Types of Trusts

There are many types of trusts, including a credit-shelter trust, a disclaimer trust, a living trust, and a testamentary trust. Choose the type of trust that is most appropriate for your situation. An estate attorney can advise you about the right type of trust for your needs.

Trusts can be either revocable or irrevocable. A *revocable trust* is one in which you have the right to end the trust or change its terms during your lifetime. Revocable trusts avoid the lengthy process of probate, but they do not protect assets from federal or state estate taxes. An *irrevocable trust* is one that cannot be changed or ended. Irrevocable trusts avoid probate and help reduce estate taxes. However, by law you cannot remove any assets from an irrevocable trust, even if you need them at some later point in your life.

Credit-Shelter Trust A credit-shelter trust is a trust that enables the spouse of a deceased person to avoid paying federal taxes on a certain amount of assets left to him or her as part of an estate. As of 2004, the exemption amount was $1.5 million. It increased to $2 million in 2006 and continues to increase to $3.5 million in 2009. As the most common estate-planning trust, the credit-shelter trust has many other names: bypass trust, residuary trust, A/B trust, exemption equivalent trust, and family trust. A single person does not need to set up a credit-shelter trust because assets passing to someone other than a spouse automatically qualify for the estate exemption amount.

As You Read

QUESTION

What are the advantages of creating a trust?

Question Answer Trusts can save your beneficiaries taxes, prevent disputes among heirs, avoid probate, help you manage your assets, ensure your wishes are heeded if you become incapacitated, and provide income for your survivors.

Disclaimer Trust A disclaimer trust is appropriate for couples who do not have enough assets to need a credit-shelter trust but who may in the future. With a disclaimer trust, the surviving spouse is left everything, but he or she has the right to disclaim, or deny, some portion of the estate. Anything that is disclaimed goes into a credit-shelter trust. This approach allows the surviving spouse to protect wealth from estate taxes.

Living Trust A living trust, also known as an *inter vivos trust,* is a property management arrangement that you establish. It allows you, as trustor, to receive benefits during your lifetime. To set up a living trust, you simply transfer some of your assets to a trustee. Then you give the trustee instructions for managing the trust while you are alive as well as after your death. A living trust has several advantages:

- It ensures privacy. A will is a public record; however, a trust is not a public record.
- The assets held in trust avoid probate at your death. This eliminates probate costs and delays.
- It is advantageous if you own property in more than one state.
- It enables you to review your trustee's performance and make changes if necessary.
- It can relieve you of management responsibilities.
- It is less likely than a will to create arguments between heirs upon your death.
- It can guide your family and doctors to follow your wishes if you become terminally ill or if you become unable to make your own decisions.

Setting up a living trust costs more money than creating a will. However, depending on your particular circumstances, a living trust can be a good estate planning option.

Teaching Activity Divide the class into four groups, assigning one of the four types of trusts to each group. Have each group research and prepare a mini-lesson on its trust and present it to the rest of the class.

Testamentary Trust A testamentary trust is established by your will and becomes effective upon your death. Such a trust can be valuable if your beneficiaries are inexperienced in financial matters. It may also be the best option if you expect your estate taxes will be high. A testamentary trust provides many of the same advantages as a living trust.

Your Estate

How does the type of joint ownership affect the distribution of an estate?

Discussion Through discussion, ensure students understand the six advantages of a living trust.

As you learned earlier in this chapter, your estate consists of everything you own. Therefore, an important step in estate planning is taking inventory of your assets. Do not forget to include in your inventory jointly owned property, life insurance policies, employee retirement benefits, money owed to you by others, and all of your personal possessions.

Some states are known as *community-property states*. Community property is any money earned by either spouse during the marriage and any property or possessions purchased with that money. It does not include assets received as gifts or through inheritances. In community-property states, each spouse owns 50 percent of the property. Thus, half of the couple's assets are included in each spouse's estate.

In non-community-property states, property is included in the estate of the spouse who owns it. The way you own property can make a significant tax difference.

STANDARD & POOR'S

Put on Your Financial Planner's Cap

If your clients just got married and you were planning their estate, why would you tell them to own property as "tenants in common"?

See the Teacher Manual for answers.

Joint Ownership

Joint ownership of property between spouses is very common. Joint ownership may also exist between parents and children or other relatives. Joint ownership may help avoid probate and inheritance taxes in some states. However, it does not avoid federal estate taxes. It may, in fact, increase the amount of federal estate taxes.

There are three types of joint ownership, each of which has different tax and estate-planning consequences.

1. You and your spouse may own property as "joint tenants with the right of survivorship."
   - The property is considered to be owned 50–50 for estate tax purposes and will automatically pass to one spouse at the other's death.
   - No estate tax is paid at the first death. However, when the surviving spouse dies, more estate taxes may be due than with a traditional marital share will.
2. You and your spouse may own property as "tenants in common."
   - Each individual is considered to own a certain share of property for tax purposes, and only your share is included in your estate.
   - Your share does not go to the other tenant in common at your death. Instead, it is included in your probate estate, and you decide who gets it.
   - Gift and estate taxes do not apply to property that belongs to spouses.
3. Married couples may own property under the form of "tenancy by the entirety."
   - Both spouses own the property.
   - When one spouse dies, the other gets the property automatically.
   - Neither spouse may sell the property without the consent of the other.

Research Assign each of the three types of joint ownership to one third of the class. Individually, students are to research the tax and estate planning consequences of their ownership type and write a one-page report.

Joint ownership is a poor substitute for a will because it provides less control over how property is distributed and taxed after death. State laws govern the types and effects of joint ownership. An attorney should be consulted on these matters.

WebQuest

Avoiding Financial Fraud

Many people with assets protect their heirs from estate problems by setting up trust funds. However, since trusts are so popular, trust preparation is a service targeted by a number of sophisticated con-artists. Learn how to avoid estate-planning fraud.

@ To continue with Task 5 of your WebQuest project, visit **finance07.glencoe.com**.

Life Insurance and Employee Benefits

If you have life insurance, the benefits of that insurance will be counted among the assets in your estate. Life insurance benefits are free of income tax, and they do not go through probate. They are also partially exempt from most state inheritance taxes. However, they are subject to federal estate taxes under certain circumstances, such as when you change beneficiaries, surrender the policy for cash, or make loans on the policy.

Death benefits from qualified employer pension plans or Keogh plans are usually excluded from an estate. One exception is if the benefits are payable to the estate. Another exception is if the beneficiary chooses a special provision for averaging income tax in lump-sum distributions.

Lifetime Gifts and Trusts

You may give part of your estate as a gift or set up a trust for your spouse or a child. Under certain conditions, such gifts and trusts are not included as part of your estate upon your death. However, if you keep any control or use of the gift or trust, it remains part of your estate and is subject to taxes. For example, if you transfer title of your home to a child but continue to live in it, the value of the home is taxed as part of your estate. Similarly, if you put property in a trust but keep some control over the income or principal, the property is included in your estate even though you may not be able to obtain it yourself.

Taxes and Estate Planning

Which government, state or federal, imposes inheritance taxes?

Federal and state governments impose various types of taxes that you must consider in estate planning. The four major types of taxes are estate taxes, estate and trust federal income taxes, inheritance taxes, and gift taxes.

Estate Taxes

An estate tax is a federal tax collected on the value of a person's property at the time of his or her death. The tax is based on the fair market value of the deceased person's investments, property, and bank accounts, less an exempt amount.

As of 2006, the exempt amount was \$2 million. This means that the "first" \$2 million is not used to compute the estate tax. Only the amount in excess of \$2 million can be considered. The exempt amount is \$3.5 million in 2009. The tax rate applied to the remaining amount is 48 percent. With careful planning, federal estate taxes can be avoided for estates over \$2 million.

After You Read

REACT

Has the information in this chapter convinced you to start your retirement planning sooner than you may have originally planned? Why or why not?

React Answer Accept all reasonable answers.

◀ DEATH AND TAXES Dealing with the financial aspects of a person's death can be a difficult burden for the heirs. *What are the various types of taxes to consider for estate planning?*

Caption Answer estate and trust federal income taxes, inheritance taxes, and gift taxes

Estate and Trust Federal Income Taxes

In addition to the federal estate tax return, owners of estates and certain trusts must file federal income tax returns with the IRS. Taxable income for estates and trusts is computed in the same manner as taxable income for individuals. Taxes must be paid quarterly on both trusts and estates.

Research Have the class research to find out what kinds of estate or inheritance taxes your state imposes. Have students share results with the class.

Inheritance Taxes

Your heirs might have to pay a tax for the right to acquire the property that they have inherited. An inheritance tax is a tax collected on the property left by a person in his or her will.

Only state governments impose inheritance taxes. Most states collect an inheritance tax, but state laws differ widely as to exemptions and rates of taxation. A reasonable range for state inheritance taxes would be 4 to 10 percent of whatever the heir receives.

Gift Taxes

Both the federal and state governments impose a gift tax, a tax collected on money or property valued at more than $11,000 given by one person to another in a single year. One way to reduce the tax liability of your estate is to reduce the size of the estate while you are alive by giving away portions of it as gifts. You are free to make such gifts to your spouse, children, or anyone else at any time. However, when doing this, be careful that you do not give away assets that you may need in your retirement.

According to federal law, you may give up to $11,000 per person per year free of any gift tax. A married couple may give up to $22,000 per person per year without paying the tax. Gifts that exceed those amounts are subject to the tax. Gift tax rates are currently the same as estate tax rates, and they are called *unified transfer tax rates*. However, gifts might be considered as part of your estate and be taxed if they were given within three years of your death. Many states have other gift tax laws as well.

Critical Thinking Ask students to think, research, and write about the following: Are estate or inheritance taxes intrinsically fair or unfair? Should the federal and state governments abolish these taxes? Students are to write coherent, clear papers to respond.

Paying the Tax

After doing everything possible to reduce your estate taxes, you may still find that taxes are due. In that case, you will have to think about the best way to help your heirs pay the taxes. The federal estate tax is due nine months after a death. State taxes, probate costs, debts, and other expenses are also usually due within that same period. These costs might result in a real financial problem for your survivors. Finding enough cash to pay taxes, debts, and other costs without causing financial hardship can be very difficult.

There are a number of ways this problem can be handled.

1. Obtain life insurance. A life insurance policy may be the best way to provide your heirs with the tax-free cash that they will need to settle your estate.
2. Save enough cash ahead of time to pay taxes and expenses when they are due. However, the cash may be subject to income tax during your lifetime and also subject to estate tax at your death.
3. Your heirs could sell assets to pay taxes. However, this could result in the loss of important sources of income.
4. Your heirs might borrow money. However, it is unusual to find a commercial lender that will lend money to pay taxes. Besides, borrowing money only prolongs the problem and adds interest costs in the process.

Caption Answer using your life insurance, using set-aside cash, selling assets, and borrowing

◀ **FOR LIFE** Considering the expense of estate taxes can mean more money or assets for your family or heirs. *What are at least two sources of funds to pay for taxes and debts when settling an estate?*

5. If your family members or beneficiaries can show they have a reasonable cause, the IRS may allow them to make deferred or installment payments on taxes that are due. However, like borrowing, making payments may prolong the problem.

Planning for the Future

Estate planning is essential not only to ensure that your assets are distributed in the way you choose, but also to make sure that your loved ones are not left with difficult or costly problems.

Planning for your estate and taxes as well as writing a will are just a few of the steps you can take to have a secure financial future for yourself and others. In addition, planning and saving for your own retirement will help ensure that your needs are met in your later years. Remember that the trade-offs, decisions, and goals that you make for yourself today affect your personal finances, which will continue to affect your life now and in the future.

Section 15.3 Assessment

See the Teacher Manual for answers.

QUICK CHECK

1. What are the four basic types of wills?
2. What is a credit-shelter trust, a disclaimer trust, and a living trust?
3. What are several strategies that you might use to arrange for paying estate taxes?

THINK CRITICALLY

4. Which format of a will—holographic or formal—is the best from a legal point of view? Why?

USE MATH SKILLS

5. **Too Much Money** Joel and Rachel Simon are both retired. They have been married for 50 years and have amassed an estate worth $2.4 million. If either of them dies between the years 2006 and 2008, the surviving spouse can receive $2 million tax-free. The amount over that exemption will be subject to federal estate tax. The couple has no trusts or other types of tax-sheltered assets.

Analyze If Joel or Rachel dies in between 2006 and 2008, how much federal estate tax would the surviving spouse have to pay, assuming that the estate is taxed at the 48 percent rate?

SOLVE MONEY PROBLEMS

6. **Cost versus Satisfaction** Irving and Irma Lansing are making plans for the distribution of their assets after they die. They have wills, but they want to make sure that they are using the right type of will to maximize the benefits for the surviving spouse and their four grown children. The estimated value of their estate is currently $1.4 million. However, most of their assets are in high-risk stocks, which can vary greatly in value depending on economic conditions and the stock market.

Write About It Help Irving and Irma by writing a summary of the benefits and drawbacks of the four main types of wills. Identify which type would be best for them.

Chapter 15 Review & Activities

See the Teacher Manual for answers.

CHAPTER SUMMARY

- The sooner you start planning and saving for retirement, the faster your assets will accumulate.
- Estimating your living expenses is the first step of retirement planning. Housing needs will depend on your desires and your health.
- Social Security provides a regular monthly income payment but is not meant to cover all retirement expenses.
- Employer pension plans include two types: A defined-contribution plan is an individual account for each employee into which an employer contributes a specific annual amount; a defined-benefit plan specifies benefits based on total earnings and years on the job.
- Personal retirement accounts include regular IRAs, Roth IRAs, SEP plans, Spousal IRAs, Rollover IRAs, Education IRAs, and Keogh plans.
- The various types of wills include simple wills, traditional marital share wills, exemption trust wills, and stated dollar amount wills.
- The several types of trusts include credit-shelter trusts, disclaimer trusts, living trusts, and testamentary trusts.
- One common characteristic of many estates is joint ownership of property between spouses.
- Estates are taxed with estate taxes, estate and trust federal income taxes, inheritance taxes, and gift taxes.

Communicating Key Terms

Imagine you are a financial planner for a company. Prepare text for a PowerPoint presentation using as many of these terms as possible to introduce the employees to estate planning.

- assisted-living facility (ALF)
- defined-contribution plan
- 401(k) plan
- vesting
- defined-benefit plan
- individual retirement account (IRA)
- Keogh plan
- annuity (insurance)
- heirs
- estate
- estate planning
- beneficiary (estate)
- will
- intestate
- trust
- probate
- executor
- guardian
- codicil
- living will
- power of attorney

Reviewing Key Concepts

1. **Identify** three ways expenses decrease at retirement.
2. **Describe** alternative living and housing arrangements for retirement.
3. **Identify** two reasons Social Security should not be a primary source of retirement funds.
4. **Define** employer-sponsored defined-contribution plans and defined-benefit plans.
5. **Explain** the advantages of the Roth IRA over a regular IRA.
6. **Explain** why creating a living will is an important part of estate planning.
7. **Describe** the major advantages of trusts.
8. **Explain** what it means to be an executor of an estate.
9. **List** some estate planning methods to reduce inheritance taxes.

See the Teacher Manual for answers.

ACADEMIC SKILLS

Science The need for retirement planning is greater in the 21st century because more people are living longer lives.

Research Find out the life expectancy for people born in the United States in each decade of the 20th century: 1900, 1910, 1920, 1930, 1940, 1950, 1960, 1970, 1980, 1990, and 2000. Then find out how long someone born today is expected to live. Make a timeline illustrating the life spans. Then list several reasons why people are living longer lives.

YOUR FINANCIAL FIGURES

Cost of Living in Retirement Pretend you are in your late 60s. With careful planning, you have about $35,000 per year for living expenses after taxes. Find a Web site that compares the cost of living in different cities.

1. **Calculate** how much you would need if you lived in U.S. cities that are attractive to retirees, such as West Palm Beach, Florida; Phoenix, Arizona; and Dallas, Texas.
2. **Compute** by using spreadsheet or presentation software to develop charts and/or graphs comparing the cost of living in different cities.

REAL-WORLD Application

Connect with Economics and Social Studies Because of longer life expectancies and declining birth rates, fewer workers are currently paying into the Social Security system than previously, and more people are in retirement for more years.

1. **Research** Find out what the American Association of Retired Persons (AARP) thinks about Social Security and various ideas to reform it.
2. **Think Critically** Is it "fair" for younger workers to fund current retirees' benefits? Do you believe you will receive Social Security benefits when you retire? Why or why not?

Internet CONNECTION

Wills and Trusts You need a lawyer to help you draw up wills and trusts. However, you can minimize the amount of time a lawyer will have to spend preparing the will or trust by organizing your documents and doing some research on your own first.

@ **Log On** Use an Internet search engine to find Web sites showing sample will and trust documents. Answer the following questions:

1. Under what circumstances is a trust essential? Do you need one currently?
2. What are some of your state's requirements for a will or trust to be valid?

BusinessWeek ONLINE

Newsclip: Social Security Reform Social Security reform has been highly debated in the news for years. Many politicians aim to change the system.

@ **Log On** Go to **finance07.glencoe.com** and open Chapter 15. Learn more about retirement saving options. Write a list of ways to help save seniors from financial hardships. Also write a list of ways to help younger people prepare for retirement.

WHAT'S YOUR FINANCIAL ID?

WHAT IS YOUR PERSONALITY?

Part of the fun of planning a successful future is considering your personal preferences. The closer you can match your activities with your personality, the more likely you are to enjoy your life. Read through the following list and write your top three characteristics on a separate sheet of paper.

____ **1.** I am steady and reliable.

____ **2.** I tend to think a lot.

____ **3.** I enjoy being by myself.

____ **4.** I almost always plan before I do something.

____ **5.** I am very emotional.

____ **6.** I love being the center of attention.

____ **7.** I enjoy drama.

____ **8.** I like to express what I feel.

____ **9.** I am always ready to get up and go.

____ **10.** I like to participate in high-action sports.

____ **11.** I am happiest when doing physical activities.

____ **12.** I find it hard to keep still.

Thinker: If all of your selections were from numbers 1–4, consider activities that use your ability to think.

Heartfelt/Feeler/Enthusiast: If all of your selections were from numbers 5–8, you are probably happiest when doing something that gives you an emotional lift.

Doer: If all of your selections were from numbers 9–12, you enjoy being active.

Adapter: If your selections were from more than one of the three sections (1–4, 5–8, or 9–12), you are versatile and could choose activities that require thinking, involve emotions, or are active.

Continue to think about the different aspects of your personality and consider what types of activities you like to do. Thinking about these things now will help you better plan for your retirement years.

Accept all reasonable answers that show student effort and an understanding of the concept.

Your Financial Portfolio

Saving for Retirement

Henri has become eligible to participate in his company's 403(b) program. He can invest from 2 to 15 percent of his salary, which is $20,000 a year. The company matches the first 5 percent at a rate of 50 percent, or 50 cents for every dollar he invests. Henri has decided to save 5 percent of his salary. Based on the current investment return of 10 percent compounded annually, Henri has calculated how much he would be able to save over 10 years, including company-matching contributions.

	Contributions	Interest	Total
Henri's contribution of 5 percent of his $20,000 salary	$1,000/year	10%	
Company contribution matching 50 percent of 5 percent of his salary	$500/year		
1st Year	$1,500	$150.00	$1,650.00
2nd Year	1,500	315.00	3,465.00
3rd Year	1,500	496.50	5,461.50
4th Year	1,500	696.15	7,657.65
5th Year	1,500	915.77	10,073.42
6th Year	1,500	1,157.34	12,730.76
7th Year	1,500	1,423.08	15,653.84
8th Year	1,500	1,715.38	18,869.22
9th Year	1,500	2,036.92	22,406.14
10th Year	1,500	2,390.61	26,296.75
Total	**$15,000**	**$11,296.75**	**$26,296.75**

Calculate

On a separate sheet of paper, calculate how much you would have in ten years if you saved $2,000 a year at an annual interest rate of 10 percent, with the company contributing $500 a year.

Accept all reasonable answers that show student effort and an understanding of the concept.

Unit 4 LAB

Get a Financial Life!

Making Retirement Plans

Overview

Carrie and David have been working and saving for their retirement for many years. Soon it will become a reality. They are looking forward to spending time with their future grandchildren, developing hobbies, traveling, volunteering, and maybe even working part-time, without having to worry about earning full-time wages. Their goal is to retire within the next five years. They need to develop a clear and organized plan for how they will spend their days, how much money their activities will cost, and where they will live.

Resources & Tools

- Internet (optional)
- Math textbook (for reference)
- Portfolio (ring binder or file folder)
- Public or school library
- Word processor

Procedures

STEP A

Step A The Process
If you were Carrie or David, how would you spend your retirement years?

1. Write a short story (one or two pages) describing how Carrie and David will spend their retirement years. Where will they live? Will they travel? Will they work? Do they have hobbies? Use your creativity and imagination.
2. Research long-term care insurance. Then help Carrie and David decide whether they should purchase it or invest their money in another way.
3. Watch a movie or TV show about people who are retired or nearing retirement age. You might rent a video or DVD of *Grumpy Old Men, Cocoon, Space Cowboys,* or a more recent film. Make a list of the hobbies and activities of the characters. Write one or two paragraphs comparing the characters' hobbies and activities to those of people you know who are teens or young adults.
4. In 2004, about 12 percent of the American population was 65 or older. By 2050, that number will increase to 21 percent. Many of these Americans are or will be living in retirement communities, assisted-living facilities, or nursing homes. As a service project, plan an activity for a group of senior citizens in your community. You might develop a craft project, a music festival, or a game day. Use your imagination. Then contact a local center and ask if you can present your activity there.

STEP B Create Your Portfolio

As you work through the process, save the results so that you can refer, review, and refine. Create a portfolio to showcase the information you collected in Step A.

1. Include your short story about Carrie and David's retirement years.
2. Present your recommendations and reasoning on whether or not Carrie and David should purchase long-term care insurance.
3. Write a summary of the movie or TV show you watched. Include the list of hobbies and activities you created and the comparison paragraph you wrote.
4. Present your plan for the senior citizens' activity. If you are able to implement it, survey the participants to find out if they enjoyed the activity. Ask how you might improve it for another time.

STEP C Mathematics

Math skills are essential for managing your own finances and planning for retirement. Also, employers look for employees who have math skills. Adding, subtracting, multiplying, dividing, working with fractions and decimals, and using algebra are the basic math skills used in the workplace.

1. Create ten word problems using basic math skills to solve financial problems from this unit. For example: David's employer matches David's contributions to his 401(k) retirement savings plan. If David contributes $250 per month to the plan, how many years must David continue to save to accumulate $90,000 without interest? ($\$250 + \$250 = \$500$; $\$500 \times 12 = \$6,000$; $\$90,000 \div \$6,000 = 15$ years)
2. Form groups of three, and as a team, solve the word problems.
3. Compile the problems and their answers into a classroom notebook. Label the notebook "Math Problems in Personal Finance." If possible, categorize the problems according to the skill (adding, subtracting, fractions, and so on).

Unit 5

Business Ownership and Planning

WebQuest Internet Project

Be Your Own Boss

Have you ever thought that you would like to be your own boss? Would you like to own your own spa, restaurant, or gas station? Business ownership is the dream of all entrepreneurs, and it is never too early to explore the opportunities. In this project, you will think about how to start or acquire your own business. You will also find out more about what entrepreneurs do, and learn where to get help on the road to success.

Log on to **finance07.glencoe.com**. Begin by reading Task 1. Then continue on your WebQuest as you study Unit 5.

Section	16.1	17.2	18.3
Page	539	559	588

BusinessWeek

FINANCE FILE

Good Works—with a Business Plan

Just a decade ago, there were virtually no B-school courses or student projects on social entrepreneurship. Today most top business schools have both.

But before such a subject can be taught, it must be defined. A social entrepreneur is one driven by a social mission, a desire to find innovative ways to solve social problems that are not being or cannot be addressed by the market or the public sector. *How to Change the World: Social Entrepreneurs and the Power of New Ideas* by David Bornstein adopts this broad definition. Well-documented cases of grassroots entrepreneurial activities to tackle such diverse social problems as child abuse, disability, illiteracy, housing, and environmental degradation give life to it.

The search for financing has sparked a wave of entrepreneurship within the field of social investment, including firms dedicated to investing in businesses that deliver solutions to social problems. Let's hope that in the process, they help restore the public's trust in the business community.

—By Laura D'Andrea Tyson

Write About It What are some examples of successful businesses that help society?

See the Teacher Manual for answer.

Log On To read the complete *BusinessWeek* article and do the *BusinessWeek* Extension activity to learn more about business ownership and financial management, go to **finance07.glencoe.com**.

CHAPTER 16
Types of Business Ownership

$ What You'll Learn

When you have completed this chapter, you will be able to:

Section 16.1

- Identify the advantages and disadvantages of a sole proprietorship.
- Explain the differences between general and limited partners.
- Identify the advantages and disadvantages of a partnership.

Section 16.2

- Describe two types of corporations.
- Summarize the process of forming a corporation.
- Discuss the advantages and disadvantages of a corporation.

Reading Strategies

To get the most out of your reading:

Predict what you will learn in this chapter.
Relate what you read to your own life.
Question what you are reading to be sure you understand.
React to what you have read.

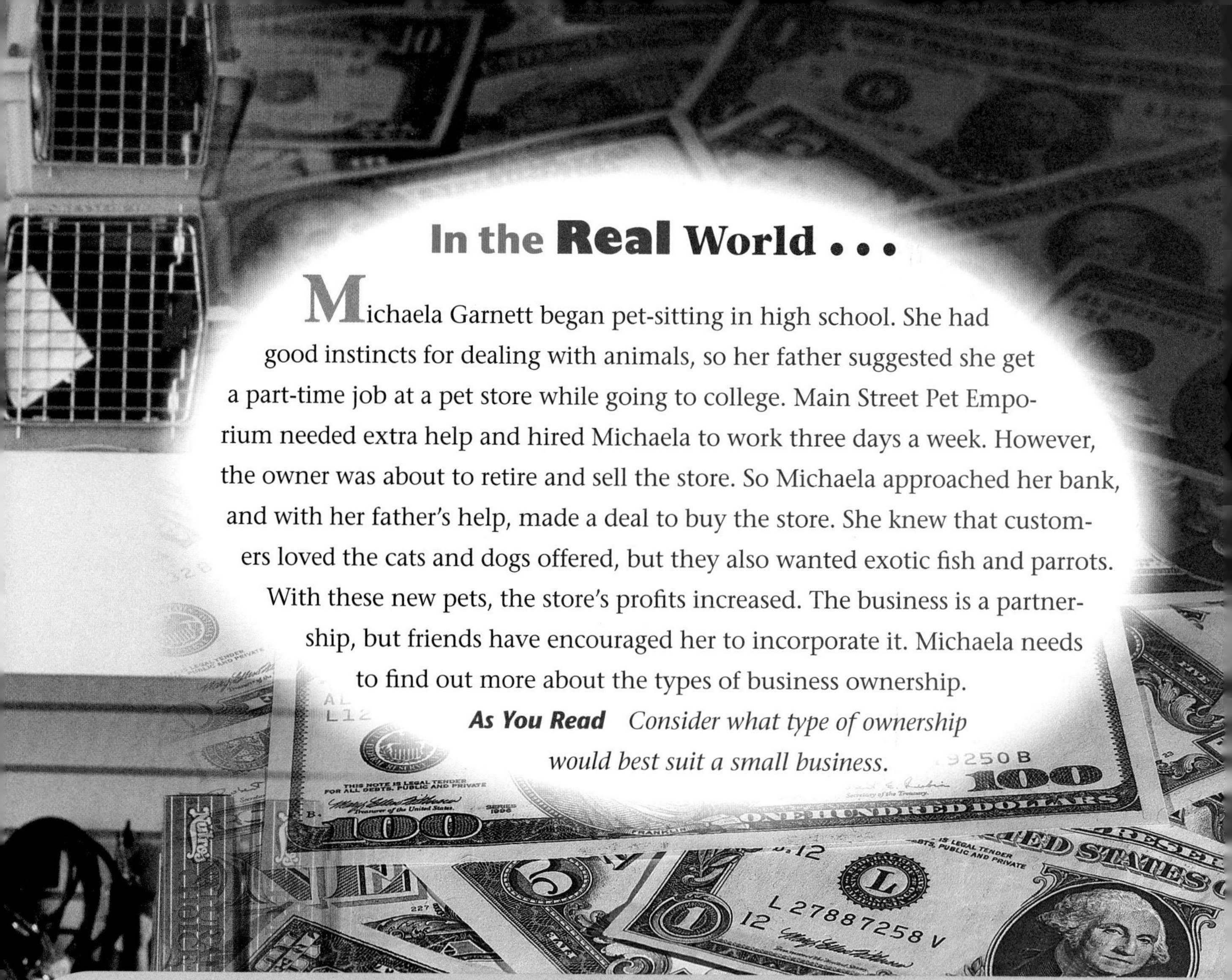

In the **Real** World . . .

Michaela Garnett began pet-sitting in high school. She had good instincts for dealing with animals, so her father suggested she get a part-time job at a pet store while going to college. Main Street Pet Emporium needed extra help and hired Michaela to work three days a week. However, the owner was about to retire and sell the store. So Michaela approached her bank, and with her father's help, made a deal to buy the store. She knew that customers loved the cats and dogs offered, but they also wanted exotic fish and parrots. With these new pets, the store's profits increased. The business is a partnership, but friends have encouraged her to incorporate it. Michaela needs to find out more about the types of business ownership.

As You Read *Consider what type of ownership would best suit a small business.*

Lesson Plan See the Teacher Manual for Chapter 16 planning guide and lesson plan.

ASK STANDARD &POOR'S

Business Ownership

Q: In a sole proprietorship, you get to keep all the profits for yourself. Why would I want to have all the hassles of setting up a corporation?

A: Each type of business structure offers advantages and disadvantages. The net income from a sole proprietorship is taxed at personal income tax rates, but a corporation's profits are taxed at lower, corporate tax rates. However, a sole proprietorship is easier to set up, so you could be in business more quickly.

Ask Yourself Why might you set up a business as a sole proprietorship?

@ Go to **finance07.glencoe.com** to complete the Standard and Poor's Financial Focus activity.

Section 16.1

Sole Proprietorship and Partnership

Focus on Reading

Read to Learn

- How to identify the advantages and disadvantages of a sole proprietorship.
- How to explain the differences between general and limited partners.
- How to identify the advantages and disadvantages of a partnership.

Main Idea

Understanding and selecting the proper form of organization for your business can be an essential factor in its success.

Key Terms

- sole proprietorship
- Employer Identification Number (EIN)
- unlimited liability
- limited life
- partnership
- partnership agreement
- general partner
- limited partner

Before You Read

PREDICT

What might be an advantage of owning your own business? A disadvantage?

Business Ownership Organization

Are there different kinds of business ownership?

Understanding how to handle your personal finances can help prepare you for managing your own business. The abilities to plan, manage, and keep track of your own money can be applied to handling a business. If you decide to start a business and manage its finances, it is important to become familiar with the different types of ownership.

When you start a business, you have a choice as to how the ownership is legally organized. Business ownership can take one of three legal forms: sole proprietorship, partnership, or corporation. It is important to select the most appropriate form of ownership that best suits your needs and the needs of your business. This section will examine the first two forms of business ownership—sole proprietorship and partnership.

Sole Proprietorship

What are the characteristics of a sole proprietorship?

The word *sole* means "single" or "one." The word *proprietor* means "owner." A **sole proprietorship**, therefore, is a business owned by one person. The sole proprietorship is the oldest and most common form of business ownership. Approximately 75 percent of all businesses in the United States today are organized as sole proprietorships. Although many people think of corporations when they think about business in the United States, the sole proprietorship is the backbone of American business.

Most sole proprietorships are small-business operations, each owned by an individual. An individual who starts a business is known as an *entrepreneur*. Many of these businesses provide services, such as auto repair, house cleaning, carpentry, or plumbing. They generally operate out of homes, small offices, or storefronts. Some sole proprietorships become quite successful, but many go out of business. In all cases, however, the owners of sole proprietorships are pursuing their dreams of running their own businesses.

For example, Debbi Fields had a dream of selling cookies. She created a highly successful business called *Mrs. Fields Cookies*. John Johnson wanted to start a magazine. So he borrowed $500 from his family and created the successful magazine *Ebony*. Even some major corporations began as risky ventures by entrepreneurs. The company Corning would not exist without Amory Houghton, and there would be no Colgate-Palmolive without the determination of William Colgate.

▲ **SMALL BUSINESS IS BIG** Small businesses have traditionally been the backbone of the American economy. *What small businesses have started in your area recently?*

Caption Answer Accept all reasonable answers.

Advantages of Sole Proprietorship

Organizing a business as a sole proprietorship has several advantages. The most important advantage is having the freedom to make all the decisions. This form of business organization also has other advantages. You receive all profits and pay tax once a year as an individual. This type of business has easy set-up, simple licensing and paperwork, and few government regulations.

Easy Set-Up A sole proprietorship is the easiest form of business organization to set up. Although local and state governments require some paperwork, you can usually complete this without much difficulty. Starting a sole proprietorship does take some effort, but because a minimal amount of documentation is required, the cost of organizing a sole proprietorship is relatively low.

Licensing In many cases, you can organize a sole proprietorship by simply obtaining a license to do business from your local or state government. You might also need to obtain a state sales tax number because you may be required to collect sales tax on any products you sell to customers.

Springboard Ask the students this question: "If you were to start a business, would you prefer to do it by yourself or with a partner? Why?"

Business Name If you are planning to operate under a business name other than your own name, you must apply for a *Certificate of Doing Business Under an Assumed Name*. This is also referred to as a *DBA*, which stands for "Doing Business As." For example, Celia Jontos wants to start a personalized wedding planning service, *Time to Remember*. In order to operate legally under this business name, Ms. Jontos will need to get a DBA certificate.

Employees If you intend to hire one or more employees to work in your business, you will need an Employer Identification Number. An **Employer Identification Number (EIN)** is a number assigned by the Internal Revenue Service, which is used for income tax purposes. Many sole proprietors hire managers and several employees. Some large companies, which are also organized as sole proprietorships, have hundreds of employees.

Motivating Students Have students name different types of businesses that interest them. Ask them if they would view running that business as a career for themselves? Why or why not?

Careers in Finance

GENERAL CONTRACTOR

Carolyn King
Self-Employed

Carolyn is a natural planner and leader. As a general contractor, she helps homeowners, landlords, and businesses construct, remodel, or repair their buildings. She may bid to take part of a job—for example, fixing a kitchen—or oversee an entire project. Carolyn must know prices and plan for expenses. Whether she handles the entire job or subcontracts parts of the job to electrical, heating, and plumbing specialists, Carolyn is responsible for the job being done on time and according to the budget. General contractors enjoy the challenge of working on different types of jobs and the satisfaction of putting together teams that are right for each project.

SKILLS:	Accounting, communication, decision-making, management, math, negotiation, organization, problem-solving, and time-management skills
PERSONAL TRAITS:	Highly motivated, leadership, able to work independently as well as with others
EDUCATION:	High school diploma or equivalent; or bachelor's degree in construction science; experience in the field; and contractor's license exam

ANALYZE Why would a general contractor need to have good money-management skills?

See the Teacher Manual for answer.

To learn more about career paths for general contractors, visit **finance07.glencoe.com**.

Extension Have the students research Debbi Fields, John Johnson, Amory Houghton, or William Colgate to find out how they actually started their businesses.

Total Control As a sole proprietor, you can run your business as you wish. This is a great advantage because you do not have to convince partners, stockholders, or other people that your business decisions are sound. You can choose what merchandise to sell or services to provide, what prices to charge, and what hours you will work. As the sole owner of your own business, you make all management and financial decisions.

Profits to Owner With a sole proprietorship, when your business makes a profit, you can keep all of it (after you pay taxes). As your business grows and becomes more successful, you will receive larger profits. A sole proprietorship allows the owner to reap the rewards of hard work and determination.

Profits Taxed Once A business organized as a sole proprietorship does not pay income taxes as a company. You as the owner must declare the profits of the business on your personal income tax return. Tax is computed on your total income for the year. If you operate your business full-time, any profits you make will be counted as taxable income. If your business operates part-time and you also have a full-time job, your taxable income will include income from your job as well as the net income from your business.

Research Ask the students to contact the IRS and find out how to obtain an EIN.

Few Government Regulations Another benefit of operating as a sole proprietorship is that you do not have to complete and file many forms and reports with the state and federal governments. There may be some government regulations regarding the particular business, but most sole proprietors experience little government red tape.

Disadvantages of Sole Proprietorship

With most choices people make, there is a positive side and a negative side. Though organizing your business as a sole proprietorship has definite advantages, this form of business organization also has several drawbacks:

- Limited capital
- Unlimited liability
- Limited human resources
- Limited life

Limited Capital When you start a sole proprietorship, the only source of working capital, besides money you borrow, is your own money. Generally, no one else helps you finance the business. Moreover, the amount of cash available to you may be limited. Adequate funding and a positive cash flow are essential for a business. Without a sufficient amount of money to establish the business, begin operations, and expand, you could have serious difficulties. See Chapter 19 for a detailed discussion on sources of funding.

Unlimited Liability A major disadvantage of a sole proprietorship is that if your business is not successful, you are responsible for all losses. **Unlimited liability** is a situation in which the owner of the business is responsible to pay the business debts out of personal assets. In other words, if your business is unsuccessful, you could lose your car, home, savings, and other assets. If your business's financial situation is bad, you might have to declare personal bankruptcy.

Starting a new business involves a high risk. More than half of all new businesses fail within five years after being established. If your business fails, your personal financial position and credit rating could be seriously damaged.

Limited Human Resources An advantage of a sole proprietorship is that you are the only decision maker in the business. However, being the only person in charge can also be a disadvantage. When you are the sole owner of a business, you cannot rely on other individuals to help carry the load.

Most people have limited knowledge and talents. Perhaps you know a lot about certain goods or services, but your basic business skills are weak. For example, if you start a painting business, you may have skills in painting, be able to identify different types of paint, and know the proper way to apply paint to different surfaces. At the same time, you may have limited business experience in pricing, record-keeping, or advertising and marketing.

$avvy Saver

Checking Account Questions

1. How much money do I need to open a personal or small business checking account?
2. What are the monthly service charges?
3. Do I need to keep a minimum amount of money in my account?
4. Will my checking account earn interest?
5. Can I sign up for overdraft protection?

Discussion Ask the students: "Why do you think, given so many disadvantages, sole proprietorships are so popular?"

As You Read

RELATE

With the skills you have now, do you think you would be able to start a sole-proprietorship business?

Poor decisions in purchasing, accounting, or marketing could ruin your business, even when you have a lot of knowledge about your product or service. A sole proprietor must be willing to hire the services of people whose different talents and skills will enhance the business.

Limited Life A sole proprietorship has a **limited life,** a situation in which a business's life span or existence is determined by the owner's life span or the owner's decision to terminate the business. The business may also legally end if sold to someone else. In that case, the new owner creates a new business in his or her name.

The Partnership

What are the characteristics of a partnership?

Some people choose to form a partnership when starting a business. A **partnership** is a business owned by two or more persons. Partners as co-owners agree voluntarily to operate the business for profit. When a partnership is formed, the partners sign a special legal agreement: A **partnership agreement** is a written document that states how the partnership will be organized. The agreement includes the following basic information:

- Names of the partners
- Name and nature of the business
- Amount of investment by each partner
- Duties, rights, and responsibilities of each partner
- Procedures for sharing profits and losses
- How assets will be divided when and if the partnership is dissolved

In a partnership you and your co-owners decide how to divide profits and losses from the business. You also outline the duties and responsibilities of each partner. All partners must agree to the conditions stated in the partnership agreement. The purpose of this written document is to prevent later disagreements among the partners.

About 5 percent of all businesses in the United States today are partnerships. However, some large companies began as partnerships before becoming corporations. For example, in 1876, an icebox maker named Abram Anderson started a partnership with a fruit merchant named Joseph Campbell. Their small partnership eventually grew to become a corporation, the Campbell Soup Company.

General Partners and Limited Partners

Within the category of partnerships, there are two basic types of partners: general partners and limited partners. In many partnerships, all partners are general partners. A **general partner** is a business partner who has decision-making authority, takes an active role in the operation of the business, and has unlimited liability for all losses or debts of the partnership. Every partnership has at least one general partner.

Critical Thinking Ask the students why every partnership has at least one general partner.

All general partners have what is known as agency power. Agency power, also known as *mutual agency*, is the right to sign contracts that are legally binding on the partnership. For example, suppose that Dylan, Juanita, and Charles form a partnership to make bookcases. Dylan goes to Clinton Wood Products and signs a contract to purchase wood from that company. Dylan acted on behalf of the business with agency power, and so the partnership is legally obligated under the contract.

A partnership can also add limited partners. A **limited partner** is a business partner who does not take an active role in decision making or in running the business. A limited partner's liability in the partnership is limited to the amount of his or her investment in the business. For example, Christa Clark, a limited partner in Low Country Furniture, invested $25,000 in the business. Christa is not involved in running the business. Moreover, her financial liability is limited to her $25,000 investment. That means if the business fails, the most she can lose is $25,000.

Teaching Activity Divide the students into groups of three or four. Allow them to select their own groups. Then have each group develop a partnership agreement that they could use when students work together on a project.

Advantages of the Partnership

Many of the advantages of a partnership are similar to the advantages of a sole proprietorship. However, instead of being the only decision maker in a business, you would share decision making with your partners. More people can generate more ideas and possibly more money. There are several advantages of a partnership:

- Easy set-up
- More skills and knowledge
- Available capital
- Total control by partners
- Profits taxed once

Discussion Ask the students to discuss the qualities they would look for in a good business partner.

Caption Answer business skills in accounting, pricing, recordkeeping, or advertising and marketing

◀ **YOU ARE THE BOSS** In a sole proprietorship, the owner makes all the decisions and takes all the responsibility. However, it is impossible for one person to be knowledgeable and skilled in all areas. *What skills and knowledge might a sole proprietor owner lack?*

▲ **PROFESSIONAL PARTNERSHIPS**
Partnerships are common among groups of professionals, such as architects, lawyers, and accountants. *Can you name groups of people in other occupations that might form partnerships?*

Caption Answer Accept all reasonable answers.

Easy Set-Up A partnership is also relatively easy to set up. Although some paperwork is required, it is generally minimal. You may need to obtain certain local or state business permits or licenses. For some types of business operations, you must also know and follow various government regulations.

The most important legal document of a partnership is the partnership agreement. All the terms and conditions of the partnership must be clearly stated in this written document. Taking care to make the agreement as complete and clear as possible can help you to avoid misinterpretations and misunderstandings between partners as the partnership and business grow.

More Skills and Knowledge The skills and knowledge needed to operate the business in a sole proprietorship are the responsibility of just one person. In a partnership, however, the various partners can contribute different skills and experience. One person may have previous experience running a similar type of business. Another partner might have extensive business or accounting experience. A third partner might have excellent sales and marketing skills. The pooling of talent and knowledge is an advantage that partnerships have over sole proprietorships.

Available Capital Several individuals in a business partnership can contribute more money to a business venture than one person acting alone with only personal assets. Moreover, if additional cash is needed to maintain or expand business operations, it can be easier to raise capital when several people are working to do so.

For example, in 1872, dry goods merchant Levi Strauss received a letter from one of his customers, a Nevada tailor named Jacob Davis. Davis had been making overalls for miners and had come up with a way to strengthen the pants by adding rivets to the seams. He wanted to patent his idea but could not afford the $68 he needed to file the papers. He wrote to Strauss to suggest that they hold the patent together. When Strauss teamed up with Davis in 1873, Levi's® jeans became a reality.

Obtaining bank financing may be more feasible when more than one individual is responsible for the loan. Banks may also be more willing to loan greater sums of money to a partnership than to a sole proprietorship because the risk is shared among the partners.

The partners' credit ratings are very important. Avoid entering a partnership agreement with anyone who has a questionable credit rating. The ability of all partners to borrow money can be an important factor in the success or failure of a business.

As You Read
QUESTION

What are two advantages of a partnership over a sole proprietorship?

Question Answer Answers might include ease of set-up, more skills and knowledge, and more available capital.

Document Detective

Learn to identify and understand the standard financial documents you will use in the real world.

See the Teacher Manual for answers.

Investigate: An Application for Employer ID Number

An IRS Form SS-4 contains the following information:

- Name and address of the business
- Type of business
- Date the business started
- Principal activity of the business

Your Motive: You may decide in the future to start your own business. When you establish a business, you are required by law to apply to the federal government for an employer identification number.

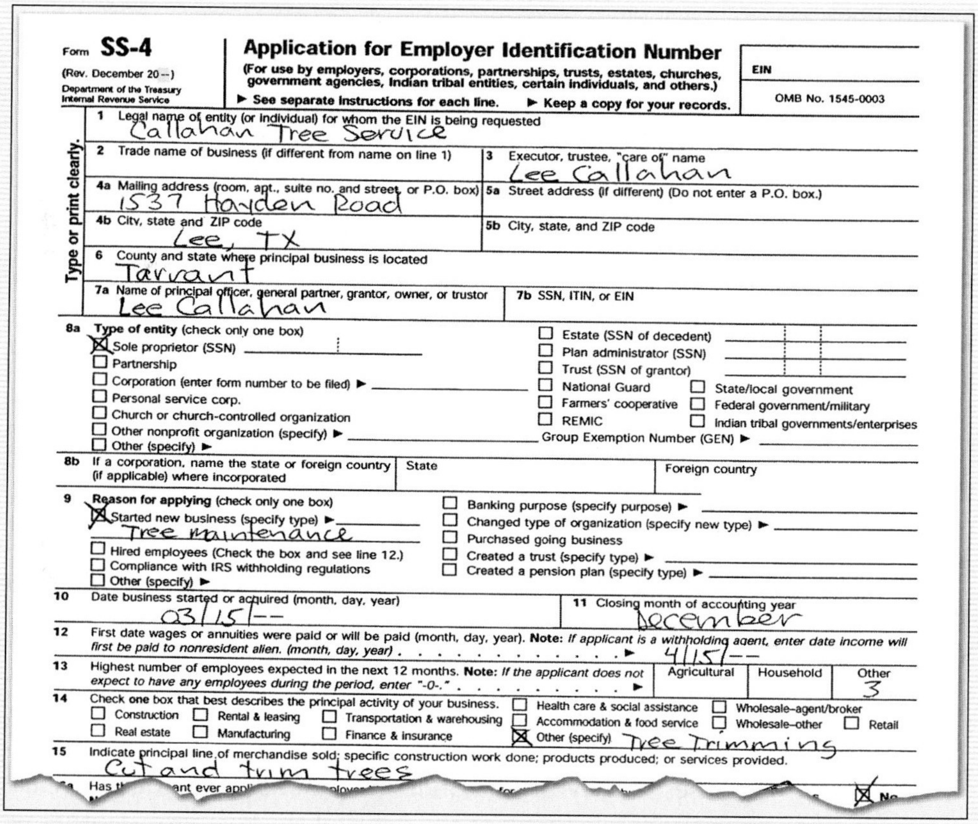

Form **SS-4** (Rev. December 20--) Department of the Treasury Internal Revenue Service

Application for Employer Identification Number

(For use by employers, corporations, partnerships, trusts, estates, churches, government agencies, Indian tribal entities, certain individuals, and others.)

► **See separate instructions for each line.** ► **Keep a copy for your records.**

EIN

OMB No. 1545-0003

Type or print clearly.

1 Legal name of entity (or individual) for whom the EIN is being requested: Callahan Tree Service

2 Trade name of business (if different from name on line 1)

3 Executor, trustee, "care of" name: Lee Callahan

4a Mailing address (room, apt., suite no. and street, or P.O. box): 1537 Hayden Road

5a Street address (if different) (Do not enter a P.O. box.)

4b City, state and ZIP code: Lee, TX

5b City, state, and ZIP code

6 County and state where principal business is located: Tarrant

7a Name of principal officer, general partner, grantor, owner, or trustor: Lee Callahan

7b SSN, ITIN, or EIN

8a **Type of entity** (check only one box)

- ☒ Sole proprietor (SSN)
- ☐ Partnership
- ☐ Corporation (enter form number to be filed) ►
- ☐ Personal service corp.
- ☐ Church or church-controlled organization
- ☐ Other nonprofit organization (specify) ►
- ☐ Other (specify) ►
- ☐ Estate (SSN of decedent)
- ☐ Plan administrator (SSN)
- ☐ Trust (SSN of grantor)
- ☐ National Guard
- ☐ Farmers' cooperative
- ☐ REMIC
- ☐ State/local government
- ☐ Federal government/military
- ☐ Indian tribal governments/enterprises
- Group Exemption Number (GEN) ►

8b If a corporation, name the state or foreign country (if applicable) where incorporated | State | Foreign country

9 **Reason for applying** (check only one box)

- ☒ Started new business (specify type) ► Tree maintenance
- ☐ Hired employees (Check the box and see line 12.)
- ☐ Compliance with IRS withholding regulations
- ☐ Other (specify) ►
- ☐ Banking purpose (specify purpose) ►
- ☐ Changed type of organization (specify new type) ►
- ☐ Purchased going business
- ☐ Created a trust (specify type) ►
- ☐ Created a pension plan (specify type) ►

10 Date business started or acquired (month, day, year): 03/15/--

11 Closing month of accounting year: December

12 First date wages or annuities were paid or will be paid (month, day, year). **Note:** *If applicant is a withholding agent, enter date income will first be paid to nonresident alien. (month, day, year)* ► 4/15/--

13 Highest number of employees expected in the next 12 months. **Note:** *If the applicant does not expect to have any employees during the period, enter "-0-."* ►

Agricultural	Household	Other
		3

14 Check **one** box that best describes the principal activity of your business.

☐ Construction ☐ Rental & leasing ☐ Transportation & warehousing ☐ Health care & social assistance ☐ Wholesale–agent/broker ☐ Real estate ☐ Manufacturing ☐ Finance & insurance ☐ Accommodation & food service ☐ Wholesale–other ☐ Retail ☒ Other (specify) Tree Trimming

15 Indicate principal line of merchandise sold; specific construction work done; products produced; or services provided: Cut and trim trees

Has th... ☒ No

Key Points: An employer sends an IRS Form SS-4 to the federal government. When received, the government assigns the employer a number. The Employer Identification Number (EIN) helps the government monitor taxes that a business is required to pay. Whenever taxes are paid, a business must provide its identification number.

Find the Solutions

1. Who should use the Form SS-4?
2. What is the purpose of this form?
3. What was the date that this business started?
4. In what state was this business incorporated?
5. What is the principal activity of the business?

STANDARD &POOR'S

Put on Your Financial Planner's Cap

After working for two years as a financial planner, you have decided to go out on your own. Determine how you want to establish your business: as a sole proprietorship, with a partner or as a limited partnership. Create a chart for each business type, comparing start-up funds, insurance needed, supplies needed, and type of advertising needed.

See the Teacher Manual for answer.

Critical Thinking Have the students brainstorm a list of situations a business owner might face that could lead to financial problems.

Total Control by Partners In a partnership the operation of the business is the sole responsibility of the general partners, who can do as they want. However, the partners are also responsible for the success or failure of the business.

Profits Taxed Once Like a sole proprietorship, a partnership is not taxed as a business. Therefore, it is not subject to state or federal income taxes. The partnership agreement states how the profits of the partnership should be divided. Each partner must pay personal income taxes to the state and federal government, based on his or her share of the profits received from the business. Thus, business profits are taxed only once.

Disadvantages of the Partnership

While a partnership can offer many advantages, a number of problems can arise when several people own and operate a business. This form of business ownership can avoid some of the problems associated with sole proprietorships, but it also has disadvantages:

- Unlimited liability
- Possible disagreement among partners
- Shared profits
- Limited life

In 1975, two young men named Bill Gates and Paul Allen formed a partnership to produce computer software. Today their company, Microsoft, is a major corporation, and Bill Gates and Paul Allen are two of the wealthiest people in the world. Microsoft is a partnership that turned into one of America's greatest success stories. However, most people never come close to this level of achievement. Many partnerships have very little success or eventually fail. Entering a partnership involves large financial risks.

Unlimited Liability Earlier in this section, you learned that the owner of a sole proprietorship has unlimited liability. The same is true of the general partners in a partnership. If the partnership loses money or has financial problems, each co-owner is personally responsible for all of the debts of the business. In other words, if your partnership fails and the debts of the business cannot be covered by its assets, you and your partners are responsible for paying the bills out of your own personal assets.

For example, two friends ask you to join them in forming a partnership. You have a large amount of personal assets. Your two partners have very few assets. If the business fails, you could end up being personally responsible for the majority of the business debts. You could even lose everything you own. It is very important to choose your business partners carefully. Know the personal financial position and credit ratings of each partner. Remember, each general partner has unlimited liability for the entire business, not just part of it.

Disagreement among Partners When several people manage a business, they may not always agree on important business decisions. A common reason for failed partnerships is that the partners have serious conflicts about how the business should operate, and they allow the business to suffer financially from these conflicts.

Shared Profits Hard work on your part may be the crucial factor in the success of the business. Nevertheless, you still must share the profits with your partners. The way in which the profits of the business are divided is outlined in the partnership agreement.

Limited Life The life of a partnership depends on the willingness and ability of the partners to continue in business together. A partnership has a limited life, and partnerships can end for a number of reasons. Perhaps a partner dies or decides to retire or withdraw from the partnership due to illness. The partners may disagree and decide to end their partnership, or they may decide to add new partners. In these situations, the original partnership dissolves. The remaining partners and any new partners should then draw up a new partnership agreement, which will create a new business.

Section 16.1 Assessment

See the Teacher Manual for answers.

QUICK CHECK

1. What is an advantage of being a sole proprietor?
2. What is the difference between a general partner and a limited partner?
3. What are several disadvantages of a partnership?

THINK CRITICALLY

4. In your opinion, what is the most important element of a partnership agreement? Explain your answer.

USE COMMUNICATION SKILLS

5. **Perturbed Partners** Lawrence and Tyrell are partners in a small retail business. They sell hats and T-shirts from a kiosk in a shopping mall. Recently they have been thinking about selling other items as well, but they cannot agree on what items to add to their product line. Their disagreements have caused the business to suffer financially.

Write About It What advice would you offer Lawrence and Tyrell to help them work out their differences? What solutions would you suggest? Write down your suggestions for them.

SOLVE MONEY PROBLEMS

6. **Business Ownership Decisions** Pamela owns a pet-sitting business. People hire her to take care of their pets when they go out of town. As part of her service, Pamela also brings in her clients' mail and waters their plants. Her business is booming, and she needs to make some critical decisions about its future.

Analyze Help Pamela decide what to do now. Should she expand her business? Add employees? Take on a partner? Make sure that you evaluate the advantages and disadvantages of each suggestion you offer as you outline your suggestions on paper.

Section 16.2

The Corporation

Focus on Reading

Read to Learn

- How to describe two types of corporations.
- How to summarize the process of forming a corporation.
- How to discuss the advantages and disadvantages of a corporation.

Main Idea

A typical form of business organization is the corporation, which is in operation all over the world.

Key Terms

- corporation
- articles of incorporation
- corporate bylaws
- corporate charter
- board of directors
- limited liability company (LLC)
- franchise

Before You Read

PREDICT

What might be an advantage of a corporation?

Springboard Have the students discuss the positive and negative images that the word *corporation* connotes to them.

What Is a Corporation?

What is the difference between a corporation and other businesses?

You have probably heard the word *corporation.* A number of large corporations exist nationally and globally, such as IBM, General Motors, Hershey Foods, Sony, Hewlett-Packard, Motorola, Xerox, and Goodyear. A corporation is another form of business ownership that is different from a sole proprietorship or a partnership.

A **corporation** is a business organization that operates as a legal entity that is separate from its owners and is treated by law as if it were an individual person. A corporation can do everything that a sole proprietorship or a partnership can do—own property, buy and sell merchandise, pay bills, and make contracts. It can also sue and be sued in the court system. About 20 percent of businesses in the United States are organized as corporations, but they produce about 90 percent of the total business revenue in the United States.

Starting a Corporation

What is the process of forming a corporation?

When you form a corporation, you create a legal entity. This process is more complex than starting a sole proprietorship or a partnership.

Paperwork and Documents

To create a corporation, you must file an application with the state for permission to operate. The application to operate as a corporation is called the **articles of incorporation**. The application includes information such as the corporate name and the type of business in which the corporation will be involved.

In addition to the articles of incorporation, you must write a set of corporate bylaws. **Corporate bylaws** are the rules by which a corporation will operate. Items in the bylaws may include how the company will elect directors of the corporation and when stockholders will meet.

When the state approves the application, it issues a corporate charter. A **corporate charter** is a license to operate a corporation. It states the purpose of the business and spells out the laws and guidelines under which the business will operate.

Issuing Stock

The ownership of a corporation is divided into units, which are shares of stock. These shares of stock are bought by people who become known as *stockholders*. Stockholders are the legal owners of the corporation. If you buy even one share of stock in Xerox, for example, you are legally an owner of the company and have all the rights of ownership. Each stockholder receives a stock certificate, which is a document that is proof of ownership. Small corporations usually have only a few stockholders. Larger corporations, such as Kodak and Verizon, have thousands of stockholders.

Closely Held Corporations A closely held, or private, corporation is one whose shares are owned by a relatively small group of people. In many cases, there are only three or four stockholders. The shares are not traded openly in stock markets. Many small and family businesses are organized as closely held corporations.

Publicly Held Corporations A publicly held corporation is one that sells its shares openly in stock markets, where anyone can buy them. Most of these corporations trade their stock on an exchange, such as the New York Stock Exchange or the American Stock Exchange. Almost all major corporations, such as Black & Decker, Intel, and American Express, are publicly held.

Going Public A closely held corporation can be opened to the general public if the stockholders decide in favor of this move. When a corporation decides to sell its stock on the open market, the decision is known as *going public*.

TechByte

Virtual Consultants
Using technology can help you plan your business strategy. Smart software allows you to strategize about how to build your business. For example, the MBA Wizard is intelligent software created with the capacity to learn. It has accurately evaluated over 20,000 business plans, and thus, its expanding knowledge is accessible to the user.

@ Read more about the MBA Wizard and write a paragraph about how smart software might help an entrepreneur write a business plan through **finance07.glencoe.com**.

Motivating Students There are do-it-yourself incorporation kits on the market. Ask the students: "Do you think it is a good idea to use one, or should an attorney be consulted to handle all the legal aspects of incorporating?" Have them explain their answers.

Caption Answer Accept all reasonable answers, but some might include that because corporations are usually large companies, they can raise more capital and produce more revenue.

◀ **CORPORATE POWER**
Corporations produce about 90 percent of all U.S. business revenue. *Why do you think this is the case?*

As You Read

RELATE

Imagine you and a few friends decide to start a business making and selling cookies decorated to order. What type of business organization would suit you best?

Advantages of the Corporation

What are the benefits of forming a corporation?

Establishing your business as a corporation has a number of advantages over a sole proprietorship and a partnership:

- Ability to raise capital
- Limited liability
- Continued life
- Separation of ownership and management

Ability to Raise Capital

A major advantage of a corporation is the ability to sell its stock and generate capital, or money. If the corporation needs money for growth, expansion, or other purposes, the company can sell additional shares of stock to raise the necessary funds. If a large amount of capital is needed to start a business, the company may begin as a closely held corporation rather than as a partnership. Examples of this kind of corporation might include an automobile dealership, a restaurant, and an amusement park.

Discussion Generate a discussion with the students on the responsibilities of the stockholder to the corporation.

Limited Liability

A great advantage to the stockholders, or owners, of a corporation is that they have limited liability. This means that if the corporation has debts or financial problems, the owners may lose only the amount of their investment—the price they paid for their stock.

Extension Have the students research what a company must do in order to go public.

▲ **WHO OWNS THAT TEAM?** Professional sports teams are operated under all forms of business ownership. Some teams are public corporations. *What would happen if a publicly owned sports team experienced a change in owners?*

Caption Answer The owners of a sports team are the stockholders. Stockholders may enter or leave the business at any time without affecting the status of the corporation.

Consider the following example: You own $20,000 worth of stock in the Family Fun Restaurant. The restaurant is not successful and goes out of business while owing $150,000 dollars to its creditors. As a stockholder, you can lose only up to $20,000, or the amount of your investment, to help repay these debts. You are not personally responsible for any debt beyond that amount. Unlike a sole proprietorship or a general partnership, a corporation leaves your personal assets protected. You are not legally responsible for all the debts owed by the corporation.

STANDARD & POOR'S

Global Financial Landscape

Standard and Poor's publishes the globally recognized S&P 500® financial index. It also gathers financial statistics, information, and news, and analyzes this data for international businesses, governments, and individuals to help them guide their financial decisions.

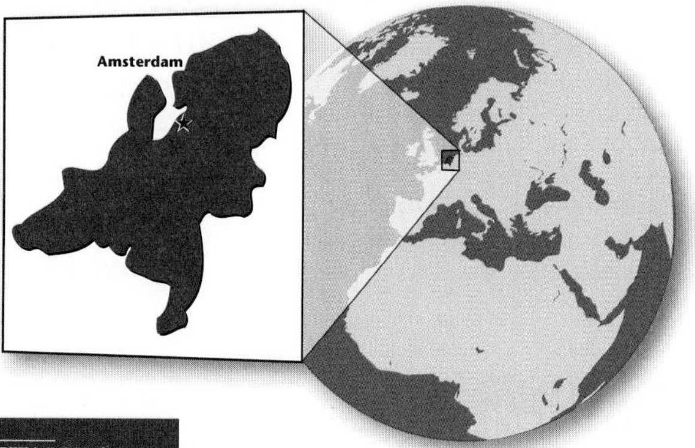

NETHERLANDS

Energy engineers have said that harnessing only 1 percent of the wind's force could produce enough electricity to run the world. By 2020, both the American and European Energy Associations predict that wind will supply 12 percent of the world's power.

The Netherlands is off to a good start. A pioneer of wind energy, the country has granted licenses for the development of wind parks on its coast. The parks will include at least 2,000 turbines, which are the modern-day versions of traditional windmills, familiar sights of the Dutch countryside. To help eliminate polluting fossil-fuel emissions, the Netherlands plans to use these powerful turbines to generate 6,000 megawatts of wind energy. (Nine megawatts can provide electricity for about 5,000 houses.)

Centuries ago there were as many as 9,000 traditional windmills in the Netherlands. Wind energy was used to pump ocean water away from the Dutch land. Today it can help to light streets and power computers.

STANDARD & POOR'S

DATABYTES

Capital	Amsterdam
Population	16,237,000
Languages	Dutch and Frisian
Currency	euro
Gross Domestic Product (GDP)	$461.4 billion (2003 est.)
GDP per capita	$28,600

Industry: Agro-industries, metal and engineering products, electrical machinery and equipment, and chemicals

Agriculture: Grains, potatoes, sugar beets, fruits, and livestock

Exports: Machinery and equipment, chemicals, fuels, and foodstuffs

Natural Resources: Natural gas, crude oil, and fertile soil

Think Globally

If a corporation used alternative sources of energy, do you think stockholders might have more or less confidence in the company? Why or why not?

See the Teacher Manual for answer.

As You Read
QUESTION

What is the advantage of separating ownership and management?

Question Answer The corporation takes advantage of skills, knowledge, and experience of various individuals.

Teaching Activity Tell the students you are going to paint the classroom. Ask each student individually what color they would like to paint the room. Then divide the class into two groups. Have each group reach a decision on the color the room should be painted. Then have each group explain the difference between making a decision by themselves and making one in a large group.

Continued Life

When a sole proprietor retires, dies, or sells his or her business to someone else, that business ceases to exist. Each time partners enter or leave a partnership, a new partnership must be created. In a corporation, however, a change of owners does not end the legal operation of the business. Stockholders may enter or leave at any time without affecting the existence of the corporation. Its legal status as a business continues indefinitely.

Separation of Ownership and Management

The owners do not run the business in most publicly held corporations. Instead, they elect a **board of directors**, a group of individuals who are responsible for overseeing the general affairs of the corporation. Corporate officers and professional managers are hired to make day-to-day decisions in running the business. Other specialists, such as lawyers and accountants, advise the professional managers. By separating management from ownership, the corporation can take advantage of the skills, knowledge, and experience of various individuals to ensure that the business will run successfully. (See **Figure 16.1** for corporate advantages.)

Figure 16.1 Corporate Advantages

Incorporating Business Even some small sole proprietorships and family businesses decide or convert to corporations to gain the benefits of incorporation.

What is a closely held corporation?

Caption Answer It is a corporation whose shares are owned by a small group of people and are not traded openly in stock markets. The owners often act as managers.

In smaller, closely held corporations, the owners often act as the managers who run the business. The separation of ownership and management usually does not occur until a company grows large and goes public. For example, Apple Computer was established originally as a partnership managed and run by its co-owners, Steve Jobs and Steve Wozniak. To expand, they formed a closely held corporation. After it became a publicly held corporation, the company hired professional managers and other specialists to run the business. (See **Figure 16.2** on pages 540–541 for an example of a publicly held corporation as well as other forms of business ownership.)

Disadvantages of a Corporation

What are the drawbacks of corporate ownership?

Though the corporate form of ownership has a number of advantages, it also has several disadvantages:

- Complex and expensive set-up
- Slow decision-making process
- Taxes

Complex and Expensive Set-Up

You have learned that sole proprietorships and partnerships are fairly easy to set up. In contrast, a great deal of work is required to create a corporation. You must complete many forms, file reports, and adhere to many laws and regulations.

As a result of the great amount of work and organization required, forming a corporation costs a large amount of money. Some costs of creating a corporation include legal fees, licensing costs, filing fees, costs of issuing stock certificates, and administrative costs.

Slow Decision-Making Process

A major disadvantage of the corporation is the slowness of the decision-making process. In sole proprietorships and partnerships, only a few people determine how the business is run. As a result, decisions may be made quickly. However, in corporations, especially large ones, many different people study the issues and discuss and debate them before making a decision. The process can take even more time if disagreements occur. Thus, corporations may not respond quickly to issues or situations that affect business.

Taxes

Another major disadvantage of a corporation concerns taxes. Because a corporation is a separate legal entity, it must pay state and federal income taxes on its profits. Dividends that stockholders receive are then taxed again.

WebQuest

Be Your Own Boss
When you are a business owner, you may need to consider incorporating. Learn about the different types of corporations from which to choose and how to incorporate your business.

@ To continue with Task 2 of your WebQuest project, visit **finance07.glencoe.com**.

Common CENTS

Shop by Phone
Instead of driving from store to store, use your telephone to see if a store has the item that you want and compare prices. You will save gas and time. Also, use the Internet to see if the store sells merchandise online. *What type of business ownership might an e-tail store have? What would be the advantage of this type of ownership for the store?*

Common Cents Accept all reasonable answers. Some may say that a start-up e-tail store might begin as a partnership.

Figure 16.2 Forms of Business Ownership

Perhaps you have wanted to open a business one day that would allow you to combine your love of a sport, interest, or hobby with a business opportunity. This kind of business can take different forms of ownership.

1

Sole Proprietorships
A hobby such as fly-fishing could turn into an ideal *sole proprietorship*. An avid fisherman could offer his or her services as a fishing guide or instructor.

2

Partnerships
Some businesses may be too large for one person to operate. For example, a floral-design business that specializes in events might be a good enterprise for a *partnership* whose owners contribute different talents.

3 Closely Held Corporations Some businesses are organized as *closely held corporations*. The owners could be a group with a common interest, such as kayaking.

4 Publicly Held Corporations Walt Disney World is part of the The Walt Disney Company, a *publicly held corporation* with thousands of stockholders.

Academic Connection

MARKETING

Businesses spend billions of dollars on advertising. The most common types of advertising media include newspapers, magazines, direct mail, billboards, television, and radio. *Select two businesses in your community—a sole proprietorship or partnership and a corporation. For each business, find an example of an advertisement for the business. Compile the ads as a class according to the type of media represented. Discuss how each form of business ownership affects the business's choice of advertising media.*

See the Teacher Manual for answer.

Research Ask the students to research when and why LLCs were first created and why they are becoming so popular.

Limited Liability Company

What is another type of ownership?

The federal government also allows another form of business ownership—a **limited liability company (LLC)**, which is a business that operates and pays taxes as a partnership but has limited liability for the owners. It combines some advantages of both the partnership and the corporation. In an LLC, the liability of the owners is limited to their investments. The profits are taxed only once. This form of business is intended for smaller businesses.

Most states allow the creation of LLCs, and they are becoming very popular. The Internal Revenue Service approves of this new form of business organization if the company is small. This form of ownership is not intended for large business operations.

Franchise

Is a franchise a form of business ownership?

A franchise is not a form of business ownership, but it is important to understand its legal status. A **franchise** is a contractual agreement to sell a company's products or services in a designated geographic area. Franchises are very popular in fast-food businesses, such as McDonald's, Subway, Burger King, Wendy's, and Taco Bell, all of which have franchises.

If you start a franchise, you first organize your business as a sole proprietorship, partnership, corporation, or LLC. You then purchase a franchise from a corporation, such as Burger King. This corporation is known as a *parent corporation*. You are now licensed, and the franchise is an asset of your business.

▲ **OWNING A FRANCHISE** Many businesses are franchises. *What are some advantages of purchasing a franchise from a corporation?*

Caption Answer Answers might include you are buying into an established business and you have access to services of a larger corporation.

Smaller franchises may cost only a few thousand dollars, but large ones, such as McDonald's and Midas Muffler, cost hundreds of thousands of dollars. The next time you dine under McDonald's golden arches, remember that the establishment is actually a business organized under one of the three forms of business ownership. The business is also a franchise and has paid a franchise fee to McDonald's.

After You Read

REACT

What are four types of business ownership?

React Answer sole proprietorships, partnerships, closely held corporations, and publicly held corporations

Choosing the Form of Ownership

Which form of business ownership is best?

No magic formula exists for deciding which form of ownership is the best. You must carefully consider the advantages and disadvantages of each. Then you can decide which one is best for your particular business and personal needs. Many people feel that a small start-up business is best established as a sole proprietorship or a partnership. These forms of ownership are easy to establish. If the business is successful, you can consider creating a corporation to gain increased capital and limited liability.

Extension Have the students make a list of all the franchises they can think of in their community. Ask if there is more than one of each and if that affects each one's success.

Section 16.2 Assessment

See the Teacher Manual for answers.

QUICK CHECK

1. What are the articles of incorporation, a corporate charter, and corporate bylaws?
2. What is a closely held corporation?
3. What are advantages of a corporation?

THINK CRITICALLY

4. What effect might an increase of stockholders have on a corporation?

USE MATH SKILLS

5. **Issuing Stock** Terrance and several partners own a dry cleaning business that operates as a closely held corporation. They want to go public and sell stock, hoping to raise enough capital to expand the business.

Calculate If the initial offering of their stock sells for $29.50 per share, how many shares of stock will they have to sell to raise $1 million?

SOLVE MONEY PROBLEMS

6. **Limited Liability?** Beverly Echo-Hawk is the sole proprietor of All Wet, a raft rental company that operates on the Colorado River. She saved $35,000 to establish the business. However, competition from other companies with better equipment has caused losses for All Wet. Beverly also owns $33,000 worth of stock in a corporation that is being managed poorly. She fears that the corporation will go out of business.

Analyze Which investment poses a greater financial risk? Why?

Chapter 16 Review & Activities

See the Teacher Manual for answers.

CHAPTER SUMMARY

- Sole proprietorships are easy to set up; the owner retains control and profits; there are few government regulations; and profits are taxed once as personal income. The disadvantages include limited capital, unlimited liability, limited human resources, and a limited life.
- In partnerships, general partners have decision-making authority, are active in the business, and have unlimited liability. Limited partners rarely take an active role in the business, and their liability is limited to their investment.
- Partnerships are easy to set up and bring more skills, knowledge, and capital to the business. Partners retain control, and profits are taxed once as personal income. Disadvantages include unlimited liability; potential disagreements; shared profits; and limited life of the business.
- Closely held corporations have shares held by a few individuals, and shares are not traded in stock markets. Publicly held corporations sell shares on stock exchanges, and shares are held by many individuals and institutions.
- To form a corporation, you must file articles of incorporation with the state in which you incorporate, and you must write corporate bylaws. The state issues a corporate charter.
- Corporations operate as legal entities separate from owners and continue no matter who owns them. Corporations issue stock; stockholders have limited liability. However, corporations are difficult and expensive to establish; decision making can be slow; and profits are taxed twice.

Communicating Key Terms

Imagine that you are a lawyer specializing in business law. Use the terms below to explain to a new client the different forms of ownership. Role-play this meeting with a partner.

- sole proprietorship
- Employer Identification Number (EIN)
- unlimited liability
- limited life
- partnership
- partnership agreement
- general partner
- limited partner
- corporation
- articles of incorporation
- corporate bylaws
- corporate charter
- board of directors
- limited liability company (LLC)
- franchise

Reviewing Key Concepts

1. **Explain** why most new businesses begin as sole proprietorships.
2. **Describe** the roles of general and limited partners in a business.
3. **Discuss** the advantage of starting a business as a partnership versus a sole proprietorship.
4. **Identify** the advantages and disadvantages of a closely held versus publicly held corporation.
5. **List** the contents of articles of incorporation.
6. **Explain** why current stockholders might oppose a corporation's decision to issue more stock.

See the Teacher Manual for answers.

ACADEMIC SKILLS

Geography Three friends who majored in biology together in college want to open up a medical laboratory. They would like to work in a smaller city to service the medical community there.

Research Look at a map of the United States as you search online for growing communities in smaller cities. Pick three possibilities for the new laboratory and choose the best form of business for this group.

YOUR FINANCIAL FIGURES

Initial Public Offerings (IPOs) "Going public" and issuing stock is neither simple nor inexpensive. Go online or use other sources to find out the average cost of an initial public offering. A stockbroker may be able to help you.

1. **Calculate** If a medium-sized software development company with a current annual net income of $10 million wants to "go public" and raise $75 million for growth and expansion, determine the total worth of stock it will have to sell to net this amount.
2. **Analyze** What factors will be involved in setting the initial stock price?

REAL-WORLD Application

Connect with Economics and Social Studies After being downsized from her job at a corporation, Mia decides to start her own business as a technical writer and editor. Her accountant thinks she should "set up shop" as a limited liability corporation. Mia decides to research this further.

1. **Research** Investigate the advantages and disadvantages of limited liability companies for someone in Mia's situation.
2. **Role-Play** With a partner, take the roles of Mia and her accountant. Prepare a list of questions for Mia to ask and answers for the accountant.

Internet CONNECTION

Running the Show Although many people feel that "being your own boss" is something they really would like to do, not everyone can handle the risks associated with entrepreneurship and sole proprietorship.

@ **Log On** Access the Small Business Administration Web site through **finance07.glencoe.com** and research the personality characteristics an entrepreneur needs to survive and thrive.

Write About It Prepare an article for the school or class newsletter describing these characteristics.

BusinessWeek ONLINE

Newsclip: The New Entrepreneurship There are more entrepreneurs today than there were 20 years ago.

@ **Log On** Go to **finance07.glencoe.com** and open Chapter 16. Learn more about what steps you need to take to build your own enterprise. Write a few sentences about what kind of business you would like to run.

WHAT'S YOUR FINANCIAL ID?

WHAT KIND OF BUSINESS?

You could start a business for virtually any activity. As you take this quiz, use your imagination. Just for fun, review the following list of businesses and choose five that you could imagine owning. Write your answers on a separate sheet of paper.

______ a. car repair
______ b. photographic studio
______ c. veterinary clinic
______ d. rock group
______ e. gourmet coffee shop
______ f. graphic artist studio
______ g. newsletter or other publishing enterprise
______ h. computer software
______ i. biotechnology lab
______ j. bed-and-breakfast inn
______ k. architectural firm
______ l. medical care
______ m. hair salon
______ n. tutoring service
______ o. detective

What do your choices say about you?

- If you selected **b, d, f, g,** or **k,** you are probably artistic. Your strongest interests are in the creative arts or working in a field that requires originality and imagination.
- If you selected **e, j, l, m,** or **n,** you are probably social. You enjoy helping others and working closely with people.
- If you selected **a, c, h, i,** or **o,** you are probably investigative. You like the challenge of making decisions and coming up with innovative solutions.

Accept all reasonable answers that show student effort and an understanding of the concept.

Were your selections from one category—artistic, social, or investigative—or from a combination of categories? Look to see if you have stronger interests in one area over another. Which types of daily activities do you prefer—artistic, social, or investigative?

Your Financial Portfolio

Setting Up a Partnership

Mary has been teaching yoga classes at a gym for the past three years. She feels she now has enough experience to open her own yoga studio. Since she is concerned about costs and responsibilities, she spoke with one of the other yoga instructors, Tony, about starting a yoga business together. Tony thinks it is a great idea. Together, they outlined their partnership plan:

Location: One of Tony's friends works at an art gallery, which has a peaceful environment and ample floor space. Mary spoke with the owner of the gallery and negotiated using the gallery weekday evenings and Saturday and Sunday mornings. Mary and Tony agreed to pay the gallery owner 25 percent of all class fees.

Competition: The only yoga classes presently being offered in the area are at the health club where they both work.

Start-Up Costs: Mary and Tony must purchase 25 yoga mats at $20 per mat. They also will have insurance costs of $1,200 per year, plus $150 in fees and licenses. They will each contribute an equal amount of money from their personal savings to open the business.

Schedule: They will begin their business with eight classes per week: one each weekday evening, two classes on Saturday morning, and one on Sunday morning. Each class will be one hour in length. They agree that each person will teach four classes a week and cover for the other during illness or vacation.

Responsibilities: Mary is responsible for maintaining accounting records and paying bills. Tony is responsible for advertising and promotion.

Revenue: They decide to charge $15 per class. They project the weekend classes might bring in 25 students at each class ($375). Weekday classes might average 5 to 10 students ($75–150). Mary and Tony agree to share revenue and expenses equally.

Creating the Partnership: To establish a legal partnership, they write a document that outlines the organization of the business, the responsibilities of each partner, and the division of profits and losses.

Analyze

What kind of business would you start with a partner? With another student, choose a business and discuss how you would share responsibilities if you started a partnership together. Ask: What ways might you finance the business? What skills and traits do each of you have that might complement each other in a partnership? On a separate sheet of paper, outline your plan, using Mary and Tony's outline as a model for your business partnership. Accept all reasonable answers that show student effort and an understanding of the concept.

CHAPTER 17
Developing a Business Plan

$ What You'll Learn

When you have completed this chapter, you will be able to:

Section 17.1

- Discuss the importance of financial management for a business.
- Explain the components of a business plan.
- Describe the aspects of a financial plan.

Section 17.2

- Explain the importance of accounting in financial management.
- Identify the primary functions of accounting.

Reading Strategies

To get the most out of your reading:

Predict what you will learn in this chapter.
Relate what you read to your own life.
Question what you are reading to be sure you understand.
React to what you have read.

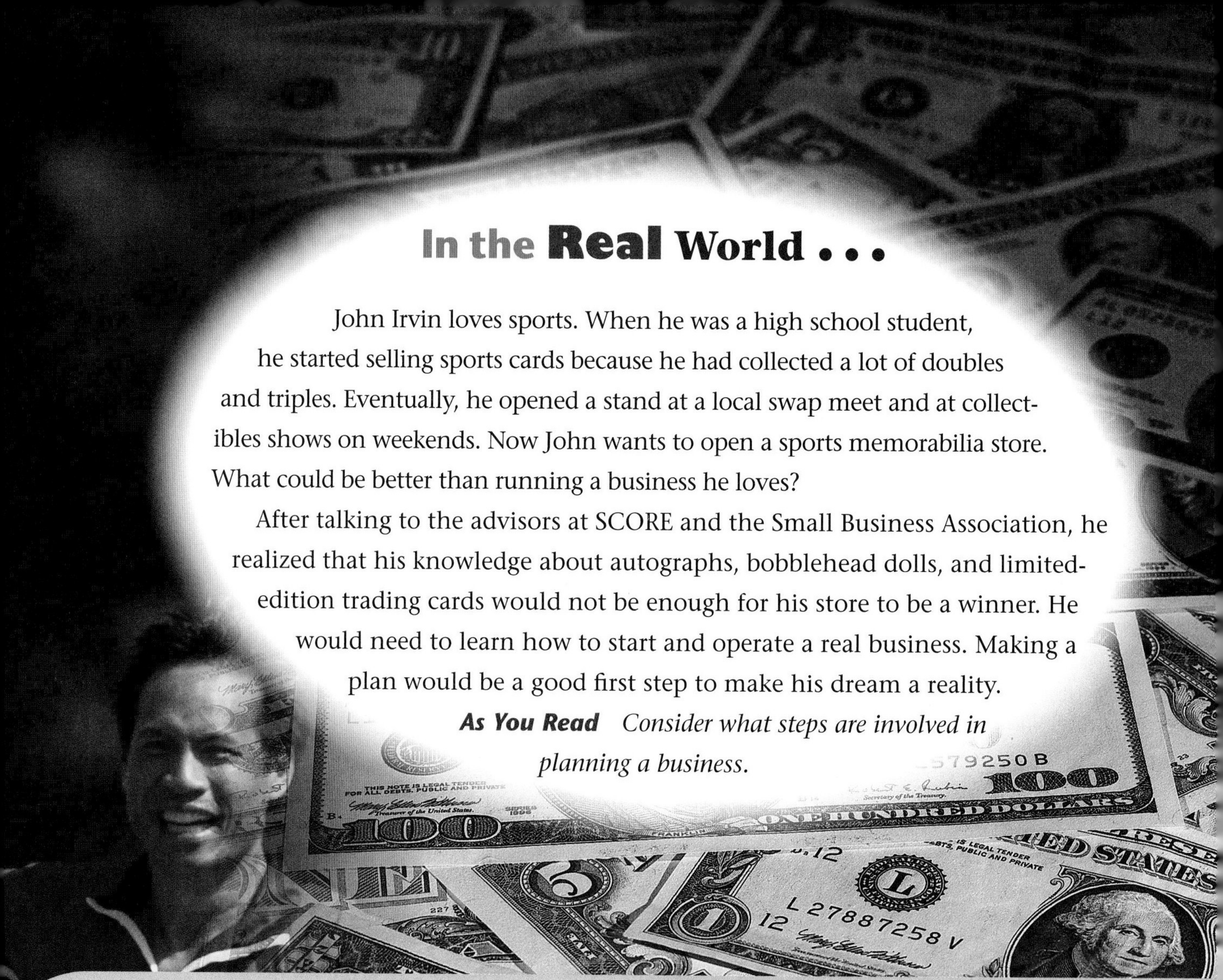

In the Real World . . .

John Irvin loves sports. When he was a high school student, he started selling sports cards because he had collected a lot of doubles and triples. Eventually, he opened a stand at a local swap meet and at collectibles shows on weekends. Now John wants to open a sports memorabilia store. What could be better than running a business he loves?

After talking to the advisors at SCORE and the Small Business Association, he realized that his knowledge about autographs, bobblehead dolls, and limited-edition trading cards would not be enough for his store to be a winner. He would need to learn how to start and operate a real business. Making a plan would be a good first step to make his dream a reality.

As You Read *Consider what steps are involved in planning a business.*

Lesson Plan See Teacher Manual for Chapter 17 planning guide and lesson plan.

ASK STANDARD & POOR'S

Business Plan

Q: My older sister and I are running a very successful business making children's birthday cakes. Since we are already doing well, why do we need a business plan?

A: Just because your business is successful now does not mean that it will remain successful. By creating a business plan, you can define clear goals for things like sales and profitability that will help you keep your business on track. Your business plan can help you to assess how inflation may affect your business over time.

Ask Yourself Can you think of any other advantages that writing up a business plan would provide?

@ Go to **finance07.glencoe.com** to complete the Standard & Poor's Financial Focus activity.

Section 17.1

Focus on Reading

Read to Learn

- How to discuss the importance of financial management for a business.
- How to explain the components of a business plan.
- How to describe the aspects of a financial plan.

Main Idea

For a business to thrive, a sound business plan and an understanding of financial management are essential.

Key Terms

- free enterprise system
- profit
- business plan
- strategic plan
- marketing plan
- financial plan

Before You Read

PREDICT

What might be included in a business plan?

Springboard Ask your students to share the ways they keep track of their personal finances. Then ask them to brainstorm the similarities and differences between the ways businesses keep track of their finances.

A Plan for Business

The Business Environment

What do all businesses have in common?

When you hear the word "business," do you think of large businesses, such as Microsoft, Ford, Coca-Cola, Disney, or IBM? Maybe you think of smaller businesses, such as your neighborhood convenience store, flower shop, or hardware store. All of these businesses, large and small, are part of the **free enterprise system**, which is an economic system in which people can choose what they buy, what they produce and sell, and where they work. Businesses in such a system must compete to attract customers.

One of the main measurements of success for a business is the amount of profit it generates. **Profit** is the amount of money earned over and above the amount spent to keep the business operating. Profit motivates most people to take the risk of starting a business. Large and small businesses must do two things to survive: 1) operate at a profit with effective financial management and 2) attract and keep individuals who will run the business.

Developing a Business Plan

What is a business plan?

Whether you are starting your own business or taking over a family business, you must first develop a business plan. A **business plan** is a written proposal that describes a new business and strategies to launch that business. It helps you focus on exactly what you want to do, how you will do it, and what you expect to accomplish. It sets goals for the business just as you set goals for yourself. A business plan is an important part of a proposal to secure funding from investors. Before they invest or loan money, they want to see that prospective owners have fully developed ideas.

Components of a Business Plan

A business plan can have as many as 15 components: an executive summary, mission statement, company description, product and service plan, management team plan, industry overview, market analysis, competitive analysis, marketing plan, operational plan, organizational plan, financial plan, growth plan, contingency plan, and supporting documents, as well as a cover page, title page, and table of contents.

Three basic parts of a business plan, that can include many of the 15 components, focus on a strategic plan, a marketing plan, and a financial plan. The overall **strategic plan** is a written outline of the business goals and the steps to take to achieve them. The second part is the **marketing plan**, a written outline of how the business will be promoted to increase customers and sales. The third part is the **financial plan,** which is a written outline of how the business will get money to start up and operate, and how the business will maintain financial operations and business records. Basically, the financial plan determines how you will keep track of your money. **Figure 17.1** illustrates the components of a business plan.

Motivating Students Ask your students: "Why is competition important in a free enterprise system?"

The Strategic Plan

Both new and ongoing businesses must have sound strategic plans to be successful. In the classic novel, *Alice in Wonderland,* Alice asks the Cheshire Cat which way she should walk. The Cheshire Cat replies, "That depends a good deal on where you want to get to." This is an appropriate observation about decision making and planning. Every person and every business needs goals and a specific course of action to achieve those goals.

Discussion Help the students understand what the word *strategic* means. Develop a definition and a list of synonyms and write them on the board.

Figure 17.1 **Business Plan Components**

The Complete Plan:

- Cover Page, Title Page, Table of Contents
- Executive Summary
- Mission Statement
- Company Description
- Product and Service Plan
- Management Team Plan
- Industry Overview
- Market Analysis
- Competitive Analysis
- Marketing Plan
- Operational Plan
- Organization Plan
- Financial Plan
- Growth Plan
- Contingency Plan
- Supporting Documents

The 3 Basic Parts:

1) Strategic Plan
Your business goals and how you will achieve them

2) Marketing Plan
How you will promote your business and increase sales in order to make it profitable

3) Financial Plan
How you will fund the creation and operation of your business, maintain financial operations, and keep business records

The Essential Business Plan Whether you are starting a business of your own, purchasing an existing business, or taking over a family business, it is a good idea to develop a business plan.

What is the purpose of a business plan?

Caption Answer It describes a new business and strategies to launch that business. It sets goals for the business and helps secure funding.

▲ **WORKING TOGETHER** Both large and small businesses can prosper and grow as neighbors. *Can you think of some large and small businesses in the same mall in your town?*

Caption Answer Accept all answers that demonstrate student effort.

Critical Thinking Ask the students if the process for goal setting is any different whether you do it for yourself or for your business.

As You Read
RELATE

What are your financial goals for the future? List at least two short-term goals that will help you reach your long-term goals.

If you are a business owner, your ultimate goal is to have a successful and profitable business. In order to realize that objective, you must first determine the strategic plan you will follow to keep the business growing and moving in the right direction.

A strategic plan is similar to a game plan you might have for your sports team. Simply saying "We want to win!" will not bring a victory. The coach must devise a plan that outlines how the team will achieve the big win. The team must work together to apply the strategies that the coach has developed. Similarly, a business owner or operator may say that he or she wants the business to succeed, but without a sound business plan, it probably will not happen. The first step in writing a strategic plan is to set goals.

Setting Goals Businesses set both short-term and long-term goals. In the business world, short-term goals are goals you expect to reach within one or two years. Long-term goals are those that may take three or more years to reach. Because long-term goals require a considerable amount of time, they may be less specific than short-term goals. You will probably revise them as you go.

Goals for businesses have the same guidelines as goals you might establish for your personal finances:

- They should be realistic.
- They should be specific.
- They should have a clear time frame.
- They should help you decide what type of action to take.

Whether you own a small convenience store in the city or run a multinational corporation such as Kodak, the goals can be similar. Common objectives might include increasing sales, adding new customers, or updating equipment.

However, goals can also differ, depending on the size of the business. For example, the goals of a small business might include buying a computer system, introducing a new line of merchandise, or moving to a better location. Medium-sized businesses may want to open more stores or begin operating online to increase sales. Larger corporations have more complex goals. They may want to expand their international markets, change distribution systems, or acquire other smaller corporations.

Businesses should design goals according to the basic guidelines, regardless of the size of the business. Goals should be well thought out and compatible with the philosophy of the business. In all cases, a business needs to determine if its goals are financially possible.

Identify Steps to Achieve Your Goals When you studied personal finance in earlier chapters, you learned that people set financial goals and then decide on ways to achieve those goals. For example, suppose that you have a short-term personal goal of making the honor roll. This is an admirable goal, but how do you accomplish it? You analyze the situation and plan your course of action. You identify specific actions you can take, such as taking better notes, doing your homework more carefully, and asking more questions in class.

Caption Answer Answers will vary but might include buying a computer system, introducing a new line of merchandise, and moving to a better location.

◀ **AIMING FOR GOALS** Businesses and individuals need financial goals. *Can you name three goals that a small business such as this one might have?*

▲ **MARKETING SELLS** With so many brands of carpet on the market, a good marketing plan will give one company an edge over the others. *Can you name some of the ways carpet companies market their products?*

Caption Answer Answers may vary but might include radio and television commercials, ads in newspapers and flyers, and offering special promotions and sales.

Teaching Activity Have the students work in pairs. Have each team select a business in your community and pretend they are the owners. Then ask each team to create two short-term and two long-term goals for its business.

Long-term goals involve more steps over a longer period of time. Suppose that your long-term goal is to become a successful graphic designer. What must you do to become a designer? You will need a career plan. Then you will have to identify short-term steps, such as taking related courses in high school, selecting schools or colleges you want to atend to attend, and completing the application process. Later you will probably focus your attention on long-term steps, such as graduating, getting a job, and acquiring professional experience. Hopefully, by taking these short-term and long-term steps, you will achieve your goal of becoming a designer.

When developing a strategic plan for your business, you should use the same technique. First, identify your short-term and long-term goals. Then create a plan that consists of specific steps toward each goal.

A Strategic Plan Case Study Mike and Erin have plans to start up an eco-friendly landscape business. They realize the importance of setting realistic, achievable goals. Because their business would be new, their short-term goals include getting a new business loan with a low interest rate, purchasing basic equipment, locating suppliers for plants and flowers, and purchasing a low-cost phone system. Long-term goals include acquiring a storage facility, purchasing a hybrid (gas/electric) vehicle to transport equipment, and increasing the number of customers by 20 percent each year.

Steps to Achieve Business Goals Mike and Erin recently graduated from high school and want to start a landscaping business. They have worked with other landscapers and have experience taking care of a variety of flowers, plants, and trees. They plan to start their business as a service, and then open a retail nursery as well.

In their strategic plan, Mike and Erin identify the steps they will take to achieve each of their goals. One of their short-term goals is to show a profit after two years. To reach that goal, they plan to increase the number of customers and keep expenses low.

STANDARD & POOR'S

Global Financial Landscape

Standard and Poor's publishes the globally recognized S&P 500® financial index. It also gathers financial statistics, information, and news, and analyzes this data for international businesses, governments, and individuals to help them guide their financial decisions.

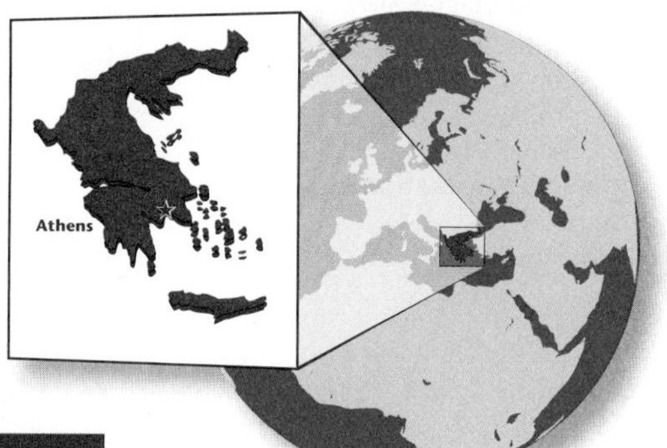

GREECE

Surrounded by the crystal-clear waters of the Aegean and Ionian Seas, Greece is one of the world's most popular travel destinations. Many tourists come for the sun and surf. Others come to see the birthplace of the Olympics and democracy, and to explore the ancient ruins that stand as tributes to the past. Dating back more than 2,500 years, Greece's glory days have become a major industry and source of income. Athens attracts the most tourists. Few could leave the capital city without visiting the Parthenon, the country's most famous national treasure. Dedicated to the Greek goddess Athena, the white marble temple sits majestically on top of a rocky hill called the Acropolis.

STANDARD & POOR'S **DATABYTES**

Capital	Athens
Population	10,988,000
Language	Greek
Currency	euro
Gross Domestic Product (GDP)	$212.2 billion (2003 est.)
GDP per capita	$19,900

Industry: Tourism, food and tobacco processing, textiles, and chemicals

Agriculture: Wheat, corn, barley, sugar beets, and beef

Exports: Food and beverages, manufactured goods, petroleum products, and chemicals

Natural Resources: Bauxite, lignite, magnesite, crude oil, and marble

Think Globally

Athens is a major tourist destination. What businesses might be successful there?

See the Teacher Manual for answer.

As You Read

QUESTION

Why is a good marketing plan necessary for any business?

Question Answer Effective marketing can increase customers and profits.

The Marketing Plan

A marketing plan outlines the ways in which you will promote your business. Promotional activities include advertising and promotions. Advertising is any paid message that a business sends about its products. Promotion is any form of communication a business uses to inform, persuade, or remind people about its products or to enhance its image. You will show a profit or expand your operations by increasing customers. Therefore, you want to communicate with as many potential customers as possible to tell them about your goods or services. For example, Mike and Erin plan to place ads with photographs of their projects in a local newspaper.

As with the creation of a strategic plan, you have to address some specific questions. If you have something to sell, how do you sell it? How do you reach people in an efficient manner? What promotions or advertising can you afford? To begin to answer these questions, you should research the existing market for your goods or services. See **Figure 17.2** for an illustration of this process.

Larger corporations may hire private marketing firms to assist them in developing marketing plans. Some corporations, such as Levi-Strauss, McDonald's, and Ford, have been very successful over the years. Effective marketing plans have allowed these corporations to introduce new products, maintain sales of existing products, and keep their names in the public eye.

Extension Have the students choose a large corporation such as Levi's®, McDonald's, Ford, or another one. Ask them to research the products that have been released during the last year. Have the students find out how the corporation introduced the products.

The Financial Plan

You have probably noticed that the elements in the strategic plan and the marketing plan involve the need for the efficient management of money. In order to make intelligent financial decisions regarding the direction and future of your business, you must record and report your finances in an orderly, consistent manner. Many people consider a financial plan to be the most important document for a successful business venture.

Sound financial decisions provide the opportunity for:

- Sales to rise
- Expenses to fall
- Profits to increase
- Assets to be acquired
- Liabilities to be paid
- Credit to expand
- Customers to increase
- New products to develop

Aspects of a Financial Plan A financial plan outlines the essential financial elements for starting and running a business. An effective plan addresses three aspects of operating your business: assets needed, purchasing methods, and daily financial operations. (See **Figure 17.3** on p. 558.)

First, it identifies the assets you will need to purchase in order to begin or continue operating the business. Assets are property or items of value owned by a business. These might include products to sell or machines, supplies, office equipment, and transportation necessary for operations.

Common Cents $35,000 × .05 = $1,750

Common CENTS

The Advertising Dollar

Many businesses, large and small, plan to spend a certain amount of their budgets (about 5 percent or more of their net sales) on promotional activities, such as advertising promotions. This expense pays off with more customers and profits. *If a surf and skateboard shop earns $35,000 a month in net sales, what might be a good annual advertising budget for the store?*

Figure 17.2 Steps to Prepare a Marketing Plan

To prepare a marketing plan, you first need to research the existing market. By seeing what is out there, you can better develop an effective marketing plan. This plan will become your road map for reaching new customers and expanding your business. Take these steps to prepare your marketing plan, an important component of your overall business plan.

1 **Assess** the competition.

2 **Identify** services offered.

4 **Identify** potential customers.

3 **Research** the current pricing and advertising.

TechByte

Business Planning Software There is a lot of software available to help the budding entrepreneur write a business plan. These programs, such as Business Plan Pro, help you develop a professional business plan for any size or type of business. Many of these programs also provide sample business plans that you can review for ideas.

@ Before you write your own business plan, listen to planning expert Tim Berry discuss the planning process and how Business Plan Pro can help you through **finance07.glencoe.com.**

Discussion Ask your students what other assets Mike and Erin might need for their business.

Second, your financial plan should address the method that you will use to acquire or purchase these items. How will your business pay for the things it needs? Do you have sufficient cash available? Should you borrow money from a bank or credit union?

The third and most important aspect of the financial plan involves the daily financial operations of the business. This feature addresses the recording, summarizing, reporting, and analyzing of your business's finances.

Identifying Needed Assets The first aspect of creating a financial plan is to identify the assets that are necessary to start the business and then to make it grow and increase its profits. Suppose that the two entrepreneurs, Mike and Erin, want to buy a computer system. The system should be able to handle their present business operations as well as increased business activity in the future. They should consider features such as processing speed, memory capacity, upgradeability, and the software that is included.

After Mike and Erin have determined the computer components that their business needs, they should analyze the prices of different systems. They will need to purchase the best system for the best price. When their analysis is complete, Mike and Erin can decide what computer system to buy. This research process should be a part of buying any major asset.

Purchasing Assets The second step of a financial plan is to determine the method to use to purchase the items. Mike and Erin need to ask several specific questions: Can they purchase the computer system with their available cash—or should they get a loan?

Figure 17.3 **The Financial Plan**

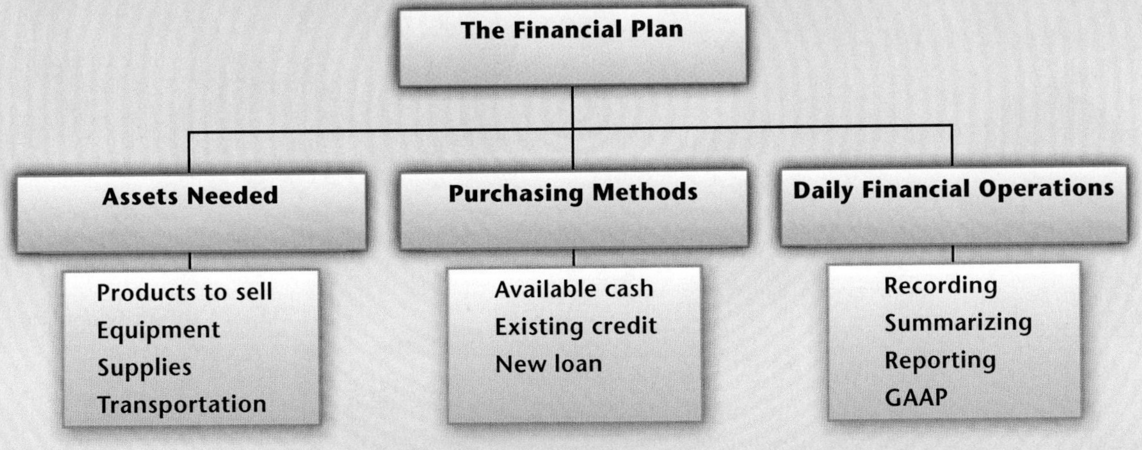

Funding Your Business Most lenders and investors require a well-organized and feasible financial plan before they will provide the money to start a business.

Why might a financial plan be the most important aspect of a business plan?

Caption Answer It outlines the essential financial elements for starting and running a business.

◀ **PRODUCT RESEARCH** Good research leads to appropriate purchases for your company. *Can you name at least five items that business owners might purchase that require product research?*

Caption Answer Answers might include cars, computers, copy machines, coffeemakers, stereo systems, etc.

Will they be able to get a reasonable interest rate? Can they take advantage of alternatives to purchasing, such as leasing? Can they get a better deal if they wait? In answering these questions, Mike and Erin will have to perform a careful analysis of their existing finances regarding their debts, available cash, and future expenses.

They must also investigate all sources of credit. Will the company that is selling them the computer extend credit to them? Should they apply for a short-term loan from a bank? By examining these and other questions, Mike and Erin are practicing effective financial management.

As a high school student, you make similar decisions about your personal finances. If you want to buy an inexpensive item, such as a CD, you might pay cash. You will give the purchase little financial consideration. However, if it is a more expensive item, such as a sound system or a used car, you should examine your situation more carefully. Consider some of the following questions: Do you really need it? What is the most you can spend? How much money do you have now? Is there anything else you might need? By considering these questions, you are performing a financial analysis of your purchase—and practicing effective financial management.

WebQuest

Be Your Own Boss

The Small Business Administration (SBA) is an agency of the federal government that helps entrepreneurs. Find out if you are ready to be an entrepreneur by taking the SBA's Are You Ready? quiz, and learn more about what it takes to start up a business.

@ To continue with Task 4 of your WebQuest project, visit **finance07.glencoe.com**.

Academic Connection

SOCIAL STUDIES/ MARKETING

Small businesses recognize that they need to sell to a broad market to expand. Imagine you are starting a business to sell a specific product or service. Choose one. As part of your marketing plan, you need to know more about who will buy your product or service. Consider what cultures will provide good markets for you. *Do research on the Internet to find three countries or cultures offering such markets. Then present your findings to the class explaining why you selected those three.*

See the Teacher Manual for answers.

As a business owner or operator, you might find that some items you want to purchase are beyond your means. You may not have enough cash. Especially when you are starting a business, you will have to accept the fact that you will not be able to obtain everything that you want immediately. You will have to work within your financial resources until your business begins to make a profit and you can afford to expand your assets. If you are working with limited resources, you must make decisions based on your need for the items and your ability to pay for them, whether with cash or credit.

Recording and Reporting Business Finances The third aspect of a financial plan involves the financial operation of a business. How will Mike and Erin keep daily financial records? Will sales cover their expenses and produce a profit? Will cash be available for unexpected costs? Will they be able to pay their bills on time?

Mike and Erin must know where their business stands financially at all times. The recording and handling of financial information, in an accurate and efficient manner, is essential. It includes using accepted accounting procedures, analyzing financial statements, controlling cash, and paying debts. If data is not recorded in a timely manner, or if the information is not analyzed correctly, inappropriate financial decisions can result. For a new business or a small existing business, this could be disastrous. Thousands of small businesses close each year due to poor financial decisions.

Section 17.1 Assessment

See the Teacher Manual for answer.

QUICK CHECK

1. Describe the three main parts of a business plan.
2. Explain why financial management is an important aspect of a successful business.
3. Identify three aspects of a financial plan.

THINK CRITICALLY

4. What might happen to a business that analyzes its finances only twice a year?

USE COMMUNICATION SKILLS

5. **Marketing Your Product** Carol and Blanca have been operating their own jewelry-making business for three months. During that time they have sold their creations to friends and relatives. However, they now want to market their products to a larger customer base.

Present Help Carol and Blanca market their jewelry by creating an advertising flyer. The flyer should be informative and persuasive.

SOLVE MONEY PROBLEMS

6. **Financial Plan Development** Santiago and his classmates want to raise money for Habitat for Humanity. Santiago plans to sell doughnuts and hot chocolate three mornings a week at school to raise funds. His teacher asks for a list of assets he will need.

Write About It Help Santiago make a list of the assets he will need to run his doughnut stand. Indicate which assets he might borrow and which ones he must buy.

Section 17.2

Financial Management

Aspects of Financial Management

What economic theories and principles should you know for effective financial management?

As you learned in the first section of this chapter, sound financial management is critical to the survival of any business. Financial management includes all aspects of operating a business. It is the glue that holds the business together. At the same time, it is the oil that helps it run smoothly. Many business functions and procedures are based on economic theories and principles. Supply and demand, pricing, market segments, and competition are just a few of the economic principles you need to know about. An understanding of basic accounting principles and procedures is also useful. You should have the financial knowledge and skills to be able to collect, summarize, and analyze financial data.

Accounting: The Backbone of Financial Management

What is accounting?

Accounting is the systematic process of recording and reporting the financial position of a business. The financial position depends on the transactions that occur in the daily operation of the business. A **transaction** is any activity that has an effect on the financial situation of a business. Every time you buy supplies, sell merchandise, buy a photocopier, or pay utility bills, your business is making a transaction. Accounting records and reports can help a business operate efficiently—and profitably—by keeping track of how much the business earns and spends.

Accounting is often referred to as the "language of business." Accounting plays a vital role in the day-to-day activities of every business. The influence of accounting is demonstrated by the fact that many of its terms have become commonplace. You have probably heard terms such as "assets," "liabilities," "expenses," "revenue," and "inventory." These are all accounting terms. Business owners use this language to communicate with other owners of the business, their creditors, and customers. They do this by issuing financial statements.

Focus on Reading

Read to Learn

- How to explain the importance of accounting in financial management.
- How to identify the primary functions of accounting.

Main Idea

To ensure effective financial management, knowledge and skills in accounting are essential.

Key Terms

- accounting
- transaction
- generally accepted accounting principles (GAAP)
- budget
- merchandise
- inventory
- cash flow
- negative cash flow

Before You Read

PREDICT

What do you think the term *cash flow* means?

Springboard Tell the students you have an idea for a business. It will be successful because you are a hard worker, and your friends will buy your product. Ask students: "Why is this not enough to ensure success?"

Document Detective

Learn to identify and understand the standard financial documents you will use in the real world.

See the Teacher Manual for answer.

Investigate: A Job Description

A job description contains the following information:

- Job title
- Description of responsibilities
- List of required skills and education

Your Motive: When you write a business plan, it is important to think about how you will build a staff of employees. You start by defining the positions and listing the qualifications of the people who will fill those positions.

Premier Building Company

Title/Compensation	Description	Job Specifications
Entrepreneur/Owner • Full time • Salary/Wage: Varies based on revenues; 20% of sales • Estimated after year one: $120,000	• Oversees all operations • Responsible for setting up all policies, procedures, and guidelines • Performs all hiring and employee evaluation functions • Responsible for setting long-and short-term organizational goals • Allocates resources	• Excellent communication skills • Ability to motivate and lead
Accountant • Part-time contract professional; 12 hours per week • Pro-rated salary: $30,000	• Responsible for supervising payroll, accounts payable, and accounts receivable functions • Responsible for, and coordinates with, vendors and subcontractors • Works with owner to obtain financing and lines of credit • Responsible for payment and compliance with local, state, and federal requirements	• Excellent verbal and written communication skills • Ability to work with others • At least 2 years experience in construction or a related service or manufacturing industry • Certification as a CPA
Director of Operations • Full time • Salary: $55,000 per year	• Develops operational procedures • Responsible for implementing all policies, procedures, and guidelines • Manages all operations and assists with hiring and employee evaluation • Troubleshoots all problems, customer service issues, and employee complaints	• Ability to work with people of all backgrounds and skills • Ability to motivate and lead • At least 4 years experience in the construction industry or 2-year degree in management • A minimum of 2 years management experience

Key Points: Job descriptions are an important part of a business plan because investors will want to know how you will staff your organization. The descriptions can be advertised in the classified section of a newspaper or magazine, or posted on Internet job sites.

Find the Solutions

1. How will the owner be compensated?
2. What skills and background are required for the job of accountant?
3. What are the job functions of the director of operations?
4. Why is the accountant's salary pro-rated over the year?
5. How much experience does the director of operations need?

GAAP

When recording and reporting financial changes in a business, owners, bookkeepers, and accountants must use a standard set of guidelines, which are referred to as **generally accepted accounting principles (GAAP)** (pronounced "gap"). If General Motors, Ford, and DaimlerChrysler all prepared their financial reports in different ways, no one could compare the three corporations financially. Using the GAAP guidelines allows investors, banks, suppliers, and government agencies to make comparisons of the financial condition of various companies. They can determine which businesses are financially stable, which ones have the highest percentage of profit, and which ones are growing the fastest.

Every business must have an accurate accounting system, either manual or computerized. Computer software programs can handle much of the basic accounting work for most businesses. By using this modern technology, owners and managers can spend more time analyzing their finances and planning for the future, and spend less time doing monotonous paperwork.

The accounting system has many functions and procedures. However, some of the most essential functions of accounting that most businesses use include budgeting, inventory, payroll, cash flow, and investments.

Budgeting

One important function of accounting is budgeting. A **budget** for a business is a formal, written statement of expected income and expenses for a future period of time. For example, the entrepreneurs Mike and Erin can write a budget to project, or predict, the amount of money they think they will earn through sales or other income in their landscaping business. They also project their production or operating costs (expenses) for the same period. The difference between these two amounts will be their projected profit or loss for the period. This gives them a glimpse into the financial future of their business. It provides the information they will need to make decisions.

To be practical, you should regularly compare a budget with actual income and expenses. If you are working with a yearly budget, you should make monthly comparisons of the budgeted amounts to the actual amounts. If the actual amounts are not reasonably close to the budgeted figures, you need to make adjustments. If the actual amounts are far greater than the projected figures, you must take immediate action to avoid further financial problems. An important aspect of financial management is to recognize a problem and take action to remedy it. Accurate, current accounting statements and reports allow you to recognize a problem when it first develops so that you can make financial decisions and take corrective measures.

STANDARD &POOR'S

Put on Your Financial Planner's Cap

Seven months ago your client opened a small business, and it is already showing a reasonable profit. She is tempted to take all the profits and have a little fun, but she knows this might not be a good idea. Think of three ways she could handle the profits.

See the Teacher Manual for answer.

Motivating Students Have students imagine they have businesses of their choice. Ask them: "What problems might you face as an owner of this type of business?"

Extension Have the students research GAAP and find out when businesses began standardizing their accounting functions according to these guidelines.

As You Read

RELATE

Businesses need well-planned budgets—and so do individuals. What income and expenses would be included in your personal budget?

▶ CONTROLLING INVENTORY Proper levels of inventory are essential for a profitable business operation. *As a business owner, what might you do if you had too many of one model of television in stock?*

Caption Answer Answers might include hold a sale or display the model prominently so customers will see it before they see other models.

Research Ask the students to visit a retail establishment in your community and find out about the inventory tracking system that it uses. Have the students share their findings with the class.

Teaching Activity Divide the class into groups and assign each group a different type of retail business in your town (fast-food restaurant, music store, clothing boutique, gas station, etc.). Ask each group to develop a list of inventory for that particular type of business.

Question Answer Having the wrong level of inventory—too much or too little—can cost a business money.

As You Read

QUESTION

Why is having proper inventory levels an important aspect of financial asset management?

Inventory

The largest asset of many businesses is the merchandise they have on hand to sell. **Merchandise** is the goods retailers buy with the intent to resell to customers. The **inventory** is the merchandise retailers have for sale. Most cash transactions involve the purchase, control, and sale of merchandise. Therefore, it is essential that inventory be carefully maintained and examined. By tracking inventory, businesses know the following facts about their merchandise:

- Amount of merchandise sold
- Merchandise that is selling well
- When to reorder merchandise
- Merchandise that should not be reordered

Amount of Inventory The wrong level, or amount, of inventory can be costly for a business. Having too little inventory means that the business may not be able to satisfy its customers' wants. For example, when you go to a store to buy CDs, and they have very few on the shelves, you might not bother to look around the store. Instead, it is likely you will go to another store to make your purchase. Lost sales mean lower profits for the store.

If inventory is too high, too much money has been spent on inventory and is not available for other things, such as a new computer system, because cash is not available. Inappropriate inventory levels, either too high or too low, are signs of poor management.

Most stores use computer programs to monitor inventory. These programs provide daily reports that detail what items have been sold, what is still available, and what must be reordered.

Payroll

While merchandise is usually the largest asset of a business, payroll is usually the largest expense of a business. Large companies such as AT&T, Coca-Cola, and American Airlines employ thousands of people. Weekly payrolls are in the millions of dollars. Some small businesses employ fewer than a hundred people, and some very small businesses might employ fewer than ten people. Whether your business is large or small, payroll is usually your greatest expense.

Because payroll involves so much cash, it is regulated by state and federal laws and must be prepared according to generally accepted accounting principles (GAAP). Most businesses use computer programs to process payroll checks, to complete payroll reports, and to examine payroll information. Efficient payroll management involves two important activities.

Determining Number of Employees First, you must determine whether you have the proper number of employees working at the proper times. Having too many employees or employees working at the wrong times means that you are paying more in wages and salaries than you should. Your payroll expense must be reduced. If you do not have enough employees or are understaffed at certain times, your company risks losing sales. Both situations are indicators of poor management.

Using GAAP The second activity that ensures efficient payroll management is using generally accepted accounting principles (GAAP) to prepare payrolls. Paychecks must be issued on time. All payroll taxes must be paid, and voluntary deductions must be taken. All payroll records should also be available for managers and owners to evaluate immediately. Accurate, complete, and readily available payroll information is essential. Chapter 21 explains more about payroll procedures and regulations.

$avvy Saver

Cutting Office Expenses

1. Write or print on the backs of used paper for interoffice notes.
2. Buy refilled ink cartridges instead of new ones (savings up to $30 each).
3. Do not use disposable coffee cups. Buy ceramic mugs for everyone.
4. Do advertising swaps for your services or products.
5. Buy used office equipment and furniture.

Discussion Ask the students to discuss why it is often very difficult for a business owner to lay off employees or add employees.

Cash Flow

Every person needs cash. Every business needs cash. Available cash often determines what a business can or cannot do. An adequate amount of available cash allows your business to pay its debts, take advantage of discounts, and pay for expansion.

In personal finance, "cash flow" refers to the amount of money that actually goes into and out of a person's wallet or bank accounts. For a business, **cash flow** is the amount of cash that is available at any given time. Money comes in, and money goes out—this is cash flow. A goal of effective financial management is to maintain a constant flow of cash through the business. This is easy to say, but it is not always easy to do. Economic and financial conditions constantly change. Sometimes sales are high, and then they may suddenly drop off. Expenses may also vary. When a business spends more money than it receives, it experiences a condition known as a **negative cash flow,** also called a *cash crunch*. When your cash flow is negative, your business suffers.

Discussion Have the students discuss the economic and financial conditions that might affect a business's cash flow.

As a student, you have probably experienced similar cash crunches. For example, suppose that you want to go to the movies on Friday night with your friends, but on Wednesday you buy the wool sweater you want. So, on Friday night, you discover that you do not have enough money to go out. For you, this is a short-term disappointment. For a business, however, a shortage of money could mean serious problems. Without a sufficient flow of cash, merchandise cannot be replaced, bills cannot be paid, and funds for future growth and expansion cannot be invested. Maintaining a positive cash flow is a primary goal of financial management.

Investments

Successful businesses invest for the future. As profits increase, money should be set aside or invested for future business needs. This reserve cash may be needed to purchase new equipment, relocate the business operation, or sell a new line of merchandise. For example, suppose that Mike and Erin form a business partnership. Their goal is to purchase a building for their landscaping business within the next five years. They should set aside a certain amount of money each year to ensure that sufficient funds will be available to buy the building or make a down payment.

Careers in Finance

BOOKKEEPER **Brad Chapman**
Longs Drugs

After moving from his hometown, Brad found it easy to find another bookkeeping job. He has always enjoyed the challenge of balancing ledgers and creating spreadsheets. The skills and experience he picked up while keeping books for a local music store seem to apply everywhere. At Longs Drugs, he balances cash registers, determines if registers are over or short, completes daily reports, and counts and deposits daily receipts. He also handles payroll, tags and logs invoices and claims, and forwards pertinent paperwork to the general offices. Other tasks of a bookkeeper might include preparing weekly gross profit study surveys and following up on returned checks.

SKILLS: Accounting, computer, math, organizational, customer-service, and problem-solving skills

PERSONAL TRAITS: Detail-oriented, discreet, honest, and likes working with numbers

EDUCATION: High school diploma or equivalent; associate degree or technical training at a college; on-the-job training

ANALYZE Why would most businesses need a bookkeeper?
See the Teacher Manual for answer.

@ To learn more about career paths for bookkeepers, visit **finance07.glencoe.com**.

Investments and Reserve Funds

Businesses need reserve cash for emergencies or unexpected costs. If equipment breaks and needs repair, sales take an unexpected drop, or a natural disaster hits your area, you will need cash. Cash reserves, also called *reserve funds,* could save your business when any type of disaster strikes.

Cash should be carefully invested and closely monitored. Investments by businesses are similar to personal savings. You should save money for unexpected bills or events, such as a broken water heater or a medical bill. You would also need to save for a new car, summer vacation, or computer for your personal needs.

After You Read

REACT

Is having a reserve fund as important as having a regular savings account? Why or why not?

React Answer Both accounts are important, but a reserve fund can save a business if disaster strikes.

The Importance of Financial Management

What are some aspects of financial management?

Businesses must make a profit and invest part of that profit for future use. Making and monitoring investments is an important aspect of financial management. In addition to investments, sound financial management relies on accounting. You will learn more about accounting functions and managing a business's finances in the remaining chapters of this book.

Extension Ask your students to brainstorm a list of unexpected costs that Mike and Erin might face once their landscaping business is up and running.

Section 17.2 Assessment

See the Teacher Manual for answers.

QUICK CHECK

1. Define the term *accounting.*
2. What are five of the most essential funtions of accounting?
3. Explain why it is important for a business to maintain and examine its inventory carefully.

THINK CRITICALLY

4. Explain why a business should have enough cash reserves.

USE MATH SKILLS

5. **Accounting Basics** You are the bookkeeper at a toy store. Last month the following transactions occurred:

Sales:	$62,500
Payroll, rent, utilities:	$16,000
Merchandise purchased:	$25,000

Analyze Did the toy store have a positive or negative cash flow?

SOLVE MONEY PROBLEMS

6. **Accounting Statements** Vince and his sister Kim own a pool cleaning service. Kim analyzes the financial statements and reports each month. Recently she has noticed that sales are slipping and that expenses seem to be out of control. They need to take corrective measures as soon as possible.

Group Analysis In small groups, work together to help Vince and Kim figure out what might be happening to their business. Come up with three suggestions for correcting the situation and present them to the class.

Chapter 17 Review & Activities

See the Teacher Manual for answers.

CHAPTER SUMMARY

- One of the measures of success for a business is the amount of profit it earns. Businesses must do two things to survive: operate at a profit with effective financial management and attract customers.
- The components of a business plan include: executive summary, mission statement, company description, product and service plan, management team plan, industry overview, market analysis, competitive analysis, marketing plan, operational plan, organizational plan, financial plan, growth plan, contingency plan, and supporting documents—plus a cover page, title page, and table of contents. The three basic parts of a business plan focus on a strategic plan, a marketing plan, and a financial plan.
- The financial plan identifies the assets you need, how you will acquire these assets, and how you will handle daily financial operations.
- Accounting is the systematic process of recording and reporting a business's financial position, including all transactions involving money.
- Accounting functions include the preparation of financial statements, auditing, budgeting, payroll, inventory, cash flow, and investments.

Communicating Key Terms

What sort of a business would you like to start someday, perhaps after working for an employer in your chosen field to gain some experience? If you were meeting with a bank loan officer to apply for a commercial loan to start your business, what would you say? Use as many terms below as you can to develop some points to discuss with the loan officer.

- free enterprise system
- profit
- business plan
- strategic plan
- marketing plan
- financial plan
- accounting
- transaction
- generally accepted accounting principles (GAAP)
- budget
- merchandise
- inventory
- cash flow
- negative cash flow

Reviewing Key Concepts

1. **Explain** how financial management is the basic foundation for business success.
2. **Describe** specific items you would include in your business's strategic, marketing, and financial plans.
3. **Identify** the three aspects of a financial plan.
4. **List** three examples of accounting transactions.
5. **Explain** why a business needs to follow generally accepted accounting principles (GAAP).

See the Teacher Manual for answers.

ACADEMIC SKILLS

Language Arts One of the main measurements of success for a business is the amount of profit it earns.

Write About It Write a paragraph explaining what is meant by this statement.

YOUR FINANCIAL FIGURES

Business Capital A primary concern of a business is its "working" capital, which is the current assets minus current liabilities. It is all assets that can be turned into cash quickly, reduced by all liabilities that must be paid within the year.

1. **Calculate** From the following partial balance sheet, calculate the company's working capital:

Assets		**Liabilities**	
Cash	$17,500	Current liabilities	$114,000
Marketable securities	93,000	Long-term debt	216,000
Accounts receivable	87,455	Partnership equity	176,955
Inventories	162,000		
Fixed assets	147,000		
Net of depreciation			

2. **Compute** Use spreadsheet software to make this calculation.

REAL-WORLD Application

Connect with Economics and Law In the late 20th and early 21st centuries, the stock value of Enron Corporation seemed to go up. However, Enron's earnings were overstated because the company used illegal accounting practices that removed negative cash flow items from the income statement. Investors lost a great deal of money when the problem was discovered.

1. **Research** Access an Internet search engine and find out how Enron hid its money-losing operations from public view.
2. **Think Critically** As a result of Enron and a few other large companies' overstatements of earnings, the federal government passed the Sarbanes-Oxley Act. Find out the requirements of the Sarbanes-Oxley Act. Do you think this Act will prevent another Enron-like scandal?

Internet CONNECTION

Web Site: Do You Need One? The successful sales of your home-baked goods through diners and coffee shops have led you to consider filling orders for custom cakes. You are considering the creation of a Web site to promote and sell your products.

Log On Use an Internet search engine to find Web sites of similar businesses. Then answer these questions: What are the advantages and disadvantages of producing and maintaining a Web site?

BusinessWeek ONLINE

Newsclip: A Shaky Ship? Despite a weak economy, a company can succeed if it adheres to a comprehensive business plan.

Log On Go to **finance07.glencoe.com** and open Chapter 17. Learn all of the elements of a business plan. Choose a corporation featured in the news. Write a sample business plan for it.

WHAT'S YOUR FINANCIAL ID?

WHAT'S YOUR BUSINESS PERSONALITY?

Businesses need employees who have all types of personalities. Which four of the following statements best describe your personality? Write your answers on a separate sheet of paper, and then add up the number of points.

_____ I prefer activities that allow me to tell other people what to do. (5 points)

_____ I can delegate responsibility. (3 points)

_____ I prefer a clear definition of my responsibilities. (1 point)

_____ I am very good at brainstorming ideas. (5 points)

_____ I am good with details. (1 point)

_____ I like to do things exactly right. (1 point)

_____ I enjoy persuading others. (5 points)

_____ I am good at planning. (3 points)

_____ I like to be in charge. (5 points)

_____ I am good at organizing. (3 points)

_____ I prefer to follow others' instructions. (1 point)

_____ I know how to give clear directions. (3 points)

Support staff: If you scored 4–8 points, you are a real team player and can provide essential support to any business enterprise.

Manager: If you scored 10–14 points, you may be on track for a management career.

Entrepreneur: If you scored 16–20 points, you may succeed by running your own business when you are ready.

Accept all reasonable answers that show student effort and an understanding of the concept.

Your Financial Portfolio

Planning for Success

For several years Tom has been going with his father to yard sales. His father buys old clocks and radios. He fixes them if they need repairs and sells them at the Millerton Flea Market. Tom wants to start his own business and organize his plans.

Oldies but Goodies

Type of business:	Selling used CDs, DVDs, videos, and video games
Location:	Millerton Flea Market
Target customers:	All ages, but mainly ages 10 to 35 for the CDs, DVDs, and videos; and ages 10 to 25 for the video games
Potential number of customers:	About 300 to 800 people visit the flea market each day, which is open Fridays through Sundays.
Competition:	No one has been selling these products at the flea market since the Albertsons moved away.
Other competition:	The nearest place to buy used CDs is about 10 miles away; three local video stores sell used DVDs, videos, and video games.
Challenges:	Getting enough products to sell: Jaimie McKerry buys surplus stock for Franklin's Discounts, and he will sell me used CDs for about $2.50 each if I buy at least 100 at a time.
Costs:	Purchasing the products, Dad will share expenses with me for renting the table ($50 for the weekend), and gas for when we go look at garage sales.
Potential profit:	I used to look at all the DVDs, CDs, and videos when Vin Albertson had his table, and he seemed to move a lot of merchandise. I think I can make a profit of $3 a unit and sell 30 to 50 units a weekend.
Background and special skills:	I have been going to garage sales with Dad for several years. There are always old DVDs, CDs, videos, and video games that I can pick up at low prices. I like negotiating when I buy and sell, and I like helping Dad at his table. I also know popular titles.

Prepare a Plan

Select a merchandising business that you think you would like to own. On a separate sheet of paper, describe the type of business, the product(s) involved, and the factors you think would make it successful. Explain why you think you could make this business a success.

Accept all reasonable answers that show student effort and an understanding of the concept.

CHAPTER 18
Developing a Financial Plan

$ What You'll Learn

When you have completed this chapter, you will be able to:

Section 18.1

- Explain start-up capital.
- Identify start-up costs.
- Describe operating capital.
- Explain projected income statements.
- Discuss the role of reserve capital.

Section 18.2

- Identify the elements of a financial plan.

Reading Strategies

To get the most out of your reading:

Predict what you will learn in this chapter.
Relate what you read to your own life.
Question what you are reading to be sure you understand.
React to what you have read.

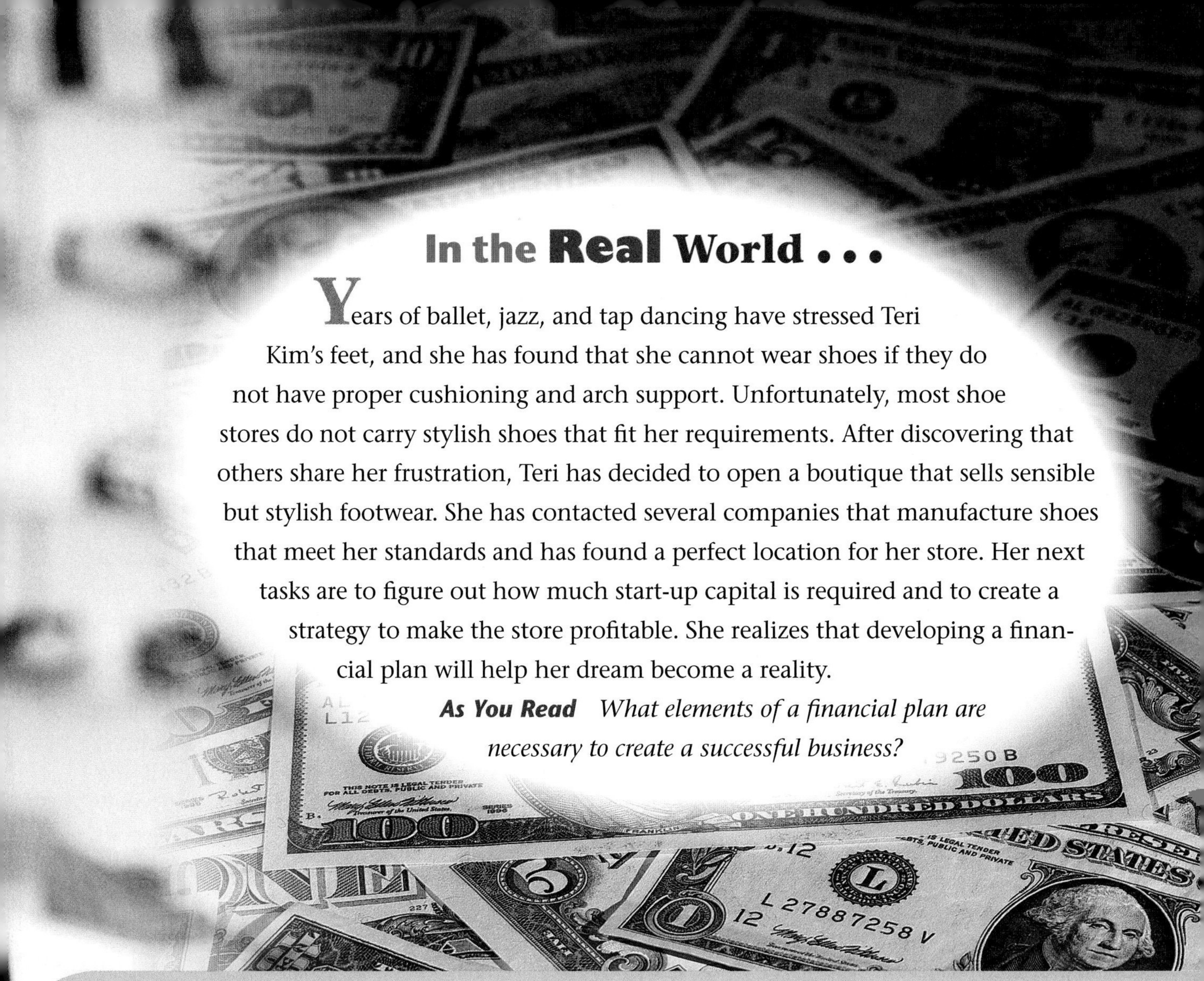

In the Real World . . .

Years of ballet, jazz, and tap dancing have stressed Teri Kim's feet, and she has found that she cannot wear shoes if they do not have proper cushioning and arch support. Unfortunately, most shoe stores do not carry stylish shoes that fit her requirements. After discovering that others share her frustration, Teri has decided to open a boutique that sells sensible but stylish footwear. She has contacted several companies that manufacture shoes that meet her standards and has found a perfect location for her store. Her next tasks are to figure out how much start-up capital is required and to create a strategy to make the store profitable. She realizes that developing a financial plan will help her dream become a reality.

As You Read *What elements of a financial plan are necessary to create a successful business?*

Lesson Plan See the Teacher Manual for Chapter 18 planning guide and lesson plan.

ASK STANDARD & POOR'S

Financial Plan

Q: Since the projections in a financial plan are just guesses, why is the plan so important? Why should I bother spending time making financial predictions that might not come true?

A: A financial plan is essential to understanding what will make your business profitable, how much cash you will need to operate the business, and the future value of the business. Even though your financial plan will need to be updated regularly, it still provides you with a solid idea of where your business should be headed.

Ask Yourself Why is it important to be able to figure out how much cash you will need to operate your business?

@ Go to **finance07.glencoe.com** to complete the Standard & Poor's Financial Focus activity.

Section 18.1

Focus on Reading

Read to Learn

- How to explain start-up capital.
- How to identify start-up costs.
- How to describe operating capital.
- How to explain projected income statements.
- How to discuss the role of reserve capital.

Main Idea

The first step in developing a financial plan is determining how much capital you will need. The next step involves creating a future financial picture of your business by developing projected financial statements.

Key Terms

- capital
- start-up capital
- start-up costs
- operating capital
- financial forecasting
- projected financial statements
- fixed expenses
- variable expenses
- reserve capital

Springboard Ask your students this question: "If you were thinking about opening a business, what planning and preparation should take place so you will be successful?"

Identifying Required Capital

Elements of a Financial Plan

Why is a financial plan an important part of a business plan?

A financial plan is often considered the most important part of an overall business plan. Without adequate planning and cash, your business may not survive. **Figure 18.1** on page 576 shows how wise financial planning can help you make your business dream a reality.

An effective financial plan enables you to determine required capital. **Capital** is the money you will need to establish a business, operate it for the first few months, and expand it once it stabilizes. The process of determining required capital will include identifying and analyzing the assets and costs that are involved in starting a new business. Once you have identified these items, you will assign an estimated dollar value to each one.

A financial plan also addresses the various sources of funding you will use to acquire or purchase the needed items. In addition, the plan outlines how you will record, summarize, and report the finances of your business. This section will examine the process of determining required capital.

Determining Required Capital

Why is it necessary to have a clear, concise, and realistic financial plan?

The first aspect of a financial plan is to determine how much capital you will need. You may be shocked at the amount of money that is required to start a business and ensure its success. The purpose of a financial plan is to give you a realistic idea of what you will need. The quality of your financial plan will affect not only the success of your business, but also your ability to qualify for financing. A clear, concise, and realistic financial plan will give lenders confidence in your business knowledge and skills.

There are three types of required capital: start-up capital, operating capital, and reserve capital. To begin a financial plan, you will need to analyze carefully all three types of required capital and estimate the amount of each needed to start up your business.

Start-Up Capital

Why do many start-up businesses fail within the first five years of operation?

The first type of required capital is **start-up capital**—the money required to start your business. Sufficient start-up capital is essential to the survival of a new business.

Establishing a business is an expensive and risky venture. The U.S. Small Business Administration reports that most small businesses fail in the first one to five years of operation. One of the reasons these businesses fail is that they lack sufficient start-up capital. If money is not available to purchase necessary merchandise or to pay current bills, a business will not survive.

Start-up capital is divided into two basic categories. The first category is the capital required to purchase the assets you will need to start your business. Before you can open the doors of your business, you will need to buy various items. These items may include equipment, display racks, and inventory.

The second category of start-up capital is **start-up costs**—the costs or fees involved in establishing your business. Start-up costs may include permits, legal and accounting fees, and security deposits. Some start-up costs are one-time expenses, such as permits, legal fees, and deposits for telephone service. Other costs are continuing expenses, such as rent, maintenance, and insurance.

Identifying Required Assets

Some assets are common to all businesses, both new and established. These are the items that most businesses need in order to operate. Other assets are unique to specific types of businesses or to certain geographic areas.

When preparing a financial plan, you will need to identify both common and unique assets. Be sure to record the types and quantities of items that you will need. To start, list the assets that are commonly needed by businesses. Assets might include office furniture, such as desks and file cabinets; computer hardware and software; display cases or shelves; store equipment, such as copiers and cash registers; merchandise inventory; transportation or delivery equipment, such as cars or vans; store and office supplies; carpeting and lighting; and security and communication systems.

Next, list the assets you will need that may be unique to your particular type of business or to your geographic area. Such assets might include unique pieces of production or repair equipment; special types of display equipment; special electronic, security, or maintenance equipment; or required health or safety equipment.

When you make these lists, it is a good idea to observe established businesses that are similar to your business, to read trade journals, and to consult with vendors in the industry. This will give you a better idea of what assets you will need for your business.

Before You Read

PREDICT

What is the difference between start-up capital and operating capital?

Motivating Students Ask the students: "How much time do you think it would take to create a financial plan for a business?"

Discussion Have the students discuss the various problems that could occur for a business owner when there is insufficient start-up capital.

$avvy Saver

Shopping for a Used Car or Van

1. Test-drive the car on streets as well as highways.
2. Have a reputable mechanic inspect the car.
3. Make sure the oil and other fluids are clean.
4. Compare the asking price with prices in newspaper ads and in *Kelley Blue Book*.
5. If you want a warranty, buy the car from a dealer instead of an individual seller.

Figure 18.1 Creating a Business

Creating a new business requires lots of preparation and hard work. By creating a thorough and realistic financial plan, you will ensure that your business has the money it needs to prosper and grow.

1 **Analyze your needs and costs.** Research the supplies your business will need and the fees and costs that you will have to pay to get started.

2 **Secure funding.** Your plan will describe how each business expense will be paid. Financial institutions will consider the accuracy of your financial plan before agreeing to lend money to your business.

3 **Plan your process.** In your financial plan, you will show how you will record, summarize, and report your business's finances once you get started.

4 **Prepare for opening.** A good financial plan will ensure that you have money to cover all the supplies and preparation necessary to open your business.

◀ **LARGE CAPITAL INVESTMENTS** Some businesses, such as patio and garden supply stores, require a great deal of start-up capital. *Can you name other types of businesses that require large amounts of capital to begin operating?*

Caption Answer Answers might include: appliance store, electronics store, auto repair or parts shop, car manufacturing plant, a construction company, computer store, swimming pool company, office supply store, and limo company.

Identifying Start-Up Costs

Next, identify and list the start-up costs for your business in your financial plan. This can be a complex task. You have to identify common start-up costs and determine which of those costs you should include in your financial plan. You must also become familiar with required local and state licenses, permits, and fees. Local trade associations, banks, and the U.S. Small Business Administration can help you identify these costs. Some common start-up costs include business insurance; legal and professional fees; licenses and permits; banking and credit card fees; marketing and advertising costs; rent and utilities security deposits; remodeling and renovation costs; and maintenance and repair expenses.

Unidentified costs are a serious problem for entrepreneurs who are beginning new businesses, so be sure to include any type of cost that you feel you may encounter in starting up your business. Too often, unexpected or hidden costs consume start-up funds. If that happens, money may not be available for other needed items.

Teaching Activity Divide the students into groups of four or five. Ask each group to choose a local business and describe what the probable start-up assets were when the business first opened.

Extension Have the students research the local licenses, permits, and/or fees required to open a gourmet grocery store in your town.

Assigning Costs to Identified Items

Once you have identified your required assets and start-up costs, you must estimate how much you will have to pay for each item. Be careful to assign a realistic dollar value to each required asset and start-up cost. If you underestimate, you may have to reduce costs in other areas, and then you may not have enough cash to pay for essential items. If this occurs often, your business may face a serious cash flow problem.

As You Read

RELATE

Think about a job you or a friend have had. What were some assets unique to that business?

Teaching Activity As a class, have the students estimate the cost of the following items for a gourmet grocery store: (1) a telephone system, (2) a computer system, (3) a fax machine, and (4) a copier. Then ask the students to research the actual prices of these pieces of equipment. Share the findings with the class and see how close the estimates were.

Play it safe by estimating on the high side. For example, suppose that your business will need a photocopier machine. You determine that it will cost between $1,400 and $1,800. When you assign costs to your required assets, you should use the higher estimate, $1,800. If you pay only $1,600 for the photocopier, you can apply the additional budgeted amount ($200) to other costs.

The final step in calculating how much money you will need to launch your business is to prepare a statement of required start-up capital. For example, Amanda Woodland is opening a new business called "The Silver Lining Gift Shop." She has developed a statement of required start-up capital. Amanda's statement is shown in **Figure 18.2.**

Amanda realizes that there will be unexpected costs and small items that she will need to purchase, which are not on this statement. But she thinks that she has identified all major required assets and start-up costs. After listing the items, she realizes that she will need approximately $90,000 in start-up capital. If Amanda had not researched and analyzed all her costs carefully, she probably would have guessed that she could start her gift shop with much less than $90,000.

Figure 18.2 **Statement of Required Start-Up Capital**

THE SILVER LINING GIFT SHOP

Statement of Required Start-Up Capital

Item	Cost	
ASSETS		
Display equipment	$11,400	
Office furniture	3,100	
Computer system	4,400	
Photocopier	1,800	
Merchandise	37,000	
Supplies	3,500	
Alarm system	2,700	
Carpet, lights, fans	12,400	
Maintenance equipment	2,900	
Total Assets		***79,200***
START-UP COSTS		
Insurance	3,100	
Professional/legal fees	2,700	
Business permits/licenses	200	
Utility deposits	700	
Advertising	1,300	
Repairs/Maintenance	2,200	
Banking fees	200	
Total Start-Up Costs		**10,400**
Total Required Start-Up Capital		**$89,600**

Counting Costs This statement can help ensure that no start-up costs are forgotten.

Why is it important to know start-up costs before opening a business?

Caption Answer Answers will vary, but students should point out that unexpected or hidden costs could use up start-up funds.

◀ **HIT OR MISS?** It is impossible to know for sure how successful your business venture will be. *What individuals or groups might you consult for reliable advice?*

Caption Answer Answers may include lawyers, accountants, small business advisers, bankers, Small Business Administration, and chambers of commerce.

Operating Capital

Why should you predict the amount of operating capital you will need?

Discussion Ask your students why they think it is not unusual to have losses when a business first opens.

After you determine how much capital you will need to start your business, you must focus on the second type of required capital. This is called **operating capital**—the amount of capital needed to operate a business for the first few months or years.

Although the sale of your products or services will generate revenue, this money is often not enough to cover business expenses and expansion plans. You will need money to purchase additional merchandise and increase sales to keep your business running. Cash must also be available to carry out your strategic plan and marketing plan.

As part of your financial plan, you must do **financial forecasting**, which is the process of estimating a business's operating capital. This future financial picture of your business is reported in **projected financial statements**—statements that predict the financial position of a business in the months and years to come. The projected financial statements will include income statements, balance sheets, and statements of cash flows.

Projected Income Statement

An income statement for a merchandising business will report revenue, cost of merchandise sold, gross profit on sales, operating expenses, and net income (or loss). This type of financial statement usually reports what happened in the previous accounting period.

In contrast, a projected income statement is an estimate of the way in which income amounts will change over the next few months or years. You create this statement before you begin business operations. This statement reveals where you expect your business to be in the future.

TechByte

Easy Planning Many entrepreneurs are skilled at sales and promoting their businesses but have trouble applying financial math. However, when you must create a financial plan to start or expand a business, technology is available to help. Financial plan software can analyze a financial situation, make projections, and create financial statements for a financial plan.

@ Read more about financial plan software and list three types of statements that it can create through **finance07.glencoe.com**.

▲ **PRICEY PROMOTIONS** Promotions are a variable marketing expense that increases or decreases depending on the success of the business. *Can you name a promotional activity that recently took place at a store near you?*

Caption Answer Accept all reasonable answers that show student effort.

Critical Thinking Have the students brainstorm a list of emergencies and opportunities for which a business might need to use its reserve capital.

Estimating figures for a projected income statement can be a challenge. You must analyze all information regarding revenue and expenses for your type of business. You can obtain this information from trade associations, vendors, local business organizations, and government agencies such as the U.S. Small Business Administration and the Bureau of the Census. The information from these sources is based on facts and averages. However, to create figures for your projected income statement, you will have to apply that information to your business and make educated guesses.

It is better to estimate projected revenues on the low side and to estimate projected expenses on the high side. This approach will allow some flexibility if sales do not reach your expectations or if expenses are higher than you had originally estimated. If you project yearly sales of between $130,000 and $150,000, use the lower estimate of $130,000. If you estimate your heating bill might be between $3,000 and $4,000, use the higher amount of $4,000.

It is important to determine the correct amount for a start-up company's expenses. Expenses are often classified as fixed or variable.

Fixed Expenses **Fixed expenses** are expenses that remain the same regardless of business activity. These might include rent, insurance, or interest on a loan. Fixed expenses are fairly easy to project because they remain constant, or fixed, for a stated length of time. For example, no matter how much your business earns from sales in a particular month, you will still pay the same amount in rent for the duration of your lease.

Variable Expenses **Variable expenses** are expenses that may change. Sometimes variable expenses can be adjusted depending on sales. Such expenses might include supplies, advertising, wages, and sometimes utilities. For example, if sales are lower than you had predicted, you could purchase fewer supplies or reduce your employees' hours. It is more difficult to project variable expenses.

Some variable expenses, such as maintenance and repairs, have nothing to do with sales. These also cannot be projected accurately. When your computer or cash register no longer works, you must have it repaired or replaced. The principal characteristic of variable expenses is that they change with business conditions and other situations.

Figure 18.3 shows a projected income statement for Skelly's Craft Shop for the first four months of operation. You can see that the statement is projecting losses in each month. This is not unusual for a new business. In fact, it is common for a new business to go for several months or even a year without reporting a profit. Notice, however, that the estimated loss for Skelly's Craft Shop decreases each month. With continued good financial management, it is likely that profits will be reported in the near future.

As You Read

QUESTION

In what way is a projected income statement different from other income statements?

Question Answer It is an estimate of the way in which income amounts will change over the next few months or years, and not a statement of what happened in previous accounting period.

Figure 18.3 **Projected Income Statement**

SKELLY'S CRAFT SHOP

Projected Income Statement

MONTH	1	2	3	4
REVENUE				
Sales	$9,000	$10,600	$12,500	$14,600
Cost of Merchandise Sold	– 5,400	– 6,400	– 7,300	– 8,700
Gross Profit on Sales	**$3,600**	**$4,200**	**$5,200**	**$5,900**
EXPENSES				
Rent	3,800	3,800	3,800	3,800
Electricity	200	200	200	200
Heat/AC	300	325	340	350
Telephone	100	140	175	195
Insurance	290	290	290	290
Maintenance/Repairs	100	160	230	250
Miscellaneous	100	140	170	200
Wages	400	490	575	680
Taxes	250	250	250	250
Supplies	475	550	630	720
Interest	510	510	530	530
Advertising	875	875	960	760
Total Expenses	**$7,400**	**$7,730**	**$8,150**	**$8,225**
Net Income /<Loss>	**<$3,800>**	**<$3,530>**	**<$2,950>**	**<$2,325>**

Forecasting Profit A projected income statement can help determine whether a company will become profitable within a reasonable amount of time.

Why is creating such a statement an important part of developing a financial plan?

Caption Answer
Answers will vary, but students should point out that the statement reveals where the owner expects his or her company's financial situation to be in the future.

Figure 18.4 shows a projected income statement for Skelly's Craft Shop for the first five years of operation. It provides a long-range view of business activity. Although the amounts are only estimates, if they are projected realistically, they may indicate the potential success of the business.

Notice that by the end of the second year, the craft shop anticipates a profit. If all goes according to projections, the business should be doing quite well within five years. This is good news for the business owners. It is also important information to include in a financial plan for banks or other financial institutions that might provide funding to the owner.

Figure 18.4 **Projected 5-Year Income Statement**

SKELLY'S CRAFT SHOP

Projected 5-Year Income Statement

YEAR	1	2	3	4	5
REVENUE					
Sales	$172,000	$224,600	$258,500	$298,000	$370,000
Cost of Merchandise Sold	−103,200	− 125,400	−147,100	−169,000	−205,000
Gross Profit on Sales	**$68,800**	**$99,200**	**$111,400**	**$129,000**	**$165,000**
EXPENSES					
Rent	45,600	47,300	48,200	51,800	55,000
Electricity	4,600	4,800	5,000	5,200	5,600
Heat/AC	3,500	3,900	4,400	4,700	5,000
Telephone	1,200	1,400	1,600	1,800	2,200
Insurance	3,500	3,600	3,700	3,800	4,000
Maintenance/Repairs	1,200	1,600	2,300	2,500	2,800
Miscellaneous	1,000	1,400	1,700	1,900	2,200
Wages	4,800	6,100	7,200	8,000	9,900
Taxes	2,900	3,500	3,900	4,200	7,600
Supplies	4,900	5,500	6,300	7,000	7,900
Interest	5,800	5,400	5,000	4,800	4,100
Advertising	5,900	5,100	4,300	4,000	5,000
Total Expenses	**$84,900**	**$89,600**	**$93,600**	**$99,700**	**$111,300**
Net Income/<Loss>	**<$16,100>**	**$9,600**	**$17,800**	**$29,300**	**$53,700**

Income Over Time This statement provides important information for financial institutions which may provide funding.

What would it mean if a company's projected 5-year income statement showed losses through all five years?

Caption Answer
An extended period of loss indicates that the business must ensure a higher income or reduce expenditures to be successful.

Projected Balance Sheet

Financial institutions will also want to see a forecast of the overall financial position of your business. You provide this with a projected balance sheet. On a projected balance sheet, you estimate the future assets, liabilities, and net worth of your business one year, three years, or five years from now. A projected balance sheet for Ramos T-Shirts is shown in **Figure 18.5.**

Review the projected balance sheet for Ramos T-Shirts, and you can see that the shop seems to be headed in the right direction. The net worth of the business is projected to increase over the next three years, with the owner's equity increasing from $37,600 at the end of the first year to $50,600 at the end of the third year. You will also notice that in this same three-year period, assets are projected to increase ($71,200 to $83,100), and liabilities are projected to decrease ($33,600 to $32,500).

Figure 18.5 **Projected 3-Year Balance Sheet**

RAMOS T-SHIRTS

Projected 3-Year Balance Sheet

YEAR	1	2	3
ASSETS			
Cash in Bank	$13,200	$15,000	$12,000
Accounts Receivable	2,300	3,100	4,000
Store Equipment	18,400	22,100	27,000
Office Equipment	7,200	6,500	6,700
Merchandise Inventory	24,900	26,000	30,000
Supplies	1,000	1,100	1,100
Computer Equipment	4,200	3,500	2,300
Total Assets	**$71,200**	**$77,300**	**$83,100**
Accounts Payable	$7,400	$8,100	$8,800
Notes Payable	26,200	25,300	23,700
Total Liabilities	**$33,600**	**$33,400**	**$32,500**
OWNER'S EQUITY			
Jon Ramos, Capital	37,600	43,900	50,600
Total Liabilities	**$71,200**	**$77,300**	**$83,100**

Assets and Expenses A projected balance sheet shows estimates of the assets, liabilities, and net worth of a start-up business.

Why is it important that the projected balance sheet shows an increase in assets?

Caption Answer
Answers might include that an increase in assets indicates that the company is moving toward becoming profitable.

Projected Statement of Cash Flows

A statement of cash flows reports how much cash a business has taken in and where the cash has gone. This document shows how the cash position of a business changed during an accounting period.

Many consider the projected statement of cash flows to be the most important projected financial statement. When you prepare a projected statement of cash flows, you analyze the amount of cash that you anticipate will be available for your business in the future. Will you have sufficient cash if your business operates on its projected path? Remember, success and growth depend on available cash.

Figure 18.6 shows a projected statement of cash flows for Westport Sporting Goods for a period of three months. You can see that the business predicts a positive cash flow for the three-month period. In other words, more money is shown coming into Westport Sporting Goods each month than is shown going out. Realize that these three months—April, May, and June—are probably a particularly high sales period for a sporting goods store. Therefore, the business might not have such a positive cash flow throughout the entire year.

Figure 18.6 Projected Statement of Cash Flows

WESTPORT SPORTING GOODS

Projected Statement of Cash Flows

	APRIL	MAY	JUNE
CASH RECEIVED			
Cash Sales	$33,500	$37,400	$39,500
Interest Income	170	175	180
Total Cash Inflow	**$33,670**	**$37,575**	**$39,680**
CASH DISBURSED			
Rent	$4,600	$4,600	$4,600
Utilities	1,300	1,375	1,420
Supplies	450	450	460
Advertising	2,800	3,000	3,700
Bank Charges/Fees	220	250	270
Interest Expense	3,400	3,300	3,200
Telephone	510	530	540
Maintenance	950	1,075	1,100
Credit Card Fees	390	425	460
Payroll	9,200	10,100	10,300
Taxes	4,800	6,000	7,300
Delivery Charges	1,040	1,260	1,290
Miscellaneous	520	600	600
Insurance	675	675	675
Total Cash Outflow	**$30,855**	**$33,640**	**$35,915**
NET OPERATING CASH FLOW	**2,815**	**3,935**	**3,765**
BEGINNING CASH BALANCE	**5,860**	**8,675**	**12,610**
ENDING CASH BALANCE	**$8,675**	**$12,610**	**$16,375**

Money to Operate Using this statement will help to determine the future health of a company.

Why do some people think this statement is one of the most important financial statements for a start-up business?

Caption Answer
Answers might include that the statement helps a business owner to determine whether the business will have enough available cash during its first few months.

◀ **CASH ONLY** When you pay for pizza to be delivered to your home, you probably pay in cash. Likewise, when merchandise is delivered to a store, the store may be required to pay for the items in cash. *What types of small businesses might have deliveries every day that require cash payments?*

Caption Answer Answers may include vegetable/fruit stores, butcher shops, grocery stores, restaurants, newsstands, or small drugstores.

Reserve Capital

Why is it important for a start-up business to have reserve capital available?

The third type of capital is called **reserve capital**—money that is set aside for unexpected costs or opportunities. Reserve capital is like cash in a personal savings account. If and when you need money, it is there.

When emergencies arise, reserve capital can be a lifeline for small businesses. Unexpected costs can occur at any time and usually require immediate attention. Examples of unexpected costs include repair bills and the expense of replacing broken equipment or lost or damaged merchandise. Without immediate access to cash to pay such costs, your business could face a serious financial problem.

Reserve capital is also needed to take advantage of business opportunities. Suppose that a competitor is going out of business and has offered you inventory at a great price if you pay for it in cash. You can use cash from your reserve fund to take advantage of the opportunity. In this situation cash must be available immediately, or the opportunity is lost. Good financial planning includes taking advantage of business opportunities when they arise.

STANDARD &POOR'S

Put on Your Financial Planner's Cap

Congratulations! You are successfully operating your own financial management company. A new client, Mrs. Brent, wants to open an old-fashioned ice cream parlor and seeks your help in preparing a projected income statement for the bank. *What questions will you need to ask her in order to prepare such a statement?*

See the Teacher Manual for answer.

In addition, business owners use reserve capital to expand and grow their businesses. For example, you might use cash from the reserve fund to buy new lines of merchandise, to expand or renovate your facilities, or to purchase more up-to-date equipment. Such forward-thinking investments allow your business to develop and become financially successful.

The amount of capital set aside in a reserve fund will vary from business to business. Many businesses set up this fund as a line of credit at the bank. This money can also come from your personal funds.

STANDARD & POOR'S

Global Financial Landscape

Standard and Poor's publishes the globally recognized S&P 500® financial index. It also gathers financial statistics, information, and news, and analyzes this data for international businesses, governments, and individuals to help them guide their financial decisions.

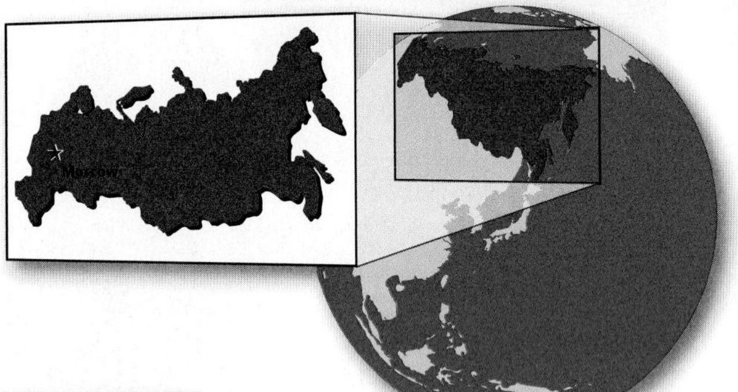

RUSSIA

Although oil is Russia's major natural resource, students may be its most important one. Each year Russia produces more than 200,000 graduates who receive degrees in the sciences. Schooled in computer science, physics, math, and engineering, they provide a foothold for Russia's economic future. However, the problem may be getting them to stay in Russia. Other countries can offer Russian scientists the powerful incentive of good salaries, something that is hard to find in Russia. For example, a professional with a postsecondary degree in Japan may earn up to $3,700 a month, whereas in Russia the same person would only make about $100 a month. In response to this trend, the Russian government has increased its monetary contributions to the field of science by 90 percent in an effort to boost salaries.

STANDARD & POOR'S **DATABYTES**

Capital	Moscow
Population	145,546,000
Language	Russian
Currency	Russian ruble
Gross Domestic Product (GDP)	$1.28 trillion (2003 est.)
GDP per capita	$8,900

Industry: Mining and extractive industries, machine building, shipbuilding, road and rail transportation equipment, and communications equipment

Agriculture: Grain, sugar beet, sunflower seed, vegetables, and beef

Exports: Petroleum and petroleum products, natural gas, wood and wood products, metals, and fur

Natural Resources: Oil, natural gas, coal, and timber

Think Globally

If you were a Russian graduate and had to choose between a good salary in a foreign country or a low salary at home, which would you choose and why?

See the Teacher Manual for answer.

Document Detective

Learn to identify and understand the standard financial documents you will use in the real world.

See the Teacher Manual for answers.

Investigate: A Personal Financial Statement

This form lists the following information:

- Name and contact information
- Assets and income
- Liabilities and loans
- Source of income
- Noteholder contact information

Your Motive: When you apply for a loan, you must present an accurate personal financial statement so that banks and lenders can review your current financial status. They want to be sure that you have resources to pay off a loan.

Personal Financial Statement

U.S. Small Business Administration — As of *April*, *20--*

Complete this form for: (1) each proprietor, or (2) each limited partner who owns 20% or more interest and each general partner, or (3) each stockholder owning 20% or more of voting stock, or (4) any person or entity providing a guaranty on the loan.

Name *Sarah Dean*	Business Phone (*303*) *555-8941*
Residence Address *10 West Cleveland Rd.*	Residence Phone (*303*) *555-1527*
City, State, & Zip Code *Twinsburg, OH 44218*	
Business Name of Applicant/Borrower *Interiors by Design*	

Assets	(Omit Cents)	Liabilities	(Omit Cents)
Cash on hand & in Banks	$ *15,000*	Accounts Payable	$ *2,500*
Savings Accounts	$ *3,000*	Notes Payable to Banks and Others (Describe in Section 2)	$ *–*
IRA or Other Retirement Account	$ *35,000*	Installment Account (Auto)	$ *2,500*
Accounts & Notes Receivable	$ *–*	Mo. Payments $ *500*	
Life Insurance-Cash Surrender Value Only (Complete Section 8)	$ *3,000*	Installment Account (Other)	$ *–*
Stocks and Bonds (Describe in Section 3)	$ *4,000*	Mo. Payments $	
Real Estate (Describe in Section 4)	$ *75,000*	Load on Life Insurance	$ *–*
Automobile-Present Value	$ *7,000*	Mortgages on Real Estate (Describe in Section 4)	$ *100,000*
Other Personal Property (Describe in Section 5)	$ *–*	Unpaid Taxes (Describe in Section 6)	$ *8,000*
Other Assets (Describe in Section 5)	$ *–*	Other Liabilities (Describe in Section 7)	$ *–*
		Total Liabilities	$ *113,000*
		Net Worth	$ *29,000*
Total	$ *142,000*	**Total**	$ *142,000*

Section 1. Source of Income		Contingent Liabilities	
Salary	$ *55,000*	As Endorser or Co-Maker	$
Net Investment Income	$	Legal Claims & Judgments	$
Real Estate Income	$	Provision for Federal Income Tax	$
Other Income (Describe below)*	$	Other Special Debt	$

Section 2. Notes Payable to Banks and Others

Name and Address of Noteholder(s) ______

Key Points: The Small Business Administration (SBA) developed a personal financial statement for loan applicants to complete when applying for an SBA loan. Similar to a personal balance sheet, the form details a person's assets, liabilities, and net worth.

Find the Solutions

1. What is the purpose of a personal financial statement?
2. What is Sarah's net worth?
3. How was her net worth calculated?
4. What is Sarah's salary?
5. Why would the SBA want to know the names and addresses of noteholders?

WebQuest

Be Your Own Boss
Learn all you can about the different ways entrepreneurs finance their start-up businesses. What you know about how to obtain financing will make the difference between the success or failure of your business.

@ To continue with Task 5 of your WebQuest project, visit **finance07.glencoe.com**.

You should not use your reserve capital for the normal operation of your business. It should be used only for unexpected costs and worthwhile business opportunities.

By keeping a reasonable amount of money in your reserve fund, you will be able to take care of your business even in crisis situations. Also, you will be able to take advantage of business opportunities that require money above and beyond the income from your business.

Using Technology

How can technology assist in preparing financial information?

Recording, summarizing, and reporting financial information can be an extremely time-consuming activity. Computers offer small business owners the ability to automate all the accounting functions. Daily, weekly, monthly, and annual reports can be generated quickly and accurately. With software and hardware being very affordable, most small businesses use some form of automated accounting.

Section 18.1 Assessment

See the Teacher Manual for answers.

QUICK CHECK

1. What are two categories of start-up capital?
2. How do you estimate the amount of operating capital needed to run a business?
3. Where is the financial information needed to create a projected income statement?

THINK CRITICALLY

4. Explain why a sound financial plan is critical to the success of a business.

USE COMMUNICATION SKILLS

5. **Projected Financial Statements** Theo and Cole have an opportunity to start a business selling sunglasses at the beach. Theo knows it is very important to develop a written financial plan for the new business. Cole, however, says that as long as they know what is going on, they do not need projected financial statements.

Write About It Write a paragraph that will help Theo convince Cole that developing a written financial plan and creating projected financial statements will help their business succeed.

SOLVE MONEY PROBLEMS

6. **Identify Start-Up Costs** Jana plans to turn her love of basketball into a business by offering summer basketball camps for children, one-on-one training for high school players, and skills assessment for college players. Jana is ready to create a financial plan for her business.

Analyze Help Jana identify the required assets and start-up costs for her business.

Section 18.2

Case Study: A Financial Plan

Starting a Business

What are some requirements to start a business?

For the past five years, Molly Singer has worked at King Point Florist, a local flower and garden store. During that time Molly learned to create fresh flower arrangements, fruit and gourmet baskets, and dried flower displays. She has read several books on floral design and has received numerous compliments on her arrangements.

Because of her work at the florist shop, Molly has experience in purchasing flowers and arrangements, advertising, pricing, sales procedures, and recordkeeping. She has taken several business courses at the local community college and has attended two seminars on running a small business.

Molly now feels that she is ready to open her own florist business. She realizes that running her own business will be very different from working for someone else. She is a little nervous about the challenges she will face as a business owner. However, she is confident that she has the knowledge and skills she needs to operate a successful flower shop.

Molly has decided to call her business "Cricket Lane Flowers." After researching locations and potential markets for a shop, she has found a small store that will fit her needs. It is located on a main street with a steady traffic flow and high visibility. No other flower shops are in the area, but there are several small businesses nearby that seem to attract customers. The store is in good condition, the monthly rent is reasonable, and the required painting and decorating should be affordable.

A Business Plan for Cricket Lane Flowers

What is an example of a business plan?

With some preliminary research completed, Molly is ready to create her business plan for Cricket Lane Flowers. Her overall business plan consists of three parts: a strategic plan, a marketing plan, and a financial plan. This section provides brief summaries of Molly's strategic and marketing plans as well as all elements of her financial plan.

Focus on Reading

Read to Learn

- How to identify the elements of a financial plan.

Main Idea

A good financial plan reflects your knowledge and skills and projects a picture of the potential financial success of your business.

Key Term

- chart of accounts

Before You Read

PREDICT

What is the advantage of having a thorough and solid financial plan?

Springboard Ask your students these questions: "How would you prepare yourself to open a business? What education do you think you would need? What type of experiences would be important?"

Motivating Students Ask the students if they think Molly is ready to open her business.

▶ **IN FULL BLOOM** Molly will need more than a good location to make her dream of a thriving flower shop come true. *What else will Molly need to build a successful new business?*

Caption Answer Answers might include: a solid business plan, including a good marketing plan, strategic plan, and financial plan; knowledge, skills, and experience in the flower business; and sufficient capital.

Teaching Activity Divide the class into groups of two or three. Ask each group to design a floor plan and decorating scheme for Cricket Lane Flowers.

Extension Have the students identify the competition Molly would face if she chose to open Cricket Lane Flowers in your community.

The Strategic Plan

For her strategic plan Molly researched the local flower market, identified the competition, and decided on the line of flowers and services that her shop will provide. After careful analysis, she set the following short-term and long-term goals.

Short-Term Goals:

- Rent a store in a good location.
- Secure a good telecommunication system.
- Computerize all accounting functions.
- Increase sales by 5 percent or more each month during the first year.
- Utilize all local advertising outlets.

Long-Term Goals:

- Increase sales by 30 percent or more in each of the first three years.
- Show a profit by the end of the second year.
- Expand inventory to include fruit and gift items.
- Develop business clients.

Molly's strategic plan also outlines the steps that she will take to achieve each of her short-term and long-term goals.

As You Read

RELATE

Which one of Molly's long-term goals do you think will be the most difficult to reach? Why?

The Marketing Plan

In her marketing plan, Molly analyzed the competition, identified advertising outlets, developed promotional activities, and established an advertising and promotion budget for Cricket Lane Flowers. The success of her sales goals depends on an effective marketing plan. At her previous job, Molly purchased advertising space in local and regional newspapers and magazines. Molly has decided to spend $2,000 in each of the first three months on advertising.

The Financial Plan

What must Molly do before she prepares her financial plan?

With her strategic and marketing plans completed, Molly is ready to develop her financial plan. As you may recall, the success of her strategic and marketing plans depends on the quality and accuracy of her financial plan.

Before preparing a financial plan, Molly must be sure that she has set realistic goals for herself and her business. She knows that although her figures are only estimates, they must be attainable. Also, Molly realizes that it will take time to earn a profit.

Background Information

To help start her business, Molly has saved money over the past five years, and her brother and sister will lend her some money. She needs to borrow additional funds, but she is confident that she will qualify for loans because of her well-established credit history. She has financed two cars and repaid her student loans. In addition, Molly uses her credit cards wisely and makes payments on time.

Molly has decided to organize her new business as a sole proprietorship. Although she will have unlimited liability, this form of ownership is easier and less costly to establish than others. She has consulted with an attorney and an accountant. Molly will continue to work with her accountant throughout the life of her business. She will need to consult him in the future regarding issues such as business expansion, tax filing, and the possibility of hiring employees.

Elements of the Financial Plan

Molly's financial plan includes the following reports:

- Statement of Required Start-Up Capital
- Projected 12-Month Income Statement
- Projected 12-Month Statement of Cash Flows
- Projected 3-Year Income Statement
- Projected 3-Year Statement of Cash Flows
- Projected 3-Year Balance Sheet

Academic Connection

LANGUAGE ARTS

A marketing plan helps a business owner to predict the cost of promoting and marketing his or her new company. An important part of developing a marketing plan is analyzing the competition. By doing so, the business owner can determine the competition's strengths and weaknesses and plan his or her marketing strategy accordingly. *Write a short essay outlining the process for evaluating potential business rivals.*

See the Teacher Manual for answer.

Critical Thinking Have the students analyze Molly's short-term and long-term goals. Then ask the students to add at least one goal to each list.

Discussion Ask the students to discuss how Molly should spend her advertising dollars.

As You Read

QUESTION

What are Molly's alternatives to setting up a business as a sole proprietorship?

Question Answer Answers might include a partnership.

Critical Thinking Ask the students to describe the advantages and disadvantages of Molly's decision to open her business as a sole proprietorship.

Molly's complete financial plan for Cricket Lane Flowers appears on the following pages. By reading and analyzing her six projected financial statements in **Figures 18.7** through **18.12** (pages 592–597), you will see how she expects her business to develop over time.

Cricket Lane Flowers
Financial Plan
Prepared by Molly Singer

Business Objective: To open and operate a financially successful flower shop.

Required Capital:	
Start-Up Capital	$89,000
Operating Capital	12,000
Reserve Capital	15,000
Total Required Capital	$116,000

Figure 18.7 Cricket Lane Flowers—Statement of Required Start-Up Capital

CRICKET LANE FLOWERS
Statement of Required Start-Up Capital

Item	Cost
ASSETS	
Refrigeration equipment	$9,600
Display equipment	8,100
Maintenance equipment	2,900
Delivery van	19,000
Office furniture	1,900
Rugs, lights, ventilation	5,200
Computer system	3,500
Phone systems	750
Photocopier	1,800
Merchandise	17,000
Supplies	1,100
Alarm system	900
Total Assets	**$71,750**
START-UP COSTS	
Rent deposit	3,500
Insurance	1,400
Building signs	3,000
Artists' fees	150
Professional/legal fees	2,200
Business permits/licenses	250
Stationery/business cards	400
Flowers/wire fees	500
Utility deposits	700
Phone lines	450
Advertising	2,000
Repairs/fix-up costs	1,800
Banking fees	200
Other	500
Total Start-Up Costs	**17,050**
Total Required Start-Up Capital	**$88,800**

Starting the Business With this statement, Molly will not forget any important start-up costs.

Do you think Molly's list of required start-up capital is accurate? Why?

Caption Answer Accept all reasonable answers that show an understanding of the concept.

Sources of Capital:	
Cash from Owner	$30,000
Personal Loans	6,000
Short-Term Commercial Loan (SBA Guaranteed)	30,000
Home Equity Loan	50,000
Total Available Capital	$116,000

Molly will invest the funds from the first three sources of capital (cash from owner, personal loans, and short-term commercial loan) in the business immediately. To cover the initial operation costs of the business, Molly has elected to use a home equity loan. As you learned in Chapter 7, a home equity loan is a loan based on the difference between the current market value of a home and the amount still owed on the mortgage. Home equity loans are an easy source of extra cash, but they must be used carefully. For example, if Molly's business were to fail, she would have difficulty repaying the loan.

Common CENTS

Saving Is Better
Spending money is easy, especially when you have a credit card. Resist the temptation to use your card to buy something you want but cannot really afford. Instead, be patient and save your money for that special item. *Why is it important to use your credit cards wisely for business or personal expenses?*

Common Cents to avoid debt and have a good credit rating

Careers in Finance

CONTROLLER **Glenn Danforth**
Lovoltech

Business math and problem solving have always interested Glenn. As the controller for a start-up semiconductor manufacturer, Glenn is responsible for all aspects of the corporation's finances. He handles banking, profit and loss statements, balance sheets, payroll, accounts payable, accounts receivable, collections, cost accounting, inventory valuation, and government filing. He also prepares and analyzes weekly cash management reports, monthly expense reports, and quarterly financial statements complete with management analysis. Because the company works with a plant in Taiwan, Glenn is in the process of learning Mandarin Chinese. He enjoys studying the different parts of the business and seeing how he can help them "add up" to a more profitable company.

SKILLS: Accounting, analytical, communication, computer, decision-making, management, math, organizational, and problem-solving skills

PERSONAL TRAITS: Discreet, flexible, good judgment, likes working with people and numbers, and tactful

EDUCATION: High school diploma or equivalent; bachelor's or master's degree in accounting, finance, or business; Certified Public Accountant certification; master's degree in business administration also recommended

ANALYZE Why would a controller need to be a good team player?
See the Teacher Manual for answer.

@ To learn more about career paths for controllers, visit **finance07.glencoe.com**.

Figure 18.8 Cricket Lane Flowers—Projected 12-Month Income Statement

CRICKET LANE FLOWERS

Projected 12-Month Income Statement

MONTH	1	2	3	4	5	6
REVENUE						
Sales	$11,000	$12,000	$13,600	$15,100	$15,800	$16,500
Cost of Merchandise Sold	4,900	5,300	5,850	6,500	6,800	7,400
Gross Profit on Sales	**$6,100**	**$6,700**	**$7,750**	**$8,600**	**$9,000**	**$9,100**
EXPENSES						
Rent	3,500	3,500	3,500	3,500	3,500	3,500
Electricity	180	180	185	185	185	185
Heat/AC	340	375	390	395	395	370
Telephone	130	140	175	205	225	225
Insurance	480	480	480	480	480	480
Maintenance/Repairs	100	130	150	150	150	155
Miscellaneous	100	140	160	180	180	180
Wages	350	400	475	500	500	600
Taxes	250	360	400	450	475	490
Supplies	460	530	590	620	640	640
Interest	680	680	680	680	680	680
Advertising	2,000	2,000	2,000	1,800	1,700	1,500
Other	100	100	100	100	100	125
Total Expenses	**$8,670**	**$9,015**	**$9,285**	**$9,245**	**$9,210**	**$9,130**
Net Income/<Loss>	**<$2,570>**	**<$2,315>**	**<$1,535>**	**<$645>**	**<$210>**	**<$30>**

Figure 18.9 Cricket Lane Flowers—Projected 12-Month Statement of Cash Flows

CRICKET LANE FLOWERS

Projected 12-Month Income Statement

MONTH	1	2	3	4	5	6
CASH RECEIPTS						
Cash Sales	$10,400	$11,900	$13,400	$15,000	$15,600	$16,500
Total Cash Receipts	**$10,400**	**$11,900**	**$13,400**	**$15,000**	**$15,600**	**$16,500**
CASH PAYMENTS						
Purchase of Merchandise	4,600	5,100	6,050	7,100	7,700	8,400
Operating Expenses	7,740	7,975	8,202	8,115	8,055	7,960
Interest Expense	680	680	680	680	680	680
Taxes	250	360	400	450	475	490
Total Cash Payments	**$13,270**	**$14,115**	**$15,335**	**$16,345**	**$16,910**	**$17,530**
NET CASH FLOW	**<$2,870>**	**<$2,215>**	**<$1,935>**	**<$1,345>**	**<$1,310>**	**<$1,030>**

Figure 18.8 Cricket Lane Flowers—Projected 12-Month Income Statement (cont'd)

CRICKET LANE FLOWERS
Projected 12-Month Income Statement

MONTH	7	8	9	10	11	12
REVENUE						
Sales	$17,000	$17,800	$18,700	$20,400	$22,300	$24,000
Cost of Merchandise Sold	7,900	8,300	9,100	9,900	11,400	12,000
Gross Profit on Sales	**$9,100**	**$9,500**	**$9,600**	**$10,500**	**$10,900**	**$12,000**
EXPENSES						
Rent	3,500	3,500	3,500	3,500	3,500	3,500
Electricity	185	190	190	190	200	200
Heat/AC	370	350	340	340	350	360
Telephone	225	240	240	250	250	250
Insurance	480	480	480	480	480	480
Maintenance/Repairs	160	160	160	175	175	175
Miscellaneous	180	190	190	190	190	190
Wages	600	700	700	800	800	900
Taxes	525	595	615	640	660	675
Supplies	660	670	670	670	680	680
Interest	680	680	680	680	680	680
Advertising	1,200	1,200	1,200	1,400	1,500	1,500
Other	125	125	125	125	100	130
Total Expenses	**$8,890**	**$9,080**	**$9,090**	**$9,440**	**$9,595**	**$9,720**
Net Income/<Loss>	**<$210>**	**<$420>**	**$510**	**$1,060**	**$1,305**	**$2,280**

Monthly Income This statement shows the progression of Cricket Lane Flowers' income.

Is there a reasonable progression of income over the 12 months?

Caption Answer
Yes, the statement does indicate a reasonable progression of income.

Figure 18.9 Cricket Lane Flowers—Projected 12-Month Statement of Cash Flows (cont'd)

CRICKET LANE FLOWERS
Projected 12-Month Income Statement

MONTH	7	8	9	10	11	12
CASH RECEIPTS						
Cash Sales	$16,500	$17,500	$18,600	$20,300	$21,400	$23,500
Total Cash Receipts	**$16,500**	**$17,500**	**$18,600**	**$20,300**	**$21,400**	**$23,500**
CASH PAYMENTS						
Purchase of Merchandise	7,500	8,300	9,000	10,100	10,600	11,900
Operating Expenses	7,685	7,805	7,795	8,120	8,225	8,365
Interest Expense	680	680	680	680	680	680
Taxes	525	595	615	640	660	675
Total Cash Payments	**$16,390**	**$17,380**	**$18,090**	**$19,540**	**$20,195**	**$21,620**
NET CASH FLOW	**$110**	**$120**	**$510**	**$760**	**$1,205**	**$1,880**
Negative Cash Flow for the 12-Month Period	**<$6,120>**					

Monthly Cash Flow A negative cash flow should progress to a positive one within a year or so.

Should Molly expect a positive cash flow by the 7th month? Why?

Caption Answer
Answers will vary, but as long as Molly's projected cash sales are accurate, then she should see a positive cash flow within the timeframe she has projected.

Figure 18.10 Cricket Lane Flowers—Projected 3-Year Income Statement

CRICKET LANE FLOWERS
Projected 3-Year Income Statement

YEAR	1	2	3
REVENUE			
Sales	$204,200	$264,000	$338,000
Cost of Merchandise Sold	95,350	122,000	159,000
Gross Profit on Sales	**$108,850**	**$142,000**	**$179,000**
EXPENSES			
Rent	42,000	42,000	43,500
Electricity	2,255	2,800	3,000
Heat/AC	4,375	5,400	5,700
Telephone	2,555	3,000	3,100
Insurance	5,760	6,000	6,300
Maintenance/Repairs	1,840	2,500	4,000
Miscellaneous	2,070	2,400	2,700
Wages	7,325	11,200	17,000
Taxes	6,135	8,200	10,000
Supplies	7,510	8,000	9,500
Interest	8,160	9,300	9,700
Advertising	19,000	15,000	14,000
Other	1,385	2,000	2,000
Total Expenses	**$110,370**	**$117,800**	**$130,500**
Net Income/<Loss>	**<$1,520>**	**$24,200**	**$48,500**

Predicting Success Molly projects the first three years of her company's income.

What is the net income increase between the first and second years?

Caption Answer
$24,200 − $1,520 = $22,680

Figure 18.11 Cricket Lane Flowers—Projected 3-Year Statement of Cash Flows

CRICKET LANE FLOWERS
Projected 3-Year Statement of Cash Flows

YEAR	1	2	3
CASH RECEIPTS			
Cash Sales	$200,600	$262,500	$330,000
Total Cash Receipts	**$200,600**	**$262,500**	**$330,000**
CASH PAYMENTS			
Purchase of Merchandise	96,350	151,000	148,000
Operating Expenses	96,075	100,300	110,800
Interest Expense	8,160	9,300	9,700
Taxes	6,135	8,200	10,000
Total Cash Payments	**$206,720**	**$268,800**	**$278,500**
NET CASH FLOW	**−$6,120**	**−$6,300**	**+$51,500**

Future Cash Flow Molly has predicted positive cash flows in three years.

How do you calculate net cash flow?

Caption Answer
Subtract the total cash payments from total cash receipts.

Figure 18.12 Cricket Lane Flowers—Projected 3-Year Balance Sheet

CRICKET LANE FLOWERS
Projected 3-Year Balance Sheet

YEAR	1	2	3
ASSETS			
Cash in Bank	$13,000	$6,700	$58,200
Accounts Receivable	2,900	4,400	12,400
Display Equipment	8,000	8,000	8,000
Refrigeration Equipment	9,000	9,000	9,000
Delivery Equipment	17,500	17,500	17,500
Office Equipment	9,100	9,100	9,100
Computer Equipment	3,000	3,000	3,000
Merchandise Inventory	21,000	51,700	43,400
Supplies	500	500	500
Total Assets	**$84,000**	**$109,900**	**$161,100**
LIABILITIES			
Accounts Payable	8,400	10,100	12,800
Notes Payable	30,000	30,000	30,000
Total Liabilities	**$38,400**	**$40,100**	**$42,800**
OWNER'S EQUITY			
Molly Singer, Capital	45,600	69,800	118,300
Total Liabilities & O.E.	**$84,000**	**$109,900**	**$161,100**

The First 3 Years Molly has used this sheet to predict the health of her company in the first three years of business.

Does it look like Cricket Lane Flowers will survive the first difficult years of operation?

Caption Answer
Answers will vary, but the projected statements seem to indicate that the business will succeed.

Accounting Procedures

Molly's accountant has set up a **chart of accounts**—a list of all the general ledger accounts that a business will use. (See Chapter 20 for more information on accounting.) This chart of accounts will provide Molly with a framework for recording and reporting her business transactions. **Figure 18.13** shows the accounts she will use.

Molly's accountant also recommended purchasing a software program to maintain Cricket Lane Flowers' accounting records, so all accounting procedures will be computerized. By using a software program, Molly will spend less time maintaining her accounting records and will have more time to run her business.

Molly will be responsible for entering all business transactions into the program. At the end of every month, the computer system will generate a trial balance, financial statements, and reports. Molly and her accountant will analyze Cricket Lane Flowers' monthly income statement, statement of cash flows, and balance sheet.

Figure 18.13 Cricket Lane Flowers—Chart of Accounts Sheet

CRICKET LANE FLOWERS
Chart of Accounts

ASSETS	**REVENUE**
101 Cash in Bank	401 Sales Revenue
105 Accounts Receivable	405 Sales Returns
110 Merchandise Inventory	
115 Supplies	**COST OF MERCHANDISE**
120 Prepaid Insurance	501 Purchases
125 Display Equipment	505 Purchases Returns
130 Refrigeration Equipment	
135 Office Equipment	**EXPENSES**
140 Computer Equipment	601 Advertising
145 Delivery Equipment	605 Bank Card Fees
	610 Delivery
LIABILITIES	615 Insurance
201 Accounts Payable	620 Interest
205 Notes Payable	625 Maintenance
	630 Miscellaneous
OWNER'S EQUITY	635 Rent
301 Molly Singer, Capital	640 Supplies
302 Molly Singer, Withdrawals	645 Utilities
303 Income Summary	650 Tax

In One Place This chart of accounts will help Molly keep track of all transactions.

Would a software program help Molly keep track of her accounts?

Caption Answer Yes, software would help Molly keep track of her accounts better than if she tried to track everything on paper.

By comparing these financial statements with statements from previous months, Molly and her accountant will be able to evaluate the financial progress and position of her business. If a financial problem is identified, her accountant will make recommendations as to what Molly needs to do to correct the problem. It is only by careful and constant financial analysis that Molly can be assured her business is growing according to the projections outlined in Cricket Lane Flowers' financial plan.

At the end of each quarter or year, her accountant will also see that all required local, state, and federal reports are submitted to the appropriate agencies.

After You Read

REACT

Do you think that you could develop a reasonable financial plan for a business using the information provided in this chapter?

React Answer Accept all reasonable answers that reference the chapter information.

Section 18.2 Assessment

See the Teacher Manual for answer key.

QUICK CHECK

1. What reports did Molly include in her financial plan?
2. Refer to Molly's projected 12-month income statement in Figure 18.8 on pages 594–595. When does Molly predict that she will begin to show a positive net income?
3. As you can see from Figure 18.9 on pages 594–595, Molly is projecting a negative cash flow of $6,120 for the first 12-month period during which she is in business. How did she arrive at this conclusion?

THINK CRITICALLY

4. Summarize the steps that Molly has taken to ensure that her financial plan will be efficient and effective.

USE MATH SKILLS

5. **Positive Predictions** One of Molly's long-term strategic goals is to increase sales by 30 percent or more in each of the first three years of business. As Molly reviews her projected income statements for the next three years, she knows that she made the "best guess" estimates for both revenue and expenses. Molly believes that she will meet or maybe even exceed her goals.

Calculate Using Figure 18.10 on page 596, calculate what Molly's projected sales would be in the second and third year if they increased 35 percent from each previous year. How might a 35 percent increase in sales impact Molly's projected expenses?

SOLVE MONEY PROBLEMS

6. **Start-Up Capital** According to Figure 18.7 on page 592, Molly will need $71,750 to purchase assets for Cricket Lane Flowers. If the bank denies her application for the short-term commercial loan of $30,000, she will not have enough money for all the assets that she has identified as necessary to begin operations.

Analyze How might Molly revise her list of assets and still have what she will need to begin to operate her business? Explain your reasoning.

Chapter 18 Review & Activities

See the Teacher Manual for answers.

CHAPTER SUMMARY

- Start-up capital includes money required for the purchase of assets needed to run a business, including inventory, equipment, furnishing, supplies, and utilities, plus start-up costs.
- Start-up costs include legal, professional, and banking fees, licenses, permits, insurance, marketing costs, and remodeling and maintenance costs. Estimates of these start-up costs should be on the high side, as new business owners often underestimate or miss some of these costs.
- Operating capital is the money needed to operate the business for the first few years. Often, revenue generated from the business is not enough to meet these costs in the first few years of business.
- Projected income statements are an estimate of the way in which income amounts will change over the next few months or years. Estimates of fixed expenses and variable expenses are included in the projected income statement. Lending institutions see these statements when you apply for commercial loans.
- Reserve capital is money set aside for unexpected costs or opportunities, similar to an emergency fund.
- The elements of a financial plan include a statement of required start-up capital, a projected 12-month income statement, a projected 12-month statement of cash flows, a projected 3-year income statement, a projected 3-year statement of cash flows, and a projected 3-year balance sheet.

Communicating Key Terms

Imagine that you are planning to open a new business. Using the terms below, prepare some notes for a meeting with a commercial loan officer at your bank regarding a business line of credit.

- capital
- start-up capital
- start-up costs
- operating capital
- financial forecasting
- projected financial statements
- fixed expenses
- variable expenses
- reserve capital
- chart of accounts

Reviewing Key Concepts

1. **Explain** the three steps in estimating start-up capital needs.
2. **List** the start-up costs of a business you would like to start someday.
3. **Explain** why operating capital estimates should be made "on the high side."
4. **Describe** some ways of estimating income and expenses in order to prepare projected income statements.
5. **Explain** how reserve capital will enable you to take advantage of business opportunities.
6. **Explain** why the projected statement of cash flows is considered the "most important financial statement" in the financial plan.

See the Teacher Manual for answers.

ACADEMIC SKILLS

Economics After visiting the wholesale flower mart, Molly, the owner of Cricket Lane Flowers, discovered that prices are going up on many of the flowers that the shop regularly purchases to sell to customers.

Plan and Budget Imagine you are the owner of Cricket Lane Flowers. Brainstorm some ways to reduce variable expenses to offset the rise in wholesale prices.

YOUR FINANCIAL FIGURES

Projecting Income As you can see on page 593, Molly, the owner of Cricket Lane Flowers, has the following sources of capital:

Cash from Owner	$30,000
Personal Loans	$6,000
Short-Term Commercial Loan	$30,000
Home Equity Loan	$50,000
Total Available Capital	$116,000

1. **Calculate** the percentage of the total available capital Molly is paying from her personal savings.
2. **Compute** using spreadsheet software to determine the percentage of total available capital from the other sources of capital.

REAL-WORLD Application

Connect with Economics In every financial undertaking, there are risks that can be controlled, and risks that cannot be controlled.

1. **Research** Go back through the chapter and look over Cricket Lane Flowers' sources of start-up and operating capital (page 592).
2. **Think Critically** What are some risks over which Molly, the company owner, has no control? How would you respond if Molly asked you for financial assistance with start-up costs? Why?

Internet CONNECTION

Round Up Your Consultants Everyone who runs a small business needs consultants to help him or her deal with various issues. A business owner may need a computer-support service or a promotional specialist.

@ **Log On** Use an Internet search engine to find several sources of such services in your town. Answer the following questions:

1. How much would it cost to obtain services from these sources?
2. Molly has $2,200 for professional and legal fees (see Figure 18.7 on page 592). If she needs $1,000 for legal fees, would the remaining $1,100 cover the cost of hiring a computer-support service?

BusinessWeek ONLINE

Newsclip: Lacking Capital Many start-up companies make investments in their businesses but lack start-up capital.

@ **Log On** Go to finance07.glencoe.com and open Chapter 18. Learn more about how to write a financial plan for your business. Explain the consequences of lacking capital.

WHAT'S YOUR FINANCIAL ID?

ARE YOU A PERSUADER?

Your personality can help guide your future. On a separate sheet of paper, write down ten of the following character traits that best describe you and find out if you are a persuader, a communicator, or an individualist.

______ a. I like meeting people.
______ b. I am friendly.
______ c. I try to avoid conflict.
______ d. I like to spend time alone.
______ e. I like to talk.
______ f. I am sensitive.
______ g. I am interested in other people.
______ h. I am upbeat.
______ i. I am enthusiastic.
______ j. I like to be active.
______ k. I have perseverance.
______ l. I am persuasive.
______ m. I let other people do what they want.
______ n. I am cautious.
______ o. I am ambitious.
______ p. I like to feel in control.
______ q. I like to plan.
______ r. I like organization.
______ s. I like to be the center of attention.

Score 3 points for each of these character traits: **a, b, e, g, h, i, j, k, l, o,** or **s**.

Individualist: If you scored 6–12 points, you might enjoy a career and hobbies that gives you independence.

Communicator: If you scored 15–21 points, you enjoy activities in which you are a team player working toward a common goal.

Persuader: If you scored 24–30 points, consider a career in sales or another field in which you can influence people.

Accept all reasonable answers that show student effort and an understanding of the concept.

Your Financial Portfolio

Start with a Plan

Three brothers, Collin, Kyle, and J.C., plan to start a house painting business. All of them have experience painting, and they have identified plenty of work in an area downtown that is being renovated. They want to know how much start-up capital they will need to get their business going and to keep it going until it is solidly established.

Start-Up Costs

One-time costs:		
Equipment: 3 ladders	$305	
Paint sprayers	120	
Rollers, brushes, drop cloths, and other supplies (ongoing supplies will be expensed per job)	250	
Down payment for van	$3,000	
Total one-time costs		**$3,675**
Continuing costs (monthly):		
Insurance	$120	
Cell phone	25	
Van loan	625	
Van maintenance and gas	100	
Total monthly costs		**$870**
Total monthly costs × 12 months		**10,440**
Total start-up costs		**$14,115**

Identify

Start-up costs depend on the type of business, the size of the business, and the amount and kind of inventory and operating expenses. Give an example of the following types of businesses: service, retail, and manufacturing. Which might have the most expensive start-up costs? Why?

Accept all reasonable answers that show student effort and an understanding of the concept.

Unit 5 LAB

Get a Financial Life!

A Business Is Born

Overview

Carrie and David Lanier have two children: Eva, age 23, and Jack, age 22. Eva and Jack graduated from college with a low amount of student loan debt, thanks to smart planning, saving, and investing by their parents. While Eva and Jack were in college, they worked and started saving their own money for a retail store they plan to open some day. They need help writing a business plan for Party Town. They will hire a bookkeeper to complete a financial plan. Their store will offer party decorations, paper goods, balloons, and games. Now it is time to begin finalizing their plan. They hope to earn money from the store profits to expand their business in the future.

Resources & Tools

- Assorted magazines and newspapers
- Internet
- Portfolio (ring binder or file folder)
- Public or school library
- Word processor

Procedures

STEP A **The Process**

Eva and Jack are aware that having a strong business and financial background will be crucial to the success of their business. Therefore, they have asked you for some advice and assistance with writing a rough draft of the first two main sections of their business plan.

1. Eva and Jack are ready to hire a bookkeeper. They have asked you to help them choose the right employee. Make a list of the skills and characteristics the new employee should have. Write a newspaper ad for the position.
2. **a)** Set up the first main section of the business plan—the strategic plan for Party Town. Include the mission statement of the company, a description of the business and product, a product plan with their short-term and long-term goals, and list the management team and their roles.
   b) Set up the second main section of the business plan—the marketing plan for Party Town. Include research and information on the target customers, the competition, advertising outlets, and ideas for promotional activities as well as a budget for advertising and promotion.
3. Write a list of the elements of a financial plan as a guide for the bookkeeper to use.
4. Identify several books, magazines, newspapers, and Web sites that could be used by someone interested in starting and managing a business.

STEP B Create Your Portfolio

As you work through the process, save the results so that you can refer, review, and refine. Create a portfolio with four sections to showcase the information that you collect in Step A.

1. Section 1 should include the newspaper ad you created for the bookkeeper position.
2. Section 2 should include the strategic plan document and the marketing plan document with any supporting research materials.
3. Section 3 should list all the elements of a financial plan in outline form.
4. The last section will be a bibliography of the resources that you identified.

STEP C Applying Technology

The globalization of the marketplace, advances in technology, and the downsizing of the workforce are trends that are transforming the workplace and the worker. Technology is providing ways for people to work anytime and anyplace. The successful workers and entrepreneurs of tomorrow must have strong technical skills and be willing to update those.

1. Research an emerging technology and its impact on the workplace and retailing. Some topics include: computers, artificial intelligence, e-books, video telephones, video conferencing, and voice and eye recognition.
2. Contact a vendor who sells the products you selected. Find out how much they cost and next year's projected sales.
3. Create a poster, brochure, or other visual aid about your selected technology. Include the features and benefits of the product. Also, note how one type of technology could be applied to Party Town.
4. Write a two-page paper outlining your predictions for the ways in which technology will affect the workplace and the economy.

Unit 6

Business Finance Basics

WebQuest Internet Project

Franchise Ownership

Buying a franchise business offers people a chance to own their own business. Franchise owners have the advantage of offering goods or services that have instant name recognition. But purchasing a franchise does not guarantee success. In this project you will investigate franchise opportunities to decide whether owning a franchise is right for you. You will learn about your obligations as a franchise owner, how to shop for opportunities, and how to ask the right questions before you invest.

@ Log on to **finance07.glencoe.com**. Begin by reading Task 1. Then continue on your WebQuest as you study Unit 6.

Section	19.1	20.1	21.1	22.1
Page	614	639	682	705

Cycling Back to the Future

When Gary Boulanger decided to open an independent bike shop in Dayton, Ohio, he sought inspiration from hometown heroes: Orville and Wilbur Wright. The famous brothers had built a bicycle company there in the 1890s before garnering greater fame as aviation pioneers.

So in January 2003, timed to coincide with the 100th anniversary of the Wright brothers' first flight, Boulanger introduced modern versions of the Wrights' Van Cleve and St. Clair models, opening Cycles Gaansari in downtown Dayton. Instead of going head-to-head with big manufacturers and retailers, Boulanger [created] his own niche with a retro line of cycles.

Boulanger says [his] shop brought in $140,000 in sales during its first year, $250,000 last year, and he expects revenue to double this year.

Boulanger stresses customer service. In turn, he says "our customers are brand loyal." To that end, he has begun selling a line of clothing and accessories with the Gaansari logo. And he began marketing a signature brand of coffee. Like the Wright Brothers before him, Gary Boulanger's business has definitely taken flight.

—By Rod Kurtz

Write About It How has Gaansari's inventory helped the business succeed?

See the Teacher Manual for answer.

Log On To read the complete *BusinessWeek* article and do the *BusinessWeek* Extension activity to help you learn more about inventory, go to **finance07.glencoe.com**.

CHAPTER 19
Sources of Funding

$ What You'll Learn

When you have completed this chapter, you will be able to:

Section 19.1

- Explain the role of entrepreneurs.
- Differentiate between start-up costs, operating costs, and reserve funds.
- Identify sources of personal and private financing.
- Discuss the options available through bank funding.
- Identify the factors banks consider to approve commercial loans.

Section 19.2

- Describe the function of the Small Business Administration.
- Identify alternative sources of funding for a business.

Reading Strategies

To get the most out of your reading:

Predict what you will learn in this chapter.
Relate what you read to your own life.
Question what you are reading to be sure you understand.
React to what you have read.

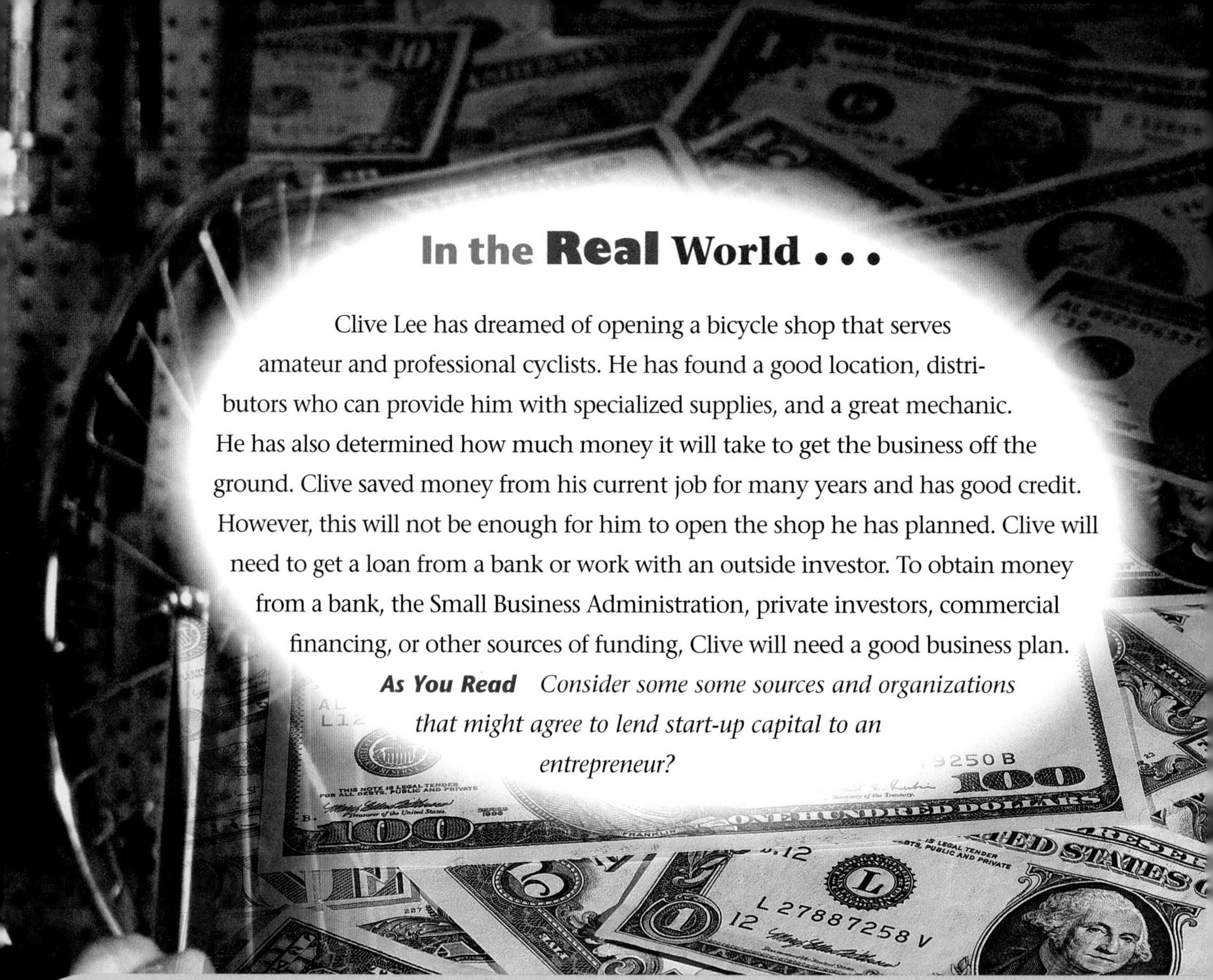

In the **Real** World . . .

Clive Lee has dreamed of opening a bicycle shop that serves amateur and professional cyclists. He has found a good location, distributors who can provide him with specialized supplies, and a great mechanic. He has also determined how much money it will take to get the business off the ground. Clive saved money from his current job for many years and has good credit. However, this will not be enough for him to open the shop he has planned. Clive will need to get a loan from a bank or work with an outside investor. To obtain money from a bank, the Small Business Administration, private investors, commercial financing, or other sources of funding, Clive will need a good business plan.

As You Read *Consider some some sources and organizations that might agree to lend start-up capital to an entrepreneur?*

Lesson Plan See the Teacher Manual for the Chapter 19 planning guide and lesson plan.

ASK STANDARD & POOR'S

Fast Cash

Q: My family runs a small business. Recently a lot of unexpected expenses came up, and now we need $4,000 in a hurry. We just expanded our business, so we have no cash in reserves. How can we obtain the money?

A: If you have outstanding (unpaid) invoices from customers whom you have billed for your products, you can take those invoices to a bank and borrow against those receivables. If you have orders to fill but need money for supplies, you can speak to a lender about a short-term commercial loan.

Ask Yourself How can a business prepare for unexpected expenses?

@ Go to **finance07.glencoe.com** to complete the Standard & Poor's Financial Focus activity.

Focus on Reading

Read to Learn

- How to explain the role of entrepreneurs.
- How to differentiate between start-up costs, operating costs, and reserve funds.
- How to identify sources of personal and private financing.
- How to discuss the options available through bank funding.
- How to identify the factors banks consider to approve commercial loans.

Main Idea

To start or expand a business, you must accurately estimate the amount of funding you will need.

Key Terms

- entrepreneur
- operating costs
- reserve fund
- private financing
- commercial debt financing
- commercial loan
- line of credit
- secured loan
- unsecured loan

Springboard Ask the students this question: "When is a business successful?"

Analyzing Financial Needs

Starting a New Business

What do you need to start a new business?

Jenny, age 8, and Matt, age 7, are going into business. They are going to set up a lemonade stand—called J & M Lemonade—in front of Matt's house. A lot of people walk down that street, which is close to a school and a park. Jenny and Matt figure that their location will provide plenty of customers. It is summer, and people are thirsty. Cold lemonade will be in demand.

Before they begin selling lemonade, however, Jenny and Matt must decide what things they will need to get their business started. In addition to lemonade, Jenny says they will need a large pitcher, a stand or table, and some cups. Matt adds a large sign, a box for their money, and some ice cubes to the list. They agree that they will also need coins to make change for customers.

As with all business operations, Jenny and Matt will need cash, equipment, and supplies, as well as goods or services to sell. How do you think they will get these items? They will probably do what you did when you were their age: They will go home and see what they can find. Their families may help them find a pitcher, a table, and some cardboard to make a sign. They may give them some coins to use for change and buy the lemonade and cups.

Soon Jenny and Matt have all the items they need, and they set up their stand. J & M Lemonade is now an active player in the free enterprise system.

Business Entrepreneurs

What does it take to become an entrepreneur?

When you were younger, you may have had a small business similar to Jenny and Matt's lemonade stand. Like Jenny or Matt, you were an entrepreneur. An **entrepreneur** is an individual who takes the risk of starting a new business. Entrepreneurs are highly motivated people who transform ideas for products or services into real-world businesses. About 80 percent of the 23 million business operations in the United States are run by one owner. Entrepreneurs are the backbone of the American economy.

High School Entrepreneurs

Would you like to be an entrepreneur? Most high school students would. In a recent Gallup poll, seven out of every ten high school students said that they would like to start a business. It is possible for a high school student to start his or her own business. For example, Fred DeLuca is one successful entrepreneur who started his business shortly after graduating from high school. In 1965, DeLuca borrowed $1,000 from a friend and opened Pete's Super Submarines, a sandwich shop in Bridgeport, Connecticut. Today you may know DeLuca's business as Subway. As of June 2005, Subway had over 23,000 restaurants in 82 countries.

Before You Read

PREDICT

Is every business owner an entrepreneur?

Funding a Business

Why do many entrepreneurs need to find outside sources for funding?

One of the major concerns when starting a business is how it will be financed. People who take on new business ventures usually need far more money than they realize.

Jenny and Matt started their lemonade stand with nothing. They had no lemonade, supplies, or cash. They funded their business with cash and other assets that their families provided. They hoped to sell several cups of lemonade and take in some money. Do you think that they made a profit? Chances are that the money they took in did not cover the cost of the lemonade and other supplies.

Motivating Students Ask if anyone in the class has a dream of becoming an entrepreneur. If so, ask the students to share their dreams and why they think this is what they want to do.

Caption Answer Answers might include cash, merchandise, and supplies.

◀ **THE AMERICAN DREAM** Anyone can start a small business. *What do you think you would need to start your own business?*

▶ FUNDING CONCERNS Successful businesses such as this one needed money to start their operations. *Where do you think you might be able to obtain money for a new business venture?*

Caption Answer Answers might include students' own funds, a bank loan, or a loan from friends or family.

Critical Thinking Ask the students how much they think it would take to start an on-campus balloon and flower shop.

Family members supported J & M Lemonade financially, but they did not expect to make a profit on their investment. They just wanted to help provide an educational and fun experience for Jenny and Matt. If it were not for their financial support, Jenny and Matt could not have started their business because other sources of funds were not available.

As a young adult, you would require funding if you decided to start your own business. Unfortunately, it is not easy to get funding for a new business from an outside source. Banks and other financial institutions are very selective about who receives loans. They also expect to get a good return on their investment.

As You Read

RELATE

Do you or your friends dream of owning your own business? What steps will it take to make those dreams come true?

Determining Needed Capital

Why is it so important to know how much money is needed to start up a business?

When you are starting a business, the first thing you must do is make a realistic estimate of how much capital you will need. As you know, capital is the money you need to establish a business, to operate it for the first few months, and to expand the business. Determining the capital needed to start up your business is one of the steps of developing a financial plan.

Start-Up Costs

The first goal in determining needed capital is to identify start-up costs. Start-up costs usually require a large amount of cash. If you attempt to estimate the costs without careful analysis, your estimate will probably be too low.

To analyze your costs, you should list everything you will require to begin to operate. Most businesses have some common start-up costs:

- Inventory needed to open the business
- Equipment, fixtures, and display cases
- Security deposit for rented space
- Advertising and promotions
- Insurance
- Professional fees (such as lawyers' fees)
- Remodeling costs (such as creating office space)
- Legal permits and licenses
- Supplies

Your next task is to assign an estimated cost to each item. Unless you list every anticipated cost, your total estimate will not be realistic.

Landscaping firms and convenience stores are different types of businesses, and each has different requirements for operating. Start-up costs vary among businesses and industries. Make sure that you research and explore the industry you are entering.

Teaching Activity As a class, make a list of Jenny and Matt's start-up costs. Then imagine Jenny and Matt have grown up and decided to open a lemonade stand in a local mall. Add any additional start-up costs that would be needed.

Careers in Finance

COMMERCIAL LOAN OFFICER

Jenny Tanner
Scott Watson & Associates, Inc.

Jenny Tanner gains satisfaction from helping small businesses and corporations become big ones. She tends to businesses and corporations that need to borrow money for new equipment or to buy property. She meets with the customers to explain the different types of loans available. After receiving a loan application from a business, she requests a credit report from a credit bureau, consults with her manager, and decides whether or not to approve the loan. As a commercial loan officer, Jenny is expected to seek out new customers.

SKILLS: Sales, presentation, communication, math, problem-solving, and organizational skills

PERSONAL TRAITS: Likes working with people and numbers, detail oriented, and self-motivated

EDUCATION: High school diploma or equivalent; bachelor's degree in finance, economics, business, or accounting; a minimum of three years' experience in a banking environment

ANALYZE How might a commercial loan officer's job differ from a personal loan officer's job?
See the Teacher Manual for answer.

@ To learn more about career paths for commercial loan officers, visit **finance07.glencoe.com**.

WebQuest

Franchise Ownership
Evaluate your personality and find out if owning a franchise business makes sense for you.

@ To continue with Task 2 of your WebQuest project, visit **finance07.glencoe.com**.

Operating Costs

Besides determining your start-up costs, you must also estimate your operating costs for the first 90 to 120 days. **Operating costs** are the ongoing expenses for operating a business.

Start-up costs and operating costs are separate cost categories. It is critical that you estimate both types of costs as accurately as possible. If you use all of your money for start-up costs, then you will not have any money available to pay your operating costs. When you start a new business, the amount you earn usually will not be enough to cover your expenses. If you cannot pay your suppliers, rent, or utility bills, your business will be in serious trouble.

When you prepare your budget for the first 90 to 120 days of business, you will include your expected income as well as your estimated monthly costs. Businesses have a number of common operating costs:

- Payroll
- Rent
- Insurance premiums
- Utility bills
- Office expenses
- Advertising
- Delivery charges
- Bank charges and other fees

Reserve Fund

Before starting a business, you will also have to estimate the amount of money you may need at a later date for growth. A **reserve fund** is money that can be made available for the future expansion of a business. You may need additional money to purchase merchandise or equipment, or perhaps to lease a truck. This money will allow for growth and help you avoid having to borrow additional capital.

Jenny and Matt's lemonade stand stayed in business for only two hours. They did not plan to operate an ongoing business. Of course, you hope that your business will have a much longer life. Therefore, careful financial planning for the future is critical. Consider other expenses when looking ahead and estimating a reserve fund:

- Additional equipment for increased business
- Advertising and other promotional costs
- Capital for any unexpected costs or decreased sales
- Maintaining a positive cash flow
- Expansion of facilities
- Getting and keeping the right amount of inventory

When you have estimated the amounts of your start-up and operating costs and your reserve fund, you will have a good idea of your business's financial needs. You will see what your cash flow will look like during the first months of operation. Then you can estimate the total amount of capital you will need to establish your business and begin to operate.

Document Detective

Learn to identify and understand the standard financial documents you will use in the real world.

See the Teacher Manual for answers.

Investigate: An Application for Business Loan

An application for a loan from the Small Business Administration (SBA) contains:

- Name and contact information
- Amount requested
- Intended use of loan
- Other outstanding federal loans or debt

Your Motive: By applying for a loan through the SBA, you will have a better chance of receiving the funding you need to start your business.

U.S. Small Business Administration

APPLICATION FOR BUSINESS LOAN

Individual: Jason True		Full Address: 1647 West Alvarez, Phoenix, AZ 85001			
Name of Applicant Business: True Business Forms				Tax I.D. No. or SSN	
Full Street Address of Business: 5743 Sun Palm Lane				Tel. No. (inc. A/C): 480-672-1853	
City: Phoenix	County: Maricopa	State: AZ	Zip: 85001	Number of Employees (Including subsidiaries and affiliates)	
Type of Business: Business to Business		Date Business Established		At Time of Application	14
Bank of Business Account and Address: First Merit #3006482-1, 5812 Tuskan Lane, Phoenix, AZ 85001				If Loan is Approved	22
				Subsidiaries or Affiliates (Separate for above)	

Use of Proceeds (Enter Gross Dollar Amount Round to the Nearest Hundreds)	Loan Requested	Use of Proceeds (Enter Gross Dollar Amount Round to the Nearest Hundreds)	Loan Request
Land Acquisition	$150,000	Pay off SBA Loans	
New Construction/ Expansion Repair	$250,000	Pay off Bank Loans (Non SBA Associated)	
Acquisition and/or Repair Machinery and Equipment		Other Debit Payment (Non SBA Associated)	
Inventory Purchase		All Other	
Working Capital (including Accounts Payable)		Total Loan Requested	$400,000
Acquisition of Existing Business		Term of Loan (Requested Mat.)	10 Yrs.

PREVIOUS SBA OR OTHER FEDERAL GOVERNMENT DEBT: If you or any principles or affiliates have 1) ever requested Government Financing or 2) are delinquent on the repayment of any Federal Debt complete the following:

Name of Agency	Original Amount of Loan	Date of Request	Approved or Declined	Balance	Current or Past Due
SBA	$100,000	6/28/20--	Approved	$12,500	Current
	$			$	

Key Points: In order to be granted a loan by the SBA, you need to provide a personal financial history, inform them of the amount of the loan you are requesting, and describe how you intend to use the funds. The example represents just a small portion of the full Application for Business Loan.

Find the Solutions

1. How many employees will this company have if the loan is approved?
2. How will this company utilize the funds?
3. What is the total amount of the loan?
4. How much does this company owe the SBA for a previous loan?
5. What is the requested term of the loan?

▶ LOCATION, LOCATION Besides having a great idea for a business, you must also find somewhere to operate it. *What features would you look for when choosing a location for a local business?*

Caption Answer Answers might include traffic, other stores in the area, parking, visibility, pedestrian traffic, area income, and rent.

$avvy Saver

Business Credit Cards Tips

1. Choose a credit card with no annual fee and low interest rates.
2. Do not mix your business and personal purchases on your business credit card.
3. Use your year-end statements from your credit card company that track and categorize your business expenses for the year.
4. Take advantage of special rewards and discounts for office supplies and travel if available.
5. Avoid using cash advance options because interest rates are higher.

Personal and Private Financing

What is the difference between personal and private financing?

After you have determined the amount of money you require, you will need to figure out how you will get it. Getting affordable and sufficient financing is often a major problem when starting or expanding a business. However, there are many sources of funding available for businesses. Initially, you will probably explore the possibility of personal financing.

Personal Financing

Many people begin small businesses with funds from their own personal assets. In fact, personal assets make up a large part of the start-up funding for most new business ventures in the United States.

The primary reason for using this method is that new small businesses often have difficulty getting affordable funding. Banks and other financial institutions are not interested in risky or unproven business ventures. You cannot just walk into a bank and tell them that you have a great idea for a new business and expect the loan officer to hand you money.

Banks are more interested in funding existing businesses that have reported profit over a period of time. These businesses are safer investments and provide banks and other financial institutions with the assurance of a good return on their money.

When starting a small business, you may have to rely on your own assets to finance the start-up and operating costs. You might use your personal savings or investments such as stocks or bonds.

You might also use loans from family members and friends to help finance the business. However, with these sources of capital, you may not have enough cash to get the business going.

Discussion Ask the students if they have ever borrowed money from family or friends. Did they pay it back? Did it cause any problems?

Consumer Loans In order to get the funds you need, consider applying for a consumer, or personal, loan. Most financial institutions require that consumer loans be secured with collateral. Collateral is a form of security (usually an asset such as a car or home) that helps guarantee that a loan will be repaid.

When you pledge collateral for a loan, the risk to the bank is reduced. As a result, you have a much better chance of getting funding and can receive better interest rates. If you cannot pay back the loan, the financial institution can take the property that you have pledged as collateral.

Home Equity Loans A home equity loan is a loan based on the difference between the current market value of a home and the amount still owed on the mortgage. A home equity loan may also be called a second mortgage. Home equity loans are fairly safe for financial institutions because they are secured by property. As a result these loans are usually easier to get than consumer loans, and some entrepreneurs who own homes use this source.

To determine the maximum amount of this type of loan, the financial institution will find out the current market value of a home and its equity. Equity is the value of the home less the current balance on the home's mortgage loan.

Suppose a house has a present market value of $175,000, and the mortgage has a balance of $65,000. The equity in the house is $110,000 ($175,000 – $65,000 = $110,000).

Banks will usually allow an owner to borrow up to 80 percent of the current market value of the home. In this example, the maximum amount the bank would loan on a home worth $175,000 would be $140,000 ($175,000 × .80 or 80% = $140,000). However, there is an existing mortgage with a current balance of $65,000. Therefore, to figure out the amount that the bank would loan, subtract the mortgage balance from $140,000. In this example, the loan cannot exceed $75,000 ($140,000 – $65,000 = $75,000).

This type of loan is available only if there is a substantial amount of equity in the property. In other words, a home must be worth a lot more than the amount owed on the mortgage.

The negative aspect of a home equity loan is that if the business fails, the owner could lose his or her home. A recent study found that more than one-half of new businesses fail during the first five years. Considering this high failure rate, you should think seriously before you finance your business with a home equity loan.

Caption Answer If the business fails, the homeowner could lose his or her home.

▼ **HOME SWEET HOME** A home equity loan can be an easy source of financing for an entrepreneur. *What risk is involved in using a home equity loan to finance a business?*

GO FIGURE — FINANCIAL MATH

A HOME EQUITY LOAN

Synopsis: Home equity loans are based on the difference between the current market value of a home and the amount still owed on the mortgage.

Example: Drew wants to apply for a home equity loan at Wilton Bank to start his new Internet company. He presently owns a home that has a market value of $160,000. He has an existing mortgage balance of $90,000. What is the maximum amount the bank will lend to Drew for a home equity loan?

Formula:

Adjusted Market Value of Home − Existing Mortgage Balance = Home Equity Loan

Solution:

A. Find the adjusted market value of the home.

Market Value	× .80 or 80%	=	Adjusted Market Value of Home
$160,000	× .80 or 80%	=	$128,000

The adjusted market value of the home is $128,000.

B. Find the maximum amount of the home equity loan.

Adjusted Market Value of Home	−	Existing Mortgage Balance	=	Home Equity Loan
$128,000	−	$90,000	=	$38,000

Wilton Bank will lend Drew up to $38,000 for a home equity loan.

YOU FIGURE

If the adjusted market value of your home is $220,000 and the existing mortgage balance is $142,000, how much would you be allowed to borrow for a home equity loan?

Answer $220,000 – $142,000 = $78,000

Private Financing

If you cannot get enough capital through personal financing, you must look to other sources. The next option might be private financing. **Private financing** is borrowing money from family or friends. This type of funding is attractive because it involves little paperwork and often requires no collateral and low, or no, interest payments. The disadvantage is that it can lead to personal conflicts if the business is unsuccessful, and you are unable to repay a loan.

Critical Thinking Ask the students this question: "Why would a bank approve an unsecured loan?"

Bank Funding

What is the difference between a secured and an unsecured loan?

If personal and private financing are insufficient, you may have to apply for a business loan to get additional money. One of your first sources for such financing is your local bank.

Commercial debt financing is borrowing money from a bank or other financial institution to fund a business. Another option is a **commercial loan**, which is a loan that finances a new or ongoing business. Larger banks give out commercial loans, but they are often interested in larger, more established business operations with revenues of millions of dollars. Therefore, when small businesses need money, smaller, local banks are their logical source.

A small bank can better relate to small business needs, and it can offer advice and assist you with other services.

Getting funding from local banks has both advantages and disadvantages. Advantages might include:

- They are highly experienced in dealing with small businesses.
- They offer a wide variety of loan plans.
- They offer advice and other business services.
- They are community-oriented and are interested in seeing local businesses succeed.

STANDARD & POOR'S

Global Financial Landscape

Standard and Poor's publishes the globally recognized S&P 500® financial index. It also gathers financial statistics, information, and news, and analyzes this data for international businesses, governments, and individuals to help them guide their financial decisions.

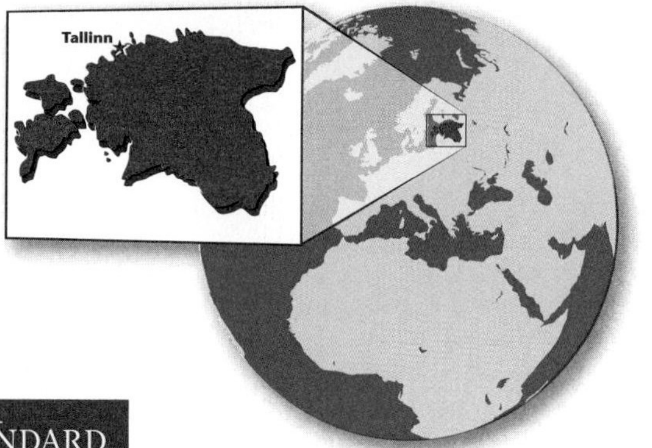

ESTONIA

After enduring Viking occupation in the 10th century and gaining independence from Russia in 1991, Estonia has come into its own. Only twice the size of the state of New Hampshire, this small country boasts one of the fastest-growing economies in Europe. An independent spirit sets the stage for success, as indicated by the fact that more than 90 percent of Estonia's businesses are privately owned.

One area of business that is experiencing rapid growth in Estonia is information technology. Government support has helped to encourage entrepreneurs to start businesses in this industry. In fact, the government has created a program called "Tiger Leap" that has connected every school in Estonia to the Internet. The government has also funded hundreds of public Internet access points to make sure its citizens are "plugged in."

STANDARD & POOR'S DATABYTES

Capital	Tallinn
Population	1,353,000
Languages	Estonian, Russian, and Ukrainian
Currency	Estonian kroon
Gross Domestic Product (GDP)	$17.3 billion (2003 est.)
GDP per capita	$12,300

Industry: Engineering, electronics, wood and wood products, and textiles

Agriculture: Potatoes, vegetables, livestock, dairy products, and fish

Exports: Machinery and equipment, wood and paper, textiles, food products, and furniture

Natural Resources: Oil, shale, peat, and phosphorites

Think Globally

How does government funding of telecommunication services benefit the entire country of Estonia?

See the Teacher Manual for answer.

▶ **BANK ON IT** A local bank may be the source of funding your business needs. *Why might a small local bank be better prepared to help a new business than a larger bank?*

Caption Answer Answers might include the idea that local banks are interested in seeing businesses succeed in their community and are prepared to offer guidance.

Disadvantages might include:

- They are closely regulated by the government. As a result, there is extensive paperwork, investigation, and documentation involved in the loan process.
- They are conservative by nature and may reject your loan if your business appears too risky.

If you and your local bank are interested in establishing a working relationship, you should know what loan options are available. All banks offer a wide variety of loans, and a good banker will recommend the loan that is best for you and your business.

Short-Term Commercial Loans

As You Read

QUESTION

What is the purpose of a short-term commercial loan?

Question Answer These loans are designed to help small businesses meet short-term financial obligations and to help with cash flow during certain times or seasons.

A short-term commercial loan is a business loan that is usually made for a term of one year or less. Most are written for 30-, 60-, or 90-day periods. These loans are typical for small businesses. They are designed to help the business meet short-term financial obligations and help with cash flow during a specific time or season. You could use the money for purchasing merchandise before a peak sales period, acquiring equipment, or paying unexpected bills.

For example, during the summer months, Durango's Ski Shop begins to prepare its inventory for the upcoming winter season. The owner, Sabrina, decides that she needs a large quantity of new skis. Because the ski shop's sales are typically low in the summer, she has to apply for temporary financing. With a short-term commercial loan, Sabrina can purchase the inventory she needs now and repay the loan with the profits from winter ski sales.

Long-Term Commercial Loans

A long-term commercial loan is a business loan that is made for a term of one to five years. These loans are normally used by larger, established businesses that require great amounts of funding. Because these are large loans, the businesses will need more time to pay them back. They may use the funds for expensive equipment, the relocation of facilities, the expansion of storage areas, or other major expenses.

New or smaller businesses might have trouble getting these loans. Banks consider such businesses to be less stable. Therefore, banks do not want to take the risk that the loan will not be repaid.

Lines of Credit

A **line of credit** is an arrangement in which bank customers can borrow a certain amount of money from the bank immediately. This makes funds available for unexpected costs or routine expenses. A store owner can borrow all or part of that money at any time and for any purpose. For example, if the plumbing breaks and costs $8,000 to repair, money is available.

The main advantage of this type of funding is that you do not pay any interest unless you access the funds. But once you borrow an amount from the line of credit, the bank will charge you interest.

The bank will review your available credit every so often. Based on your history of accessing the account and on your repayment pattern, the bank may increase or decrease the amount of credit. This type of funding is intended for short-term costs that your business may not be able to handle. For this reason, the bank also expects you to repay the money in a short period of time.

TechByte

Internet Finance Education In order to take advantage of the many loans available to entrepreneurs, you need some basic financial management skills. There are many books and resources available. You can also sign up for online courses and complete them in your spare time. Each online course is sent to you via e-mail on a daily or weekly basis and is designed to help you learn a specific skill or solve a particular problem. There are no grades or degrees, but many courses are free.

@ View a list of money- and business-related courses and list those you would like to take through **finance07.glencoe.com**.

Caption Answer a short-term commercial loan

◀ **FULL INVENTORY** A business that depends on seasonal sales will prepare its inventory in advance of the busy season. *What type of loan might such a business require?*

Secured and Unsecured Loans

A **secured loan** is a loan that is backed by collateral. Most short-term and long-term loans must be backed by collateral. Banks will hold the title to the equipment, facility, or merchandise used as collateral until the loan is repaid. Because banks must be conservative in their loan policies, most business loans are secured. Only a well-established, profitable business that has a good relationship with a bank can obtain unsecured loans. An **unsecured loan** is a loan that does not require collateral from the borrower. If an unsecured loan is approved, it is usually short-term. Because of the increased risk to the creditor, the interest rate on an unsecured loan is usually higher than on a secured loan.

Academic Connection
LANGUAGE ARTS

Successful entrepreneurs are risk takers, are goal oriented, and are independent. They also know how to secure financing to transform their ideas into products or services that will sell. *Imagine you are ready to open your business and you need to borrow $10,000 to get started. Write a letter requesting the funding from either your parents, a friend, or a bank. Be sure to describe the type of business you are going to open and why you think it will be successful.*

See the Teacher Manual for answer.

Commercial Loan Applications

What are the five C's of credit?

New and expanding small businesses often have difficulty getting necessary funding. Banks use certain standards to judge a company's financial position and determine how much risk to accept. Banks are conservative and selective as to which businesses they approve for financing.

You have already learned about the criteria banks and credit card companies use to determine your creditworthiness (see Chapter 6). When you fill out an application for credit, you must answer questions regarding your credit history, your annual income, and your valuable assets. These institutions want a complete financial picture of you.

When evaluating commercial loan applications, banks will examine these same factors as well as other information. They want a financial picture of both you and your business.

Caption Answer The bank looks for the five C's of credit—character, capacity, capital, collateral, and credit history—as well as a good business plan.

▶ **THE FIVE C'S** A loan officer will look carefully at the information you provide before deciding to grant you a commercial loan. *What criteria does a bank use to evaluate a loan request?*

The Five C's of Credit

If you apply for a commercial loan, the bank will first examine the five C's of credit: character, capacity, capital, collateral, and credit history. (See **Figure 19.1.**)

Character Banks want to make sure that you are capable of paying off the loan on time. They will consider your business experience and your dealings with other local businesses. Your prior history with the bank, your reputation in the local business community, and comments from your creditors will also be important. In addition, proof of your skills as a manager will be essential.

Capacity The bank will determine whether your business has or will have enough cash to repay the loan on time. It will also examine your sales history, statements of cash flow, and profits reported by your business.

Capital The bank will look to see whether you have invested a considerable amount of your personal assets in the business. Some financial institutions require that you use your personal assets for at least 30 percent of the capital needed to start your business.

Collateral The bank will make sure that you have enough business assets to secure the loan. Does your business own office equipment, machinery, delivery equipment, or real estate? Good collateral is also an important element for approval.

Credit History The bank will review both your personal credit history and your business credit history. It will also consider your payment history on any consumer and commercial loans you may have.

Common CENTS

Paid in Full
When you get your first credit card, use it wisely. Decide how much you can afford to charge each month and stick to that budget. Be sure to pay your bill in full every month. If you do, you will avoid high interest charges and save. *How would good use of personal credit cards help you in starting up a business in the future?*

Common Cents By building good credit, an entrepreneur would be able to secure a loan from a financial institution. Accept all reasonable answers.

Critical Thinking Ask the students if they think a bank would be interested in their personal character when deciding whether to approve their business loan.

Figure 19.1 Five C's of Credit

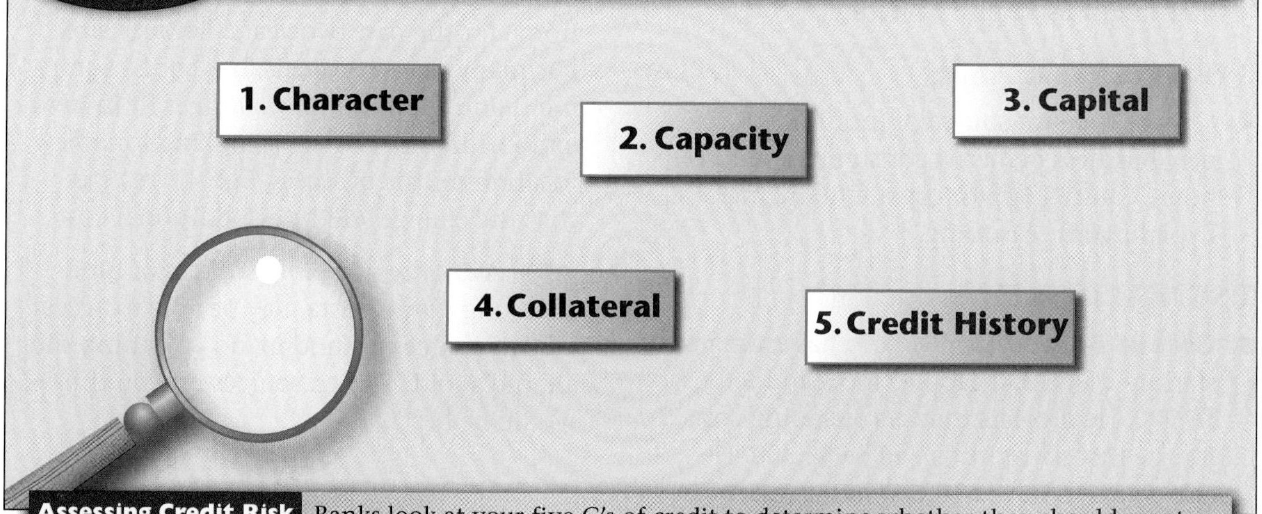

Assessing Credit Risk Banks look at your five C's of credit to determine whether they should grant you a loan.

How would you rate each one of your own five C's?

Caption Answer Accept all reasonable answers that show student effort and an understanding of the five C's of credit.

Business Plan

The bank will also examine your business plan to make sure that your business is financially sound. It looks to see whether you have a clear vision of where you want your business to go and whether you have identified the necessary steps to achieve your goals. Then the bank can better measure your financial needs.

Banks often base loan decisions on the business plan. It is vital that your plan be clear, accurate, and well planned. Include the three basic parts of a business plan that focus on a strategic plan, a marketing plan, and a financial plan. As you learned in Chapter 17, a business plan can include a variety of components, such as an executive summary, mission statement, company description, product and service plan, management team plan, industry overview, market analysis, competitive analysis, marketing plan, operational plan, organization plan, financial plan, growth plan, contingency plan, and supporting documents, as well as a cover page, title page, and table of contents. Spending extra time to make sure that your business plan has accurate information could mean the difference between getting the money you need or not.

Section 19.1 Assessment

See the Teacher Manual for answers.

QUICK CHECK

1. What is the difference between start-up costs and operating costs?

2. What are several sources of personal financing?

3. What are two ways in which a small business might use a line of credit?

THINK CRITICALLY

4. Choose the best source of funding for a new business owner: a consumer loan, a home equity loan, or private financing. Explain your reasoning.

USE MATH SKILLS

5. Cost of Borrowing Mario has estimated start-up costs for a cappuccino stand to be $8,900. He projects that his operating costs for the first six months will be $6,300. He also wants to have $10,000 in his reserve fund. Mario has saved $20,000 for his new business.

Calculate How much money will Mario need to borrow? What percentage of his total costs will he borrow?

SOLVE MONEY PROBLEMS

6. Sources of Funding Christa has operated a résumé writing service out of her home for the past two years. Because she has many new customers, her added equipment and supplies will no longer fit in her extra bedroom. Christa is looking for a new location for the business, but she realizes that the change will bring additional costs.

Analyze Identify sources of funding that Christa may be able to access. Which sources of funding do you think she should avoid? Which sources do you think would be best?

Section 19.2

Sources of Funding

Small Business Administration

What kinds of services does the Small Business Administration provide?

No matter how good your business may look on paper, banks might not provide necessary financing. This is especially true for new or start-up businesses. As a new or start-up business owner, you may not have a sound credit history or enough collateral, managerial experience, or profit from operations. Therefore, you will need some help to get your loan. To whom do you turn? Your best alternative may be the federal government.

The federal government recognizes the importance of small businesses in the American economy and, therefore, provides assistance to them. The **Small Business Administration (SBA)** is an independent agency of the federal government that offers assistance to people who are starting small businesses and to those who want to expand existing businesses. Its services include management training, organizational guidance, and assistance in getting funding.

Almost 99 percent of American business operations are considered "small businesses" under the SBA guidelines. Thousands of businesses take advantage of services offered by the SBA every year. If the SBA did not exist, many small businesses would never get the money they need.

The SBA offers many loan programs to small businesses that have a hard time getting the funding they need through other methods. If you cannot convince the bank that you are a good loan candidate and that your business will be successful, you might try one of the SBA loan programs.

SBA Guaranteed Loans

What is the benefit of receiving an SBA guaranteed loan?

The most common type of SBA loan is obtained through the Guaranteed Loan Program. To get an SBA guaranteed loan for your small business, you apply to a bank or other financial institution for a commercial loan. If the bank denies your request, you can then complete an application for an SBA loan. Your bank submits your application to the SBA under the Guaranteed Loan Program.

Focus on Reading

Read to Learn

- How to describe the function of the Small Business Administration.
- How to identify alternative sources of funding for a business.

Main Idea

Entrepreneurs can get funding through the help of the Small Business Administration and other sources.

Key Terms

- Small Business Administration (SBA)
- LowDoc Program
- business credit card
- private investor
- commercial finance company
- venture capital firm
- Small Business Investment Companies (SBICs)

Before You Read

PREDICT

What advantages might the federal government receive by operating the Small Business Administration (SBA)?

▶ FEDERAL ASSISTANCE The federal government provides help for entrepreneurs through the Small Business Administration (SBA). *How does the SBA's Guaranteed Loan Program work?*

Caption Answer If a bank denies a request for a business loan, the owner of the business can apply for an SBA loan. If the SBA approves the loan, the bank provides the funding, and the SBA guarantees a major portion of it.

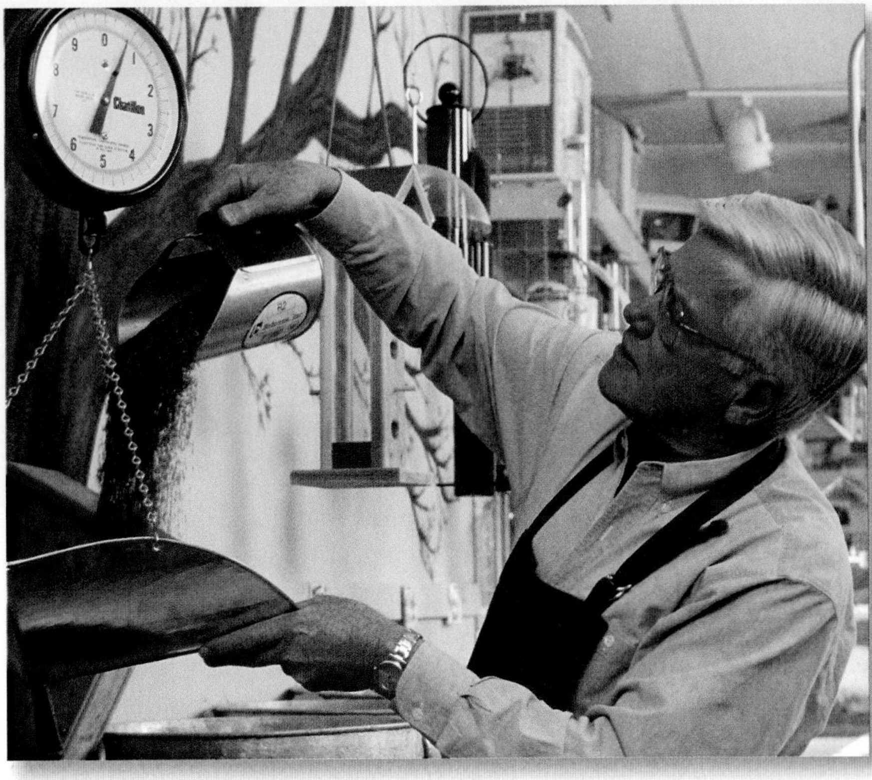

Springboard Ask the students to create a list of information the Small Business Administration might want to know before it would guarantee a loan to start a business. Have the students add to the list as they study this chapter.

The SBA examines your application. If it approves the loan, it authorizes the bank to give you the funding. The SBA then guarantees a major portion of the loan. At present the SBA will guarantee up to 85 percent of a bank loan for $150,000 or less and 75 percent of a loan for more than $150,000. The repayment period usually cannot exceed seven years.

With this guarantee by the federal government, banks are more willing to grant funding to a small business. The bank knows that if you default on the loan, the SBA will repay the majority of the money you owe. Remember, you do not borrow money from the SBA. You get your loan from a bank or some other financial institution, but the SBA guarantees a large portion of the loan.

In the past many people were frustrated by the amount of paperwork and the time it took to process loan applications through the SBA. In response, the SBA introduced the LowDoc (Low Documentation) Program in 1993. The **LowDoc Program** is a government loan program that allows businesses applying for loans of less than $150,000 to submit a one-page application with a small amount of documentation. They receive a reply within 36 hours. This program also features electronic loan processing. Loan maturity is usually 5 to 10 years or up to 25 years.

Motivating Students Explain that the SBA loan programs are designed for enterprising people who may not have the funds to start a successful business. Then ask students if they think it is possible for them to start a business if they had the money that an SBA loan might provide.

The SBA also offers a variety of other loans for specific groups or business endeavors. It has special guaranteed loan programs for international trade, pollution control, exporters, and businesses entering markets in economically depressed areas. Today the SBA is still the primary source of assistance in getting small business funding. Every year banks and other financial institutions lend billions of dollars to small business operations with SBA guarantees.

Other Sources of Funding

Why might a new business need to obtain funding from other sources?

Some business owners use personal resources or funds from family members or friends to expand their businesses. Many others use short-term commercial loans, which are often guaranteed by the SBA. However, you can also get funding through a business credit card, private investors, commercial finance companies, venture capital firms, and state and local governments.

As You Read

RELATE

Would you consider applying to the SBA for assistance if you were starting a business? Why, or why not?

Business Credit Card

In recent years financial institutions have developed alternative funding options to try to meet the needs of a wide variety of businesses. One of these options is to offer a line of credit through a business credit card. A **business credit card** is a credit card that is issued to a business rather than to an individual. The use of business credit cards has become a major source of short-term financing for small businesses. Commercial loans from financial institutions are another common source of funding.

Critical Thinking Ask the students what problems business owners might face if they use a business credit card for more than just emergencies.

Business credit cards require the business to have a good credit history. They are suitable for businesses that want to expand or cover unexpected costs, but they are generally not issued for start-up financing. A credit limit on a business credit card is usually under $15,000. The disadvantage of this quick source of funding is high interest rates, similar to those on personal credit cards. Business credit cards are good for emergencies, but balances should be paid as quickly as possible.

Visa, MasterCard, and American Express all offer small business credit cards. These cards provide discounts on travel, car rentals, and insurance. Credit card issuers also provide advice and assistance through small business publications.

Private Investors

A **private investor** is a person outside an entrepreneur's circle of friends and relatives who provides funding because he or she is interested in helping a new business to succeed. Typically called "angels," private investors will usually leave the management of the business to the owner. However, they are also interested in getting a good return on their money. This means that you may have to give them a share of ownership.

Research Have the students research the SBA to find out what services are provided, as well as when and why the SBA was started.

If you cannot locate private investors in your area, you can turn to the SBA. The SBA has set up the Angel Capital Electronic Network (ACE-Net), which is a Web site that lists small businesses that are looking for investors. The SBA screens both entrepreneurs and investors to assure reliability. Approved investors can access information on thousands of businesses. An investor chooses a business, and then the business owner and the investor can negotiate a deal.

Extension Tell your students that angels are not easy to locate. Have them research ways to find angels in your community.

As You Read
QUESTION

What are the disadvantages of borrowing money from a commerical finance company?

Question Answer Loans must be secured with collateral; the government does not regulate these companies closely; and loans have higher interest rates.

Extension Invite someone from a bank or the SBA to your class to share information with your students about the SBA programs that are available.

Commercial Finance Companies

A **commercial finance company** is a firm that lends money only to businesses. Commercial finance companies insist that all loans be secured with collateral, such as equipment or inventory. These companies are helpful to existing businesses that need short-term financing.

The government does not regulate commercial finance companies as closely as it does banks, so these companies accept more risk in granting loans. However, if a finance company grants you a riskier loan, it will charge you a higher interest rate. It is easier to get this kind of loan, but you will pay more for it.

Venture Capital Firms

A **venture capital firm** is a company that provides private funding for small businesses that need a substantial amount of immediate cash. Because these small businesses are high-risk in terms of ability to repay loans, they cannot always get adequate funding from lenders such as banks and commercial finance companies. Venture capital firms take the risk, but in turn, they often expect a large return of 25 to 40 percent on their investment.

Venture capital firms usually seek to make investments of at least $500,000. Keep in mind that the venture capital firm is not merely lending money; it is also investing in your business. Therefore, venture capital firms expect to have a voice in major business decisions and will examine a business's financial position carefully throughout the year.

Most venture capital firms are private, but the SBA created a public venture capital program—the Small Business Investment Company Program. **Small Business Investment Companies (SBICs)** are private investment firms that work with the SBA to provide longer-term funding for small businesses. The advantage in dealing with the SBIC program is that the SBA regulates lenders, and financing terms must meet SBA guidelines. If small businesses need venture capital, they usually go to SBIC firms first.

STANDARD & POOR'S

Put on Your Financial Planner's Cap

Imagine you have successfully started your new business, and you have completed six months of operations with a respectable profit. Consequently, you have decided to expand your business, but you will need an additional $125,000 in capital. Would you choose to seek this funding through a commercial finance company, a venture capital firm, or an SBIC?

See the Teacher Manual for answer.

State and Local Funding

Why do state and local governments provide funding opportunities for small businesses?

Many states provide opportunities for small businesses to get funding through a variety of programs. These funding programs are available in cities where local and state governments are encouraging individuals to open businesses in economically depressed neighborhoods. Local chambers of commerce or regional offices of the SBA can assist you.

Funding Your Dreams

Why are small businesses essential to the American economy?

The American economy has been built by entrepreneurs who were willing to take risks and explore new ventures. Ray Kroc was 52 years old when he purchased the rights to a hamburger stand owned by the McDonald brothers in San Bernardino, California. His venture would revolutionize the food industry. Robert Pittman was only 26 years old when he combined video and music and created MTV.

The funding of small businesses is essential to the American economy. Almost all of the nation's Fortune 500 companies started as small businesses. They began with little capital and obtained additional funds by using creativity. Today you can get funds through a variety of sources. Through private and public funding, you can pursue your dreams and own your own business.

After You Read

REACT

Based on what you have learned in this chapter, how would you raise start-up capital for a new business?

React Answer Accept all reasonable answers that show an understanding of the sources of funding listed in the section.

Teaching Activity Divide your students into groups and ask each group to create a chart of the other sources of funding and the advantages and disadvantages of each.

Section 19.2 Assessment

See the Teacher Manual for answers.

QUICK CHECK

1. What is the primary function of the Small Business Administration?
2. What are some alternative sources of funding for business owners?
3. How might you find venture capital for your business?

THINK CRITICALLY

4. For what types of expenses do you think a business should use a business credit card? For what expenses should a business not use a credit card? Explain.

USE COMMUNICATION SKILLS

5. **Loan Questions** Your friend Ashley is having trouble getting a loan to finance the start-up costs of her collectibles shop. Her local bank turned her down because her business idea seemed too risky.

Write About It Write a paragraph telling Ashley about alternative means of getting approval for a commercial loan. Also explain how the federal government might be able to help her.

SOLVE MONEY PROBLEMS

6. **Financing Options** Kimo owns a print shop. He offers a variety of services, including printing brochures and letterheads. He wants to expand his business by offering multimedia services. To do this, he needs \$50,000 to \$60,000. Kimo has decided to investigate a bank loan guaranteed by the SBA, private investors, and venture capital firms as sources of money for his expansion.

Write About It In a small group, analyze Kimo's prospects of receiving funding from a bank, a private investor, and a venture capital firm. Write a one-page report to help Kimo decide which funding source to explore further.

Chapter 19 Review & Activities

See the Teacher Manual for answers.

CHAPTER SUMMARY

- An entrepreneur is a person who takes the risk of starting a new business.
- Start-up costs include money for the purchase of assets needed to run a business, including inventory, equipment, furnishing, supplies, and utilities; costs such as legal, professional, and banking fees; licenses; permits; insurance; marketing costs; and remodeling and maintenance costs. Operating capital is the money needed to operate a business for the first few years. Reserve capital is money set aside for unexpected costs or opportunities.
- Sources of personal financing include personal assets, consumer loans, and home equity loans. Sources of private financing include family and friends.
- Some of the options available through bank funding are short- and long-term commercial loans, lines of credit, and secured and unsecured loans.
- The factors banks consider to approve commercial loans include the five C's: character, capacity, capital, collateral, and credit history.
- The Small Business Administration (SBA) is a major source of funding for new small businesses. This agency can also help with management training and organizational guidance.
- Other sources of funding for a business include business credit cards, private investors (angels), commercial finance companies, venture capital companies, and state and local agencies.

Communicating Key Terms

You are an entrepreneur talking with a bank loan officer about a Small Business Administration loan. Use as many of the terms below as you can to explain why the bank should give you a loan.

- entrepreneur
- operating costs
- reserve fund
- private financing
- commercial debt financing
- commercial loan
- line of credit
- secured loan
- unsecured loan
- Small Business Administration (SBA)
- LowDoc Program
- business credit card
- private investor
- commercial finance company
- venture capital firm
- Small Business Investment Companies (SBICs)

Reviewing Key Concepts

1. **Explain** why entrepreneurs are considered part of the backbone of the American economy.
2. **Identify** some differences between start-up costs, operating costs, and reserve funds.
3. **Explain** the pros and cons of taking out a home equity loan to start a business.
4. **List** one advantage and one disadvantage of secured loans, unsecured loans, and lines of credit.
5. **Describe** the five C's of credit and how they apply to a business loan.
6. **List** one reason that loans guaranteed by the Small Business Administration are a win-win situation for the entrepreneur and the lending institution.
7. **Explain** the role of a venture capital firm.

See the Teacher Manual for answers.

ACADEMIC SKILLS

Economics Assume you are a trained bookkeeper and you want to start a home-based business handling bookkeeping and tax preparation for small companies.

Write About It List the start-up and operating costs you think you will need to cover your new business.

YOUR FINANCIAL FIGURES

Start-Up Costs The following is a list of some of the start-up costs for a new, home-based word-processing business.

Computer	$1,200
Printer	$700
Office supplies	$100
Office furniture	$500

1. **Calculate** the start-up costs for this business. What percentage of the total start-up costs listed here is the computer?
2. **Compute** by using spreadsheet software to make these calculations.

REAL-WORLD Application

Connect with Economics Imagine that you are starting your own business after working in graphic design for an advertising agency for a number of years. You must take out a home equity loan to cover the $20,000 of your start-up and initial operating costs.

1. **Research** Use an Internet search engine to find interest rates for home equity loans in your area.
2. **Think Critically** Under what circumstances is a home equity loan the best choice for funding a new business?

Internet CONNECTION

Small Business Administration The Small Business Administration (SBA) is a government agency that offers assistance to small start-up businesses.

Log On Use an Internet search engine to find businesses in your area that are associated with the SBA. Answer the following questions:

1. Why do businesses become associated with the SBA?
2. What is the advantage of securing a loan from a financial source that is associated with the SBA?

BusinessWeek ONLINE

Newsclip: Finding Capital To be your own boss, you need to find capital for starting up your business. There are more options available to entrepreneurs today than in the past.

Log On Go to **finance07.glencoe.com** and open Chapter 19. Learn about different options to help you find the funding needed to start a new business. Write a paragraph about which option you would choose and why.

WHAT'S YOUR FINANCIAL ID?

ARE YOU A GO-GETTER?

Finding the money to start a business and keep it going can seem like a huge obstacle. Just for fun, take the following quiz to see if you are a go-getter who can find funding. Write your answers on a separate sheet of paper.

1. I am willing to defer getting paid in or der to see my vision succeed.

_______ Yes _______ No

2. I am willing to ask everyone I know if they want to invest in my enterprise.

_______ Yes _______ No

3. I am investigating every possibility I can think of for financing.

_______ Yes _______ No

4. I have spoken to at least one person who is a successful entrepreneur.

_______ Yes _______ No

5. I have the perseverance to reach my goals.

_______ Yes _______ No

6. My ideas are so clear that I can convince others to help me make them a reality.

_______ Yes _______ No

7. I am flexible and can readily adapt to change.

_______ Yes _______ No

Scoring:

The more "yes" answers you have, the more likely it will be that you will find funding.

Accept all reasonable answers that show student effort and an understanding of the concept.

Your Financial Portfolio

Tanya's Toys

Tanya's mother brings home rejects and remnants of towel fabric from the mill where she works. Tanya's grandmother taught Tanya how to sew the cloth into animal shapes and stuff them. Tanya and her family give these little stuffed animals as presents. She has also sold 25 of them at $8 each to raise money for the high school football team. Tanya and her friend, Lisa, have decided to start a business making and selling "Tanya's Toys." Tanya has listed the expenses of making 100 stuffed animals and the sources of funding.

Item	Cost	Source of Funding
Toweling	$25	She spoke directly to the manager at the mill, who offered a special deal of $25 payable after the animals were sold.
Sewing machines	$430	Tanya was already using the sewing machine she had at home and located another used industrial machine. She and Lisa decided they would buy the second machine after they sold 500 toys.
Other sewing equipment: Sewing shears, tape measure, patterns	$45	Tanya's grandmother offered to loan them the money to buy good sewing shears.
Supplies: Thread, eyes, buttons, ribbon, and felt to decorate the animals	$25	Tanya and Lisa decided to fund the purchase of supplies from their savings.
Wages	0	Tanya and Lisa will not pay themselves wages until they have all the equipment and supplies.

Research

What kind of business could you launch that would require minimal start-up costs? On a separate sheet of paper, use the guidelines shown above to describe and name your business and list what equipment and supplies you would need. Also indicate how you would fund your enterprise. How much would your equipment and supplies cost? How could you persuade family or friends to participate in your business?

Accept all reasonable answers that show student effort and an understanding of start-up costs and sources of funding.

CHAPTER 20 Financial Accounting

$ What You'll Learn

When you have completed this chapter, you will be able to:

Section 20.1

- Describe the accounting system.
- Identify the first five steps of the accounting cycle.
- Discuss the role of the general journal.
- Explain the purpose of posting.
- Summarize the purpose of a trial balance.

Section 20.2

- Identify items included on an income statement.
- Explain the purpose of a balance sheet.
- Define and explain the role of a statement of cash flows.

Reading Strategies

To get the most out of your reading:

Predict what you will learn in this chapter.
Relate what you read to your own life.
Question what you are reading to be sure you understand.
React to what you have read.

In the **Real** World . . .

Jessica Scott runs a small bakery. She also caters events. She has made cupcakes for graduation parties, pastries for picnics, and cakes for weddings. Her accountant tells her that she should do more catering because it is more profitable and dependable than her daily business.

Accounting records would help Jessica identify the goods and services to increase, such as take-and-bake items, biscuits for pets, and catering—as well as items to discontinue, such as low-carb donuts. Jessica has learned to trust her accountant's advice. Though she may have to stop making some of her favorite items, Jessica wants to remain profitable.

As You Read *Consider the types of accounting records a small store owner would need to understand and use.*

Lesson Plan See the Teacher Manual for Chapter 20 planning guide and lesson plan.

ASK STANDARD & POOR'S

The Accounting Cycle

Q: When I start my business, I am going to hire an accountant to keep my records. So why do I need to understand the accounting cycle?

A: A professional can help you maintain financial records. However, you still need to understand what information is represented in your financial statements and its relevance to the decisions you will need to make. Also, to communicate with your accountant, you will need to understand what he or she is talking about.

Ask Yourself Can you think of any other reasons why it is important that you understand the accounting cycle?

@ Go to **finance07.glencoe.com** to complete the Standard & Poor's Financial Focus activity.

Section 20.1

Focus on Reading

Read to Learn
- How to describe the accounting system.
- How to identify the first five steps of the accounting cycle.
- How to discuss the role of the general journal.
- How to explain the purpose of posting.
- How to summarize the purpose of a trial balance.

Main Idea
All businesses should record and summarize their financial transactions in the same way, using the accounting cycle.

Key Terms
- financial reports
- accounting period
- accounting cycle
- accounting equation
- account
- accounts receivable
- accounts payable
- double-entry accounting
- T accounts
- debit
- credit (accounting)
- journal
- general ledger
- posting
- trial balance

Springboard Ask your students to define the word *language*. Then have them list all the languages spoken in their community. Tell them they will be learning some words in the language of business—accounting.

The Accounting Cycle: The First Five Steps

The Language of Business
How is accounting used in business?

Have you ever wondered how a rap group or a rock band determines what cities to play on tour? What determines the price of tickets, and how much does a national tour cost? These questions are all answered by accountants and financial advisers.

Accounting plays a vital role in the day-to-day activities of your business—and of every business. Accounting records and reports help a business operate efficiently—and profitably—by keeping track of how much is earned and how much is spent. Accounting is so much a part of the business world that it is often called "the language of business."

The Accounting System
What is the purpose of using the accounting system?

Whether you are keeping financial records for a rock band, a neighborhood bike shop, or a major corporation, accounting principles and procedures are universal. All businesses use the same system, which follows established accounting guidelines called "generally accepted accounting principles," or GAAP. With all businesses using the same system, anyone who is interested in examining the records of a business will be able to understand its financial reports.

The accounting system is designed to collect, record, and report on financial transactions that affect a business. **Financial reports** are written records that summarize the results of financial transactions affecting a business and report its current financial position. They indicate how well your business is doing. There are many groups and individuals interested in your business's finances:

- Potential buyers
- Government agencies
- Banks or other financial institutions
- Employees and consumers

Accounting Assumptions

When you are creating the accounting books for your business, you make two assumptions about the business. The first assumption is that the business will operate as a separate unit, or business entity. This means that the records and reports of your business will be kept completely separate from your personal finances. You never mix your business finances with your personal finances.

The second assumption is that your business will make its financial reports in specific blocks of time. An **accounting period** is a block of time covered by an accounting report. The accounting period can be one month or one quarter (three months), but the most common period is one year.

During this accounting period, you record all financial transactions for your business and report the results. You engage in activities that maintain your accounting records in an orderly manner. The **accounting cycle** is the activities, or steps, that help a business keep its accounting records in an orderly manner.

In this chapter you will learn about the first five steps of the accounting cycle. In each accounting period—whether a month, a quarter, or a year—the entire accounting cycle is completed. You probably have heard news broadcasts such as: "Ford sales are up 4 percent over last quarter and up 6 percent from the same quarter last year." By using a set period of time, such as a quarter, you can compare financial reports from one period to those from another period.

Before You Read

PREDICT

What is the value of keeping day-to-day track of your financial status?

Motivating Students Ask students if they have ever seen any accounting forms used by a business? Then ask if they have ever used forms to figure out their own personal finances?

Teaching Activity Have students who have taken an accounting class form a team. Have them prepare a mini-lesson for the class emphasizing the accounting system and cycle.

The Accounting Equation

Property is anything of value that you own or control. Both people and businesses have property. You might own a CD player, a computer, clothes, a television set, or maybe a car. For a business, property could include cash, office equipment, supplies, merchandise, or vehicles. When you own an item of property, you have a legal right or financial claim to that item. In contrast, when you have control over an item, you have only the right to use it. A rented office is property, but a business does not have a financial claim to it. In accounting, property or items of value owned by your business are called *assets*.

Your equity in a piece of property is your share of its value, or your financial claim to the property. This also applies to businesses. For example, suppose that your business owns a truck valued at $16,000. You are the owner of the business, so your equity in the truck is $16,000. If the truck is completely paid for, you have financial claim to the truck. An owner's claim to the assets of a business is called *owner's equity*.

However, what if you still owe $3,000 to the Stratford Savings Bank for the truck? The truck is valued at $16,000, but the creditor (the bank) has $3,000 equity, while your equity is now only $13,000. Both you and the creditor have financial claims to (equity in) the asset.

Property	−	Creditor's Financial Claim	=	Owner's Financial Claim
$16,000	−	$3,000	=	$13,000

$avvy Saver

Accounting for Your Money

1. Put all receipts in labeled folders and file them in alphabetical order.
2. Keep a budget and review it weekly.
3. Balance your checkbook monthly.
4. Be aware of—and meet—all tax-filing deadlines.
5. Use a financial software program to track your finances.

▲ **RENTED PROPERTY** Many businesses rent space where they run their operations. *Is rented space a business asset?*

Caption Answer No, assets are property that is owned by a business. A business does not have a financial claim to property that it rents.

Creditors' claims to the assets of a business are called *liabilities*, or the debts of a business. The relationship between assets and the two types of equity (liabilities and owner's equity) is shown in the accounting equation:

Property	−	Creditor's Financial Claim	=	Owner's Financial Claim
Assets	−	Liabilities	=	Owner's Equity

Critical Thinking Ask your students: "Who really owns this truck?"

The **accounting equation** (Assets − Liabilities = Owner's Equity) is the basis for keeping all accounting records in balance. The entire system of accounting is based on this equation. As your business buys, sells, or exchanges goods and services involving many business transactions, the numbers may change. However, total assets will always equal total liabilities plus owner's equity. As you learn more, you will understand why this equation is so important.

Establishing Accounts

What are accounts?

When you set up the books of a business, you create accounts for each of the three categories in the accounting equation:

- Assets
- Liabilities
- Owner's equity

Teaching Activity Divide the class into teams. Have each team develop a song, game, or other memory method that students can use to help them remember the accounting equation and the two accounting rules.

An **account** shows the balance for a specific item, such as cash or equipment. You must look at your business and determine what accounts your business needs. Businesses create only the accounts they need for their type of business operation. The accounts used by one business may differ from the accounts used by another.

For example, Chris Archer uses the following accounts for his business, Archer Delivery Service:

Assets	Liabilities	Owner's Equity
Cash in Bank	Accounts Payable	Chris Archer, Capital
Accounts Receivable		
Office Equipment		
Delivery Equipment		

Asset Accounts

Chris has established four asset accounts. The first account shows all of the cash that enters or leaves the business. It is *Cash in Bank* because all cash received by his business is deposited in a bank account, and all cash paid out is paid by check. In accounting, both cash and checks are considered cash transactions.

The second asset account for the business is *Accounts Receivable*. **Accounts receivable** is the total amount of money owed to a business by customers. Chris completed deliveries for other companies, and they owe his business money. This account represents a future value that will eventually bring cash into the business.

Chris will use the two remaining asset accounts, *Office Equipment* and *Delivery Equipment*, when he buys equipment. If he needs other accounts for other assets, he can create them.

WebQuest

Franchise Ownership
Everyone loves ice cream. That is why there are at least 20 different franchise opportunities involving the sale of ice cream cones, dishes, and cakes. Learn more about these opportunities.

To continue with Task 3 of your WebQuest project, visit **finance07.glencoe.com**.

Careers in Finance

ACCOUNTING TEACHER

Rich Jackson
Portland Unified School District

Rich enjoys explaining, giving instruction, and providing inspiration for others. After working behind a desk as an accountant for ten years, Rich needed a change of pace. He decided to work as a teacher. Rich finds it rewarding to help his students master a skill that will be helpful to them professionally and personally. He creates lesson plans to help students learn concepts, practice transactions, and test their understanding. Teachers enjoy working with students, other teachers, parents, and administrators to foster success for students in class and life.

SKILLS:	Accounting, communication, computer, math, organizational, and time management
PERSONAL TRAITS:	Works well with people and numbers, patience, and sense of humor
EDUCATION:	Bachelor's degree in education or business education and/or a master's degree in accounting, finance, or business; experience in field

ANALYZE What skills might an accounting teacher need that an accountant may not need?
See the Teacher Manual for answer.

To learn more about career paths for accounting teachers, visit **finance07.glencoe.com**.

Common CENTS

Costly Corrections
When recording transactions manually, never erase errors. The erasure may look like an illegal cover-up. Instead, cross out the error and write the correction above it. *Accounting errors can cost businesses money. In what other ways might a business suffer as a result of accounting errors?*

Common Cents Accounting errors can result in tax problems and legal problems.

Liabilities Account

Chris listed only one liability account—*Accounts Payable.* **Accounts payable** is the amount of money owed, or payable, to the creditors of a business. The balance owed will remain in Accounts Payable until the business pays the debt.

Owner's Equity Account

The owner's equity account is identified by the owner's name, Chris Archer, followed by the word *Capital.* This account will report the owner's share of assets. Most businesses have more accounts than those presented here for Archer Delivery Service. Businesses often have many accounts, such as revenue or sales, utilities and other expenses, merchandise, payroll, and many more.

T Accounts

When accountants analyze and record business transactions, they use **double-entry accounting**, which is a system of record-keeping in which each business transaction affects at least two accounts. Remember, Archer Delivery Service has six accounts that can be used.

An efficient way to understand double-entry accounting is to use T accounts. A **T account** is a tool to increase or decrease each account that is affected by a transaction.

Account Name	
Left Side Debit	Right Side Credit

Account Name	
Left Side Debit	Right Side Credit

As you can see by this illustration, a T account has the account name at the top and has a left side and right side. An amount entered on the left side of a T account is called a **debit**. An amount entered on the right side of a T account is called a **credit**.

Rules of Debit and Credit

Debits and credits are used to record the increases or decreases in accounts affected by a business transaction. Under double-entry accounting, for each debit in one account (or accounts), there must be a credit of an equal amount in another account (or accounts).

The rules of debit and credit vary, depending on whether the account is an asset, a liability, or an owner's equity account. Regardless of the type of account, the left side is always the debit side and the right side is always the credit side. The general rules are:

- An asset account increases on the debit side and decreases on the credit side.
- Liability accounts and owner's equity accounts increase on the credit side and decrease on the debit side.

Using the Five Steps

How do businesses use the first five steps of the accounting cycle?

The accounting cycle consists of ten steps. This section describes how businesses apply and benefit from the first five activities, or steps, of the accounting cycle:

1. Collect and verify source documents.
2. Analyze each transaction.
3. Journalize each transaction.
4. Post to the general ledger.
5. Prepare a trial balance.

STANDARD & POOR'S

Put on Your Financial Planner's Cap

You are considering entering a business partnership with an accountant. What might be the advantages and disadvantages of such an arrangement?

See the Teacher Manual for answer.

Step 1: Collect and Verify Source Documents

When a business transaction occurs, a paper called a source document is prepared. A source document is evidence that a business transaction happened. Common source documents include check stubs, invoices, receipts, and memorandums. Collect and check all source documents before recording anything in your business's books.

Step 2: Analyze Each Transaction

Applying the rules of debit and credit to analyze transactions using T accounts is simple. Remember that every transaction must have a debit (or debits) and a credit (or credits) of an equal amount of money. Use these steps to analyze Transaction #1:

1. Identify the two accounts affected.
2. Classify each of the accounts.
3. Decide whether each account is increasing or decreasing.
4. Determine which account is debited and which is credited.

Transaction #1 On May 5, Archer Delivery Service purchased a photocopier for $900. Check 104 was written for the full amount.

Analysis:

1. The accounts affected are Office Equipment and Cash in Bank.
2. Both are asset accounts.
3. The business is buying office equipment. The balance in the Office Equipment account is increasing. Cash in Bank is decreasing.
4. According to the debit-credit rules, increases in asset accounts are recorded as debits. Office Equipment is debited $900. Decreases in asset accounts are recorded as credits. Cash in Bank is credited $900.

Office Equipment

Debit	Credit
+900	−

Cash in Bank

Debit	Credit
+	−900

As You Read

RELATE

Do you have a checkbook register? Do you have to stay within a budget? How do you think these activities are similar to and/or different from keeping books for a business?

Here is another example:

Transaction #2 On May 7, Archer Delivery Service bought a truck for $11,000 from Gail's Auto Land. The entire cost was financed by Wilton Bank.

Analysis:

1. The accounts affected are Delivery Equipment and Accounts Payable.
2. Delivery Equipment is an asset account. Accounts Payable is a liability account. In this transaction, the business is buying a truck.
3. The balance in the account Delivery Equipment is increasing. The balance in Accounts Payable is increasing.
4. The Delivery Equipment account is debited $11,000. Accounts Payable is credited $11,000.

Delivery Equipment		Accounts Payable	
Debit	Credit	Debit	Credit
+11,000	–	–	+11,000

Notice that both Transactions #1 and #2 have a debit to one account and a credit to another account. Every business transaction will have balancing debit and credit entries. This is how the system of double-entry accounting works.

▲ **EQUIPPED FOR BUSINESS** Expensive equipment, such as a truck for a business, is usually financed rather than paid for in full. *What types of accounts in the accounting equation are affected by financing equipment?*

Caption Answer asset and liability accounts

Document Detective

Learn to identify and understand the standard financial documents you will use in the real world.

See the Teacher Manual for answers.

Investigate: An Income Statement
An income statement contains the following information:

- Income generated
- Expenses incurred
- Profit or loss

Your Motive: If you own or work in a business, you will want to know if the business is profitable or not. If you are not bringing in enough income to offset your expenses, you will not make a profit.

General Products —Income Statement		
Year ending December 31, 2007		
Revenue		
Sales		$450,000
Costs of goods sold		250,000
Gross profit		$200,000
Operating Expenses		
Salaries	$70,000	
Advertising	12,000	
Rent	14,000	
Utilities	3,600	
Maintenance	1,200	
Insurance	1,500	
Misc.	1,000	
Total Expenses		$103,300
Net Profit		$96,700
Taxes	$48,350	
Net Profit		**$48,350**

Key Points: An income statement shows how much a company earns after it pays all its expenses, such as salaries, advertising, rent, utilities, maintenance, insurance, and other operating expenses.

Find the Solutions

1. How is gross profit calculated?
2. What time period is covered in the statement?
3. What percent of net profit does this company pay in taxes?
4. How much did it cost this company to produce the goods it sold?
5. What could this company do to increase its profits?

Discussion Ask the students to discuss how the journals or diaries they keep are similar to the journals used in accounting.

Step 3: Journalize Each Transaction

Do you keep a diary or journal? Many people do. They write down the day-to-day events that they want to remember. Businesses do the same thing. The financial events of your business are your business transactions, which you record in a journal. You use T accounts to analyze the transactions, but to record the transactions, you use a journal. A **journal** is a record of all of the transactions of a business. Business transactions are recorded in the order in which they occur. The process of recording business transactions in a journal is called *journalizing*.

A business journal uses accounting stationery. The stationery has lined columns for recording dollar amounts. You do not use commas, decimal points, or dollar signs. For example, the amount $1,846.20 is entered as shown in **Figure 20.1.**

Critical Thinking Ask the students this question: "Why is it important to enter a brief description of the transaction in the general journal?"

One of the most common accounting journals is the general journal. A general journal is an all-purpose journal in which all the transactions of a business may be recorded. When a business transaction occurs, a source document—such as a receipt or invoice—is created. Then you analyze the transaction, using T accounts, and enter it in the general journal. You record the date of the transaction, the accounts affected, and the amount of the debit and credit entries. **Figure 20.2** shows how Transactions #1 and #2 on pages 641 and 642 are entered in a general journal.

Step 4: Post to the General Ledger

By looking at a general journal, you cannot easily see what the balance is in each of your accounts. You may want to know how much cash you have, how much your business owes in accounts payable, how much office equipment you have, and most important, whether your business is making a profit.

Figure 20.1 Entry on Accounting Stationery

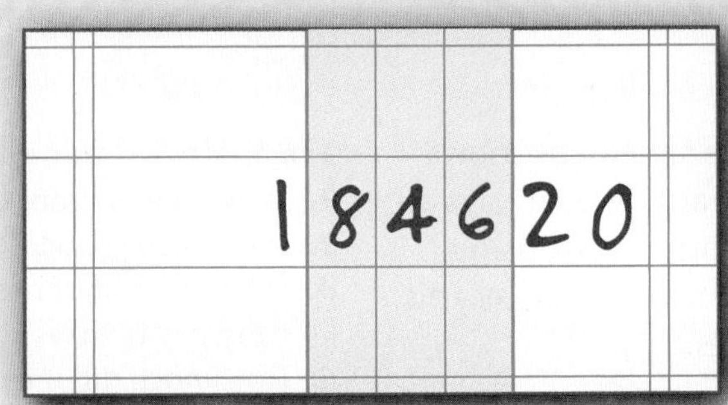

Easy Entries Accountants use a type of stationery designed for accounting procedures. **What is different about recording numbers on this stationery?**

Caption Answer You use no commas, periods, or dollar signs.

Figure 20.2 Transactions in a General Journal

GENERAL JOURNAL — PAGE 4

	DATE		DESCRIPTION	DEBIT	CREDIT	
1	May	5	*Office Equipment*	*900 00*		1
2			*Cash in Bank*		*900 00*	2
3			*Check 104*			3
4		7	*Delivery Equipment*	*11 000 00*		4
5			*Accounts Payable/Wilton Bank*		*11 000 00*	5
6			*Promissory Note*			6
7						7

Seeing the Big Picture The general journal allows businesses to record all business transactions.

What do you record in a general journal?

Caption Answer date, transaction, accounts affected, and amounts of debit and credit entries

In order to find the balance of each account, you must transfer the amounts that are in the general journal to a general ledger. A **general ledger** is a book or set of electronic files that contains the accounts used for a business. Each account has its own page. In a manual accounting system, the accounts used by a business are kept on separate pages or cards. These pages or cards are kept together in a book or file, which is the ledger. In a computerized accounting system, the electronic files of the accounts comprise the ledger. Keeping accounts together in a general ledger makes information easy to find. When you need financial statements, you can take the information from the ledger and present it as well-organized reports. **Figure 20.3** shows a blank ledger page.

Figure 20.3 The General Ledger

ACCOUNT ______ ACCOUNT NO. ______

DATE		DESCRIPTION	DEBIT	CREDIT	BALANCE	
					DEBIT	CREDIT

Keeping Track A general ledger allows a business to easily see the balance of each account.

What type of well-organized reports can you create from information in the general ledger?

Caption Answer financial statements

Figure 20.4 Posting to the General Ledger

GENERAL JOURNAL PAGE 4

	DATE		DESCRIPTION	DEBIT	CREDIT	
1	May	5	Office Equipment	900 00		1
2			Cash in Bank		900 00	2
3			Check 104			3

GENERAL LEDGER

ACCOUNT *Office Equipment* ACCOUNT NO.

DATE		DESCRIPTION	DEBIT	CREDIT	BALANCE DEBIT	BALANCE CREDIT
May	1	Balance			1 600 00	
	5		900 00		2 500 00	

ACCOUNT *Cash in Bank* ACCOUNT NO.

DATE		DESCRIPTION	DEBIT	CREDIT	BALANCE DEBIT	BALANCE CREDIT
May	1	Balance			7 318 40	
	5			900 00	6 418 40	

Detail Oriented Businesses have separate accounts for different expenses, such as equipment or cash in the bank, that must be posted to each general ledger.

What is the definition of posting?

Caption Answer It is transferring an amount from the general journal to the general ledger.

Making Entries The manual accounting system uses a ledger account form, which is accounting stationery for recording financial information about specific accounts. There are several common ledger account forms. These forms are described by the number of amount columns they have. For example, the ledger page in Figure 20.3 on page 645 is a four-column ledger account form. The four-column account form has spaces to enter the account name, the account number, the date, a description of the entry, and the posting reference.

To make entries, next to the title *Account*, you enter one of your business's account names, such as Cash in Bank. As you can see, the page has four amount columns. You use the first two amount columns to enter the debit or credit amounts from the general journal. You use the last two amount columns to enter the new account balance after you make an entry from the general journal.

The type of account determines which balance amount column you will use. For example, asset account balances are recorded on the debit side. Liability and owner's equity account balances are recorded on the credit side.

Posting is the process of recording transfers of amounts from the general journal to individual accounts in the general ledger. **Figure 20.4** shows how you would post the general journal entry for May 5 to the corresponding accounts in the general ledger.

Question Answer asset accounts

As You Read

QUESTION

What balances are recorded on the debit side?

The date you record on the account in the general ledger is the date on which the transaction occurred. You may also enter a brief description of the transaction. You then transfer the debit entry of $900 from the general journal to the account in the general ledger account called *Office Equipment*. Because this account had a previous balance of $1,600, it now has a new balance of $2,500. Remember that debit entries increase the balance in asset accounts.

You then record the credit entry to the general ledger account Cash in Bank. This amount is entered in the credit column. Cash in Bank is an asset account. Remember that credit entries decrease asset account balances. Thus, the balance in the Cash in Bank account decreases by $900. The new debit balance for Cash in Bank is $6,418.40. Both account balances are recorded on the debit side.

Final Balances At the end of an accounting period, you will post the figures from the general journal to the appropriate accounts in the general ledger. After all entries have been posted, the final balance for each account will appear on the general ledger. For example, at the end of the accounting period, the general ledger account for Office Equipment may look like **Figure 20.5.**

This account had a beginning balance of $1,600. Three debit entries were made: $900, $2,350, and $3,680. Each of these entries increased the account balance. On May 18, a credit entry of $400 decreased the balance. So, the account called *Office Equipment* has a final debit balance of $8,130.

Time to Post The size of the business, the number of transactions, and whether the business uses a manual accounting system or a computerized accounting system will affect how often posting occurs. Ideally, businesses should post daily to keep their accounts up to date.

Figure 20.5 **Journal Entries Posted to a General Ledger**

GENERAL LEDGER

ACCOUNT *Office Equipment* ACCOUNT NO. ______

DATE		DESCRIPTION	DEBIT	CREDIT	BALANCE	
					DEBIT	CREDIT
May	1	*Balance*			1 600 00	
	5		900 00		2 500 00	
	12		2 350 00		4 850 00	
	18			400 00	4 450 00	
	27		3 680 00		8 130 00	

Sample Entries A general ledger shows individual expenses and totals for each type of account.

What was the balance of this account after the credit of $400 was deducted?

Caption Answer
$4,450

Figure 20.6 A Completed Trial Balance

Archer Delivery Service Trial Balance For the Month Ended May 31, 20--		
Cash in Bank	2 891 00	
Accounts Receivable	1 370 00	
Office Equipment	8 130 00	
Delivery Equipment	4 260 00	
Accounts Payable		5 822 00
Chris Archer, Capital		10 829 00
Totals	16 651 00	16 651 00

Staying Well-Balanced A trial balance statement lists all the separate accounts for a business. **Why should the totals for the debit and credit columns be equal?**

Caption Answer They must balance so the business does not go into debt.

Extension Have the students predict what should be done if the trial balance does not balance.

Step 5: Prepare a Trial Balance

When you have journalized all your business transactions and posted each of them to the accounts in the general ledger, you need to know if the account balances are correct. Did you post all the amounts from the general journal to the general ledger accounts? Is the accounting equation still in balance?

Figure 20.7 The First Five Steps of the Accounting Cycle

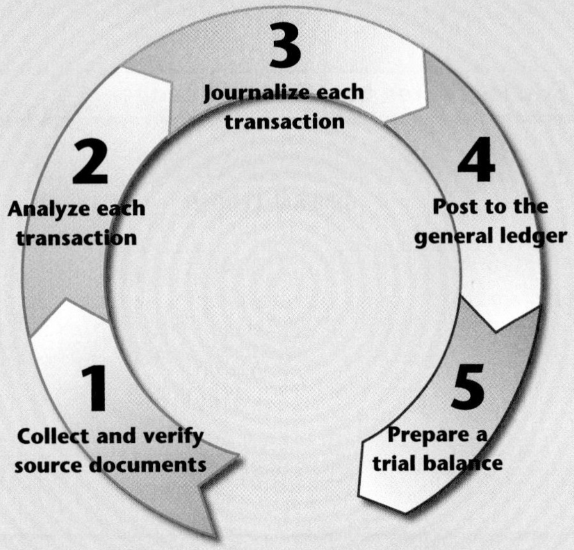

The Backbone The accounting cycle is the basis of all accounting procedures. **Why should all businesses use the same accounting system?**

Caption Answer Professionals and accountants who interact between businesses and organizations can communicate effectively and efficiently.

To answer these questions, you will prepare a trial balance. A **trial balance** is a list of all the account names for a business and their current balances. After you complete all posting, the total of all the debit balances should equal the total of all the credit balances. If the debit and credit totals are the same, then the general ledger is balanced. You can assume that the posting is complete and that the math is correct. **Figure 20.6** shows an example of a trial balance for the month of May 20--.

You will notice that the accounting equation is still balanced:

Assets = Liabilities + Owner's Equity

Keeping Records

To summarize, you have learned that businesses keep financial records according to an established set of principles and procedures. Every effective business, large and small, follows GAAP guidelines. The steps of the accounting cycle are universal. **Figure 20.7** illustrates the first five steps of the accounting cycle that were introduced in this section. Businesses generate their financial statements by following the steps of the accounting cycle.

Section 20.1 Assessment

See the Teacher Manual for answers.

QUICK CHECK

1. What are the first five steps of the accounting cycle?

2. What is recorded in a general journal?

3. How does a general ledger help you keep your business records organized?

THINK CRITICALLY

4. Suppose that you prepare a trial balance and discover that total debits do not equal total credits. What are some of the errors that you might have made?

USE COMMUNICATION SKILLS

5. The Accounting Cycle Dione teaches computer classes at a local senior citizen center. He has just been asked to teach a course on the basics of accounting for small businesses.

Write About It Write a paragraph explaining the first five steps of the accounting cycle that would help Dione begin a course outline.

SOLVE MONEY PROBLEMS

6. Account Names Jake Adams recently started Jake's Janitor Services. He cleans several office buildings in town. He borrowed money from two creditors to purchase his cleaning equipment.

Write About It Make a list of the account names that Jake might use for his cleaning business.

Section 20.2

Focus on Reading

Read to Learn

- How to identify items included on an income statement.
- How to explain the purpose of a balance sheet.
- How to define and explain the role of a statement of cash flows.

Main Idea

You need current financial statements that analyze your financial position in order to make sound financial decisions about your business.

Key Terms

- financial statements
- income statement
- cost of merchandise sold
- gross profit on sales
- net income
- balance sheet
- statement of cash flows

Before You Read

PREDICT

What do you think financial statements might tell a business owner?

Springboard Ask your students to discuss the academic skills, particularly math and language arts, that are needed in order to prepare and analyze financial statements.

Financial Statements for a Business

Financial Statements

Why are financial statements important for operating a business?

To operate a business profitably, you need to have up-to-date financial information. You cannot make decisions if you do not have the current facts. Financial statements provide this information. **Financial statements** are reports that summarize changes that result from business transactions during an accounting period. By preparing and analyzing these statements, you can see if your business is on course, having difficulty, or headed for serious trouble. Preparing financial statements is another step in the accounting cycle.

The primary financial statements are the income statement (or the statement of operations or statement of earnings) and the balance sheet. A third statement, the statement of cash flows, is also used. The sources of information for your financial statements are the final balances in the general ledger accounts. When you prepared your trial balance, you proved that the posting from the general journal to the general ledger was correct and complete. Now you have to report what happened during this accounting period.

You will now examine financial statements from a small merchandising business—Happy House Card Shop. A merchandising business is a business that buys goods, marks them up, and sells them to customers. Happy House Card Shop sells a variety of cards, gift wrapping, and small gifts bought from wholesalers or distributors.

Income Statement

At the end of an accounting period, you want to know how much money your business made or lost. You also want to know how much money you took in from sales and where the money went. You report this information on your **income statement**, which is a report of the net income or net loss for an accounting period. An income statement for a merchandising business has five sections: revenue, cost of merchandise sold, gross profit on sales, operating expenses, and net income (or loss). The amounts entered on the income statement will be the ending balances in the accounts in the general ledger. **Figure 20.8** shows an income statement.

Revenue You will notice that the beginning of the statement reports the total sales (A), or revenue, for the period. Happy House earned $292,619 in sales for the year ending December 31, 20--. This is the total amount of money that the business earned from selling merchandise to customers.

Motivating Students Ask students why they think business owners take the time and effort to keep good accounting records?

Cost of Merchandise Sold Next, the cost of the merchandise sold (B) is calculated and reported. The **cost of merchandise sold** is the amount of money the business paid for the goods that it sold to customers. To arrive at this amount, Sheila first determines the cost of merchandise in the store at the beginning of the accounting period. In this case, $83,744 was on hand. Then she adds the cost of the additional merchandise that Happy House purchased during the year, which was $205,813. This means that the store had a total of $289,557 in merchandise available to be sold.

After counting her inventory, Sheila determines that she still has $93,281 in merchandise in the store. This means that the cost of the merchandise sold is $196,276.

Discussion Ask the students to list the businesses in their community that are merchandising businesses.

Figure 20.8 Income Statement

HAPPY HOUSE CARD SHOP
Income Statement
For the Year Ended December 31, 20--

Revenue:		
Sales		292,619 (A)
Cost of Merchandise Sold:		
Merchandise on Hand Jan. 1	83,744	
Plus Merchandise Purchased	205,813	
Merchandise Available for Sale	289,557	
Minus Merchandise Still on Hand	93,281	
Total Cost of Merchandise Sold:		196,276 (B)
Gross Profit on Sales		96,343 (C)
Operating Expenses:		
Advertising Expense	2,734	
Insurance Expense	487	
Maintenance Expense	3,551	
Miscellaneous Expense	762	
Rent Expense	18,500	
Salaries Expense	26,931	
Supplies Expense	1,024	
Utilities Expense	4,107	
Total Operating Expenses:		58,096 (D)
Net Income		38,247 (E)

Vital Records An income statement is an important financial document for any business to show investors.

What amount on an income statement is also used in the general ledger?

Caption Answer amounts entered for each item

Figure 20.9 Comparison of Income Statements

HAPPY HOUSE CARD SHOP
Comparative Income Statement
For the Year Ended December 31, 20--

	Previous Year	Current Year	Dollar Change	Percent Change
Sales	283,834	292,619	+8,785	+3.10
Cost of Merchandise Sold	186,283	196,276	+9,993	+5.36
Gross Profit on Sales	97,551	96,343	–1,208	–1.24
Total Operating Expenses	61,277	58,096	–3,181	–5.19
Net Income	36,274	38,247	+1,973	+5.44

Analyzing Progress By comparing income from year to year, a business can evaluate its progress or its decline.

Did the operating expenses increase or decrease during the current year of operation for this business?

Caption Answer The expenses decreased.

Academic Connection

INTERNATIONAL FINANCE/MATH

The Internet has spurred an increase in globalization. Even small companies can now market goods worldwide. Business people need to understand how different currencies work and how to determine exchange value. The United States uses the dollar, much of Europe uses the euro, and Great Britain still uses the pound. *Using the Internet, track the exchange rate of the euro and the pound for three days, recording how many of each will equal $100.*

See the Teacher Manual for answer.

Gross Profit Sheila then subtracts the cost of the merchandise sold ($196,276) from the amount earned from sales ($292,619) to arrive at (C), the gross profit on sales ($96,343). The **gross profit on sales** is the profit made from selling merchandise before operating expenses are deducted. This is the profit Sheila made by marking up her merchandise and selling it.

Net Income **Net income** is the amount of revenue that remains after expenses for the accounting period are subtracted from the gross profit on sales. To calculate the net income for the period, Sheila subtracts the total operating expenses (D=$58,096) from the gross profit on sales (C=$96,343). For this period, Happy House Card Shop reported a net income (E) of $38,247.

Analyzing the Income Statement

You can see that Happy House made a profit. It is a good idea to compare the figures on this income statement to those on last year's statement. A comparison of condensed income statements for Happy House is shown in **Figure 20.9.** By reviewing the changes, Sheila will have an idea of how well her business is doing.

In Figure 20.9, you can see that sales increased by 3.10 percent from last year. Depending on where the business is located and on general economic conditions, this may be good. Notice that the net income rose by 5.44 percent. This could be because the business reduced total operating expenses by 5.19 percent. Sales increased, but the net income increased at a greater rate. This is an example of good financial management.

◀ **MAKING GOOD DECISIONS** Having current financial information about total sales is essential to making sound business decisions. *What kinds of financial statements would you examine to analyze a business?*

Caption Answer income statement, balance sheet, and a statement of cash flows

Another common method of analysis is to show figures on an income statement as a percentage of sales. Based on the present income statement and last year's statement from Happy House, a partial analysis is shown in **Figure 20.10.**

Last year the cost of merchandise sold was 65.63 percent of total sales. This year it increased to 67.08 percent of total sales. Sheila Henry paid more for her merchandise, but her sales did not increase at the same rate.

The gross profit on total sales decreased from 34.37 percent to 32.92 percent. Happy House sold more merchandise but lowered its percentage of gross profit. If it were not for a drop in expenses this year, the business would have reported a lower net income. This analysis provides the owner of Happy House with some of the information that she needs to make decisions regarding the store's pricing.

Critical Thinking Ask the students: "What decisions do you think Sheila will make with this information?"

Figure 20.10 **Comparison Using Percentage of Sales**

	Previous Year		Current Year	
	Amount in Dollars	Percent	Amount in Dollars	Percent
Sales	283,834	100.00	292,619	100.00
Cost of Merchandise Sold	−186,283	−65.63	−196,276	−67.08
Gross Profit on Sales	97,551	34.37	96,343	32.92

Another Way to Analyze Financial figures can also be expressed as percentages, and a business can assess and express its progress on a percentage basis.

For this business, what was the gross profit on sales percent during the previous year? Was that more or less than the current year's profit?

Caption Answer The gross profit on sales for the previous year was more at 34.37 percent.

As You Read

RELATE

Do you think Happy House should raise its prices next year? Explain your answer.

Extension Invite a business owner to class to explain how he or she uses financial statements when making business decisions.

The Balance Sheet

The other primary financial statement of a business is a balance sheet. A **balance sheet** is a report of the balances of all asset, liability, and owner's equity accounts at the end of an accounting period. The main purpose of the balance sheet is to present a business's financial position by reporting the assets of a business and the claims against those assets (creditor's claims and owner's claims). It reports what the business owns, owes, and is worth on a specific date. It is like taking a financial photo of your business on the last day of the accounting period. This is your present financial situation. The balance sheet for Happy House Card Shop is shown in **Figure 20.11.**

You learned in Section 20.1 that the basic accounting equation must always be in balance. The balance sheet represents the basic accounting equation.

Assets = Liabilities + Owner's Equity

Notice that a balance sheet consists of three sections: an asset section, a liability section, and an owner's equity section. On the Happy House balance sheet, the total assets ($211,209) equal the total liabilities ($49,092) plus the owner's equity ($162,117). This means the accounting equation is still in balance.

Figure 20.11 Balance Sheet

HAPPY HOUSE CARD SHOP
Balance Sheet
December 31, 20--

ASSETS		
Cash in Bank	35,372	
Accounts Receivable	14,201	
Merchandise Inventory	93,281	
Supplies	8,285	
Office Equipment	12,187	
Display Equipment	47,883	
TOTAL ASSETS		211,209
LIABILITIES		
Accounts Payable	42,722	
Sales Tax Payable	3,621	
Payroll Taxes Payable	2,749	
TOTAL LIABILITIES		49,092
OWNER'S EQUITY		
Sheila Henry, Capital		162,117
TOTAL LIABILITIES + OWNER'S EQUITY		211,209

Staying Afloat The balance sheet for a business must show a balanced equation in which the assets equal liabilities and owner's equity in order to stay in business.

Is this particular business in balance? Why or why not?

Caption Answer Yes, the assets of $211,209 equal the liabilities plus owner's equity of $211,209.

Analyzing the Balance Sheet

To analyze these figures, you would compare the current amounts on the balance sheet with figures from last year, as shown in **Figure 20.12.**

By examining the numbers and percentages, you can see that changes have taken place. Happy House bought various assets during the year. This is shown in various increased balances:

- Supplies
- Office Equipment
- Display Equipment

The business also has more cash and inventory on hand, and higher accounts receivable, than last year.

The balance sheet is an important financial statement, but to make wise decisions, you should always compare the financial data to a previous year's balance sheet. Remember, the financial statements provide the information about assets, liabilities, and owner's equity, but you must analyze and interpret it to make recommendations based on that information.

As You Read

QUESTION

What sections are included on a balance sheet?

Question Answer asset, liability, and owner's equity

Figure 20.12 **Comparison of Balance Sheets**

HAPPY HOUSE CARD SHOP
Comparative Balance Sheet
December 31, 20--

	Previous Year	Current Year	Dollar Change	Percent Change
ASSETS				
Cash in Bank	22,743	35,372	+12,629	+55.53
Accounts Receivable	8,338	14,201	+5,863	+70.32
Merchandise Inventory	83,744	93,281	+9,537	+11.93
Supplies	4,631	8,285	+3,654	+78.90
Office Equipment	8,958	12,187	+3,229	+36.05
Display Equipment	41,720	47,883	+6,163	+14.77
TOTAL ASSETS	**170,134**	**211,209**	**+23,075**	**+13.56**
LIABILITIES				
Accounts Payable	39,837	42,722	+2,885	+7.24
Sales Tax Payable	3,506	3,621	+115	+3.28
Payroll Taxes Payable	2,921	2,749	-172	-5.88
TOTAL LIABILITIES	**46,264**	**49,092**	**+2,828**	**+6.11**
OWNER'S EQUITY				
Sheila Henry, Capital	**123,870**	**162,117**	**+38,247**	**+30.88**

Past and Current Performance Businesses can use their balance sheets to do a comparison of profits and expenses over the years. This can help businesses pinpoint problem financial areas and make improvements.

Have this business's assets increased or decreased? Is this an improvement or not?

Caption Answer The assets have increased by 13.56 percent, which is an improvement.

Statement of Cash Flows

Why are cash flows important?

The income statement and balance sheet provide vital financial information, but neither financial statement shows how cash came into or went out of the business during the period. You will want to know how much cash is available during business operations.

You may remember that your personal cash flow is the money that actually goes in and out of your wallet and bank accounts. In a business, cash flow refers to the sources and uses of cash during an accounting period.

Understanding cash flows will help you in cash management. Suppose that your school has a big dance coming up on Friday. All of your friends are going and will probably go somewhere to eat after it is over. You will need cash for Friday night, but you will not get your paycheck from your job until Saturday. In this example, money needs to go out for the dance before money comes in from your job. You have a "cash crunch" problem.

Businesses often face similar problems. If a small business experiences a cash crunch situation, it could have serious problems. Good cash control and management means that sufficient cash is available for operating the business on a daily basis and for emergencies.

TechByte

Computerized Accounting Software
There are many options to consider when looking for computerized accounting software to help you run your business. A businessperson's decision about which one is right for his or her needs is an important choice—one that could mean the difference between success and failure. Looking for the right accounting software solution for your business can be a real challenge.

@ You can learn about free software assistance and write a paragraph explaining the process used to make the best choice through **finance07.glencoe.com**.

Cash Inflows and Outflows

A **statement of cash flows** is a financial statement that reports how much cash a business took in and where the cash went. It explains changes in the Cash in Bank account during the accounting period.

Discussion Ask the students to discuss what they do when they have a cash crunch problem. What do they think a business can do when it is in the same situation?

Caption Answer a negative cash flow

▶ **ENTERTAINMENT EXPENSES** Theatrical companies must pay for production costs well before cash from ticket sales is received. *What kind of cash flow would a theatre group experience before ticket sales begin?*

Figure 20.13 Statement of Cash Flows

HAPPY HOUSE CARD SHOP
Statement of Cash Flows
For the Year Ended December 31, 20--

Cash Flows from Operating Activities		
Cash Receipts from:		
Sales to Customers	$286,756	$286,756
Cash Payments for:		
Purchase of Merchandise	($202,928)	
Operating Expenses	(61,807)	(264,735)
Net Cash Flows from Operating Activities		$ 22,021
Cash Flows from Investing Activities:		
Cash Payments for:		
Purchase of Assets (Equipment)	($ 9,392)	
Net Cash Flows from Investing Activities		(9,392)
Cash Flows from Financing Activities:		
Net Cash Flows from Financing Activities		0
Net Increase (Decrease) in Cash		$ 12,629
Cash at Beginning of Year		22,743
Cash at End of Year		$ 35,372

Show Me the Money A business may look good on paper with assets, such as a building and equipment, but income in the form of cash is needed to pay for expenses.

What items would be considered cash inflows for this business?

Caption Answer cash receipts from sales

Cash flows include both cash inflows (cash that enters a business) and cash outflows (cash that exits a business). Cash inflows may include sales and interest earned from investments or savings. Cash outflows may include operating expenses, merchandise purchases, supplies, and interest and taxes paid.

Figure 20.13 shows the statement of cash flows for Happy House. Notice that the statement of cash flows has three sections:

- Cash Flows from Operating Activities
- Cash Flows from Investing Activities
- Cash Flows from Financing Activities

Analyzing the Statement of Cash Flows

Happy House has a positive cash flow. During the year, more cash entered the business than was paid out. The difference is $12,629.

When your business has negative cash flows, you will probably experience a lack of available cash. You may not be able to pay your bills or buy goods to resell. The business will not grow. Your statement of cash flows can be a major consideration when you want to borrow money. Potential investors and lenders want to see cash flowing into your business in a constant, positive manner.

Critical Thinking Ask the students: "Is it necessary to understand T accounts or how to manually post transactions, if you are using a computerized accounting system?" Have them justify their answers.

Computerized Accounting

How do businesses use accounting software?

Most businesses use some type of accounting software to record and report their business transactions. Even for an automated system, you still need to collect and keep your source documents. Each business transaction must be separated into its debit and credit parts. However, you will enter the transaction in the computer system by using account numbers rather than the account names. You still need to enter the amounts.

STANDARD & POOR'S

Global Financial Landscape

Standard and Poor's publishes the globally recognized S&P 500® financial index. It also gathers financial statistics, information, and news, and analyzes this data for international businesses, governments, and individuals to help them guide their financial decisions.

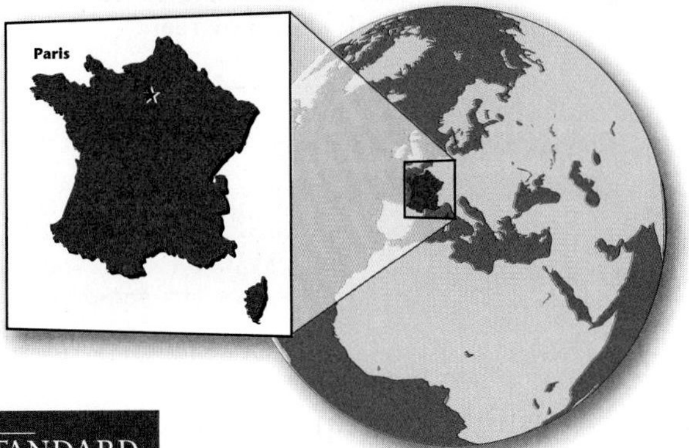

FRANCE

Telecommunication services rank as a major industry in France. The telecom sector is an important part of the French economy, making up two-thirds of French exports in manufacturing goods. These exports grew by 29 percent during the 1990s and continue to grow. One of the industry stars, France Telecom, boasts 125 million customers. The company has a global outreach to five continents and revenue of nearly $60 billion in U.S. dollars. Headquartered in Paris, France, Telecom offers the second largest wireless operation and Internet access service (called *Wannado*) in Europe.

To reach its goal as world leader in telecommunications, France Telecom has taken a page from its own book. It trains its personnel online. A computer program, called *Train Us,* matches the instruction offered for the jobs within the company. Employees can learn new skills or change career paths without leaving their desks.

STANDARD & POOR'S

DATABYTES

Capital	Paris
Population	59,771,000
Languages	French
Currency	euro
Gross Domestic Product (GDP)	$1.65 trillion (2003 est.)
GDP per capita	$27,500

Industry: Machinery, chemicals, automobiles, metallurgy, aircraft, electronics, and textiles

Agriculture: Wheat, cereals, sugar, beets, potatoes, beef, and fish

Exports: Machinery and transportation equipment, aircraft, plastics, chemicals, pharmaceuticals, and food

Natural Resources: Coal, iron ore, bauxite, fish, and timber

Think Globally

What types of functions might an accounting student need to learn from an online training course?

See the Teacher Manual for answer.

Computerized Posting

When all transactions are entered, you can "tell" the program to post all amounts to the appropriate general ledger accounts. Computerized posting is faster and eliminates accounting errors that you might make by doing it manually.

After You Read

REACT

Why is it important to understand basic accounting procedures, even if you use accounting software to manage accounts?

React Answer Accept all reasonable answers that show an understanding of the importance of having a knowledge of basic accounting principles to be able to assess accuracy.

Using Accounting Principles

What are important financial tools for businesses?

You have learned about several basic financial statements that are some of the tools used to apply the first five accounting principles. The basic accounting principles are the backbone of every business. Business owners and investors who risk their money and time depend on accurate accounting records to report the results of the operation and financial condition of their businesses. All businesses use the same practices, which help them analyze their financial positions and make effective business decisions.

Section 20.2 Assessment

See the Teacher Manual for answer keys.

QUICK CHECK

1. What items are included on an income statement of a merchandising business?
2. What is the purpose of a balance sheet?
3. Why is the statement of cash flows important to a business?

THINK CRITICALLY

4. Describe how it is possible for a business to have made a profit during the most recent accounting period but not have enough money to pay its employees this week.

USE MATH SKILLS

5. **Gross Profit** Damien is the student manager of Panther's Pen, the student store on his school campus. During the fall semester, sales (or revenue) totaled $5,420, and the cost of merchandise sold was $3,500. During the spring semester, sales were $4,890, and the cost of merchandise sold was $3,060.

Calculate What is the gross profit on sales for each semester? What is the percentage of gross profit to sales? Did profits improve from the fall semester to the spring semester?

SOLVE MONEY PROBLEMS

6. **Sharing Financial Information** Sylvia worked her way through college at a health food store. She learned about the various aspects of operating a business. When she graduated, she opened her own store, Sylvia's Smoothies. Now she is ready to add a partner to her business.

Analyze What type of financial information might Sylvia need to share with potential partners?

Chapter 20 Review & Activities

See the Teacher Manual for answers.

CHAPTER SUMMARY

- The accounting equation states that Assets − Liabilities = Owner's Equity. Accounts show the balance for a specific item. Accounts are set up as needed by a business, and may vary depending on the type of business.
- The first five steps of the accounting cycle are to collect and verify source documents, analyze each transaction, journalize each transaction, post transactions to the general ledger, and prepare a trial balance.
- Business transactions are recorded in the general journal.
- Posting to the general ledger allows you to see the balances in each account.
- A trial balance is a list of all the accounts and their current balances. All the debit balances should equal the total of all the credit balances.
- The income statement is a report of the net income or net loss for an accounting period.
- The balance sheet reports balances for all asset, liability, and owner's equity accounts at the end of an accounting period. It presents the business's financial position.
- The statement of cash flows reports how much cash your business took in and how it was used.

Communicating Key Terms

As an independent bookkeeper, you are preparing a presentation about the services you offer to someone just starting a business. Use as many terms below as you can in the presentation.

- financial reports
- accounting period
- accounting cycle
- accounting equation
- account
- accounts receivable
- accounts payable
- double-entry accounting
- T account
- debit
- credit (accounting)
- journal
- general ledger
- posting
- trial balance
- financial statements
- income statement
- cost of merchandise sold
- gross profit on sales
- net income
- balance sheet
- statement of cash flows

Reviewing Key Concepts

1. **Explain** the three parts of the accounting equation.
2. **Describe** the five steps in the accounting cycle.
3. **Explain** the rules of debit and credit.
4. **Explain** how posting to the general ledger can simplify financial reporting.
5. **Describe** a trial balance.
6. **List** items included on an income statement.
7. **Describe** reasons why a business may have a reasonable balance sheet but poor cash flow.
8. **Define** a statement of cash flows.

See the Teacher Manual for answers.

ACADEMIC SKILLS

Economics Compare and contrast the steps leading to preparing a trial balance with balancing your personal checkbook.

Write About It Write an article for your class newsletter explaining the similarities and differences in the two actions.

YOUR FINANCIAL FIGURES

Balance Comparison Below is a sample balance sheet that includes two years:

	2003	2004
Assets		
Cash	17,500	24,300
Marketable securities	93,000	88,000
Accounts receivable	87,455	68,600
Inventories	162,000	169,000
Fixed assets	147,000	138,000
Liabilities		
Current liabilities	114,000	122,000
Long-term debt	216,000	214,000
Partnership equity	176,955	151,900

1. **Calculate** How have the different items in the balance sheet changed in percentages between the end of 2003 and 2004?
2. **Compute** Use spreadsheet software to make these calculations.

REAL-WORLD Application

Connect with Communication Skills A graphic designer is starting a business. She has purchased the equipment, furniture, and supplies needed, and is working for several clients.

Role-Play Set up accounts for the graphic designer. With a partner, role-play a discussion between you, the bookkeeper, and the designer. The bookkeeper explains the accounting system set up for the business, and the designer asks questions about how it will work.

Internet CONNECTION

Accounting Software Using software saves time when generating the financial reports needed for decisions. Some early accounting software, such as Lotus 1-2-3® and Peachtree®, is still in use today in updated versions.

@ **Log On** Search the names of five different accounting software packages. Go to the Web sites for these packages.

Present How do they differ? Are some designed for particular industries? Develop a few PowerPoint slides to report the results of your research.

BusinessWeek ONLINE

Newsclip: Fuzzy Numbers Many corporations need to improve their financial reporting and disclosure techniques. Annual and quarterly profit figures are frequently inflated and may mislead investors.

@ **Log On** Go to **finance07.glencoe.com** and open Chapter 20. Find an income statement, balance sheet, and cash flow statement from any company you choose. Write down any financial inconsistencies (or "fuzzy numbers") you might find.

WHAT'S YOUR FINANCIAL ID?

DO YOU THINK LOGICALLY OR INTUITIVELY?

Which type of thinker are you—logical or intuitive? Logical thinking tends to be analytical, orderly, and consistent, sometimes based on rules or something exact. Intuitive thinking is based on insight and tends to be more approximate, symbolic, and capable of dealing with contradiction. You may have a tendency toward logical or intuitive thinking. In this quiz, there are no "right" or "wrong" answers. Choose ten of the words below that best describe your thought processes, and then write them on a separate sheet of paper.

_____ abstract
_____ ambiguous
_____ analogous
_____ analytic
_____ approximate
_____ conceptual
_____ constructive
_____ critical
_____ deductive
_____ detailed

_____ dreamy
_____ exact
_____ fantastical
_____ focused
_____ generalized
_____ imaginative
_____ impractical
_____ inferring
_____ literal
_____ logical

_____ playful
_____ poetic
_____ practical
_____ precise
_____ rational
_____ reflective
_____ specific
_____ speculative
_____ symbolic
_____ visionary

Scoring:

Give yourself 5 points if you wrote down analytic, conceptual, constructive, critical, deductive, detailed, exact, focused, literal, logical, practical, precise, rational, reflective, or specific.

Give yourself 3 points if you wrote down abstract, ambiguous, analogous, approximate, dreamy, fantastical, generalized, imaginative, impractical, inferring, playful, poetic, speculative, symbolic, or visionary.

If you scored 30–38 points, you prefer intuitive thinking.

If you scored 42–50 points, you prefer logical thinking.

Regardless of your tendencies, try alternate types of thinking. Whenever you feel you are not communicating well, consider that the other person might be using a different way of thinking.

Accept all reasonable answers that show student effort and an understanding of the concept.

Your Financial Portfolio

Income Statements

Dakota's gardening business now includes gardening for 22 homes and gardening and planting for three commercial properties. She is considering hiring Rashelle for an hourly fee to work with her so she can expand the business. To see if she can afford to hire Rashelle, she has prepared an income statement. In reviewing six months of income statements, Dakota felt she could afford to pay Rashelle, especially if she picked up some new accounts.

Dakota's Gardening
Income Statement for the Month Ended July 31, 20--

Revenue	
Regular gardening fees	$3,460
Charge for plantings	180
Charge for trimming trees	300
Total revenue	$3,940
Operating Expenses	
Buying plantings	$ 90
Truck loan	150
Equipment: new tree pruner	75
Gas expense	25
Insurance expense	35
Total expenses	$ 375
Net Income	**$3,565**

Apply

On a separate sheet of paper, choose a service business that you might like to operate. Determine what you would charge for your service. Based on your fee and services, determine what your monthly revenue and expenses would be. Using the same guidelines as shown above, prepare an income statement. Would you want to hire and supervise help or would you prefer to work alone?

Accept all income statements that show student effort and an understanding of the concept.

CHAPTER 21
Managing Payroll and Inventory

What You'll Learn

When you have completed this chapter, you will be able to:

Section 21.1
- Identify six steps in managing a payroll system.
- Describe the common methods of paying employees.
- Discuss required and voluntary payroll deductions.
- Identify the accounts used in recording payroll.

Section 21.2
- Identify information needed for an inventory control system.
- Summarize methods of determining inventory quantity.
- Explain methods used to calculate cost of inventory.
- Discuss how to analyze inventory turnover.

Reading Strategies

To get the most out of your reading:

Predict what you will learn in this chapter.
Relate what you read to your own life.
Question what you are reading to be sure you understand.
React to what you have read.

In the Real World . . .

Wendy Jansen runs a vending business, offering snacks made from potatoes. Her unique idea developed from her love of French fries. She is very knowledgeable about potatoes—white, russet, red, and more. When she told her friends about the business, they thought it was clever but impractical. However, Wendy created recipes for everything from potato-on-a-stick to sweet potato soufflé. She sells her products at fairs, music festivals, and sporting events. She does so well that she runs out of certain items. She realizes she must keep track of her stock and ingredients by using an inventory system. Otherwise, she will lose sales and the chance to grow her business into something more.

As You Read *Consider how using an inventory system makes good business sense.*

Lesson Plan See the Teacher Manual for the Chapter 21 planning guide and lesson plan.

ASK STANDARD & POOR'S

Social Security and Medicare

Q: I am only 16. Why should I pay Social Security and Medicare taxes? Those programs may not be around when I am old enough to collect.

A: It is true that Social Security programs are projected to run low on funds around the year 2025. Under the present system, the rate of return on your contributions to these programs is lower than what you might earn. However, Congress is working to ensure that Social Security will provide funds for future retirees. Also, Social Security and Medicare offer many other types of benefits including disability benefits.

Ask Yourself What can you do now to help supplement your retirement income?

@ Go to **finance07.glencoe.com** to complete the Standard & Poor's Financial Focus activity.

Section 21.1

Focus on Reading

Read to Learn

- How to identify six steps in managing a payroll system.
- How to describe the common methods of paying employees.
- How to discuss required and voluntary payroll deductions.
- How to identify the accounts used in recording payroll.

Main Idea

Managing payroll efficiently and accurately enables a business to run more effectively and profitably.

Key Terms

- payroll
- gross earnings
- salary
- hourly wage
- overtime rate
- commission
- deductions
- Federal Insurance Contributions Act (FICA)
- Social Security tax
- Medicare tax
- total gross earnings

Springboard Ask the students this question: "Why do people work?" (Most students will say to earn money.) Ask the students to explain what they know about the payroll records that a business must keep. Add to the list as you study this chapter.

Managing Payroll

The Importance of Payroll Records

Why do payroll records need to be accurate?

If you own a business, a large and important part of its accounting system will involve payroll. A **payroll** is a list of employees and the payments due to each employee for a specific period of time. The specific period of time during which you pay your employees is known as a pay period. The two most common pay periods are weekly and biweekly (every two weeks). However, some companies pay their employees only once per month.

A good payroll accounting system ensures that employees are paid on time and have the correct amounts on their paychecks. The payroll records and reports need to be very accurate. As with other accounting functions, when you process payroll information, you must follow specific guidelines. As discussed in Chapter 20, these guidelines are known as generally accepted accounting principles (GAAP). In addition to following GAAP procedures, state and federal governments issue strict guidelines for paying employees and reporting payroll information.

A business has two major goals when setting up a payroll system. The system should perform these functions:

- Collect and process all information needed to prepare and issue payroll checks.
- Maintain payroll records needed for accounting purposes and for preparing reports to government agencies.

Every payroll system has some common tasks or steps. All are important and must be done carefully, accurately, and regularly. If you pay your employees every week, you will complete all of these tasks weekly:

1. Calculate gross earnings.
2. Calculate payroll deductions.
3. Prepare payroll records.
4. Prepare paychecks.
5. Record payroll information in the accounting records.
6. Report payroll information to the government.

Calculating Gross Earnings

What is a salary and a wage?

The first step in a payroll system is to calculate the total earnings of all employees for the pay period. The total amount of money an employee earns in a pay period is the **gross earnings**. Three of the most common methods of paying employees are by salary, hourly wage, and salary plus commission.

Before You Read

PREDICT

Why do you think it is necessary to keep payroll records?

Salary

A **salary** is a fixed amount of money paid to an employee for each pay period, regardless of the number of hours worked. For example, Catherine Boggs is the manager of the shoe department at Dickinson's Department Store. She earns a fixed weekly salary of $530 even though she may work 40 hours one week and 44 hours another week. Salaries are paid to managers, supervisors, and others.

Motivating Students Ask the students who are working to discuss the ways that they keep track of their hours at work.

Hourly Wage

If you work for a local business after school and on the weekends, you probably receive an **hourly wage**, a specific amount of money paid per hour to an employee. Most temporary and part-time jobs pay an hourly wage. Many full-time jobs, such as entry-level jobs, also pay an hourly wage.

Careers in Finance

PURCHASING AGENT

Angie Strong
Rogers Corporation

Cultivating business relationships is Angie's top skill and her favorite part of her job. As a purchasing agent for a polymer and electronics manufacturer, Angie is responsible for finding good sources for products, buying the products, and negotiating the purchasing of raw materials, component parts, equipment, and more. It is Angie's job to develop relationships with suppliers, determine patterns of need, and ensure the best quality and cost of items purchased. She must also understand key market trends and issues that affect the supply of products.

SKILLS: Analytical, communication, computer, decision-making, math, organizational, negotiation, research, and sales skills

PERSONAL TRAITS: Able to handle stress, honest, likes working with people and numbers, tactful

EDUCATION: High school diploma or equivalent or bachelor's degree in business administration; experience in the field

ANALYZE How might good payroll management affect a company's purchasing abilities?
See the Teacher Manual for answer.

To learn more about career paths for purchasing agents, visit **finance07.glencoe.com**.

As You Read

RELATE

If you are currently employed, look at a recent paycheck stub and compare your gross earnings to the amount you were actually paid. What accounts for the difference?

For example, Sean McCormick works at a sporting goods outlet on weekday afternoons for $7.25 per hour. Last week he worked 20 hours, and his gross earnings were $145 ($7.25 × 20 = $145). This week he had already worked 20 hours by the end of the day on Wednesday. Sean's gross earnings vary from week to week because he works different amounts of time each week.

Employers may have hourly employees use time cards or a time clock to keep track of each day. They use this information to determine the total hours each employee worked during a pay period. At the end of each period, the employer checks the information on time cards or time sheets for accuracy. If the information is incorrect, paychecks will be inaccurate. That is a problem for both employees and employers.

Overtime Pay

According to state and federal laws, hourly-wage employees generally are paid extra when they work overtime, or more than 40 hours in a pay week. The **overtime rate**, the amount paid above the normal rate, is usually 1.5 times the employee's regular hourly wage. For example, Kelly Robinson's regular hourly wage is $7.40. If she works more than 40 hours in a given week, her overtime rate for the extra hours is $11.10 ($7.40 × 1.5 = $11.10).

Suppose that Kelly worked more than 40 hours last week. To calculate her gross earnings, multiply her regular hourly wage by 40 hours. Then you multiply the overtime rate by the number of overtime hours. By adding the results of these calculations, you can figure out her gross earnings for the week.

GO FIGURE **FINANCIAL MATH**

GROSS EARNINGS AND OVERTIME

Synopsis: Your gross earnings are the total amount of money you receive during a given pay period. Overtime, which you receive if you work more than your allotted number of hours, is 1.5 times your regular hourly rate.

Example: Kelly worked 43 hours this week. If her regular hourly wage is $7.40 and her overtime wage is $11.10, what are her gross earnings for the week?

Formula:

(Hourly Rate × Regular Hours) + (Overtime Rate × Overtime Hours) = Gross Earnings

Solution:

($7.40 × 40) + ($11.10 × 3) = Gross Earnings
$296 + $33.30 = $329.30

Kelly's gross earnings for the week are $329.30.

YOU FIGURE

If you earn $8.25 an hour and you work 47 hours in one week, what are your gross earnings?

Answer $416.66. $8.25 × 40 = $330; $8.25 × 1.5 = $12.38; $12.38 × 7 = $86.66; $330 + 86.66 = $416.66

Typically, employees might work extra hours during holiday sales or other busy periods. They might also work overtime to cover for other employees who are sick or on vacation. Remember, controlling payroll costs is an important aspect of good financial management.

Commission

A **commission** is an amount of money paid to an employee based on a percentage of the employee's sales. The more the employee sells, the more he or she is paid. Paying commissions to sales employees is a way to encourage them to increase their sales.

▲ **NINE TO FIVE** All employees are paid but not all in the same manner. Some receive a salary, some are paid an hourly wage, and some earn a salary plus commission. *What does it mean to work on salary plus commission?*

Caption Answer It means that you earn a regular salary plus a commission—an amount based on a percentage of your sales.

It is very common for employers to pay sales employees a salary plus commission. For example, Olivia Chun is paid a weekly salary of $150 plus a 5 percent commission on all merchandise she sells. This week she recorded sales of $3,725. Olivia's commission for the week is $186.25 ($3,725 × .05 or 5% = $186.25). Her gross earnings for the pay week are $336.25 ($150 + $186.25 = $336.25).

Calculating Payroll Deductions

What are some of the deductions that are taken out of employees' paychecks?

If you have ever received a payroll check, you were probably surprised to see that the amount on the check was less than you expected. **Deductions** are the various amounts that are subtracted from an employee's gross earnings. Some deductions are required by local, state, or federal law. Others are voluntary deductions. Employees choose to have these amounts withheld from, or taken out of, their gross earnings. The calculation of these deductions is the second step in a payroll system.

Critical Thinking Ask the students whether they would like to be paid on commission. Have them justify their answers.

Deductions Required by Law

As an employer, you are required by law to deduct certain payroll taxes from the gross earnings of all employees. These include federal income tax, Social Security tax, and Medicare tax. In many states additional taxes are withheld for local and state income taxes. Employers deduct these taxes from employees' paychecks and send the amounts to the appropriate government agencies.

Discussion Ask the students: "What does the federal government do with payroll tax money?"

Federal Income Tax Most people pay income tax to the federal government each year. This tax is based on their total income for the year. To ensure that people will have the money to pay these taxes, the government requires employers to withhold an amount of money from employees' paychecks each pay period. This money is sent to the government and is applied to each employee's federal income tax.

After calculating gross earnings, employers use tax tables supplied by the Internal Revenue Service (IRS) to determine the amount of federal tax to withhold from each employee's paycheck. To use the tables, employers must know how many allowances each employee is claiming. An allowance is an adjustment to the tax withheld from your paycheck. The more allowances an employee claims, the less tax will be withheld. Allowances are based on the employee's marital status and number of dependents. A single person could claim an allowance of zero or one. A married person with two children could claim an allowance of four. **Figure 21.1** shows an IRS tax table.

Figure 21.1 **Internal Revenue Service Tax Table**

SINGLE Persons—**WEEKLY** Payroll Period

If the wages are		And the number of withholding allowances claimed is										
At least	But less than	0	1	2	3	4	5	6	7	8	9	10
		The amount of income tax to be withheld is										
125	130	8	2	0	0	0	0	0	0	0	0	0
130	135	8	2	0	0	0	0	0	0	0	0	0
135	140	9	3	0	0	0	0	0	0	0	0	0
140	145	9	3	0	0	0	0	0	0	0	0	0
145	150	10	4	0	0	0	0	0	0	0	0	0
150	155	10	4	0	0	0	0	0	0	0	0	0
155	160	11	5	0	0	0	0	0	0	0	0	0
160	165	11	5	0	0	0	0	0	0	0	0	0
165	170	12	6	0	0	0	0	0	0	0	0	0
170	175	12	6	0	0	0	0	0	0	0	0	0
175	180	13	7	1	0	0	0	0	0	0	0	0
180	185	13	7	1	0	0	0	0	0	0	0	0
185	190	14	8	2	0	0	0	0	0	0	0	0
190	195	14	8	2	0	0	0	0	0	0	0	0
195	200	15	9	3	0	0	0	0	0	0	0	0
200	210	16	9	3	0	0	0	0	0	0	0	0
210	220	18	10	4	0	0	0	0	0	0	0	0
220	230	19	11	5	0	0	0	0	0	0	0	0
230	240	21	12	6	1	0	0	0	0	0	0	0
240	250	22	13	7	2	0	0	0	0	0	0	0
250	260	24	15	8	3	0	0	0	0	0	0	0
260	270	25	16	9	4	0	0	0	0	0	0	0
270	280	27	18	10	5	0	0	0	0	0	0	0
280	290	28	19	11	6	0	0	0	0	0	0	0
290	300	30	21	12	7	1	0	0	0	0	0	0
300	310	31	22	13	8	2	0	0	0	0	0	0
310	320	33	24	15	9	3	0	0	0	0	0	0
320	330	34	25	16	10	4	0	0	0	0	0	0
330	340	36	27	18	11	5	0	0	0	0	0	0
340	350	37	28	19	12	6	0	0	0	0	0	0

Paying Uncle Sam Depending on the number of allowances you claim, your employer will withhold a certain amount from your paycheck for income tax.

What is the purpose of withholding this money?

Caption Answer Answer might be to make sure that people will have the money to pay the taxes they owe each year.

For example, suppose that Eric Gaus has weekly gross earnings of \$235 and claims one allowance. According to the tax table, the amount withheld as his federal income tax is \$20. If Eric had too much withheld from his pay, the government would refund him the excess amount. If Eric had too little withheld, he would have to send the additional amount he owed to the IRS.

FICA Taxes In addition to federal income tax, employers also collect Social Security taxes for the federal government by deducting them from their employees' paychecks. The 1935 **Federal Insurance Contributions Act (FICA)** established the present Social Security system. Social Security payments are often referred to as *FICA taxes*. The FICA taxes pay for programs that provide income to certain individuals:

- The old-age and survivors' benefit programs provide income to retired persons and the spouse and dependents of a deceased worker.
- The disability insurance program provides income to people with disabilities and their families.
- The Medicare program provides health insurance benefits for people 65 or older, certain people with disabilities, and people of any age who have permanent kidney failure.

FICA includes two types of tax: Social Security tax and Medicare tax. **Social Security tax** finances the federal programs that provide retirement, disability, and life insurance benefits. **Medicare tax** is the tax that finances part of the Medicare program.

All employees pay FICA taxes based on rates established by the United States Congress. The rates can change at any time. In 2005, the FICA tax rates were 6.2 percent for Social Security and 1.45 percent for Medicare. The money from these taxes goes to the Social Security Administration, where it is put into a trust. It is then distributed to people collecting Social Security and Medicare benefits.

Academic Connection

LANGUAGE ARTS

Businesses pay their employees in different ways and with differing time periods, depending on several factors. Employees may be paid salaries, hourly wages, or salaries plus commissions, and pay periods may be weekly, biweekly, or monthly. *What types of businesses would use each payment method and pay period? Write a paragraph explaining your answers. Consider factors such as type of work performed, number of hours worked, business cash flow patterns, and any other possible factors.*

See the Teacher Manual for answer.

GO FIGURE **FINANCIAL MATH**

FICA DEDUCTION

Synopsis: FICA taxes include the Social Security tax and the Medicare tax. These taxes are used to provide income to a variety of people.

Example: What is the FICA deduction for Alex Calligros if his gross earnings for the week are \$380?

Formula:
(Gross Earnings × Social Security) + (Gross Earnings × Medicare Tax) = FICA Deduction

Solution:
(\$380 × .062) + (\$380 × .0145) = FICA Deduction

\$23.56 + \$5.51 = \$29.07

Alex's FICA taxes amount to \$29.07.

YOU FIGURE

If your gross earnings for the month are \$550, how much would be deducted from your paycheck for FICA taxes?

Answer \$42.08. (\$550 × .062) + (\$550 × .0145) = \$42.08

TechByte

Managing Cash Flow Having enough cash on hand at the right time is key when it comes to managing a growing company. The lag between the time you have to pay your suppliers and employees and the time you collect from your customers is often a problem. The solution is cash flow management. Cash flow management means delaying outlays of cash as long as possible while encouraging anyone who owes you money to pay it as quickly as possible. But how can you encourage people who owe you money to pay on time?

Learn more about software for cash flow management and write a paragraph about it through **finance07.glencoe.com**.

Extension Ask the students to create a list of other voluntary payroll deductions.

Employers use the FICA rates to calculate how much to withhold from the taxable gross earnings of each employee for each pay period. Multiply gross earnings by the Social Security tax, and then multiply gross earnings by the Medicare tax. Add these two figures to determine the FICA deduction.

State and Local Income Taxes Many states and cities tax the earnings of people who live or work within their boundaries. In some states the taxes are simply a percentage of gross earnings. In other states, the amount owed is based on tax tables similar to the federal withholding tables issued by the IRS. Where employees work and live determines how state or local taxes are taken from their gross earnings.

Voluntary Deductions

Many employers deduct other amounts of money from employees' paychecks. These deductions are voluntary, meaning that the employer will deduct these amounts only if the employee requests it. If the employee does not want the money deducted, it remains in his or her paycheck. However, once an employee requests a voluntary deduction, it is withheld from each paycheck until the employee asks his or her employer to stop taking it out. Some common voluntary deductions include:

- Health or life insurance premiums
- Union dues
- Contributions to charities
- Pensions and other retirement plans
- Direct deposits to a credit union or bank

A popular voluntary payroll deduction is a contribution to a 401(k) plan for retirement, which you learned about in Chapter 15. Many employees contribute a portion of their gross earnings to accounts in a company 401(k) plan. The funds in a 401(k) plan are tax-deferred, meaning that employees do not have to pay taxes on the money that accumulates in their 401(k) plans until they withdraw it.

Preparing Payroll Records

What information is included on a payroll register?

The third step in a payroll system is to prepare payroll records. Federal and state laws require all businesses to keep accurate payroll records. Employers are expected to:

- Calculate earnings and deductions correctly.
- Distribute employee paychecks on time.
- Keep accurate payroll records.
- Pay all taxes owed to government agencies on time.
- File all required payroll reports to government agencies on time.

To fulfill these obligations, your business needs an efficient system for collecting, recording, and summarizing payroll information.

Preparing the Payroll Register

After collecting information for the pay period, you record the data on a payroll register. The payroll register is a record that summarizes information about employee earnings and deductions for each pay period. **Figure 21.2** shows an example of a completed payroll register for Ezra's Sport Clothes.

A payroll register has three main sections pertaining to money: earnings, deductions, and net pay. The earnings section records the regular pay, overtime pay, and gross earnings of each employee for the pay period. The deductions section of the payroll register lists and totals the required and voluntary deductions withheld from each employee. The number of columns varies from business to business. The net pay section records the amount that remains after the total deductions are subtracted from gross earnings. For Ezra's Sport Clothes, the total net pay for this week's payroll is $1,338.31.

As You Read

QUESTION

What are the three main sections of a payroll register?

Question Answer earnings, deductions, and net pay

Preparing Paychecks

What are some of the benefits of direct deposit?

After checking the accuracy of the payroll register, you prepare a payroll check for each employee. This is the fourth step in a payroll system. The amount on each payroll check—often referred to as *take-home pay*—should equal the net pay listed for each employee. Along with the check, each employee receives a written or printed explanation that shows how the net pay is calculated. The stubs attached to payroll checks provide this explanation and serve as a record for employees. An example of a paycheck that lists gross earnings, deductions, and net pay is shown in **Figure 21.3** on page 674.

Teaching Activity Contact the IRS and obtain a variety of forms that businesses use to report payroll information to the government. Have the students review them and decide which ones are easy to understand and which ones are more difficult to complete.

Figure 21.2 Completed Payroll Register for Ezra's Sport Clothes

PAYROLL REGISTER

PAY PERIOD ENDING May 18 20 -- DATE OF PAYMENT May 18

	EMPLOYEE NUMBER	NAME	MAR. STATUS	ALLOW.	TOTAL HOURS	RATE	EARNINGS: REGULAR	EARNINGS: OVERTIME	EARNINGS: TOTAL	DEDUCTIONS: SOC. SEC. TAX	MED. TAX	FED. INC. TAX	STATE INC. TAX	HOSP. INS.	UNION DUES	TOTAL	NET PAY	CK. NO.	
1	3	Drummond, R.	S	0	37	7.80	288 60		288 60	17 89	4 18	35 00	5 77		5 00	67 84	220 76	186	1
2	7	Feld, D.	M	2	41	7.40	296 00	11 10	307 10	19 04	4 45	14 00	6 14	12 00		55 63	251 47	187	2
3	4	Monsalves, D.	S	0	33	8.10	267 30		267 30	16 57	3 88	32 00	5 35	7 00		64 80	202 50	188	3
4	9	Simon, J.	S	1	28	7.40	207 20		207 20	12 85	3 00	15 00	4 14		5 00	39 99	167 21	189	4
5	11	Turner, J.	S	0	42	8.20	328 00	24 60	352 60	21 86	5 11	52 00	7 05	7 00	5 00	98 02	254 58	190	5
6	6	Wyman, B.	M	2	39	7.60	296 40		296 40	18 38	4 30	14 00	5 93	12 00		54 61	241 79	191	6
24																			24
25																			25
						TOTALS	1683 50	35 70	1719 20	106 59	24 92	162 00	34 38	38 00	15 00	380 89	1338 31		

Preparing Payroll A payroll register summarizes information on employee earnings and deductions for each pay period.

What other information is recorded on the register?

Caption Answer Answers might include name, employee number, and marital status of each employee; number of allowances; total number of hours worked; hourly rate; net pay; check number; and date of payment.

Figure 21.3 **Completed Payroll Check and Stub**

Ezra's Sport Clothes
155 Gateway Blvd.
Sacramento, CA 94230

186

91-182
1721

Date May 18 *20* --

Pay to the Order of Ryan Drummond $ 220.76

Two hundred twenty dollars and 76/100 *Dollars*

American National Bank
SACRAMENTO, CALIFORNIA

Agnes Werman

⑆172109182⑆ 085 015 1189064⑈ 186

Employee Pay Statement
Detach and retain this statement.

186

Period Ending	Earnings			Deductions							Net Pay
	Regular	Overtime	Total	Social Security Tax	Med. Tax	Federal Income Tax	State Income Tax	Hosp. Ins.	Union Dues	Total	
5/18	288.60		288.60	17.89	4.18	35.00	5.70	–	5.00	67.84	220.76

Payday The amount on each payroll check—often called "take home pay"—should equal the net pay listed for each employee on the payroll register.

What were Ryan Drummond's gross earnings for the period ending May 18? What was his net pay?

Caption Answer His gross earnings were $288.60. His net pay was $220.76.

Direct Deposit

Instead of issuing paychecks, many businesses offer direct deposit of employee earnings. With direct deposit, net pay is deposited automatically in an employee's designated bank account. Employers do not have to prepare a paycheck if they offer direct deposit. However, they must give employees a written record of their payroll information.

Employees and employers generally prefer direct deposit. Employees do not have to go to the bank to deposit their paychecks; they do not risk misplacing or losing a check; and funds are usually available faster. Employers can reduce the expenses of paper and labor for processing checks by using direct deposit.

Automated Payroll Preparation

Today almost all businesses use some type of automated system to prepare payroll records. Computer-generated records provide an efficient and accurate system. Computers are affordable, and a variety of software packages is available. The employer enters the number of hours each employee worked, and the computer produces a payroll register and the paychecks.

Recording Payroll Information

What payroll information is recorded in a company's accounting records?

After you complete the payroll register and prepare individual paychecks, the payroll must be recorded in the accounting system of your business. This is the fifth step in the payroll process. In recording the payroll, you are recording only the total amounts for the pay period. The individual amounts for each employee have already been recorded on the payroll register.

The Salaries Expense Account

Each pay period, you pay out a certain amount of money to your employees in wages or salaries. The amount you pay to all employees before any deductions are taken out is called **total gross earnings**. This is a basic operating expense of your business. You record the total gross earnings in a general ledger account titled *Salaries Expense.* On the payroll register illustrated in Figure 21.2, on page 673, the total gross earnings for the period are $1,719.20.

Caption Answer Paying employees by direct deposit can reduce a company's expenses of paper and labor costs in processing checks.

▼ **CHECK IT OUT** This teacher likes the convenience of being paid by direct deposit. *What are some other reasons that a company might pay its employees by direct deposit?*

Deductions to Liabilities

The amount you deduct from employee earnings for Social Security, Medicare, and other taxes or payments is subtracted from total gross earnings. This money does not belong to your company. You must pay it to the proper agencies or organizations on behalf of your employees. Therefore, all deductions taken from employees' gross earnings immediately become liabilities of your business.

In Chapter 20, you learned that in setting up your accounting system, you create only the accounts that your business needs. These accounts are assets, liabilities, and owner's equity. The liabilities of your business are identified in the account title by the word *payable*.

Based on the deductions shown on its payroll register in Figure 21.2 on page 673, Ezra's Sport Clothes has the following liability accounts:

- Social Security Tax Payable
- Medicare Tax Payable
- Employees' Federal Income Tax Payable
- Employees' State Income Tax Payable
- Hospital Insurance Premium Payable
- Union Dues Payable

These items remain liabilities until the business makes the required payments to the government, insurance companies, local unions, and any other agencies or organizations.

STANDARD &POOR'S

Global Financial Landscape

Standard and Poor's publishes the globally recognized S&P 500® financial index. It also gathers financial statistics, information, and news, and analyzes this data for international businesses, governments, and individuals to help them guide their financial decisions.

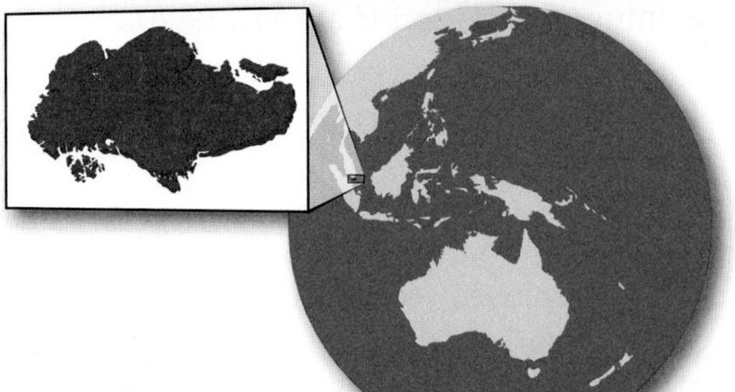

SINGAPORE

Known for centuries as the *Lion City,* Singapore might also be known as a "company town." The government involves itself in every aspect of Singapore's commerce. From international trade to trash collection, the small city-state is a study in efficiency. It is no wonder that *Fortune* magazine chose Singapore as one of the world's best places to do business. The government has threatened employers with punishment if they do not pay foreign workers on time. Many citizens believe the government knows what it is doing. Others are not so sure. Critics say that too much government control weakens the country's competitive spirit and stifles the creativity of its citizens. The concern is that this may hurt the country's economy.

STANDARD &POOR'S **DATABYTES**

Capital	Singapore
Population	4,372,000
Languages	Chinese, Malay, Tamil, English
Currency	Singapore dollar
Gross Domestic Product (GDP)	$109.1 billion (2003 est.)
GDP per capita	$23,700

Industry: Electronics, chemicals, financial services, oil drilling equipment, and petroleum refining

Agriculture: Rubber, copra, fruit, orchids, and poultry

Exports: Machinery and equipment (including electronics), consumer goods, chemicals, and mineral fuels

Natural Resources: Fish and deep-water ports

Think Globally

List some of the reasons why too much government control might have a negative effect on business.

See the Teacher Manual for answer.

Cash in Bank

After salary expenses and deductions have been recorded, the last account to be affected by payroll is Cash in Bank. Cash in Bank is the account that records all of the cash that enters or leaves the business. For the pay period shown in Figure 21.2 on page 673, the cash account is reduced by the total amount of net pay, which is $1,338.31. Your cash account balance will be reduced further as you make payments on your payroll liabilities.

▲ **KEEPING TRACK** A store such as Borders bookstore employs many people working in many different areas of the business. *How might accurate payroll records help employers manage their business expenses?*

Caption Answer Paying employees by direct deposit can reduce a company's expenses of paper and labor costs in processing checks.

Employer's Payroll Taxes

How do employers help pay for benefits such as Social Security?

The amounts in the various payroll liability accounts of a business represent the taxes that employees paid on their earnings. The state and federal governments also require employers to pay additional taxes that are based on the total taxable gross earnings each pay period. This money goes toward benefits such as Social Security and unemployment and disability insurance.

Employer's Share of FICA Taxes

Federal law requires that the employer match the total amount deducted from employees' paychecks for Social Security and Medicare. In other words, if your employee pays $25, you must pay an additional $25. In Figure 21.2 on page 673, the total Social Security tax deducted from the total gross earnings for the pay period ending May 18 was $106.59. As the employer, Ezra's Sport Clothes must match this amount ($106.59) and send the government a check totaling $213.18 ($106.59 + $106.59 = $213.18). Employers also have to match Medicare deductions with an equal amount. An employer must match and pay Social Security tax and Medicare tax for every pay period.

Federal and State Unemployment Taxes

The employer pays both federal and state unemployment taxes. The maximum federal unemployment tax is 6.2 percent on the first $7,000 of an employee's annual wages. State unemployment tax rates and maximum taxable amounts vary among states. Employers may deduct up to 5.4 percent of the state unemployment taxes from federal unemployment taxes. Most employers, therefore, pay a federal tax of 0.8 percent (6.2% − 5.4% = 0.8%) of taxable gross earnings.

GO FIGURE **FINANCIAL MATH**

UNEMPLOYMENT TAXES

Synopsis: Employers are required to pay federal and state unemployment taxes. These taxes provide income to workers who have lost their jobs.

Example: The total gross earnings of Prairie Pet Store are $3,000 for the pay period. None of the employees has reached the maximum taxable amount. How much money must the owner pay to the federal and state governments, based on the unemployment tax rates?

Formula:
(Total Gross Earnings × Federal Tax Rate) +
(Total Gross Earnings × State Tax Rate) =
Total Unemployment Taxes

Solution:

($3,000 × 0.8) + ($3,000 × .054) = Total Unemployment Taxes

$24 + $162 = $186

Prairie Pet Store will have to pay $24 to the federal government and $162 to the state government for a total of $186.

YOU FIGURE

If your company's total gross earnings for a specific pay period were $4,100, how much would you have to pay in federal and state unemployment taxes?

Answer $254.20. ($4,100 × 0.8) + ($4,100 × .054) = $254.20

To calculate the amount to pay, you multiply the total gross earnings for the pay period by the federal tax rate. Then multiply the total gross earnings for the pay period by the state tax rate. Finally, add the two figures to calculate the total amount of taxes to pay.

Reporting Payroll Information to the Government

What information is essential in filing reports to the government?

Discussion Ask students: "Why does the government impose civil or criminal penalties for not paying taxes properly?"

The amount of money a business owes government agencies must be paid according to strict guidelines, outlined in the Internal Revenue Code (IRC). Both the federal and state governments expect prompt payment along with the proper forms and reports. You must file a variety of forms to the different government agencies. Reporting information about payments to the government is the sixth and last step in the payroll process. You need current and accurate payroll information for filing the reports and making the necessary payments.

Employers must comply with employment tax rules and procedures in the IRC or risk civil or criminal penalties. The IRC addresses a number of issues:

- Determining whether the federal tax coverage rules apply
- Computing an employee's taxable wages
- Calculating the amount of employment taxes to be withheld
- Depositing the correct amount of taxes with the government
- Filing employment tax returns

Payroll Accounting in Financial Management

Why is it important to analyze payroll information regularly?

Accurate payroll records are essential for controlling business expenses. Good payroll records can pinpoint the labor cost for different areas of your business. They will also indicate how much of the total gross earnings was spent on overtime. Although overtime is justified in many cases, it may also be a sign of a poor use of employees.

Payroll is often the biggest expense of running a business. Therefore, it is very important to carefully analyze the payroll information of every pay period. Payroll costs can dramatically reduce profits. However, payroll is also an area where you can reduce expenses. Good financial management requires constant review of your payroll system.

Section 21.1 Assessment

See the Teacher Manual for answers.

QUICK CHECK

1. What are the steps of a payroll system?
2. What are the three most common methods of paying employees?
3. What are three required payroll deductions and three voluntary payroll deductions?

THINK CRITICALLY

4. Discuss some of the advantages and disadvantages of paying someone a salary instead of an hourly wage.

USE MATH SKILLS

5. **Eagle Earnings** Danielle is the payroll manager at Eagle Amos, a retail business that specializes in camping and hiking gear. She needs to determine the weekly gross earnings for several employees. Hourly employees earn overtime at a rate of 1.5 times the regular hourly rate and do not receive commission. Salaried employees earn a 4 percent commission on their sales. Danielle knows:
   - Shari worked 44 hours at $6.75/hour.
   - Rolf worked 40 hours at $7.35/hour.
   - Litisha earns a salary of $185/week and had sales totaling $1,150.

   Calculate Help Danielle with the calculations. Which employee earned the most money this week?

SOLVE MONEY PROBLEMS

6. **Growth Spurt** Alicia runs a pool cleaning service and has almost 200 clients. Her business is growing very quickly. Now Alicia must decide whether to continue paying overtime each week to her employees or to hire another employee or two. Each of Alicia's 15 employees earns an hourly wage of $7.50 and works an average of 8 hours of overtime a week.

   Calculate and Analyze Calculate how much Alicia is paying her current employees in overtime. Calculate how much it would cost for Alicia to hire an additional employee at $7.50/hour. Which would be the most cost-effective solution: hiring a new employee or continuing to pay her current employees overtime?

Section 21.2

Focus on Reading

Read to Learn

- How to identify information needed for an inventory control system.
- How to summarize methods of determining inventory quantity.
- How to explain methods used to calculate cost of inventory.
- How to analyze inventory turnover.

Main Idea

Maintaining adequate quantities of merchandise in inventory enables businesses to meet the needs of customers and manage cash flow.

Key Terms

- perpetual inventory system
- point-of-sale terminals
- periodic inventory system
- specific identification method
- first-in, first-out method (FIFO)
- last-in, first-out method (LIFO)

Before You Read

PREDICT

Why should a business manage inventory effectively?

Managing Inventory

Establishing an Inventory System

Why is it important to keep close track of inventory?

Felix Martinez owns a small bookstore in San Diego that specializes in materials about travel in the United States and other countries. Business has been very good lately. One of Felix's most challenging tasks is deciding which books to buy and keep in stock for his customers. He reviews his stock regularly to see which books sell well and which ones remain on the shelves. The decisions he makes in purchasing books can have a significant impact on his business's cash flow and profits.

When you own a business, one of the major expenses of your company is the purchasing of merchandise, or the items that you buy with the intent to resell to customers. The amount of merchandise you have on hand at any particular time is known as inventory. Inventory for a manufacturing business can include raw materials, goods in process, and finished goods. For a retail business, products or merchandise in stock, such as books, clothing, or appliances, are also considered to be inventory. Inventory is often the largest asset of a business.

In order to control the purchase and sale of merchandise for your business, you must establish an inventory control system. This system tracks the quantity and cost of merchandise purchased, the merchandise in stock, and the merchandise sold to customers. **Figure 21.4** illustrates the various stages of merchandise in a retail business. Properly tracking the flow of merchandise gives you the up-to-date information that you need to make good management decisions. The essential items of information for an inventory control system include:

- The amount of merchandise sold in each accounting period.
- Information about which items are selling well.
- Information about which items are not selling well.

Tracking and controlling inventory is also a major function of an accounting system. You cannot make good financial decisions without accurate and current inventory information.

Figure 21.4 The Stages of Merchandise

Merchandise is moving from the time you order it until the time that it is sold to a customer.

1 Ordering Merchandise Merchandise must be reordered when your inventory runs low in order to meet customer demand.

2 Storing Merchandise After you receive merchandise, it must be stored in a safe, efficient manner.

3 Displaying Merchandise Merchandise must be displayed in an appealing way that will attract customers.

4 Selling Merchandise The sale of merchandise brings in cash for your business and also reduces your inventory, which must be replenished by reordering.

WebQuest

Franchise Ownership
When you own a franchise and are in business for yourself, you will have to become a good manager of resources, time, and people. Learn more about being a good boss and business leader.

@ To continue with Task 4 of your WebQuest project, visit **finance07.glencoe.com**.

Springboard Ask the students who work to share examples of inventory management at their work location.

The Importance of Controlling Inventory

Why is having too little inventory bad for business?

Because the purchase of merchandise often requires large amounts of money, it has a great impact on cash flow. Therefore, it is essential to maintain the proper level of inventory. Your goal is to have enough merchandise to meet customer demand but not have an overstock of items.

If your inventory is too large, you may have purchased the wrong items or the wrong quantity of items. As a result, cash may not be available for operating expenses, expansion activities, or emergencies. You will also be paying more than necessary for storage. To get rid of excess inventory, you may have to sell it at a loss.

If your inventory is too low, customers will not have enough choices of merchandise. They may shop elsewhere, in which case, you lose sales. With fewer sales, your business receives less cash.

Have you ever gone to purchase something at a store only to find out that the item was out of stock? Can you remember how you felt? Disappointed customers often do not return. Satisfied customers, on the other hand, go back to businesses where they find the items they want when they want them. Therefore, maintaining an appropriate level of inventory is good business management.

Motivating Students Ask students: "Have you ever gone to a store to buy a certain product, but it was out of stock? If so, what did you do?"

Determining Amount of Inventory

What systems help determine amount of inventory in stock?

At certain points in each accounting period, businesses need to determine how much merchandise is in stock. They also need to calculate the value of the merchandise. How do you calculate the quantity of merchandise on hand at a given point?

Two accounting methods are used to determine how much merchandise is in stock: the perpetual inventory system and the periodic inventory system. Both of these systems report the quantity of merchandise available for sale to customers.

The Perpetual Inventory System

A **perpetual inventory system** is a system that keeps a constant, up-to-date record of merchandise on hand. Every time an item is sold, the item is deducted from the inventory. A perpetual inventory system allows you to determine the quantity you have on hand and the cost of the items at any time. By having current, up-to-date information, you can reorder and restock items whenever the quantity becomes low. Restocking can help avoid loss of sales.

Before the introduction of computers, this type of inventory system was impossible for most businesses to use. It was just too difficult to keep track of a large quantity of items being bought and sold. Today, however, many businesses use **point-of-sale terminals**, which are electronic cash registers. These terminals are linked to a centralized computer system that keeps track of sales.

You have probably bought an item in a store with this kind of system, where the associate passes an electronic gun or scanner over the bar code of the item you are buying. The scanner reads the bar code, you hear a beep, and the item's price appears on the screen of the point-of-sale terminal. Sales tax is automatically calculated when the items are entered. The sales slip you receive from the store lists the items you just purchased along with their prices.

In addition to recording the prices of items, point-of-sale terminals also identify the items and remove them automatically from the inventory records. When a particular item reaches a predetermined low point, the purchasing manager reorders the item so that the business does not run out of it. With such an automated system, businesses know the number of items sold and the number still on hand at all times. An example of a computer printout of a daily inventory report is shown in **Figure 21.5.**

As You Read

RELATE

Look at a receipt you received from a purchase such as clothing or a music CD. Is there an item number listed on the receipt for each item? How might a store owner use these numbers?

Critical Thinking Ask the students: "Which is worse—too much or too little inventory?" Have them explain their answers.

Figure 21.5 **Computer Printout from a Perpetual Inventory System**

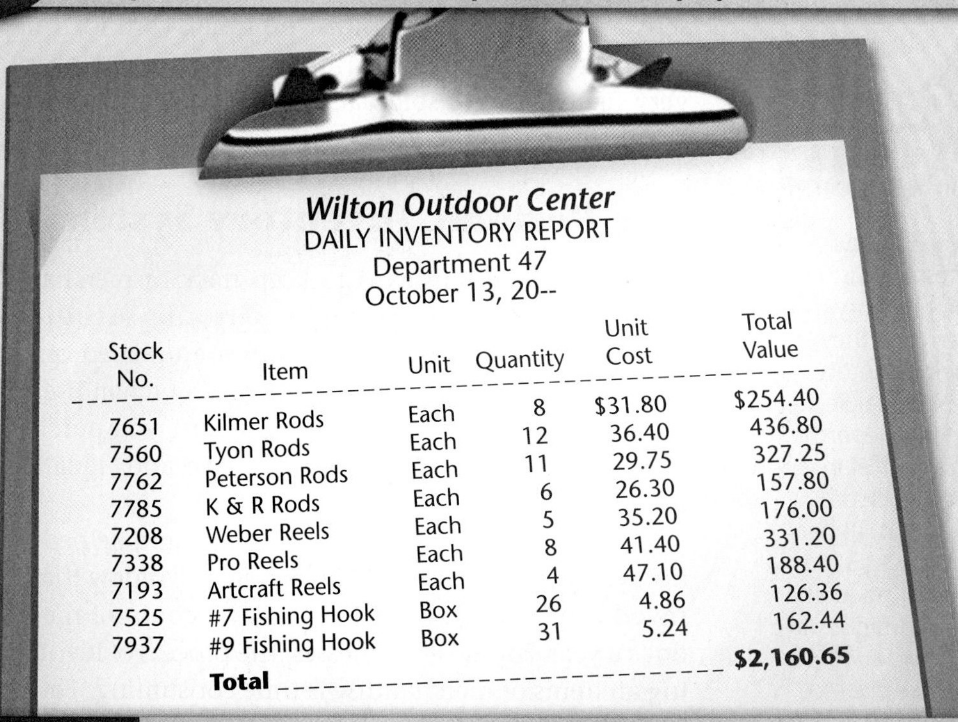

Wilton Outdoor Center
DAILY INVENTORY REPORT
Department 47
October 13, 20--

Stock No.	Item	Unit	Quantity	Unit Cost	Total Value
7651	Kilmer Rods	Each	8	$31.80	$254.40
7560	Tyon Rods	Each	12	36.40	436.80
7762	Peterson Rods	Each	11	29.75	327.25
7785	K & R Rods	Each	6	26.30	157.80
7208	Weber Reels	Each	5	35.20	176.00
7338	Pro Reels	Each	8	41.40	331.20
7193	Artcraft Reels	Each	4	47.10	188.40
7525	#7 Fishing Hook	Box	26	4.86	126.36
7937	#9 Fishing Hook	Box	31	5.24	162.44
	Total				**$2,160.65**

What's in Stock? A perpetual inventory system allows you to update inventory records every time an item is sold.

How many Peterson rods and Weber reels did Wilton Outdoor Center have in stock as of October 13?

Caption Answer Peterson rods: 11. Weber reels: 5.

▶ **SCAN IT!** Many stores use point-of-sale terminals and scanners to record sales. *What is the advantage of using this technology?*

Caption Answer With such an automated system, businesses always know the number of items sold and the number still on hand in their inventory.

Discussion Tell the students to imagine that they own a retail business and their point-of-sale terminals crashed and would not be repaired for one week. How would they handle this situation?

Common Cents 10 dressses and 5 handbags

It is difficult, but not impossible, for businesses that do not use computers to use a perpetual inventory system. Usually these businesses sell large items, such as cars or furniture. They have fewer items in stock and do not sell many items within a certain time period. As a result, they can keep track of inventory with index cards or inventory sheets that list the items in stock. When the business sells an item, someone pulls the index card for that item from an inventory box or removes the item from an inventory sheet. Because very few items are sold each day, it is possible to maintain a noncomputerized perpetual inventory system.

The Periodic Inventory System

Another system used to keep track of merchandise on hand is a periodic inventory system. A **periodic inventory system** is a system in which inventory records are updated only after someone makes an actual physical count of the merchandise on hand. You do not change inventory records every time you purchase or sell something. You count everything you have and update your inventory only after everything is counted.

Perhaps you have worked in a store and helped take inventory. If not, you may have seen a sign in a store window that read "Closed for Inventory." Businesses take a physical count of merchandise at least once a year. For most businesses, the process of identifying and counting all items of merchandise is time consuming. Therefore, inventory is usually counted when the quantity of merchandise is at its lowest point. For a seasonal business, the count occurs after the peak sales period. In a ski shop, for example, the peak sales period is November through March. You would probably take inventory in May or June, when there is less merchandise to count. After taking the physical count, you can order new merchandise for the next year.

Common CENTS

Inventory Losses
Retail businesses must consider loss of inventory due to human error as they manage their inventory levels. The National Security Survey Final Report found that causes of inventory shortages include employee theft at 48 percent, shoplifting at 32 percent, vendor fraud at 5 percent, and administrative and paper errors at 15 percent. *If a boutique carried 100 dresses and 50 designer handbags, and the store's total inventory shortage was typically 10 percent, how many of each item were lost due to shoplifting?*

Document Detective

Learn to identify and understand the standard financial documents you will use in the real world.

See the Teacher Manual for answers.

Investigate: A Paycheck Stub
A paycheck stub contains the following information:

- Name and Social Security number of employee
- Amount earned during the pay period and year-to-date
- Amount of taxes withheld from wages during the pay period and year-to-date

Your Motive: When you receive a check from your employer, a statement will be attached to the check. This statement tells you how your paycheck was calculated. Sometimes employers make mistakes in their payroll. You can check the paycheck stub to make sure the amounts are correct.

General Products
P.O. Box 27806
New York, NY 20012

Michelle Li
101 Second Street
Athens, OH 44573

SS no. 299-XX-XXXX

Period beginning: 12/24/2007	Period ending: 01/04/2008	Pay date: 01/11/2008

Pay Summary	
Earnings	$113.07
Less: Taxes	12.93
Deductions	.00
Net Check	$100.14

Earnings-to-Date	**Type**	**Rate**	**Hours**	**Current**	**Year-to-Date**
Holiday	17	6.75	3.25	21.94	89.08
Straight Time	12	6.75	13.50	91.13	368.05

Taxes	**Current**	**Year-to-Date**
Federal income tax	1.11	25.63
Social Security	7.01	65.24
Medicare	1.64	28.43
State income tax	.91	23.06
City tax	2.26	56.97

Key Points: A paycheck stub contains information for the current pay period as well as the cumulative total for the calendar year.

Find the Solutions

1. How much does Michelle make per hour?
2. Does she make more money per hour on holidays?
3. When did Michelle receive this pay?
4. How much in taxes was deducted from her paycheck?
5. What was the total amount Michelle received?

As You Read

QUESTION

Even with good inventory controls in place, why might you still want to do a physical inventory?

Question Answer to check accuracy and correct errors

Today many businesses use electronic equipment when taking a physical inventory. An employee simply enters the stock number of each item and the quantity in stock into a handheld computer. When the physical count is complete, he or she prints an up-to-date record of the inventory items.

Even if a business uses a perpetual inventory system, it must conduct a periodic physical inventory at least once a year to check the accuracy of inventory records. Errors can be made in entering inventory data when purchasing merchandise. Errors can also be made at point-of-sale terminals when the business sells merchandise. Items can be lost, stolen, or identified incorrectly. A periodic physical count ensures that accounting records are accurate and agree with what the business actually has in stock.

Determining the Cost of Inventory

Why is it important for a business to use its chosen costing method consistently?

Extension Ask the students to list the seasonal businesses that are located in their community. If these businesses were using the periodic inventory system, when would they take inventory?

You have determined the quantity of merchandise on hand. Now you need to calculate the cost of that merchandise. In other words, the inventory must be assigned a value. You could do this fairly easily if the cost of every item were always the same. However, that is unusual.

For example, Heather Martin buys certain items for her pet store several times within a single inventory period. Often the cost of these items changes during that period. Heather might buy a specific brand and size of dog food for $9 per bag in March. She might pay $12 for the same dog food in June. How can she appropriately determine the cost of the remaining bags of dog food she still has on hand? To answer this question, businesses use one of several inventory costing methods approved by GAAP guidelines. All of these methods calculate a value for inventory on hand: the specific identification costing method; the first-in, first-out method; and the last-in, first-out method.

The Specific Identification Costing Method

Critical Thinking Ask the students what could happen if errors were made when entering inventory data.

The **specific identification method** is an inventory costing method in which the exact cost of each item is determined and assigned to an item. The actual cost of each item is obtained from the invoice. This is the most accurate costing method. It is commonly used by businesses that sell a small number of items at high prices. These businesses include appliance stores, car dealerships, and furniture stores. Because every item must be researched, this costing method is not practical for most businesses. You will use it only if you have few items to track and if the cost is easy to look up.

The First-In, First-Out Costing Method

If you cannot determine the exact cost of every item in your inventory, you will have to make a good estimate. One method of estimating cost is the first-in, first-out method. The **first-in, first-out method (FIFO)** is an inventory costing system that assumes the first items purchased (first in) are the first items sold (first out). It also assumes that the items the business purchased most recently are the ones on hand at the end of the period.

For example, Matthew Lee owns a small neighborhood grocery store. One of his best-selling items is milk. Because milk is perishable, the employees stock the shelves first with the milk that was purchased first. As that milk is sold, later purchases are added at the back of the shelves. The first in are the first out.

Here is another example of how the FIFO inventory method works for Lamar's House of Music:

▲ HOW MANY? HOW MUCH? Counting inventory and determining its value is an important task for all businesses. *Why is it important to count merchandise and assign it a value?*

Caption Answer Businesses need to calculate the cost of their merchandise in order to make decisions about purchasing and related issues.

Troy DVD Player—Model #875

Date	Description	Units	Cost	Total
Feb. 4	Beginning Inventory	9	$250	= $2,250
May 12	Purchase	20	253	= 5,060
July 7	Purchase	10	258	= 2,580
Sept. 15	Purchase	12	263	= 3,156
Nov. 9	Purchase	10	265	= 2,650
Total		**61**		**$15,696**

After taking a physical inventory, the employees at Lamar's House of Music discover that there are 12 DVD players still in stock. Using the FIFO method, they assume that the 12 remaining players are the last ones the business purchased, because the "first in" are the "first out." They calculate the cost of the ending inventory as follows:

Sept. 15: 2 units @ $263	=	526
Nov. 9: 10 units @ $265	=	$2,650
Cost of ending inventory	=	$3,176

Discussion Ask the students if they know of any retail or service business in their community that uses a physical system for tracking inventory. If so, have the students find out how it is done.

$avvy Saver

Inventory at Home

1. To keep track of your assets, start a list.
2. Go room by room and write a description of each item and note serial numbers.
3. Collect a receipt and photo for each item.
4. Collect personal papers such as birth certificates.
5. Make two copies of your list to keep in a safe place.

The Last-In, First-Out Costing Method

Another method for calculating the value of your ending inventory is the last-in, first-out method. The **last-in, first-out method (LIFO)** is a costing method that assumes the last items purchased (last in) are the first items sold (first out). It also assumes that the items purchased first are still on hand at the end of the period.

For example, Stratford Stone Company sells loose stone to contractors. When new stone arrives, it is deposited on top of the existing stone. As the stone is taken from the top of the pile, the first stones sold are the last delivered. The physical flow of the company's product, therefore, is "last-in, first-out."

If the employees at Lamar's House of Music use the LIFO method for calculating the cost of DVD players, they would assume that the last players purchased were sold first. The earliest players are still in stock. This could happen if they pushed older items to the back of the shelves. Using the LIFO method, they would calculate the cost of ending inventory as follows:

Feb. 4: 9 units @ $250	=	$2,250
May 12: 3 units @ $253	=	$ 759
Cost of ending inventory	=	$3,009

Choosing a Costing Method

The cost of the ending inventory will vary, depending on which costing method you use. Notice that the inventory at Lamar's House of Music is valued at $3,176 using the FIFO method but at $3,009 using the LIFO method. Similarly, the inventory would be valued at a different amount if the store used the specific identification method.

Businesses choose the inventory costing method that seems best for their particular type of business. Once a business chooses a method, however, it must use that method consistently. Consistent reporting helps owners and creditors compare financial reports from one accounting period to another.

STANDARD &POOR'S

Put on Your Financial Planner's Cap

Imagine that you have a client who is opening a shop that will sell kitchen supplies, from stoves to spoons and everything in between. One of your tasks is to establish inventory and determine inventory control and reporting methods. Would you suggest inventory control using specific identification costing, FIFO, or LIFO?

See the Teacher Manual for answer.

Analyzing Inventory Turnover

Is it better to have high or low inventory turnover?

In order to evaluate the performance of your business, analyze current inventory information and compare it to data from previous accounting periods.

One type of analysis—the inventory turnover—is the number of times you sell your inventory in a given time period. To calculate the inventory turnover, divide the cost of the merchandise sold in a given time period by the average inventory. (The average inventory is the value of beginning inventory plus the value of ending inventory, divided by two.)

GO FIGURE — FINANCIAL MATH

AVERAGE INVENTORY

Synopsis: You need to determine the average inventory for your company in order to calculate the inventory turnover for a specific period of time.

Example: Cindy's Fine China had an inventory valued at $65,000 as of January 1, and an inventory valued at $80,000 as of December 31 of the same year. What was the store's average inventory for the year?

Formula:

$$\frac{\text{Value of Beginning Inventory} + \text{Value of Ending Inventory}}{2} = \text{Average Inventory}$$

Solution:

$$\frac{\$65{,}000 + \$80{,}000}{2} = \$72{,}500$$

The store's average inventory for the year was $72,500.

YOU FIGURE

If the value of your beginning inventory was $72,000 and the value of your ending inventory was $100,000, what was your store's average inventory for the year?

Answer $86,000. $72,000 + $100,000 ÷ 2 = $86,000

Average Inventory After you have determined the average inventory for a particular time period, you can calculate the inventory turnover. To do so, divide the cost of merchandise sold during that time period by the average inventory.

Inventory Turnover Levels A high inventory turnover means that your business has money tied up in inventory for shorter periods of time. As a result, your financing, storage, and insurance costs are reduced, which benefits your business. On the other hand, a low inventory turnover may mean that sales were lower than expected or that too many items were in stock and remained unsold.

GO FIGURE — FINANCIAL MATH

INVENTORY TURNOVER

Synopsis: Inventory turnover is the number of times you sell your inventory in a given period of time. High inventory turnover is good.

Example: Cindy's Fine China sold $200,000 of merchandise. If the store's average inventory for the period was $72,500, what was its inventory turnover?

Formula:

$$\frac{\text{Cost of Merchandise Sold}}{\text{Average Inventory}} = \text{Inventory Turnover}$$

Solution:

$$\frac{\$200{,}000}{\$\ 72{,}500} = 2.76$$

The inventory turnover for Cindy's Fine China was 2.76 times a year.

YOU FIGURE

If you sold $110,000 of merchandise and your average inventory was $80,000, what was your inventory turnover for the year?

Answer 1.38. $110,000 ÷ $80,000 = 1.38

GO FIGURE — FINANCIAL MATH

NUMBER OF DAYS IN STOCK

Synopsis: Inventory turnover is used to determine the number of days that you have merchandise in stock. If merchandise remains in stock for an increasing amount of time, you may want to rethink your purchasing practices.

Example: Inventory turnover for Cindy's Fine China was 2.76 in 2007 and 3.25 in 2006. How many days did the merchandise remain in stock each year?

Formula:

$$\frac{\text{365 Days}}{\text{Inventory Turnover}} = \text{Number of Days in Stock}$$

Solution:

$$\frac{365}{2.76} = \text{about 132 days} \quad \frac{365}{3.25} = \text{about 112 days}$$

Merchandise remained in stock for about 132 days in 2007 and for about 112 days in 2006.

YOU FIGURE

If you had an inventory turnover of 3.6 for one year, how many days did your merchandise stay in stock?

Answer 101 days. 365 ÷ 3.6 = 101 days

Extension Invite a couple of small business owners to your class. Ask them to tell the students about their inventory turnover and the decisions they make based on the inventory turnover measurement.

Days in Stock Inventory turnover is used to determine the number of days that merchandise is in stock. You calculate this figure by dividing the number of days in a calendar year (365) by inventory turnover.

If you find that your merchandise remains in stock for an increasing amount of time from one year to the next, you should investigate the reasons and decide whether to change your purchasing practices.

Stock Lists

Another tool that businesses use to plan purchases and manage inventory is stock lists. There are three types of stock lists: the basic stock list, model stock list, and never-out list.

Basic Stock List A basic stock list is a form that lists items a store should always keep in stock. A basic stock list is used for staple merchandise. For example, the basic stock list for a sporting goods store might include tennis balls, golf balls, and basketballs. The basic stock list includes the minimum amount of an item and the quantity to be reordered.

Model Stock List The model stock list is used for fashion merchandise. It is not as specific as the basic stock list. Since fashion merchandise varies more than staple merchandise, the model stock list is shorter, but it specifies quantities of each item.

Never-Out List The never-out list is used for the most popular merchandise. This list changes often. Items are added to the list as their popularity increases, and items are dropped as their sales decrease; thus, cash flow can remain steady.

Payroll, Inventory, and Cash Flow

Why should a business closely monitor its cash flow?

Blood flows through your body, keeping you healthy, active, and alive. Without a steady flow of blood, your body would not function properly, and you would eventually die. Cash has a similar effect on a business. Cash flows through the business, giving it the financial resources it needs to operate in a healthy and profitable manner. A negative cash flow might cause difficulty in a business's daily operations. A negative cash flow means that cash is not available for paying bills, restocking merchandise, or expanding the business. If this happens over an extended period of time, the business may close.

Payroll and inventory are two financial areas that have great influence on your cash flow and on the life of your business. If the inflow of cash is not sufficient to meet the demanding needs of payroll and inventory, financial problems may result. Payroll expenses must be kept to a minimum, and merchandise must be purchased with careful analysis of present and future sales markets. Careful recording, monitoring, and analysis of data involving payroll and merchandise is essential for a positive cash flow and the ability to make sound financial decisions. A successful business carefully monitors its cash flow and constantly analyzes its payroll and inventory costs.

After You Read

REACT

Why do payroll and inventory systems require more careful monitoring and analysis than other aspects of a business?

React Answer Answer might include that they affect cash flow and the ability to make sound financial decisions. Poor monitoring and analysis can result in having insufficient cash.

Section 21.2 Assessment

See the Teacher Manual for answers.

QUICK CHECK

1. What is the difference between the perpetual inventory system and the periodic inventory system?
2. What are the various costing methods?
3. Why do payroll and cash flow have such a large influence on a business's health?

THINK CRITICALLY

4. Explain when and why a business should conduct a physical count of its inventory.

USE COMMUNICATION SKILLS

5. **Inventory Analysis** Jerry's Junkyard sells used parts for Japanese cars. Recently Jerry hired you to analyze his current inventory information. Last year his inventory turnover was 16.67. This year inventory turnover has dropped to 12.5.

Analyze In groups of two or three, discuss possible causes for the change in Jerry's inventory turnover. Then offer Jerry some suggestions. What might he do to increase his inventory turnover?

SOLVE MONEY PROBLEMS

6. **Inventory Control** Aurora is planning to open a small art gallery in New York City, featuring artwork from new and emerging artists in Latin America. As she gets ready to establish her inventory system, she realizes that she will have many decisions to make regarding how to track and control her inventory.

Analyze Decide which inventory system Aurora's art gallery should use. Explain your decision. Also, which costing method should Aurora use? Explain why.

Chapter 21 Review & Activities

See the Teacher Manual for answers.

CHAPTER SUMMARY

- The six steps in managing a payroll system are: (1) calculate gross earnings; (2) calculate payroll deductions; (3) prepare payroll records; (4) prepare paychecks; (5) record payroll information in accounting records; and (6) report payroll information to the government.
- Employees are paid by fixed salary, hourly wages, and commissions based on the value of goods they sell.
- Some payroll deductions are required by law, such as income and Social Security tax. Others, such as 401(k), are voluntary.
- Payroll information is recorded in the salaries expense account. Deductions become liabilities and are recorded in separate accounts as payables.
- To establish an inventory control system, know the amount of merchandise sold, what items are selling, and what items are not.
- Perpetual inventory systems are possible with bar code scanning and point-of-sale terminals. To keep a periodic inventory system up-to-date, regular physical counts are required.
- The specific identification method works for businesses that sell few, high-priced items. For first in, first out (FIFO) costing, the first items sold are the first bought. For last in, first out (LIFO) costing, the first items sold are the last bought.
- Inventory turnover is calculated by dividing the cost of merchandise sold in a time period by the average inventory.

Communicating Key Terms

Using the terms below, write questions a store owner would ask a payroll-and-inventory service.

- payroll
- gross earnings
- salary
- hourly wage
- overtime rate
- commission
- deductions
- Federal Insurance Contributions Act (FICA)
- Social Security tax
- Medicare tax
- total gross earnings
- perpetual inventory system
- point-of-sale terminals
- periodic inventory system
- specific identification method
- first-in, first-out method (FIFO)
- last-in, first-out method (LIFO)

Reviewing Key Concepts

1. **Explain** why using computers makes the steps in the payroll system easier.
2. **Describe** the types of jobs that get paid by salary, wages, and commission.
3. **Identify** some required payroll deductions.
4. **Explain** how the rules of debit and credit apply to employee deductions.
5. **List** information needed for an inventory control system.
6. **Explain** why the perpetual inventory system is preferable for most businesses.
7. **Describe** the FIFO costing method and the LIFO costing method.
8. **Explain** inventory turnover analysis.

See the Teacher Manual for answers.

ACADEMIC SKILLS

Art The prices of merchandise are advertised on television and in print ads, and are even painted on store-front windows. Pricing is one of the most important tools retailers use to promote their businesses.

Design Choose a product that you would like to advertise in a print ad. Research the typical prices for this product and set a reduced price for a clearance sale at the mall. Using markers, crayons, paint, cut-outs from magazines, or computer graphics, create an ad displaying the product and its sale price.

YOUR FINANCIAL FIGURES

Salary vs. Commission Marika is a salesperson who earns the following amount:

Base salary: $27,000; sales commission: 6.5 percent

Monthly sales reported:

January	$10,300	April	$42,000
February	$17,000	May	$53,000
March	$35,300	June	$72,000

1. **Calculate** Marika's gross pay in salary and commissions for January through June.
2. **Compute** by using spreadsheet software to make these calculations.

REAL-WORLD Application

Connect with Government In 2005, the United States federal government started discussing the option of allowing younger workers to handle the investment of part of their Social Security contributions.

1. **Research** Access the Internet and find the reasons different groups, such as A.A.R.P., are for or against this proposal.
2. **Think Critically** What is your opinion about this issue? Explain the reasoning behind your view.

Internet CONNECTION

Just-in-Time Inventory (JIT) Industries have reduced the cost of storing and carrying inventories by requiring just-in-time inventory from their suppliers.

Log On Use the Internet to research just-in-time inventory systems and their requirements. Answer the following questions:

1. What industries seem to use this system the most?
2. How does a business's relationship with suppliers change under this system?

BusinessWeek ONLINE

Newsclip: More Demand There is demand when companies bolster their assembly lines and inventories, which eventually creates more supply.

Log On Go to finance07.glencoe.com and open Chapter 21. Learn more about how companies stock up their inventories. Think about a product that is in high demand. Write it down and compare your response with your classmates' responses.

WHAT'S YOUR FINANCIAL **ID?**

STOCKING UP ON KNOWLEDGE

Whether you plan to work for a company or imagine running your own business some day, here is a chance to test yourself on some business basics. Write your answers on a separate sheet of paper. After you finish studying the chapter, take the quiz again to see how much you have learned.

1. After federal, state, and local taxes are subtracted from a paycheck, the amount of money left is called ____b____.

a. gross pay
b. net pay
c. salary
d. wages

2. The various amounts of money that are subtracted from an employee's paycheck are called ____d____.

a. taxable incomes
b. co-payments
c. withholdings
d. deductions

3. The agency that collects federal taxes and oversees the federal income tax system is called the ____b____.

a. Social Security Administration
b. Internal Revenue Service
c. Big Brother
d. U.S. Treasury

4. A fixed amount of money that is paid to an employee for each pay period is called ____b____.

a. wage
b. salary
c. commission
d. allowance

5. The system of physically counting merchandise on hand is called ____d____.

a. spot-checking inventory system
b. unit control system
c. point-of-sale inventory system
d. periodic inventory system

6. The number of times a business sells its inventory in a given period of time is called ____d____.

a. margin
b. markup
c. unit control
d. inventory turnover

Your Financial Portfolio

Keeping Track of Inventory

Janine is helping to count inventory at her mother's jewelry store, The Silver Parrot. She thas been working on birthstone pendants. After she counted them, she looked up how many were on order. Then she filled in the number to order, based on the guideline of always keeping at least five pendants in stock.

Description	Number in Stock	Number on Order	Number to Order	
January	2	3	0	(10)
February	5	0	0	(10)
March	0	3	2	(12)
April	0	3	2	(12)
May	1	3	1	(11)
June	4	3	0	(8)
July	3	3	0	(9)
August	3	0	2	(12)
September	2	0	3	(13)
October	4	0	1	(11)
November	2	3	0	(10)
December	1	3	1	(11)

Calculate

Before the new products were ordered, Janine's mother decided to change the guideline to "always keep 15 of each pendant in stock," rather than five. On a separate sheet of paper, calculate how many additional birthstone pendants Janine should order for the store.

CHAPTER 22

Pricing, Costing, and Growth

$ What You'll Learn

When you have completed this chapter, you will be able to:

Section 22.1

- Explain how to calculate selling price.
- Identify variable and fixed costs.
- Discuss effective pricing.

Section 22.2

- Describe different forms of business growth.
- Discuss profit planning.
- Explain how to calculate target sales and margin of safety.
- Explain the importance of planning for growth.

Reading Strategies

To get the most out of your reading:

Predict what you will learn in this chapter.
Relate what you read to your own life.
Question what you are reading to be sure you understand.
React to what you have read.

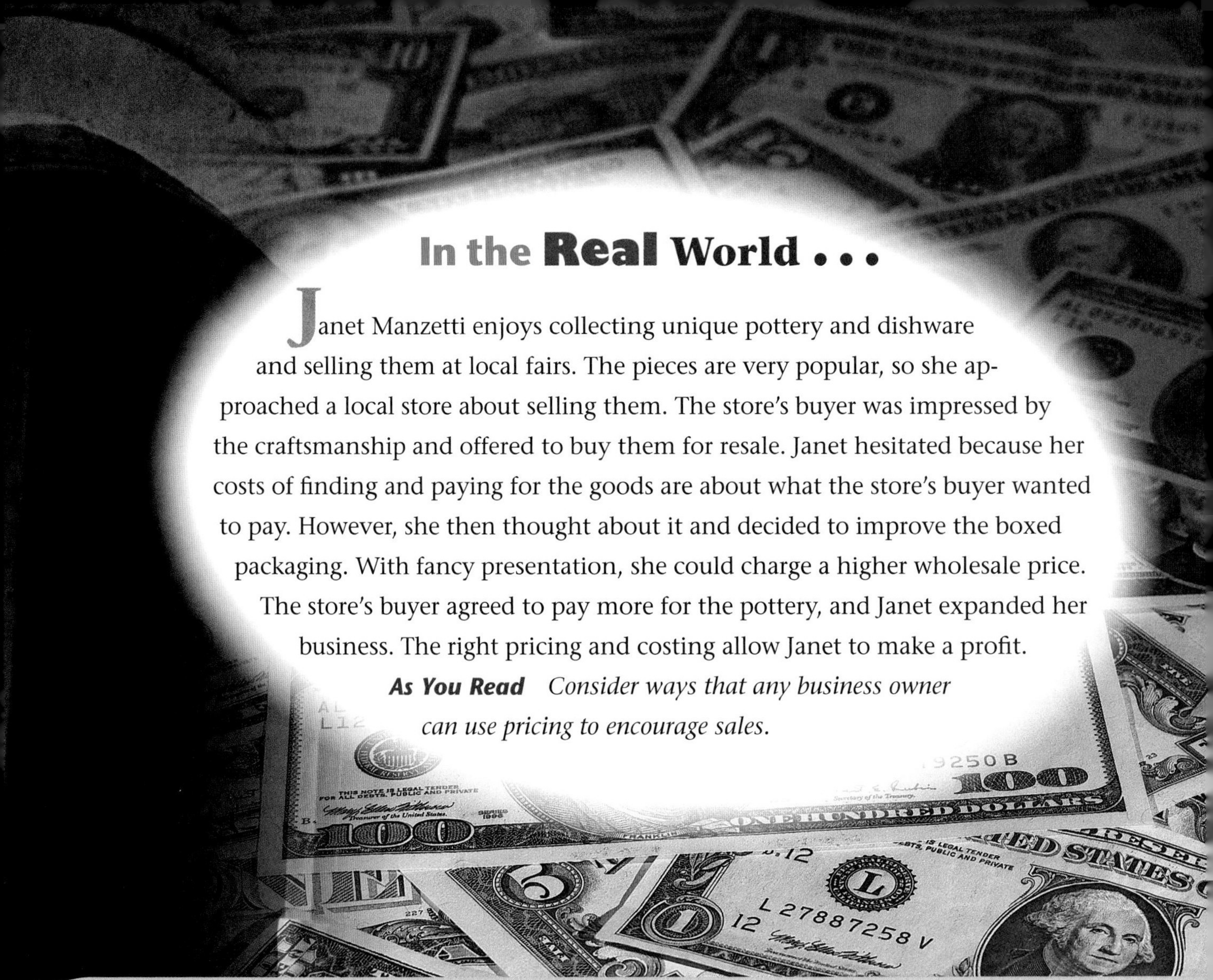

In the **Real** World . . .

Janet Manzetti enjoys collecting unique pottery and dishware and selling them at local fairs. The pieces are very popular, so she approached a local store about selling them. The store's buyer was impressed by the craftsmanship and offered to buy them for resale. Janet hesitated because her costs of finding and paying for the goods are about what the store's buyer wanted to pay. However, she then thought about it and decided to improve the boxed packaging. With fancy presentation, she could charge a higher wholesale price. The store's buyer agreed to pay more for the pottery, and Janet expanded her business. The right pricing and costing allow Janet to make a profit.

As You Read *Consider ways that any business owner can use pricing to encourage sales.*

Lesson Plan See the Teacher Manual for the Chapter 22 planning guide and lesson plan.

ASK STANDARD & POOR'S

Selling Price

Q: I started making scarves and hats for my friends for fun, but demand for them has become so high that I am thinking of selling them. How much do I charge?

A: Your selling prices should be close to what your competitors charge. Make sure that your business will be profitable at those prices. For many businesses, profit margins are only in the 10 to 15 percent range. For each $1 in sales, the business keeps ten cents—making accurate pricing essential.

Ask Yourself How do you find out what competitors charge?

@ Go to **finance07.glencoe.com** to complete the Standard & Poor's Financial Focus activity.

Section 22.1

Merchandise Pricing and Costing

Focus on Reading

Read to Learn

- How to calculate selling price.
- How to identify variable and fixed costs.
- How to discuss effective pricing.

Main Idea

Effective pricing and costing are essential factors for a business's financial success.

Key Terms

- pricing
- product cost-plus pricing
- markup
- manufacturing business
- product costing
- cost behavior
- variable costs
- direct materials
- direct labor
- fixed costs
- contribution margin
- break-even point

Before You Read

PREDICT

What factors do you think a retailer should consider when setting prices for merchandise?

Springboard Ask the students if they have ever made anything that someone else wanted to buy. Did they think of a price?

Pricing

Why is pricing important to a business?

Pricing is the process of assigning a selling price to a good or service. Price is usually expressed in monetary terms, such as $60 for a pair of shoes. It can also be expressed in non-monetary terms, such as free goods or services in exchange for the purchase of a product. The oldest form of pricing is the barter system, which involves exchanging a good or service for another good or service without the use of money. For a merchandise business, you must price goods and services appropriately for your business to succeed. If you set monetary prices too high, customers may buy from your competition—or not buy at all. If you set prices too low, you may not be able to cover your costs and operating expenses.

Goals of Pricing

Many factors influence the prices of goods and services. Pricing decisions must take into account costs, competition, and economic conditions. To make sound pricing decisions, a business owner must consider the goals of pricing.

Every business owner wants to set effective prices that yield large profits. Most businesses have three goals that act as guidelines for effective pricing:

- To obtain a given share of the market
- To generate sales that produce a specific profit
- To meet competitors' prices

In establishing prices, a business may have to prioritize these three goals. For example, suppose that a primary goal of your new outdoor sportswear business is to match your competitors' prices. You must remember that if you set your prices too low, you may not generate enough profit for your business to succeed. Suppose that the primary goal of your business is to increase profits. You can achieve your objective by selling more items at the current price or by selling the same number of items at a higher price. However, if you raise prices to increase profits, you may no longer meet competitors' prices. You must decide which pricing goals are most important to your business.

Merchandise Pricing

How do retail businesses price merchandise they sell?

Motivating Students Ask students if they have ever found the same item in different stores at different prices? Why were the prices different?

All the financial procedures you have learned so far have involved merchandising businesses. A merchandising business buys goods, marks them up, and sells them to customers, such as retail stores. Establishing selling prices in this type of business is relatively simple.

Retail Pricing Methods

A retail business sells goods or services to the final user, the consumer. One pricing method commonly used by retail businesses is product cost-plus pricing. **Product cost-plus pricing** is the process of determining an item's selling price by adding the invoice cost of the item (how much the business paid for the item) to a certain percentage of that cost. This added amount is the **markup**, which is the difference between the cost of an item to a business and the selling price of the item. This markup amount must cover all of the business's expenses and allow for a profit.

For example, Luggage World is a retail store that sells a wide variety of travel bags and suitcases. As merchandise is received, the store manager prices all bags with a 70 percent markup. Suppose that the Presidential Bag has an invoice cost of $48. The manager calculates the selling price as follows:

Purchase cost	$48.00	
Plus markup	+ 33.60	($48.00 × .70 or 70%)
Selling price	$81.60	

◀ ANNOUNCING PRICES Newspaper and magazine advertisements are sources for information on what competitors are charging for goods. *Do you think a business should always match competitors' selling prices? Why?*

Caption Answer Accept all reasonable answers.

As You Read

RELATE

Think about sales where you have "gotten a bargain." What do you think the retailer reduces to come up with a sale price?

Research Divide the students into groups of three or four. Ask each group to choose a product and research the price of that product at three different stores. Have each group share their findings with the class.

Caption Answer The store must cover all of its costs with only a few sales. This means that the store has to put a high markup on items.

Adjusting Prices

If you cannot sell an item or a line of merchandise with a particular markup, you may have to lower the selling price or discontinue stocking the item. The decision to mark up items by a certain percentage will depend on factors such as economic conditions, competition, or the season of the year.

Suppose that you purchase sweatshirts for your outdoor sportswear shop at $12 per shirt and price each one with a markup of 60 percent ($12 × .60 or 60% = $7.20). The retail price of each sweatshirt is $19.20 ($12 + $7.20 = $19.20). However, if your competitors are selling the same sweatshirts for $17.99 each, you will probably have difficulty selling your sweatshirts with a 60 percent markup. If you lower your price to be competitive, you may not earn enough profit to cover your expenses. If you cannot purchase the same sweatshirts from another supplier at a lower cost, you may have to sell a different line of sweatshirts.

The percentage of markup will vary depending on the line of merchandise you are selling. Stores (such as jewelry stores) that sell very few items in a day have higher markup percentages than stores (such as music stores) that sell many items in a day. Regardless of the product, the markup must cover expenses and generate a profit for the business.

▲ **EXPENSIVE ITEMS** A jewelry store may have only a few potential customers each day and will sell merchandise to only a small percentage of them. *Why does a jewelry store have to set high prices on its merchandise?*

Costing and Pricing in a Manufacturing Business

How does costing affect pricing for manufacturing businesses?

Critical Thinking Would the markup percentage be higher or lower than 60 percent if you sold the sweatshirt for $16.99?

Not all businesses simply purchase items, mark them up, and resell them to customers. Some businesses produce new merchandise. These businesses are called manufacturing businesses. A **manufacturing business** is a business that buys raw materials or processed goods and transforms them into finished products.

For example, if Tonya decides to sell hand-decorated handbags to her friends, her business will be a manufacturing business. She purchased a plain bag and decorated it, using paints, buttons, and sewing materials to create a desirable new item. Tonya will have to consider the cost of the materials and labor that go into the production of her first bag before she can determine an appropriate price for similar bags. Determining costs and pricing in a manufacturing business is more complicated than it is in a retail business.

Extension Ask the students if they can think of businesses in your community that emphasize the price of their products when they advertise. (Examples: a discount clothing store or a warehouse store such as SAM's Club)

Careers in Finance

CHIEF FINANCIAL OFFICER

Alberto Saenz
Cycle Gear

Alberto loves to make short-term goals that help achieve long-term ones. As the chief financial officer (CFO) for a chain of motorcycle parts, accessories, and clothing retailers, Alberto is expected to direct the company's overall financial policies, procedures, and reporting that are required to continue a 30 percent per year growth rate with increasing profitability. He manages all financial functions, including accounting, budgeting, cash flow, bank relationships, risk, inventory management, and taxes. Besides knowledge of accounting, CFOs need to know federal and state laws and regulations as well as international trade.

SKILLS: Accounting, analytical, communication, computer, decision making, math, problem solving, and long-range planning skills

PERSONAL TRAITS: Able to see the big picture, able to cope with stress, flexible, good judgment, independent, likes working with people and numbers, and tactful

EDUCATION: High school diploma or equivalent; bachelor's degree or master's degree in accounting, economics, finance, or business administration; Certified Public Accountant certification

ANALYZE Why would a CFO need to understand pricing principles?
See the Teacher Manual for answer.

To learn more about career paths for chief financial officers, visit **finance07.glencoe.com**.

Discussion As a class, create a list of manufacturing businesses in your community or state.

Product Costing

Product costing is the process of analyzing all costs involved in creating products. By product costing, you can establish a selling price that is both competitive and profitable for your business.

Product costing will help Tonya decide whether she can sell hand-decorated bags for a reasonable price. Her costs for the first bag might be low. Thus, she could make and sell similar bags at a profit. However, making the first bag could be expensive. To cover costs, she would have to set a high price. The price may be so high that no one would buy the bags. Thus, Tonya could decide that the bags are not worth making.

STANDARD & POOR'S

Global Financial Landscape

Standard and Poor's publishes the globally recognized S&P 500® financial index. It also gathers financial statistics, information, and news, and analyzes this data for international businesses, governments, and individuals to help them guide their financial decisions.

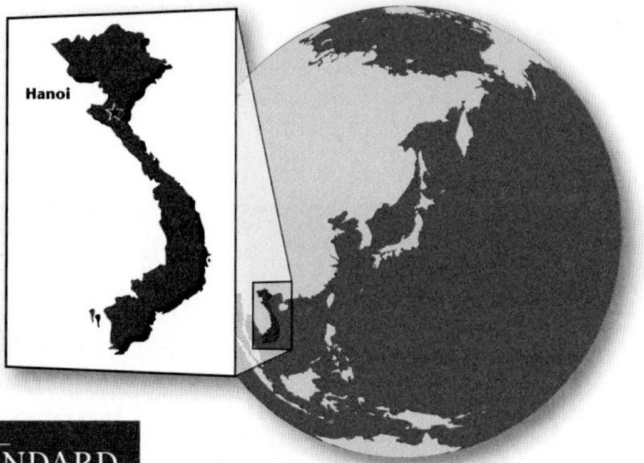

VIETNAM

The Vietnamese have a saying: "Close the past, open the future." When American troops pulled out of Vietnam at war's end in 1975, they were the enemy. Today they are welcomed as friends. The Vietnamese have opened up former war-related sites as part of The Vets' Tour, adding one more market to their soaring economy. In the last decade, the country's economy has grown 7.4 percent a year. Two of the most famous exhibits include the "Hanoi Hilton," a war prison, and the Cu Chi tunnels. This underground, 75-mile-long maze hid thousands of guerilla soldiers. Now widened to accommodate tourists, the tunnels display mess halls, meeting rooms, and a small cinema.

Tourism is a growth industry in Vietnam. Many hotels have been rated at three to four stars, and investors such as Disney are developing resorts. Focusing on cultural, ecological, and business tourism, Vietnam may attract 7.5 million visitors by 2010.

STANDARD & POOR'S **DATABYTES**

Capital	Hanoi
Population	80,786,000
Languages	Vietnamese, English, French, Chinese, Khmer, and local languages
Currency	dong
Gross Domestic Product (GDP)	$203.9 billion (2003 est.)
GDP per capita	$2,500

Industry: Food processing, garments, shoes, and machine manufacturing

Agriculture: Paddy rice, corn, potatoes, rubber, poultry, and fish

Exports: Oil, marine products, rice, coffee, and rubber

Natural Resources: Phosphates, coal, manganese, bauxite, and chromate

Think Globally
How might pricing and costing affect Vietnam's tourist industry?

See the Teacher Manual for answer.

◀ **THEY'RE HOT!** Items that are in great demand, such as barbecues during warm weather, rarely go on sale during the summer months. *What might be the reason for this?*

Caption Answer Stores can sell items such as barbecues, air conditioners, and fans without giving customers the incentive to buy just because it is a good price. Customers are motivated by other demands—recreation and heat.

Classifying Costs

What are the different types of costs to consider?

Whether you are the manager of a large business, such as General Electric, or a small business, such as a local bakery, you need complete information about costs to make smart financial decisions. You must identify your costs and determine what costs will increase, and what costs will remain the same.

Cost behavior is the way a cost changes in relation to a change in business activity. For example, as your business makes more items, some costs may increase, such as the costs of additional materials or labor. Other costs remain constant and are not influenced by the number of items you produce or the volume of sales. These costs could include rent, taxes, and insurance. In analyzing cost behavior, you will usually classify costs as variable or fixed.

Variable Costs

In product costing, **variable costs** are costs that change in direct proportion to the activity level of production. This means that if production increases, these costs will increase. If production decreases, your variable costs will decrease.

To understand cost behavior, consider the example of Windy River Creations. Wayne and Naomi are Native Americans who want to start a small business producing handmade Native American jewelry. They intend to buy metal bands, beads, leather, and other materials and make items to sell to area stores. They have rented a small shop, purchased a few pieces of equipment, bought materials and supplies, and hired two local artists to make the jewelry.

Windy River has identified three variable costs. These are (1) direct materials used to make the jewelry, (2) direct labor to create the jewelry, and (3) supplies used in processing the jewelry.

Common Cents Accept all reasonable answers that show an understanding of the concept. Possible answer might be utilities, labor, and materials.

Common CENTS

Business Expenses
When planning for expenses that will affect the prices of the products you sell, consider your operating expenses. The top ten small business expenses include: health insurance, DSL or dial-up Internet fees, cell phone fees, utilities, advertising, accounting services, voice mail, financial planning services, and collection services. *Choose a small business that you would like to own. If you were looking for ways to cut back on your business expenses, what areas would you target and why?*

Academic Connection

MATH

Imagine you have a retail business selling widgets, doodads, and thingamabobs. You want to determine the selling price for each. You have costs, such as rent and labor plus the items' wholesale costs. *Figure the markup at 70% and the price for each item:*

Item	Costs
Widgets	$1.32
Doodads	$4.80
Thingamabobs	$8.74

See the Teacher Manual for answer.

Direct Variable Costs **Direct materials** are the raw materials used to make a finished product. For Windy River's jewelry, these materials include metal, beads, leather, pins, packaging, and other items. Wayne and Naomi plan to produce five pieces of jewelry, one of which is the Sunset Bracelet. The direct materials needed to produce each bracelet cost $4.30.

Direct labor is the work required to convert raw materials into a finished product. To determine the cost of direct labor, multiply the amount of time spent to produce the item by the employee's hourly wage. Wayne and Naomi are paying their employees $12 per hour. It takes approximately 15 minutes (0.25 hours) to make the Sunset Bracelet. Therefore, the cost of direct labor per bracelet is $3 (0.25 × $12 = $3).

Wayne and Naomi now know that the cost of materials and labor needed to make the bracelet is $7.30 ($4.30 direct materials plus $3 direct labor). They must also take into account the cost of the supplies that will be consumed in the production process. This cost could include polish, wire, solder, glue, and finishing spray. Wayne and Naomi estimate that the cost of the supplies for one bracelet is $0.35. This brings the total variable cost per bracelet to $7.65, illustrated as follows:

Direct materials	$4.30
Direct labor	3.00
Supplies	0.35
Total variable cost	$7.65

As more units are made, the variable cost assigned to each unit remains the same, but the total variable cost for the business increases. When fewer units are made, total variable costs decrease. The table below shows how the total variable cost for Windy River increases or decreases depending on the number of Sunset Bracelets made.

	Unit Variable Cost				Total Variable Cost
7 Bracelets	$7.65	×	7	=	$53.55
10 Bracelets	$7.65	×	10	=	$76.50
18 Bracelets	$7.65	×	18	=	$137.70

Fixed Costs

Rent, insurance, taxes, salaries, and some utilities are examples of fixed costs. **Fixed costs** are costs that remain constant even if activity or production level changes. The total fixed cost remains the same regardless of the number of units produced.

For example, Wayne and Naomi pay $700 per month to rent the shop that Windy River occupies. Regardless of the number of bracelets produced in a month, the fixed cost of rent will remain at $700. Remember, the selling price of the bracelets must exceed all fixed costs plus all variable costs in order for Windy River to make a profit.

Extension Ask the students to discuss other fixed and variable costs that Windy River might have.

◀ **LABOR INTENSE** Many manufacturing companies use robots to assemble products. *What are some advantages of using robots instead of human beings?*

Caption Answer Students may say that using robots keeps the cost of direct labor lower than it would be by using human beings. Robots do not need benefits, do not get hurt, and do not get sick.

Selling Price

How do businesses determine the selling price for goods?

Wayne and Naomi plan to mark up the variable costs by approximately 70 percent in order to cover the fixed costs and show a profit. The total monthly fixed costs for the business are $1,400. Windy River is selling five types of jewelry, so each type must cover one-fifth, or 20 percent, of the fixed costs per month. Therefore, each type of jewelry must cover $280 in fixed costs per month ($1,400 × .20 or 20% = $280).

If the variable costs total $7.65 for each bracelet and a 70 percent markup is added, the selling price of the bracelet will be $13 ($7.65 + [$7.65 × .70 or 70%] = $13). Wayne and Naomi must determine whether this markup is sufficient. To do so, they will have to figure out how many bracelets they must sell to cover both fixed and variable costs.

The Contribution Margin

What is the contribution margin?

The **contribution margin** is the amount of money that the sale of a particular product contributes toward the payment of fixed costs and the profit of a business. The contribution margin equals total sales minus total variable costs. For example, if a product has sales of $13,000 and has variable costs totaling $7,000, it has a contribution margin of $6,000. This is the product's contribution to cover the fixed expenses and provide a profit.

Sales	$13,000	
Minus variable costs	– 7,000	
Contribution margin	$ 6,000	(Amount available for fixed expenses)

WebQuest

Franchise Ownership
What skills and abilities make a business leader effective? Learn more about leadership and imagine yourself as a great business leader.

@ To continue with Task 5 of your WebQuest project, visit **finance07.glencoe.com**.

Document Detective

Learn to identify and understand the standard financial documents you will use in the real world.

See the Teacher Manual for answers.

Investigate: A Break-Even Analysis
A break-even analysis contains the following information:
- Names of the products analyzed
- Unit pricing and fixed and variable expenses
- Calculation for number items that must be sold to break even

Your Motive: If you manage or own a retail store, you need to analyze your merchandise pricing, costs, and sales to determine when you are making a profit. The Break-Even Analysis Worksheet can help you determine profitability.

Break-Even Analysis Worksheet

Store: Sallie's Accessories
Location: 129 Fashion Way
Skokie, Illinois
Product Line: Jewelry
Period: Six months beginning June 2008

Item	Unit Price (*P*)	Variable Costs per Unit (*V*)	Fixed Costs (*F*)	Units to Breakeven (*n*) $Pn = Vn + F$
Watches	$49.99	$23.25	$2,000	75
Necklaces	$79.95	$29.50	$2,000	40
Rings		$40.00	$2,000	40
Bracelets	$19.95	$4.50	$2,000	130
Earrings	$41.50	$12.00	$2,000	68

Key Points: Fixed costs can include such expenses as rent, utilities, insurance, advertising, and administrative expenses.

Find the Solutions
1. What are the total fixed costs assigned to the jewelry department for the six-month period?
2. What is the break-even point for necklaces?
3. Which item has the highest markup?
4. What would happen to the break-even point if Sallie raised the price of the bracelets?
5. How much does a ring cost at Sallie's?

The Break-Even Point

Why do businesses that sell products want to know the break-even point?

The **break-even point** is the point at which total sales equal total costs (variable and fixed costs). The break-even point represents the sales that a business must achieve to break even, or cover all costs. At the break-even point, there is neither a profit nor a loss.

Calculating the break-even point helps a business owner predict how changes in costs and sales will affect the profit earned by the business. The break-even analysis can also determine how many units of a product must be made and sold to cover expenses.

For example, suppose that you wanted to calculate how many units of the Sunset Bracelet that Wayne and Naomi would have to sell to break even, or cover all costs. Represent the number of units needed to break even by a variable such as n. On the left side of the equation, multiply unit sales price by n. On the right side of the equation, multiply the unit variable costs by n, then add the total fixed costs. Solve for n.

Break-even sales are the sales, expressed as a dollar amount that a business must make to cover all costs. Break-even sales for the Sunset Bracelet are \$689 (53 bracelets × \$13 = \$689) per month. The following calculations show the accuracy of the math.

TechByte

Pricing Science When setting the price for a product, some businesses use product cost-plus pricing; some consider how the competition is priced; and some look at the break-even point. A variety of e-newsletters provide information covering case studies, marketing trends, and the latest product news on pricing strategy. This research can help businesses determine the best price for a product.

@ Learn more about pricing science and research and list resources through **finance07.glencoe.com**.

GO FIGURE — FINANCIAL MATH

BREAK-EVEN POINT

Synopsis: By calculating the unit variable cost of products to sell with the monthly fixed costs, a business can figure out how many units of a product must sell to break even.

Example: Windy River sells each Sunset Bracelet for \$13. The unit variable cost for the bracelet is \$7.65. The amount of monthly fixed costs that sales of the Sunset Bracelet are expected to contribute is \$280. How many units of the Sunset Bracelet must Windy River sell to break even?

Formula:

Break-Even Sales = Variable Costs + Total Fixed Costs

Unit Sales Price × n = (Unit Variable Costs × n) + Fixed Costs

Solution:

$$\$13.00n = \$7.65n + \$280.00$$
$$\$13.00n - \$7.65n = \$280.00$$
$$\$5.35n = \$280.00$$
$$n = \$280.00 \div \$5.35$$
$$n = 52.3 \text{ or } 53 \text{ bracelets}$$

To break even, Windy River must sell 53 Sunset Bracelets each month.

YOU FIGURE

Your sister is selling custom printed T-shirts at the beach on weekends. Fixed costs from sales total \$345. How many bracelets should she sell to break even if each T-shirt sells for \$20 and the unit variable cost is \$11.50 each?

Answer 41 T-shirts. \$20 - \$11.50 = \$8.50; \$345 ÷ 8.50 = 40.5 or 41 T-shirts

As You Read QUESTION

Define, in your own words, fixed costs, variable costs, and break-even point.

Question Answer Accept all reasonable answers that demonstrate students have read and understand the section.

	Total	Unit
Sales (53 × $13)	$689.00	$13.00
Less variable costs (53 × $7.65)	– $405.45	– $7.65
Contribution margin	$283.55	$ 5.35
Less fixed costs	– $280.00	
Net income	$ 3.55	

Fortunately for Wayne and Naomi, Windy River has been averaging sales of 70–80 bracelets per month for the past few months, exceeding their break-even point. At the present rate of sales, the bracelet's contribution margin is covering its share of fixed costs and is contributing to a net income for the business.

By substituting different numbers in the break-even equation, Wayne and Naomi can analyze how changes in sales price, costs, and sales volume affect profit. What if only 45 bracelets are sold? What if the variable costs increase by $2? How much profit is reported if 75 bracelets are sold? Such questions are an important part of financial analysis. If you are a business owner, you must anticipate changes in the market and be prepared with alternative plans if the changes actually occur. Using the techniques to analyze all financial possibilities and being prepared for change can help keep a business growing.

Critical Thinking Ask the students what changes in the market could occur that might impact Windy River.

Section 22.1 Assessment

See the Teacher Manual for answers.

QUICK CHECK

1. What are the basic goals that businesses use for setting prices?
2. What is the difference between variable costs and fixed costs in product costing?
3. What is the purpose of calculating the break-even point?

THINK CRITICALLY

4. Describe what might happen if a retail business sold its products to consumers for the same price it paid for them.

USE MATH SKILLS

5. **Break-Even Point** Dani sells mirrors at weekend craft shows for $75 each. She makes the mirror frames out of colored pieces of glass and ceramic tile. The mirrors are very popular, and Dani has more orders than she can fill.

Calculate Help Dani figure out how many mirrors she has to sell to break even. Dani estimates that her variable costs are $25 per mirror and her fixed costs are $1,000.

SOLVE MONEY PROBLEMS

6. **Establishing Retail Prices** Cookie Cutters is a retail store that sells a variety of kitchen gadgets and gifts. Today is your first day on the job there, and you have been asked to price the food processors that have just arrived. The manager has told you that all products have a 65 percent markup. The invoice price of one food processor is $72.

Calculate Figure out the selling price of each food processor.

Section 22.2

Planning for Growth

Sources of Business Growth

What are the different sources of business growth?

The key to all successful business operations is growth. Businesses, whether they are small sole proprietorships or large corporations, are much like people. They must grow and mature to achieve success. A business that does not grow can end up far behind its competition.

Business growth can come from many sources and can be measured in many ways. It may develop from an increase in the number of customers, sales, share of the market, employees, lines of merchandise, and (of course) profit. These are important aspects of growth for any business as well as indicators of success. However, growth should be carefully planned and directed. Sound financial planning is essential for making decisions regarding expansion.

Not every aspect of your business needs to grow every year. For a business, bigger does not necessarily mean better. If a business grows too rapidly or in the wrong area, serious financial problems may result.

Planning growth to correspond with the business's short-term and long-term goals is essential to financial success. If you have a business, short-term goals for the business reflect the areas to concentrate efforts. One year you may place an emphasis on increasing the number of customers; the following year, you may explore new lines of merchandise. As one of your target areas grows, others may also increase and grow. For example, if you concentrate on increasing your number of customers this year, your sales and profits should also report increases. Primary growth in one area often leads to secondary growth in other areas.

Customers

Adding new customers usually causes a rise in sales. More sales usually result in greater profits. Increasing the number of customers is always a primary goal in business. Acquiring new customers is often a result of two factors: effective advertising and promotions and referrals by satisfied customers. Potential customers must know where the business is located, and they must believe that buying goods and services from your business will be a positive experience. Although you may have control over your advertising and marketing programs, you have little or no control over customer referrals. Satisfying your customers' needs is the key to building a solid customer base.

Focus on Reading

Read to Learn

- How to describe different forms of business growth.
- How to discuss profit planning.
- How to calculate target sales and margin of safety.
- How to explain the importance of planning for growth.

Main Idea

To be successful, a business needs to make a profit but also must grow.

Key Terms

- target profit
- target sales
- margin of safety

Before You Read

PREDICT

In what ways do you think businesses can grow?

Springboard Write this statement on the board: "The key to successful business opportunity is growth." Ask the students to react to this statement.

Sales

Growth in sales is also a source of business growth. When sales increase, however, you must be capable of handling the larger volume so that you continue to satisfy your customers. If sales grow too quickly, and you do not have enough employees, the quality of your customer service may suffer seriously. In addition, you must be sure that you have sufficient merchandise to offer.

Market Share

A measurement of growth is the business's share of the existing market. If your business held approximately 15 percent of the potential market last year, and this year your market share has risen to 19 percent, you have achieved positive growth. This is evidence that your business is staying competitive, probably through effective advertising and promotions.

Market Development

A business can grow and expand its products to reach new locations locally, nationally, or even internationally. Franchising is one way to grow. Franchisers sell the right to operate a business under the company's name. In exchange for a fee, you the franchiser provide training, hiring, and other assistance such as manuals and market analyses.

Employees

As your market share grows and your sales increase, you must maintain an appropriate number of employees to contribute to growth. The need to hire more employees to accommodate your customers is a sign of positive growth. However, the additional employees should be utilized in the proper manner. Payroll is a major expense of your business.

Product Development

When expanding with a new line of merchandise, carefully analyze the potential market and estimate the profits to be made. Expanding for the sake of expansion is not always a source of positive growth. The new line should assure a new sales market and good profits. Unfortunately, many small businesses experience financial success only to expand to new areas that prove unprofitable.

Profits

One of the key indicators of the success of your business is the rate of growth of your profits. Making a profit is crucial to your business. Profits must grow for your business to survive. However, planning for increased profits is often easier said than done. Businesses may approach profit in several ways.

$avvy Saver

Avoiding Fees

1. Shop around for business checking accounts with low or no fees.
2. Pay your credit card and other bills in full each month on time.
3. Use a free Internet service.
4. Ask your telephone company for the best small business deal.
5. Return all equipment rentals on time to avoid late fees.

Motivating Students Ask the students if they think growth has to be planned and directed. Ask them why growth does not "just happen."

Discussion Ask the students to share positive and negative customer service experiences they have had as a consumer.

As You Read

RELATE

Can you think of a company that began offering more types of products than it had in the past?

◀ **HOW MANY CAN YOU SELL?** Stores are always faced with the problem of realistically predicting how many items can be sold. *What problem could result from stocking too many soccer balls?*

Caption Answer Soccer is a seasonal sport. Once the season is over, you would have to store most of the unsold balls until the next year.

Profit Planning

How can a business plan to make profits?

Business managers frequently evaluate cost and profit data to determine how to maximize profits. They use break-even analysis to test possible changes and to determine how those changes might affect future profits. Using the results of their analysis, managers forecast sales and plan financial activities for their business.

Extension Ask the students to find two or three advertisements (Hint: in newspapers, magazines, or mailings) that focus on acquiring you as a customer.

Setting a Target Profit

An important part of the planning process is setting goals. One common goal is to increase the amount of net income, or profit. **Target profit** is the amount of net income that a business sets as a goal. For example, you may want to expand to a new line of merchandise or possibly open another outlet or store. In order to fulfill these objectives, you will need to generate a given amount of profit.

Suppose that Wayne and Naomi want to earn a profit of $500 per month over the next six months on sales of the Sunset Bracelet. Assuming that the selling price and costs remain constant, how many bracelets would they need to sell to achieve this target profit?

Target sales is the number of units a business needs to sell to reach a target profit. The target sales equation is as follows:

Target Sales = Variable Costs + Fixed Costs + Target Profit

Question Answer Target profit is amount of net sales set as a goal, and target sales is the number of units needed to sell to reach the target profit.

As You Read

QUESTION

What is the difference between target profit and target sales?

GO FIGURE FINANCIAL MATH

TARGET SALES

Synopsis: Calculating how much product a business must sell to reach a profit is essential for success.

Example: Windy River sells each Sunset Bracelet for $13. The unit variable cost for the bracelet is $7.65. The amount of monthly fixed costs that sales of the Sunset Bracelet are expected to contribute is $280. The target profit is $500 per month. How many units of the Sunset Bracelet must Windy River sell to reach its target profit?

Formula:

Target Sales = Variable Costs + Fixed Costs + Target Profit

Unit Sales Price × n = (Unit Variable Costs × n) + Fixed Costs + Target Profit

Solution:

$13.00n	=	$7.65n + $280.00 + $500.00
$13.00n – $7.65n	+	$280.00 + $500.00
$5.35n	=	$780.00
n	=	$780.00 ÷ $5.35
n	=	145.7, or 146 bracelets

Windy River would have to sell 146 Sunset Bracelets to achieve its target profit.

YOU FIGURE

You are selling smoothies at school-sponsored sporting events. You price them at $3.50 each. The unit variable cost is $1.25 each. Your monthly fixed costs by sales should be $150. The target profit is $400 a month. How many smoothies should you sell?

Answer 244. $3.50 − $1.25 = $2.25; $150 + $400 = $550; $550 ÷ 2.25 = 244

Extension Ask the students to research a national company to find out its market share.

Using the target sales equation, you can calculate how many units a business must sell to reach its target profit. Represent the number of units needed to achieve the target profit by a variable such as *n*. On the left side of the equation, multiply the unit sales price by *n*. On the right side of the equation, multiply the unit variable costs by *n*. Then add fixed costs and the required profit. Solve for *n*.

Windy River has been selling about 70 to 80 bracelets per month, and sales have risen approximately 10 percent per month. By increasing current sales by approximately 10 percent a month for the next six months, Windy River will sell about 124 Sunset Bracelets per month by the sixth month. Assuming current sales are 70 per month, projected sales would be as follows:*

Month	1	77
	2	85
	3	94
	4	103
	5	113
	6	124

(*Assumes 10 percent increase in current sales per month.)

Teaching Activity Divide the class into groups of three or four. Ask each group to create a mini-lesson for figuring target sales and margin of safety. Have each group teach one of their lessons to another group.

Windy River would have to sell 146 bracelets per month to reach its target profit of $500. Wayne and Naomi decide that this is an unrealistic expectation. They conclude that a target profit of $400 is more realistic. Using the target sales calculation, they determine that they must sell 128 bracelets each month to achieve the goal of $400 profit per month.

Margin of Safety

When you are analyzing target sales and profits, you should consider what will happen if you do not reach your target. Your margin of safety will indicate the amount that sales can drop before the business experiences a loss. The **margin of safety** is the target sales minus the break-even sales, which indicates the amount of risk that sales will meet the break-even point. A high margin of safety suggests a minimal risk that sales will fall below the break-even point. Wayne and Naomi calculate the margin of safety for the Sunset Bracelet as follows:

Target sales (to achieve a profit of $400)	$1,664.00	128 bracelets
Less break-even sales	− 689.00	− 53 bracelets
Margin of safety	$975.00	75 bracelets

The margin of safety is $975, or 75 bracelets. This means that sales can drop by this amount below target sales before the business experiences a loss on this item. For Windy River, this target sales amount is a fairly safe venture.

Caption Answer Answers may include best-selling books, air conditioners and fans, sports team items, and school supplies.

▼ SHORT DEMAND Items such as seasonal clothes and CDs have a short selling period. Tastes in music and clothes change, and new items come out every day. *Can you name any other products that have a very short selling period?*

Put on Your Financial Planner's Cap

STANDARD &POOR'S

Imagine you are operating an athletic shoe store for teens. You plan to expand your merchandise lines. You can (a) sell shoes to other age groups, or b) sell other items to the teen market. Which expansion plan will you follow and why?

See the Teacher Manual for answer.

▲ **CONTROLLED EXPANSION** Expanding a small business such as a restaurant or boutique is good, but you should not expand too rapidly. *Can you name a business in your area that expanded but then had financial problems?*

Caption Answer Accept all reasonable answers.

The Challenges of Growth

What are the factors that might affect a business's ability to grow?

If your business is successful, it will probably grow. If you have planned effectively for growth, you will also experience growth. However, you should consider whether your business is ready or suited for growth. Several factors affect the ability of a business to grow:

- **Market characteristics**—If your niche market is too small, your business may be unable to grow. To develop further, the business must expand outside into new market areas.
- **Multiple sites**—With more than one location, you must decide where your main operations will be located. You will also need to staff your other locations.
- **Delegation**—Many small business owners are successful at starting their own businesses. However, they may not have the skills to manage others to do expanded tasks. You might consider hiring someone as a manager.
- **Industry innovation**—If your industry's growth is dependent upon innovation or constantly changing ideas and products, you will have to move ahead faster than the trends.
- **Systems and controls**—Effective systems and controls need to be in place for management, marketing, finances, and record keeping.

Planning and Growth

Why is planning so important?

As you project your business's financial prospects, you must analyze carefully where you will spend your profits. Growth is important, but only if it is carefully analyzed, planned, and controlled. Good planning will usually result in successful growth; poor planning could drive you out of business.

The following guidelines will not guarantee successful decisions, but ignoring them could result in business failure:

- Make sound financial decisions when setting short-term and long-term goals.
- Set realistic financial targets.
- Control expenses and costs.
- Analyze financial statements frequently.
- Analyze your competition.
- Evaluate current economic conditions.
- Maintain a reserve fund.

You may always have limited funds to invest for business growth. However, careful planning and financial analysis should provide you with the knowledge you will need for intelligent investment decisions and well-planned, controlled growth of your business.

After You Read

REACT

How can profits be used?

React Answer Accept all reasonable answers that show student effort and an understanding of the concept.

Extension Have the students draw a picture that describes each of the seven guidelines for growth.

Section 22.2 Assessment

See the Teacher Manual for answers.

QUICK CHECK

1. What are the common forms of business growth?
2. How is the target sales figure calculated?
3. How is margin of safety calculated?

THINK CRITICALLY

4. Explain why business growth just for the sake of growth is not wise.

USE COMMUNICATION SKILLS

5. Business Growth Lil owns an independent rug store in a small town. The Rug Rack has been open for about a year, and business has been very good. Currently she sells new and antique rugs as well as home decorating magazines. Lil thinks that it is time to add a new line of merchandise and expand her customer base.

Write About It You write an advice column for small business owners. What guidance might you give Lil regarding the goals she has set for The Rug Rack?

SOLVE MONEY PROBLEMS

6. Achieve Target Profit You have been hired by Windy River Creations as a business consultant. After analyzing the market for the company's products, you determine it is possible to earn a profit of $600 per month within the next six months on the Sunset Bracelet. Assume that the bracelet will continue to sell for $13 and that the costs will remain constant.

Calculate Figure out how many bracelets Windy River will need to sell in order to achieve this target profit.

Chapter 22 Review & Activities

See the Teacher Manual for answers.

CHAPTER SUMMARY

- In merchandising businesses, product cost-plus pricing is used: A markup based on the cost of the item is added to the actual cost. The markup percentage covers business expenses plus profit margin. In manufacturing businesses, product costing covers raw materials, plus the cost of processing them into finished products, plus profit.
- Variable costs, such as direct materials and direct labor, change in proportion to production levels. Fixed costs remain constant despite production level changes.
- By determining the contribution margin and break-even point, a business can set attractive prices that also ensure a profit for the business.
- Businesses grow by increasing customers, sales, market share, markets, number of employees, lines of merchandise, and profits.
- Profit planning occurs by setting target profit goals and estimating a margin of safety—target sales minus break-even sales.
- Target sales needed to reach a target profit is equal to variable costs, plus fixed costs, plus target profits. The margin of safety is the amount that sales can drop before the business experiences a loss. This is equal to the target sales minus the break-even sales.
- Planning for growth will enable you to grow in a controlled way and to be prepared and able to take advantage of growth opportunities when they appear.

Communicating Key Terms

Imagine you are a consultant assisting the owner of a florist shop in pricing her flowers and floral design services. Use as many of the key terms as you can to write a presentation on pricing.

- pricing
- product cost-plus pricing
- markup
- manufacturing business
- product costing
- cost behavior
- variable costs
- direct materials
- direct labor
- fixed costs
- contribution margin
- break-even point
- target profit
- target sales
- margin of safety

Reviewing Key Concepts

1. **Explain** why product cost-plus pricing would not work in a manufacturing business.
2. **Explain** why, in some cases, it may be beneficial to have more variable costs and to also reduce fixed costs.
3. **Explain** why the contribution margin is so important.
4. **Explain** why expanding into new lines of merchandise may not lead to business growth.
5. **Explain** why determining target profits is necessary to plan for business growth.
6. **Explain** why the margin of safety is so important to a business.
7. **Discuss** how your reserve fund can affect growth opportunities.

See the Teacher Manual for answers.

ACADEMIC SKILLS

Economics Clothing is often marked up more than 100 percent.

Write About It Write a paragraph explaining what this means in terms of the price you pay in the store. Include your analysis of factors that go into the price determination, other than the cost of the clothing before markup.

YOUR FINANCIAL FIGURES

Margin of Safety Target sales for Cricket Lane Flowers are $338,000 in its third year of operation. Break-even sales are estimated at $289,000 (estimated cost of goods sold + expenses for year three).

1. **Calculate** the margin of safety. Then explain your opinion of this level.
2. **Compute** as an alternative activity, using spreadsheet software to make these calculations.

REAL-WORLD Application

Connect with Economics and Business In economics, demand for a product usually grows gradually. Unfortunately, a business owner has to make large investments in lump sums to increase capacity to meet the growing demand. For example, investment in production facilities is made in large "jumps" while demand grows gradually.

1. **Role-Play** Imagine that Electro Toys has experienced great demand for its products and services, and its owner is thinking about opening two more stores, a major investment. How can she be sure that demand will continue to grow and use the additional supply she offers? With a partner, take on the roles of the shop's owner and a friend of hers who invested in her business when she first started it. They are discussing the business owner's thoughts about whether to expand.
2. **Write About It** Write a script about this discussion.

Internet CONNECTION

Competition You are considering opening a business providing home maintenance and "handyman" services. You realize that you will be competing with large plumbing repair companies and other specialists.

@ **Log On** Make a list of services you plan to offer. Then access an Internet search engine and find sources of such services in your town to evaluate the competition.

Write About It Write a marketing plan that explains how you will grow your business by promoting your services so that potential customers can differentiate you from the competition, and thus, increase your market share.

BusinessWeek ONLINE

Newsclip: The Right Price Smart pricing systems are Web-based systems that adjust prices to changing market conditions.

@ **Log On** Go to **finance07.glencoe.com** and open Chapter 22. Learn about the methods companies use to price goods. Write a list of some of your favorite things to buy and what they cost.

WHAT'S YOUR FINANCIAL ID?

CREATIVE THINKING

Successful businesses rely on a constant stream of ideas and people with the courage to present them. Do you have a lot of good ideas? Here is an opportunity to test your creative thinking. Write your answers on a separate sheet of paper.

1. Do you look for ideas?
Often Sometimes Rarely

2. Do you sometimes play "devil's advocate" as a way to stimulate others?
Often Sometimes Rarely

3. Do you challenge the rules?
Often Sometimes Rarely

4. Do you ask "what if" questions?
Often Sometimes Rarely

5. Can you motivate yourself and do what it takes to set your ideas in motion?
Often Sometimes Rarely

6. Do you use impractical ideas as stepping stones to new ideas?
Often Sometimes Rarely

7. Do you express silly ideas?
Often Sometimes Rarely

8. Do you challenge assumptions?
Often Sometimes Rarely

Scoring: Give yourself 5 points for each "often," 3 points for each "sometimes," and 0 points for each "rarely."

Beginner: If you scored 0–10 points, consider playing around with new ideas and presenting them. Ideas can be fun!

Explorer: If you scored 11–20 points, you are willing to stretch yourself.

Creator: If you scored 21–30 points, your input will be welcome on any team.

Brainstormer: If you scored 31–40 points, you take the lead in risky ideas that may result in big rewards.

Accept all reasonable answers that show student effort and an understanding of the concept.

Your Financial Portfolio

Business Expansion Magic

Under the name of Morgan the Magnificent, Victor Morgan has been performing magic since he was eight years old. Now that he is 16, he wants to branch out from school events and birthday parties for friends and family to perform professionally. He already has his own Web site and a performance video. To expand the business, he wrote down the following strategies and actions he could take:

- Make a flyer and a cover letter I can send out to potential customers.
- Contact a public relations agency and offer to do free performances in exchange for their helping me get publicity.
- Call the local newspaper and ask if someone could write an article about me.
- Contact the human resources department of local companies to let them know I am available to perform at employee functions and holiday parties.
- Contact local chambers of commerce to find out when they are having street fairs or crafts fairs.
- Contact local stores that sell or rent party supplies. Ask if I can post a flyer and if they can recommend me if anybody is looking for an entertainer.
- Contact wedding planners to see if they would recommend me to be part of the wedding entertainment.
- Stop by ice cream stores to find out if I can post a flyer.

Analyze

Pick a business in your town. On a separate sheet of paper, list eight strategies and actions that could improve or expand the business.

Accept all reasonable answers that show student effort and an understanding of the concept.

Unit 6 LAB

Get a Financial Life!

Growing a Business

Overview

Two years ago, Jack Lanier and his sister Eva opened their retail store called *Party Town.* They sell a wide variety of party decorations, paper goods, balloons, and games. The business has been a success so far. Eva and Jack have been able to meet their expenses each month and make a modest profit. Now they want to grow their business. They are interested in carrying a new line of merchandise and opening an online store with expanded inventory. With their regular customers, in addition to new Web-site customers from outside their area, they hope to gain a greater share of the market and expand their business now and in the future.

Resources & Tools

- Crayons, markers, colored pencils
- Internet (optional)
- Portfolio (ring binder or file folder)
- Public or school library
- Publication software (optional)
- Spreadsheet software (optional)
- Word processor

Procedures

STEP A **The Process**

Eva and Jack need help making a decision about what merchandise they should carry and the best type of Web site to develop.

1. Recommend a new product or line of merchandise that you think Party Town should carry. (Examples might include hard-to-find costumes, piñatas, or party favors.) Create a flyer, poster, or other visual aid describing the new product.
2. Research the competition (other party stores, discount stores, toy stores, and Internet sites), either by looking through the yellow pages or by visiting stores nearby. Describe Party Town's competition and its merchandise.
3. Interview a business owner of a similar business in town.
4. Eva and Jack also plan to sell balloon bouquets that they will make. The direct materials will cost $5.25; the direct labor per bouquet is $6; and the supply costs will be about $0.85. Assume that Party Town plans to mark up the bouquets by 80 percent. Figure out the selling price of each bouquet. If the fixed costs are $300, determine how many balloon bouquets Eva and Jack must sell to break even.
5. Help Eva and Jack set a target profit for the balloon bouquets. How many bouquets must they sell to achieve the target profit? Calculate the margin of safety for this product.
6. Research costs of starting a Web site with e-tail capability, such as costs of Internet service providers, design, and customer-service support.

STEP B Create Your Portfolio

As you work through the process, save the results so that you can refer, review, and refine. Create a professional-looking portfolio of the recommendations that you will present to Eva and Jack.

1. The first page should be a title page with the following information centered:
   Business Growth
   Presented to Eva Lanier and Jack Lanier, Owners
   Party Town
   By (Your Name)
2. The first section should include your flyer, poster, or other visual material describing the new merchandise and Web site that you have recommended to Eva and Jack.
3. The second section should present your research about the competition in your community and on the Internet.
4. The third section should include the selling price, break-even point, target profit, and margin of safety for the balloon bouquets. Include calculations. Also, include costs for operating a Web-site.

STEP C The Internet

Almost anything you want to know can be found on the Internet. It provides a vast communication network for people around the world. Students and employees must learn to use the available information wisely, ethically, and legally.

1. Write a definition for the term *ethics*.
2. Many employers have a formal policy that defines the acceptable and unacceptable uses of the Internet in the workplace. Write a policy that Eva and Jack might establish for their employees.
3. Research one legal issue that can arise when an employee uses the Internet, such as plagiarism, viruses, employers accessing employees' e-mail, or employees accessing the Internet for personal use. Write a one- to two-page paper on the issue.
4. Some people assume that everything appearing on the Internet is factual. However, this is not always the case. As a class, develop a list of ways to check the accuracy of information that you find.

Appendix: Math Skills Builder

WRITING NUMBERS AS WORDS AND ROUNDING NUMBERS

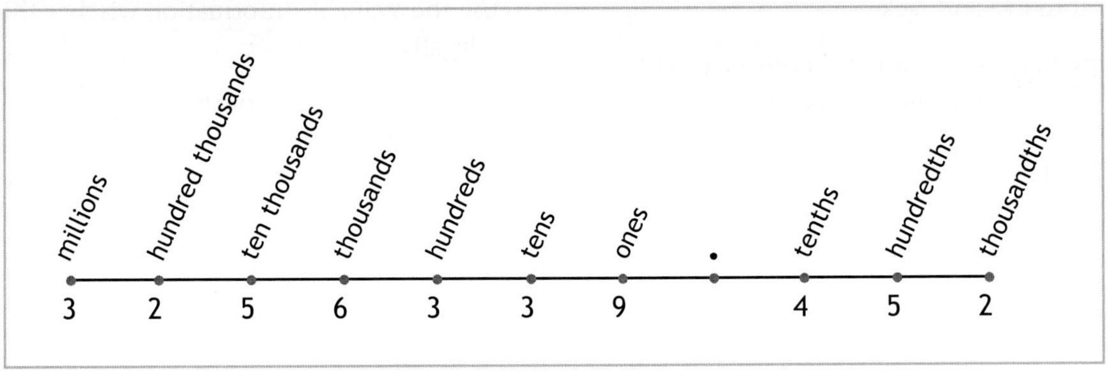

The place-value chart shows the value of each digit in the number 3,256,339.452. The place-value chart can help you write numbers.

EXAMPLE

482
8.557
$39.45

SOLUTION

four hundred eighty-two
eight and five hundred fifty-seven thousandths
thirty-nine and forty-five hundredths dollars
or thirty-nine and $^{45}/_{100}$ dollars

Place value is also used in rounding numbers. If the digit to the right of the place value you want to round is 5 or more, round up by adding 1 to the number in the place value. Then change all the digits to the right of the place value to zeros. If the number is 4 or less, round down by changing all the numbers to the right of the place value to zeros.

EXAMPLE Round 4765 to the nearest hundred.

SOLUTION

4765 — **A.** Find the digit in the hundred place. It is 7.

4765 — **B.** Is the digit to the right 5 or more? Yes.

4800 — **C.** Add 1 to the hundreds place. Change the digits to the right to zeros.

EXAMPLE Round 0.843 to the nearest tenth.

SOLUTION

0.843 — **A.** Find the digit in the tenth place. It is 8.

0.843 — **B.** Is the digit to the right 5 or more? No.

0.8 — **C.** Do not change the tenths digit. Drop the digits to the right.

WRITING NUMBERS AS WORDS AND ROUNDING NUMBERS

Dollar and cents amounts are often rounded to the nearest cent, or the hundredths place.

EXAMPLE

$26.7443
$683.1582

SOLUTION

$26.74
$683.16

PROBLEMS

Write as numbers.

1. three thousand four hundred ninety-nine — 3499
2. one hundred eleven and $^{32}/_{100}$ dollars — $111.32
3. two hundred six and eighty-eight thousandths — 206.088

Write in word form.

4. 572 — five hundred seventy-two
5. 2.897 — two and eight hundred ninety-seven thousandths
6. $325.10 — three hundred twenty-five and $^{10}/_{100}$ dollars

Round to the nearest place value shown.

7. ten thousand	327,975	330,000
8. thousand	816,777	817,000
9. hundred	26,312	26,300
10. ten	6336	6340
11. one	28.91	29
12. tenth	86.379	86.4
13. hundredth	5.5787	5.58

Round 23,793,611 to the place value shown.

14. millions — 24,000,000
15. ten millions — 20,000,000
16. thousands — 23,794,000
17. hundreds — 23,793,600
18. ten thousands — 23,790,000
19. hundred thousands — 23,800,000

Round to the nearest place value shown.

20. cent	$87.2671	$87.27
21. ten cents	$213.432	$213.40
22. one dollar	$671.98	$672.00
23. ten dollars	$5,982	$5,980
24. hundred dollars	$12,785	$12,800

APPLICATIONS

25. As an accountant for the advertising agency of Phillips & Phillips, Marcia Strasser writes many checks. Write each check amount in words.
    a. $27.83 — twenty-seven and $^{83}/_{100}$ dollars
    b. $121. 77 — one hundred twenty-one and $^{77}/_{100}$ dollars
    c. $569.14 — five hundred sixty-nine and $^{14}/_{100}$ dollars
    d. $8,721. 65 — eight thousand seven hundred twenty-one and $^{65}/_{100}$ dollars

26. Juan Sanchez, an inventory clerk for a lumber yard, often rounds inventory figures for easier handling. Round the number from the inventory list to the nearest ten.
    a. grade 1 oak — 519 ft. — 520
    b. grade 2 oak — 795 ft. — 800
    c. grade 1 pine — 323 ft. — 320
    d. grade 2 pine — 477 ft. — 480

ADDING AND SUBTRACTING DECIMALS

When adding decimals, write the addition problem in vertical form. Be sure to line up the decimal points. When adding amounts with different numbers of decimal places, write zeros in the empty decimal places.

EXAMPLE 15.27 + 16.39 + 36.19

SOLUTION

```
  15.27
  16.39
 +36.19
 ------
  67.85
```

EXAMPLE 58.2 + 3.97 + 8 + 123.796

SOLUTION

```
  58.2          58.200
   3.97          3.970
   8.            8.000
+123.796      +123.796
--------      --------
               193.966
```

When subtracting decimals, write the subtraction problem in vertical form. Be sure to line up the decimal points. When subtracting amounts with different numbers of decimal places, write zeros in the empty decimal places.

EXAMPLE 78.63 − 42.41

SOLUTION

```
  78.63
 −42.41
 ------
  36.22
```

EXAMPLE 149.9 − 28.37

SOLUTION

```
 149.9        149.90
 −28.37       −28.37
 ------       ------
              121.53
```

Adding and subtracting amounts of money is just like adding and subtracting decimals. The decimal point separates the dollars and cents. Remember to put a dollar sign in the total.

EXAMPLE $74.99 + $8.76

SOLUTION

```
 $74.99
  +8.76
 ------
 $ 83.75
```

EXAMPLE $750 − $43.29

SOLUTION

```
 $750.00
  −43.29
 -------
 $706.71
```

PROBLEMS

1. 19.87 + 32.24 + 27.55 = 79.66
2. 4.377 + 6.829 + 2.707 = 13.913
3. 8.3 + 12.78 + 322.437 = 343.517
4. 46.65 + 3.5 + 125.397 = 175.547
5. $ 2.77 + 35.96 + 10.37 = $ 49.10
6. 22.19 + 47.75 + 13.88 + 19.85 103.67
7. 0.78 + 9.82 + 36.242 + 37.4 84.242
8. 6.7 + 27.81 + 653.47 + 5.5 693.48
9. 54.32 + 0.37 + 2.5 + 0.797 57.987
10. $6.22 + $53.19 + $ .33 + $7.85 $67.59
11. $4.78 + $12.50 + $22 + $17.10 $56.38
12. 3.75 − 2.18 = 1.57
13. 376.55 − 27.42 = 349.13
14. 468.47 − 233.55 = 234.92
15. 367.05 − 219.87 = 147.18
16. $363.27 − 79.14 = $284.13

17. 547.7 – 127.6 420.10
18. 76.99 – 3.87 73.12
19. 695.13 – 428.1 267.03
20. 3076 – 2205.50 870.5
21. $300 – $5.75 $294.25
22. $445.19 – $175.76 $269.43

APPLICATIONS Complete the sales receipts by finding the subtotals and the totals.

23. a. 189.95 b. 203.25

Date	Auth. No.	Identification	Clerk	Reg./Dept.	☑ Take ❑ Send
6/1/--	86430		DL		

Qty	Class	Description	Price	Amount	
1		dress		77	98
1		jacket		85	99
2		hosiery	12.99 ea	25	98
a.	Freight charges will be included with your invoice at the time of shipping. You will be billed the published rates from UPS, US Postal Service.		Subtotal	?	
	CUSTOMER SIGNATURE X *Shelley Turner*		Tax	13	30
b.	Sales Slip		Total	?	

24. a. 879.83 b. 937.02

Date	Auth. No.	Identification	Clerk	Reg./Dept.	☑ Take ❑ Send
3/14/--	42		JR		

Qty	Class	Description	Price	Amount	
1		couch		599	95
1 pr		draperies		279	88
a.	Freight charges will be included with your invoice at the time of shipping. You will be billed the published rates from UPS, US Postal Service.		Subtotal	?	
	CUSTOMER SIGNATURE X *Betty Clark*		Tax	57	19
b.	Sales Slip		Total	?	

Complete the bank deposit slips by finding the subtotals and the total deposits.

25.

			DOLLARS	CENTS
CASH	CURRENCY		72	00
	COINS			
CHECKS	LIST SEPARATELY	95-76	413	12
		98-11	25	00
		95-13	211	10
a.	SUBTOTAL		?	
	LESS CASH RECEIVED		50	00
b.	TOTAL DEPOSIT		?	

a. 721.22
b. 671.22

26.

			DOLLARS	CENTS
CASH	CURRENCY		23	00
	COINS		7	44
CHECKS	LIST SEPARATELY	85-76	175	66
		88-11	23	33
			12	87
a.	SUBTOTAL		?	
	LESS CASH RECEIVED		75	00
b.	TOTAL DEPOSIT		?	

a. 242.30
b. 167.30

27.

			DOLLARS	CENTS
CASH	CURRENCY			
	COINS		4	75
CHECKS	LIST SEPARATELY	57-12	25	95
		57-10	38	11
	SUBTOTAL		?	
	LESS CASH RECEIVED		25	00
	TOTAL DEPOSIT		?	

a. 68.81
b. 43.81

28. You are a cashier at a coffee shop. Compute the correct change for each of the following orders.

	Customer's Order	Customer Gives You	Change
a.	$8.76	$10.00	$1.24
b.	$12.94	$15.00	$2.06
c.	$9.30	$10.50	$1.20
d.	$16.11	$20.00	$3.89
e.	$5.57	$5.75	$0.18
f.	$22.02	$25.00	$2.98
g.	$7.12	$7.15	$0.03
h.	$3.33	$5.00	$1.67
i.	$28.04	$30.04	$2.00
j.	$6.12	$10.25	$4.13

MULTIPLYING AND DIVIDING DECIMALS

When multiplying decimals, multiply as if the decimal numbers were whole numbers. Then count the total number of decimal places in the factors. This number will be the number of decimal places in the product.

EXAMPLE

$$\begin{array}{rl} 18.7 & \leftarrow \text{factor} \\ \times\ 0.34 & \leftarrow \text{factor} \\ \hline 748 & \\ 561 & \\ \hline 6358 & \leftarrow \text{product} \end{array}$$

SOLUTION

$$\begin{array}{rl} 18.7 & \leftarrow \text{1 decimal place} \\ \times\ 0.34 & \leftarrow +\ \text{2 decimal places} \\ \hline 748 & \\ 561 & \\ \hline 6.358 & \leftarrow \text{3 decimal places} \end{array}$$

If the product does not have enough digits to place the decimal in the correct position, you will need to write zeros. Start at the right of the product in counting the decimal places and write zeros at the left.

EXAMPLE

$$\begin{array}{r} 0.63 \\ \times\ 0.05 \\ \hline 315 \end{array}$$

SOLUTION

$$\begin{array}{rl} 0.63 & \leftarrow \text{2 decimal places} \\ \times\ 0.05 & \leftarrow +\ \text{2 decimal places} \\ \hline 0.0315 & \leftarrow \text{4 decimal places} \end{array}$$

When multiplying amounts of money, round the answer to the nearest cent. Remember to put a dollar sign in the answer.

EXAMPLE

$$\begin{array}{r} \$2.25 \\ \times\ 1.5 \\ \hline 3.375 \end{array}$$

SOLUTION

$$\begin{array}{rl} \$\ 2.25 & \leftarrow \text{2 places} \\ \times\ 1.5 & \leftarrow +\ \text{1 place} \\ \hline \$3.375 & \leftarrow \text{3 places} \end{array}$$

$\$2.25 \times 1.5 = \$3.375$
$= \$3.38$
rounded to the nearest cent

When multiplying by 10, 100, or 1000, count the number of zeros. Then move the decimal point to the right the same number of spaces.

EXAMPLE 8.32×100

SOLUTION $8.32 \times 100 = 8.32 = 832$ 100 has 2 zeros; move decimal 2 places.

PROBLEMS

1. $\begin{array}{r} 18.3 \\ \times\ 2.5 \\ \hline 45.75 \end{array}$
2. $\begin{array}{r} 27.5 \\ \times\ 8.2 \\ \hline 225.50 \end{array}$
3. $\begin{array}{r} 56.8 \\ \times\ 0.33 \\ \hline 18.744 \end{array}$
4. $\begin{array}{r} 88.1 \\ \times\ 0.23 \\ \hline 20.263 \end{array}$
5. $\begin{array}{r} 0.57 \\ \times\ 0.14 \\ \hline 0.0798 \end{array}$
6. $\begin{array}{r} 0.88 \\ \times\ 0.07 \\ \hline 0.0616 \end{array}$
7. $\begin{array}{r} 0.93 \\ \times\ 0.04 \\ \hline 0.0372 \end{array}$
8. $\begin{array}{r} 0.323 \\ \times\ 0.005 \\ \hline 0.001615 \end{array}$
9. $17.85 × 15.5 = $276.675 = $276.68
10. $25.24 × 6.3 = $159.012 = $159.01
11. $18.15 × 6.5 = $117.975 = $117.98
12. $14.98 × 8.7 = $130.326 = $130.33
13. 33.8 × 10 = 338
14. 55.399 × 100 = 5539.9
15. 0.518 × 1000 = 518
16. 532.788 × 10,000 = 5,327,880

MULTIPLYING AND DIVIDING DECIMALS

APPLICATION

17. Below are partial payroll records for Fanciful Flowers. Complete the records by calculating gross earnings (hourly rate x hours worked), Social Security tax (gross earnings × 0.062), Medicare tax (gross earnings × 0.0145), federal income tax (gross earnings × 0.15), and state income tax (gross earnings × 0.045). Round each deduction to the nearest cent. Find the total deductions and subtract from gross earnings to find the net pay.

	Employee	Hourly Rate	Number of Hours	Gross Earnings	Social Security Tax	Medicare Tax	Federal Inc. Tax	State Inc. Tax	Total Deductions	Net Pay
a.	M. Smith	$8.25	24	198.00	12.28	2.87	29.70	8.91	53.76	144.24
b.	R. Nash	$9.15	33	301.95	18.72	4.38	45.29	13.59	81.98	219.97
c.	C. Young	$7.75	15	116.25	7.21	1.69	17.44	5.23	31.57	84.68
d.	D. Cha	$9.15	30	274.50	17.02	3.98	41.18	12.35	74.53	199.97

When dividing decimals, if there is a decimal point in the divisor, you must move it to the right to make the divisor a whole number. Move the decimal point in the dividend to the right the same number of places you moved the decimal point in the divisor. Then divide as with whole numbers.

$$\begin{array}{rr} & 140 \\ 6 & \overline{)840} \end{array}$$

divisor 6; quotient 140; dividend 840

EXAMPLE

$3.44\overline{)15.5488}$

SOLUTION

$3.44\overline{)15.5488}$

$$\begin{array}{r} 4.52 \\ 344\overline{)1554.88} \\ -1376 \\ \hline 1788 \\ -1720 \\ \hline 688 \\ -688 \\ \hline \end{array}$$

Add zeros to the right of the decimal point in the dividend if needed.

EXAMPLE

$0.42\overline{)0.147}$

SOLUTION

$0.42\overline{)0.147}$

$$\begin{array}{r} 0.35 \\ 42\overline{)14.70} \\ -126 \\ \hline 210 \\ -210 \\ \hline \end{array}$$

zero added

When the dividend is an amount of money, remember to place the dollar sign in the quotient and round the answer to the nearest cent.

EXAMPLE

$48\overline{)\$95.12}$

SOLUTION

$$\begin{array}{r} \$1.981 \\ 48\overline{)\$95.120} \end{array}$$

$95.12 ÷ 48 = $1.98 rounded to the nearest cent.

MULTIPLYING AND DIVIDING DECIMALS

When dividing by 10, 100, or 1000, count the number of zeros in 10, 100, or 1000 and move the decimal point to the left the same number of places.

EXAMPLE

15,213.7 ÷ 1000

SOLUTION

15,213.7 ÷ 1000 = 15213.7 =15.2137 — 1000 has 3 zeros; move decimal 3 places

PROBLEMS

Round to the nearest hundredth or the nearest cent.

18. $2.7\overline{)11.61}$ 4.3
19. $1.3\overline{)7.67}$ 5.9
20. $6.2\overline{)44.02}$ 7.1
21. $0.3\overline{)1.62}$ 5.4
22. $.05\overline{)1.47}$ 29.4
23. $.04\overline{)28.4}$ 710
24. $8.3\overline{)46.99}$ 5.66
25. $3.4\overline{)178.3}$ 52.44
26. $88\overline{)\$356.68}$ \$4.05
27. $45\overline{)\$42.79}$ \$.95
28. $15\overline{)\$87.32}$ \$5.82
29. $14.1\overline{)7.823}$ 0.55

APPLICATIONS

30. Your family is looking into buying a late model, used vehicle. Calculate (to the nearest tenth) the gas mileage for the following types of vehicles.

	Type of Vehicle	Miles	Gallons of Fuel	Miles per Gallon
a.	Subcompact	631	17.8	35.4
b.	4-door sedan	471.4	16.6	28.4
c.	Minivan	405.1	18.2	22.3
d.	Compact	512.2	15.7	32.6
e.	SUV	298.1	23.2	12.8

FRACTION TO DECIMAL, DECIMAL TO FRACTION

Any fraction can be renamed as a decimal and any decimal can be renamed as a fraction. To rename a fraction as a decimal, use division. Think of the fraction bar in the fraction as meaning "divide by." For example, $^5/_8$ means "5 divided by 8." After the 5, write a decimal point and as many zeros as are needed. Then divide by 8.

EXAMPLE Change $^3/_8$ to a decimal.

SOLUTION

$$\frac{3}{8} \rightarrow \begin{array}{r} 0.375 \\ 8\overline{)3.000} \\ \underline{-24} \\ 60 \\ \underline{-56} \\ 40 \\ \underline{-40} \end{array}$$

EXAMPLE Change $^1/_5$ to a decimal.

SOLUTION

$$\frac{1}{5} \rightarrow \begin{array}{r} 0.2 \\ 5\overline{)1.0} \\ \underline{-10} \end{array}$$

If a fraction does not divide evenly, divide to one more decimal place than you are rounding to.

EXAMPLE Change $^5/_7$ to a decimal rounded to the nearest hundredth. (Divide to the thousandths place.)

SOLUTION

$$\frac{5}{7} \rightarrow \begin{array}{r} 0.714 = 0.71 \\ 7\overline{)5.000} \\ \underline{-49} \\ 10 \\ \underline{-7} \\ 30 \\ \underline{-28} \\ 2 \end{array}$$

EXAMPLE Change $^2/_7$ to a decimal rounded to the nearest thousandth. (Divide to the ten thousandths place.)

SOLUTION

$$\frac{2}{7} \rightarrow \begin{array}{r} 0.2857 = 0.286 \\ 7\overline{)2.0000} \\ \underline{-14} \\ 60 \\ \underline{-56} \\ 40 \\ \underline{-35} \\ 50 \\ \underline{-49} \\ 1 \end{array}$$

To rename a decimal as a fraction, name the place value of the digit at the far right. This is the denominator of the fraction.

$0.83 = {}^{83}/_{100}$

3 is in the hundredths place, so the denominator is 100.

$0.007 = {}^{7}/_{1000}$

7 is in the thousandths place, so the denominator is 1000.

Note that the number of zeros in the denominator is the same as the number of places to the right of the decimal point. The fraction should always be written in lowest terms.

$0.25 = {}^{25}/_{100} = {}^{1}/_{4}$

$3.375 = 3\,{}^{375}/_{1000} = 3\,{}^{3}/_{8}$

FRACTION TO DECIMAL, DECIMAL TO FRACTION

PROBLEMS

Change the fractions to decimals. Round to the nearest thousandth.

1. $^{2}/_{5}$ 0.4	2. $^{5}/_{6}$ 0.833	3. $^{4}/_{9}$ 0.444	4. $^{7}/_{10}$ 0.7
5. $^{9}/_{25}$ 0.36	6. $^{115}/_{200}$ 0.575	7. $^{1}/_{7}$ 0.143	8. $^{13}/_{40}$ 0.325
9. $^{4}/_{15}$ 0.267	10. $^{5}/_{12}$ 0.417	11. $^{11}/_{16}$ 0.688	12. $^{1}/_{4}$ 0.25

Change the fractions to decimals. Round to the nearest hundredth.

13. $^{1}/_{8}$ 0.13	14. $^{5}/_{9}$ 0.56	15. $^{33}/_{35}$ 0.94	16. $^{12}/_{25}$ 0.48
17. $^{7}/_{20}$ 0.35	18. $^{2}/_{25}$ 0.08	19. $^{15}/_{16}$ 0.94	20. $^{2}/_{9}$ 0.22
21. $^{3}/_{7}$ 0.43	22. $^{3}/_{4}$ 0.75	23. $^{1}/_{6}$ 0.17	24. $^{31}/_{32}$ 0.97

Change the decimals to fractions reduced to lowest terms.

25. 0.275 $^{11}/_{40}$	26. 0.3 $^{3}/_{10}$	27. 0.15 $^{3}/_{20}$	28. 0.8 $^{4}/_{5}$
29. 1.125 $1\,^{1}/_{8}$	30. 0.117 $^{117}/_{1000}$	31. 0.32 $^{8}/_{25}$	32. 2.5 $2\,^{1}/_{2}$
33. 44.755 $44\,^{151}/_{200}$	34. 0.005 $^{1}/_{200}$	35. 5.545 $5\,^{109}/_{200}$	36. 0.2 $^{1}/_{5}$

APPLICATIONS

37. In the past, stock prices were quoted as dollars and fractions of a dollar. Change the stock prices to dollars and cents. Round to the nearest cent.

Stock	Price	
a. AdobeSy	$61\,^{5}/_{16}$	\$61.31
b. AirTran	$4\,^{15}/_{32}$	\$4.47
c. CNET	$50\,^{3}/_{4}$	\$50.75
d. ETrade	$20\,^{1}/_{4}$	\$20.25
e. Omnipoint	$112\,^{5}/_{8}$	\$112.63
f. Qualcomm	$142\,^{1}/_{16}$	\$142.06
g. WebLink	$17\,^{13}/_{16}$	\$17.81
h. Winstar	$70\,^{23}/_{32}$	\$70.72

38. Individual bowling averages in the Southern Community League are carried to the nearest hundredth. Convert the decimals to fractions reduced to the lowest terms.

Name	Average	
a. B. Taylor	220.13	$220\,^{13}/_{100}$
b. J. Scott	217.02	$217\,^{1}/_{50}$
c. T. Anfinson	216.97	$216\,^{97}/_{100}$
d. G. Ingram	212.08	$212\,^{2}/_{25}$
e. D. Ingram	210.50	$210\,^{1}/_{2}$
f. B. Jordan	209.25	$209\,^{1}/_{4}$
g. G. Maddux	207.88	$207\,^{44}/_{50}$
h. A. Jones	205.15	$205\,^{3}/_{20}$

PERCENT TO DECIMAL, DECIMAL TO PERCENT

Percent is an abbreviation of the Latin words *per centum*, meaning "by the hundred." So percent means "divide by 100." A percent can be written as a decimal. To change a percent to a decimal, first write the percent as a fraction with a denominator of 100, then divide by 100.

EXAMPLE Change 31% to a decimal.

SOLUTION $31\% = {}^{31}/_{100} = 0.31$

EXAMPLE Change 17.3% to a decimal.

SOLUTION $17.3\% = {}^{17.3}/_{100} = 0.173$

When dividing by 100, you can just move the decimal point two places to the left. When you write a percent as a decimal, you are moving the decimal point two places to the left and dropping the percent sign (%). If necessary, use zero as a placeholder.

EXAMPLE / **SOLUTION**

A. 31% — 31% = 31. = 0.31 ← Drop % sign. ← Move decimal 2 places.

B. 7% — 7% = 07. = 0.07 ← Insert a zero as a placeholder.

To write a decimal as a percent, move the decimal point two places to the right and add a percent sign (%).

EXAMPLE / **SOLUTION**

A. 0.31 — 0.31 = 0.31 = 31 % ← Add % sign. ← Move decimal 2 places.

B. 0.07 — 0.07 = 0.07 = 7%

C. 2.5 — 2.5 = 2.50 = 250%

D. 0.008 — 0.008 = 0.008 = 0.8%

PROBLEMS

Write as decimals.

1. 35%
   0.35
2. 22%
   0.22
3. 68%
   0.68
4. 30%
   0.30
5. 49.2%
   0.492
6. 88.7%
   0.887
7. 11.5%
   0.115
8. 92.9%
   0.929
9. 322%
   3.22
10. 526%
    5.26
11. 663%
    6.63
12. 275%
    2.75
13. 9%
    0.09
14. 5%
    0.05
15. 4%
    0.04
16. 12%
    0.12
17. 7.03%
    0.0703
18. 9.02%
    0.0902
19. 2.0725%
    0.020725
20. 3.0843%
    0.030843

Write as percents.

21. 0.75
    75%
22. 0.17
    17%
23. 0.44
    44%
24. 0.26
    26%

PERCENT TO DECIMAL, DECIMAL TO PERCENT

25. 0.06
6%

26. 0.07
7%

27. 0.01
1%

28. 0.02
2%

29. 0.003
0.3%

30. 0.009
0.9%

31. 0.0045
0.45%

32. 0.0029
0.29%

33. 3.12
312%

34. 4.14
414%

35. 6.007
600.7%

36. 5.000
500%

37. 0.1
10%

38. 0.5
50%

39. 325.5
32,550%

40. 0.2015
20.15%

APPLICATIONS

41. The percent changes in retail sales were reported as a decimal in the October issue of *Retail Monthly* magazine. Change the decimals to percents.

Retail Sales

	Month	Change
a.	February	0.012
b.	March	0.006
c.	April	0.013
d.	May	0.038
e.	June	0.043
f.	July	0.011
g.	August	0.022

a. 1.2%
b. 0.6%
c. 1.3%
d. 3.8%
e. 4.3%
f. 1.1%
g. 2.2%

42. The commission rate schedule for a stockbroker is shown. Change the percents to decimals.

Commission Rate Schedule

	Dollar Amount	% of Dollar Amount
a.	\$0 – \$2,499	2.3%, minimum \$30
b.	\$2,500 – \$4,999	2.0%, minimum \$42
c.	\$5,000 – \$9,999	1.5%, minimum \$65
d.	\$10,000 – \$14,999	1.1%, minimum \$110
e.	\$15,000 – \$24,999	0.9%, minimum \$135
f.	\$25,000 – \$49,999	0.6%, minimum \$175
	\$50,000 and above	negotiated

a. 0.023
b. 0.020
c. 0.015
d. 0.011
e. 0.009
f. 0.006

PERCENT TO DECIMAL, DECIMAL TO PERCENT

43. During the National Basketball Association season, the teams had these won–lost records. The Pct. column shows the percent of games won, expressed as a decimal. Change the decimals to percents.

EASTERN CONFERENCE
Atlantic Division

	W	L	Pct.	GB	
a. Miami	28	16	.636	-	63.6%
b. New York	27	17	.614	1	61.4%
c. Philadelphia	25	21	.543	4	54.3%
d. Boston	21	25	.457	8	45.7%
e. Orlando	21	26	.447	8½	44.7%
f. New Jersey	17	29	.370	12	37.0%
g. Washington	15	31	.326	14	32.6%

Central Division

	W	L	Pct.	GB	
h. Indiana	29	15	.659	-	65.9%
i. Milwaukee	26	21	.553	4½	55.3%
j. Charlotte	24	20	.545	5	54.5%
k. Toronto	24	20	.545	5	54.5%
l. Detroit	22	23	.489	7½	48.9%
m. Cleveland	19	26	.422	10½	42.2%
n. Atlanta	17	26	.395	11½	39.5%
o. Chicago	9	34	.209	19½	20.9%

WESTERN CONFERENCE
Midwest Division

	W	L	Pct.	GB	
p. San Antonio	30	16	.652	-	65.2%
q. Utah	27	17	.614	2	61.4%
r. Minnesota	25	18	.581	3½	58.1%
s. Denver	21	22	.488	7½	48.8%
t. Houston	19	27	.413	11	41.3%
u. Dallas	18	27	.400	11½	40.0%
v. Vancouver	12	32	.273	17	27.3%

Pacific Division

	W	L	Pct.	GB	
w. L.A. Lakers	34	11	.756	-	75.6%
x. Portland	34	11	.756	-	75.6%
y. Sacramento	28	16	.636	5½	63.6%
z. Seattle	29	18	.617	6	61.7%
aa. Phoenix	26	18	.591	7½	59.1%
ab. Golden State	11	32	.256	22	25.6%
ac. L.A. Clippers	11	34	.244	23	24.4%

44. How many teams have won more than 75% of their games? 2
Who are they? L.A. Lakers and Portland

45. How many teams have won more than 50% of their games? 15

46. How many have won less than 30% of their games? 4

FINDING A PERCENTAGE

Finding a percentage means finding a percent of a number. To find a percent of a number, you change the percent to a decimal, then multiply it by the number.

EXAMPLE 30% of 90 is what number?

SOLUTION

$30\% \times 90 = n$	In mathematics, *of* means "times" and *is* means "equals." Let n stand for the unknown number.
$0.30 \times 90 = n$	Change the percent to a decimal.
$27 = n$	Multiply.
30% of $90 = 27$	Write the answer.

EXAMPLE The delivery charge is 8% of the selling price of \$145.00. Find the delivery charge.

SOLUTION

$8\% \times \$145.00 = n$
$0.08 \times \$145.00 = n$
$\$11.60 = n$
$8\% \times \$145.00 = \$11.60$ delivery charge

EXAMPLE The student had 95% correct out of 80 questions. How many answers were correct?

SOLUTION

$95\% \times 80 = n$
$0.95 \times 80 = n$
$76 = n$
$95\% \times 80 = 76$ correct

PROBLEMS

Find the percentage.

1. 25% of 60
   15
2. 45% of 80
   36
3. 40% of 30
   12
4. 33% of 112
   36.96
5. 58% of 420
   243.6
6. 50% of 422
   211
7. 3% of 100
   3
8. 2% of 247
   4.94
9. 110% of 65
   71.5
10. 7% of 785
    54.95
11. 1% of 819
    8.19
12. 4% of 19.5
    0.78
13. 185% of 95
    175.75
14. 200% of 720
    1440
15. 135% of 860
    1161
16. 120% of 3.35
    4.02
17. 4.5% of 50
    2.25
18. 1.25% of 300
    3.75
19. 33.3% of 80
    26.64
20. 67.2% of 365
    245.28

Round the answer to the nearest cent.

21. 7% of \$35.78
    \$2.50
22. 6.5% of \$80
    \$5.20
23. 10% of \$93.20
    \$9.32
24. 5.5% of \$135
    \$7.43
25. 4.25% of \$65.00
    \$2.76
26. 2.75% of \$115
    \$3.16
27. 125% of \$98
    \$122.50
28. 7.5% of \$150
    \$11.25
29. 0.3% of \$450
    \$1.35
30. 0.15% of \$125
    \$.19
31. 8.2% of \$19.89
    \$1.63
32. 5.25% of \$110.15
    \$5.78

APPLICATIONS

33. The following items appeared in a sales flyer for a major department store. Calculate the amount saved from the regular price as well as the sale price for each item. Round to the nearest cent.

	Amount Saved	Sale Price
a. Save 25% on juniors knit shirts. Reg. $18.	$4.50	$13.50
b. Save 30% on women's dresses. Reg. $69.99	$21.00	$48.99
c. Save 20% on men's shoes. Reg. $135.	$27.00	$108.00
d. Save 25% on all nursery cribs. Reg. $119.99	$30.00	$89.99
e. Save 25% on all boxed jewelry sets. Reg. $19.99	$5.00	$14.99
f. Save 30% on family athletic shoes. Reg. $59.99	$18.00	$41.99

34. Student Sean Hu received these test scores. How many answers were correct on each test?

Subject	Test Score	Number of Items	Correct Answers
a. Math	90%	80	72
b. English	70%	90	63
c. Science	80%	110	88
d. Spanish	90%	50	45
e. Government	85%	100	85

35. Sales taxes are found by multiplying the tax rate times the selling price of the item. The total purchase price is the selling price plus the sales tax. Find the sales tax and total purchase price for each selling price. Round to the nearest cent.

	Selling Price	Tax Rate	Sales Tax	Total Purchase Price
a.	$14.78	4%	$0.59	$15.37
b.	$22.50	5%	$1.13	$23.63
c.	$3.88	6%	$0.23	$4.11
d.	$95.85	6.5%	$6.23	$102.08
e.	$212.00	7.25%	$15.37	$227.37
f.	$85.06	8.25%	$7.02	$92.08
g.	$199.99	7.455%	$14.91	$214.90

AVERAGE (MEAN)

The average, or mean, is a single number used to represent a group of numbers. The average, or mean, of two or more numbers is the sum of the numbers divided by the number of items added.

EXAMPLE Find the average of 8, 5, 3, 7, and 2. Add to find the total.

SOLUTION $\frac{8 + 5 + 3 + 7 + 2}{5} = \frac{25}{5} = 5$ Divide by the number of items.

EXAMPLE Find the average of 278, 340, 205, and 235.

SOLUTION $\frac{278 + 340 + 205 + 235}{4} = \frac{1058}{4} = 264.5$

EXAMPLE Find the average of 4.3, 7.1, 1.5, 3.2, and 6.4. Round to the nearest tenth.

SOLUTION $\frac{4.3 + 7.1 + 1.5 + 3.2 + 6.4}{5} = \frac{22.5}{5} = 4.5$

EXAMPLE Find the average of \$12, \$35, \$19, \$23, \$11, and \$21. Round to the nearest dollar.

SOLUTION $\frac{\$12 + \$35 + \$19 + \$23 + \$11 + \$21}{6} = \frac{\$121}{6} = \$20.17 = \$20$

PROBLEMS

Find the average for each group.

1. 3, 5, 7, 9, 11 7
2. 25, 40, 35, 50 37.5
3. 211, 197, 132 180
4. 416, 310, 344, 430 375
5. 4.4, 2.9, 3.7, 1.8, 6.5 3.86
6. 3.6, 7.1, 4.8, 4.7, 6.3, 5.3 5.3
7. \$23, \$21, \$25, \$24, \$26 \$23.80
8. \$98, \$87, \$79, \$85, \$88, \$91 \$88

Find the average for each group. Round to the nearest hundredth or cent.

9. 8.1, 8.6, 7.7, 9.2, 5.5, 6.9, 7.3 7.61
10. 3.3, 5.8, 4.6, 2.8, 3.4, 5.2 4.18
11. \$31.70, \$33.91, \$36.17, \$33.85 \$33.91
12. \$4.37, \$3.74, \$4.90, \$5.74, \$6.11 \$4.97
13. \$55.78, \$44.20, \$43.95, \$34.36 \$44.57

AVERAGE (MEAN)

14. $121.19, $115.08, $135, $129.05, $111.88 $122.44
15. Ben Agars had bowling scores of 187, 154, and 130. What was his average? 157
16. Kelley O'Reilly's tips from being a waitress were $5.00, $5.50, $4.75, $3.00, $4.50, $2.00, $5.75, and $4.50. What was her average tip? $4.38
17. Last year, Michael Legato's telephone bills averaged $66.12 a month. What was his total bill for the year? $793.44
18. Mark Purdue recorded his math test scores this quarter. What is his average? 83.5

Test Number	1	2	3	4	5	6	7	8
Score	65	77	81	79	90	86	92	98

19. What does he need on the next test to have an average of 85? 97
20. If Mark got a 97 on test 9 and 100 on test 10, what would be his average? 86.5

APPLICATIONS

21. As captain of the school golf team, Erica Samuelson has to complete this form after each game. Help her by computing the total and the average for each golfer. She also computes the total and the team average for each game. Round to the nearest whole number.

	Golfer	Game 1	Game 2	Game 3	Total	Average
a.	Samuelson	86	78	75	239	80
b.	Haas	80	81	70	231	77
c.	Sutherland	82	77	71	230	77
d.	Beck	80	66	73	219	73
e.	McCarron	78	81	82	241	80
f.	Total	406	383	371		
g.	Team average	81	77	74		

ELAPSED TIME

To find elapsed time, subtract the earlier time from the later time.

EXAMPLE Find the elapsed time for Kaitlin Harper who worked from:
A. 4:30 P.M. to 11:45 P.M. B. 5:15 A.M. to 10:33 A.M.

SOLUTION

A. 11:45 − 4:30 = 7:15 = 7 hours 15 minutes written as 7 h: 15 min

B. 10:33 − 5:15 = 5:18 = 5 hours 18 minutes written as 5 h: 18 min

You cannot subtract 45 minutes from 30 minutes unless you borrow an hour and add it to the 30 minutes. Remember that 1 hour = 60 minutes.

EXAMPLE Find the elapsed time from 2:50 P.M. to 9:15 P.M.

SOLUTION

9:15 = 8:15 + :60 = 8:75 borrowed 1 hour
− 2:50 = − 2:50 − 2:50
6:25 = 6 h: 25 min

To find elapsed time when the time period goes past noon, add 12 hours to the later time before subtracting.

EXAMPLE Find the elapsed time from 6:00 A.M. to 3:15 P.M.

SOLUTION

3:15 = 3:15 + 12:00 = 15:15
− 6:00 = − 6:00 − 6:00
9:15 = 9 h: 15 min

EXAMPLE Find the elapsed time from 10:35 P.M. to 3:12 A.M.

SOLUTION

3:12 = 15:12 = 14:12 + :60 = 14:72
− 10:35 = − 10:35 = − 10:35 − 10:35
4:37 = 4 h: 37 min

PROBLEMS

Find the elapsed time.

1. From 2:30 P.M. to 6:35 P.M. 4 h: 5 min
2. From 1:18 P.M. to 7:25 P.M. 6 h: 7 min
3. From 4:40 A.M. to 8:57 A.M. 4 h: 17 min
4. From 3:33 a.m. to 10:47 A.M. 7 h: 14 min
5. From 3:15 A.M. to 5:20 A.M. 2 h: 5 min
6. From 1:25 P.M. to 9:05 P.M. 7 h: 40 min
7. From 7:35 P.M. to 11:12 P.M. 3 h: 37 min
8. From 8:43 A.M. to 11:30 A.M. 2 h: 47 min
9. From 6:00 A.M. to 3:30 P.M. 9 h: 30 min
10. From 10:30 A.M. to 6:45 P.M. 8 h: 15 min
11. From 5:45 A.M. to 9:16 A.M. 3 h: 31 min
12. From 1:45 A.M. to 7:05 A.M. 5 h: 20 min
13. From 6:10 P.M. to 8:08 P.M. 1 h: 58 min
14. From 3:28 A.M. to 11:16 A.M. 7 h: 48 min
15. From 2:27 P.M. to 9:11 P.M. 6 h: 44 min
16. From 3:56 P.M. to 10:22 P.M. 6 h: 26 min

ELAPSED TIME

17. From 12:07 A.M. to 7:25 A.M. 7 h: 18 min
18. From 12:35 P.M. to 6:45 P.M. 6 h: 10 min
19. From 8:10 A.M. to 4:45 P.M. 8 h: 35 min
20. From 7:45 A.M. to 5:30 P.M. 9 h: 45 min
21. From 7:00 A.M. to 3:00 P.M. 8 h
22. From 8:30 A.M. to 5:00 P.M. 8 h: 30 min
23. From 7:30 A.M. to 4:10 P.M. 8 h: 40 min
24. From 8:23 A.M. to 5:04 P.M. 8 h: 41 min
25. From 5:45 A.M. to 2:15 P.M. 8 h: 30 min
26. From 7:43 A.M. to 4:21 P.M. 8 h: 38 min
27. From 8:45 P.M. to 1:18 A.M. 4 h: 33 min
28. From 9:47 A.M. to 7:08 P.M. 9 h: 21 min
29. From 11:27 P.M. to 4:11 A.M. 4 h: 44 min
30. From 5:55 P.M. to 1:55 A.M. 8 h

APPLICATIONS

31. Jack Keegan worked from 7:15 A.M. to 5:00 P.M. How long did he work? 9 h: 45 min

32. Elena Diaz took a bus that left Cincinnati at 5:45 P.M. and arrived in Cleveland at 1:10 A.M. How long was the trip? 7 h: 25 min

33. National Delivery Service (N.D.S.) ships hundreds of packages across the United States every day by air freight. Below is an N.D.S. air freight schedule. Calculate the total transit time for each shipment. (Note that all times given are Eastern Standard Time; therefore, time zones do not need to be taken into account.)

	Shipped From	Shipped To	Departure Time	Arrival Time	Total Transit Time
a.	Chattanooga, TN	Atlanta, GA	7:35 A.M.	8:20 A.M.	45 min
b.	Chicago, IL	Houston, TX	8:10 A.M.	12:57 P.M.	4 h: 47 min
c.	Los Angeles, CA	New Orleans, LA	8:35 A.M.	2:17 P.M.	5 h: 42 min
d.	New York, NY	Cleveland, OH	5:25 P.M.	7:25 P.M.	2 h
e.	Boston, MA	Phoenix, AZ	11:45 A.M.	7:28 P.M.	7 h: 43 min
f.	Atlanta, GA	Miami, FL	7:07 A.M.	9:00 A.M.	1 h: 53 min

READING TABLES AND CHARTS

To read a table or chart, find the *column* containing one of the pieces of information you have. Look across the *row* containing the other piece of information. Read down the column and across the row. Read the information you need where the column and row intersect.

Shipping Costs

Not Over (lbs)	Zone 2 & 3	Zone 4	Zone 5	Zone 6	Zone 7
1	$4.00	$4.00	$4.00	$4.00	$4.00
2	$4.00	$4.00	$4.00	$4.00	$4.00
3	$5.10	$5.10	$5.10	$5.10	$5.10
4	$6.20	$6.20	$6.20	$6.20	$6.20
5	$7.30	$7.30	$7.30	$7.30	$7.30
6	$8.60	$8.90	$9.10	$9.45	$9.70
7	$8.70	$9.30	$9.70	$10.40	$10.90
8	$8.80	$9.70	$10.30	$11.35	$12.10
9	$8.90	$10.10	$10.90	$12.30	$13.30
10	$9.00	$10.50	$11.50	$13.25	$14.50

EXAMPLE What is the cost to ship a 6-lb package to Zone 5?

SOLUTION

a. Find the Zone 5 column. b. Find the 6-lb row.

c. Read across the 6-lb row to the Zone 5 column. The cost is $9.10.

To classify an item, find the row that contains the known data. Then read the classification from the head of the column.

Men's Body Measurement

Size	S	M	L	XL	XXL
Neck	14–14½	15–15½	16–16½	17–17½	18–18½
Chest	34–36	38–40	42–44	46–48	50–52
Waist	28–30	32–34	36–38	40–42	44–46
Reg. Sleeve	32–33	33–34	34–35	35–36	36–37
Tall Sleeve	33–34	34–35	35–36	36–37	37–38
Height	Reg. 5′8″–6′	Tall 6′1″–6′4″			

Talls: Measure 2″ longer overall, 1″ at sleeves

EXAMPLE What size shirt should a man with a 42-inch chest order?

SOLUTION

a. Find the row for the Chest measurements. b. Read across the row to 42–44.

c. Read the size at the head of the column (L). A man with a 42-inch chest should order a size L, which stands for large.

PROBLEMS

Use the shipping chart above to find the cost to ship each package to the indicated zone.

1. 3 lb, Zone 3 $5.10
2. 4 lb, Zone 7 $6.20
3. 9 lb, Zone 4 $10.10
4. 2 lb, Zone 6 $4.00
5. 6 lb, Zone 2 $8.60
6. 5 lb, Zone 5 $7.30
7. 1.5 lb, Zone 5 $4.00
8. 6.4 lb, Zone 7 $10.90
9. 8.2 lb, Zone 3 $8.90
10. 7.1 lb, Zone 6 $11.35
11. 5.8 lb, Zone 4 $8.90
12. 9.3 lb, Zone 3 $9.00

READING TABLES AND CHARTS

Use the size chart on the previous page to determine what size to order. In-between sizes should order the next size up.

13. Shorts—waist 33 32–34, M
14. Shirt—chest 37 38–40, M
15. Jacket—chest 47 46–48, XL
16. Pants—waist 43 44–46, XXL
17. Sweater—chest 43 42–44, L
18. Shirt—height 6′2″, sleeves 36 Tall, L

APPLICATIONS

19. Use the shipping chart on the previous page to determine the maximum amount a package can weigh.

	a.	b.	c.	d.	e.	f.
Shipping Zone	2	5	7	3	6	4
Shipping Cost	$7.30	$4.00	$13.30	$8.90	$7.30	$5.10
Maximum Weight	5 lb	2 lb	9 lb	9 lb	5 lb	3 lb

Use the Federal Income Tax Table to find the amount of tax withheld in questions 20–25 and the amount of wages earned in questions 26–31:

Federal Income Tax Table
MARRIED Persons—WEEKLY Payroll Period

If the wages are—		And the number of withholding allowances claimed is—							
At least	But less than	0	1	2	3	4	5	6	7
		The amount of income tax to be withheld is—							
$480	$490	$63	$56	$50	$44	$38	$32	$25	$19
490	500	64	58	52	45	39	33	27	21
500	510	66	59	53	47	41	35	28	22
510	520	67	61	55	48	42	36	30	24
520	530	69	62	56	50	44	38	31	25
530	540	70	64	58	51	45	39	33	27
540	550	72	65	59	53	47	41	34	28
550	560	73	67	61	54	48	42	36	30
560	570	75	68	62	56	50	44	37	31
570	580	76	70	64	57	51	45	39	33
580	590	78	71	65	59	53	47	40	34
590	600	79	73	67	60	54	48	42	36
600	610	81	74	68	62	56	50	43	37
610	620	82	76	70	63	57	51	45	39
620	630	84	77	71	65	59	53	46	40

	20.	21.	22.	23.	24.	25.
Income	$491.77	$501.07	$617.30	$525.00	$600.00	$531.13
Allowances	2	1	3	0	4	6
Amount Withheld	$52.00	$59.00	$63.00	$69.00	$56.00	$33.00

	Number of Allowances	Tax Withheld	Wages At least	Wages But less than
26.	5	$47	580	590
27.	2	$71	620	630
28.	3	$53	540	550
29.	1	$62	520	530
30.	4	$38	480	490
31.	0	$76	570	580

CONSTRUCTING GRAPHS

A **bar graph** is a picture that displays and compares numerical facts in the form of vertical or horizontal bars. To construct a vertical bar graph, follow these steps:

a. Draw the vertical and horizontal axes.
b. Scale the vertical axis to correspond to the given data.
c. Draw one bar to represent each quantity.
d. Label each bar and the vertical and horizontal axes.
e. Title the graph.

Metropolitan Statistical Areas Population (in millions)	
Chicago, IL	8.6
San Francisco, CA	6.6
Philadelphia, PA	6.0
Detroit, MI	5.3

EXAMPLE Construct a vertical bar graph of the given data.

SOLUTION

a. Draw vertical and horizontal axes.
b. Scale the vertical axis.
c. Draw one bar to represent each quantity.
d. Label each bar and the vertical and horizontal axes.
e. Title the graph.

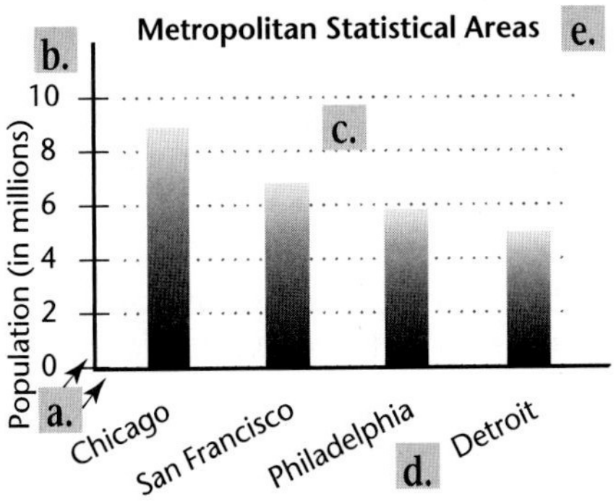

A **line graph** is a picture used to compare data over a period of time. It is an excellent way to show trends (increases or decreases). To construct a line graph, follow these steps:

a. Draw the vertical and horizontal axes.
b. Scale the vertical axis to correspond to the given data.
c. Label the axes.
d. Place a point on the graph to correspond to each item of data.
e. Connect the points from left to right.
f. Title the graph.

Percentage of Women in the Total Workforce	
1950	29.6%
1960	33.4%
1970	38.1%
1980	42.5%
1990	45.8%
2000	47.5%

EXAMPLE Construct a line graph of the given data.

SOLUTION

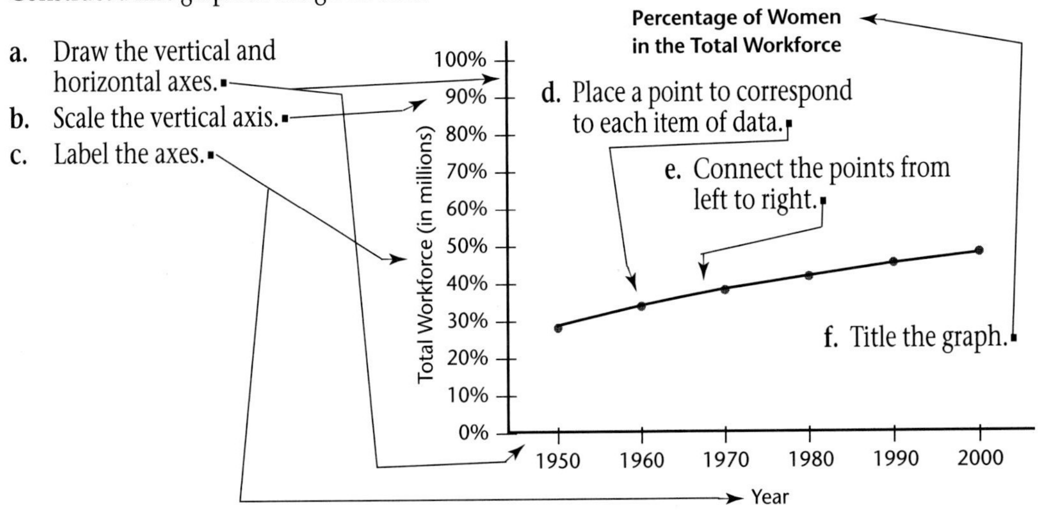

CONSTRUCTING GRAPHS

PROBLEMS

1. Construct a vertical bar graph of the given data.

Wrenn's Department Store
Total Sales by Department (in thousands)

Housewares	122
Men's Clothing	145
Women's Clothing	160
Appliances	183
Electronics	214

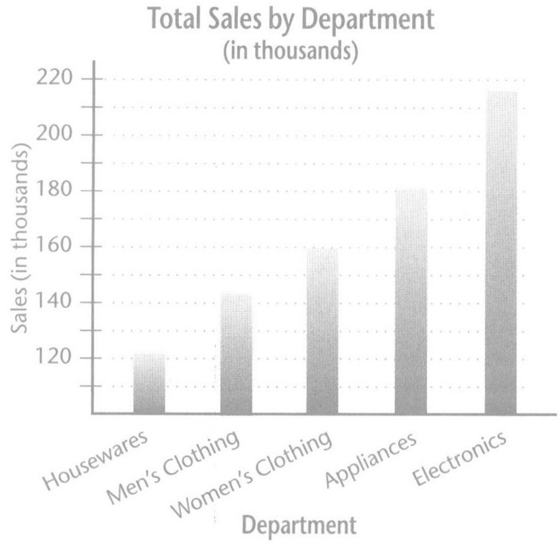

2. Read the vertical bar graph.
   a. Of the metropolitan areas listed, which is projected to have the largest population in 2033? Los Angeles
   b. Which of the metropolitan areas listed is projected to have the smallest population in 2033? Washington, DC
   c. What is Chicago's projected population for 2033? about 9 million

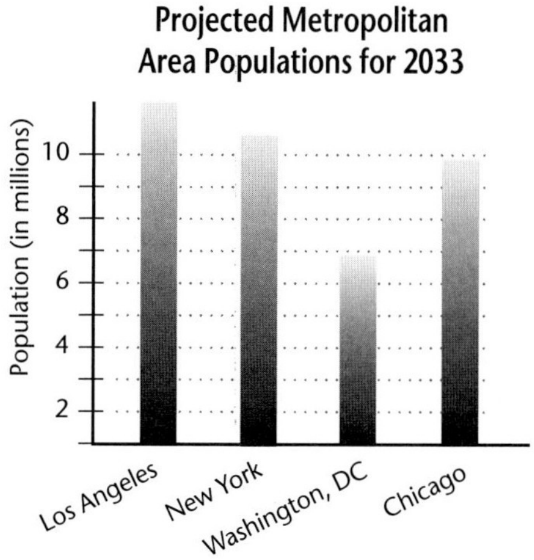

3. Construct a line graph of the given data.

Tollhouse Industries Stock

Month	Average
Jan.	16.50
Feb.	17
Mar.	16.25
Apr.	15
May	17.50
June	18

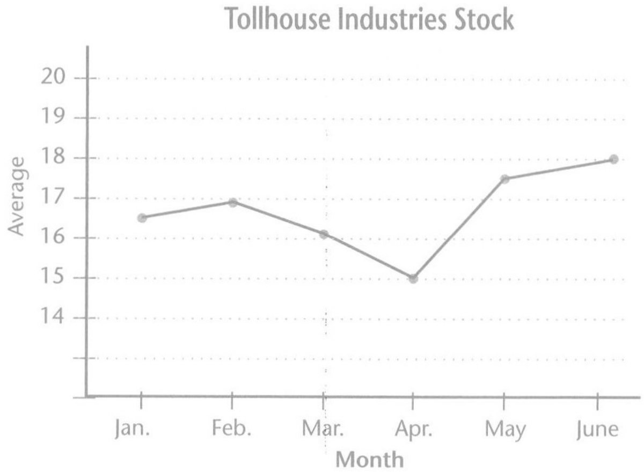

UNITS OF MEASURE

Here are abbreviations and conversions for units of measure in the customary measurement system.

Length
12 inches (in) = 1 foot (ft)
3 ft = 1 yard (yd)
5280 ft = 1 mile (mi)

Volume
2 cups (c) = 1 pint (pt)
2 pt = 1 quart (qt)
4 qt = 1 gallon (gal)

Weight
16 ounces (oz) = 1 pound (lb)
2000 lb = 1 ton (t)

Here are symbols and conversions for units of measure in the metric system.

Length
1000 millimeters (mm) = 1 meter (m)
100 centimeters (cm) = 1 m
1000 m = 1 kilometer (km)

Volume
1000 milliliters (mL) = 1 liter (L)

Mass
1000 grams (g) = 1 kilogram (kg)

To convert from one unit of measure to another, use the conversions lists above.

When converting to a smaller unit, multiply.

EXAMPLE Convert 5 feet to inches.

SOLUTION Use 12 in = 1 ft
5 ft: $5 \times 12 = 60$
5 ft = 60 in

EXAMPLE Convert 4 meters to centimeters.

SOLUTION Use 100 cm = 1 m
4 m: $4 \times 100 = 400$
4 m = 400 cm

When converting to a larger unit, divide.

EXAMPLE Convert 6 pints to quarts.

SOLUTION Use 2 pt = 1 qt
6 pt: $6 \div 2 = 3$
6 pt = 3 qt

EXAMPLE Convert 6500 grams to kilograms.

SOLUTION Use 1000 g = 1 kg
6500 g: $6500 \div 1000 = 6.5$
6500 g = 6.5 kg

PROBLEMS

Make the following conversions.

1. 12 yd to feet 36 ft
2. 8 gal to quarts 32 qt
3. 9 lb to ounces 144 oz
4. 2 ft to inches 24 in
5. 3 lb to ounces 48 oz
6. 5 L to milliliters 5000 mL
7. 2.4 km to meters 2400 m
8. 24 pt to cups 48 c
9. 3.6 kg to grams 3600 g
10. 99 in to yards 2.75 yd
11. 15 qt to gallons 3.75 gal
12. 66 oz to pounds 4.125 lb
13. 18 qt to gallons 4.5 gal
14. 24 oz to pounds 1.5 lb
15. 7000 g to kilograms 7 kg
16. 60 cm to meters 0.6 m
17. 2200 mL to liters 2.2 L
18. 350 cm to meters 3.5 m
19. 29 kg to grams 29,000 g
20. 17.3 L to milliliters 17,300 mL
21. 522 g to kilograms 0.522 kg
22. 10.122 mL to liters 0.010122 L
23. 72 cm to millimeters 720 mm
24. 432.2 cm to meters 4.322 m
25. 1 yd 7 in to inches 43 in
26. 5 ft 7 in to inches 67 in
27. 3 qt 1 pt to pints 7 pt
28. 6 lb 9 oz to ounces 105 oz
29. 4 gal 1 qt to quarts 17 qt
30. 3 yd 1 ft 5 in to inches 125 in
31. 5 gal 3 qt 1 pt to pints 47 pt
32. 3 m 57 cm 29 mm to millimeters 3599 mm

APPLICATIONS

33. How many quarts will a 6-gallon bucket hold? 24 qt
34. How many milliliters will a 2-liter bottle hold? 2000 mL
35. How many cups of coffee does a 4-quart coffeepot hold? 16 c
36. How many cups of hot chocolate will a 1.5-gallon thermos jug hold? 24 c
37. How many inches long is an 8-yard roll of aluminum foil? 288 in
38. Strawberries are sold in 1-pint containers. How many pints must be purchased to have enough for a recipe that calls for 3 cups? 2 (1.5)
39. James Jones knows that his jogging stride is about 1 meter long. The jogging trail he uses is 4.2 kilometers long. How many strides does it take him to go around the trail once? 4200
40. The cafeteria receives 49 cases of milk each day. Each case contains 24 half-pint cartons. How many gallons of milk are received each day? 73.5 gal
41. A soft drink is sold in 355 mL cans. How many liters are in a six-pack? 2.13 L
42. Katie Karanikos baked a chocolate layer cake weighing 1.5 kilograms. How many 75-gram servings can be cut from the cake? 20
43. Joan Baird ordered baseboard molding for the rooms of a new house. Joan needs to complete this chart to determine the total number of feet of molding needed. How much molding is needed?

	Length	Width	2 lengths	+ 2 widths	=	Perimeter
	12 ft	10 ft	24 ft	+ 20 ft	=	44 ft
	11 ft	8 ft	22 ft	+ 16 ft	=	38 ft
a.	11 ft	19 ft	22 ft	+ 38 ft	=	60 ft
b.	12 ft	12 ft 2 in	24 ft	+ 24 ft 4 in	=	48 ft 4 in
c.	15 ft	16 ft 8 in	30 ft	+ 33 ft 4 in	=	63 ft 4 in
d.	11 ft 8 in	12 ft 2 in	23 ft 4 in	+ 24 ft 4 in	=	47 ft 8 in
e.	12 ft 10 in	16 ft 10 in	25 ft 8 in	+ 33 ft 8 in	=	59 ft 4 in
f.	16 ft 9 in	24 ft 3 in	33 ft 6 in	+ 48 ft 6 in	=	82 ft
g.	9 ft 4 in	10 ft	18 ft 8 in	+ 20 ft	=	38 ft 8 in
h.			Total			481 ft 4 in

Glossary

A

account a record that shows the balance for a specific item, such as cash or equipment (p. 638)

accounting the systematic process of recording and reporting the financial position of a business (p. 561)

accounting cycle the activities, or steps, that help a business keep its accounting records in an orderly manner (p. 637)

accounting equation Assets – Liabilities = Owner's Equity, the basis for keeping all accounting records in balance (p. 638)

accounting period a block of time covered by an accounting report (p. 637)

accounts payable the amount of money owed, or payable, to the creditors of a business (p. 640)

accounts receivable the total amount of money owed to a business by customers (p. 639)

actual cash value the replacement cost of an item minus depreciation (p. 426)

adjustable-rate mortgage (ARM) a mortgage with an interest rate that increases or decreases during the life of the loan, also known as a "variable-payment mortgage" (p. 222)

adjusted gross income gross income after certain reductions are calculated (p. 384)

allowance an adjustment to the tax withheld from your paycheck, based on your marital status and whether you have dependents (p. 386)

amortization the reduction of a loan balance through payments made over a period of time (p. 221)

annual percentage rate (APR) the cost of credit on a yearly basis, expressed as a percentage (p. 163)

annual percentage yield (APY) amount of interest that a $100 deposit would earn, after compounding, for one year (p. 137)

annuity term sometimes used for a series of equal regular deposits to a savings account (p. 22)

annuity (insurance) a contract purchased from an insurance company that guarantees a future fixed or variable payment to the purchaser for a certain number of years or for life (p. 495)

appraisal an estimate of the current value of the property (p. 226)

aptitudes the natural abilities people possess (p. 34)

arbitration a process whereby a conflict between a customer and a business is resolved by an impartial third party whose decision is legally binding (p. 108)

articles of incorporation the application to operate as a corporation (p. 534)

assets items of value that an individual or company owns, including cash, property, personal possessions, and investments (p. 65)

assigned risk pool a group of people who cannot get motor vehicle insurance (p. 436)

assisted-living facility (ALF) a residence complex that provides personal and medical services for the elderly (p. 485)

automated teller machine (ATM) a computer terminal that allows a withdrawal of cash from an account (p. 126)

B

balance sheet a report of the balances of all asset, liability, and owner's equity accounts at the end of an accounting period (p. 654)

bank reconciliation a report that accounts for the differences between the bank statement and your checkbook balance (p. 145)

bankruptcy a legal process in which some or all of the assets of a debtor are distributed among the creditors because the debtor is unable to pay his or her debts (p. 188)

bear market market condition that occurs when investors are pessimistic about the economy and sell stocks (p. 285)

bearer bond a bond that is not registered in the investor's name (p. 310)

beneficiary (estate) a person who is named to receive a portion of someone's estate (p. 499)

beneficiary (insurance) a person named to receive the benefits from an insurance policy (p. 464)

Blue Cross an insurance company that provides hospital care benefits (p. 453)

Blue Shield an insurance company that provides benefits for surgical and medical services performed by physicians (p. 453)

blue-chip stock a safe investment that generally attracts conservative investors, usually stocks issued by the strongest and most respected companies (p. 277)

board of directors a group of individuals who are responsible for overseeing the general affairs of the corporation (p. 538)

bodily injury liability insurance that covers physical injuries caused by a vehicle accident for which the insured is responsible (p. 430)

break-even point the point at which total sales equal total costs (variable and fixed costs) (p. 707)

budget a formal, written statement of expected income and expenses for a future period of time (p. 563)

budget a plan for using money to meet wants and needs (p. 74)

budget variance the difference between the budgeted amount and the actual amount that you spend (p. 77)

bull market market condition that occurs when investors are optimistic about the economy and buy stocks (p. 285)

business credit card a credit card issued to a business rather than to an individual (p. 627)

business plan a written proposal that describes a new business and strategies to launch that business (p. 550)

C

cafeteria-style employee benefits programs that allow workers to choose the benefits that best meet their personal needs (p. 49)

capital the money you need to establish a business, operate it for the first few months, and expand it once it stabilizes (p. 574)

capital gain profit from the sale of assets such as stocks, bonds, or real estate (p. 261)

capital loss the sale of an investment for less than its purchase price (p. 262)

capitalization the total amount of stocks and bonds issued by a corporation (p. 279)

career a commitment to work in a field that you find interesting and fulfilling (p. 32)

cash flow the amount of cash that is available at any given time (p. 565)

cash flow the money that goes into and out of your wallet and bank accounts (p. 70)

cash value in a whole life policy, the accumulated savings to which you are entitled when and if you cancel the policy (p. 467)

certificate of deposit (CD) a savings alternative in which money is left on deposit for a stated period of time to earn a specific rate of return (p. 132)

chart of accounts a list of all the general ledger accounts that a business will use (p. 598)

class-action suit a legal action on behalf of all the people who have suffered the same injustice (p. 110)

closed-end credit credit as a one-time loan that you will pay back over a specified period of time in payments of equal amounts (p. 157)

closed-end fund a mutual fund with a fixed number of shares that are issued by an investment company when the fund is first organized (p. 327)

closing a meeting of the seller, the buyer, and the lender of funds, or representatives of each party, to complete the transaction (p. 223)

codicil a document that explains, adds, or deletes provisions in an existing will (p. 504)

coinsurance the percentage of the medical expenses the policyholder must pay in addition to the deductible amount (p. 447)

collateral a form of security to help guarantee that the creditor will be repaid (p. 166)

collectibles items that appeal to collectors and investors, including rare coins, works of art, antiques, stamps, rare books, comic books, sports memorabilia, rugs, ceramics, and paintings (p. 366)

collision insurance that covers damage to your vehicle when it is involved in an accident (p. 432)

commercial bank a for-profit institution that offers a full range of financial services, including checking, savings, and lending (p. 129)

commercial debt financing borrowing money from a bank or other financial institution to fund a business (p. 618)

commercial finance company a firm that lends money only to businesses (p. 628)

commercial loan a loan that finances a new or ongoing business (p. 618)

commercial property land and buildings that produce rental income (p. 353)

commission an amount of money paid to an employee based on a percentage of the employee's sales (p. 669)

common stock a unit of ownership of a company that entitles the owner, or stockholder, to voting privileges (p. 250)

compounding the process in which interest is earned on both the principal—the original amount you deposited—and on any previously earned interest (p. 136)

consumer a person who purchases and uses goods or services (p. 17)

consumer credit use of credit for personal needs (p. 154)

consumer price index (CPI) a measure of the changes in prices for commonly purchased goods and services in the United States (p. 77)

contribution margin the amount of money that the sale of a particular product contributes toward the payment of fixed costs and the profit of a business (p. 705)

convertible bond a bond that an investor can trade for shares of the corporation's common stock (p. 307)

cooperative a nonprofit organization owned and operated by its members for the purpose of saving money on the purchase of goods and services (p. 99)

cooperative education a program that allows students to enhance classroom learning with part-time work related to their majors and interests (p. 41)

co-payment a flat fee that you pay every time you receive a covered service (p. 449)

corporate bond a corporation's written pledge to repay a specific amount of money, along with interest (p. 251)

corporate bylaws the rules by which a corporation will operate (p. 534)

corporate charter a license to operate a corporation (p. 534)

corporation a business organization that operates as a legal entity that is separate from its owners and is treated by law as if it were an individual person (p. 534)

cosigning agreeing to be responsible for another person's loan payments if that person fails to make them (p. 182)

cost behavior the way a cost changes in relation to a change in business activity (p. 703)

cost of merchandise sold the amount of money the business paid for the goods that it sold to customers (p. 651)

coupon bond a bond that is registered in the owner's name for the face value only and not for interest (p. 310)

cover letter a personal letter you present along with your résumé (p. 45)

credit an arrangement to receive cash, goods, or services now and pay for them in the future (p. 154)

credit (accounting) an amount entered on the right side of a T account (p. 640)

credit rating a measure of a person's ability and willingness to make credit payments on time (p. 170)

credit union a nonprofit financial institution that is owned by its members and organized for their benefit (p. 130)

creditor an entity, such as a financial institution, merchant, or individual, that lends money (p. 154)

current yield the annual dividend of an investment divided by the current market value (p. 286)

cyclical stock stock with a market value that tends to reflect the state of the economy (p. 278)

D

debenture a bond that is backed only by the reputation of the issuing corporation, rather than by its assets (p. 306)

debit an amount entered on the left side of a T account (p. 640)

debit card a cash card that allows you to withdraw money or pay for purchases from your checking or savings account (p. 126)

deductible the set amount that a policyholder must pay per loss on an insurance policy (p. 414)

deductions the various amounts that are subtracted from an employee's gross earnings (p. 669)

deed the official document transferring ownership from seller to buyer (p. 224)

defensive stock stock that remains stable during declines in the economy (p. 278)

deficit the financial situation that occurs when more money is spent than is earned or received (p. 72)

defined-benefit plan a retirement plan that specifies the benefits an employee will receive at retirement age, based on total earnings and years on the job (p. 489)

defined-contribution plan an individual retirement account for each employee, also called an "individual account plan" (p. 488)

demand the amount of goods and services people are willing to buy (p. 14)

demographic trends tendencies of people grouped by age, gender, ethnicity, education, or income that change over time (p. 37)

direct deposit an automatic deposit of net pay to an employee's designated bank account (p. 125)

direct investment real estate investment in which the owner holds legal title to the property he or she has purchased (p. 352)

direct labor the work required to convert raw materials into a finished product (p. 704)

direct materials the raw materials used to make a finished product (p. 704)

disability income insurance coverage that provides regular cash income when you are unable to work due to a pregnancy, non-work-related accident, or illness (p. 460)

discretionary income the money left after paying for the essentials, such as food, clothing, shelter, transportation, and medication (p. 71)

diversification the process of spreading your assets among several different types of investments to reduce risk (p. 254)

dividends distributions of money, stock, or other property that a corporation pays to stockholders (p. 246)

double-entry accounting a system of recordkeeping in which each business transaction affects at least two accounts (p. 640)

down payment a portion of the total cost of an item that must be paid at the time of purchase (p. 96)

E

earnings per share a corporation's net, or after-tax, earnings divided by the number of outstanding shares of common stock (p. 287)

economics the study of the decisions that go into making, distributing, and using goods and services (p. 14)

economy the ways in which people make, distribute, and use their goods and services (p. 14)

emergency fund a savings account you can access quickly to pay for unexpected expenses or emergencies (p. 238)

Employer Identification Number (EIN) a number assigned by the Internal Revenue Service that is used for income tax purposes (p. 525)

endorsement the signature of the payee, the party to whom the check has been written (p. 144)

endowment life insurance that provides coverage for a specific period of time and pays a sum of money to the policyholder if he or she is living at the end of the endowment period (p. 468)

entrepreneur an individual who takes the risk of starting a new business (p. 610)

equity the value of the home less the amount still owed on the money borrowed to purchase it (p. 209)

equity capital money that a business gets from its owners in order to operate (p. 250)

escrow account an account where money is held in trust until it can be delivered to a designated party (p. 217)

estate all property and assets owned by an individual or group (p. 499)

estate planning the process of creating a detailed plan for managing personal assets to make the most of them while you are alive and to ensure that they are distributed wisely after your death (p. 499)

estate tax a federal tax collected on the value of a person's property at the time of his or her death (p. 381)

exclusion income that is not subject to taxes, also called "tax-exempt income" (p. 383)

executor a person who is willing and able to perform the tasks involved in carrying out a will (p. 504)

exemption a deduction from adjusted gross income for the taxpayer, the spouse, and qualified dependents (p. 385)

extension an extended deadline for filing an income tax return (p. 391)

F

face value the dollar amount that the bondholder will receive at the bond's maturity (p. 306)

Federal Insurance Contributions Act (FICA) the 1935 law that established the present Social Security system (p. 671)

Federal Reserve System the central banking organization of the United States (p. 16)

finance charge the total dollar amount you pay to use credit (p. 160)

financial forecasting the process of estimating a business's operating capital (p. 579)

financial leverage the use of borrowed funds for direct investment purposes (p. 358)

financial plan a written outline of how the business will get money to start up and operate, and how the business will maintain financial operations and business records (p. 551)

financial planner a specialist who is trained to offer specific financial help and advice (p. 257)

financial reports written records that summarize the results of financial transactions affecting a business and report its current financial position (p. 636)

financial statements reports that summarize changes that result from business transactions during an accounting period (p. 650)

first-in, first-out method (FIFO) an inventory costing system that assumes that the first items purchased (first in) are the first items sold (first out) (p. 687)

fixed costs costs that remain constant even if activity or production level changes (p. 704)

fixed expenses expenses that remain the same regardless of business activity (p. 580)

fixed-rate mortgage a mortgage with a fixed interest rate and a fixed schedule of payments, also called a "conventional mortgage" (p. 221)

401(k) plan a type of retirement savings plan funded by a portion of your salary that is deducted from your gross paycheck and placed in a special account, also called a "salary-reduction plan" (p. 488)

franchise a contractual agreement to sell a company's products or services in a designated geographic area (p. 542)

fraud dishonest business practices that are meant to deceive, trick, or gain an unfair advantage (p. 104)

free enterprise system an economic system in which people can choose what they buy, what they produce and sell, and where they work (p. 550)

future value the amount your original deposit will be worth in the future based on earning a specific interest rate over a specific period of time (p. 21)

G

general ledger a book or set of electronic files that contains the accounts used for a business (p. 645)

general partner a business partner who has decision-making authority, takes an active role in the operation of the business, and has unlimited liability for all losses or debts of the partnership (p. 528)

generally accepted accounting principles (GAAP) a standard set of guidelines used in recording and reporting financial changes (p. 563)

geographic trends tendencies of people moving from one area of the country to another as financial centers shift location (p. 37)

goals things you want to accomplish (p. 6)

good a physical item that is produced and can be weighed or measured (p. 11)

government bond the written pledge of a government or a municipality, such as a city, to repay a specific sum of money with interest (p. 251)

grace period a time period during which no finance charges will be added to your account (p. 160)

gross earnings the total amount of money an employee earns in a pay period (p. 667)

gross profit on sales the profit made from selling merchandise before operating expenses are deducted (p. 652)

growth stock stock issued by a corporation whose potential earnings may be higher than the average earnings predicted for all the corporations in the country (p. 278)

guardian the person who accepts the responsibility of caring for the children of the deceased and managing an estate for the children until they reach a certain age (p. 504)

H

hazard anything that increases the likelihood of loss through peril (p. 413)

health insurance a form of protection that eases the financial burden people may experience as a result of illness or injury (p. 444)

health maintenance organization (HMO) a health insurance plan that directly employs or contracts with selected, or preapproved, physicians and other medical professionals to provide health care services in exchange for a fixed, prepaid monthly premium (p. 454)

heirs the people who will have the legal right to your assets when you die (p. 498)

home equity loan a loan based on the difference between the current market value of a home and the amount the borrower owes on the mortgage (p. 223)

homeowners insurance coverage that provides protection for your residence and its associated financial risks (p. 419)

hourly wage a specific amount of money paid per hour to an employee (p. 667)

I

impulse buying purchasing items on the spur of the moment (p. 99)

income cash inflow, or the money you receive (p. 70)

income dividends the earnings a fund pays to shareholders (p. 341)

income statement a report of the net income or net loss for an accounting period (p. 650)

income stock stock that pays higher-than-average dividends compared to other stock issues (p. 277)

income tax tax on wages, salaries, and self-employed earnings (p. 382)

income tax return a form, such as 1040 or 1040EZ, on which a taxpayer reports how much money he or she received from working and other sources and the exact taxes that are owed (p. 383)

indirect investment a real estate investment in which a trustee is appointed to hold legal title to the property on behalf of an investor or group of investors (p. 354)

individual retirement account (IRA) a special account in which a person sets aside a portion of income for retirement (p. 490)

inflation rise in the level of prices for goods and services over time (p. 16)

informational interview a meeting with someone who works in your area of interest who can provide you with practical information about a career or company of interest (p. 43)

inheritance tax a state tax collected on the property left by a person to his or her heir(s) in a will (p. 381)

insolvency a financial state that occurs if liabilities are greater than assets (p. 69)

insurance protection against possible financial loss (p. 412)

interest the price that is paid for the use of another's money (p. 17)

interest inventories tests that help you identify the activities you enjoy the most (p. 34)

internship a position in which a person receives training by working with people who are experienced in a particular field (p. 41)

intestate a status of not having a valid will (p. 501)

inventory the merchandise retailers have for sale (p. 564)

investment liquidity the ability to buy or sell an investment quickly without substantially reducing its value (p. 249)

investment-grade bonds bonds that are issued by financially stable companies or municipalities (p. 323)

itemized deduction a specific expense, such as a medical expense, that you deduct from your adjusted gross income (p. 384)

J

job work you do mainly to earn money (p. 32)

journal a record of all of the transactions of a business (p. 644)

K

Keogh plan a retirement plan specially designed for self-employed people and their employees, also known as an "H.R.10 plan" or a "self-employed retirement plan" (p. 493)

L

landlord the person who owns the property that is rented (p. 202)

large-cap stock stock of a corporation that has issued a large number of shares of stock and has a large amount of capitalization (p. 279)

last-in, first-out method (LIFO) a costing method that assumes the last items purchased (last in) are the first items sold (first out) (p. 688)

lease a legal document that defines the conditions of the rental agreement between the tenant and the landlord (p. 205)

legal aid society a network of community law offices that provide free or low-cost legal assistance (p. 111)

liabilities the debts you owe (p. 68)

liability legal responsibility for the financial cost of another person's losses or injuries (p. 418)

limited liability company (LLC) a business that operates and pays taxes as a partnership but has limited liability for the owners (p. 542)

limited life a situation in which a business's life span or existence is determined by the owner's life span or the owner's decision to terminate the business (p. 528)

limited partner a business partner who does not take an active role in decision making or in running the business (p. 529)

line of credit an arrangement in which bank customers can borrow a certain amount of money from the bank immediately (p. 621)

line of credit the maximum amount of money a creditor will allow a credit user to borrow (p. 157)

liquid assets cash and items that can be quickly converted to cash (p. 67)

liquidity the ability to easily convert financial assets into cash without loss in value (p. 9)

living will a legal document in which you state if you want to be kept alive by artificial means if you become terminally ill and are unable to make such a decision (p. 505)

load fund a mutual fund for which you pay a commission every time you buy or sell shares (p. 328)

LowDoc Program a government loan program that allows businesses applying for loans of less than $150,000 to submit a one-page application with a small amount of documentation (p. 626)

M

managed care prepaid health plans that provide comprehensive health care to their members (p. 453)

manufacturing business a business that buys raw materials or processed goods and transforms them into finished products (p. 701)

margin of safety the target sales minus the break-even sales, which indicates the amount of risk that sales will meet the break-even point (p. 713)

market value the price at which property would sell (p. 67)

marketing plan a written outline of how the business will be promoted to increase customers and sales (p. 551)

markup the difference between the cost of an item to a business and the selling price of the item (p. 699)

maturity date the date when a bond will be repaid (p. 306)

mediation the attempt by a neutral third party to resolve a conflict between a customer and a business through discussion and negotiation (p. 108)

Medicaid a medical assistance program offered to certain low-income individuals and families (p. 458)

medical payments coverage insurance that pays the costs of minor accidental injuries to visitors on your property (p. 422)

Medicare a federally funded health insurance program available mainly to people over 65 and to people with certain disabilities (p. 456)

Medicare tax the tax that finances part of the Medicare program (p. 671)

mentor an experienced employee who serves as a teacher and counselor for a less-experienced person (p. 52)

merchandise the goods retailers buy with the intent to resell to customers (p. 564)

minimum monthly payment the smallest amount you can pay and remain a borrower in good standing (p. 168)

mobility the ability to move easily from place to place (p. 198)

money management planning how to get the most from your money (p. 60)

money market account a savings account that requires a minimum balance and earns interest that varies from month to month (p. 134)

mortgage a long-term loan extended to someone who buys property (p. 218)

mortgage bond a bond that is backed by assets of the corporation, also called a "secured bond" (p. 307)

municipal bond a security issued by a state or local government (town, city, or county) to pay for its ongoing activities (p. 317)

mutual fund an investment in which investors pool their money to buy stocks, bonds, and other securities selected by professional managers who work for an investment company (p. 252)

N

negative cash flow a situation that occurs when a business spends more money than it receives (p. 565)

negligence the failure to take ordinary or reasonable care to prevent accidents from happening (p. 413)

net asset value (NAV) the amount one share of a mutual fund is worth (p. 328)

net income the amount of revenue that remains after expenses for the accounting period are subtracted from the gross profit on sales (p. 652)

net income the income you receive (take-home pay, allowance, gifts, and interest) (p. 162)

net worth the difference between the amount that you own and the debts that you owe (p. 65)

networking making and using contacts to get job information and advice (p. 43)

no-fault system an arrangement whereby drivers who are involved in accidents collect money from their own insurance companies (p. 433)

no-load fund a mutual fund that has no commission fee (p. 329)

O

open dating a labeling method that indicates the freshness, or shelf life, of a perishable product, such as milk or bread (p. 100)

open-end credit credit as a loan with a certain limit on the amount of money you can borrow for a variety of goods and services (p. 157)

open-end fund a mutual fund with an unlimited number of shares that are issued and redeemed by an investment company at the investors' request (p. 327)

operating capital the amount of capital needed to operate a business for the first few months or years (p. 579)

operating costs the ongoing expenses for operating a business (p. 614)

opportunity cost what is given up when making one choice instead of another (p. 8)

overdraft protection an automatic loan made to an account if the balance will not cover checks written (p. 141)

over-the-counter (OTC) market a network of dealers who buy and sell the stocks of corporations that are not listed on a securities exchange (p. 292)

overtime rate the amount paid above the normal rate for overtime, usually 1.5 times the employee's regular hourly wage (p. 668)

P

par value an assigned dollar value that is printed on a stock certificate (p. 275)

participation certificate (PC) an investment in a group of mortgages that have been purchased by a government agency (p. 357)

partnership a business owned by two or more persons (p. 528)

partnership agreement a written document that states how the partnership will be organized (p. 528)

payroll a list of employees and the payments due to each employee for a specific period of time (p. 666)

penny stock stock that typically sells for less than $1 a share, although it can sell for as much as $10 a share (p. 280)

pension plan a retirement plan that is funded at least in part by an employer (p. 49)

peril anything that may possibly cause a loss (p. 413)

periodic inventory system a system in which inventory records are updated only after someone makes an actual physical count of the merchandise on hand (p. 684)

perpetual inventory system a system that keeps a constant, up-to-date record of merchandise on hand (p. 682)

personal balance sheet also a net worth statement, a financial statement that lists items of value owned, debts owed, and a person's net worth (p. 65)

personal financial planning arranging to spend, save, and invest money to live comfortably, have financial security, and achieve goals (p. 6)

personal financial statement a document that provides information about an individual's current financial position and presents a summary of income and spending (p. 65)

personal property floater additional property insurance that covers the damage or loss of a specific item of high value (p. 420)

point-of-sale terminals electronic cash registers (p. 683)

point-of-sale transaction a purchase by a debit card of a good or service at a retail store, a restaurant, or elsewhere (p. 127)

point-of-service (POS) plan a health insurance plan that combines features of both HMOs and PPOs (p. 455)

points extra charges that must be paid by the buyer to the lender in order to get a lower interest rate (p. 219)

policy a contract between an insurance company and a person by which that person joins a risk-sharing group (p. 412)

portfolio a collection of all the securities held by an investor (p. 294)

posting the process of recording transfers of amounts from the general journal to individual accounts in the general ledger (p. 646)

potential earning power the amount of money you may earn over time (p. 33)

power of attorney a legal document that authorizes someone to act on your behalf (p. 506)

precious gems rough mineral deposits (usually crystals) that are dug from the earth by miners and then cut and shaped into brilliant jewels (p. 363)

precious metals valuable ores such as gold, platinum, and silver (p. 361)

preferred provider organization (PPO) a group of doctors and hospitals that agree to provide specified medical services to members at prearranged fees (p. 455)

preferred stock a type of stock that gives the owner the advantage of receiving cash dividends before common stockholders receive cash dividends (p. 250)

premium the fee a policyholder pays for insurance (p. 412)

present value the amount of money you would need to deposit now in order to have a desired amount in the future (p. 22)

price-earnings (PE) ratio the price of one share of stock divided by a corporation's earnings per share of stock over the last 12 months (p. 287)

pricing the process of assigning a selling price to a good or service (p. 698)

principal the original amount of money you deposit (p. 20)

private corporation a company that issues stock to a small group of people, also called a "closely held corporation" (p. 272)

private financing borrowing money from family or friends (p. 618)

private investor a person outside an entrepreneur's circle of friends and relatives who provides funding because he or she is interested in helping a new business to succeed (p. 627)

private mortgage insurance (PMI) a special policy that protects the lender in case the buyer cannot make payments or cannot make them on time (p. 218)

probate the legal procedure of proving that a will is valid or invalid (p. 503)

product costing the process of analyzing all costs involved in creating products (p. 702)

product cost-plus pricing the process of determining an item's selling price by adding the invoice cost of the item (how much the business paid for the item) to a certain percentage of that cost (p. 699)

profit the amount of money earned over and above the amount spent to keep the business operating (p. 550)

projected financial statements statements that predict the financial position of a business in the months and years to come (p. 579)

property damage liability motor vehicle insurance that applies when you damage the property of others (p. 432)

prospectus a document that discloses information about a company's earnings, assets and liabilities, its products or services, a particular stock, and the qualifications of its management (p. 263)

public corporation a company that sells its shares openly in stock markets, where anyone can buy them, also called a "publicly held corporation" (p. 272)

R

rate of return the percentage of increase in the value of your savings from earned interest (p. 135)

real estate land and any structures that are on it, such as a house or other building, that a person or family owns (p. 67)

rebate a partial refund of the price of a product (p. 100)

refinance obtaining a new mortgage to replace an existing one (p. 223)

registered bond a bond registered in the owner's name by the company that issues the bond (p. 310)

renters insurance a type of insurance that covers the loss of a tenant's personal property as a result of damage or theft (p. 208)

replacement value the full cost of repairing or replacing an item (p. 426)

reserve capital money that is set aside for unexpected costs or opportunities (p. 585)

reserve fund money that can be made available for the future expansion of a business (p. 614)

résumé one- or two-page summary of your education, training, experience, and qualifications (p. 45)

retained earnings profits that a company reinvests (p. 249)

risk the chance of loss or injury (p. 412)

S

safe-deposit box a small, secure storage compartment that you can rent in a bank (p. 63)

salary a fixed amount of money paid to an employee for each pay period, regardless of the number of hours worked (p. 667)

savings and loan association (S&L) a financial institution that traditionally specialized in savings accounts and mortgage loans but now offers many of the same services as commercial banks (p. 130)

secured loan a loan that is backed by collateral (p. 622)

securities all the investments that are bought and sold on the stock market, including stocks, bonds, mutual funds, options, and commodities (p. 272)

securities exchange a marketplace where brokers who represent investors meet to buy and sell securities (p. 291)

security deposit an amount of money paid to the owner of the property by a tenant to guard against any financial loss or damage that the tenant might cause (p. 208)

serial bonds bonds that are issued at the same time but mature on different dates (p. 309)

service a task that a person or a machine performs for you (p. 11)

service contract a separately purchased agreement by the manufacturer or distributor to cover the costs of repairing an item (p. 103)

service industries businesses that provide services for a fee (p. 39)

simple interest the interest computed only on the principal, the amount that you borrow (p. 167)

sinking fund a fund to which a corporation makes deposits for the purpose of paying back a bond issue (p. 308)

Small Business Administration (SBA) an independent agency of the federal government that offers assistance to people who are starting small businesses and to those who want to expand existing businesses (p. 625)

Small Business Investment Companies (SBICs) private investment firms that work with the SBA to provide longer-term funding for small businesses (p. 628)

small claims court a court that deals with legal disputes that involve amounts below a certain limit (p. 109)

small-cap stock stock issued by a company with a capitalization of $500 million or less (p. 280)

Social Security tax the tax that finances the federal programs that provide retirement, disability, and life insurance benefits (p. 671)

sole proprietorship a business owned by one person (p. 524)

specific identification method an inventory costing method in which the exact cost of each item is determined and assigned to an item (p. 686)

speculative investment a high-risk investment that might earn a large profit in a short time (p. 243)

standard deduction an amount of money set by the IRS that is not taxed (p. 384)

standard of living a measure of quality of life based on the amounts and kinds of goods and services a person can buy (p. 32)

start-up capital the money required to start your business (p. 575)

start-up costs the costs or fees involved in establishing your business (p. 575)

statement of cash flows a financial statement that reports how much cash a business took in and where the cash went (p. 656)

stop-loss an insurance policy provision that requires the policyholder to pay all costs up to a certain amount, after which the insurance company pays 100 percent of the remaining expenses covered in the policy (p. 447)

stop-payment order a request that a bank or other financial institution not cash a particular check (p. 143)

strategic plan a written outline of the business goals and the steps to take to achieve them (p. 551)

supply the amount of goods and services available for sale (p. 14)

surplus extra money that can be spent or saved, depending on a person's financial goals and values (p. 72)

syndicate a temporary association of individuals or business firms organized to perform a task that requires a large amount of funds (p. 355)

T

T account a tool to increase or decrease each account that is affected by a transaction (p. 640)

take-home pay the amount of income left after taxes and other deductions are taken out of your gross pay (p. 71)

target profit the amount of net income that a business sets as a goal (p. 711)

target sales the number of units a business needs to sell to reach a target profit (p. 711)

tax audit a detailed examination of your tax return by the IRS (p. 401)

tax credit an amount of money that can be subtracted directly from taxes you owe (p. 386)

tax deduction an expense that you can subtract from your adjusted gross income to figure your taxable income (p. 384)

tax liability the total amount of taxes owed (p. 380)

taxable income adjusted gross income less any allowable tax deductions and exemptions (p. 384)

tax-deferred income income that is taxed at a later date (p. 261)

tax-exempt income income that is not taxed (p. 261)

tenant a person who pays for the right to live in a residence owned by someone else (p. 202)

term insurance insurance that provides protection against loss of life for only a specified term, or period of time, also called *temporary life insurance* (p. 466)

time value of money the increase of an amount of money due to earned interest or dividends (p. 19)

title insurance a type of insurance that protects the buyer in case problems with the title are found later (p. 224)

total gross earnings the amount a business pays to all employees before any deductions are taken out (p. 675)

total return a calculation that includes the annual dividend as well as any increase or decrease in the original purchase price of an investment (p. 286)

transaction any activity that has an effect on the financial situation of a business (p. 561)

trends developments that mark changes in a particular area (p. 32)

trial balance a list of all the account names for a business and their current balances (p. 649)

trust an arrangement in which a designated person known as a *trustee* manages assets for the benefit of someone else (p. 501)

U

uninsured motorist's protection insurance that covers you and your family members if you are involved in an accident with an uninsured or hit-and-run driver (p. 432)

unit pricing the use of a standard unit of measurement to compare the prices of packages that are different sizes (p. 100)

unlimited liability a situation in which the owner of the business is responsible to pay the business debts out of personal assets (p. 527)

unsecured loan a loan that does not require collateral from the borrower (p. 622)

V

values beliefs and principles you consider important, correct, and desirable (p. 7)

variable costs costs that change in direct proportion to the activity level of production (p. 703)

variable expenses expenses that may change (p. 580)

venture capital firm a company that provides private funding for small businesses that need a substantial amount of immediate cash (p. 628)

vesting the right of an employee to keep the company's contributions from company-sponsored plans, such as pensions, even if the employee no longer works for that employer (p. 489)

W

warranty a written guarantee from the manufacturer or distributor that states the conditions under which the product can be returned, replaced, or repaired (p. 101)

wealth an abundance of valuable material possessions or resources (p. 65)

whole life insurance a permanent policy for which you pay a specified premium each year for the rest of your life (p. 467)

will a legal declaration of a person's wishes regarding disposal of his or her estate after death (p. 500)

Y

yield the rate of return, usually stated as a percentage, earned by an investor who holds a bond for a certain period of time (p. 323)

Z

zero-coupon bond a bond that does not produce interest (p. 311)

Index

A

B

C

D

E

G

H

I

N

O

Q

R

S

T

Features Index

A

B

C

D

G

I

S

T

W

Photo Credits

Cover Photography: Brand X Pictures(RF)/Picture Quest.

AFP/Corbis 309; AFP/Getty Images 705; AbleStock/Royalty Free 181ml; age fotostock/SuperStock 293, 295br, 427, 681bl; Alan Abramowitz/Getty Images 426; Erik Aeder/SuperStock 461; Bruce Ayers/Getty Images 110, 450; Bill Bachman/PhotoEdit 38, 541t, 240mc; David Ball/Getty Images 366; Paul Barton/Corbis 176, 181mr, 381; Paul Barton/Getty Images 576tr; Peter Beck/Corbis 540b; Randa Bishop/Image State 80; Ed Bock/Corbis 216b, 240b, 577, 626; Cleve Bryant/PhotoEdit 317; Jeffrey Burke/Image State/Royalty Free xiii(t), 78b, 548; Jeffrey Burke/Imagestate x(t), 350; Paul Chesley/Getty Images 497; Steve Chenn/Corbis 446; Stephen Chernin/Getty Images 295t; Gianni Cigolini/Image Bank 362t; Kindra Clineff/Index Stock 128r; Jason Cohn/Reuters/Corbis 536; Stewart Cohen/Getty Images 96; Comstock Images/Alamy/Royalty Free 128l; Comstock Images/Getty Images/Royalty Free 51; Corbis/Royalty-Free viii(t), xii(t), xiv(m), 153, 196, 476, 507, 537, 559, 634, 653; Philip James Corwin/Corbis x(b), 378; Steve Craft/Masterfile 620; Will Crocker/ Image Bank 362m; Jim Cummins/Getty Images 457, 487; Robert E. Daemmrich/Getty Images 384; Tim De Waele/Corbis 606–607; Patrick De Wilde/Imagestate 365; Kayte M. Deioma/PhotoEdit 529; Tony Demin/Imagestate xi(b), 442; Palais Didler/SuperStock 700; Digital Vision/Getty Images/Royalty Free 164, 502; Melanie Einzig/Getty Images 285; Amy Etra/PhotoEdit 642, 699; Jon Feingersh/Getty Images 622; Jon Feingersh/Masterfile 576tl; Myrleen Ferguson/PhotoEdit 36bl; Fisher/Hatcher/Getty Images 210; Peter M. Fisher/Corbis 156; Tony Freeman/PhotoEdit 93, 656; Getty Images 9l; Getty Images/Royalty Free viii(b), 681ml, 240br, 236, 702; Martyn Goddard/Corbis 187; Lynn Goldsmith/Corbis 580; Larry Dale Gordon/Getty Images 484br; Spencer Grant/PhotoEdit 677; Jeff Greenberg/PhotoEdit 41, 125, 278, 553; Nick Gunderson/Getty Images 462; Charles Gupton/Corbis 422; Will Hart/PhotoEdit 33; Gavin Hellier/Imagestate 619; Chip Henderson/Getty Images 48; Hemera.com 153b, 154t, 155, 156b; Maria Hesse/Imagestate 402tl; Hirb/Index Stock 557bl; Jeremy Hoare/Life File/Getty Images 448; Jack Hollingsworth/Corbis 714; Tony Hopewell/Getty Images 179; Dave G. Houser/Corbis v(b), 30; Richard Hutchins/PhotoEdit 226; Image State 20, 140; Imagestate/Royalty Free 204, 295mr, 676, 681bl, 669; Index Stock 234–235; iStock 161, 163; Mark Junak/Getty Images 24; Wolfgang Kaehler/Corbis 382; Reed Kaestner/Imagestate 511; Zigy Kalunzny/Getty Images 480; Bonnie Kamin/PhotoEdit 129r, 273; Mitch Kezar/Getty Images 564; Helen King/Corbis 181bl; Jutta Klee/Corbis 181tr; Michael Krasowitz/Getty Images 78tr, 675; LWA-JDC/Corbis 720–721; Rich LaSalle/Getty Images 638; Mark Lewis/Getty Images xiv(t), 608; Frederic Lucano/Getty Images 8m; Willie Maldonado/Getty Images xv, 696; Manchan/Getty Images/Royalty Free 576br; Court Mast/Getty Images 169; Masterfile/Royalty Free 374–375; Francis G. Mayer/Corbis 364; Joe McBride/Corbis 118–119; Patti McConville/Getty Images xi(t), 410; Medioimages/Imagestate 333, 423; Cathy Melloan Resources/PhotoEdit 211; Bill Miles/Corbis 520–521; Benn Mitchell/Image Bank 362b; Antonio Mo/Getty Images 357; Christopher J. Morris/Corbis 277; Roy Morsch/Corbis 2–3; John Neubauer/PhotoEdit 251, 541b; Michael Newman/PhotoEdit 44, 92r, 99, 134, 402b, 403; Chris Noble/Getty Images 248; David Oliver/Getty Images xiii(b), 572; John Olsen/Corbis 576bl; Roy Ooms/Masterfile 234–235; Lisa Peardon/Getty Images 414; Jose Luis Pelaez, Inc./Corbis 9r, 116–117, 129l, 294; Photos.com/Royalty Free 167, 169; Pictor/Imagestate 279; Pluriel Phototheque/SuperStock 216t; Frank Polich/Reuters/Corbis 417; Todd Powell/Index Stock vii(t),120; Michael Prince/Corbis 08l; Patrick Ramsey/Imagestate 454; Reuters Newmedia, Inc/Corbis 295bl, 295tl; Reuters/Corbis ix(t), 270; Mark Richards/PhotoEdit 402m; Jon Riley/Getty Images 9m, 36t, 311; Elena Rooraid/ PhotoEdit 217m; David Rosenberg/Getty Images 263; Galen Rowell/Corbis 15; Norbert Schaefer/Corbis 61; Alan Schein Photography/Corbis 535; Jed & Kaory Share/Getty Images 126; Shannon Stapleton/Reuters/Corbis 616; George Shelley/Masterfile 611; H. Sitton/Corbis 146; George Shelley/Corbis 376–377; Ariel Skelley/Corbis 105, 129r, 219, 590, 466, 604–605; Don Smetzer/Getty Images v(t), 04; Bruce Smith/Corbis 554; Steve Smith/SuperStock xiv(b), 664; Lee Snider/Corbis 334; Bill Stanton/Imagestate ix(b), 304; Gerhard Steiner/Corbis 579; Tom Stewart/Corbis vi(t), 58, 159, 36tl, 518–519, 621; Mark Stone/Getty Images 251; Stockbyte Platinum/Alamy 82; Superstock Inc./SuperStock 220; SuperStock/Royalty Free 585, 713; The Cover Story/Corbis 247; ThinkStock/Royalty Free vi(b), 88; ThinkStock/SuperStock/Royalty Free 354; Wes Thompson/Corbis 617; Bob Torrez/Getty Images 216m; Susan Van Etten/PhotoEdit 552; Pablo Corral Vega/Corbis 106; Anton Venon/SuperStock 703; Victoria Blackie/Getty Images 484l; Steve Vider/Imagestate 259, 491, 555, 586, 658; Alana Wesley White/PhotoEdit vii(b), 152; Dana White/PhotoEdit 67; Marshall Williams/Imagestate xii(b), 522; Matthew Wiley/Masterfile 512; David Young Wolff/PhotoEdit 7, 36br, 240tr, 342, 484tr, 500, 557mr, 684; Alex Wong/Getty Images 557tr; Mei Yan/Masterfile 92l; Yoshikazu/Tsuno/AFP/Getty Images 557ml.